H. K. Smith
Des Arc, Ark.
1-10-91

THOSE FABULOUS SERIAL HEROINES

Their Lives and Films

by

Buck Rainey

With Introductions by

JEAN ROGERS
CAROL FORMAN

The World of Yesterday
Waynesville, North Carolina
1990

Copyright © 1990 by Buck Rainey

All rights reserved under International and Pan American Copyright Convention. No part of this book may be reproduced in any manner whatsoever without written permission from the publisher, except in the case of brief quotations in reviews and articles.

ISBN: 0-936505-10-9

Library of Congress Catalog Card Number 88-11369

Published by
The World of Yesterday
Route 3, Box 263-H
Waynesville, NC 28786
Phone (704) 648-5647

Manufactured in the United States of America

Printed on acid-free paper

THOSE FABULOUS SERIAL HEROINES

Their Lives and Films

For

ROSALVA

My Own Beautiful Heroine

And in memory of

LAURENCE AND VIOLET RAINEY

Whose Love and Quarters Made Possible the Thousands
of Hours I Spent Watching Westerns and Serials
in the Fabulous Years of My Youth

ACKNOWLEDGMENTS

Special thanks are extended to BILL MCDOWELL, BOB ROBISON, LES ADAMS, and JOSE SIMOES FILHO for significant research assistance, to BOB and CHARLES SMITH of FILM FAVORITES who enthusiastically helped in locating and supplying many of the photos used herein, and to RON DOWNEY who was instrumental in bringing about the publication of this book.
In addition, these friends assisted in various aspects of the book's preparation: Janus Barfoed, Lois Collier, Louise Currie, Carol Forman, Dorothy Gulliver, Ann Little, Louise Lorraine, Merrill T. McCord, Noel Neill, Cecilia Parker, Jean Rogers, Eileen Sedgwick, Linda Stirling, George Geltzer, Oliver G. Tucker, Nick Williams, William C. Wilson, Peggy Stewart, and Richard Braff.

TABLE OF CONTENTS

FOREWORD (Jean Rogers) XI

FOREWORD (Carol Forman) XIII

INTRODUCTION 1

PART I - SERIAL HEROINES NONPAREIL 3

    Kay Aldridge 5
    Lucile Browne 13
    Phyllis Coates 21
    Grace Cunard 29
    Carol Forman 43
    Neva Gerber 51
    Lorna Gray/Adrian Booth 65
    Dorothy Gulliver 77
    Juanita Hansen 89
    Helen Holmes 97
    Edith Johnson 107
    Anna Little 115
    Louise Lorraine 127
    Noel Neill 137
    Allene Ray 149
    Jean Rogers 159
    Ruth Roland 173
    Eileen Sedgwick 187
    Linda Stirling 199
    Aline Towne 207
    Marie Walcamp 215
    Pearl White 225

PART II - FEARLESS BEAUTIES IN DISTRESS 241

    Veda Ann Borg 243
    Lois Collier 259
    Marguerite Courtot 269
    Pauline Curley 277
    Louise Currie 283
    Grace Darmond 291
    Helen Ferguson 299
    Mary Fuller 307
    Frances Gifford 321
    Eugenia Gilbert 329

Carol Holloway 337
Natalie Kingston 345
Cleo Madison 351
Edna Murphy 361
Anne Nagel 373
Cecilia Parker 385
Arline Pretty 395
Ruth Royce 401
Marin Sais 405
Marguerite Snow 417
Peggy Stewart 425
Ruth Stonehouse 437
Jacqueline Wells/Julie Bishop 449
Kathlyn Williams 459

HONORABLE MENTION 475

BIBLIOGRAPHY 483

INDEX 495

FILMOGRAPHIES NOTE

Entries in each filmography are in chronological order according to either release date or copyright date, when at least one of these is known. Where possible, exact release dates have been used. Lacking the release date, copyright dates, if known, have been used. Usually the two dates are fairly close in time, so no effort has been made to distinguish between release and copyright dates. If neither date is known, the year of release is used and the film listed after all other films for that year for which there is a release or copyright date.

Running times are expressed in minutes where possible; otherwise, in number of reels. A reel normally is ten to fifteen minutes; thus, a five-reel film should be between fifty and seventy minutes in length.

Tailspin Tommy and the Great Air Mystery (Universal, 1935) – Jean Rogers.

FOREWORD

By

JEAN ROGERS

By now, film buffs everywhere must realize that movie serials have played a major role in the growth and development of motion pictures. Directors, writers, actors, and technicians who served their apprenticeship in serials emerged as the cinema creators of the feature films that made Hollywood the motion picture capital of the world.

In the beginning the serial budgets were low, the shooting schedules short, and in many instances the talent at all levels, while young and eager, was also green and inexperienced.

Looking back on it now, all of us who were part of the serial world realize only too well what a marvelous training ground it was. My own experience provided me with knowledge of what to do and what not to do in front of the camera. Equally important, it gave me confidence and the poise one must have to be truly professional. In retrospect, it was a training ground that paved the way for my growth as an actress and enabled me to play feature roles in major films while under long-term contract to Metro-Goldwyn-Mayer and Twentieth Century-Fox.

For me, this delightful book has been a trip down memory lane and those of you about to read it are in for a fascinating and illuminating glimpse at one of Hollywood's most exciting and rewarding periods, one I was lucky enough to be a part of.

Serial fans and the motion picture industry itself are indebted to Buck Rainey for preserving this bit of cinema history and keeping alive the memory of a fabulous era and of a type of film unequaled in its power to thrill and entertain the young at heart.

The Black Widow (Republic, 1947) – Carol Forman.

FOREWORD

by

CAROL FORMAN

The era of Serials was one when the good guys always won and the bad guys paid the price for their meanness, when life in general was a lot simpler and somehow prettier, and when good and evil were more distinguishable on screen than they are today.

Serials were the "street urchin" of the business. Agents always warned you never to admit that you had appeared in one because it would be held against you by the major studios, although many actors went on to become super stars after getting their start in these films. Some of the top producers today, also, got their early training with these serials.

My own regret, now, is that I didn't make more of them. I, too, was reaching for the top rung in the ladder and not wanting to be "type-cast," and I turned down three times more serials than I made. They were clean and decent and people got just as many thrills and excitement out of them as people now get while watching today's fare of violence, graphic gore, and ugliness.

My personal gratitude goes to Buck Rainey for finding me after all these years and for opening up my world for me again. One day I received a letter from him asking if I was the Carol Forman who appeared in **The Black Widow** serial. I couldn't believe anyone remembered me after nearly forty years! It took me many months to answer Buck. Finally, after a second letter from him, I hesitatingly picked up the phone and called him in Oklahoma. He then enlightened me to the network of fans across the country who were asking about me and wondering where I had disappeared to.

Thanks to Buck, I have been honored at film festivals and have found, to my amazement, a horde of fans who remember my modest efforts in the thrill-a-minute genre. Also, I'm scheduled to go into a film soon--playing the same kind of part I played in the serials! You'll enjoy this book and will appreciate the long hours of loving work that it took to bring it about. Buck's books and other publications have endeavored to bring back to life a type of entertainment that apparently never really died, at least in the hearts of a legion of film lovers.

The Perils of Pauline (Pathé, 1914) – Probably the most famous serial of all time.

INTRODUCTION

The last echoes of a heroine's screams as she dangles over the abyss, or lies trussed to the tracks in the path of an on-rushing locomotive, or plunges toward death in a spinning aeroplane (seconds before Continued Next Week starts an avalanche on the popcorn counter) are muted now by time. The motion picture serial, or "Cliffhanger" as it is lovingly referred to by its followers, is no more. The last one was produced in 1956.

The demise of the serial leaves the older generation of moviegoers with a sense of moroseness. An important part of our lives has disappeared. Mountains of prose have been written about this action genre, expressing the height and depth, the length and breadth of one's affection for it.

At the same time, there has been a plethora of criticism. There seems to be no in-between. Either serials have been acclaimed as magnificent entertainment or denounced as insipid and downright stupid. The two viewpoints are poles apart. Obviously, this book is for those with a fervid and lasting appreciation for the film fare that featured its comely subjects.

Motion picture serials depended for their survival on thrills, stunts, death-defying acrobatics, speed, hokum, minimum dialogue, childish plots, unsophisticated audiences, and various other elements, but in nearly every case there had to be a beautiful girl in jeopardy. And so it is with no disparagement that we categorize the ladies of this volume, a group of Hollywood actresses heretofore strangely neglected by historians--those brave, unpublicized, poorly compensated women who withstood the rigors of serial filmmaking, entering into it with a degree of risk which sometimes seemed suicidal to those who took part in them. To fall in love with them, time and time again, was an easy accomplishment for budding young romanticists.

Sophisticates generally curled a supercilious lip at serials, but a large segment of the movie-going public devoured them with a seemingly insatiable appetite. Rehashing familiar material, but doubling back on the trail with sufficient appeal to provide a pleasant swing around the box-office track, 515 serials were made between 1912 and 1956, most of which contained some combination of the standard serial ingredients: gunplay, rough-and-tumble fights, whirlwind speed, mystery figures, bizarre scientific gimmickry . . . and a pretty girl. Always a pretty girl! Often she was a damsel in distress, with little opportunity to do anything but look scared at her imminent fate, or stay decoratively in the background. Subtlety in acting was an impossibility, but some became quite adept at registering claustrophobic horror at their ends-of-chapters fate. And not a few were able to bring to serials a style and finesse that lifted them well above mediocrity. The importance of the heroine-- and sometimes harlot--in the inexorable appeal of serials from the heyday of Pearl White and Ruth Roland to the last sickly serials of the 1950s cannot be overemphasized.

After the advent of sound many of the serial ingenues became just "lovely props," without much functional value to the story. But others were given good, meaty roles and made genuine contributions to plot development and to the enjoyment of the films. Any little boy would naturally have denied it, but many of them were secretly in love with the heroines they watched week after week. Boys of all ages could imagine themselves snuggled in the arms of these pretty damsels, and the mention of their names today sends our memories reeling back over the years to a happier era when the heroines we had a crush on battled it out with the minions of satanic evil beside the conquering hero. And how our envy would be roused as the hero's protective arm would envelop our "sweetheart." Oh, the pangs of unrequited love!

In their own diminutive kingdom, their royalty was as real as that of the big-name and better paid actresses at the prestige studios, and the faithfulness of their fans was often greater. Relatively few succeeded in scaling the heights to film stardom. In the shadow of over-publicized actresses who had armies of press agents beating their drums, the young ladies who labored in the serial and "B" ranks have long been overlooked and either forgotten or ignored by film historians. Only the "over 40" film patrons who once faithfully plunked down their dimes at the box office and cheered the gals on recall most of them today. But the movie industry was blessed in a unique way by their ability, their charm, their dignity, their beauty, and, yes, sometimes their escapades as well.

In truth, serial heroines were more of an attraction than they have been given credit for. Supposedly nothing counted but continuous action in the low-budget cliffhangers, yet that action became awfully dull and monotonous after a while unless it involved a girl. Many of the girls had the beauty and personality to charm even the pre-teenagers, a sizable portion of the audience for this type of film fare. Some had that quality of passivity which poets, in more classically-minded times, considered the essence of femininity. Some came on strong and vied with the hero in the boldness of their exploits. Some had a screen persona of significance; others did not. Often their thespian skills were limited, yet the charm of their personalities would fill the void. And though they did not work at being sexy, many of the leading ladies of cliffhangers were all the more appealing for it. Jean Rogers, Frances Gifford, Allene Ray, Carol Forman, and Lucille Browne are all good examples of this understated sexuality.

Some actresses did double duty as serial heroines and Western heroines, the best known being Ruth Roland, Marie Walcamp, Ann Little, Eileen Sedgwick, Peggy Stewart, Allene Ray, and Neva Gerber. Other serial heroines spent little time on the range, but skipped around in the mouth of hell from week to week in episodic, thrill-a-minute action that saw them in jeopardy in a multitude of ways. The films may not have set new high water marks for suspense, poignance, melodrama, or mystery, but they entertained their noncritical audience so thoroughly that scenes, plots, and dialogue experienced fifty years ago remain indelibly stamped on the memories of aging fans who may not remember the grandchildren's birthdays, what the preacher said in his sermon last week, or what the movie was all about that they saw just the other evening.

This book is about a number of the more important serial heroines who were loved, supported, and fantasized about by three generations of action fans. The filmographies will be a boon to film historians and fans who have always wanted a fairly complete filmography of their favorite heroine. Many readers will be more interested in the biographical data and the photographs. The book contains much information; it is not just another "picture book."

Not every heroine can be covered in a single book--or two--or three. If your favorite heroine is not here, it is not because she is unappreciated. The ladies chosen for this volume have been selected for one or more of these reasons: (1) they were extremely popular in their day; (2) they represented a unique type of heroine; (3) they had a long career; (4) they made a significant number of action films; (5) they appeared in important cliffhangers; and (6) their careers and/or personal charisma intrigued the author. There are a number of other leading ladies who deserve to be recognized just as much as the ones selected. Limitations of space simply did not permit such a complete coverage of great serial heroines.

The ladies await us on yonder cliff and well-beaten dusty trail, lit by the glow of the bigger-than-life memories of our childhood. It's time to keep our final rendezvous with the girls we loved in our more youthful, innocent years, when all trails were downhill and shady, and led into a fantasy world of vicarious adventure, where rescuing angelic heroines from death, the "fate worse than death," and all lesser calamities seemed to be our reason for existing on a Saturday afternoon.

Get your popcorn, grab your front-row seat, and nudge aside the hero again to steal the kiss intended for him, as Finis flashes across the screen of your mind, and the curtain drops on an era that can never be experienced again.

PART I
SERIAL HEROINES NONPAREIL

The serial queens whose personal stories and film credits are presented in this chapter are the incomparables of the genre. They had "true" grit. Their charm, ability, and pulling power were irrefutable. Week after week these popular beauties were jeopardized by insidious villains bent on nefarious activities. While they never suffered the "fate worse than death" that befell later heroines in the age of X-rated entertainment, these sagacious sirens were always on the brink of disaster at the hands of madmen whose evil desires sometimes included their bodies. Most villains, however, were simply out to do them in-- by fire, auto or train crash, avalanche, explosion, bullet, stampede, knife, flood, drowning, poison, aerial disaster, or whatever expedient might be at hand.

Serials were most popular in the period from 1915 to 1928. In the years before 1925, the most successful ones usually starred a heroine rather than a hero. Pearl White, Mary Fuller, and Kathlyn Williams led the way, followed in short order by Ruth Roland, Grace Cunard, Helen Holmes, and Marie Walcamp. The person who can only remember back to the serial releases of the 1930s and '40s finds it hard to realize just how popular the old-time serials and their stars were. The girls had a tremendous following, and four-digit-weekly salaries to prove it. In the sound era, Jean Rogers, Linda Stirling, Kay Aldridge, and Lucile Browne attained some degree of popularity and recognition as serial personalities, but it was only a semblance of the charisma that silent screamers had for the naive audiences of over half a century ago.

There was no magic formula for success as a serial heroine. The ladies whose careers are presented in this book had widely varying backgrounds and abilities. Certainly one prerequisite was courage; another was stamina; another, especially in the silent era, was athletic prowess. And they had to be attractive; their loveliness and vulnerability were capitalized on. Male audiences, at least, developed a consuming affection for Jean Rogers as Dale Arden, Frances Gifford as Jungle Girl, Phyllis Coates as Panther Girl of the Congo, Kay Aldridge as Nyoka, and Anita Stewart as The Goddess. They exuded sex appeal, though, in a serial, they seldom got a chance to play a romantic scene.

But in the last analysis it was the star's personality in combination with these other attributes that determined her acceptance by serial patrons, a demanding audience. Fans might not be able to express what it was about a particular heroine that attracted them, but if she had that indefinable charisma they were inexorably drawn to her. It has been said that Gene Autry could not act, that he was a poor singer, and that he was no athlete at all. Yet as a screen cowboy he achieved a popularity far greater than that of better actors, singers, or athletes. Few successful serial heroines were great actresses, yet some great actresses who tried their hands as serial heroines failed. Peggy O'Day, Evelyn Finley, and Ruth Mix were fair athletes, yet they never made the top rung as heroines.

The ladies herein had what it took to survive as serial stars, to provide heart-chilling drama by installments, to generate excitement as they hurtled into the abyss at the end of each episode-- "continued next week."

They were eager, ambitious, determined, and hopeful. They had looks, humor, charm, vitality, and individuality. And each was peculiarly endowed by physique or temperament to withstand the rigors of fast-paced, sixteen-hour-a-day outdoor shooting schedules.

Petite Louise Lorraine, Noel Neill, and Marguerite Courtot, lady-like Marguerite Snow and Mary Fuller; reserved and bashful Allene Ray and Edith Johnson--all were embraced by serial lovers along with boisterous, athletic Ruth Roland, Marie Walcamp, and Pearl White. Fighting through cordons of crafty foemen, with or without the aid of a male companion, they made their way to happiness in spite of all the obstacles heaped before them--and if they couldn't quite make it all believable, they at least made it highly enjoyable.

Daredevils of the West (Republic, 1943) – Kay Aldridge

1 • KAY ALDRIDGE

A Buoyant Spirit, Sex Appeal, and Charm Made Her a Serial Queen of the First Magnitude

There was no question about the engaging screen personality of Kay Aldridge. She was good-looking and high-spirited, and she could be counted on to draw with her fans. In many of her Fox features she seemed to be no more than a pretty ingénue, making as little of her parts as she could without doing anything wrong. She just strolled through them, and whenever she seemed least essential the camera came in for a close-up and showed why she was in the picture business. Her youth and beauty were important assets as her expression of emotion was limited--but her virginal/sexy quality went a long way toward making up for the deficit.

Kay Aldridge was the star of **The Perils of Nyoka** (1942), one of the most celebrated serials produced in the age of sound. Republic was trying to establish a serial heroine reminiscent of Allene Ray, Pearl White, or Ruth Roland. Certainly Miss Aldridge never became as popular as those silent serial queens, but **Perils of Nyoka** could hold its own in any comparison with the vintage films.

It was the second try by Republic in this vein, preceded by Frances Gifford's **Jungle Girl** (1941). That too had been successful, and Miss Gifford, perhaps even more than Miss Aldridge, was uniquely qualified for serial stardom. But she was under contract to another studio at the time of casting for **Perils of Nyoka** and was not available for the role. Also, Republic was trying to avoid the cost of exercising its literary option with Edgar Rice Burroughs, author of the book from which **Jungle Girl** was adapted. The company wanted to make a second serial along parallel lines but with enough changes to avoid the obligation to Burroughs. Retaining Miss Gifford in the second series would have added fuel to Burroughs' contention that Republic was still using the **Jungle Girl** story without paying for the right to do so. As a result, only the name Nyoka survived from the first serial and the time frame, story, and characters were changed completely.

Miss Aldridge was contracted for four serials, and **Perils of Nyoka** was an auspicious beginning. Imperiled on nineteen major occasions, including all the endings, Nyoka jumped, rolled, swung, and fought her way along an obstacle course which included four physical combats with her arch-nemesis Vultura (played by Lorna Gray/Adrian Booth). Her leading man, Clayton Moore, still several years from immortality as the Lone Ranger, was just starting his serial career. It would end in 1954 after another eight cliffhangers had been completed. A friendly, unassuming man, he proved a good choice and, along with the many veteran character actors and director William Witney, helped her over the rough spots of her first serial, which was also her first outdoor film.

Kay was an unusual choice for top billing in a serial. She had never even seen one, and had little inkling of what was going on during the shooting. Even though she made two other serials, it was thirty years before she ever saw herself in them. She did not have an athletic background. Rather, she was one of New York's top models before going into the movies. In 1937 she was selected as one of the ten most-photographed girls in the world. All ten were brought from New York to Hollywood to appear in **Vogues of 1938**. She got $250 a week plus expenses. Before she could return to New York after filming was completed, Metro-Goldwyn-Mayer offered her a part in **Rosalie** (1937) and she remained in Hollywood to pursue a movie career.

Concurrently, she continued her modeling career, appearing in almost every top magazine in the country. When David O. Selznick saw her picture on the cover of <u>Life</u> for September 5, 1938, he wired her an offer to test for the part of Scarlett O'Hara in **Gone With the Wind**

Kay Aldridge makes the cover of Life.

(1939). She also tested for the role of Melanie but, as the world knows, the parts went to Vivien Leigh and Olivia de Havilland.

In 1939 Kay was signed by 20th Century-Fox at $250 a week, following a tour she had made with Georgia Carroll (another model, who became Mrs. Kay Kyser) for a "Cover Girls See the World" series for Redbook magazine. Her first Fox film was **Hotel for Women** (1939), in which another great serial heroine, Jean Rogers, had a principal role. Originally slated for the leading part, Kay lost out to newcomer Linda Darnell. In 1940, as "the other woman," she supported Miss Rogers in **Yesterday's Heroes**. That same year she played with Gene Autry in **Shooting High** (1940), but Marjorie Weaver was the object of the hero's affections in this film about the making of a Western movie. Kay is the heroine of the movie within a movie.

Republic Pictures fans sometimes contend that **Daredevils of the West** (1943), Kay's second serial, was among the top Western serials ever filmed, if not the best. Alan Barbour, in his book Days of Thrills and Adventure, says it was the perfect serial. Most serial historians and Western buffs would agree that it was at least exceptional in general execution. It was a straightforward Western, fast-paced, and with topnotch production values throughout. Co-starring with Miss Aldridge was Allan Lane, a veteran of two previous Republic serials and soon to become a "B" Western favorite. They were billed as "The Serial Queen" and "The Serial King."

Haunted Harbor (1944) was Republic's last serial adapted from another medium--Dayle Douglas' novel of the same name. The film story closely paralleled that of the book. Playing opposite Kay was Kane Richmond, one of the sound era's greatest serial heroes. Richmond was not at all conceited or difficult to get along with, as Allan Lane had been, and Kay found it a pleasure to work with him. Kane was the kind of man who would try to make others look good in a scene too, and their camaraderie came across effectively on screen.

Evidently Republic intended to star Kay in the serial **The Tiger Woman** (1944). The part went to Linda Stirling instead, possibly because Kay was appearing in a Broadway play at that time.

Her last two films were done for PRC as leading lady to Dave O'Brien. Designed for the dualer or double-bill market, the low-budget films were entertaining and served their purpose well. **The Man Who Walked Alone** (1945) gave Kay a rare chance to essay romantic comedy, which she had always wanted to do, and **The Phantom of 42nd Street** (1945) was a tight little mystery melodrama.

On Valentine's Day in 1945 Kay married Texas oilman Arthur Cameron and retired from acting. The marriage produced four children but after nine years the Camerons separated; they were divorced in the mid-fifties. She later married artist Richard Derby Tucker and settled in Camden, Maine. They were still married at his death in 1979.

An excellent book by Merrill T. McCord, Perils of Kay Aldridge: Life of the Serial Queen, was published in 1979 (see Selected Bibliography).

Miss Aldridge has been a guest celebrity at several film conventions, including the St. Louis Western Film Convention in 1979 and the Knoxville, Tennessee film fair in 1987. Highly popular with Western and serial buffs, she has retained the affection of her original fans while attracting new admirers with each public appearance and screening of her films.

Perils of Nyoka (Republic, 1942) – Charles Middleton, Lorna Gray, and George J. Lewis have Kay Aldridge at their mercy.

KAY ALDRIDGE Filmography

VOGUES OF 1938
(United Artists, September 17, 1937) 108 Mins.
Warner Baxter, Joan Bennett, Helen Vinson, Mischa Auer, Alan Mowbray, Jerome Cowan, Alma Kruger, Marjorie Gateson, Dorothy McNulty (Penny Singleton), Polly Rowles, Marla Shelton, Hedda Hopper, Roman Bohnen, Georgia Tapps, Virginia Verrill, Fred Lawrence, Gloria Gilbert, Olympic Trio, Wiere Brothers, Rocco and Saulters, Four Hot Shots, Victor Young and his Orchestra, *Kay Aldridge*
Director: Irving Cummings
Screenplay: Bella and Samuel Spewack
Producer: Walter Wanger

ROSALIE
(M-G-M, December 24, 1937) 122 Mins.
Nelson Eddy, Eleanor Powell, Frank Morgan, Edna May Oliver, Ray Bolger, Ilona Massey, Billy Gibert, Reginald Owen, Tom Rutherford, Clay Clement, Virginia Grey, George Zucco, Oscar O'Shea, Jerry Colonna, Janet Beecher, Tommy Bond, *Kay Aldridge*
Director: W. S. Van Dyke
Screenplay: William Anthony McGuire
Story: William Anthony McGuire, Guy Bolton
Producer: William Anthony McGuire

HOTEL FOR WOMEN
(20th Century-Fox, August 4, 1939) 83 Mins.
Ann Sothern, Linda Darnell, James Ellison, Jean Rogers, Lynn Bari, June Gale, Joyce Compton, Elsa Maxwell, John Halliday, *Kay Aldridge*, Alan Dinehart, Sidney Blackmer, Amanda Duff, Ruth Terry, Chick Chandler
Director: Gregory Ratoff
Screenplay: Kathryn Scola, Darrell Ware
Story: Elsa Maxwell, Kathryn Scola
Producer: Darryl F. Zanuck

HERE I AM A STRANGER
(20th Century-Fox, September 29, 1939) 83 Mins.
Richard Greene, Richard Dix, Gladys George, George Zucco, Brenda Joyce, Roland Young, Edward Norris, *Kay Aldridge*, Henry Kolker, Russell Gleason, Richard Bond
Director: Roy Del Ruth
Screenplay: Milton Sperling, Sam Hellman
Story: Gordon Malherbe Hillman
Associate Producer: Harry Joe Brown

FREE, BLONDE AND 21
(20th Century-Fox, March 29, 1940) 67 Mins.
Lynn Bari, Mary Beth Hughes, Joan Davis, Henry Wilcoxon, Robert Lowery, Alan Baxter, *Kay Aldridge*, Helen Ericson, Chick Chandler, Joan Valerie, Elyse Knox, Dorothy Dearing, Herbert Rawlinson, Kay Linaker, Thomas Jackson, Richard Lane, Dorothy Moore, Gwen Kenyon, Frank Coghlan, Jr., Mickey Simpson
Director: Ricardo Cortez
Screenplay: Frances Hyland
Producer: Sol M. Wurtzel

SHOOTING HIGH
(20th Century-Fox, April 26, 1940) 65 Mins.
Jane Withers, Gene Autry, Marjorie Weaver, Robert Lowery, *Kay Aldridge*, Hobart Cavanaugh, Frank M. Thomas, Jack Carson, Hamilton MacFadden, Charles Middleton, Ed Brady, Tom London, Eddie Acuff, Pat O'Malley, George Chandler
Director: Alfred E. Green
Screenplay: Lou Breslow, Owen Francis
Story: Lou Breslow, Owen Francis
Associate Producer: John Stone

GIRL IN ROOM 313
(20th Century-Fox, May 31, 1940) 56 Mins.
Florence Rice, Kent Taylor, Lionel Atwill, *Kay Aldridge*, Mary Treen, Jack Carson, Elyse Knox, Joan Valerie, Dorothy Dearing, Dorothy Moore, Jacqueline Wells, Charles C. Wilson, William Davidson
Director: Ricardo Cortez
Screenplay: Barry Trivers, Clay Adams
Story: Hilda Stone
Producer: Sol M. Wurtzel

SAILOR'S LADY
(20th Century-Fox, July 5, 1940) 66 Mins.
Nancy Kelly, Jon Hall, Joan Davis, Dana Andrews, Mary Nash, Buster Crabbe, *Kay Aldridge*, Harry Shannon, Wally Vernon, Bruce Hampton, C. D. Brown, Selmer Jackson, Edgar Dearing, Edmund MacDonald, William B. Davidson, Kane Richmond, Lester Dorr, Don Barry, George O'Hanlon, Matt McHugh, Peggy Ryan, Ward Bond, Barbara Pepper, Gaylord Pendleton, Eddie Acuff
Director: Allan Dwan
Screenplay: Frederick Hazlett Brennan
Story: Frank Wead
Producer: Sol M. Wurtzel

GIRL FROM AVENUE A
(20th Century-Fox, August 9, 1940) 73 Mins.
Jane Withers, Kent Taylor, *Kay Aldridge*, Elyse Knox, Laura Hope Crews, Jessie Ralph, Harry Shannon, Vaughn Glaser, Rand Brooks, Ann Shoemaker, George Humbert
Director: Otto Brower
Screenplay: Frances Hyland
Story: Maud Fulton,"The Brat"
Producer: Sol M. Wurtzel

YESTERDAY'S HEROES
(20th Century-Fox, September 20, 1940) 65 Mins.
Jean Rogers, Robert Sterling, Ted North, *Kay Aldridge*, Russell Gleason, Richard Lane, Edmund MacDonald, George Irving, Emma Dunn, Harry Hayden, Isabel Randolph, Pierre Watkin, Frank Sully, Mike Frankovich, Don Forbes, Bert Roach, Matt McHugh, Truman Bradley, George Meeker
Director: Herbert I. Leeds
Screenplay: Irving Cummings, Jr., William Conselman, Jr.
Story: William Brent
Producer: Sol M. Wurtzel

DOWN ARGENTINE WAY
(20th Century-Fox, October 11, 1940) 88 Mins.
Betty Grable, Don Ameche, Carmen Miranda, Charlotte Greenwood, J. Carrol Naish, Henry Stephenson, *Kay Aldridge*, Leonid Kinskey, Chris-Pin Martin, Robert Conway, Gregory Gaye, Bobby Stone, Charles Jedels, Nicholas Brothers
Directors: Darrell Ware, Karl Tunberg
Story: Rian James, Ralph Spence
Producer: Darryl F. Zanuck

Perils of Nyoka (Republic, 1942) — Kay Aldridge is menaced by Lorna Gray (Adrian Booth) and Emil Van Horn as "Satan," the gorilla.

GOLDEN HOOFS
(20th Century-Fox, February 14, 1941) 67 Mins.
Jane Withers, Charles "Buddy" Rogers, *Kay Aldridge*, George Irving, Buddy Pepper, Cliff Clark, Philipp Hurlock, Sheila Ryan, Howard Hickman
Director: Lynn Shores
Screenplay: Ben Grauman Kohn
Story: Roy Chanslor, Thomas Langan
Associate Producers: Walter Morosco, Ralph Dietrich

DEAD MEN TELL
(20th Century-Fox, March 28, 1941) 61 Mins.
Sidney Toler, Sheila Ryan, Robert Weldon, Sen Yung, Don Douglas, *Kay Aldridge*, Paul McGrath, George Reeves, Truman Bradley, Ethel Griffies, Lenita Lane, Milton Parsons
Director: Harry Lachman
Screenplay: John Larkin
Associate Producers: Walter Morosco, Ralph Dietrich

NAVY BLUES
(Warner Bros., September 13, 1941) 108 Mins.
Ann Sheridan, Jack Oakie, Martha Raye, Jack Haley, Herbert Anderson, Jack Carson, Jackie C. Gleason, Richard Lane, William T. Orr, John Ridgely, Frank Wilcox, William Justice, Ray Book, Selmer Jackson, Peggy Diggins, Georgia Carroll, Loraine Gettman (Leslie Brooks), Marguerite Chapman, *Kay Aldridge*, Claire James, Howard da Silva, Richard Travis, William Hooper, Ralph Byrd, Gig Young
Director: Lloyd Bacon
Screenplay: Jerry Wald, Richard Macaulay, Arthur T. Horman
Story: Arthur T. Horman
Producer: Hal B. Wallis

YOU'RE IN THE ARMY NOW
(Warner Bros., December 25, 1941) 79 Mins.
Jimmy Durante, Jane Wyman, Phil Silvers, Regis Toomey, Donald MacBride, George Meeker, Joseph Sawyer, William Haade, Navy Blues Sextet (*Kay Aldridge*, Peggy Diggins, Loraine Gettman, Marguerite Chapman, Georgia Carroll, Alice Talton)
Director: Lewis Seiler
Screenplay: Paul Gerard Smith, George Beatty
Associate Producer: Ben Stoloff

LOUISIANA PURCHASE
(Paramount, December 25, 1941) 98 Mins.
Bob Hope, Vera Zorina, Victor Moore, Irene Bordoni, Dona Drake, Raymond Walburn, Maxie Rosenbloom, Frank Albertson, Phyllis Ruth, Donald MacBride, Andrew Tombes, Robert Warwick, Charles LaTorre, Charles Lasky, Emory Parnell, Iris Meredith, Catherine Craig, Jack Norton, Sam McDaniel, *Kay Aldridge*, Katherine Booth, Alaine Brandes, Barbara Britton, Brooke Evans, Lynda Grey, Eleanor Stewart, Jean Wallace, Frances Gifford, Louise LaPlanche
Director: Irving Cummings
Screenplay: Jerome Chodorov, Joseph Fields
Story: B. C. DeSylva
Associate Producer: Harold Wilson

THE PERILS OF NYOKA
(Republic, June 27, 1942) 15 Chapters.
Kay Aldridge, Clayton Moore, William Benedict, Lorna Gray (Adrian Booth), Charles Middleton, Tristram Coffin, Forbes Murray, Robert Strange, George Pembroke, Georges Renavent, John Davidson, George J. Lewis, Ken Terrell, John Bagni, Kenne Duncan, Arvon Dale, John Daheim, Kuke Taylor, Tom Steele, Iron Eyes Cody, Forrest Taylor, Yakima Canutt, Art Dillard, Duke Taylor, Augie Gomez, Bud Wolfe, Robert Barron, Emil Van Horn, Herbert Rawlinson, David Sharpe, George Plues
Director: William Witney
Screenplay: Ronald Davidson, Norman S. Hall, William Lively, Joseph O'Donnell, and Joseph Poland
Assistant Director: W. J. O'Sullivan
Chapters: (1) Desert Intrigue (2) Death's Chariot (3) Devil's Crucible (4) Ascending Doom (5) Fatal Second (6) Human Sacrifice (7) Monster's Clutch (8) Tuareg Vengeance (9) Burned Alive (10) Treacherous Trail (11) Unknown Peril (12) Underground Tornado (13) Thundering Death (14) Blazing Barrier (15) Satan's Fury

THE FALCON'S BROTHER
(RKO, November 6, 1942) 63 Mins.
George Sanders, Tom Conway, Jane Randolph, Don Barclay, Cliff Clark, Edward Gargan, Eddie Dunn, Charlotte Wynters, James Newill, Keye Luke, Amanda Varela, George Lewis, Gwili Andre, Andre Charlot, Mary Halsey, Charles Arnt, Richard Martin, *Kay Aldridge*
Director: Stanley Logan
Screenplay: Stuart Palmer, Craig Rice
Producer: Maurice Geraghty

SOMETHING TO SHOUT ABOUT
(Columbia, February 25, 1943) 90 Mins.
Don Ameche, Janet Blair, Jack Oakie, William Gaxton, Cobina Wright, Jr., Veda Ann Borg, Hazel Scott, Jaye Martin, Lily Norwood, James Walker, Teddy Wilson and band, *Kay Aldridge*
Director/Producer: Gregory Ratoff
Screenplay: Lou Breslow, Edward Eliscu
Story: Fred Schiller

DAREDEVILS OF THE WEST
(Republic, May 1, 1943) 12 Chapters.
Kay Aldridge, Allan Lane, Eddie Acuff, William Haade, Robert Frazer, Ted Adams, George J. Lewis, Stanley Andrews, Jack Rockwell, Charles Miller, John Hamilton, Budd Buster, Denneth Harlan, Kenne Duncan, Rex Lease, Chief Thunder Cloud, Duke Green, Eddie Parker, Tom Steele, Jack O'Shea, George Magrill, Al Taylor, Edmund Cobb, Joe Yrigoyen, Bill Yrigoyen, Eddie Parker, Babe DeFreest, Herbert Rawlinson, Edward Cassidy, Ralph Bucko
Director: John English
Screenplay: Ronald Davidson, William Lively, Joseph Poland, Joseph O'Donnell, Basil Dickey
Associate Producer: W. J. O'Sullivan
Chapters: (1) Valley of Death (2) Flaming Prison (3) The Killer Strikes (4) Tunnel of Terror (5) Fiery Tomb (6) Redskin Raiders (7) Perilous Pursuit (8) Dance of Doom (9) Terror Trail (10) Suicide Showdown (11) Cavern of Cremation (12) Frontier Justice

DU BARRY WAS A LADY
(MGM, May, 1943) 101 Mins.
Red Skelton, Lucille Ball, Gene Kelly, Virginia O'Brien, "Rags" Ragland, Zero Mostel, Donald Meek, Douglass Dumbrille, George Givot, Louise Beavers, Tommy Dorsey and orchestra, Dick Haymes, Lana Turner, *Kay Aldridge*, Ava Gardner, Hazel Brooks, Kay Williams
Director: Roy Del Ruth
Screenplay: Irving Brecher
Story: B. G. DeSylva, Herbert Fields
Producer: Arthur Freed

HAUNTED HARBOR
(Republic, August 26, 1944) 15 Chapters.
Kay Aldridge, Kane Richmond, Roy Barcroft, Clancy Cooper, Marshall Reed, Oscar O'Shea, Forrest Taylor, Hal Taliaferro (Wally Wales), Edward Keane, George J. Lewis, Kenne Duncan, Bud Geary, Robert Homans, Duke Green, Dale Van Sickel, Tom Steele, Robert Wilke, Fred Graham, Jack O'Shea, Ken Terrell, Eddie Parker, Rico de Montez
Director: Spencer Bennet, Wallace Grissell
Screenplay: Royal Cole, Basil Dickey, Jesse Duffy, Grant Nelson, Joseph Poland
Associate Producer: Ronald Davidson
Chapters: (1) Wanted for Murder (2) Flight to Danger (3) Ladder of Death (4) The Unknown Assassin (5) Harbor of Horror (6) Return of the Fugitive (7) Journey into Peril (8) Wings of Doom (9) Death's Door (10) Crimson Sacrifice (11) Jungle Jeopardy (12) Fire Trap (13) Monsters of the Deep (14) High Voltage (15) Crucible of Justice

THE MAN WHO WALKED ALONE
(PRC, March 15, 1945) 65 Mins.
Dave O'Brien, *Kay Aldridge*, Walter Catlett, Guinn "Big Boy" Williams, Smith Ballew, Isabel Randolph, Nancy June Robinson, Ruth Lee, Chester Clute, Vivian Oakland, Vicki Saunders, Robert Hartzell, Charles Williams, Frank Melton, Eddy Waller, Don Brodie, Tom Dugan, William B. Davidson, Jack Mulhall, Tom Kennedy, Elmo Lincoln, Lloyd Ingraham
Director: Christy Cabanne
Screenplay: Robert Lee Johnson
Story: Christy Cabanne

THE PHANTOM OF 42ND STREET
(PRC, May 2, 1945) 58 Mins.
Kay Aldridge, Dave O'Brien, Alan Mowbray, Frank Jenks, Edythe Elliott, Jack Mulhall, Vera Marshe, Stanley Price, John Crawford, Cyril Delevanti, Paul Power, Robert Strange
Director: Albert Herman
Screenplay: Milton Raison
Story: Jack Harvey, Milton Raison
Associate Producers: Martin Mooney, Albert Herman

Lucile Browne

2 • LUCILE BROWNE

Unobtrusively Alluring, She Exercised a Subtle Magnetism

Lucile Browne was not Hollywood's contribution to the era of bathtub gin and flappers, à la Clara Bow, Pola Negri, or Kay Francis. She wasn't diminutive or sultry-looking, versatile, or sophisticated. Rather, she was a vivacious, blue-eyed blonde whose pretty face and natural mannerisms enabled her to captivate almost any male in the audience without much effort. Innocence was her forte and she had a faithful coterie of fans. There was a certain dignity of character about Lucile, an inner warmth that could surface on the screen in a very pleasing way.

Certainly hers is not a name that registers instantly with the average motion picture fan. But to the initiated, Lucile was the sound era's first serial queen of any real importance, preceding Jean Rogers, whose own beauty and personality were similar to Miss Browne's, and following silent-era queen Allene Ray who was also a beautiful, shy blonde.

Lucile was born in Memphis, Tennessee, in 1907 and was educated in the public schools of that city and at National Park Seminary in Washington, D.C. She studied dramatics in Memphis and modeled in New York and Chicago before joining Walton and Prye, a Chicago stock company. After playing juveniles for six months she joined Richard Bennett in Jarnegan. In 1929 she had a small role in an unidentified Pathé picture and became a Fox player in 1930, just as the industry was settling down to the production of talking pictures.

Her film beginning was auspicious, starring opposite George O'Brien in Fox's cinematization of **Last of the Duanes** (1930) by Zane Grey. But she was largely wasted in the Fox features **Soup to Nuts** (1930) and **Young as You Feel** (1931), as well as in Paramount's **Girls About Town** (1931). Lucile was, in fact, peculiarly suited to the cliffhangers and Westerns which became her specialty. She was created to be menaced, to express terror (she was one of serialdom's best screamers), to emote before a wilderness backdrop while bedlam prevailed around her.

Danger Island (1931), viewed today, would probably seem ridiculous and crude. But judging a film in the context of fifty years of subsequent technical progress is not fair to the vintage product. Saturday matinée audiences of 1931 found this story of adventure on an African island quite palatable. They looked forward each week to the exciting continuation of Lucile Browne's and Kenneth Harlan's fight against villainous Walter Miller and Beulah Hutton for a rich radium deposit. One can only conjecture about the number of men and boys who were captivated by the charm of Miss Browne and who envied the giant gorilla that carried her around the jungle before Fay Wray ever thought about **King Kong** (1933).

Battling with Buffalo Bill (1931) gave Lucile her second chance to play the Western lass. This time she was terrorized by outlaws for twelve successive weeks. Tom Tyler and Rex Bell were on hand to see that no serious harm befell her, and she had Ray Taylor as a director again. Because it was a serial, her association with Westerns was quickly established in the minds of Western addicts.

In **The Cannonball Express** (1932), a feature for Sono Art, Lucile played opposite Rex Lease in a suspenseful railroad picture. Then Universal put her into a third serial, **Airmail Mystery** (1932), opposite James Flavin. Ray Taylor was able to elicit a good performance from his principals, though the story line could easily be summarized on a postage stamp. A real-life romance developed between the stars and Lucile married James Flavin shortly after completing the film.

The Mystery Squadron (Mascot, 1933) – Lucile Browne and Bob Steele in one of the Depression era's most popular serials.

In her fourth serial Lucile shared honors with Edwina Booth as one of the Monroe sisters in Mascot's serialization of a James Fenimore Cooper classic, **The Last of the Mohicans** (1932). Harry Carey and Hobart Bosworth, an idol of the silent era, played Hawkeye and Chingachgook, respectively, while Bob Kortman was the evil Huron chief, Magua. Walter Miller was on the side of law and order for a change, as Major Duncan Heyward.

Mystery Squadron (1933) and **The Law of the Wild** (1934) were both made for Mascot and full of the thrill-a-minute action associated with a Mascot cliffhanger. In **Mystery Squadron** Lucile plays the daughter of Lafe McKee, a construction company owner whose attempts to build a power dam are plagued by The Black Ace and his gang. Bob Steele and Guinn "Big Boy" Williams are enlisted to thwart the Squadron and protect the work site. In the process of running down The Black Ace, Bob finds a little time for romancing Lucile. In the latter serial Lucile has Bob Custer as her champion, as well as Rex, King of Wild Horses, and Rin-Tin-Tin, Jr.

On a lucky Saturday, her fans could not only catch Lucile in one of her seventy-two episodic action films (all six of her serials were twelve chapters in length), but could see her as heroine in a prairie saga as well. John Wayne, Ken Maynard, Johnny Mack Brown, Tom Tyler, Gene Autry, Bob Steele, and Buffalo Bill, Jr. all vied for her affection.

Lucile and James Flavin remained happily married for over thirty years, until his death in the late 1960s or early 1970s. They had a son, William, who was a captain in the U.S. Army during the mid-1970s. Lucile appeared on screen only a few times after 1938, devoting most of her time to making a home for her husband and young son. She died on May 10, 1976, at the age of sixty-nine; her death rated only three or four sentences in Variety and other papers, but Lucile Browne will live on for as long as hearts beat in those who were serial-conscious youngsters in the early 1930s. To one small boy of many years ago, now involved in the writing of this book, she was the epitome of femininity, the standard-setter of virginal beauty, the logical successor to serial queen extraordinaire Allene Ray.

LUCILE BROWNE Filmography

LAST OF THE DUANES
(Fox, September 14, 1930) 5580 Ft.
George O'Brien, *Lucile Browne*, Myrna Loy, Nat Pendleton, Walter McGrail, James Mason, Lloyd Ingraham, James Bradbury, Jr., Willard Robertson, Blanche Frederici, Frank Campeau
Director: Alfred L. Werker
Screenplay: Ernest Pascal
Story: Zane Grey
Associate Producers: Edward Butcher, Harold B. Lipsitz

SOUP TO NUTS
(Fox, September 28, 1930) 65 Mins.
Ted Healy, Frances McCoy, Stanley Smith, *Lucile Browne*, Charles Winniger, Hallan Cooley, George Bickel, William H. Tooker, Florence Roberts, Clifford Dempsey, George Chandler, Ted Healy's Racketeers (Moe Howard, Shemp Howard, Larry Fine and Fred Sanborn)
Director: Benjamin Stoloff
Screenplay: Rube Goldberg

YOUNG AS YOU FEEL
(Fox, August 23, 1931) 73 Mins.
Will Rogers, Fifi Dorsay, Lucien Littlefield, Donald Dillaway, Terrance Ray, *Lucile Browne*, Rosalie Roy, C. Henry Gordon, John T. Murray, Brandon Hurst, Marcia Harris, Joan Standing
Director: Frank Borzage
Screenplay: Edwin Burke
Story: George Ade "Father and the Boys"

DANGER ISLAND
(Universal, August 24, 1931) 12 Chapters.
Kenneth Harlan, *Lucile Browne*, Tom Ricketts, Andy Devine, Walter Miller, Everett Brown, George Regas, Beulah Hatton, W. L. Thorne
Director: Ray Taylor
Screenplay: Basil Dickey, Ella O'Neal
Story: Henry McRae
Producer: Henry McRae
Chapters: (1) Coast of Peril (2) Death Rides the Storm (3) Demons of the Pool (4) Devil Worshippers (5) Mutiny (6) The Cat Creeps (7) The Drums of Doom (8) Human Sacrifice (9) The Devil Bird (10) Captures for Sacrifice (11) The Lion's Lair (12) Fire God's Vengeance

GIRLS ABOUT TOWN
(Paramount, October 31, 1931) 66 Mins.
Kay Francis, Joel McCrea, Lilyan Tashman, Eugene Pallette, Allen Dinehart, Lucille Webster Gleason, Anderson Lawler, *Lucile Browne*, George Barbier, Robert McWade, Louise Beavers, Adrienne Ames, Haz Howard, Claire Dodd, Patricia Caron, Judith Wood
Director: George Cukor
Screenplay: Raymond Griffith, Brian Marlowe

BATTLING WITH BUFFALO BILL
(Universal, November 23, 1931) 12 Chapters.
Tom Tyler, Rex Bell, *Lucile Browne*, William Desmond, Francis Ford, Yakima Canutt, Bud Osborne, John Beck, George Regas, Joe Bonomo, Jim Thorpe, Bobbie Nelson, Chief Thunderbird, Edmund Cobb, Fred Humes, Art Mix, Franklyn Farnum
Director: Ray Taylor
Screenplay: George Plympton
Story: Henry McRae (Based on "The Great West That Was" by William F. "Buffalo Bill" Cody)
Dialogue: Ella O'Neill
Producer: Henry McRae
Chapters: (1) Captured by the Redskins (2) Circling Death (3) Between Hostile Tribes (4) The Savage Horde (5) The Fatal Plunge (6) Trapped (7) The Unseen Killer (8) Sentenced to Death (9) The Death Trap (10) A Shot from Ambush (11) The Flaming Death (12) Cheyenne Vengeance

THE CANNONBALL EXPRESS
(Sono Art-World Wide, February 7, 1932) 63 Mins.
Tom Moore, Rex Lease, *Lucile Browne*, Leon Waycoff (Leon Ames), Ruth Renick
Director: Wallace Fox
Screenplay: Bernard McConville
Story: Bernard McConville
Producer: Fanchon Royer

King of the Arena (Universal, 1933) – Lucile Browne, Ken Maynard, and Bobby Nelson.

AIRMAIL MYSTERY
(Universal, March 23, 1932) 12 Chapters.
James Flavin, *Lucile Browne*, Wheeler Oakman, Frank Hagney, Sidney Bracey, Bruce Mitchell, Al Wilson, Walter Brennan, Nelson McDowell, Jack Holley, Matthew Betz, Ethan Laidlaw
Director: Ray Taylor
Screenplay: Basil Dickey, George Plympton, George Morgan
Story: Ella O'Neal
Associate Producer: Henry McRae
Chapters: (1) Pirate of the Air (2) Hovering Death (3) A Leap for Life (4) A Fatal Crash (5) The Hawk Strikes (6) Bridge of Destruction (7) The Hawk's Treachery (8) The Aerial Third Degree (9) Attack on the Mine (10) The Hawk's Lair (11) The Law Strikes (12) The Mail Must Go Through

THE LAST OF THE MOHICANS
(Mascot, May 17, 1932) 12 Chapters.
Harry Carey, Hobart Bosworth, Junior (Frank) Coghlan, Edwina Booth, *Lucile Browne*, Bob Kortman, Walter McGrail, Nelson McDowe, Mischa Auer, Yakima Canutt, Chief Big Tree, Joan Gale, Tully Marshall, Al Craven, Jewel Richford
Director: B. Reeves Eason, Ford Beebe
Screenplay: Colbert Clark, Jack Natteford, Ford Beebe, Wyndham Gittens
Story: James Fenimore Cooper
Producer: Nat Levine
Chapters: (1) Unknown (2) Flaming Arrows (3) Rifles or Tomahawks (4) Riding with Death (5) Red Shadows (6) The Lure of Gold (7) The Crimson Trail (8) The Tide of Battle (9) A Redskin's Honor (10) The Enemy's Stronghold (11) Paleface Magic (12) The End of the Trail

THE TEXAN
(Principal Attraction, 1932)
Jay Wilsey (Buffalo Bill, Jr.), *Lucile Browne*, Jack Mower, Bobby Nelson, Lafe McKee, Yakima Canutt, Art Mix
Director: Cliff Smith
Producer: William Pizor
(Filmed in 1930)

THE DEVIL'S BROTHER (FRA DIAVOLO)
(Roach/MGM, May 5, 1933) 88 Mins.
Stan Laurel, Oliver Hardy, Dennis King, Thelma Todd, James Finlayson, *Lucile Browne*, Arthur Pierson, Henry Armetta, Matt McHugh, Lane Chandler, Nina Quartero, Wilfred Lucas, James C. Morton, Carl Harbaugh, George Miller, Jack Hill, Tiny Sandford, Dick Gilbert, Arthur Stone, John Qualen, Edith Fellows, Jackie Taylor, Rolfe Sedan, Kay Deslys, Lilian Moore, Walter Shumway, Wilfred Lucas, Matt McHugh, Louise Carver, Leo White
Director: Hal Roach, Charles Rogers
Screenplay: Jeanie McPherson
Story: D.F.E. Auber. "Fra Diavolo"
Producer: Hal Roach
(Reissued by Astor Pictures as **Bogus Bandits**)

KING OF THE ARENA
(Universal, June 1, 1933) 61 Mins.
Ken Maynard, *Lucile Browne*, John St. Polis, Robert Kortman, James Marcus, Michael Visaroff, Frank Rice, Jack Rockwell, Bobbie Nelson, Blue Washington, Jack Mower, Iron Eyes Cody, Edward Coxen, Lafe McKee, Fred McKaye, Robert Walker, William Steele, Helen Gibson, Bud McClure, Pascale Perry, Horace B. Carpenter, Jack Kirk, Buck Bucko, Chief Big Tree, Artie Ortego, Merrill McCormack, Bob Burns, Tarzan the Horse
Director: Alan James
Screenplay: Alan James (Alvin J. Neitz)
Story: Hal Berger, Ray Bouk
Producer: Ken Maynard

DOUBLE HARNESS
(RKO, July 21, 1933) 69 Mins.
Ann Harding, William Powell, Henry Stephenson, Lilian Bond, George Meeker, Reginald Owens, *Lucile Browne*, Kay Hammond, Leigh Allen, Hugh Huntley, Wallis Clark
Director: John Cromwell
Screenplay: Jane Murfin
Story: Edward P. Montgomery
Associate Producer: Kenneth MacGowan

FLYING DOWN TO RIO
(RKO-Radio, December 29, 1933) 89 Mins.
Dolores del Rio, Gene Raymond, Raoul Rouline, Ginger Rogers, Fred Astaire, Blanche Frederici, Walter Walker, Etta Moten, Roy D'Arcy, Maurice Black, Armand Kaliz, Paul Porcasi, Reginald Barlow, Eric Blore, Franklin Pangborn, Luis Alberni, Eddie Borden, *Lucile Browne*, Mary Kornman, Clarence Muse, Movita Castaneda, Harry Semels, Gino Corrado, Wallace MacDonald, Betty Furness, Julian Rivero, Alive Ardell, The American Clippers Band, The Brazilian Turunas
Director: Thornton Freeland
Screenplay: Cyril Hume, H. W. Hanemann, Erwin Gelsey
Story: Louis Brock, based on a play by Anne Caldwell
Producer: Lou Brock

MYSTERY SQUADRON
(Mascot, December 30, 1933) 12 Chapters.
Bob Steele, Guinn "Big Boy" Williams, *Lucile Browne*, Jack Mulhall, J. Carrol Naish, Bob Kortman, Purnell Pratt, Robert Frazer, Edward Peil, Sr., Lafe McKee, Edward Hearn, Jack Perrin, Jack Mower, Lew Meehan, Wally Wales
Director: David Howard, Colbert Clark
Producer: Nat Levine
Chapters: (1) The Black Ace (2) The Fatal Warning (3) The Black Ace Strikes (4) Men of Steel (5) The Death Swoop (6) Doomed! (7) Enemy Signals (8) Canyon of Calamity (9) Secret of the Mine (10) Clipped Wings (11) The Beast at Bay (12) The Ace of Aces

ABROAD IN OLD KENTUCKY
(Masquers Club/RKO-Radio, 1933) 2 Reels
Mary Carr, Russell Simpson, *Lucile Browne*, Russell Hopton, Frank McGlynn, Jr.

HIDE-OUT
(M-G-M, August 24, 1934) 82 Mins.
Robert Montgomery, Maureen O'Sullivan, Edward Arnold, Elizabeth Patterson, Whitford Kane, Mickey Rooney, C. Henry Gordon, Muriel Evans, Edward Brophy, Henry Armetta, Herman Bing, Louise Henry, Harold Huber, *Lucile Browne*
Director: W. S. Van Dyke
Screenplay: Frances Goodrich, Albert Hackett
Story: Mauri Garshim

THE LAW OF THE WILD
(Mascot, August, 1934) 12 Chapters.
Rex (King of Wild Horses), Rin-Tin-Tin, Jr., Bob Custer, Ben Turpin, *Lucile Browne,* Richard Cramer, Ernie Adams, Edmund Cobb, Slim Whitaker, Dick Alexander, Jack Rockwell, Wally Wales, Charles King, Lafe McKee, Hank Bell, Art Mix, Bud Osborne, Glenn Strange, Silver Harr, Al Taylor, Jack Evans, Bud McClure, Herman Hack
Director: B. Reeves Eason, Armand Schaefer
Screenplay: Sherman Lowe, B. Reeves Eason
Story: Ford Beebe, John Rathmell, Al Martin
Producer: Nat Levine
Chapters: (1) The Man Killer (2) The Battle of the Strong (3) The Cross-Eyed Goony (4) Avenging Fangs (5) A Dead Man's Hand (6) Horse Thief Justice (7) The Death Stampede (8) The Canyon of Calamity (9) Robber's Roost (10) King of the Range (11) Winner Takes All (12) The Grand Sweepstakes

BRAND OF HATE
(Supreme/William Steiner, November 2, 1934) 63 Mins.
Bob Steele, *Lucile Browne,* William Farnum, Charles K. French, George "Gabby" Hayes, Jack Rockwell, Mickey Rentschiler, Archie Ricks, James Flavin
Director: Lew Collins
Screenplay: Jack Natteford
Story: Jack Natteford
Producer: A. W. Hackel

TEXAS TERROR
(Lone Star/Monogram, February 1, 1935) 51 Mins.
John Wayne, *Lucile Browne,* LeRoy Mason, George "Gabby" Hayes, Buffalo Bill, Jr. (Jay Wilsey), Bert Dillard, John Ince, Yakima Canutt, Bobbie Nelson, Fern Emmett, Henry Rocquemore, Jack Duffy, Bert O'Hara, Eddie Parker
Director: Robert N. Bradbury
Screenplay: Robert N. Bradbury
Story: Robert N. Bradbury
Producer: Paul Malvern

SECRETS OF CHINATOWN
(Northern Films, February, 1935) 63 Mins.
Nick Stuart, *Lucile Browne,* Raymond Lawrence, James Flavin, Henry Hewitson, James McGrath, Reginald Hinds, John Barnard, Arthur Legge-Willis
Director: Fred Newmeyer
Screenplay: Guy Morton
Story: Guy Morton.

RAINBOW VALLEY
(Lone Star/Monogram, March 15, 1935) 52 Mins.
John Wayne, *Lucile Browne,* George "Gabby" Hayes, LeRoy Mason, Buffalo Bill, Jr. (Jay Wilsey), Bert Dillard Lloyd Ingrahm, Lafe McKee, Fern Emmett, Henry Rocquemore, Eddie Parker, Herman Hack, Frank Ellis, Art Dillard, Frank Ball
Director: Robert N. Bradbury
Screenplay: Lindsley Parsons
Story: Lindsley Parsons
Producer: Paul Malvern

ON PROBATION
(Peerless, April, 1935) 60 Mins.
Monte Blue, *Lucile Browne,* William Bakewell, Barbara Bedford, Matthew Betz, Edward J. LeSaint, Betty Jane Graham, Arthur Loft, Henry Rocquemore, Lloyd Ingraham, King Kennedy, James "Hambone" Robinson, Henry Hall, Margaret Sealy, John Webb Dillon, Roy Rice Louise Warner
Director: Charles Hutchinson
Screenplay: Sherman L. Lowe
Story: Crane Wilbur
Producer: Sam Efrus

TUMBLING TUMBLEWEEDS
(Republic, September 5, 1935) 57 Mins.
Gene Autry, Smiley Burnette, *Lucile Browne,* Norma Taylor, George "Gabby" Hayes, Edward Hearn, Jack Rockwell, Frankie Marvin, George Cheesebro, Eugene Jackson, Charles King, Charles Whitaker, George Burton, Tom London, Cornelius Keefe, Tommy Coats, Cliff Lyons, Bud Pope, Tracy Layne, "Champion," Bud McClure, George Morrell, Oscar Gahan, Leonard Slye (Roy Rogers)
Director: Joseph Kane
Screenplay: Ford Beebe
Story: Alan Ludwig
Producer: Nat Levine

WESTERN FRONTIER
(Columbia, September 25, 1935) 59 Mins.
Ken Maynard, *Lucile Browne*, Nora Lane, Robert (Buzz) Henry, Frank Yaconelli, Otis Harlan, Harold Goodwin, Frank Hagney, Gordon S. Griffith, James Marcus, Rodney Hildebrand, Nelson McDowell, Frank Ellis, William Gould, Dick Curtis, Budd Buster, Herman Hack, Horace B. Carpenter, Oscar Gahan, Fred Parker, Charles Whitaker, Art Mix, Victor Potel, Bob Card, William McCall, Tarzan the horse
Director: Al Herman
Screenplay: Nate Gatzert
Story: Ken Maynard
Producer: Larry Darmour

THE CROOKED TRAIL
(Supreme Pictures, July 26, 1936) 59 Mins.
Johnny Mack Brown, *Lucile Browne*, John Merton, Ted Adams, Charles King, Dick Curtis, John Van Pelt, Edward Cassidy, Horace Murphy, Earl Dwire, Artie Ortego, Roger Williams
Director: S. Roy Luby
Screenplay: George Plympton
Story: George Plympton
Producer: A. W. Hackel

CHEYENNE RIDES AGAIN
(Victory, January 7, 1937) 56 Mins.
Tom Tyler, *Lucile Browne*, Jimmy Fox, Creighton Chaney (Lon Chaney, Jr.), Roger Williams, Carmen LaRoux, Edward Cassidy, Ted Lorch, Bud Pope, Francis Walker, Slim Whitaker, Merrill McCormack, Wilbur H. McCauley, Tommy Rix
Director: Bob Hill
Screenplay: Basil Dickey
Story: Basil Dickey
Producer: Sam Katzman

DEAD END
(United Artists, August 27, 1937) 93 Mins.
Sylvia Sidney, Joel McCrea, Humphrey Bogart, Wendy Barrie, Claire Trevor, Allen Jenkins, Marjorie Main, Billy Halop, Huntz Hall, Bobby Jordon, Leo Gorcey, Gabriel Dell, Bernard Punsley, Charles Peck, Minor Watson, James Burke, Ward Bond, Elizabeth Risdon, Esther Dale, George Humbert, Marcelle Corday, Jerry Cooper, Bud Gearty, Tom Ricketts, Esther Howard, Wesley Girard, Don Barry, Earl Askam, *Lucile Browne*
Director: William Wyler
Screenplay: Lillian Hellman
Story: Sidney Kingsley--"Dead End"

THE STORY OF ELIAS HOWE
(Fools Who Made History No. 1)
(Columbia, October, 1939) 11 Mins.
Richard Fiske, *Lucile Browne*, Lindsay MacHarrie
(Commentary)
Director: Jan Leman
Story: Jan Leman
Producer: Hugh McCollum

WIFE TO SPARE
(Columbia, November 20, 1947) 2 Reels
Andy Clyde, Christine McIntyre, *Lucille Browne*, Dick Wessel, Vera Lewis, Murray Alper, Heinie Conklin
Director: Edward Bernds

A WOMAN OF DISTINCTION
(Columbia, April, 1950) 85 Mins.
Ray Milland, Rosalind Russell, Edmund Gwenn, Janis Carter, Mary Jane Saunders, Francis Lederer, Jerome Courtland, Alex Gerry, Charles Evans, Charlotte Wynters, Clifton Young, Gale Gordon, Jean Willes, Wanda McKay, Elizabeth Flournoy, Harry Tyler, Billy Newell, Charles Trowbridge, Harry Strang, Donald Kerr, Mira McKinney, Leah Tyler, Lois Hall, Myron Healey, Edward Keane, *Lucile Browne*, Marie Blake, Walter Sande, Maxine Gates, Lucille Ball (Unbilled Cameo)
Director: Edward Buzzell
Screenplay: Charles Hoffman
Story: Hugh and Ian McClellan Butler
Producer: Buddy Adler

NO SAD SONGS FOR ME
(Columbia, May, 1950) 89 Mins.
Margaret Sullavan, Wendell Corey, Viveca Lindfors, Natalie Wood, John McIntire, Ann Doran, Richard Quine, Jeanette Nolan, Dorothy Tree, Raymond Greenleaf, Urylee Leonardos, Harlan Warde, Margo Woode, Harry Cheshire, Douglas Evans, Sumner Getchell, *Lucile Browne*
Director: Rudolph Mate
Screenplay: Howard Koch
Story: Ruth Southard
Producer: Buddy Adler

Phyllis Coates, one of the loveliest of serial heroines.

3 • PHYLLIS COATES

Beautiful and Talented, She Was Hollywood's Last Try at a Serial Queen

Like any other star, Phyllis Coates was neither quite unique not wholly representative. Her range of abilities was greater than that possessed by most serial and Western heroines, she was strikingly beautiful, and she was athletic enough to cope with the rigors of action films. And she was the last serial queen.

In **Panther Girl of the Congo** (1955) Phyllis received top billing over her leading man, Myron Healey. Only three serial actresses in Republic's twenty-year history had been so billed- Frances Gifford in **Jungle Girl** (1941), Kay Aldridge in **The Perils of Nyoka** (1942), and Adrian Booth in **Daughter of Don Q** (1946). Not even Linda Stirling in **The Tiger Woman** (1944) had received top-billing distinction. Possibly Republic had hoped to create in Phyllis a serial queen on the order of Pearl White, but it was a little late for that. The studio made only one more serial. In fact, only three serials were released after **Panther Girl of the Congo**, one by Republic and two by Columbia. That was it-- the end of an era and the end of the line for what had once been a profitable and popular film genre.

Certainly Phyllis was a good choice for the last-ditch effort to inject life into the cliffhanger film, for she was attractive and she could act. But the production values of the film were just not there to back her up. Both Phyllis and Myron Healey did their best, but their abilities could only go so far in overcoming the inadequacies of the low-budget, poorly scripted, stock-footage-padded film. Phyllis played Jean Evans, a photographer-guide in Africa who thwarts a scientist's attempts to mine diamonds illegally by scaring off the native population with giant crayfish he has developed.

Phyllis had received second billing to Clayton Moore in an earlier serial, also set in Africa. In **Jungle Drums of Africa** (1953) she had played the daughter of a medical missionary carrying on in her father's place after his death. She befriended Moore and his partner, who were prospecting for uranium, and they were all in constant peril from those who wanted the uranium for themselves and from the native witchdoctor who had it in for Phyllis. This serial, too, had been interesting enough to the juvenile audience, but the product itself was becoming impotent by this time.

Between the two Republic cliffhangers Phyllis had played the heroine in one of Columbia's last chapter plays, **Gunfighters of the Northwest** (1954), but the Columbia product was even shoddier than Republic's and did nothing to sustain or promote interest in the genre. It was unfortunate that such an attractive and talented girl could not have been discovered and promoted five or ten years earlier. She had what it took to become a real serial star.

In her Westerns she was believable, although she sometimes got bogged down in pedestrian screenplays. Her heroine was often the strong, self-sufficient type, but less brassy than Dale Evans' heroine. Serious film critics and historians usually relegate her to a minor place in their works, if they mention her at all.

Phyllis was perfect as the wife of George O'Hanlon in the Joe McDoakes series of one-reel comedies at Warners. She took the role in 1948 and stayed through 1953. In 1956 she returned for the final entry in the long-running series.

She also had a successful television career. Her best-remembered characterization is that of Lois Lane on the "Superman" series, before Noel Neill took over. During the summer season of 1954 she was featured as the girlfriend of Paul Gilbert on "The Duke," a series about a retired prize fighter. Her talent was utilized in such television shows as "Jewelers Showcase," "G. E. Theatre," "Death Valley Days," "Perry Mason," "The Untouch-

Jungle Drums of Africa (Republic, 1953) – Phyllis Coates and Clayton Moore (TV's "The Lone Ranger").

ables," "Rawhide," "Gunslinger," "Hennesey," and "Black Saddle."

Phyllis, whose nonprofessional name is Gypsie Ann Stell, came from Wichita Falls, Texas, where she was born in 1927. In 1948 she married film director-writer Richard Bare. The marriage failed, and in 1950 she married Robert L. Nelms, a dance band pianist, by whom she had a son, Christopher. In 1953 she was granted a divorce when she testified that Nelms had left her with no intention of returning (contending that married life was too much of a responsibility for a musician). Later she married Norman Tokar, a CBS-TV director.

In spite of her good roles in more expensively mounted productions, it is as Panther Girl and Lois Lane that she is likely to be remembered, and as Carol Bryant in **Jungle Drums of Africa** and Rio in **Gunfighters of the Northwest**. In these she provided entertainment, not art. And she can be proud that action-loving audiences accepted her open-heartedly in the closing days of the "B" film.

PHYLLIS COATES Filmography

SO YOU WANT TO BE IN POLITICS
(Warner Bros., October 2, 1948) 1 Reel
George O'Hanlon, *Phyllis Coates*, Clifton Young, Fred Kelsey
Director: Richard L. Bare

SO YOU WANT TO BE A MUSCLEMAN
(Warner Bros., July 2, 1949) 1 Reel
George O'Hanlon, *Phyllis Coates*
Director: Richard L. Bare

SO YOU'RE HAVING IN-LAW TROUBLE
(Warner Bros., August 27, 1949) 1 Reel
George O'Hanlon, *Phyllis Coates*, Clifton Young, Willard Waterman
Director: Richard L. Bare

SO YOU WANT TO HOLD YOUR HUSBAND
(Warner Bros., July 1, 1950) 1 Reel
George O'Hanlon, *Phyllis Coates*
Director: Richard L. Bare

BLUES BUSTERS
(Monogram, October 29, 1950) 64 Mins.
Leo Gorcey, Huntz Hall, Adele Jergens, Craig Stevens, Gabriel Dell, *Phyllis Coates*, Bernard Gorcey, William Benedict, David Gorcey
Director: William Beaudine
Screenplay: Charles R. Marion
Producer: Jan Grippo

OUTLAWS OF TEXAS
(Monogram, December 10, 1950) 56 Mins.
Whip Wilson, Andy Clyde, *Phyllis Coates*, Terry Frost, Tommy Farrell, Zon Murray, George DeNormand, Steve Carr, Stanley Price
Director: Thomas Carr
Screenplay: Dan Ullman
Producer: Vincent M. Fennelly

MAN FROM SONORA
(Monogram, March 11, 1951) 54 Mins.
Johnny Mack Brown, *Phyllis Coates*, Lyle Talbot, House Peters, Jr., Lee Roberts, John Merton, Stanley Price, Dennis Moore, Ray Jones, Pierce Lyden, Sam Flint, George DeNormand
Director: Lewis Collins
Screenplay: Maurice Tombragel
Producer: Vincent M. Fennelly

CANYON RAIDERS
(Monogram, April 8, 1951) 54 Mins.
Whip Wilson, Fuzzy Knight, Jim Bannon, *Phyllis Coates*, I. Stanford Jolley, Barbara Woodell, Marshall Reed, Riley Hill, Bill Kennedy
Director: Lewis Collins
Screenplay: Jay Gilgore
Producer: Vincent M. Fennelly

SO YOU WANT TO BE A COWBOY
(Warner Bros., April 14, 1951) 1 Reel
George O'Hanlon, *Phyllis Coates*
Director: Richard L. Bare

NEVADA BADMEN
(Monogram, May 27, 1951) 58 Mins.
Whip Wilson, Fuzzy Knight, Jim Bannon, *Phyllis Coates*, I. Stanford Jolley, Marshall Reed, Riley Hill, Lee Roberts, Pierce Lyden, Bill Kennedy, Bud Osborne, Stanley Price, Artie Ortego, Carl Mathews
Director: Lewis Collins
Screenplay: Joseph O'Donnell
Producer: Vincent M. Fennelly

SO YOU WANT TO BUY A USED CAR
(Warner Bros., July 28, 1951) 1 Reel
George O'Hanlon, *Phyllis Coates*, Fred Kelsey
Director: Richard L. Bare

SO YOU WANT TO BE A BACHELOR
(Warner Bros., September 22, 1951) 1 Reel
George O'Hanlon, *Phyllis Coates*, Ted Stanhope, Chester Clute, Jack Rice, Fred Kelsey
Director: Richard L. Bare

SO YOU WANT TO BE A PLUMBER
(Warner Bros., November 19, 1951) 1 Reel
George O'Hanlon, *Phyllis Coates*, Rodney Bell
Director: Richard L. Bare

THE LONGHORN
(Monogram, November 25, 1951) 70 Mins.
Bill Elliott, Myron Healey, *Phyllis Coates*, Lane Bradford, Stan Jolley, Marshall Reed, Marshall Bradford, William Fawcett, Zon Murray, Lee Roberts, John Hart, Steve Clark, Carol Henry
Director: Lewis Collins
Screenplay: Dan Ullman
Producer: Vincent M. Fennelly

STAGE TO BLUE RIVER
(Monogram, December 30, 1951) 55 Mins.
Whip Wilson, Fuzzy Knight, *Phyllis Coates*, Lee Roberts, John Hart, Lane Bradford, Pierce Lyden, Terry Frost, I. Stanford Jolley, William Fawcett, Steve Clark, Stanley Price, Bud Osborne
Director: Lewis Collins
Screenplay: Joseph Poland
Producer: Vincent M. Fennelly

SO YOU WANT TO GET IT WHOLESALE
(Warner Bros., January 12, 1952) 1 Reel
George O'Hanlon, *Phyllis Coates*, Rodney Bell, Frank Nelson, Ted Stanhope, Charles Sullivan, Richard Reeves, Jack Mower, George Penbroke
Director: Richard L. Bare

THE GUNMAN
(Monogram, April 13, 1952) 52 Mins.
Whip Wilson, Fuzzy Knight, *Phyllis Coates*, Rand Brooks, Terry Frost, Lane Bradford, I. Stanford Jolley, Gregg Barton, Russ Whiteman, Richard Avonde, Robert Bray
Director: Lewis Collins
Screenplay: Fred Myton
Producer: Vincent M. Fennelly

SO YOU'RE GOING TO A CONVENTION
(Warner Bros., June 7, 1952) 1 Reel
George O'Hanlon, *Phyllis Coates*, Connie Cezan
Director: Richard L. Bare

FARGO
(Monogram, September 7, 1952) 69 Mins.
Bill Elliott, *Phyllis Coates*, Myron Healey, Fuzzy Knight, Jack Ingram, Arthur Space, Bob Wilke, Terry Frost, Robert Bray, Tim Ryan, Florence Lake, Stanley Andrews, Richard Reeves, Gene Roth
Director: Lewis Collins
Screenplay: Joseph Poland, Jack DeWitt
Producer: Vincent M. Fennelly

CANYON AMBUSH
(Monogram, October 12, 1952) 53 Mins.
Johnny Mack Brown, *Phyllis Coates*, Lee Roberts, Dennis Moore, Denver Pyle, Pierce Lyden, Hugh Prosser, Marshall Reed, Stanley Price, Bill Koontz, Frank Ellis, Russ Whiteman, Carol Henry, George DeNormand
Director: Lewis Collins
Screenplay: Joseph Poland
Producer: Vincent M. Pennelly

SO YOU WANT TO WEAR THE PANTS
(Warner Bros., November 8, 1952) 1 Reel
George O'Hanlon, *Phyllis Coates*
Director: Richard L. Bare

INVASION USA
(American/Columbia, 1953) 74 Mins.
Gerald Mohr, Peggie Castle, Dan O'Herlihy, Robert Bice, Tom Kennedy, *Phyllis Coates*, Wade Crosby, Erik Blythe
Director: Alfred E. Green
Screenplay: Robert Smith
Producer: Robert Smith

WYOMING ROUNDUP
(Monogram, November 9, 1952) 53 Mins.
Whip Wilson, *Phyllis Coates*, Tommy Farrell, Henry Rowland, House Peters, Jr., I. Stanford Jolley, Richard Emory, Bob Wilke, Stanley Price
Director: Thomas Carr
Screenplay: Dan Ullman
Producer: Vincent M. Fennelly

FLATTOP
(Monogram, November 30, 1952) 85 Mins.
Sterling Hayden, Richard Carlson, John Bromfield, William Phipps, Keith Larsen, William Schallert, Todd Kerns, *Phyllis Coates*, Walter Coy
Director: Lesley Selander
Screenplay: Steve Fisher
Story: Steve Fisher
Producer: Walter Mirisch

THE MAVERICK
(Allied Artists, December 14, 1952) 71 Mins.
Bill Elliott, *Phyllis Coates*, Myron Healey, Richard Reeves, Terry Frost, Rand Brooks, Russell Hicks, Robert Bray, Florence Lake, Gregg Barton, Denver Pyle, Robert Wilke, Eugene Roth, Joel Allen
Director: Thomas Carr
Screenplay: Sid Theil
Producer: Vincent M. Fennelly

JUNGLE DRUMS OF AFRICA
(Republic, December 19, 1952) 12 Chapters
Phyllis Coates, Clayton Moore, Johnny Spencer, Roy Glenn, Sr., John Cason, Henry Rowland, Steve Mitchell, Bill Walker, Don Blackman, Felix Nelson, Joel Fluellen, Bill Washington, Tom Steele, Robert Davis, Roy Engel, Bob Johnson, Joe Yrigoyen, DeForest Covan, Walter Smith, Maxie Thrower
Director: Fred C. Brannon
Screenplay: Ronald Davidson
Associate Producer: Franklin Adreon
Chapters: (1) Jungle Ambush (2) Savage Strategy (3) The Beast-Fiend (4) Voodoo Vengeance (5) The Lion Pit (6) Underground Tornado (7) Cavern of Doom (8) The Water Trap (9) Trail to Destruction (10) The Flaming Ring (11) Bridge of Death (12) The Avenging River
(A feature version titled **U-238 and the Witch Doctor** was released in 1955)

The Maverick (Allied Artists, 1952) – Phyllis Coates and Bill Elliott.

MARSHAL OF CEDAR ROCK
(Republic, February 1, 1953) 54 Mins.
Allan Lane, Eddy Waller, *Phyllis Coates*, Roy Barcroft, Bill Henry, Robert Shayne, John Crawford, John Hamilton, Kenneth MacDonald, Herbert Lytton, "Black Jack" (a horse)
Director: Harry Keller
Screenplay: Albert DeMond
Story: M. Coates Webster
Associate Producer: Rudy Ralston

SO YOU WANT A TELEVISION SET
(Warner Bros., May 23, 1953) 1 Reel
George O'Hanlon, *Phyllis Coates*, Rodney Bell, Phil Van Zant, Fred Kelsey, Doris Day, Gordon MacRae
Director: Richard L. Bare

SO YOU LOVE YOUR DOG
(Warner Bros., August 1, 1953) 1 Reel
George O'Hanlon, *Phyllis Coates*
Director: Richard L. Bare

TOPEKA
(Allied Artist, August 9, 1953) 69 Mins.
Bill Elliott, *Phyllis Coates*, Rick Vallin, Fuzzy Knight, John James, Denver Pyle, Dick Crockett, Harry Lauter, Dale Van Sickel, Ted Mapes, Henry Rowland, Edward Clark
Director: Thomas Carr
Screenplay: Milton M. Raison
Producer: Vincent M. Fennelly

EL PASO STAMPEDE
(Republic, September 8, 1953) 54 Mins.
Allan Lane, Eddy Waller, *Phyllis Coates*, Stephen Chase, Roy Barcroft, Edward Clark, Tom Monroe, Stanley Andrews, William Tannen, John Hamilton, "Black Jack" (a horse)
Director: Harry Keller
Screenplay: Arthur Orloff
Associate Producer: Rudy Ralston

SO YOU THINK YOU CAN'T SLEEP
(Warner Bros., October 31, 1953) 1 Reel
George O'Hanlon, *Phyllis Coates*, Ted Stanhope, Fred Kelsey
Director: Richard L. Bare

SO YOU WANT TO BE AN HEIR
(Warner Bros., December 19, 1953) 1 Reel
George O'Hanlon, *Phyllis Coates*, Phil Van Zandt
Director: Richare L. Bare

SO YOU'RE HAVING NEIGHBOR TROUBLE
(Warner Bros., February 30, 1954) 1 Reel
George O'Hanlon, *Phyllis Coates*, Rodney Bell
Director: Richare L. Bare

GUNFIGHTERS OF THE NORTHWEST
(Columbia, April 15, 1954) 15 Chapters
Jack (Jock) Mahoney, *Phyllis Coates*, Clayton Moore, Don Harvey, Marshall Reed, Rodd Redwing, Lyle Talbot, Tommy Farrell, Lee Roberts, Terry Frost, Joe Allen, Jr., Gregg Barton, Chief Yowlachie, Pierce Lyden, John Hart, Gene Roth
Director: Spencer G. Bennet
Screenplay: Arthur Hoerl, Royal K. Cole, George H. Plympton
Producer: Sam Katzman
Chapters: (1) A Trap for the Mounties (2) Indian War Drums (3) Between Two Fires (4) Midnight Raiders (5) Running the Gauntlet (6) Mounties at Bay (7) Plunge of Peril (8) Killer at Large (9) The Fighting Mounties (10) The Sergeant Gets his Man (11) The Fugitive Escapes (12) Stolen Gold (13) Perils of the Mounted Police (14) Surprise Attack (15) Trail's End

PANTHER GIRL OF THE KONGO
(Republic, January 3, 1955) 12 Chapters
Phyllis Coates, Myron Healey, Arthur Space, John Daheim, Mike Ragan, Morris Buchanan, Roy Glenn, Sr., Archie Savage, Ramsay Hill, Naaman Brown, Dan Ferniel, James Logan, Gene Stutenroth, Fred Graham, Charles Sullivan, Steve Calvert, Keith McConnell, DeForest Covan, Daniel Elam, Wesley Gale, Alan Reynolds, Martin Wilkins, Tom Steele, Don Carlos
Director: Franklin Adreon
Screenplay: Ronald Davidson
Associate Producer: Franklin Adreon

SO YOUR WIFE WANTS TO WORK
(Warner Bros., July 14, 1956) 1 Reel
George O'Hanlon, *Phyllis Coates*, Emory Parnell
Director: Richard L. Bare

GIRLS IN PRISON
(Golden Gate/American-International, 1956) 67 Mins.
Richard Denning, Joan Taylor, Adele Jergens, Helen Gilbert, Lane Fuller, Jane Darwell, Raymond Hatton, *Phyllis Coates*, Diana Darrin, Mae Marsh, Laurie Mitchell, Diane Richards, Luana Walters, Riza Royce
Director: Edward L. Cahn
Screenplay: Lou Rusoff
Producer: Alex Gordon

CHICAGO CONFIDENTIAL
(Peerless/United Artists, September, 1957) 74 Mins.
Brian Keith, Beverly Garland, Dick Foran, Beverly Tyler, Elisha Cook, Paul Langton, Tony George, Jack Lambert, Douglas Kennedy, Gavin Gordon, *Phyllis Coates*, Jim Bannon, Dennis Moore, John Morley, Joe McGuinn, Henry Rowland, Mark Scott, Jack Kenney, John Hamilton
Director: Sidney Salkow
Screenplay: Robert T. Marcus
Producer: Robert E. Kent

I WAS A TEENAGE FRANKENSTEIN
(Santa Rosa Prod./American-International, November, 1957) 74 Mins.
Whit Bissell, *Phyllis Coates*, Robert Burton, Gary Conway, George Lynn, John Cliff, Claudia Bryar, Charles Steel, Paul Keast
Director: Herbert L. Stock
Screenplay: Kenneth Langtry
Story: Kenneth Langtry
Producer: Herman Cohen

BLOOD ARROW
(Emirau-Regal, April 1, 1958)
Scott Brady, Paul Richards, *Phyllis Coates*, Don Haggerty, Rocky Shahan, Des Slatterty, Bill McGraw, Patrick O'Moore, Jeanne Bates, Richard Gilden, John Dierkes, Diana Darrin
Director: Charles Marquis Warren
Screenplay: Fred Freiberger
Producer: Robert Stabler

CATTLE EMPIRE
(20th Century-Fox, April 15, 1958) 83 Mins.
Joel McCrea, Gloria Talbott, Don Haggerty, *Phyllis Coates*, Bing Russell, Paul Brinegar, Hal K. Dawson, Duane Gray, Richard Shannon, Charles Gray, Patrick O'Moore, Bill McGraw, Jack Lomas, Steve Raines, Rocky Shahan, Nesdon Booth, Bill Hale, Ronald Poster, Howard B. Culver, Edward Jauregui, Ted Smile
Director: Charles Marquis Warren
Story: Daniel B. Ullman

Panther Girl of the Congo (Republic, 1955) – Phyllis Coates.

INCREDIBLE PETRIFIED WORLD
(Governor Films, April, 1960) 70 Mins.
John Carradine, *Phyllis Coates*, Robert Clarke, Allen Windsor, Sheila Noonan, George Skaff, Maurice Bernard, Joe Maierhouser, Harry Raven, Lloyd Nelson, Jack Haffner
Director: Jerry Warren
Producer: Jerry Warren

THE BABY MAKER
(Robert Wise Prod./National General, October 1, 1970) 109 Mins.
Barbara Hershey, Collin Wilcox-Horne, Sam Groom, Scott Glenn, Jeannie Berlin, Lili Valenty, Helena Kallianioles, Jeff Siggins, *Phyllis Coates*, Madge Kennedy, Ray Hemphill
Director: James Bridges
Producer: Richard Goldstone

(Segments of "The Adventures of Superman" Television Series in Which Phyllis Coates Appeared)
(All in 1951)

Superman on Earth
The Haunted Lighthouse
The Case of the Talkative Dummy
The Mystery of the Broken Statues
The Monkey Mystery
A Night of Terror
The Birthday Letter
The Mind Machine
Rescue
The Secret of Superman
No Holds Barred
The Deserted Village
The Stolen Costume
Mystery in Wax
Treasure of the Incas
Double Trouble

The Runaway Robot
Drums of Death
The Evil Three
Riddle of the Chinese Jade
The Human Bomb
Czar of the Underworld
The Ghost Wolf
Crime Wave
The Unknown People (2 parter)

4 • GRACE CUNARD

A Heroine Not to Be Bound by Rules and Conventions

Her appearance in thirteen silent serials assured Grace Cunard of her status as one of the great serial performers. Her real name was Harriet Mildred Jeffries, and she was born in Columbus, Ohio, on April 8, 1893. At the age of thirteen she persuaded her mother to let her go on the road with a stock company in a play called Tora Thorne. (Her mother accompanied her.) During the next two or three years Grace gained knowledge of the stage in plays with Eddie Foy, Louis Mann, and other professionals of the day.

Around 1910 Grace received an invitation to enter the movies. Although a movie career was not socially acceptable at that time, she decided to give it a try, especially since the play she was in had folded. **The Duke's Plan** (1910) for Biograph may have been her first picture. She didn't hit it off too well with D. W. Griffith, however, and soon left Biograph to appear in many short films for Broncho, Kay-Bee, Bison, and Republic during the years 1910-1913.

In 1912 Grace made the acquaintance of Francis Ford (whose real name was Frank Feeney), older brother of director John Ford. Francis was both director and actor and, when required, scenario writer, film editor, cameraman, stagehand, and anything else that might be needed to put a motion picture together. Most of all he was an independent thinker--imaginative, flamboyant, confident, and a ready gambler with studio money.

Grace had already found that she had a flair for writing and she soon learned that she shared much in common with Ford. They worked well together. Believing that a partnership with herself as writer-actress and Ford as director-actor would prove successful, she approached him on the idea of teaming up. Like Grace, Francis disliked restraint and wanted more control as a creative artist. They bided their time until Universal invited Grace to join the company; she insisted on bringing Ford with her. The two formed a working relationship (so far as is known, there was never a romance) that was one of the longest-lasting and most successful in early Hollywood, beginning possibly with **Sundered Ties** (1912) and ending with **The Chinatown Mystery** (1928).

After the team joined Universal, things begin to pick up for them. Here they found the environment that allowed their fertile talents to grow and flower--until years later when Carl Laemmle decided it was time to cut the grass. The couple co-starred in, directed, and wrote a series of historical films, Westerns, and melodramas that included **The Battle of Bull Run** (1913), **Texas Kelly at Bay** (1913), **An Orphan of War** (1913), **The Belle of Yorktown** (1913), **In the Fall of '64** (1914), **The Bride of Mystery** (1914), **Sheridan's Pride** (1914), and **Washington at Valley Forge** (1914). **In The Mysterious Leopard Lady** (1914) Grace created her popular character My Lady Raffles, a jewel thief with a delightful devil-may-care attitude. The film proved popular and was followed by **The Mystery of the White Car** (1914), in which she played the same character. Ford played a superhuman detective out to apprehend her in both films.

Two films deserve special mention by reason of technical innovations and imagination. In **The Twin's Double** (1914) Grace played the parts of twin sisters and an unrelated look-alike. All three women were seen on the screen at the same time, thanks to cameraman Al Siegler's expertise. The film proved so popular that **The Return of the Twin's Double** (1914) appeared several months later.

In April of 1914 Grace and Francis had completed a two-reel film about spies in the Philippines, but it had not yet been released.

29

The Broken Coin (Universal, 1915) – Grace Cunard in a scene from Episode No. 11.

Isadore Bernstein, manager of the West Coast division of Universal, persuaded the two to embark on the production of a serial, using the two-reeler as the initial chapter and launching pad for the remaining episodes. Universal boss Carl Laemmle felt that he had to enter serial production to compete with Edison, Kalem, Pathé, and Thanhouser, all of which were rushing to cash in on the popularity of serials. This had started with the success of **What Happened to Mary?** (1912) and **The Adventures of Kathlyn** (1913), both tied to newspaper and magazine serializations of the same stories. Laemmle had a weakness for teams, and it was not hard to convince him that a Cunard-Ford combination might be a rewarding one. What better way to begin than with a winning team already recognized as successful in the outdoor department? The episodic action thriller seemed ideal for their talents.

When Cunard and Ford expressed enthusiasm for the idea, the two-reeler was expanded into a fifteen-chapter serial titled **Lucille Love, Girl of Mystery** (1914), with Grace playing the heroine menaced by Ford as the villain Hugo who pursued her around the world in an attempt to steal a valuable map from her. The film hit the market just ahead of Pearl White's **The Perils of Pauline** (1914). The Cunard serial boasted hundreds of players and fabulous outdoor sets, unlike the serials of the 1930s and 1940s.

The movie-going public became enmeshed in the adventures of Grace, and Universal's coffers swelled with the profits. This success prompted Carl Laemmle to commit Universal wholeheartedly to serial production, which continued through 1946--32 years, 139 serials, 1,911 pulse-pounding episodes, and roughly four million feet of film.

Grace portrayed almost every type of woman from tomboy to queen in her long series of Universal shorts with Francis Ford, but it was the serials that immortalized her in films. **The Broken Coin** (1915), in twenty-two chapters, was one of the most sensational and thrilling films produced up to that time, and its success made movie history. Ford directed, and Grace wrote the scenario based on an Emerson Hough story. Eddie Polo and Jack Holt, both on the verge of stardom themselves, had parts as heavies, as did John Ford, who soon gave up acting in favor of directing Westerns for Universal.

The Adventures of Peg o' the Ring (1916) was another popular serial directed and written by Francis and Grace, who also played the lead roles. At one point in production Carl Laemmle had them taken off the film and their roles assigned to Ruth Stonehouse and Eddie Polo, for reasons undisclosed. Cunard interceded with Laemmle and the Ford-Cunard team was reinstated. Ruth Stonehouse, who appeared in the film in a supporting role, asked for and received her release from the studio shortly thereafter.

More short films followed, and then the serial **The Purple Mask** (1916). In the story Grace is a lady Robin Hood who leaves a purple mask as her sign after each robbery. Ford is the detective bent on capturing her. In the end, of course, Grace gives up her Robin Hood life to marry Ford. Costs of production ran high and returns were disappointing. Again, Cunard and Ford had directed and written the film. They were considered unmanageable by Universal's front office and their spendthrift ways were not endearing them to Carl Laemmle, who made an attempt to break them up as a team. Grace was put into several five-reel features that did nothing to advance her career. In 1919 she was cast opposite Elmo Lincoln in **Elmo, the Mighty**, directed by Henry McRae. Her work in this serial, plus acting in and writing the long succession of shorter films, had exhausted her physically and emotionally. She was unable to do **Elmo, the Fearless** (1920), her next scheduled serial. Universal gave the part to Louise Lorraine and did not renew Grace's contract when it expired.

When she was able to face the grind again, Grace worked in the independent market. A few two-reel Westerns were made in a contracted series of twenty-six, but the company went broke. She even appeared once more with Francis Ford, in a cheap production called **The Woman of Mystery** (1922). But it was probably put together from footage shot for **The Purple Mask** (1916) and spirited away by Ford or someone else. Author Eldon Everett, who has written an excellent piece on Cunard and Ford, says that it was probably the last chapter shot for **The Purple Mask** but never delivered to the studio. Evidently it was composed mostly of superfluous footage retained by Ford for later use. Ultimately Grace worked again for Universal, appearing in several serials and features, but as a featured player, not as a star.

In 1928 Syndicate made **The Chinatown Mystery**, with direction by J. P. McGowan and story by Francis Ford. Appearing in the serial as principals were Joe Bonomo, Ruth Hiatt, and Francis Ford, while Grace Cunard, Peggy O'Day, Rosemary Theby, and Helen Gibson, along with other old-timers, ably supported. It was the last time Ford and Cunard worked together.

Grace married stuntman Jack Shannon in 1925. It was her second marriage and a lasting one. Although she worked until the early 1940s, mostly at Universal, her roles were small. Her last good part was in **Last Man on Earth** (1924), a science fiction comedy in which she was a gangster out to collect from the all-female government a ransom for the only male survivor on Earth.

On January 19, 1967, Grace Cunard died at the Motion Picture Country Home after a long bout with cancer. She was survived by her husband, Jack Shannon, and her sister, former actress Mina Cunard.

GRACE CUNARD Filmography

THE DUKE'S PLAN
(American Biograph, February 12, 1910) 1 Reel
Frank Grandin, Marion Leonard, Owen Moore, Linda Arvidson, Charles Craig, *Grace Cunard*
Director: D. W. Griffith
Screenplay: D. W. Griffith

BEFORE YORKTOWN
(Republic, December, 1911) 1 Reel
Grace Cunard

SUNDERED TIES
(Broncho, September, 1912)
Francis Ford, Red Wing, Jack Conway, *Grace Cunard*
Director: Francis Ford

CUSTER'S LAST RAID
(101 Bison, October, 1912) 3 Reels
Francis Ford, Anna Little, *Grace Cunard*, William Eagleshirt, J. Barney Sherry, Charles K. French, Lillian Christie, "Snowball," Art Acord
Director: Thomas H. Ince
Screenplay: Richard V. Spencer
Camera: Ray Smallwood

AN INDIAN LEGEND
(Broncho, October, 1912)
Grace Cunard, Francis Ford, Sherman Bainbridge
Director: Charles Giblyn
Screenplay: H. G. Stafford

HIS SQUAW
(Broncho, November, 1912) 2 Reels
Rhea Mitchell, Sherman Bainbridge, *Grace Cunard*, William Eagleshirt, Francis Ford
Director: Charles Giblyn
Screenplay: Monte Katterjohn

THE WHITE VAQUERO
(Universal, 1912) 1 Reel
Grace Cunard, Francis Ford

THE FAVORITE SON
(Kay-Bee, January, 1913) 2 Reels
Joe King, Charles Ray, *Grace Cunard*, Francis Ford
Director: Francis Ford

THE SHARPSHOOTER
(Broncho, February, 1913) 2 Reels
Charles Ray, *Grace Cunard*, Edgar Keller
Director: Charles Giblyn
Screenplay: H. G. Stafford

THE TELLTALE HAT BAND
(Kay-Bee, February, 1913)
Francis Ford, *Grace Cunard*, Helen Case, Jack Conway, Robert Stanton
Director: Francis Ford
Screenplay: C. Gardner Sullivan

THE BATTLE OF BULL RUN
(Bison, March, 1913) 3 Reels
Grace Cunard, Ray Myers, William Clifford, Victoria Forde

The Broken Coin (Universal, 1915) – Grace Cunard, Francis Ford (going out of window), Jack Holt (on floor), and John Ford (holding Grace).

TEXAS KELLY AT BAY
(Kay-Bee, March, 1913)
Francis Ford, *Grace Cunard*, Ethel Grandin
Director: Francis Ford

THE STARS AND STRIPES FOREVER
(Bison, May, 1913) 3 Reels
Grace Cunard

AN ORPHAN OF WAR
(Kay-Bee, August, 1913) 2 Reels
Francis Ford, *Grace Cunard*, Cyril Gottleib
Director: Francis Ford

CAPTAIN BILLY'S MATE
(Bison, September, 1913) 3 Reels
Francis Ford, *Grace Cunard*
Screenplay: Grace Cunard

THE SHE WOLF
(Bison, October, 1913) 3 Reels
Francis Ford, *Grace Cunard*
Screenplay: Grace Cunard

THE BLACK MASKS
(Bison, October, 1913) 2 Reels
Francis Ford, *Grace Cunard*
(Also released as **Diamond Cut Diamond**)

FROM DAWN TILL DARK
(Bison, November, 1913) 2 Reels
Francis Ford, *Grace Cunard*

THE MADONNA OF THE SLUMS
(Bison, November, 1913) 2 Reels
Grace Cunard

WYNONA'S VENGEANCE
(Bison, November, 1913) 2 Reels
Francis Ford, *Grace Cunard*, Ethel Grandin, Ray Myers
Director: Francis Ford
Screenplay: Jack Cunningham

THE BELLE OF YORKTOWN
(Domino, November, 1913) 3 Reels
Francis Ford, *Grace Cunard*, Charles Frenort
Director: Francis Ford

A WAR TIME REFORMATION
(Universal-Gold Seal, January 10, 1914) 2 Reels
Francis Ford, *Grace Cunard*
Director: Francis Ford
Screenplay: Jack Cunningham

THE UNSIGNED AGREEMENT
(Universal-Gold Seal, January 17, 1914) 2 Reels
Francis Ford, *Grace Cunard*
Director: Francis Ford
Screenplay: J. G. Hawks

IN THE FALL OF '64
(Universal-Gold Seal, January 31, 1914) 2 Reels
Grace Cunard, Francis Ford
Director: Francis Ford
Screenplay: Jack Cunningham

THE BRIDE OF MYSTERY
(Universal-Gold Seal, February 10, 1914) 3 Reels
Francis Ford, *Grace Cunard*
Director: Francis Ford
Screenplay: Grace Cunard

SHERIDAN'S PRIDE
(Universal-Joker, March 1914)
Grace Cunard
Screenplay: Grace Cunard

THE TWIN'S DOUBLE
(Universal-Gold Seal, March 10, 1914)
Francis Ford, *Grace Cunard*
Directors: Francis Ford and Grace Cunard

WON IN THE FIRST
(Universal-Joker, March, 1914)
Grace Cunard
Story: Grace Cunard

THE MYSTERIOUS LEOPARD LADY
(Universal-Gold Seal, March 24, 1914) 2 Reels
Grace Cunard, Francis Ford
Director: Francis Ford
Screenplay: Grace Cunard

HOW GREEN PAID THE RENT
(Universal-Joker, March 25, 1914) 1 Reel
Grace Cunard
Story: Grace Cunard

THE MYSTERY OF THE WHITE CAR
(Universal-Gold Seal, April 4, 1914) 2 Reels
Grace Cunard, Francis Ford
Story: Grace Cunard

WASHINGTON AT VALLEY FORGE
(Universal, April, 1914) 4 Reels
Francis Ford, *Grace Cunard*
Directors: Francis Ford and Grace Cunard
Screenplay: Francis Ford and Grace Cunard

LUCILLE LOVE, GIRL OF MYSTERY
(Universal, April 14, 1914) 15 Chaps.
Grace Cunard, Francis Ford, Harry Schumm, Ernest Shields, E. M. Keller, Eddie Boland, Wilbur Higby, Burton Law, Jean Hathaway, Billy White, Harry Ratenbury, Jack (John) Ford
Director: Francis Ford
Screenplay: Grace Cunard, Francis Ford
Story: James Keeley
Chapters: unknown

HOW GREEN SAVED HIS MOTHER-IN-LAW
(Universal-Joker, April 15, 1914) 1 Reel
Grace Cunard
Story: Grace Cunard

ROLL YOUR PEANUT
(Universal-Joker, April 15, 1914) 1 Reel
Grace Cunard
Story: Grace Cunard

THEIR VACATION
(Universal-Joker, May, 1914)
Grace Cunard
Story: Grace Cunard

THE GREAT UNIVERSAL MYSTERY
(Universal-Nestor, July 10, 1914) 1 Reel
King Baggott, Pauline Bush, Ford Sterling, William Clifford, Lois Weber, Lee Moran, Ella Hall, Hobart Henley, William Welsh, Betty Schade, Leah Baird, Howard Crampton, Al Christie, Carl Laemmle, Maurice Fleckes, Herman Fichtenberg, Allen Curtis, Clorence Lawrence, Francis Ford, Bob Leonard, Cleo Madison, Victoria Forde, Murdock MacQuarrie, Ethel Grandin, Alexander Gadin, Rupert Julian, Edna Maison, Edmund Mortimer, Frank Crane, J. C. Graham, Wilfred Lucas, F. A. Van Husan, J. V. Bryson, Henry McRae, J. Warren Kerrigan, *Grace Cunard*, Herbert Tawlinson, Phillips Smalley, Eddie Lyons, William Shay, Irene Wallace, Matt Moore, Marie Walcamp, Frank Smith, William C. Dowland, Herbert Brenon, Isadore Bernstein, Otis Turner, Bob Thornby, David Horsley, Fred Balshofer
Director: Allan Dwan
(A Promotional film for Universal)

THE TANGLE
(Powers, July, 1914)
Grace Cunard, Francis Ford

THE RETURN OF THE TWIN'S DOUBLE
(Bison, August, 1914) 3 Reels
Grace Cunard, Francis Ford

BE NEUTRAL
(Powers, October, 1914)
Grace Cunard, Francis Ford
Director: Francis Ford
Screenplay: Jack Cunningham

THE MYSTERIOUS HAND
(Bison, October, 1914) 3 Reels
Francis Ford, *Grace Cunard*

THE MYSTERIOUS ROSE
(Universal-Gold Seal, November 21, 1914) 2 Reels
Grace Cunard, Francis Ford, John Ford
Director: Francis Ford

THE GHOST OF SMILING JIM
(Universal-Gold Seal, December 12, 1914) 2 Reels
Francis Ford, *Grace Cunard*

THE CALL OF THE WAVES
(Universal-Gold Seal, December 26, 1914) 2 Reels
Grace Cunard, Francis Ford
Story: Grace Cunard

SMUGGLER'S ISLAND
(Universal, January 16, 1915) 2 Reels
Grace Cunard, Francis Ford, Harry Schumm
Director: Francis Ford

THE MYSTERY OF THE THRONE ROOM
(Universal-Gold Seal, January 21, 1915) 2 Reels
Grace Cunard, Francis Ford, Harry Schumm
Story: Grace Cunard

OLD PEG LEG'S WILL
(Bison, January, 1915) 2 Reels
Francis Ford, *Grace Cunard*

THE MADCAP QUEEN OF GREDSHOFFEN
(Universal-Gold Seal, January 23, 1915) 2 Reels
Francis Ford, *Grace Cunard*

THE HEART OF LINCOLN
(Universal-Gold Seal, February 6, 1915) 3 Reels
Francis Ford, *Grace Cunard*

THREE BAD MEN AND A GIRL
(Bison, February, 1915) 2 Reels
Grace Cunard, Francis Ford, Major Palcolagus, Lewis Short, F. J. Denecke, John York
Director: Francis Ford

THE CURSE OF THE DESERT
(Bison, February, 1915) 2 Reels
Grace Cunard, Francis Ford
Screenplay: Grace Cunard

THE GIRL OF THE SECRET SERVICE
(Universal-Gold Seal, February 20, 1915) 2 Reels
Grace Cunard, Francis Ford
Story: Florence Higgins

PHANTOM OF THE VIOLIN
(Universal-Gold Seal, March 6, 1915) 3 Reels
Francis Ford, *Grace Cunard*
Director: Francis Ford
Story: Grace Cunard

HIDDEN CITY
(Universal-Bison, March, 1915) 2 Reels
Grace Cunard, Francis Ford
Director: Francis Ford
Screenplay: Grace Cunard

AND THEY CALLED HIM HERO
(Universal-Bison, April 15, 1915) 2 Reels
Francis Ford, *Grace Cunard*
Director: Francis Ford
Screenplay: Grace Cunard
Producer: Francis Ford

THE DOORWAY OF DESTRUCTION
(Universal, Bison, April 18, 1915) 2 Reels
Francis Ford, Mina Cunard, John Ford, Howard Daniels, Harry Schumm
Director: Francis Ford
Screenplay: Grace Cunard

NABBED
(Universal-Bison, April 24, 1915) 2 Reels
Grace Cunard, Francis Ford
Story: Grace Cunard

ONE KIND OF A FRIEND
(Universal-Laemmle, May 15, 1915) 1 Reel
Grace Cunard, Francis Ford
Director: Francis Ford
Screenplay: Grace Cunard

THE BROKEN COIN
(Universal, June 21, 1915) 22 Chapters
Francis Ford, *Grace Cunard*, Harry Mann, Eddie Polo, John Ford, Mina Cunard, Harry Schumm, Ernest Shields, Jack Holt, Norman MacDonald, Reese Gardner, W. C. Canfield, Bert Wilson, Mina Cunard, Marc Fenton, Burton C. Law, William White, E. A. Clarke, G. J. Uttal, Louis Short
Director: Francis Ford
Screenplay: Grace Cunard
Producer: Emerson Hough
Chapters: (1) The Broken Coin (2) The Satan of the Sands (3) When the Throne Rocked (4) The Face at the Window (5) The Underground Foe (6) A Startling Discovery (7) Between Two Fires (8) The Prison in the Palace (9) Room 22 (10) Cornered (11) The Clash of Arms (12) A Cry in the Dark (13) War (14) On the Battlefield (15) The Deluge (16) Kitty in Danger (17) The Castaways (18) The Underground City (19) The Sacred Fire (20) Between Two Fires (21) A Timely Rescue (22) An American Queen

THE CAMPBELLS ARE COMING
(Universal-Broadway, October, 6, 1915) 4 Reels
Francis Ford, *Grace Cunard*, M. Denecke, Duke Worne, Harry Schumm, Lee Short, Jack Holt
Director: Francis Ford
Screenplay: Grace Cunard
Story: Emerson Hough
Producer: Francis Ford

HER BETTER SELF
(Universal-Victor, January 12, 1916) 2 Reels
Grace Cunard, Jack Holt, Irving Lippner, Genevieve Abbot, Roy Russell
Story: Grace Cunard
Producer: Grace Cunard

PHANTOM ISLAND
(Universal-Bison, January 28, 1916) 2 Reels
Francis Ford, *Grace Cunard*
Director: Francis Ford
Screenplay: Grace Cunard

HIS MAJESTY DICK TURPIN
(Universal-Bison, February 4, 1916) 2 Reels
Grace Cunard, Francis Ford, Jack Holt
Producer: Grace Cunard

THE HIDDEN CITY
(Universal, 1916) 2 Reels
Grace Cunard, Francis Ford, Sam Polo, Eddie Polo, Jack Ford
Director: Francis Ford
Screenplay: Grace Cunard

BORN OF THE PEOPLE
(Universal-Gold Seal, March 7, 1916) 2 Reels
Jack Holt, *Grace Cunard*, Neal Harding
Director: Grace Cunard
Screenplay: Grace Cunard
Producer: Grace Cunard

THE MADCAP QUEEN OF CRONA
(Universal-Gold Seal, March 13, 1916) 2 Reels
Francis Ford, *Grace Cunard*, Jack Holt
Director: Francis Ford

LADY RAFFLES RETURNS
(Universal, March 20, 1916) 2 Reels
Jack Connelly, *Grace Cunard*, Francis Ford, Harry Mann
Director: Francis Ford
Screenplay: Grace Cunard, Francis Ford, Harry Mann

HER SISTER'S SIN
(Universal-Rex, March 24, 1916) 1 Reel
Grace Cunard, Francis Ford
Director: Francis Ford
Screenplay: Grace Cunard
Producer: Francis Ford

THE SHAM REALITY
(Universal-Rex, April 7, 1916) 1/2 Reel
Francis Ford, *Grace Cunard*, Irving Lipner
Screenplay: Grace Cunard
Producer: Francis Ford

BEHIND THE MASK
(Universal-Bison, April 8, 1916) 2 Reels
Peter Gerald, *Grace Cunard*, Jack Holt, Francis Ford, Irving Lippner, Neal Harding, Lou Short, Robert Murdock, Burtos S. Witson
Director: Francis Ford
Screenplay: Grace Cunard

THE UNEXPECTED
(Universal-Bluebird, April, 1916) 1 Reel
Grace Cunard, Francis Ford, Jack Holt
Director: Francis Ford
Screenplay: Grace Cunard
Producer: Francis Ford

THE ADVENTURES OF PEG O' THE RING
(Universal, May 1, 1916) 15 Chapters.
Francis Ford, *Grace Cunard*, Ruth Stonehouse, Peter Gerald, Charles Gunn, G. Raymond Nye, Eddie Polo, Mark Fenton, Jean Hathaway, Irving Lippner, Jack Duffy, Lionel Bradshaw
Directors: Francis Ford, Jacques Jaccard
Screenplay: Grace Cunard
Producer: Francis Ford
Chapters: (1) The Leopard's Mark (2) A Strange Inheritance (3) In the Lion's Den (4) The Circus Mongrels (5) The House of Mystery (6) The Cry for Help or Cry of the Ring (7) The Wreck (8) Outwitted (9) The Leap (10) In the Hands of the Enemy (11) The Stampede (12) On the High Seas (13) The Clown Act (14) The Will (15) Retribution

BRENNON O' THE MOOR
(Universal-Special, August 12, 1916) 2 Reels
Francis Ford, *Grace Cunard*, Jack Holt, Jack Francis, Orin Jackson, Robert Murdock, Daddy Manley, Harry Mann
Director: Francis Ford
Screenplay: Grace Cunard
Producer: Francis Ford

THE PRINCELY BANDIT
(Universal-Bison, August 23, 1916) 2 Reels
Francis Ford, *Grace Cunard*, Jack Holt, Peter Gerald
Director: Francis Ford
Screenplay: Grace Cunard

THE ELUSIVE ENEMY
(Universal-Special/IMP, October 9, 1916) 1 Reel
Grace Cunard, Francis Ford
Director: Francis Ford
Story: Grace Cunard

THE BANDIT'S WAGER
(Universal-Big U, October 21, 1916) 1 Reel
Grace Cunard, Francis Ford
Director: Francis Ford
Story: Grace Cunard
Producers: Grace Cunard, Francis Ford

THE POWDER TRAIL
(Universal-Big U, October 28, 1916) 2 Reels
Francis Ford, *Grace Cunard*, Sherman Bainbridge
Director: Francis Ford
Screenplay: Grace Cunard
Producer: Francis Ford

THE HEROINE OF SAN JUAN
(Universal, November 14, 1916) 2 Reels
Francis Ford, *Grace Cunard*
Director: Francis Ford
Screenplay: Grace Cunard
Producer: Francis Ford

THE MAD HERMIT
(Universal-Big U, December 21, 1916) 2 Reels
Francis Ford, *Grace Cunard*
Director: Francis Ford
Screenplay: Grace Cunard

THE PURPLE MASK
(Universal, December 31, 1916) 16 Chapters
Francis Ford, *Grace Cunard*, Jean Hathaway, Peter Gerald, Jerry Ash, Mario Bianchi, John Eatherstone, John Duffy, Joe Moore, Gertrude Short, Leonard T. Claphan (Tom London), William White, Phillip Ford
Directors: Francis Ford, Grace Cunard
Screenplay: Francis Ford, Grace Cunard
Chapters: (1) The Vanished Jewels (2) Suspected (3) The Capture (4) Facing Death (5) The Demon of the Sky (6) The Silent Feud (7) The Race for Freedom (8) Secret Adventure (9) A Strange Discovery (10) House of Mystery (11) Garden of Surprise (12) The Vault of Mystery (13) The Leap (14) The Sky Monsters (15) Floating Signal (16) A Prisoner of Love

THE TERRORS OF WAR
Universal, April, 1917) 2 Reels
Grace Cunard, Francis Ford
Director: Francis Ford
Screenplay: Grace Cunard

TRUE TO THEIR COLORS
(Universal-Big U, April 23, 1917) 2 Reels
Grace Cunard, Francis Ford
Director: Grace Cunard, Francis Ford
Story: Grace Cunard, Francis Ford

UNMASKED
(Universal-Rex, May 10, 1917) 1 Reel
Francis Ford, *Grace Cunard*, Harry Schumm, Tony Jeanette
Director: Francis Ford
Screenplay: Grace Cunard
Story: Grace Cunard
Producer: Francis Ford

IN TREASON'S GRASP
(Renowned Pictures, June, 1917) 5 Reels
Francis Ford, *Grace Cunard*

CIRCUS SARAH
(Universal-Joker, September 8, 1917) 1 Reel
Grace Cunard
Director: Allen Curtis
Screenplay: Tom Gibson
Story: Allen Curtis

SOCIETY'S DRIFTWOOD
(Universal-Butterfly, October 12, 1917) 5 Reels
Grace Cunard, Joseph Girard, Charles West, William Musgrave
Director: Louis Chaudet
Story: Harvey Gates
Producer: Louis Chaudet

THE PUZZLE WOMAN
(Universal, 1917) 1 Reel
Grace Cunard, Francis Ford
Directors: Grace Cunard, Francis Ford
Story: Grace Cunard, Francis Ford

DANTE'S INFERNO
(Universal, 1917)
Grace Cunard, Francis Ford

HELL'S CRATER
(Universal, January 14, 1918) 5 Reels
Grace Cunard
Director: W. B. Pearson
Story: W. B. Pearson
Producer: Grace Cunard

THE SPAWN
(1918)
Grace Cunard

AFTER THE WAR
(Universal, January 2, 1919) 5 Reels
Grace Cunard, Edward Cecil, Herbert Prior, Dora Rogers, Gretchen Lederer, Gertrude Astor, Harry Carter, Joseph DeGrasse, L. M. Wells
Director: Joseph De Grasse
Screenplay: Harvey Gates
Story: Kingsley Benedict

ELMO, THE MIGHTY
(Universal, June 16, 1919) 18 Chaps.
Elmo Lincoln, *Grace Cunard*, Fred Starr, Virginia Craft, Ivor McFadden, James Cole, Rex De Rosselli, William A. Orlamond, Bob Reeves, Madge Hunt, Grace McClean, William Chapman, Chai Hong
Director: Henry McRae
Story: Joe Brandt, William E. Wing
Chapters: (1) The Mystery of Mad Mountain (2) Buried Alive (3) Flames of Hate (4) A Fiendish Revenge (5) The Phantom Rescue (6) The Puma's Paws (7) The Masked Pursuer (8) The Flaming Pit (9) The House of a Thousand Tortures (10) Victims of the Sea (11) The Burning Den (12) Lashed to the Rocks (13) Into the Chasm (14) The Human Bridge (15) Crashing to Earth (16) Parachute Perils (17) The Plunge (18) Unmasked

THE GIRL IN THE TAXI
(Carter De Haven/Productions/Associated First National Pictures, April 1921) 6 Reels
Mrs. Carter De Haven, Carter De Haven, King Baggot, *Grace Cunard*, Otis Harlan, Tom McGuire, Margaret Campbell, Lincoln Plumer, Freya Sterling, John Gough
Director: Lloyd Ingraham
Screenplay: Bob McGowan
Story: Stanislaus Strange, "The Girl in the Taxi"

THE MAN HATER
(Star Ranch-CBC, 1921) 2 Reels
Grace Cunard, Cole Herbert
Director: Grace Cunard
Producer: Marion H. Cohn

A DAUGHTER OF THE LAW
(Star Ranch-CBC, 1921) 2 Reels
Grace Cunard, Cole Herbert
Director: Grace Cunard
Producer: Marion H. Cohn

HER WESTERN ADVENTURE
(Star Ranch-CBC, 1921)
Grace Cunard, Cole Herbert
Director: Grace Cunard
Producer: Marion H. Cohn

GASOLINE BUCKAROO
(Star Ranch-CBC, 1921) 2 Reels
Grace Cunard, Cole Herbert
Director: Grace Cunard
Producer: Marion H. Cohn

THE HEART OF LINCOLN
(New Era Productions/Anchor, November 1, 1922) 5 Reels
Francis Ford, *Grace Cunard*, Ella Hall, William Quinn, Elmer Morrow, Lew Short
Director: Francis Ford
Producer: Francis Ford

THE WOMAN OF MYSTERY
(Nathan Hirsch-Aywon, 1922)
Francis Ford, *Grace Cunard*
Director: Francis Ford

CARMEN OF THE BORDER
(1923)
Grace Cunard

EMBLEMS OF LOVE
(Progress Productions, February 8, 1924) 7 Reels
Jack Drumier, Jane Jennings, Charles Delaney, *Grace Cunard*, Jane Thomas, Bernard Siegel, James West, Jack Driscoll, John Flowers

THE ELK'S TOOTH
(Renalles, 1924)
Lillian Hall, *Grace Cunard*
Director: Clarence Bricher
Story: Clarke Renalle

THE LAST MAN ON EARTH
(Fox Film Corp., November 2, 1924) 7 Reels
Jean Johnson, Buck Black, Maurice Murphy, William Steele, Jean Dumas, Harry Kunkinson, Fay Holderness, Earle Foxe, *Grace Cunard*, Gladys Tennyson, Derelys Perdue, Maryon Aye, Clarissa Selwynne, Pauline French, Marie Astaire
Director: J. G. Blystone
Screenplay: Donald W. Lee
Story: John D. Swain, "The Last Man on Earth"

OUTWITTED
(Independent Pictures, January 21, 1925) 5 Reels
Helen Holmes, William Desmond, J. P. McGowan, *Grace Cunard*, Alec Francis, Emily Fitzroy
Director: J. P. McGowan

THE WINKING IDOL
(Universal, March, 1926) 10 Chapters
William Desmond, Eileen Sedwick, *Grace Cunard*, Herbert Sutch, Jack Richardson, Helen Broneau, Les Sailor, Art Ortego, Dorothy Gulliver, Vanna Carroll
Director: Francis Ford
Screenplay: Arthur Henry Gooden, George Morgan
Story: Charles E. Van Loan
Chapters: (1) The Eye of Evil (2) Buzzard's Roost (3) Crashing Timbers (4) Racing for Love (5) The Vanishing Bride (6) The Torrent of Terror (7) Flames of Fear (8) The Fight at the Falls (9) In Danger of Dynamite (10) The Lost Lode

STRINGS OF STEEL
(Universal, June 28, 1926) 10 Chapters
William Desmond, Eileen Sedgwick, Albert J. Smith, George Ovey, Ted Duncan, Alphonse Martel, Arthur Morrison, *Grace Cunard*, Taylor N. Duncan, Blanche Fisher, Dorothy Gulliver
Director: Henry McRae
Screenplay: Phillip Dutton Hurn, Oscar Lund
Chapters: (1) The Voice on the Wire (2) The First Central (3) Fighting for Love (4) The Power of Might (5) Kings of the Wire (6) Voice of the Continent (7) Telephone Poles (8) War of the Wire (9) When Lightning Strikes (10) Love and Victory

FIGHTING WITH BUFFALO BILL
(Universal, August 30, 1926) 10 Chapters
Wallace MacDonald, Elsa Benham, *Grace Cunard*, Howard Truesdell, Robert E. Homans, Edmund Cobb, Cuyler Supplee
Director: Ray Taylor
Story: William F. Cody, "The Great West That Was"
Chapters: (1) Westward (2) The Red Menace (3) The Blazing Arrow (4) The Death Trap (5) The Renegade (6) The Race for Life (7) Buried Alive (8) Desperate Chances (9) The Shadow of Evil (10) At the End of the Trail

EXCLUSIVE RIGHTS
(Preferred Pictures, December 15, 1926) 6 Reels
Gayne Whitman, Lillian Rich, Gloria Gordon, Raymond McKee, Gaston Glass, *Grace Cunard*, Sheldon Lewis, Charles Mailes, Shirley Palmer, James Bradbury, Jr., Fletcher Norton, Jimmy Savo
Director: Frank O'Connor
Screenplay: Eve Unsell
Story: Jerome N. Wilson, "Invisible Government"

THE DENVER DUDE
(Universal, Pictures, February 13, 1927) 6 Reels
Hoot Gibson, Blanche Mehaffey, Robert McKim, George Summerville, Gleen Tryon, Howard Truesdell, Mathilde Brundage, Rolfe Sedan, *Grace Cunard*, Buck Carey, Pee Wee Holmes
Director: B. Reeves Eason
Screenplay: Carl Krusada, William B. Lester
Story: Earle Snell

THE RETURN OF THE RIDDLE RIDER
(Universal, March 8, 1927) 10 Chapters
William Desmond, Lola Todd, *Grace Cunard*, Tom London, Henry Barrows, Scotty Mattraw, Lewis Dayton, Norbert Myles, Howard Davies
Director: Robert Hill
Story: Arthur B. Reeve, Fred J. McConnell
Chapters: (1) The Riddle Rider Rides Again (2) A Day of Terror (3) Not a Chance (4) The Holdup (5) The River of Flame (6) The Trap (7) The Crooked Deal (8) The Rock Slide (9) The Silencer (10) Vengeance

BLAKE OF SCOTLAND YARD
(Universal, August 15, 1927) 12 Chapters
Hayden Stevenson, Gloria Gray, Monte Montague, *Grace Cunard*, Albert Hart, Wilbur Mack, Walter Brennan, George Burton, Herbert Prior, Jack Kenney
Director: Robert F. Hill
Screenplay: William Lord Wright
Chapters: (1) The Caster of Fear (2) The Spider's Web (3) The Vanishing Heiress (4) The Room Without a Door (5) Shots in the Dark (6) Ambushed (7) The Secret of the Coin (8) Into the Web (9) The Baited Trap (10) The Lady in White (11) The Closing Web (12) The Final Reckoning

HAUNTED ISLAND
(Universal, March 26, 1928) 10 Chapters
Jack Daugherty, Helen Foster, Al Ferguson, *Grace Cunard*, Myrtis Grinley, Carl Miller, Scotty Mattraw, John T. Prince, Wilbur Mack, Jon Wallace
Director: Robert F. Hill
Screenplay: Frank R. Adams
Chapters: (1) A Night of Fear (2) The Phantom Raider (3) A Trail of Terror (4) The Haunted Room (5) Buried Alive (6) A Race with Death (7) Fires of Fury (8) The Treasure Trap (9) Unmasked (10) Uncut Diamonds

MASKED ANGEL
(Chadwick/Pictures/First Division, Dist., June 29, 1928) 6 Reels
Betty Compson, Erick Arnold, Wheeler Oakman, Jocelyn Lee, *Grace Cunard*, Lincoln Plummer, Robert Homans, Jane Keckley
Director: Frank O'Connor
Screenplay: Maxine Alton
Story: Evelyn Campbell, "Remorse" or "Rescue" in Red Book
Producer: I. E. Chadwick

THE CHINATOWN MYSTERY
(Syndicate, September 1, 1928) 10 Chapters
Joe Bonomo, Ruth Hiatt, Francis Ford, George Chesebro, Sheldon Lewis, Ernest Shields, Jack Richardson, *Grace Cunard*, Rosemary Theby, Peggy O'Day, Duke Worne, Helen Gibson, Paul Malvern, Al Baffert, J. P. McGowan, Billy Ford, Paul Panzer, Harry Myers, William Clifford, Sybil Grove, Spencer Bell, Duke Green, Carl Sepulveda, Tom Curson, Rolf Sedan, Frank Moran, James Leong
Director: J. P. McGowan
Story: Francis Ford
Producer: Trem Carr
Chapters: (1) The Chinatown Mystery (2) The Clutching Claw (3) The Devil's Dice (4) The Mysterious Thirteen (5) Galloping Fury (6) The Depth of Danger (7) The Invisible Hand (8) The Wreck (9) Broken Jade (10) The Thirteenth Hour

THE PRICE OF FEAR
(Universal Pictures, October 28, 1928) 5 Reels
Bill Cody, Duane Thompson, Tom London, *Grace Cunard*, Monte Montague, Ole M. Ness, Jack Raymond
Director: Leigh Jason
Screenplay: William Lester
Story: William Lester

THE ACE OF SCOTLAND YARD
(Universal, September 30, 1929) 10 Chapters
Crauford Kent, Florence Allen, *Grace Cunard*, Monte Montague, Herbert Prior, Albert Prisco
Screenplay: Harold M. Atkinson
Story: Harold M. Atkinson
Chapters: (1) The Fatal Circlet (2) A Cry in the Night (3) The Dungeon of Doom (4) The Depths of Limehouse (5) Menace of the Mummy (6) Dead or Alive (7) Shadows of Fear (8) The Baited Trap (9) A Battle of Wits (10) The Final Judgment

UNTAMED
(M-G-M, November 23, 1929) 9 Reels
Joan Crawford, Robert Montgomery, Ernest Torrence, Homes Herbert, John Miljan, Gwen Lee, Edward Nugent, Don Terry, Gertrude Astor, Milton Fahrney, Lloyd Ingraham, *Grace Cunard*, Wilson Benge
Director: Jack Conway
Screenplay: Sylvia Thalberg, Frank Bulter
Story: Charles E. Scoggins, unidentified story

THE KISS BARRIER
(Fox Film Corp., May 31, 1930) 10 Reels
Edmund Lowe, Claire Adams, Diana Miller, Marion Harlan, Thomas Mills, Charles Clary, *Grace Cunard*
Director: R. William Neill
Screenplay: E. Magnus Ingleton
Story: Frederick and Fanny Hatton

A LADY SURRENDERS
(Universal Pictures, October 6, 1930) 10 Reels
Genevieve Tobin, Rose Hobart, Conrad Nagel, Basil Rathbone, Edgar Norton, Carmel Myers, Franklin Pangborn, Vivian Oakland, *Grace Cunard*
Director: John M. Stahl
Screenplay: Gladys Lehman
Story: John Erskine, "Sincerity, A Story of Our Time"
Producer: Carl Laemmle, Jr.

THE FOURTH HORSEMAN
(Universal, September 25, 1932) 63 Mins.
Tom Mix, Margaret Lindsay, Fred Kohler, Raymond Hatton, Rosita Marstini, Buddy Roosevelt, Edmund Cobb, Richard Cramer, Herman Nolan, Paul Shawhan, Donald Kirke, Harry Allen, Duke Lee, C. E. Anderson, Helene Millard, Martha Mattox, Frederick Howard, *Grace Cunard*, Walter Brennan, Pat Harmon, Hank Mann, Jim Corey, Delmar Watson, Fred Burns, Bud Osborne, Harry Tenbrook, Charles Sullivan, Sandy Sallee, Nip Reynolds, Henry Morris, Clyde Kinney, Jim Kinney, Ed Hendershot, Joe Balch, Augie Gomez, Frank Buskie, Art Bowden, Roy Bucko, Buck Bucko, "Tony, Jr."
Director: Hamilton MacFadden
Screenplay: Jack Dunningham
Story: Nina Wilcox Putnam
Associate Producer: Stanley Bergman

RUSTLERS OF RED DOG
(Universal, January, 1935) 12 Chapters
Johnny Mack Brown, Raymond Hatton, Joyce Compton, Walter Miller, Harry Woods, Charles K. French, Fred McKaye, William Desmond, Wally Wales, Chief Thunder Cloud, Slim Whitaker, Art Mix, Jim Corey, Bill Patton, Cliff Lyons, Tex Cooper, Ben Corbett, Hank Bell, Bud Osborne, Edmund Cobb, J. P. McGowan, Monte Montague, Lafe McKee, Artie Ortego, Jim Thorpe, Chief Thunderbird, Ann D'Arcy, Fritzi Burnette, *Grace Cunard*, Virginia Ainsworth
Director: Louis Friedlander (Lew Landers)
Screenplay: George Plympton, Basil Dickey, Ella O'Neill, Nate Gatzert, Vin Moore
Story: Nathaniel Eddy
Chapters: (1) Hostile Redskins (2) Flaming Arrows (3) Thundering Hoofs (4) Attack at Dawn (5) Buried Alive (6) Flames of Vengeance (7) Into the Depths (8) Paths of Peril (9) The Snake Strikes (10) Riding Wild (11) The Rustlers Clash (12) Law and Order

BRIDE OF FRANKENSTEIN
(Universal, May 6, 1935) 75 Mins.
Boris Karloff, Colin Clive, Valerie Hobson, Elsa Lanchester, Ernest Thesiger, O. P. Heggie, Dwight Frye, E. E. Clive, Una O'Connor, Anne Darling, Douglas Walton, Gavin Gordon, Neil Fitzgerald, Reginald Barlow, Mary Gordon, Ted Billings, Lucien Prival, John Carradine, Maurice Black, Billy Barty, Norman Ainsley, Joan Woodbury, Arthur S. Byron, Josephine McKim, Kansas DeForrest, Peter Shaw, Walter Brennan, Helen Parish, *Grace Cunard*
Director: James Whale
Screenplay: William Hurlbut, and John L. Balderston
Story: Mary Wollstonecraft Shelley
Producer: Carl Laemmle, Jr.

WINNERS OF THE WEST
(Universal, July 2, 1940) 13 Chapters
Dick Foran, Anne Nagel, James Craig, Tom Fadden, Charles Stevens, Trevor Bardette, Harry Woods, Chief Yowlachie, Edward Keane, William Desmond, Edmund Cobb, Chuck Morrison, Edgar Edwards, Jack Voglin, Roy Barcroft, Edward Cassidy, Slim Whitaker, Alan Bridge, Jack Casey, George Plues, Tex Palmer, Vyola (Viola) Vonn, James Blaine, Evelyn Selbie, Robert Long, Hank Worden, Henry Hall, James Farley, Earle Douglas, Jim Pierce, George Magrill, Bud Osborne, Paul Reed, Jack Voglin, Bob Kortman, *Grace Cunard*, Charles Murphy, Bill Hunter, Horace B. Carpenter, Dick Rush, Charles Sherlock, Harry Tenbrook, Tom London, Iron Eyes Cody, Charles Brunner, Frank Ellis, Jim Corey, Rose Plumner, Bud McClure, Universal Jack, Gene Alsace, Ken Terrell (stunt double), Eddie Parker (fight double for Foran), Cliff Lyons (riding double for Foran and Fadden), Fred Graham (double for Harry Woods)
Directors: Ford Beebe, Ray Taylor
Screenplay: George Plympton, Basil Dickey, Charles R. Condon
Producer: Henry McRae
Chapters: (1) Redskins Ride Again (2) The Wreck at Red River Gorge (3) The Bridge of Disaster (4) Trapped by Redskins (5) Death Stalks the Trail (6) A Leap for Life (7) Thundering Terror (8) The Flaming Arsenal (9) Sacrificed by Savages (10) Under Crashing Timbers (11) Bullets in the Dark (12) The Battle of Blackhawk (13) Barricades Blasted

GANG BUSTERS
(Universal, March 31, 1942) 13 Chapters
Kent Taylor, Irene Hervey, Ralph Morgan, Robert Armstrong, Richard Davies, Joseph Crehan, George Watts, George J. Lewis, Beatrice Roberts, William Desmond, *Grace Cunard*, Karl Hackett, Dale Van Sickel
Director: Ray Taylor, Noel Smith
Screenplay: Morgan B. Cox, Al Martin, Vin Martin, George H. Plympton
Story: Ford Beebe

FIREBRANDS OF ARIZONA
(Republic, December 1, 1944) 55 Minutes
Smiley Burnette, Sunset Carson, Peggy Stewart, Earle Hodgins, Roy Barcroft, Rex Lease, Tom London, Jack Kirk, Bud Geary, Bob Wilke, LeRoy Mason, Charles Morton, Fred Toones, Pierce Lyden, Frank Ellis, Frank McCarroll, Budd Buster, Bob Burns, Jack O'Shea, Hank Bell, Jess Cavin, William Desmond, *Grace Cunard*, Mazine Doyle, Pascale Perry, Bill Nestell, Bob Woodward, Phil Dunham, Horace B. Carpenter, Tom Steele, Chick Hannon, Tex Cooper, George Morrell, Bob Cason, Warner Richmond, Sherry Tansey
Director: Robert Emmett (Tansey)
Screenplay: Frances Kavanaugh
Story: Frank Simpson
Producer: Walt Mattox

GREAT STAGECOACH ROBBERY
(Republic, February 15, 1945) 56 Mins.
(Red Ryder Series)
Bill Elliott, Bobby Blake, Alice Fleming, Francis McDonald, Don Costello, Sylvia Arslan, Bud Geary, Leon Tyler, Freddie Chapman, Henry Wills, Hank Bell, Bob Wilke, John James, Tom London, Dickie Dillion, Bobby Dillion, Raymond ZeBrack, Patsy May, Chris Wren, Horace Carpenter, *Grace Cunard*, Frederick Howard
Director: Lesley Selander
Screenplay: Randall Faye
Associate Producer: Louis Gray
Producer: William J. O'Sullivan

Carol Forman

5 • CAROL FORMAN

"Queen of Serial Villainesses"

Post-World War II serial viewers were treated to a delightful plot twist when the hero of several cliffhangers was opposed by a voluptuous female rather than a male mystery figure. Even after forty years many a serial fan will fight back goosebumps at the recollection of "The Black Widow," "The Spider Lady," "Queen Khana," "Nila," and "Lasca"--a set of evil women portrayed by Carol Forman, a beautiful, sexy young actress of meritorious talent. A sort of mystique surrounded Carol as a result of the villainess roles she assayed, and many fans have long wondered what happened to this pretty young lady who could look as mean as hell, yet retain a certain virginal beauty, while directing her minions to mutilate, kill, steal, and engage in whatever other nefarious activities pleased her at the moment.

Fu Manchu had nothing on this cunning, deadly, mysterious female. Her bewitching beauty was capable of luring men's souls to the abyss of doom by the light of her wanton eyes, or of lifting their spirits with a companionable twinkling smile. Villainy was her forte. Her sexy, seductive screen persona registered well with audiences, and her talent made it all believable as she achieved serial immortality via the cliffhanger route.

It was in 1947 that Carol made her big splash as Sombra, nicknamed "The Black Widow," in Republic's serial of the same name, easily taking the limelight from heroine Virginia Lindley and hero Bruce Edwards. The part of an evil Asian ruler's daughter out to steal atomic secrets seemed tailor-made for Carol, who obviously reveled in the role. That same year she did a small but memorable part as Queen Khana in Columbia's **Brick Bradford**, a serial starring Kane Richmond. Columbia must have liked what they saw, for the following year she was cast as "The Spider Lady" in **Superman**, proving to be an able antagonist for the man of steel as she seeks to steal a reducer ray by which she plans to subjugate governments. Though Noel Neill had the heroine role as Lois Lane, it was Carol's role that was the meaty one. In the final chapter, as she tries to escape, a ray is turned on her by a vengeful henchman and the screaming villainess and her web go up in a blazing explosion that leaves no trace of the evil woman and only shattered remnants of her web. The scene was indelibly etched in the memory of many a youthful viewer, much as an earlier generation of front-row kids would always have a picture in the back of their minds of Queen Tika being disintegrated by a powerful ray machine as the Muranian Empire is destroyed in **The Phantom Empire**.

Back at Republic in 1949 Carol was again a top-billed villainess in **Federal Agents vs. the Underworld**. Her role was that of Nila, an international thief and one of the founders of Underworld, Inc. With her minions she ruthlessly murders anyone in her way as she seeks the famous Golden Hands of Kurigal, key to a great fortune. Her adversary is again Kirk Alyn, minus his Superman garb.

Carol's last serial outing came in 1952 when she teamed with Kirk Alyn for a third time in **Blackhawk**, a Columbia release. As Laska, a foreign agent working for an unidentified boss known only as "The Leader," she manages to steal a deadly electronic ray, thereby running afoul of Blackhawk and his international brotherhood, who are sworn to combat the forces of tyranny throughout the world.

I mention her serials in the very beginning because it is these that gave Carol Forman her small measure of screen immortality. Not since the silent era skullduggery of Ruth Royce had the serial genre seen a villainess of the calibre of Miss Forman, whose charisma (or consummate acting) endeared her to serial enthusiasts. Audiences

Federal Agents Vs. the Underworld (Republic, 1949) – Roy Barcroft, Carol Forman, ~~Clayton Moore~~ KIRK ALYN, Rosemary LaPlanche.

loved to hate her in the nasty roles she played, yet could not resist loving her characters because of the life she brought to them.

Her despicableness was not confined to serials; disrepute was also her speciality in feature films. But because she specialized in playing lecherous women, one naturally wondered about the woman behind the facade.

Carol Forman, whose real name was Carolyn Sawls, was born in Epes, Alabama on June 9. Like many women, she would just as soon not divulge the year. She was raised in Livingston, Alabama. Her mother, Mrs. Annabelle Sawls, made a living for herself, Carol, and Carol's sister, Ellen, by running an antique store. Carol's father was Edward Sawls, an attorney. He died when Carol was nine.

For the record, Carol is 5' 6" tall, has brown eyes, and originally had dark brown hair, as moviegoers will recall. For the last twenty years, however, Carol has dyed her hair red. In her movie days she was a size 7 and 9, but now wears a size 10. She measures 38-25-38--still not a bad package of femininity, considering that she has retained much of the beauty she possessed when she was beguiling men in her movie roles.

From earliest childhood Carol wanted to be an actress. Consequently, she availed herself of every opportunity to participate in dramatics while in school. When the family lived briefly in Sebring, Florida, Carol was active in a little theatre group.

Because of Carol's intense desire to become an actress, her mother allowed her to go to Hollywood immediately after graduation from high school, having made arrangements with a singing teacher for Carol to board and study with her. Carol also took drama lessons and soon became involved in little theatre work.

It was Carol's good fortune to have one of the most expensive "screen tests" on record--the Joan Fontaine starring picture, **From This Day**

Forward at RKO Radio. It all came about through an unconventional approach to the movies made by the film's director, John Berry, who demanded a girl who had never been in the movies before to play a clerk in a USES office in the picture. Knowing that this girl had to be a good actress, no matter how little she knew about camera technique, RKO talent scouts went hastily to the little theaters around Los Angeles to locate a candidate. They saw Carol do an excellent part in a play put on by the Penthouse Theater Guild of Pasadena and got her for the bit in the Fontaine picture. In it Carol had to be employment advisor for Mark Stevens, hero of the film, and to get angry with him because he is unreasonable with her, so the two begin shouting at each other.

Carol put over this acrimonious scene so well that various producers who saw the film bid for her to play parts in their pictures. The studio saw that the young lady ought to be signed on contract, and swiftly secured her signature on the right dotted line. Shortly afterward she was assigned as a contract player to her first regular feature picture, **Honeymoon**, with Shirley Temple and Franchot Tone, after first appearing in a Leon Errol short, **Follow That Blonde**. She quickly fell into the "bad girl" roles for which she became known.

After a year at RKO she became a free lance for the remainder of her career. She would have remained at RKO longer had she really been the bad girl she portrayed on screen, but when a powerful producer insisted that she take the "casting couch" route to retaining her RKO contract, the "good girl" ingrained in her surfaced quickly. Carol lost her contract. Sometime later, when Howard Hughes found out what had happened to her, he threw the producer's stuff out on the parking lot and barred the man from ever entering the studio again.

Carol turned down more serials than she made. In fact, she turned down three serial offers in one week, much to her regret now. It wasn't that she didn't like to do them. She did. But her agent thought they would hurt her career, as serials were frowned on by the major studios. She now wishes she had not listened to him, as she could have become a major serial queen had she continued. Ironically, serials today are revered far more than they were at the time they were made, and Carol loved doing them at the time.

Her feature westerns were confined to two with Tim Holt and one with James Warren. In each she played a somewhat wicked woman, as for example in **Under the Tonto Rim**, in which she is a half-breed Indian girl who is a heavy but who falls in love with Tim. Her television work includes appearances on "Dr. Hudson's Secret Journal," "77 Sunset Strip," "The Loretta Young Show," "The Cisco Kid," and "Files of Jeffrey Jones." She also did commercials, little theatre, and TV modeling.

In 1948 Carol was featured in **The Mozart Story**, a film which had its own unusual story. The film was being made in Austria to be released in Austria. The actors were famous opera stars in that country at the time. The film was, as the title suggests, the life story of the famous composer. When the war broke out over there Germany took over Austria, which stopped the filming. Somehow the unfinished film survived the war and was bought for peanuts by a foreign producer making films here in this country. He finished the film with American actors, but all of the singers and actors are real opera stars. The scenes that tie the story together were done by American actors. Wilton Graff played Carol's husband Antonio Salieri. Salieri was an aristocrat with power and Mozart was poor. When Mozart's music began to reach the ears of the aristocrats it was far superior to Salieri's--which was number one at the time--and Salieri did many dirty things to stop Mozart and his music. The foreign actor who played Mozart in the Austrian film was killed during the war and in piecing the film together here, they used an American double--even his nose was changed to correspond to the foreign shots. Carol had a few scenes in the film, which was released by Screen Guild.

Early in her career Carol married Robert Forman, a man 20 to 25 years her senior. Forman's Air Force career kept him apart from Carol, whose own career ambitions kept her in California, and so the marriage ultimately ended. However, the two remained close friends. Forman later retired from the Air Force as a three-star general.

Later Carol was married for six months to a writer and drama critic from Jacksonville, Florida whom Colonel Tom Parker had brought out to California. It was a marriage on the rebound and a mistake for Carol. Her third and last marriage was to William Dennis, an associate director with Russell Hayden Productions. Dennis had three young daughters by a former marriage. When the mother abandoned the children, Carol took them in and raised them as her own, giving up her career for "instant motherhood." For many years the family lived in the Texas area, then came back to California about 1977 when Bill's health deteriorated. About two years afterwards he suffered a fatal heart attack. Hospital bills and other expenses took about all of Carol's savings.

Carol Forman once again is trying for a screen or television career. The past 30 years, from a physical standpoint, have been most kind to her,

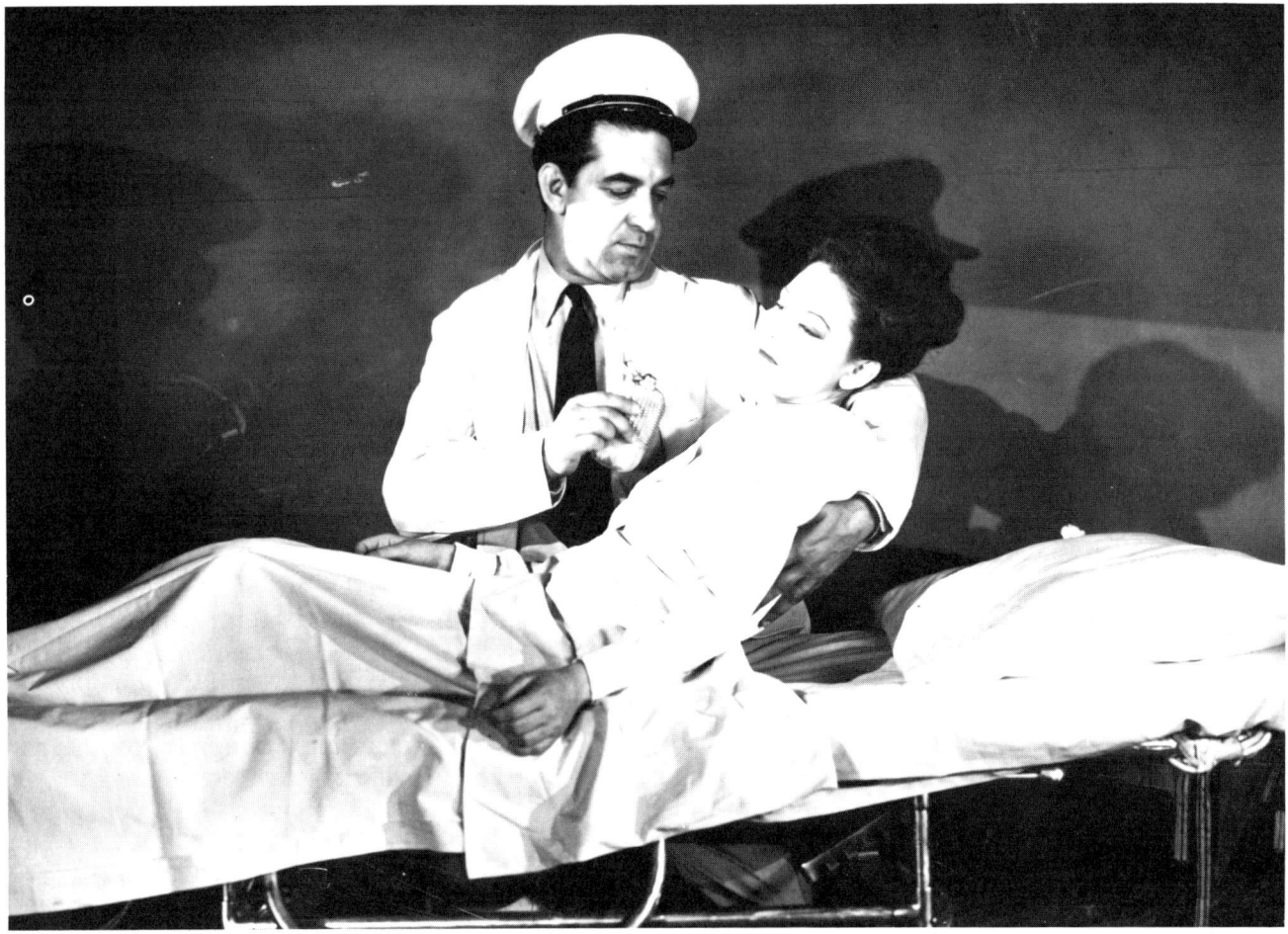

The Black Widow (Republic, 1947) – Carol Forman is aided by her henchman, Anthony Warde.

for she is still an attractive woman worthy of wolf whistles. On February 11, 1984 she was honored by the Hollywood Appreciation Society at the Masquers Club in Hollywood, and in June 1984 she appeared as a guest at the famed Memphis Film Festival. Other offers are coming in from organizations or groups that want to honor her. We can only hope that today's Hollywood will rediscover Carol Forman, reigning villainess queen of yesteryear's serial world. Feature films aside, she would be an ideal choice for some of the TV soaps, playing the same type of role she always played. Surely there is a niche for this actress who demonstrated such finesse at playing the sensuous, unvirtuous, decadent, and incorrigible female, and whose talent is only highlighted when one realizes that in real life she is a delightfully charming woman who is the antithesis of her screen personage.

CAROL FORMAN Filmography

FROM THIS DAY FORWARD
(RKO Radio, February, 1946) 95 Mins.
Joan Fontaine, Mark Stevens, Rosemary DeCamp, Henry Morgan, Wally Brown, Arline Judge, Renny McEvoy, Bobby Driscoll, Mary Treen, Queenie Smith, Doreen McGann, Erskine Sanford, *Carol Forman*
Director: John Berry
Screenplay: Hugo Butler
Adaption: Garson Kanin
Based on a novel by Thomas Bell
Producer: William Pereira

FOLLOW THAT BLONDE
(RKO Radio, September 27, 1946) 2 Reels
Leon Errol, Harry Harvey, Claire Carleton, Phil Warren, Marian Carr, Dick Elliott, *Carol Forman*, Teddy Infuhr
Director: Hal Yates

SAN QUENTIN
(RKO-Radio, October 17, 1946) 66 Mins.
Lawrence Tierney, Barton MacLane, Marian Carr, Harry Shannon, *Carol Forman*, Richard Powers (Tom Keene), Joe Devlin, Tony Barrett, Lee Bonnell, Robert Clarke, Raymond Burr
Director: Gordon M. Douglas
Screenplay: Lawrence Kimble, Arthur A. Ross, Howard J. Green
Producer: Martin Mooney
Executive Producer: Sid Rogell

NOCTURNE
(RKO Radio, November 9, 1946) 87 Mins.
George Raft, Lynn Bari, Virginia Huston, Joseph Pevney, Myrna Dell, Edward Ashley, Walter Sande, Mabel Paige, Bernard Hoffman, Queenie Smith, Mack Gray, Greta Granstedt, Lillian Bond, *Carol Forman*, Harry Harvey
Director: Edwin L. Marin
Screenplay: Jonathan Latimer
Story: Frank Fenton, Rowland Brown
Executive Producer: Jack J. Gross

THE FALCON'S ADVENTURE
(RKO Radio, December 13, 1946) 61 Mins.
Tom Conway, Madge Meredith, Edward S. Brophy, Robert Warwick, Myrna Dell, Steve Brodie, Ian Wolfe, *Carol Forman*, Joseph Crehan, Phil Warren, Tony Barrett, Harry Harvey, Jason Robards, Dave Sharpe
Director: William Berke
Screenplay: Aubrey Wisberg
Producer: Herman Schlom

CODE OF THE WEST
(RKO Radio, February 2, 1947) 57 Mins.
James Warren, Debra Alden, John Laurenz, Robert Clarke, Steve Brodie, Rita Lynn, *Carol Forman*, Harry Woods, Raymond Burr, Harry Harvey, Phil Warren, Emmett Lynn
Director: William Berke
Screenplay: Norman Houston
Story: Zane Grey
Producer: Herman Schlom

WIFE TAMES WOLF
(RKO Radio, April 25, 1947) 2 Reels
Leon Errol, Dorothy Granger, Eddie Kane, *Carol Forman*, Phil Warren, Peggy Maley, Barbara Smith
Director: Hal Yates

HONEYMOON
(RKO Radio, April, 1947) 74 Mins.
Shirley Temple, Franchot Tone, Guy Madison, Lina Romay, Gene Lockhart, Corinna Mura, Grant Mitchell, Julio Villareal, Manuel Arvide, Jose R. Goula, *Carol Forman*
Director: William Keighley
Screenplay: Michael Kanin
Based on story by Vicki Baum
Producer: Warren Duff

DESPERATE
(RKO Radio, May 20, 1947) 73 Mins.
Steve Brodie, Audrey Long, Raymond Burr, Douglas Fowley, William Challee, Jason Robards, Sr., Freddie Steele, Lee Frederick, Paul E. Burns, Ika Gruning, Larry Nunn, Robert Bray, Carl Kent, *Carol Forman*, Erville Alderson, Teddy Infuhr, Perc Launders, Ralfe Harolde, Kay Christopher, Bill Wallace, Carl Saxe, Grahame Covert, Jay Norris, Milt Kibbee, Dick Elliot, Charles Flynn, Ernie Adams, Don Kerr, Jack Baxley, Frank O'Connor, Hans Herbert
Director: Anthony Mann
Screenplay: Harry Essex, Martin Rackin
Story: Anthony Mann
Producer: Michel Kraike

THE BLACK WIDOW
(Republic, June, 1947) 13 Chapters
Bruce Edwards, Virginia Lindley, *Carol Forman*, Anthony Warde, I. Stanford Jolley, Ramsay Ames, Theodore Gottlieb, Virginia Carroll, Gene Stutenroth, Ernie Adams, Tom Steele, Dale Van Sickel, Maxine Doyle, LeRoy Mason, Sam Flint, George Douglas, Robert Barron, Carey Loftin, Bud Wolfe, Hal Landon, Robert Wilke, Peggy Wynne, Duke Green, Stanley Price, Forrest Taylor, Larry Steers, Ted Mapes, Bob Reeves, Jack O'Shea, Gil Perkins, George Chesebro, Keith Richards, Hal Landon, Robert Wilke, Stanley Price, Peggy Wynne, John Phillips, Ken Terrell, Laura Stevens, Arvon Dale, John Alban, Dave Anderson, Jerry Jerome, Richard Gordon
Directors: Spencer Bennet and Fred C. Brannon
Screenplay: Franklyn Adreon, Basil Dickey, Jesse Duffy, Sol Shor
Associate Producer: Mike Frankovich
Chapter Titles: (1) Deadly Prophecy (2) The Stolen Formula (3) Hidden Death (4) Peril in the Sky (5) The Spider's Lair (6) The Glass Guillotine (7) Wheels of Death (8) False Information (9) The Spider's Venom (10) The Stolen Corpse (11) Death Dials a Number (12) The Talking Mirror (13) A Life for a Life

Brick Bradford (Columbia, 1947) – Gene Stutenroth, Kane Richmond, Carol Forman, Robert Barron, John Merton, Pierre Watkin.

UNDER THE TONTO RIM
(RKO Radio, August 1, 1947) 61 Mins.
Tim Holt, Nan Leslie, Richard Martin, Richard Powers (Tom Keene), *Carol Forman*, Tom Barrett, Harry Harvey, Jason Robards, Sr., Lex Barker, Robert Clarke, Jay Norris, Steve Savage, Herman Hack
Director: Lew Landers
Screenplay: Norman Houston
Story: Zane Grey
Producer: Herman Schlom

BRICK BRADFORD
(Columbia, 1947) 15 Chapters
Kane Richmond, Rick Vallin, Linda Johnson, Pierre Watkin, Charles Quigley, *Carol Forman*, Jack Ingram, Fred Graham, Wheeler Oakman, Leonard Penn, John Merton, Charles King, John Hart, Helene Stanley, Nelson Leigh, Robert Barron, George DeNormand, Noel Neill, Stanley Blystone, Frank Ellis, Al Ferguson, Gene Stutenroth
Director: Spencer G. Bennet
Screenplay: George H. Plympton, Arthur Hoerl, Lewis Clay
Based upon the newspaper feature, "Brick Bradford"
Producer: Sam Katzman
Chapter Titles: (1) Atomic Defense (2) Flight to the Moon (3) Prisoners of the Moon (4) Into the Volcano (5) Bradford at Bay (6) Back to Earth (7) Into Another Century (8) Buried Treasure (9) Trapped in the Time Top (10) The Unseen Hand (11) Poison Gas (12) Door of Disaster (13) Sinister Rendezvous (14) River of Revenge (15) For the Peace of the World

SUPERMAN
(Columbia, 1948) 15 Chapters
Kirk Alyn, Noel Neill, *Carol Forman*, Tommy Bond, Pierre Watkin, George Meeker, Jack Ingram, Terry Frost, Charles Quigley, Herbert Rawlinson, Forrest Taylor, Stephen Carr, Charles King, Rusty Wescoatt, Nelson Leigh, Luana Walters, Robert Barron, Edward Cassidy, Virginia Carroll, Alan Dinehart, III, Ralph Hodges, Jack George, Tom London, Rube Schaefer, Stanley Price, Paul Stader, Reed Howes, Leonard Penn, Gene Roth, Peggy Wynn, Frank Ellis, Emmett Vogan
Directors: Spencer G. Bennet and Thomas Carr
Screenplay: Arthur Hoerl, Lewis Clay, Royal Cole
Adaptation: George H. Plympton and Joseph F. Poland
Producer: Sam Katzman
Chapter Titles: (1) Superman Comes to Earth (2) Depths of the Earth (3) The Reducer Ray (4) Man of Steel (5) A Job for Superman (6) Superman in Danger (7) Into the Electrical Furnace (8) Superman to the Rescue (9) Irresistible Force (10) Between Two Fires (11) Superman's Dilemma (12) Blast in the Depths (13) Hurled to Destruction (14) Superman at Bay (15) The Payoff

DOCKS OF NEW ORLEANS
(Monogram, March 21, 1948) 64 Mins.
Roland Winters, Virginia Dale, Mantan Moreland, John Gallaudet, Victor Sen Young, *Carol Forman*, Douglas Fowley, Harry Hayden, Howard Negley, Stanley Andrews, Emmett Vogan, Boyd Irwin, Rory Mallinson, George J. Lewis, Larry Steers, Dian Fauntelle, Ferris Taylor, Haywood Jones, Paul Conrad, Fred Miller, Frank Stephens, Eric Wilton, Forrest Matthews, Wally Walker
Director: Derwin Abrahams
Screenplay: W. Scott Darling
Producer: James S. Burkett
Based on a character created by Earl Derr Biggers

THE MOZART STORY
(Screen Guild, November, 1948) 91 Mins.
Hans Holt, Winnie Markus, Irene V. Meydendorff, Rene Deltgen, Edward Vedder, Wilton Graff, *Carol Forman*, Anthony Barr, Walther Janssen, Rosa Albach-Retty, Anita Rosar, Thea Weiss, Curt Juergens, Paul Hoerbiger, John Siebert, Richard Eybner, Eric Nicowitz, Theo Danegger, Fred Imhoff, Carl Bluhm
Director: Karl Hartl
Screenplay: Richard Billinger
Producer: Abraham Haimson

THE FEATHERED SERPENT
(Monogram, December 19, 1948) 68 Mins.
Roland Winters, Keye Luke, Victor Sen Yung, Mantan Moreland, Robert Livingston, Martin Garralaga, Nils Asther, *Carol Forman*, Beverly Jons, George J. Lewis, Leslie Dennison, Jay Silverheels
Director: William Beaudine
Screenplay: Oliver Drake
Story: Oliver Drake
Producer: James S. Burkett

FEDERAL AGENTS VS. UNDERWORLD, INC.
(Republic, January, 1949) 12 Chapters
Kirk Alyn, Rosemary LaPlanche, *Carol Forman*, Roy Barcroft, James Dale, Bruce Edwards, James Craven, Tris Coffin, Jack O'Shea, Dale Van Sickel, Tom Steele, Marshall Reed, Robert Wilke, Art Dillard, Dave Sharpe, Dave Anderson, Carey Loftin, Post Parks, Joe Yrigoyen, Bud Wolfe, Duke Taylor, Ken Terrell, Bert LeBaron, James Carlisle, John Daheim, Saul Gorss, Loren Riebe
Director: Fred C. Brannon
Screenplay: Royal K. Cole, Basil Dickey, William Lively, Sol Shor
Associate Producer: Franklin Adreon
Chapter Titles: (1) The Golden Hands (2) The Floating Coffin (3) Death in the Skies (4) Fatal Evidence (5) The Trapped Conspirator (6) Wheels of Disaster (7) The Hidden Key (8) The Enemy's Mouthpiece (9) The Stolen Hand (10) Unmasked (11) Tombs of the Ancients (12) The Curse of Kurigal

BROTHERS IN THE SADDLE
(RKO Radio, February 8, 1949) 60 Mins.
Tim Holt, Richard Martin, Steve Brodie, Virginia Cox, *Carol Forman*, Richard Powers (Tom Keene), Stanley Andrews, Robert Bray, Francis McDonald, Emmett Vogan, Monte Montague
Director: Lesley Selander
Screenplay: Norman Houston
Producer: Herman Schlom

OH, SUSANNA
(Republic, March 3, 1951) 90 Mins.
Rod Cameron, Adrian Booth, Forrest Tucker, Chill Wills, William Ching, Jim Davis, Wally Cassell, Douglas Kennedy, James Lydon, William Haade, John Compton, James Flavin, Charles Stevens, Alan Bridge, Marion Randolph, Marshall Reed, John Pickard, Ruth Brennan, Louise Kane, *Carol Forman*
Director: Joseph Kane
Screenplay: Charles Marquis Warren
Associate Producer: Joseph Kane

The Feathered Serpent (Monogram, 1948) – Carol Forman, Roland Winters, and Robert Livingston.

BLACKHAWK
(Columbia, July 1952) 15 Chapters
Kirk Alyn, *Carol Forman*, John Crawford, Michael Fox, Don C. Harvey, Rick Vallin, Larry Stewart, Weaver Levy, Zon Murray, Nick Stuart, Marshall Reed, Pierce Lyden, William Fawcett, Terry Frost, Rory Mallinson, Frank Ellis, Jack Mulhall, Frank Gerstle, Dave Sharpe
Directors: Spencer G. Bennet and Fred F. Sears
Screenplay: George H. Plympton, Royal K. Cole, Sherman L. Lowe
Based on the "Blackhawk" comic magazine created by Reed Crandall
Producer: Sam Katzman
Chapter Titles: (1) Distress Call from Space (2) Blackhawk Traps a Traitor (3) In the Enemy's Hideout (4) The Iron Monster (5) Human Targets (6) Blackhawk's Leap for Life (7) Mystery Fuel (8) Blasted from the Sky (9) Blackhawk Tempts Fate (10) Chase for Element X (11) Forced Down (12) Drums of Doom (13) Blackhawk's Daring Plan (14) Blackhawk's Wild Ride (15) The Leader Unmasked

BY THE LIGHT OF THE SILVERY MOON
(Warner Bros., May 2, 1953) 101 Mins.
Doris Day, Gordon McRae, Leon Ames, Rosemary DeCamp, Billy Gray, Mary Wickes, Russell Arms, *Carol Forman*, John Maxwell
Director: David Butler
Screenplay: Robert O'Brien, Irving Elinson
Suggested by Booth Tarkinton's Penrod stories
Producer: William Jacobs

6 • NEVA GERBER

She Vied with Allene Ray as Crown Princess of the Silent Serial

Neva Gerber is one of the top ten serial heroines of all time, yet she is one of the least known. We do know that she came from Chicago, and was educated at Immaculate Heart College. She was 5 feet 2 inches tall, had brown hair and eyes, and weighed about 115 pounds. She was making movies at Kalem as early as 1912. She was once engaged to William Desmond Taylor but the marriage never materialized; at the time of his murder on February 1, 1922, he was romantically linked with other, more famous ladies.

By 1915 Neva was at American studios playing opposite Webster Campbell in a long series of predominantly comic films. In late 1916 she appeared in her first serial--at least, her first to our knowledge. It was **The Great Secret** (1917), produced by Christy Cabanne for the Serial Producing Company organized by Louis Mayer, and released through Metro. Neva's was a small part in support of the highly popular team of Francis X. Bushman and Beverly Bayne. The serial did little to help any of the careers involved.

Neva's fortunes rose, however, when she joined Universal in late 1916. **Honor Thy Country** (1916) and **The Prodigal Widow** (1917) gave her a chance to prove herself in the popular "Gold Seal" three-reelers that Universal produced, along with "Mustang," "Butterfly," "Rex," and other brands. **Honor Thy Country** had to do with an American girl (Neva) and her father who visit a South American country where the villainous dictator makes advances to her after throwing her father in jail. Two Americans, one with the regular army and the other a soldier of fortune, have a chance to show their colors in protecting our heroine and setting things right.

The story of **The Prodigal Widow** as reviewed in one trade paper is given here to illustrate the big difference between Westerns of the pre-1930 era and those formula products often churned out in the sound era. To compare even a simple three-reeler such as this one with the "B" Western product of the late forties and early fifties reveals the depths to which the later Western film genre had sunk, and particularly the story importance of the heroine.

Paul Braintree had come West prospecting and had sought his fortunes in the mining district. His brother, Henry, had gone to Mexico and had acquired valuable oil lands--also a wife, Bina (Neva), a great flirt. Jack Winthrop, a young college student, Allen Bradley, a lawyer, and Dr. Le Rene are among her most devoted admirers.

Things have not been going very well in a financial way for Henry, and his lawyer announces his credit is no longer good. Paul pays a visit to his brother, and for the first time is attracted by a woman, but the hopelessness bewilders him. Bina recognizes a new victim and when she confesses her love, he quits his brother's house, leaving a note that business interests call him home.

Henry's affairs reach a crisis, and he chooses the easiest route, feeling that his brother has deserted him at the crucial moment. Bina wires Paul of his brother's suicide, as he has struck it rich and is celebrating in the mining camp. He goes home and blames Bina for Henry's downfall, and when she appeals to him he flings her from him and goes back West.

Bina plots to revenge herself on Paul. Dressed very elaborately she goes to the mining camp and begins a flirtation with the gambling sheriff, and is entertaining the gamblers when Paul arrives. She repulses him when he attempts to make her leave. He goes home, gets his horse, and returning to the dance hall with a gun forces her to leave the place, holding off the men and starting a fight between them to distract their attention while he takes her away.

Arrived in the wilds, he forces her to darn

The Voice on the Wire (Universal, 1917) – Ben Wilson (standing, holding man), Neva Gerber, Joseph W. Girard (man being held), Francis McDonald (man lying down)

overalls and to cook her own meals. Paul falls over a cliff, and Bina, puzzled by her own sensations, is nursing him when Allen Bradley, her husband's attorney and an old admirer of hers, arrives and tells her her fortune in Mexico has been restored. As she is wondering why the news fails to enthuse her, the gamblers arrive. She refuses Bradley, and fights for the man she finds she loves.

The Voice on the Wire (1917) was the first of nine serials that Neva made opposite Ben Wilson, and it was an auspicious beginning--well made, suspenseful, a good story (as serials go), and, most important, released by Universal, which guaranteed wide exposure. Obviously Wilson and Gerber worked well together and more serials for the two of them were inevitable. Their careers were closely linked for the next dozen years. **The Mystery Ship** (1917) followed that same year, with Henry McRae and Harry Harvey in charge of the eighteen-chapter thriller. The story was hackneyed (the heroine looking for buried treasure on a remote island), but audiences returned faithfully each week to follow the skullduggery.

During the World War I era Neva was also appearing in features and shorts. Harry Carey evidently liked her as a heroine, for she played opposite him in four Westerns in 1918 and 1919, a time when Carey was King of the Westerns at Universal. Consequently, the pictures were uncommonly rich in exciting episodes, the primitive action was in harmony with the locales of the stories, the direction was by John Ford, and the films had that extra polish that made the Cheyenne Harry series the popular vehicle that it was.

Having left Universal in mid-1919, Neva and Wilson made their next serial, **Trail of the Octopus** (1919), for Hallmark Pictures. It was unusual in that Chapter 6 was five reels in length, as contrasted with the customary two. **The Screaming Shadow** (1920), also from Hallmark, followed shortly. Chapter titles such as

"The Virgin of Death," "The Fang of the Beast," "The Crawling Horror," "Entombed Alive," and "The Vapor of Death" suggest that suspense and thrills abounded in this fifteen-chapter offering, which revolved around the secret of prolonging human life through animal gland transplants.

In 1920 Wilson and Gerber made **The Branded Four** for Select, with an unusual story by George Pyper and Hope Loring. The title refers to four babies who were mysteriously branded by a wealthy old man in such a way that the brands would surface at maturity to reveal, with the help of his diary, the hiding place of a fortune in gold. After his death, his crooked lawyer attempts to kidnap the girls, now grown, and to steal the diary. Detective Wilson always manages to see that he never gets them all together at the same time. Neva, of course, was one of the four branded beauties, and we suspect that certain members of the audience would have been more interested in examining the brands than in tracing down the gold.

After a couple of adventure features for Berwilla Films, which Wilson also produced, the two did a serial titled **The Mysterious Pearl** (1921) for Photoplay Serials, with Wilson directing and producing. While he did not act in them, he also directed and produced two Gerber features, **The Price of Youth** (1922), in which Neva played an aspiring musician, and **Impulse** (1922), a society melodrama.

In a change of pace, Neva co-starred with popular Western star Jack Perrin in Arrow's **The Santa Fe Trail** (1923), then made **In the Days of '49** (1924) with Edmund Cobb. Both were undistinguished Western serials. Subsequently she made a series of features for Wild West Films, released by Arrow. Most were with Dick Hatton. Wilson was nowhere in sight. The features were cheapies, made for and shown almost exclusively in the independent market in second-rate houses, but they promoted Neva, since she was actually better known than Hatton.

She was reunited with Wilson for one Arrow film, **Vic Dyson Pays** (1925), and then made a series of Western features for J. Charles Davis Distributing Company, with Wilson directing as well as acting. These forgotten little gems were a notch above the Hatton-Gerber films, though still inexpensive oaters destined for the independent market. Their work for Davis culminated in three Wilson-Gerber serials, which Davis had arranged for release through Vital Exchanges. The first, **The Mystery Box** (1925), was a Western of average quality with story and direction by Alvin J. Neitz. The second, called **The Power God** (1925), proved to be a good one. It was directed by Wilson, and the story revolved around a machine that could generate power without consuming fuel. Their third chapter-by-chapter thriller, **Officer 444**, was released by Goodwill Pictures after both Vital Exchanges, through which Davis released its serial products, and Davis itself collapsed and went out of business. Goodwill also took over distribution of **The Power God**. Neither cliffhanger got many bookings, as Goodwill was a small outfit with a poor distribution setup. It was unfortunate that the Davis serials met such an inglorious end, for they were not bad and Miss Gerber, as well as Wilson, deserved more recognition for her serial work.

One of the better Western features released by Goodwill Pictures in its short history was **The Fighting Stallion** (1926), starring Yakima Canutt and Neva Gerber. This time Ben Wilson directed Miss Gerber, and Yak demonstrated his stunting superiority (he was less convincing in the romantic interludes).

Wilson and Gerber had not yet walked the last mile as a screen team. For his own production company, Wilson starred in, produced, and directed seven prairie thunderers for release by Rayart, forerunner of Monogram. Naturally Miss Gerber was the leading lady. Today these are scarcely remembered, though they were satisfactory fodder for insatiable shoot-em-up appetites in the 1920s. Wilson failed to make a lasting impression as a Western hero, though he was a better actor than Al Hoxie, Bob Reeves, Fred Humes, Bob Curwood, and others whose names are still associated with standard Westerns. Both Wilson's and Gerber's fame rests primarily on serials, which are understandably better remembered than routine Western features. Many more people saw Wilson and Gerber in the continued pieces, for the serials played at some of the theatres that would not book the independent Westerns but would use the cheaper serials to supplement their program of quality Westerns from Universal, Pathé, and Fox.

In 1928 Wilson evidently called it quits as an actor. As a director he guided Miss Gerber through a few "C" films, including one called **The Lone Patrol** (1928), in which she was billed as Jean Dolores. In 1928 Neva co-starred with Wally Wales in the first, and unpublicized, all-sound serial for Ben Wilson productions. Here too she was billed as Jean Dolores. We have no idea why Neva, with a name recognized by serial audiences, would be billed under an unknown name. The serial needed all the help it could get! It was never copyrighted, never reviewed, and evidently had few playdates. In 1974 Wally Wales, commenting on the film, stated in a letter to the author that:

The Branded Four (Select, 1920)

It was about a mad inventor who could throw his voice in the air so a whole city could hear it. He then threatened the officials and people that if they didn't change their rotten ways he would destroy them and all they had. The film was made in Hollywood at the very beginning of sound when no one knew how to make a sound picture. I doubt very much it was ever released. It must have been pretty bad!

But it was released on the state rights market. Today a copy of this lost serial would be a real find, worth far more than its total production cost at the time.

The Voice from the Sky is the last credit we have for Neva Gerber under either of her screen names. It was her thirteenth serial and the twelfth in which she was the leading lady.

We wish we could report on what happened to this heroine, perhaps the most elusive and enigmatic of all the serial stars. With a demonstrable ability to survive and, in varying degrees, to prosper, Neva came out looking good no matter how odious the picture. Her films were designed to score heavily in the hinterlands as well as at Saturday matinées in the "nabes" (neighborhood theatres), and this they did. Such primitive ingredients as lust, diabolical revenge, and jealousy were handled in such a way (hopefully) as not to warp kids' thinking. The suspense of the Gerber pictures was well sustained, with all kinds of deviltry mixed in to keep the customers coming back.

We can only hope that Neva's post-screen life was a long and happy one, and that we may yet be able to unearth the details of her life and enhance her recognition as an all-time great cliffhanger queen and cowgirl.

NEVA GERBER Filmography

THE FLOWER GIRL'S ROMANCE
(Kalem, November 1912) 1 Reel
Jane Wolff, Carlyle Blackwell, William H. West, *Neva Gerber*

THE WATER RIGHT WAR
(Kalem, November, 1912) 1 Reel
Neva Gerber, Carlyle Blackwell, William H. West, Miriam Cooper

THE CASTLE OF DESPAIR
(Universal-Gold Seal, August 22, 1913) 3 Reels
Malcolm Blevins, Percy Challenger, *Neva Gerber*, Carl Von Schiller, Frederick Herrington, Virginia Corbin
Director: Ben Wilson
Story: William A. Lathrop

THE DETECTIVE'S SISTER
(Kalem, April 1914) 2 Reels
Carlyle Blackwell, *Neva Gerber*
Director: George Melford
Story: Hamilton Smith

THE FRINGE OF THE GLOVE
(Kalem, May 1914) 2 Reels
Carlyle Blackwell, *Neva Gerber*, R. C. Hadley

THE CRIMINAL CODE
(Balboa, November 1914) 3 Reels
Edwin August, *Neva Gerber*

THE HIGH HAND
(Favorite Players, 1914)
Carlyle Blackwell, *Neva Gerber*

AN EYE FOR AN EYE
(Balboa, January 1915) 4 Reels
Neva Gerber
Director: William Desmond Taylor

THE AWAKENING
(Vitagraph, April 12, 1915) 2 Reels
Neva Gerber, Montagu Love, Anita Stewart, Earle Williams
Director: Ralph Ince
Story: James Olive Curwood

NAUGHTY HENRIETTA
(American Film/Beauty, May 28, 1915)
Neva Gerber, Webster Campbell
Director: Frank Cooley
Story: Mrs. Howard Clark

THE STAY-AT-HOMES
(American Film/Beauty, June 14, 1915)
Neva Gerber, Webster Campbell
Director: Frank Cooley
Story: C. M. Brown

THE REDEMPTION OF THE JASONS
(American Film/Beauty, June 18, 1915) 1 Reel
Neva Gerber, Webster Campbell, Frank Cooley
Director: Frank Cooley

THE MOLLYCODDLE
(American Film/Beauty, June 18, 1915)
Neva Gerber, Webster Campbell
Director: Frank Cooley
Story: M. R. McKinstry

A DEAL IN DIAMONDS
(American Film/Beauty, June 19, 1915) 1 Reel
Neva Gerber, Webster Campbell
Director: Frank Cooley
Story: Abraham Nelson

THE MADONNA
(American Film/Beauty, June 19, 1915) 1 Reel
Neva Gerber, Webster Campbell
Director: Frank Cooley
Story: Mrs. E. N. Shipley

APPLIED ROMANCE
(American Film/Beauty, July 12, 1915) 1 Reel
Neva Gerber, Webster Campbell
Director: Archer MacMackin
Story: Flora B. Snyder

CUPID TAKES A TAXI
(American Film/Beauty, July 14, 1915) 1 Reel
Neva Gerber, Webster Campbell
Director: Archer MacMackin
Story: E. Ballard

HIS COLLEGE WIFE
(American Film/Beauty, July 29, 1915)
Neva Gerber, Webster Campbell
Director: Archer MacMackin
Story: Wallace McDonald

BETTY'S FIRST SPONGE CAKE
(American Film/Beauty, July 29, 1915) 1 Reel
Neva Gerber, Webster Campbell
Director: Archer MacMackin
Story: Alan E. Stone

JIMMY ON THE JOB
(American Film/Beauty, August 7, 1915)
Neva Gerber, Webster Campbell, Lucille Ward
Director: Archer MacMackin

The Santa Fe Trail (Arrow, 1923)

PLOT AND COUNTERPLOT
(American Film/Beauty, September 4, 1915)
Neva Gerber, Webster Campbell
Director: Archer MacMackin

GREEN APPLES
(American Film/Beauty, September 13, 1915) 1 Reel
Neva Gerber, Webster Campbell
Director: Archer MacMackin

THE HONEYMOONERS
(American Film/Beauty, September 13, 1915)
Neva Gerber, Webster Campbell, William Carroll, Martey Martin
Director: Archer MacMackin

HIS MYSTERIOUS PROFESSION
(American Film/Beauty, September 13, 1915)
Neva Gerber, Webster Campbell, Lucille Ward
Director: Archer MacMackin
Story: C. M. Brown

INCOGNITO
(American Film/Beauty, September 18, 1915)
Webster Campbell, *Neva Gerber*, Rae Berger, Lucille Ward, Wallace MacDonald, William Carroll
Director: Archer MacMackin

EVERYHEART
(American Film/Beauty, September 18, 1915)
Webster Campbell, *Neva Gerber*, William Carroll, John Sheehan

LOVE, MUMPS, AND BUMPS
(American Film/Beauty, September 25, 1915)
Neva Gerber, Webster Campbell, William Carroll, Lucille Ward, Rae Berger
Director: Archer MacMackin

MOTHER'S BUSY WEEK
(American Film/Beauty, October 2, 1915)
Neva Gerber, William Carroll, Webster Campbell, Rae Berger, Lucille Ward, Cupie Cavens
Director: Archer MacMackin

BILLE, THE HILLBILLY
(American Film/Beauty, October 9, 1915)
Neva Gerber, William Carroll, Lucille Ward, Webster Campbell, Teddy Lynch, Robert Miller
Director: Archer MacMackin

ALIAS JAMES, CHAUFFEUR
(American Film/Beauty, October 16, 1915)
Neva Gerber, Frank Borzage, Jimsey Maye

TOURING WITH TILLIE
(American Film/Beauty, October 23, 1915)
Frank Borzage, *Neva Gerber*, Lucille Ward
Director: Archer MacMackin

ONE TO THE MINUTE
(American Film/Beauty, October 30, 1915)
Neva Gerber, Frank Borzage, William Carroll, Rae Berger, Lucille Ward
Director: John Dillon

ALMOST A WIDOW
(American Film/Beauty, November 6, 1915) 1 Reel
Neva Gerber, Beatrice Van, Frank Borzage, Lucille Ward, William Carroll
Director: John Dillon

ANITA'S BUTTERFLY
(American Film/Beauty, November 13, 1915) 1 Reel
Neva Gerber, Frank Borzage
Director: John Dillon

CUPID BEATS FATHER
(American Film/Beauty, November 20, 1915) 1 Reel
Neva Gerber, Frank Borzage
Director: James Douglass

GETTING IN WRONG
(American-Beauty, December, 1915)
Neva Gerber, William Carroll, Lucille Ward, Jack Dillon
Director: Jack Dillon

MISCHIEF AND A MIRROR
(American-Beauty, December, 1915)
Neva Gerber, William MacDonald, Dick Rosson, William Carroll, Lucille Ward
Director: Archer MacMackin

NOBODY'S HOME
(American Film/Beauty, December 4, 1915)
Frank Borzage, *Neva Gerber*, William Carroll, Mollie Shafer, Lucille Ward, Rae Berger, Dick Rosson

MAKING OVER FATHER
(American Film/Beauty, December 11, 1915) 1 Reel
Frank Borzage, *Neva Gerber*, William Carroll

TWO HEARTS AND A THIEF
(American Film/Beauty, December 11, 1915)
Neva Gerber, Frank Borzage, Lucille Ward, Rae Berger
Director: Jack Dillon

THAT COUNTRY GAL
(American Film/Beauty, December 18, 1915)
Neva Gerber, Lucille Ward, William Carroll, Nan Christy, King Clark
Director: James Douglass

ELLA WANTED TO ELOPE
(American-Beauty, January, 1916) 1 Reel
Neva Gerber, Lucille Ward, William Carroll, Richard Rosson
Director: James Douglass

MAMMY'S ROSE
(American-Beauty, January, 1916) 1 Reel
Neva Gerber, Frank Borzage
Director: James Douglass

WON BY ONE
(American-Beauty, January, 1916)
Neva Gerber, Wallace MacDonald, Dick Rosson, Hugh Bennett
Director: Archer MacMackin

IDLE WIVES
(Universal, October, 1916) 7 Reels
Lois Weber, Phillips Smalley, Mary MacLaren, Charles Perley, *Neva Gerber*, Edward Hearn, Maude George, Eva Lewis, Ben Wilson
Director: Lois Weber, Phillips Smalley
Screenplay: Lois Weber
Story: James Oppenheim

SOCIETY HYPOCRITES
(Universal, October, 1916) 3 Reels
Ben Wilson, *Neva Gerber*, Charley Perley, Helen Leslie, Joseph Girard, F. MacQuarrie, Mina Cunard, Edward Cecil, William Welsh
Director: Ben Wilson
Screenplay: Willis and Woods

HONOR THY COUNTRY
(Universal, November 8, 1916) 3 Reels
Neva Gerber, Edward Cecil, Joseph Gerard, Rhea Haines, Charles Perley
Director: Ben Wilson
Screenplay: Alice Von Saxmar
Story: Willis Woods

THE PRODIGAL WIDOW
(Universal-Gold Seal, January 3, 1917) 3 Reels
Neva Gerber, Edward Cecil, Carl Von Schiller, Charles Perley, Clyde Benson
Director: Ben Wilson
Story: Walter Woods

THE GREAT SECRET
(Serial Producing Company/Metro, January 8, 1917) 18 Chapters
Francix X. Bushman, Beverly Bayne, Belle Bruce, Fred R. Stanton, Tom Blake, Sue Balfour, Charles Ripley, Ed Connelly, Helen Dunbar, Art Ortego, Dorothy Haydel, Charles Fang, Tammany Young, William J. Butler, *Neva Gerber*, John Clark, Lillian Sullivan, Kid Broad, Bert Keyes, Jim Quinn, William J. Calhoun, Matilda Brundage, Jack Goodman, Spike Robinson, Ed Kelly, Paddy Sullivan, Baby Ivyward, John Leach, Ed Laurence, Monte Attel, Robert Carson, Eugene Beandino, Fred Roberts, Marie De Chett
Director: Christy Cabanne
Screenplay: Christy Cabanne
Story: Fred de Gresac
Producer: Christy Cabanne
Chapters: (1) The Whirlpools of Destiny (2) The Casket of Tainted Treasure (3) The Hidden Hand (4) From Sunshine to Shadow (5) The Trap (6) The Dragon's Den (7) The Yellow Claw (8) A Clue from the Klondike (9) Cupid's Puzzle (10) The Woman and the Game (11) A Shot in the Dark (12) Caught in the Web (13) The Struggle (14) The Escape (15) The Test of Death (16) The Crafty Hand (17) The Missing Finger (18) The Great Secret

THE VOICE ON THE WIRE
(Universal, March 18, 1917) 15 Chaps.
Neva Gerber, Ben Wilson, Francis McDonald, Ernest Shields, Joseph W. Girard, Frank Tokonaga, Howard Crampton, Kingsley Benedict, Nigel De Brulier, Lim Wells, Frank MacQuarrie, Hoot Gibson
Director: Stuart Paton
Screenplay: J. Grubb Alexander
Chapters: (1) The Oriental Death Punch (2) The Mysterious Man in Black (3) The Spider's Web (4) The Next Victim (5) The Spectral Hand (6) The Death Warrant (7) The Marked Room (8) High Finance (9) A Stern Chase (10) The Guarded Heart (11) The Thought Machine (12) The Sign of the Thumb or The Fifth Victim (13) Twixt Death and Dawn (14) The Light of Dawn (15) The Living Death

LIKE WILDFIRE
(Universal-Butterfly, April 26, 1917) 5 Reels
Neva Gerber, Herbert Rawlinson, L. M. Wells, Johnnie Cook, Howard Crampton, Burton Law, Willard Wayne
Director: Stuart Paton
Screenplay: Karl Coolidge
Story: Louis Weltzenkorn, "The Ten Cent Lady"

CAUGHT IN THE ACT
(Universal-Victor, July 13, 1917) 2 Reels
Neva Gerber, Herbert Rawlinson, Willard Wayne, Frank Tokonaga, Dick Ryan, Billy Human
Director: Eugene B. Lewis
Story: T. N. Heffron

THE SPINDLE OF LIFE
(Universal-Butterfly, September 8, 1917) 5 Reels
Neva Gerber, Ben Wilson, Jessie Pratt, Ed Brady, Richard La Reno, Winter Hall, Hayward Mack, A. E. Witting, Willard Wayne
Director: George Cochrane
Screenplay: Karl R. Coolidge
Story: Sidney Robinson, "Gladstone"

THE MYSTERY SHIP
(Universal, December 1, 1917) 18 Chapters
Ben Wilson, *Neva Gerber*, Kingsley Benedict, Duke Worne, Neal Hart, Harry Archer, Elsie Jane Wilson, Phil Ford, Elsie Van Name, Nigel De Brulier
Directors: Harry Harvey, Henry McRae
Screenplay: Elsie Van Name
Story: William Parker, Blaine Pearson
Chapters: (1) The Crescent Scar (2) The Grip of Hate (3) Adrift (4) The Secret of the Tomb (5) The Fire God (6) Treachery (7) One Minute to Leave (8) Hidden Hands (9) The Black Masks (10) The Rescue (11) The Line of Death (12) The Rain of Fire (13) The Underground House (14) The Masked Riders (15) The House of Trickery (16) The Forced Marriage (17) The Deadly Torpedo (18) The Fight in Mid-Air

THE GREAT TORPEDO SECRET
(Universal-Gold Seal, February 20, 1918) 3 Reels
Herbert Rawlinson, Howard Crampton, *Neva Gerber*, Frank Tokanaga, Mrs. Crampton, Frances Mayon, Adele Woods
Director: Stuart Paton
Screenplay: E. B. Lewis

HELL BENT
(Universal, June 29, 1918)
Harry Carey, *Neva Gerber*, Duke R. Lee, Vester Pegg, Joe Harris
Director: John Ford
Screenplay: John Ford, Harry Carey
Story: Jack Ford, Harry Carey

THREE MOUNTED MEN
(Universal, October 7, 1918) 6 Reels
Harry Carey, *Neva Gerber*, Joe Harris, Harry Carter
Director: Jack (John) Ford
Story: Eugene B. Lewis

LET'S FIGHT
(Nestor, November, 1918) 1 Reel
Ben Wilson, *Neva Gerber*
Director: Ben Wilson
Story: William E. Wing

ROPED
(Universal, January 13, 1919) 6 Reels
Harry Carey, *Neva Gerber*, J. Farrell McDonald, Mollie McConnell, Arthur Shirley
Director: Jack (John) Ford
Story: Eugene B. Lewis

WHEN A WOMAN STRIKES
(British-American Pictures, March, 1919)
Rosemary Theby, Ben Wilson, *Neva Gerber*, Murdock MacQuarrie, George Nicholls, Robert Brower
Director/Story: Roy Clements

A FIGHT FOR LOVE
(Universal--Special, March 24, 1919) 6 Reels
Harry Carey, *Neva Gerber*, J. Farrell McDonald, Joe Harris, Princess Neola Mae, Mark Fenton
Director: Jack (John) Ford
Story: Eugene B. Lewis

PITFALLS OF A BIG CITY
(Fox, April 13, 1919) 5 Reels
William Scott, Gladys Brockwell, William Sheer, *Neva Gerber*, Al Fremont, Ashton Dearholt, Janis Wilson
Story: Bennett R. Cohn

BILLY'S HAT
(Universal, September, 1919) 1 Reel
Ben Wilson, *Neva Gerber*
Director: Roy Clements

TRAIL OF THE OCTOPUS
(Hallmark, October, 1919) 15 Chapters
Ben Wilson, *Neva Gerber*, William Dyer, Howard Crampton, William Carroll, Marie Pavis, Allan Garcia
Director: Duke Worne
Story: J. Grubb Alexander
Chapters: (1) The Devil's Trade-Mark (2) Purple Dagger (3) Face to Face (4) The Hand of Wang (5) The Eye of Satan (6) Behind the Mask (7) The Dance of Death (8) Satan's Soulmate (9) The Chained Soul (10) The Ape Man (11) The Red Death (12) The Poisoned Talon (13) The Phantom Mandarin (14) The House of Shadows (15) The Yellow Octopus
(**Note:** Chapter 6 is 5 reels in length, whereas the others are 2 reels)

TAILOR MAID
(Universal, December, 1919) 1 Reel
Billy Mason, *Neva Gerber*

THE SCREAMING SHADOW
(Hallmark, February 22, 1920) 15 Chapters
Ben Wilson, *Neva Gerber*, William Dyer, Howard Crampton, William Carroll, Fred Gable, Joseph W. Girard, Francis Terry, Pansy Porter, Claire Mille, Joseph Manning
Director: Duke Worne
Story: J. Grubb Alexander, Harvey Gates
Chapters: (1) A Cry in the Dark (2) The Virgin of Death (3) The Fang of the Beast (4) The Black Seven (5) The Vapor of Death (6) The Hidden Menace or The Crawling Horror (7) Into the Depths (8) The White Terror (9) The Sleeping Death (10) The Prey of Mong (11) Liquid Fire (12) Cold Steel (13) The Fourth Symbol (14) Entombed Alive (15) Unmasked

THE BRANDED FOUR
(Select, August 1, 1920) 15 Chapters
Ben Wilson, *Neva Gerber*, Joseph Girard, William Dyer, Ashton Dearholt, Pansy Porter, William Carroll, Golda Madden, Hal Wilson
Director: Duke Worne
Screenplay: Hope Loring, George W. Pyper
Story: Hope Loring, George W. Pyper
Chapters: (1) A Strange Legacy (2) The Devil's Trap (3) Flames of Revenge (4) The Blade of Death (5) Fate's Pawn (6) The Hidden Cave (7) Shanghaied (8) Mutiny (9) The House of Doom (10) Ray of Destruction (11) Buried Alive (12) Lost to the World (13) Valley of Death (14) From the Sky (15) Sands of Torment

DANGEROUS PATHS
(Berwilla/Arrow, July 1921) 5 Reels
Neva Gerber, Ben Wilson, Edith Stayart, Joseph W. Girard, Henry Van Sickle, Helen Gilmore
Director: Duke Worne
Screenplay: Joseph W. Girard
Story: Joseph W. Girard
Producer: Ben Wilson

A YANKEE GO-GETTER
(Berwilla/Arrow, July 1921) 5 Reels
Neva Gerber, James Morrison, Joseph Girard, Ashton Dearholt
Director: Duke Worne
Story: Clifford Howard, Burke Jenkins
Producer: Ben Wilson

THE MYSTERIOUS PEARL
(Photoplay Serials, December 1921) 15 Chapters
Ben Wilson, *Neva Gerber*, Ashton Dearholt, Joseph W. Girard, William A. Carroll, Charles King, Duke Worne, Charles B. Mason
Director: Ben Wilson
Screenplay: J. Grubb Alexander, Harvey Gates
Chapters: (1) The Pearl Web (2) The Brass Spectre (3) The Hand in the Fog (4) Four Black Pennies (5) Through the Door (6) The Bride of Hate (7) The Getaway (8) Broken Fetters (9) Leering Faces (10) The Graven Image (11) The Phantom Husband (12) The Door Between (13) The Living Death (14) The Sting of the Lash (15) The Pearl

THE PRICE OF YOUTH
(Berwilla/Arrow, March 15, 1922) 5 Reels
Neva Gerber, Spottiswoode Aitken, Ashton Dearholt, Charles L. King, Joseph Girard, Jack Pratt, Pietro Sosso
Director: Ben Wilson
Screenplay: Hope Loring
Story: Wyndham Martin
Producer: Ben Wilson

IMPULSE
(Berwilla/Arrow, July 15, 1922) 5 Reels
Neva Gerber, Jack Dougherty, Goldie Madden, Douglas Gerrard, Ashton Dearholt, Helen Gilmore, Miss Grey
Director: Norval MacGregor
Screenplay: J. Grubb Alexander
Producer: Ben Wilson

THE SANTA FE TRAIL
(Arrow, July 15, 1923) 15 Chaps.
Jack Perrin, *Neva Gerber*, James Welch, Elias Bullock, Wilbur McGaugh, Clark B. Coffey, Jose De La Cruz, Maria Loredo
Directors: Ashton Dearholt, Robert Dillon
Chapters: (1) Mystery of the Trail (2) Kit Carson's Daring Ruse (3) Wagon of Doom (4) The Half-Breed's Treachery (5) The Gauntlet of Death (6) Ride for Life (7) Chasm of Fate (8) Pueblo of Death (9) The Red Menace (10) A Duel of Wits (11) Buried Alive (12) Cavern of Doom (13) Scorching Sands (14) Mission Bells (15) End of the Trail

THE SEVENTH SHERIFF
(Wild West/Arrow, November 15, 1923) 5 Reels
Neva Gerber, Richard Hatton
Director: Richard Hatton

IN THE WEST
(Wild West/Arrow, December 20, 1923) 5 Reels
Neva Gerber, Richard Hatton, Arthur Morrison, Elias Bullock, Robert McKenzie
Director: George Holt
Story: George Holt

TROUBLE TRAIL
(Wild West/Arrow, January 15, 1924) 5 Reels
Neva Gerber, Richard Hatton
Director: George Holt
Screenplay: George Elwood Jenks
Story: George Elwood Jenks

SAGEBRUSH GOSPEL
(Wild West/Arrow, March 1, 1924) 5 Reels
Neva Gerber, Harry von Meter, Richard Hatton, Nellie Franzen
Director: Richard Hatton
Screenplay: Karl Coolidge
Story: Karl Coolidge

THE DAYS OF '49
(Arrow, March 15, 1924) 15 Chapters
Neva Gerber, Edmund Cobb, Ruth Royce, Wilbur McGaugh, Yakima Canutt, Charles Brinley, Clark Coffey, Al Hoxie, Elias Bullock
Directors: Jacques Jaccard, J. Marchand
Story: Karl Coolidge
Chapters: (1) Soldiers of Fortune (2) Red Men and White (3) A Night of Terror (4) The Empire Builders (5) A Web of Lies (6) Demetroff's Vow (7) Facing Death (8) Under the Bear Flag (9) A Ride of Peril (10) Yellow Metal and Blue Blood (11) Gold Madness (2) Crimson Nights (13) Vigilantes Justice (14) For Life and Love (15) Trail's End

WESTERN FATE
(Wild West/Arrow, April 1, 1924) 5 Reels
Dick Hatton, *Neva Gerber*
Director: George Holt
Screenplay: George H. Plympton
Story: George H. Plympton

THE WHIRLWIND RANGER
(Wild West/Arrow, May 1, 1924) 5 Reels
Dick Hatton, *Neva Gerber*
Director: Dick Hatton
Story: Robert McKenzie

CALIFORNIA IN '49
(Arrow, November 13, 1924) 6 Reels
(Feature version of the serial **The Days of '49**)
Edmund Cobb, *Neva Gerber*, Charles Brinley, Ruth Royce, Wilbur McGaugh, Yakima Canutt, Al Hoxie, Clark Coffey, Elias Bullock
Director: Jacques Jaccard, J. Marchand
Story: Karl Coolidge

VIC DYSON PAYS
(Ben Wilson/Arrow, January 3, 1925) 5 Reels
Ben Wilson, Archie Ricks, *Neva Gerber*, Vic Allen, Merrill McCormick, Joseph Girard, Dan Learned
Director: Jacques Jaccard
Story: William E. Wing

WARRIOR GAP
(Davis Distributing Division/Vital Exchanges, December 4, 1925) 5 Reels
Ben Wilson, *Neva Gerber*, Robert Walker, Jim Welch, Aline Goodwin, Lafe McKee, Dick Hatton, Alfred Hewston, Ruth Royce, Len Haynes, William Patten
Director: Alvin J. Neitz
Screenplay: George W. Pyper
Story: Captain Charles King, "Warrior Gap, a story of the Sioux Outbreak of '68"

TONIO, SON OF THE SIERRAS
(Davis Distributing Division, December 19, 1925) 5 Reels
Been Wilson, *Neva Gerber*, Chief Yowlachie, Jim Welch, Bob Walker, Ruth Royce, Fay Adams
Director: Ben Wilson
Story: General Charles King, "Tonio, Son of the Sierras: A Story of the Apache War"

A DAUGHTER OF THE SIOUX
(Davis Distributing Division, December 28, 1925) 5 Reels
Ben Wilson, *Neva Gerber*, Robert Walker, Fay Adams, William Lowery, Rhody Hathaway
Director: Ben Wilson
Screenplay: George W. Pyper
Story: General Charles King, "A Daughter of the Sioux: A Tale of the Indian Frontier"

THE MYSTERY BOX
(Davis Distributing Division/Vital Exchanges, December 1925) 10 Chapters
Ben Wilson, *Neva Gerber*, Lafe McKee, Robert Walker, Charles Brinley, Alfred Hollingsworth, Jack Henderson, Yakima Canutt
Director: Alvin J. Neitz
Story: Alvin J. Neitz
Chapters: (1) The Fatal Box (2) A Tragic Legacy (3) Daring Danger (4) A Leap for Life (5) Defying Fate (6) Trapped by Outlaws (7) Pendulum of Death (8) The Miracle Rider (9) Vengeance of the Mystery Box (10) Vindicated

FORT FRAYNE
(Davis Distributing Division, January 11, 1926) 5 Reels
Ben Wilson, *Neva Gerber*, Ruth Royce, Bill Patton, Lafe McKee
Director: Ben Wilson
Screenplay: George W. Pyper
Story: General Charles King, "Fort Frayne"

THE POWER GOD
(Davis Distributing Divison/Goodwill, January 1926) 15 Chapters
Ben Wilson, *Neva Gerber*, Mary Brooklyn, Mary Crane, John Battaglia
Director: Ben Wilson
Story: Rex Taylor, Harry Haven
Chapters: (1) The Ring of Fate (2) Trapped (3) The Living Dead (4) Black Shadows (5) The Death Chamber (6) House of Peril (7) Hands of the Dark (8) 59th Second (9) Perilous Waters (10) The Bridge of Doom (11) Treachery (12) The Storm's Lash (13) The Purloined Papers (14) The Flaming Menace (15) The Wages of Sin

OFFICER 444
(Davis Distributing Division/Goodwill, May 15, 1926) 10 Chapters
Ben Wilson, *Neva Gerber*, Al Ferguson, Ruth Royce, Jack Mower, Phil Ford, Lafe McKee, Francis Ford, Arthur Beckel, Harry McDonald, Frank Baker
Director: Ben Wilson
Chapters: (1) Flying Squadron (2) Human Rats (3) Trapped (4) Gassed (5) Missing (6) The Radio Ray (7) Death's Shadow (8) Jaws of Doom (9) Underground Trap (10) Justice

THE FIGHTING STALLION
(Goodwill, 1926) 5 Reels
Yakima Canutt, *Neva Gerber*, Al Ferguson, Bud Osborne, Leonard Trainer, Fred Gamble, Boy (a horse)
Director: Ben Wilson
Camera: Joseph Walker

HELL HOUNDS OF THE PLAINS
(Goodwill, 1926) 5 Reels
Yakima Canutt, *Neva Gerber*, Boy (a horse)
Director: Ben Wilson

BAITED TRAP
(Ben Wilson/Rayart, September 1926) 5 Reels
Ben Wilson, *Neva Gerber*, Al Ferguson, Monty O'Grady, Ashton Dearholt, Lafe McKee, Fang (a dog)
Director: Stuart Paton
Screenplay: George W. Pyper
Story: George W. Pyper

THE SHERIFF'S GIRL
(Ben Wilson/Rayart, October 1926) 5 Reels
Ben Wilson, *Neva Gerber*, Fang (a dog)
Director: Ben Wilson

WOLVES OF THE DESERT
(Ben Wilson/Rayart, November 1926) 5 Reels
Ben Wilson, *Neva Gerber*, Ruth Royce, Ashton Dearholt, Al Ferguson, Edward Le Neice, Fang (a dog)
Director: Ben Wilson

WEST OF THE LAW
(Ben Wilson/Rayart, December 1926) 5 Reels
Ben Wilson, *Neva Gerber*, Ashton Dearholt, Hal Walters, Cliff Lyons, Lafe McKee, Al Ferguson, Myrna Thompson, Fang (a dog)
Director: Ben Wilson

THE MYSTERY BRAND
(Ben Wilson/Rayart, January 1927) 5 Reels
Ben Wilson, *Neva Gerber*, Fang (a dog)
Director: Ben Wilson

A YELLOW STREAK
(Ben Wilson/Rayart, February 1927) 5 Reels
Ben Wilson, *Neva Gerber*, Fang (a dog)
Director: Ben Wilson

RIDERS OF THE WEST
(Ben Wilson/Rayart, March 1927) 5 Reels
Ben Wilson, *Neva Gerber*, Ed La Neice, Bud Osborne, Fang (a dog)
Director: Ben Wilson
Screenplay: Robert Dillon

THE RANGE RIDERS
(Ben Wilson/Rayart, April 1927) 5 Reels
Ben Wilson, *Neva Gerber*, Al Ferguson, Ed La Neice, Earl C. Turner, Fang (a dog)
Director: Ben Wilson
Screenplay: Robert Dillon

THE OLD CODE
(Morris R. Schlank/Anchor, November 14, 1928) 6 Reels
Walter McGrail, Lillian Rich, Cliff Lyons, Melbourne McDowell, J. P. McGowan, *Neva Gerber*, Ervin Renard, Mary Gordon, Rhody Hathaway, John Rainbow
Director: Ben Wilson
Screenplay: E. C. Maxwell
Story: James Oliver Curwood

THE LONE PATROL
(Major/Aywon, December 15, 1928) 5 Reels
William Bailey, Jean Dolores (*Neva Gerber*)

THE PHANTOM PINTO
(Major, 1928)
Edmund Cobb, *Neva Gerber*, Francis Ford

THE SADDLE KING
(Anchor, September 5, 1929) 5 Reels
Cliff (Tex) Lyons, *Neva Gerber*, Al Ferguson, Glen Cook, Cheyenne Bill (William McKechnie), Jack Casey, Irving Wafford, Victor Allen
Director: Ben Wilson
Story: Bennett R. Cohen
Camera: Robert Cline

THUNDERING THOMPSON
(Morris R. Schlank/Anchor, October 8, 1929) 5 Reels
Cheyenne Bill (William McKechnie), *Neva Gerber*, Al Ferguson, Cliff Lyons, Ed La Neice
Director: Ben Wilson
Story: Robert Dillon
Camera: Robert Cline

THE VOICE FROM THE SKY
(Ben Wilson/B.Y.B. Films, 1930) 10 Chapters
Wally Wales, Jean Dolores (*Neva Gerber*), Robert Walker, J. P. Lockney, Al Haskell, Cliff Lyons, John C. McCallum, Merle Ferris
Director: Ben Wilson
Story: Robert Dillon
Chapters: (1) Doomed (2) The Cave of Horror (3) The Man From Nowhere (4) Danger Ahead (5) Desperate Deeds (6) Trail of Vengeance (7) The Scarlet Scourge (8) Trapped by Fate (9) The Pit of Peril (10) Hearts of Steel
(This was the first all-sound serial)

Flying G-Men (Columbia, 1939) – Lorna Gray

7 • LORNA GRAY/ADRIAN BOOTH

A Beautiful Brunette Whose Endowments Won a Host of Fans

Adrian Booth, at one time queen of Republic's big-budget Westerns, could put heart into a scene while dressed in a sacklike garment and inundated by billowing clouds of dust thrown up by thundering hoofs. Even in period costumes that failed to do justice to her figure, she always looked desirable.

There was no time for temperament in her films; the scenes were shot fast and the action moved right on to the next setup. The studio seldom spent money on retakes (unless the horses relieved themselves on camera). Actors were expected to get the scene right the first time, and there was no place for prima donnas.

Adrian was born Virginia Pound on July 26, 1924, in Grand Rapids, Michigan. It was in her junior year of high school there that she entered the highly competitive personality and beauty contest from which she emerged as "Miss Michigan." That was the first step in a promising histrionic career, but at the time Adrian didn't give it a thought; she wanted to be a writer.

A shortage of funds kept her from going to college, so she took a job as social director at the New Whitcomb Hotel in St. Joseph, Michigan. A guest at the hotel was impressed with her beauty and her fine singing and urged her to go to New York to meet producer Ben Yost. The actress followed this advice and landed a job as singer and mistress of ceremonies with Yost's "Co-Eds."

While the troupe was playing in Cleveland, Ohio, she also sang with Roger Pryor and his band, who were engaged at the same theater. It was here that she was discovered by a Hollywood talent scout who brought her to the film capital for a screen test. The conclusion was that she "wasn't the type."

The actress was hurt and disillusioned, but for the first time really determined to prove her ability. She made the rounds of the casting offices for weeks and did a few modeling jobs to pay her way. After several discouraging months an agent saw her model in a fashion show, signed her, and arranged for a test at Columbia.

Miss Booth was amazed to hear that the test was successful and she soon signed a contract. She was billed as Lorna Gray until mid-1945, when she became Adrian Booth. Her first features were made in late 1938--two "B" programmers at Columbia and the femme lead in **Red River Range** (1938) on loan-out to Republic. This was a Three Mesquiteers film with John Wayne, Ray Corrigan, and Max Terhune.

Columbia used her as a foil for both The Three Stooges and Buster Keaton in two-reel comedies and as the heroine opposite Charles Starrett in a couple of cowboy flicks. She got a lot of good footage as the daughter of Boris Karloff in **The Man They Could Not Hang** (1939), and she was used advantageously in three Monogram programmers as the love interest opposite Ralph Byrd and Frank Albertson. Before leaving Columbia Adrian was featured in two of the studio's routine serials. She played the sister of an aircraft manufacturer who works with the G-men against a spy ring that is sabotaging American defense industries in **Flying G-Men** (1939). The following year she was the Western heroine who aids a Robin Hood character in his fight against The Skull and his gang in **Deadwood Dick** (1940).

In 1941, still known as Lorna Gray, she began her long association with Republic. As Vultura, exotic ruler of a band of vicious Arabs who want to obtain the tablets and treasure of Hippocrates, she made an impression on serial audiences, along with her pet gorilla Satan (actually Emil Van Horn in a gorilla suit). Of course, heroine Kay Aldridge as Nyoka triumphed in the end, and Vultura got her just deserts. But several years later Adrian was

65

Daughter of Don Q (Republic, 1946) – Kirk Alyn and Adrian Booth

on the right side of the law as the assistant to Dick Purcell playing **Captain America** (1943) in a battle against Lionel Atwill. As The Scarab, Atwill is out to kill with his "purple death," while also conspiring to steal both a life-restoring machine and a Mayan plaque that reveals the location of treasure, and to secure plans for a highly destructive dynamic vibrator. (There was quite a bit of greed in Mr. Atwill!) But Adrian and Captain America saw to it that he finally got the hot seat.

In a return to villainy Adrian portrays a beautiful adventuress who, along with George J. Lewis, LeRoy Mason, and Hal Taliaferro, attempts to steal crown jewels destined for transfer back to Europe in **Federal Operator 99** (1945). But they were foiled by the G-men headed by Marten Lamont. Having learned that crime does not pay, and with the new name of Adrian Booth, she essayed the lead in her final chapter play, **Daughter of Don Q** (1946), as an heiress under an ancient Spanish land grant. With the aid of Kirk Alyn, she attempted to keep another heir from killing all the descendants of Don Quantero so as to inherit the wealth himself.

Adrian made a "B" Western series with Monte Hale and played in assorted features from 1945 to 1948, the year she made **The Gallant Legion** with William Elliott, her first big-budget Western. Three more Westerns with Elliott followed, plus three with Rod Cameron and one with Forrest Tucker, all directed by Joseph Kane, one of Republic's best.

On June 19, 1948, she was married to Warner Bros. film star David Brian in a garden ceremony performed at the Pacific Palisades home of friends. The couple set up housekeeping in a Monterey-style house on a hillside in Sherman Oaks, California, and Adrian worked for several more years. After completing **The Sea Hornet** (1951) for Republic, she decided to retire. In later years both she and her husband became vitally interested in the City of Hope Cancer Research

Hospital and worked in its behalf. Mr. Brian has been quite ill for several years with cancer, and Adrian has remained loyally and lovingly at his side.

LORNA GRAY/ADRIAN BOOTH
Filmography

ADVENTURE IN SAHARA
(Columbia, November 15, 1938) 57 Mins.
Paul Kelly, C. Henry Gordon, *Lorna Gray*, Robert Fiske, Marc Lawrence, Dick Curtis, Stanley Brown, Alan Bridge, Raphael Bennett, Charles Moore, Dwight Frye, Stanley Andrews, Edwin Stanley, Al Herman, Blackie Whiteford, Dutch Hendrian, Harry Strange, George Chesebro, Albert Pollet, Dee Cascoigne, Rube Dalroy
Director: D. Ross Lederman
Screenplay: Maxwell Shane
Story: Sam Fuller

SMASHING THE SPY RING
(Columbia, December 20, 1938) 62 Mins.
Ralph Bellamy, Fay Wray, Regis Toomey, Walter Kingsford, Ann Doran, Warren Hull, Forbes Murray, Paul Whitney, John Tyrell, May Wallace, *Lorna Gray*
Director: Christy Cabanne
Screenplay: Arthur T. Horman, Dorrell and Stuart McGowan
Story: Dorrell and Stuart McGowan

RED RIVER RANGE
(Republic, December 22, 1938) 56 Mins.
(Three Mesquiteers Series)
John Wayne, Ray Corrigan, Max Terhune, Polly Moran, *Lorna Gray*, Kirby Grant, Sammy McKim, William Royle, Perry Ivans, Stanley Blyston, Lenore Bushman, Burr Caruth, Roger Williams, Earl Askam, Olin Francis, Edward Cassidy, Fred Toones, Bob McKenzie, Jack Montgomery, Al Taylor, Theodore Lorch
Director: George Sherman
Screenplay: Luci Ward, Stanley Roberts, Betty Burbridge
Story: Luci Ward
Based on characters created by William Colt MacDonald
Associate Producer: William Berke

THE LONE WOLF SPY HUNT
(Columbia, January 28, 1939) 67 Mins.
Warren William, Ida Lupino, Rita Hayworth, Virginia Weidler, Ralph Morgan, Tom Dugan, Don Beddoe, Leonard Carey, Ben Welden, Bryndon Tynan, Helen Lynd, Irving Bacon, Marek Windheim, Jack Norton, Dick Elliott, Dick Curtis, Marc Lawrence, Stanley Brown, James Craig, Forbes Murray, *Lorna Gray*, Edmund Cobb, I. Stanford Jolley, George DeNormand, James Blaine, Lola Jensen
Director: Peter Godfrey
Screenplay: Jonathan Latimer
Story: Louis Joseph Vance
Associate Producer: Joseph Sistrom

FLYING G-MEN
(Columbia, February, 1939) 15 Chaps.
Robert Paige, James Craig, Richard Fiske, *Lorna Gray*, Forbes Murray, Dick Curtis, Don Beddoe, Sammy McKim, Ann Doran, Nestor Paiva, George Chesebro, Bud Geary, Tom Steele, George Turner, Hugh Prosser
Directors: Ray Taylor, James W. Horne
Screenplay: Robert E. Kent, Basil Dickey, Sherman Lowe
Chapters: (1) Challenge in the Sky (2) Flight of the Condemned (3) The Vulture's Nest (4) The Falcon Strikes (5) Flight from Death (6) Phantom of the Sky (7) Trapped by Radio (8) The Midnight Watch (9) Wings of Terror (10) Flaming Wreckage (11) While a Nation Sleeps (12) Sealed Orders (13) Flame Island (14) Jaws of Death (15) The Falcon's Reward

PEST FROM THE WEST
(Columbia, June 16, 1939) 10 Mins.
Buster Keaton, *Lorna Gray*, Gino Corrado, Richard Fiske, Bud Jamison, Eddie Laughton, Ned Glass, Forbes Murray
Director: Del Lord
Screenplay: Clyde Bruckman

THE MAN THEY COULD NOT HANG
(Columbia, August 17, 1939) 72 Mins.
Boris Karloff, *Lorna Gray*, Robert Wilcox, Roger Pryor, Don Beddoe, Ann Doran, Joseph De Stanfani, Charles Trowbridge, Byron Foulger, Dick Curtis, James Craig, John Tyrell
Director: Nick Grinde
Screenplay: Karl Brown

The Stranger From Texas (Columbia, 1939) – Lorna Gray and Charles Starrett

SKINNY THE MOOCHER
(Columbia, September 8, 1939) 2 Reels
Charley Chase, Ann Doran, John T. Murray, Richard Fiske, Ben Taggart, John Tyrrell, Cy Schindell, Stanley Brown, James Craig, *Lorna Gray* (Adrian Booth)
Director: Del Lord

THOSE HIGH GREY WALLS
(Columbia, September 21, 1939) 82 Mins.
Walter Connolly, Onslow Stevens, Iris Meredith, Paul Fix, Bernerd Nedell, Oscar O'Shea, Nicholas Soussanin, Don Beddoe, Eduardu Thomajan, Delmar Watson, Claire McDowell, Lee Ford, Jack Chapin, *Lorna Gray*, William Bakewell, Robert Sterling
Director: Charles Vidor
Screenplay: Lewis Meltzer, Gladys Lehman
Story: William A. Ullman, Jr.
Producer: B. B. Kahane

BEWARE SPOOKS
(Columbia, October 24, 1939) 68 Mins.
Joe E. Brown, Mary Carlisle, Marc Lawrence, Clarence Kolb, Frank M. Thomas, Don Beddoe, Joseph Downing, *Lorna Gray*, Eddie Laughton
Director: Edward Sedgwick
Screenplay: Richard Flournoy, Albert Duffy, Brian Marlow

THREE SNAPPY PEOPLE
(Columbia, December 1, 1939) 2 Reels
(Three Stooges Series)
Moe Howard, Larry Fine, Jerry Howard, *Lorna Gray*, Don Beddoe, Bud Jamison, Ann Doran, Richard Fiske
Director: Jules White

THE STRANGER FROM TEXAS
(Columbia, December 8, 1939) 54 Mins.
Charles Starrett, *Lorna Gray*, Richard Fiske, Dick Curtis, Edmund Cobb, Bob Nolan and the Sons of the Pioneers, Al Bridge, Jack Rockwell, Hal Taliaferro, Edward J. LeSaint, Buel Bryant, Art Mix, George Chesebro
Director: Sam Nelson
Screenplay: Paul Franklin
Story: Ford Beebe, "The Mysterious Avenger"

ANDY CLYDE GETS SPRING CHICKEN
(Columbia, December 15, 1939) 2 Reels
Andy Clyde, Beatrice Blinn, Richard Fiske, Dorothy Appleby, Eva McKenzie, *Lorna Gray*, Don Beddoe, John Tyrrell, Ethelreda Leopold, Kay Vallon
Director: Jules White

CONVICTED WOMEN
(Columbia, January 31, 1940) 66 Mins.
Rochelle Hudson, Freida Inescort, June Lang, Lola Lane, Glenn Ford, Iris Meredith, *Lorna Gray*, Esther Dale, William Farnum, Mary Field, Beatrice Blinn, Dorothy Appleby, Linda Winters, Claire Rochelle
Director: Nick Grinde
Screenplay: Joseph Carole
Story: Martin Mooney, Alex Gottlieb
Producer: Ralph Cohn

BULLETS FOR RUSTLERS
(Columbia, March 5, 1940) 58 Mins.
Charles Starrett, *Lorna Gray*, Bob Nolan and the Sons of the Pioneers, Dick Curtis, Jack Rockwell, Kenneth MacDonald, Edward J. LeSaint, Francis Walker, Hal Taliaferro, Lee Frather
Director: Sam Nelson
Screenplay: John Rathmell

ROCKIN' THROUGH THE ROCKIES
(Columbia, March 8, 1940) 2 Reels
(The Three Stooges Series)
Moe Howard, Larry Fine, Jerry Howard, Linda Winters, *Lorna Gray*, Dorothy Appleby, Kathryn Sheldon
Director: Jules White

DEADWOOD DICK
(Columbia, July 19, 1940) 15 Chaps.
Don Douglas, *Lorna Gray*, Harry Harvey, Marin Sais, Lane Chandler, Jack Ingram, Charles King, Edward Cassidy, Robert Fiske, Lee Shumway, Edmund Cobb, Ed Peil, Sr., Edward Hearn, Karl Hackett, Roy Barcroft, Bud Osborne, Joe Girard, Tom London, Kenneth Duncan, Yakima Canutt, Kit Guard, Al Ferguson, Constantine Romanoff, Franklyn Farnum, Charles Hamilton, Eddie Featherstone, Jim Corey
Director: James W. Horne
Screenplay: Wyndham Gittens, Morgan B. Cox, George Morgan, John Cutting
Producer: Larry Darmour
Chapters: (1) A Wild West Empire (2) Who Is the Skull? (3) Pirates of the Plains (4) The Skull Baits a Trap (5) Win, Lose, or Draw (6) Buried Alive (7) The Chariot of Doom (8) The Secret of Number 10 (9) The Fatal Warning (10) Framed for Murder (11) The Bucket of Death (12) A Race Against Time (13) The Arsenal of Revolt (14) Holding the Fort (15) The Deadwood Express

UP IN THE AIR
(Monogram, September 9, 1940) 62 Mins.
Frankie Darro, Mantan Moreland, Marjorie Reynolds, *Lorna Gray*, Gordon Jones, Tristram Coffin, Clyde Dilson, Dick Elliott, John Holland, Charleton Young, Dennis Moore, Maxine Leslie, Alex Callam
Director: Howard Bretherton
Screenplay: Edmund Kelso
Producer: Lindsley Parsons

DRUMS OF THE DESERT
(Monogram, October 7, 1940) 64 Mins.
Ralph Byrd, *Lorna Gray*, Peter George Lynn, William Castello, Mantan Moreland, Jean Del-Val, Ann Codee, Boyd Irwin, Neyle Marx, Albert Morin, Charles Townsend, Jack Chafe, John Stark, Bud Harrison
Director: George Waggner
Screenplay: Joseph West, Dorothy Reid
Story: John T. Neville
Producer: Paul Malvern

CITY LIMITS
(Monogram, July 19, 1941) 63 Mins.
(AKA **Father Steps Out**)
Frank Albertson, Jed Prouty, *Lorna Gray*, Kathryn Sheldon, Frank Faylen, Charles Hall, John Maxwell, John Dilson, Mary Field, Paul Maxey
Director: Jean Yarborough
Screenplay: Joseph West
Producer: Lindsley Parsons

TUXEDO JUNCTION
(Republic, November 23, 1941) 71 Mins.
Leon Weaver, Frank Weaver, June Weaver, Thurston Hall, Frankie Darro, Sally Payne, Clayton Moore, *Lorna Gray*, Billy Benedict, Kenneth Lundy, Howard Hickman, Betty Blythe, Sam Flint
Director: Frank McDonald
Screenplay: Dorrell McGowan, Stuart McGowan
Associate Producer: Armand Schaefer

THE PERILS OF NYOKA
(Republic, June 22, 1942) 15 Chaps.
Kay Aldridge, Clayton Moore, William Benedict, *Lorna Gray*, Charles Middleton, Tris Coffin, Forbes Murray, Robert Strange, George Pembroke, Georges Renavent, John Davidson, George J. Lewis, Ken Terrell, John Bagni, Kenne Duncan, Arvon Dale, John Daheim, Duke Taylor, Tom Steele, Iron Eyes Cody, Forrest Taylor, Yakima Canutt, Art Dillard, Ken Terrell, Augie Gomez, Bud Wolfe, Robert Barron, Emil Van Horn, Herbert Rawlinson, David Sharpe, George Plues, Al Kikume, Leonard Hampton, Cy Slocum, George Suzanne, Dick Thane, Jack O'Shea, Carey Loftin, Duke Green, Jerry Frank
Director: William Witney
Screenplay: Ronald Davidson, Norman S. Hall, William Lively, Joseph O'Donnell, Joseph Poland
Associate Producer: W. J. O'Sullivan
Chapters: (1) Desert Intrigue (2) Death's Chariot (3) Devil's Crucible (4) Ascending Doom (5) Fatal Second (6) Human Sacrifice (7) Monster's Clutch (8) Tuareg Vengeance (9) Burned Alive (10) Treacherous Trail (11) Unknown Peril (12) Underground Tornado (13) Thundering Death (14) Blazing Barrier (15) Satan's Fury

RIDIN' DOWN THE CANYON
(Republic, December 30, 1942) 55 Mins.
Roy Rogers, George F. Hayes, Bob Nolan and the Sons of the Pioneers, (Pat Brady, Hugh and Earl Farr, Tim Spencer, and Lloyd Perryman), Dee "Buzzy" Henry, Linda Hayes, Addison Richards, *Lorna Gray*, Olin Howlin, James Seay, Hal Taliaferro, Forrest Taylor, Roy Barcroft, Art Mix, Art Dillard, "Trigger"
Director: Joseph Kane
Screenplay: Albert DeMond
Story: Robert Williams, Norman Houston
Associate Producer: Harry Grey

SO PROUDLY WE HAIL
(Paramount, July 1943) 126 Mins.
Claudette Colbert, Paulette Goddard, Veronica Lake, George Reeves, Barbara Britton, Walter Abel, Sonny Tufts, Mary Servoss, Ted Hecht, John Litel, Mary Treen, Kitty Kelly, Helen Lynd, *Lorna Gray*, Dorothy Adams, Ann Doran, Jan Wiley, James Flavin, Byron Foulger, Richard Crane, Linda Brent, William Forrest, Yvonne DeCarlo, Hugh Prosser, Eddie Dew
Director: Mark Sandrich
Screenplay: Allan Scott
Producer: Mark Sandrich

O', MY DARLING CLEMENTINE
(Republic, December 31, 1943) 68 Mins.
Roy Acuff and His Smoky Mountain Boys and Girls, The Radio Rogues, Isabel Randolph, Harry Cheshire, The Tennessee Ramblers, Frank Albertson, *Lorna Gray,* Irene Ryan, Eddie Parks, Loie Bridge, Patricia Knox, Tom Kennedy, Edwin Stanley, Emmett Vogan
Director: Frank McDonald
Screenplay: Dorrell and Stuart McGowan
Associate Producer: Armand Schaefer

CAPTAIN AMERICA
(Republic, December 1943) 15 Chapters
Dick Purcell, *Lorna Gray,* Lionel Atwill, Charles Trowbridge, Russell Hicks, George J. Lewis, John Davidson, Norman Nesbitt, Frank Reicher, Tom Chatterton, Robert Frazer, John Hamilton, Hugh Sothern, Crane Whitley, Edward Keane, John Bagni, Jay Novello, LeRoy Mason, Stanley Price, Al Ferguson, Post Parks, Ben Taggart, Jack Kirk, Jack O'Shea, Dale Van Sickel, Fred Graham, Tom London, Tom Steele, Bud Geary, Ken Terrell, Edward Cassidy, Edward Van Sloan, Kenneth Duncan, Robert Wilke, Brooks Benedict, Sam Ash, J. C. Henley, Terry Frost, Hal Craig, Paul Marion, Lynton Brent, Duke Green, Joe Yrigoyen, Ben Erway, Frank O'Connor, Herb Lytton, Robert Strange, Jerry Jerome, Gil Perkins, Wilson Benge, John Daheim, George Magrill, Charles Hutchinson, Glenn Knight, Roy Brent, Jeffrey Sayre, George DeNormand, Allen Pomeroy, Ralf Harolde, Helen Thurston, James Carlisle
Director: John English, Elmer Clifton
Screenplay: Royal Cole, Ronald Davidson, Basil Dickey, Jesse Duffy, Harry Fraser, Grant Nelson, Joseph Poland
Associate Producer: W. J. O'Sullivan
Story: Based on Captain America comic strip
Chapters: (1) The Purple Death (2) Mechanical Executioner (3) The Scarlet Shroud (4) Preview of Murder (5) Blade of Wrath (6) Vault of Vengeance (7) Wholesale Destruction (8) Cremation in the Clouds (9) Triple Tragedy (10) The Avenging Corpse (11) The Dead Man Returns (12) Horror on the Highway (13) Skyscraper Plunge (14) The Scarab Strikes (15) The Toll of Doom

THE GIRL WHO DARED
(Republic, August 5, 1944)
Lorna Gray, Peter Cookson, Grant Withers, Veda Ann Borg, John Hamilton, Willie Best, Vivien Oakland, Roy Barcroft, Kirk Alyn
Director: Howard Bretherton
Screenplay: John K. Butler
Story: Medora Field, "Blood on Her Shoe"
Associate Producer: Rudolph E. Abel

THE ADVENTURES OF KITTY O'DAY
(Monogram, January 19, 1945) 63 Mins.
Jean Parker, Peter Cookson, Tim Ryan, Ralph Sanford, *Lorna Gray,* Jan Wiley, William Forrest, Byron Foulger, Hugh Prosser, Dick Elliott, William Ruhl, Shelton Brooks
Director: William Beaudine
Screenplay: George Callahan, Tim Ryan, Victor Hammond
Story: Victor Hammond
Producer: Lindsley Parsons

FEDERAL OPERATOR 99
(Republic, February 1945) 12 Chaps.
Marten Lamont, Helen Talbot, George J. Lewis, *Lorna Gray,* Hal Taliaferro, LeRoy Mason, Bill Stevens, Maurice Cass, Kernan Cripps, Elaine Lange, Frank Jaquet, Forrest Taylor, Jay Novello, Tom London, Jack Ingram, Craig Lawrence, Rex Lease, Frederick Howard, Michael Gaddis, Edmund Cobb, Tom Steele, Stanley Price, Ernie Adams, George Chesebro, Walter Shumway, Jack O'Shea, Duke Green, Ken Terrell, Dale Van Sickel, Harry Strang, Jack George, Nolan Leary, Frank Marlowe, Jimmy Zaner, Curt Barrett
Directors: Spencer Bennet, Wallace A. Grissell, Yakima Canutt
Screenplay: Albert DeMond, Basil Dickey, Jesse Duffy, Joseph Poland
Associate Producer: Ronald Davidson
Chapters: (1) The Case of Crown Jewels (2) The Case of the Stolen Ransom (3) The Case of the Lawful Counterfeit (4) The Case of the Telephone Code (5) The Case of the Missing Expert (6) The Case of the Double Trap (7) The Case of the Golden Cat (8) The Case of the Invulnerable Criminal (9) The Case of the Torn Blueprint (10) The Case of the Hidden Witness (11) The Case of the Stradivarius (12) The Case of the Musical Clue

FASHION MODEL
(Monogram, March 2, 1945) 61 Mins.
Robert Lowery, Marjorie Weaver, Tim Ryan, *Lorna Gray*, Dorothy Christy, Dewey Robinson, Sally Yarnell, Harry Depp, Nell Craig, Edward Keane, John Valentine
Director: William Beaudine
Screenplay: Victor Hammond, Tim Ryan
Story: Victor Hammond
Associate Producer: William Strobach

TELL IT TO A STAR
(Republic, August 16, 1945) 67 Mins.
Ruth Terry, Robert Livingston, Alan Mowbray, Franklin Pangborn, Isabel Randolph, Eddie Marr, *Adrian Booth*, Frank Orth, Tom Dugan, George Chandler, Mary McCarty, William Davidson, Aurora Miranda
Director: Frank McDonald
Screenplay: John K. Butler
Story: Gerald Drayson Adams, John Krafft

DAKOTA
(Republic, December 25, 1945) 82 Mins.
John Wayne, Vera Ralston, Walter Brennan, Ward Bond, Ona Munson, Hugo Haas, Mike Mazurki, Olive Blakeney, Paul Fix, Grant Withers, Robert Livingston, Olin Howlin, Pierre Watkin, Robert Barrat, Jonathan Hale, Bobby Blake, Paul Hurst, Eddy Waller, Sarah Padden, Jack LaRue, George Cleveland, Roy Barcroft, Selmer Jackson, Claire DuBrey, Linda Stirling, *Adrian Booth*, Cliff Lyons, Rex Lease, Paul E. Burns, William Haade, Nicodemus Stewart
Director: Joseph Kane
Screenplay: Howard Estabrook, Lawrence Hazard
Story: Carl Foreman
Associate Producer: Joseph Kane

HOME ON THE RANGE
(Republic, April 18, 1946) 55 Mins.
(Magnacolor)
Monte Hale, *Adrian Booth*, Bob Nolan and the Sons of the Pioneers, Tom Chatterton, Bobby Blake, LeRoy Mason, Roy Barcroft, Kenne Duncan, Budd Buster, Jack Kirk, John Hamilton
Director: R. G. Springsteen
Screenplay: Betty Burbridge
Story: Betty Burbridge, Bernard McConville
Associate Producer: Louis Gray

VALLEY OF THE ZOMBIES
(Republic, May 24, 1946) 56 Mins.
Robert Livingston, *Adrian Booth*, Ian Keith, Thomas Jackson, Charles Trowbridge, Earle Hodgins, LeRoy Mason, William Haade, Wilton Graff, Charles Cane, Russ Clark, Charles Hamilton
Director: Philip Ford
Screenplay: Dorrell and Stuart McGowan
Story: Royal K. Cole, Sherman L. Loew
Associate Producers: Dorrell and Stuart McGowan

MAN FROM RAINBOW VALLEY
(Republic, June 15, 1946) 56 Mins.
(Magnacolor)
Monte Hale, *Adrian Booth*, Jo Ann Marlowe, Ferris Taylor, Emmett Lynn, Tom London, Bud Geary, Kenne Duncan, Doyle O'Dell, Bert Roach, The Sagebrush Serenaders (Enright Busse, John Scott, and Frank Wilder)
Director: R. G. Springsteen
Screenplay: Betty Burbridge
Associate Producer: Louis Gray

OUT CALIFORNIA WAY
(Republic, December 5, 1946) 67 Mins.
(Trucolor)
Monte Hale, *Adrian Booth*, Bobby Blake, John Dehner, Nolan Leary, Fred Graham, Tom London, Jimmy Starr, Edward Keane, Bob Wilke, Brooks Benedict, St. Luke's Choristers, Foy Willing and the Riders of the Purple Sage, and guest stars Roy Rogers, Allan Lane, Dale Evans, Donald Barry, and "Trigger"
Director: Lesley Selander
Screenplay: Betty Burbridge
Screenplay: Barry Shipman
Associate Producer: Louis Gray

DAUGHTER OF DON Q
(Republic, February 1946) 12 Chapters
Adrian Booth, Kirk Alyn, LeRoy Mason, Roy Barcroft, Claire Meade, Kernan Cripps, Jimmy Ames, Eddie Parker, Tom Steele, Dale Van Sickel, Fred Graham, Tom Quinn, John Daheim, Ted Mapes, I. Standford Jolley, Buddy Roosevelt, George Chesebro, Maxine Doyle, Virginia Carroll, Jack O'Shea, Joe Yrigoyen, George Magrill, Eddie Rocco, D'Arcy Miller, Ken Terrell, Michael Gaddis, Robert Wilke, Charles Sullivan, Matty Roubert, Frederick Howard, Betty Danko
Directors: Spencer Bennet, Fred Brannon
Screenplay: Albert DeMond, Basil Dickey, Jesse Duffy, Lynn Perkins
Associate Producer: Ronald Davidson
Chapters: (1) Multiple Murders (2) Vendetta (3) Under the Knives (4) Race to Destruction (5) Blackout (6) Forged Evidence (7) Execution by Error (8) Window to Death (9) The Juggernaut (10) Cremation (11) Glass Guillotine (12) Dead Man's Vengeance

LAST FRONTIER UPRISING
(Republic, February 1, 1947) 67 Mins.
(Trucolor)
Monte Hale, *Adrian Booth*, James Taggert, Roy Barcroft, Philip Van Zandt, Edmund Cobb, John Ince, Frank O'Conner, Bob Blair, Doye O'Dell, Foy Willing and the Riders of the Purple Sage
Director: Lesley Selander
Screenplay: Harvey Gates
Story: Jerome Odlum
Associate Producer: Louis Gray

SPOILERS OF THE NORTH
(Republic, April 24, 1947) 66 Mins.
(Trucolor)
Paul Kelly, *Adrian Booth*, Evelyn Ankers, James Millican, Roy Barcroft, Louis Jean Heydt, Ted Hecht, Harlan Briggs, Francis McDonald, Maurice Cass, Neyle Morrow
Director: Richard Sale
Screenplay: Milton H. Raison
Story: Milton H. Raison
Associate Producer: Donald H. Brown

ALONG THE OREGON TRAIL
(Republic, August 30, 1947) 64 Mins.
(Trucolor)
Monte Hale, *Adrian Booth*, Max Terhune, Clayton Moore, Roy Barcroft, Will Wright, Wade Crosby, LeRoy Mason, Tom London, Forrest Taylor, Kermit Maynard, Foy Willing and the Riders of the Purple Sage
Director: R. G. Springsteen
Screenplay: Earle Snell
Associate Producer: Melville Tucker

UNDER COLORADO SKIES
(Republic, December 15, 1947) 65 Mins.
(Trucolor)
Monte Hale, *Adrian Booth*, Paul Hurst, William Haade, John Alvin, LeRoy Mason, Tom London, Steve Darrell, Gene Evans, Ted Adams, Steve Raines, Hank Patterson, Foy Willing and the Riders of the Purple Sage
Director: R. G. Springsteen
Screenplay: Louise Rousseau
Associate Producer: Melville Tucker

EXPOSED
(Republic, September 8, 1947) 59 Mins.
Robert Armstrong, Adele Mara, *Adrian Booth*, Robert Scott, Bob Steele, William Haade, Harry Shannon, Charles Evans, Joyce Compton, Russell Hicks, Colin Campbell, Paul E. Burns, Edward Gargan, Mary Gordon, Patricia Knox
Director: George Blair
Screenplay: Royal K. Cole, Charles Moran
Story: Charles Moran
Associate Producer: William O'Sullivan

LIGHTNIN' IN THE FOREST
(Republic, March 25, 1948) 58 Mins.
Lynne Roberts, Donald Barry, Warren Douglas, *Adrian Booth*, Lucien Littlefield, Claire DuBrey, Roy Barcroft, Paul Harvey, Al Eben, Jerry Jerome, George Chandler, Eddie Dunn, Dale Van Sickel, Bud Wolfe, Hank Worden
Director: George Blair
Screenplay: John K. Butler
Story: J. Benton Cheney
Producer: Sidney Picker

CALIFORNIA FIREBRAND
(Republic, April 1, 1948) 63 Mins.
(Trucolor)
Monte Hale, *Adrian Booth*, Paul C. Hurst, Alice Tyrell, Tris Coffin, LeRoy Mason, Douglas Evans, Sarah Edwards, Dan Sheridan, Duke York, Lanny Rees, Foy Willing and the Riders of the Purple Sage
Director: Philip Ford
Screenplay: J. Benton Cheney, John K. Butler

THE GALLANT LEGION
(Republic, May 24, 1948) 88 Mins.
William Elliott, *Adrian Booth*, Joseph Schildkraut, Bruce Cabot, Andy Devine, Jack Holt, Grant Withers, Adele Mara, James Brown, Hal Landon, Russell Hicks, Hal Taliaferro, Herbert Rawlinson, Marshall Reed, Harry Woods, Trevor Bardette, John Hamilton, Iron Eyes Cody, Rex Lease, Kermit Maynard, George Chesebro, Chief Yowlachie, Noble Johnson, Glenn Strange, Jack Kirk
Director: Joseph Kane
Screenplay: Gerald Adams
Story: John Butler, Gerald Geraghty
Producer: Joseph Kane

THE PLUNDERERS
(Republic, December 1, 1948) 87 Mins.
(Trucolor)
Rod Cameron, Ilona Massey, *Adrian Booth*, Forrest Tucker, George Cleveland, Grant Withers, Taylor Holmes, Paul Fix, Francis Ford, James Flavin, Maude Eburne, Russell Hicks, Mary Ruth Wade, Louis R. Faust, Hank Bell, Rex Lease
Director: Joseph Kane
Screenplay: Gerald Geraghty, Gerald Adams
Story: James Edward Grant
Associate Producer: Joseph Kane

HIDEOUT
(Republic, March 8, 1949) 61 Mins.
Adrian Booth, Lloyd Bridges, Ray Collins, Sheila Ryan, Alan Carney, Jeff Corey, Fletcher Chandler, Don Beddoe, Charles Halton, Emory Parnell, Nana Bryant, Paul E. Burns, Douglas Evans, Smoki Whitfield
Director: Philip Ford
Screenplay: John K. Butler
Story: William Port
Associate Producer: Sidney Picker

THE LAST BANDIT
(Republic, February 25, 1949) 80 Mins.
Bill Elliott, *Adrian Booth*, Forrest Tucker, Andy Devine, Jack Holt, Minna Gombell, Grant Withers, Virginia Brissac, Stanley Andrews, Martin Garralaga, Charles Middleton, Joseph Crehan, Rex Lease, Emmett Lynn, Eugene Roth, George Chesebro, Hank Bell, Jack O'Shea, Tex Terry, Steve Clark
Director: Joseph Kane
Screenplay: Thames Williams
Story: Norman S. Hall
Associate Producer: Joseph Kane

BRIMSTONE
(Republic, August 15, 1949) 90 Mins.
Rod Cameron, *Adrian Booth*, Walter Brennan, Forrest Tucker, Jack Holt, Jim Davis, James Brown, Guinn "Big Boy" Williams, Charlita, Hal Taliaferro
Director: Joseph Kane
Screenplay: Thames Williams
Story: Norman S. Hall
Associate Producer: Joseph Kane

ROCK ISLAND TRAIL
(Republic, May 18, 1950) 90 Mins.
Forrest Tucker, Adele Mara, *Adrian Booth*, Bruce Cabot, Chill Wills, Jeff Corey, Grant Withers, Barbara Fuller, Roy Barcroft, Pierre Watkin, Olin Howlin, Emory Parnell
Director: Joseph Kane
Screenplay: James Edward Grant
Story: Frank J. Nevins, "A Yankee Dared"
Associate Producer: Paul Malvern

SAVAGE HORDE
(Republic, July 3, 1950) 90 Mins.
William Elliott, *Adrian Booth,* Grant Withers, Barbara Fuller, Noah Beery, Jim Davis, Bob Steele, Douglass Dumbrille, Will Wright, Roy Barcroft, Earle Hodgins, Stuart Hamblen, Hal Taliaferro, Lloyd Ingraham, Marshall Reed, Crane Whitley, Charles Stevens, James Flavin, Edward Cassidy, Kermit Maynard, George Chesebro, Jack O'Shea, Monte Montague, Bud Osborne, Reed Howes
Director: Joseph Kane
Screenplay: Kenneth Gamet
Story: Thames Williamson, Gerald Geraghty
Associate Producer: Joseph Kane

HOLLYWOOD GOES TO BAT
(Columbia Screen Snapshots, December 1950)
10 Mins.
Jack Carson, Dennis Morgan, Tony Martin, Robert Mitchum, David Brian, *Adrian Booth*, Sonny Tufts, Bob Crosby, Roddy McDowall, Art Linkletter, Jane Russell, Marilyn Maxwell, Rhonda Fleming
Director: Ralph Staub
Producer: Ralph Staub

OH SUSANNA
(Republic, March 3, 1951) 90 Mins.
(Trucolor)
Rod Cameron, *Adrian Booth*, Forrest Tucker, Chill Wills, William Ching, Jim Davis, Wally Cassell, Douglas Kennedy, James Lydon, William Haade, James Flavin, Charles Stevens, Alan Bridge, Marshall Reed, John Pickard
Director: Joseph Kane
Screenplay: Charles Marquis Warren
Associate Producer: Joseph Kane

YELLOW FIN
(Monogram, October 14, 1951) 74 Mins.
Wayne Morris, *Adrian Booth*, Gloria Henry, Damian O'Flynn, Gordon Jones, Paul Fierro, Nacho Galindo, Warren Douglas, Guy Zanette
Director: Frank McDonald
Screenplay: Warren D. Wandberg, Clint Johnson
Producer: Lindsley Parsons

THE SEA HORNET
(Republic, November 11, 1951) 84 Mins.
Rod Cameron, Adele Mara, *Adrian Booth*, Chill Wills, Jim Davis, Richard Jaeckel, Ellen Corby, James Brown, Grant Withers, William Ching, William Haade, Hal Taliaferro, Emil Sitka, Byron Foulger, Monte Blue, Jack Pennick
Director: Gerald Drayson Adams
Story: Gerald Drayson Adams
Associate Producer: Joseph Kane

LOVE'S A-POPPIN'
(Columbia, June 11, 1953) 2 Reels
Andy Clyde, Phil Van Zandt, Margia Dean, Dorothy Appleby, Eva McKenzie, *Lorna Gray,* Suzanne Ridgeway, Ethelreda Leopold, Kay Vallon
Director: Jules White

Dorothy Gulliver

8 • DOROTHY GULLIVER

A Blaze of Glory that Dimmed All Too Quickly

Dorothy Gulliver, at sixteen, was fresh from winning first prize in one of Universal's famous talent searches in 1926. She was soon cast as the flapper heroine in the long-running series of two-reel shorts titled The Collegians. Made over a span of four years, these films, which ran in neighborhood and small-town theatres, costarred Dorothy with George J. Lewis and Eddie Phillips. Many of the scenes were shot on the campus at either the University of California in Los Angeles or the University of Southern California. Most of the extras were college students. The series took two fellows and a girl through four years of Calford College, and was mainly sports oriented. Lewis was the sterling athlete who was always honorable and fair. Phillips was also a fine athlete, but he was inclined to break training and get into scrapes. Often Lewis took the blame and/or covered up for a contrite Phillips. Gulliver was the girl they both loved, but their rivalry was friendly.

A full-length talkie spin-off titled **College Love** (1929) was produced with the principal players near the end of the series. And though she made Westerns, serials, and dramatic films, it is The Collegians for which Dorothy Gulliver is best remembered.

Dorothy was born in Salt Lake City on September 6, circa 1910, and received her education in the public schools there. The petite, hazel-eyed brunette was in amateur dramatics before films. When she won the title "Miss Salt Lake City" in a "See America First" contest, the local Paramount distributor was ready to send her to Hollywood. But then Dorothy won a beauty and talent contest conducted by Universal, with the prize of a trip to Hollywood, a screen test, and a film contract. She appeared in bit roles in a wide variety of films before being cast in the lead in The Collegians series.

For the next five years, the happiest in her professional life, Dorothy was at Universal. In addition to the college pictures she appeared as a supporting player in **The Winking Idol** (1926) and **Strings of Steel** (1926), two William Desmond-Eileen Sedgwick serials. Her first Western of record was a Jack Hoxie oater called **The Rambling Ranger** (1927), in which she was the heroine. She appeared in subsequent Westerns starring Fred Humes, Hoot Gibson, and the dog star, Rin-Tin-Tin.

In 1928 Dorothy was selected as a Wampas Baby Star, one of thirteen young actresses named each year by leading publicists as most likely to reach superstardom.

With the advent of talkies, Dorothy free-lanced and made a number of action films which justify her inclusion in this volume. Audiences of the 1930s saw her as the heroine in quickie sagebrushers with Rex Lease, Tim McCoy, and Bill Elliott, and she played the leading lady in four serials, three of them for Nat Levine's newly organized Mascot Pictures. In **The Galloping Ghost** (1931) Dorothy played another college sweetheart, this time to Harold (Red) Grange, who is out to clear his name of game-throwing and win reinstatement on the team; in **The Phantom of the West** (1931) she aids Tom Tyler in his search for the murderer of his father; and in **The Shadow of the Eagle** (1932) she risks death with John Wayne to bring The Eagle to justice and clear her father's name. RKO's only serial, **The Last Frontier** (1932), had Dorothy as the heartthrob of fighting frontier newspaper editor Creighton Chaney (Lon Chaney, Jr.). Four years later she was one of the principals in the star-studded **Custer's Last Stand** (1936), an independently produced chapter play from Stage and Screen Films.

At the height of her career, Dorothy had a serious accident and was incapacitated for more

Dorothy Gulliver and George J. Lewis (center) in a scene from one of the many "Collegiate" films at Universal.

than a year. This resulted in fewer roles, and she decided to give up her film career. Some years later she did a number of stage plays, including a role in "Face Value" at the Laguna Summer Theatre, which won her acclaim as a comedienne. She also appeared in several television shows, but it was not until 1964 that she made her return to films in the John Cassavetes production, **Faces** (released in 1968). She played a blowsy, middle-aged woman honest enough to express her attraction for the young hustler she and her friends have picked up in a bar. The role brought her additional plaudits. More recently she appeared in **Won Ton Ton, the Dog Who Saved Hollywood** (1976).

Married to publicist Jack Proctor since the late 1940s, Dorothy lives in Hollywood and still has an interest in doing character roles. She won new fans and pleased old ones when she appeared as a guest star at the Raleigh, North Carolina film festival in the summer of 1984.

DOROTHY GULLIVER Filmography

ONE WILD TIME
(Universal-Mustang, March 20, 1926) 2 Reels
Ben Corbett, "Pee Wee" Holmes, Fay Wray, *Dorothy Gulliver*, Robert McKenzie
Director: Vin Moore
Adaptation: Robert McKenzie
Story: W. C. Tuttle

THE WINKING IDOL
(Universal, March 1926) 10 Chapters.
William Desmond, Eileen Sedgwick, Grace Cunard, Herbert Sutch, Jack Richardson, Helen Broneau, Les Sailor, Art Ortego, *Dorothy Gulliver*, Vanna Carroll, Syd Saylor, Monavana
Director: Francis Ford
Screenplay: Arthur Henry Gooden, George Morgan
Story: Charles E. Van Loan
Chapters: (1) The Eye of Evil (2) Buzzard's Roost (3) Crashing Timbers (4) Racing For Love (5) The Vanishing Bride (6) The Torrent of Terror (7) Flames of Fear (8) The Fight at the Falls (9) In Danger of Dynamite (10) The Lost Lode

STRINGS OF STEEL
(Universal, June 28, 1926) 10 Chapters.
William Desmond, Eileen Sedgwick, Albert J. Smith, George Ovey, Ted Duncan, Alphonse Martel, Arthur Morrison, Grace Cunard, Taylor N. Duncan, Blanche Fisher, *Dorothy Gulliver*
Director: Henry McRae
Story: Phillip Dutton Hurn, Oscar Lund
Chapters: (1) The Voice on the Wire (2) The First Central (3) Fighting for Love (4) The Power of Might (5) Kings of the Wire (6) Voice of the Continent (7) Telephone Poles (8) War of the Wire (9) When Lightning Strikes (10) Love and Victory

THE SHOOT 'EM UP KID
(Universal-Mustang, September 11, 1926) 2 Reels
Fred Gilman, Dorothy Gulliver, Ida Teabrook, Jim Corey
Director: Hoot Gibson
Scenario: William Lester
Story: Carol Holloway

BENSON AT CALFORD
(The Collegians Series)
(Universal-Junior Jewel, September 30, 1926) 2 Reels
George J. Lewis, Eddie Phillips, *Dorothy Gulliver*
Producer: Carl Laemmle, Jr.

FIGHTING TO WIN
(The Collegians Series)
(Universal-Junior Jewel, October 12, 1926) 2 Reels
George J. Lewis, Eddie Phillips, *Dorothy Gulliver*
Producer: Carl Laemmle, Jr.

MAKING GOOD
(The Collegians Series)
(Universal-Junior Jewel, October 19, 1926) 2 Reels
George J. Lewis, Eddie Phillips, *Dorothy Gulliver*
Producer: Carl Laemmle, Jr.

THE LAST LAP
(The Collegians Series)
(Universal-Junior Jewel, November 8, 1926) 2 Reels
George J. Lewis, Eddie Phillips, *Dorothy Gulliver*
Producer: Carl Laemmle, Jr.

AROUND THE BASES
(The Collegians Series)
(Universal-Junior Jewel, December 21, 1926) 2 Reels
George J. Lewis, Eddie Phillips, *Dorothy Gulliver*
Producer: Carl Laemmle, Jr.

FIGHTING SPIRIT
(The Collegians Series)
(Universal-Junior Jewel, December 22, 1926) 2 Reels
George J. Lewis, Eddie Phillips, *Dorothy Gulliver*
Producer: Carl Laemmle, Jr.

THE RELAY
(The Collegians Series)
(Universal-Junior Jewel, December 22, 1926) 2 Reels
George J. Lewis, Eddie Phillips, *Dorothy Gulliver*
Producer: Carl Laemmle, Jr.

THE DUDE DESPERADO
(Universal-Mustang, January 29, 1927) 2 Reels
Fred Gilman, *Dorothy Gulliver*
Director: George Hunter
Scenario: Meta C. Sterbe
Story: Rhea Mitchell

CINDER PATH
(The Collegians Series)
(Universal-Junior Jewel, January 31, 1927) 2 Reels
George J. Lewis, Eddie Phillips, *Dorothy Gulliver*
Producer: Carl Laemmle, Jr.

FLASHING OARS
(The Collegians Series)
(Universal-Junior Jewel, February 10, 1927) 2 Reels
George J. Lewis, Eddie Phillips, *Dorothy Gulliver*
Producer: Carl Laemmle, Jr.

BREAKING RECORDS
(The Collegians Series)
(Universal-Junior Jewel, February 28, 1927) 2 Reels
George J. Lewis, Eddie Phillips, *Dorothy Gulliver*
Producer: Carl Laemmle, Jr.

THE RAMBLING RANGER
(Universal, April 10, 1927) 5 Reels
Jack Hoxie, *Dorothy Gulliver*, C. E. Anderson, Monte Montague, Jr., Charles Avery, Monte Montague, Scout, Bunk
Director: Del Henderson
Screenplay: George C. Hively
Story: George C. Hively

CRIMSON COLORS
(The Collegians Series)
(Universal-Junior Jewel, May 2, 1927) 2 Reels
George J. Lewis, Eddie Phillips, *Dorothy Gulliver*
Producer: Carl Laemmle, Jr.

WINNING FIVE
(The Collegians Series)
(Universal-Junior Jewel, July 5, 1927) 2 Reels
George J. Lewis, Eddie Phillips, *Dorothy Gulliver*
Producer: Carl Laemmle, Jr.

THE DAZZLING COEDS
(The Collegians Series)
(Universal-Junior Jewel, July 12, 1927) 2 Reels
George J. Lewis, Eddie Phillips, *Dorothy Gulliver*
Producer: Carl Laemmle, Jr.

THE FIGHTING FINISH
(The Collegians Series)
(Universal-Junior Jewel, July 12, 1927) 2 Reels
George J. Lewis, Eddie Phillips, *Dorothy Gulliver*
Producer: Carl Laemmle, Jr.

SAMSON AT CALFORD
(The Collegians Series)
(Universal-Junior Jewel, October 14, 1927) 2 Reels
George J. Lewis, Eddie Phillips, *Dorothy Gulliver*
Producer: Carl Laemmle, Jr.

THE WINNING PUNCH
(The Collegians Series)
(Universal-Junior Jewel, October 14, 1927) 2 Reels
George J. Lewis, Eddie Phillips, *Dorothy Gulliver*
Producer: Carl Laemmle, Jr.

RUNNING WILD
(The Collegians Series)
(Universal-Junior Jewel, October 18, 1927) 2 Reels
George J. Lewis, Eddie Phillips, *Dorothy Gulliver*
Producer: Carl Laemmle, Jr.

SPLASHING THROUGH
(The Collegians Series)
(Universal-Junior Jewel, October 18, 1927) 2 Reels
George J. Lewis, Eddie Phillips, *Dorothy Gulliver*
Producer: Carl Laemmle, Jr.

THE WINNING GOAL
(The Collegians Series)
(Universal-Junior Jewel, October 24, 1927) 2 Reels
George J. Lewis, Eddie Phillips, *Dorothy Gulliver*
Producer: Carl Laemmle, Jr.

SLIDING HOME
(The Collegians Series)
(Universal-Junior Jewel, October 24, 1927) 2 Reels
George J. Lewis, Eddie Phillips, *Dorothy Gulliver*
Producer: Carl Laemmle, Jr.

A DOG OF THE REGIMENT
(Warner Bros., October 29, 1927) 5 Reels
"Rin-Tin-Tin," *Dorothy Gulliver*, Tom Gallery, John Peters
Director: Ross Lederman
Screenplay: Charles R. Condon
Story: Albert S. Howson, "A Dog of the Regiment"

ONE GLORIOUS SCRAP
(Universal, November 20, 1927) 5 Reels
Fred Humes, *Dorothy Gulliver*, Robert McKenzie, Francis Ford, George French, Cuyler Supplee, Benny Corbett, Gilbert "Pee Wee" Holmes, Dick L'Estrange, Scotty Mattraw
Director: Edgar Lewis
Screenplay: George H. Plympton, George Morgan
Story: Leigh Jacobson

THE SHIELD OF HONOR
(Universal, December 10, 1927) 6 Reels
Neil Hamilton, *Dorothy Gulliver*, Ralph Lewis, Nigel Barrie, Claire McDowell, Fred Esmelton, Harry Northrup, Thelma Todd, David Kirby, Joseph Girard, William Bakewell
Director: Emory Johnson
Screenplay: Leigh Jacobson, Gladys Lehman
Story: Emilie Johnson

GOOD MORNING JUDGE
(Universal, April 29, 1928) 6 Reels
Reginald Denny, Mary Nolan, Otis Harlan, *Dorothy Gulliver*, William Davidson, Bull Montana, William Worthington, Sailor Sharkey, Charles Coleman, William H. Tooker
Director: William A. Seiter
Story: Harry O. Hoyt
Screenplay: Beatrice Van
Adaptation: Earle Snell

HONEYMOON FLATS
(Universal, April 1928) 6 Reels
George Lewis, *Dorothy Gulliver*, Kathlyn Williams, Ward Crane, Bryant Washburn, Phillips Smalley, Jane Winton, Patricia Caron, Eddie Phillips
Director: Millar Webb
Screenplay: Morton Blumenstock
Story: Earl Derr Biggers, "Honeymoon Flats," in Saturday Evening Post

THE WILD WEST SHOW
(Universal, May 20, 1928) 6 Reels
Hoot Gibson, *Dorothy Gulliver*, Allan Forrest, Gale Henry, Monte Montague, Roy Laidlaw, John Hall
Director: Del Andrews
Screenplay: John B. Clymer
Adaptation: Isadore Bernstein
Story: Del Andrews, St. Elmo Boyce

THE JUNIOR YEAR
(The Collegians Series)
(Universal-Junior Jewel, July 25, 1928) 2 Reels
George J. Lewis, Eddie Phillips, *Dorothy Gulliver*
Producer: Carl Laemmle, Jr.

CALFORD vs REDSKINS
(The Collegians Series)
(Universal-Junior Jewel, July 31, 1928) 2 Reels
George J. Lewis, Eddie Phillips, *Dorothy Gulliver*
Producer: Carl Laemmle, Jr.

KICKING THROUGH
(The Collegians Series)
(Universal-Junior Jewel, August 22, 1928) 2 Reels
George J. Lewis, Eddie Phillips, *Dorothy Gulliver*
Producer: Carl Laemmle, Jr.

CALFORD IN THE MOVIES
(The Collegians Series)
(Universal-Junior Jewel, September 7, 1928) 2 Reels
George J. Lewis, Eddie Phillips, *Dorothy Gulliver*
Producer: Carl Laemmle, Jr.

PADDLING COEDS
(The Collegians Series)
(Universal-Junior Jewel, September 20, 1928) 2 Reels
George J. Lewis, Eddie Phillips, Dorothy Gulliver
Producer: Carl Laemmle, Jr.

CLEARING THE TRAIL
(Universal, October 7, 1928) 6 Reels
Hoot Gibson, *Dorothy Gulliver*, Fred Gilman, Cap Anderson, Philo McCullough, Andy Waldron, Duke Lee, Monte Montague, Universal Ranch Riders
Director: B. Reeves Eason
Adaptation: John F. Natteford
Screenplay: John F. Natteford
Story: Charles Maigne

FIGHTING FOR VICTORY
(The Collegians Series)
(Universal-Junior Jewel, October 11, 1928) 2 Reels
George J. Lewis, Eddie Phillips, *Dorothy Gulliver*
Producer: Carl Laemmle, Jr.

DEAR OLD CALFORD
(The Collegians Series)
(Universal-Junior Jewel, October 24, 1928) 2 Reels
George J. Lewis, Eddie Phillips, *Dorothy Gulliver*
Producer: Carl Laemmle, Jr.

CALFORD ON HORSEBACK
(The Collegians Series)
(Universal-Junior Jewel, November 14, 1928) 2 Reels
George J. Lewis, Eddie Phillips, *Dorothy Gulliver*
Producer: Carl Laemmle, Jr.

THE BOOKWORM HERO
(The Collegians Series)
(Universal-Junior Jewel, November 24, 1928) 2 Reels
George J. Lewis, Eddie Phillips, *Dorothy Gulliver*
Producer: Carl Laemmle, Jr.

SPEEDING YOUTH
(The Collegians Series)
(Universal-Junior Jewel, December 19, 1928) 2 Reels
George J. Lewis, Eddie Phillips, *Dorothy Gulliver*
Producer: Carl Laemmle, Jr.

THE WINNING POINT
(The Collegians Series)
(Universal-Junior Jewel, December 19, 1928) 2 Reels
George J. Lewis, Eddie Phillips, *Dorothy Gulliver*
Producer: Carl Laemmle, Jr.

FAREWELL
(The Collegians Series)
(Universal-Junior Jewel, December 19, 1928) 2 Reels
George J. Lewis, Eddie Phillips, *Dorothy Gulliver*
Producer: Carl Laemmle, Jr.

KING OF THE CAMPUS
(The Collegians Series)
(Universal-Junior Jewel, March 23, 1929) 2 Reels
George J. Lewis, Eddie Phillips, *Dorothy Gulliver*
Producer: Carl Laemmle, Jr.

THE RIVALS
(The Collegians Series)
(Universal-Junior Jewel, April 5, 1929) 2 Reels
George J. Lewis, Eddie Phillips, *Dorothy Gulliver*
Producer: Carl Laemmle, Jr.

ON GUARD
(The Collegians Series)
(Universal-Junior Jewel, April 19, 1929) 2 Reels
George J. Lewis, Eddie Phillips, *Dorothy Gulliver*
Producer: Carl Laemmle, Jr.

JUNIOR LUCK
(The Collegians Series)
(Universal-Junior Jewel, May 20, 1929) 2 Reels
George J. Lewis, Eddie Phillips, *Dorothy Gulliver*
Producer: Carl Laemmle, Jr.

THE CROSS COUNTRY RUN
(The Collegians Series)
(Universal-Junior Jewel, June 7, 1929) 2 Reels
George J. Lewis, Eddie Phillips, *Dorothy Gulliver*
Producer: Carl Laemmle, Jr.

SPORTING COURAGE
(The Collegians Series)
(Universal-Junior Jewel, June 13, 1929) 2 Reels
George J. Lewis, Eddie Phillips, *Dorothy Gulliver*
Producer: Carl Laemmle, Jr.

THE VARSITY DRAG
(The Collegians Series)
(Universal-Junior Jewel, June 27, 1929) 2 Reels
George J. Lewis, Eddie Phillips, *Dorothy Gulliver*
Producer: Carl Laemmle, Jr.

FLYING HIGH
(The Collegians Series)
(Universal-Junior Jewel, July 6, 1929) 2 Reels
George J. Lewis, Eddie Phillips, *Dorothy Gulliver*
Producer: Carl Laemmle, Jr.

COLLEGE LOVE
(Universal, July 7, 1929) 8 Reels
George Lewis, Eddie Phillips, *Dorothy Gulliver*, Churchill Ross, Hayden Stevenson, Sumner Getchel
Director: Nat Ross
Screenplay: John B. Clymer, Pierre Couderc
Story: Leonard Fields
Producer: Carl Laemmle, Jr.

ON THE SIDE LINES
(The Collegians Series)
(Universal-Junior Jewel, July 25, 1929) 2 Reels
George J. Lewis, Eddie Phillips, *Dorothy Gulliver*
Producer: Carl Laemmle, Jr.

USE YOUR FEET
(The Collegians Series)
(Universal-Junior Jewel, August 5, 1929) 2 Reels
George J. Lewis, Eddie Phillips, *Dorothy Gulliver*
Producer: Carl Laemmle, Jr.

SPLASH MATES
(The Collegians Series)
(Universal-Junior Jewel, August 19, 1929) 2 Reels
George J. Lewis, Eddie Phillips, *Dorothy Gulliver*
Producer: Carl Laemmle, Jr.

GRADUATION DAZE
(The Collegians Series)
(Universal-Junior Jewel, September 5, 1929) 2 Reels
George J. Lewis, Eddie Phillips, *Dorothy Gulliver*
Producer: Carl Laemmle, Jr.

NIGHT PARADE
(RKO, October 27, 1929) 8 Reels
Hugh Trevor, Lloyd Ingraham, *Dorothy Gulliver*, Aileen Pringle, Robert Ellis, Lee Shumway, Ann Pennington, Charles Sullivan, Walter Kane, Barney Furey, James Dugan, Nate Slott, Marie Astaire
Director: Malcolm St. Clair
Screenplay: James Gruen, George O'Hara
Story: George Abbott, Edward Paramore, and Hyatt Daab, "Ringside"
Producer: William Le Baron

PAINTED FACES
(Tiffany-Stahl, November 20, 1929) 8 Reels
Joe E. Brown, Helen Foster, Richard Tucker, William B. Davidson, Barton Hepburn, *Dorothy Gulliver*, Lester Cole, Sojin, Jack Richardson, Howard Truesdell, Baldy Belmont, Jerry Drew, Walter Jerry, Russ Dudley, Purnell Pratt, Clinton Lyle, Alma Bennett, Mabel Julienne Scott, Florence Midgley, May Wallace
Director: Albert Rogell
Adaptation: Frederic Hatton, Fanny Hatton
Story: Frances Hyland

TROOPERS THREE
(Tiffany, February 15, 1930) 9 Reels
Rex Lease, *Dorothy Gulliver*, Roscoe Karns, Slim Summerville, Tom London, Joseph Girard, Walter Perry
Directors: Norman Taurog, Reeves Eason
Screenplay: John F. Natteford
Story: Arthur Guy Empey

VOICE OF HOLLYWOOD NO. 7
(Tec-Art Studios/Tiffany, May 1930)
Jack Duffy, Johnny Mack Brown, Lillian Rich, *Dorothy Gulliver*, George J. Lewis, Mr. and Mrs. Calvin Coolidge, Mary Pickford, Mack Sennett, Antonio Moreno, Will Hay, The Duncan Sisters
Producer: Louis Lewyn

BIG HEARTED
(Pathe, June 14, 1930) 2 Reels
(Woopee Series)
Harry Gribbon, *Dorothy Gulliver*, Vivian Oakland, Ray Hughes
Director: Robert De Lacy
Adaptation: Hugh Cummings
Story: Charles Diltz
Producer: John C. Flinn
Supervision: Bill Woolfenden

UNDER MONTANA SKIES
(Tiffany, September 10, 1930) 6 Reels
Kenneth Harlan, Slim Summerville, *Dorothy Gulliver*, Nita Martan, Christian Frank, Harry Todd, Ethel Wales, Lafe McKee
Director: Richard Thorpe
Screenplay: Bennett R. Cohen, James A. Aubrey
Story: James A. Aubrey

MIND YOUR OWN BUSINESS
(Pathe, 1930)
(Melody Series)
Dorothy Gulliver, Mary Foy, John Hyams

Troopers Three (Tiffany, 1930) – Dorothy Gulliver, Rex Lease (right), and unidentified player (left).

THE PHANTOM OF THE WEST
(Mascot, January 1, 1931) 10 Chapters.
Tom Tyler, William Desmond, Tom Santschi, *Dorothy Gulliver*, Joe Bonomo, Tom Dugan, Philo McCullough, Kermit Maynard, Frank Lanning, Frank Hagney, Dick Dickinson, Halee Sullivan, Al Taylor, Ernie Adams
Director: Ross Lederman
Producer: Nat Levine
Chapters: (1) The Ghost Riders (2) The Stairway of Doom (3) The Horror in the Dark (4) The Battle of the Strong (5) The League of the Lawless (6) The Canyon of Calamity (7) The Price of Silence (8) The House of Hate (9) The Fatal Secret (10) Rogues' Roundup

IN OLD CHEYENNE
(World Wide/Sono-Art, May 25, 1931) 59 Mins.
Rex Lease, *Dorothy Gulliver*, Jay Hunt, Harry Woods, Harry Todd, Slim Whitaker, Ernie Adams
Director: Stuart Paton
Screenplay: Betty Burbridge
Producer: George Weeks

THE GALLOPING GHOST
(Mascot, September 1931) 12 Chapters.
Harold (Red) Grange, *Dorothy Gulliver*, Walter Miller, Gwen Lee, Francis X. Bushman, Jr., Tom Dugan, Theodore Lorch, Tom London, Edward Hearn, Ernie Adams, Frank Brownlee, Stepin Fetchit, Creighton Chaney (Lon Chaney, Jr.), Wilfred Lucas, Dick Dickison, Joe Mack, Edward Peil, Sr.
Director: B. Reeves Eason
Screenplay: Ford Beebe
Producer: Nat Levine

THE FIGHTING MARSHAL
(Columbia, November 25, 1931) 56 Mins.
Tim McCoy, *Dorothy Gulliver*, Mary Carr, Matthew Betz, Pat O'Malley, Edward J. LeSaint, Lafe McKee, W. A. Howell, Dick Dickinson, Bob Perry, Harry Todd, Ethan Laidlaw, Lee Shumway, Jack Ward, Blackie Whiteford
Director: Ross Lederman
Screenplay: Frank Clark
Story: Frank Clark

THE SHADOW OF THE EAGLE
(Mascot, February 1, 1932) 12 Chapters.
John Wayne, *Dorothy Gulliver*, Walter Miller, Kenneth Harlan, Richard Tucker, Pat O'Malley, Bud Osborne, Ernie Adams, Monte Montague, Yakima Canutt, Edmund Burns, Roy D'Arcy, Billy West, Edward Hearn, Lloyd Whitlock, Ivan Linow, James Bradbury, Jr.
Directors: Ford Beebe, B. Reeves Eason
Screenplay: Ford Beebe, Colbert Clark, Wyndham Gittens
Producer: Nat Levine
Chapters: (1) Unknown (2) Pinholes (3) The Eagle Strikes (4) A Man of a Million Voices (5) The Telephone Cipher (6) Code of the Carnival (7) Eagle or Vulture (8) On the Spot (9) When Thieves Fall Out (10) The Man Who Knows (11) The Eagle's Wings (12) Unknown

THE HONOR OF THE PRESS
(Mayfair, May 15, 1932) 60 Minutes.
Edward J. Nugent, Rita LaRoy, *Dorothy Gulliver*, Wheeler Oakman, Russell Simpson, John Ince, Reginald Simpson, Franklyn Farnum, Frank Parker, Vivian Fields, Charles K. French
Director: Breezy Reeves Eason
Producer: Fanchon Royer

THE PHANTOM EXPRESS
(Majestic, September 15, 1932) 70 Mins.
Sally Blane, William Collier, Jr., Eddie Phillips, Lina Basquette, Jack Pennick, Jack Mower, *Dorothy Gulliver*, Claire McDowell, Alex Axelson, Robert Ellis, Allan Forrest, Huntley Gordon, Tom O'Brien, David Rollins, Hobart Bosworth
Director: Emory Johnson
Screenplay: Laird Doyle
Story: Emory Johnson

THE LAST FRONTIER
(RKO, September 2, 1932) 12 Chapters
Creighton Chaney (Lon Chaney, Jr.), *Dorothy Gulliver*, Mary Jo Desmond, Francis X. Bushman, Jr., Joe Bonomo, Yakima Canutt, Slim Cole, Judith Barrie, Richard Neil, LeRoy Mason, Pete Morrison, Claude Peyton, Benny Corbett, Fritzi Fern, Bill Nestell, William Desmond, Leo Cooper, Walt Robbins, Ray Steel, Frank Lackteen, Fred Burns
Director: Spencer Gordon Bennet
Story: Courtney Ryley Cooper
Supvisor: Fred J. McConnell
Producer: A Van Bruen Production
Chapters: (1) The Black Ghost Rides (2) The Thundering Herd (3) The Black Ghost Strikes (4) A Single Shot (5) Clutching Hands (6) The Terror Trail (7) Doomed (8) Facing Death (9) Thundering Doom (10) The Life Line (11) Driving Danger (12) The Black Ghost's Last Ride

OUTLAW JUSTICE
(Majestic, October 1, 1932) 61 Mins.
Jack Hoxie, *Dorothy Gulliver*, Chris-Pin Martin, Donald Keith, Charles King, Kermit Maynard, Jack Trent, Walter Shumway, Jack Rockwell, Tom London, Dynamite (a horse)
Director: Armand Schaefer
Screenplay: Oliver Drake
Story: W. Scott Darling
Producer: Larry Darmour

REVENGE AT MONTE CARLO
(Mayfair, February, 1933) 63 Mins.
June Collyer, Jose Crespo, Wheeler Oakman, *Dorothy Gulliver*, Edward Earle, Lloyd Ingraham, Clarence Geldert, Lloyd Whitlock
Director: B. Reeves Eason
Screenplay/Story: Frank E. Fenton, John T. Neville
Dialogue: John Thomas Neville
Producer: Fanchon Royer

KING KONG
(RKO, April 7, 1933) 100 Mins.
Fay Wray, Robert Armstrong, Bruce Cabot, Frank Reicher, Sam Hardy, Noble Johnson, Steve Clemente, James Flavin, Victor Wong, Paul Porcasi, Russ Powell, Sandra Shaw, Ethan Laidlaw, Blackie Whiteford, Dick Curtis, Charles Sullivan, Harry Tenbrook, Gil Perkins, Vera Lewis, LeRoy Mason, Frank Mills, Lynton Brent, Jim Thorpe, George MacQuarrie, Madame Sul-te-wan, Etta (Hattie) McDaniel, Ray Turner, *Dorothy Gulliver*, Carlotti Monti, Barney Capehart, Bob Galloway, Eric Wood, Dusty Mitchell, Russ Rogers, Reginald Barlow, Merian C. Cooper, Ernest B. Schoedsack
Directors: Merian C. Cooper, Ernest B. Schoedsack
Screenplay: James A. Creelman, Ruth Rose
Story: Merian C. Cooper (credited to Edgar Wallace)
Producers: Merian C. Cooper, Ernest B. Schoedsack

CHEATING BLONDES
(Equitable/Majestic, May 1, 1933) 66 Mins.
Thelma Todd, Ralf Harolde, Inez Courtney, Milton Wallis, Mae Busch, Earl McCarthy, William Humphries, *Dorothy Gulliver*, Brooks Benedict, Eddie Featherston, Ben Savage, Edna Murphy
Director: Joseph Levering
Screenplay: Lewis B. Foster, Islen Auster

THE PECOS DANDY
(Security, 1934)
George J. Lewis, *Dorothy Gulliver*, Betty Lee, Horace B. Carpenter, Robert Walker, Clyde McClary
Director: Horace B. Carpenter or Victor Adamson (sources disagree)
Screenplay: L. W. Jefferson
Producer: Victor Adamson (Denver Dixon)

FIGHTING CABALLERO
(Superior/Merrick, 1935)
Rex Lease, *Dorothy Gulliver*, Earl Douglas, George Chesebro, Robert Walker, Wally Wales, Milburn Morante, George Morrell, Pinkey Barnes, Carl Mathews, Barney Furey, Franklyn Farnum, Marty Joyce, Paul (Frank?) Ellis
Director: Elmer Clifton
Screenplay: George Merrick, Elmer Clifton
Producer: George M. Merrick

CUSTER'S LAST STAND
(Stage and Screen, 1936) 15 Chapters.
Rex Lease, Jack Mulhall, William Farnum, Ruth Mix, Lona Andre, Reed Howes, Bobby Nelson, *Dorothy Gulliver*, Frank McGlynn, Jr., Helen Gibson, William Desmond, Nancy Caswell, Chief Thunder Cloud, Josef Swickard, Creighton Hale, Marty Joyce, George Chesebro, Milburn Morante, Ted Adams, George Morrell, Howling Wolf, Robert Walker, Walter James, Cactus Mack, Budd Buster, Carl Mathews, Art Ortego, Franklyn Farnum, Lafe McKee, Mabel Strickland, Allen Greer, Barney Furty, James Sheridan, Chick Davis, Ken Cooper, Big Tree, Iron Eyes Cody, Patter Poe, High Eagle, Carter Wayne, Ed Withrow, Whiten Sovern, Buddy Fisher, Charles Hunter, William Hunt, Walter Gable, Bill Thompson, William Bartlett, Humming Bird, Swift Eagle, Tall Tree, Little Eagle, Lone Pine, Herb Jackson, J. Spencer, White Feather, Red Star Cody
Director: Elmer Clifton
Screenplay: George A. Durlam, Eddy Graneman, Bob (William?) Lively
Producer: George M. Merrick
Chapters: (1) Perils of the Plains (2) Thunder Hoofs, (3) Fires of Vengeance (4) The Ghost Dancers (5) Trapped (6) Human Wolves (7) Demons of Disaster (8) White Treachery (9) Circle of Death (10) Flaming Arrow (11) Warpath (12) Firing Squad (13) Red Panthers (14) Custer's Last Ride (15) The Last Stand

IN EARLY ARIZONA
(Columbia, November 2, 1938) 53 Mins.
Bill Elliott, *Dorothy Gulliver*, Harry Woods, Jack Ingram, Franklyn Farnum, Frank Ellis, Art Davis, Charles King, Edward Cassidy, Slim Whitaker, Frank Ball, Tom London, Tex Palmer, Buzz Barton, Jack O'Shea, Bob Card, Chick Hannon, Oscar Gahan, Kit Guard, Al Ferguson, Lester Dorr, Bud Osborne, Cliff Lyons, Symona Boniface, Dick Dorrell, Jess Cavin, Sherry Tansey
Director: Joseph Levering
Screenplay: Nate Gatzert
Story: Nate Gatzert
Producer: Larry Darmour

NORTH OF SHANGHAI
(Columbia, January 24, 1939) 59 Mins.
James Craig, Betty Furness, Morgan Conway, Joseph Downing, Russell Hicks, *Dorothy Gulliver*, Honorable Wu, Dick Curtis, Keye Luke, E. Alyn Warren, Richard Loo, Philip Ahn, Litus Liu
Director: D. Ross Lederman
Screenplay: Maurice Rapf, Harold Buchman
Story: Maurice Rapf, Harold Buchman

LONE STAR PIONEERS
(Columbia, March 16, 1939) 56 Mins.
Bill Elliott, *Dorothy Gulliver*, Lee Shumway, Slim Whitaker, Charles King, Jack Ingram, Harry Harvey, Buzz Barton, Frank LaRue, Frank Ellis, Budd Buster, David Sharpe, Kit Guard, Merrill McCormack, Jack Rockwell, Tex Palmer
Director: Joseph Levering
Screenplay: Nate Gatzert
Producer: Larry Darmour

BORROWED HERO
(Monogram, December 5, 1941) 65 Mins.
Alan Baxter, Florence Rice, John Hamilton, Constance Worth, Wilma Francis, Richard Terry, Mary Gordon, Jerry Marlowe, Stanley Andres, George Dobbs, Paul Everton, John Maxwell, Guy Usher, Karl Hackett, Robert Fiske, Joel Friedkin, Isabel LaMal, *Dorothy Gulliver*, Eba Larson, Eddie Kane, Dudley Dickerton, James Deliso, Gene O'Donnell, Ted Stanhope, Robert Street, Charles King, Syd Saylor
Director: Lewis D. Collins
Screenplay: Earle Snell
Story: Ben Roberts, Sidney Shelton
Producer: A. W. Hackel

FACES
(Maurice McEndree/Continental, November 24, 1968) 129 Mins.
John Morley, Gena Rowlands, Lynn Carlin, Seymour Cassel, Fred Draper, Val Avery, *Dorothy Gulliver*, Joanne Moore Jordan, Darlene Conley, Gene Darfler, Elizabeth During, Dave Liazzie, Julie Gambol, James Bridges
Director: John Cassavetes
Story: John Cassavetes
Producer: Maurice McEndree
Associate Producer: Al Ruban

WON TON TON, THE DOG WHO SAVED HOLLYWOOD
(Paramount, 1976) 92 Mins.
(Color)
Bruce Dern, Madeline Kahn, Art Carney, Phil Silvers, Teri Garr, Ron Liebman, *Dorothy Gulliver*, Rhonda Fleming, The Ritz Brothers, Yvonne DeCarlo
Director: Michael Winner
Screenplay: Arnold Schilman

Juanita Hansen

9 • JUANITA HANSEN

A Leading Goddess in the Chapter Play Pantheon

Juanita Hansen, of Danish-Swedish descent, was born in either Portland, Oregon or Des Moines, Iowa in 1895 or 1897. Des Moines and 1897 are most often listed in reference books, though in interviews early in her career she mentioned Portland as her birthplace. At the age of eight she moved with her family to Los Angeles where she grew up and graduated from high school. Almost immediately after her graduation she went before the cameras as a chorus girl and bit player. Our first known credit for her is **The Love Route** (1915) for Famous Players-Lasky.

The "ultra-blonde of all screendom," she soon became one of the Mack Sennett bathing beauties. Her best role prior to going with Sennett had been in D. W. Griffith's **The Martyrs of the Alamo** (1915), a crude but veracious historical drama of tremendous action. As a Sennett beauty, Juanita was a popular favorite and was featured over most of the other girls.

In an attempt to diversify her career, Juanita talked herself into the heroine's role in American Film's war-preparedness serial **The Secret of the Submarine** (1916). But the film did not immediately project her into the thrill-a-minute genre on a permanent basis; she was soon back at Keystone doing comedies when she could not get further serious roles. Throughout 1917 she toiled in Sennett's Keystone Comedy factory, delighting audiences in such fine comedies as **Cactus Nell** (1917) and a **Clever Dummy** (1917), both with Wallace Beery and Ben Turpin, and **A Royal Rogue** (1917) with Billy Armstrong. But when she got the chance to move into non-comedy features, she signed with Universal in 1918.

Soon she was emoting with Jack Mulhall in **The Brass Bullet** (1918), released in eighteen episodes of two reels each. The popularity of this cliffhanger led to her getting the role of Lurline, a South Sea Island girl, in **The Sea Flower** (1918). Lurline, believed to be the daughter of the island drunk, was actually the daughter of the chief of the secret service, having been kidnapped as a baby. Made while the U.S. was engaged in World War I, the story concerns German spies and Al Whitman's attempts to corral them, when he isn't romancing Juanita. She was also the love interest opposite William S. Hart in **The Poppy Girl's Husband** (1919) and played Tom Mix's girl in **Rough Riding Romance** (1919). In **A Midnight Romance** (1919) she lost hero Jack Holt to Anita Stewart.

William Selig hired Juanita to star in **The Lost City** (1920), a serial released by Warner Bros. She portrayed a princess of a proud race and, with male lead George Chesebro (who later became famous for his badman roles in countless Westerns), she ran, jumped, fell, dived, crawled, and swam her way through peril after peril. The film was popular and was also released in a feature version, **The Jungle Princess** (1923). Her work convinced Pathé moguls that this graduate of the "Sennett school" was also an actress of the caliber to fill the vacant niche in their serial star department, and they put her into **The Phantom Foe** (1920) and **The Yellow Arm** (1921).

Juanita was extremely popular in 1921 and earned nearly $1500 a week. She enjoyed the "good life," particularly parties, fine clothes, and fast cars, and raced her Chalmers speedster down country roads at all hours. Her car was highly conspicuous--gray, trimmed in red, with red-spoked wheels--and so highly geared that it could make sixty in second gear and ninety in third without any trouble at all, except to the police. She was arrested so often that it was a routine event.

Physically worn out from long, hard days before the camera and all-night parties, Juanita turned to the use of cocaine, not realizing the dangers

Lost City (Warner Bros., 1920) – Juanita Hansen is probably thinking that it is not one of her better days.

involved. By the time she made **The Yellow Arm**, she was an addict. Pathé had difficulty finishing the film because of her physical condition. The studio dropped her rather than face the bad publicity of having a drug addict as their star attraction, when the trademark of the crowing rooster was supposed to signal fine, clean family entertainment throughout the world. Juanita sought help and went through several "cures" over the years.

She was finally able to secure a part in **The High Hatters** on Broadway in 1928, her addiction apparently behind her. But tragedy struck as scalding hot water poured over her as she lay unconscious in a tub--she had fainted after turning on the too-hot shower in her New York hotel bathroom. For several weeks doctors gave her morphine to ease the pain, and once again she became addicted. Most of the $118,000 she received as compensation for the hotel mishap went for hospital bills, lawyers' fees, and drugs or drug cures.

Apparently Juanita was cured again in 1934, but by this time she was just an empty shell. There was little in her face to recall the delicate beauty of Juanita Hansen, the original Mack Sennett girl, whose daredevil stunts thrilled moviegoers in the World War I years. Her spirit was gone, as well as her beauty and wealth. She traveled with carnivals, making her living by lecturing on the evils of drugs. On June 21, 1941, after being locked out of her room in a cheap hotel, Juanita took an overdose of sleeping pills in a suicide attempt. She said later, "I'm tired of fighting life. I can't stand it. I'd rather die than live." It was the low ebb of a courage which had brought her through several sieges of drug addiction.

Toward the end of her life she was a train order clerk for the Southern Pacific Railway. She died from a heart attack on September 26, 1961 in her apartment in Hollywood.

Phantom Foe (Pathé, 1920) – Juanita Hansen and unidentified player.

JUANITA HANSEN Filmography

THE LOVE ROUTE
(Famous Players, February, 1915) 4 Reels
Harold Lockwood, Winifred Kingston, Donald Crisp, Jack Pickford, *Juanita Hansen*
Director: Allan Dwan
Screenplay: Allan Dwan
Story: Edward Peple

THE FAILURE
(Reliance, May 29, 1915) 4 Reels
John Emerson, *Juanita Hansen*, A. D. Sears, Olga Gray, Augustus Carney
Director: Christy Cabanne

BETTY IN SEARCH OF A THRILL
(Bosworth, May 29, 1915) 5 Reels
Elsi Janis, Owen Moore, *Juanita Hansen*, Harry Ham, Roberta Hickman
Director: Phillips Smalley
Screenplay: Elsie Janie

THE MARTYRS OF THE ALAMO
(Fine Arts-Triangle, October 30, 1915) 5 Reels
Sam DeGrasse, Walter Long, Tom Wilson, H. D. Sears, Alfred Paget, Augustus Carney, John Dillon, Fred Burns, Ora Carew, *Juanita Hansen*
Director: W. Christy Cabanne
Supervision: D. W. Griffith
Screenplay: W. Christy Cabanne
Story: Theodosia Harris

HIS PRIDE AND SHAME
(Keystone-Triangle, March 23, 1916) 2 Reels
Ford Sterling, *Juanita Hansen*, Bobby Vernon, Bobby Dunn, Guy Woodward
Directors: Ford Sterling, Charles Chase
Story: Mack Sennett
Producer: Mack Sennett

THE SECRET OF THE SUBMARINE
(American, May 22, 1916) 15 Chapters.
Juanita Hansen, Tom Chatterton, William Tedmarsh, Lamar Johnstone, Jylda Hollis, George Clancy, Harry Edmundson, George Webb, Hugh Bennett
Director: George Sargent

THE FINISHING TOUCH
(Universal, July 21, 1916) 1 Reel
Juanita Hansen, Rex De Rosselli, Marjorie Ellison, Buddy McQuoid
Director: George Cochrane
Story: Harvey Gates

BLACK EYES AND BLUE
(Keystone/Triangle, 1916)
Juanita Hansen, Martha Trick, Billy Armstrong

GLORY
(Unity, January, 1917) 6 Reels
Juanita Hansen, Kolb and Dill (German comedians), May Cloy, Wellington Playter, William Lampe
Directors: Burton King, Francis Grandon
Screenplay: Aaron Hoffman

A ROYAL ROGUE
(Keystone/Triangle, May 1917) 2 Reels
Juanita Hansen, Billy Armstrong, Hallam Cooley, Raymond Griffith, Jack Henderson, Ray Russell, Martha Trick

DANGERS OF A BRIDE
(Keystone-Triangle, July 1917) 2 Reels
Bobby Vernon, Gloria Swanson, Robert Milliken, Jay Dwiggens, *Juanita Hansen*, Al McKinnon, Martha Trick, Fritz Schade, F. B. Cooper
Directors: Robert Kerr, Ferris Hartman

The Brass Bullet (Universal, 1918) – Juanita Hansen and Jack Mulhall.

WHOSE BABY?
(Keystone-Triangle, July 1917) 2 Reels
Bobby Vernon, Gloria Swanson, Jay Dwiggins, Martha Trick, Robert Milliken, Fritz Schade, *Juanita Hansen*
Director: Clarence Badger

BROADWAY LOVE
(Universal-Bluebird, December 26, 1917) 2 Reels
Dorothy Phillips, William Stowell, *Juanita Hansen*, Lon Chaney, Harry von Meter, Gladys Tennyson
Director: Ida May Park
Screenplay: Ida May Park
Story: W. Carey Wonderly

CACTUS NELL
(Keystone, 1917)
Ben Turpin, Chester Conklin, Wallace Beery, *Juanita Hansen*, Claire Anderson, James Donnelly

A CLEVER DUMMY
(Keystone-Triangle, 1917)
Ben Turpin, Wallace Beery, Chester Conklin, *Juanita Hansen*, Claire Anderson, James Donnelly, James Delano
Director: Herman Raymaker

THE ROUGH LOVER
(Bluebird, February 18, 1918) 5 Reels
Juanita Hansen, Franklyn Farnum, Catherine Henry, Fred Montague, Martha Mattox
Director: Joseph DeGrasse
Screenplay: Eugene B. Lewis
Story: Joseph F. Poland

FAST COMPANY
(Universal-Bluebird, March 6, 1918) 5 Reels
Franklyn Farnum, Kathlyn Griffith, Lon Chaney, Fred Montagu, *Juanita Hansen*, Edward Cecil
Director: Lynn F. Reynolds
Screenplay: Eugene Lewis, Waldemar Young
Story: John McDermott

The Lost City (Warner Bros., 1920) – Juanita Hansen at the mercy of a lecherous slave trader.

THE RISKY ROAD
(Universal, March 27, 1918) 5 Reels
Dorothy Phillips, William Stowell, George Chesebro, Edward Cecil, Joseph Girard, *Juanita Hansen*, Claire DuBrey, Sally Starr
Director: Ida May Park
Screenplay: Ida May Park
Story: Katherine Leiser Robbins, "Her Fling"

THE MATING OF MARCELLA
(Ince-Paramount, May 6, 1918) 5 Reels
Dorothy Dalton, Thurston Hall, *Juanita Hansen*, William Conklin, Donald MacDonald, Milton Ross, Spottiswoode Aitkin, Buster Irving
Director: R. William Ince
Screenplay: R. Cecil Smith
Story: Joseph Franklin Poland

THE BRASS BULLET
(Universal, August 10, 1918) 18 Chapters.
Juanita Hansen, Jack Mulhall, Charles Hill Mailes, Joseph W. Girard, Harry Dunkinson, Helen Wright, Ashton Dearholt, Charles Force, Halam Cooley
Director: Ben Wilson
Screenplay: Walter Woods
Story: Frank R. Adams
Producer: Ben Wilson
Chapters: (1) A Flying Start (2) The Muffled Man (3) The Mysterious Murder of Locked in the Tower (4) Smoked Out (5) The Mock Bride (6) A Dangerous Honeymoon (7) Pleasure Island or The Depth Bomb (8) The Magnetic Rug (9) The Room of Flame (10) A New Peril (11) Evil Waters (12) Caught by Wireless (13) $500 Reward (14) On Trial for His Life (15) In the Shadow (16) The Noose (17) The Avenger (18) The Amazing Confession

THE SEA FLOWER
(Bluebird, December 23, 1918) 5 Reels
Juanita Hansen, Al Whitman, Fred Huntley, Eugenia Besserrer, Frederick Starr, Wilson Taylor, George Pearch
Director: Colin Campbell
Screenplay: H. Tipton Steck
Story: George Hull

BREEZY JIM
(Triangle, February, 1919) 5 Reels
Crane Wilbur, *Juanita Hansen*
Director: Lorimer Johnson
Story: J. Francis Dumbar

THE POPPY GIRL'S HUSBAND
(William S. Hart/Artcraft, March 8, 1919) 5 Reels
William S. Hart, *Juanita Hansen*, Walter Long
Director: William S. Hart
Screenplay: C. Gardner Sullivan
Story: Jack Boyle
Supervision: Thomas H. Ince

A MIDNIGHT ROMANCE
(First National, March 16, 1919) 6 Reels
Juanita Hansen, Anita Stewart, Jack Holt, Edward Tilton, Elinor Hancock, Helen Yoder, Montagu Dumont
Director: Lois Weber
Screenplay: Marion Orth

ROUGH RIDING ROMANCE
(Fox, August 24, 1919) 5 Reels
Tom Mix, *Juanita Hansen*, Jack Nelson, Pat Chrisman, Sid Jordan
Director: Arthur Rosson
Screenplay: Charles Kenyon
Story: Charles Kenyon

LOMBARDI, LIMITED
(Metro, October 1, 1919) 7 Reels
Jean Acker, *Juanita Hansen*, Virginia Caldwell, Patricia Hannon, Vera Lewis, Ann May, Bert Lytell, Alice Lake
Director: Jack Conway
Director General: Maxwell Karger
Adaptation: June Mathis
Screenplay: June Mathis

THE LOST CITY
(Warner Bros., February 1920) 15 Chapters.
Juanita Hansen, George Chesebro, Frank Clark, Hector Dion, Irene Wallace, Al Ferguson, Marjorie Lake, Jack Abraham
Director: E. A. Martin
Story: Frederic Chapin
Producer: William N. Selig
Chapters: (1) The Lost Princess (2) The City of Hanging Gourds (3) The Flaming Tower (4) Jungle Death (5) The Puma's Victim (6) The Man Eater's Prey (7) The Bride of Death (8) A Tragedy in the Sky (9) In the Palace of Black Walls (10) The Tug of War (11) In the Lion's Jaw (12) The Jungle Fire (13) In the Cave of Eternal Fire (14) The Eagle's Next (15) The Lost City

THE PHANTOM FOE
(Pathé, October 17, 1920) 15 Chapters
Juanita Hansen, William N. Bailey, Warner Oland, Harry Semels, Wallace McCutcheon, Nina Cassavant, Tom Goodwin, Joe Cuny, Al Franklyn Thomas
Director: Bertram Millhauser
Screenplay: George B. Seitz
Chapters: (1) Doom (2) Disappearance of Janet Dale (3) Trail of the Wolf (4) The Open Window (5) The Tower Room (6) The Crystal Ball (7) Gun Fire (8) The Man Trap (9) The Mystic Summons (10) The Foe Unmasked (11) Through Prison Walls (12) Behind the Veil (13) Attack at the Inn (14) Confession (15) Retribution

THE YELLOW ARM
(Pathé, May 19, 1921) 15 Chapters
Juanita Hansen, Marguerite Courtot, Warner Oland, William N. Bailey, Tom Keith, Stephan Carr
Director: Bertram Millhauser
Screenplay: James Shelley Hamilton
Chapters: (1) House of Alarms (2) Vengeance of the East (3) A Strange Disappearance (4) At Bay (5) Danger Ahead (6) A Nest of Knaves (7) Into the Dead of Night (8) Smuggled Abroad (9) Kingdom of Deceit (10) The Water Peril (11) Pawns of Power (12) Price of a Throne (13) Behind the Curtain (14) The False Goddess (15) The Miracle

THE RED SNOW
(1921)
Juanita Hansen

THE ETERNAL FLAME
(Norma Talmadge/First National, September 1922) 8 Reels
Norma Talmadge, Adolphe Menjou, Wedgwood Nowell, Conway Tearle, Rosemary Theby, Kate Lester, Thomas Ricketts, Otis Harlan, Irving Cummings, *Juanita Hansen*
Director: Frank Lloyd
Screenplay: Frances Marion
Story: Honoré de Balzac, "La Duchesse de Langeais"

THE BROADWAY MADONNA
(Quality/FBO, October 29, 1922) 6 Reels
Dorothy Revier, Jack Connolly, Harry van Meter, Eugene Burr, *Juanita Hansen*, Lee Willard, Lydia Knott
Director: Harry Revier

THE JUNGLE PRINCESS
(Adolph Kremnitzer, June 6, 1923) 7 Reels
Juanita Hansen

GIRL FROM THE WEST
(Sam Warner/Aywon, September, 1923) 5 Reels
Jack Richardson, *Juanita Hansen*, Edward Sutherland
Director: Wallace MacDonald
Story: Carter De Haven

Helen Holmes

10 • HELEN HOLMES

Her Eminence in the Runaway Boxcar Realm was Uncontested

Helen Holmes did most of her screen work as the heroine of innumerable "iron horse" dramas or independent Westerns. She seems destined to be remembered for the forty-eight episodes of **The Hazards of Helen** (1914), in which she starred before relinquishing her role to Helen Gibson, who went on to make another seventy-one episodes of the long-running railroad series.

America was enchanted with the west and the railroad in that era. The accepted roles of hero and heroine had been reversed; Helen was truly a woman for her time. At her peak she almost matched Pearl White in popularity. Two brief synopses will serve to illustrate the nature of the unrelated but loosely connected one-reelers comprising **The Hazards of Helen.**

The Girl at the Throttle was the third in the series and, like the others, is a railroad saga filled with a number of fine scenes of moving trains and engines. When a hunter accidentally wounds an engineer, Helen runs a yard engine after the express, catches it, and tows it back out of danger before there is a head-on smash-up with another train. In **The Little Engineer,** episode 12, an engineer's little boy climbs onto his father's freight locomotive and starts the train out onto the single track line, down which a fast mail is coming. The passenger train has just flashed by the last signal tower, but Helen, hopping onto a gasoline section car, overtakes the freight, climbs over the cars, and sidetracks it in time to save the other train.

And so it went. Helen worked for a solid year on **The Hazards of Helen** series before leaving with her husband, director J. P. McGowan, to work for Universal. Week by week she was chasing trains or being chased by them; climbing aboard or jumping off them; struggling on the catwalks above the boxcars or cheating death as she clung perilously to the rods beneath them. She was most often cast as a girl telegrapher. But even before the series she had been having a love affair with trains in such Kalem one- and two-reelers as **The Runaway Freight** (1913), **The Operator at Black Rock** (1914), **The Car of Death** (1914), **Grouch, the Engineer** (1914), **From Peril to Peril** (1914), and **The Demon of the Rails** (1914). Helen's favorite stunt was to be tied in front of an onrushing locomotive, to be rescued by the hero just a split second before the engine thundered by. It is not surprising that she became known as the queen of the iron horse dramas.

Helen Holmes was born in Louisville, Kentucky, on either June 19 or July 7, 1892. At maturity she was five feet six inches tall and weighed 120 pounds. She had dark brown hair and hazel eyes. Chicago became her home when she was quite small, and it was there that she was educated, in St. Mary's Convent. Because her family was poor, she became a photographer's model in her youth and contributed what she could at home. When the family moved to Death Valley because of her brother's health, Helen moved there with them. Her father is believed either to have died or to have remained in Chicago to work. Helen led the life of a Bret Harte or Zane Grey character as she lived and worked in Death Valley in the Shoshone Country. After a prospecting trip with her ailing brother, she joined the Gold Rush and lived briefly among the Indians and half-breeds. After her brother's death she went to New York City looking for work. She appeared in a 1910 stage play titled The City, creating the role of Eleanor Voorhees at the Lyric Theater on Broadway.

In 1911, Helen, a buxom girl in her teens, wrote to her friend Mabel Normand, a Keystone actress, who advised her to come West. She got considerable modeling work and was the subject

The Hazards of Helen (Kalem, 1914) – Helen Holmes.

of The Santa Fe Girl, a railroad poster. Through Mabel she got work in Keystone's **Kings Court** (1912) and **Barney Oldfield's Race for Life** (1913) and was soon at Kalem as a full-fledged leading lady. A few of her better pictures were **The Battle of Fort Laramie** (1913), in which she played the Indian girl; **A Million in Jewels** (1914), as the daughter of a Rajah; **The Identification** (1914), a plain dramatic lead; and **The Conductor's Courtship** (1914), as the agent's daughter. It was at Kalem that she met director J. P. McGowan whom she married while she was working with him on **The Hazards of Helen** series.

McGowan and Holmes remained at Universal only briefly. In late 1915 McGowan formed Signal Films, with Helen signed to play in all of the productions. A releasing arrangement was entered into with Mutual. Signal's first release, a serial, was **The Girl and the Game** (1915), a smashing success with serial audiences. It was followed by **Lass of the Lumberlands** (1916), **The Railroad Raiders** (1917), and **The Lost Express** (1917), all extremely popular. Appearing with her in each of the thrillers was Leo Maloney, destined to become one of the all-time great silent Western leads.

Between the serials Helen and Leo made features--exceptionally fine features for an independent like Signal. Two of the best were **Whispering Smith** (1916) and its sequel **Medicine Bend** (1916). J. P. McGowan himself played the lead character, Whispering Smith, a virile man who fears no physical danger but is reticent in his affections. Helen is the carefree and beautiful Western girl; Paul C. Hurst is her harsh husband, foreman of a wrecking crew on a transcontinental railroad section; and Leo Maloney is Du Sang, as cruel as a soft bullet. Thomas G. Lingham is memorable as the sheriff of Medicine Bend. The principal cast is the same for both pictures. The characters are real and stirring, and easy, continuous action marks every inch of the films. Helen came off well as the faithful wife of bullying husband Hurst. The story revolves around the looting of freight cars near Medicine Bend, a typical Western railroad and mining town located at the foot of a steep declivity and noted for the frequency of the wrecks occurring there. The films were exciting and popular with World War I audiences.

Equally popular was **Judith of the Cumberlands** (1916), a story about an ancient mountain feud. Leo Maloney tries to educate the sturdy mountain men to respect the law instead of ignoring it. He is loved by Helen, the niece of Thomas Lingham, leader of a rival clan. Helen is also loved by Paul Hurst, who runs an illicit still. Things get pretty sticky before it is all over, with Maloney almost lynched by an excited mob but saved by Helen, who tricks Hurst (supposedly killed by Maloney) into revealing himself as very much alive and head of the contraband whiskey operation.

The Lost Express (1917), Helen's last Signal serial, was about a disappearing train carrying a valuable formula for granulated gasoline. It took Helen and Maloney fifteen chapters to unravel the mystery.

With the collapse of Mutual Films, Signal also folded its tent and disappeared. But Helen was soon on the screen again in a state-righted serial titled **The Fatal Fortune** (1919), released by SLK Serial Corporation. Gone were the railroad scenery and Leo Maloney. In their places were a South Seas island and Lieutenant Jack Levering. Although the fifteen episodes held up well from a production standpoint, the film was not nearly as popular as Helen's previous endeavors, as fans did not readily accept the transition from a railroad heroine to a newspaper woman in search of buried treasure on a desolate island. Also, the state-rights release meant that a much smaller number of theaters showed the film.

In 1920 Helen formed the Holmes Producing Corporation and made a contract with Warner Bros. to star in **The Tiger Band** (1920). It, too, was state-righted and received limited bookings. For the next six years she played in a number of Westerns and railroad films, sometimes as star, sometimes as co-star or supporting player. **Ghost City** (1921) was one of her better Western features, and further serial honors were earned with William Desmond in **The Riddle Rider** (1924) and with Franklyn Farnum in **Battling Brewster** (1924). State-righted programmers such as **Peril of the Rail** (1926), with Ed Hearn, and **The Open Switch** (1926), with Jack Perrin, were enjoyable respites from life's realities, but few people saw them.

Sometime around 1925 Helen and McGowan's marriage dissolved and her subsequent marriage to stuntman Lloyd Saunders heralded her retirement from the screen. Her final series had been produced by Morris Schlank's California Studio and marketed by Rayart, one of the more durable independent distributors of the 1920s.

The Saunders moved to Sonora to operate a huge ranch into which they had plowed much of their savings. Several years of bad luck forced them to give it up, and Lloyd went back on the rodeo circuit to earn much-needed money. One or two attempts by Helen to get back into the movies in the early 1930s were unsuccessful.

The years slipped by with little news of Helen until 1945, when she made the papers by becoming a Hollywood animal trainer, specializing in training dogs and cats for movie roles. In 1946 her husband died. Helen was already suffering from a heart condition at the time of Saunders' death, and for the next five years her condition deteriorated. She provided for herself by operating a small antique business until her death on July 8, 1950, from a heart attack. At her bedside when she died was her long-time friend, Helen Gibson. Miss Holmes was fifty-eight years old.

HELEN HOLMES Filmography

KINGS COURT
(Keystone, 1912)
Mabel Normand, *Helen Holmes*

BROUGHT TO BAY
(Kalem, May 13, 1913) 2 Reels
Helen Holmes, Jack Conway, Hart (Jack) Hoxie, Steve Banner, May Madden, Pete Frawley, Joe Temple, William Bruton
Director: J. P. McGowan

BARNEY OLDFIELD'S RACE FOR LIFE
(Keystone, May 31, 1913)
Mabel Normand, Mack Sennett, Ford Sterling, Hank Mann, Barney Oldfield, Al St. John, *Helen Holmes*
Director: Mack Sennett
Producer: Keystone
Camera: Lee Bartholomew & Walter Wright

THE SMUGGLER
(Kalem, July 19, 1913) 1 Reel
Alice Hollister, Charles Wells, *Helen Holmes*, William Brunton, G. A. Williams

THE FLYING SWITCH
(Kalem, July 26, 1913) 1 Reel
Helen Holmes, C. E. Edrington, G. A. Williams

A DEMAND FOR JUSTICE
(Kalem, September 20, 1913) 1 Reel
C. G. Williams, *Helen Holmes*, Leo Maloney

THE LITTLE ENGINEER
RELEASED SATURDAY, JANUARY 30th

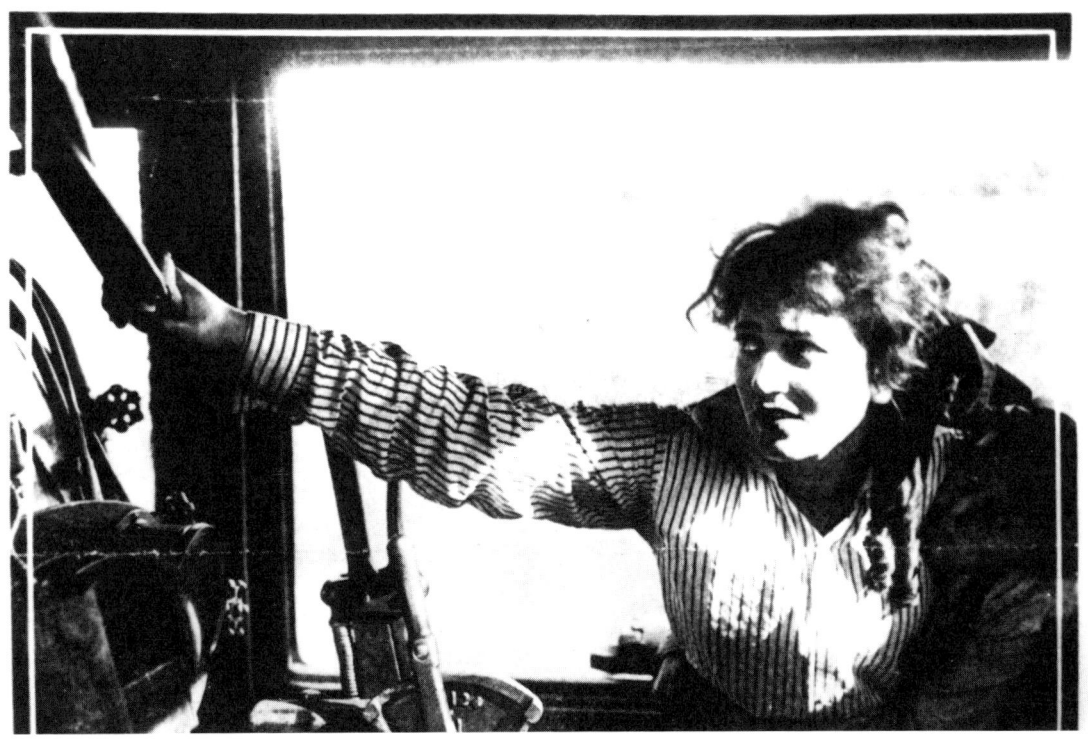

The Hazards of Helen (Kalem, 1914) – Helen Holmes is the girl telegrapher at the throttle in this episode of the long-running series.

THE BATTLE AT FORT LARAMIE
(Kalem, September 27, 1913) 2 Reels
Helen Holmes, Leo Maloney, G. A. Williams, Hart (Jack) Hoxie, Alice Dexter, Charles Gillette, Billy Gillette
Director: J. P. McGowan

THE HERMIT'S RUSE
(Kalem, October 11, 1913) 1 Reel
George Williams, *Helen Holmes*, William Brunton, Leo Maloney

THE RUNAWAY FREIGHT
(Kalem, November 8, 1913)
Helen Holmes, William Brunton, Leo Maloney

THE FOOTPRINT CLUE
(Kalem, November 29, 1913) 1 Reel
Charles Wells, *Helen Holmes*, Leo Maloney

A MILLION IN JEWELS
(Kalem, February 14, 1914) 2 Reels
Helen Holmes, William Brunton, G. A. Williams

THE STOLEN REMBRANDT
(Kalem, April 25, 1914) 2 Reels
Helen Holmes, William Brunton, Leo Maloney
Director: Leo Maloney

A MAN'S SOUL
(Kalem, May 9, 1914) 1 Reel
Helen Holmes, J. P. McGowan, Leo Maloney, Helen Schwam
Director: J. P. McGowan

THE CONDUCTOR'S COURTSHIP
(Kalem, June 20, 1914)
Helen Holmes

THE FLAW IN THE ALIBI
(Kalem, June 27, 1914) 2 Reels
Helen Holmes

A STRING OF PEARLS
(Kalem, July 4, 1914) 2 Reels
Helen Holmes

THE IDENTIFICATION
(Kalem, July 1914) 2 Reels
Helen Holmes, Hart (Jack) Hoxie, J. P. McGowan
Director: J. P. McGowan

THE OPERATOR AT BLACK ROCK
(Kalem, August 1, 1914) 2 Reels
Helen Holmes, G. A. Pulliam, Bert C. Hadley, Hart (Jack) Hoxie
Director: J. P. McGowan
Story: E. W. Matlock

THE CAR OF DEATH
(Kalem, August 29, 1914)
Helen Holmes, Hart (Jack) Hoxie

NEAR DEATH'S DOOR
(Kalem, August 1914)
Helen Holmes, Hart (Jack) Hoxie

THE OIL WELL CONSPIRACY
(Kalem, September 2, 1914)
Helen Holmes, J. P. McGowan

GROUCH, THE ENGINEER
(Kalem, September 26, 1914)
Helen Holmes, J. P. McGowan, Billy Gilett
Director: J. P. McGowan
Story: E. W. Matlock

FROM PERIL TO PERIL
(Kalem, October 10, 1914)
Helen Holmes, Charles Wells

THE DEMON OF THE RAILS
(Kalem, October 17, 1914) 1 Reel
Helen Holmes, Charles Wells
Director: J. P. McGowan
Story: E. W. Matlock

THE HAZARDS OF HELEN
(Kalem, November 13, 1914) 119 Chapters.
Helen Holmes, Helen Gibson, Robyn Adair, Ethel Clisbee, Ton Trent, G. A. Williams, Pearl Anibus, P. S. Pembroke, Roy Watson, Hoot Gibson, Hartford (Jack) Hoxie, Leo D. Maloney, Charles Mulgro, Jennie Antibus, M. J. Murchison, Bobbie Antibus, Norma Antibus, M. Z. Woods, George Routh, Billy Boy, Franklin Hall, Clement Graw, Clarence Burton, Harry Schumm, O. Pillipi, Hi Sing, Jack Messick, Richard Johnson, Thomas Means, Frank Henderson, Betty Hartigan, Hal Clements, Henry Hallam, True Boardman, E. Z. Roberts
Director: J. P. McGowan, James Davis
Story: W. Scott Darling, based on John Russell Corvell's novelized version of the play by Denman Thompson
Chapter titles of the 48 episodes that featured Miss Holmes (remaining chapters featured Helen Gibson): (1) Helen's Sacrifice (2) The Plot at the R. R. Cut (3) The Girl at the Throttle (4) The Stolen Engine (5) The Flying Freight's Captive (6) The Black Diamond Express (7) The Escape on the Limited (8) The Girl Telegrapher's Peril (9) The Leap from the Water Tower (10) The Broken Circuit (11) The Fast Mail's Danger (12) The Little Engineer (13) Escape of the Fast Freight (14) The Red Signal (15) The Engineer's Peril (16) The Open Drawbridge (17) The Death Train (18) Night Operator at Buxton (19) Railroad Raiders of '62 (20) Girl at Lone Point (21) A Life in the Balance (22) The Girl on the Trestle (23) The Girl Engineer (24) A Race for a Crossing (25) The Box Car Trap (26) The Wild Engine (27) A Friend at the Throttle (28) The Broken Train (29) A Railroader's Bravery (30) The Human Chain (31) The Pay Train (32) Near Eternity (33) In Danger's Path (34) The Midnight Limited (35) A Wild Ride (36) A Deed of Daring (37) The Girl on the Engine (38) The Fate of #1 (39) The Substitute Fireman (40) The Limited's Peril (41) A Perilous Chance (42) Train Order #45 (43) The Broken Rail (44) Nerves of Steel (45) A Girl's Grit (46) A Matter of Seconds (47) The Runaway Boxcar (48) The Water Tank Plot

HIS NEMESIS
(Kalem, November 14, 1914) 2 Reels
Helen Holmes
Director: J. P. MacGowan
Screenplay: J. P. MacGowan

THE RAJAH'S JEWELS
(Kalem, circa 1914)
Helen Holmes
(This title unverified)

THE REFRIGERATOR CAR'S CAPTIVE
(Kalem, 1914)
Helen Holmes, William Brunton
Director: J. P. McGowan

THE PAY TRAIN
(Kalem, 1914)
Helen Holmes
Director: J. P. McGowan

UNDER DESPERATION'S SPUR
(Kalem, 1914) 1 Reel
Helen Holmes, J. P. McGowan
Director: J. P. McGowan

FAST FREIGHT 3205
(Kalem 1914) 1 Reel
Helen Holmes, William Brunton
Director: William Brunton

THE METTLE OF JERRY McGUIRE
(Universal-Bison, October 29, 1915) 2 Reels
Helen Holmes, J. P. McGowan, Leo D. Maloney
Director: J. P. McGowan

A DESPERATE LEAP
(Universal-Bison, November 19, 1915) 2 Reels
Helen Holmes, Leo D. Maloney, George Perry, George Cummings, C. E. Horn, Joe Neary, G. H. Wischussen
Director: J. P. McGowan
Story: Helen Holmes

WHEN ROGUES FALL OUT
(Universal-Bison, December 17, 1915) 3 Reels
Helen Holmes, J. T. McDaniels, W. R. Weber, Leo Maloney
Director: J. P. McGowan
Story: Helen Holmes

THE GIRL AND THE GAME
(Signal/Mutual, December 27, 1915) 15 Chapters
Helen Holmes, Leo Mahoney, J. P. McGowan, George McDaniel, J. H. Farley, William Brunton, Edward Sutherland
Director: J. P. McGowan
Screenplay: J. P. McGowan, Helen Holmes
Story: Frank Hamilton Spearman
Producer: Samuel S. Hutchinson
Chapters: (1) Helen's Race with Death (2) The Winning Jump (3) A Life in Peril (4) Helen's Perilous Escape (5) The Fight at the Signal Station (6) Helen's Wild Ride (7) Spike's Awakening (8) A Race for the Right of Way (9) A Close Call (10) A Dash Through Flames (11) The Salting of Superstition Mine (12) Buried Alive (13) A Fight for a Fortune (14) Helen's Race Against Time (15) Driving the Last Spike

WHISPERING SMITH
(Signal/Mutual, June 5, 1916) 5 Reels
Helen Holmes, Belle Hutchinson, J. P. McGowan, Paul C. Hurst, Leo D. Maloney, F. M. Van Norman, Samuel Appfel, Walter Rodgers, Thomas G. Lingham, E. Howland, William Bebrens, C. U. Wells, J. E. Perkins, N. Z. Woods, G. H. Wisschussen, Chance Ward, William Brunton, Hugh Adams, Slim Roe
Director: J. P. McGowan
Story: Frank H. Spearman, "Whispering Smith"

MEDICINE BEND
(Signal/Mutual, July 3, 1916) 5 Reels
Helen Holmes, J. P. McGowan, Leo D. Maloney, Paul C. Hurst, Thomas G. Lingham
Director: J. P. McGowan
Story: Frank H. Spearman, "Whispering Smith"

JUDITH OF THE CUMBERLANDS
(Signal/Mutual, July 31, 1916) 5 Reels
Helen Holmes, Leo D. Maloney, Paul C. Hurst, Thomas G. Lingham, William Brunton, Clara Mosher, Harry Lloyd, Sam Morje, G. H. Wisschussen, J. P. McGowan
Director: J. P. McGowan
Story: Alice McGowan, "Judith of the Cumberlands"
(Rereleased in 1921 by American Film Company as **THE MOONSHINE MENACE**)

THE MANAGER OF THE B & A
(Signal/Mutual, October 1916) 5 Reels
(Reissued by American Film Co. on January 12, 1921 as **The Man From Medicine Hat**)
Helen Holmes, Leo Maloney, Paul C. Hurst, N. Z. Wood, Thomas G. Lingham, William N. Chapman, William Brunton

LASS OF THE LUMBERLANDS
(Signal/Mutual, October 23, 1916) 15 Chapters.
Helen Holmes, Thomas G. Lingham, Leo D. Maloney, Ned Chapman, Paul C. Hurst, Katherine Goodrich, F. L. Hemphill. William Behren
Directors: J. P. McGowan, Paul C. Hurst
Chapters: (1) The Lumber Pirate (2) The Wreck in the Fog (3) First Blood (4) A Deed of Daring (5) The Burned Record (6) The Spiked Switch (7) The Runaway Car (8) The Fight in Camp I (9) The Double Fight (10) The Gold Rush (11) The Ace High Loses (12) The Main Line Wreck (13) Unknown (14) The Indian's Hand (15) Retribution

THE DIAMOND RUNNERS
(Signal/Mutual, 1916) 5 Reels
Helen Holmes, Leo Maloney, Paul C. Hurst, Thomas G. Lingham
Director: J. P. McGowan
Screenplay: J. P. McGowan

THE RAILROAD RAIDERS
(Signal, April 9, 1917) 15 Chapters.
Helen Holmes, Thomas G. Lingham, Leo D. Maloney, Paul C. Hurst, William Brunton, F. L. Hemphill, William Behrens, J. P. McGowan, William Buhler, Marvin Martin
Director: J. P. McGowan
Chapters: (1) Circumstantial Evidence (2) A Double Steal (3) Inside Treachery (4) A Race for a Fortune (5) A Woman's Wit (6) The Overland Disaster (7) Mistaken Identity (8) A Knotted Cord (9) A Leap for Life (10) A Watery Grave (11) A Desperate Deed (12) A Fight for a Franchise (13) The Road Wrecker (14) The Trap (15) Mystery of the Counterfeit Tickets

THE LOST EXPRESS
(Signal, September 17, 1917) 15 Chapters.
Helen Holmes, Thomas G. Lingham, Leo D. Maloney, John McKinnon, Ed Hearn, William Brunton, Edward Hearn, John McKinnon, Will M. Chapman
Director: J. P. McGowan
Screenplay: J. P. McGowan
Story: Frederick B. Bennett
Chapters: (1) The Lost Express (2) The Destroyed Document (3) The Wreck at the Crossing (4) The Oil Well Conspiracy (5) In Deep Waters (6) High Voltage (7) The Race with the Limited (8) The Mountain King (9) The Looters (10) The Secret of the Mine (11) A Fight for a Million (12) Law Is Law or Daring Death (13) Disowned or The Escape (14) Trapped or Unmasked (15) The Found Express or Return of the Lost Express

THE FATAL FORTUNE
(SLK Serial, December 15, 1919) 15 Chapters.
Helen Holmes, Lieutenant Jack Levering, Leslie King, Bill Black, Frank Wunderlee, Floyd Buckley, Sidney Dalbrook, Nellie Lindrith, Lillian Worth
Director: Donald MacKenzie
Screenplay: Walter Richard Hall
Chapters: (1) The Trader's Secret (2) Men of Tigerish Mold (3) Tortured by Flames (4) A Climb for Life (5) The Forced Marriage (6) Desperate Chances (7) A Plunge to Death (8) A Struggle in Midair (9) The Deadly Peril (10) Sure Death (11) A Leap for Life (12) A Fiendish Plot (13) Set Adrift (14) The Hidden Treasure (15) Unmasked

THE TIGER BAND
(Holmes/Warner Bros., 1920) 15 Chapters.
Helen Holmes, Jack Mower, Dwight Crittenden, Omar Whitehead, Billy Brunton, Bert Hadley, Yukio Aoyama
Director: Gilbert P. Hamilton
Chapters: (1) Chang the Mighty (2) The Brand of Hate (3) The Stolen Engine (4) In the Power of Chang (5) The Great Leap (6) The Mysterious Friend (7) At Close Quarters (8) A Race with Death (9) A Perilous Escape (10) Trapped (11) The Informer (12) The Death Hazard (13) The Flaming Peril (14) The Masked Man's Treachery (15) The Masked Man's Claws

GHOST CITY
(Holmes/Associated Photoplays, November 23, 1921) 5 Reels
Helen Holmes, Ann Schaeffer, Leo D. Maloney, Leonard Clapham (Tom London), Jack Connolly
Director: William Bertram
Screenplay: George Rix

THE LOGGERS OF HELL ROARIN' MOUNTAIN
(American, 1921)
Helen Holmes, J. P. McGowan
Director: J. P. McGowan

A CROOK'S ROMANCE
(American, 1921) 5 Reels
Helen Holmes, J. P. McGowan
Director: J. P. McGowan

HILLS OF MISSING MEN
(Playgoers Pictures/Associated Exhibitors, February 26, 1922) 5 Reels
J. P. McGowan, Jean Perry, James Wong, Charles Brinley, Andrew Waldron, Florence Gilbert, *Helen Holmes*
Director: J. P. McGowan
Story: John B. Clymer

THE LONE HAND
(Universal, October 6, 1922) 5 Reels
Hoot Gibson, Marjorie Daw, *Helen Holmes*, Hayden Stevenson, Jack Pratt, William Welch, Robert Kortman
Director: B. Reeves Eason
Screenplay: A. P. Younger

ONE MILLION IN JEWELS
(William B. Brush/American Releasing, February 4, 1923)
Helen Holmes, J. P. McGowan, Elinor Rair, Nellie Parker Spauling, Charles Craig, Leslie Casey, Herbert Pattee
Director: J. P. McGowan

STORMY SEAS
(Continental/Associated Exhibitors, July 1, 1923) 5 Reels
J. P. McGowan, *Helen Holmes*, Leslie Casey, Harry Dalroy, Francis Seymour, Gordon Knapp
Director: J. P, McGowan
Story: Arthur W. Donaldson

40-HORSE HAWKINS
(Universal, April 21, 1924) 6 Reels
Hoot Gibson, Anne Cornwall, Richard Tucker, *Helen Holmes*, Jack Gordon Edwards, Ed Burns, Edward Sedgwick, John Judd
Director: Edward Sedgwick
Screenplay: Edward Sedgwick, Raymond L. Schrock
Story: Edward Sedgwick, Raymond L. Schrock

FIGHTING FURY
(Universal, August 24, 1924) 5 Reels
Hart (Jack) Hoxie, *Helen Holmes*, Fred Kohler, Duke R. Lee, Bert De Marc, Al Jennings, George Connors, Art Manning
Director: Clifford S. Smith
Screenplay: Idadore Bernstein
Story: Walter J. Coburn, "Triple Cross for Danger"

THE RIDDLE RIDER
(Universal, November 23, 1924) 15 Chapters
William Desmond, Eileen Sedgwick, *Helen Holmes*, Claude Payton, William N. Gould, Ben Corbett, Hughie Mack, Albert J. Smith, Margaret Royce, Yakima Canutt, Art Ortego
Director: William Craft
Screenplay: William Wing, Arthur H. Gooden, George Pyper
Story: William Wing, Arthur H. Gooden, George Pyper
Chapters: (1) The Canyon Torrent (2) Crashing (3) In the Path of Death (4) Plunged into the Depths (5) Race for a Fortune (6) Sinister Shadows (7) The Swindle (8) The Frame-up (9) False Faces (10) At the Brink of Death (11) Thundering Steeds (12) Trapped (13) The Valley of Fate (14) The Deadline (15) The Final Reckoning

BATTLING BREWSTER
(Rayart, December 1, 1924) 15 Chapters
Franklyn Farnum, *Helen Holmes*, Robert Walker, Emily Barrye, Jerome La Gasse, Lafe McKee, Leon Holmes
Director: Dell Henderson
Supervisor: George Blaisdell
Presented by: W. Ray Johnson

OUTWITTED
(Independent, January 21, 1925) 5 Reels
Helen Holmes, William Desmond, J. P. McGowan, Grace Cunard, Alec Francis, Emily Fitzroy
Director: J. P. McGowan

BARRIERS OF THE LAW
(Independent, March 27, 1925) 5 Reels
J. P. McGowan, *Helen Holmes*, William Desmond, Albert J. Smith, Norma Wills, Marguerite Clayton
Director: J. P. McGowan
Screenplay: William Lester
Story: Travers Vale

DUPED
(Independent, April 1, 1925) 5 Reels
William Desmond, *Helen Holmes*, Dorothea Wolbert, George Magrill, Ford West, James Thompson
Director: J. P. McGowan
Story: John Clymer

BLOOD AND STEEL
(Independent, May 29, 1925) 5 Reels
Helen Holmes, William Desmond, Robert Edeson, Mack V. Wright, Albert J. Smith, Ruth Stonehouse, C. L. Sherwood, Paul Walters, Walter Fitzroy
Director: J. P. McGowan
Story: George Plympton

WEBS OF STEEL
(Morris R. Schlank/Anchor, October 24, 1925) 5 Reels
Helen Holmes
Director: J. P. McGowan

THE TRAIN WRECKERS
(Morris R. Schlank/Anchor, December 1, 1925) 5 Reels
Helen Holmes, Franklyn Farnum, Nelson McDowell, Harry von Meter, James Aubrey, Park Frame, Slim Whitaker
Director: J. P. McGowan

WHISPERING SMITH
(Metropolitan/PDC, March 28, 1926) 7 Reels
H. B. Warner, Lillian Rich, John Bowers, Lilyan Tashman, Eugene Pallette, Richard Neill, James Mason, Warren Rodgers, Nelson McDowell, Robert Edeson, *Helen Holmes*
Director: George Melford
Screenplay: Elliott J. Clawson, Will M. Ritchy
Story: Frank Hamilton Spearman, "Whispering Smith"

MISTAKEN ORDERS
(Larry Wheeler/Rayart, May 5, 1926) 5 Reels
Helen Holmes, Jack Perrin, Henry Barrows, Hal Walters, Harry Tenbrook, Cecil Kellog, Mack V. Wright, Arthur Millett, Alice Belcher
Director: J. P. McGowan
Producer: Morris R. Schlank

THE OPEN SWITCH
(California Studios/Rayart, June 30, 1926) 5 Reels
Helen Holmes, Jack Perrin, Slim Whitaker, Max Ascher, Mack V. Wright, Arthur Millett, Henry Rocquemore
Director: J. P. McGowan

THE LOST EXPRESS
(Rayart, August 15, 1926) 5 Reels
Henry Barrows, Eddie Barry, Martin Turner, *Helen Holmes*, Olita Otis, Jack Mower, Lassie Lou Ahern, Fred Church, Al Hoxie
Director: J. P. McGowan
Producer: Morris R. Schlank

CROSSED SIGNALS
(Morris R. Schlank/Rayart, September 28, 1926) 5 Reels
Helen Holmes, Henry Victor, Georgie Chapman, William Lowery, Milla Davenport, Nelson McDowell, Clyde McAtee
Director: J. P. McGowan
Producer: Morris R. Schlank
Story: George Saxton

PERIL OF THE RAIL
(Morris R. Schlank/Anchor, October 30, 1926) 5 Reels
Helen Holmes, Edward Hearn, Wilfred North, Lloyd Whitlock, Dick Rush, Dan Crimmins, Norma Wills, Rex
Director: J. P. McGowan
Producer: J. P. McGowan
Story: William E. Wing

THE FAST FREIGHT
(Larry Wheeler/Rayart, 1926)
Helen Holmes
Director: J. P. McGowan

WAY OUT WEST
(M-G-M, April 9, 1937) 65 Mins.
Stan Laurel, Oliver Hardy, Sharon Lynne, James Finlayson, Rosina Lawrence, Stanley Fields, Vivien Oakland, Chill Wills and the Avalon Boys, *Helen Holmes*, Denver Dixon, Buffalo Bill, Jr. (Jay Wilsey), Jim Mason, James C. Morton, Frank Mills, Fred "Snowflake" Toones, Art Mix, Ben Corbett, Dinah (a mule), Fritzi Brunette, Jack Hill, Eddie Borden, Lester Dorr, Ham Kinsey, John Ince, Mary Gordon, Cy Slocum, Bill Wolf, Frank Montgomery, Tex Driscoll, Bobby Dunn, Flora Finch
Director: James W. Horne
Screenplay: Jack Jevne, Charles Rogers, James Parrott, Felix Adler

DUDE COWBOY
(RKO, December 12, 1941) 59 Mins.
Tim Holt, Marjorie Reynolds, Ray Whitley, Lee "Lasses" White, Louise Currie, *Helen Holmes*, Eddie Kane, Eddie Dew, Byron Foulger, Tom London, Lloyd Ingraham, Glenn Strange
Director: David Howard
Screenplay: Morton Grant
Story: Morton Grant
Producer: Bert Gilroy

THE MORE THE MERRIER
(Columbia, April 7, 1943)
Jean Arthur, Joel McCrea, Charles Coburn, Richard Gaines, Bruce Bennett, Frank Sully, Clyde Fillmore, Stanley Clements, Don Douglas, Ann Savage, Grady Sutton, Sugar Geise, Don Barclay, Shirley Patterson, Ann Doran, Mary Treen, Gladys Blake, Kay Linaker, Nancy Gray, Byron Shores, Betzi Beaton, Harrison Greene, Robert McKenzie, Vic Potel, Lon Poff, Frank LaRue, Harry Bradley, Betty McMahan, *Helen Holmes*
Director: George Stevens

Edith Johnson

11 • EDITH JOHNSON

She Braved the Scenario Writer's Wildest Fantasies with Tireless Femininity

Edith Johnson's face was smiling at people from many media before Hollywood made her a serial heroine. She was perhaps the most photographed girl in the world before making her screen debut; her picture appeared in all the leading magazines and newspapers as The Kodak Girl. Living in Rochester, New York, the home of Kodak, Miss Johnson with her madonna-like features and stylish dress soon attracted the attention of the camera company and it engaged her to pose for them. Her photogenic quality was recognized by the Selig company, and Miss Johnson was offered a position as leading lady in the company's outdoor films after she graduated from Vassar.

Her first film of record was a melodrama called **Out of Petticoat Lane** (1914), about a poor laundry girl, befriended by a wealthy engaged couple, who incurs the jealous enmity of a fellow worker. Adda Gleason was co-starred. In her second film, **The Lure of the Windigo** (1914), Edith is Annette La Clerg, the beautiful daughter of a trapper played by that grand old man of Westerns, Lafe McKee. The story, though dealing with the time-worn subject of the betrayal of innocent love and the unwritten law, was so well developed and original at the time that it is safe from any criticism of being hackneyed. Gerard McChesney (Barney Furey), a young sergeant of the Northwest Mounted Police, wins the love of Annette from her established suitor, Jacques Le Bree (Charles Wheelock). McChesney turns out to be dissolute and without moral sense; he betrays Annette and breaks his promise of returning to marry her. In her wanderings, after she and her unwelcome baby have been turned out of her father's house, Annette runs upon Kiawa (Lamar Johnstone), her old Indian friend, whose undying hate had previously been aroused against McChesney. To avenge himself he decides to lead Annette and her child to McChesney, whom he knows to be at the settlement, and to confront him with the proof of his dishonorable act. He imitates the sound of the wind through the trees and thus lures Annette, who believes in the old Creek superstition of the voice of the Windigo, mile after mile through the forest. At the settlement McChesney is forced to marry Annette and is then throttled by her brother, leaving her free to accept the love of the forgiving Jacques.

In Heart's Desire (1915), Edith's third picture, Charles Wheelock plays the son of a wealthy society leader who falls in love with his mother's secretary, played by Edith. The jealous mother discharges her and she obtains a position with a charitable organization in a neighboring town. The son learns her whereabouts from a card attached to one of the toy balloons which the organization has sent up at a lawn fete.

These films are mentioned merely to emphasize that Edith Johnson, contrary to popular opinion, was not exclusively a serial star, nor did she work only with William Duncan, whom she eventually married. After a few more Selig films, Edith moved to Universal where she appeared in films under the directorship of Henry McRae in 1916 and 1917.

Vitagraph beckoned in 1918 and Edith was cast opposite serial king William Duncan in **A Fight for Millions** (1918), an enormously popular serial which Duncan also directed. Edith demonstrated her stamina under the excruciating demands of serial production and won the approval not only of film audiences but of the rugged Duncan. Her fondness for athletics fitted her well for the hard and dangerous feats of a serial heroine. All the more remarkable is that she broke precedent for action heroines by not having spent her early years in the West, riding bareback, shooting, and swimming. Thus one of the most popular of serial teams was born. Duncan kept her

The Silent Avenger (Vitagraph, 1920) – William Duncan and Edith Johnson.

on as his permanent leading lady in both serials and features and married her in April 1921, a second marriage for both of them.

In eight serials and eight action features with Duncan, Edith Johnson attained considerable popularity with cliffhanger and adventure audiences. She won new laurels with each release, but her performances were usually overshadowed by the amazing feats of Duncan and, though popular, she never achieved the fame of Ruth Roland, Pearl White, or Allene Ray. But she was definitely a contender with Neva Gerber, Louise Lorraine, Ann Little, Marie Walcamp, Helen Holmes, Juanita Hansen, and Eileen Sedgwick for secondary honors and was one of the top dozen serial heroines of the silent era.

The Duncan-Johnson serials were topnotch film entertainment made in a day when the continued-next-week dramas were high in popularity and profitability. Duncan received as much as $10,000 a week for his chores as actor/director. Not many Hollywood actors could match that salary. A lot of money was spent on the five serials Duncan and Johnson made for Vitagraph and the three that they did for Universal. Long location jaunts away from the familiar environs near Hollywood were commonplace. Shooting schedules were extended, casts included scores of extras, scenarios were imaginative and carefully written, camera work was good, and the action moved with kaleidoscopic swiftness. Plots had unusual twists and were novel and surprising in development.

For **A Man of Might** (1919), for instance, Duncan took his intrepid company all through southern California, lower Mexico, the Arizona Desert, and as far north as San Francisco to film a story designed to jolt men out of complacency and upset the emotional equilibrium of women. Many striking scenes resulted, contributing to the dramatic impact of the film.

Duncan was unhappy with the red tape and front-office interference imposed on him at Universal and chose to retire after he and Edith finished **Wolves of the North** (1924), an exciting story of fur traders in the Northwest that featured Esther Ralston in the second female lead. The Duncans had amassed a small fortune so there was no financial reason for them to continue to face the hazards of serial making. After a vaudeville tour the couple settled down to traveling for fun and enjoying quiet family life with their three children, though Duncan accepted a few roles in the thirties (notably as Buck Connors in the Hopalong Cassidy oaters) just for the fun of it. He died on February 7, 1961. Edith lived in Los Angeles until her death on September 5, 1969. Although it had been forty-five years since her last serial, Edith Johnson was not forgotten. The press paid her due homage for her pioneering film work.

EDITH JOHNSON Filmography

NAN'S VICTORY
(Selig, August 15, 1914) 1 Reel
Edith Johnson, Franklyn Hall, Thomas Santschi, Goldie Colwell
Director: Thomas Santschi
Screenplay: Nellie Browne Duff

OUT OF PETTICOAT LANE
(Selig, November 23, 1914) 2 Reels
Edith Johnson, Adda Gleason, Goldie Colwell, Charles Wheelock
Director: F. J. Grandin
Screenplay: Gilson Willets

THE LURE OF THE WINDIGO
(Selig, December 19, 1914) 2 Reels
Edith Johnson, Lafayette (Lafe) McKee, Barney Furey, Lamar Johnstone, Charles Wheelock, Frank Mayo, Lillian Hayward, Lucile Joy
Director: F. J. Grandin
Story: Maibelle Heikes Justice

HEART'S DESIRE
(Selig, January 27, 1915) 1 Reel
Edith Johnson, Charles Wheelock
Director: F. J. Grandin
Screenplay: Wallace C. Clifton

THE VAN THORNTON DIAMONDS
(Selig, February 13, 1915) 2 Reels
Edith Johnson, Lamar Johnson, Franklyn Hall, Catherine Henry
Director: F. J. Grandin
Story: Joe Jenette

AT THE FLOOD TIDE
(Selig, July 24, 1915) 1 Reel
Edith Johnson
Director: Guy Oliver
Screenplay: Wallace C. Clifton

THE CIRCULAR STAIRCASE
(Selig, August 25, 1915)
Eugenie Besserer, Guy Oliver, *Edith Johnson*, Stella Razeto, William Howard, Anna Dodge
Director: Edward LeSaint
Story: Mary Roberts Rinehart

TOLL OF THE JUNGLE
(Selig, March, 1916) 1 Reel
Wheeler Oakman, *Edith Johnson*, Harry Lonsdale, Walter Beckwith
Director: Thomas Santschi
Screenplay: C. J. Buckley

THE CYCLE OF FATE
(Selig, March 18, 1916) 5 Reels
Bessie Eyton, Wheeler Oakman, *Edith Johnson*
Director: Marshall Neilan
Story: Marshall Neilan

BADGERED
(Selig, April, 1916) 1 Reel
Harry Mestayer, Grace Darmond, Al W. Filson, *Edith Johnson*, James Bradbury
Director: T. N. Heffron
Story: William M. Henry

THE VALIANTS OF VIRGINIA
(Selig, June, 1916) 5 Reels
Kathlyn Williams, Arthur Shirley, Edward J. Peil, Virginia Kraft, Guy Oliver, Billy Jacobs, *Edith Johnson*, Al W. Filson, James Bradbury, Harry Lonsdale, Frank Clark
Director: T. N. Heffron
Story: Hallie Erminie Rives

THE PRIVATE BANKER
(Selig, July, 1916) 3 Reels
Edith Johnson, Wheeler Oakman, Leo Pierson, Harry Lonsdale, Thomas Bates
Director: Thomas Santschi
Screenplay: J. Edward Hungerford

BEHIND THE LINES
(Universal-Bluebird, August 28, 1916) 5 Reels
Edith Johnson
Director: Henry McRae
Screenplay: Walter Woods
Story: Mary Rider

The Fast Express (Universal, 1924) – Edith Johnson, William Duncan (standing with Edith) and unidentified players.

FOR LOVE AND GOLD
(Universal-Bison, October 21, 1916) 2 Reels
Edith Johnson, Edward Hesrn, L. C. Shumway, Mark Fenton, E. N. Walleck, Charles Dorian
Director: Henry McRae
Screenplay: William Parker
Story: E. M. McCall

GUILTY
(Universal, November, 1916) 2 Reels
Harry Carey, *Edith Johnson*, E. N. Walleck, L. C. Shumway, Peggy Coudray, Lee Hill, Mark Fenton, Hector V. Sarno
Director: Henry McRae
Screenplay: William Parker
Story: Ben Cohn, William Parker

THE FIVE FRANC PIECE
(Selig, December, 1916) 2 Reels
Lafayette McKee, Charles Wheelock, *Edith Johnson*, Barney Furey
Director: F. J. Grandin
Screenplay: Myles D. Savelle

GIANT POWER
(Universal-Bison, December 19, 1916) 2 Reels
Edith Johnson
Director: Henry McRae
Story: Maxwell Ryder

THE SCARLET CRYSTAL
(Universal-Red Feather, January 20, 1917) 5 Reels
Herbert Rawlinson, Betty Schade, *Edith Johnson*, Dorothy Davenport, Gertrude Astor, Nicholas Duneau, Richard Ryan, Raymond Whitaker
Director: Charles Swickard
Story: J. Grubb Alexander

A BROTHER'S SACRIFICE
(Selig, March, 1917) 1 Reel
Lillian Hayward, Charles Wheelock, Lafayette McKee, *Edith Johnson*
Director: F. J. Grandin
Screenplay: C. Chester Wesley

STEEL HEARTS
(Universal-Bison, March 15. 1917) 2 Reels
Edith Johnson
Director: Henry McRae
Screenplay: Wright Roberts

IN THE TALONS OF AN EAGLE
(Selig, July 7, 1917)
Lafe McKee, *Edith Johnson*, Charles Wheelock, Walter Hatfield, Philo McCullough
Director: F. J. Grandon
Scenario: Gilson Willets

HANDS IN THE DARK
(Universal-Star, August, 1917) 2 Reels
J. Warren Kerrigan, *Edith Johnson*, E. N. Wallock, Rex de Rossellit
Director: Henry McRae
Screenplay: William Parker
Story: E. M. McCall

THE RIGHT MAN
(Universal, September, 1917) 2 Reels
J. Warren Kerrigan, *Edith Johnson*, E. N. Wallack, Charles Cummings, Harry Griffith
Director: Henry McRae
Screenplay: William Parker, Henry McRae
Story: E. M. McCall

THE SCARLET CAR
(Universal-Bluebird, December 4, 1917) 5 Reels
Franklyn Farnum, *Edith Johnson,* Lon Chaney, Sam DeGrasse, Al Filson, Howard Crampton
Director: Joseph DeGrasse
Screenplay: William Parker
Story: Richard Harding

THE FIGHTING GRIN
(Universal-Bluebird, January 9, 1918) 5 Reels
Franklyn Farnum, *Edith Johnson,* J. Morris Foster
Director: Joseph DeGrasse
Scenario: Charles Kenyon
Story: R. E. Bradbury, F. H. Clark

THE SHUTTLE
(Select, February, 1918) 5 Reels
Constance Talmadge, Albert Roscoe, *Edith Johnson*, E. B. Tilton, Helen Dunbar, George McDaniel, Thomas Persse, Edward Peil, Casson Ferguson
Director: Rollin S. Sturgeon
Screenplay: Margaret Turnbull, Harvey Thew
Story: Frances Hodgson Burnett

A FIGHT FOR MILLIONS
(Vitagraph, July 15, 1918) 15 Chapters.
William Duncan, *Edith Johnson*, Joe Ryan, Walter Rodgers, S. E. Jennings, Leo Maloney, Hart (Jack) Hoxie, Willie Calles, Vincente Howard, William McCall
Director: William Duncan
Screenplay: Graham Baker
Story: Albert E. Smith, Cyrus Townsend Brady
Chapters: (1) The Snare (2) Flames of Peril (3) The Secret Stockade (4) The Precipice of Horror (5) The Path of Thrills (6) The Spell of Evil (7) The Gorge of Destruction (8) In the Clutches (9) The Escape (10) The Secret Tunnel (11) The Noose of Death (12) The Tide of Disaster (13) The Engine of Terror (14) The Decoy (15) The Sealed Envelope

MAN OF MIGHT
(Vitagraph, January 1919) 15 Chapters.
William Duncan, *Edith Johnson*, Joe Ryan, Walter Rodgers, Del Harris, Frank Tokanaga, Otto Lederer, Willie Calles, George Kuva
Director: William Duncan
Screenplay: Graham Baker
Story: Albert E. Smith, C. T. Brady
Chapters: (1) The Riven Flag (2) The Leap Through Space (3) The Creeping Death (4) The Gripping Hand (5) The Human Shield (6) The Height of Torment (7) Into the Trap (8) The One Chance (9) The Crashing Horror (10) Double Crossed (11) The Ship (12) The Volcano's Prey (13) The Flood of Despair (14) The Living Catapult (15) The Rescue

SMASHING BARRIERS
(Vitagraph, September 1919) 15 Chapters.
William Duncan, *Edith Johnson*, Walter Rodgers, George Stanley, Fred Darnton, Slim Cole, William McCall, Joe Ryan, Vincente Howard, Dorothea Wolbert
Director: William Duncan
Screenplay: Graham Baker, R. Cecil Smith
Story: Albert E. Smith, Cyrus T. Brady
Chapters: (1) Test of Courage (2) Plunge of Death (3) Tree-Hut of Torture (4) Deed of a Devil (5) Living Rave (6) Downward to Doom (7) The Fatal Flight (8) The Murder Car (9) The Dynamite Tree (10) Overpowered (11) The Den of Deviltry (12) Explosive Bullets (13) Dead Fall (14) Trapped Like Rats (15) The Final Barrier

THE SILENT AVENGER
(Vitagraph, April 1920) 15 Chapters.
William Duncan, *Edith Johnson*, Jack Richardson, Virginia Nightingale, Ernest Shields, Willis L. Robards, William S. Smith
Director: William Duncan
Screenplay: Graham Baker, William B. Courtney
Story: Albert E. Smith, Cleveland Moffett
Chapters: (1) The Escape (2) Fighting Back (3) Within the Noose (4) Tearing Through (5) Blotted Out (6) The Hidden Blow (7) Dynamite Doom (8) The Crusher (9) Into the Jaws (10) Blades of Horror (11) Shot into Space (12) Facing Eternity (13) A Human Pendulum (14) The Lakes of Fire (15) The Final Trump

FIGHTING FATE
(Vitagraph, January 1921) 15 Chapters.
William Duncan, *Edith Johnson*, Ford West, Frank Weed, William McCall, George Stanley, C. L. Davidson, Burwell Hamrick, Laddie Earle, Jean Carpenter, Will Badger, Charles Dudley
Director: William Duncan
Screenplay: C. Graham Baker, William B. Courtney
Story: Albert E. Smith, Arthur P. Hankins
Chapters: (1) A Borrowed Life (2) Playing the Game (3) A Modern Daniel (4) A Desperate Dilemma (5) Double Crossed (6) The Crown Jewel Clue (7) A Demon's Bluff (8) The Treasure Hunt (9) The Air Avenger (10) The Stolen Bride (11) A Choice of Death (12) Indian Vengeance (13) Mystery Mountain (14) When Thieves Fall Out (15) Cleaning the Bolt

WHERE MEN ARE MEN
(Vitagraph, September 1, 1921) 5 Reels
William Duncan, *Edith Johnson*, George Stanley, Tom Wilson, Gertrude Wilson, Harry Lonsdale, George Kunkel, William McCall, Charles Dudley
Director: William Duncan
Screenplay: Thomas Dixon, Jr.
Story: Ralph Cummins, "The Princess of the Desert Dream"

STEELHEART
(Vitagraph, November 6, 1921) 6 Reels
William Duncan, *Edith Johnson*, Jack Curtis, Walter Rodgers, Euna Luckey, Ardeta Malino, Earl Crain, Charles Dudley
Director: William Duncan
Screenplay: Bradley J. Smollen

NO DEFENSE
(Vitagraph, December 25, 1921) 6 Reels
William Duncan, *Edith Johnson*, Jack Richardson, Henry Hebert, Mathilde Brundage, Charles Dudley
Director: William Duncan
Screenplay: C. Graham Baker
Story: J. Raleigh Davies, "The Comeback"

THE SILENT VOW
(Vitagraph, April 16, 1922) 5 Reels
William Duncan, *Edith Johnson*, Dorothy Dwan, Maud Emery, J. Morris Foster, Henry Hebert, Fred Burley, Jack Curtis, Charles Dudley
Director: William Duncan
Screenplay: Bradley J. Smollen

WHEN DANGER SMILES
(Vitagraph, October 3, 1922) 5 Reels
William Duncan, *Edith Johnson*, James Farley, Henry Hebert, Charles Dudley, William McCall
Director: William Duncan
Screenplay: Bradley J. Smollen
Story: John B. Clymer

THE FIGHTING GUIDE
(Vitagraph, October 15, 1922) 5 Reels
William Duncan, *Edith Johnson*, Harry Lonsdale, William McCall, Sidney D'Albrook, Charles Dudley, Fred De Silva, Mrs. Harry Burns
Directors: William Duncan, Don Clark
Screenplay: Bradley J. Smollen
Story: Bradley J. Smollen

PLAYING IT WILD
(Vitagraph, April 19, 1923) 6 Reels
William Duncan, *Edith Johnson*, Francis Powers, Dick La Reno, Edmund Cobb, Frank Beal, Frank Weed
Director: William Duncan
Screenplay: C. Graham Baker
Story: C. Graham Baker

SMASHING BARRIERS
(Vitagraph, June 17, 1923) 6 Reels
(Feature version of the 1919 serial of the same title)
William Duncan, *Edith Johnson*, Joe Ryan, Walter Rogers, George Stanley, Frederick Darnton, Slim Cole, William McCall
Director: William Duncan
Screenplay: Graham Baker, R. Cecil Smith, Harvey Gates
Story: Albert E. Smith, Cyrus Townsend Brady

THE STEEL TRAIL
(Universal, August 27, 1923) 15 Chapters.
William Duncan, *Edith Johnson*, Harry Carter, John Cossar, Harry Woods, Mabel Randall
Director: William Duncan
Screenplay: George Plympton, Karl Coolidge, Paul M. Bryan
Story: George Plympton, Karl Coolidge, Paul M. Bryan
Chapters: (1) Intrigue (2) Dynamite (3) Wildfire (4) Blown from the Cliff (5) Head On (6) Crushed (7) The Gold Rush (8) Judith's Peril (9) The Dam Bursts (10) The Trap (11) The Fight on the Cliff (12) The Tottering Bridge (13) Between Two Fires (14) Burning Fumes (15) Ten Seconds to Go

THE FAST EXPRESS
(Universal, March 10, 1924) 15 Chapters.
William Duncan, *Edith Johnson*, Albert J. Smith, Harry Woods, John Cossar, Harry Carter, Janet Ford, Ralph McCullough, Mabel Randall, Catherine Calhoun
Director: William Duncan
Screenplay: Frank H. Clark
Story: Courtney Ryley Cooper, "Crossed Wires"
Chapters: (1) Facing the Crisis (2) The Woman of Mystery (3) Unknown (4) The Haunted House (5) Perils of the City (6) The Cipher Message (7) The Bandit Raiders (8) The Imposter's Schem (9) The Falsely Accused (10) The Path of Danger (11) The Abduction (12) The Trial Run (13) The False Summons (14) Black Treasure (15) Retribution

WOLVES OF THE NORTH
(Universal, September 21, 1924) 10 Chapters.
William Duncan, *Edith Johnson*, Esther Ralston, Joseph W. Girard, Frank Rice, Joe Bonomo, Clarke Comstock, Edward Cecil, Harry Woods, Joe Dominguez, Dan Martin, Robert F. Homans, Leo White, Malvina Polo
Director: William Duncan
Screenplay: Frank H. Clark
Story: Katherine and Robert Pinkerton, "The Free Trader"
Chapters: (1) The Fur Pirates (2) The Wolf Pack (3) The Avalanche (4) Passions of War (5) The Blizzard (6) Flames of Peril (7) The Man Hunt (8) The Trail of Gold (9) A Trick of Fate (10) The Stolen Map

Ann Little

12 • ANNA LITTLE

Attuned to the Plains, She Was a Spirited Star in the Serial Cosmos

Anna Little was born in Sisson, California, on February 1, 1891, and educated in Chicago and Los Angeles. Until the age of sixteen, she lived mostly on a ranch at the foot of Mount Shasta. Shortly after completing her schooling she joined a stock company in California, making her first stage appearance in the chorus of a company in San Francisco. Anna was a beautiful young woman with dark brown eyes and a luxurious crop of chestnut hair. Though she was first engaged for her good singing voice, her dramatic ability was soon recognized and the following year she was playing leads.

The date of her entrance into motion pictures has long been forgotten, but it is believed that she first played with Broncho Billy Anderson at San Rafael for a short period. Her first bid to fame came during her long engagement with the New York Motion Picture Corporation (which handled the products of Bison, Kay-Bee, Broncho, and Domino) at Santa Monica, where she played a great variety of parts.

"If nobody else can do the part, give it to Anna Little" is what one director said of this versatile player, who had learned as a girl to ride, shoot, swim, and hunt in the wilderness. She had studied the red man thoroughly, and so true were her characterizations that it was difficult to believe that she was a white girl. Her most famous Indian portrayal was that of Naturich in Cecil B. DeMille's **The Squaw Man** (1918). Her sympathetic interpretation of these roles won her the friendship of chiefs, ex-chiefs, subchiefs, braves, squaws, and papooses.

She was an athletic girl, an expert horsewoman, and well equipped with vigor and strength to stand the strain of these arduous roles. Producers found her a congenial woman who adapted easily to the movie world of cowboys and horses. However, she liked to play other parts and preferred straight leads in strong dramas, for which her mature dramatic expression also fitted her. Emotional scenes came naturally to her--she could cry real tears on cue, but sometimes found it hard to smile at the proper time.

By 1914 Anna was firmly established at Universal, often working in films with Herbert Rawlinson and under the direction of Otis Turner. The best-known of these films are **The Opened Shutters** (1914) and **Called Back** (1914), both four-reelers; **Damon and Pythias** (1914), a six-reeler adapted to the screen by Allan Dwan; and **The Black Box** (1915), the first of her six serials. Most of the action in this latter film was centered on Herbert Rawlinson, as criminologist Sanford Quest, and Anna had to share the spotlight with Laura Oakley. But she managed well, as the tempo and hazards of serial production were no more demanding than those of the short Westerns she had been making. And there were more to come. In a number of Mustang Westerns released by Universal and American, Anna acquired the affectionate title of "The Darling of the Plains" as she proved her versatility in assorted characterizations and her ability as an equestrienne.

Such simple two-reelers as **The Gopher** (1915), **That Gal of Burke's** and **The Pilgrim** (1916) were popular with the audiences of 1916. Anna and her co-stars contributed some great teamwork and the action flowed along entertainingly. The stories may have been implausible, but they stepped along so briskly that the lack of probability didn't really bother the viewer.

In 1917 Anna temporarily abandoned the West and Hollywood and traveled to New York to check out the film colony there. "If you are a Westerner," she said, "and stay with the Western picture companies, you are always looked upon as just a commonplace sort of person who happened

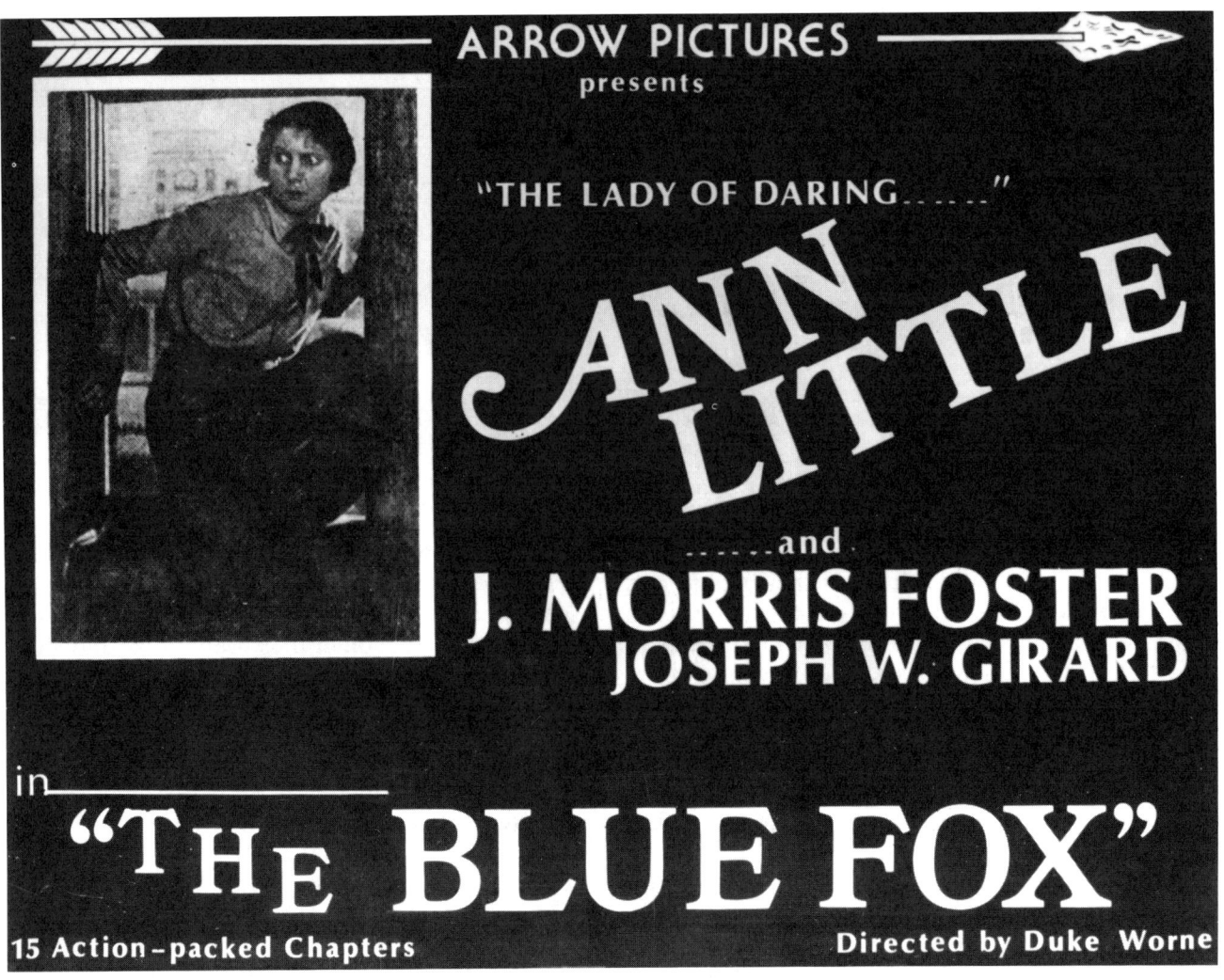

The Blue Fox (Arrow, 1921) – Ann Little

along. You come East and do a picture or two, and no matter whether or not your work is as good as it was in the West, if you go back your salary is just about double. It is the stamp of Eastern approval that counts." And Anna promptly galloped away with one of the season's most important roles, along with Anna Q. Nilsson, in Robert Warwick's **The Silent Master** (1917).

In 1917 Anna (soon dropping the a to become simply Ann) was signed by Famous Players-Lasky. She appeared in a series of superb features that included **Nan of Music Mountain** (1917), **Rimrock Jones** (1918), **Believe Me, Xantippe** (1918), **The Firefly of France** (1918), **Less Than Kin** (1918), **The Source** (1918), **The Man from Funeral Range** (1918), **Alias Mike Moran** (1918), **The Roaring Road** (1919), and **Excuse My Dust** (1920), in all as co-star to idol Wallace Reid. For Cecil B. DeMille she did **The Squaw Man** (1918), previously mentioned, giving an excellent performance as Naturich, the ill-fated Indian girl with whom Elliott Dexter falls in love and whom he marries. In the original version, made in 1914, Princess Red Wing had played the part.

Ann was twice leading lady to William S. Hart. In **Square Deal Sanderson** (1919) she is the girl in distress defended by ranger Hart. **The Cradle of Courage** (1920) is a police melodrama of old San Francisco in which reformed criminal Hart, now a cop, falls in love with his former gang chief's daughter, Ann. In **Told in the Hills** (1919) Ann co-stars with Robert Warwick in a good mountain story, notable for an exceptionally fine cast that included Wanda Hawley, Hart (Jack) Hoxie, Charles Ogle, Monte Blue, Eileen Percy, Margaret Loomis, Tom Forman, and Guy Oliver.

The serial form of film entertainment had a great hold on the public in the World War I era, and Ann was lured by National Film Corporation to star with up-and-coming Hoxie in **Lightning Brice** (1919), released by Arrow Film Corporation. All the requisites for a sure-fire serial are found as the film takes the audience out of interiors and gives them the great outdoors. Joe Brandt wrote the story following a largely conventional formula but had the foresight to give the serial a new dressing so that it appeared reasonably fresh and up to date. His mysterious figure (no serial is complete without it) is not represented as a masked monster but as a woman, a new departure. Also, the author's scheme for introducing his romance is novel to say the least. Two miners bequeath their respective children a rich secret mine. The daughter of one is made the recipient of a string, the son of the other is given a hunting knife. The mine can be located only by winding the string over the blade--the string carrying the precious information. Naturally villainy enters to complicate matters.

Lightning Brice was a success, and Arrow capitalized on Ann's popularity by rushing her into **The Blue Fox** (1921), a fifteen-chapter serial in which she portrays the daughter of a white man and an Eskimo girl. She is raised in the United States after her father is murdered by the tribe for having taken one of its women in marriage and her mother dies of grief. She returns to the northland as a grown woman determined to wreak vengeance on those who destroyed her family. The title of the film is derived from a blue fox skin in the story that holds the key to the location of a rich mine.

Next for Ann came **Nan of the North** (1922). Leonard Clapham (known later as Tom London) was the Canadian Mountie who aided Ann in thwarting the attempts of Joseph Girard and Edith Stayart to obtain the powerful substance "Tilano" from a fallen meteorite. Ann provided the love interest as the comely maiden in distress.

Ann's exuberant personality and entertaining ways were utilized effectively in Universal's **The Eagle's Talons** (1923), a direct action proposition from start to finish that introduced Fred Thomson. Stunt flyer Al Wilson and strongman Joe Bonomo headed up the supporting cast. But Ann carried off the laurels as she went through thrill after thrill, recalling Pearl White's exploits in a way that kept fans perched on the edges of their seats.

In 1925 Ann was starred in the Rayart serial, **Secret Service Saunders**, undoubtedly the weakest of her chapter plays. It is the last film credit we have for her. As to why she left films or the details of her personal life, we have little knowledge. Until her death in the spring of 1984 she lived in the Los Angeles area and is reported to have been active in Christian Science endeavors for a number of years. She preferred not to talk of her moviemaking days.

Ann Little left an indelible mark on both sagebrush and serial genres and, though she may have preferred to let go of the past, film students are not likely to let her memory slide into the abyss of forgotten photoplayers.

ANNA LITTLE Filmography

A YOUNG SQUAW'S BRAVERY
(Bison, November, 1911)
Anna Little

COWGIRLS' PRANKS
(Bison, December, 1911) 1 Reel
Anna Little, Ethel Grandin

THE CRISIS
(Bison, March, 1912) 2 Reels
Anna Little, Francis Ford, J. Barney Sherry, Ethel Grandin, William Farnum
Director: Thomas Ince

BLAZING THE TRAIL
(Bison, March, 1912)
Francis Ford, Ethel Grandin, J. Barney Sherry, *Anna Little*
Directors: Thomas Ince, E. H. Allen

THE POST TELEGRAPHER
(Bison, May, 1912) 2 Reels
William Meyers, *Anna Little*, Lillian Christy, Francis Ford, Jack Conway

A SHADOW OF THE PAST
(Republic, June, 1912)
Anna Little, Richard Stanton, J. Barney Sherry

HIS PUNISHMENT
(Bison, June, 1912)
Anna Little, Charles French, J. Barney Sherry
Director: Charles French

THE RECKONING
(Ince-Bronco, August, 1912) 1 Reel
Harold Lockwood, Ethel Grandin, Richard Stanton, *Anna Little*, Leo Maloney

THE DOCTOR'S DOUBLE
(Bison, September, 1912) 1 Reel
Harold Lockwood, *Anna Little*
Director: Fred Balshofer
Screenplay: Fred Balshofer
Supvisor: Thomas H. Ince

FOR THE HONOR OF THE SEVENTH
(Ince-Broncho, September, 1912)
Harold Lockwood, *Anna Little*, J. Barney Sherry
Director: Reginald Barker

CUSTER'S LAST RAID
(101 Bison, September, 1912) 3 Reels
Francis Ford, *Anna Little*, Grace Cunard, William Eagleshirt, J. Barney Sherry, Charles K. French, Lillian Christie, Art Acord, "Snowball"
Director: Thomas H. Ince
Screenplay: Richard V. Spencer

ON SECRET SERVICE
(Kay-Bee, November, 1912) 2 Reels
Anna Little, Robert Edeson, Walter Edwards, Frank Borzage
Director: Walter Edwards
Screenplay: Richard V. Spencer

THE ALTAR OF DEATH
(Kay-Bee, November, 1912) 2 Reels
Harold Lockwood, *Anna Little*
Director: Raymond B. West
Screenplay: Thomas H. Ince, C. Gardner Sullivan

THE CIVILIAN
(Broncho, November, 1912)
Mae Marsh, Jack Conway, Robert Stanton, *Anna Little*
Director: Fred Balshofer
Screenplay: Fred Balshofer

MARY OF THE MINES
(Broncho, November, 1912)
Anna Little, Jack Conway, Robert Stanton
Scenario: H. G. Stafford

THE PROSPECTOR'S DAUGHTER
(Broncho, December, 1912)
Anna Little, Charles French, Ethel Grandin, Ray Myers
Director: Thomas H. Ince

THE INDIAN MASSACRE
(Ince, 1912)
Anna Little, Francis Ford
Director: Thomas H. Ince

THE LITTLE TURNCOAT
(Kay-Bee, January, 1913) 2 Reels
Anna Little, Harold Lockwood
Director: Fred Balshofer
Screenplay: Fred Balshofer
Story: Mary O'Connor

THE MOSAIC LAW
(Kay-Bee, January, 1913) 2 Reels
Anna Little, Robert Edeson, Ethel Grandin, Charles French, Jack Conway
Director: Thomas H. Ince

SMILING DAN
(Kay-Bee, February, 1913)
Anna Little, Joe King
Director: Charles Miller

THE SERGEANT'S SECRET
(Broncho, March, 1913) 2 Reels
Charles Ray, Shorty Hamilton, Margaret Thompson, Richard Stanton, *Anna Little*, William Hadley

WITH LEE IN VIRGINIA
(Kay-Bee, March, 1913) 2 Reels
Anna Little, Francis Ford, Joe King, Charles K. French, Robert Edeson, Ethel Grandin, Walter Edwards
Director: Thomas H. Ince

PAST REDEMPTION
(Kay-Bee, April, 1913) 2 Reels
Anna Little

THE HOUSE OF BONDAGE
(Kay-Bee, July, 1913) 3 Reels
Anna Little, Mrs. Joe Knight, Charles Ray
Director: Raymond B. West
Screenplay: J. G. Hawks
Story: Reginald W. Kauffman

THE GREENHORN
(Broncho, September, 1913) 2 Reels
William Clifford, *Anna Little*, A. G. Vosburgh, Sherman Bainbridge
Director: Charles Giblyn
Screenplay: H. G. Stafford

THE WAIF
(Kay-Bee, September, 1913)
Anna Little
Director: Raymond B. West
Scenario: J. G. Hawks

THE SIGN OF THE SNAKE
(Kay-Bee, November, 1913)
Sherman Bainbridge, *Anna Little*, William Clifford
Director: Charles Giblyn
Screenplay: H. G. Stafford

The Black Box (Universal, 1915) – Ann Little and unidentified player.

THE FILLY
(Domino, December, 1913) 1 Reel
Bob Stanton, *Anna Little*
Story: William H. Clifford

HER LEGACY
(Kay-Bee, December, 1913)
Harold Lockwood, *Anna Little*, Edna Maison
Director: Fred Balshofer
Screenplay: Fred Balshofer

THE HEART OF AN INDIAN
(Bison, 1913)
Anna Little, J. Barney Sherry
Director: Thomas H. Ince

TRUE IRISH HEARTS
(Domino, January, 1914) 3 Reels
Thomas Chatterton, Richard Stanton, *Anna Little*

FOR THE WEARING OF THE GREEN
(Domino, March, 1914) 2 Reels
Charles Ray, *Anna Little*, Fannie Midgley

THE SQUIRE'S SON
(Kay-Bee, April, 1914) 2 Reels
Charles Ray, *Anna Little*, J. Barney Sherry, George Osborne, Jerome Storm
Director: Raymond B. West

ON THE VERGE OF WAR
(Universal-Bison, May 1914) 3 Reels
Herbert Rawlinson, *Anna Little*, Frank Lloyd
Director: Otis Turner
Story: James Dayton

ON THE RIO GRANDE
(Universal-Rex, June 1914)
Anna Little, Herbert Rawlinson, Frank Lloyd

PROWLERS OF THE WILD
(Universal-Bison, July 1914) 2 Reels
Anna Little, Herbert Rawlinson, Frank Lloyd

THE SOB SISTER
(Universal-Rex, July 25, 1914) 2 Reels
Anna Little, Herbert Rawlinson, Frank Lloyd
Director: Otis Turner
Screenplay: James Dayton
Story: Harry Care

CIRCLE 17
(Universal-Rex, August 8, 1914) 2 Reels
Herbert Rawlinson, *Anna Little*, William Worthington
Director: Otis Turner
Story: Phil Walsh

THROUGH THE FLAMES
(Universal-Rex, August 22, 1914) 2 Reels
Herbert Rawlinson, *Anna Little*, William Worthington
Director: Otis Turner

A PRINCE OF BAVARIA
(Universal-Rex, September 12, 1914) 2 Reels
Anna Little, Herbert Rawlinson

AS THE WIND BLOWS
(Universal-Rex, October 3, 1914) 2 Reels
Anna Little, William Worthington, Herbert Rawlinson

KID REGAN'S HANDS
(Universal-Rex, October 10, 1914) 2 Reels
Herbert Rawlinson, *Anna Little*
Director: Otis Turner
Story: Harry Carr

THE OPENED SHUTTERS
(Universal-Gold Seal, November 14, 1914) 4 Reels
Herbert Rawlinson, *Anna Little*, Betty Schade, William Worthington, Cora Drew, Frank Lloyd
Director: Otis Turner
Screenplay: Lois Weber
Story: Clara Louise Burnham

CALLED BACK
(Universal-Gold Seal, November 20, 1914) 4 Reels
Herbert Rawlinson, *Anna Little*, William Worthington, William J. Quinn, Allan Forrest
Director: Otis Turner
Screenplay: James Dayton
Story: Hugh Conway

THE CHORUS GIRL'S THANKSGIVING
(Universal-Rex, November 21, 1914) 2 Reels
Anna Little, Herbert Rawlinson
Story: James Dayton

A PAGE FROM LIFE
(Universal-Rex, December 12, 1914) 2 Reels
Herbert Rawlinson, *Anna Little*, Frank Lloyd, William Worthington
Director: Frank Lloyd
Screenplay: Frank Lloyd

DAMON AND PYTHIAS
(Universal, December 19, 1914) 6 Reels
Cleo Madison, *Anna Little*, William Worthington, Herbert Rawlinson, Frank Lloyd
Director: Otis Turner
Screenplay: Allan Dwan
Story: E. Bulwer Lytton

THE BIG SISTER'S CHRISTMAS
(Universal-Rex, December 26, 1914) 2 Reels
Anna Little, Herbert Rawlinson, Helen Leslie, William Worthington, Dick Rosson
Director: Otis Turner
Story: Ruth Ann Baldwin

THE BATTLE OF GETTYSBURG
(Kay-Bee, 1914)
Willard Mack, Charles French, Enid Bennett, Herschal Mayall, Walter Edwards, Frank Borzage, J. Barney Sherry, *Anna Little*, George Fisher, Frank Burke, Endi Markey
Director: Thomas H. Ince
Screenplay: C. Gardner Sullivan

THE PATHS OF GENIUS
(Kay-Bee/Mutual, 1914)
Charles Ray, *Anna Little*, Fannie Midgley, Gordon Mullins, Louis Morrison, Gretchen Lederer
Producer: Thomas Ince

THE COLONEL'S ADOPTED DAUGHTER
(Kay-Bee, February 10, 1915) 1 Reel
Anna Little

CHANGED LIVES
(Universal-Gold Seal, February 13, 1915) 3 Reels
Anna Little, Beatrice Van, Herbert Rawlinson, William Worthington, Laura Oakley
Director: Otis Turner
Screenplay: Otis Turner

THE BLACK BOX
(Universal, March 14, 1915) 15 Chapters.
Herbert Rawlinson, *Anna Little*, William Worthington, Mark Fenton, Laura Oakley, Frank MacQuarrie, Frank Lloyd, Helen Wright, Beatrice Van, Hylda Sloman, J. Edwin Brown
Director: Otis Turner
Screenplay: Otis Turner
Story: E. Phillips Oppenheimer
Producer: Otis Turner
Chapters: (1) An Apartment House Mystery (2) The Hidden Hands (3) The Pocket Wireless (4) An Old Grudge (5) On the Rack (6) The Unseen Terror (7) The House of Mystery (8) The Inherited Sin (9) Lost in London (10) The Ship of Horror (11) A Desert Vengeance (12) Neath Iron Wheels (13) Tongues of Flame (14) A Bolt from the Blue (15) The Black Box

THE GRAIL
(Universal-Laemmle, June 22, 1915) 2 Reels
William Worthington, *Anna Little*, Herbert Robinson
Director: William Worthington
Screenplay: L. V. Jefferson
Producer: William Worthington

HOMAGE
(Universal-Gold Deal, July 13, 1915) 2 Reels
Anna Little, William Worthington, Herbert Rawlinson
Director: William Worthington
Screenplay: Harvey Gates
Producer: William Worthington

THE GREAT RUBY MYSTERY
(Universal-Gold Seal, July 26, 1915) 2 Reels
Herbert Rawlinson, *Anna Little*, William Worthington
Director: Otis Turner
Screenplay: Otis Turner

THE GOPHER
(Universal-Bison, August 13, 1915) 2 Reels
Herbert Rawlinson, *Anna Little*, Hart (Jack) Hoxie
Director: William Worthington
Screenplay: Harvey Gates
Producer: William Worthington

THE SOCIAL LION
(Universal-Bison, August, 1915) 2 Reels
Herbert Rawlinson, *Anna Little*, Helen Wright, William Quinn
Director: William Worthington
Scenario: James Dayton

MISJUDGED
(Universal-Gold Seal, August 23, 1915) 3 Reels
Herbert Rawlinson, *Anna Little*, Richard Sterling, Agnes Vernon, Jack Pierce
Director: William Worthington
Story: Harvey Gates
Producer: William Worthington

THE QUEEN OF HEARTS
(Universal-Gold Seal, September 18, 1915) 3 Reels
Herbert Rawlinson, William Worthington, Barney Furey, Jack Welch, *Anna Little*
Director: William Worthington
Screenplay: Ben Cohn
Story: L. V. Jefferson

MAN AFRAID OF HIS WARDROBE
(Universal-Mustang, October 2, 1915) 3 Reels
Art Acord, *Anna Little*, E. Forrest Taylor, Lawrence Peyton, Hardy Gibson, Ashton Dearholt, A. Lester Hale
Director: William Bertram
Story: From Charles E. Van Loan's stories, "Buck Parvin in the Movies"

TWO SPOT JOE
(Mustang Photoplay-American Mutual, October 16, 1915) 2 Reels
Anna Little, Jack Richardson, E. Forrest Taylor, Louise Lester
Director: Donald MacDonald

PLAYING FOR HIGH STAKES
(Mustang Photoplay-American Mutual, October 23, 1915) 2 Reels
Anna Little, Jack Richardson, Walter Spencer, Mary Gladding, Louise Lester
Director: Donald MacDonald

THE SHERIFF OF WILLOW CREEK
(Mustang Photoplay-American Mutual, October 23, 1915) 2 Reels
E. Forrest Taylor, *Anna Little*, Jack Richardson, Louise Lester, George Webb
Director: Frank Cooley

MAN TO MAN
(Mustang Photoplay-American Mutual, November 6, 1915) 2 Reels
Jack Richardson, *Anna Little*, Jimsy Maye
Director: Donald MacDonald

THE VALLEY FEUD
(Mustang Photoplay-American Mutual, November 27, 1915) 2 Reels
Anna Little, E. Forrest Taylor, Jack Richardson, George Armstrong

BROADCLOTH AND BUCKSKIN
(Mustang Photoplay-American Mutual, November 27, 1915) 2 Reels
Anna Little, Jack Richardson, E. Forrest Taylor, Louise Lester
Director: Frank Cooley

ACCORDING TO ST. JOHN
(Mustang, December, 1915) 3 Reels
Anna Little, Jack Richardson, Tom Chatterton, Ward McAllister
Director: Tom Chatterton

THERE'S GOOD IN THE WORST OF US
(Mustang Photoplay-American Mutual, December 11, 1915) 2 Reels
Anna Little, E. Forrest Taylor

THE CACTUS BLOSSOM
(Mustang, December 25, 1915) 2 Reels
Anna Little, Frank Borzage, Dick LaReno, Chief Big Tree
Director: Tom Chatterton

WHEN THE LIGHT CAME
(Mustang, February, 1916) 3 Reels
Thomas Chatterton, *Anna Little*, George Rainey, John Farrell, Jack Richardson
Director: Thomas Chatterton

DOUBLE CROSSED
(Mustang, February, 1916) 3 Reels
Anna Little, Thomas Chatterton, Jack Richardson
Director: William Bertram

THE QUAGMIRE
(Mustang, March, 1916) 3 Reels
Anna Little, Thomas Chatterton, Jack Richardson, Perry Banks
Director: Thomas Chatterton

THE RANGER OF LONESOME GULCH
(Mustang, March, 1916) 3 Reels
Tom Chatterton, *Anna Little*, Jack Richardson
Director: Thomas Chatterton

TWO BITS
(Mustang, April, 1916) 2 Reels
Anna Little, Thomas Chatterton, Frank Borzage, Jack Richardson, Mark Thorne
Director: Thomas Chatterton

SILENT SELBY
(Mustang, April, 1916) 3 Reels
Thomas Chatterton, *Anna Little*, Jack Richardson, Dick LaReno
Director: Thomas Chatterton
Scenario: Kenneth B. Clarke

A FLICKERING LIGHT
(Mustang, April, 1916) 2 Reels
Anna Little, Frank Borzage, Jack Richardson
Director: Frank Borzage
Scenario: Carl Coolidge

THE PILGRIM
(Mustang, June 17, 1916) 2 Reels
Frank Borzage, *Anna Little*, Dick LaReno, Mary Gladding, Jack Richardson
Director: Frank Borzage
Scenario: Edward Kaugman

NUGGET JIM'S PARTNER
(Mustang, July, 1916) 2 Reels
Frank Borzage, *Anna Little*, Dick LaReno, Jack Farrell
Director: Frank Borzage
Scenario: Frank Borzage

THAT GAL OF BURKE'S
(Mustang, July 28, 1916) 2 Reels
Frank Borzage, *Anna Little*, Jack Richardson, Dick LaReno, Gordon Bennett, Queenie Rosson
Director: Frank Borzage

NELL DALE'S MEN FOLKS
(Mustang, August, 1916) 2 Reels
Anna Little, Frank Borzage, Webb Parker, Harvey Clark, Oscar Geraro, Chick Morrison
Director: Frank Borzage
Story: Kenneth B. Clarke

THE FORGOTTEN PRAYER
(Mustang, August, 1916) 3 Reels
Anna Little, Frank Borzage, Perry Banks, Jack Richardson
Director: Frank Borzage
Story: Kenneth Clarke

MATCHIN' JIM
(Mustang, September, 1916) 2 Reels
Frank Borzage, *Anna Little*, Chick Morrison, Dick LaReno, Harvey Clarke, Queenie Rosson
Director: Frank Borzage

LAND O' LIZARDS
(Mustang, September, 1916) 5 Reels
Frank Borzage, *Anna Little*, Jack Richardson, Harvey Clark, Laura Sears, Perry Banks
Director: Frank Borzage
Scenario: Kenneth B. Clarke
(Re-issued in 1922 as **Silent Shelby**)

IMMEDIATE LEE
(Mustang, November 16, 1916) 5 Reels
Frank Borzage, *Anna Little*, Chick Morrison, Jack Richardson
Director: Frank Borzage

CHANGED LIVES
(Universal-Gold Seal, 1916) 3 Reels
Anna Little, Herbert Rawlinson
Director: Otis Turner

THE SILENT MASTER
(Robert Warwick Film Corp./Mutual, May 29, 1917) 7 Reels
Anna Little, Robert Warwick, Anne Q. Nilsson, Olive Tell
Director: Leonel Perrat
Screenplay: Leonel Perret
Story: E. Phillips Oppenheim, "The Court of St. Simon"

UNDER HANDICAP
(Yorke/Metro, August 29, 1917) 8 Reels
Anna Little, W. H. Bainbridge, Lester Cuneo, William Clifford, Harold Lockwood
Director: Fred J. Balshofer
Screenplay: Fred J. Balshofer, Richard V. Spencer
Story: Jackson Gregory, "Under Handicap"

NAN OF MUSIC MOUNTAIN
(Famous Players-Lasky/Paramount, December 12, 1917) 5 Reels
Wallace Reid, *Anna Little*, Theodore Roberts, James Cruze, Charles Ogle, Raymond Hatton, Hart (Jack) Hoxie, Ernest Joy, Guy Oliver, James Mason, Horace Carpenter, Henry Woodward, Alice Marc
Director: George H. Melford
Screenplay: Beulah Marie Dix
Story: Frank H. Spearman

THE WORLD FOR SALE
(Famous Players-Lasky/Paramount, January, 1918) 5 Reels
Conway Tearle, *Ann Little*, Norbert Wicki, W. W. Bittner, Escamilio Fernandez, Maude Scofield, Joseph Donahue
Director: J. Stuart Blackton
Story: Sir Gilbert Parker

RIMROCK JONES
(Famous Players-Lasky/Paramount, January 5, 1918) 5 Reels
Wallace Reid, *Anna Little*, Guy Oliver, Gustav B. Von Seyffertitz, Charles Ogle, Paul Hurst, Fred Huntley, Edna Mae Cooper, Toto Ducrow, Ernest Joy
Director: Donald Crisp
Screenplay: Harvey F. Thew
Story: Dana Coolidge

THE HOUSE OF SILENCE
(Famous Players-Lasky/Paramount, April 1, 1918) 5 Reels
Ann Little, Adele Farrington, Winter Hall, Ernest Joy, Henry A. Barrows
Director: Donald Crisp
Screenplay: Margaret Turnbull
Story: Elwyn Barron

BELIEVE ME, XANTIPPE
(Famous Players-Lasky/Paramount, May 3, 1918) 5 Reels
Wallace Reid, *Ann Little*, Noah Beery, Donald Crisp, Theodore Roberts, Charles Ogle, James Farley, Ernest Joy, Henry Woodward, James Cruze, Winifred Greenwood, Clarence Geldart
Director: Donald Crisp
Screenplay: Olga Printzlau
Story: Frederick Ballard

THE FIREFLY OF FRANCE
(Famous Players-Lasky/Paramount, May 29, 1918) 5 Reels
Wallace Reid, *Ann Little*, Charles Ogle, Raymond Hatton, Winter Hall, Ernest Joy, William Elmer, Clarence Geldart, Henry Woodward, Jane Wolff
Director: Donald Crisp
Screenplay: Margaret Turnbull
Story: Marion Polk Angellotti

LESS THAN KIN
(Famous Players-Lasky/Paramount, July 13, 1918) 5 Reels
Ann Little, Wallace Reid, Noah Beery, Charles Ogle, Guy Oliver, Gustav B. Von Seyffertitz, Raymond Hatton, James Neill, Jane Wolff, James Cruze, Jack Herbert
Director: Cecil B. DeMille
Story: Alice Duer Miller

THE SOURCE
(Famous Players-Lasky/Paramount, August 6, 1918) 5 Reels
Wallace Reid, *Ann Little*, Noah Beery, Theodore Roberts, Raymond Hatton, Charles Ogle, James Cruze, Charles West, Nina Byron
Director: George H. Melford
Screenplay: Monte Katterjohn
Story: Clarence Budington Kelland

THE MAN FROM FUNERAL RANGE
(Famous Players-Lasky/Paramount, September 2, 1918) 5 Reels
Wallace Reid, *Ann Little*, Tully Marshall, Lottie Pickford, Willis Marks, George McDaniel, Phil Ainsworth
Director: Walter Edwards
Screenplay: Monte M. Katterjohn
Story: W. E. Wilker, "Broken Threads"

THE SQUAW MAN
(Paramount-Artcraft, December 15, 1918) 6 Reels
Elliott Dexter, Thurston Hall, Katherine MacDonald, Jack Holt, Noah Beery, *Ann Little*, Theodore Roberts, Pat Moore, Jim Mason, Tully Marshall, Herbert Standing, Edwin Stevens, Helen Dunbar, Winter Hall, Julia Faye, Pat Moore, Monte Blue, William Brunton, Charles Ogle, Guy Oliver, Jack Herbert, M. Hallward, Clarence Geldart
Director: Cecil B. DeMille
Screenplay: Beulah Marie Dix
Adaptation: From a play by Edwin Milton Royle

ALIAS MIKE MORAN
(Famous Players-Lasky/Paramount, February 1, 1919) 5 Reels
Wallace Reid, *Ann Little*, Emory Johnson, Charles Ogle, Edythe Chapman, William Elmer, Winter Hall, Jean Calhoun, Guy Oliver
Director: James Cruze
Screenplay: Will M. Richey
Story: Frederic Orrin Bartlett, "Open Sesame"

THE ROARING ROAD
(Famous Players-Lasky/Paramount, March 29, 1919) 5 Reels
Wallace Reid, *Ann Little*, Guy Oliver, Gustav B. Von Seyffertitz, Theodore Roberts, Clarence Geldart
Director: James Cruze
Screenplay: Marion Fairfax
Story: Byron Morgan

SOMETHING TO DO
(Famous Players-Lasky/Paramount, May, 1919) 5 Reels
Bryant Washburn, *Ann Little*, Robert Brower, Charles Geraco, Adele Farrington, Charles Ogle, James Mason
Director: Donald Crisp
Scenario: Will M. Ritchey
Story: Maximilian Foster

SQUARE DEAL SANDERSON
(William S. Hart/Paramount-Artcraft, June 15, 1919) 5 Reels
William S. Hart, *Ann Little*, Lloyd Bacon, Frank Whitson, Andrew Robson, Edwin Wallach
Director: William S. Hart, Lambert Hillyer
Screenplay: Lambert Hillyer
Story: Charles Alden Seltzer
Supvisor: Thomas H. Ince

TOLD IN THE HILLS
(Famous Players-Lasky/Paramount, August 15, 1919) 6 Reels
Robert Warwick, *Ann Little*, Tom Forman, Wanda Hawley, Charles Ogle, Monte Blue, Margaret Loomis, Eileen Percy, Hart (Jack) Hoxie, Jack Herbert, Guy Oliver
Director: George Melford
Screenplay: Will M. Ritchey
Story: Marah Ellis Ryan

LIGHTNING BRYCE
(National/Arrow, October 15, 1919) 15 Chapters.
Hart (Jack) Hoxie, *Ann Little*, Steve Clemente, Ben Corbett, Walter Patterson, George Champion, Slim Lucas, George Hunter, Paul C. Hurst
Director: Paul C. Hurst
Screenplay: Harvey Gates
Story: Joe Brandt
Chapters: (1) The Scarlet Moon (2) Wolf Nights (3) Perilous Trails (4) The Noose (5) The Dragon's Den (6) Robes of Destruction (7) Bared Fangs (8) The Yawning Abyss (9) The Voice of Conscience (10) Poison Waters (11) Walls of Flame (12) A Voice from the Dead (13) Battling Barriers (14) Smothering Tides (15) The End of the Trail

EXCUSE MY DUST
(Famous Players-Lasky/Paramount, March 1920) 5 Reels
Wallace Reid, Theodore Roberts, Tully Marshall, *Ann Little*, Guy Oliver, Otto Brower, James Gordon, Walter Long, Jack Herbert, Fred Huntley
Director: Sam Wood
Screenplay: Will M. Ritchey
Story: Byron Morgan, "The Bear Trap"

THE CRADLE OF COURAGE
(William S. Hart/Paramount-Artcraft, July 26, 1920) 5 Reels
William S. Hart, *Ann Little*, Gertrude Claire, Thomas Santschi, Francis Thorwald, George Williams
Director: Lambert Hillyer
Screenplay: Lambert Hillyer
Story: Frederick Bradbury

THE BLUE FOX
(Arrow, May 1921) 15 Chapters.
Ann Little, J. Morris Foster, Joseph W. Girard, Charles Mason, William La Rock, Hope Loring, Lon Seefield, Fred L. Wilson
Director: Duke Worne
Screenplay: Hope Loring
Chapters: (1) Message of Hate (2) Menace from the Sky (3) Mysterious Prisoner (4) A Perilous Ride (5) A Woman's Wit (6) A Night of Terror (7) Washed Ashore (8) A Perilous Leap (9) Lost Identity (10) In Close Pursuit (11) The Wilds of Alaska (12) The Camp of the Charkas (13) The Secret Skull (14) The Desert Island (15) Home and Happiness

NAN OF THE NORTH
(Arrow, March 1922) 15 Chapters.
Ann Little, Leonard Clapham (Tom London), Joseph W. Girard, Hal Wilson, Howard Crampton, J. Morris Foster, Edith Stayart
Director: Duke Worne
Story: Karl Coolidge
Chapters: (1) Missile from Mars (2) Fountain of Fury (3) Brink of Despair (4) In Cruel Clutches (5) On Terror's Trail (6) The Cards of Chance (7) Into the Depths (8) Burning Sands (9) Power of Titano (10) A Bolt from the Sky (11) The Ride for a Life (12) Adrift (13) Facing Death at Sea (14) The Volcano (15) Consequences

CHAIN LIGHTNING
(Ben Wilson/Arrow, April 25, 1922) 5 Reels
Norval MacGregor, Joseph W. Girard, William Carroll, Jack Dougherty, *Ann Little*
Director: Ben Wilson
Screenplay: J. Grubb Alexander, Agnes Parsons
Producer: Ben Wilson

HAIR TRIGGER CASEY
(Mustang Photoplay-American Mutual, May, 1922) 5 Reels
Frank Borzage, *Ann Little*, Chick Morrison, Jack Richardson
Director: Frank Borzage
(Retitled and reedited version of **Immediate Lee**, released in 1916)

THE EAGLE'S TALONS
(Universal, April 30, 1923) 15 Chapters.
Fred Thomson, *Ann Little*, Al Wilson, Herbert Fortier, Joseph Girard, Edith Stayart, Edward Cecil, Roy Tompkins, Joe Bonomo, Albert J. Smith, George Magrill, Jack Fowler
Director: Duke Worne
Screenplay: Anthony Coldeway, Jefferson Moffitt, Bertram Millhauser
Story: Theodore Wharton, Bertram Millhauser
Chapters: (1) House of Mystery (2) Edge of Eternity (3) Hulk of Horror (4) Daring Hearts (5) A Deal in Diplomacy (6) The Flood of Fury (7) The Road to Doom (8) Against Odds (9) A Fighting Chance (10) Into the Chasm (11) The Betrayal (12) The Sacrifice (13) Dodging the Conspirators (14) The Inferno (15) The Eagle Foiled

THE GREATEST MENACE
(J. G. Mayer/Mayer & Quinn, May 19, 1923) 7 Reels
Ann Little, Wilfred Lucas, Robert Gordon, Harry Northrup, Jack Livingston, Rhea Mitchell, Andy Maclennan, Mildred June, "Red" Kirby, Gordon Mullen, Lew Meehan
Director: Albert Rogell
Screenplay: Albert Rogell
Story: Angela C. Kaufman

SECRET SERVICE SAUNDERS
(Rayart, May 1, 1925) 15 Chapters.
Richard Holt, Ann Little, Helen Broneau, Clark Goffy, Frank Baker, Pierre Coudre, Ellis Houston
Director: Duke Worne
Scenario: Robert Dillon
Producer: Ashton Dearholt (a.k.a. Richard Holt)
Chapters: (1) The Plunge of Doom (2) The Brink of Eternity (3) Race of Death (4) The Path of Peril (5) Thunderinghoofs (6) River of Dread (7) Curse of Gold (8) Tunnel of Horror (9) Doomed (10) Heritage of Hate (11) The Brink of Despair (12) Blasted Hopes (13) Flames of Vengeance (14) Destruction Bound (15) The Final Reckoning

Louise Lorraine

13 • LOUISE LORRAINE

She Set a Pace That Successors Found Hard to Match

Louise Lorraine was one of the serial genre's greatest heroines. She played the female lead in 11 chapter plays--154 death-defying chapters. At the rate of one chapter a week, that represents three years of serial adventures in which she could be seen without any repetition.

Louise had a childlike beauty and was an accomplished actress who radiated exuberance. Her acting had spirit and honesty. Her small stature and lack of athletic background did not seem to fit her for a serial heroine, yet she carried out her roles far better than most women cast into the action arena. And surprisingly, she enjoyed making serials and Westerns.

Lorraine's first serial was **Elmo, the Fearless** (1920), a financial blockbuster for Universal in which she played Jane to Elmo Lincoln's Tarzan. Louise was only eighteen at the time. The two played The Apeman and Mate again in **The Adventures of Tarzan** (1921) for Weiss Brothers-Numa Corporation. It was Louise's only non-Universal cliffhanger. **With Stanley in Africa** (1922) kept her on the Dark Continent a while longer, this time as a young newspaper woman aiding George Walsh in his search for Doctor Livingstone.

In **The Flaming Disc** (1920), **The Radio King** (1922), and **The Diamond Master** (1929) she was battling gangsters and mad scientists who would turn the inventions of modern science to their own nefarious ends; Elmo Lincoln, Roy Stewart, and Hayden Stevenson supported respectively.

In **The Oregon Trail** (1923) she was a pioneer woman loved by trapper Art Acord, while in **The Lightning Express** (1930) she was the heroine in a more traditional Western with Lane Chandler as the hero. **A Final Reckoning** (1929) was set in Australia and had to do with Louise and Newton House, as brother and sister, finding a gold mine discovered by their father before his death. Jay Wilsey (Buffalo Bill, Jr.) lends a helping hand.

In **The Great Circus Mystery** (1925) Louise provided the love interest for strongman Joe Bonomo in an action- and animal-packed circus thriller. **The Silent Flyer** (1926) had her supporting a canine, Silver Streak, in a dog story with a Western setting produced by Nat Levine in association with California Studios. It was sold to and released by Universal. Levine would soon organize his own Mascot Pictures and produce several serials starring the more famous dogs Rin-Tin-Tin and Rin-Tin-Tin, Jr. **The Jade Box** (1930), like **The Lightning Express** (1930), was released in both silent and sound versions; Louise co-starred with Jack Perrin, with whom she had made fine Western featurettes in the early 1920s. Louise took pride in doing most of the routine dangerous sequences without a double.

Louise Lorraine was born in San Francisco on October 1, 1901. Her father was Spanish, her mother French. Her father died while Louise was still a teenager, leaving her mother with five children to care for. When Louise was about thirteen, a man taking orders for photographs called at her house in Encino, near Los Angeles, and Louise answered the door. He told her that she ought to be in pictures, and that he had a friend at the Ince Studio who would like to see her. The studio man showed up the next day and offered her a job. However, her mother would not consent, and it was some time before she did. Then Louise found work in Century comedies after first appearing in a bit role in a Clara Kimball Young feature. In these comedies she was billed as "Louise Fortune" and co-starred with Chai Hong, "The Chaplin of the Orient." Her competency as a comedienne earned her a Universal contract, followed by roles in action films.

The Great Circus Mystery (Universal, 1925) – Louise Lorraine and Joe Bonomo.

She appeared under her own name in features and featurettes in addition to serials, playing often with Jack Perrin, Hoot Gibson, and Art Acord, to whom she was married from 1925 to 1928. In 1922 she was selected as a Wampas Baby Star and in 1925 began to free-lance, though her most memorable films continued to be those made at Universal. Metro-Goldwyn-Mayer and First National both used her as leading lady in good non-Westerns, but today these features are little remembered, while "B" films remain vividly etched on aging memories. One of her last films was one of Bob Steele's earliest talkies, **Near the Rainbow's End** (1930), a real blood-and-thunder affair for Tiffany All-Talking Pictures. Louise's voice was quite satisfactory for sound films, but for other reasons she left the screen after making **Beyond the Law** (1930) with Lane Chandler. She had married for a second time in 1929 and wished to devote full time to making a home for her husband and two young babies. It was a happy marriage.

Widowed for many years, Louise lived in southern California and remained a vivacious, happy person until a lengthy illness befell her, resulting in her death in Sacramento on February 2, 1981. She had only pleasant memories of the movie career that made her a world-wide celebrity during the Roaring Twenties.

LOUISE LORRAINE Filmography

ELMO, THE FEARLESS
(Universal, February 9, 1920) 18 Chapters.
Elmo Lincoln, *Louise Lorraine*, William Chapman, Roy Watson, Frank Ellis, W. L. Barnes, Gordon McGregor, J. P. McGowan, Monte Montague
Director: J. P. McGowan
Story: Arthur Henry Goodson
Chapters: (1) Wreck of the Santiam (2) The Racing Death (3) The Life Line (4) The Flames of Death (5) The Smugglers Cave (6) The Battle Under the Sea (7) The House of Mystery (8) The Fatal Crossing (9) The Assassin's Knife (10) The Fatal Bullet (11) The Temple of the Dragon (12) Crashing Through (13) The Hand on the Latch (14) The Avalanche (15) The Burning Fuse (16) The House of Intrigue (17) The Trap (18) The Fateful Letter

THE FLAMING DISC
(Universal, November 21, 1920) 18 Chapters.
Elmo Lincoln, *Louise Lorraine*, Lee Kohlmar, Roy Watson, George Williams, Monte Montague, Jenks Harris, Fay Holderness, Fred Hamer, Bob Reeves, Lillian Lorraine
Director: Robert F. Hill
Story: Arthur Henry Goodson
Chapters: (1) Rails of Death (2) Span of Life (3) Perilous Leap (4) Fires of Hate (5) Vanishing Floor (6) Pool of Mystery (7) Circle of Fire (8) Through Walls of Steel (9) The Floating Mine (10) Spiked Death (11) The Dynamite Trail (12) The Tunnel of Flames (13) Caged In (14) The Purple Rays (15) Poisoned Waters (16) Running Wild (17) Rails of Destruction (18) End of the Trail

THE TRIGGER TRAIL
(Universal, February 7, 1921) 2 Reels
Jack Perrin, *Louise Lorraine*, Jim Corey, Starlight (a horse)
Director: Edward Laemmle
Screenplay: George W. Plympton
Story: James Edward Hungerford
Producer: Edward Laemmle

The Lightning Express (Universal, 1930) – Louise Lorraine.

THE MIDNIGHT RAIDERS
(Universal, March 16, 1921) 2 Reels
Jack Perrin, *Louise Lorraine*, Starlight (a horse)
Director: Edward Laemmle
Screenplay: Robert Dillon
Story: James Edward Hungerford

THE KNOCKOUT MAN
(Universal, March 25, 1921) 2 Reels
Jack Perrin, *Louise Lorraine*, Jim Corey, Starlight (a horse)
Director: Edward Laemmle
Screenplay: George H. Plympton
Story: Fred V. Williams
Producer: Edward Laemmle

THE OUTLAW
(Universal, April 27, 1921) 2 Reels
Jack Perrin, *Louise Lorraine*, Starlight (a horse)
Director: Edward Laemmle
Screenplay: George Morgan
Story: George Morgan

DOUBLE CROSSED
(Universal, April 1921) 2 Reels
Jack Perrin, *Louise Lorraine*
Director: Edward Laemmle

THE VALLEY OF THE ROGUES
(Universal, July 21, 1921)
Jack Perrin, *Louise Lorraine*, Starlight (a horse)
Director: Edward Laemmle
Screenplay: George Morgan
Story: George Morgan
Producer: Edward Laemmle

THE ADVENTURES OF TARZAN
(Weiss Brothers-Numa, December 1, 1921) 15 Chapters.
Elmo Lincoln, *Louise Lorraine*, Percy Pembroke, Frank Whitson, James Inslee, Lillian Worth, George Momberg, Frank Merrill, Joe Martin (orangutan), Charles Gay, Macer Bruce Sheffield, Fifi R. Lachoy, Byrd Wheeler
Director: Robert F. Hill
Adaptation: Lillian Valentine, Robert F. Hill
Screenplay: Lillian Valentine, Robert F. Hill
Chapters: (1) Jungle Romance (2) City of Gold (3) Sun Death (4) Stalking Death (5) Flames of Hate (6) The Ivory Tomb (7) The Jungle Trap (8) The Tornado (9) Fangs of the Lion (10) The Simoon (11) The Hidden Arrows (12) Dynamite Trail (13) The Jungle's Prey (14) Flaming Arrows (15) The Last Adventure

THE FIRE EATER
(Universal, December 24, 1921) 5 Reels
Hoot Gibson, *Louise Lorraine*, Walter Perry, Thomas G. Lingham, Fred Lancaster, Carmen Phillips, George Berrell, W. Bradley Ward, George A. Williams
Director: B. Reeves Eason
Screenplay: Harvey Gates
Story: Ralph Cummins, "The Badge of Fighting Hearts"

WITH STANLEY IN AFRICA
(Universal, January 23, 1922) 18 Chapters.
George Walsh, *Louise Lorraine*, Charles Mason, William Welsh, Gordon Sackville, Jack Mower, Fred Kohler
Directors: William Craft, Ed Kull
Screenplay: George H. Plympton
Story: George H. Plympton
Chapters: (1) Jaws of the Jungle (2) The Trip of the Slavers (3) Paths of Peril (4) Find Livingstone (5) The Flaming Spear (6) Lost in the Jungle (7) Trail of the Serpent (8) Pool of Death (9) Menace of the Jungle (10) The Ordeal (11) The Lion's Prey (12) The Forest of Flame (13) Buried Alive (14) The Lair of Death (15) The Good Samaritan (16) The Slave's Secret (17) The White Tribe (18) Out of the Dark

HEADIN' WEST
(Universal, February 13, 1922) 5 Reels
Hoot Gibson, Gertrude Short, Charles Le Moyne, Jim Corey, Leo White, *Louise Lorraine*, George A. Williams, Frank Whitson, Mark Fenton
Director: William J. Craft
Screenplay: Harvey Gates
Story: Harvey Gates

UP IN THE AIR ABOUT MARY
(William Watson/Associated Exhibitors, June 25, 1922) 5 Reels
Louise Lorraine, Joe Moore, Laura La Varnie, Robert Anderson
Producer: William Watson

THE RADIO KING
(Universal, October 30, 1922) 10 Chapters.
Roy Stewart, *Louise Lorraine*, Al Smith, Sidney Bracey, Clark Comstock, Ernest Butterworth, Jr., Fontaine LaRue, Slim Whitaker, Lew Meehan, Joseph North, Marion Faducha, Helen Brannean, D.J. Mitsoras, Laddie Earle, Charles Force
Director: Robert F. Hill
Screenplay: Robert Dillon
Story: Robert Dillon
Chapters: (1) A Cry for Help (2) The Secret of the Air (3) A Battle of Wits (4) Warned by Radio (5) Ship of Doom (6) S.O.S. (7) Saved by Wireless (8) The Master Wave (9) The Trail of Vengeance (10) Saved by Science

TRUE BLUE
(Century/Universal, November 2, 1922) 2 Reels
Louise Lorraine
Director: Al Herman
Story: Al Herman

THE ALTAR STAIRS
(Universal, December 4, 1922) 5 Reels
Frank Mayo, *Louise Lorraine*, Lawrence Hughes, J. J. Lance, Harry de Vere, Hugh Thompson, Boris Karloff, Dagmar Godowsky, Nick De Ruiz
Director: Lambert Hillyer
Screenplay: George Hively, Doris Schroeder, George Randolph Chester
Story: G. B. Lancaster, "The Altar Stairs"

THE GENTLEMAN FROM AMERICA
(Universal, February 19, 1923) 5 Reels
Hoot Gibson, Tom O'Brien, *Louise Lorraine*, Carmen Phillips, Frank Leigh, Jack Crane, Bob McKenzie, Albert Prisoc, Rosa Rosanova
Director: Edward Sedgwick
Screenplay: George Hull
Story: Raymond L. Schrock

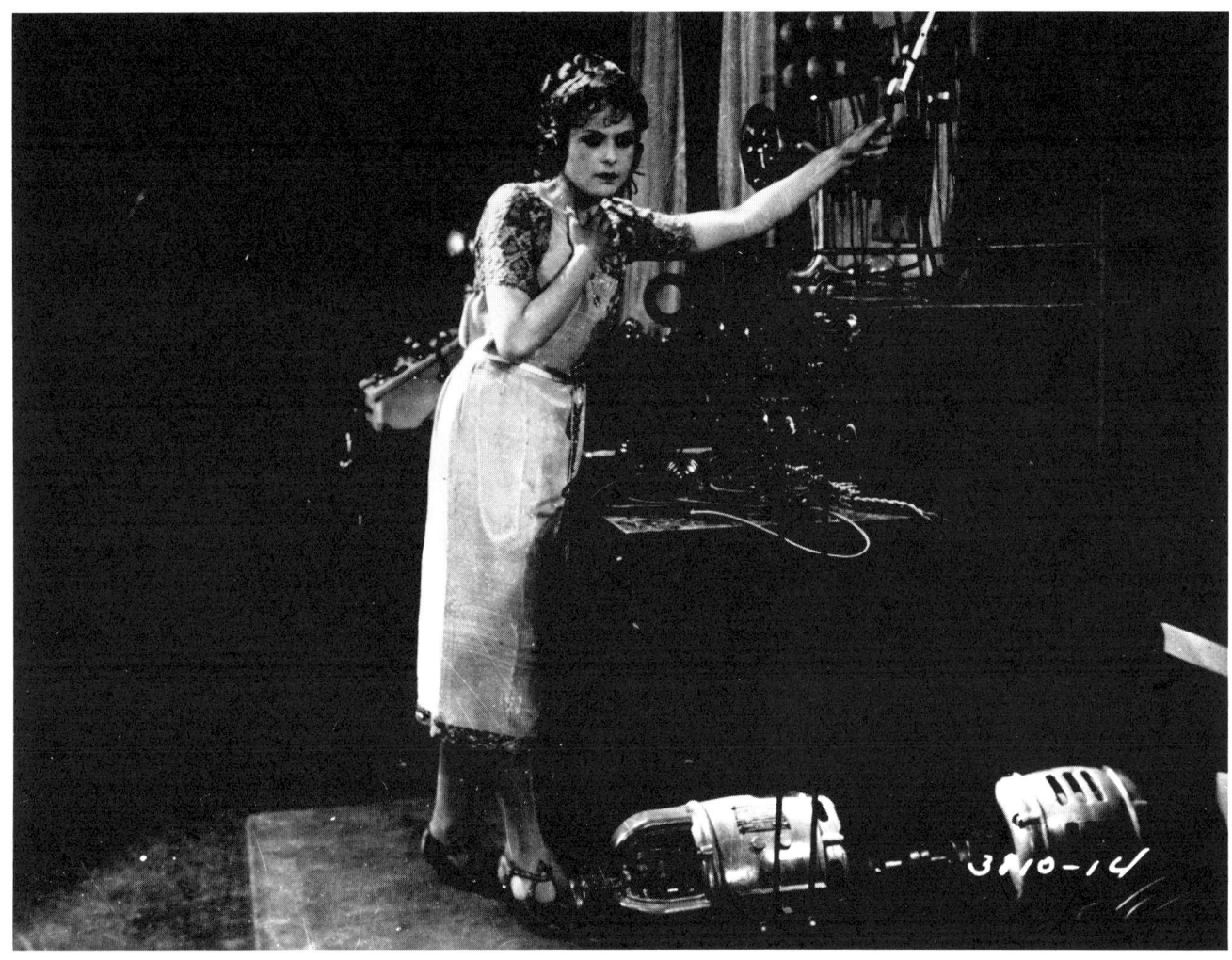

The Radio King (Universal, 1922) – Louise Lorraine.

THE OREGON TRAIL
(Universal, March 12, 1923) 18 Chapters.
Art Acord, *Louise Lorraine*, Duke R. Lee, Jim Corey, Burton C. Law, Walter Bytell, Sidney DeGray, Ruth Royce, Grace E. McLean, Dick Carter, Sidney De Grey, W. H. Rhyno, Frederic Peters
Director: Edward Laemmle
Screenplay: Anthony Coldeway, Douglas Bronston, Jefferson Moffitt
Story: Robert Dillon
Chapters: (1) Westward Ho! (2) White Treachery (3) Across the Continent (4) Message of Death (5) Wagon of Doom (6) Secret Foes (7) A Man of God (8) Seeds of Civilization (9) Justice (10) The New Era (11) A Game of Nations (12) To Save an Empire (13) Trail of Death (14) On to Washington (15) Santa Fe (16) Fate of a Nation (17) For High Stakes (18) Victory

McGUIRE OF THE MOUNTED
(Universal, July 9, 1923) 5 Reels
William Desmond, *Louise Lorraine*, Willard Louis, Vera James, J. P. Lockney, William A. Lowery, Peggy Browne, Frank Johnson, Jack Walters
Director: Richard Stanton
Screenplay: George Hively
Story: Raymond L. Schrock, George Hively

The Jade Box (Universal, 1930) – Jack Perrin is about to get clobbered as Louise Lorraine watches the fallen hoodlum.

THE GREAT CIRCUS MYSTERY
(Universal, March 9, 1925) 15 Chapters.
Joe Bonomo, *Louise Lorraine*, Robert J. Graves, Robert Seiter, Carmen Phillips, Slim Cole, Sam Polo, Albert Prisco, Monte Montague, Jackie Goodrich, Floyd Criswell, Eduardo Martini, Carlo Bernardi, Cecil Woodworth, Tui Loraine, Carlotta, Charles Magetti, Tony Brock, The Sieberling Four, Morgan Brown, Buck Russ
Director: Jay Marchant
Screenplay: George Morgan
Story: Isadore Bernstein, William Lord Wright
Chapters: (1) Pact of Peril (2) A Cry for Help (3) A Race with Death (4) The Plunge of Peril (5) The Ladder of Life (6) A Leap for Liberty (7) Harvest of Hate (8) Fires of Fate (9) Cycle of Fear (10) The Leopard Strikes (11) The Sacred Ruby (12) Dive of Destiny (13) The Leap for Liberty (14) Buried Treasure (15) The Leopard Strikes

THE VERDICT
(Phil Goldstone/Truart, April 16, 1925) 7 Reels
Lou Tellegen, *Louise Lorraine*, William Collier, Jr., Gertrude Astor, Joseph Swickard, Paul Weigel, Taylor Holmes, Stanton Heck, Elliott Dexter, George Fawcett, Gaston Glass, Walter Long
Director: Fred Windemere
Screenplay: John F. Natteford

THE WILD GIRL
(Truart Film Corp., October 10, 1925) 5 Reels
Louise Lorraine, Art Acord, Andrew Waldron, Rex (a horse), Black Beauty (a horse)
Director: William Bletcher

THREE IN EXILE
(Truart, October 30, 1925) 5 Reels
Louise Lorraine, Art Acord, Tom London, Rex (a horse). Black Beauty (a horse)
Director: Fred Windemere
Story: George Hively

BORROWED FINERY
(Tiffany, November 1925) 7 Reels
Louise Lorraine, Ward Crane, Lou Tellegen, Taylor Holmes, Hedda Hooper, Gertrude Astor, Trixie Friganza Tennant, Otto Lederer
Director: Oscar Apfel
Story: George Bronson Howard

PALS
(Truart, November 1925) 5 Reels
Louise Lorraine, Art Acord, Rex (a horse), Black Beauty (a horse), Leo Kent, Andrew Waldron
Director: John P. McCarthy
Story: George Hively

THE BLUE STREAK
(Richard Talmadge/FBO, January 31, 1926) 5 Reels
Richard Talmadge, Charles Clary, *Louise Lorraine*, Henry Herbert, Charles Hill Mailes, Victor Dillingham, Tote Du Crow
Director: Noel Mason
Screenplay: James Bell Smith
Story: James Bell Smith

THE SILENT GUARDIAN
(Truart, February 4, 1926) 5 Reels
Louise Lorraine, Harry Tenbrook, L. J. O'Connor, Art Acord, Grace Woods, Rex (a horse), Black Beauty (a horse)
Director: William Bletcher
Story: Ewart Adamson

BEHIND THE FRONT
(Famous Players-Lasky/Paramount, February 22, 1926) 6 Reels
Wallace Beery, Raymond Hatton, Mary Brian, Richard Arlen, Hayden Stevenson, Chester Conklin, Tom Kennedy, Frances Raymond, Melbourne MacDowell, *Louise Lorraine*
Director: Edward Sutherland
Screenplay: Ethel Doherty
Adaptation: Monte Brice
Story: Hugh Wiley, "The Spoils of War" in Saturday Evening Post

EXIT SMILING
(M-G-M, November 6, 1926) 7 Reels
Beatrice Lillie, Jack Pickford, Doris Lloyd, De Witt Jennings, Harry Myers, Tenen Holtz, *Louise Lorraine*, Franklin Pangborn, D'Arcy Corrigan, William Gillespie, Carl Richards
Director: Sam Taylor
Screenplay: Sam Taylor, Tim Whelan
Story: Marc Connelly

THE SILENT FLYER
(Universal, November 8, 1926) 10 Chapters.
Silver Streak (a dog), Malcolm MacGregor, *Louise Lorraine*, Thur Fairfax, Hughie Mack, Anders Randolph, Edith Yorke, Arthur Morrison, Robert Walker
Director: William Craft
Story: George Morgan
Chapters: (1) The Jaws of Death (2) Dynamited (3) Waters of Death (4) The Treacherous Trail (5) Plunge of Peril (6) Fight of Honor (7) Under Arrest (8) Flames of Terror (9) Hurled Through Space (10) Love and Glory

THE STOLEN RANCH
(Universal, December 26, 1926) 5 Reels
Fred Humes, *Louise Lorraine*, William Norton Bailey, Ralph McCullough, Nita Cavalier, Edward Cecil, Howard Truesdell, Slim Whittaker, Jack Kirk
Director: William Wyler
Screenplay: George H. Plympton
Story: Robert F. Hill

WINNERS OF THE WILDERNESS
(M-G-M, January 15, 1927) 7 Reels
(Technicolor Sequences)
Tim McCoy, Joan Crawford, Roy D'Arcy, *Louise Lorraine*, Lionel Belmore, Edward Hearn, Frank Currier, Tom O'Brien, Edward Connelly, Will R. Walling, Chief Big Tree, Jean Arthur
Director: W. S. Van Dyke
Screenplay: Josephine Chippo
Story: John Thomas Neville

HARD FISTS
(Universal, April 24, 1927) 5 Reels
Art Acord, *Louise Lorraine*, Lee Holmes, Albert J. Smith
Director: William Wyler
Adaptation: William Lester, George H. Plympton
Screenplay: William Lester, George H. Plympton
Story: Charles A. Logue, "The Grappler"

ROOKIES
(M-G-M, April 30, 1927) 7 Reels
Kari Dane, George K. Arthur, Marceline Day, *Louise Lorraine*, Frank Currier, E. H. Calvert, Tom O'Brien, Charles Sullivan, Lincoln Stedman, Gene Stone
Director: Sam Wood
Screenplay: Byron Morgan
Story: Byron Morgan

THE FRONTIERSMAN
(M-G-M, June 11, 1927) 5 Reels
Tim McCoy, Claire Windsor, Tom O'Brien, Russell Simpson, Lillian Leighton, *Louise Lorraine*, May Foster, Chief Big Tree, Frank Hagney, John Peters
Director: Reginald Barker
Screenplay: L. G. Rigby
Story: Ross B. Wills, Madeleine Ruthven

LEGIONNAIRES IN PAIRS
(FBO, February 26, 1927) 6 Reels
Al Cooke, Kit Guard, *Louise Lorraine*, Virginia Sale, John Aasen
Director: Arvid E. Gillstrom
Screenplay: Jefferson Moffitt
Story: Louis Sarecky

BABY MINE
(M-G-M, January 7, 1928) 6 Reels
Karl Dane, George K. Arthur, Charlotte Greenwood, *Louise Lorraine*
Director: Robert Z. Leonard
Screenplay: F. Hugh Harbert, Lew Lipton
Adaptation: Sylvia Thalberg
Story: Margaret May, "Baby Mine: A Domestic Farce in Three Acts"

CIRCUS ROOKIES
(M-G-M, March 31, 1928) 6 Reels
Karl Dane, George K. Arthur, *Louise Lorraine*, Sidney Jarvic, Fred Humes
Director: Edward Sedgwick
Screenplay: Richard Schayer
Story: Edward Sedgwick, Lew Lipton

CHINATOWN CHARLIE
(First National, April 15, 1928) 7 Reels
Johnny Hines, *Louise Lorraine*, Harry Gribbon, Fred Kohler, Sojin, Scooter Lowry, Anna May Wong, George Kuwa, John Burdette
Director: Charles Hines
Screenplay: Roland Asher, John Grey
Story: Owen Davis
Producer: C. C. Burr

THE WRIGHT IDEA
(C.C. Burr/First National, August 5, 1928) 7 Reels
Johnny Hines, *Louise Lorraine*, Edmund Breese, Walter James, Fred Kelsey, Henry Barrows, Henry Hebert, Charles Giblyn, Jack McHugh, J. Barney Sherry, Charles Gerrard, Betty Egan, Blanche Craig, Richard Maitland, George Irving
Director: Charles Hines
Screenplay: Jack Townley
Story: Jack Townley

SHADOWS OF THE NIGHT
(M-G-M, October 26, 1928) 7 Reels
Lawrence Gray, *Louise Lorraine*, Warner Richmond, Tom Dugan, Alphonse Ethier, Polly Moran, Flash
Director: D. Ross Lederman
Story: Ted Shane

THE DIAMOND MASTER
(Universal, February 3, 1929) 10 Chapters.
Hayden Stevenson, *Louise Lorraine*, Al Hart, Monte Montague, Louis Stern, Walter Maly
Director: Jack Nelson
Story: Jacques Futrelle, "The Diamond Master"
Chapters: (1) The Secret of the Night (2) The Diamond of Death (3) The Tunnel of Terror (4) Trapped (5) The Diamond Machine (6) The Wolf Pack (7) The Death Trap (8) Into the Flames (9) The Last Stand (10) The Reckoning

A FINAL RECKONING
(Universal, April 15, 1929) 12 Chapters.
Newton House, *Louise Lorraine*, Jay Wilsey (Buffalo Bill, Jr.), Edmund Cobb, Frank Clark
Director: Ray Taylor
Screenplay: Basil Dickey, George Morgan
Story: G. A. Henry
Chapters: (1) A Treacherous Friend (2) The Man Trap (3) Trapped (4) Face to Face (5) Ambushed (6) Unmasked (7) In Wolf's Clothing (8) An Attack in the Dark (9) A Ride for Life (10) The Blast of Death (11) The Living Bead (12) The Reward

THE MOUNTED STRANGER
(Universal, February 8, 1930) 6 Reels
Hoot Gibson, Buddy Hunter, Milton Brown, Fred Burns, James Corey, Francis Ford, Walter Patterson, Francelia Billington, *Louise Lorraine*
Director: Arthur Rosson
Screenplay: Arthur Rosson
Story: Henry Herbert Knibbs, "Ridin' Kid from Powder River"

THE JADE BOX
(Universal, March 24, 1930) 10 Chapters.
Jack Perrin, *Louise Lorraine*, Monroe Salisbury, Francis Ford, Wilbur S. Mack, Leo White, Jay Novello
Director: Ray Taylor
Story: Fred Jackson
Chapters: (1) The Jade of Jeopardy! (2) Buried Alive! (3) The Shadow Man (4) The Fatal Prophecy (5) The Unseen Death (6) The Haunting Shadow (7) The Guilty Man (8) The Grip of Death (9) Out of the Shadows (10) The Atonement

THE LIGHTNING EXPRESS
(Universal, June 2, 1930) 10 Chapters.
(Released in both silent and sound versions)
Lane Chandler, *Louise Lorraine*, Al Ferguson, Greta Granstedt, J. Gordon Russell, John Oscar, Martin Clichy, Jim Pierce, Floyd Criswell, Robert Kelly, Bob Reeves
Director: Henry McRae
Story: Frank H. Spearman, "Whispering Smith Rides"
Chapters: (1) A Shot in the Dark (2) A Scream of Terror (3) Dangerous Rails (4) The Death Trap (5) Tower of Terror (6) A Call for Help (7) The Runaway Freight (8) The Show Down (9) The Secret Survey (10) Cleared Tracks

NEAR THE RAINBOW'S END
(Tiffany, June 10, 1930) 51 Mins.
Bob Steele, *Louise Lorraine*, Lafe McKee, Al Ferguson, Alfred Hewston
Director: J. P. McGowan
Screenplay: Sally Winters
Story: Sally Winters
Producer: Trem Carr

BEYOND THE LAW
(Syndicate, November 2, 1930) 5 Reels
Robert Frazer, Lane Chandler, *Louise Lorraine*, Charles King, William Walling, Robert Greaves, Jr., Ed Lynch, Jimmy Kane, George Hackathorne, Franklyn Farnum, Harry Holden, Bob Reeves, Blackie Whiteford, Tex Phelps
Director: J. P. McGowan
Screenplay: G. A. Durlan
Story: G. A. Durlan
Producer: G. A. Durlan

MOONLIGHT AND CACTUS
(Educational, January 10, 1932) 2 Reels
Tom Patricola, Charles Judels, Charles Dorety, *Louise Lorraine*, Renée Borden
Director: William Goodrich
Story: Ernest Pagano, Jack Townley

Noel Neill

14 • NOEL NEILL

A Real Journalist Who Became a Reel Journalist

In the mid-fifties Noel Neill played Lois Lane, star reporter of the Metropolis Daily Planet, in TV's "Superman" series opposite George Reeves in his double role as Clark Kent and Superman. Noel turned out seventy-eight episodes of the popular series, after replacing Phyllis Coates, another serial and Western heroine, who had filmed the first twenty-six episodes before making another commitment which precluded her continuing in the role.

In recent years Noel has been a lecturer on college campuses, proving to be a popular speaker with those who grew up on reruns of "Superman" but who remember nothing of Noel Neill as a movie actress and serial heroine. It might surprise them to know that prior to George Reeves there was another popular Superman, just as Clayton Moore was not the original, or even the second, Lone Ranger.

Noel wanted to be a journalist from the time she was old enough to hold a pencil. She got her newspaper training from her father, David Neill, news editor of the Minneapolis Star-Tribune, and earned her first money by writing articles for Women's Wear Daily. Her newspaper career was short-lived, however.

One summer she was spotted by Bing Crosby at NBC, and he signed her to sing at his Del Mar Turf Club, in Del Mar, California. After the season there the call from Hollywood was inevitable. Noel was signed to a long-term contract by Paramount Studios and made her professional screen debut in the movie **Henry Aldrich for President** (1941) with Jimmy Lydon and Charles Smith. Other Paramount releases included **The Remarkable Andrew** (1942), **Let's Face It** (1943), **Here Come the Waves** (1944), **Rainbow Island** (1944), **The Stork Club** (1945), **Duffy's Tavern** (1945), and **The Greatest Show on Earth** (1952). In these pictures she worked with such stars as Bing Crosby, William Holden, Ray Milland, Bob Hope, Eddie Bracken, and Betty Hutton. While under contract to Paramount, she was loaned out to do the High School Hero series with Freddie Stewart, June Preisser, and Frankie Darro at Monogram.

She also hosted live television shows from an experimental station on the Paramount lot in the late 1940s, singing, emceeing, and performing in various acts for the limited Hollywood audience that had TV receivers at that time (probably not more than a few hundred).

Noel's introduction to serials came in **Brick Bradford** (1947), a Sam Katzman production for Columbia starring Kane Richmond. Linda Johnson had the female lead; Noel merely flitted in and out of scenes as a minor supporting player. However, Republic picked her up for the female lead in **Adventures of Frank and Jesse James** (1948), which starred Clayton Moore, soon to become the "Heigh-Ho, Silver" crusader, as the infamous Jesse. Sam Katzman then latched on to her again for the part of Lois Lane in the serial **Superman** (1948), the first motion picture about the comic book hero. Kirk Alyn played Superman and, along with Noel, proved to be an excellent choice.

In 1950 Republic used her again in another serial about the family of outlaw fame, **The James Brothers of Missouri**. This serial had an entirely different story line and starred Keith Richards and Robert Bice as Jesse and Frank. Noel was the heroine who needed a little help in running her stage line. However, **Atom Man vs. Superman** (1950), for Katzman and Columbia, carried on the adventures of Superman and Lois Lane, as portrayed by Kirk Alyn and Noel Neill, with Tommy Bond and Pierre Watkin again cast as Jimmy Olson and Perry White.

137

The Adventures of Frank and Jesse James (Republic, 1948) – Noel Neill and Clayton Moore.

Spencer Bennet was at the directorial helm, as he was in Superman. The serial proved profitable and highly popular with the juvenile audience, as had the first.

Twentieth Century-Fox cashed in on the popularity of the TV series by releasing five features to theatres in 1954, each made up of three edited episodes of the TV series starring Reeves and Neill. After completion of the series in 1957 Noel retired from the screen, but she reappeared in the 1970s and has recently reactivated her career. She did a cameo, along with original star Kirk Alyn, in the Warner Bros. multimillion dollar production, **Superman** (1978).

NOEL NEILL Filmography

HENRY ALDRICH FOR PRESIDENT
(Paramount, October 24, 1941) 75 Mins.
James Lydon, Charles Smith, June Preisser, Mary Anderson, Martha O'Driscoll, Dorothy Peterson, John Litel, Rod Cameron, Frank Coghlan, Jr., Lucien Littlefield, Kenneth Howell, Buddy Pepper, Vaughn Glaser, Dick Paxton, Paul Matthews, Bob Pittard, Bud (Lon) McCallister, Carmen Johnson, Helen Westcott, Rosita Butler, Georgia Lee Settle, *Noel Neill*
Director: Hugh Bennett
Screenplay: Val Burton
Producer: Sol C. Siegel

THE REMARKABLE ANDREW
(Paramount, January 19, 1942) 80 Mins.
Brian Donlevy, William Holden, Ellen Drew, Montagu Love, Porter Hall, Gilbert Emery, Brandon Hurst, George Watts, Rod Cameron, Jimmy Conlin, Richard Webb, Spencer Charters, Minor Watson, Clyde Fillmore, Thomas W. Ross, Wallis Clark, Milt Parsons, Helena Phillips Evans, Tom Fadden, Harlan Briggs, Nydia Westman, Frances Gifford, Martha O'Driscoll, *Noel Neill*
Director: Stuart Heisler
Screenplay: Dalton Trumbo
Story: Dalton Trumbo
Associate Producer: Richard Blumenthal

HENRY AND DIZZY
(Paramount, March 21, 1942) 71 Mins.
Jimmy Lydon, Mary Anderson, Charles Smith, John Litel, Olive Blakeney, Maude Eburne, Vaughn Glaser, Shirley Coates, Olin Howland, Minerva Urecal, Trevor Bardette, Carl "Alfalfa" Switzer, Warren Hymer, *Noel Neill*, Jane Cowan
Director: Hugh Bennett
Screenplay: Val Burton
Producer: Sol. C. Siegel

MISS ANNIE ROONEY
(United Artists, May 30, 1942) 84 Mins.
Shirley Temple, William Gargan, Guy Kibbee, Dickie Moore, Peggy Ryan, Roland DuPree, Gloria Holden, Jonathan Hale, Mary Field, George Lloyd, Jan Buckingham, Selmer Jackson, June Lockhart, Charles Coleman, Edgar Dearing, Virginia Sale, Shirley Mills, *Noel Neill*, Byron Foulger, Wilson Benge
Director: Edwin L. Marin
Screenplay: George Bruce
Producer: Edward Small

SALUTE FOR THREE
(Paramount, March 17, 1943) 71 Mins.
Betty Rhodes, Macdonald Carey, Marty May, Cliff Edwards, Minna Gombell, Dona Drake, *Noel Neill*, Charles Smith, Charles Williams, Walter Sande, Tony Hughes, Lorraine and Rognan, Doodles Weaver, Harry Barris, Jack Gardner, Linda Brent, Patti Brilhandte, DeDe Barrington, Frank Moran, Frederic Henry, Frank Wayne, Emmett Vogan, Eddie Dew, Edna Bennett, Franklin Parker, Blanch Payson, Isabel Withers, Frank Faylen, Eddie Coke, Billy Wayne, George Sherwood, Lynda Grey, Louise La Planche, Maxine Ardell, Christopher King, Marcella Phillips, Marjorie Deanne, Yvonne De Carlo, Alice Kirby, Tom Siedel, Ralph Montgomery
Director: Ralph Murphy
Screenplay: Doris Anderson, Curtis Kenyon, Hugh Wedlock, Jr.
Story: Art Arthur
Producer: Walter MacEwen

LET'S FACE IT
(Paramount, August 7, 1943) 76 Mins.
Bob Hope, Betty Hutton, Zasu Pitts, Phyllis Povah, Dave Willock, Eve Arden, Cully Richards, Marjorie Weaver, Dona Drake, Raymond Walburn, Andrew Tombes, Arthur Loft, Joe Sawyer, Grace Hayle, Evelyn Dockson, Andria Moreland, Kay Linaker, Frederick Nay, Joyce Compton, Florence Shirley, Barbara Pepper, Robin Raymond, Phyllis Ruth, Lionel Royce, Emory Parnell, Brooke Evans, Don Kerr, Eddie Dew, Eddie Dunn, Elinor Troy, Eleanor Prentiss, Cyril Ring, William B. Davidson, Yvonne De Carlo, *Noel Neill*, Julie Gibson, Jayne Hazard
Director: Sidney Lanfield
Screenplay: Harry Turgend
Story: Based on the musical by Dorothy and Herbert Fields and Cole Porter, and the play "Cradle Snatchers" by Norma Mitchells and Russell G. Medcraft
Producer: Fred Kohlmar

STANDING ROOM ONLY
(Paramount, January 8, 1944) 83 Mins.
Paulette Goddard, Fred MacMurray, Edward Arnold, Roland Young, Hillary Brooke, Porter Hall, Clarence Kolb, Anne Revere, Isabel Randolph, Veda Ann Borg, Marie McDonald, Josephine Whittel, Sig Arno, Boyd Davis, Roy Gordon, Herbert Hayes, Eddie Dunn, Arthur Loft, Yvonne De Carlo, *Noel Neill*, Gayne Whitman, Frank Faylen, Ethel May Halls, Georgia Backus, Grayce Hampton, Rita Gould, Forbes Murray, Edwin Stanley
Director: Sidney Lanfield
Screenplay: Darrel Ware, Karl Tunberg
Story: Al Martin
Associate Producer: Paul Jones

HENRY ALDRICH'S LITTLE SECRET
(Paramount, June 10, 1944) 75 Mins.
Jimmy Lydon, Charles Smith, Joan Mortimer, John Litel, Olive Blackeney, Ann Doran, John David Robb, Tina Thayer, Sarah Edwards, Harry Bradley, Lucille Ward, Almira Sessions, Tom Fadden, George Charleton, Byron Foulger, Fern Emmett, Dorothy Vaughn, Eddie Dunn, Hal K. Dawson, *Noel Neill*
Director: Hugh Bennett
Screenplay: Aileen Leslie
Story: Aileen Leslie
Associate Producer: Michel Kraike

ARE THESE OUR PARENTS?
(Monogram, July 15, 1944) 73 Mins.
Helen Vinson, Lyle Talbot, *Noel Neill*, Richard Byron, Emma Dunn, Addison Richards, Anthony Warde, Robin Raymond, Ian Wolfe, Jean Carlin, Claire McDowell, Emmett Vogan, Edgar Norton, Jimmy Strano
Director: William Nigh
Screenplay: Michael Jacoby
Story: Hillary Lynn
Producer: Jeffrey Bernard

OUR HEARTS WERE YOUNG AND GAY
(Paramount, September 2, 1944) 81 Mins.
Gail Russell, Diana Lynn, Charlie Ruggles, Dorothy Gish, Beulah Bondi, James Brown, Bill Edwards, Jean Heather, Alma Druger, Helen Freeman, Joy Harington, Valentine Perkins, Georges Renavent, Roland Varno, Holmes Herbert, Reginald Sheffield, Edmond Breon, Nina Koshetz, *Noel Neill*, Maxine Fife, Will Staton, Olaf Hytten, Carmelle Bergstrom, Roland Dupree, Nell Craig, Maurice Marsac, Ronnie Rondell, Alphonse Martell, Eugene Bordon, Marie McDonald, Queenie Leonard
Director: Lewis Allen
Screenplay: Sheridan Gibney
Story: Cornelia Otis Skinner, Emily Kimbrough
Associate Producer: Sheridan Gibney

HERE COME THE WAVES
(Paramount, December 23, 1944) 99 Mins.
Bing Crosby, Betty Hutton, Sonny Tufts, Ann Doran, Gwen Crawford, *Noel Neill*, Catherine Craig, Marjorie Henshaw, Harry Barris, Mae Clark, Minor Watson, Louise LaPlanche, Mona Freeman, Carlotta Jelm, Jack Norton, James Flavin, Jimmie Dundee, Babe London, Oscar O'Shea, Cyril Ring, Frances Morris, Yvonne De Carlo
Director: Mark Sandrick
Screenplay: Allen Scott, Ken Englund, Zion Myers
Producer: Mark Sandrick

RAINBOW ISLAND
(Paramount, 1944) 98 Mins.
Dorothy Lamour, Eddie Bracken, Gil Lamb, Barry Sullivan, Forrest Orr, Anne Revere, Reed Hadley, Marc Lawrence, Olga San Juan, Elena Verdugo, Iris Lancaster, Audrey Young, Louise La Planche, Rodd Redwing, Alex Montoya, Dan Seymour, Stanley Price, Yvonne DeCarlo, *Noel Neill*, Luis Alberni, Eddie Acuff, Frank Wilcox, Paul McVey
Director: Ralph Murphy
Screenplay: Walter DeLong, Arthur Phillips
Story: Seena Owen
Associate Producer: E. D. Leshin

BRING ON THE GIRLS
(Paramount, March 30, 1945) 92 Mins.
Veronica Lake, Sonny Tufts, Eddie Bracken, Marjorie Reynolds, Grant Mitchell, Johnny Coy, Peter Whitney, Alan Mowbray, Porter Hall, Thurston Hall, Lloyd Corrigan, Andrew Tombes, Frank Faylen, Huntz Hall, Norma Varden, Dorothea Kent, Jimmie Dundee, Walter Baldwin, Veda Ann Borg, *Noel Neill*, Jimmy Conlin, George Turner, Louise LaPlanche, Yvonne De Carlo, Kay Linaker, Frank Hagney, Harry Hays Morgan, Joan Woodbury, Golden Gate Quartette, Spike Jones and His City Slickers
Director: Sidney Lanfield
Screenplay: Karl Tunberg, Darrell Ware
Story: Perre Wolff
Associate Producer: Fred Kohlmar

DUFFY'S TAVERN
(Paramount, September 28, 1945) 97 Mins.
Ed Gardner, Margorie Reynolds, Barry Sullivan, Victor Moore, Charles Cantor, Eddie Green, Ann Thomas, Howard Da Silva, Billy De Wolfe, Walter Abel, Charles Quigley, Olga San Juna, Robert Watson, Frank Faylen, Matt McHugh, Emmett Vogan, Cyril Ring, *Noel Neill*, and Guest Stars: Bing Crosby, Betty Hutton, Paulette Goddard, Alan Ladd, Dorothy Lamour, Eddie Bracken, Brian Donlevy, Sonny Tufts, Veronica Lake, Arturo De Cordova, Cass Daley, Diana Lynn, Gary Crosby, Philip Crosby, Lin Crosby, Dennis Crosby, William Bendix, Maurice Rocco, James Brown, Joan Caulfield, Gail Russell, Helen Walker, Hean Heather, Barry Fitzgerald
Director: Hal Walker
Screenplay: Melvin Panama
Story: Adapted from the radio program by Ed Gardner
Associate Producer: Danny Dare

THE STORK CLUB
(Paramount, December 28, 1945) 98 Mins.
Betty Hutton, Barry Fitzgerald, Don DeFore, Robert Benchley, Bill Goodwin, Iris Adrian, Mikhail Rasumny, Mary Young, Andy Russell, Perc Launders, Mary Currier, *Noel Neill*, Gloria Donovan, Mae Busch, Pierre Watkin, Charles Coleman, Grady Sutton, Audrey Young, Anthony Caruso, Jimmy Dundee, Franklyn Farnum, Reed Howes
Director: Hal Walker
Screenplay: B. G. DeSylva, John McGowan
Producer: B. G. DeSylva

JUNIOR PROM
(Monogram, May 11, 1946) 69 Mins.
Freddie Stewart, June Preisser, Judy Clark, Warren Mills, Frankie Darro, *Noel Neill*, Jackie Moran, Abe Lyman and Orchestra, Eddie Heywood and Orchestra, Harry (The Hipster) Gibson, Murray Davis, Mira McKinney, Belle Mitchell, Milt Kibbee, Sam Flint, Charles Evans, Hank Henry, Julia Beth McMillan, The Airliners
Director: Arthur Dreifuss
Screenplay: Erna Lazarus, Hal Collins
Story: Erna Lazarus, Hal Collins
Producer: Sam Katzman

FREDDIE STEPS OUT
(Monogram, June 8, 1946) 75 Mins.
Freddie Stewart, June Preisser, Ann Rooney, Warren Mills, *Noel Neill*, Jackie Moran, Frankie Darro, Milt Kibbee, Belle Mitchell, Edythe Elliott, Murray Davis, Claire James, Douglas Fowley, Emmett Vogan, Terry Lee Carlson, Neta Geddes, Chury Reyes, Charlie Barnet and Orchestra
Director: Arthur Dreifuss
Screenplay: Hal Collins
Story: Hal Collins
Producer: Sam Katzman

HIGH SCHOOL HERO
(Monogram, September 7, 1946) 69 Mins.
Freddie Stewart, June Preisser, *Noel Neill*, Ann Rooney, Warren Mills, Jackie Moran, Frankie Darro, Milt Kibbee, Belle Mitchell, Isabelita, Douglas Fowley, Edythe Elliott, Leonard Penn, Pierre Watkin, Dick Elliott, Jan Savitt, Freddie Stack, Joe Derita
Director: Arthur Dreifuss
Screenplay: Hal Collins, Arthur Dreifuss
Story: Hal Collins, Arthur Dreisfuss
Producer: Sam Katzman

VACATION DAYS
(Monogram, January 25, 1947) 66 Mins.
Freddie Stewart, June Preisser, Frankie Darro, Warren Mills, *Noel Neill*, Milton Kibbee, Belle Mitchell, John Hart, Hugh Prosser, Terry Frost, Edythe Elliott, Claire James, Spade Cooley and His Orchestra, Jerry Wald and His Orchestra, Forrest Taylor
Director: Arthur Dreifuss
Screenplay: Hal Collins
Producer: Sam Katzman

OVER THE SANTA FE TRAIL
(Columbia, February 13, 1947) 63 Mins.
The Hoosier Hot Shots (Hezzie, Ken, Gil and Gabe), Ken Curtis, Jennifer Holt, Guy Kibbee, Guinn "Big Boy" William, The De Castro Sisters, Art West and His Sunset Riders, *Noel Neill*, Holmes Herbert, George Chesebro, Jim Diehl, Frank LaRue, Steve Clark, Julian Rivero, Nolan Leary, Bud Osborne
Director: Ray Nazarro
Screenplay: Louise Rousseau
Story: Eileen Gary
Producer: Colbert Clark

SMASH-UP
(Universal-International, March, 1947) 103 Mins.
Susan Hayward, Lee Bowman, Marsha Hunt, Eddie Albert, Carl Esmond, Carleton Young, Charles D. Brown, Janet Murdoch, Tom Chatterton, Sharyn Payne, Robert Shayne, Larry Blake, George Meeker, Erville Alderson, Bess Flowers, George Meader, Ruth Sanderson, Barbara Woodell, Alice Fleming, Virginia Carroll, Nanette Vallon, Dorothy Christy, Al Hill Jan Cravan, Frances Morris, William Gould, Ernie Adams, Ethel Wales, *Noel Neill*
Director: Stuart Heisler
Screenplay: John Howard Lawson, Lionel Wiggham
Story: Dorothy Parker, Frank Cavett
Producer: Walter Wanger

SARGE GOES TO COLLEGE
(Monogram, May 17, 1947) 63 Mins.
Freddie Stewart, June Preisser, Frankie Darro, Warren Mills, *Noel Neill*, Alan Hale, Jr., Arthur Walsh, Russ Morgan, Monte Collins, Frank Cady, Margaret Brayton, Selmer Jackson, Earl Bennett, Margaret Burt, Harry Tyler, Pat Goldin, William Forrest, Irwin Kauffman, Russ Morgan Orchestra, Jack McVea Orchestra, Candy Candino, Abe Lyman Band, Wigy Manone, Les Paul, Mary Ford, Jess Stacy, Joe Venuti, Jerry Wald
Director: Will Jason
Screenplay: Hal Collins
Story: Harry Edwards
Producer: Will Jason

Superman (Columbia, 1948) – Kirk Alyn and Noel Neill.

BRICK BRADFORD
(Columbia, December 1947) 15 Chapters.
Kane Richmond, Rick Vallin, Linda Johnson, Pierre Watkin, Charles Quigley, Jack Ingram, Fred Graham, John Merton, Leonard Penn, Wheeler Oakman, Carol Forman, Charles King, John Hart, Helene Stanley, Nelson Leigh, Robert Barron, George DeNormand, *Noel Neill*, Al Ferguson, Frank Ellis, Stanley Blystone
Director: Spencer G. Bennet
Screenplay: George Plympton, Arthur Hoerl, Lewis Clay
Story: Based on the King Features comic strip
Producer: Sam Katzman
Chapters: (1) Atomic Defense (2) Flight to the Moon (3) Prisoners of the Moon (4) Into the Volcano (5) Bradford at Bay (6) Back to Earth (7) Into Another Century (8) Buried Treasure (9) Trapped in the Time Top (10) The Unseen Hand (11) Poison Gas (12) Door of Disaster (13) Sinister Rendezvous (14) River of Revenge (15) For the Peace of the World

SMART POLITICS
(Monogram, January 3, 1948) 63 Mins.
Freddie Stewart, June Preisser, *Noel Neill*, Frankie Darro, Warren Mills, Donald MacBride, Martha Davis, Butch Stone, Don Ripps, Candy Candido, Harry Tyler, Monte F. Collins, George Offerman, Jr., George Fields, Dick Paxton, Tommy Mack, Bill Snyder, Gene Krupa and Orchestra, Cappy Barra Harmonica Boys
Director/Producer: Will Jason
Screenplay: Hal Collins
Story: Monte F. Collins, Hal Collins

MAN OR MOUSE
(Columbia, January 15, 1948) 2 Reels
Sterling Holloway, *Noel Neill*, Edgar Dearing
Director: Jules White

GLAMOUR GIRL
(Columbia, January 16, 1948) 67 Mins.
Gene Krupa and Band, Susan Reed, Virginia Grey, Michael Duane, Jimmy Lloyd, Jack Leonard, Pierre Watkin, Eugene Borden, Netta Packer, *Noel Neill*, Caroly Grey, Jeanne Bell
Director: Arthur Dreifuss
Screenplay: M. Coates Webster, Lee Gold
Story: Lee Gold
Producer: Sam Katzman

CAMPUS SLEUTH
(Monogram, April 4, 1948) 66 Mins.
Freddie Stewart, June Preisser, Warren Mills, *Noel Neill*, Bobby Sherwood, Donald MacBrdie, Stan Ross, Monty Collins, Billy Snyder, Paul Bryar, George Eldredge, Gerri Gallian, Joey Preston, Bobby Sherwood's Orchestra, Stan Ross, William Norton Bailey, Charles Campbell, Dotty D. Brown, Harry Taylor, Margaret Bert, Lane Chandler, Mildred Jorman, Jimmy Grisson, George Fields
Director: Will Jason
Screenplay: Hal Collins
Story: Max Wilson, Hal Collins
Producer: Will Jason

THE BLUE DAHLIA
(Paramount, May 8, 1948) 96 Mins.
Alan Ladd, Veronica Lake, William Bendix, Howard da Silva, Doris Dowling, Tom Powers, Hugh Beaumont, Howard Freeman, Don Costello, Will Wright, Frank Faylen, Walter Sande, Vera Marshe, Mae Busch, Gloria Williams, George Barton, Harry Barris, Paul Gustine, Roberta Jonay, Milton Kibbee, Dick Winslow, Anthony Caruso, Matt McHugh, Arthur Loft, Stan Johnson, Ernie Adams, Henry Vroom, Harry Tyler, Jack Clifford, George Sorrel, James Millican, Albert Ruiz, Charles A. Hughes, Perc Launders, Jimmie Dundee, Tom Dillon, Dick Elliott, George Carleton, *Noel Neill*, Mavis Murray
Director: George Marshall
Screenplay: Raymond Chandler
Story: Raymond Chandler
Producer: George Marshall

ARE YOU WITH IT?
(Universal-International, May 1948) 90 Mins.
Donald O'Connor, Olga San Juan, Martha Stewart, Lew Parker, Walter Catlett, Pat Dane, Ransom Sherman, Louis Da Pron, *Noel Neill*, Julie Gibson, George O'Hanlon, Eddie Parks, Raymond Largay, Jody Gilbert, Howard Negley, Charles Bedell
Director: Jack Hively
Screenplay: Oscar Brodney
Story: Based on the musical comedy by Sam Perrin and George Blazer
Producer: Robert Arthur

ADVENTURES OF FRANK AND JESSE JAMES
(Republic, June 24, 1948) 13 Chapters.
Clayton Moore, Steve Darrell, *Noel Neill*, George J. Lewis, Stanley Andrews, John Crawford, Sam Flint, House Peters, Jr., Dale Van Sickel, Tom Steele, James Dale, I. Stanford Jolley, Gene Stutenroth, Lane Bradford, George Chesebro, Jack Kirk, Steve Clark, Duke Taylor, Carey Loftin, Duke Green, Frank Ellis, Roy Bucko, Art Dillard, Ralph Bucko, Victor Cox, Fred Graham, Guy Teague, Frank O'Connor, Joe Yrigoyen, Augie Gomez, Eddie Parker, Bud Osborne, Bud Wolfe, Rosa Turich, David Sharpe, Bob Reeves, Ken Terrell, Joe Phillips
Directors: Fred Brannon, Yakima Canutt
Screenplay: Franklyn Adreon, Sol Shor, Basil Dickey
Associate Producer: Franklyn Adreon
Chapters: (1) Agent of Treachery (2) The Hidden Witness (3) The Lost Tunnel (4) Blades of Death (5) Roaring Wheels (6) Passage to Danger (7) The Secret Code (8) Doomed Cargo (9) The Eyes of the Law (10) The Stolen Body (11) Suspicion (12) Talk or Die! (13) Unmasked

SUPERMAN
(Columbia, July 1948) 15 Chaps.
Kirk Alyn, *Noel Neill*, Tommy Bond, Carol Forman, George Meeker, Jack Ingram, Pierre Watkin, Terry Frost, Charles King, Charles Quigley, Herbert Rawlinson, Forrest Taylor, Stephen Carr, Rusty Wescoatt, Nelson Leigh, Luana Walters, Edward Cassidy, Virginia Carroll, Alan Dinehart III, Ralph Hodges, Robert Barron, Gene Roth, Jack North, Tom London, Frank Ellis, Stanley Price, Paul Stader, Leonard Penn, Peggy Wynn, Emmett Vogan, Rube Schaefer, Al Wyatt
Directors: Spencer G. Bennet, Thomas Carr
Screenplay: Arthur Hoerl, Lewis Clay, Royal Cole
Story: Based on the Superman comic strip and adapted from the radio program
Producer: Sam Katzman
Chapters: (1) Superman Comes to Earth (2) Depths of the Earth (3) The Reducer Ray (4) Man of Steel (5) A Job for Superman (6) Superman in Danger (7) Into the Electrical Furnace (8) Superman to the Rescue (9) Irresistible Force (10) Between Two Fires (11) Superman's Dilemma (12) Blast in the Depths (13) Hurled to Destruction (14) Superman at Bay (15) The Payoff

MUSIC MAN
(Monogram, September 5, 1948) 66 Mins.
Freddie Stewart, Phil Brito, Jimmy Dorsey and His Orchestra, Alan Hale, Jr., June Preisser, *Noel Neill*, Grazia Marciso, Chick Chandler, Norman Leavitt, Helen Woodford, Gertrude Astor, William Norton Bailey, Roy Aversa, Herman Canotor, Paul Bradley
Director: Will Jason
Screenplay: Sam Mintz
Producer: Will Jason

THE BIG CLOCK
(Paramount, 1948) 95 Mins.
Ray Milland, Charles Laughton, Maureen O'Sullivan, Rita Johnson, Elsa Lanchester, George Macready, Harold Vermilyea, Dan Tobin, Harry Morgan, Richard Webb, Ted Van Brunt, Elaine Riley, Luis Van Rooten, Lloyd Corrigan, Douglas Spencer, *Noel Neill*
Director: John Farrow
Screenplay: Jonathan Latimer
Story: Jonathan Latimer

WHEN MY BABY SMILES AT ME
(20th Century-Fox, November, 1948) 98 Mins. (Technicolor)
Betty Grable, Dan Dailey, Jack Oakie, June Havoc, Richard Arlen, James Gleason, Venita Wade, Kenny Williams, Robert Emmett Keane, Jean Wallace, Pati Behrs, Lee MacGregor, Charles Tannen, *Noel Neill*, LuAnne Jones, Joanne Dale, Dorothy Babb, Hank Mann, Edward Clark, Charles LaTorre, Lela Bliss
Director: Walter Lang
Story: Based on the play "Burlesque" by George M. Watters and Arthur Hopkins
Producer: George Jessel

GUN RUNNER
(Monogram, January 30, 1949) 54 Mins.
Jimmy Wakely, Dub Taylor, *Noel Neill*, Mae Clark, Kenne Duncan, Steve Clark, Marshall Reed, Ted Adams, Bud Osborne, Carol Henry, Bob Woodward, Clem Fuller, Ray Jones, Ray Whitley
Director: Lambert Hillyer
Screenplay: J. Benton Cheney
Producer: Louis Gray

CACTUS CUT-UP
(RKO, April 15, 1949) 2 Reels
Leon Errol, Dorothy Granger, *Noel Neill*, Roland Morris, Ralph Peters
Director: Charles Roberts

SON OF A BADMAN
(Western Aventure/Screen Guild, April 16, 1949) 64 Mins.
Al "Lash" LaRue, Al "Fuzzy" St. John, Michael Whalen, *Noel Neill*, Zon Murray, Jack Ingram, Steve Raines, Chuck (Bob) Cason, Don Harvey, Frank Lackteen, Francis McDonald, Edna Holland, William Norton Bailey, Sandy Sanders, Doyle O'Dell
Director: Ray Taylor
Screenplay: Ron Ormond, Ira Webb
Producer: Ron Ormond

SKY DRAGON
(Monogram, May 1, 1949) 64 Mins.
Roland Winters, Keye Luke, Mantan Moreland, *Noel Neill*, Tim Ryan, Iris Adrian, Elena Verdugo, Milburn Stone, Joel Marston, Lyle Talbot, Paul Maxey, John Eldredge, Lyle Latell, Eddie Parks, Louise Franklin, George Eldredge, Bob Curtis, Charles Jordan
Director: Lesley Selander
Screenplay: Oliver Drake, Clint Johnston
Story: Clint Johnston
Producer: James S. Burkett

FORGOTTEN WOMEN
(Monogram, July 17, 1949) 65 Mins.
Elyse Knox, Edward Norris, Robert Shayne, Theodora Lynch, Veda Ann Borg, *Noel Neill*, Tim Ryan, Bill Kennedy, Warren Douglas, Selmer Jackson, Paul Frison
Director: William Beaudine
Screenplay: W. Scott Darling
Story: Jeffrey Bernard
Producer: Jeffrey Bernard

RED, HOT AND BLUE
(Paramount, November 25, 1949) 84 Mins.
Betty Hutton, Victor Mature, William Demarest, June Havoc, Jane Nigh, Frank Loesser, William Talman, Art Smith, Raymond Walburn, Onslow Stevens, Joseph Vitale, Barry Kelley, Robert Watson, Jack Kruschen, Percy Helton, Philip Van Zandt, Dorothy Abbott, Julia Faye, *Noel Neill*, Joey Ray, Betty (Julie) Adams, Lester Dorr, Harland Tucker, Billy Daniels, Bess Flowers, Tim Ryan, Jimmie Dundee, Al Ferguson, Edward Peil, Sr., Robert Kellard, Lee Phelps
Director: John Farrow
Screenplay: Hagar Wilde, John Farrow
Story: Charles Lederer
Producer: Robert Fellows

THE JAMES BROTHERS OF MISSOURI
(Republic, January 21, 1950) 12 Chapters.
Keith Richards, Robert Bice, *Noel Neill*, Roy Barcroft, Patricia Knox, Lane Bradford, Gene Stutenroth, John Hamilton, Edmund Cobb, Hank Patterson, Dale Van Sickel, Tom Steele, Lee Roberts, Frank O'Connor, Marshall Reed, Wade Ray, Nolan Leary, David Sharpe, Art Dillard, Duke Green, John Crawford, Jim Rinehart, May Morgan, Post Parks, Duke Taylor, Al Ferguson, Cactus Mack, Joe Phillips, Tommy Coats, Bert LeBaron, Ken Terrell, Ted Hubert, Robert Wilke, Ray Morgan, Hank Patterson, Ralph Bucko, Forrest Burns, Helen Griffith, Herman Hack, Chick Hannon, Chuck Roberson, Bud Wolfe, Frosty Royce, Rockey Shahan
Director: Fred C. Brannon
Screenplay: Royal Cole, William Lively, Sol Shor
Associate Producer: Franklyn Adreon (sometimes spelled Franklin)
Chapters: (1) Frontier Renegades (2) Racing Peril (3) Danger Road (4) Murder at Midnight (5) Road to Oblivion (6) Missouri Manhunt (7) Hangman's Noose (8) Coffin on Wheels (9) Dead Man's Return (10) Galloping Gunslingers (11) The Haunting Past (12) Fugitive Code

ATOM MAN VS. SUPERMAN
(Columbia, June 1950) 15 Chaps.
Kirk Alyn, *Noel Neill*, Lyle Talbot, Tommy Bond, Pierre Watkin, Jack Ingram, Don Harvey, Rusty Wescoatt, Terry Frost, Wally West, Paul Stader, George Robotham, William Fawcett, Stanley Blystone, Fred Kelsey, Jack George
Director: Spencer G. Bennet
Screenplay: George Plympton, Joseph Poland, David Mathews
Story: Based on the comic strip and the radio program
Producer: Sam Katzman
Chapters: (1) Superman Flies Again (2) Atom Man Appears (3) Ablaze in the Sky (4) Superman Meets Atom Man (5) Atom Man Tricks Superman (6) Atom Man's Challenge (7) At the Mercy of Atom Man (8) Into the Empty Doom (9) Superman Crashes Through (10) Atom Man's Heat Ray (11) Luthor's Strategy (12) Atom Man Strikes (13) Atom Man's Flying Saucer (14) Rocket of Vengeance (15) Superman Saves the Universe

ABILENE TRAIL
(Monogram, February 4, 1951) 54 Mins.
Whip Wilson, Andy Clyde, Tommy Farrell, Steve Clark, *Noel Neill*, Dennis Moore, Marshall Reed, Lee Roberts, Milburn Morante, Ted Adams, Bill Kennedy, Stanley Price, Lyle Talbot
Director: Lewis Collins
Screenplay: Harry Fraser
Producer: Vincent M. Fennelly

WHISTLING HILLS
(Frontier Pictures/Monogram, October 7, 1951) 58 Mins.
Johnny Mack Brown, Jimmy Ellison, *Noel Neill*, Lee Roberts, Pamela Duncan, I. Stanford Jolley, Marshall Reed, Bud Osborne, Pierce Lyden, Frank Ellis, Ray Jones, Merrill McCormack
Director: Derwin Abrahams
Screenplay: Fred Myton
Producer: Vincent M. Fennelly

AN AMERICAN IN PARIS
(MGM, November 9, 1951) 113 Mins.
(Technicolor)
Gene Kelly, Leslie Caron, Oscar Levant, Georges Guetary, Nina Foch, Eugene Borden, Ann Codee, Hayden Rorke, Paul Maxey, Dick Wessel, Jeanne Lafayette, *Noel Neill*, John Eldredge, Anna Q. Nilsson, Madge Blake
Director: Vincente Minnelli
Screenplay: Alan Lin
Story: Alan Jay Lerner
Producer: Arthur Freed

SUBMARINE COMMAND
(Paramount, November 1951) 87 Mins.
William Holden, Nancy Olsen, William Bendix, Don Taylor, Arthur Franz, Darryl Hickman, Peggy Webber, Moroni Olsen, Jack Gregson, Jack Kelly, Don Dunning, Jarry Pris, Charles Meredith, Philip Van Zandt, *Noel Neill*
Director: John Farrow
Screenplay: Jonathan Latimer
Story: Jonathan Latimer
Producer: Joseph Sistrom

THE GREATEST SHOW ON EARTH
(Paramount, July 1, 1952) 151 Mins.
(Technicolor)
Betty Hutton, Cornel Wilde, Charlton Heston, Dorothy Lamour, Gloria Grahame, James Stewart, Henry Wilcoxon, Emmett Kelly, Lyle Bettger, Gloria Drew, Anthony Marsh, *Noel Neill*, Hugh Prosser, Keith Richards, Mona Knox, Gertrude Messinger, Lawrence Tierney, Julia Faye, Lane Chandler, John Merton, Jimmie Dundee, Dorothy Adams, Syd Saylor, Milt Kibbee, Fred Kohler, Jr. Greta Grandstedt, Bess Flowers
Director: Cecil B. De Mille
Screenplay: Barre Lyndon, Frederic M. Frank, Theodore St. John
Story: Frank Cavett, Barre Lyndon, Frederic M. Frank
Producer: Cecil B. De Mille

MONTANA INCIDENT
(Monogram, August 10, 1952) 54 Mins.
Whip Wilson, Rand Brooks, *Noel Neill*, Peggy Stewart, Hugh Prosser, William Fawcett, Terry Frost, Marshall Reed, Lyle Talbot, Russ Whiteman, Barbara Woodell, Bruce Edwards, Stanley Price
Director: Lewis Collins
Screenplay: Dan Ullman
Producer: Vincent M. Fennelly

INVASION U.S.A.
(American Pictures/Columbia, December 1953) 74 Mins.
Gerald Mohr, Peggie Castle, Dan O'Herlihy, Robert Bice, Tom Kennedy, Wade Crosby, Phyllis Coates, Erik Blythe, Aram Katcher, *Noel Neill*
Director: Alfred E. Green
Screenplay: Franz Spencer, Robert Smith
Story: Franz Spencer, Robert Smith
Producer: Albert Zugsmith

THE LAWLESS RIDER
(United Artists, July 1, 1954) 62 Mins.
John Carpenter, Rose Bascom, Frankie Darro, Douglass Dumbrille, Frank "Red" Carpenter, *Noel Neill*, Kenne Duncan, Weldon Bascom, Bud Osborne, Lon Roberson, Bill Coontz, Bill Chaney, Roy Canada, Tap Canutt, Hank Caldwell and his Saddle Kings
Director: Yakima Canutt
Screenplay: John Carpenter
Story: John Carpenter
Producer: Alex Gordon, John Carpenter

SUPERMAN FLIES AGAIN
(20th Century-Fox, 1954)
George Reeves, *Noel Neill*, Jack Larson, John Hamilton, Robert Shayne, William Wayne, Peter Brocco, Mickey Simpson, Harry Mendoza, George Douglas, Charles Williams, Dick Crockett, Richard Lewis, Harvey Parry, Ben Welden, Billy Nelson, Dona Drake, John Daly, Lester Dorr, Lane Bradford, Selmer Jackson, Richard Reeves, Jim Hayward, Larry Blake, Mauritz Hugo, Sam Balter, Bud Wolfe, Ric Roman
Directors: Thomas Carr, George Clair
Screenplay: David Chantler
Story: A compilation of three television episodes: "Jet Ace," "The Dog Who Knew Superman," and "The Clown Who Cried"

SUPERMAN'S PERIL
(20th Century-Fox, 1954)
George Reeves, *Noel Neill*, Jack Larson, John Hamilton, Robert Shayne, Peter Whitney, Vic Perrin, Robert Bice, Murray Alper, Wesley Hudman, Saul M. Gorss, Carl H. Saxe, Dan Turner, William J. Vincent, Elisha Cook, Jr., Paul Fix, Douglas Henderson, Richard Benedict, Alfred Linder, Maruice Cass, Peter Mamakos, Sid Tomack
Director: Thomas Carr
Screenplay: Jackson Gillis
Story: A compilation of three television episodes: "The Golden Vulture," "The Semi-Private Eye," and "The Defeat of Superman"

SUPERMAN IN EXILE
(20th Century-Fox, 1954)
George Reeves, *Noel Neill*, Jack Larson, John Hamilton, Robert Shayne, Leon Askin, Joe Forte, Robert S. Carson, Philip Van Zandt, John Harmon, Don Dillaway, Gregg Barton, Sam Balter, Hayden Roarke, I. Stanford Jolley, George Chandler, Percy Helton, Carlton Young, William Newell, Nolan Leary, Sam Balter, Sterling Holloway, Joseph Vitale, Otto Waldis, Toni Carroll, Allene Roberts, Marshall Reed, Jerry Hausner
Directors: Thomas Carr, George Blair
Screenplay: David Chantler, Jackson Gillis
Story: A compilation of three television episodes: "The Face and the Voice," "The Whistling Bird," and "Superman in Exile"

SUPERMAN AND SCOTLAND YARD
(20th Century-Fox, 1954)
George Reeves, *Noel Neill*, Jack Larson, John Hamilton, Robert Shayne, Leonard Mudie, Colin Campbell, Norma Varden, Patrick Aherne, Evelyn Halpern, Clyde Cook, Jonathan Hale, Jane Frazee, Clark Howat, Thomas Moore, Frank Ferguson, Virginia Christine, Mike Ragan, John Doucette, Rudolph Anders, Frank Marlowe
Directors: George Blair, Thomas Carr
Screenplay: Jackson Gillis
Story: A compilation of three television episodes: "A Ghost for Scotland Yard," "Lady in Black," and "Panic in the Sky"

SUPERMAN AND THE JUNGLE DEVIL
(20th Century-Fox, 1954)
George Reeves, *Noel Neill*, Jack Larson, John Hamilton, Robert Shayne, Vera Marshe, Billy Gray, John Eldredge, Frank Richards, Alan Lee, Sterling Holloway, Billy Nelson, Ben Welden, Stan Jarman, Sherry Moreland, San Balter, Russell Custer, Doris Singleton, Damian O'Flynn, Nacho Galindo, James Seay, Al Kikume, Leon Lontoc, Steve Clavert, Henry A. Escalante, Bernard Gozier
Directors: Thomas Carr, George Blair
Screenplay: Peter Dixon, David Chantler, Jackson Gillis
Story: A compilation of three television episodes: "Jungle Devil," "Shot in the Dark," and "The Machine that Could Plot Crimes"

SUPERMAN
(Warner Bros. December, 1978) 143 Mins. (Technicolor) (Panavision)
Marlon Brando, Gene Hackman, Christopher Reeve, Ned Beatty, Jackie Cooper, Glenn Ford, Trevor Howard, Margot Kidder, Jack O'Halloran, Valerie Perrine, Maria Schell, Terence Stamp, Phyllis Thaxter, Susannah York, Jeff East, Marc McClure, Sarah Douglas, Vass Anderson, John Hollis, James Garbutt, Michael Gover, David Neal, William Russell, Penelope Lee, John Stuart, Alan Cullen, Lee Quigley, Aaron Smolinski, Diane Sherry, Jeff Atchson, Rex Reed, Larry Hagman, *Noel Neill*, Kirk Alyn
Director: Richard Donner
Screenplay: Mario Puzo, David Newman, Leslie Newman, Robert Benton
Story: Mario Puzo, based on characters created by Jerry Siegel and Joe Shuster
Producer: Pierre Spengher

Allene Ray

15 • ALLENE RAY

Crown Princess of the Silent Serial and a Beautiful and Talented Heroine

With all due respect to Pearl White and Ruth Roland, Allene Ray was probably the best serial heroine to grace the genre in either era, silent or sound. Certainly she was the most prolific, co-starring in sixteen cliffhangers. Our hats are off to this underrated ingenue who made a great deal of money for Pathé when serials were respectable and popular film fare.

Allene had blond hair and hazel eyes and was five feet three inches tall. She was born Allene Bunch in San Antonio, Texas, January 2, 1901. A real Lone Star girl, Allene spent her childhood on a ranch outside San Antonio, at Devine, except for brief forays into San Antonio for a season of town life.

As a child on the ranch, she had no thought of a screen career. She learned to ride a horse in fearless, reckless fashion and was called "a little ridin' fool" by the ranch hands. She could take a bucking bronco and turn him into a mild, well-mannered animal. She was equally proficient at swimming and diving. In fact, she knew every outdoor sport, including baseball.

In her late teens Allene attracted the attention of a musical comedy manager in San Antonio who offered her a part in his production. Allene could sing, and she had studied dancing in San Antonio. The idea of appearing in musical comedy appealed to her and she accepted the manager's offer.

Then, Tex O'Reilly, the O. Henry of the plains, met her and called her to the attention of actor-director Harry Myers, who was in San Antonio to make a series of two-reel Westerns. Allene was asked to play a leading role in the first of his series. This, too, appealed to Allene--more strongly, in fact, than did the stage. And her family was happier. They didn't like the idea of their daughter being in musical comedy, but pictures were different. So eighteen-year-old Allene Ray started a career as a Western heroine in 1919.

It is uncertain what her first picture was or how many two-reelers she made in the early years. But we do have a good account of **Honeymoon Ranch** (1920), a five-reeler made for Bert Lubin from a story by Tex O'Reilly. Made in the Big Bend country close to the Mexican border, it portrays the days of the old Chisholm Trail, when boundary lines were determined by the branding iron and personal arguments settled by the bullet. Harry McLaughlin is the New Yorker who falls desperately in love when he steps off a train in the West. He is forced at the point of a six-shooter to marry the object of his affection an hour later, and then obliged to whip the male members of her family and their numerous cohorts. As Blue Bonnet, daughter of outlaw Wild Bill Devlin (Tex O'Reilly), Allene steals the picture.

In 1920 Allene won the Fame and Fortune contest sponsored by Brewster Publications and appeared in **Ramon, the Sailmaker** (1920), produced in New York. She is supposed to have returned to Texas to make six Tex O'Reilly Westerns, but we cannot determine that she did. We do know she was leading lady opposite Harry McLaughlin in the O'Reilly story, **West of the Rio Grande** (1921), a five-reeler for Western Pictures, a subsidiary of the Weiss-Artclass organization. She also played the lead in **Partners of the Sunset** (1922), with Robert Frazer as her protector in a run-of-the-mill prairie saga. A few film roles followed, and then Pathé picked her up as heroine and principal star of the serial **Way of a Man** (1924), after concluding that serial audiences wanted a change from the total self-sufficiency (no romance) of Roland, White, and other contemporary cliffhanger heroines.

With her striking beauty and athletic prowess, wistful charm, and believability in romantic or dramatic interludes, Allene was a natural for the

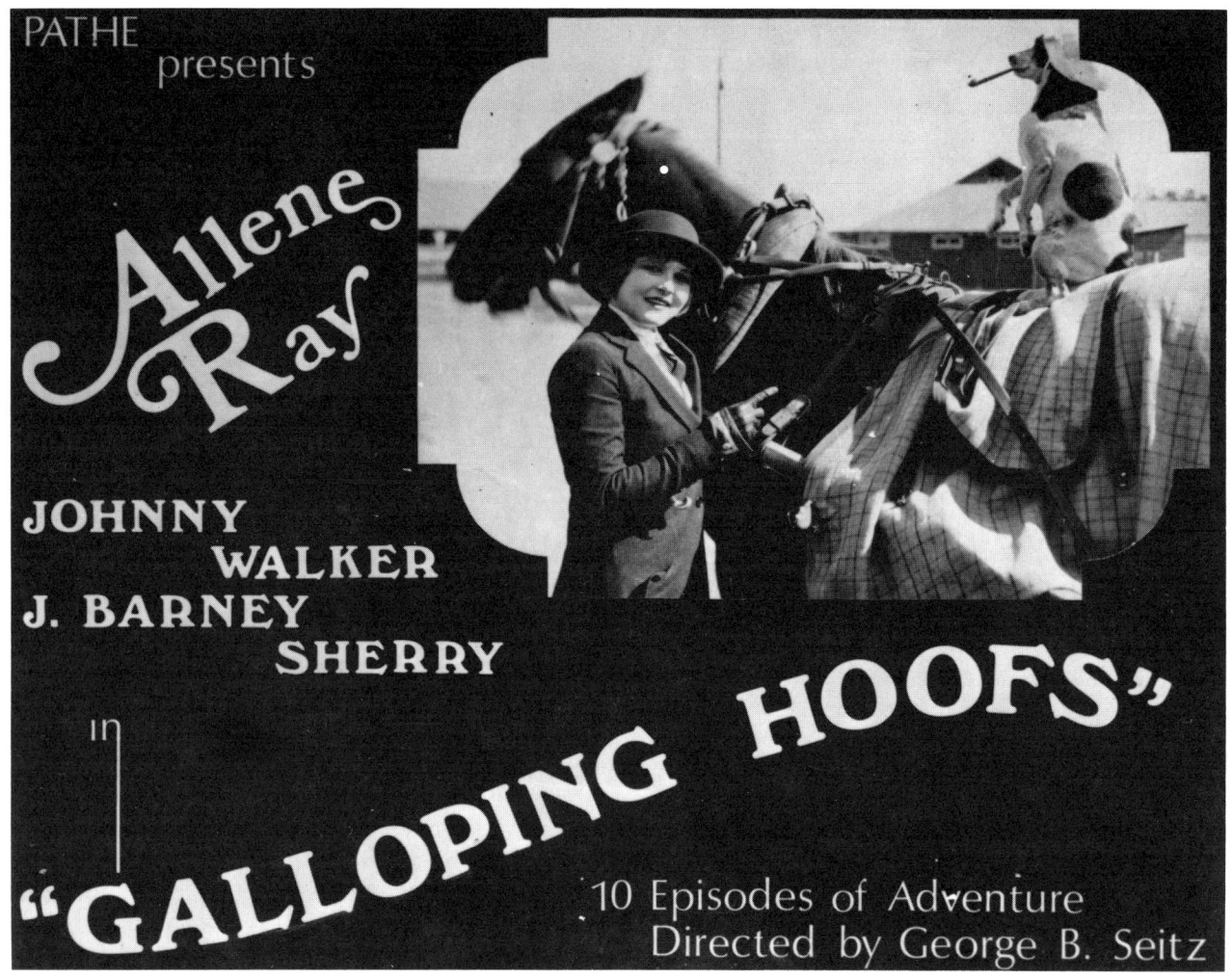

Galloping Hoofs (Pathé, 1924) – Allene Ray was the last of the silent serial queens and ranks as one of the five foremost serial heroines of all time.

serial world. She took direction well and, unlike Ruth Roland, was cooperative and friendly to everyone on a set. She was seldom known to use a double, even when she became Pathé's hottest property. Allene was definitely an introvert, but her friendly ways and sincerity quickly endeared her to colleagues. One might even say that she was the Buck Jones of her sex, a professional performer who took pride in her work, appreciated the genre that made her famous, and conducted herself in a genteel way at all times. If anyone in the serial sorority deserves to be remembered it is Allene Ray, in whom one's childhood idolization was not misplaced.

Her early films for Pathé included **Way of a Man** (1924), a good serial beginning for her; **The Fortieth Door** (1924), in which Allene plays a French girl entrapped by Mohammedans headed by lustful Frank Lackteen; **Ten Scars Make a Man** (1924), in which she was back in a Western setting, opposite Jack Mower, who had to acquire ten scars before winning her hand in marriage; and **Galloping Hoofs** (1924), a story about a treasure box and its secret, in which she had Johnnie Walker's help in overcoming the machinations of those who wanted to steal her inheritance.

In her fifth serial outing, **Sunken Silver** (1925), Pathé gave her Walter Miller as a leading man. Walter exuded virility and was a seasoned performer, having been in films since 1912. Buried treasure in the Florida Everglades was the foundation for all the excitement and skullduggery.

A hit with serial enthusiasts, the team of Miller and Ray went to bat again in **Play Ball** (1925). Spencer Gordon Bennet directed this and the eight Ray-Miller cliffhangers that followed. These included **The Green Archer** (1925), probably the finest and most popular of the Ray-Miller serials; **Snowed In** (1926), which took Ray and Miller outdoors again as they tried to capture mail robbers in the High Sierras, with considerable activity revolving around an abandoned hotel; **House Without a Key** (1926), based on a

The Green Archer (Pathé, 1925) – Allene Ray swings a wicked chair.

Charlie Chan book by Earl D. Biggers, adapted to the screen by Frank Leon Smith; **Melting Millions** (1927), where Allene and Walter Miller were reunited in a story about a young lady who is the rightful heiress to a fortune and her attempts to gain possession of it; and **Hawk of the Hills** (1927), a return to the West for Allene.

The quality of the Pathé serial, with the exception of the Ray-Miller vehicles, had slipped considerably by 1928, and the rooster trademark was being stamped on products that would not have met Pathé's former standards. But the Ray-Miller outings remained topnotch thrillers that the old rooster, had he a voice in those days, could have crowed about. Director Spencer Bennet shares credit with Ray and Miller for maintaining quality on mediocre budgets of around $90,000 to $100,000 a picture.

In 1929 Allene and Miller made **The Black Book**, their last film together and the last serial ever made by Pathé. It had been nearly a year since their previous film together, **The Terrible People**. Both stars had used the time off for vaudeville engagements. Mediocre compared to their previous serials, the story is based on the patriotic efforts of a beautiful young girl detective, opposed by a criminal coterie which includes the masterminds of evil in two countries.

Though she was the most popular serial queen of the twenties, Allene never received more than $500 a week for her labors. Pathé chose to hold down salaries and use the savings to produce better serials. That she worked as hard and as effectively as she did for so little money is a credit to her, for she literally risked her life many times, seldom letting a double take her place.

With the demise of serial production at Pathé, Allene was lured to Universal to appear in **The Indians Are Coming** (1930), a serial released in both silent and sound versions. Tim McCoy had the male lead, and Henry MacRae produced and directed. It made a million dollars for

The Hawk of the Hills (Pathé, 1927) – Allene Ray and Walter Miller.

Universal and pulled McCoy out of oblivion, but for Allene it did little. Reportedly, she had a high, squeaky voice which could not be disguised sufficiently by the early recording equipment. She made a few talkies, most notably **Overland Bound** (1930), and then dropped out of the movies.

No one seems to know much about the personal life of the movies' most prolific serial heroine or what happened to her thereafter. We have been no more successful than previous writers in tracing her. At one time she was married to a man named Larry Wheeler, and beyond that, we are in the dark. This we do know--to become enamored of Allene Ray was one of the easiest things a man or boy could do in those halcyon years just before the Great Depression.

ALLENE RAY Filmography

SQUATTER'S RIGHT
(Aywon, 1919) 2 Reels
Harry Myers, *Allene Ray*

THE TRAIL'S END
(Aywon, 1919) 2 Reels
Harry Myers, *Allene Ray*

WHEN LAD CAME HOME
(Aywon, 1919) 2 Reels
Harry Myers, *Allene Ray*

A MODERN LOCHINVAR
(Aywon, 1919) 2 Reels
Harry Myers, *Allene Ray*

THE WILDCATTER
(Aywon, 1919) 2 Reels
Harry Myers, *Allene Ray*

HONEYMOON RANCH
(Bert Lubin, 1920) 5 Reels
Allene Ray, Harry McLaughlin, John B. Hagin, Edward S. (Tex) O'Reilly, Margaret Davis, Sam White, Robin H. Townley
Director: Robert H. Townley
Story: Edward S. (Tex) O'Reilly

CROSSED TRAILS
(Méliès/Knickerbocker, 1920)
Allene Ray
Story: Edward S. (Tex) O'Reilly

RAMON, THE SAILMAKER
(Brewster, 1920)
Allene Ray

ON THE HIGH CARD
(Western Pictures/Arrow, 1921) 5 Reels
Allene Ray, Harry Myers, Tex O'Reilly, Ben Hill, Gene Baker, Charles E. Graham
Story: Edward S. (Tex) O'Reilly

WEST OF THE RIO GRANDE
(Bert Lubin, October 1921) 5 Reels
Harry McLaughlin, *Allene Ray*, John Hagin, Tex O'Reilly, Marguerite Davis, George Crazy, Sam White, Roberta Bellinger, Charles Hollman
Director: Robert H. Townley
Screenplay: Robert H. Townley
Story: Tex O'Reilly

PARTNERS OF THE SUNSET
(Western Pictures, February 1922) 5 Reels
Allene Ray, Robert Frazer, Mildred Bright, J. W. Johnston
Director: Robert H. Townley
Story: Walter Richard Hall

YOUR FRIEND AND MINE
(S-L Pictures/Metro, March 5, 1923) 6 Reels
Enid Bennett, Huntly Gordon, Willard Mack, Rosemary Theby, J. Herbert Frank, Otto Lederer, *Allene Ray*
Director: Clarence G. Badger
Screenplay: Winifred Dunn
Story: Willard Mack, "Your Friend and Mine"
Producers: Arthur H. Sawyer, Herbert Lubin

TIMES HAVE CHANGED
(Fox, October 7, 1923) 5 Reels
William Russell, Mabel Juienne Scott, Charles West, Martha Mattox, Edwin B. Tilton, George Atkinson, *Allene Ray*, Dick LaReno, Gus Leonard, Jack Curtis
Director: James Flood
Screenplay: Jack Strumwasser
Story: Elmer Holmes Davis, "Times Have Changed"

WAY OF A MAN
(Pathé, January 20, 1924) 10 Chapters.
Allene Ray, Harold Miller, Florence Lee, Bud Osborne, Chief Whitehorse, Lillian Gale, Kathryn Appleton, Chet Tyan, Lillian Adreian
Director: George B. Seitz
Story: Emerson Hough
Chapters: (1) Into the Unknown (2) Redskin and White (3) In the Toils of the Torrent (4) Lost in the Wilds (5) White Medicine (6) The Firing Squad (7) Gold! Gold! (8) The Fugitive (9) California (10) Trail's End
(Also released in a 7-reel feature version)

THE FORTIETH DOOR
(Pathé, May 25, 1924) 10 Chapters.
Allene Ray, Bruce Gordon, Anna May Wong, Frank Lackteen, David Dunbar, Frances Mann, Lillian Gale, Bernard Siegel
Director: George B. Seitz
Screenplay: Frank Leon Smith
Chapters: (1) The Secret Portal (2) Two Lockets (3) The Wedding (4) Buried Alive (5) Desert Trails (6) The Tomb of a King (7) Claws of the Vulture (8) Held for Hostage (9) The Rack (10) The Temple of the Forty doors
(Also released in a 6-reel feature version)

THE FORTIETH DOOR
(Pathé, August 17, 1924) 6 Reels
Allene Ray, Bruce Gordon, David Dunbar, Anna May Wong, Frances Mann, Frank Lackteen, Lillian Gale, Bernard Seigel, Whitehorse, Omar Whitehead, Scott McGee, Eli Stanton
Director: George B. Seitz
Screenplay: Frank Leon Smith
Story: Mary Hasting Bradley, "The Fortieth Door"
Producer: C. W. Patton

TEN SCARS MAKE A MAN
(Pathé, October 12, 1924) 10 Chapters.
Allene Ray, Jack Mower, Rose Burdick, Lillian Gale, Larry Steers, Leon De La Methé, Harry Woods
Director: William Parke
Story: Phillips Barry
Chapters: (1) Two Girls and a Man (2) Cowboy Chivalry (3) Westward Bound (4) The Cattle Raid (5) Through the Hills (6) Midnight Marauders (7) Unmasked (8) Liquid Gold (9) The Valley of the Legend (10) The End of the Quest

GALLOPING HOOFS
(Pathé, December 21, 1924) 10 Chapters.
Allene Ray, Johnnie Walker, J. Barney Sherry, Ernest Hilliard, Armand Cortez, William Nally, George Nardelli, Albert Roccardi
Director: George B. Seitz
Story: Frank Leon Smith
Chapters: (1) The Sealed Box (2) The Mountain Raid (3) Neck and Neck (4) The Duplicate Box (5) The Fateful Jump (6) Raging Waters (7) Out of the Depths (8) Ambushed (9) Tricked (10) Flying Colors

SUNKEN SILVER
(Pathé, May 10, 1925) 10 Chapters.
Allene Ray, Walter Miller, Frank Lackteen, Ivan Linow, Charlie Fang, Gordon (Spencer G.) Bennet, Frank Wunderlee, Albert Roccardi, Jean Bronte
Director: George B. Seitz
Producer: George B. Seitz
Screenplay: Frank Leon Smith
Adaptation: Frank Leon Smith
Chapters: (1) Watched (2) On Secret Service (3) The Hidden Way (4) Fangs (5) Sea Tigers (6) In Double Peril (7) Face to Face (8) The Shadow on the Stairs (9) The Secret Panel (10) The End of the Trail

PLAY BALL
(Pathé, July 19, 1925) 10 Chapters.
Allene Ray, Walter Miller, J. Barney Sherry, Harry Semels, Mary Milnor, Wally Oettel, Franklyn Hanna, Ed Maurelli
Director: Spencer G. Bennet
Screenplay: Frank Leon Smith
Story: John J. McGraw
Chapters: (1) To the Rescue (2) The Flaming Float (3) Betrayed (4) The Decoy Wire (5) Face to Face (6) The Showdown (7) A Mission of Hate (8) Double Peril (9) Into Segundo's Hands (10) A Home Plate Wedding

THE GREEN ARCHER
(Pathé, December 6, 1925) 10 Chapters
Allene Ray, Walter Miller, Burr McIntosh, Stephen Gratten, Frank Lackteen, Walter P. Lewis, Jack Tanner, Ray Allen, William Randall, Dorothy King, Wally Oettel, Tom Cameron
Director: Spencer G. Bennet
Screenplay: Frank Leon Smith
Story: Edgar Wallace
Chapters: (1) The Ghost of Bellamy Castle (2) The Midnight Warning (3) In the Enemy's Stronghold (4) On the Storm King Road (5) The Affair at the River (6) The Mystery Ship (7) Bellamy Baits a Trap (8) The Cottage in the Woods (9) The Battle Starts (10) The Smoke Clears Away

SNOWED IN
(Pathé, July 4, 1926) 10 Chapters.
Allene Ray, Walter Miller, Frank Austin, Leonard Clapham, (Tom London), John Webb Dillon, Natalie Warfield, Wally Oettel, Harrison Martell, Charles West, J. F. McCullough, Ben Walker, Bert Apling, George Albert Kingsley
Director: Spencer G. Bennet
Screenplay: Frank Leon Smith
Chapters: (1) Storm Warnings (2) The Storm Starts (3) The Coming of Redfield (4) Redfield Strikes (5) Buried (6) The Enemy's Stronghold (7) The Trap (8) Thieves' Honor (9) Daybreak (10) The End of Redfield

HOUSE WITHOUT A KEY
(Pathé, November 21, 1926) 10 Chapters.
Allene Ray, Walter Miller, Frank Lackteen, Charles H. West, John Webb Dillon, Natalie _Warfield, William Norton Bailey, E. H. Calvert, Betty Caldwell, Jack Pratt, George Kuwa, Harry Semels, John Cossar, Scott Seaton, Clifford Saum
Director: Spencer G. Bennet
Screenplay: Frank Leon Smith
Chapters: (1) The Spite Fence (2) The Mystery Box (3) The Missing Numeral (4) Suspicion (5) The Death Buoy (6) Sinister Shadows (7) The Mystery Man (8) The Spotted Menace (9) The Wrist Watch (10) The Culprit

House Without a Key (Pathé, 1926) – Allene Ray and Walter Miller.

MELTING MILLIONS
(Pathé, April 10, 1927) 10 Chapters
Allene Ray, Walter Miller, E. H. Calvert, Frank Lackteen, William N. Bailey, John J. Richardson, Bob Burns, Ernie Adams, John Cossar, William Van Dyke, Richard C. Travers, Ann Gladman, Eugenia Gilbert, Albert Roccardi, George Kuwa
Director: Spencer G. Bennet
Story: Joseph Anthony Roach
Chapters: (1) A Shot in the Dark (2) Perilous Waters (3) The Fatal Attack (4) The Heiress of Craghaven (5) The Hidden Harbor (6) Strange Voyage (7) The Mysterious Prisoner (8) The Imposter (9) The Spy (10) Exposed

HAWK OF THE HILLS
(Pathé, August 28, 1927) 10 Chapters.
Allene Ray, Walter Miller, Frank Lackteen, Paul Panzer, Wally Oettel, Jack Pratt, Jack Ganzhorn, J. Parks Jones, Fred Dana, Evangeline Russell, George Magrill, Chief Whitehorse, Harry Semels, John T. Prince, Robert Chandler, Chief Yowlatchie
Director: Spencer G. Bennet
Story: George Arthur Gray
Chapters: (1) The Outlaws (2) In the Talons of the Hawk (3) Heroes in Blue (4) The Attack (5) The Danger Trail (6) The Death Menace of Lost Canyon (7) Demons of the Darkness (8) Doomed to the Arrows (9) The House of Horror (10) The Triumph of Law and Love
(A 5-reel feature version was released March 17, 1929)

Westward Bound (Syndicate, 1930) – Allene Ray and Buffalo Bill, Jr.

THE MAN WITHOUT A FACE
(Pathé, January 15, 1928) 10 Chapters.
Allene Ray, Walter Miller, E. H. Calvert, Sojin, Jeanette Loff, Gladden James, Kathleen Chambers, Richard R. Neill, Toshiye Schioka, Richard C. Travers
Director: Spencer G. Bennet
Screenplay: Joseph Anthony Roach
Story: C. N. and Alice M. Williamson
Chapters: (1) A Perilous Mission (2) The Barrage (3) The Death Shell (4) The Abuction (5) The Mark of Crime (6) The Road of Peril (7) The Master Strikes (8) The Crime Craft (9) A Mysterious Visitor (10) Unmasked

THE YELLOW CAMEO
(Pathé, June 3, 1928) 10 Chapters.
Allene Ray, Ed Hearn, "Cyclone" (a dog), Noble Johnson, Tom London, Maurice Klein, Ed Snyder, Frank Redman, Harry Semels, Frederick Dana, Walter Shumway
Director: Spencer G. Bennet
Screenplay: George Arthur Gray
Story: George Arthur Gray
Chapters: (1) The Train Robbery (2) The Mystery Man (3) The Race for Life (4) In the Path of Doom (5) The Signal Tower (6) The Tower of Death (7) The Fangs of Fury (8) The Devil's Cauldron (9) The Underworld Peril (10) The Lost Treasure

THE TERRIBLE PEOPLE
(Pathé, August 5, 1928) 10 Chapters.
Allene Ray, Walter Miller, Wilfred North, Fred Vroom, Tom Holding, Larry Steers, Mary Foy, Alice McCormack, Allen Craven, Joy Auburn
Director: Spencer G. Bennet
Screenplay: George Arthur Gray
Story: Edgar Wallace
Chapters: (1) The Penalty (2) Disaster (3) The Claws of Death (4) Hidden Enemies (5) The Disastrous Rescue (6) The House of Peril (7) In the Enemy's Hands (8) The Dread Professor (9) The Death Trap (10 The Capture

THE BLACK BOOK
(Pathé, July 21, 1929) 10 Chapters.
Allene Ray, Walter Miller, Frank Lackteen, Paul Panzer, Marie Mosquini, Edith London, Willie Fung, Edward Cecil, John Webb Dillon, Evan Pearson, Clay de Roy, Fred Malatesta, Floyd Adams, Olga Vamma, Jock Fraser
Directors: Spencer G. Bennet, Thomas L. Storey
Screenplay: Joseph Anthony Roach
Chapters: (1) The Secret of the Vault (2) The Death Rail (3) A Shot in the Night (4) The Danger Sign (5) The Flaming Trap (6) The Black Dam (7) The Fatal Hour (8) The Mystery Mill (9) The Assassin Strikes (10) Out of the Shadows

OVERLAND BOUND
(Presidio/Raytone, April 15, 1930) 6 Reels
Leo Maloney, *Allene Ray*, Jack Perrin, Lydia Knott, Wally Wales, Charles K. French, R. J. Smith, William J. Dyer, "Bullet," "Starlight"
Director: Leo Maloney
Screenplay: Ford I. Beebe
Story: Ford I. Beebe, Joseph Kane
Producer: Leo Maloney

THE INDIANS ARE COMING
(Universal, October 20, 1930) 13 Chapters.
Tim McCoy, *Allene Ray*, Edmund Cobb, Francis Ford, Wilbur McGough, Bud Osborne, Charles Roy, Don Francis, "Dynamite" (a dog), Bob Reeves, Jim Corey, Dick Hatton, Lafe McKee
Director: Henry McRae
Screenplay: Ford Beebe, George Plympton
Story: William F. Cody, "The Great West That Was"
Producer: Henry McRae
Chapters: (1) Pals in Buckskin (2) A Call to Arms (3) A Furnace of Fear (4) The Red Terror (5) The Circle of Death (6) Hate's Harvest (7) Hostages of Fear (8) The Dagger Duel (9) The Blast of Death (10) Redskin's Vengeance (11) Frontiers Aflame (12) The Trail's End

WESTWARD BOUND
(Webb-Douglas/Syndicate, December 1, 1930) 6 Reels
Jay Wilsey (Buffalo Bill Jr.), *Allene Ray*, Buddy Roosevelt, Fern Emmett, Ben Corbett, Yakima Canutt, Tom London, Robert Walker, Pete Morrison, Henry Rocquemore, Wally Wales
Director: Harry S. Webb
Screenplay: Carl Krusada
Story: Carl Krusada

GUN CARGO
(Film Favorites, circa 1949)
Rex Lease, *Allene Ray*, William Farnum, Robert Frazer, John Ince, Gibson Gowland, Rondo Hatton, Don Azpiazu and His Havana Casino Orchestra (via stock footage from 1930's **Hell Harbor**), Smith Ballew
Director/Producer: Jack Irwin
(Note: Film also known as **Contraband Cargo**. The movie was begun in 1934 and never finished. In 1939 new scenes were added but apparently the finished product got little or no release. A decade later Film Favorites picked it up for television. The author does not know if Smith Ballew actually appears in the film of if he is merely credited to the film due to his singing on the soundtrack.)

Jean Rogers

16 • JEAN ROGERS

DIED 2-24-91

Multiple Attractions Combined to Make Her the Queen of the Serial World in the Late Thirties

Mark Lamberti, a Rogers biographer, wrote about Jean: "There is an appeal that is not the mystique of legend, nor the grace of an impeccable image on photographic film. There exists that appeal of a sensual nature, the pretty, blonde, girl next door, the American beauty of which dreams are made. Jean Rogers posesses that certain beauty."

Of all the roles played by this comely girl, fans remember best her portrayal of the enchanting Dale Arden in two of the most profitable and popular sound serials ever produced. Jean Rogers had charisma before the word was in vogue. As a boy, this writer was one of many fans who had no trouble imagining himself on a South Sea island beach with her, or carrying her down a mountainside in a blizzard to win her undying gratitude.

Jean Rogers was born Eleanor Lovegren in Belmont, Massachussets, on March 25, 1916, and educated in the public schools of that city. As a child she had exhibited a rare natural aptitude for drawing, and it had been her hope to study art in New York and perhaps abroad. Her artistic talents ran to oil painting, music, and charcoal sketching. When she graduated from Belmont High School and won a national beauty contest conducted by Charles R. Rogers, later a Universal executive in charge of production, she changed her plans for attending college.

Just before winning the contest, Jean was serving sodas in a little ice cream place in Belmont. She had not considered an acting career before the day she and her mother took a boat ride to visit friends at Nantasket, and as they disembarked she was picked out of the crowd by a man representing the Paramount beauty contest. Every day the man chose the most beautiful girl aboard the vessel as an entrant in the contest. When the boat neared Boston Harbor, he saw Jean standing gracefully against the forward rail and knew instantly that his work was over for the day.

At first Jean and her mother were reluctant to embark on such an adventure, but the scout was persuasive. The next day, more for the fun of the thing than from any real desire for a Hollywood career, Jean found herself competing for divisional honors. The contest was conducted by Charles Rogers as a way of getting new talent for his production, **Eight Girls in a Boat** (1933). Jean won the divisional honors and went to Boston to compete in the New England finals at the Metropolitan Theatre. After days of eliminations Jean was chosen as the outstanding beauty. She won first place from a group of forty-five candidates, and in July of 1933 found herself en route to Hollywood, chaperoned, of course, by her mother, Mrs. Ellen Lovegren.

They found that they liked the climate, the people, the freedom of expression in California. Upon completion of **Eight Girls in a Boat**, Jean and Mrs. Lovegren decided they'd stay in Hollywood. The vibrant young beauty had no illusions about overnight stardom. With intense earnestness, she set to work molding her career as an actress. Warner Bros. signed her to a contract, and during the following year she got a lot of dramatic schooling but no screen roles. Offered a second contract by the studio, Jean asked for her release and in May 1935 signed with Universal, which was looking for a young ingenue for the lead in **Stormy** (1935). Jean got the part without a test. However, she was put first into **Manhattan Moon** (1935) to gain experience. Asked to pick a name for herself, she thought of a young friend named Jean from her home town and of Charles Rogers, who had brought her to California--thus Jean Rogers.

It is her six serials for Universal for which she is best known and which established her as the

Flash Gordon (Universal, 1936) – Jean Rogers and Buster Crabbe in the most popular of all sound serials.

Ace Drummond (Universal, 1936) – Jean Rogers and Jackie Morrow.

reigning queen of serials in the 1935-40 era, taking over from Lucile Browne who had made her last chapter play in 1934.

Jean was a radiant lead in **Tailspin Tommy in the Great Air Mystery** (1935). Film patrons of the day got a reasonable number of thrills from watching Clark Williams (as Tailspin Tommy), Noah Beery, Jr. (as Skeeter), and Jean (as Betty Lou) in this old-fashioned aeroplane adventure. The ingredients included a mystery plane camouflaged to suggest a great eagle, roaring volcanos, dirigibles, jungle fortresses, wild animals, and cannibals. Jean had taken over the role of Betty Lou from Patricia Farr, and Clark Williams had succeeded Maurice Murphy, both changes making for a better serial than its predecessor.

The Adventures of Frank Merriwell (1936) evolved from the magazine series that ran for nearly twenty years. It's all a mixture of college athletics and a treasure hunt hampered by much villainy. As Elsie Belwood, Jean is about the best thing in the film, though John King and Don Briggs do their best.

It was **Flash Gordon** (1936) that zoomed Jean into almost instant world-wide popularity and, as history has shown, gave her screen immortality. Up to that time there had never been a serial like **Flash Gordon.** It was pure fantasy, pure escapist film fare. Sophisticates might curl a supercilious lip at the childishness of the Alex Raymond characters brought to life by the scenarists, yet it was just what the doctor ordered, evidently, for a Depression-weary public.

The role of Dale Arden was not really challenging, as Jean usually had only such lines as "Flash, look out!" and "Ooohh, Flash!" Her wardrobe was on the skimpy side; in fact, she sometimes showed enough cleavage to tempt male viewers to watch her exclusively and to let Buster Crabbe go it alone. She was not, and made no attempt to be, a siren, and was all the more appealing for it. Ming, the Merciless stalked her and so did King Vultan, as described by Raymond Stedman in his book The Serials:

Moments after the earth girl is brought to him as a prisoner, Vultan (John Lipson) begins his game by using a pet bear to terrify his prey and force her, trembling, against a wall. Then, ridding the chamber of pets and underlings, he closes in on the nearly hysterical damsel for what clearly is not the kill. The focus at the end of this chapter is not upon the more serious concurrent action--Flash's rocket, about to be blasted from the sky by one of Vultan's ray guns--but upon the predicament of Dale Arden, her slender form pressed against the wall, her midriff sucked in till it will go no farther, her bosom thrust forward to the limit of its dimensions. Shots of the approaching rocket intercut this sequence, each shift to the menaced maiden showing her breathing deeper, ever deeper, until, with Vultan only a few steps away, the closing titles suspend her agony for another week.

Ace Drummond (1936), based on the newspaper character created by Captain Eddie Rickenbacker, featured John King, Jean Rogers, and Noah Beery, Jr. as the principals, a mystery figure known as The Dragon, a sinister Russian gang, a Buddhist temple where strange things happen, mysterious electrical wizardry, and numerous aerial battles, and the result almost had to be a great serial. As Ace Drummond, John King is out to help Peggy Trainor (Jean Rogers) find her lost father, discover the location of a mountain of jade in Mongolia, and capture the mysterious Dragon who wants to stop construction of the Mongolian link necessary to establish a globe-circling airplane service.

In **Secret Agent X-9** (1937) Jean suffered the fate of many cliffhanger heroines. Because of the overshadowing hero roles, women in these films usually didn't get a chance to be anything but "up-gazers" while the big boys emoted. The plot of this serial has Secret Agent X-9 (Scott Kolk) assigned to track down the stolen Belgravian crown jewels. Rogers is Shara Graustark, for whom X-9 risks life and limb for twelve chapters.

Flash Gordon's Trip to Mars (1938) reunited most of the principals from **Flash Gordon** in a sequel many believe to be better than the first film, though made for half as much money. This time Jean was allowed to keep her natural hair coloring (light brunette) rather than appearing as a blonde, as she had in her previous outings. Jean came through in the tight places and romanced in a very understated way, earning another feather in her popularity cap while Universal scored with a box-office winner.

Jean did not appear in the third entry of the Flash Gordon trilogy made in 1940. By that time she had gotten out of her Universal contract and had gone to 20th Century-Fox. In a way, it is unfortunate that she did not work longer at Universal. Certainly she would have repeated her role as Dale Arden in the third and final Flash Gordon serial, **Flash Gordon Conquers the Universe** (1940). Since the Laemmles (Universal's bosses) wanted to keep her as their main serial heroine, she would probably have been cast in two or three others as well, clinching the title "Queen of the Sound Serials." As it is, that honor is split and shared by Jean, Lucile Browne, and Linda Stirling, with Aline Towne, Phyllis Coates, Dorothy Gulliver, and Kay Aldridge trailing as runners-up.

Though Jean was cast in features at Universal, she got the female lead only in "B" films, never in the "A" productions. Her first co-starring role in a feature film was **Stormy** (1935), a horse story with Noah Beery, Jr. as male lead. In **Conflict** (1936) she is a newspaper woman responsible for the reformation of a fighter, played by John Wayne. She was good as the daughter of Boris Karloff in **Night Key** (1937) and made competent programmers with James Dunn, Scott Kolk, William Gargan, and others. But she felt that if she stayed at Universal she would be kept in the serials and programmers indefinitely. And the studio would not raise her salary. She believed that she had enough talent and experience to move into bigger features, so she left.

She was playing in a radio soap opera for Ponds Products when her agent got her a contract at Fox. There she appeared as leading lady in more good programmers--**Inside Story** (1939), **Elsa Maxwell's Hotel for Women** (1939), **Stop, Look and Love** (1939), **Heaven with a Barbed Wire Fence** (1939), **The Man Who Wouldn't Talk** (1940), **Charlie Chan in Panama** (1940), **Viva Cisco Kid** (1940), **Yesterday's Heroes** (1940), and **Let's Make Music** (1941), the latter on loan-out to RKO. In her only "A" film, she had a minor but good role as Dean Jagger's second wife in **Brigham Young** (1940).

Jean left Fox in 1941 for the same reasons she had left Universal. She wanted a better salary and better films. She signed with Metro-Goldwyn-Mayer and got the Metro buildup and better parts.

While at 20th Century-Fox she had met Dan Winkler, Myron Selznick's assistant, and they were married but then divorced around 1942. Louis Mayer was gradually building her into a star, but when her contract came up for renewal in 1943 he insisted that her work had to have priority over her private life. Jean and Dan were planning to remarry and Mayer forbade it. She had to decide what was most important to her--stardom at M-G-M or marriage. She opted for a family life, and she and Winkler married for the second time. She did not make a film in 1944, but gave birth to

Jean Rogers and author Buck Rainey (August, 1977).

her daughter Ellen. In 1945 she made a single film, **Rough, Tough, and Ready**, with Chester Morris. In 1946 she played the female lead in a trio of films--one each for Monogram, Paramount, and Republic. In 1947 she starred in **Back Lash** for 20th Century-Fox; in 1948 she had the lead in **Speed to Spare** for Paramount and **Fighting Back** for 20th Century-Fox. Her last screen appearance was in a supporting role in **The Second Woman** (1951), just for the fun of it. By this time she was too engrossed in her family to think much about her movie career. Her mother had a long illness (she died in 1954) and Jean spent much time taking care of her as well as raising her young daughter.

By 1960 the Winklers had decided to separate. There was no divorce and no ill will. When Dan became too sick to drive himself to work, Jean became his Girl Friday. When his condition worsened he entered the Motion Picture Country Hospital. It was there that he died in early 1970.

For several years Jean worked as a journalist and thoroughly enjoyed it. She has kept up her painting and sells many of her sketches. Her fans have rediscovered her, and she has appeared at several film conventions during the last few years, much to the delight of those young enough in heart to remember their Saturdays with Jean Rogers so long ago. The romance still flourishes, though all participants, and the fantasy itself, are etched with the lines of the passing decades. Today Jean is in poor health as the result of three strokes she has suffered, but she bravely holds her chin high and faces life one day at a time, thankful for the Lord's many blessings.

JEAN ROGERS Filmography

EIGHT GIRLS IN A BOAT
(Paramount, January 5, 1933) 85 Mins.
Dorothy Wilson, Douglas Montgomery, Kay Johnson, Barbara Barondess, Ferike Boros, Walter Connolly, James Bush, Colin Campbell, Peggy Montgomery, Margaret Marquis, Marjorie Cavlier, Virginia Hall, Kay Hammond, *Jean Rogers*
Director: Richard Wallace
Screenplay: Lewis Foster, Casey Robinson
Story: Helmut Brandis

MANHATTAN MOON
(Universal, July 1935) 67 Mins.
Ricardo Cortez, Dorothy Page, Henry Mollinson, Hugh O'Connell, Luis Alberni, Henry Armetta, Regis Toomey, *Jean Rogers*, L'Estrange Millman, Irving Bacon
Director: Stuart Walker
Screenplay: Barry Trivers, Ben Kohn
Adaptation: Aben Kandel
Story: Robert Harris
Producer: Stanley Bergerman

STORMY
(Universal, October 22, 1935) 67 Mins.
Noah Beery, Jr., *Jean Rogers*, J. Farrell MacDonald, Raymond Hatton, Walter Miller, Fred Kohler, Sr., James Burtis, Charles Hunter, I. F. Costello, Curtis McPeters (Cactus Mack). Cal Short, John Jackson, Glenn Strange, Johnny Luther, Bud Osborne, Ken Cooper, James Phillips, Jack Saunders, Cecil Kellogg, Jack Shannon, Robert Homans, Wilfred Lucas, Sam McDaniel, Edmund Cobb, Charles Murphy, James Welch, Shirley Marks, Chester Gan, William Welsh, Jack Leonard, Monte Montague, W. H. Davis, Rex, the Wonder Horse
Director: Louis Freidlander (Lew Landers)
Screenplay: George Plympton, Ben Kohn
Stormy: Cherry Wilson, "Stormy"
Associate Producer: Henry McRae

TAILSPIN TOMMY IN THE GREAT AIR MYSTERY
(Universal, October 1935) 12 Chapters.
Clark Williams, Noah Beery, Jr., *Jean Rogers*, Delphine Drew, Bryant Washburn, Pat O'Brien, Helen Brown, Matthew Betz, William Desmond, Manuel Peris, Frank Mayo, Pablo Alvarez, Herbert Heywood, Charles Browne, Paul Ellis, James Burtis, Manuel Lopez, Lew Kelly
Director: Ray Taylor
Screenplay: Ray Cannon, Ella O'Neill, Basil Dickey, Robert Herschon, George Plympton
Story: Based on the comic strip by Hal Forrest
Associate Producer: Henry McRae
Chapters: (1) Wreck of the Dirigible (2) Roaring Fire God (3) Hurled From the Skies (4) Bolt from the Blue (5) The Torrent (6) Crash in the Clouds (7) Flying Death (8) Crossed and Double Crossed (9) Wings of Disaster (10) Doomed in a Dungeon (11) Desperate Chances (12) The Last Stand

FIGHTING YOUTH
(Universal, November 1935) 85 Mins.
Charles Farrell, June Martel, Andy Devine, J. Farrell MacDonald, Ann Sheridan, Eddie Nugent, Herman Bing, Phyllis Fraser, Alden Chase, Glenn Boles, Murray Kinnell, David Worth, Charles Wilson, Walter Johnson, *Jean Rogers*, Clara Kimball Young, Del Henderson
Director: Hamilton McFadden
Screenplay: Henry Johnson, Florabel Muir, Hamilton McFadden
Story: Stanley Meyer

ADVENTURES OF FRANK MERRIWELL
(Universal, January 13, 1936) 12 Chaps.
Don Briggs, *Jean Rogers*, John King, Carla Laemmle, Sumner Getchell, Wallace Reid, Jr., House Peters, Jr., Peter Gowland, Allan Herscholt, Bryant Washburn, Jr., Carlyle Blackwell, Jr., Edward Arnold, Jr., Hershell Mayall, Jr., Dickie Jones, Bentley Hewitt, Alan Bridge, Bert Young, Monte Montague, Edmund Cobb, Bud Osborne, Dick Wessell, Slim Whitaker, William Desmond, Dick Cramer, Mike Frankovitch, Nick Lucats, Walter Law, Den Corbett, Hank Bell, Robert Walker, Sam McDaniels, Yancey (Bruce) Lane, Philo McCullough, Ella Ethridge, Isobell LaMal, Viola Callaghan, Fred Sumner, William Carleton, King Baggott, Joseph DeGrasse, Jack Donovan, Carlos Montalban, Jack Hall, William Franey, Chester Gann, Vic Allen, George Pines, William L. Thorne, John Irwin, Morgan Brown, Dave O'Brien, Rain-in-the-Face, Corkey (a dog)
Director: Cliff Smith
Screenplay: George Plympton, Maurice Geraphty, Ella O'Neill, Basil Dickey
Story: Based on the Novels by Bert L. Standish
Associate Producer: Henry McRae
Chapters: (1) College Hero (2) The Death Plunge (3) Death at the Cross Roads (4) Wreck of the Viking (5) Capsized in the Cataract (6) Descending Doom (7) Monster of the Deep (8) The Tragic Victory (9) Between Savage Foes (10) Imprisoned in a Dungeon (11) The Crash in the Chasm (12) The Winning Play

Tailspin Tommy in the Great Air Mystery (Universal, 1935) – Clark Williams and Jean Rogers.

DON'T GET PERSONAL
(Universal, February 12, 1936) 64 Mins.
James Dunn, Sally Eilers, Pinky Tomlin, Spencer Charters, Doris Lloyd, George Cleveland, Lillian Harmer, Charles Coleman, George Meeker, *Jean Rogers*, Lucille Lund
Director: William Nigh
Screenplay: George Waggner, Clarence Marks, Houston Branch
Story: William Thiele, Edmund Hartman
Producer: David Diamond

FLASH GORDON
(Universal, April 6, 1936) 13 Chapters.
Buster Crabbe, *Jean Rogers*, Charles Middleton, Priscilla Lawson, John Lipson, Dick Alexander, Frank Shannon, Duke York, Earl Askam, Theodore Lorch, James Pierce, Muriel Goodspeed, Richard Rucker, Lon Poff, Lane Chandler, Lynton Brent, Glenn Strange, George Cleveland, House Peters, Jr., William Desmond, Fred Kohler, Jr., Slim Whitaker, Al Ferguson, Bob Lewis, Reed Howes, Roy Barcroft, Constantine Romaninoff
Director: Frederick Stephani
Screenplay: Frederick Stephani, Ella O'Neill, George Plympton, Basil Dickey
Story: Based on the comic strip by Alex Raymond
Associate Producer: Henry McRae
Chapters: (1) The Planet of Peril (2) The Tunnel of Terror (3) Captured by the Shark Men (4) Battling the Sea Beast (5) The Destroying Ray (6) Flaming Torture (7) Shattering Doom (8) Tournament of Doom (9) Fighting the Fire Dragon (10) The Unseen Peril (11) In the Claws of the Tigron (12) Trapped in the Turret (13) Rocketing to Earth

MY MAN GODFREY
(Universal, September 6, 1936) 95 Mins.
William Powell, Carole Lombard, Alice Brady, Eugene Pallette, Gail Patrick, Alan Mowbray, Jean Dixon, Mischa Auer, Robert Light, Pat Flaherty, Robert Perry, Franklin Pangborn, Selmer Jackson, Ernie Adams, Phyllis Crane, *Jean Rogers*, Grady Sutton, Jack Chefe, Eddie Featherston, Edward Gargan, James Flavin, Art Singley, Reginald Mason, Jane Wyman, Bess Flowers
Director: Gregory LaCava
Screenplay: Morrie Ryskind, Eric Hatch, Gregory LaCava
Story: Eric Hatch
Producer: Gregory LaCava

TWO IN A CROWD
(Universal, September 13, 1936) 82 Mins.
Joan Bennett, Joel McCrea, Elisha Cook, Jr., Alison Skipworth, Reginald Denny, Henry Armetta, Andy Clyde, Nat Pendleton, Donald Meek, Bradley Page, Robert Murphy, Matt McHugh, *Jean Rogers*, Edward Gargan, Barbara Rogers, John Hamilton, Tyler Brooke, Douglas Wood, Milburn Stone, Frank Layton, Paul Porcasi, Joe Sawyer, Paul Fix, Eddie Anderson, Eddie Kane, Nena Quartero, Alan Matthews, James C. Morton, Eddie Chandler, Henry Otho, James Flavin, James Quinn, Billy Barrud, Diana Gibson, Evelyn Selbie, Winter Hall, Jerry Mandy, Johnnie Morries, Phyllis Crane
Director: Alfred E. Green
Screenplay: Lewis Foster, Doris Malloy, Earle Snell
Story: Lewis Foster
Producer: Charles R. Rogers

ACE DRUMMOND
(Universal, October 19, 1926) 13 Chaps.
John King, *Jean Rogers*, Noah Beery, Jr., Guy Bates Post, Arthur Loft, Chester Gan, Jackie Morrow, James B. Leong, James Eagle, Selmer Jackson, Robert Warwick, Montague Shaw, Frederick Vogeding, Al Bridge, Lon Chaney, Jr., Stanley Blystone, Ed Cobb, Richard Wessel, Louis Vinzinot, Sam Ash, Hooper Atchley, Edward Parker, Diana Gibson, Russell Wade, House Peters, Jr., Lew Hicks, Edward Peil, Sr.
Directors: Ford Beebe, Cliff Smith
Screenplay: Wyndham Gittens, Norman S. Hall, Ray Trampe
Story: Based on a character created by Captain Eddie Rickenbacker
Associate Producer: Henry MacRae
Chapters: (1) Where East Meets West (2) The Invisible Enemy (3) The Doorway of Doom (4) The Radio Riddle (5) Bullets of Sand (6) Evil Spirits (7) The Trackless Trail (8) The Sign in the Sky (9) Secret Service (10) The Mountain of Jade (11) The Dragon Commands (12) The Squadron of Death (13) The World's Akin

CONFLICT
(Universal, November 29, 1936) 60 Mins.
John Wayne, *Jean Rogers*, Tommy Bupp, Eddie Borden, Frank Sheridan, Ward Bond, Harry Woods, Bryant Washburn, Frank Hagney, Lloyd Ingraham, Margaret Mann
Director: David Howard
Screenplay: Charles A. Logue, Walter Weems
Story: Jack London, "The Abysmal Brute"
Producer: Trem Carr

MYSTERIOUS CROSSING
(Universal, December 27, 1936) 56 Mins.
James Dunn, Jean Rogers, John Eldredge, Any Devine, Hobart Cavanaugh, Herbert Rawlinson, J. Farrell MacDonald, Clarence Muse, James Flavin, Jonathan Hale
Director: Arthur Lubin
Screenplay: Jefferson Parker, John Grey
Story: Fred MacIsaacs
Associate Producer: Val Paul

SECRET AGENT X-9
(Universal, February 11, 1937) 12 Chapters.
Scott Kolk, Jean Rogers, Henry Hunter, David Oliver, Larry Blake, Monte Blue, Henry Brandon, Lon Chaney, Jr., Max Hoffman, Jr., Bentley Hewlett, George Shelley, Robert Dalton, Leonard Lord, Bob Kortman, Edward Peil, Sr., Lynn Gilbert, Jack Cheatham, Eddy Waller
Directors: Ford Beebe, Cliff Smith
Screenplay: Wyndham Gittens, Norman S. Hall, Ray Trampe, Leslie Swabacher
Story: Based on the newspaper feature by Charles Flanders and Leslie Charteris; character created by Dashiell Hammett
Associate Producer: Henry McRae
Chapters: (1) Modern Pirates (2) The Ray That Blinds (3) The Man of Many Faces (4) The Listening Shadow (5) False Fire (6) The Dragnet (7) Sealed Lips (8) Exhibit A (9) The Masquerader (10) The Forced Lie (11) The Enemy Camp (12) Crime Does Not Pay

WHEN LOVE IS YOUNG
(Universal, April 4, 1937) 76 Mins.
Virginia Bruce, Kent Taylor, Walter Brennan, *Jean Rogers*, Jack Smart, Franklin Pangborn, Sterling Holloway, Greta Meyer, Christian Rub, William Tannen, Mydia Westman, David Oliver, Laurie Douglas, Bryant Washburn, Jr., Nick Long, Jr.
Director: Hal Mohr
Screenplay: Eve Greene, Joseph Fields
Story: Eleanor Griffin, "Class Prophecy" in McCall's
Associate Producer: Robert Presnell

NIGHT KEY
(Universal, May 2, 1937) 67 Mins.
Boris Karloff, *Jean Rogers*, Warren Hull, Hobart Cavanaugh, Samuel S. Hinds, Alan Baxter, David Oliver, Edwin Maxwell, Ward Bond, Frank Hagney, Frank Reicher, Ethan Laidlaw, George Cleveland
Director: Lloyd Corrigan
Screenplay: Tristram Tupper, John C. Moffitt
Story: William Pierce
Associate Producer: Robert Presnell

FLASH GORDON'S TRIP TO MARS
(Universal, May 1938) 15 Chaps.
Buster Crabbe, *Jean Rogers*, Charles Middleton, Frank Shannon, Beatrice Roberts, C. Montague Shaw, Kane Richmond, Kenne Duncan, Wheeler Oakman, Donald Kerr, Richard Alexander, Lane Chandler, Ben Lewis, Jack Mulhall, Reed Howes, Warner Richmond, Anthony Warde, Edwin Stanley, Tom Steele, Eddie Parker, Herb Holcombe, Hooper Atchley, Jerry Frank, Stanley Price, James Eagles
Directors: Ford Beebe, Robert Hill
Screenplay: Ray Trampe, Norman S. Halland, Wyndham Gittens, Herbert Dalmas
Story: Based on the comic strip by Alex Raymond
Associate Producer: Barney Sarecky
Chapters: (1) New Worlds to Conquer (2) The Living Dead (3) Queen of Magic (4) Ancient Enemies (5) The Boomerang (6) Treeman of Mars (7) Prisoner of Monga (8) Black Sapphire of Kalu (9) Symbol of Death (10) Incense of Forgetfulness (11) Human Bait (12) Ming the Merciless (13) Mirage of Magic (14) Beasts at Bay (15) An Eye for an Eye

THE WILDCATTER
(Universal, June 13, 1937) 58 Mins.
Scott Colton, *Jean Rogers*, Jack Smart, Suzanne Kaaren, Russell Hicks, Ward Bond, Wallis Clark, Jack Powell
Director: Lewis D. Collins
Screenplay: Tom Van Dyke
Associate Producer: George Owen

REPORTED MISSING
(Universal, August 15, 1937) 63 Mins.
William Gargan, Jean Rogers, Dick Purcell, Hobart Cavanaugh, Michael Fitzsimmons, Joseph Sawyer, Billy Wayne, Robert Spencer
Director: Milton Carruth
Screenplay: Jerome Chodoroff, Joseph Fields
Story: Verne Whitehead, "Channel Crossing"
Associate Producer: Milton Carruth
Producer: E. M. Asher

TIME OUT FOR MURDER
(20th Century-Fox, September 23, 1938) 60 Mins.
Gloria Stuart, Michael Whalen, Chick Chandler, Douglas Fowley, Robert Kellard, Jane Darwell, *Jean Rogers*, June Gale, Ruth Hussey, Cliff Clark, Peter Lynn, Edward Marr, Lester Matthews
Director: H. Bruce Humberstone
Screenplay: Jerry Cady
Story: Irving Reis
Associate Producer: Howard J. Green
(Previewed as **Meridian 7-1212**)

ALWAYS IN TROUBLE
(20th Century-Fox, November 4, 1938) 70 Mins.
Jane Withers, *Jean Rogers*, Arthur Treacher, Robert Kellard, Eddie Collins, Andrew Tombes, Nana Bryant, Joan Woodbury, Joseph Sawyer, Charles Lane, Pat Flaherty
Director: Joseph Santley
Screenplay: Karen DeWolf, Robert Chapin
Story: Albert Treynor, Jeff Moffit, "Down To Earth"
Associate Producer: John Stone

MARS ATTACKS THE WORLD
(Universal, November 18, 1938) 70 Mins.
Feature release of **Flash Gordon's Trip To Mars**

INSIDE STORY
(20th Century-Fox, March 10, 1939) 60 Mins.
Michael Whalen, *Jean Rogers*, Chick Chandler, Douglas Fowley, John King, Jane Darwell, June Gale, Spencer Charters, Theodore von Eltz, Cliff Clark, Charles D. Brown, Charles Lamb, Jan Duggan, Louise Carter, Bert Roach
Director: Ricardo Cortez
Screenplay: Jerry Cady
Story: Ben Ames Williams
Associate Producer: Howard J. Green

ELSA MAXWELL'S HOTEL FOR WOMEN
(20th Century-Fox, August 14, 1939) 83 Mins.
Ann Sothern, Linda Darnell, James Ellison, *Jean Rogers*, Lynn Bari, June Gale, Joyce Compton, Elsa Maxwell, John Halliday, Katherine (Kay) Aldridge, Alan Dinehart, Sidney Blackmer, Mary Healy, Amanda Duff, Chick Chandler, Gregory Gaye, Charles Wilson, Herbert Ashley, Ivan Lebedeff, Helen Ericson, Dorothy Dearing, Barnett Parker, Lillian Porter, Frances Leslie, Ruth Terry, Kay Griffith, Irma Wilsen, Brewster Twins, Alice Armand, Kay Linaker, Claire Du Brey, Charles Trowbridge, Hal K. Dawson, Helen Brown
Director: Gregory Ratoff
Screenplay: Kathryn Scola, Darrell Ware
Story: Elsa Maxwell, Kathryn Scola
Associate Producer: Raymond Griffith
(A Cosmopolitan Production)

STOP, LOOK AND LOVE
(20th Century-Fox, September 22, 1939) 57 Mins.
Jean Rogers, William Frawley, Robert Kellard, Minna Gombell, Eddie Collins, Cora Sue Collins, Jay Ward, Roger McGee, Lillian Porter
Director: Otto Brower
Screenplay: Harold Tarshis, Sada Cowan
Story: Henry Delf
Producer: Sol M. Wurtzel

HEAVEN WITH A BARBED WIRE FENCE
(20th Century-Fox, November 3, 1939) 62 Mins.
Jean Rogers, Raymond Walburn, Marjorie Rambeau, Glenn Ford, Nicholas (Richard) Conte, Eddie Collins, Ward Bond, Irving Bacon, Kay Linaker
Director: Ricardo Cortez
Screenplay: Dalton Trumbo, Leonard Hoffman, Ben Grauman Kohn
Story: Dalton Trumbo
Producer: Sol M. Wurtzel

THE MAN WHO WOULDN'T TALK
(20th Century-Fox, February 2, 1940) 72 Mins.
Lloyd Nolan, *Jean Rogers*, Onslow Stevens, Eric Blore, Mae Marsh, Richard Clark, Joan Valerie, Paul Stanton, Douglas Wood, Irving Bacon, Lester Sharff, Harlan Briggs, Elizabeth Risdon, Renie Riano
Director: David Burton
Screenplay: Robert Ellis, Helen Logan, Lester Ziffren, Edward Ettinger
Story: Holworthy Hall, Robert M. Middlemass, "Dr. Valiant"
Producer: Sol M. Wurtzel

CHARLIE CHAN IN PANAMA
(20th Century-Fox, March 1, 1940) 67 Mins.
Sidney Toler, *Jean Rogers*, Lionel Atwill, Mary Nash, Sen Young, Kane Richmond, Chris-Pin Martin, Lionel Royce, Helen Ericson, Jack La Rue, Edwin Stanley, Don Douglas, Frank Puglia, Addison Richards, Edward Keane, Lane Chandler, Eddie Acuff, Ed Gargan, Jimmy Aubrey
Director: Norman Foster
Screenplay: John Larkin, Lester Ziffren
Producer: Sol M. Wurtzel

VIVA CISCO KID
(20th Century-Fox, April 12, 1940) 70 Mins.
(Cisco Kid Series)
Cesar Romero, *Jean Rogers*, Chris-Pin Martin, Minor Watson, Stanley Fields, Nigel de Brulier, Harold Goodwrn, Francis Ford, Charles Judels
Director: Norman Foster
Screenplay: Samuel G. Engel, Hal Long
Story: Based on the O. Henry character
Producer: Sol M. Wurtzel

YESTERDAY'S HEROES
(20th Century-Fox, September 20, 1940)
Jean Rogers, Robert Sterling, Ted North, Katherine Adlridge, Russell Gleason, Richard Lane, Edmund McDonald, George Irving, Emma Dunn, Harry Hayden, Isabel Randolph, Pierre Watkin, Frank Sully, Mike Frankovich, Don Forbes, Bert Roach, Matt McHugh, Truman Bradley, George Meeker
Director: Herbert I. Leeds
Screenplay: Irving Cummings, Jr., William Conselman, Jr.
Story: William Brent
Producer: Sol M. Wurtzel

BRIGHAM YOUNG--FRONTIERSMAN
(20th Century-Fox, Dec. 27, 1940) 114 Mins.
Tyrone Power, Linda Darnell, Dean Jagger, Brian Donlevy, John Carradine, Jane Darwell, *Jean Rogers*, Moroni Olson, Willard Robertson, Mary Astor, Vincent Price, Marc Lawrence, Dickie Jones, Stanley Andrews, Frank M. Thomas, Fuzzy Knight, Selmer Jackson, Frederick Burton, Russell Simpson, Arthur Aylesworth, Chief John Big Tree, Davison Clark, Claire DuBrey, Tully Marshall, Dick Rich, Joseph Dunn, Edwin Maxwell, Edmund McDonald, George Melford
Director: Henry Hathaway
Screenplay: Lamar Trotti
Story: Louis Bromfield
Associate Producer: Kenneth MacGowan

LET'S MAKE MUSIC
(RKO-Radio, January 17, 1941) 85 Mins.
Bob Crosby, *Jean Rogers*, Elizabeth Risdon, Joseph Buloff, Joyce Compton, Bennie Bartlett, Louis Jean Heydt, Bill Goodwin, Frank Orth, Grant Withers, Walter Tetley, Benny Rubin, Jacqueline Nash, Donna Jean Dolfer, Jimmy Conlin, Beryl Vaughn, Jean Matthews, Terry Belmont, Charles Trowbridge, Marilyn Wilkins, Renee Hall, Jane Patton, Eddie Miller, Max Herman, Happy LaMare, Bob Crosby's Orchestra, featuring The Bobcats
Director: Leslie Goodwins
Screenplay: Nathanael West, Charles E. Roberts
Story: Edward Dein
Producer: Howard Benedict

DESIGN FOR SCANDAL
(M-G-M, December 1941) 85 Mins.
Rosalind Russell, Walter Pidgeon, Edward Arnold, Lee Bowman, *Jean Rogers*, Mary Beth Hughes, Guy Kibbee, Barbara Jo Allen (Vera Vague), Leon Belasco, Bobby Larson, Charles Coleman, Thurston Hall
Director: Norman Taurog
Screenplay: Lionel Houser
Producer: John W. Considine, Jr.

DR. KILDARE'S VICTORY
(M-G-M, January, 1942) 92 Mins.
Lew Ayres, Lionel Barrymore, Robert Sterling, Ann Ayars, *Jean Rogers*, Alma Kruger, Walter Kingsford, Nell Craig, Edward Gargan, Marie Blake, Frank Orth, George H. Reed, Eddie Acuff, Barry Nelson, Kirby Grant, Gus Schilling, Stuart Crawford, William Bakewell, Charlotte Winters
Director: W. S. Van Dyke II
Screenplay: Harry Ruskin, Willis Goldbeck
Producer: Joseph Harrington

SUNDAY PUNCH
(M-G-M, May, 1942) 76 Mins.
William Lundigan, Jean Rogers, Dan Dailey, Jr., Guy Kibbee, J. Carrol Naish, Connie Gilchrist, Same Levene, Leo Gorcey, "Rags" Ragland, Douglas Newland, Anthony Caruso, Tito Renaldo, Michael Brown
Director: David Miller
Screenplay: Allen Rivkin, Fay and Michael Kanin
Story: Fay and Michael Kanin
Producer: Irving Starr

PACIFIC RENDEZVOUS
(M-G-M, June, 1942) 76 Mins.
Lee Bowman, *Jean Rogers,* Mona Maris, Carl Esmond, Paul Cavanagh, Blanche Yurka, Russell Hicks, Arthur Shields, William Post, Jr., William Tannen, Frederic Worlock, Curt Bois, Felix Basch, Addison Richards, Edward Fielding
Director: George Sideny
Screenplay: Harry Kurnitz, P. J. Wolfson, George Oppenheimer
Producer: B. F. Ziedman

THE WAR AGAINST MRS. HADLEY
(M-G-M, September 1942) 86 Mins.
Edward Arnold, Fay Bainter, Richard Ney, *Jean Rogers*, Sara Allgood, Spring Byington, Van Johnson, Isobel Elson, Frances Rafferty, Dorothy Morris, Halliwell Hobbes, Connie Gilchrist, Horace McNally, Miles Mander, "Rags" Ragland, Mark Daniels, Carl "Alfalfa" Switzer
Director: Harold S. Bucquet
Screenplay: George Oppenheimer
Producer: Irving Asher

A STRANGER IN TOWN
(M-G-M, April 1943) 67 Mins.
Frank Morgan, Richard Carlson, *Jean Rogers*, Port Hall, Robert Barrat, Donald MacBride, Walter Baldwin, Andrew Tombes, Olin Howlin, Chill Wills, Irving Bacon, Eddie Dunn, Gladys Blake, John Hodiak
Director: Roy Towland
Screenplay: Isobel Lennart, William Kozlenko
Producer: Robert Sisk

SWING SHIFT MAISIE
(M-G-M, October 1943) 87 Mins.
Ann Sothern, James Craig, *Jean Rogers*, Connie Gilchrist, John Qualen, Fred Brady, Marta Linden, Donald Curtis, Celia Travers, Pierre Watkins, Lillian Yarbo, Wiere Brothers, Pamela Blake, Jacqueline White, Betty Jaynes, Kay Medford, Katharine Booth, John Hodiak, Rose Hobart, Jack Mulhall, William Bishop, James Davis
Director: Norman McLeod
Screenplay: Mary McCall, Jr., Robert Halff
Producer: George Haight

WHISTLING IN BROOKLYN
(M-G-M, December 1943) 87 Mins.
Red Skelton, Ann Rutherford, *Jean Rogers*, "Rags" Ragland, Ray Collins, Henry O'Neill, William Frawley, Sam Levene, Arthur Space, Robert Emmett O'Connor, Steve Geray, Howard Freeman, Tom Dillon
Director: S. Sylvan Simon
Screenplay: Nat Perrin
Producer: George Haight

ROUGH, TOUGH AND READY
(Columbia, March 22, 1945) 66 Mins.
Chester Morris, Victor McLaglen, *Jean Rogers*, Veda Ann Borg, Amelita Ward, Robert Williams, John Tyrell, Fred Graff, Addison Richards, William Forrest, Tex Harding, Loren Tindal, Bob Meredith, Ida Moore, Blackie Whiteford
Director: Del Lord
Screenplay: Edward T. Love
Story: Edward T. Love
Producer: Alexis Thurn-Taxis

THE STRANGE MR. GREGORY
(Monogram, January 12, 1946) 63 Mins.
Edmund Lowe, *Jean Rogers*, Don Douglas, Frank Reicher, Marjorie Hoshelle, Robert Emmett Keane, Jonathan Hale, Frank Mayo, Fred Kelsey, Jack Norton, Anita Turner, Tom Leffingwell
Director: Phil Rosen
Screenplay: Charles S. Belden
Story: Myles Connolly
Producer: Louis Berkoff

GAY BLADES
(Republic, January 25, 1946) 67 Mins.
Allan Lane, *Jean Rogers*, Edward Ashley, Frank Albertson, Anne Gillis, Robert Armstrong, Paul Harvey, Ray Walker, Jonathan Hale, Russell Hicks, Emmett Vogan, Edward Gargan, Fredrick Young
Director: George Blair
Screenplay: Albert Reich, Marcel Klauber
Story: Jack Goodman, Albert Rice
Associate Producer: George Blair

HOT CARGO
(Paramount, June 28, 1946) 57 Mins.
William Gargan, *Jean Rogers*, Philip Reed, Larry Young, Harry Cording, Will Wright, Virginia Brissac, David Holt, Dick Elliott
Director: Lew Landers (Louis Friedlander)
Screenplay: Geoffrey Holmes
Producer: William H. Pine, William C. Thomas

BACK LASH
(20th Century-Fox, March 1947) 66 Mins.
Jean Rogers, Richard Travis, Larry Blake, John Eldredge, Leonard Strong, Robert Shayne, Louise Currie, Douglas Fowley, Sara Berner, Richard Benedict, Wynne Larke, Susan Klimist
Director: Eugene Ford
Screenplay: Irving Elman
Story: Irving Elman
Producer: Sol M. Wurtzel

SPEED TO SPARE
(Paramount, May 14, 1948) 57 Mins.
Richard Arlen, *Jean Rogers*, Richard Travis, Roscoe Karns, Nanette Parks, Pat Phelan, Ian MacDonald
Director: William Berke
Screenplay: Milton Raison
Producer: William H. Pine, William C. Thomas

FIGHTING BACK
(20th Century-Fox, August 1948) 61 Mins.
Paul Langton, *Jean Rogers*, Gary Gray, Joe Sawyer, Morris Nakrum, John Kellogg, Dorothy Christy, Tommy Ivo, Lela Tyler, Pierre Watkin, Daisy (a dog)
Director: Mal St. Clair
Screenplay: John Stone
Story: John Stone
Producer: Sol M. Wurtzel

THE SECOND WOMAN
(United Artists/Popkin, March 16, 1951) 91 Mins.
Robert Young, Betsy Drake, John Sutton, Henry O'Neill, Florance Bates, Morris Carnovsky, *Jean Rogers*, Raymond Largay, Shirley Ballard, Vici Raaf, John Gallaudet, Jason Robards, Sr., Steven Geray, Jimmy Dodd, Smokey Whitfield, Cliff Clark
Director: James V. Kern
Screenplay: Robert Smith
Producer: Mort Briskin

Ruth Roland

17 • RUTH ROLAND

Beautiful and Spontaneous, She Vied with Pearl White When Screams Were Silent

Ruth Roland was the second greatest of the silent serial queens and Pearl White's only real competitor, at least until Allene Ray came along in 1924. In many respects Ruth was a far more exciting performer than Pearl, and, unlike Pearl, she was at home in Westerns. Ruth relished making the mustangers with her horse Joker, which she rode through many dangers and more than once plunged toward what seemed inevitable disaster, only to be saved by Joker's cleverness and her own quick resources. She was a girl of the outdoor--an expert equestrienne, a strong swimmer, a crack shot with the rifle and revolver, and a steady winner in tennis and golf tournaments. These accomplishments served her well in her work as a sagebrush and serial heroine. At the same time, her screen personality was attractive to audiences, though those who worked with her might have entertained a different image.

Ruth was born in San Francisco on August 26, 1892. Her mother was a professional singer and her father operated the Columbia Theatre. At the age of three-and-a-half, Ruth "went on" in Edward Holden's Cinderella at her father's theatre. She was a hit with her treble rendition of the popular ditty, "What Could the Poor Girl Do?" From that night on Ruth was an actress.

After Cinderella had enjoyed a good run, Ruth (now firmly established as a child actress) was engaged to play Little Lord Fauntleroy in the children's classic. When her parents separated, Ruth toured the East under her mother's chaperonage, appearing in stock and vaudeville as "Baby Ruth." Later she worked with the Edward Holden Company and in vaudeville's "Broadway Trio." She had a stock engagement with the Morosco Company and was the first child actress to appear in Honolulu, making such a hit that she remained for six months, playing continuously. Then she went back to San Francisco for a long engagement with the famous Belasco Company at the Alcazar Theater. When her mother died at the age of twenty-seven, eight-year-old Ruth went to live with an aunt in Los Angeles and attended school there. At sixteen she returned to the theatre, now blossomed into an ingénue. Ruth then made a successful two-year tour in her own act on the Sullivan-Considine and Majestic vaudeville circuits.

One evening a director for the old Kalem Company, which specialized in Western epics, dropped into the theatre where Miss Roland was playing. "Ah," said he, "a perfect camera type." After the performance he went back to Ruth's dressing room and talked with her. Two weeks later she reported at the Kalem studios outside of Los Angeles and went to work in early 1909, leaving the stage "flat on the lot," as they say around the circus.

Ruth's initial salary at Kalem was twenty-five dollars a week, and her first film of record was **The Old Soldier's Story** (1909). During the next three or four years she is reputed to have made more than 200 split- and one-reelers for Kalem, but titles and dates on most of these films are unknown; consequently, they do not appear in her filmography. Many of her short films were Westerns, at which she was adept, but Kalem officials soon recognized her potential for humor, and she became the company's chief comedienne. When Mack Sennett tried to entice her away Ruth was able to get her Kalem salary raised to ninety-five dollars a week.

Miss Roland's beauty, enhanced by unusual deep violet eyes, was of the athletic type, and her humor was contagious. She made people laugh when they really didn't want to. She had an ebullient nature that found fun in everything. Consequently, even the most amusing scenarios of the films intended for her proved even funnier when the result was shown upon the screen.

Ruth tired of comedies, however, and longed to do more serious things; she pointed out to the Kalem brass that she was too highly paid to be wasted in pie-throwing slapstickers. She got her way. Shortly before leaving Kalem she starred in eight segments of <u>The Girl Detective</u> series, playing a society girl who has a position as a special investigator for the police. The situation is absurd, but the stories were audience pleasers.

In early 1915 Ruth Roland moved to Balboa Feature Film Company, which had a releasing arrangement with Pathé, thus ensuring wide distribution and promotion of its product. Ruth was soon at work in the <u>Who Pays?</u> series, with Henry King (who later became an outstanding director) playing opposite her and with Mollie McConnell featured. Each of the twelve three-reel dramas was a complete story ending with a question to the audience as to who was responsible for the dilemma in which the principals found themselves. In a way, the films were a forerunner of today's soap operas, and audiences enjoyed the "jury duty" imposed on them; the films were profitable.

Following a five-reel feature titled **Comrade John** (1915), Ruth made her first true serial, **The Red Circle** (1915), about a wealthy girl reformer cursed with a family taint that caused her to commit crimes against society--a sort of lady Jekyll and Hyde. Frank Mayo was the crime specialist who loved Ruth and solved the riddle of the red circle curse.

Balboa then put Ruth into several more features, followed by a role opposite Frank Mayo in a series called <u>Who Wins?</u> The studio hoped to cash in on the popularity of the <u>Who Pays?</u> series, but problems developed and the completed series was shelved. Two years later eight of the episodes were released as **The Price of Folly** (1918), and the remaining segments were scrapped.

The Neglected Wife (1917) was Ruth's next serial, but it did little to further her career. Its dearth of action and story were more typical of a society drama than of a serial thriller.

In May 1917, Ruth was married to Lionel T. Kent. After two months they separated, but Kent remained Ruth's business manager for some years. Ruth, in fact, had much business acumen of her own. She was a "lady Gene Autry" in that she was constantly wheeling and dealing. Beneath that smooth, well-groomed exterior, she knew more about stocks and bonds than almost anyone in Hollywood. Though her acting salary eventually rose to several thousand dollars a week, the fact that she retired a millionaire was due more to her business sagacity than to her powers or income as an actress. Her acting gave her the capital with which to operate, and she used it to an advantage that would shame most businessmen. She invested early in Hollywood real estate and rarely made a mistake. She had the courage to make quick decisions involving large sums of money. Unfortunately, unlike Autry, she was often temperamental on the set and is known to have made several serials without even speaking to her leading man or director except when absolutely necessary.

Switching from Balboa to Astra, a subsidiary of Pathé, Ruth made **Hands Up** (1918), the serial that put her on the road to immortality. There were thrills aplenty in this story of an Inca tribe which believed that Ruth, a newspaper woman, was their missing princess. In 1919 Miss Roland starred in two tremendously popular cliffhangers. For Astra she made **The Tiger's Trail**, probably her most popular serial, and for her own Ruth Roland Serials, Inc. releasing through Pathé, she made **The Adventures of Ruth**.

The Tiger's Trail was a quasi Western, adapted from what was originally a city melodrama by the skillful pen of Frank Leon Smith at the insistence of Astra president Louis Gasnier. The original story from which Gilson Willets made the screen adaptation was called "The Long Arm." Smith then changed Willets' scenario into one with a Western flavor. The story revolved around the attempts of Hindu tiger worshippers and Western outlaws to cheat our heroine of rich mines that rightfully belonged to her. **The Adventures of Ruth** dealt with Ruth's attempts to recover a "peacock fan" which hid a secret important to her. The story line followed out the instructions she received on each of thirteen keys handed to her by an unknown person, according to her father's deathbed instructions.

Ruth of the Rockies (1920) concerned a Broadway waitress who flees westward after finding a trunk full of diamonds unclaimed by a thief. George Marshall directed and Al Hoxie, unbilled, did stunting for Ruth and others in the serial, although Ruth usually used Bob Rose as her stuntman for dangerous sequences. It was all strictly business to Ruth. She saw no need to take a chance if there was no money in it.

In **The Avenging Arrow** (1921) Ruth dashes around southern California trying to solve the mystery of why all her female ancestors have been killed on their twenty-first birthday. She also made **White Eagle** and **The Timber Queen** in 1921 for Hal Roach, both serials released through Pathé. **White Eagle** was standard Western stuff with mysterious riders, deep, yawning canyons, and wild horsemen taking wilder falls, as opposing factions sought to gain control of an

Haunted Valley (Pathé, 1923) – Ruth Roland.

inexhaustible pool of molten gold. But **The Timber Queen** was an excellent cliffhanger with some superb action sequences created by director Fred Jackman. The runaway boxcar episode has remained a serial action classic.

Ruth of the Range (1923) was a mediocre effort about Ruth's attempts to free her father from a group that wished to steal his formula for making "Fuelite," a substitute for coal; the story was standard but the action was plentiful. Ruth had begun to be temperamental and unsuccessfully tried to get her leading man, Bruce Gordon, fired. She also had a falling out with W. S. Van Dyke, the director hired to get the serial going again when production bogged down due to director Ernest Warde's emphasis on close-ups of Ruth rather than action. Van Dyke finally quit to take another job. To compound problems, Gilson Willets, the scenarist, died during filming, leaving only sketchy notes as to what was to happen next in the story. Frank Leon Smith had to take over and create his own riddle around existing footage and characters. He wound up as director, and Ruth's stuntman, Bob Rose, had to put on a wig and double for her in the last two episodes because Ruth went on vacation!

She made one more serial, **Haunted Valley** (1923), co-starring with Jack Daugherty. Frank Leon Smith wrote the screenplay which had Ruth, the owner of Haunted Valley, borrowing a million dollars from the villain in order to finish a dam. The terms of the loan specified that if she couldn't pay it back in three months, the villain would get Ruth, Lost River Dam, and Haunted Valley.

Ruth chose not to renew her Pathé contract. Eleven serials were more than enough for her. Her real estate transactions had made her a millionaire, and she found almost as much satisfaction in being a business woman as in facing the cameras on Joker. So she sold more real estate, invested in various enterprises, made concert tours, and did a lot of vaudeville. She made a couple of

Ruth Roland

inconsequential features for Co-Artists Productions in 1925 and played a minor role in an Anna Q. Nilsson vehicle in 1927. In 1929 she married Ben Bard, a theatre owner, and it was a happy and lasting marriage.

When sound came to the movies Ruth could not resist the temptation to try a talkie; the result was **Reno** (1930), and the critics panned her "old-fashioned" acting. Ruth hit the road again in 1931 on a nine-month tour with Franchon and Marco in a revue called "Cozy Corner." In 1935 she journeyed to Canada to make her final film, **Nine to Nine**, for Coronet Pictures. A sloppily made film with poor sound reproduction, it got little exposure in the United States through the William Steiner setup.

On September 22, 1937, at the age of forty-four, Ruth Roland died of cancer in Hollywood. She had met an enemy from whom there was no escape. But sixty-five years after her last serial was made, her status as one of the greatest cliff-hanger heroines of all time is as solid as ever.

RUTH ROLAND Filmography

THE OLD SOLDIER'S STORY
(Kalem, February 1909) 825 Ft.
Jack Conway, *Ruth Roland*, Sidney Olcott
Director: Sidney Olcott
Screenplay: Sidney Olcott

THE CARDBOARD BABY
(Kalem, December 1909) 1 Reel
George Melford, *Ruth Roland*, Robert Vignola
Director: Sidney Olcott
Screenplay: Sidney Olcott

THE INDIAN SCOUT'S VENGEANCE
(Kalem, February 1910) 1 Reel
Ruth Roland, Jack Conway
Director: Sidney Olcott
Screenplay: Sidney Olcott

HER INDIAN MOTHER
(Kalem, December 1910) 1 Reel
Jack Conway, *Ruth Roland*
Director: Sidney Olcott
Screenplay: Sidney Olcott

ARIZONA BILL
(Kalem, September 1911) 1 Reel
Ruth Roland, Jack Conway
Directors: Robert Vignola, George Melford
Screenplay: George Meldord

THE ROMANCE OF A DRY TOWN
(Kalem, 1911) Split-reel
Ruth Roland, Marshall Neilan

HOW JIM PROPOSED
(Kalem, 1911) Split-Reel
Ruth Roland, Marshall Neilan

A CHANCE SHOT
(Kalem, 1911)
Ruth Roland
Director: Pat Hartigan

WAGES OF SIN
(Kalem, circa 1911)
Ruth Roland, Marshall Neilan

THE DESERT TRAIL
(Kalem, January 1912) 1 Reel
Ruth Roland

THE TRAIL OF GOLD
(Kalem, April 1912) 1 Reel
Ruth Roland

THE PASADENA PEACH
(Kalem, April 1912) 1 Reel
Ruth Roland, Marshall Neilan, John E. Brennan

HYPNOTIC NELL
(Kalem, May 1912) 1 Reel
Ruth Roland, Edward Coxen

THE BUGLER OF BATTERY B
(Kalem, July 1912) 1 Reel
George Melford, *Ruth Roland*, Jack Conway, Marshall Neilan, Miriam Cooper
Director: George Melford
Screenplay: Emmett Campbell Hall

THE SOLDIER BROTHERS OF SUSANNA
(Kalem, July 1912) 1 Reel
Guy Coombs, Anna Q. Nilsson, Alice Joyce, George Melford, Jack Conway, *Ruth Roland*, Miriam Cooper
Director: George Melford
Screenplay: Emmett Campbell Hall

THE BEAUTY PARLOR OF STONE GULCH
(Kalem, August 1912) 1 Reel
Ruth Roland

SAVED FROM COURT MARTIAL
(Kalem, August 1912) 1 Reel
Alice Joyce, George Melford, Anna Q. Nilsson, Guy Coombs, *Ruth Roland*, Miriam Cooper
Director: George Melford
Screenplay: Marshall Neilan

FAT BILL'S WOOING
(Kalem, September 1912)
John E. Brennan, *Ruth Roland*, Virginia Chester, O. M. Gore

QUEEN OF THE KITCHEN
(Kalem, September 1912)
Ruth Roland, John E. Brennan, Edward Coxen

A HOSPITAL HOAX
(Kalem, September 1912)
John E. Brennan, Herbert Glennon, Edward Coxen, *Ruth Roland*

THE BELLE OF THE BEACH
(Kalem, October 1912) 1 Reel
Ruth Roland, Edward Coxen

DEATH VALLEY SCOTTY'S MINE
(Kalem, October 1912) 1 Reel
Walter Scott, *Ruth Roland*, Marin Sais

I SAW HIM FIRST
(Kalem, November 1912)
Ruth Roland, Marin Sais, Edward Coxen

STRONG ARM NELLIE
(Kalem, November 1912) 1 Reel
Ruth Roland, John Brennan

THE LANDLUBBER
(Kalem, November 1912)
Ruth Roland, John E. Brennan, Robert Grey

THE CHAPERON GETS A DUCKLING
(Kalem, November 1912) 1 Reel
John E. Brennan, Ed Coxen, *Ruth Roland*, Marin Sais

PULQUE PETE AND THE OPERA TROUPE
(Kalem, December 1912)
John E. Brennan, *Ruth Roland*

A MOUNTAIN TRAGEDY
(Kalem, December 1912) 1 Reel
Ruth Roland, Marshall Neilan, P. C. Hartigan, Horace Peyton

THE MISSION OF A BULLET
(Kalem, December 1912) 1 Reel
Ruth Roland, Marshall Neilan, Gavin Young

THE PEACE OFFERING
(Kalem, December 1912) 1 Reel
Ruth Roland, Marshall Neilan, John Brennan, Anita Baldwin

SI'S WONDERFUL MINERAL SPRING
(Kalem, circa 1912) 1 Reel
Ruth Roland

AN ELOPEMENT IN ROME
(Kalem circa 1912) 1 Reel
Ruth Roland

RANCH GIRLS ON A RAMPAGE
(Kalem, circa 1912) 1 Reel
Ruth Roland

RUTH ROLAND, THE KALEM GIRL
(Kalem, 1912)
Ruth Roland

THE MANICURIST AND THE MUTT
(Kalem, January 1913) 1 Reel
Ruth Roland, John Brennan, Marshall Neilan, Lord McConickie, Robert Chandler, Horace Peyton

ONE ON WILLIE
(Kalem, January 1913) 1 Reel
Ruth Roland, John Brennan, Edward Coxen, Mr. Barry

THE HORSE THAT WOULDN'T STAY HITCHED
(Kalem, January 1913) 1 Reel
John Brennan, *Ruth Roland*

ABSENT MINDED ABE
(Kalem, March 1913) 1 Reel
John Brennan, *Ruth Roland*

JONES' JONAH DAY
(Kalem, March 1913) 1 Reel
John Brennan, *Ruth Roland*, Marshall Neilan

THE INDIAN MAID'S WARNING
(Kalem, March 1913) 1 Reel
Ruth Roland, P. C. Hartigan, V. Howard

THE FIRED COOK
(Kalem, March, 1913) 1 Reel
Ruth Roland, Marshall Neilan, John Brennan

THE INDESTRUCTIBLE MR. JENKS
(Kalem, April 1913) 1 Reel
Ruth Roland, John Brennan

THE PHONY SINGER
(Kalem, April 1913) 1 Reel
Ruth Roland, John Brennan, Marshall Neilan

A COUPON COURTSHIP
(Kalem, April 1913) 1 Reel
Ruth Roland, John Brennan, Jack McDermott, Marshall Neilan

THE HASH HOUSE COUNT
(Kalem, May 1913) 1 Reel
John Brennan, *Ruth Roland*, Marshall Neilan

THE BLACK HAND
(Kalem, May 1913) 1 Reel
John Brennan, Ruth Roland, Marshall Neilan

WHEN WOMEN ARE POLICE
(Kalem, June 1913) 1 Reel
Ruth Roland, Marshall Neilan, John Brennan

PERCY'S WOOING
(Kalem, June 1913) 1 Reel
Marshall Neilan, *Ruth Roland*, John Young, John Brennan

THE RAIDERS FROM DOUBLE L RANCH
(Kalem, June 1913) 1 Reel
Ruth Roland, Francis Newburg

ENTERTAINING UNCLE
(Kalem, July 1913) 1 Reel
John Brennan, *Ruth Roland*

THE TENDERFOOT'S LUCK
(Kalem, July 1913) 1 Reel
Ruth Roland, John Brennan, Marshall Neilan

HOODOOED ON HIS WEDDING DAY
(Kalem, July 1913) 1 Reel
Ruth Roland

THE HOBO AND THE MYTH
(Kalem, September 1913) 1 Reel
Ruth Roland, John Brennan

THE TROUBLESOME TELPHONE
(Kalem, October 1913) 1 Reel
Ruth Roland, John Brennan

THE SPEED LIMIT
(Kalem, October 1913) 1 Reel
John Brennan, *Ruth Roland*, Grover Larkin

HYPNOTIZING MAMIE
(Kalem, November 1913) 1 Reel
Ruth Roland, John Brennan

THE FICKLE FREAK
(Kalem, November 1913) 1 Reel
Ruth Roland, John Brennan, George Larkin

THE LAUNDRESS AND THE LADY
(Kalem, November 1913) 1 Reel
John Brennan, *Ruth Roland*

THE GOOD OLE SUMMER TIME
(Kalem, November 1913) 1 Reel
John Brennan, *Ruth Roland*

WHILE FATHER TELEPHONED
(Kalem, November 1913) 1 Reel
John Brennan, *Ruth Roland*, George Larkin
Director: Thomas H. Hunter
Screenplay: Thomas H. Hunter

GENERAL BUNKO'S VICTORY
(Kalem, December 1913) 1 Reel
John Brennan, *Ruth Roland*

BILL'S BOARD BILL
(Kalem, December 1913) 1 Reel
John Brennan, *Ruth Roland*

THE JOKE ON JANE
(Kalem, January 1914) 1 Reel
Ruth Roland, John Brennan

ONLY ONE SHIRT
(Kalem, January 1914) 1 Reel
Ruth Roland, John Brennan, Marshall Neilan

THE MEDICINE SHOW AT STONE GULCH
(Kalem, January 1914) 1 Reel
John Brennan, *Ruth Roland*

HIRAM'S HOTEL
(Kalem, February 1914) 1 Reel
John Brennan, *Ruth Roland*, Sylvia Ashton

THE FAMILY SKELETON
(Kalem, March 1914) 1 Reel
John Brennan, *Ruth Roland*

AND THE VILLAIN STILL PURSUED HER
(Kalem, March 1914) 1 Reel
John Brennan, *Ruth Roland*

THE CONFISCATED COUNT
(Kalem, March 1914) 1 Reel
George Larkin, *Ruth Roland*

HUBBY'S NIGHT OFF
(Kalem, April 1914) 1 Reel
Ruth Roland, John Brennan

GERTIE GETS THE CASH
(Kalem, April 1914) 1 Reel
Ruth Roland, Laura Oakley

MCBRIDE'S BRIDE
(Kalem, April 1914) 1 Reel
John Brennan, *Ruth Roland*, Marshal Neilan

TIGHT SHOES
(Kalem, May 1914) 1 Reel
Ruth Roland, John Brennan, Bennet A. Molter, Augustus Chandler

REAPING FOR THE WHIRLWIND
(Kalem, June 1914) 1 Reel
Ruth Roland, John Brennan

AN ELOPEMENT IN ROME
(Kalem, June 1914) 1 Reel
Ruth Roland, John Brennan
Director: Marshall Neilan

WANTED, AN HEIR
(Kalem, July 1914) 1 Reel
Ruth Roland, Marshall Neilan, John Brennan

THE DEADLY BATTLE AT HICKSVILLE
(Kalem, July 1914) 1 Reel
Ruth Roland, Marshall Neilan

DON'T MONKEY WITH THE BUZZSAW
(Kalem, July 1914) 1 Reel
Ruth Roland, Marshall Neilan, Lloyd Hamilton, Dud Duncan

A SUBSTITUTE FOR PANTS
(Kalem, August 1914) 1 Reel
Ruth Roland, Marshall Neilan

SHERLOCK BONEHEAD
(Kalem, August 1914) 1 Reel
Ruth Roland, Marshall Neilan, Lloyd Hamilton, Dick Rosson
Director: Marshall Neilan

WHEN MEN WEAR SKIRTS
(Kalem, August 1914) 1 Reel
Ruth Roland, Marshall Neilan

THE TATTERED DUKE
(Kalem, September 1914) 1 Reel
Ruth Roland, Marshall Neilan, Lloyd Hamilton, Bud Duncan

THE SLAVERY OF FOXICUS
(Kalem, September 1914) 1 Reel
Ruth Roland, Marshall Neilan
Story: Edwin Ray Coffin

SI'S WONDERFUL MINERAL SPRING
(Kalem, October 1914) 1 Reel
Ruth Roland, Lloyd Hamilton, F. Fralick, Bud Duncan

LIZZIE, THE LIFE SAVER
(Kalem, October 1914) 1 Reel
Ruth Roland, Lloyd Hamilton, Marshall Neilan
Director: Marshall Neilan

HAM, THE PIANO MOVER
(Kalem, November 1914) 1 Reel
Ruth Roland, Lloyd Hamilton, Bud Duncan
Director: Marshall Neilan
Screenplay: Marshall Neilan

THE PEACH AT THE BEACH
(Kalem, November 1914) 1 Reel
Ruth Roland, Lloyd Hamilton, Lucille Kellar, Bud Duncan, Chance Ward, Dick Rosson
Director: Marshall Neilan

BUD, BILL, AND THE WAITER
(Kalem, December 1914) 1 Reel
Ruth Roland, Lloyd Hamilton, Bud Duncan
Director: Marshall Neilan

A MODEL WIFE
(Kalem, January 26, 1915) 1/2 Reel
Ruth Roland
(This film on same reel with **Fatty's Echo**)

THE TIP-OFF
(Balboa, January, 1915) 3 Reels
Ruth Roland, William Elliott, Lew Cody
Director: T. Hayes Hunter
Screenplay: T. Hayes Hunter

AFFAIR OF THE DESERTED HOUSE
(Kalem, February 1915) 2 Reels
(The Girl Detective Series)
Ruth Roland, Thomas Lingham, Cleo Ridgely
Director: James W. Horne

SHE WOULD BE A COWBOY
(Kalem, February 1915) 1/2 Reel
Ruth Roland

THE APARTMENT HOUSE MYSTERY
(Kalem, February, 1915) 2 Reels
(The Girl Detective Series)
Ruth Roland, Thomas Lingham, Cleo Ridgely, William H. West
Director: James W. Horne

THE DISAPPEARANCE OF HARRY WORTHINGTON
(Kalem, February 1915) 2 Reels
(The Girl Detective Series)
Ruth Roland, Thomas Lingham, Cleo Ridgely
Director: James W. Horne

THE MYSTERY OF THE THÉ DANSANT
(Kalem, February 1915) 2 Reels
(The Girl Detective Series)
Ruth Roland, Thomas Lingham, Cleo Ridgely, Knute Rahmn, Anna Lingham, Edward Clisbee
Director: James W. Horne
Story: Hamilton Smith

FOLLOWING A CLUE
(Kalem, February 1915) 2 Reels
(The Girl Detective Series)
Ruth Roland, Thomas Lingham, Cleo Ridgely
Director: James W. Horne

OLD ISAACSON'S DIAMONDS
(Kalem, February 24, 1915) 2 Reels
(The Girl Detective Series)
Ruth Roland, Paul C. Hurst, Cleo Ridgely
Director: James W. Horne

JARED FAIRFAX'S MILLIONS
(Kalem, March 6, 1915) 2 Reels
(The Girl Detective Series)
Ruth Roland, Thomas Lingham, Cleo Ridgely, Robert Gray
Director: James W. Horne

THE PURSUIT OF PLEASURE
(Balboa, March 12, 1915) 3 Reels
(Who Pays? Series)
Ruth Roland, Mollie McConnell, Henry King, Daniel Gilfeather
Story: William Ritchie

THE PRICE OF FAME
(Balboa, March 21, 1915) 3 Reels
(Who Pays? Series)
Ruth Roland, Henry King, Mollie McConnell
Director: H. M. Horkheimer

WHEN JUSTICE SLEEPS
(Balboa, March 25, 1915) 3 Reels
(Who Pays? Series)
Ruth Roland, Mollie McConnell, Henry King

THE LOVE LIAR
(Balboa, April 13, 1915) 3 Reels
(Who Pays? Series)
Ruth Roland, Mollie McConnell, Henry King
Director: Harry Harvey
Screenplay: William Ritchie

UNTO HERSELF ALONE
(Balboa, April 13, 1915) 3 Reels
(Who Pays? Series)
Ruth Roland, Mollie McConnell, Henry King

HOUSES OF GLASS
(Balboa, May 1915) 3 Reels
(Who Pays? Series)
Ruth Roland, Mollie McConnell, Henry King

BLUE BLOOD AND YELLOW
(Balboa, May 1915) 3 Reels
(Who Pays? Series)
Ruth Roland, Mollie McConnell, Henry King

TODAY AND TOMORROW
(Balboa, June 1915) 3 Reels
(Who Pays? Series)
Ruth Roland, Henry King, Mollie McConell

FOR THE COMMONWEALTH
(Balboa, June 1915) 3 Reels
(Who Pays? Series)
Ruth Roland, Henry King, Mollie McConnell

THE POMP OF EARTH
(Balboa, June 1915) 3 Reels
(Who Pays? Series)
Ruth Roland, Henry King, Mollie McConnell

THE FRUIT OF FOLLY
(Balboa, June 1915) 3 Reels
(Who Pays? Series)
Ruth Roland, Mollie McConnell, Henry King, Daniel Gilfeather, Edward Brady

TOIL AND TYRANNY
(Balboa, July 1915) 3 Reels
(Who Pays? Series)
Ruth Roland, Mollie McConnell, Henry King

COMRADE JOHN
(Balboa, October 30, 1915} 5 Reels
William Elliott, *Ruth Roland*, Lew Cody
Director: T. Hayes Hunter
Screenplay: T. Hayes Hunter
Story: Samuel Merwin, Henry Ketchell Webster

THE RED CIRCLE
(Balboa/Pathé, December 16, 1915) 14 Chapters.
Ruth Roland, Frank Mayo, Philo McCullough, Gordon Sackville, Daniel Gilfeather, Edward Peters, Mollie McConnell, Corenne Grant, Myrtle Reeves, Makato Inokuchi, Lillian West, Frank Erlanger, Andrew Arbuckle
Director: Sherwood MacDonald
Screenplay: Will M. Ritchey, H.M. Horkheimer
Chapters: (1) Nevermore (2) Pity the Poor (3) Twenty Years Ago (4) In Strange Attire (5) Weapons of War (6) False Colors (7) Third Degree or Two Captives (8) Peace at Any Price (9) Dodging the Law (10) Excess Baggage (11) Seeds of Suspicion (12) Like a Rat in a Trap (13) Branded as a Thief [14] Judgment Day

A MATRIMONIAL MARTYR
(Balboa/Pathé, April 29, 1916) 5 Reels
Ruth Roland, Andrew Arbuckle, Daniel Gilfeather, Marguerite Nichols, Henry Gray

THE SULTANA
(Balboa/Pathé, October, 1916) 5 Reels
(Colored Sequences)
Ruth Roland, William Conklin, Charles Dudley, Frank Erlanger, Daniel Gilfeather, E. T. Peters, Edward J. Brady, Gordon Sackville, R. Henry Gray

SAN DIEGO EXPOSITION OF 1916
(1916) 5 Reels
Ruth Roland, Teddy Roosevelt, and other celebrities
(Special Documentary Feature)

THE DEVIL'S BAIT
(Balboa/Fortune Photoplays, April, 1917) 4 Reels
Ruth Roland, William Conklin, Edward J. Brady, Lucy Blake, Henry King, Myrtle Reeves, Gordon Sackville, Lucille Serwill, Zada Marlo, Charles Dudley
Director: Harry Harvey
Scenario: Will M. Ritchey
Supervisors: H. M. Harkheimer and E. D. Harkheimer

THE NEGLECTED WIFE
(Balboa/Pathé, May 13, 1917) 15 Chapters.
Ruth Roland, Roland Bottomley, Corene Grant, Neil Hardin, Philo McCullough, Mollie McConnell
Director: William Bertram
Screenplay: Joseph Dunn, Will M. Ritchey
Story: Mabel Herbert Hurne
Chapters: (1) The Woman Alone (2) The Weakening (3) In the Crucible (4) Beyond Recall (5) Under Suspicion (6) On the Precipice (7) The Message on the Mirror (8) A Relentless Fate (9) Deepening Degradation (10) A Veiled Intrigue (11) A Reckless Indiscretion (12) Embittered Love (13) Revolting Pride (14) Desperation (15) A Sacrifice Supreme

THE STOLEN PLAY
(Falcon Features/General, August 31, 1917) 4 Reels
Ruth Roland, William Conklin, Edward J. Brady, Lucy Blacke, Harry Southard, Ruth Lackeye, Makato Inokuchi
Director: Harry Harvey
Screenplay: H. M. Harkheimer, E. D. Harkheimer
Story: D. F. Whitcomb

THE FRINGE OF SOCIETY
(George Backer/Pathé, 1917)
Ruth Roland, Milton Sills, Leah Baird, J. Herbert Frank, Ollie Kirby, George Larkin, Tammany Young, Jules Cowles, Jack Crane, Ricardo Cortez
Director: Robert Ellis
Screenplay: Pierre V. R. Key
Story: Pierre V. R. Key

A MESSAGE FROM RENO
(Balboa/Pathé, 1917)
Ruth Roland

THE PRICE OF FOLLY
(Pathé, March 1918) 8 Chapters.
(Film also known as **Who Wins?** It was made in 1916 but not released until 1918, and then only in 8 chapters--remaining chapters were scrapped.)
Ruth Roland, Frank Mayo, Lafe McKee, Conrad K. Arnold, Bruce Smith, Jimsy Maye, Neal Hardin
Director: Henry King
Story: Will M. Ritchie
Chapters: (1) Phantom Fame (2) Counterfeit Clues (3) The Catspaw (4) title unknown (5) title unknown (6) In Poverty's Power (7) **The Rebound** (8) The Shifting Sands

HANDS UP
(Astra/Pathé, August 18, 1918) 15 Chapters.
Ruth Roland, George Chesebro, George Larkin, Easter Walters, William A. Carroll, George Gebhardt, William E. Lawrence, Thomas Jefferson, Monte Blue
Director: James W. Horne
Screenplay: Jack Cunningham
Story: Gilson Willets
Chapters: (1) Bride of the Sun (2) The Missing Prince (3) The Phantom and the Girl (4) The Phantom Trail (5) The Runaway Bride (6) Flames of Vengeance (7) Tossed into the Torrent (8) The Fatal Jewels (9) A Leap Through Space (10) The Sun Message (11) Stranger from the Sea (12 The Silver Book (13) The Last Warning (14) The Oracle's Decree (15) The Celestial Messenger

CUPID ANGLING
(Leon Douglass Natural Color Motion Picture Co., 1918)
Ruth Roland, Albert Morrison
Director: Louis W. Chauder
Story: Leon Forrest Douglass
Distributor: W. W. Hodkinson

LOVE AND THE LAW
(Sherry Service, March, 1919) 6 Reels
Ruth Roland, Glenn White, Josephine Hill
Director: Edgar Lewis
Story: William Hamilton Osborne - "The Troop Train"
Producer: Edgar Lewis

THE TIGER'S TRAIL
(Astra/Pathé, April 20, 1919) 15 Chapters.
Ruth Roland, George Larkin, Fred Kohler, Easter Walters, Harry G. Moody, George Field, Mark Strong, Bud Osborne, Chet Ryan, Mlle. Dion, Easter Walters
Director: Robert Ellis, Paul C. Hurst
Screenplay: Arthur B. Reeve, Charles A. Logue
Story: Gilson Willets
Chapters: (1) The Tiger Worshipers (2) Glowing Eyes (3) The Human Chain (4) Danger Signals (5) The Tiger Trap (6) The Secret Assassin (7) Flaming Waters (8) Danger Ahead (9) Raging Torrent (10) Bringing in the Law (11) In the Breakers (12) The Two Amazons (13) The False Idol (14) The Mountain Hermit (15) The Tiger Face

THE ADVENTURES OF RUTH
(Ruth Roland Serials/Pathé, December 28, 1919) 15 Chapters.
Ruth Roland, Herbert Heyes, Thomas Lingham, Charles Bennett, Helen Case, William Human, Helen Deliane, Charles Belcher
Director: George Marshall
Screenplay: Gilson Willets
Chapters: (1) The Wrong Countess (2) The Celestial Maiden (3) The Bewitching Spy (4) The Stolen Picture (5) The Bank Robbery (6) The Border Fury (7) The Substitute Messenger (8) The Harem Model (9) The Cellar Gangsters (10) The Forged Check (11) The Trap (12) The Vault of Terror (13) Within Hollow Walls (14) The Fighting Chance (15) The Key to Victory

RUTH OF THE ROCKIES
(Ruth Roland Serials/Pathé, August 29, 1920) 15 Chapters.
Ruth Roland, Herbert Heyes, Thomas Lingham, Fred Burns, Norma Bichole, William Gillis, Jack Rollens, Gilbert (Pee Wee) Holmes, Harry Maynard, Al Hoxie,* Captain S. J. Bingham
Director: George Marshall
Screenplay: Frances Guihan
Story: Johnston McCulley, "Broadway Bab"
Chapters: (1) The Mysterious Trunk (2) The Inner Circle (3) The Tower of Danger (4) Between Two Fires (5) Double Crossed (6) The Eagle's Nest (7) Troubled Waters (8) Danger Trails (9) The Perilous Path (10) Outlawed (11) The Fatal Diamond (12) The Secret Order (13) The Surprise Attack (14) The Secret of Regina Island (15) The Hidden Treasure
(*Hoxie doubled for Roland and others.)

THE AVENGING ARROW
(Ruth Roland Serials/Pathé, January 13, 1921) 15 Chapters.
Ruth Roland, Ed Hearn, Frank Lackteen, Virginia Ainsworth, Vera Sisson, Otto Lederer, S. E. Jennings, William Steele, Chief Big Tree, Robert Chandler
Directors: William J. Bowman, W. S. Van Dyke
Screenplay: Jack Cunningham
Story: Arthur Preston Haskins, "The Honeymoon Quest"
Chapters: (1) Vow of Mystery (2) The Enemy Strikes (3) The Hand of Treachery (4) A Life in Jeopardy (5) The Message Stone (6) The Midnight Attack (7) The Double Game (8) The Strange Pact (9) The Auction Block (10) Outwitted (11) Dangerous Waters (12) House of Treachery (13) On Perilous Grounds (14) Shifting Sands (15) The Toll of the Desert

WHITE EAGLE
(Hal Roach-Ruth Roland Serials/Pathé, January 1, 1922) 15 Chapters.
Ruth Roland, Earle Metcalfe, Otto Lederer, Harry Girard, Frank Lackteen, Virginia Ainsworth, Bud Osborne, Gertrude Douglas, Louise Emmons, Frank Valrose, Chick Morrison, Anita Nara
Directors: W. S. Van Dyke, Fred Jackman
Screenplay: Val Cleveland
Chapters: (1) The Sign of the Trident (2) The Red Men's Menace (3) A Strange Message (4) The Lost Trail (5) The Clash of the Clans (6) The Trap (7) The Mysterious Voyage (8) The Island of Terror (9) The Flaming Arrow (10) The Cave of Peril (11) Danger Rails (12) Win or Lose (13) Clash of the Clans (14) The Pivoted Rock (15) The Golden Pool

THE TIMBER QUEEN
(Ruth Roland Serials/Pathé, July 16, 1922) 15 Chapters.
Ruth Roland, Bruce Gordon, Val Paul, Leo Willis, Frank Lackteen, Bull Montana, Al Ferguson, Otto Freez, Chris Linton
Director: Fred Jackson
Screenplay: Bertram Millhauser
Story: Val Cleveland
Chapters: (1) The Log Jam (2) The Flaming Forest (3) Guilty as Charged (4) Go Get Your Man (5) The Yukon Trail (6) The Hidden Pearl (7) Mutiny (8) The Smuggler's Cave (9) Horned Fury (10) Human Vultures (11) The Runaway Engine (12) The Abyss (13) The Stolen Wedding (14) One Day to Go (15) The Silver Lining

HAUNTED VALLEY
(Ruth Roland Serials/Pathé, May 6, 1923) 15 Chapters.
Ruth Roland, Jack Daugherty, Larry Steers, Eulalie Jenson, Francis Ford, William Ryno, Edouard Trebeal, Aaron Edwards, Noble Johnson
Director: George Marshall
Screenplay: Frank Leon Smith
Chapters: (1) Bound to the Enemy (2) Adventure in the Valley (3) Imperiled at Sea (4) Into the Earthquake Abyss (5) Flight at Lost River Dam (6) Brink of Eternity (7) Midnight Raid (8) Radio Trap (9) Ordeal of Fire (10) The 100th Day (11) Called to Account (12) Double Peril (13) To Hazardous Heights (14) In Desperate Flight (15) Disputed Treasure

RUTH OF THE RANGE
(Ruth Roland Serials/ Pathé, October 14, 1923) 15 Chapters.
Ruth Roland, Bruce Gordon, Lorimer Johnston, Ernest C. Warde, Pat Harmon, Andre Peyre, Harry De Vere, V. Omar Whitehead
Director: Ernest C. Warde
Screenplay: Frank Leon Smith
Producer: M. C. Levee
Chapters: (1) The Last Shot (2) The Seething Pit (3) The Danger Trail (4) The Terror Trail (5) The Temple Dungeon (6) The Pitfall (7) The Fatal Count (8) The Dynamite Plot (9) The Lava Crusher (10) Circumstantial Evidence (11) The Desert of Death (12) The Vital Test (13) The Molten Menace (14) The First Freight (15) Promises Fulfilled

White Eagle (Pathé, 1922) – Ruth Roland.

DOLLAR DOWN
(Co-Artists Productions/Truart, September, 1925)
6 Reels
Ruth Roland, Henry B. Walthall, Maym Kelso, Earl Schenck, Claire McDowell, Roscoe Karns, Jane Mercer, Lloyd Whitlock, Otis Harlan, Edward Borman
Director: Tod Browning
Screenplay: Fred Stowers
Story: James Courthope

WHERE THE WORST BEGINS
(Co-Artists Productions/Truart, November, 1925)
6 Reels
Ruth Roland, Alec B. Francis, Matt Moore, Grace Darmond, Roy Stewart, Derelys Perdue, Theodore Lorch, Ernie Adams, J. P. Lockeny, Robert Burns, Floyd Shakelford
Director: John McDermott
Screenplay: Joseph Anthony Roach
Story: George Frank Worts, "Out Where the Worst Begins"

SCREEN SNAPSHOTS NO. 2
(Pathé, 1925) 10 Mins.
Viola Dana, Clarence Brown, Marshall Neilan, Blanche Sweet, Lloyd Hughes, Doug Fairbanks, Mary Pickford, Aileen Pringle, Dorothy Mackaill, Claire Windsor, Bert Lytell, Herb Rawlinson, *Ruth Roland*, Madge Bellamy, Bebe Daniels
Producer: Louis Lewyn

SCREEN SNAPSHOTS
(C.B.C., August, 1926) 1 Reel
Pauline Garon, Lowell Sherman, Billie Dove, George K. Arthur, William S. Hart, Estelle Taylor, *Ruth Roland*, Tom Mix, Leatrice Joy, Charles Chaplin, Norma Shearer, Elinor Glyn, Paul Bern, Pauline Starke

THE MASKED WOMAN
(First National, January 16, 1927) 6 Reels
Anna Q. Nilsson, Holbrook Blinn, Einar Hansen, Charlie Murray, Gertrude Short, Ruth Roland, Richard Pennell, Cora Macey, Paulette Day
Director: Silvano Balboni
Story: Charles Méré, "La Femme masquée, pièce en quatre actes"

RENO
(Sono-Art, October 1, 1930) 8 Reels
Ruth Roland, Montagu Love, Kenneth Thomson, Sam Hardy, Alyce McCormick,
Edward Hearn, Doris Lloyd, Judith Vosselli, Virginia Ainsworth, Beulah Monroe, Douglas Scott, Emmett King, Henry Hall, Gayne Whitman
Director: George J. Crone
Screenplay: June Mathis
Adaptation: Harry Chandlee, Douglas W. Churchill
Story: Cornelius Vanderbilt, Jr.

NINE TO NINE
(Coronet Pictures Ltd., 1935)
Ruth Roland, Roland Drew, Doris Covert, Miriam Batista, Kenneth Duncan, M. R. Byatt, Eugene Sigoloff
(Filmed in Canada)

Eileen Sedgwick

18 • EILEEN SEDGWICK

Always in the Path of Doom, She Survived to Reign as One of the Great Serial Queens

When Mollie Malone had to have an emergency appendectomy during the production of Universal's **Lure of the Circus** (1918), Eileen Sedgwick, who had then been a minor star with the company for three years, was called in to finish the film. The script was altered, and Eileen completed the last thirteen chapters (Mollie had done the first five). The male star was Eddie Polo, and the serial was tremendously popular. It was the beginning of a career that would take Eileen through twelve cliffhangers over a ten-year period.

Eileen was cool, blonde, lovely, and poised; her initial stardom was hardly surprising. She is thought to have entered films in late 1913 or early 1914, though the first credit the author has found for her is in 1915. She was born in Galveston, Texas, in 1897 and grew up there, along with her sister Josie and her brother Edward, who also went into the movie business. Her mother and dad were stage actors, and the family toured the vaudeville circuit as "The Five Sedgwicks."

She proved competent in early comedies at Universal, and also did well in Westerns with Neal Hart and Fred Church. After her success in **Lure of the Circus** (she had earlier made a two-reeler of the same title), she made a series of Cyclone Smith shorts with action ace Eddie Polo. In **The Great Radium Mystery** (1919) she was one of two heroines (the other being Cleo Madison) but then established herself as a serial star in her own right in **The Diamond Queen** (1921).

Eileen's most famous serial seems to be **The Riddle Rider** (1924), whereas her least known is **The Spider's Net** (1926), a non-copyrighted film made for an outfit called Tenneck and released through Goodwill Pictures. Six of her twelve serials were Westerns; one, a circus story; two, jungle adventures; and three, mysteries. Ten of the twelve films were made for Universal which guaranteed them a wide market and many bookings. Assuming that **The Spider's Net** was at least ten episodes, Eileen would have been in 194 serial episodes. That is about 399 reels, since first chapters were usually three reels in length. At ten to twelve minutes per reel, Eileen would have made close to eighty hours of episodic action thrills! At one chapter per week, it would take almost four years to see all of them. No wonder her face became familiar to serial aficionados of the silent era. Her serials, though, were interspersed with her own series of short Westerns and a few features, which gave her still greater recognition.

By 1928 Eileen apparently thought that she had gotten all the mileage she could out of her own name. She began using the name Greta Yoltz, possibly to avoid having casting directors recognize her name and write her off as simply a serial and Western heroine unsuitable for dramatic parts. As Greta Yoltz she made a few films, but when Nat Levine hired her for his all-star serial **The Vanishing West** (1928), she was billed under the more familiar name.

Eileen Sedgwick retired with the coming of sound to films. She had brought a few thrills, a few stimulating moments, to audiences of her own time and would soon be forgotten by the masses. She still lives today, as she has for many decades, in quiet retirement in the suburbs of Los Angeles, preferring not to talk about her movie career. But that career did exist, and Miss Sedgwick has to be considered one of the top serial heroines in the history of the genre.

EILEEN SEDGWICK Filmography

THE EAGLE'S NEST
(Lubin, March 27, 1915) 6 Reels
Edwin Arden, Romaine Fielding, Harry Kenneth, Clark Comstock, *Eileen Sedgwick*
Director: Edwin Arden
Story: Edwin Arden, Arden Smith, "The Eagle's Nest: A Story of the 70's"
Producer: Romaine Fielding

THE MYSTERIOUS CONTRAGRAV
(Universal-Gold Seal, March 27, 1915) 2 Reels
Eileen Sedgwick
Director: Henry MacRae
Story: Henry MacRae

HIRED, TIRED AND FIRED
(Universal-IMP, January 22, 1916)
Victor Potel, Jean Bernoudy, Edward Sedgwick, *Eileen Sedgwick*
Story: Jay Hunt

SOME HEROES
(Imp., February, 1916) 1/2 reel
Victor Potel, Ed Sedgwick, Jane Bernoudy, *Eileen Sedgwick*
Director: Roy Clements
Scenario: Roy Clements

I'LL GET HER YET
(Universal, February 18, 1916) 2 Reels
Pat Rooney, Dan Duffy, Marion Bent, Jane Bernoudy, Victor Poetel, Edward Sedgwick, *Eileen Sedgwick*
Story: Roy Clements
Producer: Roy Clements

AIN'T HE GRAND?
(Imp, March, 1916) 1 Reel
Ed Sedgwick, George Barnes, Victor Potel, Jane Bernoudy, *Eileen Sedgwick*
Director: Roy Clements
Scenario: Roy Clements

THE TOWN THAT TRIED TO COME BACK
(Imp., March, 1916) 1 Reel
Victor Potel, Ed Sedgwick, Jane Bernoudy, *Eileen Sedgwick*
Director: Roy Clements
Scenario: Roy Clements

KILL THE UMPIRE
(Nestor, July, 1916) 1 Reel
Eddie Lyons, *Eileen Sedgwick*, Lee Moran, Mina Cunard
Directors: Eddie Lyons and Lee Moran
Scenario: Ben Cohn

THE PLUMBERS WATERLOO
(Universal-Victor, October 27, 1916) 1 Reel
Eileen Sedgwick, Harry Depp, Ernie Shields, Andrew Arbuckle
Director: R. M. Donaldson
Story: Harry Depp

ROOM RENT AND ROMANCE
(Victor, October, 1916) 1 Reel
Victor Potel, Ed Sedgwick, *Eileen Sedgwick*, Jane Bernoudy
Director: Roy Clements
Scenario: Roy Clements

THE EMERALD PIN
(Universal-Laemmle, November, 1916) 2 Reels
Roberta Wilson, *Eileen Sedgwick*, Gretchen Lederer, Charles Perley, Louise Owen, Myrtle Gillette
Director: Burton George
Scenario: Maie Havey
Story: E. Magnus Ingleton

GIANT POWDER
(Universal-Bison, December 19, 1916) 2 Reels
Eileen Sedgwick
Director: Henry McRae
Story: Maxwell Ryder

IT'S GREAT TO BE MARRIED
(Universal-Victor, December 23, 1916) 1 Reel
Eileen Sedgwick, Louis Mayon, Fred Church
Director: Leslie T. Peacocke
Scenario: Leslie T. Peacocke

THE HONEYMOON SURPRISE
(Victor, January, 1917) 1 Reel
Fred Church, *Eileen Sedgwick*, Charles Perley, Claire Du Brey
Director: Leslie T. Peacocke
Scenario: Leslie T. Peacocke

IT'S CHEAPER TO BE MARRIED
(Victor, January, 1917) 1 Reel
Ralph McComas, Milton Sims, *Eileen Sedgwick*
Director: Allen Curtis
Scenario: W. Warren Schoene

THE HIGH COST OF STARVING
(Victor, January, 1917) 1 Reel
Eugene Walsh, *Eileen Sedgwick*, Al McKinnon, Dolly Ohnet
Director: Leslie T. Peacocke
Scenario: Maie Havey
Story: Leslie T. Peacocke

A BARE LIVING
(Victor, February, 1917) 1 Reel
Ralph McComas, *Eileen Sedgwick*, Milton Sims, Jack Connolly
Director: Allen Curtis
Scenario: W. Warren Schoene

GOOD MORNING NURSE
(Victor, February, 1917) 1 Reel
Eileen Sedgwick, Eugene Walsh, Ralph McComas, Margaret Whistler
Director: Allen Curtis
Scenario: Maie B. Havey
Story: Leslie T. Peacocke

A WOMAN IN THE CASE
(Universal-Victor, March 13, 1917) 1 Reel
Eileeen Sedgwick, Ralph McComas, Milton Sims
Director: Allen Curtis
Story: W. Warren Schoene

THE GASOLINE HABIT
(Universal-IMP, March 28, 1917) 1 Reel
Victor Potel, *Eileen Sedgwick*

HIS FAMILY TREE
(Universal-Victor, April 1917) 1 Reel
Milton Sims, *Eileen Sedgwick*, Ralph McComas, Charles Haefeli
Director: Allen Curtis
Screenplay: Tom Gibson
Story: Tom Gibson
Producer: Allen Curtis

SWEARING OFF
(Victor, April, 1917) 1 Reel
Eileen Sedgwick, Milton Sims, Dolly Ohnet, Ralph McComas, Charles Haefli
Director: Allen Curtis
Scenario: W. Warren Schoene

THE THOUSAND-DOLLAR DROP
(Universal-Victor, April 24, 1917) 1 Reel
Ralph McComas, *Eileen Sedgwick*, Milton Sims
Story: Tom Gibson
Producer: Allen Curtis

FLAT HARMONY
(Universal-Victor, May 1, 1917) 1 Reel
Ralph McComas, *Eileen Sedgwick*, Milton Sims, Edward Brady
Director: Allen Curtis
Screenplay: Tom Gibson
Producer: Allen Curtis

DROPPED FROM THE CLOUDS
(Universal-Bison, May 14, 1917) 2 Reels
Eileen Sedgwick
Director: Henry McRae
Story: W. B. Pearson

NUMBER 10, WESTBOUND
Universal-Bison, May 19, 1917) 2 Reels
Eileen Sedgwick, Mary Fenton, Fred Church, Kingsley Benedict, T. D. Crittenden, B. Lawrence
Director: Henry McRae
Screenplay: George Hively
Story: T. Shelley Sutton
Producer: Henry McRae

NOT TOO THIN TO FIGHT
(Victor, June, 1917) 1 Reel
Eileen Sedgwick, Ralph McComas, Milton Sims, Ed Baker, Charles Haefli
Director: Allen Curtis
Scenario: W. Warren Schoene

LONE LARRY
(Universal-Bison, June 9, 1917) 2 Reels
Eileen Sedgwick, Kingsley Benedict, Vestet Pegg
Director: Henry McRae
Screenplay: Helen Starr
Story: Grant Carpenter

MAKING MONKEY BUSINESS
(Universal-Victor, June 11, 1917) 1 Reel
Ralph McComas, *Eileen Sedgwick*, Milton Sims, "Joe Martin" (an orangutan)
Director: Allen Curtis
Story: Tom Gibson
Producer: Allen Curtis

MAN AND BEAST
(Universal-Butterfly, June 25, 1917) 5 Reels
Harry Clifton, *Eileen Sedgwick*, L. M. Wells, Mrs. Witting, Parks Jones, Kingsley Benedict, "Charlie" (an elephant), "Joe Martin" (an orangutan), "Sam" (a lion), "Tom" (a leopard)
Director: Henry McRae
Screenplay: Reed Heustis

THE PAPERHANGER'S REVENGE
(Victor, July, 1917) 1 Reel
Eileen Sedgwick, Margaret Whistler, Ralph McComas, Charles Haefli
Director: Allen Curtis
Scenario: W. Warren Schoene

MONEY AND MYSTERY
(Universal-Bison, July 20, 1917) 2 Reels
Eileen Sedgwick, Kingsley Benedict, W. E. Lawrence, George Pearce, William Dyer, Martha Mattox, Mrs. G. Hernandez
Director: Henry McRae
Screenplay: Jack Cunningham
Story: Robert von Saxmar

JUNGLE TREACHERY
(Bison, August, 1917) 2 Reels
Eileen Sedgwick, Charles Brinley, Fred Church, Fred Montague, Willard Wayne
Directors: Rex Hodge and W. B. Pearson
Scenario: W. B. Pearson

THE LURE OF THE CIRCUS
(Universal-Bison, August 24, 1917) 2 Reels
Eileen Sedgwick, Fred Church
Director: W. B. Pearson
Screenplay: W. B. Pearson
Story: W. B. Pearson

THE LAST OF THE NIGHT RIDERS
(Universal, September 8, 1917) 2 Reels
Eileen Sedgwick, Fred Church
Director: Hugh Hoffman
Screenplay: Karl Coolidge
Story: Jack Cunningham, Grant Carpenter

THE LION'S LAIR
(Universal-Bison, September 20, 1917) 2 Reels
Eileen Sedgwick, T. D. Crittenden, Fred Church, Albert McQuarrie
Director: W. B. Pearson
Screenplay: George Hively
Story: W. B. Pearson

THE TEMPLE OF TERROR
(Universal-Bison, October 5, 1917) 2 Reels
T. D. Crittenden, *Eileen Sedgwick*, Fred Church, Nellie Allen, Sam Appel
Director: W. B. Pearson
Story: W. B. Pearson
Producer: W. B. Pearson

HELL'S CRATER
(Butterfly, January, 1918) 5 Reels
Grace Cunard, Ray Hanford, *Eileen Sedgwick*, George McDaniel
Director: W. B. Pearson
Story: W. B. Pearson

WATCH YOUR WATCH
(Nestor, February 25, 1918) 1 Reel
Eileen Sedgwick, Orrin C. Johnson, Ernie Shields, Jack Abbott, Lillian Concord
Director: Allen Curtis
Scenario: Charles J. Wilson, Jr.

A KITCHEN HERO
(Nestor, April, 1918) 1 Reel
Eileen Sedgwick
Director: Allen Curtis
Scenario: W. Warren Schoene

PASSING THE BOMB
(Nestor, June, 1918) 1 Reel
Eileen Sedgwick, Ralph McComas, Milton Sims
Director: Allen Curtis
Scenario: Tom Gibson

QUICK TRIGGERS
(Universal, June 6, 1918) 2 Reels
Neal Hart, Gypsy Hart, *Eileen Sedgwick*

THE BUTLER'S BLUNDER
(Universal-Nestor, June 19, 1918) 1 Reel
Eileen Sedgwick, Ralph McComas, Milton Sims, Charles Haefeli
Director: Allen Curtis
Story: W. Warren Schoene

OH, MAN!
(Universal-Nestor, June 24, 1918) 1 Reel
Eileen Sedgwick, Ed Baker, Milton Sims, Anna Hernandez, Charles Haefeli, Dolly Ohonet, Ralph McComas
Director: Allen Curtis
Screenplay: Tom Gibson

REPEATING THE HONEYMOON
(Nestor, July, 1918) 1 Reel
Eileen Sedgwick, Charles King
Director: Leslie T. Peacocke
Scenario: Leslie T. Peacocke

Lure of the Circus (Universal, 1917)

TRAIL OF NO RETURN
(Universal, July 30, 1918) 2 Reels
Neal Hart, *Eileen Sedgwick*, Joseph Rickson, Dick LaReno
Director: Harry Harvey
Screenplay: Nan Blair
Story: Shelby Sutton

ROPED AND TIED
(Universal, August 6, 1918) 2 Reels
Eileen Sedgwick, Neal Hart, Joe Rickson, Lola Wright
Screenplay: Karl Coolidge
Story: E. P. Maxwell

THE HUMAN TIGER
(Universal, Septembtr 10, 1918) 2 Reels
Eileen Sedgwick, Fred Church, Frank Lanning
Story: C. B. Hoadley

NAKED FISTS
(Universal, September 19, 1918) 2 Reels
Neal Hart, *Eileen Sedgwick*, Sam Polo, Dick La Reno, Joseph Rickson, Dark Cloud

ALL FOR GOLD
(Universal, September 23, 1918) 2 Reels
Eileen Sedgwick, Fred Church, Betty Schade, T. B. Crittenden
Director: T. Shelley Sutton
Story: T. Shelley Sutton

LURE OF THE CIRCUS
(Universal, November 18, 1918) 18 Chapters.
Eddie Polo, *Eileen Sedgwick*, Mollie Malone, Harry Carter, Noble Johnson, Frederick Starr, Duke R. Lee, Charles Hill Mailes, James Gordon, Andrew Waldron, Fred Montague, Sidney Deane
Director: J. P. McGowan
Screenplay: Hope Loring
Story: William Wing
Chapters: (1) The Big Tent (2) The Giant's Leap (3) Beaten Back (4) The Message on the Cuff (5) The Lip Reader (6) The Aerial Disaster (7) The Charge of the Elephant (8) The Human Ladder (9) The Flying Loop (10) A Shot for Life (11) The Dagger (12) A Strange Escape (13) A Plunge for Life (14) Flames (15) The Stolen Record (16) The Knockout (17) A Race with Time (18) The Last Trick

THE FICKLE BLACKSMITH
(Nestor, November 25, 1918) 1 Reel
Eileen Sedgwick, Ralph McComas, Doley Ohnet
Story: W. Warren Schoene

THE SHOPLIFTER
(Nestor, 1918) 1 Reel
Eileen Sedgwick, Ralph McComas, Martin Sims
Director: Allen Curtis
Scenario: Tom Gibson

A PRISONER FOR LIFE
(Universal, April 22, 1919) 2 Reels
Eddie Polo, *Eileen Sedgwick*

A PHANTOM FUGITIVE
(Universal, May 1, 1919) 2 Reels
Eddie Polo, *Eileen Sedgwick*, Joe La Cruz
Director: Jacques Jaccard
Story: Jacques Jaccard, Marie Walcamp

THE WILD RIDER
(Cyclone Smith Series)
(Universal, May 12, 1919) 2 Reels
Eddie Polo, *Eileen Sedgwick*
Director: Jacques Jaccard
Story: Jacques Jaccard, Milton Moore

CYCLONE SMITH'S COMEBACK
(Cyclone Smith Series)
(Universal, May 21, 1919) 2 Reels
Eddie Polo, *Eileen Sedgwick*
Director: Jacques Jaccard
Story: Jacques Jaccard

A PISTOL POINT PROPOSAL
(Cyclone Smith Series)
(Universal, May 28, 1919) 2 Reels
Eddie Polo, *Eileen Sedgwick*
Director: George Holt
Screenplay: Karl Coolidge
Story: J. A. Alexander

CYCLONE SMITH PLAYS TRUMPS
(Cyclone Smith Series)
(Universal, June, 1919) 2 Reels
Eddie Polo, *Eileen Sedgwick*, Ruby Lafayette, Leonard Clapham (Tom London), Charles Downs, Bob Anderson
Director: Jacques Jaccard
Story: Jacques Jaccard, George Hively

THE GREAT RADIUM MYSTERY
(Universal, October 13, 1919) 18 Chapters.
Cleo Madison, Robert Reeves, *Eileen Sedgwick*, Robert Kortman, Ed Brady, Jeff Osborne, Robert Gray, Gordon McGregor, Fred Hamer
Director: Robert Bradwell, Robert F. Hill
Screenplay: Frederick Bennett
Chapters: (1) The Mystic Stone (2) The Death Trap (3) The Fatal Ride (4) The Swing for Life (5) The Torture Chamber (6) The Tunnel of Doom (7) A Flash in the Dark (8) In the Clutches of the Mad Man (9) The Roaring Volcano (10) Creeping Flames (11) Perils of Doom (12) Shackled (13) The Scalding Pit (14) Hemmed In (15) The Flaming Arrow (16) Over the Cataract (17) The Wheels of Death (18) Liquid Flames

LOVE'S BATTLE
(Climax Films, 1920)
Eileen Sedgwick, Joe Moore
Director: William J. Craft

PUTTING IT OVER
(Universal, 1920) 2 Reels
Eileen Sedgwick

THE WHITE RIDER
(1920)
Eileen Sedgwick

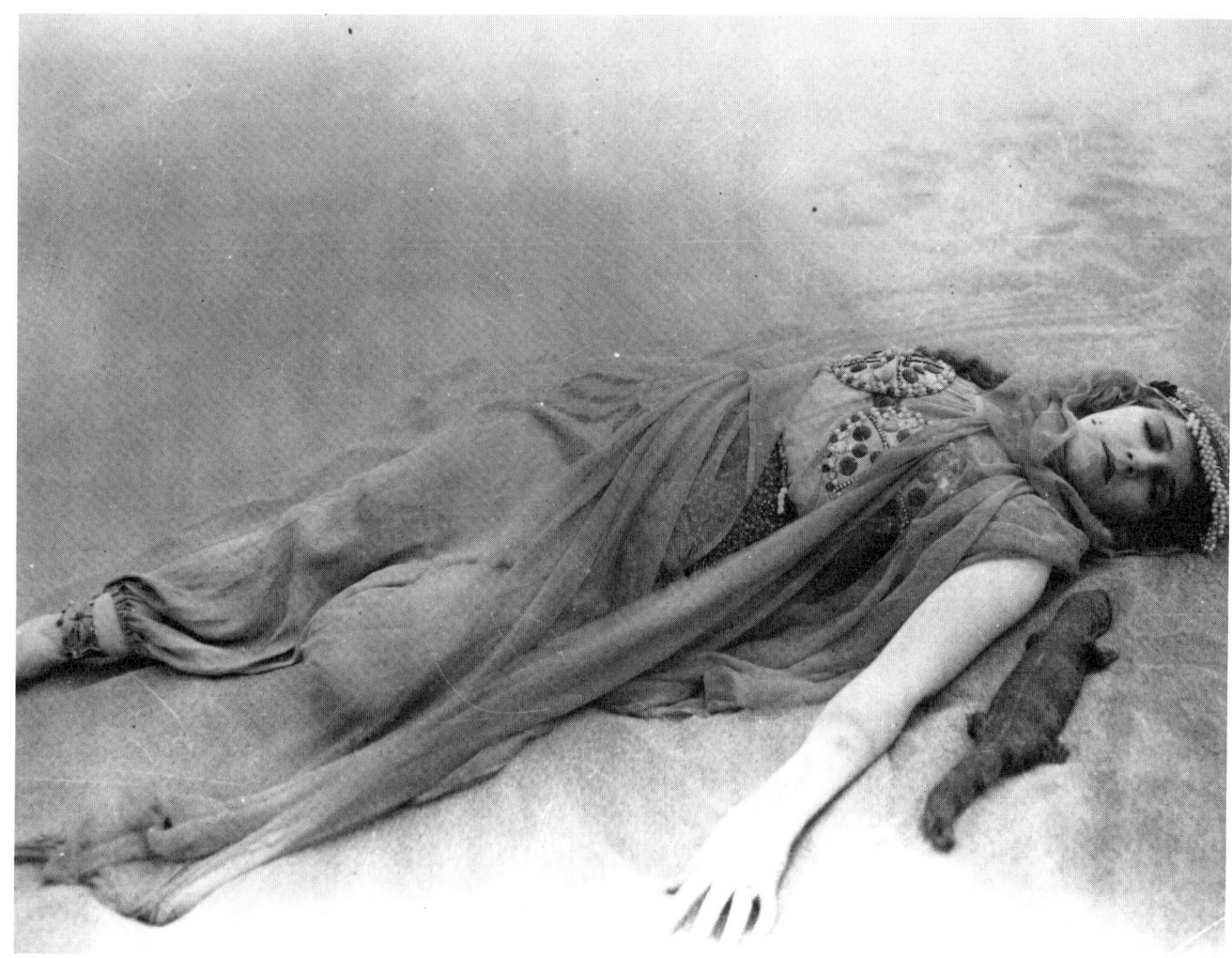

The Diamond Queen (Universal, 1921) – Eileen Sedgwick.

THE DIAMOND QUEEN
(Universal, March 15, 1921) 18 Chapters.
Eileen Sedgwick, George Chesebro, Al Smith, Frank M. Clark, Lew Short, Josephine Scott, Burton Wilson, Alfred Fisher
Director: Ed Kull
Screenplay: George W. Pyper
Adaptation: Robert F. Roden, George W. Pyper
Story: Jacques Futrelle, "The Diamond Master"
Chapters: (1) Vow of Vengeance (2) Plunge of Doom (3) Perils of the Jungle (4) Fires of Hate (5) Tide of Destiny (6) The Colossal Game (7) An Amazing Ultimatum (8) In Merciless Clutches (9) A Race with Rogues (10) The Betrayal (11) In Torture's Grip (12) The Kidnapping (13) Weird Walls (14) The Plunge (15) The Decoy (16) The Dip of Death (17) The Hand of Fate (18) The Hour of Reckoning

THE HEART OF ARIZONA
(Universal, June 4, 1921) 2 Reels
Eileen Sedgwick
Director: Edward Kull
Screenplay: George H. Plympton
Story: George H. Plympton

THE GIRL IN THE SADDLE
(Universal, June 17, 1921) 2 Reels
Eileen Sedgwick
Director: Edward Kull
Story: George Morgan

THE SHADOW OF SUSPICION
(Universal, July 1, 1921) 2 Reels
Eileen Sedgwick
Director: Edward Kull
Screenplay: George H. Plympton
Story: George H. Plympton

Terror Trail (Universal, 1921) – Eileen Sedgwick and George Larkin.

TERROR TRAIL
(Universal, July 1921) 18 Chapters.
Eileen Sedgwick, George Larkin, Albert J. Smith, Barney Furey, Theodore Brown, Pierre Dourdec
Director: Edward Kull
Screenplay: Edward Kull, John W. Grey, George H. Plympton
Story: Edward Kull, John W. Grey, George H. Plympton
Chapters: (1) The Mystery Girl (2) False Clues (3) The Mine of Menace (4) The Door of Doom (5) The Bridge of Disaster (6) The Ship of Surprise (7) The Palace of Fear (8) The Peril of the Palace (9) The Desert of Despair (10) Sands of Fate (11) The Menace of the Sea (12) The Isle of Eternity (13) The Forest of Fear (14) The Lure of the Jungle (15) The Jaws of Death (16) The Storm of Despair (17) The Arm of the Law (18) The Final Reckoning

A WOMAN'S WIT
(Universal, November 13, 1921) 2 Reels
Eileen Sedgwick
Director: Edward Kull
Screenplay: George Morgan
Story: George Morgan

DREAM GIRL
(Universal, November 29, 1921) 2 Reels
Eileen Sedgwick
Director: Edward Kull
Story: Edward Kull, George Morgan

ARREST NORMA MACGREGOR
(World/Rialto, November 30, 1921) 5 Reels
Joe Moore, *Eileen Sedgwick*

A BATTLE OF WITS
(Universal, December 16, 1921) 2 Reels
Eileen Sedgwick
Director: Edward Kull
Screenplay: George Morgan, George H. Plympton
Story: George Morgan, George H. Plympton

THE NIGHT ATTACK
(Universal, December 24, 1921) 2 Reels
Eileen Sedgwick, Percy Pembroke, Richard Daniels
Director: Edward Kull
Screenplay: George H. Plympton
Story: George H. Plympton

FALSE BRANDS
(World/Pacific, Februray 14, 1922) 5 Reels
Joe Moore, *Eileen Sedgwick*, C. W. Williams, Robert Kentman
Director: William J. Craft
Screenplay: Harry Chandlee, William B. Laub
Story: William J. Craft

JUDGEMENT
(World, February 15, 1922) 6 Reels
Joe Moore, *Eileen Sedgwick*

WOLF PACK
(World/Rialto, March 16, 1922) 5 Reels
Joe Moore, *Eileen Sedgwick*, S. W. Williams, Robert Kortman
Director: William Craft

MAKING GOOD
(Sanford, February 12, 1923) 5 Reels
Pete Morrison, *Eileen Sedgwick*

IN THE DAYS OF DANIEL BOONE
(Universal, June 25, 1923) 15 Chapters.
Jack Mower, *Eileen Sedgwick*, Duke R. Lee, Charles Binley, Albert J. Smith, Ruth Royce, Frank Farrington, Herschell Mayall, Jack Lewis
Director: William Craft
Screenplay: Jefferson Moffitt
Story: Paul Bryan, Jefferson Moffitt
Chapters: (1) His Country's Need (2) At Sword's Point (3) Liberty or Death (4) Foiling the Regulators (5) Perilous Paths (6) Trapped (7) In the Hands of the Enemy (8) Over the Cliff (9) The Flaming Forest (1) Running the Gauntlet (11) The Wilderness Trail (12) The Fort in the Forest (13) The Boiling Springs (14) Chief Blackfish Attacks (15) Boone's Triumph

SCARRED HANDS
(H. B. Productions/Madoc Sales, September 1, 1923) 5 Reels
Cliff Smith, *Eileen Sedgwick*
Director: Cliff Smith

WHEN LAW COMES TO HADES
(Sanford, September 1923) 5 Reels
Noah Beery, *Eileen Sedgwick*, Edward W. Borman

BEASTS OF PARADISE
(Universal, October 1, 1923) 15 Chapters.
William Desmond, *Eileen Sedgwick*, William N. Gould, Ruth Royce, Margaret Morris, Jim Welsh, Clarke Comstock, Joe Bonomo, Slim Cole, Alfred Fisher, Gordon McGregor, William J. Welsh
Director: William Craft
Screenplay: Val Cleveland
Story: Val Cleveland
Chapters: (1) The Mystery Ships (2) The Unseen Peril (3) The Typhoon (4) The Sea Rider (5)The Tidewater Trap (6) The Alligator Attacks (7) The Deluge (8) The Mutiny (9) Ship Aflame (10) The Mad Elephant Charge (11) Smothered in the Sand (12) Millions in Gold (13) Into the Bloodhound's Jaws (14) Into the Whirlpool (15) The Trail's End

THE LONE ROUNDUP
(Universal, May 1, 1924) 2 Reels
Jack Daugherty, *Eileen Sedgwick*
Director: Ernst Laemmle
Screenplay: Arthur H. Gooden
Story: Arthur H. Gooden

THE RIDDLE RIDER
(Universal, November 23, 1924) 15 Chapters.
William Desmond, *Eileen Sedgwick*, Helen Holmes, Claude Payton, William N. Gould, Ben Corbett, Hughie Mack, Albert J. Smith, Margaret Royce, Yakima Canutt, Art Ortego
Director: William Craft
Screenplay: William Wing, Arthur H. Gooden, George Pyper
Story: William Wing, Arthur H. Gooden, George Pyper
Chapters: (1) The Canyon Torrent (2) Crashing Doom (3) In the Path of Death (4) Plunged Into the Depths (5) Race for a Fortune (6) Sinister Shadows (7) The Swindle (8) The Frame-up (9) False Faces (10) At the Brink of Death (11) Thundering Steeds (12) Trapped (13) The Valley of Fate (14) The Deadline (15) The Final Reckoning

DANGEROUS ODDS
(Independent, April 7, 1925) 5 Reels
Bill Cody, *Eileen Sedgwick*, Milton Fahrney, Claude Payton, Monte Collins, Al Hallett, Art Ortega
Director: William J. Craft
Producer: Jesse Goldburg

FIGHTING RANGER
(Universal, May 11, 1925) 18 Chapters.
Jack Daugherty, *Eileen Sedgwick*, Al Wilson, William Welsh, Bud Osborne, Charles Avery, Frank Lanning, Sam Polo, Slim Cole, Gladys Roy
Director: Jay Marchant
Story: F. J. McConnell, George W. Pyper
Chapters: (1) The Intruder (2) The Frame-up (3) The Secret Trail (4) Falsely Accused (5) The Betrayal (6) The Lost Fortune (7) Cattle Wolves (8) Under Fire (9) Man to Man (10) The Fatal Message (11) Hidden Fangs (12) False Friends (13) Stolen Secrets (14) Steeds of the Sky (15) Yaqui Gold (16) Left for Dead (17-18) Unknown

THE SAGEBRUSH LADY
(H. T. Henderson/Chesterfield, October 1, 1925) 5 Reels
Eileen Sedgwick, Bernie Corbett, Jack Richardson, Eddie Barry, William Steele
Director: H. B. Carpenter, Horace Davey
Screenplay: Carle Cooly

GIRL OF THE WEST
(H. T. Henderson/Chesterfield, December 1, 1925) 5 Reels
Eileen Sedgwick
Director: Alvin J. Neitz

BEYOND ALL ODDS
(H. T. Henderson/Chesterfield, February, 1926) 5 Reels
Eileen Sedgwick, Carlos Silvera, Ray Childs, Theodore Henderson, Les Bates, Lew Heehan, Alfred Hewston, D. Maley
Director: Alvin J. Neitz

THE WINKING IDOL
(Universal, March 1926) 10 Chapters.
William Desmond, *Eileen Sedgwick*, Grace Cunard, Herbert Sutch, Jack Richardson, Helen Broneau, Les Sailor, Art Ortego, Dorothy Gulliver, Vanna Carroll
Director: Francis Ford
Screenplay: Arthur Henry Gooden, George Morgan
Story: Charles E. Van Loan
Chapters: (1) The Eye of Evil (2) Buzzard's Roost (3) Crashing Timbers (4) Racing for Love (5) The Vanishing Bride (6) The Torrent of Terror (7) Flames of Fear (8) The Fight at the Falls (9) In Danger of Dynamite (10) The Lost Lode

THUNDERING SPEED
(Chesterfield, May 1926) 5 Reels
Eileen Sedgwick
Director: Alvin J. Neitz
Producer: H. T. Henderson

STRINGS OF STEEL
(Universal, June 28, 1926) 10 Chapters.
William Desmond, *Eileen Sedgwick*, Albert J. Smith, George Ovey, Ted Duncan, Alphonse Martel, Arthur Morrison, Grace Cunard, Taylor N. Duncan, Blanche Fisher, Dorothy Gulliver
Director: Henry McRae
Story: Phillip Dutton Hurn, Oscar Lund
Chapters: (1) The Voice on the Wire (2) The First Central (3) Fighting for Love (4) The Power of Might (5) Kings of the Wire (6) Voice of the Continent (7) Telephone Poles (8) War of the Wire (9) When Lightning Strikes (10) Love and Victory

LIGHTNIN' STRIKES
(Tenneck, September 1, 1926)
Eileen Sedgwick, "Lightnin'" (a dog)

LIGHTNIN' WINS
(Tenneck, October 4, 1926)
Eileen Sedgwick, "Lightnin'" (a dog), Gary Cooper
Director: Hans Tiesler

LIGHTNIN' FLASHES
(Tenneck, November 1, 1926)
Eileen Sedgwick, "Lightnin'" (a dog)

TIN HATS
(M-G-M, November 28, 1926) 7 Reels
Conrad Nagel, Claire Windsor, George Cooper, Bert Roach, Tom O'Brien, *Eileen Sedgwick*
Director: Edward Sedgwick
Adaptation: Lew Lipton, Donald W. Lee
Story: Albert Lewin

LURE OF THE WEST
(Chesterfield, November, 1926) 5 Reels
Eileen Sedgwick, Lee Bates, Ray Childs, D. Maley, Alfred Newston, Elsie Bower, Carlos Silvers
Director: Alvin J. Neitz
Story: Alvin J. Neitz
Producer: H. T. Henderson

TEMPLE OF TERROR
(Fred Balshofer, 1926) 5 Reels
Fred Church (Montana Bill), *Eileen Sedgwick*

FURY
(Tenneck, February 1, 1927)
Eileen Sedgwick, "Lightnin'" (a dog)

FANGS
(Tenneck, February 15, 1927)
Eileen Sedgwick, "Lightnin'" (a dog)

SPEED
(Tenneck, March 1, 1927)
Eileen Sedgwick, "Lightnin'" (a dog)

WHEN DANGER CALLS
(Camera Pictures/Lumas, September 23, 1927) 5 Reels
William Fairbanks, *Eileen Sedgwick*, Ethan Laidlaw, Sally Long, Donald MacDonald, Hank Mann
Director: Charles Hutchison
Story: Ben Allah

THE SPIDER'S NET
(Tenneck/Goodwill, 1927)
Eileen Sedgwick, Gary Cooper, Robert Walker, Tom London, Harry Semels, Frank Lackteen, Wilbur McGaugh, William A. Lovery, Hal Water, "Lightnin'" (a dog)
Producer: Hans Tirsler
(**Notes:** This film was a serial put together from the earlier films starring Eileen Sedgwick and "Lightnin'." Published books on the films of Gary Cooper do not credit him to this serial, though he was in it. The reason for the non-credit is that few film historians know that this independent serial was even made. It had very limited distribution on the states-right market. The number of chapters or their titles have not been determined.)

GIRL IN EVERY PORT
(Fox, February 26, 1928) 6 Reels
Victor McLaglen, Maria Casajuana, Natalie Joyce, Dorothy Mathews, Elena Jurado, Louise Brooks, Francis McDonald, Phalba Morgan, Felix Valle, Greta Yoltz (*Eileen Sedgwick*), Leila Hyams, Robert Armstrong, Sally Rand, Natalie Kingston, Caryl Lincoln
Director: Howard Hawks
Scenario: Seton I. Miller
Screenplay: James K. McGuinness
Story: Howard Hawks

WHITE FLAME
(I. H. Adam/Biltmore, March 20, 1928) 6 Reels
Mahlon Hamilton, William V. Mong, *Eileen Sedgwick*

HOT HEELS
(Universal, May 13, 1928) 6 Reels
Glenn Tryon, Patsy Ruth Miller, Greta Yoltz (*Eileen Sedgwick*), James Bradbury, Sr., Rod Sloan, Lloyd Whitlock
Director: William James Craft
Screenplay: Harry O. Hoyt
Story: Harry O. Hoyt

BEAUTIFUL BUT DUMB
(Tiffany-Stahl, August 1, 1928) 7 Reels
Patsy Ruth Miller, Charles Byer, George E. Stone, Shirley Palmer, Greta Yoltz (*Eileen Sedgwick*), William Irving, Harvey Clark
Director: Elmer Clifton
Screenplay: J. F. Natteford
Story: J. F. Natteford

THE VANISHING WEST
(Mascot, October 15, 1928) 10 Chapters
Jack Daugherty, Leo Maloney, Jack Perrin, Yakima Canutt, William Fairbanks, *Eileen Sedgwick*, Fred Church, Mickey Bennett, Helen Gibson, Harry Lorraine, Aaron Edwards, Bob Burns, Tom Bay, Ed Waldron
Director: Richard Thorpe
Screenplay: Wyndham Gittens
Producer: Nat Levine
Story: Karl Krusada and William Lester
Chapters: (1) The Trail to Yesterday (2) The Flaming Trap (3) Thundering Hoofs (4) The Balance of Fate (5) The Chasm of Danger (6) Roaring Wheels (7) The Phantom Roper (8) The Tunnel of Terror (9) The Fatal Second (10) The End of the Trail

YELLOW CONTRABAND
(Pathé, October 28, 1928) 6 Reels
Leo Maloney, Greta Yoltz (*Eileen Sedgwick*), Noble Johnson, Tom London, Joseph Rickson, Robert Burns, Vester Pegg, Walter Patterson, Bill Patton, Bud Osborne, Frank Ellis, Tom Forman
Director: Leo Maloney
Screenplay: Ford Beebe
Story: Ford Beebe

Linda Stirling

19 • LINDA STIRLING

Fantasizing About This Lively Queen of Republic Serials Was Easy for Boys of All Ages

Linda Stirling's special forte as a motion picture actress of the forties was serials and Westerns. She had a likeable, simple, and unaffected personality. Her sensuality was less blatant than that of Rita Hayworth, Ava Gardner, or Marilyn Monroe, but it was there.

Unlike many others in the serial and Western genre, Linda showed considerable intelligence (in a slightly self-conscious way) as she went about overcoming the vicissitudes created by Republic's script writers. Esprit de corps was never better on a set than when Linda was playing the heroine. She was an actress of unusual beauty, vitality, and enthusiasm.

Today, the former "Tiger Woman" is more at home in the classroom with Shakespeare than she is in the man-made jungles of the studio backlot. It has been four decades since she was last menaced by The Crimson Ghost, The Purple Monster, and other assorted villains on the old Republic lot. The only villains now are those English students who try her patience by not doing their term papers. She gave up the cardboard jungle long ago for the chalkboard jungle and is now a college English teacher.

Linda was born in Long Beach, California, on October 11, 1921. Her father was in the furniture and real estate businesses. She always wanted to be an actress and took dancing lessons from the age of three and piano lessons from the age of five. This was de rigeur for grace and culture in those days. She began drama lessons at age twelve and spent a lot of time at the Long Beach Community Players Theatre. Though her father opposed her desire to become an actress, he allowed her to study at Ben Bard's Academy of Dramatic Art in Los Angeles for two years following her high school graduation. By chance she met a photographer who asked her to pose, which she did in exchange for pictures. Other photographers began to call her and she soon had an agent and was in great demand as a model for live fashion shows. The modeling provided her entrée into films, as in **The Powers Girl** (1943) where she was one of the models. Republic execs saw her on a magazine cover and called her in to audition for **The Tiger Woman** (1944). Thus began Linda's life as the forties' best-known serial queen.

Undoubtedly **The Tiger Woman** was Linda's most popular episodic drama and also one of Republic's top money-makers. She seemed to have all the essential requisites for a serial heroine --athletic prowess, beauty, bravery, acting talent, and that special charisma that caused audiences to empathize with her. She was quickly compared to Frances Gifford, whom Republic had earlier hoped would revive the serial queen title, but who made only one serial before moving on to other things.

Zorro's Black Whip (1944) gave Linda a chance to play a masked character in a Western serial. Audiences found her just as attractive as a masquerading newspaper woman in the Wild West as she had been as the white princess of the Amazon. Next came a devil-and-the-deep-blue-sea adventure called **Manhunt of Mystery Island** (1945), with a weaker male hero in Richard Bailey but an exceptionally virile villain in Roy Barcroft, who played Captain Mephisto.

Interestingly, Republic followed parallel courses for both of its popular serial queens, Linda and Kay Aldridge. Both started with a jungle yarn, followed by a Western and then a sea drama. But whereas Kay bowed out of serial production and never got into Westerns at Republic, Linda continued to carry the Republic banner through three more serials and a number of Westerns. **The Purple Monster Strikes** (1945), her fourth chapter play, dealt with a new realm in the

The Tiger Woman (Republic, 1944) – Looks like that arrow just missed one of the features that made Linda Stirling so appealing. George J. Lewis is the hero.

Republic serial domain, the depths of outer space. Linda's role as Sheila Layton was more subdued than those of her previous outings. Roy Barcroft was the Martian Purple Monster and Dennis Moore the hero who, along with Linda, was frequently imperiled. In **The Crimson Ghost** (1946) Linda and Charles Quigley battle more earthly creatures who are bent on stealing the Cyclotrode, or atom smasher. I. Stanford Jolley plays the Ghost, while Clayton Moore, still several years away from his Lone Ranger role, plays his lieutenant. But in **Jesse James Rides Again** (1947) Clayton is the hero/outlaw in a plot set in the nether world between fact and fiction. Linda plays Ann Bolton, whose interests he protects, but the part was a weak one that did not allow her the footage or dramatic scenes that she deserved in her final serial role.

Fans are apt to remember Linda's ten Western features at Republic, especially **Santa Fe Saddlemates** (1945), in which she played a dance-hall girl and sang two songs. Commenting on the Westerns, Linda has said:

We shot most of the outdoor stuff at Iverson's Ranch, and I can still remember every physical aspect of it--the rocks, the trails, the bushes, everything. I had no skill whatsoever with horses, and more than once the crew would find me sprawled in the dust or crumpled in the bushes somewhere after my horse had run away with me.

I remember once Spencer Bennet asked me if I could do a running insert. I said sure, although I had no idea what it was. To my dismay, I found out. My horse took it as a personal challenge to outrun the camera truck, and I went along for the ride, taking in the scenery from every possible angle as I was bounced around from side to side and end to end on that galloping beast. Horses and I never really got on a first-name basis or shared social lives.

Another facet of Linda's career was the stage. In **Decision** (1945) she played a young political liberal who supports her future father-in-law when he is accused of advancing subversive socialist ideas as a school administrator. In **Angel Face** (1947) she was a wisecracking girl who had been deserted by the man she loved and hides her deep hurt behind a breezy, joking facade. **Russet**

Mantle (1948) presented her as a girl who shocks her conventional family by saying outrageous things in a desperate effort to break away from their smug, self-satisfied way of life. In **The Browning Version** (1956) Linda played the evil wife, a subtle, understated role, while in **Ladies in Retirement** (1956) she had a very dramatic role as the lead. In **No Exit** (1957) she did Inez, the Lesbian, and in **Country Girl** (1958) she played Georgie Elgin.

In 1946 Linda married Sloan Nibley, one of Republic's scenario writers. It was a third marriage for both. Still happily married, they now have two grown children. She left Republic in 1948 to have her first baby, then went to television in 1952 after her second son was born. She worked in TV until 1961, appearing in numerous shows including "Mr. District Attorney," "Dr. Christian," "The Real McCoys," "City Detective," "I Led Three Lives," "The Joan Blondell Show," "Heinz 57 Series," "The Public Defender," "The Man Behind the Badge," "The Line Up," "Cavalcade Theatre," "The Adventures of Wyatt Earp," and "On Trial."

In 1959 and 1960 Linda attended Los Angeles City College on a part-time basis for self-enrichment. By 1961 she was definitely hooked on college and entered The University of California at Los Angeles as a full-time student. Almost before she realized the turn in her life, she had gotten a master's degree and become a teacher of English and drama at Glendale College.

Linda Stirling is a very beautiful and gifted actress whose talent was wasted to some extent in the low-budget action films at Republic (though serial and Western fans were certainly delighted that fate had pushed her in that direction). As a queen of the episodic action genre, Linda, like Ruth Roland and Pearl White before her, will be remembered longer than many dramatic actresses.

LINDA STIRLING Filmography

THE POWERS GIRL
(United Artists, January 15, 1943) 93 Mins.
George Murphy, Anne Shirley, Carole Landis, Dennis Day, Benny Goodman and Orchestra, Alan Mowbray, Jean Ames, Mary Treen, Helen MacKellar, Harry Shannon, Jayne Hazard, *Linda Stirling*, George Chandler, Willie Best, Minerva Urecal, Jack Daley, Peggy Lee, Jack Baxley
Director: Norman Z. McLeod
Screenplay: Edwin Moran, Harry Segall
Story: William A. Pierce, Malvin Wald--based on the book by John R. Powers
Producer: Charles R. Rogers

THE TIGER WOMAN
(Republic, March 1944) 12 Chapters.
Allan Lane, *Linda Stirling*, Duncan Renaldo, George J. Lewis, LeRoy Mason, Crane Whitley, Robert Frazer, Rico de Montez, Stanley Price, Nolan Leary, Kenne Duncan, Tom Steele, Duke Green, Eddie Parker, Ken Terrell, Cliff Lyons, Charles Hayes, Bud Geary, John Daheim, Bud Wolfe, Frank Marlowe, Georges Renavent, Tom London, Marshall Reed, Fred Graham, Al Ferguson, Dale Van Sickel, Rex Lease, Roy Darmour, Bert LeBaron, Paul Gustine, Carey Loftin, Walt LaRue, Herman Hack, Babe DeFreest, Augie Gomez, Harry Smith, Catherine McLeod, Joe Molina
Directors: Spencer Bennet, Wallace Grissell
Screenplay: Royal Cole, Ronald Davidson, Basil Dickey, Jesse Duffy, Grant Nelson, Joseph Poland
Associate Producer: W. J. O'Sullivan
Chapters: (1) Temple of Terror (2) Doorway to Death (3) Cathedral of Carnage (4) Echo of Eternity (5) Two Shall Die (6) Dungeon of the Doomed (7) Mile-a-Minute Murder (8) Passage to Peril (9) Cruise to Cremation (10) Target for Murder (11) The House of Horror (12) Triumph over Treachery

THE SAN ANTONIO KID
(Republic, August 16, 1944) 59 Mins.
Bill Elliott, Bobby Blake, Alice Fleming, *Linda Stirling*. Tom London, Duncan Renaldo, Earle Hodgins, Glenn Strange, LeRoy Mason, Jack Kirk, Bob Wilke, Cliff Parkinson, Jack O'Shea, Henry Wills, Tom Steele, Tex Terry, Pascale Perry, Herman Hack, Bud Geary, Roy Bucko, Joe Garcia
Director: Howard Bretherton
Screenplay: Norman S. Hall
Story: Based on the Fred Harman comic strip
Associate Producer: Stephen Auer.

SHERIFF OF SUNDOWN
(Republic, November 7, 1944) 57 Mins.
Allan Lane, *Linda Stirling*. Max Terhune, Twinkle Watts, Duncan Renaldo, Roy Barcroft, Herbert Rawlinson, Bud Geary, Jack Kirk, Tom London, Bob Wilke, Kenne Duncan, Herman Hack, Jack O'Shea, Carl Sepulveda, Rex Lease, Nolan Leary, Horace B. Carpenter, Cactus Mack, Neal Hart, Chick Hannon, Foxy Callahan, Duke Greene
Director: Lesley Selander
Screenplay: Norman S. Hall
Associate Producer: Stephen Auer

The Crimson Ghost (Republic, 1946) – Clayton Moore is apparently trying to make a point with Linda Stirling.

VIGILANTES OF DODGE CITY
(Republic, November 15, 1944) 54 Mins.
Bill Elliott, Bobby Blake, Alice Fleming, *Linda Stirling,* LeRoy Mason, Hal Taliaferro, Tom London, Stephen Barclay, Bud Geary, Kenne Duncan, Bob Wilke, Horace B. Carpenter, Stanley Andrews, Herman Hack
Director: Wallace Grissell
Screenplay: Norman S. Hall, Anthony Coldeway
Story: Norman S. Hall, based on the Fred Harman comic strip
Associate Producer: Stephen Auer

ZORRO'S BLACK WHIP
(Republic, December 16, 1944) 12 Chapters.
George J. Lewis, *Linda Stirling.* Lucien Littlefield, Francis McDonald, Hal Taliaferro, John Merton, John Hamilton, Tom Chatterton, Tom London, Jack Kirk, Jay Kirby, Si Jenks, Stanley Price, Tom Steele, Duke Green, Dale Van Sicke, Cliff Lyons, Roy Brent, Joe Yrigoyen, Forrest Taylor, Bill Yrigoyen, Marshall Reed, Augie Gomez, Carl Sepulveda, Horace B. Carpenter, Herman Hack, Carey Loftin, Cliff Parkinson, Duke Taylor, Nolan Leary, Post Parks, Robert Wilke, Vinegar Roan, Babe DeFreest
Directors: Spencer Bennet, Wallace Grissell
Screenplay: Basil Dickey, Jesse Duffy, Grant Nelson, Joseph Poland
Story: Based on the character created by Johnston McCulley
Chapters: (1) The Masked Avenger (2) Tomb of Terror (3) Mob Murder (4) Detour to Deat (5) Take off That Mask! (6) Fatal Gold (7) Wolf Pack (8) The Invisible Victim (9) Avalanche (10) Fangs of Doom (11) Flaming Juggernaut (12) Trail of Treachery

DAKOTA
(Republic, December 25, 1944) 82 Mins.
John Wayne, Vera Ralston, Walter Brennan, Ward Bond, Ona Munson, Hugo Haas, Mike Mazurki, Olive Blakeney, Nicodemus Stewart, Paul Fix, Grant Withers, Robert Livingston, Olin Howlin, Pierre Watkin, Robert Barrat, Jonathan Hale, Bobby Blake, Paul Hurst, Eddy Waller, Sarah Padden, Jack LaRue, George Cleveland, Selmer Jackson, Claire Dubrey, Roy Barcroft, Yakima Canutt, William Haade, *Linda Stirling*. Adrian Booth, Larry Thompson, Dorothy Christy, Cay Forester, Jack Roper, Cliff Lyons, Fred Graham, Houseley Stevenson, Rex Lease, Michael Visaroff, Hector Sarno, Dick Wessell, Betty Shaw, Al Murphy, Victor Varconi, Paul E. Burns, Arthur Miles, Eugene Borden, Martha Carroll
Director: Joseph Kane
Screenplay: Lawrence Hazard
Adaptation: Howard Estabrook
Story: Carl Forman
Associate Producer: Joseph Kane

MANHUNT OF MYSTERY ISLAND
(Republic, January 1945) 15 Chapters.
Richard Bailey, *Linda Stirling*, Roy Barcroft, Kenne Duncan, Forrest Taylor, Forbes Murray, Jack Ingram, Harry Strang, Edward Cassidy, Frank Alten, Lane Chandler, Russ Vincent, Dale Van Sickel, Tom Steele, Duke Green, Si Jenks, Fred Graham, Eddie Parker, Duke Taylor, Frederick Howard
Directors: Spencer Bennet, Wallace A. Grissell, Yakima Canutt
Screenplay: Albert DeMond, Basil Dickey, Jesse Duffy, Grant Nelson, Joseph Poland
Associate Producer: Ronald Davidson
Chapters: (1) Secret Weapon (2) Satan's Web (3) The Murder Machine (4) The Lethal Chamber (5) Mephisto's Mantrap (6) Ocean Tomb (7) The Death Drop (8) Bombs Away (9) The Fatal Flood (10) The Sable Shroud (11) Satan's Shadow (12) Cauldron of Cremation (13) Bridge to Eternity (14) Power Dive to Doom (15) Fatal Transformation

THE TOPEKA TERROR
(Republic, January 26, 1945) 55 Mins.
Allan Lane, *Linda Stirling*, Roy Barcroft, Earle Hodgins, Twinkle Watts, Bud Geary, Frank Jacquet, Jack Kirk, Tom London, Eve Novak, Hank Bell, Bob Wilke, Monte Hale, Jess Cavan, Herman Nolan, Fred Graham, Tom Smith, Herman Hack, Bill Wolfe, Horace B. Carpenter, Jack O'Shea
Director: Howard Bretherton
Screenplay: Patricia Harper, Norman S. Hall
Story: Patricia Harper
Associate Producer: Stephen Auer

SHERIFF OF CIMARRON
(Republic, February 28, 1945) 56 Mins.
Sunset Carson, *Linda Stirling*, Olin Howlin, Riley Hill, Jack Kirk, Jack Ingram, Bob Wilke, Edward Cassidy, George Chesebro, Dickie Dillon, Tom London, Jack O'Shea, Sylvia Arslan, Henry Wills, Hal Price, Carol Henry
Director: Yakima Canutt
Screenplay: Bennett R. Cohen
Associate Producer: Thomas Carr

SANTA FE SADDLEMATES
(Republic, June 2, 1945) 56 Mins.
Sunset Carson, *Linda Stirling*, Olin Howlin, Roy Barcroft, Rex Lease, Bud Geary, Kenne Duncan, George Chesebro, Bob Wilke, Henry Wills, Forbes Murray, Frank Jacquet, Josh (John) Carpenter, Edmund Cobb, Nolan Leary, Fred Graham, George Magrill, Jack O'Shea, Carol Henry, Billy Vincent, Horace B. Carpenter, Bill McCall, Bud Wolfe, Neal Hart, Kansas Moehring, Bob Reeves, Chick Hannon, Bill Nestell, Rose Plummer
Director: Thomas Carr
Associate Producer: Thomas Carr
Screenplay: Bennett R. Cohen

THE PURPLE MONSTER STRIKES
(Republic, October 6, 1945) 15 Chapters.
Dennis Moore, *Linda Stirling*, Roy Barcroft, James Craven, Bud Geary, Mary Moore, John Davidson, Joe Whitehead, Emmett Vogan, George Carleton, Kenne Duncan, Rosemonde James, Monte Hale, Wheaton Chambers, Frederick Howard, Anthony Warde, Ken Terrell, Fred Graham, John Daheim, Tom Steele, Cliff Lyons, Robert Blair, Carey Loftin, Henry Wills, Dale Van Sickel, George Chesebro, Robert Wilke, Polly Burson, Babe DeFreest
Directors: Spencer Bennet, Fred Brannon
Screenplay: Royal Cole, Albert DeMond, Basil Dickey, Joseph Poland, Barney Sarecky
Associate Producer: Ronald Davidson
Chapters: (1) The Man in the Meteor (2) The Time Trap (3) Flaming Avalanche (4) The Lethal Pit (5) Death on the Beam (6) The Demon Killer (7) The Evil Eye (8) Descending Doom (9) The Living Dead (10) House of Horror (11) Menace from Mars (12) Perilous Plunge (13) Fiery Shroud (14) The Fatal Trail (15) Take-Off to Destruction

The Tiger Woman (Republic, 1944) – Linda Stirling, Duncan Renaldo, and Allan Lane.

THE CHEROKEE FLASH
(Republic, December 13, 1945) 58 Mins.
Sunset Carson, *Linda Stirling*, Tom London, Roy Barcroft, John Merton, Bud Geary, Frank Jacquet, Fred Graham, Joe McGuinn, Pierce Lyden, James Lynn, Bud Osborne, Edmund Cobb, Herman Hack, Bill Wolfe, Hank Bell, Chick Hannon, Roy Bucko, Buck Bucko, George Sowards, George Chesebro
Director: Thomas Carr
Screenplay: Betty Burbridge
Associate Producer: Bennett Cohen

WAGON WHEELS WESTWARD
(Republic, December 21, 1945) 56 Mins.
(Red Ryder Series)
Bill Elliott, Bobby Blake, Alice Fleming, *Linda Stirling*, Roy Barcroft, Emmett Lynn, Jay Kirby, Dick Curtis, George J. Lewis, Bud Geary, Tom London, Kenne Duncan, George Chesebro, Tom Chatterton, Frank Ellis, Bob McKenzie, Jack Kirk

Director: R. G. Springsteen
Screenplay: Earle Snell
Story: Gerald Geraghty
Associate Producer: Sidney Picker

THE MADONNA'S SECRET
(Republic, February 16, 1946) 79 Mins.
Francis Lederer, Gail Patrick, Ann Rutherford, Edward Ashley, *Linda Stirling*, John Litel, Leona Roberts, Michael Hawks, Clifford Brooke, Pierre Watkin, Will Wright, Geraldine Wall, John Hamilton
Director: William Thiele
Screenplay: Bradbury Foote, William Thiele
Associate Producer: Stephen Auer

THE CRIMSON GHOST
(Republic, May 1, 1946) 12 Chapters.
Charles Quigley, *Linda Stirling*, Clayton Moore, I. Stanford Jolley, Kenne Duncan, Forrest Taylor, Emmett Vogan, Sam Flint, Joseph Forte, Stanley Price, Wheaton Chambers, Tom Steele, Dale Van Sickel, Rex Lease, Fred Graham, Bud Wolfe, Bill Wilkus, Ken Terrell, Duke Taylor, George Magrill, Eddie Rocco, John Daheim, Loren Riebe, Rose Plummer, Bill Yrigoyen, Virginia Carroll, Carey Loftin, Dick Rush, Rod Bacon, Robert Wilke, Eddie Parker, Joe Yrigoyen
Directors: William Witney, Fred Brannon
Screenplay: Albert DeMond, Basil Dickey, Jesse Duffy, Sol Shor
Associate Producer: Ronald Davidson
Chapters: (1) Atomic Peril (2) Thunderbolt (3) The Fatal Sacrifice (4) The Laughing Skull (5) Flaming Death (6) Mystery of the Mountain (7) Electrocution (8) The Slave Collar (9) Blazing Fury (10) The Trap that Failed (11) Double Murder (12) The Invisible Trail

THE INVISIBLE INFORMER
(Republic, August 19, 1946) 57 Mins.
Linda Stirling, William Henry, Adele Mara, Peggy Stewart, Tom London, Gerald Mohr, Donia Bussey, Claire DuBrey, Tristram Coffin, Charles Lane, Cy Kendall, Francis McDonald
Director: Philip Ford
Screenplay: Sherman L. Loew
Story: Gerald Drayson Adams
Associate Producer: William J. O'Sullivan

THE MYSTERIOUS MR. VALENTINE
(Republic, September 3, 1946)
William Henry, *Linda Stirling*, Virginia Christine, Thomas Jackson, Barbara Wooddell, Kenne Duncan, Virginia Brissac, Lyle Latell, Ernie Adams, Tristram Coffin, Arthur Space, Robert Bice
Director: Phil Ford
Screenplay: Milton Raison
Associate Producer: Donald H. Brown

RIO GRANDE RAIDERS
(Republic, September 9, 1946) 56 Mins.
Sunset Carson, *Linda Stirling*, Bob Steele, Tom London, Tristram Coffin, Edmund Cobb, Jack O'Shea, Tex Terry, **Kenne Duncan**, Al Taylor, Fred Burns, Roy Bucko, Blackie Whiteford
Director: Thomas Carr
Screenplay: Norton S. Parker
Associate Producer: Bennett Cohen

JESSE JAMES RIDES AGAIN
(Republic, March 21, 1947) 13 Chapters.
Clayton Moore, *Linda Stirling*, Roy Barcroft, John Compton, Tristram Coffin, Tom London, Holly Bane, Edmund Cobb, Gene Stutenroth, LeRoy Mason, Edward Cassidy, Dave Anderson, Eddie Parker, Tom Steele, Dale Van Sickel, Robert Blair, Ted Mapes, Tex Terry, Gil Perkins, Tex Palmer, Casey McGregor, Emmett Lynn, Charles Morton, Watson Downs, Duke Taylor, Monte Montague, Lee Shumway, Carey Loftin, Loren Riebe, Frank Marlowe, Herman Hack, Chuck Roberson, Carl Sepulveda, Ken Terrell, Bert LeBaron, Pascale Perry, Nellie Walker, Chester Conklin, Tommy Coates, George Chesebro, Bud Wolfe, Tom Chatterton, Charles King, Robert Riordan, Howard Mitchell, Dick Alexander, Keith Richards, Victor Cox, Helen Griffith, Don Summers
Directors: Fred C. Brannon, Thomas Carr
Screenplay: Franklyn Adreon, Basil Dickey, Jesse Duffy, Sol Shor
Associate Producer: Mike Frankovich
Chapters: (1) The Black Raiders (2) Signal for Action (3) The Stacked Deck (4) Concealed Evidence (5) The Corpse of Jesse James (6) The Traitor (7) Talk or Die! (8) Boomerang (9) The Captured Raider (10) The Revealing Torch (11) The Spy (12) Black Gold (13) Deadline at Midnight

THE PRETENDER
(Republic, August 16, 1947) 69 Mins.
Albert Dekker, Catherine Craig, Charles Drake, Alan Carney, *Linda Stirling*, Tom Kennedy, Selmer Jackson, Charles Middleton, Ernie Adams, Ben Welden, John Bagni, Stanley Ross, Forrest Taylor, Greta Clement, Peggy Wynne, Eula Guy, Cay Forrester, Peter Michael, Michael Mark, Dorothy Scott
Director: W. Lee Wilder
Screenplay: Don Martin, Doris Miller
Story: Don Martin
Producer: W. Lee Wilder

Aline Towne

20 • ALINE TOWNE

Queen of a Crumbling and Decaying Empire

Aline Towne played the lead in five Republic serials, yet she is less recognized and appreciated than many of her colleagues. Though competent enough, she did not have that special magnetism of such serial heroines as Kay Aldridge, Linda Stirling, Phyllis Coates, Frances Gifford, Adrian Booth, and Lynne Roberts. She was never given a unique character to portray, as was the case with Aldridge as Nyoka, Stirling as Tiger Woman, or Coates as Panther Girl. Even Carol Forman, who essayed the role of The Black Widow in the serial of the same name, is probably remembered by more moviegoers than Miss Towne, who was given the traditional subservient woman's role and had few chances of obtaining superior film footage, dialogue, or wardrobe.

In **The Invisible Monster** (1950) she is an insurance investigator assigned to work with Richard Webb in tracking down the Phantom Ruler (Stanley Price), a power-mad genius with the secret of invisibility. She plays a lady rancher opposite Ken Curtis in **Don Daredevil Rides Again** (1951). This serial was made, according to Jack Mathis in his excellent book Valley of the Cliffhangers, "to match the extensive library clips earmarked for recycling to maintain the serial's ecological viability in a regressing wasteland of theater attendance . . . born out of a need to suppress inflationary production costs through the exploitation of stock footage from previous Zorro serials, but without benefit of the Zorro name."

Radar Men from the Moon (1952) finds her as the assistant to Commando Cody (George Wallace) fighting to thwart the ruler of the Moon (Roy Barcroft) in his plot to overthrow Earth, while in **Zombies of the Stratosphere** (1952) she is assistant to Judd Holdren, an executive in the Inter-Planetary Patrol. The story had to do with alien creatures attempting to displace Earth from its orbit through a gigantic atomic explosion, so that their planet could move into the vacuum and enjoy the more favorable climate. In her final episodic action thriller, **Trader Tom of the China Seas** (1954), she plays a nurse who, with Trader Tom (Harry Lauter), becomes involved in political intrigue and insurgency on a South Seas island after World War II.

Each of these serials was twelve chapters in length--a total of sixty episodes. To anyone seeing all five serials, Aline's features became familiar, but she never had the following or the stories to lift her out of the "ordinary" classification of heroines who always looked helpless and weak. The serials themselves were mundane affairs made in the waning days of the genre on crimped budgets. Quality had slipped perceptibly and Aline never had a chance. Nor did her few feature films lead to anything, though she continued to work as an actress into the 1970s.

Today, ironically, the serials which were churned out on poverty budgets in record time have outlived most of the productions of the big studios. The nostalgia craze has enveloped the serial and "B" Western, and they enjoy a new popularity with film collectors and fans throughout the world. As the female lead in five cliffhangers and several "B" Westerns, Miss Towne will be seen, remembered, and written about for years to come.

The Invisible Monster (Republic, 1950) – Aline Towne and Richard Webb.

ALINE TOWNE Filmography

THE VANISHING WESTERNER
(Republic, March 31, 1950) 60 Mins.
Monte Hale, Paul C. Hurst, *Aline Towne*, Roy Barcroft, Arthur Space, Richard Anderson, William Phipps, Don Haggerty, Dick Curtis, Rand Brooks, Edmund Cobb, Harold Goodwin
Director: Philip Ford
Screenplay: Bob Williams
Associate Producer: Melville Tucker

HARBOR OF MISSING MEN
(Republic, April 1950) 60 Mins.
Richard Denning, Barbra Fuller, Steven Geray, *Aline Towne*, Percy Helton, George Zucco, Paul Marion, Ray Teal, Robert Osterloh, Fernanda Eliseu, Gregory Gay, Jimmy Kelly, Barbara Stanley, Neyle Morrow, Charles LaTorre
Director: T. G. Springsteen
Screenplay: John K. Butler
Associate Producer: Sidney Picker

INVISIBLE MONSTER
(Republic, May 1950) 12 Chapters.
Richard Webb, *Aline Towne*, Lane Bradford, Stanley Price, John Crawford, George Meeker, Keith Richards, Dale Van Sickel, Tom Steele, Marshall Reed, Forest Burns, Eddie Parker, Frank O'Connor, Charles Sullivan, Howard Mitchell, Bud Wolfe, Guy Teague, Carey Loftin, David Sharpe, Duke Taylor, George Magrill, George Volk, Douglas Evans, Ken Terrell, Harold Goodwin, Tom Monroe
Director: Fred C. Brannon
Screenplay: Ronald Davidson
Associate Producer: Franklyn Adreon
Chapters: (1) Slaves of the Phantom (2) The Acid Clue (3) The Death Car (4) Highway Holocaust (5) Bridge to Eternity (6) Ordeal by Fire (7) Murder Train (8) Window of Peril (9) Trail to Destruction (10) High Voltage Danger (11) Death's Highway (12) The Phantom Meets Justice (Reedited into the feature film **Slaves of the Invisible Monster**)

Radar Men From the Moon (Republic, 1952) – Aline Towne and George Wallace.

HIGHWAY 301
(Warner Bros. November 1950) 82 Mins.
Steve Cochran, Virginia Grey, Gaby Andre, Edmon Ryan, Robert Webber, Wally Cassell, *Aline Towne*, Richard Egan, Edward Norris
Director: Andrew Stone
Associate Producer: Andrew Stone
Producer: Bryan Foy

ROUGH RIDERS OF DURANGO
(Republic, January 30, 1951) 60 Mins.
Allan Lane, Walter Baldwin, *Aline Towne*, Steve Darrell, Ross Ford, Denver Pyle, Stuart Randall, Hap Price, Tom London, Russ Whiteman, Dale Van Sickel, Bob Burns, "Black Jack" (a horse)
Director: Fred C. Brannon
Screenplay: M. Coates Webster
Associate Producer: Gordon Kay

DON DAREDEVIL RIDES AGAIN
(Republic, September 1, 1951) 12 Chaps.
Ken Curtis, *Aline Towne*, Roy Barcroft, Lane Bradford, Robert Einer, John Cason, I. Stanford Jolley, Hank Patterson, Lee Phelps, Sandy Sanders, Guy Teague, Tom Steele, Mike Ragan, Cactus Mack, Art Dillard, Joe Phillips, Roy Bucko, Bud Osborne, Saul Gorss, Gene Stutenroth, James Magill, David Sharpe, Charles Horvath, Dale Van Sickel, Jack Ingram, Carey Loftin, Tex Terry, Herman Hack, Bob Reeves, Gene Christopher, Tony DeMario, Don Harvey
Director: Fred C. Brannon
Screenplay: Ronald Davidson
Associate Producer: Franklyn Adreon
Chapters: (1) Return of the Don (2) Double Death (3) Hidden Danger (4) Retreat to Destruction (5) Cold Steel (6) The Flaming Juggernaut (7) Claim Jumper (8) Perilous Combat (9) Hostage of Destiny (10) Marked for Murder (11) The Captive Witness (12) Flames of Vengeance

Don Daredevil Rides Again (Republic, 1951) – Aline Towne and Ken Curtis.

I CAN GET IT FOR YOU WHOLESALE
(20th Century-Fox, 1951)
Susan Hayward, Dan Dailey, George Sanders, Barbara Whiting, Ross Elliott, Marvin Kaplan, Sam Jaffe, Randy Stuart, *Aline Towne,* Vicki Cummings, Richard Lane, Harry Von Zell
Director: Michael Gordon
Producer: Sol C. Siegel
Screenplay: Abraham Polansky
Based on novel by Jerome Weidman

PURPLE HEART DIARY
(Columbia, 1951) 75 Mins.
Frances Langford, Judd Holdren, Ben Lessey, Tony Romano, Rory Mallinson, Selmer Jackson, Lyle Talbot, *Aline Towne,* Bret King, Warren Mills, Larry Stewart, Joel Marson, Richard Grant, Douglas F. Bank, William Klein, Harry Guardino, Marshall Reed, George Offerman, Jr., Steve Pendleton
Director: Richard Quine
Screenplay: William Sackheim
Story: Based on Frances Langford's syndicated column
Producer: Sam Katzman

Trader Tom of the China Seas (Republic, 1954) – Aline Towne and Harry Lauter.

RADAR MEN FROM THE MOON
(Republic, February 1952) 12 Chaps.
George Wallace, *Aline Towne*, Roy Barcroft, William Bakewell, Clayton Moore, Peter Brocco, Bob Stevenson, Don Walters, Tom Steele, Dale Van Sickel, Wilson Wood, Noel Cravat, Baynes Barron, Paul McGuire, Ted Thorpe, Dick Cogan, Stephen Gregory, Paul Palmer, Harry Hollins, Carey Loftin, Jack O'Shea, Billy Dix, William Marke, Claude Dunkin, Sam Sebby, Arthur Walsh, Joe Bailey, Guy Teague, Dick Rich, Tony Merrill, John Marshall, Ken Terrell
Director: Fred C. Brannon
Screenplay: Ronald Davidson
Associate Producer: Franklyn Adreon
Chapters: (1) Moon Rockets (2) Molten Terror (3) Bridge of Death (4) Flight to Destruction (5) Murder Car (6) Hills of Death (7) Human Targets (8) The Enemy Planet (9) Battle in the Stratosphere (10) Mass Execution (11) Planned Pursuit (12) Take-off to Eternity

(Reedited into the feature film **Retik, The Moon Menace**)

CONFIDENCE GIRL
(United Artists, June 1952) 81 Mins.
Tom Conway, Hillary Brooke, Eddie Marr, John Gallaudet, Jack Kruschen, Dan Riss, Paul Livermore, *Aline Towne*, Charlie Collins, Helen Van Tuyl, Bruce Edwards, Tyler McVey, Paul Guilfoyle, Walter Kingsford, Yvonne Peattie, Joe Allen, John Phillips, Leo Cleary, Pamela Duncan, Barbara Woodell, Edmund Cobb
Director: Andrew L. Stone
Screenplay: Andrew L. Stone
Producer: Andrew L. Stone

ZOMBIES OF THE STRATOSPHERE
(Republic, July 1952) 12 Chaps.
Judd Holdren, *Aline Towne*, Wilson Wood, Lane Bradford, Stanley Waxman, John Crawford, Craig Kelly, Ray Boyle, Leonard Nimoy, Tom Steele, Dale Van Sickel, Roy Engel, Jack Harden, Paul Stader, Gayle Kellogg, Jack O'Shea, Robert Garabedian, Jack Mack, Robert Strange, Floyd Criswell, Davison Clark, Paul Gustine, Henry Rowland, Clifton Young, Norman Willis, George Magrill, Frank Alten
Director: Fred C. Brannon
Screenplay: Ronald Davidson
Associate Producer: Franklyn Adreon
Chapters: (1) The Zombie Vanguard (2) Battle of the Rockets (3) Undersea Agents (4) Contraband Cargo (5) The Iron Executioner (6) Murder Mine (7) Death on the Waterfront (8) Hostage for Murder (9) The Human Torpedo (10) Flying Gas Chamber (11) Man vs.Monster (12) Tomb of the Traitors
(Reedited into the feature film **Satan's Satellites**)

A BLUEPRINT FOR MURDER
(20th Century-Fox, February 1953) 76 Mins.
Joseph Cotten, Jean Peters, Gary Merrill, Catherine McLeod, Jack Kruschen, Barney Phillips, Fred Ridgeway, Joyce McCluskey, Mae Marsh, Harry Carter, Jonathan Hole, Walter Sande, Tyler McVey, Teddy Mangean, *Aline Towne*, Ray Hyke, Charles Collins, Eugene Borden, Carleton Young, Grandon Rhodes, Herb Butterfield, George Melford
Director: Andres Stone
Screenplay: Andrew Stone
Producer: Michael Abel

TRADER TOM OF THE CHINA SEAS
(Republic, 1953) 12 Chaps.
Harry Lauter, *Aline Towne*, Lyle Talbot, Robert Shayne, Fred Graham, Richard Reeves, Tom Steele, John Crawford, Dale Van Sickel, Victor Sen Yung, Jan Arvan, Ramsay Hill, George Selk, Charley Phillips, Bill Hudson, Budd Buster, Saul Gorss, Ken Terrell, Richard Alexander, Duane Thorsen, Robert Bice, Charles Sullivan, Rush Williams, Steve Conte, Bill Chandler
Director: Franklyn Adreon
Screenplay: Ronald Davidson
Associate Producer: Franklyn Adreon
Chapters: (1) Sea Saboteurs (2) Death Takes the Deck (3) Five Fathoms Down (4) On Target! (5) The Fire Ship (6) Collision! (7) War in the Hills (8) Native Execution (9) Mass Attack (10) Machine Murder (11) Underwater Ambush (12) Twisted Vengeance

JULIE
(Arwin/Metro, September 1956) 109 Mins.
Doris Day, Louis Jourdan, Barry Sullivan, Frank Lovejoy, Jack Kelly, Ann Robinson, Barney Phillips, Jack Druschen, John Gallaudet, Carlton Young, Hank Patterson, Ed Hinton, Harlan Warde, *Aline Towne*, Eddie Marr, Mae Marsh
Director: Andrew L. Stone
Screenplay: Andrew L. Stone
Producer: Martin Melcher

GUNS DON'T ARGUE
(Visual Drama, 1957) 92 Mins.
Myron Healey, Jim Davis, Lyle Talbot, Jean Harvey, Paul Dubov, Sam Edwards, Richard Crane, Tamar Cooper, Baynes Baron, Doug Wilson, Regina Gleason, Jeanne Carmen, Lash LaRue, Sydney Mason, Ralph Moody, Ann Morriss, *Aline Towne*, Jeanne Bates, Hellen Van Tuyl, Knobby Schaeffer, Russell Whitney, Coulter Irwin, Robert Kendall, Sam Flint, Bill Baldwin
Directors: Bill Karn, Richard C. Kahn
Screenplay: Phillips H. Lord, William J. Faris
Associate Producer: Terry Turner
Producer: William J. Faris

THE BRASS BOTTLE
(Universal-Scarus/Universal, February 12, 1964) 89 Mins.
(Eastman Color)
Tony Randall, Burl Ives, Barbara Eden, Kamala Devi, Edward Andrews, Richard Erdman, Kathie Browne, Ann Doran, Philip Ober, Parley Baer, Howard I. Smith, Lulu Porter, Alex Gerry, Herb Virgran, Alan Dexter, Robert Liev, Jan Arvan, Nora Marlowe, *Aline Towne*
Director: Harry Keller
Screenplay: Oscar Brodney
Story: F. Anstey, "The Brass Bottle"
Producer: Robert Arthur

SEND ME NO FLOWERS
(Martin Melcher/Universal, October 14, 1964) 100 Mins.
(Technicolor)
Rock Hudson, Doris Day, Tony Randall, Clint Walker, Edward Andrews, Patricia Barry, Hal March, Paul Lynde, Clive Clerk, Dave Willock, *Aline Towne*, Helen Winston, Christine Nelson
Director: Norman Jewison
Screenplay: Julius J. Epstein
Story: Norman Barasch, Carroll Moore, "Send Me No Flowers"
Executive Producer: Martin Melcher
Producer: Harry Kelly

A GUIDE FOR THE MARRIED MAN
(20th Century-Fox, May 25, 1967) 92 Mins.
Walter Matthau, Inger Stevens, Sue Ann Langdon, Jackie Russell, Robert Morse, Elaine Devry, *Aline Towne*, Claire Kelly, Eve Brent, Marvin Brady
Director: Gene Kelly
Screenplay: Frank Tarloff
Story: Frank Tarloff, "A Guide for the Married Man, as Told to Frank Tarloff"
Producer: Frank McCarthy

SONG OF NORWAY
(ABC Pictures/Cinerama Releasing, November 4, 1970) 142 Mins.
Toraly Maurstad, Florence Henderson, Christina Schollin, Frak Porretta, Harry Secombe, Robert Morley, Edward G. Robinson, Elizabeth Larner, Oscar Homolka, Frederick Jaeger, Henry Gilbert, Richard Wordsworth, Bernard Archard, *Aline Towne*, Nan Munro
Director: Andrew L. Stone
Screenplay: Andrew L. Stone
2nd Unit Director: Yakima Canutt
Story: Milton Lazarus, Robert Wright, George Forrest, "Song of Norway"
Producer: Andrew L. and Virginia Stone

Marie Walcamp

21 • MARIE WALCAMP

The Great Adventuress of the Screen

Marie Walcamp, born in Denison, Ohio, on July 27, 1894, was one of the most admired serial queens of the twenties. She earned the title "The Great Adventuress of the Screen" in a string of Universal serials. Her proficiency in nearly every branch of outdoor sport helped to make her a prime favorite with that portion of the audience that demanded action as well as beauty from its heroines. It seemed that there was nothing too dangerous for her to attempt; she fearlessly leaped from careening automobiles into foaming chasms and just as fearlessly played with wild animals.

Marie is the girl who fell over the 150-foot cliff and clung to a bit of ledge until the hero was lowered by his ankles to pull her to safety. She laughed at being abducted through the window of a speeding passenger train onto a galloping horse's back; enjoyed being leaped over by an irritable lion while the camera clicked; and trained a horse to turn a somersault at racing speed (with her on its back) so she could do a picture fall and laugh about it afterward.

Marie was not beautiful, though she was a striking blonde; it was her individuality that made her remarkable. Slightly over five feet tall and weighed around 130 pounds, her athletic training showed in every line of her small, sturdy figure.

Before entering movies she was a standout in musical comedy for four years with Weber and Fields, Kolb and Dill, De Wolf Hopper, and Held and Frank Daniel. She also spent intervals in stock, that reliable school for all branches of acting. Laura Oakley, an actress much admired by Marie, advised her to try for pictures and introduced her to Henry McRae, who put her to work in bit roles as a regular stock player. In her first two weeks she earned ninety dollars a week, a large sum to Marie. She gladly turned her back on musical comedy, one-night stands, and general discomforts.

Her earliest work was in late 1912 or early 1913 in the comedies of Lyons and Moran. By 1914 she was being featured with William Clifford in a variety of two-reelers, most of which were action-oriented. In 1916 she appeared prominently in chapters 10-13 of **Patria** (1917), the war-preparedness propaganda serial starring Irene Castle. Marie played the part of Bess Morgan, one of her aides. However, because of a delayed release of Patria, Marie's own starring vehicle, **Liberty** (1916), was released first. **Liberty** (also known as **Liberty, a Daughter of the U.S.A.**) was the first Western serial ever made and quickly won the approval of audiences. Marie, as Liberty, and Jack Holt, as Captain Rutledge of the Texas Rangers, were convincing in their portrayals. They received ample support from Neal Hart, Eddie Polo, and L. M. Wells, but the action in this pioneering Western chapter play sagged in many spots as the story unfolded. The film did, however, establish Marie as one of the top athletic stars of the cinema world.

In the next several years Marie starred in a number of short Western and action films, and in a few features. It was as Tempest Cody that Marie gained her Western laurels in a series of two-reelers for Universal. But her greatest fame came via the serials. In 1917 she made **The Red Ace**; in 1918, **The Lion's Claw;** in 1919, **The Red Glove**; and in 1920, **The Dragon's Net.** Each was a smashing success. Universal made special efforts to build Marie into a popular serial queen, and plot complications and artistic presentation represented an advance in the adventure serial. Settings were elaborate, and location jaunts to faraway places were not uncommon, a contrast to the era when serial filming crews seldom got more than a hundred miles from the studio.

The Red Ace (1917) was set in the wilds of Canada and the thrills were as wild as the setting.

Marie braved every conceivable misfortune to prove that her family was the victim of foreign machinations and innocent of stealing platinum for transmission to the enemies of the U.S. The overall construction and execution of this photoplay made it superior to **Liberty**, and Miss Walcamp's popularity with the fans climbed.

The Lion's Claw (1918), in eighteen two-reel episodes, was probably Marie's most popular serial. During the shooting she was attacked by one of the lions used in the film and bore a scar for the rest of her life. This serial, too, had a World War I backdrop, the story centering around a group of English people trapped in the African jungle. Marie was involved in a plot hatched by the Central Powers to bring about a holy war among the African peoples.

Marie was no stranger to jungle pictures, having previously starred in the two-reelers **The Jungle Queen** (1915), **A Daughter of the Jungle** (1915), **The Terrors of the Jungle** (1915), **The Jungle Master** (1914), and **From the Lion's Jaws** (1914). For the most part, plots were negligible, mere threads of interest on which to hang the incidents featuring lions, leopards, chimpanzees, and snakes.

Marie was keeping her identification with Westerns intact in such outings as **A Railroad Bandit** (1916), a splendid two-reeler written by Wright Roberts. A bandit organization, a box of gold bullion, and some attractive mountain scenic effects are among the ingredients. The action is good, including some stirring stunts of various kinds. **The Indian's Lament** (1917) was directed by Henry McRae and starred Marie as Bess Conolly, loved by both good guy Lee Hill and bad guy E. N. Wallack, and respected by Noble Johnson in his role as Sleepy Horse, an Indian mistreated by Indian agent Wallack. An even meatier role was essayed by Marie in **Tongues of Flame** (1919), in which she plays Teresa, a dance hall girl who has killed her lover in a fit of jealousy. On her way to jail she escapes in the Carquinez Woods and is befriended by L'Eau Dormonte (Al Whitman), an educated half-breed who lives in the hollow trunk of one of the great redwoods. The sheriff (Alfred Allen) grows jealous of Dormonte, who he thinks has stolen the love of Nellie Wynn (Lilly Clarke), and stumbles upon Teresa while waiting for his rival. Then Dormonte discovers that the sheriff is his own father. Events move fast, but the fates write the final chapter of the tangled romance, for fire sweeps the woods and the trio finds a pyre in the great redwoods that stood long before man.

Marie's popularity increased with **The Red Glove** (1919), an eighteen-chapter thriller directed by J. P. McGowan and based on Douglas Grant's "The Fifth Ace." But it was **The Dragon's Net** (1920) that proved to be her finest serial. Subtitles stated that the scenes laid in China, Japan, and the Philippines were actually filmed in those lands and the atmosphere maintained did not belie that declaration. The settings and surroundings were generally excellent and the prevailing spirit impressed serial enthusiasts. Thematically, the film was out of the ordinary, the story centering about a set of eight lotus leaves made of gold. A formula for perpetual life could be gleaned from an inscription to be determined only from the entire set. The efforts of a crooked old fellow who secures one of the leaves from the heroine by trickery and then tries to obtain the other seven is the basis of the tale. The search leads Marie and a male adventurer across the Pacific.

There was much action in the production, which was adapted from the novel **The Petals of Lao-Tze**, by J. Allen Dunn. Henry McRae was responsible for the screen version. Harlan Tucker, Marie's former partner in the Morosco Theatre of Los Angeles, was second in the cast. While filming scenes in Tokyo, Marie and Harlan were married.

After **The Dragon's Net** Marie Walcamp made only a few more pictures before retiring to devote herself to domestic and non-movie pursuits. In 1927 she came out of retirement to play a principal role in FBO's **In a Moment of Temptation** (1927), then gave up moviemaking for good. She died November 17, 1936, her passing scarcely noticed by those who had once thrilled to her screen exploits. But true-blue serial buffs will always remember Marie as one of the heroines who molded the genre in its early years, and Western aficionados will not forget her Tempest Cody shoot-em-ups when the roll of great Western heroines is prepared.

MARIE WALCAMP Filmography

FROM THE LION'S JAWS
(Universal-Bison, March 14, 1914)
William Clifford, *Marie Walcamp*
Director: Henry McRae
Screenplay: Henry McRae

IN THE WOLF'S FANGS
(Universal-Bison, March 21, 1914) 2 Reels
Marie Walcamp, William Clifford

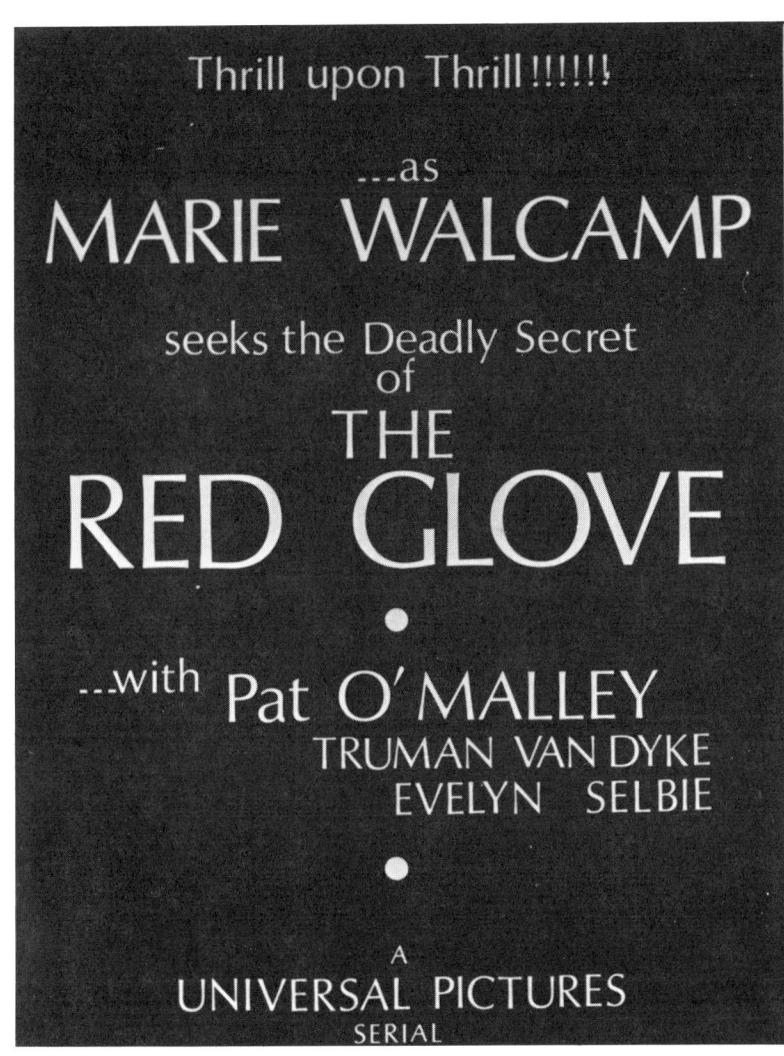 

The Red Glove (Universal, 1919) – Marie Walcamp.

WON IN THE CLOUDS
(Universal, April 11, 1914) 3 Reels
Herbert Rawlinson, *Marie Walcamp*, Rex de Rosselli, Essie Fay, Frank Lloyd
Director: Otis Turner
Screenplay: Otis Turner

THE GREAT UNIVERSAL MYSTERY
(Universal-Nestor, July 10, 1914) 1 Reel
King Baggot, Pauline Bush, Ford Sterling, William Clifford, Lois Weber, Lee Morna, Ella Hall, Hobart Henley, William Welsh, Betty Schade, Leah Baird, Howard Crampton, Al Christie, Carl Laemmle, Maurice Flecks, Herman Fichtenberg, Allen Curtis, Florence Lawrence, Francis Ford, Bob Leonard, Cleo Madison, Victoria Forde, Murdock MacQuarrie, Ethel Grandin, Alexander Gadin, Rupert Julian, Edna Maison, Edmund Mortimer, Frank Crane, J. C. Graham, Wilfred Lucas, F. A. Van Jusan, J. V. Bryson, Henry McRae, J. Warren Kerrigan, Grace Cunard, Herbert Rawlinson, Phillips Smalley, Eddie Lyons, William Shay, Iren Wallace, Matt Moore, *Marie Walcamp*, Frank Smith, William C. Dowlan, Herbert Brenon, Isadore Berstein, Otis Turner, Bob Thornby, David Horsley, Fred Balshofer
Director: Allan Dwan
(A promotional film for Universal)

OLANA OF THE SOUTH SEAS
(Universal-Bison, July 18, 1914)
Marie Walcamp, William Clifford

RESCUED BY WIRELESS
(Universal-Bison, August 15, 1914) 2 Reels
William Clifford, *Marie Walcamp*, Sherman Bainbridge
Director: Henry McRae
Screenplay: Henry McRae

THE LAW OF THE LUMBERJACK
(Universal-Bison, August 22, 1914) 2 Reels
William Clifford, Sherman Bainbridge, *Marie Walcamp*, Val Paul

OUR ENEMY'S SPY
(Universal-Bison, September 19, 1914) 3 Reels
Marie Walcamp, William Clifford

THE PHANTOM LIGHT
(Universal-Bison, October 3, 1914) 2 Reels
Marie Walcamp, William Clifford
Story: Margaret Oswald

THE MOON CHILD
(Universal-Bison, October, 1914)
Marie Walcamp, William Hart Crane, J. Barney Sherry
Director: Henry McRae
Screenplay: H. G. Stafford

THE SILENT PERIL
(Universal-Bison, November 7, 1914) 2 Reels
Marie Walcamp, William Clifford

THE JUNGLE MASTER
(Universal-Bison, November 14, 1914) 2 Reels
Marie Walcamp, Rex de Rosselli, William Clifford, Val Paul
Director: Henry McRae
Screenplay: H. G. Stafford
Story: Rex de Rosselli

THE BRAND OF HIS TRIBE
(Universal-Bison, November 21, 1914) 2 Reels
William Clifford, Val Paul, *Marie Walcamp*
Director: Henry McRae
Screenplay: H. G. Stafford

THE TRAIL BREAKERS
(Universal-Bison, December 5, 1914) 2 Reels
William Clifford, Rex de Rosselli, Val Paul, *Marie Walcamp*, Sherman Bainbridge
Director: Henry McRae

THE LAW OF THE RANGE
(Universal-Bison, December 26, 1914) 3 Reels
Marie Walcamp, William Clifford, Sherman Bainbridge, Rex de Rosselli, Val Paul, Lule Warrenton
Director: Henry McRae
Screenplay: H. G. Stafford
Story: Wayne Groves Barrows

CUSTER'S LAST SCOUT
(Universal-Bison, 1914) 2 Reels
Marie Walcamp, William Clifford, Alfred Chapman
Director: Henry McRae

THE GOVERNOR MAKER
(Universal-Bison, January 9, 1915) 2 Reels
William Clifford, *Marie Walcamp*, Doris Pawn

THE CRIME OF THOUGHT
(Powers, January 23, 1915) 1 Reel
William Clifford, *Marie Walcamp*, Sherman Bainbridge
Story: Sherman Bainbridge

THE TERRORS OF THE JUNGLE
(Universal-Bison, February 6, 1915) 2 Reels
William Clifford, *Marie Walcamp*, Rex de Rosselli, Sherman Bainbridge, Lule Warrenton, "Baby" Wilson

THE LOST LEDGE
(Universal-Bison, February 27, 1915) 2 Reels
William Clifford, *Marie Walcamp*, Sherman Bainbridge

THE BLOOD OF THE CHILDREN
(Universal-Gold Seal, March 5, 1915) 2 Reels
Rex de Rosselli, William Clifford, *Marie Walcamp*
Director: Herny McRae
Screenplay: Bess Meredyth

THE BLOOD OF HIS BROTHER
(Universal-Bison, April 29, 1915) 2 Reels
Rex de Rosselli, Wellington Playter, *Marie Walcamp*, Sherman Bainbridge
Director: Henry McRae
Screenplay: Henry McRae

THE TORRENT
(Universal-Bison, May 3, 1915) 2 Reels
Wellington Playter, *Marie Walcamp*
Director: Henry McRae
Screenplay: Henry McRae

THE OAK-LAWN HANDICAP
(Universal-Bison, May 25, 1915) 2 Reels
William Clifford, *Marie Walcamp*, Rex de Rosselli
Director: Henry McRae
Screenplay: H. G. Stafford

The Red Ace (Universal, 1917) – Marie Walcamp has her name above the title, a feat few serial heroines achieved after 1930.

THE CIRCUS GIRL'S ROMANCE
(Universal-Bison, June 4, 1915) 2 Reels
Rex de Rosselli, *Marie Walcamp*, Sherman Bainbridge, Wellington Playter
Director: Henry McRae
Screenplay: Hugh Weir

THE JUNGLE QUEEN
(Universal-Bison, June 5, 1915) 2 Reels
Marie Walcamp, Wellington Playter, Sherman Bainbridge
Director: Henry McRae
Screenplay: Henry McRae

THE TEST OF A MAN
(Universal-Bison, June 18, 1915)
Wellington Playter, *Marie Walcamp*, Sherman Bainbridge
Director: Henry McRae
Screenplay: Hugh Weir

THE TOLL OF THE SEA
(Universal-Bison, July 8, 1915) 2 Reels
Sherman Bainbridge, *Marie Walcamp*, Wellington Playter
Director: Henry McRae
Story: Henry McRae, Don Meaney

A MEXICAN SPY IN AMERICA
(Universal-Bison, July 11, 1915)
Marie Walcamp, William Clifford
Director: Henry McRae
Screenplay: Henry McRae

A DAUGHTER OF THE JUNGLES
(Universal-Bison, July 23, 1915) 2 Reels
Marie Walcamp, Wellington Playter, Rex de Rosselli, Sherman Bainbridge, Betty Schade
Director: Henry McRae
Screenplay: Henry McRae

CHASING THE LIMITED
(Universal-Bison, August 6, 1915) 2 Reels
Wellington Playter, Betty Schade, *Marie Walcamp*, Kingsley Benedict
Director: Henry McRae
Story: Julius Grinnel Furthmann

CORAL
(Universal-Bison, August 27, 1915) 4 Reels
Marie Walcamp, Wellington Playter
Director: Henry McRae
Screenplay: Olga P. Clark

THE SURRENDER
(Universal-Bison, September 10, 1915) 3 Reels
Marie Walcamp, W. Marks, Seymour Zeliff, Helen Wright, Clarence Burton, Joseph Singleton
Director: Harold Entwhistle
Screenplay: L. V. Jefferson

THE YELLOW STAR
(Universal-Bison, October 8, 1915) 3 Reels
Marie Walcamp, Frank Newbury
Director: J. P. McGowan
Story: Randall Parrish

A FIGHT TO A FINISH
(Universal-Bison, October 15, 1915) 3 Reels
Marie Walcamp, C. E. Horn, George Cummings, Kinglsey Benedict, Fred Church
Director: J. P. McGowan
Screenplay: Helen Holmes

PATSY OF THE CIRCUS
(Universal, 1915) 2 Reels
Marie Walcamp, William F. "Buffalo Bill" Cody
Director: Henry McRae

HOP, THE DEVIL'S BREW
(Universal-Bluebird, January 18, 1916) 5 Reels
Phillips Smalley, Lois Weber, *Marie Walcamp*, Juan de la Cruz, Norman Hammond
Director: Phillips Smalley
Screenplay: Lois Weber
Story: Rufus Steele

DISCONTENT
(Universal-Gold Seal, January 25, 1916) 2 Reels
J. Edward Brown, Charles Hammond, Katherine Griffith, *Marie Walcamp*, Alva Blake, John R. Hope, Juan de la Cruz
Director: Phillips Smalley, Lois Weber
Producer: The Smalleys
Story: Lois Weber

THE FLIRT: A NAMORADEIRA
(Universal-Bluebird, March 1, 1916) 5 Reels
Marie Walcamp, Fred Church, Antrim Short, Grace Benham, Olga Crane, Nannine Wright, Juna de la Cruz, Paul Bryon, Robert Lawler
Director: Phillips Smalley
Screenplay: Lois Weber
Story: Booth Tarkington

JOHN NEEDHAM'S DOUBLE
(Universal-Bluebird, March 17, 1916) 5 Reels
Marie Walcamp, Tyrone Power
Directors: Phillips Smalley, Lois Weber
Screenplay: Olga Printzlau
Story: Joseph Hatton

WHERE ARE MY CHILDREN?
(Universal, April 27, 1916) 5 Reels
Tyrone Power, Helen Riaume, *Marie Walcamp*, Cora Drew, Rene Rogers, A. D. Blake, Juan de la Cruz, Norman Hammond, William J. Hope, Marjorie Blynn, William Haben
Directors: Phillips Smalley, Lois Weber
Screenplay: Lois Weber
Story: Lucy Payton, Franklin Hall
Producer: The Smalleys

TAMMANY'S TIGER
(Bison, June, 1916) 2 Reels
Marie Walcamp, Lee Hill, H. Griffith, L. C. Shumway, E. N. Wallack
Director: Henry McRae
Scenario: Henry McRae
Story: Wright Roberts

A RAILROAD BANDIT
(Universal-Bison, June 17, 1916) 2 Reels
Lee Hill, *Marie Walcamp*, L. C. Shumway
Director: Henry McRae
Story: Wright Roberts

ONDA OF THE ORIENT
(Universal-Gold Seal, July 28, 1916) 3 Reels
Marie Walcamp, Lee Shumway, E. Walleck, Duke Worne, Eddie Polo, Charles Dorian
Director: Henry McRae
Story: Ben Cohn, Walter Woods

THE HUMAN PENDULUM
(Universal-Bison, July, 1916) 3 Reels
Marie Walcamp, E. N. Wallock, Lee Hill, L. C. Shumway, Ivor McFadden
Director: Henry McRae
Screenplay: Frank Wiltermood
Story: Henry McRae

LIBERTY
(Universal, August 14, 1916) 20 Chapters
Marie Walcamp, Jack Holt, Neal Hart, B. Raymond Nye, L. M. Wells, Eddie Polo, Hazel Buckham, Roy Stewart, Maude Emory, Bertram Grassby, Charles Bringly, Leonard Clapham (Tom London)
Directors: Jacques Jaccard, Henry McRae
Screenplay: Jacques Jaccard
Story: W. B. Pearson
Chapters: (1) The Fangs of the Wolf (2) Riding with Death (3) American Blood (4) Dead or Alive (5) Love and War (6) The Desert of Lost Souls (7) Liberty's Sacrifice (8) Clipped Wings (9) A Daughter of Mars (10) The Buzzard's Prey (11) The Devil's Triumph (12) For the Flag (13) Strife and Sorrow (14) A Modern Joan of Arc (15) Flag of Truce (16) Court-Martialed (17) A Trail of Blood (18) The Wolf's Nemesis (19) An Avenging Angel (20) A Daughter of the U.S.A.

THE SILENT TERROR
(Universal, circa 1916)
Marie Walcamp

THE QUEST OF VIRGINIA
(Universal, circa 1916)
Marie Walcamp

A JUNGLE TRAGEDY
(Universal-Big U, January, 1917) 2 Reels
Marie Walcamp

PATRIA
(International Film Service/Pathe, January 14, 1917) 15 Chapters
Irene Castle, Warner Oland, Milton Sills, Floyd Buckley, *Marie Walcamp*, George Maharoni, Allen Murnane, Dorothy Green, Wallace Beery, Nigel Barrie, Charles Brimley, Jack Holt, George Lessey, M. W. Rale, Leory Baker, Rudolph Valentino, Dick Stewart
Directors: Theodore and Leo Wharton (Ithaca scenes), Jacques Jaccard (Hollywood scenes)
Screenplay: J. B. Clymer, Louis Joseph Vance, Charles W. Goddard
Story: Louis Joseph Vance, "The Last of the Fighting Channings"
Chapters: (1) Last of the Fighting Channings (2) The Treasure (3) Winged Millions (4) Double Crossed (5) The Island God Forgot (6) Alias Nemesis (7) Red Dawn (8) Red Night (9) Cat's Paw and Scapegoat (10) War in the Dooryard (11) Sunset Falls (12) Peace on the Border or Peace Which Passeth All Understanding (13) Wings of Death (14) Border Peril (15) For the Flag

THE INDIAN'S LAMENT
(Universal-Gold Seal, February 13, 1917) 3 Reels
Marie Walcamp, Noble Johnson, Lee Hill, E. N. Wallace, Nanine Wright
Director: Henry McRae
Screenplay: Walter Woods
Story: Noble Johnson

STEEL HEARTS
(Universal-Bison, March 31, 1917) 2 Reels
Marie Walcamp, E. C. Wallack, L. C. Shumway, Lee Hill, Gypsy Sontoris
Director: Henry McRae
Screenplay: Wright Roberts

HER GREAT MISTAKE
(Universal-Big U, April, 1917) 2 Reels
Marie Walcamp

THE KIDNAPPED BRIDE
(Universal-Bison, April, 1917) 2 Reels
E. N. Wallack, Lois White, *Marie Walcamp*, Lee Hill, L. C. Shumway, Marc Fenton
Director: Henry McRae
Screenplay: Wright Roberts
Story: Wright Roberts

THE FLIRT
(Pathé, October 19, 1917)
Marie Walcamp, Snub Pollard, Harold Lloyd

THE RED ACE
(Universal, October 22, 1917) 16 Chapters
Marie Walcamp, Larry Peyton, Yvette Mitchell, Bobby Mack, L. M. Wells, Charles Brindley, Miriam Shelby, Noble Johnson, Harry Archer, Nellie Allen
Director: Jacques Jaccard
Screenplay: Jacques Jaccard
Chapters: (1) Silent Terror (2) Lure of the Unattainable (3) A Leap for Liberty (4) The Undercurrent (5) In Mid-Air (6) Fighting Blood (7) The Lion's Claws (8) Lair of the Beast (9) A Voice from the Dead or Voice from the Past (10) Hearts of Steel (11) The Burning Span (12) Overboard (13) New Enemies (14) The Fugitives (15) Hell's Riders (16) Virginia's Triumph

THE LION'S CLAW
(Universal, April 6, 1918) 18 Chapters
Marie Walcamp, Thomas Lingham, Gertrude Astor, Alfred Allen, Edwin August, Leonard Clapham, Harry Von Meter, Frank Lanning, Roy Hanford, Neal Hart, Rex de Rosselli, Sam Polo
Directors: Jacques Jaccard, Harry Harvey
Screenplay: W. B. Pearson, Jacques Jaccard
Chapters: (1) A Woman's Honor (2) Beasts of the Jungle (3) Net of Terror (4) A Woman's Scream (5) The Secret Document (6) The Dungeon of Terror (7) Quicksand (8) Into the Harem (9) The Human Pendulum (10) Escape thru the Flames (11) Caught in the Toils (12) The Spies' Cave (13) In Disguise (14) Hell Let Loose (15) Bridge of the Beast (16) The Jungle Pool (17) The Well of Horror or The Danger Pit (18) The Doom of Rej Hari, or Triumph

THE WHIRLWIND FINISH
(Universal, September 18, 1918) 2 Reels
Marie Walcamp, Harry Blake, Clara Horton, E. N. Wallock
Director: Henry McRae
Story: Mrs. A. G. Robinson

TONGUES OF FLAME
(Universal-Bluebird, December 2, 1918) 5 Reels
Marie Walcamp, Al Whitman, Alfred Allen, Hugh Sutherland, J. P. Wilde, Lilly Clarke
Director: Colin Campbell
Screenplay: Lanier Bartlett
Story: Bret Harte, "In the Carquinez Woods"

THE RED GLOVE
(Universal, March 17, 1919) 18 Chapters
Marie Walcamp, Pat O'Malley, Truman Van Dyke, Evelyn Selbie, Alfred Allen, Andrew Waldron, Thomas Lingham, Leon de la Mothe, William Dyer, Edgar Allen, Leon Kent
Director: J. P. McGowan
Screenplay: Hope Loring
Story: Douglas Grant, "The Fifth Ace"
Chapters: (1) Pool of Lost Souls (2) Claws of the Vulture (3) The Vulture's Vengeance (4) Passing of Gentleman Geoff (5) At the Mercy of a Monster (6) Flames of Death (7) A Desperate Chance (8) Facing Death (9) A Leap for Life (10) Out of Death's Shadow (11) In the Depths of the Sea (12) In Death's Grip (13) Trapped (14) The Lost Millions (15) The Mystery Message (16) In Deadly Peril (17) The Rope of Death (18) Run to Earth

A PHANTOM FUGITIVE
(Universal, May 1, 1919) 2 Reels
Eddie Polo, *Marie Walcamp*
Director: Jacques Jaccard
Story: Jacques Jaccard, Marie Walcamp

TEMPEST CODY HITS THE TRAIL
(Spur & Saddles Series, No. 1)
(Universal, September 1, 1919) 2 Reels
Marie Walcamp, Robert Anderson, Charles Brinley, Ben Corbett, Leonard Trainor, Slim Pagette, Archie Ricks, Eugenie Forde, A. MacPherson
Director: Jacques Jaccard
Screenplay: George Hively
Story: Jacques Jaccard, George Hively

TEMPEST CODY FLIRTS WITH DEATH
(Spur & Saddles Series, No. 2)
(Universal, September 8, 1919) 2 Reels
Marie Walcamp, Robert Anderson, Charles Brinley
Director: Jacques Jaccard
Screenplay: George Hively
Story: Jacques Jaccard, George Hively

TEMPEST CODY RIDES WILD
(Spur & Saddles Series, No. 3)
(Universal, September 15, 1919) 2 Reels
Marie Walcamp, Robert Anderson, Charles Brinley, Ben Corbett, Gabe Price
Director: Jacques Jaccard
Screenplay: George Hively
Story: Jacques Jaccard, George Hively

TEMPEST CODY'S MAN HUNT
(Spur & Saddles Series, No. 4)
(Universal, September 22, 1919) 2 Reels
Marie Walcamp
Director: Jacques Jaccard
Screenplay: George Hively
Story: Jacques Jaccard, George Hively

TEMPEST CODY PLAYS DETECTIVE
(Spur & Saddles Series, No. 5)
(Universal, September 30, 1919) 2 Reels
Marie Walcamp, Carl Miller, Jack Walters, Betty Srack
Director: George Holt
Screenplay: George Hively
Story: Jacques Jaccard

TEMPEST CODY GETS HER MAN
(Spur & Saddles Series, No. 6)
(Universal, October 6, 1919) 2 Reels
Marie Walcamp
Director: George Holt
Screenplay: Anthony Coldeway
Story: Dorothy Rockfort

TEMPEST CODY TURNS THE TABLES
(Spur & Saddles Series, No. 7)
(Universal, October 13, 1919) 2 Reels
Marie Walcamp, Carl Miller, Arizona Brady
Director: George Holt
Screenplay: George Hively
Story: Karl Coolidge, George Hively

TEMPEST CODY BUCKS THE TRUST
(Spur & Saddles Series, No. 8)
(Universal, October 20, 1919) 2 Reels
Marie Walcamp, Frank Braidwood, Bert Sprotte, Madge Hunt, John Linge
Director: George Holt
Screenplay: George Hively
Story: George Hively

TEMPEST CODY, KIDNAPPER
(Spur & Saddles Series, No. 9)
(Universal, October 27, 1919) 2 Reels
Marie Walcamp, Beulah Booker, Frank Braidwood, Harry Schumm
Director: Henry McRae
Screenplay: Wycliffe A. Hill
Story: Dorothy Rockfort

THE DRAGON'S NET
(Universal, August 23, 1920) 12 Chapters
Marie Walcamp, Harlan Tucker, Otto Lederer, Wadsworth Harris
Director: Henry McRae
Screenplay: Henry McRae
Story: J. Allen Dunn, "The Petals of Lao-Tze"
Chapters: (1) The Mysterious Murder (2) Thrown Overboard (3) A Watery Grave (4) Into the Chase (5) A Jump for Life (6) Captured in China (7) The Unseen Foe (8) Trailed to Peking (9) On the Great Wall of China (10) The Train of Death (11) The Shanghai Peril (12) The Unmasking

THE BLOT
(Lois Weber/F. B. Warren, September 4, 1921) 7 Reels
Philip Hubbard, Margaret McWade, Claire Windsor, Louis Calhern, *Marie Walcamp*
Director: Lois Weber
Producer: Lois Weber

TREASURE CANYON
(Sunset/Aywon, January 1924) 5 Reels
J. B. Warner, *Marie Walcamp*

A DESPERATE ADVENTURE
(Independent, June 20, 1924) 5 Reels
Franklyn Farnum, *Marie Walcamp*, Priscilla Bonner
Director: J. P. McGowan
Story: James Ormont

WESTERN VENGEANCE
(Independent, July 20, 1924) 5 Reels
Franklyn Farnum, Doreen Turner, *Marie Walcamp*, Jim Corey, Martin Turner, Mack V. Wright, Pete
Director: J. P. McGowan
Story: James Ormont

IN A MOMENT OF TEMPTATION
(R-C Pictures/FBO, September 18, 1927) 6 Reels
Charlotte Stevens, Grant Withers, Cornelius Keefe, *Marie Walcamp*, Kit Guard, Tom Ricketts, John MacKinnon
Director: Philip Carle
Screenplay: Julia Crawford
Story: Laura Jean Libbey

Pearl White

22 • PEARL WHITE

The Silent Serial's Reigning Queen, She Showed Them How to Do It

With the release of **The Perils of Pauline** (1914), the motion picture serial came into its own. A whole new genre was fashioned on the success of this crudely made chapter play and its phenomenally popular star, formerly a little-known comedienne with Crystal. Though Mary Fuller, Kathlyn Williams, and Grace Cunard preceded her as serial heroines, it was Pearl White who captivated the world with her performance of the hair-raising scenes written for her.

Strangely enough, it was in New Jersey, not Hollywood, that Pearl earned screen immortality. There, without benefit of doubles, she raced across rooftops to escape the clutches of the hooded terror, leaped from speeding trains, tumbled down stairways, disappeared through trapdoors, and swarmed up fire escapes. And it was there that she endured the desperate hazards of the mill saw, the onrushing flood waters, the leaps from the bridges, fires, explosions, and the jutting rocks of the Palisades. She could scuffle with a dozen ruffians without so much as mussing the blonde wig that hid her auburn hair and became her trademark. She was Pearl White, a woman uniquely fitted to fill the need of millions of people living humdrum lives for escapist entertainment and vicarious thrills.

Pearl Fay White's serial escapades and uninhibited personal life fulfilled the dreams of both the sweatshop working girls and the small town belles who wished for balls and marcelled Charles Dana Gibson boy friends. She is one of the few silent picture stars to achieve a permanent place in American folklore.

The facts surrounding Pearl's childhood are clouded. Myth and fact have become so intertwined that it is impossible to unravel them. Pearl herself created and perpetuated many of the myths; her own autobiography, <u>Just Me</u> (Doran Company, 1919), has to be read with many reservations. But it is safe to say that no career in studio or stage history was more crowded with adventure than Pearl White's.

Pearl was born in Greenridge, Missouri, a small community near Sedalia, on March 4, 1889, but grew up in Springfield. Her father was at various times a farmer, a realtor, and an insurance man. Her mother died when Pearl was three.

In her autobiography Pearl states that she ran away from home at the age of fourteen and worked for several weeks in a circus, earning room and board and eight dollars a week. This story has been neither confirmed nor discredited. Pearl claimed that a broken collar bone sustained in a fall from the trapeze bar soon forced her to return home.

At fifteen Pearl went to work in a print shop that turned out theatre programs. Her job was to feed paper bags to a press from early morning until six at night. One story has it that the same hand injured in the circus was caught and crushed by the press.

Pearl wanted a chance to play on the stage, and she made that chance for herself. Fearing her father, a stern, unsympathetic man, she continued to work in the shop by day while playing small parts at night. That way she could still give him money, and he wouldn't be angry with her. She had to act; there was something in her that demanded expression and made her willing to endure a great deal.

When she reached eighteen she left home and joined the Trousedale Stock Company, which traveled throughout Missouri, Kansas, and Oklahoma. While appearing in a play in Oklahoma City she married Victor Sutherland, one of the actors, on October 12, 1907. The marriage was dissolved in 1914, just as Pearl was catching on as a movie star. For three years Pearl traveled with various shows throughout the South, and it has been

The Perils of Pauline (Pathé, 1914) – Pearl White.

suggested that some of them were nothing more than medicine shows. Stranded with a show in South Carolina, she worked her way to Cuba as a stewardess, emptying slop jars and making beds. In a cheap Cuban dance hall she sang American songs under the name of "Miss Mazie" and picked up the pesos the Cubans flung at her. Evidently she split early from Sutherland, though they did not divorce until 1914. She would never talk about the marriage.

Pearl moved on to South America with her tawdry costume of red, white, and blue to sing in the dance halls and casinos until homesickness drove her back north. Tired and penniless, she returned to her father's house in Springfield, finding work with a dressmaker and then as a nursemaid in a family where she was blissfully happy because she had plenty to eat.

It is little wonder that Pearl White emerged with few illusions, a frank materialist. At an age when youth steps out into life, she had already lived it. She eventually hit the road again with a stock company and only a sense of humor kept her from quitting. The failure of her voice while appearing in Connecticut in an old-fashioned melodrama led her to the silent cinema and the rest her throat needed. Her first job was with Pat Powers, who placed her on the payroll at thirty dollars a week. Her first movie of record is **The Girl from Arizona** (1910). After about eighteen months with Powers, Pearl accepted a job at Lubin but was fired within a few months. Pathé picked her up, and she achieved a degree of popularity and recognition there, enough so that Crystal hastened to put her under contract to appear exclusively as a commedienne. She got top billing, and the titles of films often included her name, which helped to establish her identity.

A series of short comedies for Crystal followed, and by mid-1913 Pearl was not only a well-known film star but had accumulated $6,000, which she was determined to spend on a good time in Europe. After six lively months on the Continent, she returned to Crystal and was grinding out more comedies when she met an old friend, Theodore Wharton, who was now working for Pathé. Through Wharton she met Louis Gasnier, who was preparing to film **The Perils of Pauline** (1914). He liked Pearl, was familiar with her Crystal work, and felt she was just the woman to play Pauline. Pearl accepted his offer of extensive publicity and $250 a week, and starred in what was destined to be the most famous episodic cliffhanger of all time.

Serial buffs are probably familiar with the many stories about the risks Pearl took in filming, and the fact that she only used a double when it was physically impossible for her to perform the action required. Her most serious accident occurred in her very first serial, **The Perils of Pauline**, when she sustained a bad back injury in falling down a flight of stairs. This injury plagued Pearl in later years and may have been a contributing cause to her early death at forty-nine.

The Exploits of Elaine (1914), **The New Exploits of Elaine** (1915), and **The Romance of Elaine** (1915) followed in short order, making big money for Pathé. Pearl became the studio's leading money-maker and her salary skyrocketed to between $3,000 and $5,000 a week. More serials followed, including **The Iron Claw** (1916), **Pearl of the Army** (1916), **The Fatal Ring** (1917), **The House of Hate** (1918), **The Lightning Raider** (1919), and **The Black Secret** (1919), all of them successful.

The Lightning Raider, it might be added, was acclaimed as the best serial that Pathé had ever produced, in fact, the best in the entire field. Hyperbole, perhaps, but it was a good film nevertheless. Bertram Millhauser and George B. Seitz, respectively author and director, utilized every single foot of film in each episode. No action was wasted, and the mental and physical clash of the opposing factions was gripping.

Pearl White was perhaps the best-known woman in the world. Since the silent screen had no language barriers, her following was international. She lived better than most real-life queens, enjoying the many luxuries an annual income of $250,000 to $300,000 could provide her. By today's standards that income would equal better than $1 million a year in purchasing power. Wallace Davies characterized Pearl aptly when he wrote:

All accounts of Pearl add up to a person who was frank, friendly, warm-hearted, humorous, sometimes given to practical jokes, fond of shooting craps with the workmen in the studio, and possessed of a vivid vocabulary when annoyed. Her voice, rough and hoarse, suggested both a lack of genteel background and a history of throat trouble such as had supposedly propelled her into pictures in the first place. Never temperamental, she was popular with associates because of her cooperativeness and willingness to work hard.

In 1918 Pearl married Major Wallace McCutcheon, a much-decorated, battle-scarred veteran of World War I who had previously made a few films for Kalem and Lubin. The marriage lasted long enough for them to appear in **The Black Secret** (1919), before Pearl was lured by William Fox to join his studio and to make a series of features that were largely in the style of drawing room comedy (hardly the type to appeal to her followers). McCutcheon appeared with Pearl in **The Thief** (1920), but the war had worked insidious changes in him. One day he walked out of the Lambs Club and disappeared completely. Pearl White's need for romance was thwarted again, and in 1921 she obtained a divorce. Months later, McCutcheon was discovered in a sanitarium in Washington, D.C. The deadly gas of war and two bullet wounds had slowly undermined him. He committed suicide in Hollywood in January of 1928.

Pearl made ten lackluster films for Fox in 1920-22, but features were not her forte, and they did not achieve anything like the success of her serials.

In 1922 Pearl went to live in France, where she owned a country villa and a town house. She traveled extensively after announcing that she had become tired of "being swung from cliffs and dropped from burning houses down into sewers." Her eyesight had also been impaired by the studio lights. But her desire for retirement did not long survive the attractions and plaudits of Paris. There she drew crowds to the Montmartre Music Hall in a revue called "Tu Perds La Boule" and later, at a reputed $3,000 a week, she did a successful London revue in which she costarred with George Carney. She became a notable figure at racetracks and night clubs, appeared in other European theatres, and made a tour to Asia Minor and Egypt. She made world headlines by spending time in an Alpine convent, "in search of her soul."

George Seitz lured her back to the States for one last serial, **Plunder** (1923), in which she starred mainly as a favor to him. The film centered on a skyscraper in New York City beneath which was a hidden treasure which the villain sought to obtain by any possible means. The serial was successful, as were all of those made by Pearl, but it was not her best. The back injury suffered in making **Perils of Pauline** was giving her more trouble than ever, and it was painful for her to subject herself to the rigors of her work. Her last picture was a feature titled **Terror** (1924), filmed in France and released in the United States as **The Perils of Paris**.

On Miss White's final visit to the United States in 1937, three Hollywood studios offered to promote her return to the screen. She turned them down, commenting, "Why should I make a comeback? I have plenty of money: I'm happy now. Why should I go to Hollywood? Do I look crazy?"

Pearl White died of a liver ailment at the age of forty-nine on August 4, 1938, in the American Hospital in Neuilly, France. Only a dozen people were in attendance when she was buried in the Possy cemetery. Much of her estate, valued at close to half a million dollars, was willed to charitable institutions.

Not one of Pearl's movies was made in California, nor is she known to have visited the state. But Hollywood profited by her pioneering efforts as the silent screen's most popular heroine, and every cliffhanger produced after 1915 -- regardless of locale--was influenced by the example set by vivacious and daring Pearl White.

PEARL WHITE Filmography

THE GIRL FROM ARIZONA
(Pathé, May 21, 1910) 1 Reel
Pearl White, Crane Wilbur
Director: Joseph A. Golden
Screenplay: Anthony Coldeway

THE MISSING BRIDEGROOM
(Powers, July 26, 1910)
Pearl White

TOMMY GETS HIS SISTER MARRIED
(Pathé, July 29, 1910) 850 Ft.
Pearl White, Crane Wilbur
Director: Joseph A. Golden
Screenplay: Henry Otto

HER PHOTOGRAPH
(Pathé, August 20, 1910) 1 Reel
Pearl White, Crane Wilbur
Director: Joseph A. Golden
Screenplay: Henry Otto

THE HOODOO
(Pathé, October 1, 1910) 1 Reel
Pearl White, Crane Wilbur
Director: Joseph A. Golden
Screenplay: Anthony Coldeway

A SUMMER FLIRTATION
(Pathé, October 15, 1910) 1 Reel
Pearl White, Crane Wilbur
Director: Joseph A. Golden
Screenplay: Anthony Coldeway

THE NEW MAGDALENE
(Powers, November 26, 1910) 1 Reel
Pearl White, Paul Panzer
Director: Joseph A. Golden
Screenplay: Pierce Kingsley
Story: Wilkie Collins

THE WOMAN HATER
(Powers, November 26, 1910)
Pearl White, Stuart Holmes

THE MAID OF NIAGARA
(Pathé, December 3, 1910) 1 Reel
Pearl White, Paul Panzer
Director: Joseph A. Golden
Screenplay: Pierce Kingsley

WHEN THE WORLD SLEEPS
(Powers, December 3, 1910)
Pearl White

THE COUNT OF MONTE CRISTO
(Powers, January 14, 1911)
Pearl White

HOME SWEET HOME
(Powers, March, 1911) 1 Reel
Pearl White
Director: Joseph A. Golden
Screenplay: J. C. Whitcomb

HELPING HIM OUT
(Lubin, April 20, 1911) 1 Reel
Pearl White
Director: Joseph A. Golden
Screenplay: Bertram Millhauser

ANGEL OF THE SLUMS
(Powers, May, 1911) 1 Reel
Pearl White
Director: Joseph A. Golden
Screenplay: Bertram Millhauser

HIS BIRTHDAY
(Lubin, July 1, 1911) 1 Reel
Pearl White
Director: Joseph A. Golden
Screenplay: Henry Otto

MEMORIES OF THE PAST
(Pathé, August 20, 1911)
Pearl White

THROUGH THE WINDOW
(Pathé, August 23, 1911)
Pearl White, Octavia Handworth

THE REPORTER
(Pathé, November 11, 1911) 1 Reel
Pearl White

THE LOST NECKLACE
(Pathé, November 23, 1911) 1 Reel
Jack Smith, *Pearl White*, Octavia Handworth
Director: Joseph A. Golden
Screenplay: Bertram Millhauser

THE POWER OF LOVE
(Pathé, 1911)
Pearl White, Crane Wilbur

FOR THE HONOR OF THE NAME
(Powers, 1911) 1 Reel
Pearl White

THE ARROWMAKER'S DAUGHTER
(Pathe, August 7, 1912) 1 Reel
Pearl White, Paul Panzer

THE GIRL IN THE NEXT ROOM
(Crystal, October 6, 1912) 1 Reel
Pearl White
Director: Joseph A. Golden
Screenplay: Alex Frank

HER DRESSMAKER'S BILLS
(Crystal, October 13, 1912) 1 Reel
Pearl White

BELLA'S BEAUS
(Crystal, October 20, 1912)
Pearl White, Chester Barnett
Director: Phillips Smalley

A PAIR OF FOOLS
(Crystal, October 26, 1912)
Pearl White

OH, SUCH A NIGHT
(Crystal, November 3, 1912) 1 Reel
Pearl White
Director: Joseph A. Golden
Screenplay: Henry Otto

THE GYPSY FLIRT
(Crystal, November 10, 1912) 1 Reel
Pearl White
Director: Joseph A. Golden
Screenplay: Anthony Coldeway

THE CHORUS GIRL
(Crystal, November 16, 1912) 1 Reel
Pearl White, Chester Barnett
Director: Phillips Smalley

LOCKED OUT
(Crystal, December 1, 1912) 1 Reel
Pearl White, Chester Barnett
Director: Joseph A. Golden
Screenplay: Bertram Millhauser

A TANGLED MARRIAGE
(Crystal, December 8, 1912)
Pearl White

THE MIND CURE
(Crystal, December 15, 1912)
Pearl White, Chester Barnett
Director: Phillips Smalley

HIS WIFE'S STRATAGEM
(Crystal, December 22, 1912) 1 Reel
Pearl White, Chester Barnett

HER VISITOR
(Crystal, December 29, 1912)
Pearl White, Claude Belmont

MAYBLOSSOM
(Pathé, 1912)
Pearl White, Hal Forde

Pearl White.

HER KID SISTER
(Crystal, January 5, 1913)
Pearl White

HEROIC HAROLD
(Crystal, January 12, 1913) 1 Reel
Pearl White

A DIP INTO SOCIETY
(Crystal, January 19, 1913)
Pearl White

PEARL'S ADMIRERS
(Crystal, January 26, 1913)
Pearl White, Chester Barnett
Director: Phillips Smalley

WITH HER RIVAL'S HELP
(Crystal, February 2, 1913)
Pearl White, Chester Barnett
Director: Phillips Smalley

ACCIDENT INSURANCE
(Crystal, February 9, 1913)
Pearl White

STRICTLY BUSINESS
(Crystal, February 16, 1913)
Pearl White, Chester Barnett
Director: Phillips Smalley

THAT OTHER GIRL
(Crystal, February 23, 1913)
Pearl White, Chester Barnett
Director: Phillips Smalley

A NIGHT IN TOWN
(Crystal, March 2, 1913) 1 Reel
Pearl White, Chester kBarnett
Director: Phillips Smalley

WHO IS THE GOAT?
(Crystal, March 8, 1913)
Pearl White, Chester Barnett
Director: Phillips Smalley

KNIGHTS AND LADIES
(Crystal, March 9, 1913) 1 Reel
Pearl White, Chester Barnett
Director: Phillips Smalley

LOVERS THREE
(Crystal, March 23, 1913) 1 Reel
Pearl White, Chester Barnett
Director: Phillips Smalley

THE DRUMMER'S NOTE BOOK
(Crystal, March 30, 1913) 1 Reel
Pearl White, Chester Barnett
Director: Phillips Smalley

OUR PARENTS-IN-LAW
(Crystal, April 5, 1913)
Pearl White, Chester Barnett
Director: Phillips Smalley

PEARL AS A CLAIRVOYANT
(Crystal, April 6, 1913)
Pearl White, Chester Barnett
Director: Phillips Smalley

THE VEILED LADY
(Crystal, April 13, 1913)
Pearl White
Director: Phillips Smalley

TWO LUNATICS
(Crystal, April 20, 1913)
Pearl White, Chester Barnett
Director: Phillips Smalley

FORGETFUL FLOSSIE
(Crystal, April 27, 1913)
Pearl White, Chester Barnett
Director: Phillips Smalley

HIS AWFUL DAUGHTER
(Crystal, May 3, 1913) 1 Reel
Pearl White, Chester Barnett
Director: Phillips Smalley

WHEN LOVE IS YOUNG
(Crystal, May 3, 1913)
Pearl White, Chester Barnett
Director: Phillips Smalley

PEARL AS A DETECTIVE
(Crystal, May 4, 1913)
Pearl White, Chester Barnett
Director: Phillips Smalley

HOMLOCK SHERMES
(Crystal, May 18, 1913) 1 Reel
Pearl White
Director: Phillips Smalley

TOODLEUMS
(Crystal, May 25, 1913)
Pearl White, Chester Barnett
Director: Phillips Smalley

WHERE CHARITY BEGINS
(Crystal, May 24, 1913)
Pearl White, Chester Barnett
Director: Phillips Smalley

MARY'S ROMANCE
(Crystal, June 3, 1913) 1 Reel
Pearl White, Chester Barnett
Director: Phillips Smalley

THE NEW TYPIST
(Crystal, June 8, 1913)
Pearl White, Chester Barnett
Director: Phillips Smalley

A CALL FROM HOME
(Crystal, June 17, 1913) 1 Reel
Pearl White, Chester Barnett
Director: Phillips Smalley

WILL POWER
(Crystal, June 22, 1913)
Pearl White, Chester Barnett
Director: Phillips Smalley

WHO IS IN THE BOX?
(Crystal, June 28, 1913)
Pearl White, Chester Barnett
Director: Phillips Smalley

MUCHLY ENGAGED
(Crystal, June 28, 1913)
Pearl White, Chester Barnett
Director: Phillips Smalley

AN HOUR OF TERROR
(Crystal, June 28, 1913) 1 Reel
Pearl White, Chester Barnett
Director: Phillips Smalley

TRUE CHIVALRY
(Crystal, July 5, 1913)
Pearl White, Chester Barnett
Director: Phillips Smalley

THE GIRL REPORTER
(Crystal, July 6, 1913) 1 Reel
Pearl White, Chester Barnett
Director: Phillips Smalley

PEARL'S DILEMMA
(Crystal, July 13, 1913)
Pearl White, Chester Barnett
Director: Phillips Smalley

COLLEGE CHUMS
(Crystal, July 19, 1913) 1 Reel
Pearl White, Chester Barnett
Director: Phillips Smalley

THE HALL ROOM GIRLS
(Crystal, July 20, 1913) 1 Reel
Pearl White, Chester Barnett
Director: Phillips Smalley

THE BROKEN SPELL
(Crystal, July 22, 1913)
Pearl White, Chester Barnett
Director: Phillips Smalley

THE PAPER DOLL
(Crystal, July 29, 1913)
Pearl White, Chester Barnett
Director: Phillips Smalley

STARVING FOR LOVE
(Crystal, August 2, 1913) 1 Reel
Pearl White, Chester Barnett
Director: Phillips Smalley

WHAT PAPA GOT
(Crystal, August 3, 1913)
Pearl White, Chester Barnett
Director: Phillips Smalley

A CHILD'S INFLUENCE
(Crystal, August 5, 1913) 1 Reel
Pearl White, Chester Barnett
Director: Phillips Smalley

OH! YOU SCOTCH LASSIE
(Crystal, August 10, 1913)
Pearl White, Chester Barnett
Director: Phillips Smalley

PEARL AND THE TRAMP
(Crystal, August 17, 1913)
Pearl White, Chester Barnett
Director: Phillips Smalley

CAUGHT IN THE ACT
(Crystal, August 19, 1913)
Pearl White, Chester Barnett, Claude Belmont
Director: Phillips Smalley

A GREATER INFLUENCE
(Crystal, August 19, 1913)
Pearl White
Director: Phillips Smalley

HIS AUNT EMMA
(Crystal, August 23, 1913) 1 Reel
Pearl White, Chester Barnett, Claude Belmont
Director: Phillips Smalley

THAT CRYING BABY
(Crystal, August 23, 1913)
Pearl White, Chester Barnett, Joe Belmont
Director: Phillips Smalley

MUCH ADO ABOUT NOTHING
(Crystal, September 2, 1913)
Pearl White, Chester Barnett
Director: Phillips Smalley

THE HAND OF PROVIDENCE
(Crystal, September 6, 1913) 1 Reel
Pearl White, Chester Barnett
Director: Phillips Smalley

LOST IN THE NIGHT
(Crystal, September 7, 1913)
Pearl White, Chester Barnett
Director: Phillips Smalley

PLEASING HER HUSBAND
(Crystal, September 9, 1913)
Pearl White, Chester Barnett
Director: Phillips Smalley

A NEWS ITEM
(Crystal, September 16, 1913)
Pearl White, Chester Barnett, Claude Belmont
Director: Phillips Smalley

MISPLACED LOVE
(Crystal, September 21, 1913)
Pearl White, Chester Barnett
Director: Phillips Smalley

PEARL AND THE POET
(Crystal, September 23, 1913)
Pearl White, Chester Barnett, Claude Belmont
Director: Phillips Smalley

HIS LOST GAMBLE
(Crystal, September 28, 1913) 1 Reel
Pearl White, Chester Barnett
Director: Phillips Smalley

DRESS REFORM
(Crystal, October 7, 1913)
Pearl White, Chester Barnett
Director: Phillips Smalley

THE WOMAN AND THE LAW
(Crystal, October 12, 1913)
Pearl White, Chester Barnett
Director: Phillips Smalley

PEARL'S MISTAKE
(Crystal, October 14, 1913)
Pearl White, Chester Barnett
Director: Phillips Smalley

WILLIE'S GREAT SCHEME
(Crystal, October 18, 1913)
Pearl White, Chester Barnett
Director: Phillips Smalley

HEARTS ENTANGLED
(Crystal, October 19, 1913)
Pearl White, Chester Barnett
Director: Phillips Smalley

A HIDDEN LOVE
(Crystal, October 25, 1913)
Pearl White, Chester Barnett
Director: Phillips Smalley

ROBERT'S LESSON
(Crystal, October 26, 1913)
Pearl White, Chester Barnett
Director: Phillips Smalley

THE RICH UNCLE
(Crystal, October 28, 1913)
Pearl White, Chester Barnett
Director: Phillips Smalley

THE FATAL PLUNGE
(Eclectic, November 2, 1913)
Pearl White
Story: Pierre Mangnier

GIRLS WILL BE BOYS
(Crystal, November 4, 1913) 1 Reel
Pearl White, Chester Barnett
Director: Phillips Smalley

OUT OF THE GROVE
(Crystal, November 8, 1913)
Pearl White
Director: Phillips Smalley

WHEN DUTY CALLS
(Crystal, November 9, 1913)
Pearl White
Director: Phillips Smalley

PALS
(Pathé, November 9, 1913) 1 Reel
Pearl White, Crane Wilbur

DAISY WINS THE DAY
(Pathé, November 9, 1913)
Pearl White

AT THE BURGLAR'S COMMAND
(Pathé, November 11, 1913)
Pearl White

OH! YOU PEARL
(Crystal, November 11, 1913)
Pearl White, Chester Barnett
Director: Phillips Smalley

HER SECRETARIES
(Crystal, November 15, 1913)
Pearl White, Chester Barnett
Director: Phillips Smalley

OUT OF THE GRAVE
(Crystal, November 16, 1913)
Pearl White
Director: Phillips Smalley

THE CABARET SINGER
(Crystal, November 23, 1913) 1 Reel
Pearl White, Chester Barnett
Director: Phillips Smalley

HUBBY'S NEW COAT
(Crystal, November 24, 1913)
Pearl White, Chester Barnett
Director: Phillips Smalley

THE CONVICT'S DAUGHTER
(Crystal, November 30, 1913) 1 Reel
Pearl White, Chester Barnett
Director: Phillips Smalley

A WOMAN'S REVENGE
(Crystal, December 7, 1913)
Pearl White, Chester Barnett
Director: Phillips Smalley

PEARL'S HERO
(Crystal, December 9, 1913)
Pearl White, Chester Barnett
Director: Phillips Smalley

FIRST LOVE
(Crystal, December 14, 1913) 1 Reel
Pearl White
Director: Phillips Smalley

THE SOUBRETTE
(Crystal, December 16, 1913)
Pearl White
Director: Phillips Smalley

THE HEART OF AN ARTIST
(Crystal, December 21, 1913) 1 Reel
Pearl White
Director: Phillips Smalley

THE LIFTED VEIL
(Crystal, December 27, 1913)
Pearl White
Director: Phillips Smalley

LURE OF THE STAGE
(Crystal, December 28, 1913)
Pearl White
Director: Phillips Smalley

THE KITCHEN MECHANIC
(Crystal, December 30, 1913)
Pearl White
Director: Phillips Smalley

SHADOWED
(Crystal, January 6, 1914) 1 Reel
Pearl White, Chester Barnett
Director: Phillips Smalley

THE RING
(Crystal, January 11, 1914) 1 Reel
Pearl White
Director: Phillips Smalley

IT MAY COME TO THIS
(Crystal, January 13, 1914)
Pearl White
Director: Phillips Smalley

A FATHER'S DEVOTION
(Crystal, January 18, 1914)
Pearl White
Director: Phillips Smalley

THE SHADOW OF CRIME
(Crystal, January 25, 1914)
Pearl White
Director: Phillips Smalley

OH! YOU PUPPY
(Crystal, January 27, 1914) 1 Reel
Pearl White
Director: Phillips Smalley

A GRATEFUL OUTCAST
(Crystal, February 1, 1914) 1 Reel
Pearl White
Director: Phillips Smalley

WHAT DIDN'T HAPPEN TO MARY
(Crystal, February 3, 1914) 1 Reel
Pearl White
Director: Phillips Smalley

FOR A WOMAN
(Crystal, February 8, 1914)
Pearl White
Director: Phillips Smalley

GETTING REUBEN BACK
(Crystal, February 10, 1914) 1 Reel
Pearl White, Claude Belmont
Director: Phillips Smalley

McSWEENEY'S MASTERPIECE
(Crystal, February 14, 1914) 1 Reel
Pearl White
Director: Phillips Smalley

A SURE CURE
(Crystal, February 15, 1914)
Pearl White
Director: Phillips Smalley

LIZZIE AND THE ICEMAN
(Crystal, March 8, 1914) 1 Reel
Pearl White
Director: Phillips Smalley

GOING SOME
(Crystal, March 31, 1914) 1 Reel
Pearl White, Chester Barnett
Director: Phillips Smalley

THE PERILS OF PAULINE
(Pathé, March 31, 1914) 20 Chapters
Pearl White, Crane Wilbur, Paul Panzer, Edward Jose, Francis Carlyle, Eleanor Woodruff, Clifford Bruce, Sam Ryan, Donald MacKenzie, Jack Standing, Louis Gasnier, Joe Cuny, Charles Revada, Frank Redman, Sr.
Directors: Louis Gasnier, Donald McKenzie
Scenario: George B. Seitz
Story: Charles Goddard
Producers: Leopold and Theodore Wharton
Chapters: Apparently, as originally released, the serial did not have chapter titles. Subsequently, however, chapter titles were written and issued with the chapters by several different sources. For example, Chapter 1 has been titled both "The Breath of Dead Centuries" and "Through Air and Fire," and Chapter 2 has been titled "The Will" as well as "Goddess of the Far West." Other titles used with various episodes are: Pauline Takes the First Trick; Owen Wins the First Game; The Pirate and Pauline; The Treasure Hunters; A Flirty Buccaneer; The Courteous Reception; Baskinell's Quarry; Kaboff's Wild Horse; From Cloud to Cliff; Old Grigsby House Pays Penance; Double Cross Ranch; The Great White Queen; The Death Stone; Sophie McCallan's Wedding; Palmer Comes Back; A Hot Young Comet; Owen Offers a Reward; Owen Makes a Reputation; The Guest of Honor; Submarine B-2; A Paper Chase; and The Mummy's Last Warning.

THE LADY DOCTOR
(Crystal, April 5, 1914) 1 Reel
Pearl White
Director: Phillips Smalley

GET OUT AND GET UNDER
(Crystal, April 7, 1914) 1 Reel
Pearl White
Director: Phillips Smalley

A TELEPHONE ENGAGEMENT
(Crystal, May 5, 1914) 1 Reel
Pearl White
Director: Phillips Smalley

THE MASHERS
(Crystal, May 16, 1914) 1 Reel
Pearl White
Director: Phillips Smalley

THE DANCING CRAZE
(Crystal, May 19, 1914)
Pearl White
Director: Phillips Smalley

EASY MONEY
(Crystal, June 2, 1914) 1 Reel
Pearl White
Director: Phillips Smalley

THE GIRL IN PANTS
(Crystal, June 27, 1914) 1 Reel
Pearl White
Director: Phillips Smalley

HER NEW HAT
(Crystal, June 30, 1914) 1 Reel
Pearl White
Director: Phillips Smalley

WHAT PEARL'S PEARLS DID
(Crystal, July 14, 1914) 1 Reel
Pearl White
Director: Phillips Smalley

WILLIE'S DISGUISE
(Crystal, August 11, 1914)
Pearl White, Chester Barnett
Director: Phillips Smalley

EAST LYNN IN BUGVILLE
(Crystal, September, 1914) 1 Reel
Pearl White
Director: Phillips Smalley

SOME COLLECTORS
(Crystal, October 13, 1914)
Pearl White
Director: Phillips Smalley

OH! YOU MUMMY
(Crystal, November 17, 1914)
Pearl White
Director: Phillips Smalley

THE EXPLOITS OF ELAINE
(Pathé, December 29, 1914) 14 Chapters.
Pearl White, Creighton Hale, Arnold Daly, Sheldon Lewis, Floyd Buckley, Edwin Arden, Ramon Owens, Lee Roy Barker, Bessie Wharton, William Riley, Robin Towney, Lionel Barrymore
Directors: Louis Gasnier, George B. Seitz
Screenplay: Arthur B. Reeve, C. W. Goddard
Producers: Leopold and Theodore Wharton
Chapters: (1) The Clutching Hand (2) The Twilight Sleep (3) The Vanishing Jewels (4) The Frozen Safe (5) The Poisoned Room (6) The Vampire (7) The Double Trap (8) The Hidden Voice (9) The Death Ray (10) The Life Current (11) The Hour of Three (12) The Blood Crystals (13) The Devil Worshippers (14) The Reckoning

A LADY IN DISTRESS
(Superba/Warners, January 3, 1915)
Pearl White
Director: Phillips Smalley

THE NEW EXPLOITS OF ELAINE
(Pathé, April 5, 1915) 10 Chapters.
Pearl White, Creighton Hale, Arnold Daly, Edwin Arden, M. W. Rale, Bessie Wharton, Gazelle March, Ah Ling Foo
Director: George B. Seitz
Scenario: Charles W. Goddard, George B. Seitz
Story: Arthur B. Reeve
Producers: Leopold and Theodore Wharton
Chapters: (1) The Serpent Sign (2) The Cryptic Ring (3) The Watching Eye (4) The Vengeance of Wu Fang (5) The Saving Circles (6) Spontaneous Combustion (7) The Ear in the Wall (8) The Opium Smugglers (9) The Tell-Tale Heart (10) Shadows of War

THE ROMANCE OF ELAINE
(Pathé, June 14, 1915) 12 Chapters.
Pearl White, Creighton Hale, Arnold Daly, Lionel Barrymore, Bessie Wharton
Director: George B. Seitz
Scenario: Charles W. Goddard, George B. Seitz, Bertram Millhauser
Story: Arthur B. Reeve
Producers: Leopold and Theodore Wharton
Chapters: (1) The Lost Torpedo (2) The Gray Friar (3) The Vanishing Man (4) The Submarine Harbor (5) The Conspirators (6) The Wireless Detective (7) The Death Cloud (8) The Search Light Gun (9) The Life Chain (10) The Flash (11) The Disappearing Helmet (12) The Triumph of Elaine

THE KING'S GAME
(Pathé, January 7, 1916)
Pearl White, George Probert, Sheldon Lewis, Nora Moore, George Parks
Story: George B. Seitz, "The King's Game"
Producer: Arnold Daly

HAZEL KIRKE
(Pathé, February 8, 1916)
Pearl White, William Riley Hatch, Bruce McRae, Allen Murnane, Creighton Hale, Florence Edney
Adaptation: Stelle Mackaye

THE IRON CLAW
(Pathé, February 27, 1916) 20 Chapters.
Pearl White, Creighton Hale, Sheldon Lewis, Harry Fraser, J. E. Dunn, Carey Lee, Clare Miller, Henry G. Sell, Edward Jose, E. Cooper Willis, Allan Walker, Bertrand Gudgeon
Directors: Edward Jose, George B. Seitz
Scenario: George B. Seitz
Story: Arthur Stringer
Producers: Leopold and Theodore Wharton
Chapters: (1) The Vengeance of Legar (2) The House of Unhappiness (3) The Cognac Mask (4) The Name and the Game (5) The Incorrigible Captive (6) The Spotted Warning (7) The Hooded Helper (8) The Stroke of 12 (9) Arrows of Hate (10) The Living Dead (11) The Saving of Dan O'Mara (12) The Haunted Canvas (13) The Hidden Face (14) The Plunge for Life (15) The Double Resurrection (16) The Unmasking of Davy (17) The Vanishing Fair (18) The Green-Eyed God (19) The Cave of Despair (20) The Triumph of the Laughing Mask

PEARL OF THE ARMY
(Pathé, December 3, 1916) 15 Chapters.
Pearl White, Ralph Kellard, Marie Wayne, Floyd Buckley, Theodore Friebus, W. T. Carleton, Joe Cuny
Director: Edward Jose
Scenario: G. M. McConnell, George B. Seitz
Chapters: (1) The Traitor (2) Found Guilty (3) The Silent Menace (4) War Clouds (5) Somewhere in Grenada (6) Major Brent's Perfidy (7) For the Stars and Stripes (8) International Diplomacy (9) The Monroe Doctrine (10) The Silent Army (11) A Million Volunteers (12) The Foreign Alliance (13) Modern Buccaneers (14) The Flag Despoiler (15) The Colonel's Orderly

MAYBLOSSOM
(Astro, April 8, 1917)
Pearl White, Niles Welch, Hal Ford, Fuller Mellish
Director: Edward Jose

THE FATAL RING
(Pathé, July 8, 1917) 20 Chapters.
Pearl White, Earle Fox, Warner Oland, Floyd Buckley, Casare Gravaina, Ruby Horrman, Henry G. Sell, Mattie Ferguson, Richard La Marr, Bert Starkey, Louis J. O'Connor, Harriet Reller, Mrs. Spencer Bennet
Director: George B. Seitz
Scenario: Bertram Millhauser
Story: Fred Jackson
Chapters: (1) The Violet Diamond (2) The Crushing Wall (3) Borrowed Identity (4) The Warning on the Ring (5) Danger Underground (6) Rays of Death (7) The Signal Lantern (8) The Switch in the Safe (9) The Dice of Death (10) The Perilous Plunge (11) The Short Circuit (12) A Desperate Chance (13) A Dash for Arabia (14) The Painted Safe (15) The Dagger Duel (16) The Double Disguise (17) The Death Weight (18) The Subterfuge (19) The Cryptic Maze (20) The End of the Trail

THE HOUSE OF HATE
(Pathé, March 10, 1918) 20 Chapters
Pearl White, Antonio Moreno, Floyd Buckley, Peggy Shanor, Paul Dillon, John Gilmour, John Webb Dillon, Joe Cuny, Paul Glerget, Ruby Hoffman, Helene Chadwick, Louis Wolheim
Director: George B. Seitz
Scenario: Bertram Millhauser
Story: Arthur B. Reeve, Charles A. Logue
Chapters: (1) The Hooded Terror (2) The Tiger's Eye (3) A Woman's Perfidy (4) The Man From Java (5) Spies Within (6) A Living Target (7) Germ Menace (8) The Untold Secret (9) Poisoned Darts (10) Double Crossed (11) Haunts of Evil (12) Flashes in the Dark (13) Enemy Aliens (14) Underworld Allies (15) The False Signal (16) The Vial of Death (17) The Death Switch (18) At the Pistol's Point (19) The Hooded Terror Unmasked (20) Following Old Glory

THE LIGHTNING RAIDER
(Pathé, January 5, 1919) 15 Chapters
Pearl White, Warner Oland, Harry G. Sell, Ruby Hoffman, William Burt, Frank Redman, Nellie Burt, Sam Kim, Henrietta Simpson
Director: George B. Seitz
Screenplay: George B. Seitz, Bertram Millhauser
Chapters: (1) The Ebony Block (2) The Counterplot (3) Underworld Terrors (4) Through the Doors of Steel (5) The Brass Key (6) The Mystic Box (7) Meshes of Evil (8) Cave of Dread (9) Falsely Accused (10) The Baited Trap (11) Bars of Death (12) Hurled into Space (13) The White Roses (14) Cleared of Guilt (15) Wu Fang Atones

THE BLACK SECRET
(Pathé, November 9, 1919) 15 Chapters
Pearl White, George B. Seitz, Walter McGrail, Wallace McCutcheon, Harry Gsell, Marjorie Milton, Harry Semels
Director: George B. Seitz
Scenario: Bertram Millhauser
Story: Robert W. Chambers, "In Secret"
Chapters: (1) The Great Secret (2) Marked for Death (3) The Gas Chamber (4) Below the Waterline (5) The Acid Bath (6) The Unknown (7) The Betrayal (8) A Crippled hand (9) Woes of Deceit (10) Inn of Dread (11) The Death Studio (12) The Chance Trail (13) Wings of Mystery (14) The Hidden Way (15) The Secret Host

THE WHITE MOLL
(Fox, July 24, 1920) 8 Reels
Pearl White, Richard C. Travers, J. Thornton Baston, Eva Gordon, William Harvey, Walter Lewis, Blanch Davenport, Charles Slatter, John Woodford, George Pauncefort, John P. Wade
Director: Harry Millarde
Scenario: E. Lloyd Sheldon
Story: Frank L. Packard

THE TIGER'S CUB
(Fox, October 16, 1920) 6 Reels
Pearl White, Thomas Carrigan, J. Thornton Baston, John Davidson, Frank Evans, John Woodford, Ruby Hoffman, Albert Tavernier
Director: Charles Giblyn
Scenario: Paul H. Sloane
Story: George Goodchild

THE THIEF
(Fox, December 11, 1920) 6 Reels
Pearl White, Charles Waldron, Wallace McCutcheon, George Howard, Sidney Herbert, Dorothy Cummings, Anthony Merlo
Director: Charles Giblyn
Scenario: Max Marcin, Paul H. Sloane
Story: Henri Bernstein

THE MOUNTAIN WOMAN
(Fox, January 23, 1921) 6 Reels
Pearl White, Corliss Giles, Richard C. Travers, George Barnum, Warner Richmond, John Webb Dillon, J. Thornton Baston, Charles Graham
Director: Charles Giblyn
Scenario: Ashley T. Locke

KNOW YOUR MEN
(Fox, March 13, 1921) 6 Reels
Pearl White, Wilfred Lytell, Downing Clarke, Harry C. Browne, Estar Banks, Byron Douglas, William Eville
Director: Charles Giblyn
Scenario: Paul H. Sloane

BEYOND PRICE
(Fox, May 8, 1921) 5 Reels
Pearl White, Vernon Steel, Nora Reed, Arthur Gordini, Louis Haines, Maude Turner Gordon, Byron Douglas, Ottola Nesmith, Dorothy Walters, Dorothy Allen, J. Thornton Baston, Charles Sutton
Director: J. Searle Dawley
Scenario: Paul H. Sloane
Story: Paul H. Sloane

VIRGIN PARADISE
(Fox, September 4, 1921) 8 Reels
Pearl White, Robert Elliott, J. Thornton Baston, Alan Edwards, Henrietta Floyd, Grace Beaumont, Mary Beth Barnelle, Lynn Pratt, Lewis Seeley, Charles Sutton, Hal Clarendon
Director: J. Searle Dawley
Story: Hiram Percy Maxim

ANY WIFE
(Fox, January 1, 1922) 5 Reels
Pearl White, Holmes Herbert, Gilbert Emery, Lawrence Johnson, Augustus Balfour, Eulalie Jensen
Director: Herbert Brenon
Story/Scenario: Julia Tolsva

THE BROADWAY PEACOCK
(Fox, February 19, 1922) 5 Reels
Pearl White, Joseph Striker, Doris Eaton, Harry Southard, Elizabeth Garrison
Director: Charles J. Barbin
Story/Scenario: Julia Tolsva

WITHOUT FEAR
(Fox, April 16, 1922) 5 Reels
Pearl White, Robert Elliott, Charles Mckay, Marie Burke, Robert Agnew, Macey Harlam
Director: Kenneth Webb
Scenario: Paul H. Sloane

Plunder (Pathé, 1923) – Perhaps Pearl White needs to tidy up the house a bit before guests arrive.

PLUNDER
(Pathé, January 28, 1923) 15 Chapters.
Pearl White, Harry Semels, Warren Krech (Warren William), Tom McIntyre, J. Elwood Pool, Wally Oettel, William Naly, Charles Revada
Director: George B. Seitz
Adaptation: Bertram Millhauser
Chapters: (1) The Bandaged Man (2) Held by the Enemy (3) The Hidden Thing (4) Ruin (5) To Beat a Knave (6) Heights of Hazard (7) Mocked from the Grave (8) The Human Target (9) Game Clear Through (10) Against Time (11) Spunk (12) Under the Floor (13) Swamp of Lost Souls (14) The Madman (15) A King's Ransom

TERROR
(Epinay Films, June 25, 1924)
(Filmed in France)
Pearl White, Robert Lee, Arlette Marchal, Henry Baudin, Martin Mitchell, Paul Vermoyal
Director: Edward Jose
(Released in the U.S. under the title **The Perils of Paris**)

PART II

FEARLESS BEAUTIES IN DISTRESS

Another bevy of beauties constituted what might be considered the second echelon of serial heroines. They were not necessarily less talented than those mentioned in chapter two; they simply made fewer or less important serials. Therefore, their entrenchment as serial stars was not as solid as that of the first group. Kathlyn Williams, for example, made only one serial in her long, illustrious career, but because of its cinematic importance she is included in this group. Her **The Adventures of Kathlyn** (1913) was the forerunner of the cliffhanger-type serials in which heroine or hero is in jeopardy at the end of each chapter. Mary Fuller is included because she starred in the first serial, **What Happened to Mary?** (1912), then went on to do a sequel, **Who Will Marry Mary?** (1913). These were made before the serial had developed into the familiar jeopardy endings and the continuation of a single story. In the infancy of the motion picture serial each episode was complete in itself; only the character continued, much as in the television series of today.

Most of these heroines are from the silent era, the Golden Age of the Serial Queen. In many instances they were stars or co-stars, and as such they played an integral part in the story. In the sound era most of the girls had to take a back seat to the hero, and their participation was often limited to providing feminine pulchritude and a few screams here and there as a lively musical agitato accentuated the action they precipitated. However, there were exceptions, and a few serial heroines appeared after 1930 who could hold their own with the silent screamers.

Two generations of moviegoers were thrilled by comely heroines from the group whose careers are discussed herein. Although their ranking and popularity as serial heroines is slightly less than that of those discussed in Part I, they were still important serial performers. A study of their careers should prove to be a nostalgic journey for many readers who fondly recall their own early years as front-row youngsters, whistling and stomping as these thrill-a-minute girls faced peril after peril.

Veda Ann Borg

23 • VEDA ANN BORG

A Tough Exterior Hid a Twenty-four-Carat Heart

With part of a rib and pieces of earlobe making up her new nose, Veda Ann Borg, the actress who literally lost her face in an automobile wreck, became a movie star again after a long, uphill climb from near death.

When she went through the windshield of actor Dick Purcell's roadster in a head-on collision the night of August 7, 1939, the broken glass sheared her features away and replaced one of Hollywood's most beautiful faces with a mass of raw flesh. She was slashed beyond recognition, and most of her nose was cut off. Purcell and the driver of the other car were not hurt as badly.

It was feared that Veda would not live, but she did. She was put in touch with Dr. Josif Ginsberg, a famed plastic surgeon. There was a piece of glass in her left eye, and it was feared she would lose her sight. The doctor fixed her eye first, then went to work on what used to be her face. She spent eight months in the hospital, was swathed in bandages for months, and endured ten operations. The doctor removed a piece of her rib to build up a new nose; for cartilage he took pieces of her earlobes.

Warner Bros., with whom she had a contract, was kind. The studio footed the bill for her enormous hospital expenses. But, her face rebuilt, Veda was dropped when her contract expired. Though the surgeon had done a magnificent job in reconstructing her features, the studio thought she would not photograph well. Thus Veda, who a year before had been the subject of a big buildup by Warners, which was promoting her as another Garbo, was suddenly out on the street looking for work.

But we have started in the middle of the story. To begin at the beginning, Veda Ann Borg (her real name) was born in West Roxbury, Massachusetts. Her father, Gottfried Borg, was a painter and decorator who had immigrated from Sweden. But Veda was strictly a hot dog-and-Coke-type American, as Samuel Goldwyn and director Joseph L. Mankiewicz recognized years later when they cast her as Vivian Blaine's showgirl friend in **Guys and Dolls** (1955), in which Veda was as Runyonesque a Broadway character as they make them.

After finishing high school, Veda went to work as a model in a department store. As the result of her photo being sent to Paramount offices in New York, Veda was tested and signed in 1936. She was sent to Hollywood to appear in **Three Cheers for Love** (1936), a minor musical in which she played a cheating wife, but Paramount thought she had little talent and didn't take up her option. She moved over to Warner Bros. and appeared in small roles for two years. In 1939 she was making her first big movie, **One More Tomorrow** (and getting the publicity treatment that Ann Sheridan later received), when her accident occurred.

Between operations on her face Larry Darmour offered her the female lead opposite Victor Jory in Columbia's **The Shadow** (1939). first of the two serials for which continued-next-week fans fondly remember her. It was a thrilling chapter play, and the Saturday matinee audiences readily accepted Veda, who worked hard at all the stunting and swashbuckling. But although the cameraman did what he could to hide the scars, she didn't photograph well. More surgery and a few insignificant parts followed. Then Gregory Ratoff gave her the part of Akim Tamiroff's mistress in **The Corsican Brothers** (1941), a turning point in her career, and saw to it that special care was taken in lighting her. Because Virginia Grey was ill and could not accept the part, Veda played the blonde gun moll in Metro-Goldwyn-Mayer's **The Penalty** (1941), boosting her career still further. As Edward

The Shadow (Columbia, 1940) – Victor Jory and Veda Ann Borg.

Arnold's mistress, Veda received better reviews than anyone else in the cast. Commenting on the film later, Veda said, "It was getting tough paying the bills and I'd arranged to get a job in a department store. But on my final call at Metro, the casting office was in a dither because Virginia Grey was ill and had to be replaced in **The Penalty.** Benny Thau saw me and had a test made, and he and Jack Chertok, the producer, gave me the part."

In 1942 she married a wealthy playboy named Paul Herrick, but the marriage was short-lived, reports having it that the break came because Veda would not abandon her career to live the quiet, domestic life.

The Penalty established a new image for Veda. In **Honky Tonk** (1941) she was a raucous lady barber. Director Gregory Ratoff gave her important roles in **Two Yanks in Trinidad** (1942) and **Something to Shout About** (1943), and the song "Be My Little Bumblebee" in **Irish Eyes are Smiling** (1944). Her role as a burlesque queen in this musical helped convince Hollywood that Veda was just as beautiful as she had been before her shattering accident. Betty Grable requested her for her best friend in **Mother Wore Tights** (1947).

Veda gave a sprightly performance as Vivian Blaine's showgirl buddy in Goldwyn's **Guys and Dolls** (1955). and an outstanding one as an ex-drinker waitress in a brief scene with Susan Hayward in **I'll Cry Tomorrow** (1956). She practically stole the film in **Big Jim McLain** (1952) with John Wayne.

Western buffs will probably remember her in **The Law Comes to Texas** (1936), **Melody Ranch** (1940), **Marked Trails** (1945), **Rider from Tucson** (1950), **The Kangaroo Kid** (1950), **Bitter Creek** (1954), **Frontier Gambler** (1956), and **Naked Gun** (1956). Certainly serial aficionados will recall her fondly as Cora in Columbia's **Jungle Raiders** (1945), and many whose cinema tastes run in a different vein will respect her contributions to such "A" pictures as **San Quentin** (1947). **Bitter Sweet** (1940), and **Over the Wall** (1938). But it is for a multitude of "B" programmers that she is best remembered. As a tough, wise-cracking blonde in whodunits and minor melodramas, she endeared herself to a loyal following.

In 1945, while working on a film with Victor MacLaglen, she met Andrew, the actor's son, who was assistant director on the film. They were married in May of 1946. She miscarried in 1947, but gave birth to a son, Andrew, Jr., in 1954, a few months after the couple separated. She and MacLaglen were divorced in June, 1957, after three years of court battles. She retained custody of her son and her mother moved in with them.

Veda was a stock performer on the "Abbott and Costello" TV series, along with Joyce Compton, during the 1952-54 seasons, and could also be seen in many other television shows. Her screen appearances tapered off during the 1950s. Her last film was **The Alamo** (1960), in which she played a dramatic role as Blind Nell. Thereafter she retired. In 1970 she learned that she had cancer and underwent treatments, to no avail. She died on August 16, 1973, and was cremated quietly. Her elderly mother was placed in a nursing home, and her son went to live with his father.

Veda Ann Borg was at her best playing women of strong character, not necessarily of high morals. Given one of those unrewarding roles that sometimes crop up when the female lead part is small, Veda Ann had no equal. Her touch was simply surer and lighter than that of any of the others.

VEDA ANN BORG Filmography

THREE CHEERS FOR LOVE
(Paramount, 1936) 65 Minutes.
Eleanor Whitney, Robert Cummings, William Frawley, Elizabeth Patterson, Roscoe Karns, John Halliday, Grace Bradley, *Veda Ann Borg*, Louis Da Pron, Olympe Brande, Billy Lee
Director: Ray McCarey
Screenplay: Barry Trivers
Story: George Marion, Jr.
Producer: A. M. Botsford

MEN IN EXILE
(First National, April 4, 1937) 61 Minutes.
Dick Purcell, June Travis, Alan Baxter, Margaret Irving, Victor Varconi, Olin Howlin, *Veda Ann Borg*, Norman Willis, Carlos De Valdez, Alec Harford, John Alexander, Demitris Emanuel
Director: John Farrow
Screenplay: Roy Chanslor
Story: Roy Chanslor
Supervisor: Bryan Foy

KID GALAHAD
(Warner Bros., May 29, 1937) 101 Minutes.
Edward G. Robinson, Bette Davis, Humphrey Bogart, Wayne Morris, Jane Bryan, Harry Carey, William Haade, Soledad Jiminez, Joe Cunningham, Ben Welden, Joseph Crehan, *Veda Ann Borg*, Frank Faylen, Harland Tucker, Bob Evans, Hank Hankinson, Bob Nestell, Jack Kranz, George Blake, Charlie Sullivan, Joyce Compton, Emmett Vogan, I. Stanford Jolley, Don DeFore, Milton Kibbee, Horace McMahon, Eddie Chandler
Director: Michael Curtis
Screenplay: Seton I. Miller
Story: Francis Wallace
Associate Producer: Samuel Bischoff

THE CASE OF THE STUTTERING BISHOP
(First National, June 5, 1937) 70 Minutes.
Donald Woods, Ann Dvorak, Anne Nagel, Linda Perry, Craig Reynolds, Gordon Oliver, Joseph Crehan, Helen MacKellar, Edward McWade, Tom Kennedy, Mira McKinney, Frank Faylen, Douglas Wood, *Veda Ann Borg*, George Lloyd, Selmer Jackson
Director: William Clemens
Screenplay: Don Ryan, Kenneth Gamet
Story: Erle Stanley Gardner
Supervisor: Bryan Foy

MARRY THE GIRL
(Warner Bros., July 1, 1937) 68 Minutes.
Mary Boland, Frank McHugh, Carol Hughes, Allen Jenkins, Mischa Auer, Alan Mowbray, Hugh O'Connell, Tom Kennedy, Dewey Robinson, Teddy Hart, Olin Howlin, Arthur Aylesworth, William B. Davidson, Charles Judels, Irving Bacon, Louis Mason, Louise Stanley, Bess Flowers, *Veda Ann Borg*
Director: William McGann
Screenplay: Sig Herzig, Pat C. Flick, Tom Reed
Story: Edward Hope
Producer: Hal B. Wallis

THE SINGING MARINE
(Warner Bros., July 3, 1937) 105 Minutes.
Dick Powell, Doris Weston, Hugh Herbert, Lee Dixon, Jane Darwell, Allen Jenkins, George "Doc" Rockwell, Larry Adler, Ross King, Marcia Ralston, Guinn "Big Boy" Williams, *Veda Ann Borg*, Jane Wyman, Berton Churchill, Eddie Acuff, Henry O'Neill, Addison Richards, James Robbins, Miki Morita, Pierre Watkin
Director: Ray Enright
Screenplay: Delmar Daves
Story: Delmar Daves
Supervisor: Lou Edelman

PUBLIC WEDDING
(Warner Bros., July 10, 1937) 61 Minutes.
Jane Wyman, William Hopper, Dick Purcell, Marie Wilson, Berton Churchill, James Robbins, Raymond Hatton. *Veda Ann Borg*, Zeni Vatoria
Director: Nick Grinde
Screenplay: Roy Chanslor, Houston Branch
Story: Houston Branch
Supervisor: Bryan Foy

SAN QUENTIN
(First National, August 7, 1937) 70 Minutes.
Pat O'Brien, Ann Sheridan, Humphrey Bogart, Barton MacLane, Joseph Sawyer, *Veda Ann Borg*, James Robbins, Joseph King, Gordon Oliver, Garry Owen, Marc Lawrence, Emmett Vogan, William Pawley, Al Hill, Max Wagner, George Lloyd, Ernie Adams
Director: Lloyd Bacon
Screenplay: Peter Milne, Humphrey Cobb
Story: John Bright, Robert Tasker
Supervisor: Sam Bischoff

DANCE, CHARLIE, DANCE
(First National, August 14, 1937) 64 Minutes.
Stuart Erwin, Jean Muir, Glenda Farrell, Allen Jenkins, Addison Richards, Charles Foy, Chester Clute, Mary Treen, Colette Lyons, Tommy Wonder, Frank Faylen, Robert Homans, Harvey Clark, Olive Olson, *Veda Ann Borg*
Director: Frank McDonald
Screenplay: Crane Wilbur, William Jacobs
Story: George Kaufman, "The Butter and Egg Man"
Supervisor: Bryan Foy

CONFESSION
(First National, August 28, 1937) 86 Minutes.
Kay Francis, Ian Hunter, Basil Rathbone, Jane Bryan, Donald Crisp, Mary Maguire, Dorothy Peterson, Laura Hope Crews, Ben Welden, Robert Barratt, *Veda Ann Borg*, Helen Valkis, Anderson Lawlor
Director: Joe May
Screenplay: Julius Epstein, Margaret Levino
Story: Hans Rameau, "Mazurka"
Supervisor: Henry Blanke

VARSITY SHOW
(Warner Bros., September 4, 1937)
Dick Powell, Fred Waring and his Pennsylvanians, Ted Healy, Rosemary Lane, Priscilla Lane, Walter Catlett, Johnny Davis, Mable Todd, Buck and Bubbles, Sterling Holloway, Scotty Bates, George McFarlane, Polly McClintock, Lee Dixon, Halliwell Hobbs, Roy Atwell, Ed Murphy, Ben Welden, Emma Dunn, *Veda Ann Borg*
Director: William Keighley
Screenplay: Jerry Wald, Richard Macauly
Story: Sig Herzig, Warren Duff
Supervisor: Lou Edelman

ALCATRAZ ISLAND
(Warner Bros., November 6, 1937) 61 Minutes.
John Litel, Mary Maguire, Ann Sheridan, Gordon Oliver, Dick Purcell, Ben Welden, Addison Richards, George E. Stone, Vladimir Sokoloff, Peggy Bates, Doris Lloyd, Anderson Lawlor, Charles Trowbridge. Ellen Clany, Edward Keane, Matty Fain, *Veda Ann Borg*, Walter Young, Ed Stanley, Lane Chandler
Director: William McGann
Screenplay: Crane Wilbur
Story: Crane Wilbur, "Alcatraz"
Supervisor: Bryan Foy

IT'S LOVE I'M AFTER
(Warner Bros., November 20, 1937) 90 Minutes.
Leslie Howard, Bette Davis, Olivia de Havilland, Patric Knowles, Eric Blore, George Barbier, Bonita Granville, Spring Byington, Irving Bacon, Georgia Caine, *Veda Ann Borg*, E. E. Clive, Valerie Bergere, Sarah Edwards, Thomas Pogue, Grace Fields, Harvey Clark, Ed Mortimer, Thomas Mills, Lionel Belmore, Ellen Clancy
Director: Archie Mayo
Screenplay: Casey Robinson
Story: Maurice Hanline, "Gentleman After Midnight"
Supervisor: Harry Joe Brown

SUBMARINE D-1
(Cosmopolitan/First National, November 27, 1937) 101 Minutes.
Pat O'Brien, George Brent, Wayne Morris, Frank McHugh, Doris Weston, Henry O'Neill, Dennie Moore, *Veda Ann Borg*, Regis Toomey, Broderick Crawford, John Ridgely, Owen King, Wally Maher, Jerry Fletcher
Director: Lloyd Bacon
Screenplay: Frank Wead, Warren Duff, Lawrence Krimble
Story: Frank Wead, "Submarine 262"
Supervisor: Lou Edelman

MISSING WITNESSES
(First National, December 11, 1937) 60 Minutes.
John Litel, Dick Purcell, Jean Dale, Raymond Hatton, Sheila Bromley, William Haade, Ben welden, Harland Tucker, Jack Mower, John Harron, Michael Mark, Earl Gunn, Louis Natheaux, *Veda Ann Borg*
Director: William Clemens
Screenplay: Kenneth Gamet, Don Ryan
Story: Kenneth Gamet, Don Ryan
Supervisor: Bryan Foy

SHE LOVED A FIREMAN
(Warner Bros., December 18, 1937) 57 Minutes.
Dick Foran, Robert Armstrong, Ann Sheridan, Eddie Acuff, *Veda Ann Borg*, May Beatty, Eddie Chandler, Ted Oliver, Lane Chandler, Pat Flaherty
Director: John Farrow
Screenplay: Morton Grant, Carlton Sand
Story: Morton Grant, Carlton Sand
Producer: Bryan Foy

OVER THE WALL
(Warner Bros., April 2, 1938) 66 Minutes.
Dick Foran, June Travis, John Litel, Dick Purcell, *Veda Ann Borg*, George E. Stone, Ward Bond, John Hamilton, Jonathan Hale, Tommy Bupp, Robert Homans, Mabel Hart, Raymond Hatton, Alan Davis, Eddie Chandler
Director: Frank MacDonald
Screenplay: Crane Wilbur, George Bricker
Story: Lewis E. Lawes
Producer: Bryan Foy

THE LAW COMES TO TEXAS
(Columbia, April 16, 1939) 61 Minutes.
Bill Elliott, *Veda Ann Borg*, Charles King, Bud Osborne, Charles "Slim" Whitaker, Leon Beaumon, Edmund Cobb, Paul Everton, Lee Shumway, Frank Ellis, Jack Ingram, Frank LaRue, David Sharpe, Forrest Taylor, Budd Buster, Lane Chandler, Dan White, Ben Corbett
Director: Joseph Levering
Screenplay: Nate Gatzert
Story: Nate Gatzert
Producer: Larry Darmour

A MIRACLE ON MAIN STREET
(Columbia, October 20, 1939) 78 Minutes.
Margo, Walter Abel, Lyle Talbot, Wynne Gibson, *Veda Ann Borg*, William Collier, Sr., Jane Darwell, Pat Flaherty, George Humbert, Jeanne Kelly (Jean Brooks), Susan Miller
Director: Steven Sekely
Screenplay: Frederick Jackson
Story: Samuel Ornitz, Boris Ingster
Producer: Jack Skirball

CAFE HOSTESS
(Columbia, November 30, 1939) 63 Minutes.
Preston Foster, Wynne Gibson, Ann Dvorak, Peggy Shannon, Douglas Fowley, Arthur Loft, Bruce Bennett, Eddie Acuff, Bradley Page Linda Winters, Beatrice Blinn, Dick Wessel, *Veda Ann Borg*
Director: Sidney Salkow
Screenplay: Harold Shumate
Story: Tay Garnett, Howard Higgin

THE SHADOW
(Columbia, January 1940) 15 Episodes
Victor Jory, *Veda Ann Borg,* Roger Moore, Robert Fiske, J. Paul Jones, Jack Ingram, Charles Hamilton, Edward Piel, Sr., Frank LaRue, Dick Botiller, Kit Guard, Charles King, Griff Barnett, Eddie Featherstone, Lew Sargeant, Philip Ahn, Charles K. French, Marin Sais, Franklyn Farnum
Director: James W. Horne
Screenplay: Joseph Poland, Ned Dandy, Joseph O'Donnell
Adapted from the Mutual radio program and based upon stories in "Shadow Magazine"
Chapter Titles, (1) The Doomed City (2) The Shadow Attacks (3) The Shadow's Peril (4) In the Tiger's Lair (5) Danger Above (6) The Shadow's Trap (7) Where Horror Walks (8) The Shadow Rides the Rails (9) The Devil in White (10) The Underground Trap (11) Chinatown at Dark (12) Murder by Remote Control (13) The Wheels of Death (14) The Sealed Room (15) The Shadow's Net Closes

I TAKE THIS OATH
(PRC, May 20, 1940) 67 Minutes.
Gordon Jones, Joyce Compton, Craig Reynolds. J. Farrell MacDonald, Robert Homans, Guy Usher, Mary Gordon, Sam Flint, Brooks Benedict, Edward Peil, Sr., Budd Buster, *Veda Ann Borg*
Director: Sherman Scott (Sam Newfield)
Screenplay: George Bricker
Story: William A. Ullman, Jr.
Producer: Sigmund Neufeld

LAUGHING AT DANGER
(Monogram, August 12, 1940) 63 Minutes.
Frankie Darro, Mantan Moreland, Joy Hodges, George Houston, Kay Sutton, Guy Usher, Lillian Elliott, *Veda Ann Borg*, Betty Compson, Rolfe Sedan, Maxine Leslie, Ralph Peters, Gene O'Donnell
Director: Howard Bretherton
Screenplay: Joseph West
Story: Joseph West
Producer: Lindsley Parsons

DR. CHRISTIAN MEETS THE WOMEN
(RKO, September 5, 1940) 68 Minutes.
Jean Hersholt, Dorothy Lovett, Edgar Kennedy, Rod LaRocque, Frank Albertson, Marilyn Merrick, Maude Eburne, *Veda Ann Borg*, Lelah Tyler, William Gould, Heine Conklin, Phyllis Kennedy, Bertha Priestley, Diedra Vale, Julie Carter
Director: William McGann
Screenplay: Marian Orth
Producer: William Stephens

GLAMOUR FOR SALE
(Columbia, September 27, 1940) 57 Minutes.
Anita Louise, Roger Pryor, June MacCloy, Frances Robinson, Don Beddoe, Paul Fix, Arthur Loft, *Veda Ann Borg*, Myra Marsh, Evelyn Young, Madelon Grayson, Ann Doran, Ruth Fallow, Lynn Browing, Dorothy Fay, Jeanne Hart, Bonnie Bennett
Director: D. Ross Lederman
Screenplay: John Bright

BITTER SWEET
(M-G-M, November 8, 1940) 92 Minutes.
Jeanette MacDonald, Nelson Eddy, George Sanders, Felix Bressart, Lynne Carver, Ian Hunter, Edward Ashley, Diana Lewis, Curt Bois, Fay Holden, Sig Rumann, Janet Beecher, Charles Judels, *Veda Ann Borg*, Herman Bing, Greta Meyer, Colin Campbell, Hans Conreid, Sam Harris, Gino Corrado, June Wilkins, Louis Natheaux, Mauriel Goodspeed, Davison Clark, William Tannen, Paul E. Burns, Jeff Corey, Howard Lang
Director: W. S. Van Dyke
Screenplay: Lester Samuels
Story: Noel Coward
Producer: Victor Saville

MELODY RANCH
(Republic, November 15, 1940) 83 Minutes.
Gene Autry, Jimmy Durante, Ann Miller, Barton MacLane, Barbara Allen (Vera Vague), George "Gabby" Hayes, Jerome Cowan, Mary Lee, Joe Sawyer, Horace MacMahon, Clarence Wilson, Billy Benedict, Ruth Gifford, Maxine Ardell, *Veda Ann Borg*, George Chandler, Jack Ingram, Horace Murphy, Lloyd Ingraham, Billy Bletcher (Voice only), Jim Corey, Dick Elliott, Herman Hack, Buck Bucko, Elizabeth "Tiny" Jones, Jane Keckley, Frank Hagney, Jack Montgomery, Priscilla Bonner, Tom London, John Merton, Edmund Cobb, Charles "Slim" Whitaker, Curley Dresden, Art Mix, George Chesebro, Jack Kirk, Merrill McCormack, Wally West, Tex Cooper, Chick Hannon, Tom Smith, Carl Cotner, Bob Wills, Frankie Marvin, Joe Yrigoyen, Champion
Director: Joseph Santley
Screenplay: Jack Moffitt, F. Hugh Herbert
Associate Producer: Sol C. Siegel

BEHIND THE NEWS
(Republic, December 20, 1940) 75 Minutes.
Lloyd Nolan, Doris Davenport, Frank Albertson, Robert Armstrong, Paul Harvey, Charles Halton, Eddie Conrad, Harry Tyler, Dick Elliott, Archie Twitchell, *Veda Ann Borg*, Milton Parsons
Director: Joseph Santley
Screenplay: Isabel Dawn, Boyce DeGaw
Story: Dore Schary, Allen Rivkin
Associate Producer: Robert North

ARKANSAS JUDGE
(Republic, January 28, 1941) 72 Minutes.
Weaver Brothers and Elviry (Leon, Frank and June Weaver), Roy Rogers. Spring Byington, Pauline Moore, Frank M. Thomas, *Veda Ann Borg*, Eily Malyon, Loretta Weaver, Minerva Urecal, Beatrice Maude, Harrison Greene, Barry Macollum, George Rosener, Monte Blue, Frank Darien, Russell Hicks, Edwin Stanley
Director: Frank McDonald
Screenplay: Dorrell and Stuart McGowan
Story: Irving Stone, "False Witness"
Associate Producer: Armand Schaefer

THE PENALTY
(M-G-M, March 14, 1941) 81 Minutes.
Edward Arnold, Lionel Barrymore, Marsha Hunt, Robert Sterling, Gene Reynolds, Emma Dunn, *Veda Ann Borg,* Richard Lane, Gloria De Haven, Grant Mitchell, Phil Silvers, Warren Ashe, William Haade, Ralph Byrd, Edgar Barrier
Director: Harold S. Bucquet
Screenplay: Harry Ruskin
Story: Martin Berkeley

I'LL WAIT FOR YOU
(M-G-M, May 16, 1941) 71 Minutes.
Robert Sterling, Marsha Hunt, Virginia Weidler, Paul Kelly, Fay Holden, Henry Travers, Don Costello, Carol Hughes, Reed Hadley, Ben Weldon, Theodore von Eltz, Leon Belasco, Mitchell Lewis, *Veda Ann Borg*
Director: Robert B. Sinclair
Screenplay: Gus Trosper
Story: Mauri Grashin
Producer: Edwin Knopf

THE GET-AWAY
(M-G-M, June 13, 1941) 89 Minutes.
Robert Sterling, Charles Winninger, Donna Reed, Henry O'Neil, Dan Dailey, Jr., Don Douglas, Ernest Whitman, Grant Withers, Chester Gan, Charles Wagenheim, Guy Kingsford, Marry Fain, *Veda Ann Borg*
Director: Edward Buzzell
Screenplay: Wells Root, W. R. Burnett
Story: J. Walter Ruben, Wells Root
Producer: J. Walter Ruben

THE PITTSBURGH KID
(Republic, August 29, 1941) 76 Minutes.
Billy Conn, Jean Parker, Dick Purcell, Alan Baxter, *Veda Ann Borg,* Jonathan Hale, Ernest Whitman, John Kelly, Etta McDaniel, Dick Elliott, John Harmon, Robert Barron, Arthur Donovan, Henry Armstrong, Freddie Steele, Jack Roper, Sam Balter, Dan Tobey
Director: Jack Townley
Screenplay: Earl Felton
Story: Octavius Roy Cohen
Associate Producer: Armand Schaefer

DOWN IN SAN DIEGO
(M-G-M, September, 1941) 70 Minutes.
Bonita Granville, Ray McDonald, Dan Dailey, Jr., Dorothy Morris, Leo Gorcey, Henry O'Neill, Stanley Clements, *Veda Ann Borg*
Director: Robert B. Sinclair
Screenplay: Harry Clark, Franz G. Spencer
Story: Franz G. Spencer
Producer: Frederick Stephani

HONKY TONK
(M-G-M, October, 1941) 105 Minutes.
Clark Gable, Lana Turner, Frank Morgan, Claire Trevor, Marjorie Main, Albert Dekker, Henry O'Neill, Chill Wills, *Veda Ann Borg,* Douglas Wood, Betty Blythe, Harry Worth, Lew Harvey, Yakima Canutt
Director: Jack Conway
Screenplay: Marguerite Roberts, John Sanford
Producer: Pandro S. Berman

THE CORSICAN BROTHERS
(United Artists, November 29, 1941) 112 Minutes.
Douglas Fairbanks, Jr., Ruth Warrick, Akim Tamiroff, J. Carrol Naish, H. B. Warner, John Emery, Henry Wilcoxin, Gloria Holden, Walter Kingsford, Nana Bryant, Pedro de Cordoba, *Veda Ann Borg*, William Farnum, Sarah Padden, Manart Kippen, Ruth Robinson, Belle Mitchell
Director: Gregory Ratoff
Screenplay: George Bruce, Howard Estabrook
Story: Alexandre Dumas
Producer: Edward Small

DUKE OF THE NAVY
(PRC, January 23, 1942) 63 Minutes
Ralph Byrd, *Veda Ann Borg*, Stubby Kruger, Herbert Corthell, Margaret Armstrong, Val Stanton, Paul Bryar, Sammy Cohen, Red Knight, Lester Towne, William Beaudine, Jr., Zack Williams
Director: William Beaudine
Screenplay: Gerald D. Adams, William Beaudine
Story: Gerald D. Adams, William Beaudine
Producer: John T. Coyle

TWO YANKS IN TRINIDAD
(Columbia, March 26, 1942) 84 Minutes.
Pat O'Brien, Brian Donlevy, Janet Blair, Donald MacDride, Roger Clark, John Emery, Frank Jenks, Frank Sully, *Veda Ann Borg*, Clyde Fillmore, Dick Curtis, Sig Arno
Director: Gregory Ratoff
Screenplay: Sy Bartlett, Richard Carroll, Harry Segall
Producer: Samuel Bischoff

ABOUT FACE
(United Artists/Roach, April 17, 1942) 43 Minutes.
William Tracy, Joe Sawyer, Jean Porter, Marjorie Lord, Margaret Dumont, *Veda Ann Borg*, Joe Cunningham, Harold Goodwin, Grank Faylen, Dick Wessell, Charles Lane
Director: Kurt Neumann
Screenplay: Eugene Conrad, Edward E. Seabrook
Producer: Fred Guiol

SHE'S IN THE ARMY
(Monogram, May 15, 1942) 63 Minutes.
Lucile Gleason, *Veda Ann Borg*, Marie Wilson, Lyle Talbot, Robert Lowery, Maxine Leslie, Charlotte Henry, John Holland, Marcella Richards, Warren Hymer
Director: Jean Yarbrough
Screenplay: Sidney Shelton, George Bricker
Producer: T. H. Richmond

LADY IN A JAM
(Universal, June 19, 1942) 91 Minutes.
Irene Dunne, Patric Knowles, Ralph Bellamy, Eugene Pallette, Samuel S. Hinds, Queenie Vassar, Jane Garland, Edward McWade, Robert Homans, Charles Lane, Hobart Cavanaugh, Mira McKinney, Sarah Padden, Clara Blandick, Sam Underwood, Kathleen Howard, Mona Barrie, *Veda Ann Borg*, Josephine Whittell, Kitty O'Neil, Claire Whitney, Isobel LaMal, Russell Hicks, Irving Bacon, Hardie Albright, Fuzzy Knight, Eddie Fetherstone, Robert Emmett Keane, Charles Cane, Holmes Herbert, Garry Owen, Reed Hadley, Rex Lease, Charles Colemen, Phyllis Kennedy, Syd Saylor, Ruth Warren, Eddie Dunn, Chief Thunder Cloud, Eddy Chandler, Lester Dorr, Al Bridge, Dick Alexander, Billy Benedict, Bess Flowers, Casey MacGregor
Director: Gregory La Cava
Screenplay: Eugene Thackery, Frank Cockrell, Otto Lovering
Producer: Gregory La Cava

I MARRIED AN ANGEL
(M-G-M, July 9, 1942) 84 Minutes.
Jeanette MacDonald, Nelson Eddy, Edward Everett Horton, Binnie Barnes, Reginald Owen, Douglass Dumbrille, Mona Maris, Janis Carter, Inez Cooper, Leonid Kinskey, Anne Jeffreys, Marion Rosamond, *Veda Ann Borg*
Director: W. S. Van Dyke II
Screenplay: Anita Loos
Story: Adapted From the Vaszary Janos play by Richard Rodgers and Lorenz Hart
Producer: Hunt Stromberg

SOMETHING TO SHOUT ABOUT
(Columbia, February 25, 1943) 90 Minutes.
Don Ameche, Janet Blair, Jack Oakie, William Gaxton, Cobina Wright, Jr., *Veda Ann Borg*, Hazel Scott, Jayne Martin, Lily Norwood, James "Chuckles" Walker, Kay Aldridge
Director: Gregory Ratoff
Screenplay: Lou Breslow, Edward Eliscu
Story: Fred Schiller

MURDER IN TIMES SQUARE
(Columbia, April 1, 1943) 65 Minutes.
Edmund Lowe, Marguerite Chapman, John Litel, William Wright, Bruce Bennett, Esther Dale, *Veda Ann Borg*, Gerald Mohr, Sidney Blackmer, Leslie Denison, Douglas Leavitt, George McKay
Director: Lew Landers (Louis Friedlander)
Screenplay: Paul Gangelin
Story: Stuart Palmer
Producer: Colbert Clark

FALSE FACES
(Republic, May 28, 1943) 56 Minutes.
Stanley Ridges, Bill Henry, Rex Williams, *Veda Ann Borg*, Janet Shaw, Joseph Crehan, Chester Clute, John Maxwell, Dick Wessell, Billy Nelson, Etta McDaniel, Nicodemus Stewart
Director: George Sherman
Screenplay: Curt Siodmak
Associate Producer: George Sherman

ISLE OF FORGOTTEN SINS
(PRC, August 15, 1943) 82 Minutes.
John Carradine, Gale Sondergaard, Sidney Toler, Frank Fenton, *Veda Ann Borg*, Rita Quigley, Rick Vallin, Betty Amann, Tala Birell, Patti McCarty, Marian Colby, William Edmonds
Director: Edgar G. Ulmer
Screenplay: Raymond L. Schrock
Story: Raymond L. Schrock
Producer: Peter R. Van Duinen

REVENGE OF THE ZOMBIES
(Monogram, September 17, 1943) 61 Minutes.
John Carradine, Robert Lowery, Gale Storm, *Veda Ann Borg*, Mantan Moreland, Mauritz Hugo, Bob Steele, James Baskett, Madame Sul-Te-Wan, Sybil Lewis, Robert Cherry
Director: Steve Sekely
Screenplay: Edmund Kelso, Van Norcross
Producer: Lindsley Parsons

THE GIRL FROM MONTEREY
(PRC, October 4, 1943) 58 Minutes.
Armida, Edgar Kennedy, *Veda Ann Borg*, Jack LaRue, Terry Frost, Anthony Caruso, Charles Williams, Bryant Washburn, Guy Zanett, Wheeler Oakman
Director: Wallace Fox
Screenplay: Arthur Hoerl
Story: George Green, Robert Gordon
Producer: Jack Schwarz

THE UNKNOWN GUEST
(Monogram, October 22, 1943) 65 Minutes.
Victor Jory, Pamela Blake, Harry Hayden, Emory Parnell, Nora Cecil, Lee "Lasses" White, Paul Fix, Ray Walker, Edwin Mills, *Veda Ann Borg*
Director: Kurt Neumann
Screenplay: Philip Jordan
Story: Maurice Franklin (Maurice and Franklin King)
Producer: Maurice and Franklin King

SMART GUY
(Monogram, December 17, 1943) 63 Minutes.
Rick Vallin, Bobby Larson, *Veda Ann Borg*, Wanda McKay, Jack Larue, Mary Gordon, Paul McVey, Addison Richards, Roy Darmour, John Dawson
Director: Lambert Hillyer
Screenplay: Charles R. Marion, John W. Krafft
Producer: John T. Coyle

STANDING ROOM ONLY
(Paramount, January, 1944) 83 Minutes.
Paulette Goddard, Fred MacMurray, Edward Arnold, Roland Young, Hillary Brook, Porter Hall, Clarence Kolb, Anne Revere, Isabel Randolph, *Veda Ann Borg,* Marie MacDonald, Josephine Whittell, Sig Arno, Boyd Davis, Roy Gordon, Herbert Heyes, Eddie Dunn, Arthur Loft, Yvonne DeCarlo, Noel Neill, Frank Faylen, Ethel May Halls, Forbes Murray, Edwin Stanley
Director: Sidney Lanfield
Screenplay: Darrel Ware, Karl Tunberg
Story: Al Martin
Associate Producer: Paul Jones

DETECTIVE KITTY O'DAY
(Monogram, May 13, 1944) 63 Minutes.
Jean Parker, Peter Cookson, Tim Ryan, *Veda Ann Borg*, Edward Gargan, Douglas Fowley, Herbert Heyes, Pat Gleason, Olaf Hytten
Director: William Beaudine
Screenplay: Victor Hammond, Tim Ryan
Story: Victor Hammond
Producer: Lindsley Parsons

MARKED TRAILS
(Monogram, July 29, 1944) 58 Minutes.
Hoot Gibson, Bob Steele, *Veda Ann Borg*, Ralph Lewis. Mauritz Hugo, Steve Clark, Charles Stevens, Lynton Brent, Bud Osborne, George Morell, Allen B. Sewall, Ben Corbett, John L. (Bob) Cason,
Director: J. P. McCarthy
Screenplay: J. P. McCarthy, Victor Hammond
Producer: William Strobach

THE GIRL WHO DARED
(Republic, August 5, 1944) 56 Minutes.
Lorna Gray, Peter Cookson, Grant Withers, *Veda Ann Borg*, John Hamilton, Willie Best, Vivien Oakland, Roy Barcroft, Kirk Alyn
Director: Howard Bretherton
Screenplay: John K. Butler
Story: Medora Field, "Blood on Her Shoe"
Associate Producer: Rudolph E. Abel

THE BIG NOISE
(20th Century-Fox, October, 1944) 74 Minutes.
Stan Laurel, Oliver Hardy, Arthur Space, Doris Merrick, *Veda Ann Borg*, Bobby Blake, Esther Howard, James Bush, Philip Van Zandt, Beal Wong, Jack Norton, Robert Dudley, Charles Wilson, Francis Ford, George Melford, Frank Fenton, Del Henderson, Edgar Dearing, Selmer Jackson, Harry Hayden, Julie Carter, Sarah Edwards, Emmett Vogan, Ken Christy, Billy Bletcher
Director: Malcolm St. Clair
Screenplay: W. Scott Darling
Producer: Sol M. Wurtzel

IRISH EYES ARE SMILING
(20th Century-Fox, October, 1944) 90 Minutes.
Monty Wooley, June Haver, Dick Haymes, Anthony Quinn, Beverly Whitney, Maxie Rosenbloom, *Veda Ann Borg*, Clarence Kolb, Blanche Thebon, Leonard Warren, Marian Martin, George Chandler, Eddie Acuff, Minerva Urecal, Arthur Hohl, J. Farrell MacDonald, Charles Williams, Art Foster, Emmet Vogan, Pat O'Malley, Mary Gordon, Kenny Williams
Director: Gregory Ratoff
Screenplay: Earl Baldwin, John Tucker Battle
Story: E. A. Ellington
Producer: Damon Runyon

THE FALCON IN HOLLYWOOD
(RKO, December, 1944) 67 Minutes.
Tom Conway, Barbara Hale, *Veda Ann Borg*, John Abbott, Sheldon Leonard, Konstantin Shayne, Emory Parnell, Frank Jenks, Jean Brooks, Rita Corday, Walter Soderling, Usaf Ali, Robert Clarke, Patti Brill, Bryant Washburn, George Dendrmand, Perc Launders, Wheaton Chambers, Bert Moorhouse, Chester Clute, Chili Williams
Director: Gordon Douglas
Screenplay: Gerald Geraghty
Producer: Maurice Geraghty

FOG ISLAND
(PRC, February 15, 1945) 70 Minutes.
George Zucco, Lionel Atwill, Jerome Cowan, Sharon Douglas, *Veda Ann Borg,* John Whitney, Jacqueline DeWitt, Ian Keith, George Lloyd
Director: Terry Morse
Screenplay: Pierre Gendron
Story: Bernadine Angus
Associate Producer: Terry Morse

WHAT A BLONDE
(RKO-Radio, February, 1945) 71 Minutes.
Leon Errol, Richard Lane, Michael St. Angel, Elaine Riley, *Veda Ann Borg,* Lydia Bilbrook, Clarence Kolb, Ann Shoemaker, Chef Milani, Nancy Marlow, Rosemary LaPlanche, Virginia Belmont, Patti Brill, Emory Parnell, Larry Wheat, Dorothy Vaughn, Jason Robards
Director: Leslie Goodwins
Screenplay: Charles E. Roberts
Story: Oscar Brodney
Producer: Ben Stoloff

ROUGH, TOUGH AND READY
(Columbia, March 22, 1945) 66 Minutes.
Chester Morris, Victor McLaglen, Jean Rogers, *Veda Ann Borg*, Amelita Ward, Robert Williams, John Tyrell, Fred Graff, Addison Richards, William Forrest, Tex Harding, Loren Tindal, Bob Meredith, Ida Moore, Blackie Whiteford
Director: Del Lord
Screenplay: Edward T. Lowe
Story: Edward T. Lowe
Producer: Alexis Thurn-Taxis

BRING ON THE GIRLS
(Paramount, March 30, 1945) 92 Minutes (Technicolor)
Veronica Lake, Sonny Tufts, Eddie Bracken, Marjorie Reynolds, Grant Mitchell, Johnny Coy, Peter Whitney, Alan Mowbray, Porter Hall, Thurston Hall, Lloyd Corrigan, Sig Arno, Joan Woodbury, Andrew Tombes, Frank Faylen, Huntz Hall, William Moss, Noram Varden, Dorothea Kent, *Veda Ann Borg*, Jimmy Dundee, Noel Neill, Yvonne De Carlo, Kay Linaker, Frank Hagney, Louise LaPlanche, George Turner, Walter Baldwin, Jimmy Conlin, Spike Jones and His City Slickers, The Golden Gate Quartette
Director: Sidney Lanfield
Screenplay: Karl Tunberg, Darrell Ware
Story: Pierre Wolff
Associate Producer: Fred Kohlmar

DON JUAN QUILLIGAN
(20th Century-Fox, June, 1945) 75 Minutes
William Bendix, Joan Blondell, Phil Silvers, Anne Revere, B. S. Pully, Mary Treen, John Russell, *Veda Ann Borg*, Thurston Hall, Cara Williams, Richard Gaines, Hobart Cavanaugh, Rene Carson, George Macready, Helen Freeman, Charles Cane, Anthony Caruso, Eddie Acuff, Joel Friedkin, Charles Marsh, Emmett Vogan, James Flavin, John Albright, Charles D. Brown, Lee Phelps, Tom Dugan, Carey Harrison, Genevieve Bell, Jimmy Conlin
Director: Frank Tuttle
Screenplay: Arthur Kober, Frank Gabrielson
Story: Herbert Clyde Lewis
Producer: William LeBaron

SCARED STIFF
(Paramount, June 22, 1945) 64 Minutes.
Jack Haley, Ann Savage, Barton MacLane, *Veda Ann Borg,* Arthur Aylesworth, George E. Stone, Lucien Littlefield, Paul Hurst, Robert Emmett Keane, Eily Malyon, Buddy Swan, Roger Pryor
Director: Frank McDonald
Screenplay: Geoffrey Home, Maxwell Shane
Story: Geoffrey Home, Maxwell Shane
Producers: William H. Pine, William C. Thomas

NOB HILL
(20th Century-Fox, July, 1945) 95 Minutes
George Raft, Joan Bennett, Vivian Blaine, Peggy Ann Garner, Alan Reed, B. S. Pully, Edgar Barrier, Mike Mazurki, The Three Swifts, William Haade, Nestor Pavia, *Veda Ann Borg,* Arthur Loft, Chick Chandler, Rory Calhoun, Sven-Hugo Borg, Byron Foulger, Benson Fong, Joe Bernard, Chief Thunder Cloud, Frank Orth, Lester Dorr, George Anderson, Don Costello, Beal Wong, Charles Cane, Arthur Loft, Harry Shannon, Ralph Peters, Harry Strang, Harry Harvey, Will Stanton, Syd Saylor, Almira Sessions, Edward Keane, Eddie Hart, George Lloyd, Sam Flint, J. Farrell McDonald
Director: Henry Hathaway
Screenplay: Wanda Tuchock, Norman Reilly Raine
Producer: Andre Daven
Story: Eleanore Griffin

DANGEROUS INTRUDER
(PRC, August 21, 1945) 62 Mins.
Charles Arnt, *Veda Ann Borg,* Richard Powers (Tom Keene), Fay Helm, John Rogers, Jo Ann Marlowe, Helena P. Evans, Roberta Smith, George Sorrel, Forrest Taylor, Eddie Rocco
Director: Vernon Keays
Screenplay: Martin M. Goldsmith
Story: Philip MacDonald, F. Ruth Howard
Associate Producer: Martin Mooney

JUNGLE RAIDERS
(Columbia, September 14, 1945) 15 Episodes
Kane Richmond, *Veda Ann Borg*, Eddie Quillan, Carol Hughes, Janet Shaw, John Elliott, Jack Ingram, Charles King, Ernie Adams, I. Stanford Jolley, Kermit Maynard, Budd Buster, George Turner, Nick Thompson, Jimmy Aubrey, Ted Adams, P. J. Kelly, Alfredo Desa, Jack Gordon
Director: Lesley Selander
Screenplay: Ande Lamb, George Plympton
Producer: Sam Katzman
Chapter Titles: (1) Mystery of the Lost Tribe (2) Primitive Sacrifice (3) Prisoners of Fate (4) Valley of Destruction (5) Perilous Mission (6) Into the Valley of Fire (7) Devil's Brew (8) The Dagger Pit (9) Jungle Jeopardy (10) Prisoners of Peril (11) Vengeance of Zara (12) The Key to Arzec (13) Witch Doctor's Treachery (14) The Judgement of Rama (15) The Jewels of Arzec

LOVE, HONOR AND GOODBYE
(Republic, September 15, 1945) 87 Minutes
Virginia Bruce, Edward Ashley, Victor McLaglen, Nils Asther, Helen Broderick, *Veda Ann Borg,* Jacqueline Moore, Robert Greig, Victoria Horne, Ralph Dunn, Theresa Lyon
Director: Albert S. Rogell
Screenplay: Arthur Phillips, Lee Loeb, Dick Irving Hyland
Story: Art Arthur, Albert S. Rogell
Associate Producer: Harry Grey

LIFE WITH BLONDIE
(Columbia, December 13, 1945) 70 Minutes.
Penny Singleton, Arthur Lake, Larry Simms, Marjorie Kent, Jonathan Hale, Ernest Truex, Marc Lawrence, *Veda Ann Borg*, Jack Rice, Bobby Larson, Doug Fowley, George Tyne, Edward Gargan, Francis Pierlot, Ray Walker, Eddie Acuff, Robert Ryan, Steve Benton
Director: Abby Berlin
Screenplay: Connie Lee
Producer: Burt Kelly

AVALANCHE
(PRC, June 20, 1946) 70 Minutes.
Bruce Cabot, Roscoe Karns, Helen Mowery, *Veda Ann Borg*, Regina Wallace, John Good, Philip Van Zandt, Eddie Parks, Wilton Graff, Harry Hays Morgan, Eddie Hyans, Eddy Waller, Syd Saylor
Director: Irving Allen
Screenplay: Andrew Holt
Producer: Pat De Cicco

ACCOMPLICE
(PRC, September 26, 1946) 67 Minutes.
Richard Arlen, *Veda Ann Borg*, Michael Branden, Earle Hodgins, Edward Earle, Tom Dugan, Marjorie Manners, Francis Ford, Herbert Rawlinson, Sherry Hall
Director: Walter Colmes
Screenplay: Irving Elman, Frank Gruber
Story: Frank Gruber, "Simon Lash, Private Detective"
Producer: John K. Teaford

WIFE WANTED
(Monogram, October 19, 1946) 73 Minutes.
Kay Francis, Paul Cavanagh, Robert Shayne, *Veda Ann Borg*, Teala Loring, Edgar Hayes, John Gallaudet, Jonathan Hale, Tim Ryan, Barton Yarborough, Paul Everton, Selmer Jackson, Barbara Woodell, Anthony Warde, Elaine Lange, Joe Green, Sara Berner, George Carleton, John Hamilton, Mabel Todd, Will Stanton, Buddy Gorman
Director: Phil Karlson
Screenplay: Caryl Coleman, Sidney Sutherland
Story: Robert Callahan
Producer: Jeffrey Bernerd, Kay Francis

I LOVE MY HUSBAND, BUT!
(M-G-M, December 7, 1946) 1 Reel
(A Pete Smith Specialty)
Dave O'Brien, *Veda Ann Borg*, Dorothy Short
Director: David Barclay
Producer: Pete Smith

THE FABULOUS SUZANNE
(Republic, December 15, 1946) 71 Minutes.
Barbara Britton, Rudy Vallee, Otto Kruger, Richard Denning, Bill Henry, *Veda Ann Borg*, Irene Agay, Grady Sutton, Frank Darien, Harry Tyler, Eddie Fields, Al Hammer
Director: Steve Sekely
Screenplay: Tedwell Chapman, Randall Faye
Story: William Bowers, Tedwell Chapman
Producer: Steve Sekely

THE PILGRIM LADY
(Republic, January 22, 1947) 67 Minutes.
Lynne Roberts, Warren Doublas, Alan Mowbray, *Veda Ann Borg*, Clarence Kolb, Helen Freeman, Doris Merrick, Russell Hicks, Ray Walker, Charles Coleman
Director: Lesley Selander
Screenplay: Dane Lussier
Story: Dane Lussier
Associate Producer: William J. O'Sullivan

BIG TOWN
(Paramount, May 23, 1947) 60 Minutes.
Philip Reed, Hillary Brooke, Robert Lowery, *Veda Ann Borg*, Byron Barr, Charles Arnt, Nana Bryant, Frank Fenton, Roy Gordon, Eddie Parks, Nella Walker, Thomas Jackson, Richard Lydon, Daisy DeWitt
Director: William C. Thomas
Screenplay: Geoffrey Homes
Story: Geoffrey Homes, Maxwell Shane
Based on the radio program "Big Town"
Producers: William C. Thomas, William H. Pine

THE BACHELOR AND THE BOBBY-SOXER
(RKO, September 4, 1947) 95 Minutes
Ray Collins, Cary Grant, Myrna Loy, Shirley Temple, Rudy Vallee, Harry Davenport, Johnny Sands, Don Beddoe, Lillian Randolph, *Veda Ann Borg*, Dan Tobin, Ransom Sherman, Carol Hughes, William Bakewell, Irving Bacon, Ian Bernard, Gregory Gay, Marilyn Mercer, Kay Christopher, Myra Marsh
Director: Irving Reis
Screenplay: Sidney Sheldon
Producer: Dore Schary

MOTHER WORE TIGHTS
(20th Century-Fox, September, 1947) 107 Mins.
Betty Grable, Dan Dailey, Mona Freeman, Connie Marshall, Vanessa Brown, Robert Arthur, Sara Allgood, William Frawley, Ruth Nelson, Anabel Shaw, Michael Dunne, George Cleveland, *Veda Ann Borg*, Sig Rumann, Lee Patrick, Señor Wences, Maude Eburne, William Forrest, Kathleen Lockhart, Chick Chandler, Frank Orth, Harry Chesire, Billy Greene, David Thursby, Anne Baxter (Narrator)
Director: Walter Lang
Screenplay: Lamar Trotti
Story: Miriam Young
Producer: Lamar Trotti

BLONDE SAVAGE
(Eagle-Lion, November 22, 1947) 62 Minutes
Leif Erickson, Gale Sherwood, *Veda Ann Borg,* Douglass Dumbrille, Frank Jenks, Matt Willis, Ernest Whitman, Gay Forrest, John Dehner, James Logan, Arthur Foster, Alex Fraser, Eve Whitney
Director: S. K. Seeley
Screenplay: George Bache
Producer: Lionel J. Toll

JULIA MISBEHAVES
(M-G-M, October, 1948) 99 Minutes
Greer Garson, Walter Pidgeon, Peter Lawford, Elizabeth Taylor, Ceasr Romero, Lucile Watson, Nigel Bruce, Mary Boland, Reginald Owen, Henry Stephenson, Aubrey Mather, Ian Wolfe, Fritz Feld, Phyllis Morris, *Veda Ann Borg,* Ruth Hall, Jimmy Aubrey, Joi Lansing
Director: Jack Conway
Screenplay: William Ludwig, Harry Ruskin, Arthur Wimperis
Story: Margery Sharpe
Producer: Everett Riskin

CHICKEN EVERY SUNDAY
(20th Century-Fox, December, 1948) 91 Minutes
Dan Dailey, Celeste Holm, Coleen Townsend, Alan Young, Natalie Wood, William Frawley, Connie Gilchrist, William Callahan, *Veda Ann Borg,* Porter Hall, Whitney Bissell, Katherine Emory, Roy Roberts, Hal K. Dawson, Percy Helton, Mary Field, Francis Pierlot, Wilson Wood, Eddie Laughton, Frank Meredith, Jack Daley, Anthony Sydes, Loren Raker, Hiti Tsiang, Junius Matthews, Dick Ryan, Ruth Rickaby, Edward Keane, Jack Kirkwood
Director: George Seaton
Screenplay: George Seaton, Valentine Davies
Story: Julius J. Epstein, Phillip G. Epstein, Rosemary Taylor
Producer: William Perlberg

MISSISSIPPI RHYTHM
(Monogram, May 29, 1949) 68 Minutes
Jimmie Davis, Lee "Lasses" White, James Flavin, *Veda Ann Borg*, Sue England, Guy Beach, Paul Maxey, Paul Bryar, Joel Marston, Duke York, Jim Dill, Lyle Talbot, Lillian Lindsco, Wheaton Chambers, Charlie Jordan, Aileen Dixon, Bill Burt, Larry Rio, Peeme Elmo
Director: Derwin Abrahams
Screenplay: Gretchen Darling
Producer: Lindsley Parsons

FORGOTTEN WOMEN
(Monogram, July 17, 1949) 65 Minutes
Elyse Knox, Edward Norris, Robert Shayne, Theodora Lynch, *Vedà Ann Borg*, Noel Neill, Tim Ryan, Bill Kennedy, Warren Douglas, Selmer Jackson
Director: William Beaudine
Screenplay: W. Scott Darling
Story: Jeffrey Bernard
Producer: Jeffrey Bernard

ONE LAST FLING
(Warner Bros., August 6, 1949) 74 Minutes
Alexis Smith, Zachary Scott, Douglas Kennedy, Ann Doran, Ransom Sherman, *Veda Ann Borg*, Jim Backus, Helen Westcott, Barbara Bates, Jody Gilbert
Director: Peter Godfrey
Screenplay: Richard Flournoy, William Sackheim
Story: Herbert Clyde Lewis
Producer: Saul Elkins

RIDER FROM TUCSON
(RKO-Radio, June, 1950) 60 Minutes
Tim Holt, Richard Martin, Elaine Riley, Douglas Fowley, *Veda Ann Borg*, Robert Shayne, William Phipps, Harry Tyler, Marshall Reed, Stuart Randall, Luther Crockett, Dorothy Vaughn
Director: Lesley Selander
Screenplay: Ed Earl Repp
Story: Ed Earl Repp
Producer: Herman Schlom

THE KANGAROO KID
(United Artists, October 22, 1950) 73 Minutes
Jock O'Mahoney, *Veda Ann Borg*, Guy Doleman, Douglass Dumbrille, Martha Hyer, Alec Kellaway, Alan Gifford, Grant Taylor, Frank Ransom, Haydee Seldon, Clarrie Woodlands
Director: Lesley Selander
Story: Anthony S. veitch
Producer: Howard C. Brown
(Filmed in Australia)

HOLD THAT LINE
(Monogram, March 23, 1952) 64 Minutes
Leo Gorcey, Huntz Hall, John Bromfield, *Veda Ann Borg,* Mona Knox, Gloria Winters, Taylor Homes, Bernard Gorcey, Gil Stratton, Jr., David Condon, Bennie Bartlett, Francis Pierlot, Pierre Watkin, Bob Nichols, Paul Bryar, Bob Peoples, Byron Foulger, George J. Lewis, Al Eben, Tom Hanlon
Director: William Beaudine
Screenplay: Tim Ryan, Charles R. Marion
Producer: Jerry Thomas

AARON SLICK FROM PUNKIN CRICK
(Paramount, April 12, 1952) 95 Minutes
(Technicolor)
Alan Young, Dinah Shore, Robert Merrill, Adele Jergens. Minerva Urecal, Martha Stewart, Fritz Feld, *Veda Ann Borg*, Chick Chandler
Director: Claude Binyon
Screenplay: Claude Binyon
Story: Walter Benjamin Hare
Producers: William Perlberg, George Seaton

BIG JIM MCLAIN
(Warner Bros., August 30, 1952) 90 Minutes.
John Wayne, Nancy Olson, James Arness, Alan Napier, *Veda Ann Borg*, Gayne Whitman, Hal Baylor, Robert Keys, Hans Conreid, John Hubbard, Mme. Soo Young, Dan Liu, Paul Hurst, Vernon McQueen, Sarah Padden
Director: Edward Ludwig
Screenplay: James Edward Grant
Story: Richard English, Eric Taylor
Producer: Robert Fellows

A PERILOUS JOURNEY
(Republic, April 5, 1953) 90 Minutes
Vera Ralston, David Brian, Scott Brady, Charles Winninger, Hope Emerson, Eileen Christy, Leif Erickson, *Veda Ann Borg,* Virginia Grey, Dorothy Ford, Ben Cooper, Kathleen Freeman, Barbara Hayden, Paul Pierro, Angela Greene, John Dierkes, Fred Graham, Trevor Bardette, Richard Reeves, Charles Evans, Philip Van Zandt, Byron Foulger, Denver Pyle, Harry Tyler, Emil Sitka, Jack O'Shea, Frank Hagney, Stanley Blystone, Dick Alexander, Charles Cane, Gloria Clark
Director: R. G. Springsteen
Screenplay: Richard Wormser
Associate Producer: William J. O'Sullivan

MISTER SCOUTMASTER
(20th Century-Fox, September 1, 1953) 87 Mins.
Cilfton Webb. Edmund Gwenn, George "Foghorn" Winslow, Frances Dee, *Veda Ann Borg,* Orley Lindgren, Jimmy Moss, Sammy Ogg, Jimmy Hawkins, Skip Torgerson, Dee Aaker, Jon Gardiner, Amanda Randolph, Teddy Infuhr, Harry Seymour, Sarah Selby, Mickey Little, Bob Sweeney, Robert Williams, Steve Brent, Bill McKenzie
Director: Henry Levin
Screenplay: Leonard Praskins, Barney Slater
Story: Rice E. Cochran
Producer: Leonard Goldstein

HOT NEWS
(Allied Artists, October 11, 1953) 61 Minutes
Stanley Clements, Gloria Henry, Ted de Corsica, *Veda Ann Borg,* Scotty Beckett, Carl Milletaire, James Flavin, Hal Baylor, Paul Bryar, Myron Healey
Director: Edward Bernds
Screenplay: Charles R. Marion, Ellwood Ullman
Producer: Ben Schwalb

THREE SAILORS AND A GIRL
(Warner Bros., December 26, 1953) 98 Minutes
(Technicolor)
Jane Powell, Gordon MacRae, Gene Nelson, Sam Levene, Jack E. Leonard, George Givot, *Veda Ann Borg,* Archer MacDonald, Raymond Greenleaf, Henry Slate, Mickey Simpson, Elizabeth Flournoy, Dick Simmons, Philip Van Zandt, Al Hill, Guy Hearn, Paul Burke, Grandon Rhodes, Alex Gerry, Murray Alper, Merv Griffin, King Donovan, Bess Flowers and Burt Lancaster (unbilled bit)
Director: Roy Del Ruth
Screenplay: Roland Kibbee, Devery Freeman
Story: George S. Kaufman, "The Butter and Egg Man"
Producer: Sammy Cahn

BITTER CREEK
(Westwood/Allied Artists, March, 1954) 74 Minutes
Bill Elliott, Carleton Young, Beverly Garland, *Veda Ann Borg,* Claude Akins, Jim Hayward, John Harmon, John Pickard, Forrest Taylor, Mike Ragan, Dan Mummert, Zon Murray, John Larch, Jane Easton, Florence Lake, Earle Hodgins, Joe Devlin
Director: Thomas Carr
Screenplay: George Waggner
Producer: Vincent M. Fennelly

LOVE ME OR LEAVE ME
(M-G-M, June 10, 1955) 122 Minutes
(Technicolor)
Doris Day, James Cagney, Cameron Mitchell, Robert Keith, Tom Tully, Harry Bellaver, Richard Gaines, Peter Leeds, Claude Stroud, Audrey Young, John Harding, Dorothy Abbott, *Veda Ann Borg,* Claire Carleton, James Drury, Richard Simmons, Dale Van Sickel, Johnny Day, Roy Engle
Director: Charles Vindor
Screenplay: Daniel Fuchs
Story: Daniel Fuchs
Producer: Joe Pasternak

YOU'RE NEVER TOO YOUNG
(Paramount, August, 1955) 102 Minutes
(Technicolor) (VistaVision)
Dean Martin, Jerry Lewis, Diana Lynn, Nina Foch, Raymond Burr, Mitzi McCall, *Veda Ann Borg,* Margery Maude, Romo Vincent, Nancy Kulp, Milton Frome, Donna Percy, Emory Parnell, James Burke, Tommy Ivo, Whitey Haupt, Mickey Finn, Peggy Moffitt, Isabel Randolph, Hans Conreid, Stanley Blystone, Bob Morgan, Louis Lorimer, Richard Simmons
Director: Norman Taurog
Screenplay: Sidney Sheldon
Story: Edward Childs Carpenter, Fannie Kilbourne
Producer: Paul Jones

GUYS AND DOLLS
(M-G-M/Goldwyn, 1955) 149 Minutes
(Eastman Color) (CinemaScope)
Marlon Brando, Jean Simmons, Frank Sinatra, Vivian Blaine, Robert Keith, Stubby Kaye, B. S. Pully, Johnny Silver, Sheldon Leonard, Danny Dayton, George E. Stone, Regis Toomey, Kathryn Givney, *Veda Ann Borg,* Mary Hokanson, Joe McTurk, Kay Kuter, Stapleton Kent, Renee Renor, Matt Murphy, Harry Wilson, Earle Hodgins, Harry Tyler, Major Sam Harris, Franklyn Farnum, Frank Richards, John Indrisano, Julian Rivero, The Goldwyn Girls (Larri Thomas, Jana Darlyn, June Kirby, Madelyn Darrow, Barbara Brent)
Director: Joseph L. Mankiewicz
Screenplay: Joseph L. Mankiewicz
Story: Damon Runyon
Based on the musical by Jo Swerling and Abe Burrows
Producer: Samuel Goldwyn

I'LL CRY TOMORROW
(M-G-M, January, 1956) 117 Minutes
Susan Hayward, Richard Conte, Eddie Albert, Jo Van Fleet, Don Taylor, Ray Danton, Margo, Virginia Gregg, Don Barry, David Kasday, Carole Ann Campbell, Peter Leeds, Tol Avery, Guy Wilderson, Tim Carey, Charles Tannen, Ken Patterson, Voltaire Perkins, George Lloyd, Nora Marlowe, Stanley Farrar, Harlan Warde, Peter Brocco, Bob Dix, Anthony Jochim, Kay English, Eve McVeagh, *Veda Ann Borg,* Gail Ganley, Robert B. Williams, Bob Hopkins, Vernon Rich, Herbert C. Lytton, George Selk, Cherrio Meredith
Director: Daniel Mann
Screenplay: Helen Deutsch, Jay R. Kennedy
Story: Lillian Roth, Mike Connolly, Gerold Frank
Producer: Lawrence Weungarten

FRONTIER GAMBLER
(Associated Releasing, September 1, 1956) 70 Minutes.
John Bromfield, Coleen Gray, Kent Taylor, Jim Davis, Margia Dean, *Veda Ann Borg,* Tracey Roberts, Stanley Andrews, Roy Engel, Nadene Ashdown, Frank Sully, Pierce Lyden, Ewing Brown, Rick Vallin, John Merton, Helen Jay
Director: Sam Newfield
Screenplay: Orville Hampton
Story: Orville Hampton
Producer: Sigmund Neufeld

NAKED GUN
(Associated Releasing, November, 1956) 69 Minutes
Willard Parker, Mara Corday, Barton MacLane, *Veda Ann Borg,* Billy House, Morris Ankrum, Chick Chandler, Bill Phillips, Tom Brown, Tony McCoy, Timothy Carey, X. Brands, Steve Rains. Jim Hayward, Rick Vallin, Elena Di Vinci, Jody McCrea, Bill Ward, Morry Ogden, Helen Jay, Doris Simons
Director: Edward Dew
Screenplay: Ron Ormond, Jack Lewis
Story: Ron Ormond, Jack Lewis
Producer: Ron Ormond

THE WINGS OF EAGLES
(M-G-M, February 22, 1957) 109 Minutes
(Technicolor)
John Wayne, Maureen O'Hara, Dan Dailey, Ward Bond, Ken Curtis, Edmund Lowe, Ken Tobey, James Todd, Barry Kelley, Sig Rumann, Henry O'Neill, Willis Bouchey, Dorothy Jordan, Peter Ortiz, Louis Jean Heydt, Tige Andrews, Dan Borzage, William Tracy, Harlan Warde, Jack Pennick, *Veda Ann Borg,* Bill Henry, Alberto Morin, Mimi Gibson, Evelyn Rudie, Charles Trowbridge, Mae Marsh, Fred Graham, Stuart Holmes, Olive Carey, Major Sam Harris, Chuck Roberson, Cliff Lyons
Director: John Ford
Screenplay: Frank Fenton, William Wister Haines
Based on the life and writing of Frank W. Wead
Producer: Charles Schnee

THE FEARMAKERS
(United Artists, November, 1958) 83 Minutes
Dana Andrews, Dick Foran, Mel Torme, Marilee Earle, *Veda Ann Borg,* Kelly Thordson, Roy Gordon, Robert Fortier
Director: Jacques Tourneur
Screenplay: Elliot West, Chris Appleby
Story: Darwin L. Teilhet
Producer: Martin Lancer

THUNDER IN THE SUN
(Paramount, May 1, 1959) 81 Minutes
(Eastman Color)
Susan Hayward, Jeff Chandler, Jacques Bergerac, Blanche Yurka, Carl Esmond, Fortunio Bonanova, Felix Locher, *Veda Ann Borg*
Director: Russell Rouse
Screenplay: Russell Rouse
Story: Guy Trosper, James Hill
Producer: Clarence Greene

THE ALAMO
(United Artists, October, 1960) 192 Minutes
(Technicolor) (Todd-AO)
John Wayne, Richard Widmark, Laurence Harvey, Richard Boone, Frankie Avalon, Linda Cristal, Chill Wills, Carlos Arruza, Joan O'Brien, Pat Wayne, Olive Carey, Hank Worden, *Veda Ann Borg,* Guinn "Big Boy" Williams, Joseph Calleia, Ken Curtis, Denver Pyle, Alissa Wayne, Julian Trevino, Bill Henry, John Dierkes, Chuck Roberson, Jack Pennick, Fred Graham
Director: John Wayne
Screenplay: James Edward Grant
Producer: John Wayne

24 • LOIS COLLIER

Possessed of Youthful Buoyancy and Undeniable Charm, She Could Be Counted on to Beautify the Femme Lead Excellently

Playing "Pam Courtney" in the inconsequential African romp **Jungle Queen** (1945), a Universal serial, was a curvaceous, strikingly young actress named Lois Collier, whose warm personality exuded from the screen without benefit of any secret aura to lend glamour to her image. She was only what she seemed to be, a well-bred, demure, sweet girl-next-door type. Her role as the girl out to rescue her explorer father from the African wilds, aided by Americans Edward Norris and Eddie Quillan, was somewhat overshadowed by Ruth Roman's characterization of "Lothel," the mysterious jungle queen who befriended Lois's party, but Miss Collier's wistful charm did not escape many in the serial's audience.

In 1941-42 Lois had filled the heroine's role in six of Republic's "Three Mesquiteers" program oaters starring Bob Steele, Tom Tyler, and Rufe Davis, handling her chores admirably. Although these films will never be known for the sweep of their climactic battles or for the emotions radiated by the principals, they are nevertheless fondly remembered by western aficionados. Slickly-made "B's," they entertained those audiences who lived from one Saturday to the next awaiting the heroes of the range to beat the stuffins out of the dastardly scallywags who would mistreat a horse, defile the school marm, or sell firewater to the redskins.

Lois's first appearance before the cameras had been in 1938 as a bit player in **Desperate Adventure**, but her next three years had been spent going to school, having her teeth straightened, doing radio work, and going to a drama coach before becoming a resident heroine at Republic.

After a modicum of success as a contract player at Universal from 1943 to 1950, Lois returned to Republic as feminine lead in the cliffhanger **Flying Disc Man from Mars** (1950), playing "Helen Hall," secretary to Walter Reed, the hero who combats the intruder from outer space who has designs on the Earth. She did exceedingly well with a role that allowed her little opportunity to emote.

Lois may not have had an opportunity for many striking and powerful characterizations, and the critical contingent was prone to write her off along with most other cliffhanger and western ingenues, but she was an accomplished actress with a charm decidedly her own. One can hardly say that her influence in the western and serial genres was monumental, but she was positively stunning--an elfin creature who presented a most enchanting effect and injected a little vitality into the blood stream of most males.

It was Lois's voice that led her from the comparative obscurity of a small South Carolina town to the bright lights of the cinema's capital, but the other elements of her personality--her big blue eyes, her cameo profile, her slim graceful body, and her unusual talent for acting--kept her there for nearly fifteen years.

Though the studio publicity departments added three years to her age by listing her birth year as 1919, Lois was actually born on March 21, 1922 in Salley, South Carolina. Her real name was Madelyn Earle Jones, and she is of Welsh-English-Irish descent. She stood only 5 feet 1 inch and weighed barely 100 pounds when working in pictures.

When she was a very little girl Lois wanted to be a missionary to China. Then she began taking part in school and Sunday school plays--yes, she, too, was an angel--and the first thing she knew, she had developed a full-fledged yearning for a stage career. She was fortunate enough to have a mother who sympathized with her child's ambition, and when Lois was 14 her mother let her have a brief course of dramatic study in New York. After that,

Lois Collier and "Whitey" – "Boston Blackie" television series.

Lois naturally starred in school dramatic activities, and when the voice of opportunity reached Salley, South Carolina, it fell not on deaf ears.

It was Lois' mother, Mrs. Ruth Jones, a newspaperwoman, who first heard the golden voice. She sent her daughter's picture and a letter to Columbia Broadcasting System for entry in an audition contest for a part in a radio production called "Hollywood in Person." Lois finally won, and that was the end of Madelyn Earle Jones. The part she played in the radio play was a character named "Lois Collier," and with the permission of CBS she adopted that for her professional name. Lois had been attending Limesone College at Gaffney, South Carolina, but her professional career interfered with graduation.

The CBS job lasted three months. Then she played "Carol" in Irene Rich's show, "Dear John." Interspersed were frequent appearances with the Lux Radio Theater, and some short engagements in stage leads with Los Angeles and Hollywood theater. A more memorable performance was that of "Eileen" in Irving Berlin's "This Is The Army." In fact, it was that part which led to her screen contract with Universal.

Always conscious that it was her voice that first won her recognition, Lois never ceased to study vocal problems and to develop her singing ability. Her rendition of the "Poor Wandering One" aria from "The Pirates of Penzance" and the male chorus number, "A Policeman's Lot" in **Girl on the Spot** (Universal, 1946) suggests that Universal overlooked a real bet when they cast Lois in mostly non-singing parts. She invariably got good reviews and it is regrettable that neither Universal or Republic really promoted her as they should have. **Ladies Courageous** (Universal, 1944), in which she played an aviatrix, aptly demonstrated her acting ability. She had a great deal to offer the screen, but she never got a chance at the meaty roles that would have escalated her career, even though she always registered pleasantly as the love interest.

After her seven-year contract with Universal ended, Lois teamed up with Kent Taylor in the "Boston Blackie" television series. Production started in 1950 and continued for four years. And it is for her role as "Mary" in this series that she is remembered by many TV fans unfamiliar with her screen career. Lois made many personal appearances in connection with the promotion of this show.

Lois was also the first "Miss Emmy" chosen by the Academy of TV Arts and Sciences--the gal who presented Emmys to winners. But she herself was awarded "The Billboard Award for Outstanding Achievement in TV Films," voted by the TV Film Industry, as the best actress on a non-network mystery series for the Boston Blackie series of 1953-54.

On the personal front, Miss Collier was married to a young Hollywood bank official in the early 1940s, but the couple found their careers were not compatible, and in 1944 there was a divorce. Since 1957 she has been married to a very successful Los Angeles attorney. The couple travel extensively--in fact, they have been to the Orient 22 times! It seems her husband has a client there with whom he must frequently consult. But they have also traveled over most of Asia and Europe. Lois is appreciative of her career and the fame it brought her, but today she has no desire to renew that career. She's perfectly content in being a happily married woman with diverse interests and the health and money to pursue them. However, the fond memories of those Republic and Universal days will always be with her.

LOIS COLLIER Filmography

A DESPERATE ADVENTURE
(Republic, August 6, 1938) 67 Minutes
Ramon Novarro, Marian Marsh, Eric Blore, Margaret Tallichet, Andrew Tombes, Maurice Case, Rolfe Sedan, Gloria Rich, *Lois Collier*
Director: John H. Auer
Screenplay: Hans Kraly, M. Coates Webster

OUTLAWS OF THE CHEROKEE TRAIL
(Republic, September 10, 1941) 56 Minutes
Bob Steele, Tom Tyler, Rufe Davis, *Lois Collier,* Tom Chatterton, Rex Lease, Joel Friedkin, Roy Barcroft, Philip Trent, Peggy Lynn, Bud Osborne, Chief Yowlachie, John James, Lee Shumway, Karl Hackett, Chuck Morrison, Billy Burtis, Griff Barnette, Bud Geary, Al Taylor, Henry Wills, Sarah Padden, Iron Eyes Cody, Cactus Mack
Director: Les Orlebeck
Screenplay: Albert DeMond
Associate Producer: Louis Gray
Based on characters created by William Colt MacDonald

A Night in Casablanca (United Artists, 1946) – Lois Collier.

GAUCHOS OF ELDORADO
(Republic, October 24, 1941) 56 Minutes
Bob Steele, Tom Tyler, Rufe Davis, *Lois Collier,* Duncan Renaldo, Norman Willis, Yakima Canutt, Rosani Galli, William Ruhl, Tony Roux, Ray Bennett, Edmund Cobb, Eddie Dean, Bud Geary, John Merrill Holmes, Terry Frost, John Merton, Virginia Farmer, Si Jenks, Ted Mapes, Bob Woodward, Ray Jones, Horace B. Carpenter
Director: Les Orlebeck
Story: Earle Snell
Associate Producer: Louis Gray
Based on characters created by William Colt MacDonald

WEST OF CIMARRON
(Republic, December 15, 1941) 56 Minutes.
Bob Steele, Tom Tyler, Rufe Davis, *Lois Collier,* James Bush, Guy Usher, Hugh Prosser, Cordell Hickman, Roy Barcroft, Budd Buster, Mickey Rentschiler, John James, Bud Geary, Stanley Blystone
Director: Les Orlebeck
Screenplay: Albert Demond, Don Ryan
Associate Producer: Louis Gray
Based on characters created by William Colt MacDonald

RAIDERS OF THE RANGE
(Republic, March 18, 1942) 55 Minutes.
Bob Steele, Tom Tyler, Rufe Davis, *Lois Collier,* Frank Jacquet, Fred Kohler Jr., Dennis Moore, Tom Chatterton, Charles Miller, Max Walzman, Hal Price, Charles Phillips, Bud Geary, Jack Ingram, Al Taylor, Chuck Morrison, Joel Friedkin, Bob Woodward, Tom Steele, Monte Montague, Ken Terrell, Dick Alexander, Cactus Mack, John Cason
Director: John English
Associate Producer: Barry Shipman
Story: Albert DeMond
Associate Producer: Louis Gray
Based on characters created by William Colt MacDonald

WESTWARD HO
(Republic, April 24, 1942) 56 Minutes
Bob Steele, Tom Tyler, Rufe Davis, Evelyn Brent, Donald Curtis, *Lois Collier,* Emmett Lynn, John James, Tom Siedel, Jack Kirk, Kenne Duncan, Milton Kibbee, Edmund Cobb, Monte Montague, Al Taylor, Bud Osborne, Jack Montgomery, Horace B. Carpenter, John L. Cason, Jack O'Shea, Ray Jones, Tex Palmer, Curley Dresden, Budd Buster
Director: John English
Screenplay: Morton Grant, Doris Schroeder
Story: Morton Grant
Associate Producer: Louis Gray
Based on characters created by William Colt MacDonald

THE PHANTOM PLAINSMEN
(Republic, June 16, 1942) 65 Minutes
Bob Steele, Tom Tyler, Rufe Davis, *Lois Collier,* Robert O. Davis, Charles Miller, Alex Callam, Monte Montague, Henry Roland, Richard Crane, Jack Kirk, Edward Cassidy, Vince Barnett, Lloyd Ingraham, Al Taylor, Bud Geary, Herman Hack
Director: John English
Screenplay: Robert Yost, Barry Shipman
Story: Robert Yost
Associate Producer: Louis Gray
Based on characters created by William Colt MacDonald

MY SON THE HERO
(PRC, April 5, 1943) 68 Minutes.
Patsy Kelly, Roscoe Karns, Joan Blair, Maxie Rosenbloom. Carol Hughes, Luis Alberni, Joseph Allen Jr., *Lois Collier,* Nick Stuart, Al St. John
Director: Edgar G. Ulmer

GET GOING
(Universal, June, 1943) 62 Minutes.
Robert Paige, Grace McDonald, Vera Vague, Walter Catlett, *Lois Collier,* Maureen Cannon, Milburn Stone, Jennifer Holt, Nana Bryant, Frank Faylen, Wally Vernon
Director: Jean Yarbrough
Screenplay: Warren Wilson
Associate Producer: Will Cowan

SHE'S FOR ME
(Universal, December, 1943) 61 Minutes.
Grace McDonald, David Bruce, *Lois Collier,* George Dolenz, Charles Dingle, Helen Brown, Douglas Wood, Leon Belasco, Mantan Moreland, Charles Coleman, Frank Faylen, Charles Trowbridge, Ray Corrigan, Grace Hayle, Carol Hughes, Eddie Bruce, Frank Penny, Gerald Pierce, Teddy Infuhr
Director: Reginald Le Borg
Screenplay: Henry Blankfort
Associate Producer: Frank Gross

COBRA WOMAN
(Universal, January, 1944) 71 Minutes.
Maria Montez, Jon Hall, Sabu, Lon Chaney Jr., Edgar Barrier, *Lois Collier,* Mary Nash, Samuel S. Hinds, Moroni Olsen, Carmen D' Antonio, Robert Barron, Vivian Austin, Beth Dean, Paulita Arvizu, Fritz Leiber, Belle Mitchell, John Bagni, Eddie Parker, Dale Van Sickel, George Magrill
Director: Robert Siodmak
Screenplay: Gene Lewis, Richard Brooks
Story: W. Scott Darling
Producer: George Wagner

LADIES COURAGEOUS
(Universal, February, 1944) 88 Minutes.
Loretta Young, Geraldine Fitzgerald, Anne Gwynne, Diana Barrymore, Evelyn Ankers, Philip Terry, David Bruce, *Lois Collier,* June Vincent, Samuel S. Hinds, Richard Fraser, Frank Jenks, Janet Shaw, Kane Richmond, Ruth Roman, Dennis Moore, Steve Brodi
Director: John Rawlins
Screenplay: Norman Reilly Raine
Story: Norman Reilly Raine
Producer: Walter Wanger

FOLLOW THE BOYS
(Universal, March, 1944) 122 Minutes.
Vera Zorina, Grace McDonald, Charles Grapewin, Charles Butterworth, Ramsey Ames, and a long list of guest stars. *Lois Collier* appears in the Hollywood Victory Committee sequence with Maria Montez, Gloria Jean, Louise Albritton, Evelyn Ankers, and others
Director: A. Edward Sutherland
Screenplay: Lou Breslow and Gertrude Purcell
Associate Producer: Albert L. Rockett
Producer: Charles K. Feldman

WEIRD WOMAN
(Universal, March, 1944) 64 Minutes.
Lon Chaney Jr., Anne Gwynne, Evelyn Ankers, Ralph Morgan, Elisabeth Risdon, *Lois Collier,* Elizabeth Russell, Harry Hayden, Phil Brown, Jackie Lou Harding, Hanna Kaapa
Director: Reginald LeBorg
Screenplay: Brenda Weisberg
Story: Fritz Leiber, "Conjure Wife"
Adaptation: Scott Darling
Associate Producer: Oliver Drake

JUNGLE WOMAN
(Universal, June, 1944) 54 Minutes.
J. Carrol Naish, Evelyn Ankers, Milburn Stone, *Lois Collier,* Richard Davies, Eddie Hyans Jr., Samuel S. Hinds, Douglass Dumbrille, Nana Bryant, Christian Rub, Richard Powers (Tom Keene), Pierre Watkin, Alex Craig, Julie London
Director: Reginald LeBorg
Screenplay: Bernard Schubert, Henry Sucher, Edward Dein
Story: Henry Sucher
Associate Producer: Will Cowan

JUNGLE QUEEN
(Universal, January 1945) 13 Chapters
Lois Collier, Edward Norris, Eddie Quillan, Douglas Dumbrille, Ruth Roman, Tala Birell, Clarence Muse, Napoleon Simpson, Cy Kendall, Clinton Rosemond, Oliver Prickett, Lumsden Hare, Lester Matthews, Budd Buster, Emmett Smith, Jim Basquette, Crane Whitley, George Eldridge, Edmund Cobb, Cyril Delevanti, John Merton
Directors: Ray Taylor, Lewis D. Collins
Screenplay: George H. Plympton, Ande Lamb, Morgan B. Cox
Chapters: (1) Invitation to Danger (2) Jungle Sacrifice (3) The Flaming Mountain (4) Wildcat Stampede (5) The Burning Jungle (6) Danger Ship (7) Trip-Wire Murder (8) The Mortar Bomb (9) Death Watch (10) Execution Chamber (11) The Trail to Doom (12) Dragged Under (13) The Secret of the Sword

A NIGHT IN CASABLANCA
(Loma Vista Films/United Artists, May 10, 1945) 85 Minutes
Marx Brothers (Groucho, Harpo, Chico), Lisette Verea, *Lois Collier,* Charles Drake, Dan Seymour, Ruth Roman, Sig Rumann
Director: Archie Mayo
Producer: David Loew

Jungle Queen (Universal, 1945) – Lois Collier, with youthful buoyancy and undeniable charm, beautified the femme lead excellently.

PENTHOUSE RHYTHM
(Universal, June, 1945) 60 Minutes
Kirby Grant, *Lois Collier*, Edward Norris, Maxie Rosenbloom, Eric Blore, Minna Gombel, Edward S. Brophy, Judy Clark, Marion Martin, Donald McBride, Henry Armetta, Jimmy Dodd, Bobby Worth, Paul Hurst
Director: Eddie Cline
Screenplay: Stanley Roberts, Howard Dimsdale
Story: Min Selvin, Stanley Roberts
Producer: Frank Gross

THE NAUGHTY NINETIES
(Universal, June, 1945) 76 Minutes
Bud Abbott, Lou Costello, Alan Curtis, Rita Johnson, *Lois Collier*, Henry Travers, Joe Sawyer, Joe Kirk, Barbara Pepper, Jack Norton, The Rainbow Four, John Hamilton, Ed Gargan, Ben Johnson, Rex Lease, William Desmond, Arthur Loft, Tom Fadden, Sam McDaniel, Lillian Yarbo, Jack Rice
Director: Jean Yarbrough
Screenplay: Edmund L. Hartmann, John Grant, Edmund Joseph, Hal Fimberg
Producer: Edmund L. Hartmann, John Grant

THE CRIMSON CANARY
(Universal, November, 1945) 64 Minutes
Noah Beery Jr., *Lois Collier*, John Litel, Steven Geray, Claudia Drake, Christine MacIntyre, Steve Brodie, Danny Morton, Jimmy Dodd, John Kellogg, Arthur Space, Oscar Pettiford
Director: John Hoffman
Screenplay: Henry Blankfort, Peggy Phillips
Story: Peggy Phillips
Associate Producer: Henry Blankfort
Executive Producer: Bob Faber

GIRL ON THE SPOT
(Universal, February, 1946) 76 Minutes
Lois Collier, Jess Barker, George Dolenz, Fuzzy Knight, Ludwig Stossel, Richard Lane, Donald MacBride, Edward S. Brophy, Billy Newell, Ralph Sanford, Carol Hughes, Joseph Crehan, John Hamilton
Director: William Beaudine
Screenplay: Dorcas Cochran, Jerry Warner
Story: George Blake, Jack Hartfield
Associate Producer: George Blake

THB CAT CREEPS
(Universal, October, 1946) 60 Minutes
Noah Beery Jr., *Lois Collier,* Paul Kelly, Douglas Dumbrille, Fred Brady, Rose Hobart, Jonathan Hale, Vera Lewis, Tris Clive, William B. Davidson
Director: Erle C. Kenton
Screenplay: Edward Dein, Jerry Werner
Story: Gerald Geraghty
Associate Producer: Will Cowan
Executive Producer: Howard Welsh

WILD BEAUTY
(Universal, December, 1946) 59 Minutes
Lois Collier, Don Porter, Jacqueline deWit, George Cleveland, Robert Wilcox, Robert "Buzzy" Henry, Dick Curtis, Eva Puig, Pierce Lyden, Roy Brent, Isabel Withers, Wild Beauty (a horse)
Director: Wallace W. Fox
Screenplay: Adele Buffington
Producer: Wallace W. Fox

SLAVE GIRL
(Universal, July, 1947) 80 Minutes
Yvonne De Carlo, George Brent, Broderick Crawford, Albert Dekker, *Lois Collier,* Andy Devine, Carl Esmond, Arthur Treacher, Philip Van Zandt, Trevor Bardette, George J. Lewis, Jack Ingram, Rex Lease, Eddie Dunn, Dan Seymour, June Marlowe, Nobel Johnson, Harold Goodwin
Director: Charles Lamont
Screenplay: Michael Fessier and Ernest Pagano
Producer: Michael Fessier and Ernest Pagano

ARTHUR TAKES OVER
(20th Century Fox, May 1948) 63 Minutes
Lois Collier, Richard Crane, Skip Homeier, Ann H. Todd, Jerome Cowan, Barbara Brown, William Bakewell, Howard Freeman, Joan Blair, Almira Sessions
Director: Malcolm St. Clair
Screenplay: Mauri Grashin
Producer: Sol M. Wurtzel

OUT OF THE STORM
(Republic, August 25, 1948) 61 Minutes
James Lydon, *Lois Collier*, Marc Lawrence, Richard Travis, Robert Emmett Keane, Helen Wallace, Harry Hayden, Roy Barcroft, Charles Lane, Iris Adrian, Byron Foulger, Claire DuBrey, Smoki Whitfield, Charlie Sullivan, Rex Lease
Screenplay: John K. Butler
Story: Gordon Rigby
Associate Producer: Sidney Picker

MISS MINK OF 1949
(20th Century-Fox, March 1949) 69 Minutes
Jimmy Lydon, *Lois Collier*, Richard Lane, Barbara Brown, Paul Guilfoyle, June Storey, Grandon Rhodes, Walter Sande, Don Kohler, Vera Marsh, Dorothy Granger, Iris Adrian
Director: Glenn Tyron
Screenplay: Arnold Belgard
Producer: Sol M. Wurtzel

HUMPHREY TAKES A CHANCE
(Monogram, June 4, 1950) 74 Minutes
Leon Errol, Joe Kirkwood Jr., Gil Lamb, Tom Neal, *Lois Collier,* Jack Kirkwood, Andrew Tombes, Robert Coogan, Tim Ryan, Victoria Horne, Iris Adrian, Eddie Gribbon
Screenplay: Jeff Anjan
Story: Jeff Anjan
Producer: Hal H. Chester
Based on characters created by Ham Fisher

FLYING DISC MAN FROM MARS
(Republic, January, 1951) 12 Chapters
Walter Reed, *Lois Collier*, Gregory Gay, James Craven, Harry Lauter, Richard Irving, Sandy Sanders, Michael Carr, Dale Van Sickel, Tom Steele, George Sherwood, Jimmy O'Gatty, John DeSimone, Lester Dorr, Dick Cogan, Clayton Moore, Dick Crockett, Bill Wilkus, Guy Teague, Ken Terrell, Barry Brooks, Saul Gorss, Chuck Hamilton, John Daheim
Director: Fred C. Brannon
Screenplay: Ronald Davidson
Associate Producer: Franklin Adreon
Chapters: (1) Menace from Mars (2) The Volcano's Secret (3) Death Rides the Stratosphere (4) Execution by Fire (5) The Living Projectile (6) Perilous Mission (7) Descending Doom (8) Suicidal Sacrifice (9) The Funeral Pyre (10) Weapons of Hate (11) Disaster on the Highway (12) Volcanic Vengeance
(Re-edited into feature film **MISSILE MONSTERS**)

RHYTHM INN
(Monogram, February 11, 1951) 73 Minutes
Kirby Grant, Jane Frazee, Charles Smith, Fritz Feld, Ralph Sanford, Armida, Anson Weeks, *Lois Collier*, Ames and Arno, Ramon Brothers
Director: Paul Landres
Screenplay: William Rayno
Story: William Rayno
Producer: Lindsley Parsons

Marguerite Courtot.

25 • MARGUERITE COURTOT

A Striking Teenage Star Who Was as Wholesome as the Proverbial Girl Next Door

Back in 1901 a New York newspaper held a contest to decide the burning question of whether American or English children were prettier. The first prize of $100 went to a golden-haired girl only four years old--and the Americans had it! Everyone, including the judges (or should one say especially the judges), smiled at her, captivated by this pre-Shirley Temple child who was soon to become one of the youngest leading women on the screen.

Marguerite Gabrielle Courtot was born in Summit, New Jersey, of French parentage on August 20, 1897. After winning the baby contest, she learned to dance at the insistence of Mother Courtot, who had wisely invested in her daughter's future by using the prize money to pay for dancing lessons. Marguerite danced and posed until she was twelve, at which time she was sent abroad, to Lausanne, Switzerland, to be educated in a convent. When she returned to America, she posed for Harrison Fisher as the ideal young American girl. She also kept up her dancing, and when she wasn't studying with a governess, she was posing for children's frocks for Messrs. Davis and Sanford, photographers.

Mr. Davis was a friend of the family's, and he advised that Marguerite could have great success as a photoplayer. When there was no parental objection, he introduced her to the officials of the Kalem Company. They seemed equally impressed and requested Mrs. Courtot's permission for Marguerite to accompany their Florida company to Jacksonville that fall. But Mrs. Courtot, wiser than most mothers of flattered children, felt that if her daughter was to have a career, an education would be the only real foundation, and she kept her in school.

While the company was in Florida, studio heads did not forget the promising little New Jersey girl, and letters kept coming back asking for a reversal of the maternal decision. Mrs. Courtot was firm, but in June, 1912, during summer vacation, she permitted Marguerite to work as an extra in the famous studio in Cliffside, New Jersey. In a few short months this eager young lady was doing leads, and at sixteen she was one of the hottest properties on the Kalem lot. (She had played her first lead at fifteen, in **The War Correspondent** [1913], embarrassed and a little confused in the love scenes.)

During most of her moviemaking days Marguerite lived in Weehawken, New Jersey, that strange place that sounds like the cry of a wild bird in distress. Raised in the studio, she became a favorite there. Hers was a demure prettiness, and her manners were ladylike. She looked like an illustration from a fashionable woman's magazine on "how the young girl should dress." Despite the youthfulness that was her chief charm, and her fascinating facility in comedy--an inheritance from her Gallic ancestors, no doubt--Marguerite preferred strong plays of emotional and problematic tendency. However, she loved real comedies too, when the humor was genuine and not a lot of silliness. One of her favorite comedy films was **The Adventure of Briarcliff** (1915), made with Tom Moore, her most frequent leading man in her early career. They made nearly a score of films together at Kalem, mostly adventure/drama, with **Barefoot Boy** (1914) (considered by Marguerite as one of her finest pieces of work), **The First Commandment** (1915), **The Secret Room** (1915), and **The Black Ring** (1915) among the best.

Prior to teaming with Moore, Marguerite played the demanding role of Zoe in **The Octoroon** (1913) when she was only fifteen years old. She followed up with successes in **A Celebrated Case** (1914) and **The Green Rose** (1914). Her performance as Kathlyn in the latter film was

269

Pirate Gold (Pathé, 1920) – Marguerite Courtot and George B. Seitz.

considered outstanding by critics.

By late 1915 Tom Moore had ceased to be Marguerite's leading man, and it was Richard Purdom who provided the heroics as she charmed her way through the sixteen one-reel episodes of **The Ventures of Marguerite** (1915) (hardly a serial in the sense of the suspenseful, action-packed chapter plays of the 1930s and '40s). It was more like a series of unconnected short stories.

Marguerite spent winters in Jacksonville during her stay with Kalem. She, her mother, and an older sister maintained an apartment on Tallyrand Avenue just two blocks from the Kalem studio, an apartment usually swarming with masculine admirers. During the summers in the north Miss Courtot was usually at the Cliffside Studio in New Jersey, having the time of her life as an outdoor girl caught up in tennis, swimming, dancing, and driving.

The Kalem days were pleasant for Marguerite. Like all the old companies, Kalem was like a family. One didn't hear much about salaries, and none of the players had contracts. After The Ventures series Marguerite got an offer from Famous Players-Lasky and left Kalem with some reluctance, and certainly against the desires of the Kalem people.

Rolling Stones (1916), Marguerite's initial film for her new employers, was an adaptation of the Edgar Selwyn stage success. Owen Moore co-starred in a fast-moving story of the underworld and of ordinary, honest people. The tale is about the reclamation of a young man who goes to the end of his rope, takes the wrong advice, comes under the spell of a good young woman (Courtot), and at the vital moment elects to travel the right road.

Moore and Courtot were matched again in **The Kiss** (1916), a dramatic comedy of polite society. Moore is an American aviator on furlough from foreign service, and Marguerite is Louise, his grandmother's companion, who (along with a dozen other girls) is very much in love with the lion of the hour.

During World War I there was a recruiting office for the marines in Weehawken, and Marguerite would help out there. When the sergeant who did the desk work was ordered to France, Marguerite volunteered to take his place. It took all her time, so she had to drop her studio work. Then she made tours and sold war savings stamps. Few men could resist their patriotic duty when confronted by this lovely young woman with auburn hair that looked like molten gold in the sunlight. She even "adopted" a group of Middle Western soldiers and wrote them all once a week while they were abroad. Her war-time work kept her away from the screen for about a year.

Courtot's first postwar movie was **The Perfect Lover** (1919), followed by **Teeth of the Tiger** (1919). Then came the film that started her on the road to serial immortality, **Bound and Gagged** (1919). George B. Seitz co-starred and directed, and Frank Leon Smith did the scenario. The film was successful, and the trio followed up with **Pirate Gold** (1920), also a comedy melodrama in ten chapters. In **Velvet Fingers** (1920) the length was extended to fifteen chapters, and Seitz also took over the writing, in addition to directing and co-starring. Marguerite's last serial outing was as one of the three principals (along with Juanita Hansen and Warner Oland) in **The Yellow Arm** (1921), a money-making thriller with an oriental flavor.

On September 25, 1922, after a year in production, **Down to the Sea in Ships** (1922) was premiered at the Olympia Theater in New Bedford, Massachusetts. Long at twelve reels, it was filmed on the open sea and in New Bedford. During production Marguerite and co-star Raymond McKee fell in love, and they were married not long afterward. A few films followed for Marguerite, but she soon gave up her career to devote full time to being Mrs. Raymond McKee. The McKees remained married for over sixty years, long making their home in Hawaii, where Raymond died in October, 1984.

MARGUERITE COURTOT Filmography

THE SWAMP FOX
(Kalem, circa 1912) 3 Reels
Marguerite Courtot, Guy Coombs

THE WAR CORRESPONDENT
(Kalem, March 1, 1913) 1 Reel
Harry Millarde, *Marguerite Courtot*, Robert Vignola

THE AMERICAN PRINCESS
(Kalem, March, 1913) 1 Reel
Alice Joyce, Tom Moore, E. L. Davenport, Naomi Childers, E. P. Gibbs, *Marguerite Courtot*
Director/Screenplay: Marshall Neilan

THE GRIM TOLL OF WAR
(Kalem, March, 1913) 2 Reels
Hal Clements, Guy Coombs, Anna Q. Nilsson, *Marguerite Courtot*, Storm V. Boyd
Director: George Melford
Scenario: Emmett Campbell Hall

THE WARTIME SIREN
(Kalem, March, 1913) 1 Reel
Alice Hollister, Guy Coombs, Henry Hallam, *Marguerite Courtot*
Director: George Melford
Scenario: George Melford

THE FIRE-FIGHTING ZOWAVES
(Kalem, April, 1913)
Guy Coombs, *Marguerite Courtot*, Harry Millarde, Henry Hallam
Director: George Melford
Scenario: George Melford

THE FIGHTING CHAPLIN
(Kalem, April, 1913) 1 Reel
Guy Coombs, *Marguerite Courtot*, Stuart Holmes
Director: George Melford
Scenario: Emmett Campbell Hall

SHENANDOAH
(Kalem, June, 1913) 3 Reels
Anna Q. Nilsson, Robert Vignola, Alice Hollister, Henry Hallan, *Marguerite Courtot*, Guy Coombs, Hal Clements
Director: Kenean Buel
Story: Bronson Howard

BREAKING INTO THE BIG LEAGUE
(Kalem, August, 1913) 2 Reels
Harry Millarde, *Marguerite Courtot,* Henry Hallam

THE FATAL LEGACY
(Kalem, September, 1913) 2 Reels
James Vincent, Anna Q. Nilsson, Marguerite Courtot

THE RIDDLE OF THE TIN SOLDIER
(Kalem, October, 1913) 2 Reels
Alice Joyce, Henry Hallam, *Marguerite Courtot*
Story: Hugh C. Weir

THE VAMPIRE
(Kalem, October 11, 1913) 3 Reels
Bert French, Alice Hollister, Harry Millarde, *Marguerite Courtot*, Robert Vignola
Directors: Sidney Olcott, Thomas Hayes Hunter
Scenario: Thomas Hayes Hunter, Robert Vignola

THE OCTOROON
(Kalem, November, 1913) 3 Reels
Guy Coombs, *Marguerite Courtot*, Alice Joyce
Director: Sidney Olcott
Scenario: Gene Gaunthier
Story: Dion Boucicault

A CELEBRATED CASE
(Kalem, February, 1914) 4 Reels
Alice Joyce, Guy Coombs, Alice Hollister, *Marguerite Courtot*, James B. Ross, Harry Millarde
Director: George Melford
Scenario: Gene Gaunthier
Story: D'Ennery and Cormon

FRANCIS MARION, THE SWAMP FOX
(Kalem, April, 1914) 3 Reels
Guy Coombs, *Marguerite Courtot*

THROUGH THE FLAMES
(Kalem, June, 1914) 2 Reels
Guy Coombs, *Marguerite Courtot*, Alice Hollister, Harry Millarde

THE SHOW GIRL'S GLOVE
(Kalem, June, 1914) 2 Reels
Alice Joyce, Alice Hollister, *Marguerite Courtot*, Harry Millarde

KIT, THE ARKANSAS TRAVELER
(Kalem, September, 1914) 3 Reels
Alice Hollister, *Marguerite Courtot*, Jere Austin, James B. Ross, Ben Walker, Sam Stillwell
Director: Kenean Buel
Story: Frank Chanfrau

BAREFOOT BOY
(Kalem, September, 1914) 3 Reels
Marguerite Courtot, Alice Hollister, Tom Moore, Robert Walker
Director: Robert Vignola
Scenario: Robert Vignola
Story: Mrs. Owen Bronson

THE GREEN ROSE
(Kalem, September, 1914) 1 Reel
Alice Joyce, *Marguerite Courtot*
Director: Kenean Buel

FATE'S MIDNIGHT HOUR
(Kalem, September, 1914)
Alice Joyce, *Marguerite Courtot*
Director: Kenean Buel
Story: Frederick E. Lindsey

THE GIRL AND THE STOWAWAY
(Kalem, October, 1914) 2 Reels
Alice Joyce, Tom Moore, William Bestman, *Marguerite Courtot*
Director: Kenean Buel
Story: C. Doty Hobart

THE RIDDLE OF THE GREEN UMBRELLA
(Kalem, October, 1914) 2 Reels
Alice Joyce, James B. Ross, *Marguerite Courtot*, Jere Austin, Guy Coombs
Director: Kenean Buel

THE GIRL AND THE EXPLORER
(Kalem, November 25, 1914) 1 Reel
Tom Moore, *Marguerite Courtot*, Makoto Inokuchi
Director: Tom Moore
Story: C. Doty Hobart

THE PRODIGAL
(Kalem, December, 1914) 2 Reels
Tom Moore, *Marguerite Courtot*

THE BLACK SHEEP
(Kalem, December, 1914) 2 Reels
Tom Moore, *Marguerite Courtot*, Robert Ellis, Frances Lincoln, Herbert Conley, Charlotte Courtot, Richard Purdon
Director: Tom Moore

HOME RUN BAKER'S DOUBLE
(Kalem, 1914) 2 Reels
Frank "Home Run" Baker, *Marguerite Courtot*
Director: Kenean Buel

THE ADVENTURES OF BRIARCLIFF
(Kalem, January, 1915) 2 Reels
Marguerite Courtot, Tom Moore

THE CABARET SINGER
(Kalem, January, 1915) 2 Reels
Marguerite Courtot, Tom Moore
Director: Tom Moore
Scenario: Tom Moore

THE SECRET ROOM
(Kalem, February, 1915) 2 Reels
Tom Moore, *Marguerite Courtot*, Robert Ellis, Ethel Clifton, Paton Gibbs, Betty Peterson
Director: Tom Moore

THE FIRST COMMANDMENT
(Kalem, March, 1915) 3 Reels
Tom Moore, *Marguerite Courtot*, Robert Ellis, Lowell R. Stark, Austin Webb, Marie Wells, William Calhoun
Director: Tom Moore
Story: Harry O. Hoyt

POISON
(Kalem, March, 1915) 2 Reels
Tom Moore, *Marguerite Courtot*

THE GIRL AND THE BACHELOR
(Kalem, April, 1915) 2 Reels
Tom Moore, *Marguerite Courtot*

THE THIRD COMMANDMENT
(Kalem, April, 1915) 3 Reels
Tom Moore, *Marguerite Courtot*, Robert Ellis, Warner Richman, Richard Purdon
Director: Tom Moore

THE BLACK RING
(Kalem, May, 1915) 3 Reels
Tom Moore, *Marguerite Courtot*

PREJUDICE
(Kalem, May, 1915)
Tom Moore, *Marguerite Courtot*, Robert Ellis, Richard Lyle, Herbert Conley
Director: Tom Moore
Story: Harry Hoyt

THE SEVENTH COMMANDMENT
(Kalem, July, 1915) 3 Reels
Marguerite Courtot

IN DOUBLE HARNESS
(Kalem, July, 1915) 2 Reels
Tom Moore, *Marguerite Courtot*
Director: Tom Moore

FOR HIGH STAKES
(Kalem, July, 1915) 2 Reels
Marguerite Courtot, Tom Moore
Story: Harry O. Hoyt

THE VANDERHOFF AFFAIR
(Kalem, September, 1915) 4 Reels
Hal Forde, *Marguerite Courtot*, Henry Hallam, T. J. Dow, Helen Lindroth, Robert Vignola, Frances Cappeliano
Director: Robert Vignola

BY WHOSE HAND?
(Kalem, October, 1915) 2 Reels
Harland Moore, *Marguerite Courtot*, Richard Purdon, Robert Vaughn
Story: Hamilton Smith

THE VENTURES OF MARGUERITE
(Kalem, October 29, 1915) 16 Chapters
Marguerite Courtot, Richard Purdon, E. T. Roseman, Paul Sherman, Bradley Barker, Edwin Brandt, William Sherwood, Julia Hurley, Phil Hardy, Helen Lindroth, Frank Holland, Robert Vaughn, Harry Edwards, F. B. Vernoy, Walter McEwen, Anna Reader, Otto Niemeyer, Freeman Barnes, William Sherwood, H. E. Barrows, Freeman Barnes, Stella Jenno, A. Lever, Eleanor Lewis, Lois Howell, R. A. Bennett, Joseph Sullivan, Roland Bottomley, Forrest Cummings, Hassen Mussali
Directors: Hamilton Smith, John E. Mackin, Robert Ellis
Chapter Titles: (1) When Appearances Deceive (2) The Rogue Syndicate (3) The Kidnapped Heiress (4) The Veiled Priestess (5) A Society Schemer (6) The Key to a Fortune (7) The Ancient Coin (8) The Secret Message (9) The Oriental's Plot (10) The Spy's Ruse (11) The Crossed Clues (12) The Tricksters (13) The Sealskin Coat (14) The Lurking Peril (15) The Fate of America (16) The Trail's End

THE FATE OF AMERICA
(Kalem, January, 1916)
Marguerite Courtot, Richard Purdon, Arthur Albertson, Robert Ellis, H. G. Hockey, Mae Miksecek
Director: Robert Ellis
Scenario: Howard Irving Young

THE SEALSKIN COAT
(Kalem, January, 1916)
Marguerite Courtot, Bob Ellis, Richard Purdon, Tom J. Evans
Director: Robert Ellis
Scenario: Otto Hoffman

THE TRICKSTERS
(Kalem, January, 1916)
Marguerite Courtot, Roland Bottomley, Robert Ellis, Richard Purdon, Homer Burress
Director: R. E. Cummings
Scenario: Otto Hoffman

THE LURKING PERIL
(Kalem, January, 1916)
Marguerite Courtot, Richard Purdon, Arthur Albertson, Robert Ellis, H. G. Hockey, Florence Pendleton
Director: Robert Ellis
Scenario: Howard Irving Young

THE TRAIL'S END
(Kalem, January, 1916) 1 Reel
Marguerite Courtot, Richard Purdon, Arthur Albertson, Robert Ellis, H. G. Hockey
Director: Robert Ellis
Scenario: Howard Irving Young

THE DEAD ALIVE
(Gaumont, February, 1916) 5 Reels
Marguerite Courtot, Sidney Mason, Henry W. Pemberton, James Levering
Director: Henry J. Vernot
Scenario: Henry J. Vernot

FEATHERTOP
(Gaumont, April, 1916) 5 Reels
Marguerite Courtot, James Levering, Gerald Griffin, Mathilde Baring, Charles Graham, Sidney Mason, John Reinhardt
Director: Henry J. Vernot
Scenario: Paul M. Bryan

ROLLING STONES
(Famous Players-Lasky, August 21, 1916)
Marguerite Courtot, Owen Moore, D. Maley, Alan Hale, Gretchen Hartman, W. J. Butler, Ida Fitzhugh, Russell Bassett
Director: Dell Henderson
Story: Edgar Selwyn

THE KISS
(Famous Players-Lasky, October 19, 1916) 5 Reels
Marguerite Courtot, Owen Moore, Virginia Hammond, Adolph Menjou, Gus Weinberg
Director: Dell Henderson
Story: Elizabeth Frazer

CRIME AND PUNISHMENT
(Arrow-Gold Rooster, February 25, 1917) 5 Reels
Marguerite Courtot, Lydia Knott, Derwent Hall Caine, Carl Gerard, Cherrie Coleman, Sidney Bracy, Robert Cummings

THE NATURAL LAW
(France Films, November, 1917) 7 Reels
Marguerite Courtot, Howard Hall, George Larkin, Jack Ellis, Charles H. France, Lila Blow, Gordon Gray, Leah Peck
Director: Charles H. France
Story: Howard Hall

THE UNBELIEVER
(Edison, February 15, 1918) 7 Reels
Marguerite Courtot, Raymond McKee, Kate Lester, Frank De Vernon, Mortimer Martini, Blanche Davenport, Gertrude Norman, Erich von Stroheim, Thomas Holcomb
Director: Alan Crosland
Story: Mary Raymond Shipman Andrews, "The Three Things" (Produced with the cooperation of the U.S. Marine Corps)

THE PERFECT LOVER
(Selznick, August 25, 1919) 5 Reels
Eugene O'Brien, *Marguerite Courtot*
Director: Ralph Ince
Scenario: Edmund Goulding
Story: Lelia Burton Wells, "The Naked Truth"

BOUND AND GAGGED
(Pathé, October 26, 1919) 10 Chapters
Marguerite Courtot, George B. Seitz, Frank Redman, Nellie Burt, Joe Cuny, Harry Semels, Harry Stone, Tom Goodwin, John Reinhard
Director: George B. Seitz
Story: Frank Leon Smith
Chapter Titles: (1) The Wager (2) Overboard (3) Help, Help (4) An Unwilling Princess (5) Held for Ransom (6) Out Again, In Again (7) The Fatal Error (8) Arrested (9) A Harmless Princess (10) Hopley Takes the Liberty

TEETH OF THE TIGER
(Paramount-Artcraft, November 2, 1919) 5 Reels
David Powell, *Marguerite Courtot,* Charles Gerrald, Myrtle Stedman, Templar Saxe, Joseph Herbert, Charles L. MacDonald, Riley Hatch, Frederick Burton
Director: Chet Whitney
Scenario: Roy Sommerville
Story: Maurice Lablanc

PIRATE GOLD
(Pathé, August 15, 1920) 10 Chapters
Marguerite Courtot, George B. Seitz, Frank Redman, William Burt, Joe Cuny, Harry Stone, Harry Semels, Matthew Betz
Director: George B. Seitz
Story: Frank Leon Smith
Chapter Titles: (1) In Which Hoey Buys a Map (2) Dynamite (3) The Dead Man's Story (4) Treasure at Last (5) Drugged (6) Kidnapped (7) Under Suspicion (8) Knifed (9) The Double Cross (10) Defeat and Victory

ROGUES AND ROMANCE
(Pathé, December 2, 1920)
Marguerite Courtot, June Caprice, George Seigmann, George B. Seitz, Harry Semels, William P. Burt, Frank Redman, Anita Brown
Director: George B. Seitz
Story: George B. Seitz

VELVET FINGERS
(Pathé, December 5, 1920) 15 Chapters
George B. Seitz, *Marguerite Courtot*, Tommy Carr, Harry Semels, Lucille Lennox, Frank Redman, Joe Cuny, Al Franklyn Thomas
Director: George B. Seitz
Story: George B. Seitz
Chapter Titles: (1) To Catch a Thief (2) The Face Behind the Curtain (3) The Hand from Behind the Door (4) The Man in the Blue Spectacles (5) The Deserted Pavilion (6) Unmasked (7) The House of 1000 Veils (8) Aiming Straight (9) The Broken Necklace (10) Shots in the Dark (11) The Other Woman (12) Into Ambush (13) The Hidden Room (14) The Trap (15) Out of the Web

THE YELLOW ARM
(Pathé, May 19, 1921) 15 Chapters
Juanita Hansen, *Marguerite Courtot*, Warner Oland, William N. Bailey, Tom Keith, Stephan Carr, Al Franklyn Thomas
Director: Bertram Millhauser
Screenplay: James Shelly Hamilton
Chapter Titles: (1) House of Alarms (2) Vengeance of the East (3) A Strange Disappearance (4) At Bay (5) Danger Ahead (6) A Nest of Knaves (7) Into the Dead of Night (8) Smuggled Aboard (9) Kingdom of Deceit (10) The Water Peril (11) Pawns of Power (12) Price of a Throne (13) Behind the Curtain (14) The False Goddess (15) The Miracle

BEYOND THE RAINBOW
(R-C Pictures, February 19, 1922) 7 Reels
Harry Morey, Billie Dove, Virginia Lee, Diana Allen, James Harrison, Macey Harlam, Rose Coghlan, William Tooker, George Fawcett, *Marguerite Courtot*, Edmund Breese, Walter Miller, Charles Craig, Clara Bow, Huntly Gordon
Director: William Christy Cabanne
Adaptation: Eustace Hale Ball, Loila Brooks
Story: Solita Solano, "The Price of Feathers"

THE CRADLE BUSTER
(Patuwa Pictures/American Releasing, March 19, 1922) 6 Reels
Glenn Hunter, *Marguerite Courtot*, Mary Foy, William H. Tooker, Lois Blaine, Osgood Perkins, Townsend Martin, Beatrice Morgan
Director: Frank Tuttle
Scenario: Frank Tuttle
Story: Frank Tuttle
Producers: Frank Tuttle, Fred Waller, Jr.

DOWN TO THE SEA IN SHIPS
(Whaling Film Corp./Hodkinson, November, 1922) 12 Reels
William Walcott, William Cavanaugh, Leigh R. Smith, Elizabeth Foley, Thomas White, Juliette Courtot, Clarice Vance, Curtis Pierce, Ada Laycock, *Marguerite Courtot*, Clara Bow, James Turfler, Pat Hartigan, Capt. James A. Tilton, J. Thornton Baston, Raymond McKee
Director: Elmer Clifton
Scenario: John L. E. Pell
Story: John L. E. Pell

JACQUELINE, OR BLAZING BARRIERS
(Pine Tree Pictures/Arrow, March 19, 1923) 7 Reels
Marguerite Courtot, Helen Rowland, Gus Weinberg, Effie Shannon, Lew Cody, Joseph Depew, Russell Griffin, J. Barney Sherry, Edmund Breese, Edria Fisk, Sheldon Lewis, Charles Fang, Paul Panzer, Taxie
Director: Dell Henderson
Adaptation: Thomas F. Fallon, Dorothy Farnum
Story: James Oliver Curwood, "Jacqueline," in <u>Good Housekeeping</u>

OUTLAWS OF THE SEA
(John Brunton/American Releasing, March 30, 1923) 5 Reels
Pierre Gendron, *Marguerite Courtot*, Gordon Standing, Herbert Pattee
Director: Jack Okey

THE STEADFAST HEART
(Distinctive Pictures/Goldwyn-Cosmopolitan Dist., October 7, 1923) 7 Reels
Marguerite Courtot, Miriam Battista, Joseph Striker, Joseph Depew, Hugh Huntley, Jerry Devine, William B. Mack, Sherry Tansy, Mary Alden, William Black, Mario Majeroni, Harlan Knight, Walter Lewis, Louis Pierce, Mildred Ardin, Helen Strickland, Leslie Hunt
Director: Sheridan Hall
Adaptation: Philip Lonegran
Story: Clarence Budington Kelland, "The Steadfast Heart"

MEN, WOMEN AND MONEY
(Lester Park, August 15, 1924) 5 Reels
Walter Miller, *Marguerite Courtot*

26 • PAULINE CURLEY

A Diminutive Damsel Frequently in Distress, to the Delight of Film Fans

Pauline Curley was born in Holyoke, Massachusetts, on December 19, probably around 1895. She was educated at Professional Children's School in New York City, and was already a child actress in 1914-15, with the lead in "Polygamy" at Brady's Playhouse in New York City. Her stage career began at age five in stock and vaudeville, and she toured the country in "A Daddy by Express." Her mother was a stage and screen actress.

Pauline stood 5 feet 4 inches tall, weighed 115 pounds, and had a fair complexion, blonde hair, and hazel eyes. We know very little about the personal life of this young ingenue, who is best remembered for three films--two serials and one feature. The serials were **The Invisible Hand** (1920) and **The Veiled Mystery** (1920), both fine examples of the melodramatic serial for which Vitagraph was noted. Antonio Moreno starred in them. The feature was **Bound in Morocco** (1918), opposite Douglas Fairbanks (one of his popular swashbucklers).

Pauline played the heroine in several of the Leo Maloney Range Rider two-reel Westerns and some Jack Perrin features. She also made a Tom Mix oater and several features with minor cowboys Bill Patton, Al Ferguson, Kit Carson, and Bud Osborne for small hole-in-the-wall producing firms. Though she was on the Hollywood scene for a dozen years or more, she never made much of a splash, and by 1928 her career as a leading woman was at an end. Perhaps she remained in Hollywood to join the nameless ranks of extras; we do not know. We like to think, however, that she married, retired from the screen, and lived happily ever after.

Pauline Curley.

PAULINE CURLEY Filmography

THE BETTER WAY
(Ramo, February 22, 1913) 1 Reel
Mary Alden, Jack Hopkins, James F. Ayres, *Pauline Curley*
Director: Wray Bartlett Physioc

THE CALL OF THE ROAD
(Ramo, June 21, 1913)
Pauline Curley

THE DANCING DOLL
(Kalem, October 9, 1915) 3 Reels
Vivian Wessell, Wayne Nunn, E. T. Roseman, George Moss, Harland B. Moore, *Pauline Curley*
Story: Howard Irving Young

LIFE WITHOUT SOUL
(Ocean Photoplays, November, 1915) 5 Reels
Percy D. Standing, Lucy Cotton, William A. Cohill, Jack Hopkins, Josephine Marshall, Sue Balfour, *Pauline Curley*, David McCauley, George De Carlan, Violet De Buccari
Director: Joseph W. Smiley
Scenario: Jesse J. Goldburg
Story: Mary Shelley

THE FALL OF THE ROMANOFFS
(Illidor Pictures, August 31, 1917)
Edward Connolly, Alfred Hickman, Conway Tearle, Chris Craig, Nance O'Neill, *Pauline Curley*
Director: Herbert Brenon

CASSIDY
(Triangle, October 21, 1917) 5 Reels
Dick Rosson, Frank Currier, *Pauline Curley*, Mac Alexander, Eddie Sturgis, John O'Connor
Director: Arthur Rosson
Supervisor: Allan Dwan

THE SQUARE DECEIVER
(Yorke-Metro, November 26. 1917) 5 Reels
Harold Lockwood, *Pauline Curley*, William Clifford, Dora Mills Adams, Kathryn Hutchison, Betty Marvin, Dick Le Strange, E. P. Sullivan, Lester Cuneo
Director: Fred J. Balshofer
Story: Francis Perry Elliott, "Love Me for Myself Alone"
Adaptation: Fred J. Balshofer, Richard Spencer

A CASE AT LAW
(Triangle, December, 1917) 5 Reels
Riley Hatch, *Pauline Curley*, Dick Rosson, Jack Dillon, Ed Sturgis
Director: Arthur Rosson
Supervisor: Allan Dwan
Story: William Dudley Pelley

HER BOY
(Metro, February, 1918) 5 Reels
Effie Shannon, Niles Welch, *Pauline Curley*, Pat O'Malley, James T. Galloway, Violet Axzelle, George F. Demarest, Charles Riegel, Charles W. Sutton, William A. Bechtel, Robert Chandler, Edmund Wright, Anthony Byrd, S. McAlpin, J. C. Bates, Ferike Boros
Director: George Irving
Scenario: Albert Shelby Le Vino
Story: H. Carey Wonderly

THE LANDLOPER
(Yorke/Metro, March 25, 1918) 5 Reels
Harold Lockwood, *Pauline Curley*, William Clifford, Stanton Heck, Gertrude Maloney, Bert Starkey
Director: George Irving
Story: Holman Day
Adaptation: Fred J. Balshofer
Scenario: John B. Clymer

LEND ME YOUR NAME
(Yorke/Metro, May 29, 1918) 5 Reels
Harold Lockwood, Bessie Eyton, *Pauline Curley*, Bert Starkey, Stanton Heck, Peggy Prevost, Harry DeRoy
Director: Fred J. Balshofer
Screenplay: John Clymer, Fred J. Balshofer
Story: Francis Perry Elliott

BOUND IN MOROCCO
(Artcraft/Famous Players-Lasky, August 5, 1918) 5 Reels
Douglas Fairbanks, *Pauline Curley*, Frank Campeau, Tully Marshall, Edythe Chapman, Jay Dwiggins, Marjorie Daw
Director: Allan Dwan
Producer: Douglas Fairbanks
Story: Allen Dwan

THE MAN BENEATH
(Haworth Pictures/R-C, June 10, 1919) 5 Reels
Sessue Hayakawa, Helen Jerome Eddy, *Pauline Curley*, Fanny Ridgley, Jack (John) Gilbert, Fontaine LaRue, Wedgewood Nowell
Director: William Worthington
Scenario: Edmund Mitchell

The Veiled Mystery (Vitagraph, 1920)

THE SOLITARY SIN
(Solitary Sin Corp., July, 1919) 6 Reels
Jack Mulhall, Helene Chadwick, *Pauline Curley*, Anne Schaefer, Edward Cecil, Gordon Griffith, Leo Pierson, Milla Davenport, Dorothea Wolbert, Edward Jobson, Kate Lester, Irene Aldwyn, Charles Spere, Arthur Redden
Director: Fred Sullivan
Story: George D. Watters

TURN IN THE ROAD
(Artcraft/Famous Players-Lasky, 1919)
George Nichols, Helen Jerome Eddy, *Pauline Curley*, Lloyd Hughes, Ben Alexander, Winter Hall
Director: King Vidor

THE INVISIBLE HAND
(Vitagraph, January, 1920) 15 Chapters
Antonio Moreno, *Pauline Curley*, Brinsley Shaw, Jay Morley, Sam Polo, George Mellcrest, Gordon Sackville, Charles G. Rich
Director: William J. Bowman
Story: Albert E. Smith, C. T. Brady
Screenplay: Graham Baker
Chapters: (1) Setting the Snare (2) T.N.T. (3) Winged Death (4) Gassed (5) Dodging Disaster (6) The Closing Jaw (7) The Submarine Cave (8) Outwitted (9) A Heathen Sacrifice (10) Fender of Flesh (11) Flirting with Death (12) Dungeon of Despair (13) Plunging Peril (14) A Modern Mazeppa (15) Closing the Net
(Note: Chapter 1 is 3 reels in length; others are 2 reels)

THE VALLEY OF TOMORROW
(American Film Co., January 5, 1920) 6 Reels
Pauline Curley
Director: Emmett J. Flynn
Story: Stephen Fox

LOVE APPLE
(Robertson-Cole, 1920)
Pauline Curley

THE UNSEEN HAND
(Vitagraph, 1920)
Pauline Curley

THE VEILED MYSTERY
(Vitagraph, September, 1920) 15 Chapters
Antonio Moreno, *Pauline Curley*, H. A. Barrows, Nenette de Courcy, W. L. Rogers, George Reed, George Cooper, W. S. Smith, Valeria Olivo
Directors: F. J. Frandon, Webster Cullison, William J. Bowman
Story: Albert Smith, Cleveland Moffett
Scenario: Graham Baker
Adaptation: William B. Courtney
Chapters: (1) The Menace (2) The Quicksand (3) The Sea Demon (4) Trapped in Mid-Air (5) The Well of Despair (6) The Fiery Furnace (7) Human Targets (8) The Span of Death (9) A Slide for Life (10) A Demon's Device (11) The Smoke of Doom (12) A Climax of Hate (13) The Sinister Stroke (14) The Veil's Secret (15) The Accounting

HANDS OFF
(Fox, April 3, 1921) 5 Reels
Tom Mix, *Pauline Curley*, Charles K. French, Lloyd Bacon, Frank Clark, Sid Jordan, William McCormick, Virginia Warwick, J. Webster Dill, Marvin Loback
Director: George E. Marshall
Scenario: Frank Howard
Story: William MacLeod Raine

JUDGE HER NOT
(Harmony/Sunnywest, July 9, 1921)
Jack Livingston, *Pauline Curley*
Director: George Edward Hall
Scenario: George Edward Hall

THE VENGEANCE TRAIL
(Aywon, 1921)
Al Ferguson, *Pauline Curley*

THE PRAIRIE MYSTERY
(Bud Osborne/Truart, August 15, 1922) 5 Reels
Bud Osborne, *Pauline Curley*, Pearl May Norton, Ben Hall, Harry Gerald, Hazel Evans, Norma Willis, Nora Curley, Monte Collins
Director: George Edward Hall

BORDER LAW
(Malobee/Pathé, December 14, 1922) 2 Reels
(Range Rider Series)
Leo Maloney, *Pauline Curley*, Bud Osborne
Director: Leo Maloney
Story: Leo Maloney, Ford Beebe
Scenario: Leo Maloney, Ford Beebe

SMOKED OUT
(Malobee/Pathé, February 17, 1923) 2 Reels
(Range Rider Series)
Leo Maloney, *Pauline Curley*
Director: Leo Maloney
Scenario: Leo Maloney, Ford Beebe
Story: Leo Maloney, Ford Beebe

DOUBLE CINCHED
(Malobee/Pathé, February 23, 1923) 2 Reels
(Range Rider Series)
Leo Maloney, *Pauline Curley*, Chief Whitehorse, Noah Hendricks, Bud Osborne, Harry Belmour
Directors: Leo Maloney, Ford Beebe
Screenplay: Leo Maloney, Ford Beebe
Story: Leo Maloney, Ford Beebe

LOST, STRAYED OR STOLEN
(Malobee/Pathé, February 23, 1923) 2 Reels
(Range Rider Series)
Leo Maloney, *Pauline Curley*, Tommy Grimes, Bud Osborne, Chief Whitehorse
Directors: Leo Maloney, Ford Beebe
Screenplay: Leo Maloney, Ford Beebe
Story: Leo Maloney, Ford Beebe

THE DESERT SECRET
(H. & B. Film Co./Madoc Sales, May 24, 1924) 5 Reels
Bill Patton, *Pauline Curley*
Director: Frederick Reel, Jr.
Story: Frederick Reel, Jr.
Producer: Kenneth J. Bishop

MIDNIGHT SECRETS
(Robert J. Horner/Rayart, October 1, 1924) 5 Reels
George Larkin, Ollie Kirby, *Pauline Curley*, Jack Richardson
Director: Jack Nelson

Thunderbolt's Tracks (Rayart, 1927) – Pauline Curley, Jack Perrin, Billy Lamar (Buzz Barton), Henry Tenbrook, Ruth Royce (background).

SHACKLES OF FEAR
(J. J. Fleming/Davis Distributing Division, November 15, 1924) 5 Reels
Al Ferguson, *Pauline Curley*, Fred Dayton, Les Bates, Frank Clark, Bert DeVore, Paul Emery
Director: Al Ferguson

THE TRAIL OF VENGEANCE
(J. J. Fleming/Davis Distributing Division, December 15, 1924) 6 Reels
Al Ferguson, *Pauline Curley*
Director: Al Ferguson

THE LAFFIN' FOOL
(Morris R. Schlank/Rayart, February, 1927) 5 Reels
Jack Perrin, *Pauline Curley*, Billy Lamar (Buzz Barton), Thelma Daniels, Al Ferguson, Jack Henderson, Bud Duncan, Will Hayes, "Starlight"

THUNDERBOLT'S TRACKS
(Morris R. Schlank/Rayart, April, 1927) 5 Reels
Jack Perrin, *Pauline Curley*, Billy Lamar (Buzz Barton), Jack Henderson, Harry Tenbrook, Ethan Laidlaw, Ruth Royce, "Starlight"
Directors: J. P. McGowan, Bennett Cohn
Scenario: Bennett Cohn

CODE OF THE RANGE
(Morris R. Schlank/Rayart, May 6, 1927) 5 Reels
Jack Perrin, Nelson McDowell, *Pauline Curley*, Lew Meehan, Chic Olsen, "Starlight"
Directors: Bennett Cohn, Morris R. Schlank
Story: Cleve Meyer

DEVIL DOGS
(Morris R. Schlank/Anchor-Crescent, August 23, 1928) 6 Reels
Alexander Alt, *Pauline Curley*, Stuart Holmes, Ernest Hillard, J. P. McGowan
Director: Fred Windermere
Adaptation: Adele Buffington

POWER
(Pathé, Sleptember 23, 1928) 7 Reels
William Boyd, Alan Hale, Jacqueline Logan, Jerry Drew, Joan Bennett, Carol Lombard, *Pauline Curley*
Director: Howard Higgin
Story: Tay Garnett
Assistant Directors: Robert Fellows

HIS GREATEST BATTLE
(Robert J. Horner/Aywon, May, 1925) 5 Reels
Jack Randall, Kit Carson, Jack Richardson, *Pauline Curley*, John Pringle, Gladys Moore, Louis Moniago
Director: Robert J. Horner

RIDIN' WILD
(Robert J. Horner/Aywon, September 16, 1925) 5 Reels
Kit Carson, *Pauline Curley*, Jack Richardson, Walter Maley, C. L. James
Director: Leon De La Mothe
Story: Robert J. Horner, Matilda Smith

COWBOY COURAGE
(Robert J. Horner/Aywon, November 7, 1925) 5 Reels
Kit Carson, *Pauline Curley*, Gordon Sackville
Director: Robert J. Horner

WALLOPING KID
(Robert J. Horner/Aywon, January 5, 1926) 5 Reels
Kit Carson, Jack Richardson, Dorothy Ward, Frank Whitson, Al Kaufman, Jack Herrick, *Pauline Curley*
Director: Robert J. Horner

TWIN SIX O'BRIEN
(Robert J. Horner/Aywon, February 19, 1926) 5 Reels
Kit Carson, *Pauline Curley*
Director: Robert J. Horner

PONY EXPRESS RIDER
(Robert J. Horner/Aywon, March 27, 1926) 5 Reels
Kit Carson, *Pauline Curley*
Director: Robert J. Horner

THE MILLIONAIRE ORPHAN
(Fred Balshofer, May 26, 1926) 5 Reels
William Barrymore, Jack Richardson, Hal Ferner, *Pauline Curley*, Rex McIllvaine
Director: Robert J. Horner

WEST OF THE RAINBOW'S END
(George Blaisdell/Rayart, August 13, 1926) 5 Reels
Jack Perrin, *Pauline Curley*, Billy Lamar (Buzz Barton), James Welch, Milburn Moranti, Chief Whitehorse, "Starlight", "Rex"
Director: Bennett Cohn
Scenario: Daisy Kent
Story: Victor Rousseau

PRINCE OF THE SADDLE
(Fred Balshofer, November 11, 1926) 5 Reels
Fred Church (Montana Bill), *Pauline Curley*, Boris Bullock (Kit Carson/William Barrymore)

TWO-FISTED BUCKAROO
(Fred Balshofer, December 24, 1926) 5 Reels
Fred Church (Montana Bill), *Pauline Curley*

27 • LOUISE CURRIE

Emerging from the Multitude of Ingénues, She Made a Name for Herself

Louise Currie's modest claim to fame is founded on two better-than-average serials, several Westerns, a few "A" features, and a number of "B" programmers. Though there was nothing in particular to set her apart from other cliffhanger heroines, Louise was competent, and her good looks and pleasing manner insured her acceptance by Saturday matinee audiences.

As Betty Wallace, Louise achieved a small degree of film immortality in Republic's highly successful, pioneering fantasy **The Adventures of Captain Marvel** (1941), which starred Tom Tyler as the world's mightiest mortal as portrayed in Whiz comics. Superb special effects by the Lydecker brothers, unusually good casting, a well-written script, good direction, and excellent stunt work, particularly by Dave Sharpe, got results. The film is rated as Republic's best chapter play by many serial buffs. Louise's identity with the genre was strengthened by the release of **The Masked Marvel** (1943), which contained bounteous thrills and great stunt work by Tom Steele as the hero. Though not as well-produced as **The Adventures of Captain Marvel**, the film gave Louise a far better part--she appeared in almost every scene.

Louise was born in Oklahoma City, the daughter of Mr. and Mrs. Charles W. Gunter; her father was a bank president. She attended schools in Washington, D.C. and Bronxville, New York before entering Sarah Lawrence College. There she became interested in films and was invited by Max Reinhardt, discoverer of many famous stars, to join his drama workshop in Hollywood. She stayed for two years, starring in many of the shows he produced. Then she was signed by agent Sue Carol, who got her the heroine role in Columbia's Charles Starrett vehicle, **The Pinto Kid** (1941). Other Westerns followed with Tim Holt, Bob Steele, Kirby Grant, Gene Autry, and Eddie Dean. **Gun Town** (1946) gave Louise her finest acting opportunity in Westerns, and it remains her favorite film. She plays a mannish Calamity Jane-type character, with much cracking of a bullwhip.

During her movie years Louise supplemented her income by working as an interior decorator, a field she is still in today as head of Louise Currie Interiors of Los Angeles. Commenting on her work, she says, "It is fascinating; it takes me into many homes, many interesting people's lives, and many fabulous countries, as I not only do interior designing but buy antiques in foreign countries as well. It is stimulating, creative, and rewarding, in spite of the many difficulties and headaches which are inevitable in this custom-type of endeavor."

After **Second Chance** (1948) with Kent Taylor, Louise left the screen to concentrate her efforts entirely on decorating and designing. She has been married to architectural designer John Good for many years, and they have two sons, one daughter, and six grandchildren.

LOUISE CURRIE Filmography

BILLY THE KID OUTLAWED
(PRC, July 20, 1940) 52 Mins.
(Billy the Kid Series)
Bob Steele, Al St. John, *Louise Currie,* Carleton Young, John Merton, Joe McGuinn, Ted Adams, Walter McGrail, Hal Price, Kenne Duncan, Reed Howes, George Chesebro, Steve Clark, Budd Buster, Sherry Tansey, Jack Ingram, Carl Sepulveda
Director: Peter Stewart (Sam Newfield)
Screenplay: Oliver Drake
Story: Oliver Drake
Producer: Sigmund Neufeld

Stardust on the Sage (Republic, 1942) – Louise Currie and Gene Autry.

BILLY THE KID'S GUN JUSTICE
(PRC, December 27, 1940) 59 Mins.
(Billy the Kid Series)
Bob Steele, Al St. John, *Louise Currie,* Carleton Young, Charles King, Rex Lease, Ted Adams, Kenne Duncan, Forrest Taylor, Al Ferguson, Karl Hackett, Edward Pail, Sr., Julian Rivero, Blanca Vischer, Joe McGuinn, George Morrell
Director: Peter Stewart (Sam Newfield)
Screenplay: Joseph O'Donnell
Producer: Sigmund Neufeld

THE PINTO KID
(Columbia, February 5, 1941) 61 Mins.
Charles Starrett, *Louise Currie,* Bob Nolan, Paul Sutton, Hank Bell, Francis Walker, Ernie Adams, Jack Rockwell, Roger Grey, Dick Botiller, Steve Clark, Frank Ellis, Sons of the Pioneers
Director: Lambert Hillyer
Screenplay: Fred Myton
Story: Fred Myton
Producer: Jack Fier

ADVENTURES OF CAPTAIN MARVEL
(Republic, February, 1941) 12 Chapters
Tom Tyler, Frank Coghlan, Jr., William Benedict, *Louise Currie,* Robert Strange, Harry Worth, Gerald Mohr, Bryant Washburn, John Davidson, George Pembroke, Peter George Lynn, Reed Hadley, Jack Mulhall, Kenne Duncan, Nigel de Brulier, John Bagni, Carleton Young, Leyland Hodgson, Stanley Price, Ernest Sarracino, Tetsu Komai, Paul Lopez, Wilson Benge, Jerry Jerome, Dick Crockett, Chuck Morrison, Francis Sayles, Eddie Dew, Loren Riebe, Earl Bunn, George Suzanne, Edward Cassidy, Ted Mapes, Frank Marlowe, Armand Cortes, Ken Terrell, Major Sam Harris, Loren Riebe, Duke Taylor, Lynton Brent, Augie Gomez, Al Taylor, Curley Dresden, Henry Willis, Steve Clemente, Al Kikume, Bud Geary, Marten Lamont, Carl Zwolsman, Ray Hanson, Frank Wayne, David Sharpe
Directors: William Witney, John English
Screenplay: Ronald Davidson, Norman S. Hall, Arch B. Heath, Joseph Poland, Sol Shor
Associate Producer: Hiram S. Brown, Jr.
Chapter Titles: (1) Curse of the Scorpion (2) The Guillotine (3) Time Bomb (4) Death Takes the Wheel (5) The Scorpion Strikes (6) Lens of Death (7) Human Targets (8) Boomerang (9) Dead Man's Trap (10) Doom Ship (11) Valley of Death (12) Captain Marvel's Secret

CITIZEN KANE
(RKO-Radio, September 5, 1941) 119 Mins.
Orson Welles, Dorothy Comingore (Linda Winters), Joseph Cotten, Everett Sloane, George Coulouris, Ray Collins, Ruth Warrick, Erskine Sanford, William Alland, Agnes Moorehead, Richard Baer, Paul Stewart, Fortunio Bonanova, Joan Blair, Buddy Swan, Harry Shannon, Georgia Backus, Al Eben, Charles Bennett, Philip van Zandt, Milton Kibbee, Tom Curran, Sonny Bupp, Irving Mitchell, Edith Evanson, Arthur Kay, Tudor Williams, Herbert Corthell, Alan Ladd, *Louise Currie,* Walter Sande, Arthur O'Connell, Benny Rubin, Edmund Cobb, Frances Neal, Ellen Lowe, Gus Schilling, Gino Corrado
Director: Orson Welles
Screenplay: Herman J. Mankiewicz, Orson Welles
Producer: Orson Welles

LOOK WHO'S LAUGHING
(RKO Radio, November 21, 1941) 78 Mins.
Edgar Bergen, Fibber McGee and Molly (Jim and Marian Jordan), Lucille Ball, Lee Bonnell, Dorothy Lovett, Harold Peary, Isabel Randolph, Walter Baldwin, Neil Hamilton, Charles Halton, Harlow Wilcox, Spencer Charters, Jed Prouty, George Cleveland, Bill Thompson, Sterling Holloway, Florence Wright, Harlan Briggs, Arthur Q. Bryan, Dell Henderson, Jack George, Matty Kemp, *Louise Currie,* Donald Kerr
Director: Allan Dwan
Screenplay: James V. Kern
Producer: Allan Dwan

DOUBLE TROUBLE
(Monogram, November 27, 1941) 63 Min.
Harry Langdon, Charles Rogers, Catherine Lewis, *Louise Currie,* Benny Rubin, Mira McKinney, Frank Jacquet, Wheeler Oakman, David Cavendish, Dave O'Brien, Eddie Kane, Dick Alexander, Ruth Hiatt, Guy Kingsford, Fred Santley, Richard Cramer, Art Hamberger
Director: William West
Screenplay: Jack Natteford
Producer: Dixon R. Harwin, Barney Sarecky

DUDE COWBOY
(RKO-Radio, December 12, 1941) 59 Mins.
Tim Holt, Marjorie Reynolds, Ray Whitley, Lee "Lasses" White, *Louise Currie,* Helen Holmes, Eddie Kane, Eddie Dew, Byron Foulger, Tom London, Lloyd Ingraham, Glenn Strange
Director: David Howard
Screenplay: Morton Grant
Story: Morton Grant
Producer: Bert Gilroy

The Ape Man (Monogram, 1943) – Louise Currie and Bela Lugosi.

THE BASHFUL BACHELOR
(RKO, March 20, 1942) 79 Mins.
Lum and Abner (Chester Lauck and Norris Goff), Zasu Pitts, Grady Sutton, Oscar O'Shea, *Louise Currie*, Constance Purdie, Irving Bacon, Earle Hodgins, Benny Rubin
Director: Malcolm St. Clair
Screenplay: Chandler Sprague
Story: Chester Lauck, Norris Goff
Producer: Jack William Votion

STARDUST ON THE SAGE
(Republic, May 25, 1942) 65 Mins.
Gene Autry, Smiley Burnette, Bill Henry, Edith Fellows, *Louise Currie*, George Ernest, Emmett Vogan, Vince Barnett, Betty Farrington, Roy Barcroft, Tom London, Rex Lease, Frank Ellis, Edward Cassidy, Fred Burns, Frank LaRue, Franklyn Farnum, Edward Cobb, Jerry Jerome, Merrill McCormack, Bert LeBaron, Monte Montague, George DeNormand, Bill Jamison, Jimmy Fox, George Sherwood, William Nestell, Frank O'Connor, Griff Barnett, Frankie Marvin, Lee Shumway, Champion"
Director: William Morgan
Screenplay: Betty Burbridge
Story: Dorrell and Stuart McGowan
Associate Producer: Harry Grey

TIREMAN, SPARE MY TIRES
(Columbia, June 4, 1942) 2 Reels
Harry Langdon, *Louise Currie*, Emmett Lynn, Vernon Dent, Bud Jamison
Director: Jules White

HIS WEDDING SCARE
(Columbia, January 15, 1943) 2 Reels
El Brendel, *Louise Currie*, Monty Collins, Vernon Dent, Dudley Dickerson, Lloyd Bridges, Stanley Blystone, Eddie Laughton, Chester Conklin, Snub Pollard, Stanley Brown
Director: Del Lord

A BLITZ ON THE FRITZ
(Columbia, January 22, 1943) 2 Reels
Harry Langdon, *Louise Currie*, Douglas Leavitt, Vernon Dent, Bud Jamison, Beatrice Blinn, Jack "Tiny" Lipson, Blanche Payson, Charles Berry, Al Hill, Al Thompson, Joe Palma, Stanley Blystone, Kit Guard, Bud Fine
Director: Jules White

THE APE MAN
(Monogram, March, 1943) 64 Mins.
Bela Lugosi, *Louise Currie*, Wallace Ford, Henry Hall, Minerva Urecal, Emil Van Horn, J. Farrell MacDonald, Wheeler Oakman, Ralph Littlefield, Jack Mulhall, Charles Jordan
Director: William Beaudine
Screenplay: Barney Sarecky
Story: Karl Brown, "They Creep in the Dark"
Producers: Sam Katzman, Jack Dietz

THE MASKED MARVEL
(Republic, September, 1943) 12 Chapters
William Forrest, *Louise Currie*, Johnny Arthur, Rod Bacon, Richard Clarke, Anthony Warde, David Bacon, Tom Steele, Gayne Whitman, Bill Healy, Howard Hickman, Kenneth Harlan, Thomas Louden, Eddie Parker, Duke Green, Dale Van Sickel, Wendell Niles, Lester Dorr, George Pembroke, Stanley Price, John Daheim, Eddie Phillips, Ken Terrell, Allen Pomeroy, Crane Whitley, Forbes Murray, Robert Wilke, Bill Cody, Nolan Leary, Lynton Brent, Lee Roberts, Joe Yrigoyen, Fred Graham. Duke Green, Roy Barcroft, Herbert Rawlinson, Edward Van Sloan, George J. Lewis, Harry Woods, Brooks Benedict, George Suzanne, Sam Flint, Sam Ash, Jack O'Shea, Nora Lane, Harold Kruger, Bud Geary, Tom London, Frank O'Connor, Ernie Adams, Charles Hutchison, Betty Miles, Thom Metzetti, Preston Peterson, Pat O'Shea
Director: Spencer Bennet
Screenplay: Roy Cole, Ronald Davidson, Basil Dickey, Jesse Duffy, Grant Nelson, George Plympton, Joseph Poland
Associate Producer: W. J. O'Sullivan
Special Effects: Howard Lydecker
Chapter Titles: (1) The Masked Crusader (2) Death Takes the Helm (3) Dive to Doom (4) Suspense at Midnight (5) Murder Meter (6) Exit to Eternity (7) Doorway to Destruction (8) Destined to Die (9) Danger Express (10) Suicide Sacrifice (11) The Fatal Mistake (12) The Man Behind the Mask

VOODOO MAN
(Monogram, February 21, 1944) 62 MIns.
Bela Lugosi, John Carradine, George Zucco, Wanda McKay, *Louise Currie*, Michael Ames, Ellen Hall, Terry Walker, Mary Currier, Claire James, Henry Hall, Dan White, Pat McKee, Mici Goty
Director: William Beaudine
Screenplay: Robert Charles
Story: Robert Charles
Producers: Sam Katzman, Jack Dietz

MILLION DOLLAR KID
(Monogram, February 28, 1944) 65 Mins.
Leo Gorcey, Huntz Hall, Gabriel Dell, Billy Benedict, *Louise Currie*, Noah Beery, Sr., Iris Adrian, Robert Greig, Herbert Heyes, Johnny Duncan, Stanley Brown, Patsy Moran, Mary Gordon, Al Stone, David Durand, Bud Borman, Jimmy Strand, Pat Costello
Director: Wallace Fox
Screenplay: Frank Young
Story: Frank Young
Producers: Sam Katzman, Jack Dietz

FORTY THIEVES
(United Artists, June 23, 1944) 60 Mins.
(Hopalong Cassidy Series)
William Boyd, Andy Clyde, Jimmy Rogers, *Louise Currie*, Douglass Dumbrille, Kirk Alyn, Herbert Rawlinson, Robert Frazer, Glenn Strange, Jack Rockwell, Bob Kortman, Hal Taliaferro
Director: Lesley Selander
Screenplay: Michael Wilson, Bernie Kamins
Based on characters created by Clarence E. Mulford
Producer: Harry Sherman

SENSATIONS OF 1945
(United Artists, June 30, 1944) 86 Mins.
Eleanor Powell, Dennis O'Keefe, C. Aubrey Smith, Eugene Pallette, Mimi Forsythe, Lyle Talbot, Hubert Castle, W. C. Fields, Sophie Tucker, Dorothy Donegan, The Christians, Pallenberg Bears, Cab Calloway Band, Woody Herman Band, David Lichine, Richard Hegeman, Marie Blake, Stanley Andrews, *Louise Currie*, Betty Wells, Bert Roach, Grandon Rhodes, Earle Hodgins, Constance Purdy, Joe Devlin, George Humbert, Wendell Niles, Anthony Warde, Gene Rodgers, Ruth Lee, Les Paul Trio, The Copelands, Mel Hall, The Johnson Brothers
Director: Andrew Stone
Screenplay: Dorothy Bennett, Andrew Stone
Story: Frederick Jackson
Producer: Andrew Stone

PRACTICALLY YOURS
(Paramount, March, 1945) 90 Mins.
Claudette Colbert, Fred MacMurray, Gil Lamb, Cecil Kellaway, Robert Benchley, Tom Powers, Jane Frazee, Rosemary De Camp, Isabel Randolph, Mikhail Rasumny, Arthur Loft, Edgar Norton, Donald MacBride, Donald Kerr, Will Wright, Don Barclay, Earle Hodgins, Yvonne De Carlo, *Louise Currie*, Louise La Planche, Tom Kennedy, Kitty Kelly, Stanley Andrews, Jack Clifford, Gladys Blake, Dorothy Granger, Isabel Withers, George Carleton, Byron Barr, Roy Brent, George Turner, Hugh Beaumont, John James, George Melford, Nell Craig
Director: Mitchell Leisen
Screenplay: Norman Krasna
Producer: Mitchell Leisen

LOVE LETTERS
(Paramount, October 26, 1945) 101 Mins.
Jennifer Jones, Joseph Cotten, Ann Richards, Anita Louise, Cecil Kellaway, Gladys Cooper, Byron Barr, Robert Sully, Reginald Denny, Ernest Cossart, James Milligan, Lumsden Hare, Winifred Harris, Ethel May Halls, Matthew Boulton, David Clyde, Ian Wolfe, Alec Craig, Arthur Hohl, *Louise Currie*, Constance Purdy, Catherine Craig
Director: William Dieterle
Screenplay: Ayn Rand
Story: Chris Massie
Producer: Hal B. Wallis

GUN TOWN
(Universal, January 18, 1946) 57 Mins.
Kirby Grant, Fuzzy Knight, Lyle Talbot, Claire Carleton, *Louise Currie*, Dan White, Ray Bennett, Earle Hodgins, George Morrell, Tex Cooper, Merrill McCormack
Director: Wallace Fox
Screenplay: William Lively
Producer: Wallace Fox

WILD WEST
(PRC, December 1, 1946) 73 Mins.
(Cinecolor)
Eddie Dean, Roscoe Ates, Al LaRue, Robert "Buzzy" Henry, Sarah Padden, *Louise Currie*, Jean Carlin, Lee Bennett, Terry Frost, Warner Richmond, Lee Roberts, Bob Allen, Chief Yowlachie, Bob Duncan, Frank Pharr, John Bridges, Al Ferguson, Bud Osborne, "Flash"
Director: Robert Emmett Tansey
Screenplay: Frances Kavanaugh
Producer: Emmett Tansey

BACK LASH
(20th Century-Fox, March, 1947) 66 Mins.
Jean Rogers, Richard Travis, Larry Blake, John Eldredge, Leonard Strong, Robert Shayne, *Louise Currie*, Douglas Fowley, Sara Berner, Richard Benedict, Wynne Larke, Susan Klimist
Director: Eugene Forde
Screenplay: Irving Elman
Story: Irving Elman
Producer: Sol M. Wurtzel

THREE ON A TICKET
(PRC, April 5, 1947) 64 Mins.
Hugh Beaumont, Cheryl Walker, Paul Bryar, Ralph Dunn, *Louise Currie*, Gavin Gordon, Charles Quigley, Douglas Fowley, Noel Cravat, Charles King, Brooks Benedict
Director: Sam Newfield
Screenplay: Fred Myton
Story: Brett Halliday
Producer: Sigmund Neufeld

THE CRIMSON KEY
(20th Century-Fox, July, 1947) 76 Mins.
Kent Taylor, Doris Dowling, Dennis Hoey, *Louise Currie*, Ivan Triesault, Arthur Space, Vera Marshe, Edwin Rand, Bernadene Hayes, Victoria Horne, Douglas Evans, Ann Doran, Victor Sen Yung, Milton Parsons, Marietta Canty, Chester Clute
Director: Eugene Forde
Screenplay: Irving Elman
Story: Irving Elman
Producer: Sol M. Wurtzel

SECOND CHANCE
(20th Century-Fox, September, 1947) 62 Mins.
Kent Taylor, *Louise Currie*, Dennis Hoey, Larry Blake, Ann Doran, John Eldredge, Paul Guilfoyle, William Newill, Guy Kingsford, Charles Flynn, Eddie Fetherston, Francis Pierlot, Betty Compson
Director: James S. Tinling
Screenplay: Arnold Belgard
Story: Lou Breslow, John Patrick
Producer: Sol M. Wurtzel

THE CHINESE RING
(Monogram, December, 1947) 67 Mins.
Ronald Winters, Mantan Moreland, Warren Douglas, Victor Sen Yung, *Louise Currie,* Phillip Ahn, Byron Foulger, Thayer Roberts, Jean Wong, Chabing, Paul Bryar, George L. Spaulding, Charmienne Harker, Thornton Edwards, Spencer Chan, Kenneth Chuck, Lee Tong Foo, Richard Wang
Director: William Beaudine
Screenplay: Scott Darling
Producer: James S. Burkett
(Reviewed as "The Red Hornet")

AND BABY MAKES THREE
(Columbia, December, 1949) 83 Mins.
Robert Young, Barbara Hale, Robert Hutton, Janis Carter, Billie Burke, Nicholas Joy, Lloyd Corrigan, Howland Chamberlain, Melville Cooper, *Louise Currie*, Grandon Rhodes, Katherine Warren, Joe Sawyer, Mary Treen, Teddy Infuhr, Vernon Dent, Theresa Harris, Barbara Woodell, John Doucette, Victor Sen Yung
Director: Henry Levin
Screenplay: Lou Breslow, Joseph Hoffman
Story: Lou Breslow, Joseph Hoffman
Producer: Robert Lord

QUEEN FOR A DAY
(United Artists/Stillman, July 7, 1951) 107 Mins.
"The Gossamer World" Sequence: Phyllis Avery, Darren McGavin, Rudy Lee, Frances E. Williams, Joan Winfield, Lonny Burr, Tristram Coffin, Jiggs Wood, Casey Folks, George Sherwood
"High Diver" Sequence: Adam Williams, Kasia Orzazewski, Albert Ben-Astar, Tracey Roberts, Larry Johns, Bernard Szold, Joan Sudlow, Grace Lenard, Leonard Nemoy, Danny Davenport Madge Blake
"Horsie" Sequence: Edith Meiser, Dan Tobin, Jessie Cavitt, Douglas Evans, Don Shelton, *Louise Currie*, Sheila Watson, Minna Phillips, Byron Keith
Broadcast Studio: Jack Bailey, Jim Morgan, Fort Pearson, Melanie York, Cynthia Corley, Kay Wiley, Helen Mowery, Dian Fauntelle
Director: Arthur Lubin
Screenplay: Seton I. Miller
Story: Faith Baldwin, "The Gossamer World"
John Ashworth, "High Diver"
Dorothy Parker, "Horsie"
Producer: Robert Stillman

Grace Darmond.

28 • GRACE DARMOND

A Model of Femininity for Her Time

Timidity, sensitivity, shyness have traditionally been admirable qualities in a woman--not only admirable, but lovable as well. And Grace Darmond had all these qualities. Her personality was quintessentially feminine by traditional standards. In the early twenties she was the type of girl whom a man would instinctively choose to be his wife. Dependent and trustful, she lacked the touch of hardness which sometimes becomes associated with the woman who makes her own way in the world.

Grace was of medium height and slender build. Her features were as perfectly modeled as those of a Greek statue, and her dark, doe-like eyes were very striking. Her modesty was only one of Miss Darmond's appealing characteristics, none of which, however, seemed to qualify her for serial stardom.

No incident of her career sheds so much light on the timidity she had to fight as that which occurred when she first appeared in front of the camera. She had attended a private school in Springfield, Illinois, and, as so often happens, had caught the fever to go on the stage. In Grace's case it was compelling enough to make her overcome her natural shyness and apply for a role, and she got a part in "Editha's Burglar". Colonel Selig of the Selig Company met her and asked her to play in his films. At that time Grace was so young that she did not have the beautifully rounded figure she developed at maturity. And her role demanded that she put on tights and a chorus girl's costume. Grace was petrified. She dressed in her costume and hid herself under a long cloak until the scene was called. When she walked shivering onto the set, Colonel Selig gave one look and gasped, "Good heaven, Grace, I didn't know you were knock-kneed!"

"I'm not," protested Grace, proving her point by standing up straight. She had been so shocked at the idea of appearing in tights that she had drawn her knees as close together as she could in an effort to hide them.

Grace was born in Toronto, Canada, in 1898. Her father was a concert violinist. After his death, she and her mother went to Chicago, where she appeared on the stage, and where she met Selig. Her first picture was a comedy, **When the Clock Went Wrong** (1914). After about a year with Selig she went to Astra Film Corporation, releasing through Pathé, to star in **The Shielding Shadow** (1916), a suspenseful serial about a mantle of invisibility; its fifteen chapters were written by George Seitz.

By 1918 Grace was a star at Vitagraph, playing an assortment of roles, and in 1919 she worked for several studios. But her two big features of that year were for Paramount: **The Valley of the Giants** opposite Wallace Reid and **Behind the Door** as female lead with Hobart Bosworth.

In 1920 she played one of the two female leads opposite King Baggot in Burston's serial thriller, **The Hawk's Trail**. That same year she played again with Hobart Bosworth in Paramount's **Below the Surface**. But her career never really shifted into high gear, and she was soon back in the serial genre with **The Hope Diamond Mystery** (1921) for Kosmik and **A Dangerous Adventure** (1922) for Warner Bros. She drifted into vamp roles and was often the "other woman" in love triangles, until she decided she had had enough of filmmaking and quit the business with the advent of talkies.

We have no knowledge of Grace's activities from 1928 until her death at age sixty-five on October 7, 1963. She had been undergoing treatment for a lung ailment at the Motion Picture Country Hospital, although she died at her home. The actress left instructions that her body be donated to the University of Southern California Medical School.

Remembered today more for the serials than for the features she made, Grace was the first female star ever photographed in color, back in 1917.

Grace Darmond.

GRACE DARMOND Filmography

YOUR GIRL AND MINE
(Selig, October 31, 1914) 7 Reels
Olive Wyndham, Katherine Kaeired, Sidney Booth, John Charles, Anna Howard, Katherine Henry, Clara Smith, *Grace Darmond,* Margaret Collier
Director: Giles Warren
Scenario: Gilson Willets

WHEN THE CLOCK WENT WRONG
(Selig, 1914)
Grace Darmond

THE MILLIONAIRE BABY
(Selig-Red Seal, May 19, 1915) 6 Reels
Harry Mestayer, John Charles, *Grace Darmond,* Mrs. C. A. Marston, Charlotte Stevens, Frederick Hand
Director: Lawrence Marston
Scenario: Gilson Willets
Story: Anna Katherine Green

A TEXAS STEER
(Selig, July 24, 1915)
Tyrone Power, *Grace Darmond,* Frances Bayless, John Charles, Mrs. Tyrone Power, Russell Fulton, Walter Roberts, Ralph Johnson, James West, Frank Weed, Charles Huntington, Elmer Jerome, Isabell Randolph, William Castelatt
Director: Giles R. Warren
Story: Charles A. Hoyt

THE HOUSE OF A THOUSAND CANDLES
(Selig, August 14, 1915) 6 Reels
Grace Darmond, Harry Mestayer, George Backus, John Charles, Edgar Nelson, Effinham Pinto, Forrest Robinson, Mary Robson, Gladys Samms, Emma Glenwood
Director: T. N. Heffron
Scenario: Gilson Willets
Story: Meredith Nicholson

A BLACK SHEEP
(Selig, October, 1915) 5 Reels
Otis Harlan, James Bradbury, *Grace Darmond,* Rita Gould, John Charles, John D. Murphy, Fred Morley, Lou Kelso, Jack Rollins, Emma Glenwood, Virginia Ainsworth, Myrtle Healy
Director: T. N. Heffron
Scenario: Gilson Willets
Story: Charles Hoyt

THE GULF BETWEEN
(Lubin, March 9, 1916) 3 Reels
Grace Darmond, Niles Welch
Producer: Edward Sloman
Story: Tom Gibson

HER DREAM OF LIFE
(Selig, April, 1916) 1 Reel
Harry Mestayer, *Grace Darmond*
Director: Frank R. Beal
Scenario: Lottie S. Beckelman

WIVES OF THE RICH
(Selig, April, 1916) 3 Reels
Harry Mestayer, *Grace Darmond,* Lafayette McKee, Lillian Hayward, Emma Glenwood
Director: T. N. Heffron
Scenario: Allen Curtis Mason

A STRANGER IN NEW YORK
(Selig, April 22, 1916) 3 Reels
Otis Harlan, Robert Bolder, John Charles, Emma Glenwood, *Grace Darmond*
Director: T. N. Heffron
Scenario: Gilson Willets

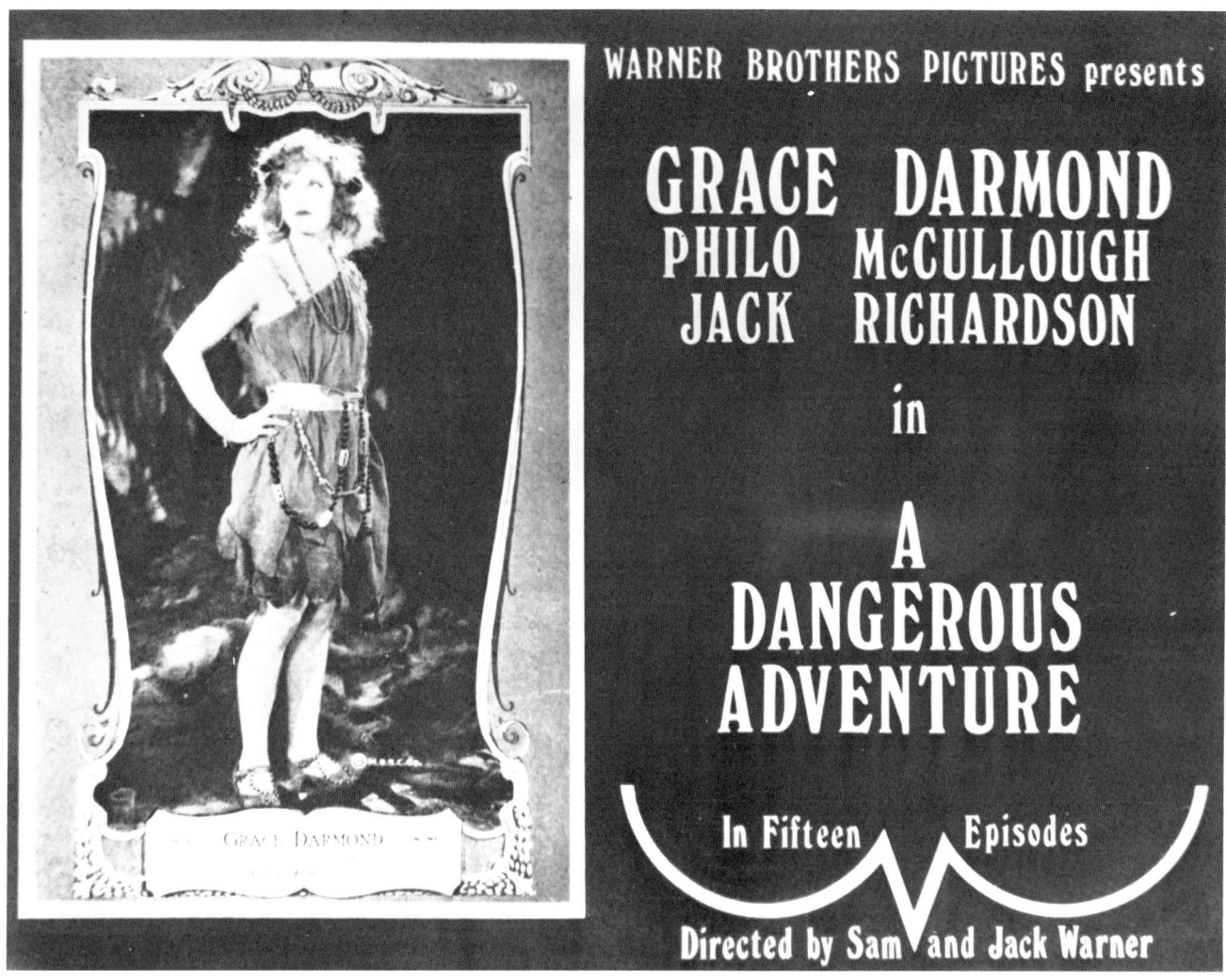

A Dangerous Adventure (Warner Bros., 1922) – Grace Darmond.

TEMPERANCE TOWN
(Selig, June 5, 1916) 3 Reels
Otis Harlan, *Grace Darmond*, John Charles, James Bradbury, Leslie J. King
Director: T. N. Heffron
Scenario: Gilson Willets
From the play by Charles Hoyt

THE SHIELDING SHADOW
(Astra/Pathé, October 1, 1916) 15 Chapters
Grace Darmond, Leon Bary, Ralph Kellard, Madeline Traverse, Lionel Brahm, Frankie Mann, Leslie King, Halian Mostyn, Madeline Francine
Directors: Louis Gasnier, Donald MacKenzie
Screenplay: George B. Seitz
Story: Randall Parrish
Chapters: (1) The Treasure Trove (2) Into the Depths (3) The Mystic Defender (4) The Earthquake (5) Through Bolted Doors (6) The Disappearing Shadow (7) The Awakening (8) The Haunting Hand (9) The Incorrigible Captive (10) The Vanishing Mantle (11) The Great Sacrifice (12) The Stolen Shadow (13) The Hidden Menace (14) Absolute Black (15) The Final Chapter

IN THE BALANCE
(Vitagraph, December, 1917) 5 Reels
Grace Darmond, Earle Williams, Denton Vane, Robert Gaillard, Miriam Miles, Templar Saxe, Julia Swayne Gordon
Director: Paul Scardon
Scenario: Garfield Thompson
Story: E. Phillips Oppenheim

THE CRUCIBLE OF LIFE
(General Enterprises, 1917) 7 Reels
Grace Darmond, Frank O'Connor, Jack Sherrill, Winifred Harris, Edwin Forsberg
Director: Harry Lambart
Story: Bartley Campbell

THE OTHER MAN
(Vitagraph, January 24, 1918) 5 Reels
Grace Darmond, Harry Morey, Florence Deshon, Frank Norcross, Jessie Stevens, Stanley Walpole, Mrs. Chapin
Director: Paul Scardon
Scenario: Paul Scardon
Story: Rex Taylor, Irma Whelpley Taylor

THE GULF BETWEEN
(The Technicolor Motion Picture Co., February, 1918) 8 Reels
Grace Darmond, Niles Welch, Herbert Fortier, Violet Axzelle
Director: Ray Physioc
Supervisor: C. A. Willat
Scenario: Anthony Kelly
Story: J. Parker Read, Jr.

AN AMERICAN LIVE WIRE
(Vitagraph, March, 1918) 5 Reels
Grace Darmond, Earle Williams, Hal Clements, Claire Toner, Orral Humphrey, Margaret Bennett, Malcolm Blevins
Director: Thomas R. Mills
Scenario: William Addison Lathrop
Story: O. Henry, "The Lotus and the Bottle"

THE SEAL OF SILENCE
(Vitagraph, April 23, 1918) 5 Reels
Earle Williams, *Grace Darmond,* Kathleen Kirkham, Bobby Connelly
Director: Thomas R. Mills
Scenario: William Addison
Story: William Addison

THE GIRL IN HIS HOUSE
(Vitagraph, June 15, 1918) 5 Reels
Grace Darmond, Earle Williams
Director: Thomas R. Mills
Scenario: Katherine Reed
Story: Harold MacGrath

WIVES OF MEN
(Pioneer, August 5, 1918) 7 Reels
Florence Reed, *Grace Darmond,* Frank Mills
Director: John M. Stahl
Story: John M. Stahl

A DIPLOMATIC MISSION
(Vitagraph, September 18, 1918) 5 Reels
Grace Darmond, Earle Williams
Director: Jack Conway
Story: Don Bartlett

THE MAN WHO WOULDN'T TELL
(Vitagraph, November 30, 1918) 5 Reels
Grace Darmond, Earle Williams
Director: James Young
Story: Bess Meredyth

THE HIGHEST TRUMP
(Vitagraph, February 3, 1919) 5 Reels
Earle Williams, *Grace Darmond,* Robert Byrem, John Cossar, C. H. Geldart, Robert Bolder, Miles McCarty
Director: James Young
Story: H. H. Van Loan, Earle Williams

A GENTLEMAN OF QUALITY
(Vitagraph, February 15, 1919) 5 Reels
Earle Williams, *Grace Darmond,* Kathryn Adams
Director: James Young
Scenario: Edward J. Montagne
Story: Frederic Van Rensselaer Dey

THE VALLEY OF THE GIANTS
(Paramount-Artcraft, July 24, 1919) 5 Reels
Wallace Reid, *Grace Darmond,* Noah Beery, Ralph Lewis, Will Brunton, Charles Ogle, Alice Taafe, Kay Laurel, Hart (Jack) Hoxie, Virginia Fultz, William H. Brown
Director: James Cruze
Scenario: Marion Fairfax
Story: Peter B. Kyne

BEHIND THE DOOR
(Paramount, November 5, 1919) 7 Reels
Hobart Bosworth, *Grace Darmond,* Lloyd Hughes, Wallace Beery, Jane Novak, Gibson Gowland
Director: Irvin Willat
Scenario: Luther Reed
From the play by Gouverneur Morris

WHAT EVERY WOMAN WANTS
(Mutual, 1919)
Grace Darmond, Forrest Stanley, Wilfred Lucas, Claire du Brey, Percy Challenger

AN AMERICAN ACE
(Vitagraph, 1919)
Grace Darmond, Earle Williams
Director: James Young

THE MAN WHO CAME BACK
(Vitagraph, 1919)
Grace Darmond

INVISIBLE DIVORCE
(National Pictures, Janaury 2, 1920) 6 Reels
Leatrice Joy, Walter McGrail, *Grace Darmond*, Walter Miller, Tom Bates
Directors: Thomas Mills, Nat Deverich
Scenario: Katherine Reed
Story: Leila Burton Wells

THE HAWK'S TRAIL
(Burston, January 13, 1920) 15 Chapters
King Baggot, Rhea Mitchell, *Grace Darmond*, Harry Lorraine, Fred Windermere, Stanton Heck, George Siegmann, Carmen Phillips, Nigel De Brulier, Edna Robinson, Carl Stockdale, Sylvia Jocelyn, Billy White, Art Belasco, Leo White
Director: W. S. Van Dyke
Screenplay: John B. Clymer
Story: Nan Blair
Chapters: (1) False Faces (2) The Superman (3) Yellow Shadows (4) Stained Hands (5) House of Fear (6) Room Above (7) The Bargain (8) The Phantom Melody (9) The Lure (10) The Swoop (11) One Fatal Step (12) Tides that Tell (13) Face to Face (14) The Substitute (15) The Showdown

EVEN AS EVE
(First National, January 20, 1920) 6 Reels
Grace Darmond
Directors: E. A. Rolfe, Chester Devonde
Story: Robert W. Chambers

THE SERVANT IN THE HOUSE
(H. O. Davis, March 1, 1920) 9 Reels
Grace Darmond
Director: Jack Conway
Scenario: Lanier Barlett
Story: Charles Rann Kennedy

BELOW THE SURFACE
(Ince Paramount, May 3, 1920) 7 Reels
Hobart Boxworth, *Grace Darmond*, Lloyd Hughes, George Webb, Gladys George, Edith York, J. P. Lockney, George Clair
Director: Irvin Willat
Scenario: E. Magnus Ingleton
Story: Luther Reed

SO LONG, LETTY
(Robertson-Cole, November 4, 1920) 6 Reels
T. Roy Barnes, *Grace Darmond*, Colleen Moore, Harry Myers
Director: Al Christie
Adaptation: Richard Ellison
Story: Elmer Harris, Oliver Morosco
From the musical comedy by Oliver Morosco and Earl Carroll

THE HOPE DIAMOND MYSTERY
(Kosmik, March, 1921) 15 Chapters
Grace Darmond, George Chesebro, Harry Carter, William Marian, Boris Karloff, Carmen Phillips, William Puckley, May Yohe, Frank Seka, Ethel Shannon, Harry Archer, Arthur Clayton
Director: Stuart Paton
Screenplay: Charles Goddard, John B. Clymer
Story: May Yohe
Chapters: (1) The Hope Diamond Mystery (2) The Vanishing Hand (3) The Forged Note (4) The Jewel of Sita (5) A Virgin's Love (6) The House of Terror (7) Flames of Despair (8) Yellow Whisperings (9) The Evil Eye (10) In the Spider's Web (11) The Cup of Fear (12) The Ring of Death (13) The Lash of Hate (14) Primitive Passions (15) An Island of Destiny

SEE MY LAWYER
(Christie/R-C Pictures, March 13, 1921) 6 Reels
T. Roy Barnes, *Grace Darmond*, Lloyd Whitlock, Jean Acker, Ogden Crane, Tom McGuire, J. P. Lockney, Lincoln Plumer, Bert Woodruff, Eugenie Ford
Director: Al Christie
Scenario: W. Scott Darling
Story: Max Marcin, "See My Lawyer: a Play"

INDISCRETION
(Pioneer, May 27, 1921)
Herbert Rawlinson, *Grace Darmond*
Director: William Davis
Producer: A. J. Bimberg

WHITE AND UNMARRIED
(Famous Players-Lasky/Paramount, June 12, 1921) 5 Reels
Thomas Meighan, Jacqueline Logan, *Grace Darmond*, Walter Long, Lloyd Whitlock, Fred Vroom, Marian Skinnet, Georgie Stone, Jack Herbert
Director: Tom Forman
Scenario: Will M. Ritchey
Story: John D. Swain, "Billy Kane, White and Unmarried"

THE BEAUTIFUL GAMBLER
(Universal, June 1921) 5 Reels
Grace Darmond, Jack Mower, Harry van Meter, Charles Brinley, Herschel Mayall, Willis Marks
Director: William Worthington
Scenario: Hope Loring
Story: Peter B. Kyne

THE SONG OF LIFE
(Louis B. Mayer/First National, January 2, 1922) 7 Reels
Gaston Glass, *Grace Darmond*, Georgia Woodthorpe, Richard Headrick, Arthur Stuart Hull, Wedgewood Nowell, Edward Peil, Fred Kelsey, Claude Payton
Director: John M. Stahl
Scenario: Bess Meredyth
Story: Frances Irene Reels

HANDLE WITH CARE
(Rockett/Associated Exhibitors, January 22, 1922) 5 Reels
Grace Darmond, Harry Myers, James Morrison, Landers Stevens, William Austin, William Courtleigh, Patsy Ruth Miller
Director: Philip E. Rosen
Scenario: Will M. Ritchie
Story: Charles Belmont Davis, "Handle With Care"

A DANGEROUS ADVENTURE
(Warner Bros., February 25, 1922) 15 Chapters (Re-released as a 7-reel feature in the Fall of 1922)
Grace Darmond, Philo McCullough, Jack Richardson, Robert Agnew, Rex De Roselli, Derelys Perdue, Mabel Stark, Captain J. R. Riccarde, Omar Whitehead, Josephine Hill
Directors: S. L. Warner, J. L. Warner
Screenplay: Sam Warner
Story: Frances Guihan
Chapters: (1) The Jungle Storm or The Stolen Medal (2) Sacrifice (3) The Lion Pit (4) Brandon's Revenge (5) At the Leopard's Mercy (6) The Traitor (7) The Volcano (8) The Escape (9) The Leopard's Cave (10) The Jungle Water Hole (11) The Hippopotamus Swamp (12) The Lion's Prey (13) In the Tiger's Lair (14) The Treasure Cave (15) The Rescue
(Note: Chapter 1 is 3 reels long; others are 2 reels)

I CAN EXPLAIN
(S-L Pictures/Metro, March 20, 1922) 5 Reels
Gareth Hughes, Bartine Burkett, *Grace Darmond*, Herbert Hayes, Victor Potel, Nelson McDowell, Edwin Wallock, Albert Breig, Harry Lorraine, Tina Modotti, Sidney D'Albrook, Stanton Heck, William H. Brown
Director: George D. Baker
Adaptation: Edgar Franklin
Story: Edgar Franklin, "Stay Home"

THE MIDNIGHT GUEST
(Universal, March 19, 1923) 5 Reels
Grace Darmond, Mahlon Hamilton, Clyde Fillmore, Pat Harmon, Mathilde Brundage
Director: George Archainbaud
Scenario: Rupert Julian
Adaptation: A. P. Younger
Story: Rupert Julian

DAYTIME WIVES
(R-C Pictures/FBO, September 2, 1923) 7 Reels
Derelys Perdue, Wyndham Standing, *Grace Darmond*, William Conklin, Edward Hearn, Katherine Lewis, Kenneth Gibson, Christina Mott, Jack Carlyle, Craig Biddle, Jr.
Director: Emile Chautard
Adaptation: Wyndham Gittens, Helmer Bergman
Story: Lenore Coffee, John Goodrich

GOLD MADNESS
(Perfect/Principal, October 2, 1923) 6 Reels
Guy Bates Post, Cleo Madison, Mitchell Lewis, *Grace Darmond*
Director: Robert T. Thornby
Scenario: Fred Kennedy Myton
Story: James Oliver Curwood, "The Man from Ten Strike"

THE HERO
(Preferred, 1923)
Grace Darmond, Gaston Glass
Director: Louis Gasnier
Scenario: Eve Unsell
Story: Gilbert Emery

THE WHEEL OF FORTUNE
(Anchor, 1923)
Grace Darmond
Director: Leslie Peacock
Story: Grace Darmond

DISCONTENTED HUSBAND
(Columbia/CBC, January 15, 1924) 6 Reels
James Kirkwood, Cleo Madison, *Grace Darmond*, Arthur Rankin, Vernon Steele, Carmelita Geraghty, Baby Muriel McCormac
Director: Edward J. LeSaint
Story: Evelyn Campbell
Producer: Harry Cohn

ALIMONY
(R-C Pictures/FBO, February 3, 1924) 7 Reels
Grace Darmond, Warner Baxter, Ruby Miller, William A. Carroll, Jackie Saunders, Clyde Fillmore, Herschel Mayall. Alton Brown
Director: James W. Horne
Adaptation: Wyndham Gittens, E. Magnus Ingleton
Story: Ashley T. Locke

THE GAIETY GIRL
(Universal-Jewel, July 21, 1924) 8 Reels
Mary Philbin, Joseph J. Dowling, William Haines, James O. Barrows, De Witt Jennings, Freeman Wood, Otto Hoffman, *Grace Darmond*, Thomas Ricketts, William Turner, Duke R. Lee, George B. Williams, Roy Laidlaw
Director: King Baggot
Scenario: Bernard McConville
Adaptation: Frank Beresford, Melville Brown
Story: Ida Alexa Ross Wylie, "The Inheritors"
Producer: Carl Laemmle

FLATTERY
(Mission/Chadwick, February 15, 1925) 6 Reels
John Bowers, Marguerite De La Motte, Alan Hale, *Grace Darmond*, Edwards Davis, Louis Morrison, Larry Steers
Director: Tom Forman
Story: H. H. Van Loan
Supvisor: Norman Walker

THE GREAT JEWEL ROBBERY
(Ince/Kerman, November 24, 1925) 5 Reels
Herbert Rawlinson, *Grace Darmond*, Frank Darmond, Carlton Griffin, Marcella Daly, Chester Conklin
Director: John Ince

WHERE THE WORST BEGINS
(Co-Artists/Truart, November, 1925) 6 Reels
Ruth Roland, Alec B. Francis, Matt Moore, *Grace Darmond*, Roy Stewart, Derelys Perdue, Theodore Lorch, Ernie Adams, J. P. Lockney, Robert Burns, Floyd Shackelford
Director: John McDermott
Adaptation: Joseph Anthony Roach
Story: George Frank Worts, "Out Where the Worst Begins"

THE PAINTED FLAPPER
(Chadwick, 1925)
James Kirkwood, Pauline Garon, Kathlyn Williams, Claire Adams, *Grace Darmond*, Hallan Cooley, Johnny Harron, Al Roscol, Crauford Kent
Director: John Corman
Story: Alan Pearl

HER BIG ADVENTURE
(Kerman/A. G. Steen, January 5, 1926) 5 Reels
Herbert Rawlinson, *Grace Darmond*, Vola Vale, Carlton Griffin, William Turner, Edward Gordon
Director: John Ince

MIDNIGHT THIEVES
(Kerman/A. G. Steen, February 26, 1926) 5 Reels
Herbert Rawlinson, *Grace Darmond*

THE NIGHT PATROL
(Richard Talmadge-Carlos/FBO, March 14, 1926) 6 Reels
Richard Talmadge, Rose Blossom, Mary Carr, Gardner James, Josef Swickard, *Grace Darmond*, Victor Dillingham. Arthur Conrad
Director: Noel Mason Smith
Scenario: Frank Howard Clark
Story: Frank Howard Clark
Producer: Richard Talmadge

HONESTY--THE BEST POLICY
(Fox, August 8, 1926) 5 Reels
Rockliffe Fellowes, Pauline Starke, Johnnie Walker, *Grace Darmond*, Mickey Bennett, Mack Swain, Albert Gran, Johnnie Walker, Dot Farley, Heinie Conklin
Directors: Chester Bennett, Albert Ray
Scenario: L. G. Rigby
Story: Howard Hawks

HER MAN O'WAR
(De Mille Pictures/PDC, August 23, 1926) 6 Reels
Jetta Goudal, William Boyd, Jimmie Adams, *Grace Darmond*, Kay Deslys, Frank Reicher, Michael Vavitch, Robert Edeson, Junior Coghlan
Director: Frank Urson
Scenario: Charles Logue
Supervisor: C. Gardner Sullivan
Story: Fred Jackson, "Black Marriage"

THE MARRIAGE CLAUSE
(Universal-Jewel, September 12, 1926) 8 Reels
Francis X. Bushman, Billie Dove, Warner Oland, Henri La Garde, *Grace Darmond*, Caroline Snowden, Oscar Smith, Andre Cheron, Robert Dudley, Charles Meakin
Director: Lois Weber
Adaptation: Lois Weber
Story: Dana Burnet, "Technic"

WIDE OPEN
(Sharlin/Sunset, January 14, 1927) 5 Reels
Dick Grace, *Grace Darmond*, Lionel Belmore, Ernest Hilliard
Director: John Wesley Grey
Scenario: John Wesley Grey

THE HOUR OF RECKONING
(Ince/George H. Davis, September, 1927) 6 Reels
John Ince, Herbert Rawlinson, *Grace Darmond*, Harry Von Meter, Virginia Castleman, John J. Darby, Edwin Middleton
Director: John Ince
Story: Frederic Chapin

WAGES OF CONSCIENCE
(Superlative/Hi-Mark, December 24, 1927) 5 Reels
Herbert Rawlinson, *Grace Darmond*, John Ince, Henri La Garde, Margaret Campbell, Jasmine
Director: John Ince
Scenario: Mrs. George Hall
Story: Mrs. George Hall

LIFE IN HOLLYWOOD No. 2
(1927) 10 Mins.
Maurice Tourneur, Colleen Moore, Ben Lyon, George Seigman, Carmelita Geraghty, Gaston Glass, Herb Rawlinson, Al St. John, *Grace Darmond*, Lloyd Hamilton, Ruth Hyatt

29 • HELEN FERGUSON

A Breezy Personality and Determination Augmented Her Modest Talents

Helen Ferguson was among the first crop of Wampas Baby Stars in 1922, at which time she had been in the movies for about eight years. Although the first credits we have for her are in 1917, she is thought to have started in movies in Chicago in 1914 with the Essanay Studios when she was thirteen. She was born in 1901.

Miss Ferguson's career might be dismissed as inconsequential, were it not for the fact that she was the leading lady in three good serials and a handful of action features opposite the big guns of the celluloid range.

During her career she played the love interest opposite such rugged he-men as Hoot Gibson, Harry Carey, Lefty Flynn, Richard Talmadge, and Hobart Bosworth, but it was in the films of Buck Jones and William Russell, both Fox stars at the time, that she made her biggest mark in features. She married Russell in 1925, but he died in 1929. In 1930 she married banker Richard L. Hargreaves, who had once been the husband of Grace Bryan, daughter of William Jennings Bryan. The marriage lasted until his death from a heart attack in 1941. Miss Ferguson did not remarry.

Among Helen's best features was **Challenge of the Law** (1920), a well-built drama of the Canadian Northwest that starred William Russell as Sergeant Bruce Cavanaugh of the Royal Northwest Mounted Police and Helen as Madeline Du Barre, a French-Canadian girl whose father was hunted by the law. There are some unusual situations when the story shifts to the American desert, where Russell is forced to choose between love and duty as all participants face death from thirst.

Burning Daylight (1920), based on the Jack London story, was another good film for Helen, though she shared the spotlight with Gertrude Astor. She made four features with Buck Jones,

Helen Ferguson.

two of which were Westerns. In the Harry Carey starrer **The Freeze-Out** (1921), directed by John Ford, she was the schoolmarm for whom Carey cleans up a sin-ridden town. In **Double Dealing** (1923), one of Hoot Gibson's few non-Westerns, Helen is the servant girl who wins his love and helps him to outmaneuver crooks who seek to take his valuable property. **In Old California** (1929) featured Helen as a Spanish girl in an unusual Western love triangle; she turns out to be the sister of one of her suitors and the other one is gunning for her father. In **The Isle**

Wild West (Pathé, 1925) – Helen Ferguson and Jack Mulhall.

of Hope (1925) she plays a captain's daughter who is stranded on a desert isle with Richard Talmadge, who plays a wealthy yachtsman in search of buried treasure. As expected in any Talmadge movie, the film was one exciting thrill after another.

In the first of her serials she plays opposite Jack Mulhall in Pathé's **Wild West** (1925), actually produced on the 101 Ranch in Oklahoma. The story combined all the elements of the Wild West and circus life. Since the story was about a stranded tent show and required a lot of circus paraphernalia, trained animals, and wide open spaces, the ranch was an ideal place to film, as it was the winter quarters of the 101 Ranch Show. The Pathé company spent three months there making the serial. At the time there were 900 people on the 101 Ranch, and many of them appeared in the film. The performances in roping, trick riding, bronc riding, and bulldogging were staged on the rodeo grounds with such celebrities of the show world as Nowata "Slim" Richardson, world champion bucking bronco rider, and Buck Lucas, world champion bulldogger. It was a fair Western chapter play and a little different in its story.

Casey of the Coast Guard (1926) was also a Pathé serial, with Helen co-starred with George O'Hara in a routine sea yarn about the Coast Guard's attempts to stamp out smuggling, contraband, and aliens. **The Fire Fighters** (1927) was another average-quality serial put out by Universal. Jack Daugherty is firefighter Cap Fallon and Helen, the love of his life.

Helen gave up the movies in 1929 to become a stage actress; she appeared in the legitimate theatre for four years with modest success. In 1933 she became a full-time publicist and for the next thirty-four years she was a powerhouse in Hollywood, with such clients as Barbara Stanwyck, Loretta Young, Pat O'Brien, Henry Fonda, Robert Taylor, Jeanette MacDonald, Franchot Tone, Joel

McCrea, Miriam Hopkins, Eva Gabor, Billie Burke, and hundreds of others. Her reputation was that of a perceptive, hard-driving, result-getting force amid the Hollywood tinsel, fiercely protecting her brood against any intruder--even the press. Her clients swore by her; many of them were represented by her for two decades or longer. Helen made a lot of money and her West Los Angeles home, a gracious Georgian Colonial, was a showplace. With Loretta Young, she co-authored the book The Things I Had to Learn, published by Bobbs-Merrill in 1961.

In 1967 Helen retired to Palm Desert. In late 1976 she moved to Clearwater, Florida, suffering from a circulatory disorder. On March 14, 1977, she died there at the age of seventy-six. Funeral services and burial were in Glendale, California.

HELEN FERGUSON Filmography

SUNDAYING IN FAIRVIEW
(Essanay, May, 1917) 2 Reels
Rod LaRoque, *Helen Ferguson*, Mark Ellison
Director: Lawrence C. Windom
Scenario: Charles J. McGuirk

FILLING HIS OWN SHOES
(Essanay-Black Cat, June, 1917) 65 Minutes
Rod La Rocque, Hazel Daly, Bryant Washburn, Lydia Datzell, Virginia Valli, *Helen Ferguson*, Louise Long, Harry Dunkinson
Director: Harry Beaumont
Story: Henry C. Rowland

THE GOLDEN IDIOT
(Essanay, July, 1917) 65 Minutes
Bryant Washburn, Virginia Valli, Arthur Metcalf, Julian Barton, Robert Bolder, William Brotherhood, *Helen Ferguson*
Director: Arthur Berthelet
Adaptation: H. Tipton Steck
Story: Robert Rudd Whiting

THE GIFT OF GAB
(Essanay, November 17, 1917) 65 Mins.
Helen Ferguson, Jack Gardner
Director: W. S. Van Dyke
Adaptation: H. Tipton Steck

THE GAMBLERS
(Vitagraph, July 31, 1919) 6 Reels
Harry T. Morey, Agnes Ayres, Charles Kent, *Helen Ferguson*, Eric Mayne, George Majeroni, George Backus, Jane Jennings
Director: Paul Scardon
Scenario: Sam Taylor
Story: Charles Klein

THE LOST BATTALION
(MacManus, September 6, 1919) 8 Reels
Major-General Alexander "Go-To-Hell" Whittlesey, Private Kroteschinsky, Major McMurtry, Gaston Glass, *Helen Ferguson*, Jack McLean
Director: Henry King
Scenario: Charles Logue

SHOD WITH FIRE
(Fox, February 20, 1920) 5 Reels
William Russell, *Helen Ferguson*, Betty Schade
Director: Emmett Flynn
Scenario: J. Anthony Roach
Story: Harold Titus

BURNING DAYLIGHT
(Metro, May 20, 1920) 5 Reels
Bosworth Hobart, Gertrude Astor, *Helen Ferguson*, Edmund Breese, Lauford Davidson, Frank Hagney, William V. Mong, Mitchell Lewis, Alfred Allen, Edmund E. Carewe, Lew Morrison
Director: Edward Sloman
Scenario: A. S. LeVino
Story: Jack London

GOING SOME
(Goldwyn Pictures, June 19, 1920) 6 Reels
Maurice Flynn, *Helen Ferguson*, Lillian Langdon, Walter Hiers, Cullen Landis, Willard Lewis, Ethel Grey Terry
Director: Harry Beaumont
Scenario: Laurence Trimble
Story: Rex Beach
Suggested by the play by Rex Beach and Paul Armstrong
Producer: Presented by Samuel Goldwyn

THE ROMANCE PROMOTERS
(Vitagraph, October 6, 1920) 5 Reels
Helen Ferguson, Earle Williams, Otis Harlan
Director: Chester Bennett
Scenario: Harvey Thew
Story: L. H. Robbins

CHALLENGE OF THE LAW
(Fox, October 10, 1920) 5 Reels
William Russell, *Helen Ferguson*, Arthur Morrison James Farley, Fred Malatesta, Robert Klein, D. I. Mitsoris
Director: Scott Dunlap
Scenario: Dennison Clift, Scott Dunlap
Story: Lloyd Sheldon

JUST PALS
(Fox, November 14, 1920) 5 Reels
Buck Jones, *Helen Ferguson*, George Stone, Duke R. Lee, William Buckley, Edwin Booth Tilton, Eunice Murdock Moore, Slim Padgett, Bert Apling, Pedro Leon, Ida Tenbrook, John J. Cooke, Helen Field
Director: John Ford
Screenplay: Paul Schofield
Story: E. McDermott

THE RIGHT WAY
(Thomas Mott Osborne-Producers Security, February 28, 1921) 7 Reels
Edward Davis, Helen Lindroth, Joseph Marquis, Vivienne Osborne. Sidney D'Albrook, Annie Ecleston, *Helen Ferguson*, Elsie McLeod, Tammany Young, Thomas Brooks
Director: Sidney Olcott
Scenario: Basil Dickey

THE FREEZE-OUT
(Universal, April 9, 1921) 5 Reels
Harry Carey, *Helen Ferguson*, Joe Harris, Charles Le Moyne, J. Farrell McDonald, Lydia Yeammans Titus
Director: Jack (John) Ford
Scenario: Harry C. Fowler

STRAIGHT FROM THE SHOULDER
(Fox, June 19, 1921) 6 Reels
Buck Jones, *Helen Ferguson*, Norman Selby, Frances Hatton, Herschel Mayall, Yvette Mitchell, G. Raymond Nye, Glen Cavender, Dan Crimmins, Albert Knott, Lewis King
Director: Bernard Durning
Scenario: John Montague
Story: Roy Norton

TO A FINISH
(Fox, August 21, 1921) 5 Reels
Buck Jones, *Helen Ferguson*, G. Raymond Nye, Norman Selby, Herschel Mayall
Director: Bernard J. Durning
Scenario: Jack Strumwasser
Story: Jack Strumwasser

MAKING THE GRADE
(David Butler/Western Pictures, September 1, 1921) 5 Reels
David Butler, *Helen Ferguson*, William Walling, Lillian Lawrence, Jack Cosgrove, Alice Wilson, Otto Lederer, Jack Rollins
Director: Fred J. Butler
Adaptation: A. P. Younger
Story: Wallace Irwin, "Sophie Semenoff"

DESERT BLOSSOMS
(Fox, November 13, 1921) 5 Reels
William Russell, *Helen Ferguson*, Wilbur Higby, Willis Robards, Margaret Mann, Dulcie Cooper, Charles Spere, Gerald Pring
Director: Arthur Rosson
Scenario: Arthur J. Zellner
Story: Kate Corbaley

MISS LULU BETT
(Famous Players-Lasky/Paramount, November 13, 1921) 7 Reels
Lois Wilson, Milton Sills, Theodore Roberts, *Helen Ferguson*, Mabel Van Buren, May Giraci, Clarence Burton, Ethel Wales, Taylor Graves, Charles Ogle
Director: William C. de Mille
Adaptation: Clara Beranger
Story: Zona Gale, "Miss Lulu Bett"

THE CALL OF THE NORTH
(Famous Players-Lasky/Paramount, November 27, 1921) 5 Reels
Jack Holt, Madge Bellamy, Noah Beery, Francis McDonald, Edward Martindel, *Helen Ferguson*, Jack Herbert
Director: Joseph Henabery
Adaptation: Jack Cunningham
Story: Stewart Edward White, "Conjuror's House"

ACCORDING TO HOYLE
(David Butler/Western Pictures, May 6, 1922) 5 Reels
David Butler, *Helen Ferguson*, Phil Ford, Fred J. Butler, Harry Todd, Buddy Ross, Hal Wilson
Director: W. S. van Dyke
Scenario: John B. Clymer
Story: Clyde C. Westover, Lottie Horner

ROUGH SHOD
(Fox, June 4, 1922) 5 Reels
Charles Jones, *Helen Ferguson*, Ruth Renick, Maurice B. Flynn, Jack Rollins, Charles Le Moyne
Director: B. Reeves Eason
Scenario: Jack Strumwasser
Story: Charles Alden Seltzer, "West"

THE CRUSADER
(Fox, September 10, 1922) 5 Reels
William Russell, Gertrude Claire, *Helen Ferguson*, Fritzi Brunette, George Webb, Carl Grantvoort
Director: Howard M. Mitchell
Scenario: William K. Howard, Jack Strumwasser
Story: Alan Sullivan, "The Crusader"

HUNGRY HEARTS
(Goldwyn, November 26, 1922) 7 Reels
Bryant Washburn, *Helen Ferguson*, E. A. Warren, Rosa Rosanova, George Siegmann, Otto Lederer, Millie Schottland, Bert Sprotte, A. Budin, Edwin B. Tilton
Director: E. Mason Hopper
Scenario: Julien Josephson
Story: Anzie Yezierska, "Hungry Hearts"

THE FLAMING HOUR
(Universal, December 12, 1922) 5 Reels
Frank Mayo, *Helen Ferguson*, Melbourne MacDowell, Charles Clary, Albert MacQuarrie, Tom Kennedy
Director: Edward Sedgwick
Scenario: George Randolph Chester
Story: Lillian Chester

THE FAMOUS MRS. FAIR
(Louis B. Mayer/Metro, February 19, 1923) 8 Reels
Myrtle Stedman, Huntly Gordon, Marguerite De La Motte, Cullen Landis, Ward Crane, Carmel Myers, *Helen Ferguson*, Lydia Yeamans Titus, Dorcas Matthews, Frankie Bailey, Josephine Kirkwood, Muriel Beresford, Eva Mudge, Kathleen Chambers, Peggy Blackwood, Coast Artillery Corps Soldiers-Fort MacArthur
Director: Fred Niblo
Adaptation: Frances Marion
Scenario: Frances Marion
Story: James Grant Forbes, "The Famous Mrs. Fair"
Producer: Louis B. Mayer

BRASS
(Warner Bros., March 4, 1923) 9 Reels
Monte Blue, Marie Prevost, Harry Myers, Irene Rich, Frank Keenan, *Helen Ferguson*, Miss Du Pont, Cyril Chadwick, Margaret Seddon, Pat O'Malley, Edward Jobson, Vera Lewis, Harvey Clark, Gertrude Bennett, Ethel Grey Terry, Bruce Puerin
Director: Sidney A. Franklin
Scenario: Julien Josephson
Adaptation: Julien Josephson
Story: Charles Gilman Norris, "Brass: A Novel of Marriage"
Producer: Harry Rapf

WITHIN THE LAW
(Joseph M. Schenck/First National, April 29, 1923) 8 Reels
Norma Talmadge, Lew Cody, Jack Mulhall, Eileen Percy, Joseph Kilgour, Arthur S. Hull, *Helen Ferguson*, Lincoln Plummer, Thomas Ricketts, Ward Crane, Catherine Murphy, De Witt Jennings, Lionel Belmore, Eddie Boland
Director: Frank Lloyd
Adaptation: Frances Marion
Story: Bayard Veiller, "Within the Law"

DOUBLE DEALING
(Universal, May 21, 1923) 5 Reels
Hoot Gibson, *Helen Ferguson*, Betty Francisco, Eddie Gribbon, Gertrude Claire, Otto Hoffman, Frank Hayes, Jack Dillon
Director: Henry Lehrman
Scenario: George C. Hull, George W. Pyper

THE UNKNOWN PURPLE
(Carlos/Truart, October, 1923) 7 Reels
Henry B. Walthall, Alice Lake, Stuart Holmes, *Helen Ferguson*, Frankie Lee, Ethel Grey Terry, James Morrison, Johnny Arthur, Richard Wayne, Brinsley Shaw, Mike Donlin
Director: Roland West
Adaptation: Roland West, Paul Schofield
Story: Roland West, Carlyle Moore, "The Unknown Purple"

WHY GET MARRIED
(Laurel Associated Exhibitors, February 20, 1924)
Andree Lafayette, Jack Perrin, *Helen Ferguson*, Bernard Randall, Max Constant, William H. Turner, Edwin Booth Tilman, Orpha Alba
Director: Paul Cazeneuve
Story: William M. Conselmen

THE RIGHT OF THE STRONGEST
(Zenith/Selznick Dist., April, 1924) 7 Reels
E. K. Lincoln, *Helen Ferguson*., George Seigmann, Tom Santschi, Robert Milasch, F. B. Phillips, Tully Marshall, James Gibson, Coy Watson, Gertrude Norman, Milla Davenport, June Elvidge, Winter Hall, Niles Welch, Beth Kosick, Leonard Clapham
Director: Edgar Lewis
Adaptation: Doty Hobart
Story: Frances Nimmo Greene

RACING LUCK
(Grand-Asher/Associated Exhibitors, May 11, 1924) 6 Reels
Monty Banks, *Helen Ferguson*, Martha Franklin, D. J. Mitsoras, Lionel Belmore, Francis McDonald, William Blaisdell, Al Martin, Al Thompson, Ed Carlie, Scaduto
Director: Herman C. Raymaker
Story: Jean Havez, Lex Neal

THE VALLEY OF HATE
(Russell Productions, June 20, 1924) 5 Reels
Raymond McKee, *Helen Ferguson*, Earl Metcalf, Wilfred Lucas, Ralph Yearsley, Helen Lynch, Frank Whitson
Director: Russell Allen
Story: Harry Farnsworth MacPherson
Continuity: George Hively

NEVER SAY DIE
(Douglas MacLean/Associated Exhibitors, August 31, 1924) 6 Reels
Douglas MacLean, Lillian Rich, *Helen Ferguson*, Hallam Cooley, Lucian Littlefield, Tom O'Brien, Andre Lanoy, Wade Boteler, Eric Mayne, William Conklin, George Cooper
Director: George J. Crone
Scenario: Raymond Cannon
Story: William H. Post, William Collier, "Never Say Die"

CHALK MARKS
(Peninsula/PDC, September 14, 1924) 7 Reels
Marguerite Snow, Ramsey Wallace, June Elvidge, Lydia Knott, Rex Lease, *Helen Ferguson*, Priscilla Bonner, Harold Holland, Verna Mercereau, Fred Church, Lee Willard
Director: John G. Adolfi
Producer: Frank E. Woods

THE CLOUD RIDER
(Van Pelt-Wilson/FBO, February 15, 1925) 5 Reels
Al Wilson, Virginia Lee Corbin, Harry von Meter, *Helen Ferguson*, Frank Rice, Melbourne MacDowell, Brinsley Shaw, Frank Tomick, Boyd Monteith, Frank Clark
Director: Bruce Mitchell
Scenario: L. V. Jefferson
Story: Al Wilson

MY NEIGHBOR'S WIFE
(Elfelt/Davis Distributing Division, May 21, 1925) 6 Reels
E. K. Lincoln, *Helen Ferguson*, Edwards David, Herbert Rawlinson, William Russell, William Bailey, Chester Conklin, Tom Santschi, Mildred Harris, Douglas Gerard, Margaret Loomis, Ralph Faulkner, Philippe De Lacy
Director: Clarence Geldert
Story: James Oliver Curwood, "The Other Man's Wife"

THE SCARLET WEST
(Frank J. Carroll/First National, July 26, 1925) 9 Reels
Robert Frazer, Clara Bow, Robert Edeson, Johnny Walker, Walter McGrail, Gaston Glass, *Helen Ferguson*, Ruth Stonehouse, Martha Francis, Florence Crawford
Director: John G. Adolfi
Scenario: Anthony Paul Kelly
Story: A. B. Heath, "The Scarlet West"

NINE AND THREE-FIFTHS SECONDS
(A. G. Steen, August 5, 1925) 6 Reels
Charles Paddock, *Helen Ferguson*, George Fawcett, Jack Giddings, Peggy Schaffer, G. Raymond Nye, Otis Harlan
Director: Lloyd B. Carleton
Scenario: Roy Clements

THE ISLE OF HOPE
(Richard Talmadge/FBO, August 16, 1925) 6 Reels
Richard Talmadge, *Helen Ferguson*, James Marcus, Bert Strong, Howard Bell, Edward Gordon, George Reed
Director: Jack Nelson
Scenario: James Bell Smith
Story: James Bell Smith

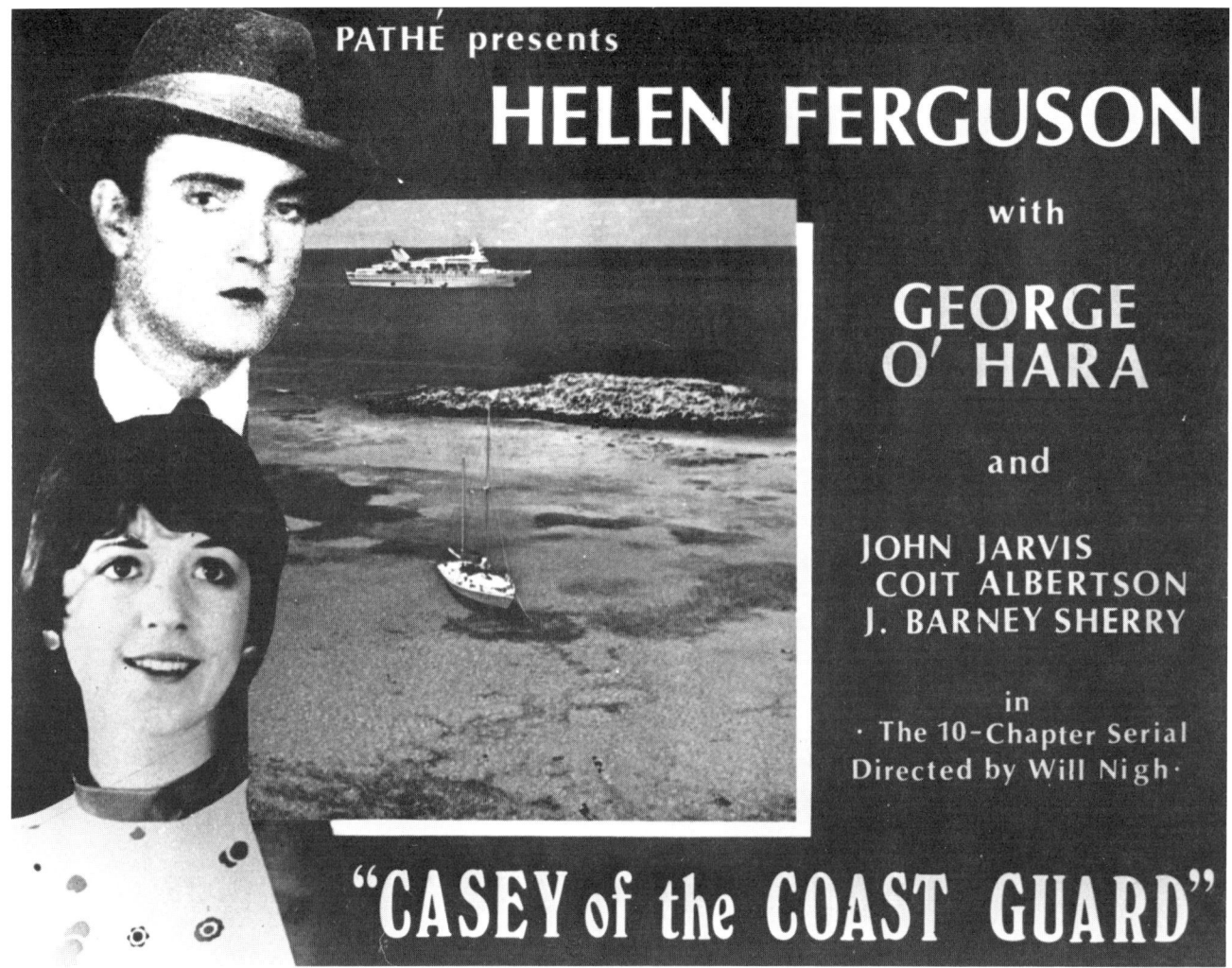

Casey of the Coast Guard (Pathé, 1926).

WILD WEST
(Pathé, September 27, 1925) 10 Chapters
Jack Mulhall, *Helen Ferguson,* Eddie Phillips, George Burton, Milla Davenport, Virginia Warwick, Gus Saville, Buck Lucas, Nowatta Slim Richardson, Fred Burns, Larry Steers, Dan Dix, Inez Gomez
Director: Robert F. Hill
Screenplay: J. F. Natteford
Chapter Titles: (1) The Land Rush (2) On the Show (3) The Outlaw Elephant (4) Ride 'em Cowboy! (5) The Rustler's Stampede (6) The Diamond Girl (7) The Champion Cowboy (8) Under the Buffalo (9) Stolen Evidence (10) The Law Decides
(Note: Chapter 1 is 3 reels in length; others are 2 reels)

CASEY OF THE COAST GUARD
(Pathé, February 14, 1926) 10 Chapters
Helen Ferguson, George O'Hara, John Jarvis, J. Barney Sherry, Coit Albertson, Robert Craig, James Mack, Joseph Marba, Roland Plander, William P. Burt
Director: Will Nigh
Chapter Titles: (1) The Smugglers' Ruse (2) Shots in the Dark (3) Watchful Waiting (4) Under Suspicion (5) The Gas Chamber (6) Shot from the Depths (7) Contraband Channels (8) Smuggled Aliens (9) Meshes of the Law (10) Caught in the Net

THE FIRE FIGHTERS
(Universal, January 17, 1927) 10 Chapters
Jack Daugherty, *Helen Ferguson*, Wilbur McGaugh, Lafe McKee, Albert Hart, Florence Allen, Robert Irwin, Milt Brown, George German
Director: Jacques Jaccard
Story: John A. Moroso, "Cap Fallon, Firefighter"
Chapter Titles: (1) For Life and Liberty (2) Paths of Peril (3) The Crimson Terror (4) Out of the Past (5) The False Alarm (6) Fighting Fate (7) Plunge of Peril (8) Face to Face (9) Wanted for Murder (10) The Reckoning

CHEATERS
(Tiffany, February 1, 1927) 6 Reels
Pat O'Malley, *Helen Ferguson*, George Hackathorne, Lawford Davidson, Claire McDowell, Helen Lynch, Hefnie Conklin, Alphonz Ethier, Max Davidson, Edward Cecil, William O'Brien
Director: Oscar Apfel
Continuity: W. C. Clifford
Story: Harry D. Kerr

TAXI! TAXI!
(Universal, April 24, 1927) 7 Reels
Edward Everett Horton, Marian Nixon, Burr McIntosh, Edward Martindel, *Helen Ferguson*, William V. Mong, Lucien Littlefield, Freeman Wood
Director: Melville W. Brown
Adaptation: Raymond Cannon
Continuity: Melville W. Brown
Story: George Weston, "Taxi! Taxi!"

JAWS OF STEEL
(Warner Bros., September 10, 1927) 6 Reels
Rin-Tin-Tin, Jason Robards, *Helen Ferguson*, Mary Louise Miller, Jack Curtis, Robert Perry, George Connors
Director: Ray Enright
Scenario: Charles R. Condon
Story: Gregory Rogers

IN OLD CALIFORNIA
(Audible Pictures, September 1, 1929) 6 Reels
Henry B. Walthall, *Helen Ferguson*, George Duryea, Ray Hallor, Orral Humphrey, Larry Steers, Richard Carlyle, Harry Allen, Louis Stern, Paul Ellis, Carlotta Monta, Gertrude Short, Gertrude Chorre, Ray Hazlor
Director: Burton King
Scenario: Arthur Hoerl
Story: Fred Hart

FINDER KEEPERS
(Vitaphone/Warner Bros., 1929)
Helen Ferguson, John Litel

SCARLET PAGES
(First National, September 28, 1930) 9 Reels
Elsie Ferguson, John Halliday, Marion Nixon, Grant Withers, Daisy Belmore, De Witt Jennings, William Davidson, Wilbur Mack, Charlotte Walker, *Helen Ferguson*, Donald MacKenzie, Jean Bary, Neely Edwards, Fred Kelsey
Director: Ray Enright
Screenplay: Walter Anthony
Story: Samuel Shipman, John B. Hymer, "Scarlet Pages"

30 • MARY FULLER

Demureness Characterized the Screen's First Serial Heroine

One can argue the finer points about labeling a group of short films built around specific characters as either a series or a serial. Suffice it to say that not all serials in the early years had cliffhanger endings (and Frank Buck's **Jungle Menace** of 1937 reverted in a small way to the nonclimactic ending). Many of the pre–World War I serials were complete stories with no relation to other episodes except through the characters and perhaps a broad plot. With this thought in mind, there is a good argument for giving credit for the first serial to Gene Gauntier, who starred in numerous short films designated as The Adventures of the Girl Spy (1908-1909).

Film historians, though, are prone to give credit to Mary Fuller as the serial genre's first exponent and to **What Happened to Mary?** (1912) as either the first serial or, if not that, at least the forerunner of the serial per se. Cliffhanger endings were two or three years away, but **What Happened to Mary?** had many of the other characteristics later identified with serials, chief of which was a multitude of thrills in each episode.

What Happened to Mary? (a prophetic title indeed, considering the mystery that later grew up around the actress) came about through an arrangement between Edison Films and McClure's Ladies World magazine, whereby Edison would produce a series of one-reel films to be released simultaneously with the publication of the same stories in the magazine. It was hoped that this device would increase both the magazine's circulation and theatre attendance. The idea worked beautifully. Ladies World jumped ahead in the circulation war with its competitors and Edison realized a nice profit on the films.

The interest shown by theatre patrons, which led them to go again and again to see what happened to Mary, was largely due to Mary's own ability to penetrate, comprehend, and reproduce a character

Mary Fuller.

who reached out and gripped common sympathy. There was very little opportunity for emotional display in the continued story on the screen, but Mary went ahead and made the most of her part. Thus she contributed materially to nation-wide curiosity as to what would next befall the story's heroine.

The success of the venture gave the necessary impetus to later serial endeavor, and directly motivated William Selig to produce **The Adventures of Kathlyn** (1913) in conjunction with the Chicago Tribune. Then E. A. McManus of the Hearst newspapers and Louis Gasnier of

Who Will Marry Mary? (Edison, 1913) – Mary Fuller.

Pathé followed with the fabulously successful **The Perils of Pauline** (1914). Ladies World gave full credit to **What Happened to Mary?** for boosting its circulation to well over one million copies monthly, and when the serial came to an end plans were made for a sequel, which came out the following year under the title **Who Will Marry Mary?** (1913). Another joint effort of the magazine and Edison Films, it involved a contest run in conjunction with the film to enhance the interest of readers and viewers. Whereas **What Happened to Mary?** was composed of twelve one-reel segments, **Who Will Marry Mary?** contained only six.

Mary Fuller's entrance into motion pictures had not been the result of planning and preparation. She was on her way south to spend an old-fashioned Christmas with her parents when she was stranded in New York, because the theatrical troupe of which she was a member broke up. She thought then of moving pictures and made a fearful tryout at the Vitagraph studio. She was put to work in one-reelers, the first of record being **Leah the Forsaken** (1908) with Maurice Costello. After perhaps a dozen films for Vitagraph, Mary transferred her talents to Edison and made a long series of split- and one-reelers, often with Marc McDermott as leading man, that placed her high in popularity. She usually got good publicity. For example, exhibitors were exhorted to bill **Elektra** (1910) like a circus: "It will draw bigger crowds than any film you have ever had." **Aida** (1911), adapted from the opera by Verdi, proved one of her more successful films, but almost as popular were **The Three Musketeers** (1911), **Mary Stuart** (1913), and **Comedy and Tragedy** (1914). Occasional forays into action films resulted in such titles as **The Luck of Roarin Camp** (1910), **The Daisy Cowboy** (1911), **The Girl and the Outlaw** (1913), **A Daughter of the Wilderness** (1913), and **The Viking Queen** (1914).

In 1914 Mary made her third serial, **The Active Life of Dolly of the Dailies.** That same year she was rated tops in popularity in a Motion Picture Story magazine contest, along with J. Warren Kerrigan, Earle Williams, Alice Joyce, and Carlyle Blackwell.

Mary was known as temperamental, intense, emotional, and even poetic. She was a shy, retiring person, but respected by those who worked with her. Doubles were practically unheard of when she made her films, and it was she who did the things audiences saw on the screen, such as sliding down a rope from a seventh-story window and falling the last ten feet as the rope snapped. What they didn't see, though, were her badly blistered hands.

Universal beckoned in 1914, and Mary cast her lot with the young company, graduating into three- and five-reel features before she retired in 1916, desiring, as she put it, "to rest, forget, and study." She did, however, return for a single Lasky production, **The Long Trail** (1917), in which Lou Tellegen was her leading man. After that she just dropped out of sight. Her whereabouts became a mystery that many journalists and fans sought to unravel, without success. But in 1924 an enterprising Photoplay magazine writer, Frederick James Smith, spent three months seaching for her. He finally found Mary living in seclusion with her mother in Washington, D.C. Reluctantly, she gave him an interview. In response to the question, "Why did you hide yourself away so carefully?," she is quoted as saying:

I wanted to rest, forget, study. I was very fortunate in the old days. Salaries were not like those of today, but I invested all my money--and invested it carefully. I am comfortably fixed--financially, at least--for the rest of my life. I never need worry on that score.

I have made several trips around the world. I have studied. Particularly, I have been interested in art and music. I think that I have broadened myself, at least in a measure. That's one reason why I feel that I would like to try pictures again. When I left the studios for the last time, I was tired, terribly tired. Picture making then was a hard, driving thing. It wore you down and sapped your vitality. I felt I must rest--and that I would never get enough rest. Now that I have built up a reserve of vitality, the old lure of the studios has returned to me. I may be disillusioned but I want to try.

No record can be found of any further film work for Mary Fuller. Evidently she reconsidered and decided not to try a comeback.

At the time of the Smith interview (1924) she was still unmarried, explaining that she hadn't yet found the right man. She dropped from sight once more, as quickly as she had surfaced. "What happened to Mary?" has been asked innumerable times by film buffs, but no answers have been forthcoming. Did anyone ever marry Mary? Rumor had it that she was living in Los Angeles in the 1940s, but no one offered any proof. She became more elusive than Howard Hughes. And so the question "What happened to Mary?" remains unanswered.

MARY FULLER Filmography

LEAH THE FORSAKEN
(Vitagraph, October, 1908) 1 Reel
Mary Fuller, Maurice Costello
Director: Van Dyke Brooke
Story: Ritter Von Mosenthal

THE STAGE-STRUCK DAUGHTER
(Vitagraph, October, 1908) 1 Reel
Mary Fuller
Director: Van Dyke Brooke

THE FLOWER GIRL OF PARIS
(Vitagraph, December, 1908) 1 Reel
Mary Fuller
Director: Van Dyke Brooke

A SISTER'S LOVE
(Vitagraph, January, 1909) 1 Reel
Mary Fuller
Director: Van Dyke Brooke

JESSIE, THE STOLEN CHILD
(Vitagraph, February, 1909) 1 Reel
Mary Fuller
Director: Van Dyke Brooke

KING LEAR
(Vitagraph, March, 1909) 1 Reel
Maurice Costello, Julia Arthur, Edith Storey, *Mary Fuller*
Director: William V. Ranous
Scenario: Eugene Mullin
Story: William Shakespeare
Supervisor: J. Stuart Blackton

THE FOUNDLING
(Vitagraph, June, 1909) 1 Reel
Mary Fuller
Director: Van Dyke Brooke

LOCHINVAR
(Edison, July, 1909) 790 Ft.
Marc McDermott, *Mary Fuller*, Harold Shaw
Director: Searle Dawley
Scenario: Searle Dawley
Story: Sir Walter Scott

HANSEL AND GRETEL
(Edison, October, 1909) 630 Ft.
Mary Fuller, Cecil Spooner
Director: J. Searle Dawley
Story: The Brothers Grim
Supervisor: Edwin S. Porter

BLUEBEARD
(Edison, November, 1909) 400 Ft.
Charles Ogle, *Mary Fuller*
Director: J. Searle Dawley
Scenario: J. Searle Dawley
Story: Charles Perroult

A ROSE OF THE TENDERLOIN
(Edison, November, 1909) 1 Reel
Mary Fuller, Harold Shaw, Robert Brower
Director: J. Searle Dawley
Scenario: Bannister Merwin
Story: Edward W. Townsend

THE HOUSE OF CARDS
(Edison, December, 1909) 1 Reel
Mary Fuller, Marc McDermott
Director: Edwin S. Porter
Scenario: Edwin S. Porter

THE ENGINEER'S ROMANCE
(Edison, January, 1910) 670 Ft.
Mary Fuller, Marc McDermott
Director: Edwin S. Porter
Scenario: Bannister Merwin

THE LUCK OF ROARING CAMP
(Edison, January, 1910) 490 Ft.
J. Barney Sherry, *Mary Fuller*
Director: Edwin S. Porter
Scenario: Edwin S. Porter
Story: Bret Harte

FRANKENSTEIN
(Edison, March, 1910) 1 Reel
Charles Ogle, Augustus Phillips, *Mary Fuller*
Director: J. Searle Dawley
Scenario: J. Searle Dawley
Story: Mary W. Shelley

MICHAEL STROGOFF
(Edison, April, 1910) 1 Reel
Mary Fuller, Charles Ogle, Marc McDermott, Harold Shaw
Director: J. Searle Dawley
Scenario: J. Searle Dawley
Story: Jules Verne

FOR HER SISTER'S SAKE
(Edison, April, 1910) 520 Ft.
Florence Turner, *Mary Fuller*, Charles Ogle
Director: Edwin S. Porter
Scenario: Edwin S. Porter

SISTERS
(Edison, May, 1910) 1 Reel
Mary Fuller, Florence Turner
Director: Bannister Merwin
Scenario: Bannister Merwin

THE PRINCESS AND THE PEASANT
(Edison, May, 1910) 1 Reel
Mary Fuller, Marc McDermott
Director: J. Searle Dawley
Scenario: Bannister Merwin

THE LADY AND THE BURGLAR
(Edison, August, 1910) 1 Reel
Mary Fuller, Marc McDermott
Director: Bannister Merwin
Scenario: Bannister Merwin

FROM TYRANNY TO LIBERTY
(Edison, August, 1910) 1 Reel
Marc McDermott, George A. Lessey, *Mary Fuller*
Director: J. Searle Dawley
Scenario: J. Searle Dawley
Story: Francis Scott Key

ONONKO'S VOW
(Edison, October, 1910) 1 Reel
Mary Fuller
Director: Edwin S. Porter
Scenario: Edwin S. Porter
Story: Bret Harte

THE HOUSE OF THE SEVEN GABLES
(Edison, October, 1910) 1 Reel
Mary Fuller
Director: J. Searle Dawley
Scenario: J. Searle Dawley
Story: Nathaniel Hawthorne

ARMS AND THE WOMAN
(Edison, December, 1910) 1 Reel
Mary Fuller, Charles Ogle
Director: Bannister Merwin
Scenario: Bannister Merwin

A STAGE ROMANCE
(Edison, February, 1911)
Mary Fuller
Director: Bannister Merwin
Scenario: Bannister Merwin

AIDA
(Edison, May, 1911)
Mary Fuller, Marc MacDermott, Miriam Nesbitt
Directors: Oscar Apfel, J. Searle Dawley
Adaptation: From the opera by Giuseppe Verdi

IN THE DAYS OF CHIVALRY
(Edison, June, 1911) 1 Reel
Mary Fuller, Marc McDermott, Mabel Trunnelle
Director: J. Searle Dawley

THE STAR SPANGLED BANNER
(Edison, June, 1911) 1 Reel
Mary Fuller, Mabel Trunnelle, Gertrude McCoy, Ben Wilson, Ralph Ince, Charles Ogle, Charles M. Seay, William H. West
Director: J. Searle Dawley

TRADING WITH MOTHER
(Edison, July, 1911) 500 Ft.
Mary Fuller, Yale Boss, Marc McDermott

THE SWITCHMAN'S TOWER
(Edison, July, 1911) 1 Reel
Herbert Prior, *Mary Fuller*, Edna May Weick, James Gordon

TWO OFFICERS
(Edison, August, 1911)
Mary Fuller, Marc McDermott, Sydney Booth

THE MODERN BIANAS
(Edison, August, 1911) 1 Reel
Mary Fuller, Harold M. Shaw, Charles Ogle, Louise Sydmeth

THE PROFESSOR AND THE NEW HAT
(Edison, August, 1911) 1/2 Reel
William West, *Mary Fuller*, Edwin Clarke
Director: Bannister Merwin
Scenario: Bannister Merwin

THE SURGEON'S TEMPTATION
(Edison, August, 1911) 1 Reel
Charles Ogle, Sydney Booth, *Mary Fuller*

THE SILENT TONGUE
(Edison, August, 1911)
Mary Fuller, Harry Eytinge, Charles White
Director: Bannister Merwin
Scenario: Bannister Merwin

THREE MUSKETEERS
(Edison, August, 1911) 2 Reels
Sydney Booth, Herbert Delmar, Jack Chagnon, Harold Shaw, William Bechtel, Mirian Nesbitt, *Mary Fuller*, Robert Brower, Herbert Barrington, Marc McDermott, Carey Lee
Director: J. Searle Dawley
Story: Alexandre Dumas

FOUL PLAY
(Edison, September, 1911) 3 Reels
Robert Brower, Harold M. Shaw, Marc McDermott, William H. West, Charles Ogle, *Mary Fuller*, Frank Gheen
Story: Charles Reade

AT THE THRESHOLD OF LIFE
(Edison, October, 1911) 1 Reel
Mary Fuller, Marc McDermott, Edward O'Connor, Mrs. William Bechtel, Kathleen Coughlin, Leonie Flugrath, Yale Boss, Harriette Mendel

A CONSPIRACY AGAINST THE KING
(Edison, October, 1911) 1 Reel
Walter Edwin, Robert Brower, *Mary Fuller*, Harold M. Shaw
Director: J. Searle Dawley
Story: H. B. Marriott Watson, "The Cockerel"

THE REFORM CANDIDATE
(Edison, October, 1911) 1 Reel
Robert Brower, Miriam Nesbitt, Charles Ogle, Harold M. Shaw, Charles M. Seay, *Mary Fuller*

A MODERN CINDERELLA
(Edison, November, 1911) 1 Reel
Mary Fuller, Darwin Karr, Mabel Trunnelle, Sidney Booth, Harold M. Shaw

THE GHOSTS'S WARNING
(Edison, November, 1911) 1 Reel
Marc McDermott, *Mary Fuller*, William Wadsworth, Miriam Nesbitt, Ethel Browning, Darwin Karr

THE AWAKENING OF JOHN BOND
(Edison, November, 1911) 1 Reel
Harold M. Shaw, Bigelow Cooper, Miriam Nesbitt, *Mary Fuller*, Philip Tannura, Kathleen Coughlin, Joseph M. Levering
Director: Charles Brabin
Scenario: Bannister Merwin

THE DAISY COWBOY
(Edison, November, 1911) 1 Reel
Mary Fuller, Wadsworth Harris, Mrs. Wallace Erskin, John R. Cumpson, William Wadsworth, Edward O'Connor, Edward Boulden

AN INTERNATIONAL HEART BREAKER
(Edison, December, 1911) 1 Reel
William H. West, *Mary Fuller*, Yale Brenner, James Gordon, Laura Sawyer
Director: J. Searle Dawley

THIRTY DAYS AT HARD LABOR
(Edison, January, 1912) 1 Reel
Robert Brower, *Mary Fuller*, Harold M. Shaw, William Wadsworth
Story: O. Henry, "Halberdier of the Little Rheischloss"

A QUESTION OF SECONDS
(Edison, January, 1912) 665 Ft.
Charles Ogle, *Mary Fuller*, Harold M. Shaw, Richard Neil

THE BACHELOR'S WATERLOO
(Edison, January, 1912) 1 Reel
Harold M. Shaw, *Mary Fuller*, Edward Boulder

THE STOLEN NICKEL
(Edison, January, 1912) 1 Reel
Yale Boss, Robert Conness, *Mary Fuller*, Phillip Tannura, Edna May Weick
Director: Bannister Merwin
Scenario: Bannister Merwin

THE JEWELS
(Edison, January, 1912) 1 Reel
Harold M. Shaw, *Mary Fuller*, Miriam Nesbitt

THE DUMB WOOING
(Edison, April, 1912) 1 Reel
Mary Fuller, Marc McDermott, Barry O'Moore, Yale Brenner, Charles Ogle
Director: Will Louis
Scenario: Bannister Merwin

THE LITTLE WOOLEN SHOE
(Edison, April, 1912) 1 Reel
Mary Fuller, Marc McDermott
Scenario: Bannister Merwin

AN UNUSUAL SACRIFICE
(Edison, April, 1912) 1 Reel
Mary Fuller, Augustus Phillips, Barry O'Moore

THE CONVICT'S PAROLE
(Edison, May, 1912) 1 Reel
Mary Fuller, Marc McDermott
Director: Edwin S. Porter
Scenario: Bannister Merwin
Story: Melvin G. Winstock

THE LITTLE BRIDE OF HEAVEN
(Edison, June, 1912) 1 Reel
Mary Fuller, Edna Hammond, Florence Klotz
Story: Mary Imloy Taylor

MASTER AND PUPIL
(Edison, June, 1912) 1 Reel
Harry Furniss, *Mary Fuller*, William Wadsworth
Director: J. Searle Dawley
Scenario: Augustus Phillips

PARTNERS FOR LIFE
(Edison, June, 1912) 1 Reel
Mary Fuller, Augustus Phillips, Jeanie MacPherson
Director: J. Searle Dawley
Story: Bannister Merwin

WHAT HAPPENED TO MARY?
(Edison, July 16, 1912) 12 Chapters
Mary Fuller, Bliss Milford, Marc McDermott, Charles Ogle, Barry O'Moore, Bigelow Cooper, William Wadsworth, Miriam Nesbitt, Harold Shaw, Henry Eytinge, Walter Edwin, Yale Banner, James Smith, Carey Lee, Arthur Housman, Ben Wilson, May Abbey, Edna Flugrath
Directors: Walter Edwin, J. Searle Dawley
Scenario: Bannister Merwin, James Oppenheim
Chapters: (1) The Escape from Bondage (2) Alone in New York (3) Mary in Stageland (4) The Affair at Raynor's (5) A Letter to the Princess (6) A Clue to Her Parentage (7) False to Their Trust (8) A Will and a Way (9) A Way to the Underworld (10) The High Tide of Misfortune (11) A Race to New York (12) Fortune Smiles
(Each chapter only 1 reel in length)

THE HARBINGER OF PEACE
(Edison, August, 1912) 1 Reel
Robert Brower, *Mary Fuller*, William West, George Lessey, Mrs. Wallace Erskine, James Gordon, Gertrude Norman
Scenario: Robert Brower

MR. PICKWICK'S PREDICAMENT
(Edison, August, 1912) 1 Reel
Charles Ogle, *Mary Fuller*, Marc McDermott
Director: J. Searle Dawley
Story: Charles Dickens, "The Pickwick Papers"

MARTIN CHUZZLEWIT
(Edison, August, 1912) 3 Reels
Marc McDermott, William West, Harold Shaw, Marion Brooks, Guy Hedlund, Miriam Nesbitt, *Mary Fuller* (?), Charles Ogle (?) (the participation of Fuller and Ogle in this film has not been definitely established)
Director: Oscar Apfel, J. Searle Dawley
Story: Charles Dickens

THE GOVERNOR
(Edison, September, 1912) 1 Reel
Mary Fuller, Charles Ogle, Willis Secord, Walter Edwin, Augustus Phillips, George Lessey
Scenario: Bannister Merwin

SALLY ANN'S STRATEGY
(Edison, November, 1912) 675 Ft.
Alice Washburn, *Mary Fuller*, Charles Ogle, William Bechtel, Bigelow Cooper
Director: Walter Edwin
Scenario: Bannister Merwin
Story: Louis Alvord

HIS MOTHER'S HOPE
(Edison, November, 1912) 1 Reel
George Lessey, Barry O'Moore, Bessie Learn, Gertrude McCoy, Louise Sydmeth, *Mary Fuller*, William Porter

FOG
(Edison, December, 1912)
Mary Fuller, Marc MacDermott, Miriam Nesbitt
Director: Bannister Merwin
Scenario: Bannister Merwin

HOW A HORSESHOE UPSET A HAPPY FAMILY
(Edison, December, 1912) 475 Ft.
Edward O'Connor, Alice Washburn, Mrs. William Bechtel, *Mary Fuller*, Yale Boss, Arthur Housman
Story: Louise Sydmeth

FOR HER
(Edison, December, 1912) 1 Reel
Mary Fuller, Charles Ogle, William H. West, Harry Beaumont, Robert Brower, Bigelow Cooper
Director: Bannister Merwin
Scenario: Bannister Merwin

IT IS NEVER TOO LATE TO MEND
(Edison, January, 1913) 2 Reels
Mary Fuller, Harry Beaumont
Director: Charles M. Seay
Scenario: Charles M. Seay
Story: Charles Reade

LEONIE
(Edison, January, 1913) 1 Reel
Mary Fuller, Augustus Phillips, Miriam Nesbitt, Mrs. Wallace Erskine, Mrs. William Bechtel, Harry Beaumont, George Lessey, Walter Edwin
Director: Bannister Merwin
Scenario: Bannister Merwin

THE AMBASSADOR'S DAUGHTER
(Edison, January, 1913) 1 Reel
Charles Ogle, *Mary Fuller*, Marc McDermott, Robert Brower, Miriam Nesbitt, George Lessey
Director: Bannister Merwin
Scenario: Bannister Merwin

THE PRINCESS AND THE MAN
(Edison, January, 1913) 1 Reel
Miriam Nesbitt, Augustus Phillips, Marc McDermott, Charles Ogle, *Mary Fuller*, Richard Ridgeley, Bigelow Cooper, Robert Brower
Director: Charles J. Brabin
Scenario: Bannister Merwin

THE MINISTER'S TEMPTATION
(Edison, February, 1913) 1 Reel
Augustus Phillips, *Mary Fuller*, Robert Brower
Director: Charles Brabin
Story: Sydney Booth

KATHLEEN MAVOURNEEN
(Edison, March, 1913) 1 Reel
Mary Fuller, Marc McDermott, Augustus Phillips, William H. West, Gertrude McCoy, H. Linson, M. Gripp
Director: Charles Brabin
Scenario: Charles Brabin
Story: Dion Boucicault

THE DEAN'S DAUGHTERS
(Edison, March, 1913) 1 Reel
Mary Fuller, Elsie McLeod, Robert Brower, Marc McDermott
Director: Walter Edwin
Scenario: Bannister Merwin

WITH THE EYES OF THE BLIND
(Edison, March, 1913) 1 Reel
Mary Fuller, Charles Ogle, Marc McDermott, Robert Brower, William West, Mrs. Erskine
Director: Walter Edwin
Scenario: Bannister Merwin

THE ELDER BROTHER
(Edison, March, 1913) 1 Reel
William H. West, *Mary Fuller*, Harry Beaumont, Richard Tucker
Director: Bannister Merwin
Scenario: Anne and Bannister Merwin

WHEN THE RIGHT MAN COMES ALONG
(Edison, April, 1913) 1 Reel
Mary Fuller, Arthur Housman, Richard Ridgeley, Bliss Milford
Director: Walter Edwin
Scenario: Mary Fuller

THE PROPHECY
(Edison, April 24, 1913) 1 Reel
Charles Ogle, *Mary Fuller*, Marion Weeks, Richard Ridgeley, Marc McDermott, Mary Clowes, Cora Williams
Director: Walter Edwin
Scenario: Mary Fuller

WHEN GREEK MEETS GREEK
(Edison, May, 1913) 1 Reel
Mary Fuller, Charles Ogle, Barry O'Moore
Director: Walter Edwin
Scenario: Mary Fuller

AN ALMOND-EYED MAID
(Edison, May, 1913) 1 Reel
Mary Fuller, Richard Tucker, Gertrude McCoy
Director: Walter Edwin
Story: Dora M. Lynn

THE TRANSLATION OF A SAVAGE
(Edison, May, 1913) 1 Reel
Mary Fuller, Richard Tucker, Gertrude McCoy, Betty Emerson, Richard Ridgeley, Barry O'Moore, Bigelow Cooper, Mrs. Wallace Erskins, Robert Brower
Director: Walter Edwin
Scenario: Charles H. France
Story: Sir Gilbert Parker

MERCY MERRICK
(Edison, June, 1913) 1 Reel
Mary Fuller, Robert Brower, Bigelow Cooper, Gertrude McCoy, Mrs. Wallace Erskine, Richard Tucker
Director: Walter Edwin
Scenario: Charles Brabin

MARY STUART
(Edison, June, 1913) 3 Reels
Mary Fuller, Marc MacDermott, Bigelow Cooper, Miriam Nesbitt, Richard Neill, Elizabeth Miller, Wallace Scott, Charles Ogle, Charles Sutton, Robert Brower, Edward Boulden, Julian Reed, William West
Director: J. Searle Dawley
Scenario: J. Searle Dawley
Story: Friedrich Schiller

ALL ON ACCOUNT OF A PORTRAIT
(Edison, June, 1913) 1 Reel
Mary Fuller, Benjamin F. Wilson, Yale Boss
Director: C. J. Williams
Scenario: Mark Swan

WHO WILL MARRY MARY?
(Edison, July 26, 1913) 6 Chaps.
Mary Fuller, Harry Beaumont, Miriam Nesbitt, Marc McDermott, Harold Shaw, William Wadsworth, May Abbey, Richard Tucker, Ben Wilson
Director: Walter Edwin
Scenario: Ida Damon
Chapters: (1) A Proposal from the Duke (2) A Proposal from the Spanish Don (3) A Proposal from the Sculptor (4) A Proposal from Nobody (5) A Proposal Deferred (6) A Proposal from Mary
(Each chapter only 1 reel in length)

THE ROMANCE OF ROWENA
(Edison, July, 1913) 1 Reel
Mary Fuller, Frank Lyon, Mrs. Wallace Erskine, Edward O'Connor
Director: C. Jay Williams
Scenario: Bannister Merwin

THE ROBBERS
(Edison, July, 1913) 1 Reel
Mary Fuller, Barry O'Moore, Robert Brower, Ben Wilson, Charles Ogle, Edward Mack, Harry Kendall
Directors: Walter Edwin, J. Searle Dawley
Story: Friedrich Schiller

JOYCE OF THE NORTH WOODS
(Edison, August, 1913) 2 Reels
Mary Fuller, Augustus Phillips
Director: Ashley Miller
Story: Harriet T. Comstock

A LIGHT ON TROUBLED WATERS
(Edison, September, 1913) 1 Reel
Mary Fuller, Augustus Phillips
Director: Walter Edwin
Story: Monte M. Katterjohn

THE GIRL AND THE OUTLAW
(Edison, October, 1913) 1 Reel
Mary Fuller, Augustus Phillips
Story: Frank McGlynn

A WOODLAND PARADISE
(Edison, October, 1913) 1 Reel
Mary Fuller, Harry Beaumont
Director: Walter Edwin
Scenario: Mary Fuller

A DAUGHTER OF THE WILDERNESS
(Edison, October, 1913) 1 Reel
Augustus Phillips, *Mary Fuller*, Richard Neill, Frank McGlynn

ELISE, THE FORESTER'S DAUGHTER
(Edison, October, 1913) 1 Reel
Mary Fuller, Augustus Phillips, Harry Beaumont
Story: Bliss Milford

A FACE FROM THE PAST
(Edison, October, 1913) 2 Reels
Mary Fuller, Augustus Phillips, Frank McGlynn
Director: Walter Edwin
Story: Frank Blighton

A TUDOR PRINCESS
(Edison, December, 1913) 2 Reels
Mary Fuller, Ben Wilson, Robert Brower, Charles Ogle
Director: J. Searle Dawley
Scenario: Monte M. Katterjohn

A LONELY ROAD
(Edison, December, 1913) 1 Reel
Mary Fuller, Gertrude McCoy, Charles Ogle
Story: Y. Spinner

THE ACTIVE LIFE OF DOLLY OF THE DAILIES
(Edison, January 31, 1914) 12 Chaps.
Mary Fuller, Yale Boss, Charles Ogle, Harry Beaumont, Gladys Hulette, William H. West, Edwin Clark, Richard Neil, Miriam Nesbitt
Director: Walter Edwin
Chapters: (1) The Perfect Truth (2) The Ghost of Mother Eve (3) An Affair of Dress (4) Putting One Over (5) The Chinese Fan (6) On the Heights (7) The End of the Umbrella (8) A Tight Squeeze (9) A Terror of the Night (10) Dolly Plays Detective (11) Dolly at the Helm (12) The Last Assignment

THE NECKLACE OF RAMESES
(Edison, January, 1914) 3 Reels
Marc MacDermott, Miriam Nesbitt, Rex Hitchcock, *Mary Fuller*
Director: Charles Brabin
Story: Charles Vernon

THE PERFECT TRUTH
(Edison, January, 1914) 1 Reel
Mary Fuller, William H. West, Edwin Clark
Director: Walter Edwin
Story: Acton Davies

THE GHOST OF MOTHER EVE
(Edison, February, 1914) 1 Reel
Mary Fuller
Director: Walter Edwin
Story: Acton Davies

COMEDY AND TRAGEDY
(Edison, February, 1914) 2 Reels
Mary Fuller, Marc MacDermott, Augustus Phillips
Director: Walter Edwin
Scenario: Walter Edwin

AN AFFAIR OF DRESS
(Edison, March, 1914) 1 Reel
Mary Fuller
Director: Walter Edwin

PUTTING ONE OVER
(Edison, March, 1914) 1 Reel
Mary Fuller
Director: Walter Edwin

A PRINCESS OF THE DESERT
(Edison, April, 1914) 1 Reel
Marc McDermott, *Mary Fuller*, Harry Beaumont
Director: Walter Edwin
Scenario: Mary Fuller

ON THE HEIGHTS
(Edison, April, 1914) 1 Reel
Mary Fuller, Gladys Hulette
Director: Walter Edwin

WHEN EAST MET WEST IN BOSTON
(Edison, April, 1914) 1 Reel
Marc MacDermott, *Mary Fuller*, Herbert Prior
Director: Walter Edwin
Story: Y. Spinner

FREDERICK THE GREAT
(Ediosn, April, 1914) 2 Reels
Charles Sutton, Barry O'Moore, Robert Brower, Charles Grady, Richard Neill, John Sturgeon, *Mary Fuller*, Bliss Milford, William H. West
Director: Walter Edwin
Scenario: Walter Edwin

THE END OF THE UMBRELLA
(Edison, April, 1914) 1 Reel
Mary Fuller
Director: Walter Edwin

A TIGHT SQUEEZE
(Edison, May, 1914) 1 Reel
Mary Fuller, Dan Mason
Director: Walter Edwin
Story: Acton Davies

LOST--A PAIR OF SHOES
(Edison, May, 1914) 1 Reel
Harry Beaumont, *Mary Fuller*
Director: Preston Kendall
Scenario: Harry Beaumont

A TERROR OF THE NIGHT
(Edison, June, 1914) 1 Reel
Mary Fuller
Director: Walter Edwin
Story: Acton Davies

DOLLY PLAYS DETECTIVE
(Edison, June, 1914) 1 Reel
Mary Fuller, Yale Boss, Duncan McRae
Director: Walter Edwin

DOLLY AT THE HELM
(Ediosn, July, 1914) 1 Reel
Mary Fuller, Charles Ogle, Carlton King, Yale Boss
Director: Walter Edwin

THE LAST ASSIGNMENT
(Edison, July, 1914) 1 Reel
Mary Fuller
Director: Walter Edwin

THE VIKING QUEEN
(Edison, August, 1914) 2 Reels
Mary Fuller, Charles Ogle

HIS BIG CHANCE
(Universal-Victor, October, 1914) 1 Reel
Charles Ogle, *Mary Fuller*

A GIRL OF THE PEOPLE
(Universal-Victor, November, 1914) 2 Reels
Mary Fuller

THE HEART OF THE NIGHT WIND
(Universal-Victor, November, 1914) 2 Reels
Mary Fuller, Charles Ogle, Ed Mortimer
Director: Walter Edwin
Story: Virgil E. Roe

A LONELY SALVATION
(Universal-Victor, November, 1914) 2 Reels
Mary Fuller, Charles Ogle

HEART OF THE HILLS
(Universal-Victor, December, 1914) 3 Reels
Mary Fuller, Charles Ogle
Director: Walter Edwin
Story: Hal Reid

THE VIRTUOSO
(Universal-Victor, December, 1914)
Mary Fuller
Scenario: Mary Fuller

MY LADY HIGH AND MIGHTY
(Universal-Victor, January, 1915) 2 Reels
Mary Fuller, Charles Ogle, Richard Benton
Story: Elaine Sterne

HIS GUARDIAN ANGEL
(Universal-Victor, January, 1915) 2 Reels
Mary Fuller, Charles Ogle

THE BRIBE
(Universal-Victor, January, 1915)
Charles Ogle, *Mary Fuller*

EVERYGIRL
(Universal-Victor, February, 1915)
Mary Fuller, Charles Ogle

THE LAUGH THAT DIED
(Universal-Victor, March, 1915)
Mary Fuller, Matt Moore, Charles Ogle
Director: Lorimer Johnston
Story: Raymond L. Schrock

THE MASTER MUMMER
(Edison, March, 1915) 3 Reels
Mary Fuller
Director: Walter Edwin
Scenario: Walter Edwin
Story: B. Phillips Oppenheim

MARY'S DUKE
(Universal-Victor, March, 1915) 3 Reels
Mary Fuller, Matt Moore, Mrs. Charles G. Craig, Etienne Girardot
Director: Lucius Henderson
Story: Elaine Sterne

THE RUSTLE OF A SKIRT
(Universal-Victor, March 3, 1915)
Mary Fuller, Matt Moore, Richard Benton
Story: Raymond L. Schrock

THE HONOR OF THE ORMSBYS
(Universal-victor, April, 1915) 3 Reels
Charles Ogle, *Mary Fuller*, Matt Moore
Director: M. Henderson
Story: William Addison Lathrop

A WITCH OF SALEM TOWN
(Universal-Victor, May 17, 1915) 2 Reels
Mary Fuller, Curtis Benton
Director: L. J. Henderson
Story: Margaret Hovey

THE GIRL WHO HAD A SOUL
(Universal-Victor, May, 1915) 3 Reels
Mary Fuller, Mrs. Charles Craig, Matt Moore, Curtis Benton
Director: Lucius Henderson
Scenario: Elaine Sterne

THE JUDGEMENT OF MEN
(Universal-Victor, May, 1915) 1 Reel
Mary Fuller
Director: L. J. Henderson
Story: William Addison Lathrop

CIRCUS MARY
(Universal-Victor, June, 1915) 3 Reels
Mary Fuller, Matt Moore, Charles Ogle, Etienne Girardot
Director: Lucius C. Henderson
Story: William Addison Lathrop

A DAUGHTER OF THE NILE
(Universal-Victor, June, 1915) 3 Reels
Mary Fuller, Matt Moore
Director: Lucius Henderson
Story: Hlaine Sterne

THE LITTLE WHITE VIOLET
(Universal-Victor, July, 1915) 2 Reels
Mary Fuller, Pedro de Cordoba
Director: Lucius G. Henderson
Story: Olga Printzlau Clark

JEANNE OF THE WOODS
(Universal-Victor, July, 1915) 1 Reel
Mary Fuller, Pedro de Cordoba, Charles Ogle
Director: Lucius Henderson
Story: William Addison Lathrop

THE TAMING OF MARY
(Universal-Victor, August, 1915) 1 Reel
Mary Fuller
Director: Lucius Henderson
Story: Robert F. Hill

UNDER SOUTHERN SKIES
(Universal, September, 1915) 5 Reels
Mary Fuller, Charles Ogle, Clara Byers, Bert Busby, Milton Sills, William Heidloff, John Ridgway, Paul Panzer, Marie Shotwell, Mary Moore, Harry Blakemore, Nellie Slattery, Margaret Well, Marie Weirman
Director: Lucius Henderson
Scenario: William Addison Lathrop
Story: Lottie Blair Parker

THE WOMAN WHO LIED
(Universal-Victor, October, 1915) 3 Reels
Mary Fuller, Paul Panzer, Milton Sills, William Heidoff, Charles Ogle, Edna Hunter, Eldine Stuart
Director: Lucius Henderson
Scenario: Olga Printzlau Clark

LIL NOR'WESTERN
(Universal-Victor, November, 1915) 3 Reels
Mary Fuller, Paul Panzer, Glenn White, R. F. Hill, Ralph Belmont
Director: Lucius Henderson

THE TALE OF THE C
(Universal-Victor, December, 1915) 3 Reels
Mary Fuller, Paul Panzer, Marie Shotwell, Charles Ogle
Director: Lucius Henderson
Story: Elaine Sterne

A SEA MYSTERY
(Universal-Victor, January, 1916) 1 Reel
Robert Lee, *Mary Fuller*, Paul Panzer, Ralph Belmont
Scenario: M. B. Havey

THE HEART OF A MERMAID
(Victor, January, 1916) 3 Reels
Mary Fuller, Glen White, Paul Panzer, Sydell Dowling, Marie Shotwell
Director: Lucius Henderson
Scenario: Elaine Sterne

MADAME CUBIST
(Victor, February, 1916) 2 Reels
Mary Fuller, Curtis Benton, Herbert Grey, Clifford Grey
Director: Lucius Henderson
Scenario: Elaine Sterne

THROWN TO THE LIONS
(Universal-Red Feather, March, 1916) 5 Reels
Mary Fuller, Finita DeSopia, Joe W. Girard, Clifford Gray, Emil Hick, Augustus Phillips
Scenario: Norbert Lusk
Story: Wallace Irwin

THE LITTLE FRAUD
(Victor, April, 1916) 1 Reel
Mary Fuller, Marcus Moriarty, Harry Hillard, Bob Hill
Director: Lucius Henderson
Scenario: Elizabeth R. Carpenter

THE GIRL WHO FEARED DAYLIGHT
(Victor, April, 1916) 2 Reels
Mary Fuller, Edna Pendleton, Clifford Gray, Curtis Benton, William Welch
Director: Lucius Henderson
Scenario: Norbert Lusk
Story: Arthur J. Levy

THE HUNTRESS OF MEN
(Universal-Red Feather, May, 1916) 5 Reels
Mary Fuller, Joseph W. Girard, Sidney Bracey
Director: Lucius Henderson
Scenario: Catherine Carr
Story: J. Vere Tyler

THE THREE WISHES
(Victor, May, 1916) 1 Reel
Mary Fuller, Augustus Phillips, Mrs. Ford
Director: Lucius Henderson
Scenario: Samuel Greiner

THE LIMOUSINE MYSTERY
(Victor, May, 1916) 2 Reels
Mary Fuller, Joseph W. Girard, Anthony Merlo, Bert Busby, William Welsh
Director: Lucius Henderson
Scenario: Catherine Carr
Story: Leslie T. Peacocke

THE SCARLET MARK
(Victor, June, 1916) 2 Reels
Mary Fuller, Mrs. J. H. Brundage, Joseph W. Girard, Matty Roubert, Anthony Merlo
Director: Lucius J. Henderson
Scenario: Catherine Carr
Story: Amy Vorhaus

BEHIND THE VEIL
(Victor, June, 1916) 2 Reels
Mary Fuller, Inez Marcel, Niles Welch, Johnnie Walker
Director: Lucius J. Henderson
Scenario: Catherine Carr
Story: Elizabeth R. Carpenter

THE GARDEN OF SHADOWS
(Universal, July, 1916) 2 Reels
Mary Fuller, Niles Welch, Violet Axzell
Director: Lucius Henderson
Scenario: Olga Printzlau

A SPLASH OF LOCAL COLOR
(Universal-Gold Seal, July, 1916) 2 Reels
Mary Fuller, Joseph W. Girard, Charles Slattery, Ed Murphy
Director: Lucius Henderson
Scenario: Catherine Carr
Story: Clifford F. Ivins

THE TRAIL OF CHANCE
(Universal-Bison, August 12, 1916) 2 Reels
Mary Fuller, A. G. Corbel, John Walker, Joseph G. Girard, Andy Clark
Director: Lucius Henderson
Adaptation: Catherine Carr
Story: Amy Vorhaus

STOLEN HONORS
(Universal, October, 1916) 1 Reel
Mary Fuller

THE LONG TRAIL
(Paramount-Artcraft, June, 1917) 5 Reels
Mary Fuller, Lou Tellegan
Director: Howell Hansell
Story: Eve Unsell

PUBLIC BE DAMNED
(Public Rights Film Corp./Select, June, 1917) 5 Reels
Mary Fuller, Charles Richmon, Chester Barnett, Joe Smiley, Russell Bassett
Director/Scenario: S. E. V. Taylor

THE BEAUTIFUL IMPOSTER
(Universal-Star, July, 1917) 2 Reels
Mary Fuller, Clara Beyers, Nellie Slattery, Johnnie Walker
Director: Lucius Henderson
Scenario: Catherine Carr

THE UNTAMED
(Universal-Star, July, 1917) 2 Reels
Mary Fuller, William Welsh, Johnnie Walker, Helen Slosson
Director: Lucius Henderson
Scenario: Catherine Carr
Story: Leslie T. Peacocke

TO THE HIGHEST BIDDER
(Universal-Star, August, 1917) 2 Reels
Mary Fuller, Clara Beyers, Averill Harris
Director: Lucius Henderson
Scenario: Catherine Carr
Story: Emmett Campbell Hall

Frances Gifford.

31 • FRANCES GIFFORD

Jungle Pulchritude at its Finest

Although some pretty good roles were to come Frances Gifford's way at Paramount and M-G-M, her claim to screen immortality was achieved on loan-out to Republic for a single film, **Jungle Girl** (1941). Ironically, this 15-chapter serial, a highly lucrative cliffhanger for the rising San Fernando Valley serial factory, has been out of circulation since its first release, as the result of an agreement with the Edgar Rice Burroughs estate. We can only hope that this fine serial--an artistic masterpiece of its kind--will someday be available on tape or in 16mm format so that film buffs can thrill again as Frances Gifford breaks through the jungle on her elephant and swings **Tarzan**-like through the trees. A sensational, natural beauty, Frances proved to be the screen jungle's most alluring inhabitant. So popular was this continued-next-week effort and so associated with it was Miss Gifford that she deserves her place in this volume on the basis of the one serial outing.

Jungle Girl (1941) was a return to the serial queen concept, with an athletic female assaying the main role and the leading man a secondary one. It was the first of six serials in which Republic would feature the heroine in the title. Through directors William Witney and John English, Republic produced one of the classic serials in the forty-five year history of the genre.

Technically, **Jungle Girl** was a superb serial, but it was the twenty-one year old star who gave it its vibrance. Unfortunately, Paramount would not loan her to Republic for the sequel, **The Perils of Nyoka** (1942). She did, however, again assume a jungle role a couple of years later in RKO's **Tarzan Triumphs** (1943). As Zandra, the queen of a lost Arabic tribe, she provided a new twist for the long-running Johnny Weissmuller series in that it was the first of the "Jane-less" Tarzan films.

Mary Frances Gifford was born on December 7, 1919 in Long Beach, California, the only child of Clarence Gifford, an electrical company superintendent, and Gladys Gifford, a teacher at the San Diego State Normal School. Frances attended the Fremont Grammar School, Thomas Jefferson Junior High, and Woodrow Wilson High School in Long Beach. She was valedictorian of her graduating class and a member of the school's honorary scholastic society. As a speaker on behalf of youth causes, she made a local reputation for herself and was in regular demand for speeches before service clubs.

Frances had made application to the University of California at Los Angeles as a pre-legal student when, at age 16, she had a chance to visit the Goldwyn Studio with a friend during filming of **Come and Get It** (1936). A studio executive saw her and asked her if she would care to take a screen test. Naturally she thought it would be a great idea. For her photographic test she was instructed to walk across a stage gracefully to a mirror and then turn around slowly, surveying herself from all angles. The director had her rehearse the action several times; when he told her to "try it once more," she didn't know that the camera was turning. At the end of the scene she looked at herself in the mirror and stuck out her tongue derisively. The Goldwyn brass liked what they saw on film, including the grimace, and signed her.

Frances remained at Goldwyn for six months, posing for bathing suit and other cheesecake art but getting before the camera only once, as a poolside bathing beauty in **Woman Chases Man** (1937). She transferred to RKO, but it was the same old story of being photographed for glamour and fashion stills without getting very many acting assignments. Small parts in **New Faces of 1937** (1937), **The Big Shot** (1939), **Stage Door** (1937), **Living on Love** (1937), and

Jungle Girl (Republic, 1941) – Gerald Mohr and Frances Gifford.

Sky Giant (1938) comprised her RKO output.

Frances married actor James Dunn on Christmas Day, 1938 and temporarily retired from her less-than-successful screen career. Retirement was not to be permanent, however. In 1939 she had a bit in Mr. Smith Goes to Washington (1939) at Columbia and, in 1940, got her first significant parts by co-starring with her husband in two quickie films for Producers Distributing Corporation. Before the second film was released the company underwent a name change and the second feature was released as a Producers Releasing Corporation (PRC) film. In Mercy Plane (1940) Gifford is an aviatrix who continually beats Dunn in air races, while in Hold that Woman (1940) she is the girlfriend of Dunn, a repossession agent. Variety reported that she "passed muster," but was critical of Dunn.

Her marriage was deteriorating and she had about decided to go to UCLA to begin the law career she almost started four years earlier when Walt Disney chose her for the part of a Disney studio worker in his part-live action feature The Reluctant Dragon (1941). Paramount liked what they saw and put her under contract.

Luckily for serial aficionados, Paramount loaned Frances to Republic for Jungle Girl, widely publicized as being an Edgar Rice Burroughs creation and as the first serial starring a heroine since the silent days. Subsequently she did a variety of roles at Paramount, some ten in all, but none was particularly memorable, although the sagebrush coterie would perhaps argue for the superiority of Tombstone, the Town Too Tough to Die (1942), Border Vigilantes (1941), and American Empire (1942).

Following her stint with Weissmuller in Tarzan Triumphs (1943), Frances joined M-G-M, where she quickly impressed fans and studio alike with her talents in such films as Our Vines Have Tender Grapes (1945), She Went to the Races (1945), Little Mister Jim (1946),

The Arnelo Affair (1947), and **Luxury Liner** (1948). M-G-M gave her a lot of publicity and better and better roles until her unfortunate automobile accident in 1948. She and Benny Thau, M-G-M Vice-President, were on the way to Lake Arrowhead when the crash occurred. No one in the two cars was seriously hurt except Frances, who sustained head injuries. The seriousness of those injuries was not known at the time. She seemed to recover. M-G-M announced plans for future pictures for her, but they did not materialize. The studio cut back on contract players and Gifford was one of the victims. She did not make another picture until 1950, when she played with Bing Crosby in **Riding High.** Then there was a three-year lapse before **Sky Commando** (1953), her last film. She did some early TV, such as Fireside Theatre and G. E. Theatre, but very little was seen of her.

By 1958 her head injuries (or at least it has so been reported) had taken their toll on her and she was admitted to Camarillo State Hospital, a facility specializing in mental disorders. That was the last the public heard of this fine actress for over twenty-five years. No writers had been able to find out whether or not she was still a patient of the hospital. Then, in the August 1983 issue of Hollywood Studio Magazine a letter to the editor from Frances Gifford appeared, informing the reader that she was indeed alive and well and living in Pasadena, CA, where she said she did volunteer typing for the Pasedena Public Library. A picture of Frances purportedly taken in 1983, was also published. It does appear to be Frances Gifford, allowing for an extra quarter-century.

Colin Briggs, writing in the December 1983 issue of Hollywood Studio Magazine, reports an exclusive interview with Miss Gifford. He writes that she has a keen sense of humor with a husky, infectious laugh and that she is seemingly content at last. According to Mr. Briggs she worked for and was involved with many charitable organizations during 1979-1982, in addition to the library work already mentioned, and that she is now working for the American Cancer League.

It is nice to know that our wholesome, beautiful "Jungle Girl" is well and happy.

FRANCES GIFFORD Filmography

WOMAN CHASES MAN
(United Artists, May, 1937) 71 Mins.
Miriam Hopkins, Joel McCrea, Charles Winninger, Erik Rhodes, Ella Logan, Leona Mariele, Broderick Crawford, Charles Halton, William Jaffrey, *Frances Gifford*
Director: John Blystone
Screenplay: Joseph Anthony, Manuel Seff, David Hertz
Producer: Samuel Goldwyn

NEW FACES OF 1937
(RKO-Radio, June, 1937) 105 Mins.
Joe Penner, Milton Berle, Parkyakarkus, Harriet Hilliard, William Brady, Jerome Cowan, Thelma Leeds, Lorraine Krueger, Tommy Mack, Bert Gordon, Patricia Wilder, Richard Lane, Dudley Clements, William Corson, George Rosener, Dewey Robinson, Harry C. Bradley, Brian Sisters, Derry Deane, Eddie Rio, Loria Brothers, Ann Miller, The Three Chocolateers, The Four Playboys, *Frances Gifford*, Mary Louise Smith, Betty Johnson, Harriet Brandon, Beatrice Schute, Juanita Fields, Cynthia Westlake
Director: Leigh Jason
Screenplay: Nat Perrin, Philip G. Epstein, Irving S. Brecher
Adaptation: Harold Kusell, Harry Clork, Howard J. Green
Story: George Bradshaw, "Shoestring"
David Freeman, "A Day at the Brokers"
Producer: Edward Small

THE BIG SHOT
(RKO-Radio, July, 1937) 66 Mins.
Guy Kibbee, Cora Witherspoon, Dorothy Moore, Gordon Jones, Russell Hicks, Frank M. Thomas, Dudley Clements, George Irving, Maxine Jennings, Barbara Pepper, Tom Kennedy, John Kelly, Eddie Gribbon, Al Hill, Donald Kirke, *Frances Gifford*
Director: Edward Killy
Screenplay: Arthur T. Horman, Bert Kranet
Story: Lawrence Poble, Thomas Ahearn

LIVING ON LOVE
(RKO-Radio, October, 1937) 60 Mins.
James Dunn, Whitney Bourne, Joan Woodbury, Solly Ward, Tom Kennedy, Franklin Pangborn, *Frances Gifford*
Director: Lew Landers
Screenplay: Franklin Coen
Story: John Wells
Producer: Maury Cohen

Tombstone–The Town Too Tough to Die (Paramount, 1942) – Kent Taylor, Frances Gifford, Richard Dix, and Don Castle.

STAGE DOOR
(RKO-Radio, 1937)
Katharine Hepburn, Ginger Rogers, Adolphe Menjou, Gail Patrick, Constance Collier, Andrea Leeds, Samuel S. Hinds, Lucille Ball, Pierce Watkin, Franklin Pangburn, Elizabeth Dunne, Phyllis Kennedy, Grady Sutton, Jack Carson, Ann Miller, Lynton Brent, Ralph Forbes, Mary Forbes, Jean Rouverol, Frank Reichey, *Frances Gifford*, Larry Steers, Harry Strong
Director: Gregory La Cava
Screenplay: Morrie Ryskind, Anthony Veiller
Story: Edna Ferber, George S. Kaufman
Producer: Pandro S. Berman

SKY GIANT
(RKO-Radio, June, 1938) 80 Mins.
Richard Dix, Chester Morris, Joan Fontaine, Harry Carey, Paul Guilfoyle, Robert Strange, Max Hoffman, Jr., Vicki Lester, William Corson, James Bush, Edwin Marr, Harry Campbell, *Frances Gifford*
Director: Lew Landers
Screenplay: Lionel Houser
Story: Lionel Houser
Producer: Robert Sisk

MR. SMITH GOES TO WASHINGTON
(Columbia, November 19, 1939) 125 Mins.
Jean Arthur, James Stewart, Claude Rains, Edward Arnold, Guy Kibbee, Thomas Mitchell, Eugene Pallette, Beulah Bondi, H. B. Warner, Harry Carey, Astrid Allwyn, Ruth Donnelly, Grant Mitchell, Porter Hall, Baby Dumpling, H. V. Kalterborn, Pierre Watkin, Charles Lane, William Demarest, Dick Elliott, Billy Watson, Delmar Watson, John Russell, Harry Watson, Gary Watson, *Frances Gifford*
Director: Frank Capra
Screenplay: Sidney Buchman
Story: Lewis R. Foster
Producer: Frank Capra

A FUGITIVE FROM JUSTICE
(Warner Bros., June, 1940) 54 Mins.
Roger Pryor, Lucile Fairbanks, Eddie Foy, Jr., Sheila Bromley, Morgan Conway, Donald Douglas, John Gallaudet, Lottie Williams, Joe Devlin, Steven Darrell, John Harmon, Robert E. O'Connor, Thomas Jackson, Eddy Chandler, Ed Keane, Willis Claire, Gus Glasmire, Bernie Pilot, George Lloyd, Michael Conroy, *Frances Gifford*
Director: Terry Morse
Screenplay: Alex Gottlieb
Story: Leonard Neubauer
Producer: Bryan Foy

HOLD THAT WOMAN
(PRC, July 15, 1940) 64 Mins.
James Dunn, *Frances Gifford*, George Douglas, Martin Spellman, Rita LaRoy, Eddie Fetherstone, Guy Usher, Paul Bryar
Director: Sherman Scott
Story: Raymond L. Schrock, William Pierce
Adaptation: George Bricker
Producer: Sigmund Neufeld

MERCY PLANE
(Producers Distributing Corp., October, 1940) 72 Mins.
James Dunn, *Frances Gifford*, Matty Fain, William Pawley, Harry Harvey, Forbes Murray, Edwin Miller, Duke York
Director: Richard Harlan
Screenplay: William Lively
Associate Producer: Sigmund Neufeld

BORDER VIGILANTES
(Paramount, April 18, 1941) 62 Mins.
William Boyd, Russell Hayden, Andy Clyde, Victor Jory, Morris Ankrum, *Frances Gifford*, Ethel Wales, Tom Tyler, Hal Taliaferro, Jack Rockwell, Britt Wood, Hank Worden, Hank Bell, Edward Earle, Al Haskell, Curley Dresden, Chuck Morrison, Ted Wells
Director: Derwin Abrahams
Screenplay: J. Benton Cheney
Based on characters created by Clarence E. Mulford
Producer: Harry Sherman

WEST POINT WIDOW
(Paramount, May, 1941) 63 Mins.
Anne Shirley, Richard Carlson, Richard Denning, *Frances Gifford*, Maude Eburne, Janet Beecher, Cecil Kellaway, Archie Twitchell, Lillian Randolph, Patricia Farr, Sharon Lynne, Deanna Jean Hall, Eddie Conrad
Director: Robert Stodmak
Screenplay: F. Hugh Herbert, Hana Kraly
Story: Anne Wormser
Producer: Sol C. Siegel
Associate Producer: Colbert Clark

JUNGLE GIRL
(Republic, June, 1941) 15 Chapters
Frances Gifford, Tom Neal, Trevor Bardette, Gerald Mohr, Eddie Acuff, Frank Lackteen, Tommy Cook, Robert Barron, Bud Geary, Al Kihume, Al Taylor, Joe McGuinn, Jerry Frank, Ken Terrell, Yakima Canutt, David Sharpe, Duke Green, Harry Smith, Tom Steele, Duke Taylor, Helen Thurston
Director: William Witney, John English
Screenplay: Ronald Davidson, Norman S. Hall, William Lively, Joseph O'Donnell, Alfred Batson
Based on Edgar Rice Burroughs', "Jungle Girl"
Associate Producer: Hiram S. Brown
Chapters: (1) Death by Voodoo (2) Queen of Beasts (3) River of Fire (4) Treachery (5) Jungle Vengeance (6) Tribal Fury (7) The Poison Dart (8) Man Trap (9) Treasure Tomb (10) Jungle Killer (11) Dangerous Secret (12) Trapped (13) Ambush (14) Diamond Trail (15) Flight to Freedom

THE RELUCTANT DRAGON
(RKO-Radio, July, 1941) 73 Mins.
Robert Benchley, *Frances Gifford*, Buddy Pepper, Nana Bryant, Clarence Nash, Florence Gill, Hamilton McFadden, Alan Ladd, Maurice Murphy, Jean Fenwick, Jimmy Lusk Verna Hillie, Walt Disney, Norm Ferguson, Ward Kimbell
Director: Alfred Werker
Screenplay: Ted Sears, Al Perkins, Larry Clemmons, Bill Cottrell, Harry Clork
Producer: Walt Disney

LOUISIANA PURCHASE
(Paramount, December 25, 1941) 98 Mins.
Bob Hope, Vera Zorina, Victor Moore, Irene Bordoni, Dona Drake, Raymond Walburn, Maxie Rosenbloom, Frank Albertson, Phyllis Ruth, Donald MacBride, Andrew Tombes, Robert Warwick, Charles LaToree, Charles Lasky, Emory Parnell, Iris Meredith, Catherine Craig, Jack Norton, Sam McDaniel, Kay Aldridge, Katherine Booth, Eleanor Stewart, Jean Wallace, *Frances Gifford*, Louise LaPlanche
Director: Irving Cummings
Screenplay: Jerome Chodorov, Joseph Fields
Story: B. C. DeSylva
Associate Producer: Harold Wilson

THE REMARKABLE ANDREW
(Paramount, March, 1942) 80 Mins.
William Holden, Ellen Drew, Brian Donlevy, Rod Cameron, Richard Webb, Porter Hall, *Frances Gifford*, Nydia Westman, Montagu Love, George Watts, Brandon Hurst, Spencer Charters, Minor Watson, Milton Parsons
Director: Stuart Heisler
Screenplay: Dalton Trumbo
Story: Dalton Trumbo
Producer: Richard Blumenthal

BEYOND THE BLUE HORIZON
(Paramount, May, 1942) 76 Mins.
Dorothy Lamour, Richard Denning, Jack Haley, Patricia Morison, Walter Abel, Helen Gilbert, Elizabeth Patterson, Edward Fielding, Gerald Oliver Smith, Frank Reicher, Abner Biberman, Charles Stevens, Charles Cane, Bill Telask, *Frances Gifford*
Director: Alfred Santell
Associate Producer: Monta Bell
Screenplay: Frank Butler
Based on story by E. Lloyd Sheldon, Jack DeWitt

TOMBSTONE--THE TOWN TOO TOUGH TO DIE
(Paramount, June 13, 1942) 79 Mins.
Richard Dix, Kent Taylor, Edgar Buchanan, *Frances Gifford*, Don Castle, Clem Bevins, Victor Jory, Rex Bell, Chris-Pin Martin, Jack Rockwell, Charles Stevens, Hal Taliaferro, Wallis Clark, James Ferrara, Paul Sutton, Dick Curtis, Harvey Stephens, Charles Middleton, Don Curtis, Beryl Wallace
Director: William McGann
Screenplay: Albert Shelby LeVino, Edward E. Paramore
Story: Dean Franklin, Charles Beisner
Producer: Harry Sherman

THE GLASS KEY
(Paramount, October 15, 1942) 85 Mins.
Brian Donlevy, Veronica Lake, Alan Ladd, Bonita Granville, Richard Denning, Joseph Calleia, William Bendix, *Frances Gifford*, Donald McBride, Margaret Hayes, Moroni Olsen, Eddie Marr, Arthur Loft, George Meader, Eddie Marr, Joe McGuinn, Frank Hagney, Joseph King
Director: Stuart Heisler
Screenplay: Jonathan Latimer
Story: Dashiell Hammett
Associate Producer: Fred Kohlmar

MY HEART BELONGS TO DADDY
(Paramount, October, 1942) 78 Mins.
Richard Carlson, Martha O'Driscoll, Cecil Kellaway, *Frances Gifford*, Florence Bates, Mabel Paige, Velma Borg, Cecil Cunningham, Paul Stanton, Maurice Cass, Francis Pierlot, Charles Wilson, Fern Emmett, Mary Currier, Edward Gargan, Isabel Withers, Chick Chandler, Mary Treen, Dorothy Granger
Director: Robert Siodmak
Screenplay: F. Hugh Herbert

AMERICAN EMPIRE
(United Artists, December 11, 1942)
Richard Dix, Leo Carrillo, Preston Foster, *Frances Gifford*, Guinn (Big Boy) Williams, Robert Barrat, Jack LaRue, Cliff Edwards, Guy Rodin, Chris-Pin Martin, Rich Webb, William Farnum, Etta McDaniel, Hal Taliaferro, Tom London
Director: William McGann
Screenplay: J. Robert Bren, Gladys Atwater, Ben Crauman Kohn
Producer: Harry Sherman

HENRY ALDRICH GETS GLAMOUR
(Paramount, December, 1942) 72 Mins.
Jimmy Lydon, Charles Smith, John Litel, Olive Blackeney, Diana Lynn, *Frances Gifford*, Gail Russell, Vaughn Glaser, Anne Rooney
Director: Hugh Bennett
Screenplay: Edwin Blum, Aleen Leslie
Producer: Walter MacEwen
Associate Producer: Jules Schermer

STAR SPANGLED RHYTHM
(Paramount, December 31, 1942) 99 Mins.
Betty Hutton, Eddie Bracken, Victor Moore, Anne Revere, Walter Abel, Case Daley, MacDonald Carey, Gil Lamb, William Haade, Tom Dugan, Paul Porcasi, Richard Loo, James Millican, Eddie Dew, Rod Cameron, Bob Hope, Fred MacMurray, Ray Milland, Franchot Tone, Lynne Overman, Dorothy Lamour, Veronica Lake, Paulette Goddard, *Frances Gifford*, Alan Ladd, Mary Martin, William Bendix, Jerry Colonna, Ellen Drew, Cecil B. DeMille, Betty Rhodes, Walter Catlett
Director: George Marshall
Screenplay: Harry Tugend
Associate Producer: Joseph Sistrom

TARZAN TRIUMPHS
(RKO-Radio, January 20, 1943)
Johnny Weissmuller, Johnny Sheffield, *Frances Gifford*, Stanley Ridges, Sig Ruman, Pedro de Cordoba, Philip Van Zandt, Stanley Brown, Rex Williams, Cheta
Director: William Thield
Producer: Sol Lesser
Based on books by Edgar Rice Burroughs

CRY HAVOC
(M-G-M, October, 1943)
Margaret Sullavan, Ann Sothern, Joan Blondell, Fay Bainter, Marsha Hunt, Ella Raines, *Frances Gifford*, Diana Lewis, Heather Angel, Dorothy Morris, Connie Gilchrist, Gloria Grafton, Fely Franquelli
Director: Richard Thorpe
Producer: Edwin Knopf

MARRIAGE IS A PRIVATE AFFAIR
(M-G-M, August, 1944) 116 Mins.
Lana Turner, James Craig, John Hodiak, *Frances Gifford*, Hugh Marlowe, Natalie Schafer, Keenan Wynn, Herbert Rudley, Paul Cavanaugh, Morris Ankrum, June Green, Tom Drake, Shirley Patterson, Rev. Neal Dodd, Nana Bryant, Cecilia Callejo, Virginia Briassac, Byron Foulger, Addison Richards
Director: Robert Z. Leonard
Screenplay: David Hertz, Leonore Coffee
Story: Judith Kelly
Producer: Pandro Berman

THRILL OF A ROMANCE
(M-G-M, May, 1945) 103 Mins.
Van Johnson, Esther Williams, *Frances Gifford*, Henry Travers, Spring Byington, Lauritz Melchior, Carleton G. Young, Ethel Griffies, Donald Curtis, Jerry Scott, Fernando Alvarado, Helene Stanley, Vince Barnett, Billy House, Joan Fay Macaboy, Tommy Dorsey and his Orchestra
Director: Richard Thorpe
Producer: Joe Pasternak
Music Adaptation: Georgie Stoll

SHE WENT TO THE RACES
(M-G-M, October, 1945) 87 Mins.
James Craig, *Frances Gifford*, Ava Gardner, Edmund Gwenn, Sig Ruman, Reginald Owen, J. M. Kerrigan, Charles Halton, Chester Clute, Frank Orth, Joe Hernandez
Director: Willis Goldbeck
Screenplay: Lawrence Hazard
Based on a story by Alan Friedman and De Vallon Scott
Producer: Frederick Stephani

OUR VINES HAVE TENDER GRAPES
(M-G-M, 1945) 105 Mins.
Edward G. Robinson, Margaret O'Brien, James Craig, Agnes Moorehead, Jackie "Butch" Jenkins, Morris Carnovsky, *Frances Gifford*, Sara Haden, Louis Jean Heydt, Francis Pierlot, Greta Granstedt, Arthur Space, Elizabeth Russell, Dorothy Morris, Charles Middleton, Arthur Hohl, Abigail Adams, Johnny Berkes, Rhoda Williams
Director: Roy Rowland
Screenplay: Dalton Trumbo
Story: George Victor Martin
Producer: Robert Sisk

OUT OF THE MONEY
(M-G-M, January, 1946)
James Craig, *Frances Gifford*, Ava Gardner, Edmund Gwenn, Sig Ruman, Reginald Owen, J. M. Kerrigan, Charles Halton, Frank Orth, Chester Clute
Director: Willis Goldbeck
Screenplay: Lawrence Hazard
Story: Alan Friedman, De Vallon Scott

LITTLE MISTER JIM
(M-G-M, May, 1946) 93 Mins.
Jackie "Butch" Jenkins, James Craig, *Frances Gifford*, Luana Patten, Spring Byington, Chingway Lee, Laura La Plante, Henry O'Neill, Morris Ankru, Celia Travers, Ruth Brady, Sharon McManus, Buz Buckley, Carol Nugent, Jean Van
Director: Fred Zinnerman
Screenplay: George Bruce
Based on novel by Tommy Wadelton
Producer: Orville O. Dull

THE ARNELO AFFAIR
(M-G-M, February, 1947) 88 Mins.
John Hodiak, George Murphy, *Frances Gifford*, Dean Stockwell, Eve Arden, Warner Anderson, Lowell Gilmore, Michael Brandon, Ruth Brady, Ruby Dandridge, Joan Woodbury
Director: Arch Oboler
Screenplay: Arch Oboler
Producer: Jerry Bressler

LUXURY LINER
(M-G-M, August, 1948) 97 Mins.
George Brent, Jane Powell, Lauritz Melchior, *Frances Gifford*, Marina Koshetz, Xavier Cugat and Orchestra, Thomas E. Breen, Richard Derr, John Ridgeley, The Pied Pipers, Connie Gilchrist
Director: Richard Whorf
Screenplay: Gladys Lehman, Richard Connell
Producer: Joe Pasternak

RIDING HIGH
(Paramount, December, 1950) 112 Mins.
Bing Crosby, Coleen Gray, Charles Bickford, *Frances Gifford*, Raymond Walburn, William Demarest, Clarence Muse, Margaret Hamilton, Douglas Dumbrille, Ward Bond, Charles Lane, Frankie Darro, Paul Harvey, Marjorie Lord, Marjorie Hosheile, Rand Brooks, Willard Waterman, Jimmy Gleason, Dub Taylor
Director: Frank Capra
Additional dialogue by Melville Shavelson, Jack Rose
Based on story by Mark Hellinger
Producer: Frank Capra

SKY COMMANDO
(Columbia, August, 1953) 69 Mins.
Dan Duryea, *Frances Gifford*, Touch Conners, Michael Fox, William R. Klein, Freeman Morse, Dick Paxton, Selmer Jackson, Dick Lerner, Morris Ankrum, Paul McGuire
Director: Fred F. Sears
Screenplay: Samuel Newman
Story: William Sackheim, Arthur Orloff, Samuel Newman
Producer: Sam Katzman

32 • EUGENIA GILBERT

Another Lovely Ingenue from Poverty Row Who Faced Awful Perils

If Eugenia Gilbert were to be remembered for only a single film, it would probably be **Perils of the Jungle** (1927), the independent serial produced by Weiss Brothers Artclass Pictures. It was crude enough to have that strange charm such pictures sometimes exert, and that makes them remembered for some reason other than quality of story, acting, direction, cast or settings. The story has Eugenia and her screen father searching for hidden treasure in the depths of the African jungle, aided by hero Frank Merrill and menaced by Albert J. Smith. Mediocre film fare, it was still fascinating for the undiscriminating patron.

If one chose not to put **Perils of the Jungle** at the top of the list, then **The Crimson Flash** (1927) would probably be the choice. A Pathé serial, it had wider distribution than **Perils of the Jungle** and contained enough mystery elements to keep the customers coming back each week (which really wasn't any great trick in 1927; the public was going to go to the movies no matter what.) Eugenia was the girl friend of secret service agent Cullen Landis in the Pathé outing and, like all serial heroines, managed to get herself in some terrible predicaments. The Rooster trademark almost assured the film's success.

Probably a few serial lovers would cast a vote for either **The Police Reporter** (1928) or **The Mysterious Airman** (1928) as her best film. Both were intriguing. And, of course, her features with various cowboys, especially Leo Maloney, made a greater impression on some film fans than did the continued pieces.

Today Eugenia is all but forgotten except by a faithful few diehard fans and historians; she faded from the movie scene with the coming of sound.

Eugenia Gilbert.

EUGENIA GILBERT Filmography

A CERTAIN RICH MAN
(Great Authors/Hodkinson, May, 1921) 6 Reels
Carl Gantvoort, Claire Adams, Robert McKim, Jean Hersholt, Joseph J. Dowling, Lydia Knott, Frankie Lee, Mary Jane Irving, Harry Lorraine, J. Gunnis Davis, Charles Colby, Walter Perry, Fleming Pitts, Grace Pike, *Eugenia Gilbert*, Gordon Dumont, Edna Pennington
Director: Howard Hickman
Story: William Allen White, "A Certain Rich Man"
Producer: Benjamin G. Hampton

THE MAN OF THE FOREST
(Zane Grey/Hodkinson, June, 1921) 7 Reels
Carl Gantvoort, Claire Adams, Robert McKim, Jean Hersholt, Harry Lorraine, *Eugenia Gilbert*, Frank Hayes, Charlotte Pierce, Charles B. Murphy, Frederick Starr, Tote Du Crow
Scenario: Howard Hickman, Richard Schayer, W. H. Clifford
Story: Zane Grey, "The Man of the Forest"
Producer: Benjamin B. Hampton

THE MAN FROM DOWNING STREET
(Vitagraph, April 2, 1922) 5 Reels
Earle Williams, Charles Hill Mailes, Boris Karloff, Betty Ross Clarke, Kathryn Adams, Herbert Prior, *Eugenia Gilbert*, James Butler, George Stanley
Director: Edward Jose
Scenario: Bradley J. Smollen
Story: Clyde C. Westover, Lottie Horner, Florine Williams

THE HALF BREED
(Oliver Morosco/First National, June, 1922) 6 Reels
Wheeler Oakman, Ann May, Mary Anderson, Hugh Thompson, King Evers, Joseph Dowling, Lew Harvey, Herbert Pryor, Sidney De Gray, Nick De Ruiz, Leela Lane, *Eugenia Gilbert*, Carl Stockdale, Evelyn Selbie, Dorris Deane, Albert S. Lloyd, George Kuwa
Director: Charles A. Taylor
Scenario: Charles A. Taylor
Story: H. D. Cottrell, Oliver Morosco, "Half Breed"

WILDCAT JORDAN
(Phil Goldstone, July 1, 1922) 5 Reels
Richard Talmadge, *Eugenia Gilbert*, Harry von Meter, Jack Waltemeyer
Director: Al Santell

SOULS IN BONDAGE
(Sanford, September, 1923) 7 Reels
Pat O'Malley, Cleo Madison, Otto Lederer, *Eugenia Gilbert*, Frank Hayes, Gene Crosby, Peter Howard, Leon Artigue
Director: William H. Clifford
Story: William H. Clifford

THE BACK TRAIL
(Universal, June 16, 1924) 5 Reels
Jack Hoxie, Alton Stone, *Eugenia Gilbert*, Claude Payton, William Lester, William McCall, Buck Connors, Pat Harmon
Director: Clifford Smith
Scenario: Isadore Bernstein
Story: Walter J. Coburn

SINNERS IN SILK
(M-G-M, September 1, 1924) 6 Reels
Adolphe Menjou, Eleanor Boardman, Conrad Nagel, Jean Hersholt, Edward Connelly, Jerome Patrick, John Patrick, Hedda Hopper, Miss Du Pont, Virginia Lee Corbin, Bradley Ward, Dorothy Dwan, Frank Elliott, Ann Luther, Peggy Elinor, *Eugenia Gilbert*, Mary Akin, Estelle Clark
Director: Hobart Henley
Scenario: Carey Wilson
Story: Benjamin Glazer

THE SEA SQUAWK
(Sennett-Pathé, October 2, 1924) 2 Reels
Harry Langdon, *Eugenia Gilbert*, Christian Frank, Charlotte Mineau, Leo Sulky, Bud Rose
Director: Harry Edwards
Story: Mack Sennett
Producer: Mack Sennett

THE GREAT DIAMOND MYSTERY
(Fox, October 5, 1924) 5 Reels
Shirley Mason, Jackie Saunders, Harry Von Meter, John Cossar, Philo McCullough, Jector V. Sarno, William Collier, Jr., *Eugenia Gilbert*, Mary Mayo, Hardee Kirkland
Director: Denison Clift
Scenario: Thomas Dixon, Jr.
Story: Shannon Fife

Perils of the Jungle (Artclass, 1927)

SO THIS IS MARRIAGE
(M-G-M, November 24, 1924) 7 Reels
Conrad Nagel, Eleanor Boardman, Lew Cody, Clyde Cook, Edward Connelly, John Boles, Warner Oland, Mabel Julienne Scott, Miss Du Pont, John Patrick, Claire De Lorez, Shannon Day, Jack Edwards, Estelle Clark, Thelma Morgan, Francis McDonald, *Eugenia Gilbert*, Sidney Bracey, Tom O'Brien, Philip Sleeman, Gloria Heller
Director: Hobart Henley
Scenario: John Lynch, Alice D. G. Miller
Story: Carey Wilson

FLAMES OF DESIRE
(Fox, November 30, 1924) 6 Reels
Wyndham Standing, Diana Miller, Richard Thorpe, Frank Leigh, George K. Arthur, Jackie Saunders, Frances Beaumont, Hayford Hobbs, Charles Clary, *Eugenia Gilbert*
Director: Denison Clift
Scenario: Denison Clift, Reginald G. Fogwell
Story: Ouida, "Strathmore"

THE WILD GOOSE CHASER
(Pathé, December 11, 1924) 2 Reels
Ben Turpin, Madeline Hurlock, Trilby Clark, Jack Cooper, *Eugenia Gilbert*, Dot Farly, Charles Dorety
Director: Lloyd Bacon
Producer: Mack Sennett

A BROADWAY BUTTERFLY
(Warner Bros., January 15, 1925) 7 Reels
Dorothy Devore, Louise Fazenda, Willard Louis, John Roche, Cullen Landis, Lilyan Tashman, Wilfred Lucas, *Eugenia Gilbert*, Margaret Seddon
Director: William Beaudine
Scenario: Darryl F. Zanuck
Story: Darryl F. Zanuck

THE SCARLET HONEYMOON
(Fox, March 22, 1925) 5 Reels
Shirley Mason, Pierre Gendron, Allan Sears, J. Farrell MacDonald, Rose Tapley, Maine Geary, *Eugenia Gilbert*, Eric Mayne, Eulalie Jensen
Director: Alan Hale
Scenario: E. Magnus Ingleton
Story: Fannie Davis

TRANSCONTINENTAL LIMITED
(Chadwick, February 4, 1926) 7 Reels
Johnnie Walker, *Eugenia Gilbert,* Alec B. Francis, Edith Yorke, Bruce Gordon, Edward Gillace, George Ovey, Eric Mayne, James Hamel
Director: Nat Ross
Adaptation: Hampton Del Ruth

BEYOND THE ROCKIES
(Independent/FBO, February 21, 1926) 5 Reels
Bob Custer, *Eugenia Gilbert*, David Dunbar, Bruce Gordon, Milton Ross, Eddie Harris, Max Holcomb, Roy Laidlaw, Max Asher
Director: Jack Nelson
Adaptation: William E. Wing
Continuity: William E. Wing
Story: J. Edward Leihead
Producer: Jesse J. Goldburg

THE TEST OF DONALD NORTON
(Chadwick, March 1, 1926) 7 Reels
George Walsh, Tyrone Power, Robert Graves, *Eugenia Gilbert*, Evelyn Selbie, Mickey Moore, Virginia True Boardman, Jack Dillon, Virginia Marshall
Director: B. Reeves Eason
Scenario: Adele Buffington

WILD TO GO
(R-C Pictures/FBO, April 18, 1926) 5 Reels
Tom Tyler, Frankie Darrow, Fred Burns, Ethan Laidlaw, Earl Haley, *Eugenia Gilbert*, Sitting Bull (a dog)
Director: Robert De Lacy
Adaptation: F. A. E. Pine
Story: F. A. E. Pine

VALLEY OF BRAVERY
(Independent/FBO, May 16, 1926) 5 Reels
Bob Custer, *Eugenia Gilbert*, Tom Bay, William Gillespie, Ernie Adams, Art Ortego
Director: Jack Nelson
Scenario: Carl Krusada, James Ormont
Story: E. Lanning Masters

HAIR TRIGGER BAXTER
(Independent/FBO, September 5, 1926) 5 Reels
Bob Custer, *Eugenia Gilbert*, Lew Meehan, Murdock MacQuarrie, Fannie Midgley, Jim Corey, Ernie Adams, Hugh Saxon
Director: Jack Nelson
Continuity: Paul M. Bryan
Story: James Ormont
Producer: Jesse J. Goldburg

LADDIE
(Gene Stratton Porter/FBO, September 26, 1926) 7 Reels
Viola Dana, Tom Forman, Vera Gordon, Kathleen Myers, Nat Carr, Stanley Taylor, Carroll Nye, Aggie Herring, *Eugenia Gilbert*
Director: James W. Horne
Scenario: Gerald C. Duffy
Story: Leon De Costa, "Kosher Kitty Kelly"

THE MAN FROM THE WEST
(Universal, October 13, 1926) 5 Reels
Art Acord, *Eugenia Gilbert*, Irvin Renard, William Welsh, Vin Moore, Dick Gilbert, Georgie Grandee, Eunice Vin Moore
Director: Albert Rogell
Scenario: Harrison Jacobs
Story: Josephine Dodge
Adaptation: Harrison Jacobs

OBEY THE LAW
(Columbia, November 5, 1926) 6 Reels
Bert Lytell, Edna Murphy, Hedda Hopper, Larry Kent, Sarah Padden, *Eugenia Gilbert,* William Welsh
Director: Alfred Raboch
Story: Max Marcin, "Obey the Law"

THE LONG LOOP ON THE PECOS
(Leo Maloney/Pathé, January 9, 1927) 6 Reels
Leo Maloney, *Eugenia Gilbert*, Frederick Dana, Albert Hart, Tom London, Bud Osborne, Chet Ryan, William Merrill McCormick, Robert Burns, Dick La Reno, Murdock MacQuarrie
Director: Leo Maloney
Scenario: Ford I. Beebe
Story: W. D. Hoffman

THE MAN FOR HARDPAN
(Leo Maloney/Pathé, March 6, 1927) 6 Reels
Leo Maloney, *Eugenia Gilbert*, Rosa Gore, Murdock MacQuarrie, Paul Hurst, Ben Corbett, Albert Hart
Director: Leo D. Maloney
Scenario: Ford I. Beebe
Story: Ford I. Beebe

The Mysterious Airman (Artclass, 1928).

MELTING MILLONS
(Pathé, April 10, 1927) 10 Chapters
Allene Ray, Walter Miller, E. H. Calvert, Frank Lackteen, William N. Bailey, John J. Richardson, Bob Burns, Ernie Adams, John Cossar, William Van Dyke, Richard C. Travers, Ann Gladman, *Eugenia Gilbert*, Albert Roccardi
Director: Spencer G. Bennet
Story: Joseph Anthony Roach
Chapters: (1) A Shot in the Dark (2) Perilous Waters (3) The Fatal Attack (4) The Heiress of Craghaven (5) The Hidden Harbor (6) A Strange Voyage (7) The Mysterious Prisoner (8) The Imposter (9) The Spy (10) Exposed

DON DESPERADO
(Leo Maloney/Pathé, May 8, 1927) 6 Reels
Leo Maloney, *Eugenia Gilbert*, Frederick Dana, Charles Bartlett, Chief Whitehorse, Bud Osborne, Allen Watt, Morgan Davis, Harry W. Ramsey
Director: Leo Maloney
Scenario: Ford I. Beebe
Story: Ford I. Beebe

THE CRIMSON FLASH
(Pathé, June 19, 1927) 10 Chapters
Cullen Landis, *Eugenia Gilbert*, Tom Holding, J. Barney Sherry, Walter P. Lewis, Ivan Linow, Mary Gardner, Tony Hughes, Gus De Weil, Ed Roseman, Howard Carey
Director: Arch B. Heath
Story: George Arthur Gray
Screenplay: Paul Fairfax Fuller
Chapters: (1) A Shot in the Night (2) The Ghost Takes a Hand (3) When Thieves Fall Out (4) Decoyed (5) Held in Bondage (6) Checkmate (7) The Shadow of the Menace (8) Into the Trap (9) The Flaming Menace (10) The End of the Trail

PERILS OF THE JUNGLE
(Weiss Brothers Artclass, July, 1927) 10 Chapters
Eugenia Gilbert, Frank Merrill, Bobby Nelson, Milburn Moranti, Albert J. Smith, Will Herman, Walter Maly, Harry Belmore, Frank Hurtee
Director: Jack Nelson
Chapters: (1) Jungle Trails (2) The Jungle King (3) The Elephant's Revenge (4) At the Lion's Mercy (5) The Sting of Death (6) The Trail of Blood (7) The Feast of Vengeance (8) The Leopard's Trap (9) The Gorilla's Bride (10) The Tiger's Den

THE SWELL-HEAD
(Columbia, August 5, 1927) 6 Reels
Ralph Graves, Johnnie Walker, *Eugenia Gilbert*, Mildred Harris, Mary Carr, Tom Dugan
Director: Ralph Graves
Screenplay: Robert Lord
Producer: Harry Cohn

BORDER BLACKBIRDS
(Leo Maloney/Pathé, August 28, 1927) 6 Reels
Leo Maloney, *Eugenia Gilbert*, Nelson McDowell, Joseph Rickson, Bud Osborne, Frank Clark, Morgan Davis, Tom London, Don Coleman, Allen Watt
Director: Leo Maloney
Scenario: Ford I. Beebe
Story: Ford I. Beebe

BY WHOSE HAND?
(Columbia, September 15, 1927) 6 Reels
Ricardo Cortez, *Eugenia Gilbert*, J. Thornton Baston, Tom Dugan, Edgar Washington Blue, Lillian Leighton, William Scott, John Steppling, De Sacia Mooers
Director: Walter Lang
Scenario: Marion Orth
Story: Marion Orth
Producer: Harry Cohn

THE BOSS OF RUSTLER'S ROOST
(Leo Maloney/Pathé, January 22, 1928) 5 Reels
Don Coleman, Ben Corbett, Tom London, Albert Hart, Dick Hatton, Frank Clark, William Bertram, Chet Ryan, *Eugenia Gilbert*
Director: Leo Maloney
Scenario: Ford I. Beebe
Story: W. D. Hoffman
Producer: Leo Maloney

THE APACHE RAIDER
(Leo Maloney/Pathé, February 12, 1928) 6 Reels
Leo Maloney, *Eugenia Gilbert*, Don Coleman, Tom London, Jack Ganzhorn, Frederick Dana, Joan Renee, William Merrill McCormick, Robert C. Smith, Walter Shumway, Murdock MacQuarrie, Whitehorse, Robin Williamson, Dick La Reno, Robert Burns, Allen Watt
Director: Leo Maloney
Scenario: Ford I. Beebe
Story: William Dawson Hoffman, "The Border Raider"

THE BRONC STOMPER
(Leo Maloney/Pathé, February 26, 1928) 6 Reels
Don Coleman, Ben Corbett, Tom London, Bud Osborne, Frank Clark, Frederick Dana, Whitehorse, Ray Walters, Robert Burns, Florence Lee, *Eugenia Gilbert*
Director: Leo Maloney
Adaptation: Ford I. Beebe
Scenario: Ford I. Beebe
Story: Barr Cross

THE POLICE REPORTER
(Weiss Brothers Artclass, March 1, 1928) 10 Chapters
Walter Miller, *Eugenia Gilbert.*, William A. Lowery, Robert Belcher, Kenneth Duncan
Director: Jack Nelson
Story: Arthur B. Reeve
Supervisor: George M. Merrick
Chapters: (1) The Phantom (2) Code of the Underworld (3) The Secret Tube (4) The Flaming Idol (5) The Phantom's Trap (6) The Girl Who Dared (7) The Wharf Rate (8) The Mystery Room (9) In the Phantom's Den (10) The Law Wins

AFTER THE STORM
(Columbia, April 19, 1928) 6 Reels
Hobart Bosworth, *Eugenia Gilbert*, Charles Delaney, Maude George, George Kuwa, Linda Loredo
Director: George B. Seitz
Adaptation: Will M. Ritchey
Continuity: Will M. Ritchey
Story: Harold Shumate
Producer: Harry Cohn

THE MYSTERIOUS AIRMAN
(Weiss Brothers Artclass, June 1, 1928) 10 Chapters
Walter Miller, *Eugenia Gilbert,* Robert Walker, Eugene Burr, Dorothy Talcott, James A. Fitzgerald, C. H. Allen, Ray Childs, Hugh Blair, Arthur Morrison, Hamilton Morse
Director: Harry Revier
Screenplay: Arthur B. Reeve
Chapters: (1) The Winged Avenger (2) The Sky Writer (3) The Girl who Flew Alone (4) The Smoke Screen (5) The Air Raid (6) The Vampire Pilot (7) The Faker Pilot (8) The Air Raft (9) The Hidden Ranger (10) Mystery Pilot X

THE DANGER RIDER
(Universal, November 18, 1928) 6 Reels
Hoot Gibson, *Eugenia Gilbert,* B. Reeves Eason, Monte Montague, King Zany, Frank Beal, Milla Davenport, Bud Osborne
Director: Henry MacRae
Scenario: Arthur Statter
Story: Wynn James

THE PHANTOM CITY
(Charles R. Rogers/First National, December 23, 1928) 6 Reels
Ken Maynard, *Eugenia Gilbert,* James Mason, Charles Mailes, Jack McDonald, Blue Washington, Tarzan (a horse)
Director: Albert Rogell
Story: Adele S. Buffington

MOVIE NIGHT
(Hal Roach/M-G-M, April 1, 1929) 2 Reels
Charles Chase, *Eugenia Gilbert,* Edith Fellows, Spec O'Donnell, Stanley J. Sanford
Director: Lew Foster
Story: Leo McCarey

COURTIN' WILDCATS
(Universal, December 22, 1929) 6 Reels
Hoot Gibson, *Eugenia Gilbert,* Harry Todd, Joseph Girard, Monte Montague, John Oscar, Jim Corey, James Farley, Peter Morrison, Joe Bonomo
Director: Jerome Storm
Scenario: Dudley McKenna
Story: William Dudley Pelley, "Courtin's Calamity"

Carol Holloway.

33 • CAROL HOLLOWAY

Sex Appeal, Courage, and Personality Made Her a Popular Heroine

Carol Holloway's bright record of adventurous work well done in four melodramatic serials assured her a niche in the history of that genre, and her several Westerns gave her some claim to recognition in that closely-knit film fraternity.

Little is known about this unusually pretty girl. She was the daughter of a college professor, of Scottish descent, and was born in Williamstown, Massachusetts, and educated in Franklin, Massachusetts. She was noted for her blue eyes-- not gray blue, or violet, or light blue, but the true azure blue. Her hair was dark brown and her coloring needed no help from make-up. She was of medium height, with a slender build, full lips, and an expressive face.

Carol had a stage career with the Carleton Stock Company and appeared on the New York stage in a production of "Everywoman." She worked at several studios before joining Vitagraph. Once there, she plunged whole-heartedly into the rough-and-tumble of serial production, professing to like the outdoor work. She fell into just about every body of water in California, from San Francisco Bay to the Los Angeles River (when it was a river). She once remarked that she had climbed every rock that anybody in the state of California had ever heard of. But she enjoyed the adventures, the outdoor work, and the fame that serials brought her.

Carol's first film of record was **A Strange Melody** (1914) for Lubin. Subsequently, she worked mainly for American Film Company before moving to Vitagraph, where her first film was **The Fighting Trail** (1917), a fifteen-chapter cliffhanger starring William Duncan. The team of Holloway and Duncan was a popular one, and they made two features, **Dead Shot Baker** (1917) and **The Tenderfoot** (1917), as well as a second serial, **Vengeance and the Woman** (1917). But the team was split up for some reason, with Duncan acquiring Edith Johnson as co-star in his future serials, while Carol was cast opposite Antonio Moreno in **The Iron Test** (1918) and **The Perils of Thunder Mountain** (1919), both popular serials of the World War I era. After that she left Vitagraph to work at several studios, playing opposite Tom Mix, Tom Tyler, Harry Carey, and Hoot Gibson in cactus capers.

With the coming of sound, Carol's career nose-dived into obscurity. She got bit parts and extra work and could be seen as late as 1940 in **Emergency Squad**, the last film credit we have for her. We have been unable to determine what happened to her after that. Sadly, Carol was just one more example of a heartthrob of Hollywood's youth who was cast aside as the industry grew to maturity.

CAROL HOLLOWAY Filmography

A STRANGE MELODY
(Lubin, March, 1914) 2 Reels
Carol Holloway, Joseph Smiley
Scenario: Clay M. Greene

THE VIOLINIST
(Eclair, October, 1914) 2 Reels
Carol Holloway, F. Sumner

A GAME OF WITS
(Eclair, December, 1914) 2 Reels
Carol Holloway, Fred Sumner, E. Redmond, Ernest Evers

A GENTLEMAN OF LEISURE
(Lasky, March, 1915)
Wallace Eddinger, *Carol Holloway*, Billy Elmer
Director: George Melford
Scenario: Cecil B. DeMille
Story: John Stapleton, P. G. Wodehouse

Carol Holloway.

HER MOTHER'S SECRET
(Lubin, June, 1915)
John Smiley, *Carol Holloway*, Clarence Elmer, Frankie Mann
Story: Bessie Minier

SECRETARY OF FRIVOLOUS AFFAIRS
(American Film/Mutual, July 12, 1915)
May Allison, Hal Clements, *Carol Holloway*, Wallace MacDonald, William Enfe, Carl von Schiller, Josephine Ditt, Lucy Payton, Harold Lockwood
Director: Thomas Ricketts
Scenario: Thomas Ricketts
Story: May Futrelle

AIDED BY THE MOVIES
(American Film/Beauty, October, 1915) 1 Reel
Carol Holloway, John Sheehan, Nan Christie, John Steppling, Dick Rosson
Director: James Douglass

AN AUTO-BUNGALOW FRACAS
(American Film/Beauty, October, 1915) 1 Reel
John Sheehan, *Carol Holloway*, John Steppling, Dick Rosson, Rae Berger
Director: James Douglass

DESERTED AT THE AUTO
(American Film/Beauty, October, 1915) 1 Reel
Carol Holloway, John Sheehan, Bessie Banks, Dick Rosson
Director: John Dillon

BILLY VAN DEUSEN'S CAMPAIGN
(American Film/Beauty, October, 1915)
John Steppling, *Carol Holloway*, John Sheehan, Bessie Banks, Rae Berger
Director: Archer MacMackin

JOHNNY THE BARBER
(American Film/Beauty, November 13, 1915)
John Sheehan, *Carol Holloway*, Rae Berger
Director: John Dillon

THE DRUMMER'S TRUNK
(American Film/Beauty, November 20, 1915)
John Steppling, *Carol Holloway*, John Sheehan
Director: James Douglass

BILLY VAN DEUSEN AND THE MERRY WIDOW
(American Film/Beauty, November 27, 1915)
John Steppling, *Carol Holloway*
Director: Archer MacMackin

BILLY VAN DEUSEN'S SHADOW
(Beauty, December, 1915)
John Steppling, *Carol Holloway*, Marie Van Tassel

THE FIRST QUARREL
(Beauty, December, 1915)
John Sheehan, *Carol Holloway*, Chance Ward, Beatrice Van, Rae Berger
Director: James Douglass

A GIRL, A GUARD, AND A GARRET
(American Film/Beauty, December 11, 1915) 1 Reel
Carol Holloway, John Sheehan, William Carroll, John Steppling, Rae Berger
Director: Archer MacMackin

MAKING A MAN OF JOHNNY
(American Film/Beauty, December 18, 1915)
Carol Holloway, John Sheehan, John Steppling
Director: James Douglass

KIDDEES, KIDS AND KIDDO
(American Film/Beauty, December 25, 1915)
John Sheehan, *Carol Holloway*, John Steppling, Clifford Callis
Director: Jack Dillon

JOHNNIE'S BIRTHDAY
(Beauty, January, 1916)
John Sheehan, *Carol Holloway*, John Steppling
Director: James Douglass

SOME NIGHT
(Beauty, January, 1916)
Carol Holloway, John Sheehan, Bessie Banks, George Ahearn, Marty Martin
Director: Jack Dillon

BILLY VAN DEUSEN'S WEDDING EVE
(Beauty, January, 1916)
John Steppling, *Carol Holloway*, John Sheehan, Edna Frawley, Hugh Bennett, Bessie Banks
Director: Archer MacMackin

BILLY VAN DEUSEN AND THE VAMPIRE
(Beauty, January, 1916)
John Steppling, John Sheehan, *Carol Holloway*
Director: Archer MacMackin

THE BATTLE OF CUPIDOVICH
(Beauty, February, 1916) 1 Reel
Dick Rosson, *Carol Holloway*, John Steppling, John Sheehan, Mary Talbot
Director: Archer MacMackin

TOO MUCH MARRIED
(Beauty, February, 1916) 1 Reel
Carol Holloway, John Sheehan, John Steppling, Lucille Ward
Director: Jack Dillon

CUPID AND COHEN'S
(Beauty, March, 1916) 1 Reel
Carol Holloway, Johnny Sheehan, Dixie Stuart, Rea Berger, Dick Rosson
Director: Arthur MacMackin

A GAY BLADE'S LAST SCRAPE
(Beauty, March, 1916)
John Sheehan, *Carol Holloway*, Mary Talbot, Rea Berger, George Clancy, Edna Frawley, Dixie Stewart
Director: Archie MacMackin

JOHNNY'S JUMBLE
(Beauty, March, 1916) 1 Reel
John Sheehan, *Carol Holloway*, John Steppling, Marie Van Tassell, Mary Talbot, Rae Berger, Dick Rosson
Director: Archer MacMackin

BILLY VAN DEUSEN'S MUDDLE
(Beauty, March, 1916)
John Steppling, *Carol Holloway*, John Sheehan, Queenie Rosson, Dixie Stuart, Dick Rosson, Mary Talbot
Director: Archer MacMackin

NUMBER PLEASE?
(Beauty, April, 1916)
Carol Holloway, John Sheehan, John Steppling, Mary Talbot, Dick Rosson
Director: Archer MacMackin

PEANUTS AND POWDER
(Beauty, April, 1916)
Carol Holloway, John Sheehan, John Steppling, Mary Talbot, Rea Berger
Director: Archer MacMackin

A TRUNK AN' TROUBLE
(Beauty, April, 1916) 1 Reel
John Sheehan, *Carol Holloway*, Dick Rosson, Queenie Rosson, Earl Montgomery, Al Thompson
Director: Archer MacMackin

BILLY VAN DEUSEN'S ANCESTRY
(Beauty, May, 1916)
John Steppling, *Carol Holloway*, John Sheehan, Robert Klein
Director: Archer MacMackin

BILLY VAN DEUSEN'S FIANCEE
(Beauty, May, 1916)
John Steppling, John Sheehan, *Carol Holloway*
Director: Archer MacMackin
Scenario: Al Santell

BUGS AND BUGLES
(Beauty, May, 1916)
Carol Holloway, John Sheehan, John Steppling, Alexander McClure, Meta Drinkwitz, Dick Rosson
Director: Archer MacMackin

SKELLY'S SKELETON
(Beauty, May, 1916)
Carol Holloway, John Sheehan, John Steppling, Dick Rosson, John Gough
Director: Archer MacMackin
Scenario: Al Santell

BILLY VAN DEUSEN'S EGG-SPENSIVE ADVENTURE
(Beauty, June, 1916)
John Steppling, *Carol Holloway*, John Sheehan, Dick Rosson
Director: Archer MacMackin

BILLY VAN DEUSEN'S OPERATION
(Beauty, June, 1916)
John Steppling, *Carol Holloway*, John Sheehan, Dick Rosson, Robert Klein
Director: Archer MacMackin

THE HOUSE ON HOCUM HILL
(Beauty, June, 1916)
John Sheehan, *Carol Holloway*, John Steppling, Dick Rosson, John Gough
Director: Archer MacMackin

IN THE LAND OF THE TORTILLA
(Beauty, July, 1916)
Carol Holloway, John Sheehan, John Gough, John Steppling, Dick Rosson
Director: Archer MacMackin

TWO SLIPS AND A MISS
(Beauty, July, 1916) 1 Reel
Carol Holloway, John Sheehan, John Steppling, Meta Drinkwitz
Director: Archer MacMackin

WHEN ADAM HAD 'EM
(Beauty, July, 1916) 1 Reel
Carol Holloway, John Sheehan, John Steppling, Mary Talbot, Al Santell
Director: Archer MacMackin
Scenario: Al Santell

BILLY VAN DEUSEN, THE CAVE MAN
(Beauty, August, 1916) 1 Reel
John Steppling, *Carol Holloway*, John Sheehan, Dick Rosson
Director: Archer MacMackin
Scenario: Al Santell

THAT SHARP NOTE
(Beauty, October, 1916) 2 Reels
Carol Holloway, John Sheehan, John Steppling, Vera Sisson, Robert Klein, Dick Rosson, Earl Montgomery

THE PRODIGAL UNCLE
(La Salle, April, 1917) 2 Reels
Carol Holloway, Jean Otto
Director: M. de la Parelle

THE FIGHTING TRAIL
(Vitagraph, September 10, 1917) 15 Chapters
William Duncan, *Carol Holloway*, George Holt, Joe Ryan, Walter Rodgers, Fred Burns
Director: William Duncan
Chapters: (1) The Priceless Ingredient (2) The Story of Ybarra (3) Will Yaqui Joe Tell? (4) The Other Half (5) The Torrent Rush (6) The Ledge of Despair (7) The Lion's Prey (8) Strands of Doom (9) The Bridge of Death (10) The Sheriff (11) Parched Trails (12) The Desert of Torture (13) The Water Trap (14) The Trestle of Horrors (15) Out of the Flame

DEAD-SHOT BAKER
(Vitagraph, October 6, 1917) 5 Reels
William Duncan, *Carol Holloway*, J. W. Ryan, S. E. Jennings, R. C. Rogers, Otto Lederer, Charles Wheelock
Story: Alfred Henry Lewis
Director: William Duncan
Screenplay: George H. Plympton

THE TENDERFOOT
(Vitagraph, December 2, 1917) 5 Reels
William Duncan, *Carol Holloway*, Florence Dye, Joe Ryan, Walter L. Rodgers, Charles Wheelock, Hattie Buskirk, Fred Forrester
Director: William Duncan
Story: Alfred Henry Lewis

VENGEANCE AND THE WOMAN
(Vitagraph, December 24, 1917) 15 Chapters
William Duncan, *Carol Holloway*, George Holt, Tex Allen, Vincente Howard, Fred Burns, S. E. Jennings, Walter Rodgers
Director: William Duncan
Story: Albert E. Smith, Cyrus Townsend Brady
Screenplay: Garfield Thompson, Edward J. Montagne
Chapters: (1) The Oath (2) Loaded Dice (3) The Unscaled Peak (4) The Signalling Cipher (5) The Plunge of Destruction (6) Lure of Hate (7) Wolf Trap (8) Mountain of Devastation (9) Buried Alive (10) The Leap for Life (11) The Cavern of Terror (12) The Desperate Chance (13) Sands of Doom (14) The Hand of Fate (15) The Reckoning

THE JEST OF TALKY JONES
(Vitagraph, August, 1918) 2 Reels
Carol Holloway, William Lester, Robert Burns, Hattie Buskirk, Charles Force

The Iron Test (Vitagraph, 1918) – Carol Holloway, Antonio Moreno.

THE IRON TEST
(Vitagraph, October 21, 1918) 15 Chapters
Antonio Moreno, *Carol Holloway*, Hart (Jack) Hoxie, Barney Furey, Chet Ryan, Frank Jonasson, Charles G. Rich, Jack Waltemeyer
Director: R. N. Bradbury, Paul C. Hurst
Story: Albert E. Smith, Cyrus Townsend Brady
Scenario: Graham Baker
Chapters: (1) Ring of Fire (2) Van of Disaster (3) Blade of Hate (4) The Noose (5) Tide of Death (6) Fiery Fate (7) The Whirling Trap (8) The Man Eater (9) The Pit of Lost Hope (10) In the Coils (11) The Red Mask's Prey (12) The Span of Terror (13) Hanging Peril (14) Desperate Odds (15) Riding with Death

THE PERILS OF THUNDER MOUNTAIN
(Vitagraph, May 27, 1919) 15 Chapters
Antonio Moreno, *Carol Holloway*, Kate Price, Jack Waltemeyer, George Stanley, A. D. Regnier, Tote Durrow
Directors: R. N. Bradbury, W. J. Bauman
Scenario: Graham Baker
Story: Albert E. Smith, Cyrus Townsend Brady
Chapters: (1) The Spear of Malice (2) The Bridle Trap (3) Teeth of Steel (4) Cave of Terror (5) The Cliff of Treachery (6) The Tree of Torture (7) The Lightning Lure (8) The Iron Clutch (9) Prisoner of the Deep (10) The Flaming Sacrifice (11) In the Ocean's Grip (12) The Rushing Horror (13) The River of Dread (14) The Hut of Disaster (15) Fate's Verdict

THE DECEIVER
(Arrow, December, 1920) 5 Reels
Jean Hersholt, *Carol Holloway*, Lee Hill, Bert Sprotte, William Dills
Directors: Jean Hersholt, Louis H. Moomaw

A GOOD BAD MAN
(CBC, 1920) 2 Reels
Pete Morrison, *Carol Holloway*

THE SAPHEAD
(Metro, October 18, 1920) 7 Reels
Buster Keaton, William H. Crane, *Carol Holloway*, Irving Cummings, Beulah Booker, Jeffrey Williams, Edward Jobson, Edward Alexander, Jack Livingston, Edward Connolly, Odette Tyler, Katherine Albert, Henry Holte, Alfred Hollingsworth, Henry Clauss
Director: Herbert Blache
Scenario: June Mathis
Adaptation: Bronson Howard
Story: Winchell Smith, Victor Mapes, "The New Henrietta"

TWO MOONS
(Fox, December 19, 1920) 5 Reels
Buck Jones, *Carol Holloway*, Gus Saville, Edward Peil, Bert Sprotte, Slim Podgett, William Ellingford, Dick La Reno, May Foster, Billy Fay, Jim O'Neil, Eunice Murdock Moore, Edwin Booth Tilton, Louis Fitzroy, Eleanor Gilmore
Director: Edward J. LeSaint
Adaptation: Edward J. LeSaint
Story: Robert Welles Ritchie

"IF ONLY" JIM
(Universal, February 28, 1921) 5 Reels
Harry Carey, *Carol Holloway*, Ruth Royce, Duke Lee, Roy Coulson, Charles Brinley, George Bunny, Joseph Hazelton, Minnie Prevost, Thomas Smith, Pal (a dog)
Director: Jacques Jaccard
Scenario: George C. Hull
Story: Philip Verrill Mighels, "Bruvver Jim's Baby"

THE SEA LION
(Hobart Bosworth/Associated, December 5, 1921) 5 Reels
Hobart Bosworth, Emory Johnson, Bessie Love, *Carol Holloway*, Florence Carpenter, Charles Clary, Jack Curtis, Richard Morris, J. Gordon Russell
Director: Rowland V. Lee
Scenario: Joseph Franklin Poland
Story: Emilie Johnson

TRAILIN'
(Fox, December 11, 1921) 5 Reels
Jay Morley, Cecil Van Auker, J. Farrell MacDonald, *Carol Holloway*, Tom Mix, Eva Novak, Bert Sprotte, James Gordon, Sid Jordan, William Duvall, Duke Lee, Harry Dunkinson, Al Fremont, Bert Handley
Director: Lynn F. Reynolds
Adaptation: Lynn F. Reynolds
Story: Max Brand, "Trailin'"

DANGEROUS LOVE
(1921)
Carol Holloway, Harry von Meter, Marguerite Clayton, Spottiswoode Aitken, Frank Losee

UP AND GOING
(Fox, April 2, 1922) 5 Reels
Cecil Van Auker, *Carol Holloway*, Helen Field, Marion Feducha, Tom Mix, Eva Novak, William Conklin, Sidney Jordan, Tom O'Brien, Pat Chrisman, Paul Weigel
Scenario: Lynn Reynolds
Story: Tom Mix, Lynn Reynolds

RICH MEN'S WIVES
(Preferred/Al Lichtman Corp., August 19, 1922) 7 Reels
House Peters, Claire Windsor, Rosemary Theby, Gaston Glass, Myrtle Stedman, Richard Headrick, Mildred June, Charles Clary, *Carol Holloway*, Martha Mattox, William Austin
Director: Louis J. Gasnier
Scenario: Louis Zellner
Story: Frank Dazey, Agnes Christine Johnston

GOSSIP
(Universal, March 12, 1923) 5 Reels
Gladys Walton, Ramsey Wallace, Albert Prisco, Greeman Wood, *Carol Holloway*
Director: King Baggot
Scenario: Hugh Hoffman
Story: Edith Barnard Delano, "Gossip"

CORDELIA THE MAGNIFICENT
(Samuel Zierler/Metro, April 30, 1923) 7 Reels
Clara Kimball Young, Huntley Gordon, *Carol Holloway*, Lloyd Whitlock, Jacqueline Gadsden, Lewis Dayton, Mary Jane Irving, Catherine Murphy, Elinor Hancock
Director: George Archainbaud
Scenario: Frank S. Beresford
Story: Leroy Scott, "Cordelia the Magnificent"

THE RAMBLIN' KID
(Universal, September 3, 1923) 6 Reels
Hoot Gibson, Laura LaPlante, Harold Goodwin, William Welch, W. T. McCulley, Charles K. French, G. Raymond Nye, *Carol Holloway*, Goober Glenn, George King, Gyp Streeter
Director: Edward Sedgwick
Scenario: E. Richard Schayer
Story: Earl Wayland Bowman, "The Ramblin' Kid"

WHY WOMEN REMARRY
(John Gorman/Associated Photoplays, October 30, 1923) 5 Reels
Milton Sills, Ethel Grey Terry, William Lowery, Marion Feducha, *Carol Holloway*, Jeanne Carpenter, Wilfred Lucas, Clarissa Selwynne, James Barton, Anita Simons, George Hayes, Thomas McGuire, Maine Geary W. B. Clarke, Robert Walker
Director: John Gorman
Story: Van A. James

THE LOVE PIRATE
(Richard Thomas/FBO, November, 1923) 5 Reels
Melbourne MacDowell, Carmel Myers, Charles Force, Kathryn McGuire, Clyde Fillmore, John Tonkey, *Carol Holloway*, Edward W. Borman, Spottiswoode Aitken
Director: Richard Thomas
Adaptation: William Lester

BEAU BRUMMELL
(Warner Bros., March 30, 1924) 10 Reels
John Barrymore, Mary Astor, Willard Louis, Carmel Myers, Irene Rich, Alec B. Francis, William Humphreys, Richard Tucker, Andre de Beranger, Clarissa Selwynne, John J. Richardson, Claire De Lorez, Michael Dark, Templar Saxe, James A. Marcus, Betty Brice, Roland Rushton, *Carol Holloway*, Kate Lester, Rose Dione
Director: Harry Beaumont
Adaptation: Dorothy Farnum
Story: Clyde Fitch, "Beau Brummell: A Play in Four Acts"

THE RAINBOW TRAIL
(Fox, May 24, 1925) 6 Reels
Tom Mix, Anne Cornwall, George Bancroft, Lucien Littlefield, Mark Hamilton, Vivian Oakland, Thomas Delmar, Fred De Silva, Steve Clemente, Doc Roberts, *Carol Holloway*, Diana Miller
Director: Lynn Reynolds
Adaptation: Lynn Reynolds
Story: Zane Grey, "The Rainbow Trail"

JAKE THE PLUMBER
(R-C Pictures/FBO, October 16, 1927) 6 Reels
Jess Devorska, Sharon Lynn, Rose Rosanova, Ann Brody, Bud Jamison, *Carol Holloway*, William H. Tooker, Dolores Brinkman, Eddie Harris, Fanchon Frankel
Director: Edward I. Lubby
Continuity: James J. Tynan
Story: Edward I. Lubby

THE CHEROKEE KID
(FBO, October 30, 1927) 5 Reels
Tom Tyler, Sharon Lynn, Jerry Pembroke, Robert Burns, Robert Reeves, Ray Childs, James van Horn, *Carol Holloway*
Director: Robert De Lacy
Adaptation: Oliver Drake
Continuity: Oliver Drake
Story: Joseph Kane

CHICKEN A LA KING
(Fox, June 9, 1928) 7 Reels
Nancy Carroll, George Meeker, Arthur Stone, Ford Sterling, Frances Lee, *Carol Holloway*
Director: Henry Lehrman
Scenario: Izola Forrester, Mann Page
Story: Wallace A. Mannheimer, Isaac Paul, Harry Wagstaff Gribble, "Mr. Romeo"

THE SIGN OF THE CROSS
(Paramount, December 3, 1932) 124 Mins.
Fredric March, Claudette Colbert, Elissa Landi, Charles Laughton, Ian Keith, Harry Beresford, Arthur Hohl, Tommy Conlon, Vivian Tobin, Ferdinand Gottscholk, Joyzelle Joyner, Nat Pendleton, William V. Mong, Harold Healy, Robert Alexander, Robert Manning, Joe Bonomo, Otto Lederer, Lillian Leighton, Lane Chandler, Wilfred Lucas, Jerome Storm, Gertrude Norman, Florence Turner, Horace B. Carpenter, Ynez Seabury, *Carol Holloway*
Director: Cecil B. DeMille
Adaptation: Waldemar Young, Sidney Buchman
Screenplay: Waldemar Young, Sidney Buchman
Story: Wilson Barrett, Karl Struss
Producer: Cecil B. DeMille

WAY OUT WEST
(M-G-M/Roach, April 16, 1937) 65 Mins.
Stan Laurel, Oliver Hardy, James Finlayson, Sharon Lynne, *Carol Holloway*, Rosina Lawrence, The Avalon Boys (Chill Wills, Art Green, Walter Trask, Don Brookins), Stanley Fields, James Mason, Vivien Oakland, Mary Gordon, Jack Hill, Tex Driscoll, Fred Toones, Denver Dixon (Al Adamson), Ben Corbett, Buffalo Bill, Jr. (Jay Wilsey), Helen Holmes, Lester Dorr, John Ince, Fritzi Brunette, Bill Wolfe
Director: James W. Horne
Screenplay: Charles Rogers, Felix Adler, James Parrott
Story: Jack Jevne, Charles Rogers
Producer: Stan Laurel (for Hal Roach)

THE BIG BROADCAST OF 1938
(Paramount, February 18, 1938) 97 Mins.
W. C. Fields, Martha Raye, Dorothy Lamour, Shirley Ross, Lynne Overman, Bob Hope, Ben Blue, Leif Erikson, Grace Bradley, Rufe Davis, Patricia Wilder, Lionel Pape, Dorothy Howe (Virginia Vale), Russell Hicks, Kirsten Flagstad, Tito Guizar, Shep Fields and His Rippling Rhythm Orchestra, Wilfred Pelletier, Leonid Kinsky, Archie Twitchell, James Craig, Richard Denning, Rex Moore, Bernard, Punsley, James Conlin, Irving Bacon, Mary MacLaren, *Carol Holloway*, Gertrude Astor, Robert Allen, Bud Geary
Director: Mitchell Leisen
Screenplay: Walter DeLeon, Francis Martin, Ken Englund
Story: Frederick Hazlitt Brennan
Adaptation: Howard Lindsay, Russell Crouse
Producer: Harlan Thompson

THE NIGHT OF NIGHTS
(Paramount, December 1, 1939) 85 Mins.
Pat O'Brien, Olympe Bradna, Roland Young, Reginald Gardiner, George E. Stone, Murray Alper, Frank Sully, Russ Powell, Doodles Weaver, D'Arcy Corrigan, Wyndham Standing, Charles Miller, Pat O'Malley, Frank Shannon, Ronnie Rondell, Russell Coller, Joe Gilbert, Frank Melton, Hal Belfer, Ken Terrell, Gene Clark, Jimmy Fawcett, George Suzanne, Terry Shero, *Carol Holloway*, Sue Moore, Mary Gordon, Dorothea Wolbert, Oscar O'Shea, Theodore von Eltz, G. L. Sherwood, Helen Millard, Aileen Pringle, Laura Treadwell
Director: Lewis Milestone
Screenplay: Donald Ogden Stewart
Producer: George Arthur

EMERGENCY SQUAD
(Paramount, January 5, 1940) 58 Mins.
William Henry, Louise Campbell, Richard Denning, Robert Paige, John Marston, Anthony Quinn, John Miljan, Joseph Crehan, Catherine Proctor, James Seay, Lillian Elliott, Jack Kennedy, Weldon Heyburn, Stanley Blystone, Kenneth Duncan, Wilfred Roberts, Barbara Barondess, Henry Blair, Jimmy Dundee, Pat O'Malley, Donald Curtis, Sam Ash, Oscar Rudolph, Walter Tetley, Jack Egan, Darryl Hickman, Maude Fealy, Tommy Bupp, Sonny Bupp, Willard Kent, Frank Shannon, Zeffie Tilbury, Jim Pierce, Walter Fenner, Howard Mitchell, Norma Nelson, Eduardo Thomajan, Georgia Simmons, Pop Byron, Wade Boteler, Oscar Hendrian, George Bunny, George Humbert, George McKay, *Carol Holloway*, Ivan Miller, Rex Moore
Director: Edward Dmytryk
Screenplay: Garnett Weston, Stuart Palmer
Based on an idea by Robert Musel and Michael Raymond

34 • NATALIE KINGSTON

Anyone for a Swing Through the Trees?

Natalie Kingston is best known for the two Tarzan serials she made at the end of the silent era. **Tarzan, the Mighty** (1928) starred Frank Merrill as Tarzan and Natalie as Mary Trevor, forerunner of Jane. In **Tarzan, The Tiger** (1929) she became the familiar Jane, with Merrill as Tarzan again. Both Universal serials proved extremely popular with audiences. Less popular was **Pirates of Panama** (1929), in which she was cast opposite Jay Wilsey, better known as Buffalo Bill, Jr.

Natalie was on the stage before entering films in 1923, and her early picture work was in Mack Sennett comedies. She could never seem to get her career off the ground, even though great things were predicted for her in 1927 when she was selected as a Wampas Baby Star. But her thirty-chapter swing through the jungle as Tarzan's mate, plus her twelve-chapter defiance of the Panamanian pirates, guaranteed her a place in serialdom (and remembrance by a select fraternity of movie fans with memories like elephants for their own favorites). Greater and more successful actresses have been forgotten, but Natalie lives on in that continued-next-week world kept alive by those who choose to relive the happier moments of childhood.

Natalie Kingston.

NATALIE KINGSTON Filmography

THE DAREDEVIL
(Mack Sennett/Pathé, November 23, 1923)
Harry Langdon, *Natalie Kingston*

YUKON JAKE
(Mack Sennett/Pathé, May 6, 1924) 2 Reels
Ben Turpin, *Natalie Kingston*, Madeline Hurlock, Kalla Pasha, The Sennett Bathing Beauties
Director: Del Lord
Story: Mack Sennett
Producer: Mack Sennett

ALL NIGHT LONG
(Mack Sennett/Pathé, October 29, 1924)
Harry Langdon, *Natalie Kingston*
Producer: Mack Sennett

THE REEL VIRGINIAN
(Mack Sennett/Pathé, December 3, 1924) 2 Reels
Ben Turpin, *Natalie Kingston*, Madeleine Hurlock
Directors: Edgar Kennedy, Reggie Norris
Producer: Mack Sennett

FEET OF MUD
(Mack Sennett/Pathé, December 3, 1924) 2 Reels
Harry Langdon, *Natalie Kingston*, Yorke Sherwood, Vernon Dent, Malcolm Waite
Director: Harry Edwards
Producer: Mack Sennett

ROMEO AND JULIET
(Mack Sennett, 1924) 2 Reels
Alice Day, Madeleine Hurlock, Ben Turpin, *Natalie Kingston*

HIS MARRIAGE WOW
(Mack Sennett/Pathé, December 26, 1924) 2 Reels
Harry Langdon, *Natalie Kingston*, William McCall, Vernon Dent
Director: Harry Edwards
Producer: Mack Sennett

REMEMBER WHEN?
(Mack Sennett/Pathé, February 13, 1925) 2 Reels
Harry Langdon, *Natalie Kingston*, Vernon Dent
Director: Harry Edwards
Producer: Mack Sennett

LUCKY STARS
(Mack Sennett/Pathé, July 20, 1925) 2 Reels
Harry Langdon, *Natalie Kingston*, Vernon Dent
Director: Harry Edwards
Producer: Mack Sennett
Story: Mack Sennett

BOOBS IN THE WOODS
(Mack Sennett, 1925) 2 Reels
Vernon Dent, *Natalie Kingston*, Harry Langdon

SOLDIER MAN
(Mack Sennett/Pathé, April 28, 1926) 2 Reels
Harry Langdon, *Natalie Kingston*, Frank Whitson
Director: Harry Edwards
Story: Mack Sennett
Producer: Mack Sennett

WET PAINT
(Famous Players-Lasky/Paramount, May 3, 1926) 6 Reels
Raymond Griffith, Helene Costello, Bryant Washburn, *Natalie Kingston*, Henry Kolker
Director: Arthur Rosson
Scenario: Lloyd Corrigan
Story: Reginald Morris

LOST AT SEA
(Tiffany, August 15, 1926) 7 Reels
Huntly Gordon, Lowell Sherman, Jane Novak, *Natalie Kingston*, Billy Kent Schaefer, Joan Standing, William Walling, Rev. Neal Dodd, Buddy (a dog)
Director: Louis J. Gasnier
Producer: Phil Goldstone
Scenario: Esther Shulkin

DON JUAN'S THREE NIGHTS
(Henry Hobart/First National, September 4, 1926) 7 Reels
Lewis Stone, Shirley Mason, Malcolm McGregor, Myrtle Stedman, Betty Francisco, Kalla Paha, Alma Bennett, *Natalie Kingston*, Marie Carillo, Jed Prouty, Madeline Hurlock, Gertrude Astor
Director: John Francis Dillon
Screenplay: Clara Beranger
Story: Ludwig Biro, "Don Juans drei Nachte"

KID BOOTS
(Famous Players-Lasky/Paramount, October 4, 1926) 9 Reels
Eddie Cantor, Clara Bow, Billie Dove, Lawrence Gray, *Natalie Kingston*, Malcolm Waite, William Worthington, Harry von Meter, Fred Esmelton
Director: Frank Tuttle
Screenplay: Tom Gibson
Scenario: Luther Reed
Story: William Anthony McGuire, Otto Harback, J. P. McCarthy, "Kid Boots"

THE SILENT LOVER
(First National, November 21, 1926) 7 Reels
Milton Sills, *Natalie Kingston*, William Humphrey, Arthur Edmund Carewe, William V. Mong, Viola Dana, Claude King, Charlie Murray, Arthur Stone, Alma Bennett, Montagu Love
Director: George Archainbaud
Scenario: Carey Wilson
Story: Lajos Biro, "Dear Legioner"

THE NIGHT OF LOVE
(Samuel Goldwyn/United Artists, January 22, 1927) 8 Reels
Ronald Colman, Vilma Banky, Montagu Love, *Natalie Kingston*, John George, B. Hyman, Gibson Gowland, Laska Winters, Sally Rand
Director: George Fitzmaurice
Adaptation: Lenore J. Coffee
Scenario: Lenore J. Coffee
Story: Pedro Calderon de la Barca

The Pirates of Panama (Universal, 1929) – Natalie Kingston seems undisturbed by the peg-legged, bearded corpse at her right or the two pirates behind her as she reads a letter from home.

LOVE MAKES 'EM WILD
(Fox, March 6, 1927) 6 Reels
Johnny Harron, Sally Phipps, Ben Bard, Arthur Houseman, J. Farrell MacDonald, *Natalie Kingston*, Albert Gran, Florence Gilbert, Earle Mohan, Coy Watson, Jr., Noah Young, William B. Davidson
Director: Albert Ray
Scenario: Harold Shumate
Story: Florence Ryerson, "Willie the Worm"

LONG PANTS
(Harry Langdon/First National, March 26, 1927) 6 Reels
Harry Langdon, Gladys Brockwell, Al Roscoe, Alma Bennett, Frankie Darro, Priscilla Bonner, *Natalie Kingston*, John Darrow, Betty Francisco, Ruth Hiatt, William "Bud" Jamison
Director: Frank Capra
Adaptation: Robert
Story: Arthur Ripley

HIS FIRST FLAME
(Mack Sennett/Pathé, May 3, 1927) 6 Reels
Harry Langdon, Ruth Hiatt, *Natalie Kingston*, Vernon Dent, William "Bud" Jamison, Dot Farley
Director: Harry Edwards
Scenario: Arthur Ripley, Frank Capra

LOST AT THE FRONT
(John McCormick/First National, May 29, 1927) 6 Reels
George Sidney, Charlie Murray, *Natalie Kingston*, John Kolb, Max Asher, Brooks Benedict, Ed Brady, Harry Lipman, Nita Martan, Nina Romano
Director: Del Lord
Scenario: Hampton Del Ruth
Producer: Frank Griffin

FRAMED
(First National, June 19, 1927) 6 Reels
Milton Sills, *Natalie Kingston*, E. J. Radcliffe, Charles Gerrard, Edward Peil, Burr McIntosh, Natli Barr, John Miljan
Director: Charles J. Brabin
Adaptation: Mary O'Hara
Continuity: Mary O'Hara
Story: George W. Sutton, Jr., "The Dawn of My Tomorrow"
Producer: Ray Rockett

FIGURES DON'T LIE
(Paramount/Famous Players-Lasky, October 8, 1927) 6 Reels
Esther Ralston, Richard Arlen, Ford Sterling, Doris Hill, Blanche Payson, *Natalie Kingston*
Director: Edward Sutherland
Screenplay: Ethel Doherty, Louise Long
Adaptation: Grover Jones
Story: B. F. Ziedman

THE HARVESTER
(R-C Pictures/FBO, November 7, 1927) 8 Reels
Orville Caldwell, *Natalie Kingston*, Will R. Walling, Jay Hunt, Lola Todd, Edward Hearn, Fanny Midgley
Director: Leo Meehan
Scenario: Dorothy Yost
Story: Gene Stratton Porter, "The Harvester"

GIRL IN EVERY PORT
(Fox, February 26, 1928) 6 Reels
Victor McLaglen, Maria Casajuana, Natalie Joyce, Dorothy Mathews, Elena Jurado, Louise Brooks, Francis McDonald, Phalba Morgan, Felix Valle, Greta Yoltz (Eileen Sedgwick). Leila Hyams, Robert Armstrong, Sally Rand, *Natalie Kingston*, Caryl Lincoln
Director: Howard Hawks
Scenario: Seton I. Miller
Story: Howard Hawks
Screenplay: James K. McGuinness

THE PORT OF MISSING GIRLS
(Brenda, March 1928) 8 Reels
Barbara Bedford, Malcolm McGregor, *Natalie Kingston*, Hedda Hopper, George Irving, Wyndham Standing, Charles Gerard, Paul Nicholson, Edith Yorke, Bodil Rosing, Rosemary Theby, Lotus Thompson, Amber Norman
Director: Irving Cummings
Scenario: Howard Estabrook
Story: Howard Estabrook

STREET ANGEL
(Fox, April 9, 1928) 10 Reels
Janet Gaynor, Charles Farrell, Alberto Rabagliati, Gino Conti, Guido Trento, Henry Armetta, Louis Liggett, Milton Dickinson, Helena Herman, *Natalie Kingston*, David Kashner, Jennie Bruno
Director: Frank Borzage
Scenario: Marion Orth
Adaptation: Philip Klein, Henry Roberts Symonds
Story: Monckton Hoffe, "Christilenda"

PAINTED POST
(Fox, July 1, 1928) 5 Reels
Tom Mix, *Natalie Kingston*, Philo McCullough, Al St. John, Fred Gamble, Tony (a horse)
Director: Eugene Forde
Scenario: Buckleigh F. Oxford
Story: Harry Sinclair Drago

TARZAN, THE MIGHTY
(Universal, August 13, 1928) 15 Chapters
Frank Merrill, *Natalie Kingston*, Al Ferguson, Robert Nelson, Lorimer Johnston
Director: Jack Nelson, Ray Taylor
Story: Edgar Rice Burroughs
Chapters: (1) The Terror of Tarzan (2) The Love Cry (3) The Call of the Jungle (4) The Lion's Leap (5) Flames of Hate (6) The Fiery Pit (7) The Leopard's Lair (8) The Jungle Traitor (9) Lost in the Jungle (10) Jaws of Death (11) A Thief in the Night (12) The Enemy of Tarzan (13) Perilous Paths (14) Facing Death (15) The Reckoning

RIVER OF ROMANCE
(Paramount/Famous Players-Lasky, June 29, 1929) 8 Reels
Charles "Buddy" Rogers, Mary Brian, June Collyer, Henry B. Walthall, Wallace Beery, Fred Kohler, *Natalie Kingston*, Walter McGrail, Anderson Lawler, Mrs. George Fawcett, George Reed
Director: Richard Wallace
Screenplay: Ethel Doherty
Adaptation: Dan Totheroh, John V. A. Weaver
Story: Booth Tarkington, "Magnolia"

PIRATES OF PANAMA
(Universal, July 8, 1929) 12 Chapters
Jay Wilsey (Buffalo Bill, Jr.), *Natalie Kingston*, Al Ferguson, George Ovey, Mary Sutton, Otto Bibbler
Director: Ray Taylor
Scenario: Arthur Henry Gooden, George Morgan
Story: William McLeod Raine
Chapters: (1) Pirates Gold (2) Mutiny (3) The Treasure Chest (4) The Pirates' Secret (5) Vengeance (6) Trapped by the Tide (7) The Shadow of Death (8) The Menacing Swamp (9) The Signal of Hope (10) Two Lives for One (11) The Price of Greed (12) The Greatest Treasure

HOLD YOUR MAN
(Universal, September 15, 1929) 6 Reels
Laura LaPlante, Walker Kolk, Eugene Borden, Mildred Van Dorn, Walter F. Scott, *Natalie Kingston*
Director: Emmett J. Flynn
Continuity: Harold Shumate
Story: Maxine Alton

TARZAN, THE TIGER
(Universal, December 9, 1929) 15 Chapters
Frank Merrill, *Natalie Kingston*, Lillian Worth, Al Ferguson, Sheldon Lewis, Frank Lanning
Director: Henry McRae
Scenario: Ian McClosky Heath
Story: Edgar Rice Burroughs, "The Jewels of Opar"
Chapters: (1) Call of the Jungle (2) The Road to Opar (3) The Altar of the Flaming God (4) The Vengeance of La (5) Condemned to Death (6) Tantor, the Terror (7) In Deadly Perio (8) Loop of Death (9) Flight of Werper (10) Prisoner of the Apes (11) The Jaws of Death (12) The Jewels of Opar (13) A Human Sacrifice (14) Tarzan's Rage (15) Tarzan's Triumph

THE SWELLHEAD
(Tiffany, March 20, 1930) 7 Reels
James Gleason, Johnny Walker, Marion Shilling, *Natalie Kingston*, Paul C. Hurst, Freeman Wood, Lillian Elliott
Director: James Flood
Scenario: Richard Cahoon, Adele Buffington
Story: A. P. Younger, "Cyclone Hickey"

HER WEDDING NIGHT
(Paramount, September 18, 1930) 9 Reels
Clara Bow, Ralph Forbes, Charles Ruggles, "Skeets" Gallagher, Geneva Mitchell, Rosita Moreno, *Natalie Kingston*, Wilson Benge, Lillian Elliott
Director: Frank Tuttle
Screenplay: Henry Myers
Story: Avery Hopwood, "Little Miss Bluebeard"
Associate Producer: E. Lloyd Sheldon

UNDER TEXAS SKIES
(Syndicate, November 15, 1930) 5 Reels
Bob Custer, *Natalie Kingston*, Bill Cody, Lane Chandler, Tom London, Bob Roper, William McCall, Joe Marba, Ted Adams
Director: J. P. McGowan
Screenplay: G. A. Durlan
Story: G. A. Durlan
Producers: Harry S. Webb, F. E. Douglas

FORGOTTEN
(Invincible, 1933) 65 Mins.
Lee Kohlmar, June Clyde, William Collier, Jr., Leon Waycoff (Ames), Selmer Jackson, Natalie Moorhead, *Natalie Kingston*, Otto Lederer, Tom Ricketts, Jean Hersholt, Jr.
Director: Richard Thorpe
Screenplay: Harry Sauber
Story: Harry Sauber
Producer: Maury M. Cohen

HIS PRIVATE SECRETARY
(Showmen's Pictures, 1933) 60 Mins.
Evalyn Knapp, John Wayne, Reginald Barlow, Alac B. Francis, Arthur Hoyt, *Natalie Kingston*, Patrick Cunning, Al St. John, Hugh Kidder, Mickey Rentschler
Director: Philip H. Whitman
Screenplay: John Francis Natteford
Story: Lew Collins
Producer: Sam Katzman

Cleo Madison.

35 • CLEO MADISON

A Gal Who Could Be Counted on to Do Her Job in a Competent, Workmanlike Manner

Cleo Madison's claim to serial fame rests on **The Trey O' Hearts** (1914) and **The Great Radium Mystery** (1919), both products of Universal's serial factory.

The Trey O'Hearts had the usual quota of hair-raising thrills crammed into its fifteen chapters and an excellent leading man in George Larkin, who subsequently built a reputation in a number of serials and action films. But its real claim to uniqueness was that Cleo played a double role-- that of twin sisters, one good, one bad. She measured up to the challenge admirably.

Unlike most later serials, **The Trey O' Hearts** was designed primarily as adult entertainment, not as Saturday matinee fare for the kiddies. Judith was the wicked sister who, along with her embittered, crippled father, tried to kill hero Larkin whose dead father was blamed for the affliction of the old man. Rose was the opposite of her sister and father. Not only was she a lovable person, but she was in love with Larkin. Much confusion results from the fact that the two girls are identical twins. In the course of things Judith falls in love with Larkin too, and in the final chapter, when Rose marries Larkin and is killed when a bolt of lightning strikes the chapel, Judith is able to take her place while Larkin is unconscious from the accident. When he regains consciousness, Larkin thinks he is being nursed and comforted by his wife Rose. Thus the heroine died, and the repentant villainess lived with the man she had come to love, with the hero and the world never the wiser.

The Great Radium Mystery (1919) made its chief pitch for acceptance on the basis of Cleo's name, which by then carried some weight with theatre audiences. The action content of the eighteen chapters is reflected in such titles as "The Death Trap," "The Fatal Ride," "The Swing for Life," "The Torture Chamber," "The Tunnel of

The Trey O' Hearts (Universal, 1914) – Cleo Madison.

Doom," "In the Clutches of the Mad Man," "The Roaring Volcano," "The Scalding Pit," and "Over the Cataract." The cast also boasted Bob Reeves, Eileen Sedgwick, Robert Kortman, and Ed Brady, each of whom achieved a modicum of success in the action field. And it was the first serial on which Robert F. Hill was given directorial duties. He subsequently became a top-flight serial director.

Cleo Madison was born in Bloomington, Illinois, but soon moved to California. Little is known of her personal life, but around 1910 she presented herself at the stage door of a theater in Santa Barbara and secured work with the company, then rehearsing for a tour. By the time the company was ready for the road, Cleo had advanced so rapidly that she was given the leading role. Before long she was manager. She continued upon the stage for several years and played with such artists as Virginia Harned and James K. Hackett, noted thespians of the day. Ultimately, a company was organized to star her and she played the big vaudeville circuits in such well-known successes as "The Bishop's Carriage," "Paid in Full," "The Great Divide," and "Wildfire."

When Cleo returned home to California in 1913 for a vacation, she found a growing art, right in her line, just outside the door. Motion pictures had begun to make quite a noise--in a silent sort of way. Influenced by an invalid younger sister to whom she was devoted, and because she was tired of the road, Cleo went out to the old Universal lot and obtained work easily on the basis of her stage successes.

Her first film of record was **His Pal's Request** (1913), believed to be a one-reeler. Two-reelers with Wallace Reid, J. Warren Kerrigan, and George Larkin, among others, followed. And along with just about everyone else on the lot, she appeared in Universal's one-reel promotional film, **The Great Universal Mystery** (1914). Because of the fabulous success of **What Happened to Mary** (1912), **The Adventures of Kathlyn** (1913), and **The Perils of Pauline** (1914), Universal rushed to get on the bandwagon to serial popularity and fortunes. Its first was **Lucille Love, Girl of Mystery** (1914), which established the serial team of Francis Ford and Grace Cunard. The second was **The Trey O' Hearts** (1914), which also went over big, and Cleo found herself much in demand thereafter, although she was cast in only one other serial.

Cleo quickly won a place of distinction as an emotional actress, scoring success after success in the productions of Otis Turner. She and Lon Chaney, not yet known as "The Man of a Thousand Faces," made several good films together: **The Sin of Olga Brandt** (1914), **The Pine's Revenge** (1915), **The Fascination of the Fleur De Lis** (1915), **Alas and Alack** (1915), and **A Mother's Atonement** (1915), in which she played the dual roles of mother and daughter.

Cleo became a triple threat in 1915, turning her talents to directing and producing in addition to acting. She had become temperamental after her success in **The Trey O' Hearts**, and wanted to direct her own pictures. Early directorial efforts included **Liquid Dynamite** (1915), **The Ring of Destiny** (1915), and **The Power of Fascination** (1915), which had up-and-coming Jack Holt as her male lead. Cleo could also write a scenario when she put her mind to it, as, for example, **Her Bitter Cup** (1916), a five-reel feature. As a director, Cleo met with only moderate success. Had she limited herself to acting, her career might have prospered more, and without the pressures to which she subjected herself.

Cleo could handle Westerns as well as anything else. In **Dolores, Lady of Sorrows** (1914) she plays a Mexican girl who thwarts the villain's nefarious schemes. **Sealed Orders** (1914) finds her as a nice girl lured to a Western bordello. J. Warren Kerrigan is the hero, and the film is replete with roof-top chases, à la Ken Maynard, and a fierce gun-fighting episode as Cleo's honor is protected. In **The Guilty One** (1916) she is a Western lass with plenty of pluck who helps the hero clear himself with the law.

Tear-jerker melodramas seemed especially suited to Cleo, and she handled them effectively. For example, in **When the Wolf Howls** (1916) she plays the pregnant wife of a poverty stricken artist. Cleo is obsessed with the idea that she is a millstone around her husband's neck and decides to take poison and free him. Unknown to her, he has sold a painting and hidden the check in a little sock Cleo had made for the baby. In an adjoining room, he waits impatiently for Cleo's joyful discovery of the money as she is about to drink from the bottle of poison. Finally, unable to stand the suspense any longer, he rushes in to put the sock containing the check into Cleo's hands, unaware that the bottle she has dropped at his sudden appearance is filled with poison.

In another film of the tear-jerker type, **The Girl Who Lost** (1917), Cleo is a chorus girl supporting her younger sister whose ambition is to be an actress. When Cleo has to go on the road, she leaves her sister, Frances, in care of the landlady. But Frances becomes dissatisfied, seeks employment, and before long has sacrificed her honor. When Cleo returns, she learns that her young sister is about to become a mother and determines to avenge her. Chance makes her acquainted with the son of the man who despoiled Frances. The son, Hayden, is engaged to Millicent, a nice girl. Insidiously, Cleo wins his affections, until he is willing to throw Millicent aside. Cleo then delivers her ultimatum to the father, who wants his son married to Millicent; either he will marry her sister, or she will marry Hayden. The father decides he will right the wrong. Though Cleo has learned to love the son, she now has to give him up in order that her sister may be happy.

To Another Woman (1916) was also designed to bring handkerchiefs to the ladies' eyes. William Mong is no longer in love with his wife, Cleo, who spends all her time taking care of their child, a frail little girl. Mong seeks diversion with a fast woman, who talks him into having Cleo committed to a sanitarium. Mong bribes the head of the sanitarium and Cleo is taken away. Some months later a new assistant arrives at the sanitarium and discovers that she is sane; after a number of setbacks, he is able to help her escape, and she ultimately confronts her husband and his mistress, who by this time is living in her home and mistreating her child. Cleo reproaches her husband and leaves with the child; the other woman, thinking that she is no longer in favor, kills Mong. Cleo is then free to marry the young doctor who helped her. Such films were popular in the World War I era, and Cleo worked steadily.

When the field broadened and studios began springing up almost overnight, Cleo found herself much in demand. She starred in such productions as **The Romance of Tarzan** (1918), **The Girl from Nowhere** (1919), the previously mentioned serial **The Great Radium Mystery** (1919), **The Price of Redemption** (1920), and **The Lure of Youth** (1921). Constant effort brought on a nervous breakdown, which forced her to retire to private life for more than year. But with her health restored, and still possessing the talent and personality which made her a distinctive favorite for so many years, she came back to make several films in 1923 and '24, including **Gold Madness** (1923), an adaptation of the James Oliver Curwood story titled "The Man from Ten Strike." Cleo left the screen in 1924. Why, or what she did thereafter, is unknown to the author.

On March 11, 1964, at the age of eighty-one, Cleo suffered a fatal heart attack in Burbank, California, leaving her sister as her closest surviving relative.

CLEO MADISON Filmography

THE TRAP
(Universal-Powers, October 3, 1913) 2 Reels
Cleo Madison, Lon Chaney
Director: Edwin August

HIS PAL'S REQUEST
(Universal-Powers, October 11, 1913)
Cleo Madison

THE HEART OF A CRACKSMAN
(Universal-Powers, 1913)
Wallace Reid, *Cleo Madison*, James Neill, Ed Brady, Marcia Moore
Directors: Willis Lobards, Wallace Reid
Scenario: Wallace Reid

THE BUCCANEERS
(Universal-Gold Seal, 1913) 3 Reels
Joseph Singleton, David M. Hartford, *Cleo Madison,* Antrim Short, Frank Lloyd
Director: Otis Turner
Supervisor: Frank Lloyd

UNDER THE BLACK FLAG
(Universal-Gold Seal, 1913) 3 Reels
David M. Hartford, *Cleo Madison,* Joseph Singleton, Frank Lloyd, Howard Hickman
Director: Otis Turner

CAPTAIN KIDD
(Universal-101 Bison, 1913) 3 Reels
David M. Hartford, Joseph Singleton, *Cleo Madison,* Frank Lloyd, Howard Hickman
Director: Otis Turner

SHADOWS OF LIFE
(Universal-Rex, 1913) 2 Reels
Lois Weber, Rupert Julian, *Cleo Madison,* Frank Lloyd, Phillips Smalley
Directors: Phillips Smalley and Lois Weber
Supervisor: Lois Weber and H. J. Clawson

THE MAN BETWEEN
(Universal-Victor, February 28, 1914) 2 Reels
J. Warren Kerrigan, *Cleo Madison*

HEARTS AND FLOWERS
(Universal-Victor, March 9, 1914) 2 Reels
J. Warren Kerrigan, Edith Bostwick, *Cleo Madison*, George Periolat, Billy Abbott

SEALED ORDERS
(Universal-Victor, March 28, 1914) 2 Reels
J. Warren Kerrigan, *Cleo Madison*
Story: Eugene Manlove Rhodes

DOLORES D'ARADA, LADY OF SORROW
(Universal-Bison, April 11, 1914) 2 Reels
Cleo Madison

THE HILLS OF SILENCE
(Universal-101 Bison, May 16, 1914) 3 Reels
Cleo Madison, Frank Lanning, Beatrice Van, Edwin Alexander, Ray Gallagher

THE STRENUOUS LIFE
(Universal-Joker, May 23, 1914) 1 Reel
Cleo Madison, Mae Talbot Winchell, Edward Sloman, William Dale, George Larkin

JUDITH FINDS THE TRAIL OF THE FUGITIVES.

The Trey O' Hearts (Universal, 1914) – Cleo Madison.

THE FEUD
(Universal-Powers, May 29, 1914) 2 Reels
Cleo Madison, George Larkin

THE LAST OF THEIR RACE
(Universal-Powers, June 20, 1914) 2 Reels
Cleo Madison

THE LOVE VICTORIOUS
(Universal-Powers, June 26, 1914) 2 Reels
Cleo Madison, May E. Benson
Director: Wilfred Lucas
Story: Bess Meredyth

THE MYSTERY OF WICKHAM HALL
(Universal-Powers, July 4, 1914) 3 Reels
Cleo Madison
Story: Bess Meredyth

THE GREAT UNIVERSAL MYSTERY
(Universal-Nestor, July 10, 1914) 1 Reel
King Baggott, Pauline Bush, Ford Sterling, William Clifford, Lois Weber, Lee Moran, Ella Hall, Hobart Henley, William Welsh, Betty Schade, Leah Baird, Howard Crampton, Al Christie, Carl Laemmle, Maurice Fleckes, Francis Ford, Bob Leonard, *Cleo Madison,* Victoria Forde, Murdock MacQuarrie, Phillips Smalley, Eddie Lyons, Marie Walcamp, Fred Balshofer, Irene Wallace, Edna Maison
Director: Allan Dwan
(a promotional film for Universal)

THE SEVERED HAND
(Universal-Powers, July 11, 1914) 3 Reels
Cleo Madison, George Larkin, Edwin Alexander, Edward Sloman, Frank Lanning, William V. Mong
Story: Bess Meredyth

THE TREY O'HEARTS
(Universal-Gold Seal, August 1, 1914) 15 Chapters
George Larkin, *Cleo Madison,* Edward Sloman, Roy Hanford, Tom Welsh, Charles Brinley, Doris Pawn, George Bacus
Directors: Wilfred Lucas and Henry McRae
Scenario: Bess Meredyth
Story: Louis Joseph Vance
Chapters: (1) Flower of the Flame (2) White Water (3) The Sea Venture (4) Dead Reckoning (5) The Sunset Tide (6) The Crack O'Doom (7) Stalemate (8) The Mock Rose (9) As the Crow Flies (10) Steel Ribbons (11) The Painted Hills (12) Mirage (13) The Jaws of Death (14) The First Law (15) The Last Trump

THE MASTER KEY
(Universal, November 28, 1914) 15 Chapters
Robert Leonard, Ella Hall, Harry Carter, Jean Hathaway, Alfred Hickman, Wilbur Higby, Charles E. Manly, Jack Holt, Jim Corey, Alan Forest, Mack V. Wright, Rupert Julian, Edward A. Mills, *Cleo Madison,* Robert Chandler, Marc Robbins
Director: Robert Leonard
Scenario: Calder Johnston
Story: John Fleming Wilson
Supervisor: Otis Turner
Chapters: (1) Gold Madness (2) A Shipwreck and Wrecked Hopes (3) The Ghost Appears (4) Over the Divide (5) The Lost Vein (6) Wilkerson Strikes (7) The Battle in the Dark (8) The Struggle on the Roof (9) Arrested for Murder (10) The Fight for the Mine (11) The Secret of the Chest (12) The Quest for the Idol (13) A Queer Alliance (14) The God Takes Toll (15) Fate Unlocks the Doors

THE SIN OF OLGA BRANDT
(Universal-Rex, December, 1914) 2 Reels
Cleo Madison, Lon Chaney, William C. Dowlan, Pauline Bush
Director: Joseph De Grasse

DAMON AND PYTHIAS
(Universal, December, 1914) 6 Reels
Herbert Rawlinson, William Worthington, *Cleo Madison*, Ann Little, Frank Lloyd
Director: Otis Turner
Scenario: Allan Dwan
Story: E. Bulwer Lytton

THE MEXICAN'S LAST RAID
(Universal-Nestor, 1914) 1 Reel
Cleo Madison, Frank Lloyd, Victoria Forde, J. Farrell MacDonald

UNJUSTLY ACCUSED
(Universal-101 Bison, 1914) 2 Reels
William Ellingsford, *Cleo Madison*, David M. Hartford, Frank Lloyd
Director: David M. Hartford
Supervisor: Frank Lloyd

THE LAW OF HIS KIND
(Universal-Rex, 1914) 2 Reels
Rex de Rosselli, Herbert Rawlinson, *Cleo Madison*, Frank Lloyd
Supervisor: Phillip Walsh

THE DEAD LINE
(Universal-Nestor, 1914) 1 Reel
Allan Forrest, *Cleo Madison*, Frank Lloyd, David M. Hartford

A WOMAN'S DEBT
(Universal-Gold Seal, January 9, 1915) 2 Reels
Cleo Madison, Joe King

THE MYSTERY WOMAN
(Universal, January 30, 1915) 2 Reels
Cleo Madison, Joe King, Edward Sloman
Story: Bess Meredyth

THE CRYSTAL
(Universal, 1915)
Cleo Madison, William Dyer, Francis McDonald

HAUNTED HEARTS
(Universal-Gold Seal, February, 1915) 2 Reels
Cleo Madison, Joseph King, Edward Sloman
Director: W. T. McCulley

THEIR HOUR
(Universal-Gold Seal, February, 1915) 2 Reels
Cleo Madison, Wilfred Lucas, Zoe Beck, Buster Emmons
Story: Bess Meredyth

THE MOTHER INSTINCT
(Universal-Bison, March 10, 1915) 3 Reels
Cleo Madison, Joseph King, Edward Sloman
Director: Wilfred Lucas
Scenario: Bess Meredyth
Story: Mrs. Haines V. Reed

DIANA OF EAGLE MOUNTAIN
(Universal-101 Bison, March 13, 1915) 2 Reels
Cleo Madison, Ray Hanford, Joe King, Edward Sloman
Director: W. T. McCulley

THE DUCHESS
(Universal-Gold Seal, March 19, 1915) 3 Reels
Cleo Madison, Joe King
Director: W. T. McCulley
Scenario: Helen Bailey

HUMAN MENACE
(Universal-Gold Seal, March 23, 1915) 2 Reels
Cleo Madison
Director: Wilfred Lucas
Screenplay: Bess Meredyth

WILD IRISH ROSE
(Universal-Gold Seal, April 5, 1915) 2 Reels
Cleo Madison, Joseph King
Director: Charles Giblyn
Scenario: George H. Hall

THE WHIRLING DISC
(Universal-Gold Seal, April 20, 1915) 2 Reels
Cleo Madison, Joe King, Ray Hanford, Albert MacQuarrie
Director: Charles Giblyn
Screenplay: H. G. Stafford

THE FAITH OF HER FATHERS
(Universal-Gold Seal, April 28, 1915) 3 Reels
Cleo Madison, Joe King, Murdock MacQuarrie
Director: Charles Giblyn
Screenplay: Isador Bernstein
Story: Bruno Lessing

THE DANCER
(Universal-Gold Seal, May 12, 1915) 3 Reels
Cleo Madison, Joseph King, Charles Giblyn
Director: Charles Giblyn
Scenario: Ida May Park

THE WAYS OF A MAN
(Universal-Gold Seal, June 12, 1915) 2 Reels
Cleo Madison, Hobart Henley, Ray Hanford
Director: Charles Giblyn

THE PEOPLE OF THE PIT
(Universal-Gold Seal, July 6, 1915) 2 Reels
Joseph King, *Cleo Madison,* Ray Hanford, Agnes Vernon
Director: Charles Giblyn
Scenario: Grant Carpenter

THE FLIGHT OF A NIGHT BIRD
(Universal-Gold Seal, July 20, 1915) 2 Reels
Hobart Henley, *Cleo Madison,* Agnes Vernon
Director: Charles Giblyn
Scenario: H. G. Stafford

A FIERY INTRODUCTION
(Universal-Gold Seal, August 14, 1915) 2 Reels
Cleo Madison, S. J. Bingham, Ray Hanford, Arthur Moon
Director: Charles Giblyn
Scenario: H. G. Stafford
Story: Julius G. Furthmann

EXTRAVAGANCE
(Universal-Gold Seal, August 16, 1915) 3 Reels
Cleo Madison, Adele Farrington, Wyndham Standing, Hobart Henley
Director: Charles Giblyn
Story: Hugh Weir

THE PINE'S REVENGE
(Universal-Rex, September 11, 1915) 2 Reels
Cleo Madison, Arthur Shirley, Lon Chaney, Millard K. Wilson
Director: Joseph De Grasse
Scenario: Nell Shipman, "The King's Keeper"

AGNES KEMPLERS SACRIFICE
(Universal-Rex, September 12, 1915) 2 Reels
Hobart Henley, Jean Hathaway, *Cleo Madison,* Hilda Sloman, Ray Hanford, Agnes Vernon, Baby French
Story: Tom Lewis

THE FASCINATION OF THE FLEUR DE LIS
(Universal-Rex, September 16, 1915) 3 Reels
Cleo Madison, Lon Chaney, M. K. Wilson, Arthur Shirley
Director: Joseph De Grasse
Scenario: Bess Meredyth

ALAS AND ALACK
(Universal-Rex, October 2, 1915) 1 Reel
Cleo Madison, Arthur Shirley, Margaret Whisler, Lon Chaney
Director: Joseph De Grasse
Story: Ida May Park

A MOTHER'S ATONEMENT
(Universal-Rex, October 17, 1915) 3 Reels
Cleo Madison, Lon Chaney, Ben Rothwell, Millard K. Wilson, Wyndham Standing, Arthur Shirley, Miss Standing
Director: Joseph De Grasse
Story: Ida May Park

LIQUID DYNAMITE
(Universal-Rex, November 14, 1915) 1 Reel
Cleo Madison, Thomas Chatterton, Mr. Abbott
Director: Cleo Madison
Scenario: Olga Printzlau Clark
Story: Joe King

THE RING OF DESTINY
(Universal-Rex, November 20, 1915) 2 Reels
Cleo Madison, Joseph King, Hoot Gibson, William Gettinger
Director: Cleo Madison
Scenario: Olga Printzlau
Story: Marshall Stedman

THE POWER OF FASCINATION
(Universal-Rex, December 3, 1915) 1 Reel
Cleo Madison, Jack Holt, Thomas Chatterton, Carrie Fowler, Jack Francis, Jack Wells
Story: Charles Saksby
Producer: Cleo Madison

A SOUL ENSLAVED
(Universal, January, 1916) 5 Reels
Cleo Madison, Irma Sorter, Tom Chatterton, Douglas Gerrard, Lule Warrenton, Marguerite Gibson, Alfred Allen
Director: Cleo Madison
Scenario: Olga Printzlau
Story: Adele Farrington

HIS RETURN
(Universal-Rex, January 3, 1916) 1 Reel
Cleo Madison, Jack Bryce, Mae Gaston, Raymond Russell, Helen Wright
Director: Cleo Madison
Scenario: Helen Bailey
Story: Helen Bailey
Producer: Cleo Madison

HER DEFIANCE
(Universal-Rex, January 7, 1916) 2 Reels
Cleo Madison, Ted Duncan, Edward Hearn, Willis Marks, Adele Farrington
Director/Producer: Cleo Madison
Scenario: Harvey Gates

A HEARTS CRUCIBLE
(Universal, March 18, 1916) 5 Reels
Cleo Madison, William V. Mong, Edward Hearn, Margaret Whitler, Ray Hanford
Directors: Cleo Madison, Kathleen Kerrigan

HER BITTER CUP
(Universal-Red Feather, April 17, 1916) 5 Reels
Cleo Madison, Adele Farrington, William V. Mong, Edward Hearn, Ray Hanford, Lule Warrenton
Directors: Cleo Madison and Joe King
Scenario: Cleo Madison
Story: Kathleen Kerrigan
Producer: Cleo Madison

ELEANOR'S CATCH
(Universal-Rex, April 24, 1916) 1 Reel
Cleo Madison, Edward Hearn, Lule Warrenton, William V. Mong, Margaret Whistler, Ray Hanford, Harry Mann
Director: Cleo Madison
Scenario: William V. Mong
Story: William V. Mong
Producer: Cleo Madison

VIRGINIA
(Universal-Rex, May 15, 1916) 1 Reel
Cleo Madison, Margaret Whistler, William V. Mong, Edward Hearn, Ray Hanford
Director: Cleo Madison
Story: Ida M. Evans
Scenario: Harvey Gates
Producer: Cleo Madison

WHEN THE WOLF HOWLS
(Universal-Rex, June 6, 1916) 1 Reel
Cleo Madison, Bertram Grassly, William V. Mong
Director: Cleo Madison
Scenario: W. V. Mong
Story: Charles Sommerville
Producers: Cleo Madison, W. V. Mong

ALIAS JANE JONES
(Universal-Laemmle, June 8, 1916) 2 Reels
Cleo Madison, William Mong, Ray Hanford, Margaret Whistler, Georgia French, Helen Bailey, Edward Hearn
Director: Cleo Madison
Story: William Mong

THE CRIMSON YOKE
(Universal-Rex, July 6, 1916) 2 Reels
Jack Mulhall, *Cleo Madison,* Frank MacQuarrie, William V. Mong, Helen Wright
Directors: Cleo Madison, W. V. Mong
Scenario: C. E. Hall, Harvey Gates
Story: C. E. Hall, Harvey Gates
Producers: Cleo Madison

A DEAD YESTERDAY
(Universal-Rex, July 9, 1916) 2 Reels
Hobart Henley, Jean Hathaway, *Cleo Madison*, Hilda Sloman, Ray Hanford, Agnes Vernon, Baby French
Director: Charles Giblyn
Screenplay: Tom Lewis

CROSS PURPOSES
(Universal-Rex, July 15, 1916) 1 Reel
Cleo Madison, Jack Connelly, Jessie Arnold, William Canfield
Director: William Worthington
Scenario: Bess Meredyth
Story: Bess Meredyth
Producer: William Worthington

PRISCILLA'S PRISONER
(Universal-Big U, July 18, 1916) 2 Reels
Cleo Madison, Charles Gunn, Ray Hanford, Mrs. Grassby, Wadsworth Harris, Frank MacQuarrie
Director: Cleo Madison
Scenario: Harvey Gates
Story: Harvey Gates
Producer: Cleo Madison

THE GIRL IN LOWER 9
(Universal-Big U, July 21, 1916) 1 Reel
Cleo Madison, Charles Gunn, William V. Mong
Directors: Cleo Madison, William V. Mong
Scenario: William B. Mong
Story: William B. Mong
Producers: Cleo Madison, William V. Mong

THE GUILTY ONE
(Universal-Bison, July 28, 1916) 2 Reels
Cleo Madison, William V. Mong, A. E. Witting, Charles Gunn, Bertram Grassby, L. M. Wells, B. T. Henderson
Director: Cleo Madison
Scenario: Harvey Gates
Story: R. E. Bradbury
Producers: Cleo Madison, William V. Mong
(Film also known as **Along the Malibu**)

TILLIE, THE LITTLE SWEDE
(Universal-Big U, July, 1916)
Cleo Madison, William V. Mong, Charles Gunn
Directors: Cleo Madison, William V. Mong
Scenario: William V. Mong

ALONG THE MALIBU
(Bison, August, 1916) 2 Reels
Cleo Madison, L. M. Wells, William V. Mong, Bertram Grassby, Charles Gunn, B. T. Henderson
Directors: Cleo Madison, William V. Mong
Scenario: Harvey Gates
Story: R. Bradbury

TRIUMP OF TRUTH
(Universal-Big U, August 23, 1916) 2 Reels
Cleo Madison, Tom Chatterton, Seymour Zeliff, J. F. Abbott
Director: Cleo Madison
Scenario: Harvey Gates
Story: J. F. Abbott

TO ANOTHER WOMAN
(Universal-Rex, September 13, 1916) 2 Reels
Cleo Madison, William V. Mong, Georgia French, Ray Hanford, Margaret Whister, Edward Hearn
Directors: Cleo Madison, William V. Mong
Scenario: Harvey Gates
Story: Harvey Gates
Producers: Cleo Madison, William V. Mong

THE CHALICE OF SORROW
(Universal-Bluebird, September 28, 1916) 5 Reels
Cleo Madison, Wedgewood Nowell, Blanche White, Charles Cummings, Jack Holt
Director: Rex Ingram
Adaptation: Rex Ingram

BLACK ORCHIDS
(Universal-Bluebird, December 22, 1916) 5 Reels
Cleo Madison, Richard La Reno, Francis McDonald, Wedgewood Nowell, Howard Crampton, William J. Dyer
Director: Rex Ingram
Adaptation: Rex Ingram

THE DARING CHANGE
(Universal-Bison, January 9, 1917) 2 Reels
Cleo Madison, William V. Mong, Harry Griffith, Harry Holden, Betty Human, Miss Cunard (Grace Cunard?)
Director: William V. Mong
Story: Harvey Gates

THE GIRL WHO LOST
(Universal-Red Feather, March 3, 1917) 3 Reels
Cleo Madison, Roberta Wilson, Molly Malone, Jack Nelson, Daniel Leighton, Lydia Y. Titus
Director: George Cochrane
Scenario: Bess Meredyth
Story: Colder Johnstone

THE SORCERESS
(Universal-Rex, April, 1917) 1 Reel
Herbert Rawlinson, *Cleo Madison*

THE WEB
(Universal-Star, July 11, 1917) 2 Reels
Cleo Madison, Jack Nelson, Gretchen Lederer, George Pearce
Director: George Cochrane
Scenario: Harvey Gates
Story: Katherine Kingsbury

THE WOMAN WHO WOULD NOT PAY
(Universal-Star, August 4, 1917) 2 Reels
Cleo Madison, Frank Whitson, Bertram Grassby, Daniel Leighton
Director: Ruth Ann Baldwin
Screenplay: Ruth Ann Baldwin
Story: E. M. Ingleton

FLAME OF THE WEST
(Universal, September 7, 1918) 2 Reels
Cleo Madison, L. M. Wells, Charles Gunn, William V. Mong, Bertram Grassby, B. T. Henderson

THE ROMANCE OF TARZAN
(National, September, 1918)
Elmo K. Lincoln, Enid Markey, *Cleo Madison,* Thomas Jefferson, Monte Blue, Colin Kenny
Director: Wilfred Lucas
Scenario: Bess Meredyth
Story: Edgar Rice Burroughs
Producer: William Parsons

THE GIRL FROM NOWHERE
(National Film Corp., June 9, 1919)
Cleo Madison, Winifred Lucas, Wilfred Lucas
Directors: Bess Meredyth, Wilfred Lucas
Scenario: Bess Meredyth, Wilfred Lucas

THE GREAT RADIUM MYSTERY
(Universal, October 13, 1919) 18 Chapters
Cleo Madison, Robert (Bob) Reeves, Eileen Sedgwick, Robert Kortman, Ed Brady, Jeff Osborne, Robert Gray, Gordon McGregor, Fred Hamer
Directors: Robert Broadwell, Robert F. Hill
Screenplay: Frederick Bennett
Chapters: (1) The Mystic Stone (2) The Death Trap (3) The Fatal Ride (4) The Swing for Life (5) The Torture Chamber (6) The Tunnel of Doom (7) A Flash in the Dark (8) In the Clutches of the Mad Man (9) The Roaring Volcano (10) Creeping Flames (11) Perils of Doom (12) Shackled (13) The Scalding Pit (14) Hemmed In (15) The Flaming Arrow (16) Over the Cataract (17) The Wheels of Death (18) Liquid Flames

THE PRICE OF REDEMPTION
(Metro, September 1, 1920) 6 Reels
Cleo Madison, Bert Lytell, Seena Owen, Landers Stevens, Edward Cecil, Arthur Morrison, Wilbur Higby, Grant Merrill
Director: Dallas M. Fitzgerald
Screenplay: June Mathis
Story: I. A. R. Wylie, "The Temple of Dawn"

THE LURE OF YOUTH
(Metro, January 10, 1921) 6 Reels
Cleo Madison, William Conklin, Gareth Hughes, Lydia Knott, William Courtwright, Helen Werr
Director: Philip E. Rosen
Scenario: Luther Reed
Story: Luther Reed
Producer: Bayard Veller

LADIES MUST LIVE
(Mayflower Photoplay Corp./Paramount, October 30, 1921) 8 Reels
Robert Ellis, Mahlon Hamilton, Betty Compson, Leatrice Joy, Hardee Kirkland, Gibson Gowland, Jack Gilbert, *Cleo Madison,* Snitz Edwards, Lucille Hutton, Lule Warrenton, William V. Mong, Jack McDonald, Marcia Manon, Arnold Gregg
Director: George Loane Tucker
Adaptation: George Loane Tucker
Story: Alice Duer Miller

A WOMAN'S WOMAN
(Albion Prod./Allied Producers and Distributors, September 24, 1922) 8 Reels
Mary Alden, Alouise Lee, Dorothy Mackaill, Holmes E. Herbert, Albert Hackett, Rod La Rocque, Horace James, *Cleo Madison,* Donald Hall, J. Barney Sherry
Director: Charles Giblyn
Scenario: Raymond Schrock
Story: Nalbro Isadorah Bartley

THE DANGEROUS AGE
(Louise B. Mayer Prod./Associated First National, November, 1922) 7 Reels
Lewis Stone, *Cleo Madison,* Edith Roberts, Ruth Clifford, Myrtle Stedman, James Morrison, Helen Lynch, Lincoln Stedman, Edward Burns, Richard Tucker
Director: John M. Stahl
Scenario: J. G. Hawks, Bess Meredyth
Story: Frances Irene Reels

SOULS IN BONDAGE
(Sanford, September, 1923) 7 Reels
Pat O'Malley, *Cleo Madison,* Otto Lederer, Eugenia Gilbert, Frank Hayes, Gene Crosby, Peter Howard, Leon Artigue
Director: William H. Clifford
Story: William H. Clifford

GOLD MADNESS
(Perfect/Principal, October 2, 1923) 6 Reels
Guy Bates Post, *Cleo Madison,* Mitchell Lewis, Grace Darmond
Director: Robert T. Thornby
Scenario: Fred Kennedy Myton
Story: James Oliver Curwood, "The Man from Ten Strike"

DISCONTENTED HUSBANDS
(Columbia/C. B. C. Film Sales, January 15, 1924) 6 Reels
James Kirkwood, *Cleo Madison,* Grace Darmond, Arthur Rankin, Vernon Steele, Carmelita Geraghty, Baby Muriel McCormac
Director: Edward J. Le Saint
Story: Evelyn Campbell
Producer: Harry Cohn

THE LULLABY
(R-C Pictures/FBO, January 20, 1924) 7 Reels
Jane Novak, Robert Anderson, Fred Malatesta, Dorothy Brock, *Cleo Madison,* Otis Harlan, Peter Burke, Lydia Yeamans Titus
Director: Chester Bennett
Scenario: Hope Loring, Louis D. Lighton
Story: Lillian Ducey

TRUE AS STEEL
(Goldwyn Pictures/Metro-Goldwyn Distributing Corp., April 20, 1924) 7 Reels
Aileen Pringle, Huntley Gordon, *Cleo Madison,* Eleanor Boardman, Norman Kerry, William Haines, Louise Fazenda, Louis Payne, William H. Crane, Raymond Hatton, Lucien Littlefield
Director: Rupert Hughes
Scenario: Rupert Hughes
Story: Rupert Hughes

UNSEEN HANDS
(Encore Pictures/Associated Exhibitors, May 25, 1924) 6 Reels
Wallace Beery, Joseph J. Dowling, Fontaine La Rue, Jack Rollins, *Cleo Madison,* Jim Corey, Jamie Gray
Director: Jacques Jaccard
Producer: Walker Coleman

THE ROUGHNECK
(Fox, November 30, 1924) 8 Reels
George O'Brien, Billie Dove, Harry T. Morey, *Cleo Madison,* Charles A. Sellon, Anne Cornwall, Harvey Clark, Maryon Aye, Edna Eichor, Buddy Smith
Director: Jack Conway
Scenario: Charles Kenyon
Story: Robert William Service

36 • EDNA MURPHY

Transplanted from Manhattan, She Flourished Out West

You didn't have to know her name to be certain that Edna Murphy was Irish. Her hair was fair and her eyes the color of Irish lakes. Her ancestry was also evident in quick flashes of humor and the buoyant spirit and charm of Ireland's favored sons and daughters.

Edna was born on 106th Street in New York City on November 17, 1899. She was educated at Bay Ridge High School and Manual Training High School in Brooklyn. Before she graduated from Manual Training High School, Edna was posing for commercial photographers as the pretty girl who wore the latest thing in gowns and hats. This work, in turn, led to her engagement as a model for Lajaren Hiller. From the Hiller studio she started her screen career, playing the lead with Alice Joyce in **To the Highest Bidder** (1918).

Later she was the vamp in **Over the Hill** (1920) and a featured player in **The North Wind's Malice** (1920). Fox gave her the starring role in **Fantomas** (1920), a twenty-chapter thriller that kept the kids unnerved in that glorious, uncomplicated period following World War I. Tinted sequences, a mystery ship, a haunted hotel, ghostly creatures, fire and water thrills, plenty of fights, and other action ingredients made it a typical, if not a great serial. Fantomas (Edward Roseman) was a supercriminal who could disguise himself so that no one recognized him. Offering to give up his life of crime if the police will leave him alone, he becomes enraged when the police reject his offer and vows to terrorize New York, his first act being to kidnap Professor Harrington (Lionel Adams), father of Ruth Harrington (Edna Murphy). Johnnie Walker is Edna's fiancé and John Willard is the relentless detective, Dixon.

Edna also costarred with Johnnie Walker in **Live Wires** (1921), after which came the ingénue leads in **What Love Will Do** (1921)

Caught Bluffing (Universal, 1922) – Edna Murphy.

and **The Jolt** (1921).

It was in 1922 that she signed with Universal and was put into a couple of Hoot Gibson Westerns. In 1923 Pathé cast her as the lead in **Her Dangerous Path,** a disjointed but interesting serial in which Edna played a different type of woman in each episode, and pursued the different paths that fate might dictate for such a woman.

Pathé liked Edna and put her into the lead in two more serials: **Leatherstocking** (1924), an

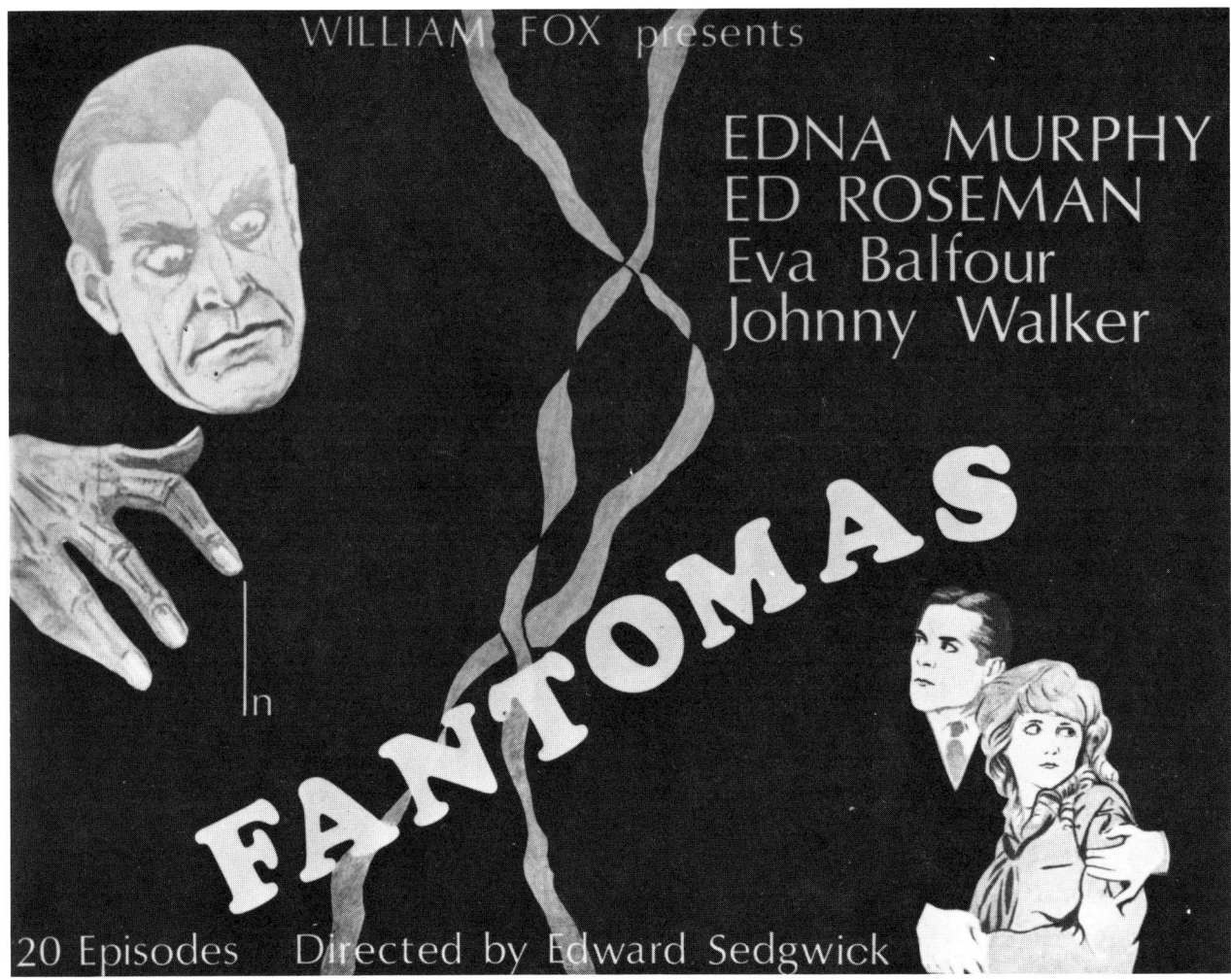

Fantomas (Fox, 1920).

adaptation of James Fenimore Cooper's classic novels, and **Into the Net** (1924), a New York City police story that had Jack Mulhall as the hero and second lead. Miss Murphy's four serials were definitely her own--she was the principal player. Thus, early in her career, she earned her right to inclusion in this tribute to cliffhanger heroines. She made one more serial later in her career, for Universal. Titled **Fingerprints** (1931), it concerned smugglers and the secret service, with Edna the love object of both good guy Kenneth Harlan and bad guy Gayne Whitman.

Edna married director Mervyn LeRoy in 1930 and apparently retired from the screen in 1933. She died on August 3, 1974.

EDNA MURPHY Filmography

TO THE HIGHEST BIDDER
(Vitagraph, July 13, 1918) 5 Reels
Alice Joyce, *Edna Murphy*
Director: Tom Terriss
Story: Florence Morse Kingsley

PUPPY LOVE
(Selznick, 1919) 1 or 2 Reels
Edna Murphy

EASY MONEY
(Selznick, 1919) 1 or 2 Reels
Edna Murphy

Finger Prints (Universal, 1931) – Kenneth Harlan (left), Edna Murphy, and player.

A PHILISTINE IN BOHEMIA
(Vitagraph, February 20, 1920) 2 Reels
Edna Murphy
Director: Howard Griffith
Scenario: Robert A. Sanborn
Story: O. Henry (pseud. of William Sydney Porter)

THE NORTH WIND'S MALICE
(Goldwyn, August 7, 1920) 7 Reels
Tom Santschi, Jane Thomas, Bessie Wheeler, *Edna Murphy,* Joseph King, Walter Abel, William Strauss, Vera Gordon
Director: Carl Harbaugh, Paul Bern
Story: Rex Beach
Producer: Samuel Goldwyn, Rex Beach

OVER THE HILL
(Fox, September 26, 1920) 11 Reels
Mary Carr, Johnnie Walker, *Edna Murphy,* William Welsh, Phyllis Diller, Sheridan Tansey, Stephen Carr, Louella Carr, Rosemary Carr, Jerry Devine, Dorothy Allen, Noel Tearle, John Dwyer, Wallace Ray, James Sheldon, May Beth Carr, Vivienne Osborne, Nellie Parker
Director: Harry Millarde
Adaptation: Paul H. Sloane

THE BRANDED WOMAN
(First National, October, 1920)
Norma Talmadge, Percy Marmont, George Fawcett, Gaston Glass, *Edna Murphy,* Vincent Serrano
Director: Albert Parker
Screenplay: Anita Loos, Albert Parker
Story: Oliver D. Bailey, "Branded"

FANTOMAS
(Fox, December 19, 1920) 20 Chapters
Edna Murphy, Edward Rossman, Johnnie Walker, Eva Halfour, Lionel Adams, John Willard, Irving Brooks, Ben Walker, Henry Armette, Rita Ragan
Director: Edward Sedgwick
Screenplay: Edward Sedgwick, George Eshenfelder
Story: Based on characters created by Marcel Allain and Pierre Souvestre
Chapters: (1) On the Stroke of 9 (2) The Million Dollar Reward (3) The Triple Peril (4) Blades of Terror (5) Heights of Honor (6) Altar of Sacrifice (7) Flames of Sacrifice (8) At Death's Door (9) The Haunted Hotel (10) The Fatal Card (11) The Phantom Sword (12) The Danger Signal (13) On the Count of 3 (14) The Blazing Train (15) The Sacred Necklace (16) The Phantom Shadow (17) The Price of Fang Wu (18) Double-Crossed (19) The Hawk's Prey (20) The Hell Ship

DYNAMITE ALLEN
(Fox, Pebruary 20, 1921) 5 Reels
George Walsh, *Edna Murphy,* Dorothy Allen, Carola Parsons, Byron Douglas, J. Thornton Baston, Nellie Parker Spalding, Mrs. Lottie Ford, Brigham Royce, Frank Nelson, Billy Gilbert
Director: Dell Henderson
Story/Scenario: Thomas F. Fallon

LIVE WIRES
(Fox, July 17, 1921) 5 Reels
Johnnie Walker, *Edna Murphy,* Alberta Lee, Frank Clark, Bob Klein, Hayward Mack, Wilbur Higby, Lefty James
Director: Edward Sedgwick
Scenario: Jack Strumwasser
Story: Charles E. Cooke, Edward Sedgwick

PLAY SQUARE
(Fox, August 14, 1921) 5 Reels
Johnnie Walker, *Edna Murphy,* Hayward Mack, Laura LaPlante, Jack Brammall, Wilbur Highby, Nanine Wright, Harry Todd, Al Fremont
Director: William K. Howard
Scenario/Story: Jack Strumwasser

WHAT LOVE WILL DO
(Fox, September 11, 1921) 5 Reels
Edna Murphy, Johnnie Walker, Glen Cavender, Barbara Tennant, Richard Tucker, Edwin B. Tilton
Director: William K. Howard
Scenario: Jack Strumwasser
Story: L. G. Rigby

THE JOLT
(Fox, November 20, 1921) 5 Reels
Edna Murphy, Johnnie Walker, Raymond McKee, Albert Prisco, Anderson Smith, Wilson Hummell, Lule Warrenton
Director: George E. Marshall
Scenario: Jack Strumwasser
Story: George E. Marshall, Jack Strumwasser

EXTRA! EXTRA!
(Fox, March 5, 1922) 5 Reels
Edna Murphy, Johnnie Walker, Herschel Mayall, Wilson Hummell, John Steppling, Gloria Woodthorpe, Theodore von Eltz, Edward Johnson
Director: William K. Howard
Scenario: Arthur J. Zellner
Story: Julien Josephson

THE ORDEAL
(Pamous Players-Lasky/Paramount, May 21, 1922) 5 Reels
Clarence Burton, Agnes Ayres, Conrad Nagel, *Edna Murphy,* Anne Schaefer, Eugene Corey, Adele Parrington, Edward Mertindel, Shannon Day, Claire Du Brey
Director: Paul Powell
Scenario: Beulah Marie Dix
Story: Somerset Maugham

DON'T SHOOT
(Universal, August 21, 1922) 6 Reels
Herbert Rawlinson, William Dyer, Harvey Clarke, Wade Boteler, Margaret Campbell, *Edna Murphy,* George Fisher, Tiny Sanford, Duke Lee, Mrs. Bertram Grassby, Fred Kelsey, L. J. O'Connor
Director: Jack Conway
Scenario: George Hively
Story: George Bronson Howard

PAID BACK
(Universal, August 28, 1922) 5 Reels
Gladys Brockwell, Mahlon Hamilton, Stuart Holmes, Lillian West, Kate Price, *Edna Murphy,* Arthur Stuart Hull, Wilfred Lucas
Director: Irving Cummings
Scenario: Hope Loring
Story: Louis Duryea Lighton

THE GALLOPING KID
(Universal, September 11, 1922) 5 Reels
Hoot Gibson, *Edna Murphy,* Lionel Belmore, Leon Bary, Jack Walters, Percy Challenger
Director: Nat Ross
Scenario: A. P. Young, Arthur Statter
Story: William Henry Hamby

Into the Net (Pathé, 1924) – Edna Murphy and players.

CAUGHT BLUFFING
(Universal, September 18, 1922) 5 Reels
Frank Mayo, *Edna Murphy,* Wallace MacDonald, Jack Curtis, Andrew Arbuckle, Ruth Royce, "Bull" Durham, Jack Walters, Scott Turner, Martin Best, Tote Du Crow
Director: Lambert Hillyer
Scenario: Charles Sarver
Story: Jack Bechdolt, "Broken Chains" in Argosy magazine

RIDIN' WILD
(Universal, November 19, 1922) 5 Reels
Hoot Gibson, *Edna Murphy,* Wade Boteler, Jack Walker, Otto Hoffman, Wilton Taylor, Bert Wilson, Gertrude Claire, William Welsh
Director: Nat Ross
Continuity: Roy Myers, Edward T. Lowe, Jr.
Story: Roy Myers

NOBODY'S BRIDE
(Universal, March 18, 1923) 5 Reels
Herbert Rawlinson, *Edna Murphy,* Alice Lake, Harry von Meter, Frank Brownlee, Sidney Bracey, Phillips Smalley, Robert Dudley, Lillian Langdon
Director: Herbert Blanche
Scenario: Albert Kenyon
Story: Evelyn Campbell

THE MAN BETWEEN
(Finis Fox/Associated Exhibitors, July 15, 1923) 6 Reels
Allan Forrest, *Edna Murphy,* Fred Malatesta, Vola Vale, Kitty Bradbury, Philo McCullough, Doreen Turner
Director: Finis Fox
Scenario: Lois Zellner

HER DANGEROUS PATH
(Pathé, August 12, 1923) 10 Chaps.
Edna Murphy, Charles Parrott (Charles Chase), Hayford Hobbs, William Moran, Percy Pembroke, William Gillespie, Glen Tryon, Ray Myers, Colin Kenny, Ed Baker, Fred McPherson, Frank Lackteen, Sam Lufkin, Fong Wong
Director: Roy Clements
Scenario: Frank Howard Clark
Producer: Hal Roach
Chapters: (1) What the Sands Told (2) Fetters of Gold (3) At the Brink (4) Should She Become a Politician's Wife? (5) Should She Marry an Artist? (6) Should She Marry a Rancher? (7) Should She Become a Society Reporter? (8) Should She Marry a Scientist? (9) Should She Become Assistant to a Detective? (10) unknown

GOING UP
(Douglas MacLean/Associated Exhibitors, September 30, 1923) 6 Reels
Douglas MacLean, Hallam Cooley, Arthur Stuart Hull, Francis McDonald, Hughie Mack, Wade Boteler, John Steppling, Mervyn LeRoy, Marjorie Daw, *Edna Murphy*, Lillian Langdon
Director: Lloyd Ingraham
Scenario: Raymond Griffith
Story: Otto Harbach, Louis A. Hirch

AFTER THE BALL
(Renco/FBO, January 27, 1924) 7 Reels
Gaston Glass, Miriam Cooper, Thomas Guise, Robert Frazer, *Edna Murphy,* Eddie Gribbon
Director: Dallas M. Fitzgerald
Scenario: James Colwell
Screenplay: Charles K. Harris
Story: Charles K. Harris

DAUGHTERS OF TODAY
(Sturgeon-Hubbard/Selznick Distributing, February 2, 1924) 7 Reels
Patsy Ruth Miller, Ralph Graves, *Edna Murphy,* Edward Hearn, Philo McCullough, George Nichols, Gertrude Claire, Phillips Smalley, Zasu Pitts, H. H. Herbert, Fontaine La Rue, Truman Van Dyke, Dorothy Wood, Marjorie Bonner
Director: Rollin Sturgeon
Story: Lucien Hubbard

LEATHERSTOCKING
(Pathé, March 23, 1924) 10 Chaps.
Edna Murphy, Harold Miller, David Dunbar, Prank Lackteen, Chief Whitehorse, Vincent Markowski (Tom Tyler). Ray Myers, James H. Pierce, Lillian Hall, Aline Goodwin, Emily Barrye
Director: George B. Seitz
Story: Robert Dillon
Based on novels by James Fenimore Cooper
Producer: C. W. Patton
Chapters: (1) The Warpath (2) The Secret Trail (3) The Hawk's Eyes (4) The Paleface Law (5) Ransom (6) The Betrayal (7) Rivenoak's Revenge (8) Out of the Storm (9) The Panther (10) Mingo Torture

THE KING OF WILD HORSES
(Hal Roach/Pathé, April 6, 1924) 5 Reels
"Rex" (King of Wild Horses), *Edna Murphy,* Charles Parrott (Charley Chase), Sidney De Gray, Leon Bary, Pat Hartigan, Frank Butler, Sidney D'Albrook
Director: Fred Jackman
Story/Producer: Hal Roach
Scenario: Carl Himm

THE WHITE MOTH
(Maurice Tourneur/First National, May 11, 1924) 7 Reels
Barbara La Marr, Conway Tearle, Charles De Roche, Ben Lyon, *Edna Murphy,* Josie Sedgwick, Kathleen Kirkham, William Orlamond
Director: Maurice Tourneur
Scenario: Izola Forrester
Adaptation: Albert Shelby LeVino
Producer: M. C. Levee

INTO THE NET
(Pathé, August 3, 1924) 10 Chaps.
Edna Murphy, Jack Mulhall, Constance Bennett, Bradley King, Frank Lackteen, Frances Landau, Harry Semels, Tom Goodwin, Paul Porter, Tom Blake
Director: George B. Seitz
Screenplay: Frank Leon Smith
Story: Richard H. Enright (As New York City Police Commissioner, he was given screen credit only as a goodwill gesture for his cooperation in the filming)
Chapters: (1) The Shadow of the Web (2) The Clue (3) Kidnapped (4) Hidden Talons (5) The Raid (6) The House of the Missing (7) Ambushed (8) The Escape (9) To the Rescue (10) In the Toils

A MAN MUST LIVE
(Famous players-Lasky/Paramount, January 19, 1925) 7 Reels
Richard Dix, Jacqueline Logan, George Nash, *Edna Murphy,* Charles Boyer, Dorothy Walters, William Ricciardi, Arthur Houseman, Lucius Henderson, Jane Jennings
Director: Paul Sloane
Scenario: James Ashmore Creelman
Story: Ida Alexa Ross Wylie, "Jungle Law" in Good Housekeeping

LENA RIVERS
(Chord/Arrow, May 31, 1925) 9 Reels
Earle Williams, Johnnie Walker, Gladys Hulette, *Edna Murphy,* Marcia Harris, Doris Rankin, Irma Harrison, Frank Sheridan, Herman Lish, Harlan Knight, William T. Hayes, Frank Andrews
Director: Whitman Bennett
Adaptation: Dana Rush
Story: Mary Jane Holmes

WILDFIRE
(Distinctive/Vitagraph, June 7, 1925) 7 Reels
Aileen Pringle, *Edna Murphy,* Holmes Herbert, Edmund Breese, Antrim Short, Tom Blake, Lawford Davidson, Arthur Bryson, Will Archie, Edna Morton
Director: T. Hayes Hunter
Story: George V. Hobart, George H. Broadhurst

LYING WIVES
(Ivan Players, June 13, 1925) 7 Reels
Clara Kimball Young, Richard Bennett, Madge Kennedy, *Edna Murphy,* Niles Welch, J. Barney Sherry, Buddy Harris, Bee Jackson
Director/Story: Ivan Abramson
Story: Ivan Abramson

THE POLICE PATROL
(Gotham/Lumas, August 28, 1925) 6 Reels
James Kirkwood, *Edna Murphy,* Edmund Breese, Bradley Barker, Prankie Evans, Joseph Smiley, Robert McKim, Blanche Craig, Edward Roseman, Tammany Young, Charles Craig, James Laffey, Monya Andree
Director: Barton King
Scenario: Victoria Moore
Story: A. Y. Pearson

ERMINE AND RHINESTONES
(Jans Productions, October 1, 1925) 6 Reels
Edna Murphy, Niles Welch, Ruth Stonehouse, Coit Albertson, Sally Crute, Bradley Barker, Marguerite McNully
Director: Burton King
Continuity: William B. Laub
Story: Louise Winter
Producer: Herman F. Jans

HIS BUDDY'S WIFE
(Associated Exhibitors, October 4, 1925) 6 Reels
Glenn Hunter, *Edna Murphy,* Gordon Begg, Harlan Knight, Cora Williams, Flora Pinch, Blanche Davenport, Douglas Gilmore
Director/Scenario: Tom Terriss
Story: T. Howard Kelly

CLOTHES MAKE THE PIRATE
(Sam E. Rork/First National, November 9, 1925) 9 Reels
Leon Errol, Dorothy Gish, Nita Naldi, George F. Marion, Tully Marshall, Prank Lawler, *Edna Murphy,* James Rennie, Walter Law, Reginald Burlow
Director: Maurice Tourneur
Scenario: Marion Fairfax
Story: Holman Francis Day

THE LITTLE GIANT
(Universal, January 3, 1926) 7 Reels
Glenn Hunter, *Edna Murphy,* David Higgins, James Bradbury, Jr., Jean Jarvis, Leonard Meeker, Louise Mackintosh, Thomas McGuire, Dodson Mitchell, Peter Raymond
Director/Adaptation: William Nigh
Scenario: Walter De Leon
Story: Hugh MacNair Kahler, "Once a Peddler" in Saturday Evening Post

WIVES AT AUCTION
(True Story, April 17, 1926) 6 Reels
Edna Murphy, Gaston Glass
Director/Story: Elmer Clifton
Adaptation: Lewis Allen Browne

COLLEGE DAYS
(Tiffany, October 15, 1926) 8 Reels
Marceline Day, Charles Delaney, James Harrison, Duane Thompson, Brooks Benedict, Kathleen Key, *Edna Murphy,* Robert Homans, Crauford Kent, Charles Wellesley, Gibson Gowland, Lawford Davidson, Pat Harmon, William A. Carroll
Director: Richard Thorpe
Story/Scenario: A. P. Younger

OBEY THE LAW
(Columbia, November 5, 1926) 6 Reels
Bert Lytell, *Edna Murphy,* Hedda Hopper, Larry Kent, Sarah Padden, Eugenia Gilbert, William Welsh
Director: Alfred Raboch
Story: Max Marcin

OH! WHAT A NIGHT!
(Sterling, November 5, 1926) 5 Reels
Raymond McKee, *Edna Murphy,* Charles K. French, Ned Sparks, Jackie Coombs, Hillard Karr, Frank Alexander
Director: Lloyd Ingraham
Scenario: Colin Clements
Story: Florence Ryerson

45 MINUTES FROM BROADWAY
(Roach/Pathé, December 26, 1926) 2 Reels
Glen Tyron, Charlotte Mineau, Rube Clifford, Sue O'Neil (Molly O'Day), Theda Bara, Our Gang (Mickey Daniels, Scooter Lowry, Allan Hoskins, Jackie Condon, Jay R. Smith, Johnny Downs, Joe Cobb), Oliver Hardy, *Edna Murphy,* Jerry Mandy, Ham Kinsey, Bud Brandenberg, Jack Hill, Stan Laurel, Al Hallet, Stanley (Tiny) Sandford, The Hal Roach Bathing Beauties
Director: Fred L. Guiol
Story/Producer: Hal Roach

TARZAN AND THE GOLDEN LION
(R-C/FBO, January 2, 1927) 6 Reels
James Pierce, Frederic Peters, *Edna Murphy,* Harold Goodwin, Liu Yu-Ching, Dorothy Dunbar, D'Arcy Corrigan, Boris Karloff, Robert Bolder,
Director: J. P. McGowan
Scenario: William E. Wing
Story: Edgar Rice Burroughs

McFADDEN'S FLATS
(Asher-Small-Roberts/FNP, February 6, 1927) 8 Reels
Charlie Murray, Chester Conklin, *Edna Murphy,* Larry Kent, Aggie Herring, DeWitt Jennings, Cissy Fitzgerald, Dorothy Dwan, Freeman Wood, Dot Farley, Leo White, Harvey Clark
Director: Richard Wallace
Producer: Edward Small
Scenario: Charles Logue
Adaptation: Jack Wagner, Jack Jeune, Rex Taylor
Story: Gus Hill, "McFadden's Row of Flats"

THE VALLEY OF HELL
(M-G-M, February 19, 1927) 5 Reels
Francis McDonald, *Edna Murphy,* William Steele, Anita Garvin, Joe Bennett
Director: Clifford S. Smith
Story: Isadore Bernstein

BURNT FINGERS
(J. C. Barnstyn/Pathé, February 20, 1927) 6 Reels
Eileen Percy, Ivan Doline, *Edna Murphy,* Wilfred Lucas, George O'Hara, Jane Jennings, J. Moy Bennett, Jimmie Ward
Director: Maurice Campbell
Story/Scenario: Maurice Campbell, G. Marion Burton

ALL ABOARD
(B & H Enterprises/First National, May 1, 1927) 7 Reels
Johnny Hines, *Edna Murphy,* Dot Farley, Henry Barrows, Frank Hagney, Babe London, Sojin, James Leonard
Director: Charles Hines
Story: Matt Taylor

ROSE OF THE BOWERY
(David M. Hartford/American Cinema, May 15, 1927) 6 Reels
Johnnie Walker, *Edna Murphy,* Mildred Harris
Director: Bertram Bracken
Adaptation: Bertram Bracken, Walter Griffin

SILVER COMES THROUGH
(R-C/FBO, May 29, 1927) 6 Reels
Fred Thomson, *Edna Murphy,* William Courtright, Harry Woods, Mathilde Brundage, "Silver King" (a horse)
Director/Adaptation: Lloyd Ingraham
Story: Frank M. Clifton

MODERN DAUGHTERS
(Trem Carr/Rayart, May, 1927) 6 Reels
Edna Murphy, Bryant Washburn, Ernest Hilliard, Virginia Lyons, Jack Fowler, Hazel Flint
Director: Charles J. Hunt
Story/Scenario: Stuart Woodhouse

THE BLACK DIAMOND EXPRESS
(Warner Bros, June 1, 1927) 6 Reels
Monte Blue, *Edna Murphy,* Myrtle Stedman, Claire McDowell, Carroll Nye, William Demarest, J. W. Johnston
Director: Howard Bretherton
Screenplay: Harvey Gates
Story: Darryl Zanuck, Mark Canfield

DEARIE
(Warner Bros., June 18, 1927) 6 Reels
Irene Rich, William Collier, Jr., *Edna Murphy*, Anders Randolf, Richard Tucker, Arthur Rankin, David Mir, Douglas Gerrard, Violet Palmer
Director: Archie Mayo
Scenario: Anthony Coldeway
Story: Carolyn Wells

THE SILENT HERO
(Duke Worne/Rayart, August, 1927) 6 Reels
Robert Frazer, *Edna Murphy*, Ernest Hilliard, Joseph Girard, Harry Allen
Director: Duke Worne
Scenario: George W. Pyper
Story: H. H. Van Loan

THE CRUISE OF THE HELLION
(Duke Worne/Rayart, September 10, 1927) 7 Reels
Donald Keith, *Edna Murphy*, Tom Santschi, Sheldon Lewis, Sailor Sharkey, Charles K. French, Francis Ford, Martin Turner
Director: Duke Worne
Story/Scenario: George W. Pyper

HIS FOREIGN WIFE
(William Wallace Cook/Pathé, November 27, 1927) 5 Reels
Edna Murphy, Wallace MacDonald, Charles Clary, Elsie Bishop, Lee Shumway
Director/Story: John P. McCarthy
Scenario: Albert DeMond

WILFUL YOUTH
(Dallas M. Fitzgerald/Peerless, December 19, 1927) 6 Reels
Edna Murphy, Kenneth Harlan, Jack Richardson, Walter Perry, James Aubrey, James Florey, Eugenie Forde, Arthur Morrison, Barbara Luddy
Director: Dallas M. Fitzgerald
Continuity: Ada McQuillan, Gladys Gordon
Story: Edith Sessions Tupper, "Whispering Pines"

ACROSS THE ATLANTIC
(Warner Bros., February 25, 1928) 7 Reels
Monte Blue, *Edna Murphy*, Burr McIntosh, Robert Ober
Director: Howard Bretherton
Adaptation: Harvey Gates
Story: John Ransom

THE SUNSET LEGION
(Famous Players-Lasky/Paramount, April 21, 1928) 7 Reels
Fred Thomson, William Courtright, *Edna Murphy*, Harry Woods, "Silver King" (a horse), Jim Corey, Lew Meehan
Directors: Lloyd Ingraham, Alfred L. Werker
Story/Scenario: Frank M. Clifton

A MIDNIGHT ADVENTURE
(Duke Worne/Rayart, May, 1928) 6 Reels
Cullen Landis, *Edna Murphy*, Ernest Hilliard, Jack Richardson, Allan Sears, Virginia Kirkley, Maude Truax, Ben Hall, Betty Caldwell, Tom O'Grady, Fred Kelsey
Director: Duke Worne
Story/Scenario: Arthur Hoerl

MY MAN
(Warner Bros., December 15, 1928) 12 Reels
Fanny Brice, Guinn (Big Boy) Williams, *Edna Murphy*, Andre De Segurola, Richard Tucker, Billy Seay, Arthur Hoyt, Ann Brody, Clarissa Selwynne
Director: Archie Mayo
Scenario: Robert Lord
Story: Mark Canfield

THE BACHELOR'S CLUB
(Oscar Price/Parthenon, January S, 1929) 6 Reels
Richard Talmadge, Barbara Worth, *Edna Murphy*, Edna Ellsmere, Talbot Henderson, Herbert Hayes, Barry Palmer
Director: Noel Mason
Scenario: Betty Moore

THE GREYHOUND LIMITED
(Warner Bros., February 9, 1929) 7 Reels
Monte Blue, *Edna Murphy*, Grant Withers, Lucy Beaumont, Ernie Shields, Lew Harvey
Directors: Howard Bretherton, Albert S. Howson
Scenario: Anthony Coldeway

STOLEN KISSES
(Warner Bros., February 23, 1929) 7 Reels
May McAvoy, Hallam Cooley, Reed Howes, Claude Gillingwater, *Edna Murphy*, Arthur Hoyt, Agnes Franey, Phyllis Crane
Director: Ray Enright
Adaptation: Edward T. Lowe, Jr.
Story: Franz Supee

KID GLOVES
(Warner Bros., March 23, 1929) 7 Reels
Conrad Nagel, Lois Wilson, Edward Harle, *Edna Murphy*, Maude Turner, Richard Cramer, Tommy Dugan, John Davidson
Director: Ray Enright
Scenario: Robert Lord
Story: Fred Myton

THE SAP
(Warner Bros., November 9, 1929) 9 Reels
Edward Everett Horton, Alan Hale, Patsy Ruth Miller, Russell Simpson, Jerry Mandy, *Edna Murphy*, Louise Carver, Franklin Pangborn
Director: Archie Mayo
Screenplay: Robert Lord
Story: William A. Grew

LITTLE JOHNNY JONES
(First National, November 17, 1929) 8 Reels
Eddie Buzzell, Alice Day, *Edna Murphy*, Robert Edeson, Wheeler Oakman, Raymond Turner, Donald Reed
Director: Mervyn LeRoy
Story: George M. Cohan

THE SHOW OF SHOWS
(Warner Bros., November 20, 1929) 15 Reels
Frank Fay, William Courtenay, H. B. Warner, Hobart Bosworth, Marian Nixon, *Edna Murphy*, Sally O'Neill, Myrna Loy, Alice Day, Patsy Ruth Miller, Ben Turpin, Noah Beery, Wheeler Oakman, Ruth Clifford, Carmel Myers, Viola Dana, Shirley Mason, Ethlyne Clair, William Collier, Grant Withers, William Bakewell, Chester Conklin, Douglas Fairbanks Jr., Jack Mulhall, Chester Morris, Lois Wilson, Gertrude Olmstead, Jacqueline Logan, Monte Blue, Armida, John Barrymore, Richard Barthelmess, Sally Blane, Betty Compson, Dolores Costello, Lila Lee, Molly O'Day, Rin-Tin-Tin, Alberta Vaughn, Loretta Young, Alice White
Director: John G. Adolfi
Supervisor: Darryl F. Zanuck

SECOND CHOICE
(Warner Bros., January 4, 1930) 7 Reels
Dolores Costello, Chester Morris, Jack Mulhall, *Edna Murphy,* Charlotte Merriam, Ethlyne Clair, James Clemmons, Edward Martindel, Henry Stockbridge, Anna Chance
Director: Howard Bretherton
Scenario: Joseph Jackson
Story: Elizabeth Alexander

LUMMOX
(Feature Productions/United Artists, January 18, 1930) 9 Reels
Winifred Westover, Dorothy Janis, Lydia Titus, Ida Darling, Ben Lyon, Myrta Bonillas, Cosmo Kyrle Bellew, Anita Bellew, Robert Ullman, Clara Langsner, William Collier Jr., *Edna Murphy,* Torben Meyer, Myrtle Stedman, William Bakewell, Sidney Franklin
Director: Herbert Brenon
Adaptation: Elizabeth Meehan
Story: Fannie Hurst

WIDE OPEN
(Warner Bros., February 1, 1930) 7 Reels
Edward Everett Horton, Patsy Ruth Miller, Louise Fazenda, Vera Lewis, T. Roy Barnes, E. J. Ratclife, Louise Beavers, *Edna Murphy,* Frank Beal, Vincent Barnett, Lloyd Ingraham, Bobby Gordon, Fred Kelsey, Robert Dudley
Director: Archie Mayo
Scenario: James A. Starr, Arthur Caesar
Story: Edwin Bateman Morris, "The Narrow Street"

DANCING SWEETIES
(Warner Bros., July 19, 1930) 7 Reels
Grant Withers, Sue Carol, Eddie Phillips, *Edna Murphy,* Sid Silvers, Tully Marshall, Margaret Seddon, Kate Price, Vincent Barnett, Dora Dean, Ada Mae Vaughn, Eddie Clayton, Joe Young, Billy Bletcher, Barnett and Clark
Director: Ray Enright
Adaptation: Gordon Rigby, Joseph Jackson
Story: Harry Fried, "Three Flights Up"

BEHIND OFFICE DOORS
(RKO, January 15, 1931) 86 Minutes
Mary Astor, Robert Ames, Ricardo Cortez, Kitty Kelly, *Edna Murphy*, Catherine Dale Owen, Charles Sellon, William Morris, Dorothy Granger
Director: Melville Brown
Screenplay: Cary Wilson
Story: Alan Brener Schultz, "Private Secretary"

FINGERPRINTS
(Universal, March 3, 1931) 10 Chapters
Kenneth Harlan, *Edna Murphy,* Gayne Whitman, Gertrude Astor, Monte Montague, William Thorne, William Worthington
Director: Ray Taylor
Screenplay: George Morgan, George Plympton, Basil Dickey
Story: Arthur B. Reeve
Producer: Henry McRae
Chapters: (1) The Dance of Death (2) A Fugitive of Fear! (3) Toll of the Sea! (4) The Sinister Shadow (5) The Plunge of Peril (6) The Finger of Fate (7) The Depths of Doom (8) The Thundering Terror (9) Flames of Fury (10) The Final Reckoning

ANYBODY'S BLONDE
(Action, October 30, 1931) 59 Minutes
Reed Howes, Dorothy Revier, *Edna Murphy,* Henry B. Wathall, Lloyd Whitlock, Arthur Houseman, Pat O'Malley, Gene Morgan, Nita Marten
Director: Frank Strayer
Story/Screenplay: Betty Burbridge

FORGOTTEN WOMEN
(Monogram, December 1, 1931) 67 Minutes
Marion Shilling, Rex Bell, Beryl Mercer, Carmelita Geraghty, *Edna Murphy,* Virginia Lee Corbin, Edward Earle, Jack Carlyle, Edward Kane, G. D. Wood (Gordon Demain)
Director: Richard Thorpe
Scenario: Adele Buffington, Wellyn Totman

GIRL OF THE RIO
(RKO-Radio, January 15, 1932) 69 Minutes
Dolores Del Rio, Leo Carrillo, Norman Poster, Ralph Ince, Lucile Gleason, *Edna Murphy,* Stanley Fields, Frank Campeau, Roberta Gale
Director: Herbert Brenon
Screenplay: Elizabeth Meehan
Story: Willard Mack, "The Dove" (a play)
Based on a story by Gerald Beaumont

CHEATING BLONDES
(Equitable/Majestic, May 1, 1933) 66 Minutes
Thelma Todd, Ralf Harolde, Inez Courtney, Milton Wallis, Mae Busch, Earl McCarthy, William Humphries, Dorothy Gulliver, Brooks Benedict, Eddie Featherston, Ben Savage, *Edna Murphy*
Director: Joseph Levering
Screenplay: Lewis B. Foster, Islen Auster
Story: Gertie Wentworth Smith
Producer: Larry Darmour

Anne Nagel.

37 • ANNE NAGEL

A Lack of Uniqueness Hampered Her Career

Anne Nagel, who appeared in motion pictures spanning nearly twenty years, died July 6, 1966 of cancer in Sunray North Convalescent Hospital in Los Angeles following surgery in early June.

The pretty wide-eyed beauty's earliest ambition was to be a nun, but before she was sixteen Anne Nagel was already well on her way towards her career of playing sophisticated comedy roles in pictures.

Born Anna Dolan in Boston, Massachusetts on September 30, 1915, she was early encouraged by her parents to be a nun. When she had finished high school her father, Joseph D. Dolan, credit manager for the Revere Sugar Refinery in Boston, enrolled her in Notre Dame Academy. There she began her preparation to enter the church and on a part-time basis worked as a commercial photographer's model in Boston.

By the time she was in her teens, Anne's stepfather, Curtis F. Nagel, a technicolor expert, had signed a long-term contract as director at Tiffany-Stahl Studios. Anne became definitely interested in the movies and upon graduation from Notre Dame started to learn the acting business in a Boston stock company. The company was presenting revivals of old plays in the Shubert Theatre, and Anne acquired much valuable experience in portraying the time-tried character roles.

Anne ultimately came to California and acted in the technicolor short subjects directed by her stepfather. She broke into feature-length productions as a dancer in silent pictures. For the record, she stood 5'4" in height, generally weighed around 110 pounds, and had blue eyes and brown hair. She danced in George White Scandals and appeared in niteries before making her sound film bow in **I Loved You Wednesday** (1933).

She quickly won light comedy assignments in such films as **Stand Up and Cheer** (1934), **King of Hockey** (1936), **A Bride for Henry** (1937), and **Should a Girl Marry?** (1939). One of her first major roles was in **Here Comes Carter** (1936), opposite Ross Alexander, whom she married shortly after completing the film. A year later, however, Alexander committed suicide. Nagel generally provided a passable performance, though she sometimes failed to measure up to possibilities, and alternated between leads and supporting roles, mostly in medium and low-budget features.

The Green Hornet (1939) was Anne's first venture into serialdom. Within the limitations of the field and budget, she acquitted herself creditably as the girlfriend of the hero, although a less erratic screenplay would have helped. In the sequel, **The Green Hornet Strikes Again** (1940), she repeats her role of Lenore Case and effectively shows the whites of her eyes in tight places. Both serial entries are typical thrillers that move along nicely and are paced with action all the way, but lack any particular originality. They were strictly formula stuff from beginning to end, albeit enjoyable escapist entertainment.

Winners of the West (1940) got Anne into the wild west in one of Universal's slick chapter plays. Action is the attraction, and there are hair-breadth escapes aplenty and enough cliffhanging to keep fans of this genre white-knuckled throughout almost the entire thirteen chapters. Anne projected a naturalness in the cliffhanger environs that was immediately discernible by the audience.

Don Winslow of the Navy (1941), the next serial outing for Nagel, was exciting cinematic escapism, and it went down well with popcorn and coke. However, Nagel's role was secondary to that of Claire Dodd, with whom she shared heroine honors. Anne projected wholesomeness and beauty, but she fell a little short on screen presence, i.e., the quality of simply being noticed in a scene when she wasn't the focal point of the

Winners of the West (Universal, 1940) — left to right are James Craig, Dick Foran, Anne Nagel, and Tom Fadden.

action. In this particular serial the scripwriters did not provide her a role that would be forever etched in audiences' minds.

Nagel's last serial, **The Secret Code** (1942), had her playing the reporter girlfriend of The Black Commando, a masked protector of justice. Her air of self-assurance, an indication that she was more than capable of the task at hand, came across much better on the screen in this one.

In features such as **Diamond Frontier** (1940), **Man Made Monster** (1941), **Mutiny in the Arctic** (1941), and **The Dawn Express** (1942) Anne performed well in the lead female role, easily conveying the qualities of attractiveness and vulnerability. However, she was more often cast as a "second banana" to another ingénue.

Miss Nagel hit the newspapers in 1947 with a $350,000 suit against her former physicians, charging they had sterilized her during a routine operation for removal of her appendix eleven years earlier. In 1951 she was back in the headlines in a fight with her husband of ten years, Air Force Lt. Col. James H. Keenan, over money and marriage. She finally was awarded a divorce but lost out in an alimony bid. It was revealed during the proceedings that she had spent time in a hospital for alcoholism.

By 1950 Miss Nagel's career was going nowhere and she left films. It cannot be said that she left an indelible mark on filmdom. She didn't. But thanks to the five serials she made, she is an inseparable element of the total serial tradition and is to be admired for her sheer durability.

ANNE NAGEL Filmography

I LOVED YOU WEDNESDAY
(Fox, June, 1933) 77 Minutes
Warner Baxter, Elissa Landi, Victor Jory, Miriam Jordan, Laura Hope Crews, *Anne Nagel*
Directors: Henry King, William C. Menzies
Screenplay: Philip Klein, Horace Jackson
From the stage play by Molly Ricardel and William DuBois

COLLEGE HUMOR
(Paramount, June 23, 1933) 80 Minutes
Bing Crosby, Jack Oakie, Mary Carlisle, Mary Kornman, Joseph Sauers (Joe Sawyer), Lona Andre, Jimmy Conlon, James Donlin, James Burke, Lumsden Hare, Churchill Ross, Robert Quirk, Jack Kennedy, Howard Jones, Eddie Nugent, Grady Sutton, Toby Wing, David O'Brien, Frank Jenks, Wade Boteler, *Anne Nagel,* Herman Brix (Bruce Bennett), George Burns, Gracie Allen, Marjorie Reynolds
Director: Wesley Ruggles
Screenplay: Frank Butler
Story: Dean Fales

STAND UP AND CHEER
(Fox, March, 1934) 80 Minutes
Warner Baxter, Madge Evans, James Dunn, Sylvia Froos, John Boles, Shirley Temple, Ralph Morgan, Jimmy Dallas, Aunt Jemima, Nick (Dick) Foran, Nigel Bruce, Stepin Fetchit, *Anne Nagel*
Director: Hamilton MacFadden
Story Idea: Will Rogers, Philip Klein
Dialogue: Ralph Spence
Producer: Winfield Sheehan
Associate Producer: Lew Brown

BULLETS OR BALLOTS
(First National, June, 1936) 81 Minutes
Edward G. Robinson, Joan Blondell, Barton MacLane, Humphrey Bogart, Frank McHugh, Joseph King, Richard Purcell, George E. Stone, Louise Beavers, Joseph Crehan, Henry O'Neill, Gilbert Emery, Henry Kolker, Herbert Rawlinson, Rosalind Marquis, Norman Willis, Frank Faylen, Alice Lyndon, Victoria Vinton, Addison Richards, Harry Watson, Jerry Madden, Al Hill, Max Wagner, Milton Kibbee, Jack Goodrich, *Anne Nagel,* Gordon (Bill) Elliott, Virginia Dabney, Carlyle Moore, Jr.
Director: William Keighley
Screenplay: Seton I. Miller
Story: Martin Mooney, Seton I. Miller
Associate Producer: Louis F. Edeiman

CHINA CLIPPER
(First National, July, 1936) 10 Reels
Pat O'Brien, Beverly Roberts, Ross Alexander, Humphrey Bogart, Marie Wilson, Henry B. Walthall, Joseph Crehan, Joseph King, Addison Richards, Ruth Robinson, Carlyle Moore Jr., Lyle Moraine, Dennis Moore, Wayne Morris, Alexander Cross, William Wright, Kenneth Harlan, *Anne Nagel,* Marjorie Weaver, Milburn Stone, Owen King
Director: Raymond Enright
Screenplay: Frank Wead
Story: Frank Wead

HOT MONEY
(Warner Bros., July, 1936) 68 Minutes
Ross Alexander, Beverly Roberts, Joseph Cawthorn, Paul Gratetz, Andrew Tombes, Harry Burns, Ed Conrad, *Anne Nagel,* Frank Orth, Cy Kendall, Andre Beranger, Joe Cunningham, Addison Richards, Charley Foy, R. Emmett Keane, Ed Stanley
Director: William McGann
Screenplay: William Jacobs
From an idea by Aben Kandel

LOVE BEGINS AT 20
(First National/Warner Bros., September, 1936) 57 Minutes
Warren Hull, Patricia Ellis, Hugh Herbert, Hobart Cavanaugh, Dorothy Vaughan, Clarence Wilson, Robert Gleckler, Mary Treen, *Anne Nagel,* Arthur Aylesworth, Saul Gorse
Director: Frank McDonald
Screenplay: Tom Reed, Dalton Trumbo
Based on the stage play "Broken Dishes" by Martin Flavin

HERE COMES CARTER
(First National/Warner Bros., October, 1936) 60 Minutes
Ross Alexander, Glenda Farrell, *Anne Nagel,* Craig Reynolds, George E. Stone, Hobart Cavanaugh, John Sheehan, Joseph Crehan, Dennis Moore, Norman Willis, John T. Murray
Director: William Clemens
Story: M. Jacoby
Screenplay: Ray Chanslor

The Secret Code (Columbia, 1942) – Anne Nagel and players.

KING OF HOCKEY
(First National/Warner Bros., November, 1936)
6 Reels
Dick Purcell, *Anne Nagel,* Marie Wilson, Wayne Morris, George E. Stone, Joseph Crehan, Gordon Hart, Ann Gilles, Dora Clemant, Guy Usher, Garry Owen, Max Hoffmann, Jr., Andre Beranger, Frank Faylen, Frank Bruno, Harry Davenport
Director: Noel Smith
Story/Screenplay: George Bricker

GUNS OF THE PECOS
(First National/Warner Bros., January 2, 1937)
65 Minutes
Dick Foran, *Anne Nagel,* Gordon (Bill) Elliott, Gordon Hart, Joseph Crehan, Eddie Acuff, Robert Middlemass, Gaby Fay (Fay Holden), Monte Montague, Milt Kibbee, Bud Osborne, Cliff Saum, Henry Othro, Bob Burns, Douglas Wood, Glenn Strange, Gene Alsace, Bob Woodward, Frank McCarroll, Jack Kirk, Ray Jones
Director: Noel Smith
Screenplay: Harold Buckley
Story: Anthony Coldeway
Producer: Bryan Foy

THE CASE OF THE STUTTERING BISHOP
(First National/Warner Bros., June 5, 1937) 70 Minutes
Donald Woods, Ann Dvorak, *Anne Nagel,* Linda Perry, Craig Reynolds, Gordon Oliver, Joseph Crehan, Helen MacKellar, Edward McWade, Tom Kennedy, Mira McKinney, Frank Faylen, Douglas Wood, Veda Ann Borg, George Lloyd, Selmer Jackson
Director: William Clemens
Screenplay: Don Ryan, Kenneth Gamet
Story: Erle Stanley Gardner
Supervisor: Bryan Foy

HOOSIER SCHOOLBOY
(Monogram, July 7, 1937) 62 Minutes
Mickey Rooney, *Anne Nagel,* Frank Shields, Edward Pawley, William Gould, Bradley Metcalf, Dorothy Vaughn
Director: William Nigh
Adaptation: Robert Lee Johnson
Story: Edward Eggleston
Producer: Ken Goldsmith

ESCAPE BY NIGHT
(Republic, September, 1937) 67 Minutes
William Hall, *Anne Nagel,* Dean Jagger, Steffi Dunn, Ward Bond, Murray Alper, Charles Waldron, George Meeker, Bill (a dog)
Director: Hamilton McFadden
Screenplay: Harold Shumate
Producer: Harold Shumate

A BRIDE FOR HENRY
(Monogram, September 27, 1937) 58 Minutes
Anne Nagel, Warren Hull, Henry Mollison, Claudia Dell, Betty R. Clark, Harrison Green
Director: William Nigh
Screenplay: Dean Spencer
Story: Josephine Bentham
Producer: Dorothy Reid

FOOTLOOSE HEIRESS
(First National/Warner Bros., September, 1937) 7 Reels
Craig Reynolds, Ann Sheridan, *Anne Nagel,* William Hopper, Hugh O'Connor, Teddy Hart, Hal Neiman, Frank Orth, William Elberhardt, Lois Chesney
Director: William Clemens
Story: Robertson White

SHE LOVED A FIREMAN
(First National/Warner Bros., October, 1937) 57 Minutes
Dick Foran, Ann Sheridan, Robert Armstrong, Eddie Acuff, Veda Ann Borg, May Beatty, Eddie Chandler, Lane Chandler, Ted Oliver, Pat Flaherty, *Anne Nagel*
Director: Johnny Farrow
Story: Carlton Sand, Morton Grant

THE ADVENTUROUS BLONDE
(First National/Warner Bros., November, 1937) 60 Minutes
Glenda Farrell, Barton MacLane, *Anne Nagel,* Tom Kennedy, George E. Stone, Natalie Moorhead, William Hopper, Anderson Lawlor, Charley Foy, Bobby Watson, Charles Wilson, Virginia Brissac, Leland Hodgson, Raymond Hatton, Frank Shannon, James Conlon, Granville Owen, Walter Young, George Guhl, Al Herman
Director: Frank McDonald
Screenplay: Robertson White and David Diamond

THREE LEGIONEERS
(General Films, 1937)
Donald Meek, Stanley Fields, Robert Armstrong, Fifi D'Orsay, *Anne Nagel,* Maurice Black, Leonid Snegoff, Herbie Freeman, Man Mountain Dean
Director: Hamilton MacFadden

SALESLADY
(Monogram, February 2, 1938) 65 Minutes
Anne Nagel, Weldon Heyburn, Harry Davenport, Harry Hayden, Ruth Fellows, Kenneth Harlan, Doris Rankin, John St. Pollis
Director: Arthur Greville Collins
Screenplay: Marion Orth
Story: Kubec Glasman, "Nothing Down"
Producer: Ken Goldsmith

MYSTERY HOUSE
(First National/Warner Bros., May, 1938) 56 Minutes
Dick Purcell, Ann Sheridan, *Anne Nagel,* William Hopper, Anthony Averill, Dennis Moore, Hugh O'Connell, Ben Weldon, Sheila Bromley, Elspeth Dudgeon, Anderson Lawlor, Trevor Bardette
Director: Noel Smith
Screenplay: Sherman L. Lowe, Robertson White
Story: Mignon C. Eberhart

UNDER THE BIG TOP
(Monogram, August 31, 1938) 63 Minutes
Anne Nagel, Marjorie Main, Jack LaRue, Grant Richards, George Cleveland, Herbert Rawlinson, Rolfe Sedan, Betty Compson, Fred "Snowflake" Toones, Harry Harvey, Charlene Wyatt, Speed Hansen
Director: Karl Brown
Screenplay: Marion Orth
Story: Marion Orth
Producer: Charles J. Bigelow

GANG BULLETS
(Monogram, November 16, 1938) 63 Minutes
Robert Kent, *Anne Nagel,* Charles Trowbridge, Morgan Wallace, J. Farrell MacDonald, John T. Murray, Arthur Loft, John Merton, Donald Kerr, Carleton Young, Isabell Lamal, Benny Bartlett, Joan Barclay, Jack O'Shea, Cully Richards, Duke York
Director: Lambert Hillyer
Screenplay/Story: John T. Neville
Producer: E. B. Derr

CONVICT'S CODE
(Monogram, January 18, 1939) 63 Minutes
Robert Kent, *Anne Nagel,* Sidney Blackmer, Victor Killien, Carleton Young, Howard Hickman, Harry Strang, Maude Eburne, Ben Alexander, Pat Flaherty, Joan Barclay
Director: Lambert Hillyer
Screenplay: John Krafft
Producer: E. B. Derr

SHOULD A GIRL MARRY
(Monogram, June 8, 1939) 61 Minutes
Anne Nagel, Warren Hull, Mayo Methot, Weldon Heyburn, Lester Mathews, Helen Brown, Sarah Padden, Robert Elliott
Director: Lambert Hillyer
Screenplay: David Silverstein and Gaye Newberry
Producer: E. B. Derr

UNEXPECTED FATHER
(Universal, August, 1939) 78 Minutes
Sandy, Mischa Auer, Dennis O'Keefe, Shirley Ross, Joy Hodges, Donald Briggs, Mayo Methot, *Anne Nagel,* Dorothy Arnold, Anne Gwynne, Richard Lane, Paul Guilfoyle, Jane Darwell, Spencer Charters, Dorothy Vaughn, Ed Stanley, Frank Reicher
Director: Charles Lamont
Screenplay: Leonard Spigelgass and Charles Grayson
Story: Leonard Spigelgass

THE GREEN HORNET
(Universal, November, 1939) 13 Chapters
Gordon Jones, *Anne Nagel,* Wade Boteler, Keye Luke, Philip Trent, Walter McGrail, John Kelly, Gene Rizzi, Douglas Evans, Ralph Dunn, Arthur Loft, Edward Earle, Cy Kendall, Alan Ladd, Ann Doran, Anne Gwynne, Jerry Marlowe, Joe Crehan, Selmer Jackson, Stanley Andrews, Fred Vogeding, Clyde Dilson, Eddie Dunn, Eddie Keane, Ben Taggart, George Lloyd, Joe Whitehead, Ray Bailey, John Harmon, James Blaine, Kenneth Harlan, Don Rowan, Robert Brister, Guy Usher, Monte Montague, Wallace Gregory, Lane Chandler, Reed Howes, Edward LeSaint, Paul Seardon, Robert Long, James Farley, Bill Pagan, Edward Cassidy, Karl Hackett, Wilson Benge, Myrtis Crinley, Bill Hunter, Tom Mizer, Jack Donovan, Kernan Cripps, Chuck Morrison, John Pine, Robert Kortman, Jack Carr, Michael O'Hara, Heinie Conklin, Colin Kenny, Edgar Edwards, Charles McMurphy, Sigfrid Tor, Charles Sullivan
Directors: Ford Beebe and Ray Taylor
Screenplay: George Plympton, Basil Dickey, Morrison C. Wood, Lyonel Margolies
Associate Producer: Henry MacRae
Based on the radio serial "The Green Hornet"
Chapters: (1) The Tunnel of Terror (2) The Thundering Terror (3) Flying Coffins (4) Pillar of Flames (5) The Time Bomb (6) Highways of Peril (7) Bridge of Disaster (8) Dead or Alive (9) The Hornet Trapped (10) Bullets and Ballots (11) Disaster Rides the Rails (12) Panic in the Zoo (13) Doom of the Underworld

LEGION OF LOST FLYERS
(Universal, November, 1939) 63 Minutes
Richard Arlen, Andy Devine, *Anne Nagel,* William Lundigan, Guinn (Big Boy) Williams, Ona Munson, Jerry Marlowe, Leon Ames, Theodore Von Eltz, Leon Belasco, Dave Willock, Jack Carson, Edith Mills, Pat Flaherty, Eddy Waller
Director: Christy Cabanne
Screenplay: Maurice Tombragel
Story: Ben Pivar

CALL A MESSENGER
(Universal, November, 1939) 65 Minutes
Billy Halop, Huntz Hall, Robert Armstrong, Mary Carlisle, *Anne Nagel,* Victor Jory, Larry "Buster" Crabbe, El Brendel, Jimmy Butler, George Offerman, The Little Tough Guys, William Benedict, David Gorcey
Director: Arthur Lubin
Screenplay: Arthur T. Horman
Story: Sally Sandlin and Michael Kraike

MY LITTLE CHICKADEE
(Universal, February, 1940) 92 Minutes
W. C. Fields, Mae West, Joseph Calleia, Dick Foran, Margaret Hamilton, George Moran, Si Jenks, James Conlin, Gene Austin, Russell Hall, Otto Heimel, Eddie Butler, Bing Conley, Fuzzy Knight, *Anne Nagel,* Ruth Donnelly, Willard Robertson, Donald Meek, William B. Davidson, Addison Richards, Jackie Searle, Wade Boteler, Hank Bell, Lane Chandler, Alan Bridge, Delmar Watson, Chester Gan, Lita Chevret, Walter McGrail, John Kelly, Bud Harris, Bob McKenzie, Joe Whitehead, Slim Gaut
Director: Edward Cline
Screenplay: W. C. Fields, Mae West
Producer: Lester Cowan

BLACK FRIDAY
(Universal, March, 1940) 70 Minutes
Boris Karloff, Bela Lugosi, Stanley Ridges, *Anne Nagel,* Anne Gwynne, Virginia Brissac, Edmund MacDonald, Paul Fix, Raymond Bailey, Jack Mulhall, Murray Alper, Joe King, John Kelly
Director: Arthur Lubin
Screenplay: Kurt Siodmak, Eric Taylor
Story: Kurt Siodmak, Eric Taylor

MA, HE'S MAKING EYES AT ME
(Universal, April, 1940) 61 Minutes
Tom Brown, Constance Moore, *Anne Nagel,* Richard Carle, Elisabeth Risdon, Fritz Feld, Larry Williams, Jerome Cowan, Vivian Fay, Peggy Chamberlain, Frank Mitchell, Marie Greene, Wade Boteler, Eddie Acuff, Henry Rocquemore, Grace Hayle, Dora Clemant, Mary Field, Fay McKenzie, Kitty McHugh, Stanley Blystone, Mary Currier, Michael Mark
Director: Harold Schuster
Screenplay: Charles Grayson, Edmund L. Hartmann
Story: Ed Sullivan, "Fashions for Sale"

HOT STEEL
(Universal, June, 1940) 64 Minutes
Richard Arlen, Andy Devine, Peggy Moran, *Anne Nagel,* Donald Briggs, Joe Besser, Robert Emmett O'Connor, Wade Boteler, Edward McWade, William Wayne
Director: Christy Cabanne
Screenplay: Clarence Upson Young and Maurice Tombragel
Story: Maurice Tombragel

WINNERS OF THE WEST
(Universal, July 2, 1940) 13 Chapters
Dick Foran, *Anne Nagel,* James Craig, Tom Fadden, Charles Stevens, Trevor Bardette, Harry Woods, Chief Yowlatchie, Edward Keane, William Desmond, Edmund Cobb, Roy Barcroft, Chuck Morrison, Edgar Edwards, Jack Voglin, Edward Cassidy, Slim Whitaker, Alan Bridge, George Plues, Tex Palmer, Bud McClure, Dick Rush, Vyola Vonn, James Blaine, Evelyn Selbie, Robert Long, Hank Worden, Henry Hall, James Farley, Earle Douglas, Jim Pierce, GeorgeMagrill, Bud Osborne, Paul Reed, Bob Kortman, Grace Cunard, Bill Hunter, Horace B. Carpenter, Charles Sherlock, Harry Tenbrook, Tom London, Iron Eyes Cody, Charles Brunner, Frank Ellis, Fred Graham, Eddie Parker, Cliff Lyons, Ken Terrell, Gene Alsace, Rose Plummer
Directors: Ford Beebe, Ray Taylor
Screenplay: George Plympton, Basil Dickey, Charles R. Condon
Producer: Henry MacRae
Chapters: (1) Redskins Ride Again (2) The Wreck at Red River Gorge (3) The Bridge of Disaster (4) Trapped by Redskins (5) Death Stalks the Trail (6) A Leap for Life (7) Thundering Terror (8) The Flaming Arsenal (9) Sacrificed by Savages (10) Under Crashing Timbers (11) Bullets in the Dark (12) The Battle of Blackhawk (13) Barricades Blasted

DIAMOND FRONTIER
(Universal, September, 1940) 71 Minutes
Victor McLaglen, John Loder, *Anne Nagel,* Philip Dorn, Cecil Kellaway, Francis Ford, J. Anthony Hughes, Ferris Taylor, Lionel Belmore, Hugh Sothern, Sigfried Arno, Dewey Robinson
Director: Harold Schuster
Screenplay: Edmund L. Hartmann, Stanley Rubin
Producer: Marshall Grant

THE GREEN HORNET STRIKES AGAIN
(Universal, October 8, 1940) 15 Chapters
Warren Hull, Keye Luke, Wade Boteler, *Anne Nagel,* Eddie Acuff, Pierre Watkin, Joe A. Devlin, William Hall, Dorothy Lovett, Jay Michael, Montague Shaw, Roy Barcroft, Arthur Loft, James Seay, Charles Miller
Directors: Ford Beebe, John Rawlins
Associate Producer: Henry MacRae
Based on the radio serial "The Green Hornet" created by Fran Striker
Chapters: (1) Flaming Havoc (2) The Plunge of Peril (3) The Avenging Heavies (4) A Night of Terror (5) Shattering Doom (6) The Fatal Flash (7) Death in the Clouds (8) Human Targets (9) The Tragic Crash (10) Blazing Fury (11) Thieves of the Night (12) Crashing Barriers (13) The Flaming Inferno (14) Racketeering Vultures (15) Smashing the Crime King

ARGENTINE NIGHTS
(Universal, October, 1940) 75 Minutes
The Ritz Brothers, The Andrews Sisters, Constance Moore, George Reeves, Peggy Moran, *Anne Nagel,* Kathryn Adams, Ferike Boros, Paul Porcasi
Director: Albert S. Rogell
Story: J. Robert Bren, Gladys Atwater
Screenplay: Arthur T. Horman, Ray Golden, Sid Kuller
Producer: Ken Goldsmith

THE INVISIBLE WOMAN
(Universal, January, 1941) 73 Minutes
Virginia Bruce, John Barrymore, John Howard, Charles Ruggles, Oscar Homolka, Charles Lane, Margaret Hamilton, Thurston Hall, Mary Gordon, Kathryn Adams, *Anne Nagel,* Maria Montez, Kay Leslie, Ed Brophy, Shemp Howard, Donald MacBride, Eddie Conrad, Kitty O'Neil, Kay Linaker, Sarah Edwards, Harry C. Bradley, Kernan Cripps
Director: A. Edward Sutherland
Screenplay: Robert Lees, Fred Rinaldo, Gertrude Purcell
Story: Kurt Siodmak, Joe May

MEET THE CHUMP
(Universal, February, 1941) 60 Minutes
Hugh Herbert, Lewis Howard, Jeanne Kelly (Jean Brooks), *Anne Nagel,* Kathryn Adams, Shemp Howard, Richard Lane, Andrew Tombes, Hobart Cavanaugh, Charles Halton, Martin Spellman, Ed Gargan, Iris Adrian, Michael Gaddis
Director: Edward F. Cline
Screenplay: Alex Gottlieb
Story: Hal Hudson, Otis Garrett

MAN-MADE MONSTER
(Universal, March, 1941) 60 Minutes
Lionel Atwill, Lon Chaney, Jr., *Anne Nagel,* Frank Albertson, Samuel S. Hinds, William Davidson, Ben Taggart, Connie Bergen, Ivan Miller, Chester Gan, George Meader, Frank O'Connor, John Dilson, Byron Foulger, Russell Hicks, Douglas Evans
Director: George Waggner
Screenplay: Joseph West
Story: H. J. Essex, "The Electric Man" (also written by Sid Schwartz and Len Golos)

MUTINY IN THE ARCTIC
(Universal, May, 1941) 64 Minutes
Richard Arlen, Andy Devine, *Anne Nagel,* Addison Richards, Don Terry, Oscar O'Shea, Harry Cording
Director: John Rawlins
Screenplay: Maurice Tombragel, Victor McLeod
Story: Paul Huston

SEALED LIPS
(Universal, July, 1941) 62 Minutes
William Gargan, June Clyde, John Litel, *Anne Nagel,* Mary Gordon, Ralf Harolde, Joe Crehan, Addison Richards, Russell Hicks, Ed Stanley, Charles Lane, William Gould, Walter Sande, Joe Downing, Paul Bryar
Director: George Waggner
Screenplay: George Waggner

NEVER GIVE A SUCKER AN EVEN BREAK
(Universal, October, 1941) 70 Minutes
W. C. Fields, Gloria Jean, Leon Errol, Billy Lenhart, Kenneth Brown, *Anne Nagel,* Franklin Pangborn, Mona Barrie, Margaret Dumont, Susan Miller, Charles Lang, Nell O'Day, Irving Bacon, Claud Allister, Leon Belasco, Emil Van Horn, Billy Wayne, Minerva Urecal, Jody Gilbert, Al Hill, William Gould, Emmett Vogan, Jack Lipson, Dave Willock, Duke York, Eddie Bruce, Lloyd Ingraham, Dick Alexander, Jack Roper, Charles Lane, Frances Morris, Irene Colman, Kathryn Sheldon, James Morton, Carlotta Monti, Frank Austin, James Sullivan
Director: Edward Cline
Screenplay: John T. Neville, Prescott Chaplin
Story: Otis Criblecoblis (W. C. Fields)

DON WINSLOW OF THE NAVY
(Universal, December, 1941) 12 Chapters
Don Terry, Walter Sande, John Litel, Claire Dodd, *Anne Nagel,* Samuel S. Hinds, Wade Boteler, Kurt Hatch, Robert Barron, Peter Leeds, Herbert Rawlinson, Ben Taggart, Lane Chandler, John Holland, Ethan Laidlaw, Arthur Loft, Kink Thane, Paul Scott, Frank Lackteen, Jerry Mandy
Director: Ford Beebe, Ray Taylor
Screenplay: Paul Huston, Griffin Jay
Based on the newspaper feature "Don Winslow of the Navy" by Frank V. Martinek
Chapters: (1) The Human Torpedo (2) Flaming Death (3) Weapon of Horror (4) Towering Doom (5) Trapped in the Dungeon (6) Menaced by Man Eaters (7) Bombed by the Enemy (8) The Chamber of Doom (9) Wings of Destruction (10) Fighting Fathoms Deep (11) Caught in the Caverns (12) The Scorpion Strangled

ROAD AGENT
(Universal, December 19, 1941) 60 Minutes
Dick Foran, Leo Carrillo, Andy Devine, Anne Gwynne, Richard Davies, *Anne Nagel,* John Gallaudet, Samuel S. Hinds, Morris Ankrum, Reed Hadley, Emmett Lynn, Ernie Adams, Lew Kelly
Director: Charles LaMont
Screenplay: Morgan Cox, Arthur Strawn
Story: Sherman Lowe, Arthur St. Claire
Associate Producer: Ben Pivar

THE MAD DOCTOR OF MARKET STREET
(Universal, January, 1942) 61 Minutes
Lionel Atwill, Una Merkel, Nat Pendleton, Claire Dodd, Richard Davies, Hardie Albright, *Anne Nagel,* John Eldredge, Ray Mala, Nobel Johnson, Rosina Galli, Al Kikume, Milton Kibbee, Byron Shores, Tani Marsh, Billy Bunkley
Director: Joseph H. Lewis
Screenplay: Al Mortin

STAGECOACH BUCKAROO
(Universal, February 13, 1942) 58 Minutes
Johnny Mack Brown, Fuzzy Knight, Nell O'Day, *Anne Nagel,* Herbert Rawlinson, Glenn Strange, Ernie Adams, Henry Hall, Lloyd Ingraham, Kermit Maynard, Frank Brownlee, Jack C. Smith, Harry Tenbrook, Frank Ellis, Blackie Whiteford, Hank Bell, Jim Corey, Ray Jones, William Nestell, Carl Sepulveda
Director: Ray Taylor
Screenplay: Al Martin
Story: Arthur St. Clair, "Shotgun Messenger"
Associate Producer: Will Cowan

THE DAWN EXPRESS
(PRC, March 22, 1942)
Michael Whalen, *Anne Nagel,* William Bakewell, Constance Worth, Jack Mulhall
Director: Albert Herman
Screenplay: Arthur St. Claire
Story: Arthur St. Claire
Producer: George M. Merrick, Max Alexander

THE MAD MONSTER
(PRC, May, 1942) 77 Minutes
Johnny Downs, George Zucco, *Anne Nagel,* Sarah Padden, Glenn Strange, Gordon Demain, Mae Busch, Reginald Barlow, Robert Strange, Henry Hall, Edward Cassidy, Eddie Holden, John Elliott, Charles Whitaker, Gil Patric
Director: Sam Newfield
Screenplay: Fred Myton
Producer: Sigmund Neufeld

NAZI SPY RING
(PRC, May, 1942) 63 Minutes
Michael Whalen, *Anne Nagel,* William Bakewell, Constance Worth, Hans von Twardowski, Jack Mulhall, George Pembroke, Kenneth Harlan, Robert Frazer, Hans von Morhart, Michael Vallin, William Costello
Director: Albert Herman
Screenplay: Arthur St. Claire
Producer: George M. Merrick, Max Alexander

THE SECRET CODE
(Columbia, September 4, 1942) 15 Chapters
Paul Kelly, *Anne Nagel,* Clancy Cooper, Trevor Bardett, Robert O. Davis, Gregory Gay, Louis Donath, Eddie Parker, Beal Wong, Jackie Dalya, Alex Callam, Eddie Woods, Lester Dorr, Franklyn Farnum
Director: Spencer G. Bennet
Screenplay: Basil Dickey, Leighton Brill, Robert Beche
Producer: Larry Darmour
Chapters: (1) Enemy Passport (2) The Shadows of the Swastika (3) Nerve Gas (4) The Sea Spy Strikes (5) Wireless Warning (6) Flaming Oil (7) Submarine Signal (8) The Missing Key (9) The Radio Bomb (10) Blind Bombardment (11) Ears of the Enemy (12) Scourge of the Orient (13) Pawn of the Spy Ring (14) Dead Men of the Deep (15) The Secret Code Smashed

WOMEN IN BONDAGE
(Monogram, January 10, 1944)
Gail Patrick, Nancy Kelly, Gertrude Michael, *Anne Nagel,* Tala Birell, Mary Forbes, Maris Wrixon, Gisela Werbiseck, Rita Quigley, Francine Bordeaux, Una Franks Bill Henry, H. B. Warner, Alan Baxter, Roland Varno, Felix Basch, Ralph Linn, Frederic Brunn, Gesisla Werbiseck
Director: Steve Sekely
Screenplay: Houston Branch
Story: Frank B. Wisbar
Producer: Herman Millakowsky

MURDER IN THE MUSIC HALL
(Republic, April 10, 1946) 84 Minutes
Vera Hruba Ralston, William Marshall, Helen Walker, Nancy Kelly, William Gargan, Ann Rutherford, Julie Bishop, Jerome Cowan, Edward Norris, Paul Hurst, Frank Orth, Jack LaRue, James Craven, Fay McKenzie, Tom London, Joe Yule, Mary Field, *Anne Nagel,* Ilka Gruning, Inez Palange, William Austin, Spec O'Donnell, Billy Vernon, Nolan Leary, LeRoy Mason, Brooks Benedict, Lee Phelps, Virginia Carroll, Lillian Bronson, Wheaton Chambers, John Weld, James Farley
Director: John English
Screenplay: Frances Hyland, Laszlo Gorog
Story: Arnold Phillips, Maria Matray
Producer: Herman Millakowsky

THE TRAP
(Monogram, 1947) 68 Minutes
Sidney Toler, Mantan Moreland, Victor Sen Yung, Tanis Chandler, Larry Blake, Kirk Alyn, Rita Quigley, *Anne Nagel,* Helen Gerald, Howard Negley, Lois Austin, Barbara Jean Wong, Minerva Urecal, Margaret Brayton, Bettie Best, Jan Bryant, Walden Boyle
Director: Howard Bretherton
Producer: James S. Burkett
Screenplay: Miriam Kissinger

TRAFFIC IN CRIME
(Republic, 1946) 55 Minutes
Kane Richmond, Adele Mara, *Anne Nagel,* Wilton Graft, Roy Barcroft, Arthur Loft, Wade Crosby, Dick Curtis, Harry V. Cheshire, Bob Wilke, Charles Sullivan
Director: Les Selander
Associate Producer: Donald H. Brown

BLONDIE'S HOLIDAY
(Columbia, July, 1947) 60 Minutes
Penny Singleton, Arthur Lake, Larry Simms, Marjorie Kent, Jerome Cowan, Grant Mitchell, Sid Tomack, Mary Young, Jeff York, Bobby Larson, Jody Gilbert, Jack Rice, Alyn Lockwood, Eddie Acuff, Tim Ryan, *Anne Nagel,* Rodney Bell
Director: Abby Berlin
Screenplay: Constance Lee
Based on comic strip by Chic Young

SPIRIT OF WEST POINT
(Film Classics, September, 1947) 77 Minutes
Felix "Doc" Blanchard, Glenn Davis, Tom Harmon, Robert Shayne, *Anne Nagel,* Alan Hale, Jr., Tanis Chandler, Margaret Wells, Franklin Parker, Allan Sacks, Michael Brown, Lee Bennett, M. A. Lightman
Director: Ralph Murphy
Screenplay: Tom Reed
Story: Mary Howard
Producers: John W. Rogers, Harry Joe Brown

AN INNOCENT AFFAIR
(United Artists, August, 1948) 89 Minutes
Fred MacMurray, Madeleine Carroll, Charles "Buddy" Rogers, Rita Johnson, Louise Albritton, Alan Mowbray, Mike Romanoff, Pierre Watkin, William Tannen, James Seay, Matt McHugh, Marie Blake, Susan Miller, *Anne Nagel,* Eddie LeBaron, Jane Weeks
Director: Lloyd Bacon
Screenplay: Lou Breslow, Joseph Hoffman
Producer: James Nasser

FAMILY HONEYMOON
(Universal, December, 1948) 90 Minutes
Claudette Colbert, Fred MacMurray, Rita Johnson, Lillian Bronson, William Daniels, Gigi Perreau, Jimmy Hunt, Peter Miles, Hattie McDaniel, Chill Wills, Catharine Doucet, Paul Harvey, Irving Bacon, Chick Chandler, Wally Brown, Frank Jenks, Almira Sessions, Holmes Herbert, John Gallaudet, Wilton Raff, Fay Baker, O. Z. Whitehead, Lorin Raker, Sarah Edwards, *Anne Nagel*
Director: Claude Binyon
Screenplay: Dane Lussier
Story: Homer Croy
Producers: John Beck, Z. Wayne Griffin

PREJUDICE
(New World/Motion Picture Sales Corp., February, 1949) 55 Minutes
David Bruce, Mary Marshall, Tommy Ivo, Bruce Edwards, Barbara Billingsley, James Seay, Joe Crehan, Billy Kimbley, Jimmy Conlin, Sharon McManus, *Anne Nagel,* Frank Cady, Mira McKinney, Grace Field, Ruth Clifford, Kay Christopher, John Dehner, Buddy Swan, Margaret Bert, Belle Mitchell, Clarence Hennecke
Director: Edward L. Cahn
Screenplay: Jarvis Couillard, Ivan Goff, Ben Roberts
Story: Jarvis Couillard
Producer: Paul F. Heard

ARMORED CAR ROBBERY
(RKO Radio, June 8, 1950) 67 Minutes
Charles McGraw, Adele Jergens, William Talman, Douglas Fowley, Steve Brodie, Don McGuire, Don Haggerty, James Flavin, *Anne Nagel,* Linda Johnson, James Bush
Director: Richard Fleisher
Screenplay: Earl Felton, Gerald Drayson Adams
Story: Robert Angus, Robert Leeds
Producer: Herman Schlom

Cecilia Parker.

38 • CECILIA PARKER

Her Wistful Charm and Golden-Haired Beauty Were Peculiarly Suited to the 1930s

Cecilia Parker, a strikingly beautiful blonde with large brown eyes, was born at Fort William, Ontario, Canada, on April 26; her year of birth is subject to debate, having been variously reported between 1905 and 1915. (Cecilia herself prefers not to say.) Her father was a British army man. She moved to Hollywood with her parents when she was a child and was educated by private tutors, at the Blessed Sacrament Parochial School, and at the Convent of the Immaculate Heart.

She started her film career as an extra and had been in pictures for a year when she was signed to a Fox contract. Sol Wurtzel, general superintendent at Fox, had seen her in a small part in Frank Borzages's **Young As You Feel (1931)** and ordered a screen test. The test so impressed Winfield Sheehan, vice-president and general manager of the studio, that he ordered her signed to a contract the next day.

In late 1937 Cecilia made her first of twelve Andy Hardy films at Metro-Goldwyn-Mayer, playing the older sister of Mickey Rooney. Today she is remembered by general audiences mainly for these pictures, but Western and serial followers remember her as the wistful charmer in "B" Westerns of the 1930s with George O'Brien, Rex Bell, Buck Jones, Ken Maynard, and John Wayne--fine little Westerns made before the genre's long-lasting illness began. They also remember the three serials that were so entertaining to front-row kids during the depression years when a dime and a vivid imagination could carry one into a world of fantasy.

The Jungle Mystery (1932) was hokum, but great fun--and what a cast! Tom Tyler, William Desmond, Noah Beery, Jr., Carmelita Geraghy, Philo McCullough, and Onslow Stevens were also featured. Cecilia survived all sorts of skulduggery and animal hazards to emerge relatively unscathed. Our heroine experienced equally harrowing dangers in **The Lost Special** (1932), all about a mining train and its cargo of gold. Then she was back in the jungle again in **The Lost Jungle** (1934), aided by wild animal trainer Clyde Beatty in overcoming both human and animal obstacles to find a lost professor on an uncharted island.

Cecilia was very much like Jean Rogers and Lucile Browne in both looks and histrionics. Serial patrons of the time liked their heroines fair, shapely, reticent, vulnerable, modest, spirited, engaging, and chaste, seasoned with not a little sensuality. Cecilia measured up well.

Her big break at M-G-M came in Greta Garbo's **The Painted Veil** (1934), and in the years before Andy Hardy she had memorable roles in **Ah! Wilderness** (1934) and **Old Hutch** (1936), both with Wallace Beery, and **Naughty Marietta** (1936) with Nelson Eddy and Jeanette MacDonald. Her last Western was **Roll Along Cowboy** (1937), with Smith Ballew at Fox.

Cecilia retired in 1942 to devote her energies to her family (she had married actor Dick Baldwin in 1938). They now have three grown children, two sons and a daughter, and operate a real estate business in Ventura County, California. She came out of retirement in 1958 to make **Andy Hardy Comes Home,** but promptly retired once more, preferring her real life role of wife, mother, and grandmother. However, she recalls her Western and serial days as happy ones, and the stars and character actors she worked with as among the nicest people in Hollywood.

The Lost Jungle (Mascot, 1934) – Cecilia Parker and Clyde Beatty.

CECILIA PARKER Filmography

WOMEN OF ALL NATIONS
(Fox, May 31, 1931) 72 Minutes
Victor McLaglen, Edmund Lowe, Greta Nissen, El Brendel, Fifi Dorsay, Marjorie White, T. Roy Barnes, Bela Lugosi, Humphrey Bogart, Joyce Compton, Jesse De Vorska, Charles Judels, *Cecilia Parker*
Director: Raoul Walsh
Scenario: Barry Connors
Story: Barry Connors

YOUNG AS YOU FEEL
(Fox, August 23, 1931) 73 Minutes
Will Rogers, Fifi Dorsay, Lucien Littlefield, Donald Dillaway, Terrance Ray, Lucile Browne, Rosalie Roy, C. Henry Gordon, John T. Murray, Brandon Hurst, Marcia Harris, Joan Standing, *Cecilia Parker*
Director: Frank Borzage
Scenario: Edwin Burke
Story: George Ade, "Father and the Boys"

RAINBOW TRAIL
(Fox, January 3, 1932) 60 Minutes
George O'Brien, *Cecilia Parker,* Roscoe Ates, James Kirkwood, Minna Gombell, Landers Stevens, Ruth Donnelly, Robert Frazer, Niles Welch, William L. Thorne
Director: David Howard
Screenplay: Barry Connors, Philip Klein
Story: Zane Grey

THE GAY CABALLERO
(Fox, February 14, 1932) 60 Minutes
George O'Brien, Victor McLaglen, *Cecilia Parker,* Weldon Heyburn, Linda Watkins, Conchita Montengro, C. Henry Gordon, Willard Robertson, Wesley Giraud
Director: Alfred Werker
Screenplay: Barry Connors, Philip Klein
Story: Tom Gill

MYSTERY RANCH
(Fox, July 1, 1932) 65 Minutes
George O'Brien, *Cecilia Parker,* Charles Middleton, Roy Stewart, Charles Stevens, Forrest Harvey, Virginia Herdman, Noble Johnson, Russell Powell
Director: David Howard
Screenplay: Al Cohn
Story: Stewart Edward White, "The Killer"

JUNGLE MYSTERY
(Universal, September 12, 1932) 12 Chapters
Tom Tyler, *Cecilia Parker,* Noah Beery, Jr., William Desmond, Philo McCullough, Carmelita Geraghty, Onslow Stevens, Frank Lackteen, Beulah Hutton, Sam Baker
Director: Ray Taylor
Screenplay: Ella O'Neal, Basil Dickey, George Plympton, George Morgan
Story: Talbot Mundy, "The Ivory Trail"
Chapters: (1) Into the Dark Continent (2) The Ivory Trail (3) The Death Scream (4) Poisoned Fangs (5) The Mystery Cavern (6) Daylight Doom (7) The Jaws of Death (8) Trapped by the Enemy (9) The Jungle Terror (10) Ambushed (11) The Lion's Prey (12) Buried Treasure

TOMBSTONE CANYON
(World Wide, December 25, 1932) 62 Minutes
Ken Maynard, *Cecilia Parker,* Lafe McKee, Sheldon Lewis, Frank Brownlee, Jack Clifford, George Gerwing, Edward Piel, Sr., George Chesebro, Jack Kirk, Merrill McCormack, Bud McClure, "Tarzan"
Director: Alan James
Screenplay/Story: Claude Rister
Producers: Burt Kelly, Sam Bischoff, William Saal

THE LOST SPECIAL
(Universal, December, 1932) 12 Chapters
Frank Albertson, *Cecilia Parker,* Ernie Nevers, Caryl Lincoln, Francis Ford, Frank Glendon, Tom London, Al Ferguson, Edmund Cobb, George Magrill, Joe Bonomo, Harold Nelson, Jack Clifford, Reb Russell (bit)
Director: Henry McRae
Screenplay: Ella O'Neill, George Plympton, Basil Dickey, George Morgan
Story: Arthur Conan Doyle
Associate Producer: Henry MacRae
Chapters: (1) The Lost Special (2) Racing Death (3) The Red Lantern (4) Devouring Flames (5) The Lightning Strikes (6) The House of Mystery (7) The Tank Room Terror (8) The Fatal Race (9) Into the Depths (10) The Jaws of Death (11) The Flaming Forest (12) Retribution

UNKNOWN VALLEY
(Columbia, May 5, 1933) 69 Minutes
Buck Jones, *Cecilia Parker,* Bret Black, Carlota Warwick, Arthur Wanzer, Wade Boteler, Frank McGlynn, Charles Thurston, Ward Bond, Gaylord Pendleton, Alf James, "Silver"
Director: Lambert Hillyer
Screenplay: Lambert Hillyer
Story: Donald W. Lee

RAINBOW RANCH
(Monogram, July 25, 1933) 55 Minutes
Rex Bell, *Cecilia Parker,* Bob Kortman, Henry Hall, George Nash, Gordon DeMain, Phil Dunham, Jerry Storm, Tiny Sanford, Van Galbert, Jackie Hoefley
Director: Harry Fraser
Screenplay: Phil Dunham
Story: Harry O. Jones (Harry Fraser)
Producer: Trem Carr

THE FUGITIVE
(Monogram, August, 1933) 56 Minutes
Rex Bell, *Cecilia Parker,* George F. Hayes, Robert Kortman, Tom London, Gordon DeMaine, Phil Dunham, Theordore Lorch, Dick Dickinson, Earl Dwire, George Nash
Director: Harry Fraser
Adaptation: Harry O. Jones (Harry Fraser)
Story: Harry O. Jones (Harry Fraser)

THE TRAIL DRIVE
(Universal, September 4, 1933) 60 Minutes
Ken Maynard, *Cecilia Parker,* William Gould, Wally Wales, Ben Corbett, Lafe McKee, Alan Bridge, Bob Kortman, Frank Rice, Fern Emmett, Jack Rockwell, Slim Whitaker, Frank Ellis, Hank Bell, Edward Coxen, Bob Reeves, Art Mix, Jack Kirk, Buck Bucko, Roy Bucko, Bud McClure, "Tarzan"
Director: Alan James
Screenplay: Nate Gatzert
Story: Ken Maynard, Nate Gatzert
Producer: Ken Maynard

RIDERS OF DESTINY
(Lone Star/Monogram, October 10, 1933) 58 Minutes
John Wayne, *Cecilia Parker,* George Hayes, Forrest Taylor, Al St. John, Earl Dwire, Heinie Conklin, Lafe McKee, Horace B. Carpenter, Yakima Canutt, Hal Price, Si Jenks, "Duke"
Director: Robert N. Bradbury
Screenplay: Robert N. Bradbury
Story: Robert N. Bradbury
Producer: Paul Malvern

The Fugitive (Monogram, 1933) – Cecilia Parker, Rex Bell, Tom London (extreme left), George F. Hayes (center), Robert Kortman (right) and unidentified player.

HIS WEAK MOMENT
(Educational, October 13, 1933) 2 Reels
Andy Clyde, *Cecilia Parker,* Bruce Riley, Fern Emmett, Esther Muir,
Spec O'Donnell, Bud Jamison
Director: Harry J. Edwards
Story: Harry J. Edwards

SECRET SINNERS
(Mayfair, November 2, 1933) 70 Minutes
Jack Mulhall, Sue Carol, Nick Stuart, *Cecilia Parker,* Armand Kaliz, Natalie Moorhead, Bert Roach, Gertrude Short, Eddie Kane, William Humphries, Tom Ricketts, Paul Ellis, Lillianna Leighton, Phillips Smalley, Lee Zahler, The Three Harmonettes
Director: Wesley Ford
Screenplay: F. McGrew Willis
Story: F. McGrew Willis
Producer: Wesley Ford

FROZEN ASSETS
(Educational, November 17, 1933) 2 Reels
Andy Clyde, Eddie Phillips, *Cecilia Parker,* Harry Bradley, Fern Emmett, Josephine Hall, Spec O'Donnell
Director: Harry J. Edwards
Story: Ernest Pagano, Ewart Adamson, C. Edward Roberts

GUN JUSTICE
(Universal, December 16, 1933) 59 Minutes
Ken Maynard, *Cecilia Parker,* Hooper Atchley, Walter Miller, Jack Rockwell, Francis Ford, Fred McKaye, William Dyer, Jack Richardson, Ed Coxen, William Gould, Sheldon Lewis, Lafe McKee, Ben Corbett, Slim Whitaker, Hank Bell, Blackie Whiteford, Horace B. Carpenter, Bob McKenzie, Frank Ellis, Bud McClure, Roy Bucko, Buck Bucko, Pascale Perry, Jack Ward, "Tarzan"
Director: Alan James
Screenplay: Robert Quigley
Story: Robert Quigley
Producer: Ken Maynard

THE OLD GYPSY CUSTOM
(Educational, January 12, 1934) 2 Reels
Andy Clyde, John Sheehan, *Cecilia Parker,* Addie McPhail, Lloyd Hamilton, Fern Emmett, Spec O'Donnell, Betty Boyd
Director: Harry J. Edwards
Story: Ernest Pagano, Ewart Adamson. C. Edward Roberts, N. T. Barrows

THE MAN TRAILER
(Columbia, March 24, 1934) 59 Minutes
Buck Jones, *Cecilia Parker,* Arthur Vinton, Clarence Geldert, Lew Meehan, Steve Clark, Charles West, Dick Botiller, Artie Ortego
Screenplay: Lambert Hillyer

THE LOST JUNGLE
(Mascot, March, 1934) 12 Chapters
Clyde Beatty, *Cecilia Parker,* Syd Saylor, Warner Richmond, Edward J. LeSaint, Wheeler Oakman, Mickey Rooney, Lloyd Whitlock, Max Wagner, Lionel Backus, Jack Carlyle, Wes Warner, Jim Corey, Harry Holman, Lew Meehan, Maston Williams, Crauford Kent, Lloyd Ingraham, Ernie Adams, Wally Wales, Slim Whitaker, Frank Lanning, Charlie Williams, Hagenback-Wallace Circus Wild Animals, George F. Hayes
Directors: Armand Schaefer, David Howard
Screenplay: Barney Sarecky, David Howard, Armand Schaefer, Wyndham Gittens
Story: Sherman Lowe, Al Martin
Chapters: (1) Noah's Ark Island (2) Nature in the Raw (3) Hypnotic Eye (4) Pit of Crocodiles (5) Gorilla Warfare (6) Battle of Beasts (7) Tiger's Prey (8) Lion's Brood (9) Eyes of the Jungle (10) Human Hyenas (11) The Gorilla (12) Take Them Back Alive

HONOR OF THE RANGE
(Universal, April 16, 1934) 61 Minutes
Ken Maynard, *Cecilia Parker,* Fred Kohler, Jack Rockwell, Frank Hagney, James Marcus, Franklyn Franum, Al Bridge, Jack Kirk, Art Mix, Eddie Barnes, Albert J. Smith, Charles Whitaker, Fred McKaye, Wally Wales, Hank Bell, Lafe McKee, William Patton, Bud McClure, Nelson McDowell, Ben Corbett, Pascale Perry, Jack Ward, Roy Bucko, Buck Bucko, Fred Burns, "Tarzan"
Director: Alan James
Screenplay: Nate Gatzert
Story: Nate Gatzert
Producer: Ken Maynard

I HATE WOMEN
(Goldsmith, May 10, 1934) 70 Minutes
Wallace Ford, June Clyde, Bradley Page, Fuzzy Knight, Alexander Carr, Bobby Watson, Eleanor Hunt. Douglas Fowley, *Cecilia Parker,* Billy Erwin, Margaret Mann, Kernan Cripps, James Mack, Philo McCullough, Fred Toones ("Snowflake"), Shirley Lee, Joey Rae, Pat Harmon, Dorothy Vernon, Charles Saxton, James Quinn
Director: Aubrey H. Scotto
Screenplay: Mary E. McCarthy
Story: Mary E. McCarthy

THE PAINTED VEIL
(M-G-M, November 20, 1934) 83 Minutes
Greta Garbo, Herbert Marshall, George Brent, Warner Oland, Jean Hersholt, Bodil Rosing, Katherine Alexander, *Cecilia Parker,* Soo Young, Forrester Harvey
Director: Richard Boleslawsky
Screenplay: John Meehan, Salka Viertel, Edith Fitzgerald
Story: W. Somerset Maugham
Producer: Hunt Stromberg

HERE IS MY HEART
(Paramount, December 28, 1934) 77 Minutes
Bing Crosby, Kitty Carlisle, Roland Young, Alison Skipworth, Reginald Owen, William Frawley, *Cecilia Parker,* Marian Mansfield, Charles E. Arnt, Akim Tamiroff, Arthur Houseman, Cromwell McKechnie, Albert Petit, Charles Wilson
Director: Frank Tuttle
Screenplay: Edwin Justin Mayer, Harlan Thompson
Story: Alfred Savior
Producer: Louis D. Lighton

The Lost Jungle (Mascot, 1934) – Cecilia Parker comforts Clyde Beatty.

ENTER MADAME
(Paramount, January 2, 1935) 83 Minutes
Elissa Landi, Cary Grant, Lynn Overman, Sharon Lynne, Frank Albertson, *Cecilia Parker,* Wilfred Hari, Michelette Burani, Paul Porcasi, Adrian Rosley, Torbem Meyer, Harold Berquist, Wallis Clark, Fred Malatesta, Tony Merlo, Dick Kline, Gino Corrado, Diana Lewis
Director: Elliott Nugent
Screenplay: Charles Brackett, Gladys Lehman
Story: Gilga Varesi, Dorothea Donn-Byrne

NAUGHTY MARIETTA
(M-G-M, March 6, 1935) 106 Minutes
Jeanette MacDonald, Nelson Eddy, Frank Morgan, Elsa Lanchester, Douglass Dumbrille, Joseph Cawthorn, *Cecilia Parker,* Walter Kingsford, Greta Meyer, Akim Tamiroff, Harold Huber, Edward Brophy, Olive Carey, Walter Long, Pat Farley, William Desmond, Edward Hearn, Edmund Cobb, Edward Norris, Cora Sue Collins, Guy Usher
Director: W. S. Van Dyke
Screenplay: John Lee Mahin, Frances Goodrich, Albert Hackett
Story: Based on the operetta by Rita Johnson Young
Producer: Hunt Stromberg

AH! WILDERNESS
(M-G-M, November 25, 1935) 101 Minutes
Wallace Beery, Lionel Barrymore, Aline MacMahon, Eric Linden, *Cecilia Parker,* Mickey Rooney, Spring Byington, Charles Grapewin, Frank Albertson, Edward Nugent, Bonita Granville, Helen Flint
Director: Clarence Brown
Screenplay: Albert Hackett, Frances Goodrich
Story: Eugene O'Neill
Producer: Hunt Stromberg

LA FIESTA DE SANTA BARBARA
(Technicolor)
(M-G-M, 1935) 2 Reels
Gary Cooper, Buster Keaton, Harpo Marx, Judy Garland, *Cecilia Parker,* Chester Conklin, Maria Gambarelli, Leo Carrillo, Warner Baxter, Robert Taylor, Binnie Barnes, Ida Lupino, Edmund Lowe, Toby Wing, Adrienne Ames, Mary Carlisle, Irvin S. Cobb, Ted Healy, Ralph Forbes, Joe Morrison, Gilbert Roland, Rosalind Keith, Steffi Duna, Shirley Ross
Director: Pete Smith
Producer: Louis Lewyn

HIGH SCHOOL GIRL
(Bryan Foy, 1935) 53 Minutes
Helen MacKellar, Mahlon Hamilton, *Cecilia Parker,* Carlyle Moore, Jr., Noel Warwick, Treva Scott, Crane Wilbur, Mildred Gover, Arthur Wanzer, Eula Gay, Frank LaRue
Director: Crane Wilbur
Screenplay: Wallace Thurman
Story: Wallace Thurman
Producer: Bryan Foy

THREE LIVE GHOSTS
(M-G-M, January 10, 1936) 70 Minutes
Richard Arlen, Beryl Mercer, Claude Allister, Charles McNaughton, *Cecilia Parker,* Dudley Digges, Nydia Westman, Jonathan Hale, Lillian Cooper, Robert Greig
Director: H. Bruce Humberstone
Screenplay: C. Gardner Sullivan
Story: Frederick S. Isham

THE MINE WITH THE IRON DOOR
(Columbia, May 15, 1936) 66 Minutes
Richard Arlen, *Cecilia Parker,* Henry B. Wathall, Stanley Fields, Spencer Charters, Charles Wilson, Barbara Bedford, Horace Murphy
Director: David Howard
Screenplay: Don Swift, Daniel Jarrett
Story: Harold Bell Wright
Producer: Sol Lesser

BELOW THE DEADLINE
(Chesterfield, June 8, 1936) 64 Minutes
Cecilia Parker, Russell Hopton, Theodore Von Eltz, Thomas Jackson, Warner Richmond, John St. Polis, Robert Frazer, Charles Delaney, Kathryn Sheldon, Robert Homans, Jack Gardner, Al Thompson, Sidney Payne, Phyllis Crane, Charles McAvoy, Harry Hearn, Jack Shutta, Francis Sayles, True Boardman, Henry Hall
Director: Charles Lamont
Screenplay/Story: Ewalt Adamson
Producer: George R. Batcheller

OLD HUTCH
(M-G-M, September 25, 1936) 80 Minutes
Wallace Beery, *Cecilia Parker,* Eric Linden, Elizabeth Patterson, Robert McWade, Caroline Perkins, Julia Perkins, Delmar Watson, James Burke, Virginia Grey, Donald Meek
Director: J. Walter Ruben
Screenplay: George Kelly
Story: Garret Smith, "Old Hutch Lives It Up"

SINS OF THE CHILDREN
(Grand National, October 4, 1936) 83 Minutes
Eric Linden, *Cecilia Parker,* Henry Kolker, Charles Richman, Olive Tell, Harry Beresford, Roger Imhoh, Clara Blandick, Robert Warrick, Warner Richmond, Donald Kirke, Stanley Andrews
Director: Duncan Mansfield
Screenplay: Karl Brown
Story: Charles Monroe Shelton
Producer: B. F. Ziedman

A FAMILY AFFAIR
(M-G-M, March 19, 1937) 67 Minutes
Lionel Barrymore, Mickey Rooney, *Cecilia Parker,* Eric Linden, Charley Grapewin, Spring Byington, Julie Haydon, Sara Haden, Allen Vincent, Margaret Marquis, Selmer Jackson, Harlan Briggs
Director: George B. Seitz
Screenplay: Kay Van Riper
Story: Aurania Rouverol, "Skidding"
Producers: Lucien Hubbard, Samuel Marx

GIRL LOVES BOY
(Grand National, March 27, 1937) 77 Minutes
Eric Linden, *Cecilia Parker,* Roger Imhof, Dorothy Peterson, Bernandine Hayes, Rollo Lloyd, Spencer Charters, Buster Phelps, Patsy O'Connor, Sherwood Bailey, William Burrud
Director: Duncan Mansfield
Screenplay: Duncan Mansfield, Carroll Graham
Story: Karl Brown, Hinton Smith
Producer: B. F. Ziedman

HOLLYWOOD COWBOY
(RKO, May 28, 1937) 64 Minutes
George O'Brien, *Cecilia Parker,* Maude Eburne, Joe Caits, Frank Milan, Charles Middleton, Lee Shumway, Walter DePalma, William Royle, Al Hill, Frank Hagney, Al Herman, Dan Wolheim, Slim Balch, Sid Jordan, Lester Dorr, Harold Daniels, Robert Walker, Donald Kerr, Hal Price, Jack Evans
Director: Ewing Scott
Screenplay: Dan Jarrett, Ewing Scott
Producer: George A. Hirliman

DAMAGED LIVES
(Weldon, June, 1937)
Diane Sinclair, Lyman Williams, *Cecilia Parker,* George Irving, Almeda Fowler, Jason Robards, Marceline Day, Charlotte Merriam, Murray Kinnell, Harry Meyers
Director: Edgar Ulmer
Story: Donald Davis, Edgar Ulmer

SWEETHEART OF THE NAVY
(Grand National, June 18, 1937) 65 Minutes
Eric Linden, *Cecilia Parker,* Roger Imhof, Cully Richards, Bernadine Hayes, Henry Rocquemore, Don Barclay, Jason Robards, Art Miles, Reed Howes, Eddy Waller, John T. Murray, Yance Carroll, Etta McDaniel
Director: Duncan Mansfield
Screenplay: Carroll Graham
Story: Carroll Graham, Jay Straus
Producer: B. F. Ziedman

ROLL ALONG COWBOY
(Principal/20th Century-Fox, October 18, 1937) 55 Minutes
Smith Ballew, *Cecilia Parker,* Stanley Fields, Gordon Bill Elliott, Wally Albright, Jr., Ruth Robinson, Frank Milan, Monte Montague, Bud Osborne, Harry Bernard, Budd Buster, Buster Fite and his Six Saddle Tramps, Frank Ellis, Herman Hack, "Sheik"
Director: Gus Meins
Screenplay: Dan Jarrett
Story: Zane Grey
Producer: Sol Lesser

YOU'RE ONLY YOUNG ONCE
(M-G-M, December 10, 1937) 78 Minutes
Lewis Stone, *Cecilia Parker,* Mickey Rooney, Fay Holden, Frank Craven, Ann Rutherford, Eleanor Lynn, Ted Pearson, Sara Haden, Charles Judels, Selmer Jackson, Oscar O'Shea
Director: George B. Seitz
Screenplay: Kay Van Riper
Story: Aurania Rouverol
Producer: Harry Rapf

JUDGE HARDY'S CHILDREN
(M-G M, March 25, 1938) 78 Minutes
Lewis Stone, Mickey Rooney, *Cecilia Parker,* Fay Holden, Betty Ross Clark, Ann Rutherford, Robert Whitney, Jacqueline Laurent, Ruth Hussey, Jonathan Hale, Janet Beecher, Leonard Penn, Boyd Crawford, Edward Earle, Don Douglas
Director: George B. Seitz
Screenplay: Kay Van Riper

LOVE FINDS ANDY HARDY
(M-G-M, July 22, 1938) 90 Minutes
Mickey Rooney, Lewis Stone, Judy Garland, *Cecilia Parker,* Fay Holden, Lana Turner, Ann Rutherford, Betty Ross Clark, Marie Blake, Don Castle, Gene Reynolds, Mary Howard, Raymond Hatton, Rand Brooks, William Bakewell
Director: George B. Seitz
Screenplay: William Ludwig
Producer: Lou Ostrow

OUT WEST WITH THE HARDYS
(M-G-M, November 25, 1938) 84 Minutes
Lewis Stone, Mickey Rooney, *Cecilia Parker,* Fay Holden, Ann Rutherford, Sara Haden, Don Castle, Virginia Weidler, Gordon Jones, Ralph Morgan, Nana Bryant, Tom Neal, Anthony Allan, Thurston Hall
Director: George B. Seitz
Screenplay: Kay Van Riper, Agnes Christine Johnston, William Ludwig

BURN 'EM UP O'CONNOR
(M-G-M, January 13, 1939) 67 Minutes
Dennis O'Keefe, *Cecilia Parker,* Nat Pendleton, Harry Carey, Addison Richards, Charles Grapewin, Alan Curtis, Tom Neal, Tom Collins, Frank Orth, Frank M. Thomas, Si Jenks
Director: Edward Sedgwick
Screenplay: Milton Merlin, Byron Morgan
Story: Sir Malcolm Campbell
Producer: Harry Rapf

THE HARDYS RIDE HIGH
(M-G-M, April 21, 1939) 80 Minutes
Lewis Stone, Mickey Rooney, *Cecilia Parker,* Fay Holden, Ann Rutherford, Sara Haden, Virginia Grey, Minor Watson, John King, John T. Murray, Halliwell Hobbes, George Irving, Aileen Pringle, Marsha Hunt, Don Castle
Director: George B. Seitz
Screenplay: Agnes Christine Johnston, Kay Van Riper, William Ludwig
Producer: Lou Ostrow

ANDY HARDY GETS SPRING FEVER
(M-G-M, July 21, 1939) 85 Minutes
Lewis Stone, Mickey Rooney, *Cecilia Parker,* Fay Holden, Ann Rutherford, Sara Haden, Helen Gilbert, Terry Kilburn, John T. Murray, George Breakston, Charley Peck, Sidney Miller, Addison Richards, Robert Kent, Byron Foulger
Director: W. S. Van Dyke
Screenplay: Kay Van Riper

JUDGE HARDY AND SON
(M-G-M, December 22, 1939) 87 Minutes
Lewis Stone, Mickey Rooney, *Cecilia Parker,* Fay Holden, Ann Rutherford, Sara Haden, June Preisser, Marie Ouspenskaya, Henry Hull, Martha O'Driscoll, Leona Maricle, George Breakston, Marie Blake, Edna Holland, Egon Brecher, Jack Mulhall
Director: George B. Seitz
Screenplay: Carey Wilson
Story: Carey Wilson
Producer: Lou Ostrow

ANDY HARDY MEETS DEBUTANTE
(M-G-M, July 5, 1940) 86 Minutes
Mickey Rooney, Lewis Stone, Judy Garland, *Cecilia Parker,* Ann Rutherford, Fay Holden, Diana Lewis, George Breakston, Sara Haden, Addison Richards, Gladys Blake, Cy Kendall, George Lessey, Clyde Wilson, Edwin Stanley, Harry Tyler, Claire DuBrey, Lester Dorr, Pat Flaherty, Marjorie Gateson, Forbes Murray
Director: George B. Seitz
Screenplay: Annalee Whitmore, Thomas Seller
Producer: J. J. Cohn

GAMBLING DAUGHTERS
(PRC, August 1, 1941) 67 Minutes
Cecilia Parker, Roger Pryor, Robert Baldwin, Gale Storm, Sig Arno, Janet Shaw, Charles Miller, Eddie Foster, Alfred Hall, Judy Kilgore, Gertrude Messinger, Roberta Smith, Marvelle Andre
Director: Max Nosseck
Screenplay: Joel Kaye, Arnold Phillips
Story: Sidney Shelton, Ben Roberts
Producer: T. H. Richmond

THE COURTSHIP OF ANDY HARDY
(M-G-M, March, 1942) 93 Minutes
Lewis Stone, Mickey Rooney, *Cecilia Parker,* Fay Holden, Ann Rutherford, Sara Haden, Donna Reed, William Lundigan, Frieda Inescort
Director: George B. Seitz
Screenplay: Agnes Christine Johnston

GRAND CENTRAL MURDER
(M-G-M, May, 1942) 71 Minutes
Van Heflin, Patricia Dane, *Cecilia Parker,* Virginia Grey, Samuel S. Hinds, Sam Levine, Connie Gilchrist, Mark Daniels, Horace McNally, Tom Conway, Betty Wells, George Lynn, Millard Mitchell
Director: S. Sylvan Simon
Screenplay: Peter Ruric
Story: Sue Macveigh
Producer: B. F. Ziedman

SEVEN SWEETHEARTS
(M-G-M, 1942) 82 Minutes
Kathryn Grayson, Van Heflin, Marsha Hunt, *Cecilia Parker,* Peggy Moran, Diana Lewis, S. Z. Sakall, Isobel Elsom, Carl Esmond, Louise Beavers, Donald Meek, Lewis Howard
Director: Frank Borzage
Screenplay: Walter Reisch
Producer: Joe Pasternak

ANDY HARDY'S DOUBLE LIFE
(M-G-M, December 12, 1942) 92 Minutes
Mickey Rooney, Lewis Stone, *Cecilia Parker,* Fay Holden, Ann Rutherford, Sara Haden, William Lundigan, Robert Pittard, Bobby Blake, Susan Peters, Manton Moreland, Frank Coghlan, Jr.
Director: George B. Seitz
Screenplay: Agnes Christine Johnston

ANDY HARDY COMES HOME
(M-G-M, August, 1958) 80 Minutes
Mickey Rooney, Patricia Breslin, Fay Holden, *Cecilia Parker,* Sara Haden, Joey Foreman, Jerry Colonna, Vaughn Taylor, Frank Ferguson, Tom Duggan, Jeannie Baird, Gina Gillespie, Jimmy Bates, Teddy Rooney
Director: Howard W. Koch
Screenplay: Edward Everett Hutshing, Robert Morris Donley
Producer: Red Doff

A Woman in Grey (Serico, 1920) – Arline Pretty.

39 • ARLINE PRETTY

She Worked Competently and Steadily in the Indie Market Arena to Make a Name that Has Weathered the Years

Arline Pretty (her actual name) was gaiety, youth, and irrepressible good spirits personified. Moreover, she had brains, sincerity of purpose, and a firm belief in the efficacy of hard work. Though she was attractive enough on the surface, she also had a loveliness within that sparkled forth and enhanced her physical beauty, speaking in her gentle voice and friendly, sympathetic smile. Star dust never rained down upon her, but she had her own coterie of loyal fans and won a degree of lasting recognition as a result of her roles in three popular silent cliffhangers.

Arline, named by her mother (a musician) for a character in **The Bohemian Girl,** was born in Washington, D.C., on September 5, 1893. She attended public schools and a private finishing school before joining the Columbia Stock Company to play ingénue parts and leads for three years. Later she appeared with Charles Hanaford in Shakespearean plays. Arline had light brown hair and gray eyes, measured 5 feet 5 inches in height, and weighed 125 pounds.

Miss Pretty is believed to have made her screen debut in 1913 with a small company based in Tampa, Florida. The first credits we have uncovered for her are in mid-1914 for Universal, working with King Baggot in a series of short films. Later she switched to Vitagraph, and it was here that she co-starred in **The Secret Kingdom** (1917), a Graustarkian serial whose locations alternated between the mythical kingdom and the American West. It almost turned out to be her last film as well as her first serial, for she jumped out of a four-story window before the cue, and workers just barely grabbed the rope attached to her body in time to stop her fall twenty feet from the Brooklyn pavement.

One of Arline's best feature roles was opposite Douglas Fairbanks in **In Again, Out Again** (1917). As Janie Smith, the deputy sheriff's daughter, she kept the hero busy getting into jail so that he could be near her; her protective father wouldn't allow her outside the jailhouse grounds.

For Pathé, Miss Pretty made **The Hidden Hand** (1917), a typical serial of the time, but also typically profitable. And for Serico she headed up the cast of **A Woman in Grey** (1920), her best and most memorable serial. Adapted from a book by English authors C. N. and A. M. Williamson, it was not simply the usual hairbreath-escape film. Behind all the sliding wall panels, mysterious staircases, sinister hands, and general mayhem there was a very good story. Miss Pretty was definitely the attraction of this fine example of the silent serial at its best--made when writers still had faith in the genre's appeal and future, and audiences shared that faith by their reappearance week after week at theatres around the world.

Arline Pretty continued in pictures for many years, but after the coming of sound she worked mainly as an extra at M-G-M, seldom earning a credit in the cast listings. But in those few years when she was a popular player, she earned and saved enough to provide for herself in leaner times, and did not meet the fate of so many actresses. She enjoyed good health for most of her life and lived to the age of ninty-two, her death occurring in Los Angeles on April 14, 1978.

ARLINE PRETTY Filmography

LOVE'S JUSTICE
(Tampa/Warner's Features, 1913) 3 Reels
Edwin Carewe, *Arline Pretty,* Bernard MacQwen, Jack Bonavita
Director: Frank Whitman

THE OLD GUARD
(Universal-IMP, 1914) 2 Reels
King Baggot, *Arline Pretty*

THE BAITED TRAP
(Universal-IMP, June 27, 1914) 2 Reels
King Baggot, *Arline Pretty*, Frank Smith, Howard Crampton
Story: Monte M. Katterjohn

ONE BEST BET
(Universal-IMP, June 27, 1914) 2 Reels
King Baggot, *Arline Pretty*

THE SILENT VALLEY
(Universal-IMP, September 7, 1914) 2 Reels
King Baggot, *Arline Pretty*, Frank Smith
Director: King Baggot
Story: George Hall

THE MAN WHO WAS MISUNDERSTOOD
(Universal-IMP, September 12, 1914) 2 Reels
King Baggot, Mrs. Walker, *Arline Pretty*, Ben Hall
Story: George Edwards Hall

THE TURN OF THE TIDE
(Universal-IMP, October 31, 1914) 2 Reels
King Baggot, *Arline Pretty*, Frank Smith
Director: George Lessey

HUMAN HEARTS
(Universal-IMP, November 21, 1914) 3 Reels
King Baggot, *Arline Pretty*
Director: King Baggot
Story: Hal Reid

THE TREASURE TRAIN
(Universal-IMP, November 28, 1914) 2 Reels
King Baggot, *Arline Pretty*

THE MILL STREAM
(Universal-IMP, December 12, 1914) 2 Reels
King Baggot, *Arline Pretty*, Robert Hill

AN ORIENTAL ROMANCE
(Universal-IMP, February 13, 1915) 2 Reels
King Baggot, *Arline Pretty*, Ned Riardon, Frank Smith
Director: George Lessey

THE FIVE-POUND NOTE
(Universal-IMP, March 6, 1915) 2 Reels
King Baggot, *Arline Pretty*, Frank Smith

PRESSING HIS SUIT
(Universal-IMP, March 20, 1915)
King Baggot, *Arline Pretty*

ONE NIGHT
(Universal-IMP, March 20, 1915)
King Baggot, *Arline Pretty*

THE MAN WHO FOUND HIMSELF
(Brady/World, April 16, 1915) 5 Reels
Robert Warwick, Paul McAllister, *Arline Pretty*, E. M. Kimball, Douglas MacLean, Charles Dungan, Madge Evans, Ruth Finley, Leone Morgan, Alec B. Francis, John Hines, Walter Miller, Louis R. Grisel, George Ingleton, Phyllis Haseltine, Martin Faust, Dick Neill, D. J. Flanagan, Fred C. Truesdell
Director: Frank Crane
Story: George Broadhurst, "The Mills of the Gods"

AT THE BANQUET TABLE
(Universal-IMP, April 24, 1915) 2 Reels
King Baggot, *Arline Pretty*, Ned Riardon
Director: George Lessey
Scenario: Harvey Gates

A LIFE IN THE BALANCE
(Universal-IMP, May 29, 1915) 2 Reels
King Baggot, *Arline Pretty*
Story: Anthony Kelly

BROWN'S SUMMER BOARDERS
(Vitagraph, September 9, 1915) 1 Reel
Jay Dwiggins, *Arline Pretty*, Thomas R. Mills, Garry McGarry, Charles Eldridge, Edwina Robbins
Director: George Ridgwell
Story: Sarie Coolidge Rask

SIS
(Vitagraph, October 6, 1915) 1 Reel
Arline Pretty, Thomas Mills, Garry McGarry, Jay Dwiggins, Edwina Robbins, Florence Natal
Director: George Ridgwell
Story: William Addison Lathrop

THE THIRTEENTH GIRL
(Broadway Star/Vitagraph, December 25, 1915) 3 Reels
Arline Pretty, Julia Swayn Gordon, Lillian Burns, Robert Whitworth, Arthur Cozine, Frank Currier
Director: Theodore Marston
Story: Frances Aymar Mathews, "Where Did Lottie Go?"

THE MILLIONAIRE ENGINEER
(Universal-IMP, January, 1916) 2 Reels
King Baggot, Bessie Toner, Frank Smith, *Arline Pretty*, Ned Riardon
Director: George Lessey

THE SURPRISES OF AN EMPTY HOTEL
(Vitagraph, January, 1916) 4 Reels
Arline Pretty
Director: Theodore Marston
Story: Archibald Clavering Gunter
Screenplay: Jasper Ewing Brady

THE DAWN OF FREEDOM
(Vitagraph, July 27, 1916) 5 Reels
Charles Richman, *Arline Pretty,* Billie Billings, James Morrison, Thomas Mills, Templar Saxe, Edward Elkas
Director: Theodore Marston, Paul Scardon
Screenplay: Marguerite Bertsch
Adaptation: Marguerite Bertsch
Story: William Hurlburt

MRS. WARREN'S BROTHER
(Vitagraph, 1916)
Arline Pretty

THE SECRET KINGDOM
(Vitagraph, January 1, 1917) 15 Chapters
Charles Richman, Dorothy Kelly, *Arline Pretty,* Joseph Kilgour, Ned Finley, Charles Wellesley, William Dunn, Robert Whitworth, De Jalma West
Directors: Theodore Marston, Charles J. Brabin
Screenplay: Basil Dickey
Story: Louis Joseph Vance
Chapters: (1) Land of the Intrigue (2) Royalty at Red Wing (3) Sealed Packet (4) Honorable Mr. Oxenham (5) Carriage Call #101 (6) Human Flotsam (7) Ghost Ship (8) Rum Cay (9) Swamp Adder (10) A Goat Without Horns (11) The White Witch (12) The Shark's Nest (13) The Tragic Masque (14) The Portrait of a King (15) The Tocsin

IN AGAIN, OUT AGAIN
(Douglas Fairbanks/Artcraft, April 24, 1917) 5 Reels
Douglas Fairbanks, *Arline Pretty,* Bull Montana, Walter Walter, Arnold Lucy, Helen Greene, Homer Hunt, Ada Gilman, Albert Parker, Frank Lalor, Betty Tyrel, Spike Robinson
Director: John Emerson
Scenario: Anita Loos

THE HIDDEN HAND
(Pathé, November 25, 1917) 15 Chapters
Doris Kenyon, Sheldon Lewis, *Arline Pretty,* Mahlon Hamilton, Henry Sedley
Director: James Vincent
Story: Arthur B. Reeve, Charles W. Goddard
Chapters: (1) The Gauntlet of Death (2) Counterfeit Faces (3) The Island of Dread (4) The False Locket (5) The Air-Lock (6) The Flower of Death (7) The Fire Trap (8) Slide for Life (9) Jets of Flame (10) Cogs of Death (11) Trapped by Treachery (12) Eyes in the Wall (13) Jaws of the Tiger (14) The Unmasking (15) The Girl of the Prophecy

THE SCARLET SHADOW
(Universal, February 14, 1919) 6 Reels
Arline Pretty
Director: Robert Z. Leonard
Scenario: Harvey F. Thew
Story: Lorne H. Fontaine, Katherine Leister Robbins

THE CHALLENGE OF CHANCE
(Continental, July 1, 1919) 7 Reels
Jess Willard (Heavyweight boxing champion), *Arline Pretty*
Director: Harry Revier
Story: Roy Somerville

A WOMAN IN GREY
(Serico, January 22, 1920) 15 Chapters
Arline Pretty, Henry G. Sell, Fred Jones, Margaret Fielding, James A. Heenan, Ann Brodie, Violet de Bicardi, Adelaine Fitzgallen, Jane Mair, Jack Newton, J. W. Driscoll, Jack Manning, Walter Chapin
Director: James Vincent
Story: C. N. and A. N. Williamson
Chapters: (1) The House of Mystery (2) The Dagger of Death (3) The Trap of Steel (4) The Strangle Knot (5) The Chasm of Fear (6) The Grip of Fate (7) At the Mercy of Flames (8) The Drop to Death (9) Burning Strands (10) House of Horrors (11) Fight for Life (12) Circumstantial Evidence (13) The Secret Chamber (14) Pages of the Past (15) Exonerated

THE VALLEY OF DOUBT
(Select, May 3, 1920) 6 Reels
Arline Pretty
Director: Burton George
Scenario: R. Cecil Smith
Story: Willard Mack

LIFE
(Famous Players-Lasky/Paramount, July 19, 1921) 5 Reels
Herbert Bruce, Nita Naldi, Jack Mower, J. H. Gilmore, Rod LaRocque, *Arline Pretty,* Leonard Meeker, Curtis Cooksey, Effingham Pinto, Geoffrey Stein
Director: Travers Vale
Story: Thompson Buchanan, William A. Brady

CROSSED CURRENTS
(Art & Science, 1921)
Arline Pretty

THE WAGES OF SIN
(Art & Science, February 2, 1922) 7 Reels
Jean Grabriel, *Arline Pretty,* Pearl Shepard

WHEN THE DEVIL DRIVES
(Leah Baird/Associated Exhibitors, June 4, 1922) 5 Reels
Leah Baird, *Arline Pretty,* Richard Tucker, Vernon Stell, Katherine Lewis
Director: Paul Scardon
Scenario: Leah Baird
Story: Leah Baird

BETWEEN TWO HUSBANDS
(Mark M. Dintenfass/Alexander, October 23, 1922) 5 Reels
Jean Grabriel, *Arline Pretty*

LOVE IN THE DARK
(Metro, November 20, 1922) 6 Reels
Viola Dana, Cullen landis, *Arline Pretty,* Bruce Guerin, Edward Connelly, Margaret Mann, John Harron, Charles West
Director: Harry Beaumont
Scenario: J. G. Hawks
Story: John Moroso, "Page Tim O'Brien"

STORMSWEPT
(Robert Thornby/FBO, February 18, 1923) 5 Reels
Wallace Beery, Noah Beery, Virginia Browne Faire, *Arline Pretty,* Jack Carlyle
Director: Robert Thornby
Scenario: Winifred Dunn
Story: H. H. Van Loan

THE WHITE FLOWER
(Famous Players-Lasky-Paramount, February 25, 1923) 6 Reels
Betty Compson, Edmund Lowe, Edward Martindel, *Arline Pretty,* Sylvia Ashton, Arthur Hoyt, Leon Barry, Lily Philips, Reginald Carter, Maui Kaito
Director: Julia Crawford
Adaptation: Julia Crawford
Story: Julia Crawford

BUCKING THE BARRIER
(Fox, April 1, 1923) 5 Reels
Dustin Farnum, *Arline Pretty,* Leon Bary, Colin Chase, Hayford Hobbs, Sidney D'Albrook
Director: Colin Campbell
Scenario: Jack Strumwasser
Story: George Goodchild

TIPPED OFF
(Harry A. McKenzie/Playgoers, August 14, 1923) 5 Reels
Arline Pretty, Harold Miller, Tom Santschi, Noah Beery, Stuart Holmes, Zella Gray, Tom O'Brien, Bessie Wong, James Alamo, Jimmie Truax, Si Wilcox, James Wang, Scotty MacGregor
Director: Finis Fox
Story: Frederick Reel, Jr.

ROUGED LIPS
(Metro, August 20, 1923) 6 Reels
Viola Dana, Tom Moore, Nola Luxford, Sidney De Gray, *Arline Pretty,* Francis Powers, Georgia Woodthorpe, Burwell Hamrick
Director: Harold Shaw
Adaptation: Tom J. Hopkins
Story: Rita Weiman, "Upstage"

A FOOL'S AWAKENING
(Metro, January 28, 1924) 6 Reels
Harrison Ford, Enid Bennett, Alec Francis, Mary Alden, Lionel Belmore, Harry Northrup, Evelyn Sherman, John Sainpolis, Pauline French, Edward Connelly, D. R. O. Hatswell, Mark Fenton, *Arline Pretty,* Lorimer Johnston
Director: Harold Shaw
Adaptation: Tom J. Hopkins
Story: William John Locke, "The Tale of Triona"

THE GIRL ON THE STAIRS
(Peninsula/PDC, November 16, 1924) 7 Reels
Patsy Ruth Miller, Frances Raymond, *Arline Pretty,* Shannon Day. Niles Welch, Freeman Wood, Bertram Grassby, Michael Dark, George Periolat
Director: William Worthington
Adaptation: Elmer Harris
Story: Winston Bouve

BARRIERS BURNED AWAY
(Encore/Associated Exhibitors, January 4, 1925) 7 Reels
Mabel Ballin, Eric Mayne, Frank Mayo, Wanda Hawley, Wally Van, *Arline Pretty,* Lawson Butt, Tom Santschi, Harry T. Morey, James Mason, J. P. Lockney, Mrs. Charles Craig, William V. Mong, Pat Harmon, Frankie Mann
Director: W. S. Van Dyke
Story: Leah Baird
Scenario: Leah Baird
Source: Edward Payson Roe

THE PRIMROSE PATH
(Arrow, September 15, 1925) 6 Reels
Wallace MacDonald, Clara Bow, *Arline Pretty,* Stuart Holmes, Pat Moore, Tom Santschi, Lydia Knott, Templar Saxe
Director: Harry O. Hoyt
Screenplay: Leah Baird
Story: E. Lanning Masters

VIRGIN LIPS
(Columbia, July 25, 1928) 6 Reels
Olive Borden, John Boles, Marshall Ruth, Alexander Gill, Richard Alexander, Erne Veo, Harry Semels, *Arline Pretty,* William Tooker
Director: Elmer Clifton
Scenario: Dorothy Howell
Story: Charles Beahan

Ruth Royce

40 • RUTH ROYCE

Forever the Villainess, Danger Lurked in the Curve of Her Smiling Lips

It seemed that Ruth Royce was always presiding over a lair of evil. Hers was not a virginal appeal; she usually played the part of a ruthless, conniving female who preyed at the altar of misfortune frequented by the male of the species. She could sometimes be sexy in her attempts to lure the hero into her web of death, danger, or degradation, but seldom did she show a spark of human kindness. Hers was the attraction of complete, unnerving dominance--her screen lovers never believed that a woman could be so purely evil. Fascinated, they always discovered too late that she was. Her attraction was definitely of the soiled and shop-worn type. She excelled in "other woman" roles and especially as the brainy female out to destroy anyone and everything that stood in the way of her greed. Seldom did she have redeeming qualities.

Naturally, this was just Ruth's screen persona. Off screen, she was a warm, friendly person. She stood five feet six inches tall and had black hair and blue eyes. In 1921 she is supposed to have appeared in a series of Northwest Mountie two-reelers, as heroine or blackguard, but this has not been verified.

Ruth's calculating viciousness was employed only in budget oaters and serials, and it was in the latter that she earned her right to recognition here. She never played the ingénue in either feature or serial, but she contributed her unique acting talents to seven cliffhangers, constantly booed, berated, hissed, and hated by the kids who resented her attempts to give their hero and his girlfriends a hard time--or, on rare occasions, applauded when she turned out to be a tarnished angel.

Ruth was born in Cersailles, Missouri on February 6, 1893 and died on May 7, 1971.

RUTH ROYCE Filmography

LITTLE BROTHER OF THE RICH
(Universal-Broadway, August 26, 1915) 5 Reels
Frank Mayo, J. Barney Sherry, *Ruth Royce*
Director: Otis Turner
Adaptation: Hobart Bosworth
Story: Joseph Mekill Patterson

THE SPLENDID SIN
(Fox, September 7, 1919) 5 Reels
Madlaine Travers, Charles Clary, Jean Calhoun, Wheeler Oakman, Elinor Hancock, George Hackathorn, *Ruth Royce,* Edwin Booth Tilton
Director: Howard M. Mitchell
Scenario: Denison Clift
Story: E. Forst

THE VANISHING DAGGER
(Universal, June 7, 1920) 18 Chapters
Eddie Polo, Thelma Percy, Leah Cross, Laura Oakley, G. Norman Hammond, Arthur Jarvis, Ray Ripley, *Ruth Royce,* Thomas Lingham, Peggy O'Dare, Karl Silvera, Texas Watts, Leslie T. Peacocke, J. P. McGowan
Directors: Ed Kull, Eddie Polo
Scenario: Hope Loring, George W. Pyper
Story: Hope Loring, Jacques Jaccard, Milton Moore
Chapters: (1) The Scarlet Confession (2) The Night of Terror (3) In Death's Clutches (4) On the Trail of the Dagger (5) The End of the Rustlers (6) A Terrible Calamity (7) Plunged to His Doom (8) In Unmerciful Hands (9) Ferocious Foes (10) When London Sleeps (11) A Race to Scotland (12) An Evil Plot (13) Spears of Death (11) Walls of Doom (15) The Great Pendulum (16) Beneath the Sea (17) Beasts of the Jungle (18) Silver Linings

BLUE STREAK McCOY
(Universal, August 16, 1920) 5 Reels
Harry Carey, Lila Leslie, Charles Arling, B. Reeves Eason, Olive Fuller Golden, Ray Ripley, Charles Le Moyne, *Ruth Royce,* Ben Alexander
Director: B. Reeves Hason
Screenplay: Harvey Gates
Story: H. H. Van Loon

"IF ONLY" JIM
(Universal, February 28, 1921) 5 Reels
Harry Carey, Carol Holloway, *Ruth Royce,* Duke Lee, Roy Coulson, Charles Brinley, George Bunny, Joseph Hazelton, Minnie Prevost, Thomas Smith, "Pal" (a dog)
Director: Jacques Jaccard
Scenario: George C. Hull
Story: Philip Verrill Mighels, "Bruvver Jim's Baby"

ALL DOLLED UP
(Universal, March, 1921) 5 Reels
Gladys Walton, Edward Hearn, Richard Norton, Florence Turner, Helen Bruneau, Fred Malatesta, *Ruth Royce,* John Goff, Frank Norcross, Muriel Godfrey Turner, Lydia Yeamans Titus
Director: Rollin Sturgeon
Scenario: A. P. Younger
Story: John Colton

THE MAN TRACKERS
(Universal, July, 1921) 5 Reels
George Larkin, Josephine Hill, Al Smith, Barney Purey, *Ruth Royce,* Harold Holland, Ralph Pee McCullough
Director: Edward Kull
Scenario: George Plympton
Story: Edward Kull, George Plympton

PERILS OF THE YUKON
(Universal, July 24, 1922) 15 Chapters
William Desmond, Laura LaPlante, *Ruth Royce,* Clark Comstock, Joseph W. Girard, Fred R. Stanton, Joe McDermott, George A. Williams, Mack Wright, Princess Neela, Chief Harris
Directors: Perry Vekroff, Jay Marchant, J. P. McGowan
Scenario: George Morgan, George Plympton
Story: George Morgan, George Plympton
Chapters: (1) The Fangs of Jealousy (2) Doomed (3) Tricked by Fate (4) Master and Man (5) Terrors of the North (6) The Menace of Death (7) Trapped by Fire (8) Hurled into Space (9) The Gold Rush (10) The Valley of Death (11) A Race for Life (12) The Path of Doom (13) Martial Law (14) The Trail of Vengeance (15) The Final Reckoning

IN THE DAYS OF BUFFALO BILL
(Universal, September 11, 1922) 18 Chapters
Art Acord, Dorothy Woods, Duke R. Lee, *Ruth Royce,* Joel Day, George A. Williams, Jay Morley, Otto Nelson, Pat Harmon, Jim Corey, Burton C. Law, Joe Hazelton, William P. DeVaull, Charles Colby, G. B. Philips, Clark Comstock, Burt Frank, William Moran
Director: Edward Laemmle
Scenario: Robert Dillon
Story: Robert Dillon
Chapters: (1) Bonds of Steel (2) In the Enemies' Hands (3) The Spy (4) The Sword of Grant and Lee (5) The Man of the Ages (6) Prisoners of the Sioux (7) Shackles of Fire (8) The Last Shot (9) From Tailor to President (10) Empire Builders (11) Perils of the Plains (12) The Hand of Justice (13) Trails of Peril (14) The Scarlet Doom (15) Men of Steel (16) The Brink of Eternity (17) A Race to the Finish (18) Driving the Golden Spike

CAUGHT BLUFFING
(Universal, September 18, 1922) 5 Reels
Frank Mayo, Edna Murphy, Wallace MacDonald, Jack Curtis, Andrew Arbuckle, *Ruth Royce,* "Bull" Durham, Jack Walters, Scott Turner, Martin Best, Tote Du Crow
Director: Lambert Hillyer
Scenario: Charles Sarver
Story: Jack Bechdolt, "Broken Chains"

IN THE DAYS OF DANIEL BOONE
(Universal, June 25, 1923) 15 Chapters
Jack Mower, Eileen Sedgwick, Duke R. Lee, Charles Brinley, Albert J. Smith, *Ruth Royce,* Frank Farrington, Jack Lewis, Herschell Mayall
Director: William Craft
Scenario: Jefferson Moffitt
Story: Paul Bryan, Jefferson Moffitt
Chapters: (1) His Country's Need (2) At Sword's Point (3) Liberty or Deat (4) Foiling the Regulators (5) Perilous Paths (6) Trapped (7) In the Hands of the Enemy (8) Over the Cliff (9) The Flaming Forest (10) Running the Gauntlet (11) The Wilderness Trail (12) The Fort in the Forest (13) The Boiling Springs (14) Chief Blackfish Attacks (15) Boone's Triumph

BEAST OF PARADISE
(Universal, October 1, 1923) 15 Chapters
William Desmond, Eileen Sedgwick, William N. Gould, *Ruth Royce,* Margaret Morris, Jim Welsh, Clarke Comstock, Joe Bonomo, Slim Cole, Alfred Fisher, Gordon McGregor, William J. Welsh
Director: William Craft
Scenario: Val Cleveland
Story: Val Cleveland
Chapters: (1) The Mystery Ships (2) The Unseen Peril (3) The Typhoon (4) The Sea Raider (5) The Tidewater Trap (6) The Alligator Attacks (7) The Deluge (8) The Mutiny (9) Ship Aflame (10) The Mad Elephant Charge (11) Smothered in the Sand (12) Millions of Gold (13) Into the Bloodhound's Jaws (14) Into the Whirlpool (15) The Trail's End

DAYS OF '49
(Arrow, March 15, 1924) 15 Chapters
Neva Gerber, Edmund Cobb, *Ruth Royce,* Wilbur McGaugh, Yakima Canutt, Charles Brinley, Clark Coffey, Elias Bullock, Al Hoxie
Directors: Jacques Jaccard, J. Marchland (some souces also credit Ben Wilson as co-director)
Story: Karl Coolidge
Chapters: (1) Soldiers of Portune (2) Red Men and White (3) A Night of Terror (4) The Empire Builders (5) A Web of Lies (6) Demetroff's Vow (7) Facing Death (8) Under the Bear Flag (9) A Ride of Peril (10) Yellow Metal and Blue Blood (11) Gold Madness (12) Crimson Nights (13) Vigilantes Justice (14) For Life and Love (15) Trail's End

RIDERS OF THE PLAINS
(Arrow, October 1, 1924) 15 Chapters
Jack Perrin, Marilyn Mills, *Ruth Royce,* Charles Brinley, Kingsley Benedict, Running Elk, Robert Miles, Rhody Hathaway, Clark Comstock, Boris Karloff, "Starlight" (a horse)
Director: Jacques Jaccard
Story: Karl Coolidge, Jacques Jaccard
Chapters: (1) Red Shadows (2) Dangerous Hazards (3) A Living Death (4) Flames of Fury (5) Morgan's Raid (6) Out of the Past (7) A Fighting Gamble (8) A Prisoner of War (9) Pawns of Destiny (10) Riding for Life (11) In Death's Shadow (12) Flaming Vengeance (13) Thundering Hoofs (11) Red Talons (15) The Reckoning (Note: Chapter 1 is 3 reels in length; others, two)

CALIFORNIA IN '49
(Arrow, November 13, 1924) 6 Reels
Neva Gerber, Edmund Cobb, *Ruth Royce,* Wilbur McGaugh
(Feature version of **Days of '49**)
Director: Jacques Jaccard
Story: Karl Coolidge

THE EMPTY SADDLE
(Lariet/Vitagraph, March 28, 1925) 5 Reels
Pete Morrison, Betty Goodwin, Bud Osborne, Lew Meehan, Eugene Washer, *Ruth Royce,* Barney Furey, "Blackie" (a horse)
Director: Harry S. Webb
Story: Forrest Sheldon
Producer: Harry S. Webb

ACTION GALORE
(Action/Weiss Brothers Artclass, November 3, 1925) 5 Reels
Buddy Roosevelt, Toy Gallagher, Charles Williams, Joe Rickson, Jack O'Brien, *Ruth Royce,* Raye Hamilton
Director: Robert Eddy

WARRIOR GAP
(Davis Distributing Division, December 4, 1925) 5 Reels
Ben Wilson, Neva Gerber, Robert Walker, Jim Welch, Aline Goodwin, Lafe McKee, *Ruth Royce,* Dick Hatton, Alfred Hewston, Len Haynes, William Patten
Director: Alvin J. Neitz (Alan James)
Scenario: George W. Pyper
Story: Charles King

TONIO, SON OF THE SIERRAS
(Davis Distributing Division, December 19, 1925) 5 Reels
Ben Wilson, Neva Gerber, Chief Yowlachie, Jim Welch, *Ruth Royce,* Bob Walker, Fay Adams
Director: Ben Wilson
Story: Charles King

FORT FRAYNE
(Davis Distributing Division, January 11, 1926) 5 Reels
Ben Wilson, Neva Gerber, *Ruth Royce,* Bill Patton, Lafe McKee
Director: Ben Wilson
Adaptation: George W. Pyper
Story: Charles King

OFFICER 444
(Goodwill, May 15, 1926) 10 Chapters
Ben Wilson, Neva Gerber, *Ruth Royce,* Al Ferguson, Jack Mower, Phil Ford, Lafe McKee, Francis Ford, Arthur Beckel, Harry McDonald, Frank Baker
Director: Francis Ford
Screenplay: Francis Ford
Chapters: (1) Flying Squadron (2) Human Rats (3) Trapped (4) Gassed (5) Missing (6) The Radio Ray (7) Death's Shadow (8) Jaws of Doom (9) Underground Trap (10) Justice

RAWHIDE
(Action/Associated Exhibitors, May 23, 1926) 5 Reels
Buffalo Bill, Jr. (Jay Wilsey), Al Taylor, Molly Malone, Joe Rickson, Charles Whitaker, Harry Todd, *Ruth Royce,* Lafe McKee
Director: Richard Thorpe
Scenario: Frank L. Inghram
Story: Ralph Cummins

WOLVES OF THE DESERT
(Ben Wilson/Rayart, November, 1926) 5 Reels
Ben Wilson, Neva Gerber, *Ruth Royce,* Ashton Dearholt, Al Ferguson, Edward La Neice, Fangs (a dog)
Director: Ben Wilson
Story: George W. Pyper
Supervisor: Ashton Dearholt
Producer: Ben Wilson

THE GALLANT FOOL
(Duke Worne/Rayart, December, 1926) 5 Reels
Billy Sullivan, Hazel Deane, Ruth Boyd, *Ruth Royce,* Frank Baker, Jimmy Aubrey, Ferdinand Schumann-Heink, Robert Waler
Director: Duke Worne
Story: George W. Pyper
Scenario: George W. Pyper

THUNDERBOLT'S TRACKS
(Morris R. Schlank/Rayart, April, 1926) 5 Reels
Jack Perrin, Pauline Curley, Jack Henderson, Billy Lamar, Harry Tenbrook, *Ruth Royce,* Ethan Laidlaw, "Starlight" (a horse)
Director: J. P. McGowan, Bennett Cohn
Scenario: Bennett Cohn

CODE OF THE COW COUNTRY
(Action/Pathé, June 19, 1927) 5 Reels
Buddy Roosevelt, Hank Bell, Elsa Benham, Melhourne MacDowell, Sherry Tansey, Richard Neill, Walter Maly, Frank Hollis, *Ruth Royce*
Director: Oscar Apfel
Scenario: Betty Burbridge
Story: Wilton West

41 • MARIN SAIS

Gutsy Independence Under the Western Sky

Marin Sais, the vivacious heroine of innumerable Kalem pictures, was a descendant of one of the finest old Spanish families of early California. She was born in 1887 on the Rancho Olompali in Marin County (for which she was named), just across the bay from San Francisco. Her father was a Spaniard, her mother, an Englishwoman. Miss Sais, who stood 5 feet 3 inches tall, weighed 115 pounds, and had brown hair and hazel eyes, was educated at Notre Dame, San Jose, and Notre Dame, Santa Clara. She planned to pursue a career in opera.

While appearing in the East and winning countless admirers with her superb voice, something happened to endanger that voice and she was forced to abandon her plans. Histrionic ability replaced the operatic ambitions and she was quickly at work in comedies for Vitagraph in their Eastern studios. Later she spent about six months at Bison 101, then joined Kalem as a dramatic actress. Success came quickly after that. Early Westerns included **How Texas Got Left** (1911), **The Tenderfoot's Troubles** (1912), **The Attack at Rocky Pass** (1913), **The Big Horn Massacre** (1913), and **The Tragedy of Bear Mountain** (1915). After her success in **The Pitfall** (1915) Marin was cast in **Stingaree** (1915), playing Ethel Porter, estranged sweetheart of Irving Randolph, known in Australia as the bandit Stingaree, a Robin Hood-like character played by True Boardman. A set of unfortunate circumstances causes both principals in the story to leave London at the end of Chapter 1; they reappear in Australia, where the story unfolds. Boardman has been falsely accused of murder by his brother, who wants the family fortune, and has fled to avoid imprisonment. He takes up a new life as a bandit, in partnership with Howie, played by Paul C. Hurst, who is instrumental in bringing the two lovers together again. Marin's departure from London has been the result of family misfortunes necessitating her employment, and she finds a position as companion to an Australian lady. Thus the stage is set for a multitude of adventures in the back country of Australia.

The Girl from Frisco (1915) was a far better series for Marin. Not only did it run for twenty-five episodes of two reels each, but Marin was definitely the star and True Boardman, as her fiancé, Congressman John Wallace, was the secondary star. Marin plays Barbara Brent, a girl of the West. Each episode is a complete story in itself, but the characters are continuing. For example, in Chapter 21 she is out to expose a faker calling himself Daniel II, who is preaching doomsday and taking over his followers' possessions. In Chapter 23 she and her fiancé are caught in the middle of a feud between cattlemen and homesteaders, and in Chapter 24 Marin is responsible for capturing a Hindoo cook who has murdered the owner of a neighboring ranch and cast suspicion on Jose, a vaquero. The series was popular and established Marin as a Western personality.

In **The Social Pirates** (1915) series, Marin shared top billing with Ollie Kirkby, and this time True Boardman was the villain of the piece. As in most of her Kalem series she had able support provided in this instance by Thomas Lingham, Paul C. Hurst, and Frank Jonasson. Marin and Ollie, Mona and Mary respectively, are two embittered women who vow to stop scoundrels who prey on helpless women. Brief synopses of two episodes are presented here to show the nature of this unusual series.

In Chapter 1, Mona and Mary save Stella, a former chorus girl, from death, and after hearing her pitiful story determine to deal justice to Holbrook, a fashionable man-about-town, and cause him to right the wrong he has committed.

The American Girl series (Kalem, 1917) – Marin Sais.

Mona places herself in Holbrook's path, and he becomes smitten with her, planning in his vanity to use her as he had Stella.

At a New Year's Eve party Mona and Holbrook, by well-planned accident, meet Mary, and the combined parties decide to finish the night at The Little Monte Carlo, a supposedly fashionable gambling house which has really been fitted out by the two women as a trap for Holbrook. The first step in their scheme is successful; Holbrook is separated from a good deal of money, which sets him up as a ready victim to the further snares of the sharp-witted girls. In succeeding scenes, Holbrook is induced to make Stella his bride, a step that he thinks he is taking voluntarily and to aid his own selfish plans.

In Episode Two James Harrasford (played by Thomas Lingham) is another conceited man-about-town who trifles with women's affections. Mona and Mary set out to teach him a lesson. Mona succeeds in becoming acquainted with him and declares that she is a Corsican living with her younger sister. Harrasford calls on Mona, and his fickle affections lead him into the trap of showing too much attention to Mary. A number of thrilling events keep Harrasford in a daze of excitement between the two girls, who (as temperamental Corsicans) are intense in love and hate. Finally Harrasford plans to flee with Mary, and arranges to meet her at ten o'clock at his apartment. At ten o'clock the bell rings--and Mona appears. She is closely followed by a detective, who forces from her a confession that she has killed Mary in her jealous rage. Harrasford--facing arrest as an accomplice--secretly passes a bribe to the detective who allows him to escape when they reach the street. Harrasford has barely turned the corner in his panic-stricken flight when Mona and the detective join in a hearty laugh. Moments later, Mary arrives to help rejoice over the success of the plan to humble the conceited heartbreaker.

Marin had no chance to display her horsemanship in this series. Off screen, however, she was busy building up her ranch at Lund, Utah, and all her spare money was going to purchase blooded horses, pigs, cows, and chickens.

The American Girl (1917) series followed, as America was plunged into the First World War. As Madge King, Marin was the central figure in an indeterminate number of two-reelers of the Old West, all melodramatic and featuring much riding and fighting. In **The Secret of Lost Valley** (1917), for instance, Marin pursues the villain on horseback, lassoes him à la Hoot Gibson, and drags him back to face justice.

In another story, **The Golden Eagle Trail** (1917), Marin and her followers round up a gang of bandits and a man who stole the bandits' loot, two bags of twenty-dollar gold pieces, by following a trail of Golden Eagles that have leaked from one of the bags. **The Lost Legion of the Border** (1917) had many strong points and one weak one. But there is enough action, stirring horsemanship, and sustained interest to overlook the point where Marin fights a contrived and unbelievable gun duel with a badman. The story is the now-familiar one of the retired outlaw who wants to form a republic of his own, comprising all the old bandits west of the Rockies.

For fast-moving, thrill-a-minute action, one would not need to look further than **The Vulture of Skull Mountain** (1917), in which ranch girl Madge King is menaced by The Vulture (Ronald Bradbury) and imprisoned in his secret torture chamber under a rude shack used as a hideout. Not to be outdone, her father (Frank Jonasson) has been held up on a trail over Skull Mountain by two outlaws and tied up under a five-ton boulder balanced on a plank over his head. Meanwhile, a kidnapped girl is being held hostage by the Vulture, and hunchback Charlie (Edward Clisbee) is lurking about to make things unpleasant for hero Larry Kerwin (Edward Hearn). In the final scene, Marin rides up behind a rig driven by the fleeing Vulture as it takes a corner on two wheels, bringing down her man, while her fiancé and father ride on to stop the runaway rig bearing the kidnapped girl. A lot of action and story was crammed into this two-reeler, which also had Jack Hoxie (then known as Hart Hoxie) in the role of a wealthy cattleman.

Not quite as fast-moving, but amply so, was **The Pot O'Gold** (1917) in which Marin attempts to keep the only paper in the little town of San Reno from biting the dust by burying a pot of gold near the town and running clues to its whereabouts in the Herald. Discovering a buried skull and a photo of a small child in the process of burying the gold, Marin and friends set out to solve a mysterious murder. **Sagebrush Law** (1917) was a common story of lawlessness in a Western town, including a vigilante committee, a hanging, the robbery of a post office, the murder of one innocent onlooker, and the framing of another--just your ordinary, garden-variety shoot-em-up. Edward Hearn played second lead to Marin in the series and was an enjoyable hero.

In her last series for Kalem, which was about to close its doors forever on picture making, Marin co-starred once more with True Boardman, this time in the fifteen chapters of **The Further Adventures of Stingaree** (1917). Marin is again Ethel Porter to Boardman's Irving Randolph/Stingaree, but Hal Clements takes the role of Howie formerly played by Paul Hurst. The story begins back in London where Stingaree has been cleared of the murder charges that drove him from the city in the first series. Finding that his deceased brother has squandered the family fortune, he realizes he cannot, as a penniless man, marry his fiancée Ethel. His old friend Howie comes from Australia to warn him that government officers are on his trail with a warrant for his arrest. He persuades Stingaree to return to Australia with him. And, as before, Ethel soon follows to share in the wild Australian adventures which culminate in their reunion.

With the demise of Kalem Marin free-lanced for several years, her career seemingly on the wane. But in 1920 she played opposite Jack Hoxie in Arrow's **Thunderbolt Jack** and won new laurels as a Western heroine in the popular serial. She also married the big Oklahoma cowboy and rodeo rider who had previously played minor parts in some of her films at Kalem. Several features with Jack followed, but when he got a job with Universal she was forced to remain in independent productions. Marin had two daughters by him, but the marriage was not a blissful one and the two were divorced about 1925. Marin subsequently worked in several of Jack's Universal Westerns as the "second woman." In the late twenties she worked only in minor roles, and with the coming of talkies she settled down to character roles.

MARIN SAIS Filmography

TWELFTH NIGHT
(Vitagraph, February 2, 1910) 1 Reel
Julia Swayne Gordon, Charles Kent, Florence Turner, Edith Storey, Tefft Johnson, *Marin Sais,* William Humphrey, James Young
Scenario: Eugene Mullin
Supervisor: J. Stuart Blackton
Story: William Shakespeare

HOW TEXAS GOT LEFT
(Kalem, November, 1911) 1 Reel
Marin Sais

THE TENDERFOOT'S TROUBLES
(Kalem, February, 1912) 1 Reel
Marin Sais

DEATH VALLEY SCOTTY'S MINE
(Kalem, October, 1912) 1 Reel
Walter Scott, Ruth Roland, *Marin Sais*

THE CHAPERON GETS A DUCKLING
(Kalem, November, 1912) 1 Reel
John E. Brennan, Ed Coxen, Ruth Roland, *Marin Sais*

DAYS OF '49
(Kalem, November, 1912) 1 Reel
Carlyle Blackwell, *Marin Sais*

THE LAST BLOCKHOUSE
(Kalem, January, 1913) 2 Reels
Carlyle Blackwell, William H. West, Paul Hurst, Knute Rahm, *Marin Sais,* C. Rhys Pryce
Director: George Melford

THE REDEMPTION
(Kalem, February, 1913) 2 Reels
William H. West, Carlyle Blackwell, Jane Wolfe, Paul C. Hurst, Knute Rahm, *Marin Sais*

THE MOUNTAIN WITCH
(Kalem, February, 1913) 1 Reel
Jane Wolfe, Carlyle Blackwell, *Marin Sais*

THE BUCKSKIN COAT
(Kalem, February, 1913) 1 Reel
Marin Sais

THE ATTACK AT ROCKY PASS
(Kalem, March, 1913) 1 Reel
Marin Sais, Carlyle Blackwell
Director: George Melford
Story: H. K. Harris

THE CALIFORNIA OIL CROOKS
(Kalem, April, 1913) 1 Reel
Marin Sais

THE CIRCLE OF FATE
(Kalem, May, 1913) 1 Reel
Marin Sais

THE BATTLE FOR FREEDOM
(Kalem, May, 1913) 2 Reels
William H. West, Jane Wolfe, *Marin Sais,* Carlyle Blackwell, C. Rhys Pryce, Knute Rahmn, Ed Clisbee
Director: George Melford

THE SCHEME OF SHIFTLESS SAM SMITH
(Kalem, June 7, 1913) 1 Reel
John Brennan, *Marin Sais*

ON THE BRINK OF RUIN
(Kalem, June 14, 1913) 1 Reel
Marin Sais, Paul Hurst, William H. West

THE STRUGGLE
(Kalem, June 21, 1913) 2 Reels
Marin Sais, Caryle Blackwell, William H. West, Paul C. Hurst
Director: George Melford
Story: Henry Albert Phillips

THE BANDIT'S CHILD
(Kalem, June, 1913) 1 Reel
Marin Sais

THE GIRL AND THE GANGSTER
(Kalem, July, 1913)
Carlyle Blackwell, *Marin Sais,* Jane Wolfe

THE SKELETON IN THE CLOSET
(Kalem, August 9, 1913) 2 Reels
Carlyle Blackwell, William H. West, Paul Hurst, *Marin Sais*

THE INVADERS
(Kalem, August 23, 1913) 2 Reels
Paul C. Hurst, Jane Wolfe, *Marin Sais,* Carlyle Blackwell, William H. West, Charles French, James Horne, Knute Rahm, Rhys Pryce
Director: George Melford
Story: John Lloyd

TROOPER BILLY
(Kalem, September, 1913) 2 Reels
Marin Sais
Story: Frederick Paulding

THE BIG HORN MASSACRE
(Kalem, December 27, 1913) 2 Reels
William H. West, *Marin Sais,* Paul C. Hurst, Hart (Jack) Hoxie, Billie Rhodes, Edeard Clisbee, Ernest Garcia

THE SHADOW OF GUILT
(Kalem, January, 1914) 2 Reels
Marin Sais

TRAPPED
(Kalem, January, 1914) 2 Reels
Marin Sais

THE MASTER ROGUE
(Kalem, April, 1914) 2 Reels
George Melford, William H. West, *Marin Sais*

THE DEATH SIGN OF HIGH NOON
(Kalem, April, 1914) 1 Reel
Marin Sais, William H. West, Jane Wolfe, Paul C. Hurst

THE BARRIER OF IGNORANCE
(Kalem, May 30, 1914) 2 Reels
George Melford, *Marin Sais*, Jane Wolfe, William H. West, Paul C. Hurst, Cleo Ridgley

THE QUICKSANDS
(Kalem, June 6, 1914) 2 Reels
Marin Sais

THE PRIMITIVE INSTINCT
(Kalem, August 15, 1914) 2 Reels
Marin Sais
Director: George Melford

THE RAJAH'S VOW
(Kalem, August, 1914) 2 Reels
Marin Sais

THE ETERNAL BOND
(Kalem, 1914)
Marin Sais

THE POTTER AND THE CLAY
(Kalem, September 19, 1914)
Marin Sais, Douglas Gerrard, Cleo Ridgely, Elise Maison, Jane Wolfe
Director: George Melford
Story: Mrs. Owen Bronson

KING OF CHANCE
(Kalem, September, 1914) 3 Reels
Marin Sais, Douglas Gerrard

THE PRISON STAIN
(Kalem, October 31, 1914) 2 Reels
Marin Sais, Paul C. Hurst, Frank Jonasson, William H. West

THE WINNING WHISKERS
(Kalem, December 19, 1914)
Lloyd V. Hamilton, *Marin Sais*, Bud Duncan, Marshall Neilan

THE DERELICT
(Kalem, December, 1914) 2 Reels
Douglas Gerrard, *Marin Sais*, Mildred Gordon, Frank Jonasson, Jane Wolfe Edward Clisbee, William H. West
Director: George Melford
Story: James W. Horne

THE SMUGGLERS OF LONE ISLE
(Kalem, December, 1914) 2 Reels
Marin Sais

THE FATAL OPAL
(Kalem, December, 1914) 2 Reels
Marin Sais, Douglas Gerrard, William H. West, Paul C. Hurst, Cleo Ridgley
Director: George Melford

COOKY'S ADVENTURE
(Kalem, January, 1915)
Chance E. Ward, *Marin Sais*, Jennie Lee, Bud Duncan
Director: Chance E. Ward

THE TRAGEDY OF BEAR MOUNTAIN
(Kalem, January 25, 19195) 2 Reels
Jane Wolfe, *Marin Sais*, Paul C. Hurst, Cleo Ridgley, Douglas Gerrard, Frank Jonasson, William H. West

THE WAITRESS AND THE BOOBS
(Kalem, January, 1915) 1 Reel
Marin Sais

INSURANCE NIGHTMARE
(Kalem, February, 1915) 1 Reel
Marin Sais, Charles Inslee, A. Munden
Director: Chance E. Ward

HAM AMONG THE REDSKINS
(Kalem, March, 1915)
Lloyd V. Hamilton, Bud Duncan, *Marin Sais*

AM IN THE HAREM
(Kalem, March, 1915)
Lloyd V. Hamilton, Bud Duncan, *Marin Sais*
Director: Chance E. Ward
Story: Hamilton Smith

OTTA COIN'S GHOST
(Kalem, April, 1915)
Lloyd V. Hamilton, Bud Duncan, *Marin Sais*

THE SOCIAL PIRATES
(Kalem, April, 1915) 15 Episodes
Marin Sais, Ollie Kirby, E. Forrest Taylor, Frank Jonasson, Rupert Dell, Edward Clisbee, Thomas Lingham, Paul C. Hurst, B. Furey, Ruth Snyder, True Boardman
Director: James W. Horne
Chapters: (1) The Little Monte Carlo (2) The Corsican Sisters (3) The Parasite (4) War of Wits (5) The Millionaire Plunger (6) The Master Swindlers (7) A Rogue's Nemesis (8) Sauce for the Gander (9) The Missing Millionaire (10) Unmasking a Rascal (11) The Finger of the Teller (12) The Disappearance of Helen Minter (13) In the Service of the State (14) The Music Swindlers (15) Black Magic

THE CLAIRVOYANT SWINDLERS
(Kalem, May 15, 1915) 2 Reels
Marin Sais
Story: Hamilton Smith

THE CLOSED DOOR
(Kalem, May 22, 1915)
Marin Sais, Thomas Lingham, Ollie Kirby

THE FIGURE IN BLACK
(Kalem, May 22, 1915) 2 Reels
Marin Sais, Ollie Kirby, Paul C. Hurst

THE MONEY LEECHES
(Kalem, June 5, 1915) 2 Reels
Marin Sais, Arthur Shirley, William H. West, Thomas Lingham

THE SECRET WELL
(Kalem, June 5, 1915) 2 Reels
Marin Sais
Story: Hamilton Smith

THE VANISHING VASES
(Kalem, June 12, 1915) 2 Reels
Marin Sais, Frank Jonasson, Ollie Kirby, Arthur Shirley, William H. West

THE STRAIGHT AND NARROW PATH
(Kalem, June 17, 1915) 2 Reels
Marin Sais, Frank Jonasson, Ollie Kirby, Arthur Shirley
Director: James W. Horne
Story: Harry O. Hoyt

THE VIVISECTIONIST
(Kalem, June 19, 1915) 2 Reels
Marin Sais, Frank Jonasson, William H. West, Paul C. Hurst, Thomas Lingham
Director: James W. Horne

THE ACCOMPLICE
(Kalem, June 26, 1915) 2 Reels
Marin Sais, Thomas Lingham, William H. West
Director: James W. Horne
Story: C. Doty Hobart

THE DISAPPEARING NECKLACE
(Kalem, July 24, 1915) 2 Reels
Marin Sais, Charles Cummings, William H. West, Ollie Kirby, Frank Jonasson
Director: James W. Horne
Story: Hamilton Smith

THE FRAME-UP
(Kalem, July, 1915) 2 Reels
Ollie Kirby, *Marin Sais*

THE STRANGLER'S CORD
(Kalem, July, 1915) 2 Reels
William H. West, Thomas Lingham, Ollie Kirby, *Marin Sais,* Charles Cummings

WHEN THIEVES FALL OUT
(Kalem, September 11, 1915) 2 Reels
Frank Jonasson, Paul C. Hurst, *Marin Sais,* True Boardman
Story: Hamilton Smith

THE MAN IN IRONS
(Kalem, September, 1915)
William H. West, Ollie Kirby, True Boardman, *Marin Sais,* Paul C. Hurst, Thomas Lingham, Frank Jonasson
Director: James W. Horne
Story: Hamilton Smith

THE WOLF'S PREY
(Kalem, September, 1915) 2 Reels
William H. West, Ollie Kirby, *Marin Sais,* Frank Jonasson
Story: Hamilton Smith

UNDER OATH
(Kalem, September, 1915) 2 Reels
True Boardman, *Marin Sais,* Thomas Lingham, Frank Jonasson
Director: James W. Horne
Story: Hamilton Smith

THE DREAM SEEKERS
(Kalem, November 6, 1915)
William H. West, *Marin Sais,* Frank Jonasson, Thomas Lingham, True Boardman
Director: James W. Horne

THE PITFALL
(Kalem, November 6, 1915) 4 Reels
Marin Sais, Frank Jonasson, Thomas Lingham, Edward Clisbee, Paul C. Hurst, True Boardman, James W. Horne
Director: James W. Horne
Story: Howard Irving Young

STINGAREE
(Kalem, November 24, 1915) 12 Chapters
True Boardman, *Marin Sais,* Paul C. Hurst, Thomas Lingham, Frank Jonasson, William Brunton, James W. Horne, Ollie Kirby, Edward Clisbee, Joseph Barber, Jack Lott, Hoot Gibson, Janet Rambeau
Director: James W. Horne
Scenario: James W. Horne
Story: E. W. Hornung
Producer: James W. Horne
Chapters: (1) An Enemy of Mankind (2) A Voice in the Wilderness (3) The Black Hole of Glenrenald (4) To the Vile Dust (5) A Bushranger at Bay (6) The Taking of Stingaree (7) The Honor of the Road (8) The Purification of Mulfers (9) The Duel in the Desert (10) The Villain Worshipper (11) The Moth and the Star (12) The Darkest Hour

THE GIRL FROM FRISCO
(Kalem, 1916) 25 Chapters
Marin Sais, True Boardman, Frank Jonasson, Ronald Bradbury, Edward Clisbee, Josephine West, Steve Murphy, Karl Formes, Jr., Barney Furey, Jack Hutchison, E. Forrest Taylor, Hart (Jack) Hoxie, Jack McDonald
Director: James W. Horne
Story: Robert Welles Ritchie
Chapters: (1) The Fighting Heiress (2) The Turquois Conspiracy (3) The Oil Field Plot (4) Tiger Unchained (5) The Ore Plunderers (6} The Treasure of Cibola (7) The Gun Runners (8) A Battle in the Dark (9) The Web of Guilt (10) The Reformation of Dog Hole (11) The Yellow Hand (12) Harvest of Gold (13) The Son of Cain (14) The Witch of the Dark House (15) The Mystery of the Brass Bound Chest (16) Fight for Paradise Valley (17) Border Wolves (18) The Poisoned Dart (19) The Stain of Chuckawalla (20) On the Brink of War (21) False Prophet (22) The Resurrection of Gold Bar (23) The Homesteaders' Feud (24) The Wolf of Los Alamos (25) The Dominion of Fernandez

THE MYSTERIES OF THE GRAND HOTEL
(Kalem, 1916)
(A series--number of episodes undetermined)
Marin Sais, True Boardman, Ollie Kirby, Charles Cummings, William H. West, Thomas Lingham, Frank Jonasson
Director: James W. Horne
Story: Hamilton Smith

WITCH OF THE DARK HOUSE
(Kalem, 1916) 1 Reel
Marin Sais

THE DARKEST HOUR
(Kalem, 1916)
Marin Sais

THE GOLDEN EAGLE TRAIL
(Kalem, March, 1917) 2 Reels
(The American Girl Series)
Marin Sais, Edward Hearn, Frank Jonasson, Ronald Bradbury, Edward Clisbee
Director: James W. Horne
Story: Frederick R. Bechdolt

THE SECRET OF THE LOST VALLEY
(Kalem, March, 1917) 2 Reels
(The American Girl Series)
Marin Sais, Frank Jonasson, Ronald Bradbury, Edward Clisbee, Knute Rahn, Hart (Jack) Hoxie, Grace Johnson
Story: Frederick R. Bechdolt
Director: James W. Horne

THE LOST LEGION OF THE BORDER
(Kalem, March, 1917) 2 Reels
(The American Girl Series)
Marin Sais, Frank Jonasson, Edward Hearn, Ronald Bradbury, Edward Clisbee
Director: James Horne
Story: Frederick R. Bechdolt

THE VULTURES OF SKULL MOUNTAIN
(Kalem, April, 1917) 2 Reels
(The American Girl Series)
Marin Sais, Frank Jonasson, Edward Hearn, Ronald Bradbury, Edward Clisbee, Hart (Jack) Hoxie
Director: James Horne
Story: Frederick R. Bechdolt

THE POT O'GOLD
(Kalem, June, 1917) 2 Reels
Marin Sais, Frank Jonasson, Edward Hearn, R. E. Bradbury, Edward Clisbee
Director: James Horne
Story: Frederick R. Bechdolt

SAGEBRUSH LAW
(Kalem, June, 1917) 2 Reels
(The American Girl Series)
Marin Sais, Frank Jonasson, Edward Hearn, R. F. Bradbury, Knute Rahm, Edward Clisbee
Director: James Horne
Story: Frederick R. Bechdolt

TREASURE OF CIBOLA
(Kalem, 1917) 2 Reels
(The American Girl Series)
Marin Sais, Frank Jonasson, Edward Hearn
Director: James Horne
Story: Frederick R. Bechdolt

HOLE IN THE MOUNTAIN
(Kalem, 1917) 2 Reels
(The American Girl Series)
Marin Sais, Frank Jonasson, Edward Hearn
Director: James Horne
Story: Frederick R. Bechdolt

FALSE PROPHET
(Kalem, 1917) 2 Reels
(The American Girl Series)
Marin Sais, Frank Jonasson, Edward Hearn
Director: James Horne
Story: Frederick R. Bechdolt

MANHUNT AT SAN REMO
(Kalem, 1917) 2 Reels
(The American Girl Series)
Marin Sais, Frank Jonasson, Edward Hearn
Director: James Horne
Story: Frederick R. Bechdolt

THE FIGHTING HEIRESS
(Kalem, 1917) 2 Reels
(The American Girl Series)
Marin Sais, Edward Hearn, Frank Jonasson
Director: James Horne
Story: Frederick R. Bechdolt

PHANTOM MINE
(Kalem, 1917) 2 Reels
Marin Sais, Edward Hearn, Frank Jonasson
Director: James Horne
Story: Frederick R. Bechdolt

THE MAN FROM TIA JUANA
(Kalem, 1917) 2 Reels
(The American Girl Series)
Marin Sais, Edward Hearn, Hart (Jack) Hoxie
Director: James Horne
Story: Frederick R. Bechdolt

THE FURTHER ADVENTURES OF STINGAREE
(Kalem, June, 1917) 15 Chapters
True Boardman, *Marin Sais,* Paul C. Hurst, Frank Jonasson, Ollie Kirby, Thomas Lingham, Edward Clisbee, Edythe Sterling, Barney Furey, G. A. Williams, Frank M. Clark, Jack Lott, Hal Clements, Jack Waltemeyer
Director: Paul C. Hurst
Screenplay: Joseph F. Poland
Story: E. W. Hornung
Chapters: (1) The Fugitive Passenger (2) A Model Marauder (3) A Double Deception (4) An Eye for an Eye (5) Mark of Stingaree (6) Through Fire and Water (7) An Order of the Court (8) Tracking of Stingaree (9) A Bushranger's Strategy (10) Poisoned Cup (11) Arrayed with the Enemy (12) The Jackaroo (13) At the Sign of the Kangaroo (14) The Stranger at Dumcrieff (15) A Champion of the Law

THE CITY OF DIM FACES
(Paramount-Lasky, July 6, 1918) 5 Reels
Sessue Hayakawa, Doris Pawn, *Marin Sais,* James Cruze, Winter Hall
Director: George Melford
Scenario: Frances Marion

HIS BIRTHRIGHT
(Haworth/Robertson-Cole, August 4, 1918) 5 Reels
Sessue Hayakawa, Maym Kelso, Tauru Aoki, *Marin Sais,* Howard Davies, Mary Anderson, Sydney DeGrey, Harry Von Meter
Director: William Worthington
Scenario: Dennison Clift and Sessue Hayakawa

BONDS OF HONOR
(Haworth/Robertson-Cole, October 31, 1918) 5 Reels
Sessue Hayakawa, Tauru Aoki, *Marin Sais,* Dagmar Godowsky, Herschal Mayall, Toyo Fujita, M. Fushida
Director: William Worthington
Screenplay: Clara Whipple

THE VANITY POOL
(Universal, October, 1918) 6 Reels
Mary MacLaren, Thomas Holding, Anna Q. Nilsson, Franklyn Farnum, *Marin Sais,* Winter Hall
Director: Ida May Park
Scenario: Ida May Park
Story: Nalbro Bartley

THE GRAY WOLF'S GHOST
(R-C, October, 1919) 5 Reels
H. B. Warner, *Marin Sais*, Edward Peil, Rita Stanwood, Violet Schram, Hector V. Sarno
Director: Park Frame (?)
Story: Bret Harte, "Maruja"

THUNDERBOLT JACK
(Arrow, November 1, 1920) 10 Chapters
Jack Hoxie, *Marin Sais,* Al Hoxie, Chris Frank, Steve Clements, Edith Stayart
Director: Murdock MacQuarrie, Francis Ford
Screenplay: Joe Brandt
Supervisor: Ben Wilson
Chapters: (1) The Thunderbolt Strikes (2) Eight to One (10) Dungeon of Death
(No information uncovered on other chapter titles)

DEAD OR ALIVE
(Unity Photoplays/Arrow, March, 1921) 5 Reels
Jack Hoxie, *Marin Sais,* Joseph Girard, C. Ray Florhe, Wilbur McGaugh, Evelyn Nelson
Director: Dell Henderson
Producer: Ben Wilson

THE SHERIFF OF HOPE ETERNAL
(Ben Wilson Prod./Arrow, March, 1921) 5 Reels
Jack Hoxie, *Marin Sais,* Joseph Girard, William Dyer, Bee Monson, Theodore Brown, Wilbur McGaugh
Director: Ben Wilson
Producer: Ben Wilson

THE BROKEN SPUR
(Ben Wilson Prod./Arrow, July, 1921) 5 Reels
Jack Hoxie, Evelyn Nelson, Jim Welch, Wilbur McGaugh, Edward Berman, Harry Rattenberry, *Marin Sais*
Director: Ben Wilson

RIDERS OF THE LAW
(Sunset, December 15, 1922) 5 Reels
Jack Hoxie, *Marin Sais,* Thomas Lingham, Jack Pierce, Pat Harmon, Frank Rice
Director: Robert North Bradbury
Screenplay: Robert North Bradbury

GOOD MEN AND BAD
(F. W. Kraemer/American Releasing Corp., July 14, 1923) 5 Reels
Marin Sais, Steve Carrie, Merrill McCormick, George Cuyton, Faith Hope
Director: Merrill McCormick
Scenario: William Lester
Story: William Lester

BEHIND TWO GUNS
(Sunset, May 15, 1924) 5 Reels
J. B. Warner, Hazel Newman, *Marin Sais,* Jay Morley, Jim Welch, Otto Lederer, William Calles, Jack Waltemeyer, Emily Gerdes, Bartlett A. Carle, Robert North Bradbury
Director: Robert N. Bradbury
Story: Robert N. Bradbury

THE HELLION
(Sunset, July 15, 1924) 5 Reels
J. B. Warner, *Marin Sais,* Boris Karloff, Aline Goodwin, William Lester
Director: Bruce Mitchell
Screenplay: Bruce Mitchell

THE MEASURE OF A MAN
(Universal, October 14, 1924) 5 Reels
William Desmond, Albert J. Smith, Francis Ford, *Marin Sais,* William J. Dyer, Bobby Gordon, Harry Tenbrook, Zala Davis, William Turner, Mary McAllister
Director: Arthur Rosson
Screenplay: Wyndham Gittnes
Scenario: Isadore Bernstein
Story: Norman Duncan

A ROARING ADVENTURE
(Universal, February 8, 1925) 5 Reels
Jack Hoxie, Mary McAllister, *Marin Sais,* J. Gordon Russell, Jack Pratt, Francis Ford, Margaret Smith
Director: Clifford S. Smith
Continuity: Percy Heath
Adaptation: Isadore Bernstein
Story: Jack Rollens, "The Tenderfoot"

THE RED RIDER
(Universal, August 2, 1925) 5 Reels
Jack Hoxie, Mary McAllister, Jack Pratt, Natalie Warfield, *Marin Sais,* William McCall, Francis Ford, George Connors, Frank Lanning, Clark Comstock, Duke R. Lee, Chief Big Tree, William Welsh, Virginia True Boardman
Director: Clifford S. Smith
Story: Isadore Bernstein

THE WILD HORSE STAMPEDE
(Universal, September 5, 1926) 5 Reels
Jack Hoxie, Fay Wray, William Steele, *Marin Sais,* Clark Comstock, Jack Pratt, George Kesterson (Art Mix), Bert De Marc, Monte Montague, "Scout," "Bunk"
Director: Albert Rogell
Scenario: Doris Malloy
Story: W. C. Tuttle, "Blind Trails"

ROUGH AND READY
(Universal, January 9, 1927) 5 Reels
Jack Hoxie, Ena Gregory, Jack Pratt, William A. Steele, Monte Montague, Clark Comstock, *Marin Sais,* Bert De Marc, "Scout," "Bunk"
Director: Albert Rogell
Continuity: William Lester
Story: Gardner Bradford

MEN OF DARING
(Universal, June 5, 1927) 7 Reels
Jack Hoxie, Ena Gregory, *Marin Sais,* Francis Ford, James Kelly, Ernie Adams, Robert Milash, Bert Lindley, Bert Apling, William Malan, John Hall, Joseph Bennett, "Scout," "Bunk"
Director: Albert Rogell
Scenario: Marion Jackson
Story: Marion Jackson

THE FIGHTING THREE
(Universal, July 3, 1927) 5 Reels
Jack Hoxie, Olive Hasbrouck, *Marin Sais,* Fanny Warren, William Malan, Buck Connors, William Dyer, Henry Roquemore, William Norton Bailey, "Scout," "Bunk"
Director: Albert Rogell
Scenario: William Lester
Story: William Lester

A SON OF THE DESERT
(F. W. Kraemer/American Releasing Corp., February 11, 1928) 5 Reels
William Merrill McCormick, *Marin Sais,* Robert Burns, Faith Hope, James Welsh
Director: William Merrill McCormick

COME AND GET IT
(FBO, February 3, 1929) 6 Reels
Bob Steele, Jimmy Quinn, Betty Welsh, Jay Morley, James B. Leong, Harry O'Connor, *Marin Sais,* William Welsh
Director: Wallace Fox
Scenario: Frank Howard Clark

THE FIGHTING COWBOY
(California Motion Pictures/Superior Talking Pictures, 1933) 58 Minutes
Buffalo Bill, Jr., Genee Boutell, Allen Holbrook, William Ryno, *Marin Sais,* Tom Palky, Bart Carre, Jack Evans, Boris Bullock, Ken Broeker, Betty Butler, Hamilton Steele, Clyde McClary, Ernest Scott, Bud Baxter, Jack Bronston
Director: Denver Dixon (Victor Adamson)
Screenplay: L. V. Jefferson
Story: L. V. Jefferson
Producer: Victor Adamson

WHEELS OF DESTINY
(Universal, February 19, 1934) 64 Minutes
Ken Maynard, Dorothy Dix, Philo McCullough, Fred McKay, Jay Wilsey (Buffalo Bill, Jr.), Fred Sale, Jr., Jack Rockwell, Frank Rice, Nelson McDowell, William Gould, Ed Coxen, Merrill McCormack, Slim Whitaker, Hank Bell, Robert Burns, Artie Ortego, Wally Wales, Jack Evans, Helen Gibson, Bud McClure, Fred Burns, Chief Big Tree, Roy Bucko, *Marin Sais,* Chuck Baldra, Arkansas Johnny, Bobby Dunn, Blackjack Ward, Al Taylor
Director: Alan James
Screenplay/Story: Nate Gatzert
Producer: Ken Maynard

RAWHIDE ROMANCE
(Superior Talking Pictures, 1934)
Buffalo Bill, Jr., Genee Boutell, Lafe McKee, Si Jenks, Bart Carre, Boris Bullock, Jack Evans, *Marin Sais,* Clyde McClary, Ken Broeker
Director: Victor Adamson (Denver Dixon)
Screenplay: L. V. Jefferson
Producer: Victor Adamson (Denver Dixon)

THE PACE THAT KILLS
(Willis Kent, December, 1935)
Lois January, Noel Madison, Sheila Manners, Lois Lindsay, Charles Delaney, Frank Shannon, Gaby Fay, Eddie Phillips, *Marin Sais,* Maury Peck, Frank Collins, Nona Lee, Dick Botiller
Director: William O'Connor

TELL YOUR CHILDREN
(G & H, 1938)
Lillian Miles, Thelma White, Carleton Young, Dorothy Short, Kenneth Craig, Pat Royale, Warren McCullon, Joe Forte, William Royal, Walter McGrail, Edward Earle, Frank O'Connor, Ted Wraye, Mary McLarne, Ed Mortimer, *Marin Sais,* Harry Harvey, Jr., Edward LeSaint, Dan Wolheim, Lester Dorr, Phil Dunham, Billy Franey, Dave O'Brien
Director: Louis Gasnier

PIONEER TRAIL
(Columbia, July 15, 1938) 59 Minutes
Jack Luden, Joan Barclay, Slim Whitaker, Leon Beaumon, Hal Taliaferro, *Marin Sais,* Eve McKenzie, Hal Price, Dick Botiller, Tom London, Tex Palmer, Art Davis, Fred Burns, Bob McKenzie, "Tuffy" (a dog)
Director: Joseph Levering
Story: Nate Gatzert
Screenplay: Nate Gatzert
Producer: Larry Darmour

PHANTOM GOLD
(Columbia, August 31, 1938) 56 Minutes
Jack Luden, Beth Marion, Barry Downing, Charles Whitaker, Hal Taliaferro, Art Davis, Jimmy Robinson, Jack Ingram, Buzz Barton, *Marin Sais,* Tex Palmer, Jack O'Shea, "Tuffy" (a dog)
Director: Joseph Levering
Screenplay: Nate Gatzert
Story: Nate Gatzert
Producer: Larry Darmour

RIDERS OF THE FRONTIER
(Monogram, August 16, 1939) 58 Minutes
Tex Ritter, Jack Rutherford, Hal Taliaferro, Jean Joyce, *Marin Sais,* Mantan Moreland, Olin Francis, Roy Barcroft, Merrill McCormack, Maxine Leslie, Nolan Willis, Nelson McDowell, Charles King, Forrest Taylor, Robert Frazer, "White Flash"
Director: Spencer Bennet
Screenplay: Jesse Duffy, Joseph Levering
Story: Jesse Duffy, Joseph Levering
Producer: Edward Finney

THE MAD EMPRESS
(Warner Bros., December, 1939) 95 Minutes
Medea Novara, Lionel Atwill, Conrad Nagel, Guy Bates Post, Jason Robards, Sr., Frank McGlynn, Sr., Evelyn Brent, Claudia Dell, Gustave von Seyffertitz, Martin Garralaga, Julian Rivero, Duncan Renaldo, *Marin Sais,* Rene de Luguro, Robert Frazer, George Regas, Gracilla Romero
Director: Miguel G. Torres
Story: Miguel G. Torres
Producer: Miguel G. Torres
Screenplay: Jean Bart, Jerome Ghodorov, Miguel G. Torres
(Film also known as **Juarez and Maximillian**)

DEADWOOD DICK
(Columbia, July 19, 1940) 15 Chapters
Don Douglas, Lorna Gray (Adrian Booth), Harry Harvey, *Marin Sais,* Lane Chandler, Jack Ingram, Charles King, Ed Cassidy, Robert Fiske, Lee Shumway, Edmund Cobb, Edward Peil, Edward Hearn, Karl Hackett, Roy Barcroft, Bud Osborne, Joe Girard, Tom London, Kenne Duncan, Yakima Canutt, Fred Kelsey, Edward Cecil, Kit Guard, Al Ferguson, Constantine Romanoff, Franklyn Farnum, Charles Hamilton, Jim Corey, Eddie Featherstone
Director: James W. Horne
Screenplay: Wyndham Gittens, Morgan B. Cox, George Morgan, John Cutting
Producer: Larry Darmour
Chapters: (1) A Wild West Empire (2) Who Is the Skull? (3) Pirates of the Plains (4) The Skull Baits a Trap (5) Win, Lose, or Draw (6) Buried Alive (7) The Chariot of Doom (8) The Secret of Number Ten (9) The Fatal Warning (10) Framed for Murder (11) The Bucket of Death (12) A Race Against Time (13) The Arsenal of Revolt (14) Holding the Fort (15) The Deadwood Express

BILLY THE KID IN SANTA FE
(PRC, July 11, 1941) 56 Minutes
Bob Steele, Al St. John, Rex Lease, *Marin Sais,* Dennis Moore, Karl Hackett, Steve Clark, Hal Price, Charles King, Frank Ellis, Dave O'Brien, Kenne Duncan, Curley Dresden, Tex Palmer
Director: Sherman Scott (Sam Newfield)
Screenplay: Joseph O'Donnell
Producer: Sigmund Neufeld

FRONTIER OUTLAWS
(PRC, March 4, 1944) 56 Minutes
Buster Crabbe, Al St. John, Frances Gladwin, *Marin Sais,* Charles King, Jack Ingram, Kermit Maynard, Edward Cassidy, Emmett Lynn, Budd Buster, Frank Ellis
Director: Sam Newfield
Screenplay: Joe O'Donnell
Producer: Sigmund Neufeld

ENEMY OF WOMEN
(Monogram, August 21, 1944)
Claudia Drake, Paul Andor, Donald Woods, H. B. Warner, Sigrid Gurie, Ralph Morgan, Gloria Stuart, Robert Barrat, Beryl Wallace, Byron Foulger, Lester Dorr, Craig Whitley, Charles Halton, *Marin Sais,* Howard Johnson, Gene Stutenroth, George Meader, Dell Henderson
Director: Alfred Zeisler
Screenplay/Story: Alfred Z. Eisler, Herbert O. Phillips
Producer: W. R. Frank

OATH OF VENGEANCE
(PRC, December 9, 1944) 57 Minutes
Buster Crabbe, Al St. John, Mady Lawrence, Jack Ingram, Charles King, *Marin Sais*, Karl Hackett, Kermit Maynard, Hal Price, Frank Ellis, Budd Buster, Jimmy Aubrey
Director: Sam Newfield
Screenplay: Fred Myton
Producer: Sigmund Neufeld

BELLS OF ROSARITA
(Republic, June 19, 1945) 68 Minutes
Roy Rogers, George F. Hayes, Dale Evans, Adele Mara, Grant Withers, Janet Martin, Syd Saylor, Addison Richards, Edward Cassidy, Roy Barcroft, Kenne Duncan, Rex Lease, Earle Hodgins, Bob Wilke, Ted Adams, Wally West, Bob Nolan and the Sons of the Pioneers, Robert Mitchell Boychoir, "Trigger," Poodles Hanaford, Helen Talbot, Hank Bell, Forbes Murray, Tom London, *Marin Sais,* Jack Richardson, and guest stars Bill Elliott, Allan Lane, Donald Barry, Robert Livingston, and Sunset Carson
Director: Frank McDonald
Screenplay: Jack Townley
Associate Producer: Eddy White

PRAIRIE RUSTLERS
(PRC, November 7, 1945) 56 Minutes
Buster Crabbe, Al St. John, Evelyn Finley, Karl Hackett, Bud Osborne, *Marin Sais,* I. Stanford Jolley, Kermit Maynard, Herman Hack, George Morrell, Tex Cooper, Dorothy Vernon
Director: Sam Newfield
Screenplay: Fred Myton
Story: Fred Myton
Producer: Sigmund Neufeld

RIDE, RYDER, RIDE
(Equity/Eagle Lion, February 1, 1949) 60 Minutes
Jim Bannon, Don Kay Reynolds, Emmett Lynn, Peggy Stewart, Gaylord Pendleton, Jack O'Shea, Jean Budinger, *Marin Sais,* Stanley Blystone, William Fawcett, Billy Hammond, Edwin Max, Steve Clark
Director: Lewis D. Collins
Screenplay: Paul Franklin
Producer: Jerry Thomas

ROLL, THUNDER, ROLL
(Equity/Eagle Lion, August 27, 1949) 60 Minutes
Jim Bannon, Don Kay Reynolds, Emmett Lynn, *Marin Sais,* Glenn Strange, Nancy Gates, I. Stanford Jolley, Lee Morgan, Lane Bradford, Steve Pendleton, Charles Stevens, William Fawcett, Dorothy Latt, Joe Green, Rocky Shahan, Carol Henry, George Chesebro, Jack O'Shea
Director: Lewis D. Collins
Screenplay: Paul Franklin
Producer: Jerry Thomas

THE FIGHTING REDHEAD
(Equity/Eagle Lion, October 12, 1949) 55 Minutes
Jim Bannon, Don Kay Reynolds, Emmett Lynn, *Marin Sais,* Peggy Stewart, John Hart, Lane Bradford, Forrest Taylor, Lee Roberts, Bob Duncan, Sandy Sanders, Billy Hammonds, Ray Jones
Director: Lewis D. Collins
Screenplay: Paul Franklin, Jerry Thomas
Producer: Jerry Thomas

COWBOY AND THE PRIZEFIGHTER
(Equity/Eagle Lion, December 15, 1949) 59 Minutes
Jim Bannon, Don Kay Reynolds, Emmett Lynn, *Marin Sais,* Lou Nova, Don Haggerty, Karen Randle, John Hart, Marshall Reed, Forrest Taylor, Lane Bradford, Bud Osborne, Steve Clark, Ray Jones
Director: Lewis D. Collins
Screenplay: Jerry Thomas
Producer: Jerry Thomas

THE GREAT JESSE JAMES RAID
(Lippert, July 17, 1953) 73 Minutes
Willard Parker, Barbara Payton, Tom Neal, Wallace Ford, James Anderson, Jim Bannon, Richard Cutting, Barbara Woodell, *Marin Sais,* Earle Hodgins, Tom Walker, Joan Arnold, Helene Hayden, Steve Pendleton, Bob Griffin, Robin Moore, Ed Russell, Rory Mallison
Director: Reginald Le Borg
Screenplay: Richard Landau
Producer: Robert L. Lippert, Jr.

42 • MARGUERITE SNOW

Peg o' the Movies

Probably any discussion of the film career of Marguerite "Peggy" Snow should begin with **The Million Dollar Mystery** (1914), Thanhouser's fabulously successful twenty-three-chapter serial produced in cooperation with the Chicago Tribune during the period of the newspaper circulation wars. The film returned $1.5 million on an investment of $125,000, making it one of the most financially successful cliffhangers ever produced. It was a real thriller in its day, with production techniques well ahead of those in **The Perils of Pauline** (1914), produced the same year by Pathé. Thanhouser was one of the most distinctive of the independent companies and this was its first serial. In fact, only a dozen serials had been produced before by anyone! The company hit the financial jackpot on its first try.

Florence LaBadie, James Cruze, Alfred Norton, and Marguerite had the principal roles, with Marguerite playing the Countess Olga, a co-conspirator with those who hoped to steal a million dollars from its hiding place in Chilton Manor, the home of millionaire Stanley Hargreave (Alfred Norton). Thanhouser offered a reward of $10,000 for the essay giving the best solution to the hiding place of the money concealed in The House of Mystery. Interest in the contest was kept alive by having William J. Burns, head of the renowned International Detective Agency, give clues to the public through a national movie magazine. The contest gimick, like the serial, was a success, and many firms subsequently used contests to exploit their product.

Thanhouser tried its luck again by casting Marguerite and Cruze in a sequel called first **Zudora,** then **Zudora in the Twenty Million Dollar Mystery,** and finally just **The Twenty Million Dollar Mystery** (1914). The second outing fell far short of its predecessor's success, but it was still a suspenseful, entertaining forty reels (later re-edited by Arrow and released in 1919 as a ten-chapter serial renamed **The Demon Shadow**).

Marguerite was born in Salt Lake City in 1892, then moved with her family to Savannah, Georgia, where she spent several years. Her father was William G. Snow, a minstrel comedian for twenty-five years with the team of Snow and West, and as such he traveled constantly. Marguerite was still a small child when he died, and she and her mother went to live in Denver. She spent most of her childhood and received her education at the Loretta Heights Academy.

She also studied drama under Marguerite Fealy, Maude Fealy's mother, and during the summer of 1906 played one or two small parts with the stock company at Elitch's Gardens, Denver. Her real stage debut occurred on February 11, 1907, at the Crawford Theatre in Wichita, Kansas; she played Mlle. Danglars in "Monte Cristo," supporting James O'Neill.

Next season Miss Snow did the title role in Henry W. Savage's production of "The College Widow," and in 1909 she made her Broadway debut in the role of Elsa in "The Devil" at the Garden Theatre. After that came a season in stock work divided between Grand Rapids, Michigan, and Wheeling, West Virginia, and in the fall of 1910 she was seen at the Bijou Theatre with Thomas Jefferson in "The Other Fellow." This play having failed, she turned her thoughts toward filmmaking.

Miss Snow has said:

My going into pictures was largely accidental. A girl friend of mine was posing for the Thanhouser people and she suggested one day that I accompany her, just to see how motion pictures were made. While watching the work, Mr. Thanhouser asked me if I would like to appear in a picture which they were about to take. Largely for the fun of the thing, I said I would, and I was pressed into immediate service, costume, makeup, and all, in a picture called Baseball in Bloomers (1911). Suddenly the director called out, 'Everybody into the machine and out into the country for pictures.' 'What!' I cried, 'Go out-of-doors in such a costume and in winter weather like this? Not for me!' And I immediately took off my costume and returned to New York. A week later, however, my telephone rang and there was Mr. Thanhouser speaking, urging me to appear in a picture, His Younger Brother, and adding, 'It is all indoor work this time.' So I consented, and was a member of the company for about six months.

In the summer of 1911 Marguerite returned temporarily to the stage as leading woman of the stock company at the Belasco Theatre, Washington, D.C. At this time she played the title role in "Peter Pan," Kathie in "Old Heidelberg," Nora Brewster in "Waterloo," Glory Quayle in "The Christian," and Helen Heye in "The Lottery Man." But she soon took up picture work again, first as a regular lead with the Kinemacolor company, and then as a star for Thanhouser, which she rejoined.

After making her decision to remain in pictures permanently she received offers for excellent theatrical engagements--leads in such plays as "The Bird of Paradise" and "The Butterfly on the Wheel"--but she resolutely turned them all down. Marguerite played opposite James Cruze for the first time in **She** (1911), a two-reeler (nearly all of her subsequent pictures through 1914 were opposite him). Their better-known films were **Lucile** (1912), **Dr. Jekyll and Mr. Hyde** (1912), and **Joseph in the Land of Egypt** (1914), which at four reels was Marguerite's longest film up to that time. Her only other four-reeler for Thanhouser was **The Patriot and the Spy** (1915), made just before she quit the studio to journey west to Hollywood.

James Cruze and Marguerite were married about 1913, and a daughter, Julia, was born to them. The marriage was dissolved, however, in 1923, about the time that Cruze scored his directorial success with **The Covered Wagon.**

Marguerite made most of her West Coast pictures, all full-length features, for the Metro organization, later to combine with Goldwyn Productions and Mayer Films to form the powerful Metro-Goldwyn-Mayer Studios.

In 1918 Marguerite made her third and final serial, **The Eagle's Eye,** a Wharton-American Production with a World War I setting. The story centered on the attempts of King Baggot, as head of a criminology club, and Marguerite, as a secret service agent, to rout German spies. Shortly after its release the war ended, and people were not interested in war-related or propaganda movies. As a consequence, **The Eagle's Eye** had fewer bookings than most serials and lost money, a fault of the story rather than of the stars or the production qualities of the film.

The last film credit we have for Marguerite Snow is **Kit Carson Over the Great Divide** (1925), a fine Western in the Roy Stewart series for Anthony J. Xydias. In 1925 she married Neely Edwards, a stage and film comedian. Apparently, Marguerite was content to settle down to the domestic life after marrying Edwards. In 1956 she underwent a kidney operation which seemed successful, but a year later complications set in which resulted in her death on February 17, 1958, at the Motion Picture Country Home. She was buried at Forest Lawn Memorial Park.

MARGUERITE SNOW Filmography

BASEBALL AND BLOOMERS
(Thanhouser, January, 1911) 1 Reel
William Garwood, *Marguerite Snow*

THE OLD CURIOSITY SHOP
(Thanhouser, January 21, 1911) 1 Reel
Frank Crane, Harry Benham, *Marguerite Snow,* Alphonse Ethier, William Bowman
Director: Theodore Marston
Scenario: Theodore Marston
Story: Charles Dickens

HIS YOUNGER BROTHER
(Thanhouser, March 18, 1911) 1 Reel
Marguerite Snow

LORNA DOANE
(Thanhouser, June 24, 1911) 1 Reel
Frank Crane, *Marguerite Snow,* William Garwood, William Russell
Director: Theodore Marston
Scenario: Theodore Marston
Story: Richard D. Blackmore

THE PIED PIPER OF HAMELIN
(Thanhouser, July 29, 1911) 1 Reel
Frank Crane, *Marguerite Snow,* James Cruze, William Garwood, Mignon Anderson
Director: Theodore Marston
Scenario: Theodore Marston
Story: Robert Browning

THE HONEYMOONERS
(Thanhouser, September 17, 1911) 1 Reel
Marguerite Snow, William Garwood

THE LADY FROM THE SEA
(Thanhouser, December 9, 1911) 1 Reel
Marguerite Snow, William Russell, William Garwood, Henry Benham, Irma Taylor
Director: Theodore Marston
Scenario: Theodore Marston
Story: Henrik Ibsen

THE TOMBOY
(Thanhouser, December 16, 1911) 1 Reel
Marguerite Snow, Harry Benham, Marie Eline

SHE
(Thanhouser, December 23, 1911) 2 Reels
Marguerite Snow, James Cruze, William C. Cooper, Horace Holly, Irma Taylor, Henry Benham, Alphonse Ethier
Director: Theodore Marston
Scenario: Theodore Marston
Story: Sir Rider Haggard

FLYING TO FORTUNE
(Thanhouser, March 23, 1912)
James Cruze, Florence LaBadie, *Marguerite Snow,* George Nicholls

MY BABY'S VOICE
(Thanhouser, March 23, 1912)
Marguerite Snow, Florence LaBadie, Helen Eline

FOR SALE--A LIFE
(Thanhouser, March 23, 1912)
Marguerite Snow, James Cruze, Joseph Graybill

INTO THE DESERT
(Thanhouser, April 13, 1912) 1 Reel
Marguerite Snow, James Cruze, William Russell

THE SALESLADY
(Thanhouser, May 4, 1912)
Marguerite Snow, Florence LaBadie, William Russell

LOVE'S MIRACLE
(Thanhouser, May 4, 1912) 1 Reel
Marguerite Snow, James Cruze

JILTED
(Thanhouser, May 11, 1912)
Marguerite Snow, Florence LaBadie, William Russell

THE RING OF A SPANISH GRANDEE
(Thanhouser, May 18, 1912)
Marguerite Snow, Florence LaBadie, James Cruze, William Russell, Joseph Graybill

WHOM GOD HATH JOINED
(Thanhouser, May 25, 1912)
Marguerite Snow, James Cruze, Florence LaBadie

DOTTIE'S NEW DOLL
(Thanhouser, June 1, 1912)
Marguerite Snow, Florence LaBadie

UNDER TWO FLAGS
(Thanhouser, July 9, 1912) 2 Reels
Katherine Horn, Florence La Badie, Alphonse Ethier, William Russell, Harry Benham, James Cruze, *Marguerite Snow*, William Garwood, William Bauman
Director: Theodore Marston
Screenplay: Theodore Marston
Story: Quida

LUCILE
(Thanhouser, August 24, 1912) 3 Reels
Marguerite Snow, James Cruze, Florence LaBadie, William Russell, Mignon Anderson, William Garwood
Director: Theodore Marston
Scenario: Theodore Marston
Story: Owen Meredith

THE MAIL CLERK'S TEMPTATION
(Thanhouser, September 14, 1912) 1 Reel
Marguerite Snow

AND THE GREATEST OF THESE IS CHARITY
(Thanhouser, September 21, 1912) 1 Reel
James Cruze, *Marguerite Snow*

UNDINE
(Thanhouser, September 21, 1912) 2 Reels
Florence LaBadie, William Russell, James Cruze, *Marguerite Snow*
Director: Theodore Marston
Scenario: Theodore Marston
Story: F. de la Motte Fouque

PUT YOURSELF IN HIS PLACE
(Thanhouser, October 26, 1912)
William Garwood, *Marguerite Snow,* William Russell, Jean Darnell, David Thompson, Ann Drew, James Cruze, Mignon Anderson
Director: Theodore Marston
Scenario: Theodore Marston
Story: Charles Reade

THE FOREST ROSE
(Thanhouser, November 23, 1912) 2 Reels
Marguerite Snow, Fred Vroom, William Russell
Director: Theodore Marston
Scenario: Theodore Marston
Story: Emerson Bennett

BRAINS VS BRAWN
(Thanhouser, December 14, 1912)
Riley Chamberlain, *Marguerite Snow,* Harry Benham

THE STAR OF BETHLEHEM
(Thanhouser, December 24, 1912) 3 Reels
William Russell, Florence LaBadie, Harry Benham, James Cruze, *Marguerite Snow*
Director: Theodore Marston
Scenario: Theodore Marston

DR. JEKYLL AND MR. HYDE
(Thanhouser, 1912)
Marguerite Snow, James Cruze, Harry Benham
Director: Lucious Henderson
Story: Robert Louis Stevenson

A MILITANT SUFFRAGETTE
(Thanhouser, 1912)
Marguerite Snow

THE DOVE IN THE EAGLE'S NEST
(Thanhouser, February 1, 1913) 2 Reels
Marguerite Snow, James Cruze

WHEN THE STUDIO BURNED
(Thanhouser, February 8, 1913)
The Thanhouser Kid, The Thanhouser Kidlet, *Marguerite Snow,* James Cruze
Director: Theodore Marston
Scenario: Lloyd Lonergan

THE IDOL OF THE HOUR
(Thanhouser, March 15, 1913)
Marguerite Snow, James Cruze

FOR HER BOY'S SAKE
(Thanhouser, March 29, 1913)
Marguerite Snow, James Cruze, William Garwood, Victory Bateman, William Russell

WHEN GHOST MEETS GHOST
(Thanhouser, April 12, 1913)
Marguerite Snow, James Cruze

THE MARBLE HEART
(Thanhouser, May 17, 1913) 2 Reels
James Cruze, *Marguerite Snow,* Florence LaBadie
Story: Charles Silby

THE CAGED BIRD
(Thanhouser, June 7, 1913) 1 Reel
Marguerite Snow, William Garwood

TANNHAUSER
(Thanhouser, July 19, 1913) 3 Reels
James Cruze, *Marguerite Snow,* Florence LaBadie, William Russell

THE GIRL AT THE CABARET
(Thanhouser, August 16, 1913) 1 Reel
Harry Benham, *Marguerite Snow,* The Thanhouser Kidlet, Dorothy Benham

PEGGY'S INVITATION
(Thanhouser. December 20, 1913)
Marguerite Snow, William Russell, Carrie L. Hastings, Lila Chester

CARMEN
(Thanhouser, 1913)
Marguerite Snow

THE DANCER
(Thanhouser, February 10, 1914) 2 Reels
Marguerite Snow, Arthur Bower, The Thanhouser Kidlet, Carey Hastings, Justus D. Barnes, N. S. Wood

JOSEPH IN THE LAND OF EGYPT
(Thanhouser, February 14, 1914) 4 Reels
James Cruze, *Marguerite Snow*
Director: Eugene Moore

THEIR BEST FRIEND
(Thanhouser, February 28, 1914)
Marguerite Snow, Morris Foster, Justus D. Barnes

A WOMAN'S LOYALTY
(Thanhouser, May 9, 1914) 2 Reels
Marguerite Snow

THE DOG OF FLANDERS
(Thanhouser, May 23, 1914) 2 Reels
Marguerite Snow, Mignon Anderson

THE MILLION DOLLAR MYSTERY
(Thanhouser, June 22, 1914) 23 Chapters
Florence LaBadie, *Marguerite Snow,* James Cruze, Frank Farrington, Sidney Bracy, Creighton Hale, Mitchell Lewis, Irving Cummings, Nick Wood, Alfred Norton, Lila Chester, Donald Gallagher, The Fairbanks Twins, Eugene Moore, Claire Krall, William A. Sullivan, Baby Julie Cruze, Albert Froome, Nick Wood, Carey Hastings, Arthur Bauer
Director: Howell Hansell
Story: Harold MacGrath
Chapters: (1) The Airship in the Night (2) The False Friend (3) A Leap in the Dark (4) The Top Floor Flat (5) At the Bottom of the Sea (6) The Coaching Party of the Countess (7) The Doom of the Auto Bandits (8) The Wiles of a Woman (9) The Leap from an Ocean Liner (10) unknown (11) In the Path of the Fast Express (12-14) unknown (15) The Borrowed Hydroplane (16) Drawn into the Quicksand (17) A Battle of Wits (18-21) unknown (22) The Million Dollar Mystery (23) The Mystery Solved
(Rereleased in 1918 in six reels by Randolph Film Corporation)

FROM WASH TO WASHINGTON
(Thanhouser, August 8, 1914)
Marguerite Snow, James Cruze

ZUDORA (THE TWENTY MILLION DOLLAR MYSTERY)
(Thanhouser, November 23, 1914) 20 Chapters
James Cruze, *Marguerite Snow,* Harry Benham, Sidney Bracy, Helen Badgley, Frank Farrington, Mary Elizabeth Forbes, Jane Fairbanks, Morgan Niblack, Helen Badgley
Director: Howell Hansell
Scenario: Lloyd Lonergan, F. W. Doughty
Story: Daniel Carson Goodman
Chapters: (1) The Mystic Message of the Spotted Collar (2) The Mystery of the Sleeping House (3) The Mystery of the Dutch Cheese Maker (4) The Secret of the Haunted Hills (5) The Case of the Perpetual Glare (6) The Case of the McWinter Family (7) The Mystery of the Lost Ships (8) The Foiled Elopement, or the Mystery of the Chang Case (9) Kidnapped or the The Mystery of the Missing Heiress (10) The Gentlemen Crooks and the Lady (11) A Message from the Heart (12) A Bag of Diamonds (13) The Secret of Dr. Munn's Sanatorium (14) The Missing Million (15) The Robbery of the Ruby Coronet (16) The Battle of the Bridge (17) The Island of Mystery (18) The Cipher Code (19) The Prisoner in the House (20) The Richest Woman of the World

THE HEART OF THE PRINCESS MARSARI
(Thanhouser, May 22, 1915) 2 Reels
Marguerite Snow, James Cruze, Harry Benham

THE ANGEL IN THE MASK
(Thanhouser, May 29, 1915) 1 Reel
Boyd Marshall, *Marguerite Snow*

DAUGHTER OF KINGS
(Thanhouser, May 29, 1915)
Marguerite Snow, Harry Benham

THE PATRIOT AND THE SPY
(Thanhouser, June 12, 1915) 4 Reels
James Cruze, *Marguerite Snow,* Alphonse Ethier

THE SECOND IN COMMAND
(Quality/Metro, July 26, 1915) 5 Reels
Marguerite Snow, Francis X. Bushman
Story: Clyde Fitch

THE SILENT VOICE
(Quality/Metro, September 13, 1915) 6 Reels
Francis X. Bushman, *Marguerite Snow,* Lester Cuneo, Helen Dunbar, Ann Drew, Miss C. Henry, Frank Bacon, William Clifford
Director: William Bowman, Fred Balshofer
Scenario: William Bowman
Story: Jules Eckert Goodman

ROSEMARY
(Quality/Metro, December 17, 1915) 5 Reels
Marguerite Snow, Paul Gilmore, Virginia Kraft, William Glifford, George F. Hernandez, Frank Bacon, Maurice Cytron
Director: William Bowman, Fred J. Balshofer
Scenario: William Bowman
Story: John Drew

A CORNER IN COTTON
(Quality/Metro, March, 1916) 5 Reels
Marguerite Snow, Frank Dayton, Lester Cuneo, Helen Dunbar, William Clifford, Zella Call, Howard Truesdell, John Goldsworthy, Wilfred Roger
Directors: Fred J. Balshofer, Howard Truesdell
Scenario: Anita Loos

THE HALF MILLION BRIDE
(Columbia/Metro, April, 1916) 5 Reels
Hamilton Revelle, *Marguerite Snow,* John Smiley, Carl Brickert, Ferdinand Tidmarsh
Director: Edgar Jones
Scenario: Harry O. Hoyt
Story: William Hamilton Osborne

NOTORIOUS GALLAGHER (a.k.a. **HIS GREAT TRIUMPH**)
(Columbia/Metro, June 1, 1916) 5 Reels
William Nigh, *Marguerite Snow,* Robert Elliott, Roy Applegate, David Thomas, Martin J. Faust, Julius Cowles, Citta Cameron
Producer: William Nigh
Director: William Nigh
Story: William Nigh

THE FADED FLOWER
(Ivan Films, August, 1916) 6 Reels
Marguerite Snow, Arthur Donaldson, Rose Coghlan, Alma Hanlon, Edward Mackay
Director: Ivan Abramson
Scenario: Ivan Abramson

BROADWAY JONES
(Paramount/Artcraft, March 17, 1917) 6 Reels
Marguerite Snow, George M. Chan
Director: Joseph Kaufman
Based on the play by George M. Cohan

THE FIRST LAW
(Pathé, July 28, 1918)
Irene Castle, Antonio Moreno, *Marguerite Snow,* J. H. Gilmour, Edward J. Connelly
Director: Laurence McGill
Scenario: Roy Sommerville
Story: Gilson Willets

THE EAGLE'S EYE
(Wharton/American, March 27, 1918) 20 Chapters
King Baggot, *Marguerite Snow,* William N. Bailey, Florence Short, Bertram Marburgh, Paul Everton, John P. Wade, Fred Jones, William Cavanaugh, George Lessey, Louise Hotelling, Leroy L. Baker
Directors: George A. Lessey, Wellington Playter
Chapters: (1) Hidden Death (2) The Naval Ball Conspiracy (3) The Plot Against the Fleet (4) Von Rintelen, the Destroyer (5) The Strike Breeders (6) The Plot Against Organized Labor (7) Brown Port Folio (8) The Kaiser's Death Messenger (9) The Munitions Campaign (10) The Invasion of Canada (11) The Burning of Hopewell (12) The Canal Conspirators (13) The Reign of Terror (14) The Infantile Paralysis Epidemic (15) The Campaign Against Cotton (16) The Raid of the U-53 (17) Germany's U-Base in America (18) The Great Hindu Conspiracy (19) The Menace of the I.W.W. (20) The Great Decision

IN HIS BROTHER'S PLACE
(Metro, July 19, 1919) 5 Reels
Marguerite Snow, Hale Hamilton, Emmett King, Ruby Lafayette
Director: Harry L. Franklin
Scenario: A. S. LeVino
Supervisor: Maxwell Karger

THE DEMON SHADOW
(Thanhouser/Arrow, 1919) 10 Chapters
Marguerite Snow, James Cruze
(See **Zudora [The Twenty Million Dollar Mystery]** for additional credits; this film is a re-edited version.)

THE WOMAN IN ROOM 13
(Goldwyn, January 30, 1920) 5 Reels
Pauline Frederick, Richard Tucker, Joan Clary, Sydney Ainsworth, Kate Lester, *Marguerite Snow,* Robert McKim
Director: Frank Lloyd
From the play by Samuel Shipman and Max Marcin

FELIX O'DAY
(Hampton/Pathé, September, 1920)
H. B. Warner, *Marguerite Snow,* Lillian Rich, Ray Ripley, Karl Formes, Jr., George Williams
Director: Robert Thornby
Scenario: Fred Myton
Story: F. Hopkinson Smith

THE GREAT SHADOW
(Adanac Productions of Canada/Selznick, 1920)
Marguerite Snow, Tyrone Power, Sr., David Pidgeon
Director: Harley Knowles
Producer: George Brownridge

LAVENDER AND OLD LACE
(Renco/Hodkinson, June, 1921) 6 Reels
Marguerite Snow, Seena Owen, Louis Bennison, Victor Potel, Zella Ingraham, Lillian Elliott, James Corrigan
Director: Lloyd Ingraham
Story: Myrtle Reed

THE VEILED WOMAN
(Renco/Hodkinson, September 3, 1922) 6 Reels
Marguerite Snow, Edward Coxen, Landers Stevens, Lottie Williams, Ralph McCullough, Charlotte Pierce
Director: Lloyd Ingraham
Scenario: David Kirkland
Story: Myrtle Reed, "A Spinner in the Sun"

CHALK MARKS
(Peninsula/PDC, September 14, 1924) 7 Reels
Marguerite Snow, Ramsey Wallace, June Elvidge, Lydia Knott, Rex Lease, Helen Ferguson, Priscilla Bonner, Harold Holland, Verna Marcereau, Fred Church, Lee Willard
Director: John G. Adolfi
Producer: Frank E. Woods

SAVAGES OF THE SEA
(Hercules/Barsky, February 17, 1925) 5 Reels
Frank Merrill, Melbourne MacDowell, *Marguerite Snow,* Danny Hoy, Clarence Burton
Director: Bruce Mitchell
Scenario: William E. Wing

KIT CARSON OVER THE GREAT DIVIDE
(Sunset/Aywon, September 3, 1925) 6 Reels
Roy Stewart, Henry B. Walthall, *Marguerite Snow,* Sheldon Lewis, Earl Metcalfe, Charlotte Stevens, Jack Mower, Arthur Hotaling, Lew Meehan, Billy Franey, Nelson McDowell
Director: Frank S. Mattison
Scenario: Frank S. Mattison
Producer: Anthony J. Xydias

Peggy Stewart.

43 • PEGGY STEWART

The Sweetheart of the Republic Lot in the Mid-1940s and a Special Favorite of Sagebrush Fans

Beauteous Peggy Stewart is one of the nicest gals ever to ride the busy trails of Iverson's and Corrigan's ranches or the back lots of Republic and Columbia. She looked wistfully into the eyes of a cowboy stalwart at Lone Pine as cameras rolled in the last decade of the programmer Western. Luckier than most cowgirls who disappeared over the horizon when the sun set on the hoss opera, Peggy remained active in the enter- tainment field and has been a popular favorite at many Western film festivals in recent years. Displaying unflagging vitality and a disarming sense of humor, her salt-and-pepper hair is the only clue that more than thirty years have passed since she rode dusty trails beside the screen's popular cowboys.

Peggy was born on June 5, 1923, in West Palm Beach, Florida. Her parents were John O'Rourke and the former Frances McCampbell, both from Bessemer, Alabama. A sister, Patricia, who later became Mrs. Wayne Morris, was born to the couple a year earlier. When Peggy was very young the O'Rourkes divorced, and she and her sister moved with their mother to Chattanooga for a year, then to Brookwood Hills, Georgia, a suburb of Atlanta. It was here that Peggy's mother married John Stewart, a successful attorney, who gave the girls his name. As a result of this marriage, a daughter, Frances, was born to the Stewarts.

Peggy attended Atlanta grade schools and the Marken Professional School. Her summers were spent at a YWCA camp near Tallulah Falls, Georgia, where she, along with her sister, spent hours perfecting her swimming skill. Both became swimmers of Olympic caliber. For two consecutive years Peggy won the Georgia Junior Championship for free-style swimming (1934-35).

When Peggy was twelve Mrs. Stewart took all three girls with her to California to vacation and to attend the wedding of her brother. Accompanying them was Peggy's grandmother from West Palm Beach. While there Peggy enrolled in Neely Dickson's Dramatic School. Two months later, when it was time to return home, she was so much in love with drama school and California that she talked her mother into letting her stay on the condition that her grandmother stay with her. Her grandmother was willing, so home went the other Stewarts while Peggy and her maternal grandmother, Elizabeth LaValle McCampbell, stayed on at the Alto Nido Apartments. Also living there was character actor Henry O'Neill, under contract to Warner Brothers, but on loan-out to Paramount for the Western **Wells Fargo** (1937). Henry liked Peggy, and knowing that Paramount was looking for a girl to play Alice McKay, the daughter of Joel McCrea and Frances Dee, he recommended her to director Frank Lloyd, telling Frank that Peggy still had the Southern accent needed for the role. Peggy was tested and got the part.

After completing **Wells Fargo** Peggy had important roles in four 1938 films: **Little Tough Guys, That Certain Age, White Banners,** and **Little Tough Guy in Society. Everybody's Hobby** followed in 1939.

Peggy married actor Donald Barry in 1940 while he was making **The Adventures of Red Ryder,** the serial that catapulted him to fame. She was only seventeen. Their marriage lasted four years and produced one son, Michael. During her marriage she made only three films, but when it ended she signed with Republic after Herb Yates, studio boss, saw her first Western, **Tucson Raiders** (1944), one of the entries in the Bill Elliott "Red Ryder" series. Don Barry had gotten her the female lead.

Peggy was no stranger to horses; she had been riding since she was a child in Atlanta and had

Peggy Stewart and Sunset Carson.

been in competition for the Judy King Stables. It was all English riding where the contestants were judged on equestrianship--elbows tucked in, stirrups swinging free, back straight. But riding was hardly done that way at Republic, and stunt woman Polly Burson, who did most of Peggy's doubling, helped her to look more like a Western cowgirl.

For three years Peggy was happy as part of the Republic "family." She made twenty-four Westerns--seven with Bill Elliott, eight with Sunset Carson, five with Allan Lane, one with Roy Rogers, and one with Gene Autry. The other two were the serials, **The Phantom Rider** (1946) with Robert Kent, and **Son of Zorro** (1946) with George Turner. Typical of the slick westerns being turned out by Republic in the mid-forties, these serials gave Peggy ample opportunity to emote in harrowing situations and to become a familiar face to audiences for twenty-seven weeks.

When Republic scheduled her to appear in another serial, Peggy balked. She didn't like serials, preferring the six-day Westerns which at least gave her a fresh costume, a new hairdo, and a frequent change of leading men. She also had a hankering to play in non-Western "B" pictures like those featuring Adele Mara and Ruth Terry. Yates said "no deal"-- she was too valuable to the studio in the shoot-em-ups. From his point of view, not moving her off the range made good buisness sense. Her acting and riding ability saved the studio money and helped them make a nice profit on the Westerns, so Yates was not inclined to tamper with an investment that was paying off. But Peggy wanted out and decided to request her release. Yates finally let her go with his blessing, but Republic officials sent her a bill for something like $130 for things they said she owed for. Bill Elliott proceeded to write up a bill for close to $500 that she presented to the studio for all the extra hours she had put in. Wisely, Republic's accounting department dropped its claim, saying it had all been a mathematical mistake.

As a free lance, Peggy found it hard to find work in non-Westerns, since everyone thought of her as strictly a Western ingénue. She was soon back in sagebrushers opposite Al "Lash" LaRue, Whip Wilson, Jim Bannon, Charles Starrett, Guy Madison, and Bill Elliott. And even though she had tried to get out of further serials at Republic, she wound up making two at Columbia, each a notch below the Republic standard. **Tex Granger** (1948) was a weak effort featuring Robert Kellard, hardly a convincing cowpoke, while **Cody of the Pony Express** (1950) featured stuntman-turned-actor Jock O'Mahoney, a believable man of the range, in a far better saga of the West.

After **Six Gun Decision** (1953) Peggy decided to quit movie work for a while to see if she couldn't break out of the Western typecasting. She accepted employment at NBC as assistant casting director and remained in the job for three years, leaving to have her second child, Abigail, by second husband Buck Young. A son, Gregory, arrived in due time and Peggy interspersed television roles with domestic ones. Among her television credits are appearances in "Have Gun, Will Travel," "Wyatt Earp," "Wild Bill Hickok," "The Cisco Kid," "Range Rider," "The Virginian." Obviously, Peggy did not escape Westerns. All told, she has appeared in nearly a hundred television shows and has done several commercials.

A great love of Peggy's is the legitimate theatre, in which she has been active. In 1974 she was nominated for an award for best supporting actress by the Los Angeles Drama Critics Circle for her work in "Picnic." Other plays included "The Great American Family," "Girls in a Turkish Bath," "George Washington, American," "Accidentally Yours," "John Brown's Body," and "Love and Roses."

Probably Peggy's most unusual role in films came in **Terror in the Wax Museum** (1972), in which she played a Cockney charwoman. She spent weeks practicing the Cockney speech patterns required, with the assistance of English friends and her associates in Lieux Dressler's Patio Playhouse, an actor-training center where she worked and studied for several years.

Today Peggy is one of Hollywood's best boosters, and one does not doubt her sincerity, enthusiasm, and love for the acting profession. Her eyes sparkle with enthusiasm as she talks of the entertainment industry. As a goodwill ambassador for her profession she is unbeatable, with a charisma that invariably draws film fans to her wherever she appears.

This author is in full accord with historians Nick Williams and John Stoginski who, in summing up their impressions of Miss Stewart, have said:

She has a personality like pink champagne--both sparkling and sweet. She has a genuine interest in other people. She likes to know what your thoughts are. Instantly she can make you feel like a friend of long standing rather than a new acquaintance. Charming? Although we attempt to eschew triteness, perhaps you will permit us just one sentence which describes her high degree of charm. She could charm a bird off its nest. She is witty, fun loving, and has a delightful sense of humor. Certainly at this point in her career Peggy Stewart, if she desired, would be entitled to a certain amount of aloofness, but she isn't aloof. She is a warm, wonderful, outgoing person. And now you know why we call her Peg of Our Hearts.

Peggy and her husband live in Studio City, California and are still active professionally. She has been a frequent guest at film festivals in Nashville, Memphis, Charlotte, Atlanta, and Los Angeles, and the fans never tire of her. They always want this spunky lass back.

PEGGY STEWART Filmography

WELLS FARGO
(Paramount, December 31, 1937) 115 Minutes
Joel McCrea, Bob Burns, Francis Dee, Lloyd Nolan, Henry O'Neill, Mary Nash, Ralph Morgan, Porter Hall, John Mack Brown, Jack Clark, Clarence Kolb, Robert Cummings, Granville Bates, Harry Davenport, Frank Conroy, Brandon Tynan, *Peggy Stewart,* Bernard Siegel, Stanley Pields, Jane Dewey, Frank McGlynn, Sr., David Durand, Scotty Beckett, Jimmy Butler, Dorothy Tennant, Clare Verdera, Howard Earle, Henry Brandon, Harry B. Stafford, Lucien Littlefield, Helen Dickson, Jerry Tucker, Babs Nelson, Rebecca Wassam, Ronnie Cosbey, Hrville Alderson, Louis Natheaux, Paul Newlan, Shirley Coates
Director: Frank Lloyd
Screenplay: Paul Schofield, Gerald Geraghty, Frederick Jackson
Story: Stuart N. Lake
Producer: Frank Lloyd

LITTLE TOUGH GUY
(Universal, July 22, 1938) 85 Minutes
Robert Wilcox, Helen Parrish, Marjorie Main, Jackie Searle, *Peggy Stewart,* Helen MacKellar, Edward Pawley, Olin Howlin, Pat C. Flick, Billy Halop, Huntz Hall, Gabriel Dell, Bernard Punsley, Hally Chester, David Gorcey, Edward Cheman, Eleanor Hanson, Charles Trowbridge, Selmer Jackson, Buster Phelps, George Billings, Ben Taggart, William Ruhl, Hooper Atchley, Clara Macklin Blore, Jason Robards, John Fitzgerald, Richard Selzer, Monte Montague, Frank Bischell, Johnny Green
Director: Harold Young
Screenplay: Gilson Brown, Brenda Weisberg
Story: Brenda Weisberg
Producer: Ken Goldsmith

WHITE BANNERS
(Warner Bros., July 25, 1938) 90 Minutes
Claude Rains, Fay Bainter, Jackie Cooper, Bonita Granville, Henry O'Neill, Kay Johnson, James Stephenson, J. Parrell MacDonald, William Pawley, Edward Pawley, John Ridgely, Edward McWade, Mary Field, *Peggy Stewart*
Director: Hdmond Goulding
Screenplay: Lenore Coffee, Cameron Rogers, Abem Finkel
Story: Lloyd C. Douglas
Associate Producer: Henry Blanke

THAT CERTAIN AGE
(Universal, October 7, 1938) 95 Minutes
Deanna Durbin, Melvyn Douglas, Jackie Cooper, Irene Rich, Nancy Carroll, John Halliday, Juanita Quigley, Jackie Searl, Charles Coleman, *Peggy Stewart,* Grant Mitchell
Director: Edward Ludwig
Screenplay: Bruce Manning
Story: F. Hugh Herbert
Producer: Joe Pasternak

LITTLE TOUGH GUYS IN SOCIETY
(Universal, November 25, 1938) 70 Minutes
Mischa Auer, Mary Boland, Edward Everett Horton, Helen Parrish, Jackie Searl, *Peggy Stewart,* Harold Huber, David Oliver, Frankie Thomas, Harris Berger, Hally Chester, Charles Duncan, David Gorcey, Billy Benedict, Lon McCallister
Director: Erle C. Kenton
Screenplay: Edward Eliscu, Mortimer Offner
Story: Edward Eliscu, Mortimer Offner
Associate Producer: Max H. Golden

MAN ABOUT TOWN
(Paramount, July 7, 1939) 85 Minutes
Jack Benny, Dorothy Lamour, Edward Arnold, Binnie Barnes, Phil Harris, Eddie "Rochester" Anderson, Monty Wooley, Isabel Jeans, Betty Grable, E. E. Clive, Leonard Mudie, *Peggy Stewart,* Patti Sacks, The Pina Troupe, Matty Maineck Orchestra, Merrill Abbott Dancers
Director: Mark Sandrich
Screenplay: Morrie Ryskind
Story: Morrie Ryskind, Allan Scott, Zion Meyers
Producer: Arthur Hornblow, Jr.

EVERYBODY'S HOBBY
(First National, August 26, 1939) 54 Minutes
Irene Rich, Henry O'Neill, Jackie Moran, Aldrich Bowker, Jean Sharon, John Ridgeley, *Peggy Stewart,* Jackie Morrow, Fredric Tozere, Albert Morin, Nat Carr, Sidney Bracy, Jack Mower, Don Rowan
Director: William McGann
Screenplay: Kenneth Gamet, William W. Brockaway
Story: William W. Brockaway

ALL THIS AND HEAVEN TOO
(Warner Bros., July 13, 1940) 143 Minutes
Bette Davis, Charles Boyer, Jeffrey Lynn, Barbara O'Neill, Virginia Weidler, Helen Westley, Walter Hampden, Henry Daniell, Harry Davenport, George Coulouris, Montagu Love, Janet Beecher, June Lockhart, Ann Todd, Richard Nichols, Fritz Leiber, Ian Keith, Sybil Harris, Hdward Fielding, Mary Anderson, Ann Gillis, *Peggy Stewart,* Victor Kilian
Director: Anatole Litvak
Screenplay: Casey Robinson
Story: Rachel Field
Producer: Hal B. Wallis

BACK STREET
(Universal, February 27, 1941) 89 Minutes
Charles Boyer, Margaret Sullivan, Richard Carlson, Frank McHugh, Tim Holt, Frank Jenks, Esther Dale, Samuel S. Hinds, *Peggy Stewart,* Nell O'Day, Kitty O'Neill, Nella Walker, Cecil Cunningham, Marjorie Gateson, Dale Winter, Irving Bacon
Director: Robert Stevenson
Screenplay: Bruce Manning, Felix Jackson
Story: Fannie Hurst
Producer: Bruce Manning

SLEEPYTIME GAL
(Republic, March 5, 1942) 82 Minutes
Judy Canova, Tom Brown, Billy Gilbert, Ruth Terry, Thurston Hall, Elisha Cook, Jr., Jerry Lester, Mildred Coles, Harold Huber, Fritz Feld, Frank Sully, Jimmy Ames, Jay Novello, *Peggy Stewart*, Skinney Ennis and his Band
Director: Albert J. Rogell
Screenplay: Art Arthur, Albert Duffy, Max Lief
Story: Mauri Grashin, Robert T. Shannon
Associate Producer: Albert J. Cohen

GIRLS IN CHAINS
(PRC, May 17, 1943) 72 Minutes
Arline Judge, Roger Clark, Robin Raymond, Barbara Pepper, Dorothy Burgess, Clancy Cooper, Allan Byron (Jack Randall), Patricia Knox, Sidney Melton, Russell Gaige, Emmett Lynn, Richard Clarke, Betty Blythe, *Peggy Stewart*, Beverly Boyd, Bob Hill, Henry Hall, Mrs. Gardner Crane, Crane Whitley, Francis Ford
Director: Edgar G. Ulmer
Screenplay: Albert Reich
Story: Edgar G. Ulmer
Producer: Peter Van Duinen

TUCSON RAIDERS
(Republic, May 14, 1944) 55 Minutes
Bill Elliott, George "Gabby" Hayes, Bobby Blake, Alice Fleming, *Peggy Stewart*, Ruth Lee, LeRoy Mason, Stanley Andrews, John Whitney, Bud Geary, Karl Hackett, Tom Steele, Tom Chatterton, Edward Howard, Edward Cassidy, Fred Graham, Frank McCarroll, Kenne Duncan, Marshall Reed, Bert LeBaron, Fred Pershing, Joe Yrigoyen, Charles Sullivan, Neal Hart, Ted Wells, Carey Loftin, Foxy O'Callahan
Director: Spencer Bennet
Screenplay: Anthony Coldeway
Story: Jack O'Donnell
Assistant Director: Yakima Canutt
Associate Producer: Eddy White

SILVER CITY KID
(Republic, July 20, 1944) 55 Minutes
Allan Lane, *Peggy Stewart*, Wally Vernon, Twinkle Watts, Harry Woods, Frank Jacquet, Glenn Strange, Lane Chandler, Bud Geary, Tom Steele, Tom London, Jack Kirk, Sam Flint, Frank McCarroll, Hal Price, Edward Piel, Sr., Fred Graham, Frank O'Connor, Horace B. Carpenter
Director: John English
Story: Bennett Cohen
Screenplay: Taylor Caven
Associate Producer: Stephen Auer

STAGECOACH TO MONTEREY
(Republic, September 15, 1944) 55 Minutes
Allan Lane, *Peggy Stewart*, Wally Vernon, Twinkle Watts, Tom London, LeRoy Mason, Roy Barcroft, Kenne Duncan, Bud Geary, Carl Sepulveda, Jack O'Shea, Jack Kirk, Fred Graham, Henry Wills, Cactus Mack, Herman Hack, Jim Mitchell, Bob Wilke, Al Taylor
Director: Lesley Selander
Screenplay: Norman S. Hall
Associate Producer: Stephen Auer

CHEYENNE WILDCAT
(Republic, September 30, 1944) 56 Minutes
Bill Elliott, Bobby Blake, Alice Fleming, *Peggy Stewart*, Francis McDonald, Roy Barcroft, Tom London, Tom Chatterton, Kenne Duncan, Bud Geary, Jack Kirk, Sam Burton, Bud Osborne, Bob Wilke, Rex Lease, Tom Steele, Charles Morton, Forrest Taylor, Franklyn Farnum, Wee Willie Keeler, Universal Jack, Tom Smith, Horace B. Carpenter, Rudy Bowman, Prank Ellis, Steve Clark, Bob Burns, Jack O'Shea, Dickie Dillon, Fred Graham
Director: Lesley Selander
Screenplay: Randall Faye
Associate Producer: Louis Gray

CODE OF THE PRAIRIE
(Republic, October 6, 1944) 56 Minutes
Smiley Burnette, Sunset Carson, *Peggy Stewart*, Weldon Heyburn, Tom Chatterton, Roy Barcroft, Bud Geary, Tom London, Jack Kirk, Tom Steele, Bob Wilke, Frank Ellis, Rex Lease, Henry Wills, Ken Terrell, Charles King, Nolan Leary, Hank Bell, Karl Hackett, Jack O'Shea, Horace B. Carpenter
Director: Spencer Bennet
Story: Albert DeMond, Anthony Coldeway
Associate Producer: Louis Gray

FIREBRANDS OF ARIZONA
(Republic, December 1, 1944) 55 Minutes
Smiley Burnette, Sunset Carson, *Peggy Stewart*, Barle Hodgins, Roy Barcroft, Rex Lease, Tom London, Jack Kirk, Bud Geary, Bob Wilke, LeRoy Mason, Fred Toones, Pierce Lyden, Budd Buster, Bob Burns, Jack O'Shea, Hank Bell, Frank Ellis, Frank McCarroll, Charles Morton, Jess Cavan, Bob Woodward
Director: Lesley Selander
Screenplay: Randall Faye
Associate Producer: Louis Gray

SHERIFF OF LAS VEGAS
(Republic, December 31, 1944) 55 Minutes
Bill Elliott, Bobby Blake, Alice Fleming, *Peggy Stewart,* Selmer Jackson, William Haade, Jay Kirby, John Hamilton, Kenne Duncan, Bud Geary, Jack Kirk, Dickie Dillon, Frankie McCarroll, Freddie Chapman, Artie Ortego, Doc Adams
Director: Lesley Selander
Screenplay: Norman S. Hall
Associate Producer: Stephen Auer

UTAH
(Republic, March 21, 1945) 78 Minutes
Roy Rogers, George "Gabby" Hayes, Dale Evans, *Peggy Stewart,* Beverly Lloyd, Grant Withers, Bob Nolan and the Sons of the Pioneers, Jill Browning, Vivien Oakland, Hal Taliaferro, Jack Rutherford, Emmett Vogan, Edward Cassidy, Forrest Taylor, Horace B. Carpenter, "Trigger" (a horse)
Director: John English
Screenplay: Jack Townley, John K. Butler
Story: Gilbert Wright, Betty Burbridge
Associate Producer: Donald H. Brown

THE VAMPIRE'S GHOST
(Republic, May 21, 1945) 59 Minutes
John Abbott, Charles Gordon, *Peggy Stewart,* Grant Withers, Adele Mara, Emmett Vogan, Roy Barcroft, Martin Wilkins, Frank Jacquet, Jimmy Aubrey, Zack Williams, Floyd Schackelford, George Carlton, Fred Howard
Director: Lesley Selander
Story: Leigh Brackett
Screenplay: John K. Butler, Leigh Brackett
Associate Producer: Rudolph E. Abel

OREGON TRAIL
(Republic, July 14, 1945) 55 Minutes
Sunset Carson, *Peggy Stewart,* Frank Jacquet, John Merton, Mary Carr, Si Jenks, Earle Hodgins, Tom London, Kenne Duncan, Bud Geary, Lee Shumway, Steve Winston, Henry Wills, Cactus Mack, Tex Terry, Bud Osborne, Monte Hale, Rex Lease, Horace B. Carpenter, Tommy Coates, George Magrill, Sheila Stuart, Jamesson Shade
Director: Thomas Carr
Screenplay: Betty Burbridge
Story: Frank Gruber
Associate Producer: Bennett Cohen

BANDITS OF THE BADLANDS
(Republic, September 14, 1945) 55 Minutes
Sunset Carson, *Peggy Stewart,* Si Jenks, Monte Hale, John Merton, Forrest Taylor, Wade Crosby, Jack Ingram, Fred Graham, Alan Ward, Bob Wilke, Tex Terry, Jack O'Shea, Jack Kirk, Horace B. Carpenter, Charles Stevens, Charlie Sullivan, Henry Wills, Marshall Reed
Director: Thomas Carr
Screenplay: Doris Schroeder
Associate Producer: Bennett Cohen

MARSHAL OF LAREDO
(Republic, October 7, 1945) 56 Minutes
Bill Elliott, Bobby Blake, Alice Fleming, *Peggy Stewart,* Tom London, George Carleton, Wheaton Chambers, Tom Chatterton, George Chesebro, Don Costello, Bud Geary, Robert Grady, Sarah Padden, Jack O'Shea, Lane Bradford, Ken Terrell, Dorothy Granger, Dick Scott, Mary Arden, Jack Kirk
Director: R. G. Springsteen
Screenplay: Bob Williams
Associate Producer: Sidney Picker

ROUGH RIDERS OF CHEYENNE
(Republic, November 1, 1945) 56 Minutes
Sunset Carson, *Peggy Stewart,* Mira McKinney, Wade Crosby, Monte Hale, Michael Sloane, Kenne Duncan, Tom London, Eddy Waller, Jack O'Shea, Bob Wilke, Tex Terry, Jack Rockwell, Rex Lease, Hank Bell, Henry Wills, Cactus Mack, Artie Ortego, Jack Luden
Director: Thomas Carr
Screenplay: Elizabeth Beecher
Associate Producer: Bennett Cohen

THE TIGER WOMAN
(Republic, November 16, 1945) 61 Minutes
Adele Mara, Kane Richmond, Richard Fraser, *Peggy Stewart,* Cy Kendall, Beverly Loyd, Gregory Gay, John Kelly, Addison Richards, Donia Bussey, Frank Reicher, Garry Owen
Director: Philip Ford
Screenplay: George Carleton Brown
Story: John A. Dunkel
Associate Producer: Dorrell and Stuart McGowan

THE PHANTOM RIDER
(Republic, January 26, 1946) 12 Chapters
Robert Kent, *Peggy Stewart,* LeRoy Mason, George J. Lewis, Kenne Duncan, Hal Taliaferro, Chief Thunder Cloud, Tom London, Roy Barcroft, Monte Hale, John Hamilton, Hugh Prosser, Jack Kirk, Rex Lease, Tommy Coats, Joe Yrigoyen, Bill Yrigoyen, Jack O'Shea, Walt LaRue, Cliff Parkinson, Carl Sepulveda, Art Dillard, Bud Bailey, George Carleton, Dale Van Sickel, Tom Steele, George Chesebro, Wayne Burson, Cliff Lyons, Post Parks, Fred Graham, Bob Duncan, Augie Gomez, Robert Wilke, John Roy, Cactus Mack, Eddie Parker, Ted Mapes, Duke Taylor, Hal Price, James Linn, Tex Cooper, Henry Wills
Directors: Spencer G. Bennet, Fred Brannon
Screenplay: Albert DeMond, Basil Dickey, Jesse Duffy, Lynn Perkins, Barney Sarecky
Associate Producer: Ronald Davidson
Chapters: (1) The Avenging Spirit (2) Flaming Ambush (3) Hoofs of Doom (4) Murder Masquerade (5) Flying Fury (6) Blazing Peril (7) Gauntlet of Guns (8) Behind the Mask (9) The Captive Chief (10) Beasts at Bay (11) The Death House (12) The Last Stand

CALIFORNIA GOLD RUSH
(Republic, February 1, 1946) 60 Minutes
Bill Elliott, Bobby Blake, Alice Pleming, *Peggy Stewart,* Russell Simpson, Dick Curtis, Joel Friedkin, Kenne Duncan, Monte Hale, Tom London, Dickie Dillon, Jack Kirk, Mary Arden, Budd Buster, Frank Ellis, Neal Hart, Jim Mitchell, Jess Cavan, Silver Harr, Herman Hack, Pascale Perry, Freddie Chapman, Nolan Leary, Ben Johnson
Director: R. G. Springsteen
Screenplay: Bob Williams
Associate Producer: Sidney Picker

DAYS OF BUFFALO BILL
(Republic, Pebruary 8, 1946) 57 Minutes
Sunset Carson, *Peggy Stewart,* Tom London, James Craven, Rex Lease, Edmund Cobb, Eddie Parker, Michael Sloane, Jay Kirby, George Chesebro, Edward Cassidy, Frank O'Connor, Pascale Perry, Kit Guard, Tex Cooper, Tommy Coates, Jess Cavan, Roy Bucko
Director: Thomas Carr
Screenplay: William Lively, Doris Schroeder
Associate Producer: Bennett Cohen

SHERIFF OF REDWOOD VALLEY
(Republic, March 29, 1946) 57 Minutes
Bill Elliott, Bobby Blake, Bob Steele, Alice Fleming, *Peggy Stewart,* Arthur Loft, James Craven, Tom London, Kenne Duncan, Bud Geary, John Wayne Wright, Tom Chatterton, Budd Buster, Frank McCarroll
Director: R. G. Springsteen
Screenplay: Earle Snell
Associate Producer: Sidney Picker

ALIAS BILLY THE KID
(Republic, April 17, 1946) 56 Minutes
Sunset Carson, *Peggy Stewart,* Tom London, Roy Barcroft, Russ Whiteman, Tom Chatterton, Tex Terry, Pierce Lyden, James R. Linn, Stanley Price, Edware Cassidy, Steve Clark
Director: Thomas Carr
Screenplay: Betty Burbridge, Earle Snell
Story: Norman Sheldon
Associate Producer: Bennett Cohen

RED RIVER RENEGADES
(Republic, July 29, 1946) 55 Minutes
Sunset Carson, *Peggy Stewart,* Bruce Langley, Tom London, LeRoy Mason, Kenne Duncan, Ted Adams, Edmund Cobb, Jack Rockwell, Tex Terry
Director: Thomas Carr
Screenplay: Norman S. Hall
Associate Producer: Bennett Cohen

CONQUEST OF CHEYENNE
(Republic, July 29, 1946) 56 Minutes
Bill Elliott, Bobby Blake, Alice Fleming, *Peggy Stewart,* Jay Kirby, Milt Kibbee, Tom London, Emmett Lynn, Kenne Duncan, George Sherwood, Frank McCarroll, Jack Kirk, Tom Chatterton, Ted Mapes, Jack Rockwell
Director: R. G. Springsteen
Screenplay: Earle Snell
Story: Bert Horswell and Joseph Poland
Associate Producer: Sidney Picker

THE INVISIBLE INFORMER
(Republic, August 19, 1946) 57 Minutes
Linda Stirling, William Henry, Adele Mara, *Peggy Stewart,* Tom London, Gerald Mohr, Donia Bussey, Claire DuBrey, Tris Coffin, Charles Lane, Cy Kendall, Francis McDonald
Director: Philip Ford
Story: Gerald Drayson Adams
Screenplay: Sherman L. Lowe
Associate Producer: William J. O'Sullivan

STAGECOACH TO DENVER
(Republic, December 23, 1946) 56 Minutes
Allan Lane, Bobby Blake, Martha Wentworth, Roy Barcroft, *Peggy Stewart,* Emmett Lynn, Ted Adams, Edmund Cobb, Tom Chatterton, Bobbie Hyatt, George Chesebro, Edward Cassidy, Wheaton Chambers, Forrest Taylor, Britt Wood, Tom London, Stanley Price
Director: R. G. Springsteen
Screenplay: Earle Snell
Associate Producer: Sidney Picker

SON OF ZORRO
(Republic, January 18, 1947) 13 Chapters
George Turner, *Peggy Stewart,* Roy Barcroft, Edward Cassidy, Ernie Adams, Stanley Price, Edmund Cobb, Ken Terrell, Wheaton Chambers, Fred Graham, Eddie Parker, Si Jenks, Jack O'Shea, Jack Kirk, Tom Steele, Dale Van Sickel, Mike Frankovich, Pierce Lyden, Rocky Shahan, Ted Admas, Gil Perkins, Tex Terry, Tom London, Art Dillard, Joe Phillips, George Bell, Duke Taylor, Charles King, Post Parks, Cactus Mack, Bud Wolfe, Newton House, Frank O'Connor, Ted Mapes, Al Ferguson, Tommy Ryan, Carl Sepulveda, Herman Hack, George Chesebro, John Dahiem, Howard Mitchell, Doc Adams, Ralph Bucko, Joe Balch, Roy Bucko, Tommy Coats, Frank Ellis, Silver Harr, Pascale Perry
Director: Spencer Bennet, Pred C. Brannon
Screenplay: Franklyn Adreon, Basil Dickey, Jesse Duffy, Sol Shor
Associate Producer: Ronald Davidson
Chapters: (1) Outlaw Country (2) The Deadly Millstone (3) Fugitive from Injustice (4) Buried Alive (5) Water Trap (6) Volley of Death (7) The Fatal Records (8) Third Degree (9) Shoot to Kill (10) Den of the Beast (11) The Devil's Trap (12) Blazing Walls (13) Checkmate

TRAIL TO SAN ANTONE
(Republic, January 25, 1947) 67 Minutes
Gene Autry, *Peggy Stewart,* Sterling Holloway, John Duncan, Tris Coffin, Bill Henry, Dorothy Vaughn, Edward Keane, Ralph Peters, Cass County Boys, "Champion" (a horse)
Director: John English
Screenplay: Jack Nattleford, Luci Ward
Associate Producer: Armand Schaefer

VIGILANTES OP BOOMTOWN
(Republic, February 15, 1947) 56 Minutes
Allan Lane, Bobby Blake, Martha Wentworth, Roscoe Karns, Roy Barcroft, *Peggy Stewart,* George Turner, Eddie Lou Simms, Bobby Barber, George Chesebro, George Lloyd, Ted Adams, John Dehner, Earle Hodgins, Harlan Briggs, Budd Buster, Jack O'Shea, Tom Steele
Director: R. G. Springsteen
Screenplay: Earle Snell
Associate Producer: Sidney Picker

RUSTLERS OF DEVIL'S CANYON
(Republic, July 1, 1947) 58 Minutes
Allan Lane, Bobby Blake, Martha Wentworth, *Peggy Stewart,* Arthur Space, Emmett Lynn, Roy Barcroft, Tom London, Harry Carr, Pierce Lyden, Forrest Taylor, Budd Buster
Director: R. G. Springsteen
Screenplay: Earle Snell
Associate Producer: Sidney Picker

TEX GRANGER
(Columbia, April 1, 1948) 15 Chapters
Robert Kellard, *Peggy Stewart,* Robert "Buzz" Henry, Smith Ballew, Jack Ingram, I. Stanford Jolley, Terry Frost, Jim Diehl, Britt Wood, Bill Brauer, William Fawcett, Stanley Blystone, John Hart, Charles King, Edmund Cobb, Charles Whittaker, Al Ferguson, Eddie Parker
Director: Derwin Abrahams
Screenplay: Arthur Hoerl, Lewis Clay, Harry Fraser, Royal Cole
Based on the "Tex Granger" stories in Calling All Boys and Tex Granger comics
Producer: Sam Katzman
Chapters: (1) Tex Finds Trouble (2) Rider of Mystery Mesa (3) Dead or Alive (4) Dangerous Trails (5) Renegade Pass (6) A Crooked Deal (7) The Rider Unmasked (8) Mystery of the Silver Ghost (9) The Rider Trapped (10) Midnight Ambush (11) Renegade Roundup (12) Carson's Last Draw (13) Blaze Takes Over (14) Riding Wild (15) The Rider Meets Blaze

DEAD MAN'S GOLD
(Western Adventure/Screen Guild, September 10, 1948) 60 Minutes
Lash LaRue, Al "Fuzzy" St. John, *Peggy Stewart,* John Cason, Terry Frost, Lane Bradford, Pierce Lyden, Steve Keys, Cliff Taylor
Director: Ray Taylor
Screenplay: Ron Ormond, Ira Webb
Story: Ron Ormond, Ira Webb
Producer: Ron Ormond

FRONTIER REVENGE
(Western Adventure/Screen Guild, December 17, 1948) 55 Minutes
Lash LaRue, Al "Fuzzy" St. John, *Peggy Stewart,* Jim Bannon, Ray Bennett, Sarah Padden, Jimmie Martin, Jack Hendricks, Lee Morgan, Sandy Sanders, Billy Dix, Cliff Taylor, Steve Raines, Bud Osborne, George Chesebro, Forrest Matthews, Kermit Maynard, Ray Henderson
Director: Ray Taylor
Screenplay: Ray Taylor
Producer: Ron Ormond

RIDE, RYDER, RIDE
(Equity/Eagle Lion, February, 1949) 59 Minutes
Jim Bannon, Don Kay Reynolds, Emmett Lynn, *Peggy Stewart,* Marin Sais, Gaylord Pendleton, Jack O'Shea, Jean Budinger, Stanley Blystone, William Fawcett, Billy Hammond, Edwin Max, Steve Clark
Director: Lewis D. Collins
Screenplay: Paul Franklin
Producer: Jerry Thomas

DESERT VIGILANTE
(Columbia, April 8, 1949)
Charles Starrett, Smiley Burnette, *Peggy Stewart,* Tris Coffin, The Georgia Crackers, George Chesebro, Jack Ingram, Mary Newton, Paul Campbell, Tex Harding, I. Stanford Jolley, Ted Mapes
Director: Fred F. Sears
Screenplay: Earle Snell
Producer: Colbert Clark

THE FIGHTING REDHEAD
(Equity/Eagle Lion, October, 1949) 55 Minutes
Jim Bannon, Don Kay Reynolds, Emmett Lynn, Marin Sais, *Peggy Stewart,* John Hart, Lane Bradford, Forrest Taylor, Lee Roberts, Bob Duncan, Sandy Sanders, Billy Hammond, Ray Jones
Director: Lewis Collins
Screenplay: Paul Franklin, Jerry Thomas
Producer: Jerry Thomas

HOLLYWOOD VARIETIES
(Lippert, January 15, 1949) 60 Minutes
Robert Alda, The Hoosier Hot Shots, *Peggy Stewart,* Lois Ray, Britt Wood, Dolores Parker, Sammy Wolfe, Shaw & Lee, Glenn Vernon and Eddie Ryan, De Pina Troupe, Sandy and his Seals, Paul Gordon, Shavo Sherman, Charles Cirillo, Cliff Taylor, Three Rio Brothers, Twirl, Whirl and a Girl, The Four Dandies, Hector and his Pals, Johnson Brothers, The Eight Carlyle Dancers
Director: Paul Landres
Producers: June Carr, Paul Schreibman

CODY OF THE PONY EXPRESS
(Columbia, April 6, 1950) 15 Chapters
Jock O'Mahoney, Dickie Moore, *Peggy Stewart,* William Fawcett, Tom London, Helena Dare, George J. Lewis, Pierce Lyden, Jack Ingram, Rick Vallin, Frank Ellis, Ross Elliott, Ben Corbett, Rusty Westcoatt, Michael Whalen, Hugh Prosser, Frank Yaconelli
Director: Spencer G. Bennet
Screenplay: David Matthews, Lewis Clay, Charles Condon
Story: George Plympton, Joseph F. Poland
Producer: Sam Katzman
Chapters: (1) Cody Carries the Mail (2) Captured by Indians (3) Cody Saves a Life (4) Cody Follows a Trail (5) Cody to the Rescue (6) The Fatal Arrow (7) Cody Gets his Man (8) Revenge Raiders (9) Frontier Law (10) Cody Tempts Fate (11) Trouble at Silver Gap (12) Cody Comes Through (13) Marshal of Nugget City (14) Unseen Danger (15) Cody's Last Ride

MESSENGER OF PEACE
(Roland Reed/Astor, June 1, 1950) 87 Minutes
John Beal, *Peggy Stewart,* Paul Guilfoyle, Fred Hasler, Raphael Bennett, Maude Prickett, Al Bridges, Elizabeth Kerr, William Gould, Edythe Elliott, Brooks Shayne, Joe Brown, Jr.
Director: Frank Strayner
Screenplay: Glenn Tyron
Story: Henry Rische
Producer: Roland Reed

PRIDE OF MARYLAND
(Republic, January 18, 1951) 60 Minutes
Stanley Clements, *Peggy Stewart,* Frankie Darro, Joe Sawyer, Robert Barrat, Harry Shannon, Duncan Richardson, Stanley Logan, Joseph Crehan, Emmett Vogan, Clyde Cook, Donald Kerr, Guy Bellis
Director: Philip Ford
Screenplay/Story: John K. Butler
Associate Producer: William Lackey

Kansas Territory (Monogram, 1952) – I. Stanford Jolley, Lane Bradford, Stanley Price, Pierce Lyden, Peggy Stewart, and Bill Elliott.

THE BLACK LASH
(Western Adventure, January 2, 1952) 55 Minutes
Lash LaRue, Al "Fuzzy" St. John, *Peggy Stewart,* Kermit Maynard, Ray Bennett, Byron Keith, Jimmie Martin, John Cason, Clarke Stevens, Bud Osborne, Roy Butler, Larry Barton
Director: Ron Ormond
Screenplay: Kathy McKeel
Producer: Ron Ormond

KANSAS TERRITORY
(Monogram, May 4, 1952) 65 Minutes
Bill Elliott, *Peggy Stewart,* House Peters, Jr., Fuzzy Knight, Lane Bradford, I. Stanford Jolley, Lyle Talbot, Stanley Andrews, Marshall Reed, Terry Frost, John Hart, William Fawcett, Lee Roberts, Ted Adams, Pierce Lyden
Director: Lewis D. Collins
Screenplay: Dan Ullman
Producer: Vincent M. Fennelly

MONTANA INCIDENT
(Monogram, August 10, 1952) 54 Minutes
Whip Wilson, Rand Brooks, Noel Neill, *Peggy Stewart,* Hugh Prosser, William Fawcett, Terry Frost, Marshall Reed, Lyle Talbot, Russ Whitemand, Barbara Woodell, Bruce Edwards, Stanley Price
Director: Lewis D. Collins
Screenplay: Dan Ullman
Producer: Vincent M. Fennelly

SIX-GUN DECISION
(Newhall/Allied Artists, November 15, 1953) 54 Minutes
Guy Madison, Andy Devine, Don Haydon, Gloria Saunders, Fred Kohler, Jr., *Peggy Stewart*, Lyle Talbot, Zon Murray, Mike Vallon, Park MacGregor, Fred Hoose, Robert Bice, Tom Steele
Director: Frank McDonald
Screenplay: Bill Raynor
Producer: Wesley E. Barry
(Compiled from two "Wild Bill Hickok" television episodes Border City Election and Pony Express vs. Telegraph)

WHEN THE CLOCK STRIKES
(United Artists, June 10, 1961) 72 Minutes
James Brown, Merry Anders, Henry Corden, Roy Barcroft, *Peggy Stewart*, Jorge Moreno, Francis De Sales, Max Mellinger, Eden Hartford, Jack Kenney
Director: Edward L. Cahn
Screenplay: Dallas Gaultois
Producer: Robert E. Kent

THE CLOWN AND THE KID
(Harvard/United Artists, December 27, 1961) 65 Minutes
John Lupton, Mike McGreevey, Don Keefer, Mary Webster, Mary Adams, *Peggy Stewart*, Barry Kelley, Ken Mayer, Charles G. Martin, Victor French, James Parnell, Edith Evanson
Director: Edward L. Cahn
Screenplay: Herbert Abbott Spiro, Jerry Sackheim
Producer: Robert E. Kent.

THE WAY WEST
(United Artists, May 21, 1967) 122 Minutes
Kirk Douglas, Robert Mitchum, Richard Widmark, Lola Albright, Michael Witney, Stubby Kaye, Sally Field, Katherine Justice, Michael McGreevey, Connie Sawyer, Harry Carey, Jr., Elizabeth Fraser, William Lundigan, Anne Barton, Roy Barcroft, Eve McVeagh, Jack Elam, Hal Lynch, Timothy Scott, John Mitchum, Roy Glenn, Patric Knowles, Nick Cravat, Gary Morris, Eddie Little Sky, *Peggy Stewart*, Michael Keep, Clarke Gordon, Ken Murray, Paul Wexler, James Burke, Everett Creach
Director: Andrew V. McLaglen
Screenplay: Ben Maddlow, Mitch Lindemann
Story: A. B. Guthrie, Jr.
Producer: Harold Hecht

THE ANIMALS
(XYZ Prods./Levitt-Pickman Film Corp., October, 1971) 88 Minutes
Henry Silva, Keenan Wynn, Michele Carey, John Anderson, Joseph Turkel, Pepper Martin, Bobby Hall, William Bryant, *Peggy Stewart*, Peter Hellman, Michael Carr, Steve Michel De France, Fred Clark, Dean Casper, Henry Kendrick, Francesca Jarvis, Les Hoyle, Neil Summers, Mike Cooper, John Dennis, Jack Wade Cox, Bryan West
Director: Ron Joy
Screenplay: Hy Mizrahi
Executive Producer: Hy Mizrahi
Producer: Richard Bakalyan

THE STRANGER
(Bing-Crosby Prod., February 26, 1973) 2 hours
Glenn Corbett, Cameron Mitchell, Sharon Acker, Lew Ayres, George Coulouris, Steve Franken, Dean Jagger, Tim O'Connor, Jerry Douglas, Arch Whiting, H. M. Wynant, Virginia Gregg, Buck Young, Steven Marlo, William Bryant, Margaret Field, Philip Manson, Alan Foster, Ben Wright, *Peggy Stewart*, Gregg Shannon, Jon Blake, William Harlow, James Chandler, Heather McCoy, Jeanne Bates, Kathleen M. Schultz
Director: Lee H. Katzin
Screenplay: Gerald Sanford
Executive Producer: Andrew J. Fenady
Producer: Alan A. Armer

TERROR IN THE WAX MUSEUM
(Cinerama Releasing Corp., May, 1973) 93 Minutes
Ray Milland, Broderick Crawford, Elsa Lanchester, Maurice Evans, Shani Wallis, John Carradine, Louis Hayward, Patric Knowles, Mark W. Edwards, Steven Mario, Nicole Shelby, *Peggy Stewart*
Director: George Fenady
Screenplay: Jameson Brewer
Story/Producer: Andrew J. Fenady

BLACK OAK CONSPIRACY
(New World, March, 1977) 92 Minutes
Jesse Vint, Karen Carlson, Albert Salmi, Seymour Cassel, Douglas V. Fowley, Robert F. Lyons, Mary Wicox, James Gammon, Janus Blyth, Will Hare, Jeremy Foster, *Peggy Stewart*, Jo Anne Strauss, Vic Perrin, Darby Hinton, Dana Derfus, Bill Cross
Director: Bob Kelljan
Screenplay: Hugh Smith, Jesse Vint
Story: Hugh Smith
Producer: Jesse Vint, Tom Clark

DONNER PASS: THE ROAD TO SURVIVAL
(Schick Sunn Classics, October 24, 1978) 2 hours
Robert Fuller, Andrew Prine, Michael Callan, Diane McBain, John Anderson, John Doucette, Cynthia Eilbacher, Royal Dano, Gregory Walcott, Lance LeGault, Whit Bissell, *Peggy Stewart,* Robert Carricart, Rudy Diaz, Elaine Daniels, Michael Ruud, Jorge Moreno, Rick Jury, John Hansen, Paul Grace
Director: James L. Conway
Screenplay: S. S. Schweitzer
Executive Producer: Charles E. Sellier, Jr.
Producer: James Simmons

THE CAPTURE OF GRIZZLY ADAMS
(Charles E. Seiller Prods./Taft International, February 21, 1982)
Dan Haggerty, Chuck Connors, Kim Darby, Noah Beery, Jr., Keenan Wynn, June Lockhart, *Peggy Stewart*, Sidney Penny, G. W. Bailey
Story: Arthur Hennemann
Executive Producer: Charles E. Seiller

44 • RUTH STONEHOUSE

A Multifaceted Talent Who Dignified the Cliff and Cactus Melodrama

Ruth Stonehouse was born in 1893 in Chicago and started her career at the age of eight, as a dancer in Douglas, Arizona. Later she became a partner, with Broncho Billy Anderson (Max Aronson) in the ownership of the Essanay Studios in Chicago and was one of the company's top female stars, making more than a hundred films during her six-year tenure.

In 1916 she signed with Universal, where she often wrote and directed the short films in which she starred. Her serial roles were undistinguished. There seems to be some doubt as to whether she did or did not appear in **The Adventures of Peg o' the Ring** (1916). She was supposed to appear as an aerial artist beginning with chapter 6, replacing Grace Cunard, while Eddie Polo was to replace Francis Ford. Cunard and Ford were having trouble with their co-workers and with Universal's boss, Carl Laemmle. However, it is believed that they patched up their differences with Universal and completed the remaining chapters, which does not exclude Stonehouse and Polo from having been featured. A check with various sources indicates that they did appear in the serial, and that Stonehouse was the third-listed principal. In **The Master Mystery** (1919), a serial from Octagon Films starring magician Harry Houdini, Ruth has the second female role. Marguerite Marsh is listed first. But in **The Masked Rider** (1919) she is the leading lady opposite Harry Myers in a Western serial from Arrow Films.

Ruth retired with the demise of the silent film, though she continued to write scenarios for a while. At the time of her death on May 12, 1941, she was married to Felix Hughes. Her husband, a businessman, was a brother of author Rupert Hughes. The cause of Ruth's death was a cerebral hemorrhage; she was forty-eight years old. She had been active in club work and was a past chairman of the Women's Auxiliary Council of the Children's Home Society. She had no children herself.

Ruth Stonehouse.

RUTH STONEHOUSE Filmography

MR. WISE, INVESTIGATOR
(Essanay, July, 1911) 1 Reel
Sidney Ainsworth, Victor Potel, *Ruth Stonehouse*
Director: E. Mason Hopper
Scenario: E. Mason Hopper

TWILIGHT
(Essanay, September 6, 1912) 1 Reel
Francis X. Bushman, Martha Russell, *Ruth Stonehouse*, Harry Mainhall

BILLY McGRATH'S LOVE LETTERS
(Essanay, September, 1912) 1 Reel
John Steppling, Beverly Bayne, Joseph Allen, Eleanor Kahn, Eleanor Blanchard, Dolores Cassinelli, E. H. Calvert, Augustus Carney, C. Hitchcock, *Ruth Stonehouse*

NEPTUNE'S DAUGHTER
(Essanay, September 17, 1912) 1 Reel
Martha Russell, Francis X. Bushman, Harry Cashman, *Ruth Stonehouse*, William Walters
Director: W. Christy Cabanne
Scenario: W. Christy Cabanne
Story: F. de la Motte Fouque

SUNSHINE
(Essanay, October, 1912) 1 Reel
Ruth Stonehouse, Harry Mainhall, Harry Cashman
Director: T. W. Wharton

THE END OF THE FEUD
(Essanay, October, 1912) 1 Reel
Martha Russell, Francis X. Bushman, Helen Dunbar, *Ruth Stonehouse*, Harry Mainhall, William Walters, Harry Cashman, Bryant Washburn

FROM THE SUBMERGED
(Essanay, November, 1912) 1 Reel
Ruth Stonehouse, E. H. Calvert, Dolores Gassinelli
Director: Theodore K. Wharton
Scenario: Theodore K. Wharton

THE STAIN
(Essanay, November, 1912) 1 Reel
E. H. Calvert, Lily Branscomb, Walter Hitchcock, *Ruth Stonehouse*, Billy Mason, Bryant Washburn

MR. HUBBY'S WISH
(Essanay, November, 1912) 1 Reel
Augustus Carney, Eleanor Blanchard, Lily Branscombe, *Ruth Stonehouse*, Dolores Cassinelli

CHAINS
(Essanay, November 5, 1912) 1 Reel
Ruth Stonehouse, Francis X. Bushman, Bryant Washburn
Scenario: Louella O. Parsons

THE SHADOW OF THE CROSS
(Essanay, December, 1912) 1 Reel
Ruth Stonehouse, E. H. Calvert, Bryant Washburn

GIUSEPPE'S GOOD FORTUNE
(Essanay, December, 1912) 1 Reel
E. H. Calvert, Augustus Carney, *Ruth Stonehouse*, John Steppling, Eleanor Blanchard, Dolores Cassinelli, Howard Missimer, Bryant Washburn, Mary Height

THE VIRTUE OF RAGS
(Essanay, December, 1912) 1 Reel
Francis X. Bushman, Helen Dunbar, Bryant Washburn, Howard Missimer, *Ruth Stonehouse*, Margaret Steppling, Dolores Cassinelli
Director: Theodore Wharton
Scenario: Theodore Wharton

REQUITED LOVE
(Essanay, December, 1912) 1 Reel
Ruth Stonehouse

THE THIRTEENTH MAN
(Essanay, January, 1913) 1 Reel
Francis X. Bushman, *Ruth Stonehouse*, Raymond Whitney, Bryant Washburn, William Walt

THE BROKEN HEART
(Essanay, January, 1913) 1 Reel
Ruth Stonehouse, Bryant Washburn, Lillian Drew, William Walters, Dolores Cassinelli, Howard Missimer, Helen Dunbar
Director: Harry McRae Webster

AN OLD, OLD SONG
(Essanay, March, 1913) 1 Reel
William Walters, *Ruth Stonehouse*, Bryant Washburn, Whitney Raymond

A BOTTLE OF MUSK
(Essanay, March, 1913) 1 Reel
William Walters, *Ruth Stonehouse*, Bryant Washburn, Whitney Raymond

THE PATHWAY OF YEARS
(Essanay, March, 1913) 1 Reel
Francis X. Bushman, Ruth Hennessy, *Ruth Stonehouse*

THE SPY'S DEFEAT
(Essanay, March 13, 1913) 2 Reels
Francis X. Bushman, *Ruth Stonehouse*, Frank Dayton, Lillian Drew, William Walters
Director: Harry McRae Webster
Scenario: Harry McRae Webster

A WOLF AMONG LAMBS
(Essanay, March, 1913) 1 Reel
Ruth Stonehouse, Dolores Cassinelli, Alan Holubar, Bryant Washburn, Helen Dunbar

THE LITTLE MOTHER
(Essanay, April, 1913) 1 Reel
Ruth Stonehouse, E. H. Calvert

THE UNKNOWN
(Essanay, April, 1913) 1 Reel
E. H. Calvert, *Ruth Stonehouse*, Dolores Cassinelli, Helen Dunbar

A WOMAN'S WAY
(Essanay, May, 1913) 1 Reel
E. H. Calvert, *Ruth Stonehouse*, Gertrude Scott

EASY PAYMENTS
(Essanay, June, 1913) 1 Reel
Ruth Stonehouse, Norman Fowler, Clara Smith

HOME SPUN
(Essanay, July, 1913) 1 Reel
Richard C. Travers, Robert Boulder, Clara Smith, Thomas Commerford, *Ruth Stonehouse*

THE WORLD ABOVE
(Essanay, August, 1913) 1 Reel
Ruth Stonehouse, E. H. Calvert, Richard C. Travers, Lillian Drew

BROKEN THREADS UNITED
(Essanay, August, 1913) 2 Reels
Thomas Commerford, Doris Mitchell, Richard C. Travers, *Ruth Stonehouse*, E. H. Calvert, Jules Ferror

IN CONVICT'S GARB
(Essanay, September, 1913) 2 Reeels
E. H. Calvert, Richard C. Travers, *Ruth Stonehouse*, Bryant Washburn
Director: Harry McRae Webster
Scenario: Harry McRae Webster

A RAY OF GOD'S SUNSHINE
(Essanay, September, 1913) 1 Reel
Ruth Stonehouse, E. H. Calvert, Thomas Commerford

THREE SCRAPS OF PAPER
(Essanay, October, 1913) 1 Reel
Ruth Stonehouse, E. H. Calvert, Thomas Commerford, Eleanor Kahn

THY WILL BE DONE
(Essanay, October, 1913) 1 Reel
E. H. Calvert, *Ruth Stonehouse*, Eleanor Kahn

THE MAN OUTSIDE
(Essanay, November, 1913) 1 Reel
Harry Mainhall, *Ruth Stonehouse*

THE HEART OF THE LAW
(Essanay, December, 1913) 1 Reel
E. H. Calvert, *Ruth Stonehouse*, Richard C. Travers

LET NO MAN PUT ASSUNDER
(Essanay, 1913) 1 Reel
Ruth Stonehouse, Bryant Washburn, Francis X. Bushman, John Steppling, Joseph Allen

HEARTS AND FLOWERS
(Essanay, January, 1914) 1 Reel
Francis X. Bushman, Eleanor Kahn, *Ruth Stonehouse*

THE HOUR AND THE MAN
(Essanay, January 9, 1914) 2 Reels
Francis X. Bushman, *Ruth Stonehouse*, Clara Smith, William Bailey

THE HAND THAT ROCKS THE CRADLE
(Essanay, January, 1914) 1 Reel
Ruth Stonehouse, Richard C. Travers, Harry Mainhall

THE CONQUEROR
(Essanay, January, 1914) 1 Reel
Ruth Stonehouse, Bryant Washburn, William Bailey

THE GRIP OF CIRCUMSTANCES
(Essanay, January, 1914) 2 Reels
Bryant Washburn, E. H. Calvert, *Ruth Stonehouse*, Thomas Commerford, Angela Dolores, Richard C. Travers
Director: E. H. Calvert

THE OTHER GIRL
(Essanay, February 20, 1914) 2 Reels
Ruth Stonehouse, Francis X. Bushman

LET NO MAN ESCAPE
(Essanay, February, 1914) 2 Reels
Ruth Stonehouse, William Bailey, Richard C. Travers, John H. Cossar, Eleanor Kahn, Baby Madden

THE LONG COLD NIGHT
Essanay, February, 1914) 1 Reel
Ruth Stonehouse

THE COUNTER-MELODY
(Essanay, March, 1914) 1 Reel
Ruth Stonehouse, E. H. Calvert

THE PRICE OF HIS HONOR
(Essanay, April, 1914)
Richard C. Travers, *Ruth Stonehouse,* Lillian Drew, Helen Dunbar

A MAN FOR A' THAT
(Essanay, April 24, 1914) 2 Reels
Francis X. Bushman, *Ruth Stonehouse*

ASHES OF HOPE
(Essanay, May, 1914) 2 Reels
Francis X. Bushman, *Ruth Stonehouse,* E. H. Calvert

AN ANGEL UNAWARE
(Essanay, May, 1914) 1 Reel
Ruth Stonehouse, Gerda Holmes, Richard C. Travers

BLOOD WILL TELL
(Essanay, May, 1914) 3 Reels
Ruth Stonehouse, Francis X. Bushman
Director: Theodore Wharton
Scenario: Harry McRae Webster

THE DARLING YOUNG PERSON
(Essanay, June, 1914) 1 Reel
Ruth Stonehouse, Richard C. Travers

TRINKETS OF TRAGEDY
(Essanay, July 3, 1914) 2 Reels
Francis X. Bushman, *Ruth Stonehouse,* E. H. Calvert

NIGHT HAWKS
(Essanay, July 3, 1914) 2 Reels
Francis X. Bushman, *Ruth Stonehouse,* Ralph Holmes

THE MOTOR BUCCANEERS
(Essanay, July, 1914) 2 Reels
Francis X. Bushman, *Ruth Stonehouse,* Thomas Commerford, William Robinson, M. C. Von Betz, John H. Cossar, Ralph Holmes, Arthur Steinguard
Story: Edward Franklin

NO. 28 DIPLOMAT
(Essanay, August, 1914)
Ruth Stonehouse, Richard C. Travers, Minor Watson, Gerda Holmes
Director: Harry Botter
Story: Edward T. Lowe

THE FABLE OF LUTIE (THE FALSE ALARM)
(Essanay, September, 1914) 1 Reel
Ruth Stonehouse
Story: George Ade

SPARKS OF FATE
(Essanay, September 18, 1914) 2 Reels
Ruth Stonehouse, Bryant Washburn, Francis X. Bushman

A SPLENDID DISHONOR
(Essanay, September, 1914) 2 Reels
Francis X. Bushman, *Ruth Stonehouse,* Bryant Washburn, Lester Cuneo

WHITE LIES
(Essanay, September, 1914) 1 Reel
Richard C. Travers, *Ruth Stonehouse*
Story: H. Tipton Steck

THE REAL AGATHA
(Essanay, September, 1914) 2 Reels
Oscar G. Briggs, *Ruth Stonehouse,* Helen Dunbar
Director: Richard C. Travers
Story: Edith Huntington Mason

MOTHER O'DREAMS
(Essanay, October, 1914) 1 Reel
Ruth Stonehouse, Gerda Holmes, Richard C. Travers, Bryant Washburn
Story: James Oppenheim

AN UNPLANNED ELOPEMENT
(Essanay, October 27, 1914) 2 Reels
Francis X. Bushman, *Ruth Stonehouse,* E. H. Calvert
Director: E. H. Calvert
Story: H. Tipton Steck

THE SERVANT QUESTION
(Essanay, November, 1914) 1 Reel
Ralph Holmes, *Ruth Stonehouse*, Leo White, Lillian Drew

THE BATTLE OF LOVE
(Essanay, December 19, 1914) 3 Reels
Francis X. Bushman, *Ruth Stonehouse*
Story: Mrs. Woodrow Wilson

THE GIRL FROM THUNDER MOUNTAIN
(Essanay, December, 1914) 2 Reels
Ruth Stonehouse, Richard C. Travers

SURGEON WARREN'S WARD
(Essanay, December, 1914) 2 Reels
Richard C. Travers, *Ruth Stonehouse*, Bryant Washburn

THE MASKED WRESTLER
(Essanay, 1914) 2 Reels
Francis X. Bushman, Beverly Bayne, Bryant Washburn, *Ruth Stonehouse*, Paul Raas
Director: E. H. Calvert

NEARLY MARRIED
(Essanay, 1914) 1 Reel
Ruth Stonehouse, Bryant Washburn, True Boardman

ONE WONDERFUL NIGHT
(Essaney, 1914) 4 Reels
Francis X. Bushamn, Beverly Bayne, Bryant Washburn, Helen Dunbar, E. H. Calvert, Lillian Drew, *Ruth Stonehouse*, Thomas Cummerford, John Cossar, Leo White, Robert Bolder, Charles Hitchcock, Richard C. Travers, Cyril Leonard, Frank Dayton, Rapley Holmes, Harry Mainhall, Howard Watrous, Ed Babille, Matthew C. von Betz
Director: E. H. Calvert

THE LIEUTENANT GOVERNOR
(Essanay, January, 1915) 2 Reels
Eugene O'Brien, *Ruth Stonehouse*, Lester Cuneo, Joseph Byron Totten, Harry Dunkinson, John Cossar, Sidney Ainsworth

MISJUDGED MR. HARTLEY
(Essanay, January, 1915) 1 Reel
Bryant Washburn, *Ruth Stonehouse*, Helen Dunbar, Mabel Forrest

THE CREED OF THE KLAN
(Essanay, January, 1915) 1 Reel
Ruth Stonehouse, Bryant Washburn, Rapley Holmes, Lillian Drew

THIRD HAND HIGH
(Essanay, January, 1915) 2 Reels
Ruth Stonehouse, Bryant Washburn, Camille D'Arcy, Richard Travers, Sidney Ainsworth, E. H. Calvert
Story: Duffild Osborne

A ROMANCE OF THE NIGHT
(Essanay, February, 1915) 1 Reel
Ruth Stonehouse, E. H. Calvert, Richard C. Travers

AN AMATEUR PRODIGAL
(Essanay, February, 1915) 2 Reels
Ruth Stonehouse, Joseph Byron Totten, Lester Cuneo
Story: Albert Payson Terhune

THE SURPRISE OF MY LIFE
(Essanay, February, 1915) 1 Reel
Bryant Washburn, *Ruth Stonehouse*, Thomas Commerford, Frank Dayton, Lester Cuneo

THE DANCE AT ALECK FONTAINE'S
(Essanay, February, 1915) 1 Reel
Richard Travers, Ralph Johnson, *Ruth Stonehouse*
Story: Henry Oyen

MAN IN MOTLEY
(Essanay, March, 1915) 1 Reel
Harry Dunkinson, *Ruth Stonehouse*, Richard C. Travers
Director: E. H. Calvert
Story: I. A. R. Wylie

THE FABLE OF THE DIVINE SPARK THAT HAD A SHORT CIRCUIT
(Essanay, March, 1915) 1 Reel
Ruth Stonehouse
Story: George Ade

THE FABLE OF THE GALUMPTIOUS GIRL
(Essanay, March, 1915) 1 Reel
Ruth Stonehouse
Story: George Ade

THE WOOD NYMPH
(Essanay, March, 1915) 2 Reels
Ruth Stonehouse, Richard C. Travers
Director: E. H. Calvert
Story: Eleanor Talbot Kindread

THE CONFLICT
(Essanay, March, 1915) 2 Reels
Richard C. Travers, Sidney Ainsworth, *Ruth Stonehouse,* Lillian Drew

THE PROFLIGATE
(Essanay, April, 1915) 3 Reels
E. H. Calvert, *Ruth Stonehouse,* Bryant Washburn
Story: Arthur Hornblow

A NIGHT IN KENTUCKY
(Essanay, April, 1915) 2 Reels
Ruth Stonehouse
Story: Crittendon Marriott

THE ROMANCE OF AN AMERICAN DUCHESS
(Essanay, May 26, 1915) 2 Reels
Ruth Stonehouse, Sydney Ainsworth, Estelle Scott, Gloria Swanson, Richard Travers
Story: Adapted from The Smart Set magazine

THE FABLE OF THE HIGHROLLER AND THE BUZZING BLONDINE
(Essanay, May, 1915) 1 Reel
Bryant Washburn, *Ruth Stonehouse,* Leota Chrider
Story: George Ade

OTHERWISE BILL HARRISON
(Essanay, May, 1915) 2 Reels
Joseph Byron Totten, *Ruth Stonehouse*

THE FABLE OF THE TWO SENSATIONAL FAILURES
(Essanay, May, 1915) 1 Reel
Lloyd Holton, *Ruth Stonehouse*
Story: George Ade

ABOVE THE ABYSS
(Essanay, May, 1915) 2 Reels
Richard C. Travers, *Ruth Stonehouse,* Mayme Gehrue, Sidney Ainsworth, Helen Dunbar

THE SLIM PRINCESS
(Essanay, May 24, 1915) 4 Reels
Francis X. Bushman, *Ruth Stonehouse,* Wallace Beery, Harry Dunkinson, Bryant Washbur
Director: E. H. Calvert
Screenplay: Edward T. Lowe
Story: George Ade

THE GILDED CAGE
(Essanay, June, 1915) 1 Reel
Betty Scott, *Ruth Stonehouse,* Bryant Washburn, Louise Crolius, John Thorn
Story: Edward T. Lowe, Jr.

A DIGNIFIED FAMILY
(Essanay, June, 1915) 3 Reels
Ruth Stonehouse, Edmund Cobb, Grant Foreman, Eugene Acker

TEMPER
(Essanay, July, 1915) 3 Reels
Ruth Stonehouse, Henry B. Walthall, Ernest Maupain, Wanda Howard
Story: H. S. Sheldon

THE CALL OF YESTERDAY
(Essanay, July, 1915) 1 Reel
Bryant Washburn, *Ruth Stonehouse,* John Cossar, Florence Oberle, Thomas Commerford

WHEN MY LADY SMILES
(Essanay, August, 1915) 3 Reels
Ruth Stonehouse, Thomas Commerford, Florence Oberle, Richard Tabor
Story: Edward T. Lowe, Jr.

DOES THE WOMAN FORGET?
(Essanay, August, 1915) 1 Reel
Ruth Stonehouse, Edward C. Cobb, William Belmont

THE FABLE OF HAZEL'S TWO HUSBANDS AND WHAT BECAME OF THEM
(Essanay, September, 1915) 1 Reel
Ruth Stonehouse, Charles J. Stine, Eugene Acker
Director: Richard Foster Baker
Story: George Ade

DARLING DANDY
(Essanay, September 18, 1915) 3 Reels
Ruth Stonehouse, John Lorenz, John Thorn

A PHANTOM HUSBAND
(Essanay, October 7, 1915) 5 Reels
Ruth Stonehouse, J. P. Wild, Charles Gunn, Evelyn Driskell, Don Likes
Director: Ferris Hartman
Scenario: George D. Proctor

INHERITANCE
(Essanay, October, 1915) 3 Reels
Bryant Washburn, *Ruth Stonehouse,* Sidney Ainsworth, Florence Oberle, John Cossar
Director: Clement Haston
Story: Joseph A. Roach

THE SPIDER
(Essanay, October, 1915) 2 Reels
John A. Lorenz, *Ruth Stonehouse,* Hugh E. Thompson
Director: Laurence Windom
Story: James Francis Dwyer

MISS FRECKLES
(Essanay, October, 1915) 2 Reels
Ruth Stonehouse, Marion Skinner, Frank Dayton
Director: Charles H. Ashley
Story: H. Tipton Steck

THE CRIMSON WING
(Essanay, November, 1915) 6 Reels
E. H. Calvert, *Ruth Stonehouse,* Beverly Bayne, Bryant Washburn, Betty Scott, Harry Dunkinson, John Cossar, Grant Foreman
Director: E. H. Calvert
Story: Hobart C. Chatfield-Taylor

THE PAPERED DOOR
(Essanay, November 13, 1915) 3 Reels
Ruth Stonehouse, Edmund Cobb, Thurlow Brewer, Peggy Sweeney
Director: Laurence C. Windom
Story: Mary Roberts Rinehart

THE ALSTER CASE
(Essanay, December, 1915) 5 Reels
Bryant Washburn, John Cossar, *Ruth Stonehouse,* Anna Lee, Louise Crolius, Betty Scott, Arthur W. Bates, Roderick LaRoque, Beatrice Styler
Director: J. Charles Haydon
Story: Rufus Gilmore

BROUGHT HOME
(Essanay, December 28, 1915) 3 Reels
Ruth Stonehouse, Richard C. Travers, Billy Harper, Edmund Cobb, Frances Raymond, Dorcas Dale
Director: Laurence C. Windom

ANGELS UNAWARE
(Essanay/General, January 11, 1916) 2 Reels
Ruth Stonehouse, Edmund Cobb, Madge Kearns, Grant Foreman

DESTINY
(Essanay/General, January 29, 1916) 3 Reels
Bryant Washburn, *Ruth Stonehouse,* Edmund Cobb, Charles J. Stine, Rod LaRocque

THE ADVENTURES OF PEG O' THE RING
(Universal, May 1, 1916) 15 Chapters
Francis Ford, Grace Cunard, *Ruth Stonehouse,* Peter Gerald, Charles Munn, G. Raymond Nye, Eddie Polo, Mark Fenton, Jean Hathaway, Irving Lippner, Jack Duffy, Jack (John) Ford, Lionel Bradshaw
Director: Francis Ford, Jacques Jaccard
Screenplay: Grace Cunard
Chapters: (1) The Leopard's Mark (2) A Strange Inheritance (3) In the Lion's Den (4) The Circus Mongrels (5) The House of Mystery (6) The Cry for Help (7) The Wreck (8) Outwitted (9) The Leap (10) In the Hands of the Enemy (11) The Stampede (12) On the High Seas (13) The Clown Act (14) The Will (15) Retribution
(NOTE: There is doubt as to whether Stonehouse and Polo appeared in the final release prints. They were scheduled to replace Cunard and Ford when the latter two walked out in a dispute with Universal. After several weeks Cunard and Ford returned to work and a lot of completed footage was scrapped as the screenplay was changed numerous times. The extent of film footage of Stonehouse and Polo, if any, cannot be determined.)

THE 'PHONE MESSAGE
(Universal-Rex, July 22, 1916) 1 Reel
Ruth Stonehouse, Allen Holubar, Jack Holt
Director: Allen Holubar

LOVE NEVER DIES
(Universal-Bluebird, October 10, 1916) 5 Reels
Ruth Stonehouse, Franklyn Farnum
Director: William Worthington
Story: Harvey Gates

KINKAID, GAMBLER
(Universal-Red Feather, December, 1916) 5 Reels
Ruth Stonehouse, R. A. Cavin, Raymond Whittaker, Noble Johnson, Harry Mann, Harry Griffith, J. H. Knowles, Jean Hersholt
Director: Raymond Wells
Scenario: Fred Myton
Story: Raymond Wells

LOVE AFLAME
(Universal-Red Feather, January 16, 1917) 5 Reels
Ruth Stonehouse, Jack Mulhall, Jean Hersholt
Director: Raymond Wells
Scenario: Fred Myton
Story: Raymond Wells

FIGHTING FOR LOVE
(Universal-Red Feather, January, 1917) 5 Reels
Ruth Stonehouse, Jack Mulhall, Noble Johnson, J. F. Brisco, Ruby Marshall
Director: Raymond Wells
Scenario: Fred Myton

SAINTLY SINNER
(Universal-Bluebird, February 5, 1917) 5 Reels
Ruth Stonehouse, Jean Hersholt, Jack Mulhall, Henry Devries, Raymond Whittaker
Director: Raymond Wells
Scenario: Eugene S. Lewis
Story: L. H. Hutton

THE HEART OF MARY ANN
(Universal-Victor, February 9, 1917) 1 Reel
Ruth Stonehouse
Director: Ruth Stonehouse
Scenario: Fred Myton
Story: Ruth Stonehouse

DOROTHY DARES
(Universal-Victor, March 3, 1917) 2 Reels
Ruth Stonehouse, Mr. Witting, Mrs. Witting, Martha Maddox, Jack Dill
Director: Ruth Stonehouse
Scenario: Fred Myton

MARY ANN IN SOCIETY
(Universal-Victor, May 10, 1917)
Ruth Stonehouse, Lydia Titus, Edith Kessler
Director: Ruth Stonehouse
Scenario: Fred Myton
Story: Ruth Stonehouse
Producer: Ruth Stonehouse

TACKY SUE'S ROMANCE
(Universal-Rex, May 21, 1917) 2 Reels
Ruth Stonehouse
Director: Ruth Stonehouse
Story: Tom Gibson

THE STOLEN ACTRESS
(Universal-Gold Seal, May 28, 1917) 3 Reels
Chester Bennett, *Ruth Stonehouse*, George Webb, Wadsworth Harris, Lydia Y. Titus, Alfred Allen, Jane Bernoudy, Eugene Walsh
Director: Ruth Stonehouse
Story: Fred Jackson

PUPPY LOVE
(Universal-Victor, June 7, 1917) 1 Reel
Ruth Stonehouse, Josephine Crowell, Lila Lee, Lydia Yeamans Titus, Dave Kershaw
Director: Ruth Stonehouse
Story: Ruth Stonehouse

DAREDEVIL DAN
(Universal-Victor, June 23, 1917) 1 Reel
Ruth Stonehouse
Director: Ruth Stonehouse
Scenario: Charles Wilson, Jr.
Story: Ruth Stonehouse

A LIMB OF SATAN
(Universal-Gold Seal, June 26, 1917) 3 Reels
Ruth Stonehouse, Jack Webster Dill, Chester Bennett, Mrs. Witting, Mrs. Pratt, Wadsworth Harris, Martha Mattox, Helen Wright
Director: Ruth Stonehouse
Scenario: Elizabeth Mahoney

FOLLOW THE GIRL
(Universal-Butterfly, July 26, 1917) 5 Reels
Roy Stewart, *Ruth Stonehouse*, Jack Dill, Claire DuBrey, Alfred Allen
Director: Louis Chaudet
Story: Fred Myton

THE WINNING PAIR
(Universal-Gold Seal, August, 1917) 3 Reels
Roy Stewart, *Ruth Stonehouse*
Director: Louis Chaudet
Story: Hugene B. Lewis

THE EDGE OF THE LAW
(Universal-Butterfly, September 14, 1917) 5 Reels
Ruth Stonehouse, Lydia Yeamans Titus, Lloyd Whitlock
Director: Louis Chaudet
Adaptation: Harvey Gates
Story: Maude Pettus, "The Gentle Ill Wind"

A WALLOPING TIME
(Universal-Victor, September 27, 1917) 1 Reel
Ruth Stonehouse, Harry Mann, Grace Marvin, Lydia Yeamans Titus
Director: Ruth Stonehouse
Scenario: Fred Myton
Story: Ruth Stonehouse

THE PHANTOM HUSBAND
(Triangle, October 7, 1917) 5 Reels
Ruth Stonehouse, J. P. Wild, Charles Gunn, Estelle Lasheur, Evelyn Driskell, Don Likes, Mary McIvor
Director: Ferris Hartman
Scenario: George D. Proctor

ROSALIND AT REDGATE
(Universal, February, 1919) 3 Reels
Ruth Stonehouse, C. M. McDowell, Larry Peyton, Martha Mattox
Scenario: Giles R. Warren
Story: Meredith Nicholson

THE MASTER MYSTERY
(Octagon, March, 1919) 15 Chapters
Harry Houdini, Marguerite Marsh, *Ruth Stonehouse,* William Pike, Charles Graham, Edna Britton, Floyd Buckley
Director: Burton King
Story: Arthur B. Reeve, Charles A. Logue
Chapters: (1) Living Death (2) The Iron Terror (3) The Water Peril (4) The Test (5) The Chemist's Shop (6) The Mad Genius (7) Barbed Wire (8) The Challenge (9) The Madagascan Madness (10) The Binding Ring (11) The Net (12) The Death Noose (13) The Flash of Death (14) The Tangled Web (15) Bound at Last or The Unmasking of the Automaton

THE MASKED RIDER
(Arrow, May, 1919) 15 Chapters
Harry Myers, *Ruth Stonehouse,* Paul Panzer, Boris Karloff, Edna M. Holland, Marie Treador, Blanche Gillespie, Robert Tober, Jack Chapman, George Murdock, George Cravey
Director: Aubrey M. Kennedy
Story: Aubrey M. Kennedy
Producer: William Steiner
Chapters: (1) The Hole in the Wall (2) In the Hands of Pancho (3) The Capture of Juanita (4) The Kiss of Hate (5) The Death Trap (6) Pancho Plans Revenge (7) The Fight on the Dam (8) The Conspirators Foiled (9) The Exchange of Prisoners (10) Harry's Perilous Escape (11) To the Rescue (12) The Imposter (13) Coals of Fire (14) In the Desert's Grip (15) Retribution

THE FOURFLUSHER
(Metro, August 25, 1919) 5 Reels
Ruth Stonehouse, Hale Hamilton, Fred M. Malatesta, Harry Holden, Ralph Bell, Robert Badger, Louis Fitzroy, Effie Conley
Director: Harry L. Franklyn
Adaptation: A. S. LeVino
Story: Izola Forrester, Mann Page

PARLOR, BEDROOM AND BATH
(Metro, July 12, 1920) 5 Reels
Eugene Pallette, *Ruth Stonehouse*
Director: Edward Dillon
Screenplay: June Mathis, A. P. Younger
Scenario: From a play by C. W. Bell and Mark Swan

THE HOPE
(Metro, August 28, 1920) 6 Reels
Jack Mulhall, Mary Astor, *Ruth Stonehouse,* Marguerite De La Motte, Frank Elliott
Director: Herbert Blanche
Scenario: A. S. LeVino
Story: Prom a play by Cecil Raleigh and Harry Hamilton

CONRAD IN QUEST OF HIS YOUTH
(Paramount, November 8, 1920)
Kathlyn Williams, Edward Sutherland, Thomas Meighan, Mabel Van Buren, *Ruth Stonehouse,* Maym Kelso, Bertram Johns, Margaret Loomis, Sylvia Ashton, Charles Ogle, Ruth Rennick
Director: William De Mille
Scenario: Olga Printzlau
Story: Leonard Merrick

ARE ALL MEN ALIKE?
(Metro, November 8, 1920) 6 Reels
May Allison, Wallace MacDonald, *Ruth Stonehouse,* Lester Cuneo, Emanuel Turner
Director: Philip E. Rosen
Adaptation: A. P. Younger
Story: Arthur Stringer, "The Waffle Iron"

I AM GUILTY
(J. Parker Reed Jr./Associated Producers, May, 1921) 7 Reels
Louise Glam, Mahlon Hamilton, Claire DuBrey, Joseph Kilgour, *Ruth Stonehouse,* May Hopkins, George Cooper, Mickey Moore, Frederic De Kovert
Director: Jack Nelson
Scenario: Bradley King
Story: Bradley King

DON'T CALL ME LITTLE GIRL
(Realart, June, 1921) 5 Reels
Mary Miles Minter, Winifred Greenwood, *Ruth Stonehouse,* Jerome Patrick, Edward Falnagan, Fannie Midgley
Director: Joseph Henabery
Scenario: Edith Kennedy
Story: Catherine Chrisholm Cushing, "Jerry"

THE FLASH
(Clinton/Russell, January, 1923) 5 Reels
George Larkin, *Ruth Stonehouse*
Director: William J. Craft
Story: George Hively

FLAMES OF PASSION
(Premium/Independent, March 1, 1923) 5 Reels
George Larkin, *Ruth Stonehouse,* Frank Whitson, Al Ferguson, Frank Whitlock, Laura Anson, Karl Silvera
Director: William J. Craft
Story: George Hively

LIGHTS OUT
(R-C/FBO, November 11, 1923) 7 Reels
Ruth Stonehouse, Walter McGrail, Marie Astaire, Theodore von Eltz, Ben Deely, Hank Mann, Ben Hewlett, Mabel Van Buren, Fred Kelsey, Chester Bishop, Max Ascher
Director: Al Santell
Story: Paul Dickey, Mann Page
Adaptation: Rex Taylor

THE WAY OF THE TRANSGRESSOR
(Premium/Independent, December, 1923) 5 Reels
George Larkin, *Ruth Stonehouse,* Frank Whitson, Al Ferguson, Laura Anson, Carl Silvera, William Vaughn Moody
Director: William J. Craft

A GIRL OF THE LIMBERLOST
(Gene Stratton Porter/FBO, April 28, 1924) 6 Reels
Gloria Grey, Emily Fitzroy, Arthur Currier, Raymond McKee, Arthur Millet, Cullen Landis, Gertrude Olmstead, Alfred Allen, Virginia Boardman, Myrtle Vane, Jack Daugherty, *Ruth Stonehouse,* Baby Pat O'Malley, Buck Black, Newton Hall, Lisamae Grey
Director: James Leo Meehan
Scenario: Gene Stratton Porter

BROKEN BARRIERS
(Metro-Goldwyn, August 18, 1924) 6 Reels
James Kirkwood, Norma Shearer, Adolphe Menjou, Mae Busch, George Fawcett, Margaret McWade, Robert Agnew, *Ruth Stonehouse,* Robert Frazer, Winifred Bryson, Vera Reynolds, Edythe Chapman, George Kuwa
Director: Reginald Barker
Scenario: Sada Cowan, Howard Higgin
Story: Meredith Nicholson

STRAIGHT THROUGH
(Universal, April 5, 1925) 5 Reels
William Desmond, Marguerite Clayton, Albert J. Smith, *Ruth Stonehouse,* Frank Brownlee, Bill Gillis, George F. Marion
Director: Arthur Rosson
Story: Charles Logue

A TWO-FISTED SHERIFF
(Ben Wilson/Arrow, April 12, 1925) 5 Reels
Yakima Canutt, *Ruth Stonehouse,* Art Walker, Cliff Davidson, Jack Woods, Joe Rickson
Directors: Ben Wilson, Ward Hayes
Story: George W. Pyper

FIFTH AVENUE MODELS
(Universal-Jewel, April 26, 1925) 7 Reels
Mary Philbin, Norman Kerry, Josef Swickard, William Conklin, Rosemary Theby, Rose Dione, Robert Brower, Betty Francisco, Helen Lynch, George B. Williams, Jean Hersholt, Bob McKenzie, *Ruth Stonehouse,* Lee Moran, Mike Donlin
Director: Svend Gade
Story: Muriel Hine Coxen, "The Best in Life"
Adaptation: Olga Printzlau

THE FUGITIVE
(Arrow, May 3, 1925) 5 Reels
Ruth Stonehouse, Wilbur McGaugh, Ben Wilson, Natalie La Supervia, Joseph Girard, Helene Rosson
Director: Ben Wilson
Story: Jacques Jaccard

BLOOD AND STEEL
(Independent, May 29, 1925) 5 Reels
Helen Holmes, William Desmond, Robert Edeson, Mack V. Wright, Albert J. Smith, *Ruth Stonehouse,* C. L. Sherwood, Paul Walters, Walter Fitzroy
Director: J. P. McGowan
Story: George Plympton

THE SCARLET WEST
(Frank K. Carroll/First National, July 26, 1925) 9 Reels
Robert Frazer, Clara Bow, Robert Edeson, Johnny Walker, Walter McGrail, Gaston Glass, Helen Ferguson, *Ruth Stonehouse*, Martha Francis, Florence Crawford
Director: John G. Adolfi
Scenario: Anthony Paul Kelly
Story: A. B. Heath

ERMINE AND RHINESTONES
(Jans Productions, October 1, 1925) 6 Reels
Hdna Murphy, Niles Welch, *Ruth Stonehouse*, Coit Albertson, Sally Crute, Bradley Barker, Marguerite McNulty
Director: Burton King
Story: Louise Winter

FALSE PRIDE
(True Story/Astor, November, 1925) 6 Reels
Owen Moore, Faire Binney, *Ruth Stonehouse*, J. Barney Sherry, Bradley Barker, Pauline Armitage, Jane Jennings
Director: Hugh Dierker
Story: Lewis Allen Browne

THE WIVES OF THE PROPHET
(J. A. Fitzgerald/Lee-Bradford, January, 1926) 7 Reels
Orville Caldwell, Alice Lake, Violet Morsereau, Harlan Knight, *Ruth Stonehouse*, Warner Richmond, Maurice Costello, Ed Roseman, Mary Thurman
Director: J. A. Fitzgerald
Story: Opie Percival Read

BROKEN HOMES
(True Story, February 15, 1926) 6 Reels
Gaston Glass, Alice Lake, J. Barney Sherry, Jane Jennings, *Ruth Stonehouse*
Director: Hugh Dierker
Adaptation: Lewis Allen Browne

THE LADYBIRD
(Chadwick/First Division, March 7, 1927) 7 Reels
Betty Compson, Malcolm McGregor, Sheldon Lewis, Hank Mann, Leo White, John Miljan, *Ruth Stonehouse*, Joseph Girard, Jean De Briac, Mathew Matron
Director: Walter Lang
Scenario: John F. Natteford
Story: William Dudley Pelley

POOR GIRLS
(Columbia, May 5, 1927) 6 Reels
Dorothy Revier, Edmund Burns, *Ruth Stonehouse*, Lloyd Whitlock, Marjorie Bonner
Director: William Craft
Screenplay: William Branch
Story: Sophie Bogen

THE SATIN WOMAN
(Gotham/Lumas, August 1, 1927) 7 Reels
Mrs. Wallace Reid, Rockliffe Fellowses, Alice White, John Miljan, Laska Winters, Charles Post, *Ruth Stonehouse*, Gladys Brockwell, Ethel Wales
Director: Walter Lang
Scenario: Walter Lang
Story: Walter Lang

THE APE
(Milt Collins/Collwyn, March 28, 1928) 5 Reels
Gladys Walton, *Ruth Stonehouse*, Basil Wilson, Bradley Barker
Director: B. C. Rule

THE DEVIL'S CAGE
(Chadwick, June S, 1928) 6 Reels
Pauline Garon, *Ruth Stonehouse*, Donald Keith, Armand Kaliz, Lincoln Stedman
Director: Wilfred Noy
Scenario: Isadore Bernstein
Story: Isadore Bernstein

Jacqueline Wells/Julie Bishop.

45 • JACQUELINE WELLS/JULIE BISHOP

Unhampered by Pride, She Doggedly Gave Her Best to Each Role

In 1941 Jacqueline Wells, tired of the kind of roles she had been playing, left Hollywood briefly to vacation in Wisconsin, there becoming affiliated with the Peninsula Players of Door County. Upon returning to Hollywood she changed her name to Julie Bishop and with her agent began a round of studio casting offices.

The trek ended at Warner Brothers, where she was placed under contract. Subsequently the attractive redheaded star achieved a measure of fame in a number of prestigious films at the giant North Hollywood studio, proving to be an actress of considerable talent.

But it was as Jacqueline Wells, prior to 1941, that the winsome beauty earned the respect and admiration of those audiences frequenting the lower-priced theatres playing serials and low-budget melodramas.

Jacqueline Brown was born in Denver, Colorado on August 30, 1914. Soon thereafter her parents moved to Dallas, Texas and later to Los Angeles. Her dad was a prominent businessman with diverse interests.

As early as 1923 Jacqueline was appearing in films and in 1926 made her first serial, **The Bar-C Mystery,** at Pathé. Shortly afterwards she left the screen to concentrate on her schooling.

Jacqueline was educated at two Los Angeles girls schools--Westlake and Kenwood. Also, she studied dancing under Theodore Kosloff, and dramatics at the Pasadena Community Playhouse. It was while she was appearing in one of the playhouse presentations that a talent scout spotted her, signed her to a contract and immediately launched her as a new screen find--Jacqueline Wells.

At age 18 she was appearing in the two-reel comedies of Hal Roach, as well as playing the sister of Noah Beery, Jr. in **Heroes of the West** (1932), a Universal serial revolving about the attempts of a gang to stop construction of a railroad. Onslow Stevens is the engineer who comes to the aid of Jacqueline and Noah and their father, the railroad contractor. For some unknown reason, Jacqueline was billed as Diane Duval this time around, a fact not appreciated today by Jacqueline. Though she will sign autographs as Julie Bishop or Jacqueline Wells, she will not sign by her third screen name of Duval.

Shortly after **Heroes of the West** hit the market, two other serials followed. In **Clancy of the Mounted** (1932) Sergeant Tom Clancy's (Tom Tyler) brother is framed for a murder and Tom has to go after him. Outlaws responsible for the frame are also the ones responsible for the murder of Ann Louise's (Jacqueline) father, discoverer of a gold mine. Tom saves Ann from the badmen and is eventually able to clear his brother, dispose of the villain, and claim Ann as his fiancée.

In **Tarzan, the Fearless** (1933) Jacqueline's last serial, Tarzan (Buster Crabbe) aids Mary Brooks (Jacqueline) and a friend in the search for Mary's father, who is a prisoner of the people of Zor, god of the Emerald Fingers. Mary's guide secretly desires to obtain a lost jungle treasure and to have Mary and is aided by another ruffian in his endeavors. The followers of Zor further complicate the situation by trying to kill everyone. However, Tarzan triumphs and, though he speaks no English, wins Mary as his mate.

These serials were memorable ones that usually found Jacqueline or the hero teetering on the brink of disaster from week to week. Jacqueline was not a lively, activist heroine in the way that Kathlyn Williams or Pearl White were. Her roles were not flamboyant, but her presence in a scene could hardly be ignored, no matter what was happening. It projected as if by magic.

Going on to play routine leads in a variety of roles, Jacqueline developed into an attractive and

Tarzan, the Fearless (Principal, 1933) – Jacqueline Wells and Buster Crabbe.

competent leading lady and, as Julie Bishop, rose to prominence in the 1940s.

A marriage to Walter Booth Brooks III, socialite and journalist, ended in a divorce in May, 1939. Brooks did not contest the divorce in which Miss Wells charged cruelty. The couple had wed in Santa Barbara on May 16, 1936. In July, 1944, after attaining stardom as Julie Bishop, Jacqueline married Lieutenent Colonel (later General) Clarence A. Shoop, who later became an RKO executive, in Falls Church, Virginia. The marriage was a lasting one, and two children were born to the union. Son Stephen became an Air Force jet pilot and daughter Pamela, an actress. General Shoop died in the 1960s and Jacqueline married a well-to-do Beverly Hills surgeon, Dr. William Bergin, in 1968.

Retired since 1957, Jacqueline paints and does charity work. She sometimes longs to return to acting, but her husband prefers that she not work.

JACQUELINE WELLS/JULIE BISHOP
Filmography

CHILDREN OF JAZZ
(Famous Players Lasky, July 8, 1923) 6 Reels
Theodore Kosloff, Ricardo Cortez, Robert Cain, Eileen Percy, Irene Dalton, Alec B. Francis, Frank Currier, Snitz Edwards, Lillian Drew, *Jacqueline Wells*
Director: Jerome Storm
Adaptation: Beulah Marie Dix
Story: Harold Brighouse, "Other Times" (a play)

MAYTIME
(B.P. Schulberg/Preferred, November 16, 1923) 8 Reels
Ethel Shannon, Harrison Ford, William Norris, Clara Bow, Wallace MacDonald, Josef Swickard, Martha Mattox, Robert McKim, *Jacqueline Wells*
Director: Louis Gassnier
Adaptation: Olga Printzlau
Story: Rida Johnson Young, Cyrus Wood

DOROTHY VERNON OF HADDON HALL
(United Artists, March 15, 1924) 10 Reels
Mary Pickford, Anders Randolf, Marc MacDermott, Mme. Daumery, Allan Forrest, Wilfred Lucas, Clare Eames, Estelle Taylor, Courtenay Foote, Colin Kenny, Lottie Pickford Forrest, *Jacqueline Wells*
Director: Marshall Neilan
Screenplay: Waldemar Young
Story: Charles Major

CAPTAIN BLOOD
(Vitagraph, September 21, 1924) 11 Reels
J. Warren Kerrigan, Jean Paige, Charlotte Merriam, James Morrison, Allan Forrest, Bertram Grassby, Otis Harlan, Jack Curtis, Wilfrid North, Otto Matiesen, Robert Bolder, Templar Saxe, Henry Barrows, Boyd Irwin, Henry Hebert, Miles McCarthy, Tom McGuire, Frank Whitson, Helen Howard, Robert Milash, William Eugene, George Williams, Omar Whitehead, Muriel Paull, George Lewis, *Jacqueline Wells*
Director: David Smith
Scenario: Jay Pilcher
Story: Rafael Sabatini

THE GOLDEN BED
(Famous Players Lasky, January 19, 1925) 9 Reels
Lillian Rich, Vera Reynolds, Henry Walthall, Rod LaRocque, Theodore Kosloff, Warner Baxter, Robert Cain, Julia Faye, Robert Edeson, *Jacqueline Wells,* Mary Jane Irving, Charles Clary
Director: Cecil B. DeMille
Screenplay: Jeanie Macpherson

CLASSIFIED
(First National, October 11, 1925) 7 Reels
Corinne Griffith, Jack Mulhall, Ward Crane, Carroll Nye, Charles Murray, Edythe Chapman, *Jacqueline Wells,* George Sidney, Bernard Randall
Director: Alfred Santell
Story: Edna Ferber

THE HOME MAKER
(Universal, November 22, 1925) 8 Reels
Alice Joyce, Clive Brook, Billy Kent Schaeffer, George Fawcett, Virginia Boardman, Maurice Murphy, *Jacqueline Wells,* Frank Newburg, Margaret Campbell, Martha Mattox, Alfred Fisher, Alice Flower, Elaine Ellis
Director: King Baggot
Scenario: Mary O'Hara

THE BAR-C MYSTERY
(Pathé, April 25, 1926) 10 Chapters
Wallace MacDonald, Dorothy Phillips, Ethel Clayton, Philo McCullough, Johnny Fox, Violet Schram, Fred de Silva, Victor Potel, Fred Kohler, Billie Bletcher, *Jacqueline Wells,* Francis McDonald, Tom London, Al Hart, Jim Corey
Director: Robert F. Hill
Screenplay: William Sherwood
Story: Raymond Spears, "Janie of the Waning Glories"
Chapters: (1) A Heritage of Danger (2) Perilous Paths (3) The Midnight Raid (4) Wheels of Doom (5) Thundering Hoofs (6) Against Desperate Odds (7) Back from the Missing (8) Fight for a Fortune (9) The Wolf's Cunning (10) A Six-Gun Wedding

THE FAMILY UPSTAIRS
(Fox, August 29, 1926) 6 Reels
Virginia Valli, Allan Simpson, J. Farrell MacDonald, Lillian Elliott, Edward Piel, Jr., Dot Farley, Cecille Evans, *Jacqueline Wells*
Director: J. G. Blystone
Scenario: L. G. Rigby

SKIP THE MALOO!
(Hal Roach/M-G-M, September 26, 1931) 2 Reels
Charley Chase, *Jacqueline Wells,* Gale Henry, Dell Henderson, Eddie Dunn, Leo Willis, Fern Emmett, Harry Bernard, Jerry Mandy
Director: James Parrott
Dialogue: H. M. Walker

SCAREHEADS
(Capital, 1931)
Richard Talmadge, *Jacqueline Wells* (Julie Bishop), Gareth Hughes, King Baggott, True Boardman
Director: Noel Mason

ANY OLD PORT
(Hal Roach/M-G-M, March 5, 1932) 2 Reels
Stan Laurel and Oliver Hardy, *Jacqueline Wells,* Walter Long, Harry Bernard, Arthur Housman, Charlie Hall, Robert Burns, Sam Lufkin, Dick Gilbert
Director: James Horne
Dialogue: H. M. Walker

THE KNOCKOUT
(Hal Roach/M-G-M, March 5, 1932) 2 Reels
Mickey Daniels, Grady Sutton, Eddie Morgan, Gordon Douglas, Mary Kornman, *Jacqueline Wells,* Harry Bernard, Spec O'Donnell
Directors: Anthony Mack, Lloyd French
Dialogue: H. M. Walker

YOU'RE TELLING ME
(Hal Roach/M-G-M, April 16, 1932) 2 Reels
Mickey Daniels, Grady Sutton, Gordon Douglas, *Jacqueline Wells,* Betty Bolen, Billy Gilbert, Louise Beavers, May Wallace
Directors: Anthony Mack, Lloyd French
Dialogue: H. M. Walker

IN WALKED CHARLEY
(Hal Roach/M-G-M, April 23, 1932) 2 Reels
Charley Chase, *Jacqueline Wells,* Gertrude Astor, Dell Henderson, Billy Gilbert, Eddie Dunn, Harry Bernard
Director: Warren Doane
Dialogue: H. M. Walker

HEROES OF THE WEST
(Universal, June 20, 1932) 12 Chapters
Noah Beery, Jr., Diane Duval *(Jacqueline Wells),* Onslow Stevens, William Desmond, Martha Mattox, Philo McCullough, Harry Tenbrook, Frank Lackteen, Edmund Cobb, Jules Cowles, Francis Ford, Thunderbird, Lafe McKee, Grace Cunard
Director: Ray Taylor
Screenplay: George Plympton, Basil Dickey, Joe Roach
Story: Peter B. Kyne, "The Tie That Binds"
Chapters: (1) Blazing the Trail (2) The Red Peril (3) The Avalanche (4) A Shot from the Dark (5) The Hold-Up (6) Captured by the Indians (7) Flaming Arrows (8) Frontier Justice (9) The Iron Master (10) Thundering Death (11) Thundering Hoofs (12) End of the Trail

CLANCY OF THE MOUNTED
(Universal, January, 1933) 12 Chapters
Tom Tyler, *Jacqueline Wells,* William Desmond, Rosalie Roy, Francis Ford, Earl McCarthy, Tom London, Edmund Cobb, William Thorne, Leon Duval, Al Ferguson, Frank Lanning, Fred Humes, Monte Montague, Frank Lackteen, Steve Clemente
Director: Ray Taylor
Screenplay: Basil Dickey, Harry O. Hoyt, Ella O'Neill
Story: Based on the poem by Robert W. Service
Producer: Henry MacRae
Chapters: (1) Toll of the Rapids (2) Brother Against Brother (3) Ambuscade (4) The Storm (5) A Desperate Chance (6) The Wolf's Fangs (7) The Night Attack (8) Crashing Timber (9) Fingerprints (10) The Breed Strikes (11) The Crimson Jacket (12) Journey's End

TARZAN, THE FEARLESS
(Principal, August 11, 1933) 12 Chapters
Buster Crabbe, *Jacqueline Wells,* E. Alyn Warren, Edward Woods, Philo McCullough, Matthews Betz, Frank Lackteen, Mischa Auer, Carlotta Monti, Symonia Boniface, Darby Jones, Al Kikume, George DeNormand
Director: Robert F. Hill
Screenplay: Basil Dickey, George Plympton, Walter Anthony
Producer: Sol Lesser
Based on characters created by Edgar Rice Burroughs
Chapters: (1) The Dive of Death (2) The Storm God Strikes (3) Thundering Death (4) The Pit of Peril (5) Blood Money (6) Voodoo Vengeance (7) Caught by Cannibals (8) The Creeping Terror (9) Eyes of Evil (10) The Death Plunge (11) Harvest of Hate (12) Jungle Justice

TILLIE AND GUS
(Paramount, October 17, 1933) 6 Reels
W. C. Fields, Edgar Kennedy, Allison Skipworth, Baby LeRoy, *Jacqueline Wells,* Barton MacLane
Director: Francis Martin
Screenplay: Walter DeLeon, Francis Martin
Story: Rupert Hughes
Producer: Douglas MacLean

ALICE IN WONDERLAND
(Paramount, December 22, 1933) 90 Minutes
Charlotte Henry, Richard Arlen, Roscoe Ates, William Austin, Gary Cooper, Jack Duffy, Louise Fazenda, W. C. Fields, Alec B. Francis, Skeets Gallagher, Cary Grant, Lillian Harmer, Raymond Hatton, Sterling Holloway, Edward Everett Horton, Roscoe Karns, Baby LeRoy, Lucien Littlefield, Mae Marsh, Polly Moran, Jack Oakie, Edna May Oliver, George Ovey, Leon Errol, May Robson, Charlie Ruggles, Jackie Searle, Alison Skipworthy, Ned Sparks, Ford Sterling, *Jacqueline Wells,* Billy Bevan, Billy Barty
Director: Norman McLeod
Screenplay: Joseph L. Mankiewicz
Story: Lewis Carroll
Producer: Louis D. Lighton

THE BLACK CAT
(Universal, May, 1934) 65 Minutes
Boris Karloff, Bela Lugosi, *Jacqueline Wells,* David Manners, Lucille Lund, Egon Brecher, Henry Armetta, Anna Duncan, John Carradine, Herman Bing, Andre Cheron, Luis Alberni, Albert Conti, Harry Cording, George Davis, Alphonse Martell, Tony Marlow, Paul Weigel, Michael Mark, King Baggott, Paul Panger
Director: Edgar C. Ulmer
Screenplay: Peter Ruric
Story: Edgar C. Ulmer, Peter Ruric
Producer: Carl Laemmle

KISS AND MAKE UP
(Paramount, June, 1934) 70 Minutes
Cary Grant, Genevieve Tobin, Helen Mack, E. E. Horton, Lucien Littlefield, Mona Maris, Rafael Storm, *Jacqueline Wells,* Wampas Baby Stars
Director: Harlan Thompson
Screenplay: Harlan Thompson, George Marion, Jr.
Adaptation: Jane Hinton, Jean Negulesco
Based on the play by Stephen Bekeffi

HAPPY LANDING
(Monogram/First Division, August, 1934) 60 Minutes
Ray Walker, *Jacqueline Wells,* William Farnum, Noah Beery, Hyram Hoover, Morgan Conway, Warner Richmond
Director: R. N. Bradbury
Screenplay: Stuart Anthony
Story: Stuart Anthony

SQUARE SHOOTER
(Columbia, January 21, 1935) 57 Minutes
Tim McCoy, *Jacqueline Wells,* Erville Alderson, Charles Middleton, John Darrow, Slim Whitaker, Fern Emmett, Nelson McDowell, Frank Rice, Ralph Lewis, Robert Walker, Murdock McQuarrie
Director: Harry S. Webb
Story: Rose Gordon
Screenplay: Jayne Regan, Carl Krusada
Producer: Bernard B. Ray

CORONADO
(Paramount, November 29, 1935) 76 Minutes
Johnny Downs, Betty Burgess, Jack Haley, Eddy Duchin, Jameson Thomas, Berton Churchill, Nella Walker, James Burke, Andy Devine, James Carson, *Jacqueline Wells,* Leon Errol
Director: Norman McLeod
Screenplay: Don Hartman, Frank Butler
Story: Brian Hooker, Don Hartman
Producer: William LeBaron

THE BOHEMIAN GIRL
(M-G-M, February 14, 1936) 70 Minutes
Stan Laurel, Oliver Hardy, Thelma Todd, *Jacqueline Wells,* Darla Hood, James Finlayson, Mae Busch, Antonio Moreno, Harry Bowen, Zeffie Tilbury, William P. Carlton, Harry Bernard, Mitchell Lewis, Andrea Leeds, Margaret Mann, Harold Switzer, James C. Morton, Eddie Borden, Sam Lufkin, Sam Lufkin, Bob O'Conor, Bobby Dunn, Felix Knight, Dick Gilbert, Leo Willis, Jack Hill, Lane Chandler, Arthur Rowlands, Rita Dunn, Eddy Chandler
Directors: James W. Horne, Charles Rogers
Story: Alfred Bunn
Producer: Hal Roach

NIGHT CARGO
(Marcy, 1936)
Jacqueline Wells, Lloyd Hughes, Walter Miller, Lloyd Whitlock, George Regas, Jimmy Aubrey, John Ince, Carlotta Monti
Director: Charles Hutchison

THE FRAME-UP
(Columbia, May, 1937) 6 Reels
Paul Kelly, *Jacqueline Wells,* George McKay
Director: D. Ross Lederman
Screenplay: Harold Shumate
Story: Richard E. Wormser

GIRLS CAN PLAY
(Columbia, June, 1937) 59 Minutes
Jacqueline Wells, Charles Quigley, Rita Hayworth, John Gallaudet, George McKay, Gene Morgan, Patricia Farr, Guinn Williams, Joseph Crehan, John Tyrrell, Richard Terry, James Flavin
Director: Lambert Hillyer
Screenplay: Lambert Hillyer
Story: Albert DeMond

COUNSEL FOR CRIME
(Columbia, September, 1937)
Otto Kruger, Douglass Montgomery, *Jacqueline Wells,* Thurston Hall, Nana Bryant, Gene Morgan, Marc Lawrence, Robert Warwick, Stanley Fields
Director: John Brahm
Screenplay: Fred Niblo, Jr., Grace Neville, Lee Loeb, Harold Buchman
Story: Harold Shumate

PAID TO DANCE
(Columbia, November 4, 1937) 55 Minutes
Don Terry, *Jacqueline Wells,* Rita Hayworth, Arthur Loft, Paul Stanton, Paul Fix, Louise Stanley, Ralph Byrd, Dorothy Wray, Ruth Hilliard, Bess Flowers, Beatrice Blinn, Dick Curtis, Jane Hamilton, Al Herman
Director: C. C. Coleman, Jr.
Screenplay: Robert E. Kent
Story: Leslie T. White
Associate Producer: Ralph Cohn

TORTURE SHIP
(Producers Releasing, 1937)
Lyle Talbot, Irving Pichel, *Jacqueline Wells,* Sheila Bromley, Russel Hopton, Anthony Averill, Wheeler Oakman, Adia Kuznetzoff, Stanley Blystone, Leander De Cardova
Director: Victor Halperin

BLUEBEARD'S 8TH WIFE
(Paramount, March, 1938) 85 Minutes
Claudette Colbert, Gary Cooper, Edward Everett Horton, David Niven, Elizabeth Patterson, Herman Bing, Warren Hymer, Franklin Pangborn, Armand Cortes, Rolfe Sedan, Lawrence Grant, Lionel Pane, Tyler Brooke, Tom Ricketts, Barlowe Borland, Charles Hatton, *Jacqueline Wells*
Director: Ernst Lubitsch
Screenplay: Charles Brackett, Billy Wilder
Based on the play by Alfred Savoir
Producer: Ernst Lubitsch

FLIGHT INTO NOWHERE
(Columbia, April 19, 1938) 61 Minutes
Jack Holt, *Jacqueline Wells,* Dick Purcell, James Burke, Karen Sorrell, Fritz Leiber, Howard Hickman, Robert Fiske, Hector Sarno
Director: Lewis D. Collins
Screenplay: Jefferson Parker, Gordon Rigby
Story: William Bloom, Clarence Jay Schneider
Producer: Larry Darmour

HIGHWAY PATROL
(Columbia, May, 1938)
Robert Paige, *Jacqueline Wells,* Robert Middlemass, Arthur Loft, Alan Bridge, Eddie Foster, George McKay, Eddie Laughton, Ann Doran
Director: C. C. Coleman, Jr.
Screenplay: Robert E. Kent, Stuart Anthony
Story: Lambert Hillyer
Associate Producer: Wallace MacDonald

SPRING MADNESS
(M-G-M, October, 1938) 66 Minutes
Maureen O'Sullivan, Lew Ayres, Ruth Hussey, Burgess Meredith, Ann Morriss, Joyce Compton, *Jacqueline Wells,* Frank Albertson, Truman Bradley, Marjorie Gateson, Renee Riano, Sterling Holloway, Dick Baldwin
Director: S. Sylvan Simon
Screenplay: Edward Chodorov
Based on the play by Phillip Barry
Adaptation: Eleanor Golden, Eloise Barrangon
Producer: Edward Chodorov

MY SON IS A CRIMINAL
(Columbia, February, 1939) 60 Minutes
Alan Baxter, *Jacqueline Wells,* Gordon Oliver, Willard Robertson, Joseph King, Eddie Laughton, John Tyrrell
Director: C. C. Coleman, Jr.
Screenplay: Arthur T. Horman

BEHIND PRISON GATES
(Columbia, July, 1939) 63 Minutes
Brian Donlevy, *Jacqueline Wells,* Joseph Crehan, Paul Fix, George Lloyd, Dick Curtis, Richard Fiske
Director: Charles Berton
Screenplay: Arthur T. Horman

THE KANSAS TERRORS
(Republic, October 6, 1939) 57 Minutes
Bob Livingston, Raymond Hatton, Duncan Renaldo, *Jacqueline Wells,* Howard Hickman, George Douglas, Frank Lackteen, Myra Marsh, Yakima Canutt, Ruth Robinson, Dick Alexander, Merrill McCormack, Artie Ortego, Curley Dresden, Al Haskell
Director: George Sherman
Screenplay: Jack Natteford, Betty Burbridge
Story: Luci Ward
Based on characters created by William Colt MacDonald
Associate Producer: Harry Grey

MY SON IS GUILTY
(Columbia, December 28, 1939) 63 Minutes
Bruce Cabot, Harry Carey, *Jacqueline Wells,* Glenn Ford, Wynne Gibson, Don Beddoe, John Tyrell, Bruce Bennett, Dick Curtis, Edgar Buchanan
Director: Charles Barton
Screenplay: Harry Shumate, Joseph Carole
Story: Karl Brown

GIRL IN ROOM 313
(20th Century-Fox, May 31, 1940) 56 Minutes
Florence Rice, Kent Taylor, Lionel Atwill, Katharine Aldridge, Mary Treen, Jack Carson, Elyse Knox, Joan Valerie, Dorothy Dearing, Dorothy Moore, *Jacqueline Wells,* Charles C. Wilson, William Davidson
Director: Ricardo Cortez
Screenplay: Barry Trivers, Clay Adams
Story: Hilda Stone
Producer: Sol M. Wurtzel

THE RANGER AND THE LADY
(Republic, July 30, 1940) 59 Minutes
Roy Rogers, George Hayes, *Jacqueline Wells,* Harry Woods, Henry Brandon, Noble Johnson, Si Jenks, Ted Mapes, Yakima Canutt, Chuck Baldra, Herman Hack, Chick Hannon, Art Dillard, "Trigger"
Director: Joseph Kane
Associate Producer: Joseph Kane
Screenplay: Stuart Anthony, Gerald Geraghty

YOUNG BILL HICKOK
(Republic, October 21, 1940) 59 Minutes
Roy Rogers, George Hayes, *Jacqueline Wells,* John Miljan, Sally Payne, Archie Twitchell, Monte Blue, Hal Taliaferro, Ethel Wales, Jack Ingram, Monte Montague, Iron Eyes Cody, Fred Burns, Frank Ellis, Slim Whitaker, Jack Kirk, Hank Bell, Henry Wills, Dick Elliott, William Desmond, John Elliott, Jack Rockwell, Bill Wolfe, Tom Smith
Director: Joseph Kane
Screenplay: Olive Cooper, Norton S. Parker
Associate Producer: Joseph Kane

BACK IN THE SADDLE
(Republic, March 14, 1941) 73 Minutes
Gene Autry, Smiley Burnette, Mary Lee, Edward Norris, *Jacqueline Wells,* Addison Richards, Arthur Loft, Edmund Elton, Joe McGuinn, Edmund Cobb, Robert Barron, Reed Howes, Stanley Blystone, Curley Dresden, Fred Toones, Frank Ellis, Jack O'Shea, Victor Cox, Herman Hack, Bob Burns, Buck Bucko, "Champion"
Director: Lew Landers
Screenplay: Richard Murphy, Jesse Lasky, Jr.
Associate Producer: Harry Grey

THE NURSE'S SECRET
(Warner Bros.-First National, May, 1941) 56 Minutes
Lee Patrick, Regis Toomey, *Julie Bishop*,* Ann Edmonds, George Campeau, Clara Blandick, Charles D. Waldron, Charles Trowbridge, Leonard Modie, Virginia Brissac, Frank Reicher, George Caine, Keith Douglas, Faye Emerson, Lucia Carroll
Director: Noel M. Smith
Screenplay: Anthony Coldeway
Story: Mary Roberts Rinehart

(*From this point forward Jacqueline Wells used the name Julie Bishop)

INTERNATIONAL SQUADRON
(Warner Bros.-First National, August 13, 1941)
James Stephenson, Ronald Reagan, *Julie Bishop,* Cliff Edwards, Reginald Denny, Olympe Bradna, William Lundigan, John Ridgely, Joan Perry, Selmer Jackson, Holmes Herbert, Crawford Kent, Charles Irwin
Director: Lothar Mendes
Screenplay: Barry Trivers
Story: Frank Wead

WILD BILL HICKOK RIDES
(Warner Bros.-First National, January 31, 1942) 82 Minutes
Constance Bennett, Bruce Cabot, Warren William, Betty Brewer, Walter Catlett, Ward Bond, Howard de Silva, Frank Wilcox, Faye Emerson, *Julie Bishop,* Lucia Carroll, Russell Simpson, Cliff Clark, J. Farrell MacDonald, Lillian Yarbo, Trevor Bardette, Elliott Sullivan, Dick Botiller, Ray Teal
Director: Ray Enright
Screenplay: Charles Grayston, Paul Gerald Smith, Raymond Schrock

I WAS FRAMED
(Warner Bros.-First National, April, 1942) 63 Minutes
Julie Bishop, Michael Ames, Regis Toomey, Patty Hale, John Harmon, Aldrich Bowker, Roland Drew, Oscar O'Shea, Wade Boteler, Howard Hickman, Norman Willis, Hobart Bosworth, Guy Usher, Sam McDaniel
Director: D. Ross Lederman
Screenplay: Robert E. Kent
Based on an idea by Jerome Odlum

LADY GANGSTER
(Warner Bros.-First National, April, 1942) 62 Minutes
Faye Emerson, *Julie Bishop,* Frank Wilcox, Roland Drew, Jackie C. Gleason, Ruth Ford, Virginia Brissac, Dorothy Vaughan, Dorothy Adams, DeWolf Hopper, Vera Lewis, Herbert Rawlinson, Peggy Diggins, Charles Wilson, Bill Phillips, Frank Mayo, Leah Baird
Director: Florian Roberts
Screenplay: Anthony Coldeway
Based on a play by Dorothy Mackaye and Carlton Miles

ESCAPE FROM CRIME
(Warner Bros.-First National, May, 1942) 51 Minutes
Richard Travis, *Julie Bishop,* Jackie C. Gleason, Frank Wilcox, Rex Williams, Wade Boteler, Charles Wilson, Paul Fix, Ruth Ford, John Hamilton, Ann Corcoran, Ben Taggart
Director: D. Ross Lederman
Screenplay: Raymond L. Schrock
Story: Danny Ahearn

BUSSES ROAR
(Warner Bros.-First National, August 18, 1942) 59 Minutes
Richard Travis, *Julie Bishop,* Charles Drake, Eleanor Parker, Elisabeth Fraser, Richard Fraser, Peter Whitney, Frank Wilcox, Willie Best, Rex Williams, Harry Lewis, Bill Kennedy, George Meeker, Vera Lewis, Harry C. Bradley, Chester Gan, Leah Baird, Lottie Williams
Director: D. Ross Lederman

THE HIDDEN HAND
(Warner Bros.-First National, September, 1942) 68 Minutes
Craig Stevens, Elizabeth Fraser, *Julie Bishop,* Frank Wilcox, Cecil Cunningham, Ruth Ford, Roland Drew, Marion Hall, Milton Parsons, Tom Stevenson, Willie Best, Wade Boteler, George Guhl, Stuart Holmes
Director: Ben Stoloff
Screenplay: Anthony Coldeway, Raymond Schroek
Based on the play by Rufus King

THE HARD WAY
(Warner Bros.-First National, September, 1942) 111 Minutes
Ida Lupino, Dennis Morgan, Joan Leslie, Jack Carson, Gladys George, Faye Emerson, Paul Cavanaugh, Leona Maricle, Roman Bohnen, Ray Montgomery, *Julie Bishop,* Nestor Paiva, Joan Woodbury, Ann Doran, Thurston Hall, Charles Judels, Lou Lubin, Jody Gilbert
Director: Vincent Sherman
Screenplay: Daniel Fuchs, Peter Viertel
Producer: Jerry Wald

ACTION IN THE NORTH ATLANTIC
(Warner Bros.-First National, May 17, 1943) 127 Minutes
Humphrey Bogart, Raymond Massey, Alan Hale, *Julie Bishop,* Ruth Gordon, Sam Levine, Dane Clark, Peter Whitney, Dick Hogan, Minor Watson, J. M. Kerrigan, Kane Richmond, William von Brincken, Chick Chandler, George Offerman, Jr., Don Douglas, Art Foster, Ray Montgomery, Glenn Strange, Creighton Hale, Elliott Sullivan, Alec Craig, Ludwig Stossel, Dick Wessel, Frank Puglia, Iris Adrian, Irving Bacon, James Flavin
Director: Lloyd Bacon
Screenplay: John Howard Lawson
Producer: Jerry Wald

PRINCESS O'ROURKE
(Warner Bros.-First National, September 21, 1943)
Olivia de Havilland, Robert Cummings, Charles Coburn, Jack Carson, Jane Wyman, Harry Davenport, Gladys Cooper, Minor Watson, Nan Wynn, Curt Bois, Ray Walker, David Clyde, Nana Bryant, Ruth Ford, *Julie Bishop,* Frank Puglia
Director: Norman Krasna

NORTHERN PURSUIT
(Warner Bros.-First National, November 13, 1943) 94 Minutes
Errol Flynn, *Julie Bishop,* Helmut Dantine, John Ridgely, Gene Lockhart, Tom Tully, Bernard Nedell, Warren Douglas, Monte Blue, Alec Craig, Russell Hicks, Kurt Krueger, Tom Fadden, Bill Kennedy, Fred Kelsey, George Lynn, John Forsythe, John Alvin, Robert Kent, Robert Hutton, Milt Kibbee, Hugh Prosser, James Mullican, Ken Christy, Donald Kerr, Jack Perrin, Richard Alden, John Royce
Director: Raoul Walsh
Screenplay: Frank Gruber, Alvah Bessie
Story: Leslie T. White
Producer: Jack Chertok

RHAPSODY IN BLUE
(Warner Bros.-First National, June, 1945) 143 Minutes
Robert Alda, Joan Leslie, Alexis Smith, Charles Coburn, *Julie Bishop,* Albert Basserman, Morris Carnovsky, Rosemary De Camp, Oscar Levant, Paul Whiteman, Al Jolson, George White, Hazel Scott, Anne Brown, Tom Patricola, Herbert Rudley, John B. Hughes, Mickey Roth, Darryl Hickman, Charles Halton, Andrew Tombes, Gregory Goluboff, Walter Soderling, Eddie Marr, Theodore von Eltz, Bill Kennedy, Robert Shayne, Oscar Loraine, Johnny Downs, Ernest Golm, Martin Noble, Hugo Kirchhoffer, Will Wright
Director: Irving Rapper
Screenplay: Howard Koch, Elliott Paul
Story: Sonya Levien
Producer: Jesse L. Lasky

YOU CAME ALONG
(Paramount, July, 1945) 102 Minutes
Robert Cummings, Lizabeth Scott, Don Defore, Charles Drake, *Julie Bishop,* Kim Hunter, Robert Sully, Helen Forrest, Rhys Williams, Franklin Pangborn, Minor Watson, Howard Freeman, Andrew Tombes, Rex Lease
Director: John Farrow
Screenplay: Robert Smith, Ayn Rand
Story: Robert Smith
Producer: Hal Wallis

IDEA GIRL
(Universal, February, 1946) 60 Minutes
Jess Barker, *Julie Bishop,* George Dolenz, Alan Mowbray, Joan Fulton, Laura Deane Dutton, Virginia Christine, Lane Chandler, Tim Ryan, Norman Leavett, Grady Sutton, Barton Yarbrough, Maurice Cass, Garry Owen, Ferris Taylor, Matt Willis, Sarah Padden
Director: Frank Skinner
Screenplay: Charles R. Marton
Story: Gladys Shelley

CINDERELLA JONES
(Warner Bros.-First National, February, 1946) 88 Minutes
Joan Leslie, Robert Alda, *Julie Bishop,* William Prince, S. Z. Sakall, Edward Everett Horton, Charles Dingle, Ruth Donnelly, Elisha Cook, Jr., Hobart Cavanaugh, Charles Arnt, Chester Clute, Ed Gargan, Margaret Early, Johnny Mitchell, Mary Dean, Monte Blue, Marianne O'Brien, Marian Martin
Director: Busby Berkeley
Screenplay: Charles Hoffman
Story: Philip Wiley
Producer: Alex Gottlieb

MURDER IN THE MUSIC HALL
(Republic, April 10, 1946) 84 Minutes
Vera Hruba Ralston, William Marshall, Helen Walker, Nancy Kelly, William Gargan, Ann Rutherford, *Julie Bishop,* Jerome Cowan, Edward Norris, Paul Hurst, Frank Orth, Jack LaRue, James Craven, Fay McKenzie, Tom London, Joe Yule, Mary Field, Anne Nagel, Ilka Gruning, Inez Palange, William Austin, Spec O'Donnell, Billy Vernon, Nolan Leary, LeRoy Mason, Brooks Benedict, Lee Phelps, Virginia Carroll, Lillian Bronson, Wheaton Chambers, John Weld, James Farley
Director: John English
Screenplay: Frances Hyland, Laszlo Gorog
Story: Arnold Phillips, Maria Matray
Producer: Herman Millakowsky

LAST OF THE REDMEN
(Columbia, August 1, 1947) 77 Minutes
Jon Hall, Michael O'Shea, Evelyn Ankers, *Julie Bishop,* Buster Crabbe, Rick Vallin, Buzz Henry, Guy Hedlund, Frederick Worlock, Emmett Vogan, Chief Many Treaties
Director: George Sherman
Screenplay: Herbert Dalmas, George Plympton
Story: James Fenimore Cooper, "Last of the Mohicans"
Producer: Sam Katzman

HIGH TIDE
(Monogram, October 11, 1947) 70 Minutes
Don Castle, Lee Tracy, Anabel Shaw, *Julie Bishop,* Douglas Walton, Regis Toomey, Anthony Warde, Wilson Wood, Francis Ford, George Ryland, Argentina Brunetti
Director: John Reinhardt
Screenplay: Robert Presnell, Sr.
Story: Raoul Whitfield
Producer: Jack Wrather

DEPUTY MARSHAL
(Lippert, October 28, 1949) 60 Minutes
Jon Hall, Frances Langford, Dick Foran, *Julie Bishop,* Joe Sawyer, Russell Hayden, Clem Bevins, Vince Barnett, Mary Gordon, Kenne Duncan, Stanley Blystone, Roy Butler, Wheaton Chambers, Forrest Taylor, Tom Greenway, Ted Adams
Director: William Berke
Screenplay: William Berke
Producer: Robert L. Lippert

SANDS OF IWO JIMA
(Republic, December 14, 1949) 109 Minutes
John Wayne, John Agar, Adele Mara, Forrest Tucker, Wally Cassell, James Brown, Richard Webb, Arthur Franz, *Julie Bishop,* James Holden, Peter Coe, Richard Jaeckel, Bill Murphy, George Tyne, Hal Fieberling, John McGuire, Martin Milner, Leonard Gumley, William Self, Dorothy Ford, Dick Jones, David Clarke
Director: Allan Dwan
Screenplay: Harry Brown and James Edward Grant
Story: Harry Brown
Associate Producer: Edmund Grainger

WESTWARD THE WOMEN
(M-G-M, January 11, 1952) 116 Minutes
Robert Taylor, Denise Darcel, John McIntire, *Julie Bishop,* Hope Emerson, Marilyn Erskine, Lenore Lonergan, Henry Nakamura, Beverly Dennis, Renata Vanni, Bruce Cowling, George Chandler, Guido Martufi
Director: William A. Wellman
Screenplay: Charles Schnee
Story: Frank Capra
Producer: Dore Schary

SABRE JET
(United Artists, 1953) 96 Minutes
Robert Stack, Coleen Grey, *Julie Bishop,* Richard Arlen, Amanda Blake, Kathleen Crowley, Ray Montgomery
Director: Louis King
Screenplay: Dale Eunson, Katherine Albert
Story: Carl Krueger

THE HIGH AND THE MIGHTY
(Warner Bros., July 3, 1954) 147 Minutes
John Wayne, Claire Trevor, Laraine Day, Robert Stack, Jan Sterling, Phil Harris, Robert Newton, David Brian, Paul Kelly, Sidney Blackmer, *Julie Bishop,* Pedro Gonzales-Gonzales, John Howard, Wally Brown, William Campbell, Ann Doran, John Qualen, Paul Fix, George Chandler, Joy Kim, Michael Wellman, Douglas Fowley, Regis Toomey, Carl Switzer, Robert Keys, William DeWolf Hopper, William Schallert, Julie Mitchum, Karen Sharpe, John Smith, Doe Avedon
Director: William A. Wellman
Screenplay: Ernest K. Gann
Story: Ernest K. Gann, "The High and the Mighty"

HEADLINE HUNTERS
(Republic, August, 1955) 70 Minutes
Rod Cameron, *Julie Bishop,* Ben Cooper, Raymond Greenleaf, Chubby Johnson, John Warburton, Nacho Galindo, Virginia Carroll, Howard Wright, Stuart Randall, Edward Colmans, Joe Besser
Director: William Witney
Screenplay: Frederic Louis Fox, John K. Butler
Associate Producer: William J. O'Sullivan

THE BIG LAND
(Warner Bros., February 23, 1957) 93 Minutes
Alan Ladd, Virginia Mayo, Edmond O'Brien, Anthony Caruso, *Julie Bishop,* John Qualen, Don Castle, David Ladd, Jack Wrather, Jr., George J. Lewis, James Anderson, Don Kelly, Charles Watts
Director: Gordon Douglas
Story: Frank Gruber
Screenplay: David Dortort, Martin Rackin
Associate Producer: George C. Bertholon

46 • KATHLYN WILLIAMS

A Mature Woman Who Showed Charm, Courage, and Poise in Every Conceivable Peril

Kathlyn Williams is identified first with her famous role as Cherry Malotte in **The Spoilers** (1914). She made this dance-hall girl of the North so splendidly human, so superbly alive, that the role still stands out as one of the achievements of her career. But the reputation she gained for this film is less than that emanating from **The Adventures of Kathlyn** (1913), the forerunner of all cliffhanger-type serials. In collaboration with the Chicago Tribune, Colonel William Selig produced and released the serial concurrently with the Tribune's publication of each chapter's story. This was at the time of the great circulation wars, and the Tribune was fighting for its life. The idea was not original with Selig or the Tribune; it had just been done by Edison and McClure's Ladies World with **What Happened to Mary?** (1912), as discussed in the entry on Mary Fuller. But Selig's idea was to pull even more fans to the theatre (and subscribers to the paper) by making an adventure film filled with wild animals and thrills that would act as a magnet to draw the masses hungry for vicarious adventure.

Selig had already made a number of one- and two-reelers with Kathlyn and others featuring wild animals. The new serial was so popular that, according to author Kalton Lahue, "Couples danced to a hesitation waltz named in her honor, sipping Kathlyn cocktails between sets; the ladies wore Kathlyn-style coiffures and hats, while the gents carried a postcard pose of their favorite film star." Over 50,000 copies of the postcard were sold in Chicago, the home of Selig Pictures, in a matter of days. The Tribune's circulation went up ten per cent, Miss Williams' name became a household word, and Colonel Selig not only made a profit on his pioneer serial but proceeded to make a whole series of films using what came to be called the Selig Zoo (later the nucleus for the famed San Diego Zoo), with Kathlyn starring in many of these wild animal flicks.

Kathlyn had a way with animals. Author Bess Burgess, writing in the January, 1917, issue of Photoplay, said, "Any young woman who will sit down in a bathing suit and try to convince a large and vicious looking lion that he is wrong, as Kathlyn Williams is doing, must be a woman of courage and poise. And Kathlyn Williams is." Kathlyn, in fact, did love animals and maintained quite a menagerie herself at her Beverly Hills estate. One writer who knew her remarked, "Had Noah's Ark been hit by a submarine, all the notes that have ever emanated from the minds of the world's brainiest diplomats would not have consoled Kathlyn Williams, for she is the lover of animals such as I have never had the pleasure of meeting in all my life."

The following remarks by Kathlyn herself, as recorded in an interview published in the January, 1917 issue of Motion Picture Classic, illustrate her feelings for the creatures she worked with for several years in such films as **Lost in the Jungle** (1911), **Rescued by Her Lions** (1911), **Harbor Island** (1912), **A Wise Old Elephant** (1913), **Thor, Lord of the Jungles** (1913) **The Leopard's Foundling** (1914), **The Lady of the Tigers** (1914), and **In Tune with the Wild** (1914).

I have never had an animal turn upon me, no matter how treacherous its nature. Every one of the many accidents I have figured in was always due to some outside cause.

At the studio the folks always say that I am a superwoman in my control over animals, but this I have always regarded as flattery. Animals are just like humans; sincerity and kindness are just as effective--and, I believe, even more so--with animals as with human beings. If you can convince an animal that you are its friend, your problem is solved. The lash may get you

Kathlyn Williams.

temporary results, but the day is bound to come when a turned back will mean injury. Animals, just like persons, will obey through fear, but only as long as you can keep fear in their hearts.

As an instance, I might cite the case of a particularly ferocious lion that was often used in connection with animal pictures. The keeper never dared go near him unless he held the lash and watched every move of the beast. I tried a different method. Every day I would go to his cage and feed him a little tidbit, always speaking in a loving way. After a while he began to know me. Every time I neared the cage, he would leap up and come to the bars, whereupon I would give him a bite to eat as a reward.

I was suddenly called away, and after a few months returned to the studio. To the surprise of all my friends, the lion expressed real delight even when he heard my voice as I started to visit him at the cage. Although the keeper and others shouted warnings as I proceeded to start to pat him through the bars, I did so in perfect confidence. Somehow or other, I just felt that the beast could treat me only as I treated him. I was not disappointed. As frisky as a kitten, he rolled on his back and leaped about as if in joy of seeing me again, alternately licking my hand, and, playfully taking it between his sharp teeth, he softly crushed it as a tame cat would, never injuring me in the least. On seeing my success in handling the animal, the keeper became satisfied that he finally had tamed the wild one. Duplicating my action, he placed his hand between the bars, in an attempt to stroke his head, but with sad results.

With a snarl, the lion leaped at the extended hand and bit it, tearing off several fingers. My power over the beast, however, improved daily. Soon I was able to enter the cage with him. In due time he appeared in my pictures, and never has he made an attempt to do me any harm.

Kathlyn Williams was a western girl, reportedly born in Butte, Montana, on May 31, 1888. Doubt has been expressed about the year of her birth, some historians believing it was several years earlier because of her sudden "aging" in the early 1920s. Her father was Norwegian, her mother, Welsh. No doubt when she left Butte to conquer the world, she never dreamed that she'd go through life pursued by a couple of hundred assorted wild animals.

She began her stage career as a child, and early became the protégée of Senator W. A. Clarke, a man always quick to help talent in its development. She attended Wesleyan University, then studied at the Empire School of Acting in New York, later appearing in a number of well-known stage plays in the city and on tour.

Coming to Los Angeles, Miss Williams became a member of the famous old Belasco stock company and was also with Willard Mack in Salt Lake City. Pictures came along about that time, and she joined the Biograph Company under D. W. Griffith in 1919 as an accomplished actress. In 1910, however, she shifted to Selig and quickly became the company's leading actress, scoring in **Two Orphans** (1911), **The Adventures of Captain Kate** series (1911), **The Adventures of Kathlyn** (1913), and **The Spoilers** (1914). Her screen persona was that of an unspoiled girl as natural and genuine as a child, keenly alive and with a diversity of absorbing interests. Lovely blonde hair, deep blue eyes, exquisite coloring, and a relaxed naturalness with both man and beast were enough to give her the charisma that kept her working for an enthusiastic public.

Her Westerns were few but good, and the stories were varied. **Chip of the Flying U** (1914) seems to be her best-remembered and most-publicized Selig Western besides **The Spoilers**, whereas **The U.P. Trail** (1919), for Zane Grey Pictures, was her most engaging one.

In 1915 Kathlyn made several hits--**The Ne'er Do Well, The Carpet from Bagdad, The Rosary, Sweet Alyssum**, and **Thou Shalt Not Covet**--each feature length and directed by Colin Campbell. It was her best year.

In March, 1913, Kathlyn had married actor Victor Kainer. The marriage collapsed but it did produce her only child, a son named after his father. In 1916 she married Charles Eyton, an actor-producer later to be studio manager for Lasky's. This marriage lasted until 1918, after which she remained single. Her son Victor died in 1922 while on a trip to China with Kathlyn.

Kathlyn left Selig in late 1916 to join the Oliver Morosco Photoplay Company, where she reigned as a major dramatic actress until 1921.

Redeeming Love (1916), directed by William D. Taylor, was her first hit. Twice she starred in Cecil B. DeMille epics, **The Whipsering Chorus** (1918) and **We Can't Have Everything** (1918). For William de Mille she did **The Tree of Knowledge** (1919), **The Prince Chap** (1920), and **Conrad in Quest of His Youth** (1920). Popular Wallace Reid was her co-star in **Big Timber** (1917) and **The Thing We Love** (1918); she played opposite Roy Stewart in **Just a Wife** (1920); and she brought vivid emotion to her dual portrayals of mother and daughter in **The Cost of Hatred** (1917).

After 1921 Kathlyn played major supporting roles through much of the decade, since she was then too old to play ingénues with conviction. She was believable as an older woman and competent

Kathlyn Williams – star of **The Adventures of Kathlyn** (Selig, 1914), the first serial to introduce "hold-over" suspense which whetted the viewer's desire to see the next installment.

in each role she essayed.

Having made only a few talkies, Kathlyn retired from the screen in 1934 to travel, enjoy a peaceful life pursuing her many hobbies, and entertain socially now and then. A car accident in 1949 cost her a leg, and she spent much of her remaining life in a wheelchair. Kathlyn died from a heart attack on September 24, 1960.

Throughout her career she held the respect and admiration of both public and associates. Known as "The Selig Girl" and "The Bernhardt of the Screen," Kathlyn was also known as the diplomat of Hollywood. Her winsome smile and a nature devoid of any sign of temperament won her many friends. She had serenity and poise--not the artificial poise of the movies, but the poise of character.

Doubtless, much of Miss Williams's success as an actress was due to her own charming womanliness, her beauty, her sincerity, and her dignity. But her rare intelligence gave her the power to discern the dramatic values of her roles in every social realm. She had an unusual capacity for identifying herself with her characters, and her work was always finely tempered, subtle, and well balanced. The wholehearted manner in which she interpreted the woman who has made a mistake, the shallow society leader, and the girl of the early West, all displayed her splendid understanding of the feminine mind and heart.

KATHLYN WILLIAMS Filmography

THE POLITICIAN'S LOVE STORY
(Selig, February, 1909)
Kathlyn Williams, Lee Dougherty, Florence Lawrence

LINES OF WHITE ON A SULLEN SEA
(Biograph, October 20, 1909) 1 Reel
Linda Arvidson, Kate Bruce, Del Henderson, Florence Laurence, Arthur Johnson, Jeanie Macpherson, James Kirkwood, *Kathlyn Williams,* Owen Moore, Billy Quirk, Harriet Quimby, Dorothy West, George Nicholls, Charles West
Director: D. W. Griffith
Scenario: Stanner E. V. Taylor, D. W. Griffith

GOLD IS NOT ALL
(Biograph, March 28, 1910) 1 Reel
Linda Arvidson, Marion Leonard, Bel Henderson, Mack Sennett, Gladys Egan, Kate Bruce, Alfred Paget, W. Crystie Miller, Gertrude Robinson, Charles Craig, Henry B. Walthall, *Kathlyn Williams*
Director: D. W. Griffith
Scenario: Stanner B. V. Taylor

THOU SHALT NOT
(Biograph, April, 1910) 1 Reel
Henry Walthall, Marion Leonard, *Kathlyn Williams*, Charles H. West, George O. Nicholls, Chrystie Miller, Gladys Egan, Dell Henderson, Linda Arvidson, Dorothy West
Director: D. W. Griffith

A ROMANCE OF THE WESTERN HILLS
(Biograph, April, 1910) 1 Reel
Mary Pickford, Alfred Paget, Arthur Johnson, Dorothy West, *Kathlyn Williams*, Charles H. West, Kate Bruce
Director: D. W. Griffith

THE FIRECHIEF'S DAUGHTER
(Selig, June, 1910) 1 Reel
Kathlyn Williams
Director: Frank Boggs

MEZEPPA
(Selig, July, 1910) 1 Reel
Tom Santschi, *Kathlyn Williams*
Director: Frank Boggs

THE CURSE OF THE RED MAN
(Selig, February, 1911) 1 Reel
Tom Santschi, *Kathlyn Williams*
Director: Frank Boggs
Scenario: Lanier Bartlett

THE WITCH OF THE EVERGLADES
(Selig, April, 1911) 1 Reel
Kathlyn Williams
Director: Otis Turner

IN OLD CALIFORNIA, WHEN THE GRINGOS CAME
(Selig, May 6, 1911) 1 Reel
Kathlyn Williams, Tom Santschi, Tom Mix
Director: Frank Boggs
Scenario: Lanier Bartlett

THE ROSE OF OLD ST. AUGUSTINE
(Selig, June 1, 1911) 1 Reel
Kathlyn Williams, Charles Clary, W. H. Stowell, Tom Mix, Frank Weed, True Boardman, Vera Hamilton, Harrison Gray
Director: Otis Turner

JIM AND JOE
(Selig, June 3, 1911) 1 Reel
Kathlyn Williams
Director: Hal Williams
Story: Hal Reid

BACK TO THE PRIMITIVE
(Selig, May 11, 1911)
Kathlyn Williams, Tom Santschi, Charles Clary, Joseph Girard
Director: Frank Boggs
Screenplay: Edward McWade

TEN NIGHTS IN A BAR ROOM
(Selig, June, 1911) 2 Reels
Kathlyn Williams, Charles Clary
Director: Frank Boggs
Story: T. S. Arthur, William Pratt

CAPTAIN KATE
(Selig, July 13, 1911) 1 Reel
Kathlyn Williams, Charles Clary, Frank Weed, Frank Smith, Tom Mix, Tom Anderson
Director: Otis Turner

LIFE ON THE BORDER
(Selig, August, 1911) 1 Reel
Kathlyn Williams

DAD'S GIRLS
(Selig, September 12, 1911) 1 Reel
Kathlyn Williams, Olive Stokes, Frank Weed, Charles Clary, Tom Mix, Stan Twist, Will Stowell, Louis Pierce
Director: Otis Turner
Story: Otis Turner

THE WHEELS OF JUSTICE
(Selig, September 14, 1911) 1 Reel
Charles Clary, Frank Weed, William Duncan, William Stowell, *Kathlyn Williams*, S. Jones, George Cox, Lillian Leighton, Virginia Ames, Rex (a dog)
Director: Otis Turner

MAUD MULLER
(Selig, September, 1911) 1 Reel
Kathlyn Williams, Charles Clary
Story: John Greenleaf Whittier

TWO ORPHANS
(Selig, September, 1911) 3 Parts
Kathlyn Williams, Winnifred Greenwood, Myrtle Stedman, Lillian Leighton, Adrienne Kroell, Leighton Stark, James O'Burrell, Tom J. Corrigan, Charles Clary, Vera Hamilton, Miles McCarthy, Rex De Rosselli, Frank Weed, Will Stowell, Tom I. Comberford, Louis Fierce
Director: Otis Turner
Scenario: Otis Turner
Story: d'Ennery and Dumanoir
Supervisor: Francis Boggs

HOW THEY STOPPED THE RUN ON THE BANK
(Selig, October, 1911) 1 Reel
Kathlyn Williams, George Cox, Charles Clary, Hobart Bosworth, Tom Santschi
Director: Otis Turner
Scenario: Lanier Bartlett

THE TOTEM MARK
(Selig, 1911)
Kathlyn Williams, Tom Santschi, Charles Clary
Director: Frank Boggs
Screenplay: Edward McWade

LOST IN THE JUNGLE
(Selig, 1911)
Kathlyn Williams, Tom Santschi, Charles Clary
Director: Frank Boggs
Screenplay: Edward McWade

RESCUED BY HER LIONS
(Selig, 1911)
Kathlyn Williams, Tom Santschi, Charles Clary
Director: Frank Boggs
Screenplay: Edward McWade

THE BROTHERHOOD OF MAN
(Selig, February, 1912) 1 Reel
William Duncan, Myrtle Stedman, *Kathlyn Williams*

SONS OF THE NORTHWOODS
(Selig, March, 1912) 1 Reel
Charles Clary, *Kathlyn Williams*, Frank Weed, William Stowell

WHEN THE HEART RULES
(Selig, April, 1912) 1/2 Reel
Kathlyn Williams, Charles Clary, Edgar Wynn

DRIFTWOOD
(Selig, April, 1912) 1 Reel
Kathlyn Williams, Myrtle Stedman, William Duncan, Frank Weed

THE DEVIL, THE SERVANT AND THE MAN
(Selig, April, 1912) 1 Reel
Kathlyn Williams, William Stowell, Charles Clary, Harry Lonsdale

THE GIRL WITH THE LANTERN
(Selig, May, 1912) 1 Reel
Kathlyn Williams

THE ADOPTED SON
(Selig, June, 1912) 1 Reel
Kathlyn Williams, Winnifred Greenwood, Adrienne Knoell, Charles Clary, Denton Vane

THE LAST DANCE
(Selig, June, 1912) 1 Reel
Winnifred Greenwood, Charles Clary, *Kathlyn Williams*
Scenario: Kathlyn Williams

THE GIRL AT THE CUPOLA
(Selig, August, 1912) 1 Reel
Kathlyn Williams, Charles Clary, L. J. Commerford, Frank Wead, Vera Hamilton, Evelyn Allen

AN UNEXPECTED FORTUNE
(Selig, August, 1912) 1 Reel
Charles Clary, William Duncan, Frank Weed, Lester Cuneo, Walter Roberts, *Kathlyn Williams*, Clara Reynolds Smith, Adrienne Kroell, Harry Lonsdale

AS THE FATES DECREE
(Selig, September, 1912) 1 Reel
Kathlyn Williams, Gladys Wayne, William Stowell

HARBOR ISLAND
(Selig, December, 1912) 1 Reel
Kathlyn Williams, Harold Lockwood, Henry Otto, Frank Richardson, Anny Dodge, Hobart Bosworth, George Hernandez, Frank Clark, Robert Greene
Director: Lem B. Parker
Scenario: Walter Nichols

THE LIPTON CUP: INTRODUCING SIR THOMAS LIPTON
(Selig, January, 1913) 1 Reel
Kathlyn Williams, Harold Lockwood, Robert B. Green, Henry Otto, Baby Lillian Wade, Sir Thomas Lipton
Director: Lem B. Parker
Scenario: Lem B. Parker

THE ARTIST AND THE BRUTE
(Selig, January, 1913) 1 Reel
Kathlyn Williams, Hobart Bosworth, Al Garcia
Story: Otto Breitkreutz

THE GOVERNOR'S DAUGHTER
(Selig, January, 1913) 1 Reel
Kathlyn Williams, Eugenie Besserer, Harold Lockwood, Henry Otto, William Hutchinson, Lem B. Parker
Director: Lem B. Parker
Scenario: Maibelle Heikes Justice

A LITTLE CHILD SHALL LEAD THEM
(Selig, January, 1913) 1 Reel
Harold Lockwood, *Kathlyn Williams*, Baby Lillian Wade, Henry Otto, Daisy Prideaux
Director: Lem B. Parker
Scenario: M. B. Gardner

TWO MEN AND A WOMAN
(Selig, February, 1913) 1 Reel
Kathlyn Williams, Harold Lockwood, Henry Otto
Director: Lem B. Parker
Scenario: Lem B. Parker

WITH LOVE'S EYES
(Selig, April, 1913) 1 Reel
Kathlyn Williams, Harold Lockwood, Al Garcia, Al W. Filson, Henry Otto, Lillian Hayward
Director: Lem B. Parker
Scenario: Emmett C. Hall

A WISE OLD ELEPHANT
(Selig, April, 1913) 2 Reels
Kathlyn Williams, Hobart Bosworth, Herbert Rawlinson, Al W. Filson, Toddles (an elephant)
Director: Colin Campbell
Story: J. Edward Hungerford

THE BURGLAR WHO ROBBED DEATH
(Selig, April, 1913) 1 Reel
Kathlyn Williams, Harold Lockwood, Baby Lillian Wade, Al Garcia, Dorothy Arnold, Daisy Prideaux, Jessie Wyckoff, Lillian Clark
Director: Lem B. Parker
Scenario: Lanier Bartlett

THEIR STEPMOTHER
(Selig, April, 1913) 1 Reel
Kathlyn Williams, Baby Lillian Wade, Harold Lockwood, Utahna La Reno, Jessie Wycoff
Director: E. A. Martin
Scenario: Hettie Gray Baker

LIEUTENANT JONES
(Selig, May 10, 1913)
Harold Lockwood, *Kathlyn Williams*, Robert Ghandler, Al Garcia, Eugenie Besserer, Al W. Filson
Director: Lem B. Parker
Scenario: F. Sample

THE STOLEN MELODY
(Selig, May, 1913) 1 Reel
Al W. Filson, Al Garcia, *Kathlyn Williams*, Harold Lockwood
Director: Lem B. Parker

THE GIRL AND THE JUDGE
(Selig, May 29, 1913) 1 Reel
Kathlyn Williams, Herbert Rawlinson, Hobart Bosworth, Eugenie Besserer, Gertrude Arnold
Director/Scenario: Lem B. Parker

WOMEN--PAST AND PRESENT
(Selig, May, 1913) 1 Reel
Kathlyn Williams, Harold Lockwood, Eugenie Besserer, Al Garcia
Director/Scenario: Lem B. Parker

MRS. HILTON'S JEWELS
(Selig, June, 1913) 1 Reel
Kathlyn Williams, Henry W. Otto
Story: Maibelle Heikes Justice

SONGS OF TRUCE
(Selig, June 12, 1913) 1 Reel
Kathlyn Williams, Tom Santschi, Tom Mix
Director: Colin Campbell
Story: Hettie Gray Baker

THE TREE AND THE CHAFF
(Selig, July 11, 1913) 1 Reel
Kathlyn Williams, Barney Furey, Al W. Filson
Director: Lem B. Parker
Story: Marc H. Jones

MAN AND HIS OTHER SELF
(Selig, July 21, 1913)
Kathlyn Williams, Tom Santschi
Director/Story: Lem B. Parker

THE YOUNG HUNTER
(Selig, 1913)
Kathlyn Williams, Tom Santschi

THE SHUTTLE OF FAITH
(Selig, 1913)
Kathlyn Williams, Tom Santschi

A MANSION OF MISERY
(Selig, August, 1913)
Kathlyn Williams, Harold Lockwood, Al Garcia, Henry W. Otto, H. A. Livingston
Director/Scenario: Lem B. Parker

THE FLIGHT OF THE CROW
(Selig, August 13, 1913) 2 Reels
Kathlyn Williams, Henry W. Otto, H. A. Livingston, William Hutchinson, Harold Lockwood
Director: E. A. Martin
Scenario: Arthur Preston Hankins

A CHILD OF THE SEA
(Selig, August 20, 1913) 2 Reels
Kathlyn Williams, Harold Lockwood, Herbert Rawlinson, Al W. Filson, Tom Lawton, William Hutchinson, Lillian Hayward, Baby Lillian Wade
Director: Lem B. Parker
Scenario: Edward McWade

THE YOUNG MRS. EAMES
(Selig, September 20, 1913) 2 Reels
Kathlyn Williams, Harold Lockwood, Hobart Bosworth, Ethyl Davis
Director: Francis J. Grandin
Scenario: Kathlyn Williams

WHEN MAY WEDS DECEMBER
(Selig, October, 1913) 1 Reel
Kathlyn Williams, Tom Santschi
Director: Frances J. Grandin
Scenario: Gilson Willets

THE CONSCIENCE FUND
(Selig, October, 1913) 2 Reels
Kathlyn Williams, Tom Santschi
Director: Francis J. Grandin
Scenario: Gilson Willets

THE TIDE OF DESTINY
(Selig, November, 1913)
Harold Lockwood, *Kathlyn Williams*, William Brown, Baby Lillian Wade, Anna Dodge
Director: Lem B. Parker
Scenario: Ruth H. Morris

THE LOVE OF PENELOPE
(Selig, November, 1913)
Harold Lockwood, *Kathlyn Williams*, Hobart Bosworth, William Brown
Director: Francis J. Grandin
Scenario: Maibelle Heikes Justice

THOR, LORD OF THE JUNGLES
(Selig, November, 1913) 3 Reels
Kathlyn Williams, Charles Clary, Thomas Santschi, Lafayette (Lafe) McKee, William Holland
Director: Colin Campbell
Scenario: Edward McWade
Story: James Oliver Curwood

THE ADVENTURES OF KATHLYN
(Selig, December 29, 1913) 13 Chapters
Kathlyn Williams, Tom Santschi, Charles Clary, William Carpenter, Goldie Colwell, Edmund Cobb, Lafe McKee, Edwin L. Wallock, Franklin Hall, C. J. Murphy, Guy Oliver
Director: Francis J. Grandin
Story: Gilson Willets
Chapters: (1) The Unwelcome Throne (2) The Two Ordeals (3) In the Temple of the Lion (4) The Royal Slave (5) A Colonel in Chains (6) Three Bags of Silver (7) The Garden of Brides (8) The Cruel Crown (9) The Spellbound Multitude (10) The Warrior Maid (11) The Forged Parchment (12) The King's Will (13) The Court of Death
(Reissued in 1916 as an 8-reel feature)

THE SPOILERS
(Selig, April 14, 1914) 9 Reels
William Farnum, *Kathlyn Williams*, Bessie Eyton, Frank Clark, Jack E. McDonald, Thomas Santschi, Wheeler Oakman, W. H. Ryno
Director/Scenario: Colin Campbell
Story: Rex Beach

THE LEOPARD'S FOUNDLING
(Selig, June 11, 1914) 2 Reels
Kathlyn Williams, Charles Clary, Lillian Wade, Tom Santschi
Director: F. J. Grandin
Story: Maibelle Heikes Justice
Producer: Kathlyn Williams

CARYL OF THE MOUNTAINS
(Selig, June 20, 1914) 1 Reel
Kathlyn Williams, Tom Santschi, Harry Lonsdale, Roy Watson
Director: Tom Santschi
Story: James Oliver Curwood

HIS FIGHT
(Selig, June 20, 1914) 1 Reel
Tom Mix, Tom Santschi, *Kathlyn Williams*
Director/Screenplay: Colin Campbell

A WOMAN LAUGHS
(Selig, July 2, 1914) 2 Reels
Kathlyn Williams, Charles Clary
Director: Norval MacGregor
Story: W. E. Wing

THE SPECK ON THE WALL
(Selig, July 31, 1914) 2 Reels
Kathlyn Williams, Wheeler Oakman
Director/Scenario: Colin Campbell
Story: James Oliver Curwood

IN TUNE WITH THE WILD
(Selig, July, 1914) 3 Reels
Kathlyn Williams, Edwin Wallock, William Stowell, Lillian Wade
Director/Scenario: H. A. Martin

CHIP OF THE FLYING U
(Selig, August 12, 1914)
Tom Mix, *Kathlyn Williams*, Frank Clark, Wheeler Oakman, Bessie Eyton, Fred Huntley
Director: Colin Campbell
Screenplay: Bertha Mugay Sinclair (B. M. Bower)

THE LONESOME TRAIL
(Selig, September 2, 1914)
Tom Mix, *Kathlyn Williams*
Director: Colin Campbell
Screenplay: Bertha M. Bower

HEARTS AND MASKS
(Selig, October 1, 1914) 3 Reels
Kathlyn Williams, Charles Clary, Wheeler Oakman, Eugenie Besserer, Harold Lockwood
Director/Screenplay: Colin Campbell
Story: Harold McGrath

THE WOMAN OF IT
(Selig, October, 1914)
Kathlyn Williams, Wheeler Oakman, Charles Clary
Director/Scenario: Colin Campbell

THE TRAGEDY THAT LIVED
(Selig, October 24, 1914) 1 Reel
Kathlyn Williams, Wheeler Oakman, Charles Clary, Eugenia Besserer
Director/Scenario: Colin Campbell
Story: James Oliver Curwood

HER SACRIFICE
(Selig, October 24, 1914) 1 Reel
Kathlyn Williams, Wheeler Oakman, Charles Clary
Director/Scenario: Colin Campbell

Chip of the Flying U (Selig, 1914) – Kathlyn Williams, Tom Mix, and Wheeler Oakman.

THE STORY OF THE BLOOD RED ROSE
(Selig, October 24, 1914) 3 Reels
Kathlyn Williams, Wheeler Oakman, Charles Clary, Hugenie Besserer, Frank Clark, Camille Astor
Director: Colin Campbell
Scenario: Lanier Bartlett
Story: James Oliver Curwood

THE LOSING FIGHT
(Selig, November 7, 1914) 1 Reel
Kathlyn Williams, Charles Clary, Wheeler Oakman, Frank Clark
Director/Scenario: Colin Campbell

THE SOUL MATE
(Selig, November 19, 1914) 1 Reel
Tom Mix, *Kathlyn Williams*
Director: F. J. Grandin
Screenplay: Mark Bearden

THE LADY OF THE TIGERS
(Selig, November 28, 1914) 1 Reel
Kathlyn Williams, Frank Clark, Lamar Johnstone
Director: Thomas Parsons
Scenario: Gilson Willets

TILL DEATH US DO PART
(Selig, December 8, 1914) 2 Reels
Kathlyn Williams, Wheeler Oakman, Charles Clary
Director/Scenario: Colin Campbell
Story: James Oliver Curwood

THE FLOWER OF FAITH
(Selig, December 10, 1914) 2 Reels
Kathlyn Williams, Tom Mix
Director: F. J. Grandin
Screenplay: Will M. Hough

THE NE'ER DO WELL
(Selig, December 18, 1914) 10 Reels
Kathlyn Williams, Wheeler Oakman, Harry Lonsdale
Director/Scenario: Colin Campbell
Story: Rex Beach

THE VISION OF THE SHEPHERD
(Selig, January 16, 1915) 2 Reels
Kathlyn Williams, Wheeler Oakman, Frank Clark, Eugenie Besserer
Director: Colin Campbell
Story: Malcolm Douglas

THE CARPET FROM BAGDAD
(Selig, May 13, 1915) 5 Reels
Kathlyn Williams, Charles Clary, Wheeler Oakman, Guy Oliver, Eugenie Besserer, Frank Clark, Harry Lonsdale, Fred Huntley
Director: Colin Campbell
Story: Harold McGrath

THE ROSARY
(Selig, June 16, 1915) 7 Reels
Kathlyn Williams, Wheeler Oakman, Charles Clary, Anna Dodge
Story: Edward E. Rose

EBB TIDE
(Selig, June 26, 1915) 3 Reels
Kathlyn Williams, Wheeler Oakman, Harry Lonsdale, Martha Boucher
Director: Colin Campbell
Scenario: Lanier Bartlett
Story: Robert Louis Stevenson

A SULTANA OF THE DESERT
(Selig, September 25, 1915) 2 Reels
Kathlyn Williams, Tom Santschi
Director: Tom Santschi
Scenario: Kathlyn Williams

SWEET ALYSSUM
(Selig, October 18, 1915) 5 Reels
Tyrone Power, *Kathlyn Williams,* Edith Johnson, Wheeler Oakman, Frank Clark, Harry Lonsdale, Jean Frazer
Director: Colin Campbell
Scenario: Gilson Willets
Story: Charles Major

THE COQUETTE'S AWAKENING
(Selig, November 27, 1915) 2 Reels
Kathlyn Williams, Harry DeVere, Guy Oliver, Charles Le Moyne
Director: Frank Beal
Story: Will M. Hough

THOU SHALT NOT COVET
(Selig, February, 1916) 5 Reels
Kathlyn Williams, Guy Oliver
Director: Colin Campbell
Story: James Oliver Curwood

NUMBER 13, WESTBOUND
(Selig, March 4, 1916) 3 Reels
Kathlyn Williams, Guy Oliver, Fred Hearn, Lillian Hayward
Director: Frank Beal
Story: Elliott Flower

THE DEVIL, THE SERVANT, AND THE MAN
(Selig, April, 1916) 3 Reels
Kathlyn Williams, Guy Oliver, Jean Fraser, Lillian Hayward, Vivian Reed, James Bradbury
Director: Frank Beal
Scenario: Anthony McGuire

THE RETURN
(Selig, July 3, 1916) 3 Reels
Kathlyn Williams, Guy Oliver, Wellington Playter, Vivian Reed, Sidney Smith, Harry Lonsdale
Director: T. N. Heffron
Story: W. E. Wing

THE BRAND OF CAIN
(Selig, December, 1916) 2 Reels
Kathlyn Williams, Harry Lonsdale, Wheeler Oakman
Director: Colin Campbell
Scenario: Wallace C. Clifton

REDEEMING LOVE
(Morosco, December 28, 1916) 5 Reels
Kathlyn Williams, Thomas Holding, Wyndham Standing, Herbert Standing, Jane Keckley, Helen J. Eddy, Dom Bailey
Director: William D. Taylor

THE DEVIL STONE
(Selig, 1916)
Kathlyn Williams, Guy Oliver, Jean Fraser, Vivian Reed, Lillian Hayward, James Bradbury
Director: Frank Beal

SWEET LADY PEGGY
(Selig, 1916)
Kathlyn Williams

OUT OF THE WRECK
(Morosco/Paramount, March 8, 1917)
Kathlyn Williams, William Clifford, William Conklin, Stella Razelo, William Jefferson
Director: William D. Taylor
Scenario: Gardner Hunting
Story: Maude Erve Corsan

THE COST OF HATRED
(Famous Players-Lasky/Paramount, April 9, 1917) 5 Reels
Kathlyn Williams, Theodore Roberts, Tom Forman, J. W. Johnston, Jack Holt, Charles Ogle, Walter Long, Horace B. Carpenter, Mayme Kelso, Louise Mineveh
Director/Producer: George H. Melford
Scenario: Beulah Marie Dix

BIG TIMBER
(Morosco/Paramount, June 15, 1917) 5 Reels
Wallace Reid, *Kathlyn Williams*, Joe King, Alfred Page, Helen Bray, William Desmond
Director: William D. Taylor
Scenario: Gardner Hunting
Story: Bertrand W. Sinclair

IN THE AFRICAN JUNGLE
(Selig, July, 1917) 2 Reels
Edwin Wallock, *Kathlyn Williams*, William Stowell
Director: E. A. Martin
Scenario: E. A. Martin

PIONEER DAYS
(Selig, September, 1917) 2 Reels
Lafayette McKee, Charles Clary, Adrienne Kroell, *Kathlyn Williams*
Director: Oscar Eagle
Scenario: C. E. Nixon

THE THING WE LOVE
(Famous Players-Lasky/Paramount, January 28, 1918) 5 Reels
Wallace Reid, *Kathlyn Williams*, Tully Marshall, Mayme Kelso, Charles Ogle, William Elmer
Director: Lou Tellegen
Scenario: Harvey Thew
Story: H. B. and M. G. Daniel

NUMBER 13, WESTBOUND
(Selig, March, 1918) 3 Reels
Kathlyn Williams, Guy Oliver, Fred Hearn, Lillian Hayward
Director: Frank Beal
Scenario: Elliott Flower

THE WHISPERING CHORUS
(Famous Players-Lasky/Paramount, March 28, 1918) 6 Reels
Raymond Hatton, *Kathlyn Williams*, Edythe Chapman, Elliott Dexter, Noah Beery, Guy Oliver, John Burton, J. Parks Jones, Tully Marshall, W. H. Brown, James Neill, Gustav von Seyffertitz, Walter Lynch, Edna May Cooper, Julia Faye
Director/Producer: Cecil B. DeMille
Scenario: Jeanie Macpherson
Story: Perley Poore Sheehan

THE HIGHWAY OF HOPE
(Famous Players-Lasky/Paramount, April 28, 1918) 5 Reels
Kathlyn Williams
Director: Howard Estabrook
Scenario: Harvey Gates
Story: Willard Mack

WE CAN'T HAVE EVERYTHING
(Famous Players-Lasky/Paramount, July 7, 1918) 6 Reels
Kathlyn Williams, Elliott Dexter, Wanda Hawley, Sylvia Breamer, Thurston Hall, Raymond Hatton, Tully Marshall, Theodore Roberts, James Neill, Ernest Joy, Billy Elmer, Charles Ogle, Sylvia Ashton
Director/Producer: Cecil B. DeMille
Scenario: William C. de Mille
Story: Rupert Hughes

THE BETTER WIFE
(C.K.Y./Select, June 21, 1919) 5 Reels
Clara Kimball Young, *Kathlyn Williams*, Ben Alexander, Nigel Barrie, Irving Cummings, Lillian Walker
Director: William P. S. Earle
Story: Lenore Coffee, "The Love Quest"

A GIRL NAMED MARY
(Famous Players-Lasky/Paramount, October 23, 1919) 5 Reels
Marguerite Clark, *Kathlyn Williams*, Wallace MacDonald
Director: Walter Edwards
Scenario: Alice Eyton
Story: Juliet Wilbor Tompkins

THE TREE OF KNOWLEDGE
(Paramount-Artcraft, November 25, 1919) 5 Reels
Robert Warwick, *Kathlyn Williams,* Wanda Hawley, Tom Forman, Winter Hall, Irving Cummings, Clarence Geldart, Lola O'Connor, William Brown
Director: William C. de Mille
Scenario: Margaret Turnbull
Story: R. C. Carton (Richard Claude Critchett)

THE U. P. TRAIL
(Zane Grey Pictures/Hodkinson, 1919)
Roy Stewart, *Kathlyn Williams,* Robert McKim, Joseph J. Dowling, Marguerite De La Motte, Frederick Starr, Charles Murphy, Virginia Caldwell, Walter Perry
Director: Jack Conway
Story: Zane Grey
Producer: B. B. Hampton

JUST A WIFE
(National, February 23, 1920) 5 Reels
Roy Stewart, *Kathlyn Williams,* Leatrice Joy, Albert Van, William West
Director: Howard Hickman
Scenario: Katherine Reed
Story: Eugene Walters

THE PRINCE CHAP
(Famous Players-Lasky/Paramount, June 1, 1920) 6 Reels
Thomas Meighan, *Kathlyn Williams,* Charles Ogle, Lila Lee, May Giracci, Peaches Jackson, Casson Ferguson, Ann Forrest, Lillian Leighton, Bertie Johns, Florence Hart
Director/Producer: William C. de Mille
Scenario: Olga Printzlau
Story: Edward Henry Peple

CONRAD IN QUEST OF HIS YOUTH
(Famous Players-Lasky/Paramount, November 8, 1920) 6 Reels
Thomas Meighan, Mabel Van Buren, *Kathlyn Williams,* Mayme Kelso, Bertram Johns, Margaret Loomis, Sylvia Ashton, Charles Ogle, Eddie Sutherland, Ruth Renick
Director: William C. de Mille
Scenario: Olga Printzlau
Story: Leonard Merrick

HER KINGDOM OF DREAMS
(First National, November 30, 1920) 7 Reels
Anita Stewart, Mahlon Hamilton, *Kathlyn Williams,* Tom Santschi, Anna Q. Nilsson, Edwin Stevens, Tully Marshall, Thomas Jefferson, Robert McKim, Wesley Barry, Thomas Holding, Spottiswoode Aitken, Ralph Graves, Frank Currier
Director: Marshall Neilan
Story: Louise Prevost

DOUBLE SPEED
(Famous Players-Lasky/Paramount, December 15, 1920) 5 Reels
Wanda Hawley, Wallace Reid, Theodore Roberts, Lucien Littlefield, Tully Marshall, Guy Oliver, *Kathlyn Williams*
Director: Sam Wood
Scenario: Clara Genevieve Kennedy
Story: J. Stewart Woodhouse

FORBIDDEN FRUIT
(Famous Players-Lasky/Paramount, February 12, 1921) 8 Reels
Agnes Ayres, Clarence Burton, Theodore Roberts, *Kathlyn Williams,* Forrest Stanley, Theodore Kosloff, Shannon Day, Bertram Johns, Julia Faye
Director: Cecil B. DeMille
Scenario: Jeanie Macpherson
Story: Jeanie Macpherson, Cecil B. DeMille
Producer: Cecil B. DeMille

HUSH
(Equity/Jans Film Service, February, 1921) 6 Reels
Clara Kimball Young, J. Frank Glendon, *Kathlyn Williams,* Jack Pratt, Bertram Grassby, Gerard Alexander, Beatrice Le Plante, John Underhill
Director: Harry Garson
Story: Sada Cowan

A PRIVATE SCANDAL
(Realart/Paramount, June, 1921) 5 Reels
May McAvoy, Bruce Gordon, Ralph Lewis, *Kathlyn Williams,* Lloyd Whitlock, Gladys Fox
Director: Chester M. Franklin
Scenario: Eve Unsell
Story: Hector Turnbull

EVERYTHING FOR SALE
(Realart/Paramount, September 25, 1921) 5 Reels
May McAvoy, Eddie Sutherland, *Kathlyn Williams,* Edwin Stevens, Richard Tucker, Betty Schade, Dana Todd, Jane Keckley
Director: Frank O'Connor
Scenario: Hector Turnbull
Story: Hector Turnbull

MORALS
(Realart/Paramount, November, 1921) 5 Reels
May McAvoy, William P. Carleton, Marian Skinner, Nicholas De Ruiz, Starke Patterson, William Lawrence, *Kathlyn Williams,* Bridgetta Clark, Sidney Bracey
Director: William D. Taylor
Adaptation: Julia Crawford Ivers
Story: William John Locke, "The Morals of Marcus Ordeyme"

A MAN'S HOME
(Selznick/Select, December, 1921) 7 Reels
Harry T. Morey, *Kathlyn Williams,* Faire Binney, Margaret Seddon, Grace Valentine, Roland Bottomley, Matt Moore
Director: Ralph Ince
Scenario: Edward J. Montagne
Story: Anna Steese Richardson, Edmund Breese

A VIRGINIA COURTSHIP
(Realart/Paramount, December, 1921) 5 Reels
May McAvoy, Alec B. Francis, Jane Keckley, L. M. Wells, Casson Ferguson, *Kathlyn Williams,* Richard Tucker, Guy Oliver, Verne Winter
Director: Frank O'Connor
Scenario: Edfrid A. Bingham

CLARENCE
(Famous Players-Lasky/Paramount, October 15, 1922) 7 Reels
Wallace Reid, Agnes Ayres, May McAvoy, *Kathlyn Williams,* Edward Martindel, Robert Agnew, Adolphe Menjou, Bertram Johns, Dorothy Gordon, Mayme Kelso
Director: William C. de Mille
Scenario: Clara Beranger
Story: Booth Tarkington

THE WORLD'S APPLAUSE
(Famous Players-Lasky/Paramount, January 14, 1923) 8 Reels
Bebe Daniels, Lewis Stone, *Kathlyn Williams,* Adolphe Menjou, Brandon Hurst, Bernice Frank, Mayme Kelso, George Kuwa, James Neill
Director: William de Mille
Scenario/Story: Clara Beranger

SOULS FOR SALE
(Goldwyn, March 27, 1923) 8 Reels
Eleanor Boardman, Mae Busch, Barbara La Marr, Richard Dix, Frank Mayo, Lew Cody, Arthur Hoyt, David Imboden, Roy Atwell, William Orlamond, Aileen Pringle, Eve Southern, Sylvia Ashton, Fred Kelsey, Jed Prouty, William Haines, T. Roy Barnes, Barbara Bedford, Hobart Bosworth, Charles Chaplin, Chester Conklin, Elliott Dexter, Alice Lake, Bessie Love, ZaSu Pitts, Milton Sills, Anita Stewart, *Kathlyn Williams,* Blanche Sweet, Erich von Stroheim, King Vidor, Florence Vidor, Johnny Walker, George Walsh, Claire Windsor
Director/Story: Rupert Hughes
Adaptation: Rupert Hughes

TRIMMED IN SCARLET
(Universal, April 9, 1923) 5 Reels
Kathlyn Williams, Roy Stewart, Lucille Rickson, Robert Agnew, David Torrence, Phillips Smalley, Eve Southern, Bert Sprotte, Grace Carlyle, Raymond Hatton, Philo McCullough
Director: Jack Conway
Scenario: Edward T. Lowe, Jr.
Story: William Hurlbut

BROADWAY GOLD
(Edward Dillon/Truart, July 29, 1923) 7 Reels
Elaine Hammerstein, Elliott Dexter, *Kathlyn Williams,* Eloise Goodale, Richard Wayne, Harold Goodwin, Henry Barrows, Marshall Neilan
Director: Edward Dillon, J. Gordon Cooper
Adaptation: Kathryn Harris
Story: William Carey Wonderly

THE SPANISH DANCER
(Famous Players-Lasky/Paramount, October 7, 1923) 9 Reels
Pola Negri, Antonio Moreno, Wallace Beery, *Kathlyn Williams,* Gareth Hughes, Adolphe Menjou, Edward Kipling, Dawn O'Day, Charles A. Stevenson, Robert Agnew
Director: Herbert Brenon
Adaptation: June Mathis, Beulah Marie Dix
Story: Adolphe Philippe Dennery, Phillippe Francois Pinel

WHEN A GIRL LOVES
(Halperin/Associated Exhibitors, April 20, 1921) 6 Reels
Agnes Ayres, Percy Marmont, Robert McKim, *Kathlyn Williams,* John George, Mary Alden, George Siegmann, Ynez Seabury, William Orlamond, Ross Rosanova, Leo White
Director: Victor Hugo Halperin

WANDERER OF THE WASTELAND
(Famous Players-Lasky/Paramount, June 21, 1924) 6 Reels
Jack Holt, Noah Beery, George Irving, *Kathlyn Williams,* Billie Dove, James Mason, Richard R. Neill, James Gordon, William Corroll, Willard Cooley
Director: Irvin Willat
Scenario: George C. Hull, Victor Irvin
Story: Zane Grey

SINGLE WIVES
(Corinne Griffith/First National, July 27, 1924) 8 Reels
Corinne Griffith, Milton Sills, *Kathlyn Williams,* Phyllis Haver, Phillips Smalley, Jere Austin, Lou Tellegen, Henry B. Walthall, John Patrick
Director: George Archainbaud
Scenario: Marion Orth
Story: Earl Hudson

THE ENEMY SEX
(Famous Players-Lasky/Paramount, August 25, 1924) 8 Reels
Betty Compson, Percy Marmont, Sheldon Lewis, Huntley Gordon, De Witt Jennings, William H. Turner, *Kathlyn Williams,* Dot Farley, Ed Faust, Pauline Bush
Director: James Cruze
Scenario: Walter Woods, Harvey Thew
Story: Owen Johnson, "The Salamander"

THE CITY THAT NEVER SLEEPS
(Famous Players-Lasky/Paramount, September 28, 1924) 6 Reels
Louise Dresser, Ricardo Cortez, *Kathlyn Williams,* Virginia Lee Corbin, Pierre Gendron, James Farley, Ben Hendricks, Vondell Darr
Director: James Cruze
Scenario: Walter Woods, Anthony Coldeway
Story: Leroy Scott, "Mother O'Day"

THE PAINTED FLAPPER
(Chadwick, October 15, 1924) 6 Reels
James Kirkwood, Pauline Garon, Crauford Kent, *Kathlyn Williams,* Claire Adams, Hal Cooley, John Harron, Maine Geary, Anita Simons, Al Roscoe, Carlton Griffin, Pauline French
Director: John Gorman
Story: Alan Pearl

LOCKED DOORS
(Famous Players-Lasky/Paramount, January 5, 1925) 7 Reels
Betty Compson, Theodore Roberts, Theodore von Eltz, *Kathlyn Williams,* Robert Edeson, Elmo Billings
Director: William C. de Mille
Scenario: Clara Beranger
Story: Clara Beranger

THE BEST PEOPLE
(Famous Players-Lasky/Paramount, November 9, 1925) 6 Reels
Warner Baxter, Esther Ralston, *Kathlyn Williams,* Edwards Davis, William Austin, Larry Steers, Margaret Livingston, Joseph Striker, Margaret Morris, Ernie Adams
Director: Sidney Olcott
Screenplay: Bernard McConville
Story: David Gray, Avery Hopwood

THE WANDERER
(Famous Players-Lasky/Paramount, February 1, 1926) 9 Reels
Greta Nissen, William Collier, Jr., Ernest Torrence, Wallace Beery, Tyrone Power, Kathryn Hill, *Kathlyn Williams,* George Rigas, Holmes Herbert, Snitz Edwards
Director: Raoul Walsh
Scenario: James T. O'Donohoe
Story: Maurice V. Samuels

SALLY IN OUR ALLEY
(Columbia, September 3, 1927) 6 Reels
Shirley Mason, Richard Arlen, Alec B. Francis, Paul Panzer, William H. Strauss, *Kathlyn Williams,* Florence Turner, Harry Crocker
Director: Walter Lang
Story: Edward Clark

WE AMERICANS
(Universal-Jewel, May 6, 1928) 9 Reels
George Sidney, Patsy Ruth Miller, George Lewis, Eddie Phillips, Beryl Mercer, John Boles, Albert Gran, Michael Visaroff, *Kathlyn Williams,* Edward Martindel, Josephine Dunn, Daisy Belmore, Rosita Marstini, Andy Devine, Flora Bramley, Jake Bleifer
Director: Edward Sloman
Adaptation: Alfred A. Cohn
Story: Milton Herbert Gropper, Max Siegel

OUR DANCING DAUGHTERS
(Cosmopolitan/M-G-M Distributing, September 1, 1928) 9 Reels
Joan Crawford, John Mack Brown, Nils Asther, Dorothy Sebastian, Anita Page, *Kathlyn Williams,* Edward Nugent, Dorothy Cumming, Huntly Gordon, Evelyn Hall, Sam De Grasse
Director: Harry Beaumont
Story: Joseph Lovett

HONEYMOON FLATS
(Universal, December 30, 1928) 6 Reels
George Lewis, Dorothy Gulliver, *Kathlyn Williams,* Ward Crane, Bryant Washburn, Phillips Smalley, Jane Winton, Patricia Caron, Eddie Phillips
Director: Millard Webb
Scenario: Morton Blumenstock
Story: Joseph Franklin Poland
Source: Earl Derr Biggers

A SINGLE MAN
(M-G-M, January 12, 1929) 7 Reels
Lew Cody, Aileen Pringle, Marceline Day, Edward Nugent, *Kathlyn Williams,* Aileen Manning
Director: Harry Beaumont
Screenplay: F. Hugh Herbert, George O'Hara
Story: Hubert Henry Davies

HER HUSBAND'S WOMEN
(Famous Players-Lasky/Paramount, June 28, 1929) 2 Reels
Kathlyn Williams, Harrison Ford
Director: A. Leslie Pearce
Adaptation: Alfred A. Cohn
Story: Florence Ryerson

THE SINGLE STANDARD
(M-G-M, July 29, 1929) 8 Reels
Greta Garbo, Nils Asther, John Mack Brown, Dorothy Sebastian, Lane Chandler, Robert Castle, Mahlon Hamilton, *Kathlyn Williams,* Zeffie Tilbury
Director: John S. Robertson
Scenario: Josephine Lovett
Story: Adele Rogers St. Johns

WEDDING RINGS
(First National, December 29, 1929) 7 Reels
H. B. Warner, Lois Wilson, Olive Borden, Hallam Cooley, James Ford, *Kathlyn Williams,* Aileen Manning
Director: William Beaudine
Scenario: Ray Harris
Story: Ernest Pascal, "The Dark Swan"

ROAD TO PARADISE
(First National, July 20, 1930) 9 Reels
Loretta Young, Jack Mulhall, George Barraud, Raymond Hatton, Purnell Pratt, *Kathlyn Williams,* Dot Parley, Winter Hall, Ben Hendricks, Jr., Georgette Rhodes, Fred Kelsey
Director: William Beaudine
Adaptation: F. Hugh Herbert
Story: Dodson Mitchell, Zelda Sears, "Cornered"

DADDY LONG LEGS
(Fox, June 7, 1931) 73 Minutes
Janet Gaynor, Warner Baxter, Una Merkel, John Arledge, Claude Gillingwater, Edwin Maxwell, Effie Ellsler, Kendall MacComas, Louise Glosser Hale, Elizabeth Patterson, Sheila Mannors, *Kathlyn Williams*
Director: Alfred Santell
Scenario: Sonya Levien
Story: Jean Webster

UNHOLY LOVE
(Hollywood Pictures, June 1, 1932) 77 Minutes
H. B. Warner, Lila Lee, Beryl Mercer, Lyle Talbot, Ivan Lebedeff, Joyce Compton, Jason Robards, *Kathlyn Williams*
Director: Albert Ray
Producer: M. H. Hoffman

THE BIG RACE
(Showmen's Pictures, December 1, 1933) 68 Minutes
Boots Mallory, John Darrow, Frankie Darro, Phillips Smalley, *Kathlyn Williams,* Paul Hurst, Georgia O'Dell, James Flavin, Richard Terry (Jack Perrin), Skipper Zellan, Horace B. Carpenter, Ted Adams
Director: Fred Newmeyer
Story/Screenplay: Hugh Cummings

RENDEZVOUS AT MIDNIGHT
(Universal, March, 1935) 60 Minutes
Ralph Bellamy, Valerie Hobson, Catherine Doucet, Irene Ware, Helen Jerome Eddy, *Kathlyn Williams,* Vivien Oakland, Purnell Pratt, W. P. Carleton, Arthur Vinton, Edgar Kennedy, William Arnold, Galle Arnold, Katherine Williams, Katherine Hall, William Ruel, James Bush
Director: Christy Cabanne
Screenplay: Gladys Unger, Ferdinand Reyher
Story: Gastano Bazio, "The Silver Fox"
Producer: Lou L. Ostrow

HONORABLE MENTION

Many women have essayed serial roles, either as leading lady or supporting player. Though the following is not a complete list of all those who have appeared in significant roles in serials, it does represent the majority, and the work of these competent women is hereby acknowledged. The number and letter following the name indicate how many serials the actress appeared in and whether she was the featured heroine (F) or supporting player (S). For example, the entry for Florence Allen reads "Allen, Florence, 2F, 1S"--meaning that she was the featured heroine in two serials and a supporting player in one.

Those heroines already discussed in Parts One and Two are not included in this list.

We wish it were possible to present the career stories and filmographies of many of the heroines listed here who have not been discussed. Some of them had very interesting careers; for example, Ruth Hall, Shirley Grey, Carol Hughes, Nora Lane, Blanche Mehaffey, Kay Hughes, and Clara Kimball Young. Unfortunately, not everyone's career can be covered in the confines of a single volume. But our hats are off to these remarkable actresses.

Abbey, May, 1S
Abbott, Gypsy, 1S
Adair, Janice, 1S
Adair, Robyn, 1S
Adams, Jane, 2F
Adams, Kathryn, 1F
Adrian, Lillian, 1S
Ahans, Carol, 1S
Ainslee, Ann, 1S
Ainslee, Mary, 1F
Ainsworth, Virginia, 3S
Alba, Maria, 1F
Alberta, Laura, 1S
Allen, Barbara, 1S

Allen, Florence, 2F, 1S
Allen, Maude Pierce, 1S
Allen, Nellie, 1S
Alphin, Patricia, 1S
Ames, Ramsay, 2F, 1S
Anderson, Claire, 1F
Anderson, Eve, 1F
Anderson, Mary, 1F
Anderson, Nellie, 1S
Andre, Dorothy, 1S
Andre, Lona, 1F
Angelus, Muriel, 1F
Anibus, Pearl, 1S
Antibus, Jennie, 1S
Antibus, Norma, 1S
Appleton, Kathryn, 1S
Armbruster, April, 1S
Armida, 1S
Arnold, Dorothy, 1F
Arthur, Jean, 1F
Arvan, Jan, 1S
Astor, Gertrude, 6S
Auborn, Joy, 2S

Badgley, Helen, 1S
Bailey, Mildred, 1S
Baird, Leah, 1F
Baldwin, Ann, 1S
Balfour, Eve, 1S
Balfour, Sue, 1S
Barclay, Joan, 2F
Barrie, Judith, 1S
Bates, Jeanne, 1F
Bayless, Mary, 1S
Bayne, Beverly, 1F
Beck, Lillian, 1S
Beharano, Julia, 1S
Bellamy, Madge, 1F
Belmont, Virginia, 1F
Benedict, Frances, 1S

Benham, Elsa, 1F
Benham, Grace, 1S
Bennett, Constance, 1S
Bennett, Fran, 1F
Bennett, Helen, 2S
Bergen, Constance, 1S
Bestar, Barbara, 1F
Beveridge, Kittoria, 1S
Bichole, Norma, 1S
Billings, Billie, 1S
Blair, Joan, 1S
Blake, Pamela, 4F
Blinn, Beatrice, 1S
Blossom, Rose, 1F
Boardman, Virginia True, 1S
Bonifice, Symona, 3S
Bonnel, Cecile, 2S
Booth, Edwina, 1F
Brannean, Helen, 1S
Brent, Evelyn, 1F, 1S
Brice, Rosetta, 1S
Briscoe, Lottie, 1F
Brissac, Virginia, 1S
Britton, Edna, 1F
Brodie, Ann, 1S
Broneau, Helen, 2S
Bronte, Jean, 1S
Brooklyn, Mary, 1S
Brooks, Myra, 1S
Brooks, Norma, 1F
Brown, Anita, 1S
Brown, Helen, 1S
Bruce, Belle, 1S
Brundage, Matilda, 1S
Bryan, Ruth, 1S
Bryant, Joyce, 2F
Buckham, Hazel, 1S
Buckingham, Lillian, 1S
Bunt, Nellie, 1S
Burdict, Rose, 1S
Burke, Billie, 1F
Burns, Lillian, 1S
Burns, Marion, 1S
Burson, Polly, 2S
Burt, Nellie, 2S
Burte, Genevieve, 1S
Burton, Charlotte, 1F, 1S
Busch, Mae, 1S

Caldwell, Betty, 1S
Calhoun, Catherine, 1S
Callaghan, Viola, 1S
Calles, Willa, 2S
Campbell, Flo, 1S
Caprice, June, 1S
Carew, Ora, 1S
Carpenter, Jean, 1S

Carroll, Vanna, 1S
Carroll, Virginia, 5S
Case, Helen, 1S
Cassavant, Nina, 1S
Castle, Irene, 1F
Caswell, Nancy, 1S
Chadwick, Helene, 2S
Chambers, Kathleen, 1S
Chapman, Marguerite, 1F
Charleson, Mary, 1F
Chester, Lila, 1S
Childers, Ethel, 1S
Chorre, Gertrude, 1S
Christensen, Mary, 1S
Christian, Helen, 1F
Christine, Virginia, 2S
Christy, Dorothy, 1F, 1S
Claire, Ethlyne, 2F
Claire, Gertrude, 1S
Clancy, Ellen, see Shaw, Janet
Clark, Judy, 2F
Clark, Mamo, 1F
Clarke, Mae, 1F
Clayton, Ethel, 1F
Clayton, Marguerite, 2F
Clements, Marjory, 1S
Clifford, Kathleen, 1F
Clifford, Ruth, 1F
Clisbee, Ethel, 1S
Codee, Ann, 1S
Cody, Inez, 1S
Coe, Vivian, 1F
Collier, Lois, 2F
Colwell, Goldie, 1S
Compson, Betty, 1F
Compton, Joyce, 1F
Conway, Lita, 1F
Cooper, Edna May, 1S
Cooper, Rosemary, 1S
Corby, Ellen, 1S
Corcoran, Ethel, 2S
Costello, Helen, 1F
Craft, Virginia, 1S
Cramer, Jennie, 1S
Crane, Mary, 1S
Cranston, Mary, 1S
Crinley, Myrtis, 1S
Cross, Leah, 1S
Cunard, Mina, 1S
Curtis, Beatrice, 1S

Dalya, Jacqueline, 1S
Daniels, Thelma, 1S
Danko, Betty, 1S
D'antonio, Carmen, 1S
D'arcy, Ann, 1S
Darcy, Sheila, 1F, 1S

Dare, Doris, 1S
Dare, Helena, 1S
Darling, Ann, 1S
Darling, Grace, 1F
Darr, Vondell, 1F
Daube, Belle, 1S
Davenport, Milla, 2S
Davis, Ruth, 1S
Dea, Gloria, 1F
Dean, Doris, 1F
Dean, Jean, 1F
Dean, Priscilla, 1F
Deane, Hazel, 1F
Deane, Shirley, 1S
Deas, Leilani, 1S
de Bicari, Violet, 1S
de Briac, Jean, 1S
Dechett, Maria, 1S
de Courey, Nenette, 1S
Deer, Diana, 1S
De La Motte, Marguerite, 1S
Deliane, Helen, 1S
Dell, Claudia, 1F
Desmond, Mary Jo, 1S
Deste, Luli, 1S
Deverell, Helen, 1S
Devote, Dorothy, 1S
Dialene, Helen, 1S
Diamond, Jean, 1S
Dione, Rose, 1S
Dodd, Claire, 1S
Dome, Agnes, 1S
Dominguez, Beatrice, 1S
Donald, Dorothy, 1S
Doran, Ann, 1S
Douglas, Gertrude, 1S
Doyle, Maxine, 1F, 3S
Drake, Peggy, 1F
Drew, Delphine, 1S
Drew, Elizabeth, 1S
Drury, Norma, 1S
Dumbar, Helen, 1F
Dumo, Evelyn, 1S
Dupre, Louise, 2S
Duprez, June, 1S
Durkin, Grace, 1S
D'use, Margot, 1S
Dwyer, Ruth, 1F, 1S

Earl, Margaret, 1S
Earle, Josephine, 1S
Edy, Grace, 1S
Ellison, Marjorie, 1S
Emmons, Louise, 1S
Emory, Maude, 2S
Ethridge, Ella, 1S
Evans, Muriel, 1F

Evers, Ann, 1S

Fair, Virgina Brown, 1F
Fairbanks, Jane, 1S
Fairchild, Madeline, 1S
Falken, Jinx (Falkenburg), 1F
Farr, Patricia, 1F
Fauntelle, Dian, 1F
Fay, Dorothy, 1F, 1S
Fenwick, Jean, 1S
Ferguson, Mattie, 1S
Fern, Fritzi, 1S
Field, Elinor, 2F
Field, Mary, 1S
Fielding, Margaret, 2S
Finley, Evelyn see Whitney, Eve
Fisher, Blanche, 1S
Fitzgallen, Adelaine, 1S
Fitzroy, Emily, 1S
Fleming, Alice, 1S
Flowers, Bess, 1F, 1S
Flugrath, Edna, 1S
Forbes, Mary Elizabeth, 1S
Ford, Janet, 1S
Forde, Eugenie, 1S
Forrestor, Ava, 1F
Foster, Helen, 1F
Fox, Lucy, 2F
Foy, Mary, 1S
Francine, Madeline, 1S
Frank, Catherine, 1S
Franklin, Gloria, 1F

Gale, Jean, 1S
Gale, Joan, 1F, 1S
Gale, Lillian, 4S
Gale, Margaret, 1F
Galya, Jacqueline, 1S
Gardner, Mary, 1S
Gasnier, Louise, 1S
Gaston, Mae, 1S
Gay, Marjorie, 1F
Gaye, Audrey, 1S
Gaze, Gwen, 1F
George, Maude, 1S
Geraghty, Carmelita, 1S
Gibson, Diana, 1F, 2S
Gibson, Helen, 1F, 3S
Gibson, Julie, 1F
Gilbert, Lynn, 1F, 1S
Giraci, Mae, 1S
Gittelsen, June, 1S
Gladman, Ann, 1S
Golden, Olive Fuller, 1S
Gomez, Inez, 1S
Goodrich, Katherine, 1S
Gordon, Eva, 1S

Gordon, Julia, 2S
Gould, Rita, 1S
Grandin, Ethel, 1F
Granger, Dorothy, 1S
Granstedt, Greta, 2S
Grant, Corene, 3S
Grant, Mary, 2S
Gray, Gloria, 1F
Gray, Jennifer, 2S
Green, Dorothy, 1S
Green, Helen, 1F, 1S
Grey, Olga, 1S
Grey, Shirley, 1F
Griffith, Helen, 2S
Griley, Helen, 1S
Grinley, Myrtis, 1S
Grove, Ethel, 1S
Grove, Sybil, 1S
Gwynne, Anne, 2S

Hackett, Florence, 2S
Hackett, Jeanette, 1S
Haines, Mary, 1S
Hale, Georgia, 1F
Hall, Ella, 1F, 1S
Hall, Lois, 2F
Hall, Ruth, 1F
Halop, Florence, 1S
Hammerstein, Elaine, 1S
Hansen, Eleanor, 1F
Hansen, Juanita, 5S
Harris, Evelyn, 1S
Harrison, Lottie, 1S
Hart, Gypsy, 1S
Hart, Helen, 1S
Hartigan, Betty, 1S
Hartman, Greta, 1S
Hastings, Ann, 1S
Hathaway, Jean, 4S
Haydel, Dorothy, 1S
Hazard, Jayne, 1S
Henry, Charlotte, 1F
Herbert, Dorothy, 1S
Herndon, Irene, 1S
Herrick, Virginia, 1F
Hervey, Irene, 1F
Hiatt, Ruth, 1F
Hill, Josephine, 1F, 2S
Hillie, Verna, 1F
Hobart, Rose, 1S
Hoffman, Ruby, 4S
Holderness, Fay, 1S
Holland, Edna, 1S
Hollis, Hylda, 1S
Holt, Jennifer, 2F
Holt, Ula, 1F
Hopkins, Mae, 1S

Horne, Victoria, 2S
Howard, June, 1F
Howe, Betty, 3S
Hughes, Carol, 1F, 1S
Hughes, Catherine, 1F
Hughes, Kay, 2F
Hulette, Gladys, 1S
Humphrey, Ola, 1F
Hunter, Edna, 1F
Hutton, Beulah, 2S

Ince, Ada, 1F
Irving, Mary Jane, 1S
Irwin, Frances, 1S
Irwin, Lucille, 1F
Isley, Phyllis (Jennifer Jones), 1F

James, Claire, 2S
James, Rosemonde, 1S
Jenno, Stella, 1S
Jenson, Eulalie, 1F
Jepp, Mary, 1S
Jergens, Adele, 1F
Jocelyn, Sylvia, 1S
Johnson, Linda, 1F
Jones, Jennifer, see Isley, Phyllis
Joy, Gloria, 1F

Kane, Marjorie, 1S
Karina, Sandra, 1S
Kay, Mary Ellen, 1F
Keckley, Jane, 2S
Keefe, Zena, 1F, 1S
Kelley, Mary, 1S
Kelly, Dorothy, 1F
Kelly, Jeanne, 1F, 1S
Kennedy, Daun, 2F
Kent, Catherine, 1S
Kenyon, Doris, 1F
King, Dorothy, 1S
King, Mollie, 2F
Kingston, Muriel, 1F
Knapp, Evalyn, 1F
Knights, Margaret, 1S
Knox, Elyse, 1F
Knox, Patricia, 1S
Kornman, Mary, 1F

La Badie, Florence, 1F
Lackaye, Helen, 1S
Laemmle, Carla, 1S
Lake, Marjorie, 1S
Lalande, Martha, 1S
LaMal, Isobel, 1S
La Marr, Margaret, 1S
Landau, Frances, 1S
Landis, Carole, 1F

Landis, Margaret, 1S
Landowaka, Lona, 1S
Lane, Brenda, 1F
Lane, Lola, 1F
Lane, Magda, 1F
Lane, Nora, 1F, 2S
Lange, Elaine, 1F
Langston, Ruth, 2S
La Planche, Rosemary, 2F
La Plante, Laura, 2F
LaRoux, Carmen, 1F
LaRue, Emily, 1S
Lawrence, Edna, 1S
Lawson, Priscilla, 1S
Lea, Flora, 1S
Lederer, Gretchen, 1S
Lee, Florence, 3S
Lee, Gwen, 1S
Lennox, Lucille, 1S
Lewis, Eleanor, 1S
Lincoln, Carl, 1F
Lind, Myrtle, 1F
Lindley, Virginia, 1F
Lindrith, Nellie, 1S
Lindroth, Helen, 1S
Lingham, Anna, 1S
Livingston, Margaret, 1F
Loff, Jeanette, 1S
Logan, Gwendolyn, 1S
Logan, Jacqueline, 1F
London, Edith, 1S
Long, Sally, 1F
Longworth, Josephine, 2S
Lord, Marjorie, 1F
Loredo, Linda, 1S
Loring, Hope, 1S
Lorraine, Lillian, 1F, 1S
Loveridge, Margaret, 1F
Lovett, Dorothy, 1S
Ludwig, Phyllis, 1S
Lund, Lucille, 1F, 1S
Luther, Anne, 2F

Macmillian, Violet, 1S
Madden, Golda, 1S
Mair, Jane, 1S
Maison, Edna, 1S
Mallory, Boots, 1F
Malone, Florence, 1F
Malone, Molly, 1F
Mann, Frances, 1S, 1F
March, Gazelle, 1S
Maris, Mona, 1F
Marlowe, June, 1F
Marsh, Joan, 1F
Marsh, Marguerite, 2F
Marshall, Tina, 1S

Marson, Truda, 1S
Marstini, Madam, 1S
Marston, Vivian, 1S
Martin, Jill, 1S
Martin, Marion, 1S
Mason, Edna, 1S
Mason, Shirley, 1F
Mason, Vivian, 1F
Mathews, Carole, 1F
Mattex, Martha, 1S
Maureice, Ruth, 1S
Maurice, Mary, 1S
May, Kathleen, 1S
Mayburn, Margaret, 1S
Mayo, Edna, 1F
McAllister, Mary, 1F
McConnell, Gladys, 2F
McConnell, Mollie, 3S
McCormack, Alice, 1S
McDonald, Inez, 1F
McGuire, Kathryn, 1F
McKay, Wanda, 1F
McKenzie, Eva, 1S
McLean, Grace, 1S
McLeod, Catherine, 1S
Meade, Claire, 1S
Mehaffey, Blanche, 1F
Meredith, Iris, 3F
Miles, Betty, 1S
Miller, Claire, 1S
Mills, Marilyn, 1F
Milnor, Mary, 1S
Milton, Marjorie, 1S
Mitchell, Belle, 2S
Mitchell, Doris, 1F
Mitchell, Helen, 1S
Mitchell, Rhea, 2F
Mitchell, Yvette, 1S
Mix, Ruth, 1F, 2S
Montgomery, Mabel, 1S
Montgomery, Peggy, 1S
Monti, Carlotta, 1S
Moore, Cleo, 1F
Moore, Constance, 1F
Moore, Mary, 1S
Moore, Mildred, 1F
Moore, Pauline, 1F
Morales, Carmen, 1F
Morris, Frances, 1S
Morris, Margaret, 3F, 1S
Morrow, Susan, 1F
Mosquini, Marie, 1S
Myers, Carmel, 1F
Myers, Katherine, 1F

Nara, Anita, 1S
Neal, Ella, 1F

Neela, Princess, 1S
Nelson, Merlyn, 1S
Nesbitt, Mirian, 1F, 3S
Nightengale, Virginia, 1S
Nova, Hedda, 1F
Novak, Jane, 1S

Oakley, Laura, 1F, 2S
O'Brien, Gypsy, 1S
O'Brien, Jean, 1S
O'Connor, Kathleen, 2F
O'Dare, Peggy, 1S
Olivio, Valerio, 4S
Olmstead, Gertrude, 1F
Olonova, Olga, 1S
Ornellas, Loni, 1S
Orr, Helen, 1S

Padden, Sarah, 2S
Page, Jean, 1F
Palmer, Patricia, 1S
Palmer, Shirley, 1F
Parrish, Helen, 1F
Paterson, Shirley, 1F
Pavis, Marie, 2S
Pawn, Doris, 1S
Payton, Gloria, 1S
Pearson, Virginia, 1S
Percy, Eileen, 1F
Percy, Thelma, 1F
Perdue, Derelys, 1F, 1S
Perkins, Jean, 1S
Phelps, Vonda, 1S
Phillips, Carmen, 6S
Phillips, Dorothy, 1F
Phillips, Norma, 1S
Pickford, Lottie, 1F
Pilsbury, Helen, 1S
Plumer, Rose, 5S
Polo, Malvina, 2S
Porter, Corrine, 1F
Porter, Jean, 1S
Porter, Pansy, 2S
Powers, Jule, 1S
Price, Kate, 1F

Quimby, Margaret, 2F

Ralston, Esther, 2F, 2S
Ralston, Marcia, 1S
Rambeau, Janet, 1S
Ramsey, Ethel, 1S
Randall, Mabel, 1S
Randle, Karen, 1F
Randolph, Jane, 1S
Rayford, Alma, 1F
Razeto, Stella, 1S

Reader, Anna, 1S
Reed, Vivian, 1F
Reeves, Myrtle, 2S
Reller, Harriet, 1S
Rhodes, Betty Jane, 1F
Rich, Gloria, 1S
Rich, Vivian, 2F
Richards, Adrienne, 1S
Rickaby, Ruth, 1S
Ricksen, Lucille, 1S
Ridgely, Cleo, 1F
Rio, Joanne, 1F
Ritchie, Ethel, 1S
Roadman, Betty, 1S
Roberts, Beatrice, 4S
Roberts, Lynne, 2F
Robertson, Lolita, 1F
Robinson, Edna, 1S
Robinson, Frances, 2F
Roma, Rita, 1F
Roman, Ruth, 1S
Rose, Mary T., 1S
Ross, Betsy King, 2F
Rowe, Eileen, 1F
Roy, Gladys, 1S
Roy, Rosalie, 1S
Royce, Margaret, 1S
Rozelle, Rita, 1S
Rubey, Lucille, 1S
Ruby, Mary, 1S
Russell, Evangeline, 2S
Rutherford, Ann, 1F

Saunders, Alice, 1S
Saunders, Jackie, 1F
Schaefer, Ann, 1S
Scholfield, Eileen, 1S
Schram, Karla, 1F
Schram, Violet, 3S
Scott, Josephine, 1S
Sebastian, Dorothy, 1F
Sedgewick, Edna, 1S
Sedgwick, Josie, 2F
Selbie, Evelyn, 1S
Seymour, Clarine, 1S
Shannon, Ethel, 1S
Shanor, Peggy, 1F, 3S
Shaw, Janet (Ellen Clancy), 2F
Shea, Gloria, 1F
Shelley, Camille, 1S
Shelby, Miriam, 1S
Shelton, Maria, 1F
Shepard, Elaine, 1F
Shepard, Pearl, 1S
Sherman, Paula, 1S
Sherry, Clarice, 1S
Shilling, Marion, 2F

Shipman, Helen, 1S
Shockley, Marion, 1F
Short, Dorothy, 2F
Short, Florence, 1S
Short, Gertrude, 1S
Shotwell, Maria, 1S
Simpson, Henrietta, 1S
Sinclair, Ethel, 1S
Sisson, Vera, 1S
Sloman, Hylda, 1S
Small, Ann, 1S
Smith, Ruth, 1S
Smith, Willetta, 1S
SooHoo, Eleanor, 1S
Sothern, Jean, 1F
Spellman, Leora, 1S
Spinner, Marilyn, 1S
Stanley, Helene, 1S
Stanley, Louise, 1F
Stapp, Marjorie, 1S
Stark, Mabel, 1S
Stayart, Edith, 3S
Steadman, Vera, 1S
Sterling, Edythe, 1S
Stewart, Anita, 2F
Stewart, Eleanor, 1F
Strickland,- Mabel, 1S
Stuart, Jean, 1F
Sullivan, Hallee, 1S
Sullivan, Lillian, 1S
Sutton, Gertrude, 1S
Sutton, Mary, 1S

Talbot, Helen, 2F
Talcott, Dorothy, 1S
Tattersall, Viva, 1F
Taylor, Norma, 1F
Teague, Frances, 1F
Terry, Ethel Grey, 1S
Terry, Frances, 1S
Thayer, Julia, 1S
Theby, Rosemary, 2F, 1S
Thomas, Olive, 1S
Thompson, Lotus, 2F
Thornton, Edith, 2F, 1S
Thrower, Maxine, 1S
Thurston, Helen, 5S
Todd, Lola, 2F, 1S
Traverse, Madeline, 1S
Treador, Marie, 1S
Tropic, Marie, 1S
Tucker, Lillian, 1S
Turich, Rosa, 1S

Urecal, Minerva, 1S
Uzzell, Corrine, 1S

Valentine, Grace, 1S
Van, Beatrice, 1S
Vance, Jane, 1F
Vance, Virginia, 1S
Vanna, Olga, 1S
Van Name, Elsie, 2S
Vaughn, Alberta, 1F
Volding, Louise, 1S
Vonn, Viola, 1S

Walker, Lillian, 1F
Walker, Nellie, 1S
Wallace, Irene, 1F
Walters, Luana, 4S
Walthall, Anna May, 1S
Ward, Amelita, 1F
Warfield, Natalie, 2S
Warwick, Virginia, 1S
Watts, Peggy, 1S
Wayne, Carole, 1F
Wayne, Marie, 1S
Weaver, Marjorie, 1F
West, Josephine, 1F, 2S
West, Lillian, 1S
Weston, Doris, 1F
Wharton, Bessie, 1S
Whitney, Eve (Evelyn Finley), 1S
Whitney, Shirley, 1S
Wilde, Lois, 1F
Wiley, Jan, 3F
Williams, Cora, 1S
Wilson, Diana, 1S
Wilson, Lois, 1F
Wolbert, Dorothea, 1S
Wong, Anna May, 1S
Wood, Jeane, 1S
Woodbury, Joan, 1F
Woodruff, Eleanor, 1S
Woods, Dorothy, 1F
Woodthorpe, Georgia, 1S
Woodward, Jill, 1S
Worth, Constance, 1F
Worth, Lillian, 4S
Wright, Florence, 1S
Wright, Helen, 3S
Wright, Jean, 1S
Wright, Nanine, 1F
Wrixon, Maria, 1S
Wynne, Peggy, 2S

Yohe, May, 1S
Yorke, Edith, 1S
Young, Clara Kimball, 2F, 3S

Zimlich, Celeste, 1S

REFERENCES

--GENERAL--

Adams, Les, and Rainey, Buck. Shoot-Em-Ups: The Complete Reference Guide to Westerns of the Sound Era. New Rochelle, N.Y.: Arlington House Publishers, 1978. 633 pp. reprint, Metuchen, N.J.: Scarecrow Press, 1985.

Barbour, Alan G. Days of Thrills and Adventure. New York: Macmillan Co., 1970. 168 pp.

_____. Cliffhanger. New York: A & W Publishers, 1977. 248 pp.

Beck, Calvin Thomas. Scream Queens: Heroines of the Horrors. New York: Macmillan Co., 1978. 344 pp.

Bonomo, Joe. The Strongman. New York: Bonomo Studios, 1968.

Casali, Edgar. "Birth of the Serial and its European Development." Classic Film Collector, No. 45, Winter, 1974, p. X-l, 13.

Cline, William C. In the Nick of Time. Jefferson, N.C.: McFarland & Co., Inc., 1984. 281 pp.

Cohn, Alfred A. "Harvesting the Serial." Photoplay, Vol. XI, No. 3, February, 1917, pp. 19-26.

Couto, Carlos de Paula. "Universal Serial Stars of the Silent Era." Classic Film Collector, No. 48, Fall, 1975, pp. 24-28.

Edmonds, L. G. Big U: Universal in the Silent Days. Cranbury, N.J.: A. S. Barnes & Co., 1977. 162 pp.

Fernett, Gene. Hollywood's Poverty Row. Satellite Beach, Fla.: Coral Reef Publishing Co., 1973. 163 pp.

_____. Next Time Drive off the Cliff. Cinememories Pub. Co., 1968. 205 pp.

Fitzgerald, Michael G. Universal Pictures. New Rochelle, N.Y.: Arlington House Publishers, 1977. 766 pp.

Geltzer, George. "40 Years of Cliffhanging." Films in Review, VIII, February, 1957, pp. 60-67.

Halliwell, Leslie. <u>Halliwell's Filmgoer's Companion,</u> 8th Edition, Charles Scribner's Sons, New York, 1984.

Harmon, Jim, and Glut, Donald F. <u>The Great Movie Serials.</u> New York: Doubleday & Co., 1972. 384 pp.

Kinnard, Roy. <u>Fifty Years of Serial Thrills,</u> Metuchen, N.J.: Scarecrow Press, 1983.

Lahue, Kalton C. <u>Bound and Gagged.</u> Cranbury, N.J.: A. S. Barnes & Co., 1986. 352 pp.

_____. <u>Ladies in Distress.</u> Cranbury, N.J.: A. S. Barnes & Co., 1971. 334 pp.

Laube, Chris. "Before the Serials Spoke." <u>Classic Images</u>, No. 69, May, 1980, p. 22.

Lauritzen, Einar, and Lundquist, Gunnar. <u>American Film-Index 1908-1915.</u> Stockholm: Film-Index, 1976. 704 pp.

_____. <u>American Film-Index 1916-1920.</u> Stockholm: Film-Index, 1983.

Manski, Albert. "Silver Screen Memories: The Serials." <u>Classic Images</u>, No. 132, June, 1986, p. 55.

Mathis, Jack. <u>Valley of the Cliffhangers.</u> Northbrook, Ill.: Jack Mathis Advertising Co., 1975. 448 pp.

Miller, Don. <u>"B" Movies.</u> New York: Curtis Books, 1973. 350 pp.

<u>Motion Pictures 1912-1939: Catalog of Copyright Entries.</u> Washington, D.C.: Copyright Office, the Library of Congress, 1951. 1256 pp.

Munden, Kenneth W. (Executive Editor). <u>The American Film Institute Catalog: Feature Films 1921-1930.</u> New York: R. R. Bowker Company, 1971. 1653 pp.

Ragan, David. <u>Who's Who in Hollywood 1900-1976.</u> New Rochelle, N.Y.: Arlington House Publishers, 1976. 864 pp.

Slide, Anthony. "The Kalem Serial Queens." <u>Silent Picture</u>, No. 1, Winter 1968-'69, pp. 7-10.

_____. <u>The Big V: A History of the Vitagraph Company.</u> Metuchen, N.J.: The Scarecrow Press, 1976. 224 pp.

_____. <u>Early American Cinema.</u> The Tantivy Press, 1970. 192 pp.

Smith, Frank Leon. "The Man Who Made Serials." <u>Films in Review</u>, VII, October, 1956, pp. 375-383.

Stedman, Raymond William. <u>The Serials: Suspense and Drama by Installment.</u> Norman, Okla.: University of Oklahoma Press, 1971. 514 pp.

Stewart, John. <u>Filmarama: The Formidable Years, 1893-1919.</u> Metuchen, N.J.: The Scarecrow Press, 1975. 394 pp.

Swann, Thomas Burnett. <u>The Heroine or the Horse.</u> New York: A. S. Barnes & Co., 1977. 134 pp.

Truitt, Evelyn Mack. <u>Who Was Who on Screen</u>, New York: R. R. Bowker Company, 1977.

Uselton, Roi A. "The Wampas Baby Stars." <u>Films in Review</u>, XXI, February, 1970, pp. 73-97.

Van Buren, Walter C. "Serial Queens of the Silent Screen." <u>Memory Lane</u>, I, No. 7, May, 1980, pp. 41-46.

Wade, Peter. "A Little of Everything--And Then Some More." <u>Motion Picture Classics,</u> January, 1917.

Weaver, John T. <u>Forty Years of Screen Credits 1929-1969.</u> 2 vols. Metuchen, N.J.: The Scarecrow Press, 1970. 1458 pp.

Weiss, Ken and Goodgold, Ed. <u>To Be Continued.</u> New York: Bonanza Books, 1972. 341 pp.

Wing, Ruth, ed. <u>The Bluebook of the Screen.</u> Hollywood: The Blue Book of the Screen, Inc., 1924.

--SPECIFIC STARS--

KAY ALDRIDGE

"Kay Aldridge." <u>Screen Thrills</u>, I, Nos. 11 & 12, July, 1979.

Dellinger, Paul. "Kay Aldridge's Next Chapter." <u>Cliffhanger</u>, No. 1, Winter, 1983, pp. 23-33.

Krohn, Lou. "Kay Aldridge, Republic Serial Queen." <u>Screen Thrills and The Nostalgia Monthly</u>, No. 9 (Premier Issue).

McCord, Merrill T. <u>Perils of Kay Aldridge: Life of the Serial Queen.</u> Washington, D.C.: Alhambra Publishers, 1979.

Shoenberger, Jim. "A Visit with Kay Aldridge." <u>Norm's Serial News</u>, Chp. 10, February, 1988, pp. 4-5.

VEDA ANN BORG

"Actress Veda Ann Borg Sues for Divorce." <u>Los Angeles Times</u>, February 26, 1957.

Crivello, Kirk. "Passing Parade/Veda Ann Borg." <u>Hollywood Studio Magazine</u>, February, 1978.

Othman, Frederick C. "Face Her Fortune Again." <u>Hollywood Citizen-News</u>, Friday, March 14, 1941.

Parsons, Louella O. "Veda Borg Wins Divorce." <u>Los Angeles Examiner</u>, November 12, 1945.

Ringold, Gene. "Veda Ann Borg." <u>Films in Review</u>, XVI, No. 3, March, 1965 pp. 188-190.

"Veda Ann Borg." Samuel Goldwyn Productions, Inc. Publicity Release.

"Veda Ann Borg Accepts New Divorce Settlement." <u>Los Angeles Times</u>, May 14, 1957.

"Veda Ann Borg Fails to Get Her Divorce Decree." <u>Los Angeles Times</u>, May 7, 1957.

"Veda Ann Borg's Divorce Battle Takes New Turn." <u>Los Angeles Times</u>, August 30, 1955.

"Veda Ann, McLaglen in Alimony Tiff." <u>Los Angeles Examiner</u>, May 7, 1957.

LUCILE BROWNE

"Converging on Lucile Browne." <u>Those Enduring Matinee Idols</u>, I, Chp. 4, April-May, 1970, pp.39, 48.

PHYLLIS COATES

"Director Weds Actress." <u>Los Angeles Times</u>, April 2, 1948.

"Phyllis Coates." Monogram Pictures Publicity Department, September, 1951.

"Phyllis Coates of TV Divorces Band Pianist." <u>Los Angeles Times</u>, October 2, 1953.

"She Married the Boss." <u>Los Angeles Times</u>, August 28, 1955.

LOIS COLLIER

"Actress Loses $700 Clothes." <u>Los Angeles Examiner</u>, November 3, 1952.

"Actress Wins Divorce." <u>Los Angeles Herald</u>, September 2, 1943.

"Court Defends Wife Criticism." <u>Los Angeles Times</u>, September 3, 1943.

"Lois Collier, Actress, Given Final Decree of Divorce." <u>Los Angeles Herald</u>, September 6, 1944.

"Lois Collier, Attorney Wed, Leave for New York." <u>Los Angeles Examiner</u>, September 29, 1957.

"Lois Collier Biography." Universal Studio Publicity Department, March 20, 1945.

"Lois Collier Gets Divorce." <u>Los Angeles Examiner</u>, September 3, 1943.

"Lois Collier of Films Wed to Bob Oakley." <u>Los Angeles Times</u>, August 18, 1945.

MARGUERITE COURTOT

"Courtot: Well, Who Is She?" <u>Photoplay</u>, June, 1915, pp. 120-121.

Howard, Lillian. "How I Teach My Gows to Act." <u>Photoplay</u>, February, 1916, pp. 89-91.

"Marguerite Courtot." <u>Motion Picture Magazine</u>, June, 1915, p. 116.

Smith, Agnes. "She Hates Broadway." <u>Photoplay Magazine</u>, February, 1920, pp. 118-119.

GRACE CUNARD

Everett, Eldon K. "The Great Grace Cunard-Francis Ford Mystery." <u>Classic Film Collector</u>, No. 39, Summer, 1973, pp. 22-25.

LOUISE CURRIE

Jackson, Gregory R., Jr. "Serial World Interviews Louise Currie." <u>Serial World</u>, No. 7, Summer, 1976, pp. 18-22.

GRACE DARMOND

Darmond, Grace. "How I Became a Photoplayer." Motion Picture Classic, February, 1916, p. 40.

"Grace Darmond Obituary." Variety, October 9, 1963.

de Roos, Robert. "Hollywood's Mother Hen." TV Guide, November 4, 1961, pp. 28-30.

CAROL FORMAN

Breeden, Ab. "Ab Breeden in Hollywood." Wrangler's Roost, No. 70, 1984.

Rainey, Buck. "Carol Forman Reminisces." Serial World, No. 37, Spring, 1984, pp. 3-10.

MARY FULLER

Fulbright, Tom. "Tribute to the Ladies World." Classic Film Collector, No. 28, Fall, 1970, p. 10.

Fuller, Mary. "My Summer Vacation." Photoplay, June 6, 1915, pp. 111-114.

Harrison, Louis Reeves. "What Happened to Mary?" The Moving Picture World, July 5, 1913, p. 26.

"Mary Fuller." Motion Picture Magazine, May, 1915.

Smith, Frederick James. "Photoplay Finds Mary Fuller." Photoplay Magazine, circa 1924.

FRANCES GIFFORD

Biggs, Colin. "The Survivors of Cry Havoc." Hollywood Studio Magazine, XVI, No. 12, December, 1983, pp. 12-15.

"Biography of Frances Gifford." Paramount Studio publicity release, June, 1949. 3 pp.

Cassa, Anthony. "Frances Gifford: Waiting for the Morning." Hollywood Studio Magazine, XVI, No. 4, March, 1983, pp. 31-32.

DeMarco, Mario. "Serial Bits." Tribute, III, No. 4, July/August, 1984, p. 39.

Feret, Bill. "Lure of the Tropics." Hollywood Studio Magazine, XVI, No. 4, March, 1984, pp. 26-27.

"Frances Gifford." Metro-Goldwyn-Mayer Studio publicity release, 1943.

Gifford, Frances. "A Letter From Frances Gifford." Hollywood Studio Magazine, XVI, August, 1983, p. 4.

McClelland, Doug. "The Perils of Frances Gifford." Cliffhanger, No. 2, Spring, 1983, pp. 20-32.

Redelings, Lowell E. "The Hollywood Scene." Hollywood Citizen-News, June 6, 1946.

Smith, Darr. Untitled column, Los Angeles Daily News, October 21, 1949.

LORNA GRAY/ADRIAN BOOTH

"Adrian Booth," Publicity Sheet, Library, Academy of Motion Picture Arts and Sciences, Hollywood, CA (undated).

Scott, John L. "Adrian Booth, Western Star, Shoots for Helen Morgan Role," Los Angeles Times, May 1, 1949.

DOROTHY GULLIVER

Breeden, Ab. "Ab Breeden in Hollywood: Dorothy Gulliver." Wrangler's Roost, No. 69, April, 1984, pages unnumbered.

Collura, Joe. "Dorothy Gulliver: Western Heroine Corrals Fans in Raleigh," Classic Images, No. 113, November, 1984, pp. 23-21.

Hoaglin, Jess J. "Where Are They Today?" The Hollywood Reporter, July 6, 1972.

Hoaglin, Jess L. "Down Memory Lane/Dorothy Gulliver." Hollywood Studio Magazine, Vol. 5, No. 9, June, 1982, p. 50.

Thomas, Kevin. "Wampas Baby Gets New Career Start in 'Faces'." Los Angeles Times, Friday, January 3, 1969.

JUANITA HANSEN

Fulbright, Tom. "Juanita Hansen, The Poppyseed Girl." Classic Film Collector, No. 23, Spring, 1969, p. 10.

Thayer, John H. "Star Sheen of 1916." Classic Film Collector, No. 58, Spring, 1978, pp. 8-9.

Weitzel, Edward. "When Juanita Hansen, New Pathé Star, First Met a Quintette of Lions." The Moving Picture World, January 24, 1920, p. 579.

HELEN HOLMES

Everett, Eldon. "Ford Beebe Recalls Helen Holmes and J. P. McGowan." Classic Images, No. 86, August, 1982, p. 34.

Irvine, Clarke. "Helen Holmes." Motion Picture World, January 16, 1916.

Parsons, Louella O. "Helen Holmes Dies at 58." Los Angeles Examiner, July 10, 1950.

"Rites Set for 'Hazards of Helen' Star." Los Angeles Daily News, July 10, 1950.

Thayer, John E. "Proudly We Hail." Classic Film Collector, No. 57, Winter, 1977, p. 8.

CAROL HOLLOWAY

Peltret, Elizabeth. "When the Celluloid Clock Strikes Twelve." Motion Picture Magazine, June, 1919, pp. 69-70.

EDITH JOHNSON

Rainey, Buck. "The Film Career of William Duncan." Classic Film Collector, No. 55, Summer, 1977, pp. 24-26.

Winship, Mary. "To Be Continued--." Photoplay Magazine, March, 1921, pp. 45-46.

NATALIE KINGSTON

Harwood, John. "Tarzans and Janes." Classic Film Collector, II, p. 5.

ANN LITTLE

"Anna Little." Motion Picture Magazine, March, 1915, p. 108.

"Anna Little, of the Mustang Company." Motion Picture Magazine, March, 1916, pp. 112-113.

Bartlett, Randolph. "Little Miss Lochinvar." Photoplay, May, 1917.

Knight, Mac. "Ann Little and the 1980 Cinevent." Classic Images, August, 1982, pp. 11, 19.

Shirk, Adam Hull. "Ann Little and the Great Desire." Motion Picture Classic, January, 1919, pp. 36-37.

LOUISE LORRAINE

Gassaway, Gordon. "Louise of the Lions." Motion Picture Classic, July, 1922, pp. 36-37, 79.

Lahue, Kalton C. "Continued Next Week--Louise Lorraine." Classic Film Collector, No. 13, Fall-Winter, 1965, p. 5.

"Louise Lorraine." Classic Images, No. 75, 1981, p. 16.

"Louise Lorraine." Metro-Goldwyn-Mayer Publicity Department, circa 1927.

CLEO MADISON

"Cleo Madison." Motion Picture World, April 14, 1914.

EDNA MURPHY

"Edna Murphy." Goldwyn Pictures Publicity Department, circa 1920.

"Edna Murphy." New York City American, May 7, 1925.

Stanley, May. "Says She'll Never Marry An Actor." Photoplay, March, 1925, p. 49.

ANNE NAGEL

"Actress Stymies Officer Hubby's Bid for Divorce." Hollywood Citizen-News, February 8, 1957.

"Anne Nagel." Hollywood Reporter, April 12, 1966. (obituary)

"Anne Nagel." Universal Studio Publicity Department, February, 1941.

"Anne Nagel." Variety, July 8, 1966. (obituary)

"Anne Nagel Asks $350,000 for Alleged Sterilization." Los Angeles Daily News, December 23, 1947.

"Anne Nagel Answered in Suit Over Operation." Los Angeles Times, January 23, 1948.

"Anne Nagel Blocks Mate on Final Divorce Decree." Los Angeles Mirror-News, February 7, 1957.

"Anne Nagel Fights Colonel Over Money and Marriage." Los Angeles Examiner, February 7, 1957.

"Anne Nagel Loses Out in Alimony Bid." Los Angeles Times, February 8, 1957.

"Anne Nagel Puts Divorce Aside to Hear Mate." Los Angeles Times, May 23, 1951.

"Anne Nagel Requiem Set Monday." Hollywood Citizen-News, July 8, 1966.

"Anne Nagel Suit Charges Surgery Left Her Barren." Los Angeles Times, December 23, 1947.

"Anne Nagel Wins Delayed Action Divorce." Los Angeles Times, May 26, 1951.

"Anne Nagel's Mate Tries to Avert Divorce." Los Angeles Daily News, May 22, 1951.

"Final Divorce Blocked by Actress Anne Nagel." Los Angeles Times, February 7, 1957.

"Final Rites Set for Actress Anne Nagel." Los Angeles Times, July 8, 1966.

"Husband Sued by Actress Anne Nagel." Los Angeles Times, April 12, 1951.

"Sterilized, Says Actress in Action Seeking $350,000." Los Angeles Times, December 23, 1947.

CECILIA PARKER

"Color Biography of Cecilia Parker." Fox Film Studio Publicity, March, 1931.

Hoaglin, Jess L. "Where Are They Now?" Hollywood Reporter, April 13, 1975.

Jordan, Don and Connor, Edward. "Judge Hardy and Family." Films in Review, XXV, No. 1, January, 1974, pp. 1-10.

ARLINE PRETTY

Dowling, Gary. "Arline Pretty Was Born That Way." Photoplay, June, 1917, p. 74.

Montanye, Lillian. "The Pretty Miss Pretty." Motion Picture Classic, November, 1919, p. 60.

"Services for Arline Pretty, 92, Star of Silent Movies, Slated." Los Angeles Times, April 19, 1978.

ALLENE RAY

"A Little Riding Fool." Photoplay, February, 1921, p. 44.

Connor, Edward. "The Serial Lovers." Films in Review, VI, August-September, 1955, pp. 328-332.

Montanye, Lillian. "The Lone Star Girl." Motion Picture Classic, April, 1921, pp. 26, 68.

Shipley, Glenn. "Allene Ray, Top Serial Star." Classic Images, No. 148, October, 1987, p. 43.

JEAN ROGERS

"Jean Rogers." Universal Studios Publicity Department, September, 1936.

Kinnard, Roy. "Interview: Jean Rogers." Fifty Years of Serial Thrills, Scarecrow Press, Metuchen, New Jersey, 1983, pp. 182-191.

Lamberti, Mark E. "Jean Rogers, Second Feature Lady." Remember When, No. 16, 1974.

_____. "Jean Rogers." Epic, I, No. 1, September, 1977, pp. 51-15.

Sulski, Jim. "The Girl Who Was Dale Arden." Fantastic Films, II, No. 2, June, 1979, pp. 56-61.

RUTH ROLAND

Bruner, Frank V. "Along Came Ruth." Motion Picture Classic, July, 1919.

Everett, Eldon K. "Ruth Roland, Queen of the Cliffhangers." Classic Film Collector, circa 1974, pp. 54-55.

Gebhart, Myrtle. "The Real Ruth Roland." Picture Play, December, 1926.

Geltzer, George. "Ruth Roland." Films in Review, XI, No. 9, November, 1960, pp. 539-548.

Goldbeck, Willis. "The Primitive." Motion Picture Magazine, December, 1921.

Groves, Gloria. "A Real Vaudeville Equilibrist." Photoplay, April, 1919.

Hall, Alice. "Roughing It with Ruth Roland." Pictures and Picturegoer, June, 1921.

Katchmer, George. "The Screen Girl of Action, Ruth Roland." Classic Images, No. 123, October, 1985, pp. 23-26.

"Miss Ruth Roland." Moving Picture World, March 7, 1914.

"A New Kalem Star." Moving Picture World, December 5, 1914.

Peterson, Elizabeth. "Comrad Ruth." Motion Picture Classic, April, 1917.

Rainey, Buck. "Ruth Roland." Serial World, Nos. 35-36, Summer 1983, p. 21 and Winter 1984, pp. 20-21 (Two parts).

"Revelations of Ruth Roland." Pictures and Picturegoer, January, 1927.

Roland, Ruth. "Personality in Dress." Photoplay, June, 1915.

_____. "What a Home Means to Me." Motion Picture Magazine, November, 1915.

"Ruth Roland." Moving Picture World, July 11, 1914.

"Ruth Roland." Moving Picture World, July 24, 1915.

"Ruth Roland Up-to-Date." Pictures and Picturegoer, October 27, 1917.

St. Johns, Adele Rogers. "Just a Good Business Man." Photoplay, August, 1922.

MARIN SAIS

Ames, Hector. "Marin Sais, the Farmer Girl of the Screen." Motion Picture Classic, June, 1917, p. 37.

"A Little Lesson in Spanish." Photoplay, March, 1917, p. 81.

PEGGY STEWART

Coons, Minard. "An Interview with Peggy Stewart." Film Collector's Registry, No. 57, November, 1974, pp. 5-9.

Oakley, Vic. "Peggy Stewart." Wrangler's Roost, No. 55.

Stewart, Peggy. "The Republic Years." Those Enduring Matinee Idols, III, Chp. 27, No. 7, 1974, pp. 409-411.

Williams, Bob. "Cinema Saddlemates." Asheboro, North Carolina Courier/Tribune, Sunday, Februrary 16, 1986.

Williams, Nick and Stoginski, John. "Peg of Our Hearts." Western Film Collector, I, No. 6, January, 1974, pp. 10-19, 35.

LINDA STIRLING

Rainey, Buck. "A Conversation with Linda Stirling, Sensuous Siren of the Serials." Film Collector's Registry, No. 71, December, 1976, pp. 3-7.

Stirling, Linda. "My Life as a Serial Queen." Movie Digest, May, 1973, pp. 44-49.

Williams, Bob. "Cinema Saddlemates." Asheboro, North Carolina Courier/Tribune, Sunday, February 16, 1986.

RUTH STONEHOUSE

Harleman, G. P. "News of Los Angeles and Vicinity." The Moving Picture World, December 15, 1917.

"Silent Film Star's Last Rites Awaited." Hollywood Citizen-News, May 14, 1941, p. 12.

MARIE WALCAMP

Bell, James. "Is It Impossible? Marie'll Do It." Photoplay, November, 1916, p. 49.

Everett, Eldon K. "Moments with Movies." <u>Classic Images</u>, No. 89, November, 1982, pp. 51-52.

Peterson, Elizabeth. "The Serial Girl--Marie Walcamp." <u>Motion Picture Magazine</u>, September, 1919, pp. 82-83.

Remont, Fritzi. "Marie: The Mystic." <u>Motion Picture Classic</u>, January, 1920, pp. 48-49, 72.

JACQUELINE WELLS/JULIE BISHOP

"Film Actress Given Divorce." <u>Los Angeles Times</u>, May 13, 1939.

"Jacqueline Wells Is Granted Divorce." <u>New York Herald</u>, May 12, 1939.

"Julie Bishop Biography." Warner Brothers Publicity Department. Undated.

"Julie Bishop, Film Actress, Bride of Lieut. Col. Shoop." <u>Los Angeles Examiner</u>, July 25, 1944.

PEARL WHITE

"Always Just Escaping Death." <u>Pictures and Picturegoer</u>, July 27, 1918.

Bacon, George Vaux. "The Girl on the Cover." <u>Photoplay</u>, January, 1916.

Bruner, Frank V. "What Sort of a Fellow Is Pearl White?" <u>Photo-Play Journal</u>, February, 1919.

_____, "The Real Pearl White." <u>Motion Picture Magazine</u>, July, 1919., pp. 32-33, 102.

Condon, Mabel. "The Real Perils of Pauline." <u>Photoplay</u>, October, 1914.

Davies, Wallace E. "Truth About Pearl White." <u>Films in Review</u>, November, 1959, pp. 537-548.

Dino, Tom. "The Heroine of the Cliffs." <u>Classic Film Collector</u>, No. 14, Spring, 1966, p. 13.

Everett, Eldon K. "Bertram Milhauser Remembers Pearl White." <u>Classic Images</u>, No. 83, 1982, p. 25.

_____. "A Postscript to Pearl White." <u>Classic Film Collector</u>, No. 55, Summer, 1977, pp. 48-49.

Eyck, John Ten. "Speaking of Pearls." <u>Photoplay</u>, September, 1917.

Fletcher, Adele Whitely. "Reconsidering Pearl." <u>Motion Picture Magazine</u>, February, 1921.

Hall, Alice. "The Ninety-Nine Lives of Pearl White." <u>Pictures and Picturegoer</u>, February, 1921.

Howe, Herbert. "A Star in Search of Her Soul." <u>Photoplay</u>, June, 1923.

Johaneson, Bland. "Good-By Boys, I'm Through." <u>Photoplay</u>, April, 1924.

Johnson, Julian. "The Girl on the Cover." <u>Photoplay</u>, April, 1920.

Lochbiler, Don. "Hiss the Villain, Cheer Pearl." <u>Classic Film Collector</u>, No. 26, Winter, 1970, p. EX4.

Mackenzie, Donald. "Chapter From Unpublished Book on Pearl White." Classic Film Collector, No. 26, Winter, 1970, pp. 6, 13.

Mullett, Mary B. "The Heroine of a Thousand Dangerous Stunts." American Magazine, May, 1918.

"Pearl White." Moving Picture World, January 23, 1915.

"Pearl White." Pictures and Picturegoer, October 9, 1920.

"Pearl White Dead: Ex-Star of Movies." New York Times, August 5, 1938.

Rainey, Buck. "Pearl White." Serial World, Nos. 34-35, Spring 1983, pp. 42-45 and Summer 1983, p. 20 (Two parts).

Reynolds, Roger. "When Pauline Had Her Perils." Classic Film Collector, (date undetermined).

"This Little Girl Is Iridescent Pearl White." Photoplay, March, 1925.

Sheridan, Oscar M. "Pearl in Paris." Pictures and Picturegoer, November, 1923.

Smith, Frank Leon. "Pearl White and Ruth Roland." Films in Review, December, 1960.

Smith, Frederick. "A Pearl in the Rough." Motion Picture Classic, January, 1919, pp. 16-19, 72.

Stainton, Walter R. "Pearl White in Ithaca." Films in Review, May, 1951.

Sterling, Ray. "Pearl White--Woman Wizard." Photo-play World, May, 1919.

Wade, Peter. "A Little of Everything--and Then Some More." Motion Picture Classic, January, 1917.

White, Pearl. "Putting It Over." Motion Picture Magazine, February, 1917 pp. 61-62.

"Why I Like to Work for Uncle Sam." Pictures and Picturegoer, October 5, 1918.

KATHLYN WILLIAMS

Ames, Hector. "Kathlyn Williams Builder." Motion Picture Magazine, July, 1916.

Burgess, Beth. "The Lady of the Lions Reconsiders." Photoplay, January, 1917.

Carter, Aline. "Untouched by Ennui." Motion Picture Magazine, August, 1921, pp. 53-54, 99.

Denton, Frances. "Kathlyn's Memory Box." Photoplay, November, 1917.

DeWitt, Bodeen. "Kathlyn Williams." Films in Review, Vol. XXXV, February, 1984, pp. 67-79.

Howe, Herbert. "The Diplomat of Hollywood." Photoplay, September, 1924, p. 63.

"Popular Players." The Moving Picture World, August 23, 1913.

Rubin, Sam. "Kathlyn Williams." Classic Film Collector, XIV, Spring, 1966, p. 9.

Schmid, Peter Gridley. "An Animal Chat with Kathlyn Williams." Motion Picture Classic, January, 1917, pp. 33-34, 36.

Smith, Bertha H. "Nervy Movie Lady." Sunset, June, 1914.

INDEX OF FILM TITLES

-A-
Aaron Slick From Punkin Crick (1952), 256
Abilene Trail (1951), 146
About Face (1942), 250
Above the Abyss (1915), 442
Abroad in Old Kentucky (1933), 17
Absent Minded Abe (1913), 178
Accident Insurance (1913), 231
Accomplice (The) (1915), 410
Accomplice (1946), 254
According to Hoyle (1922), 302
Ace Drummond (1936), 161, 162, 166
Ace of Scotland Yard (The) (1929), 40
Across the Atlantic (1928), 369
Action Galore (1925), 403
Action in the North Atlantic (1943), 456
Active Life of Dolly of the Dailies (The) (1914), 309, 315
Adopted Son (The) (1912), 465
Adventure in Sahara (1938), 67
Adventures of Briarcliff (The) (1915), 269, 272
Adventures of Captain Kate (The) (1911), 461
Adventures of Captain Marvel (The) (1941), 283, 285
Adventures of Frank and Jesse James (1948), 137, 138, 144
Adventures of Frank Merriwell (The) (1936), 161, 164
Adventures of Kathlyn (The) (1913), 241, 307, 352, 459, 461, 462, 467
Adventures of Kitty O'Day (The) (1945), 71
Adventures of Peg o' the Ring (The) (1916), 29, 36, 437, 443
Adventures of Red Ryder (The) (1940), 425
Adventures of Ruth (The) (1919), 174, 182
Adventures of Tarzan (The) (1921), 127, 130
Adventures of the Girl Spy (1908-'09), 307
Adventurous Blonde (The) (1937), 377
Affair of Dress (An) (1914), 315
Affair of the Deserted House (1915), 180
After the Ball (1924), 366
After the Storm (1928), 334
After the War (1919), 37

Agnes Kempler's Sacrifice (1915), 356
Ah! Wilderness (1934), 385, 390
Aida (1911), 308, 311
Aided by the Movies (1915), 338
Ain't He Grand? (1916), 188
Airmail Mystery (1932), 13, 16
Alamo (The) (1960), 245, 258
Alas and Alack (1915), 352, 356
Alcatraz Island (1937), 246
Alias Billy the Kid (1946), 431
Alias, James, Chauffeur (1915), 57
Alias Jane Jones (1916), 357
Alias Mike Moran (1918), 116, 124
Alice in Wonderland (1933), 452
Alimony (1924), 297
All Aboard (1927), 368
All Dolled Up (1921), 402
All for Gold (1918), 191
All Night Long (1924), 345
All on Account of a Portrait (1913), 314
All This and Heaven Too (1940), 428
Almond-Eyed Man (An) (1913), 314
Almost a Widow (1915), 57
Along the Malibu (1916), 358
Along the Oregon Trail (1947), 73
Alster Case (The) (1915), 443
Altar Stairs (The) (1922), 130
Always in Trouble (1938), 167
Am in the Harem (1915), 409
Amateur Prodigal (An) (1915), 441
Ambassador's Daughter (The) (1913), 313
American Ace (An) (1919), 294
American Girl (The) (1917), 406, 407, 411, 412
American Empire (1942), 322, 326
American in Paris (An) (1951), 146
American Live Wire (1918), 294
American Princess (The) (1913), 271
And Baby Makes Three (1949), 289
And the Greatest of These Is Charity (1912), 419
And the Villain Still Pursued Her (1914), 179
And They Called Him Hero (1915), 35
Andy Clyde Gets Spring Chicken (1939), 69
Andy Hardy Comes Home (1958), 385, 393

Andy Hardy Gets Spring Fever (1939), 392
Andy Hardy Meets Debutante (1940), 393
Andy Hardy's Double Life (1942), 393
Angel in the Mask (The) (1915), 421
Angel of the Slums (1911), 228
Angel Unaware (An) (1914), 440
Angels Unaware (1916), 443
Animals (The) (1971), 435
Anita's Butterfly (1915), 57
Any Old Port (1932), 451
Any Wife (1922), 238
Anybody's Blonde (1931), 371
Apache Raider (The) (1928), 334
Apartment House Mystery (1915), 180
Ape (The) (1928), 447
Ape Man (The) (1942), 286, 287
Applied Romance (1915), 55
Are All Men Alike? (1920), 445
Are These Our Parents? (1944), 140
Are You With It? (1948), 143
Argentine Nights (1940), 380
Arizona Bill (1911), 176
Arkansas Judge (1941), 249
Armored Car Robbery (1950), 383
Arms and the Woman (1910), 311
Arnelo Affair (The) (1947), 323, 328
Around the Bases (1926), 79
Arrest Norma MacGregor (1921), 194
Arrowmaker's Daughter (The) (1912), 229
Arthur Takes Over (1948), 266
Artist and the Brute (The) (1913), 465
As the Fates Decree (1912), 465
Ashes of Hope (1914), 440
At the Banquet Table (1915), 396
At the Burglar's Command (1913), 234
At the Flood Tide (1915), 109
At the Threshold of Life (1911), 311
Atom Man vs. Superman (1950), 137, 145
Attack at Rocky Pass (The) (1913), 405, 408
Auto-Bungalow Fracas (An) (1915), 338
Avalanche (1946), 254
Avenging Arrow (The) (1921), 174, 183
Awakening (The) (1915), 55
Awakening of John Bond (The) (1911), 312

-B-

Baby Maker (The) (1970), 27
Baby Mine (1928), 134
Bachelor and the Bobbysoxer (1947), 254
Bachelor's Club (The) (1929), 369
Bachelor's Waterloo (The) (1912), 312
Back in the Saddle (1941), 455
Back Lash (1947), 163, 170, 288
Back Street (1941), 428
Back to the Primitive (1911), 464
Back Trail (The) (1924), 330
Badgered (1916), 109
Baited Trap (The) (1914), 396

Baited Trap (The) (1926), 62
Bandits of the Badlands (1945), 430
Bandit's Child (The) (1913), 408
Bandit's Wager (The) (1916), 36
Bar-C Mystery (The) (1926), 449, 451
Bare Living (A) (1917), 189
Barefoot Boy (1914), 269, 272
Barney Oldfield's Race for Life (1913), 98, 99
Barrier of Ignorance (The) (1914), 409
Barriers Burned Away (1925), 399
Barriers of the Law (1925), 104
Baseball and Bloomers (1911), 418
Bashful Bachelor (The) (1942), 286
Battle at Fort Laramie (The) (1913), 98, 100
Battle for Freedom (The) (1913), 408
Battle of Bull Run (The) (1913), 29, 31
Battle of Cupidovich (The) (1916), 339
Battle of Love (The) (1914), 441
Battle of Wits (A) (1921). 195
Battling Brewster (1924), 99, 104
Battling with Buffalo Bill (1931), 13, 15
Be Neutral (1914), 34
Beast of Paradise (1923), 195, 403
Beau Brummell (1924), 343
Beautiful But Dumb (1928), 197
Beautiful Gambler (The) (1921), 295
Beautiful Imposter (The) (1917), 319
Beauty Parlor of Stone Gulch (The) (1912), 177
Before Yorktown (1911), 31
Behind Office Doors (1931), 370
Behind Prison Gates (1939), 454
Behind the Door (1919), 291, 294
Behind the Front (1926), 133
Behind the Lines (1916), 109
Behind the Mask (1916), 36
Behind the News (1940), 248
Behind the Veil (1916), 318
Behind Two Guns (1924), 413
Believe Me, Xantippe (1918), 116, 123
Bella's Beaus (1912), 229
Belle of the Beach (The) (1912), 177
Belle of Yorktown (The) (1913), 29, 33
Bells of Rosarita (1945), 416
Below the Deadline (1936), 391
Below the Surface (1920), 291, 295
Benson at Calford (1926), 79
Best People (The) (1925), 473
Better Way (The) (1913), 278
Better Wife (The) (1919), 470
Betty in Search of a Thrill (1915), 91
Betty's First Sponge Cake (1915), 55
Between Two Husbands (1922), 398
Beware Spooks (1939), 69
Beyond All Odds (1926), 196
Beyond Price (1921), 238
Beyond the Blue Horizon (1942), 326
Beyond the Law (1930), 128, 135

Beyond the Rainbow (1922), 275
Beyond the Rockies (1926), 332
Big Broadcast of 1938 (The) (1938), 344
Big Clock (The) (1948), 144
Big Hearted (1930), 83
Big Horn Massacre (The) (1913), 405, 408
Big Jim McLain (1952), 244, 256
Big Land (The) (1957), 458
Big Noise (The) (1944), 252
Big Race (The) (1933), 474
Big Shot (The) (1939), 321, 323
Big Timber (1917), 461, 470
Big Town (1947), 254
Bille, the Hillbilly (1915), 57
Bill's Board Bill (1913), 179
Billy McGrath's Love Letters (1912), 438
Billy the Kid in Santa Fe (1941), 415
Billy the Kid Outlawed (1940). 283
Billy the Kid's Gun Justice (1940), 285
Billy Van Deusen and the Merry Widow (1915), 338
Billy Van Deusen and the Vampire (1916), 339
Billy Van Deusen, the Cave Man (1916), 340
Billy Van Deusen's Ancestry (1916), 339
Billy Van Deusen's Campaign (1915), 338
Billy Van Deusen's Egg-Spensive Adventure (1916), 340
Billy Van Deusen's Fiancee (1916), 339
Billy Van Deusen's Muddle (1916), 339
Billy Van Deusen's Operation (1916), 340
Billy Van Deusen's Shadow (1915), 338
Billy Van Deusen's Wedding Eve (1916), 339
Billy's Hat (1919), 59
Bitter Creek (1954). 244, 256
Bitter Sweet (1940), 245, 248
Black Book (The) (1929). 151, 157
Black Box (The) (1915). 115, 120
Black Cat (The) (1934), 453
Black Diamond Express (The) (1927), 368
Black Eyes and Blue (1916), 91
Black Friday (1940), 379
Black Hand (The) (1913), 178
Black Lash (The) (1952), 434
Black Masks (The) (1913), 32
Black Oak Conspiracy (1977), 435
Black Orchids (1916), 358
Black Ring (The) (1915), 269, 273
Black Secret (The) (1919), 227, 238
Black Sheep (The) (1914), 272
Black Sheep (A) (1915), 292
Black Widow (The) (1947), XII, XIII, 43, 46, 47
Blackhawk (1952), 43, 50
Blake of Scotland Yard (1927), 39
Blitz on the Fritz (A) (1943), 287
Blonde Savage (1947), 255
Blondie's Holiday (1947), 382
Blood and Steel (1925), 104, 446

Blood Arrow (1958), 26
Blood of His Brother (1915), 218
Blood of the Children (1915), 218
Blood Will Tell (1914), 440
Blot (The) (1921), 223
Blue Blood and Yellow (1915), 181
Blue Dahlia (The) (1948), 143
Blue Fox (The) (1921), 116, 124
Blue Streak (The) (1926), 133
Blue Streak McCoy (1920), 402
Bluebeard (1909), 310
Bluebeard's 8th Wife (1938), 454
Blueprint for Murder (A) (1953). 212
Blues Busters (1950), 23
Bogus Bandits (1931), 17
Bohemian Girl (The), 453
Bonds of Honor (1918), 412
Boobs in the Woods (1925), 346
Bookworm Hero (The) (1928), 82
Border Blackbirds (1927), 334
Border Law (1922), 280
Border Vigilantes (1941), 322, 325
Born of the People (1916), 35
Borrowed Finery (1925), 132
Borrowed Hero (1941), 87
Boss of Rustler's Roost (The) (1928), 334
Bottle of Musk (A) (1913), 438
Bound and Gagged (1919), 271, 274
Bound in Morocco (1918), 277, 278
Brains Vs. Brawn (1912), 420
Brand of Cain (The) (1916). 469
Brand of Hate (1934), 18
Brand of His Tribe (1914), 218
Branded Four (The) (1920), 53, 54, 60
Branded Woman (The) (1920), 363
Brass (1923), 303
Brass Bottle (The) (1964), 212
Brass Bullet (The) (1918), 89, 92, 93
Breaking into the Big League (1913), 271
Breaking Records (1927), 80
Breezy Jim (1919), 94
Brennon o' the Moor (1916), 36
Bribe (The) (1915), 316
Brick Bradford (1947), 43, 48, 137, 143
Bride for Henry (A) (1937), 373, 377
Bride of Frankenstein (1935), 41
Bride of Mystery (The) (1914), 29, 33
Brigham Young–Frontiersman (1940), 162, 169
Brimstone (1949), 74
Bring on the Girls (1945), 140, 252
Broadway Butterfly (A) (1925), 331
Broadway Gold (1923), 472
Broadway Jones (1917), 422
Broadway Love (1917), 92
Broadway Madonna (The) (1922), 95
Broadway Peacock (The) (1922), 238
Broken Barriers (1924), 446

497

Broken Coin (The) (1915), 30, 32, 35
Broken Heart (The) (1913), 438
Broken Homes (1926), 447
Broken Spell (The) (1913), 232
Broken Spur (The) (1921), 413
Broken Threats United (1913), 439
Bronc Stomper (The) (1928), 334
Brotherhood of Man (The) (1912), 464
Brothers in the Saddle (1949), 49
Brother's Sacrifice (A) (1917), 111
Brought Home (1915), 443
Brought to Bay (1913), 99
Brown's Summer Boarders (1915), 396
Buccaneers (The) (1913), 353
Bucking the Barrier (1923), 398
Buckskin Coat (The) (1913), 408
Bud, Bill, and the Waiter (1914), 180
Bugler of Battery B (1912), 177
Bugs and Bugles (1916), 339
Bullets for Rustlers (1940), 69
Bullets or Ballots (1936), 375
Burglar Who Robbed Death (The) (1913), 465
Burn 'Em Up O'Connor (1939), 392
Burning Daylight (1920), 299, 301
Burnt Fingers (1927), 368
Busses Roar (1942), 456
Butler's Blunder (The) (1918), 190
By the Light of the Silvery Moon (1953), 50
By Whose Hand? (1915), 273
By Whose Hand? (1927), 334

-C-

Cabaret Singer (The) (1913), 234
Cabaret Singer (The) (1915), 272
Cactus Cut-Up (1949), 144
Cactus Nell (1917), 89, 92
Cafe Hostell (1939), 247
Caged Bird (The) (1913), 420
Calford in the Movies (1928), 81
Calford on Horseback (1928), 81
Calford Vs. Redskins (1928), 81
California Firebrand (1948), 74
California Gold Rush (1946), 431
California in '49 (1924), 61, 403
California Oil Crooks (The) (1913), 408
Call A Messenger (1939), 378
Call From Home (A) (1913), 232
Call of the North (The) (1921), 302
Call of the Road (The) (1913), 278
Call of the Waves (The) (1914), 34
Call of Yesterday (The) (1915), 442
Called Back (1914), 115, 120
Campbells Are Coming (The) (1915), 35
Campus Sleuth (1948), 143
Cannonball Express (The) (1933), 13, 15
Canyon Ambush (1952), 24
Canyon Raiders (1951), 23
Captain America (1943), 66, 71

Captain Billy's Mate (1913), 32
Captain Blood (1924), 451
Captain Kate (1911), 464
Captain Kidd (1913), 353
Capture of Grizzly Adams (The) (1982), 436
Car of Death (The) (1914), 97, 101
Cardboard Baby (The) (1909), 176
Carmen (1913), 420
Carmen of the Border (1923), 38
Carpet From Bagdad (The) (1915), 461, 469
Caryl of the Mountains (1914), 467
Case at Law (1917), 278
Case of the Stuttering Bishop (The) (1937), 245, 376
Casey of the Coast Guard (1926), 300, 305
Cassidy (1917), 278
Castle of Despair (The) (1913), 55
Cat Creeps (The) (1946), 266
Cattle Empire (1958), 26
Caught Bluffing (1922), 361, 365, 402
Caught in the Act (1913), 233
Caught in the Act (1917), 58
Celebrated Case (A) (1914), 269, 272
Certain Rich Man (A) (1921), 330
Chain Lightning (1922), 125
Chains (1912), 438
Chalice of Sorrow (The) (1916), 358
Chalk Marks (1924), 304, 423
Challenge of Chance (The) (1919), 397
Challenge of the Law (1920), 299, 301
Chance Shot (A) (1911), 176
Changed Lives (1916), 122
Chaperon Gets a Duckling (The) (1912), 177, 408
Charlie Chan in Panama (1940), 162, 168
Chasing the Limited (1915), 220
Cheaters (1927), 306
Cheating Blondes (1933), 86, 371
Cherokee Flash (The) (1945), 204
Cherokee Kid (The) (1927), 343
Cheyenne Rides Again (1937), 19
Cheyenne Wildcat (1944), 429
Chicago Confidential (1957), 26
Chicken A La King (1928), 343
Chicken Every Sunday (1948), 255
Child of the Sea (A) (1913), 466
Children of Jazz (1923), 450
Child's Influence (A) (1913), 233
China Clipper (1936), 375
Chinatown Charlie (1928), 134
Chinatown Mystery (The) (1928), 29, 31, 39
Chinese Ring (1947), 289
Chip of the Flying U (1914), 461, 467, 468
Chorus Girl (The) (1912), 229
Cinder Path (1927), 79
Cinderella Jones (1946), 457
Circle of Fate (The) (1913), 408
Circular Staircase (The) (1915), 109

Circus Girl's Romance (The) (1915), 219
Circus Mary (1915), 317
Circus Rookies (1928), 134
Circus Sarah (1917), 37
Citizen Kane (1941), 285
City Limits (1941), 70
City of Dim Faces (The) (1918), 412
City That Never Sleeps (The) (1924), 473
Clairvoyant Swindlers (The) (1915), 410
Clancy of the Mounted (1932), 449, 452
Clarence (1922), 472
Classified (1925), 451
Clearing the Trail (1928), 81
Clever Dummy (A) (1917), 89, 92
Closed Door (The) (1915), 410
Clothes Make the Pirate (1925), 367
Cloud Rider (The) (1925), 304
Clown and the Kid (The) (1961), 435
Cobra Woman (1944), 264
Code of the Cow Country (1927), 404
Code of the Prairie (1944), 429
Code of the Range (1927), 281
Code of the West (1947), 47
Cody of the Pony Express (1950), 427, 433
College Chums (1913), 232
College Days (1926), 367
College Humor (1933), 375
College Love (1929), 77, 83
Come and Get It (1929), 414
Come and Get It (1936), 321
Comedy and Tragedy (1914), 308, 315
Comrade John (1915), 174, 181
Conductor's Courtship (The) (1914), 98, 100
Confession (1937), 246
Confidence girl (1952), 211
Confiscated Count (The) (1914), 179
Conflict (The) (1915), 442
Conflict (1936), 162, 166
Conqueror (The) (1914), 439
Conquest of Cheyenne (1946), 431
Conrad in Quest of His Youth (1920), 445, 461, 471
Conscience Fund (The) (1913), 466
Conspiracy Against the King (A) (1911), 311
Contraband Cargo (1949), 157
Convicted Women (1940), 69
Convict's Code (1939), 378
Convict's Daughter (The) (1913), 234
Convict's Parole (The) (1912), 312
Cooky's Adventure (1915), 409
Coquette's Awakening (The) (1915), 469
Coral (1915), 220
Cordelia the Magnificent (1923), 342
Corner in Cotton (A) (1916), 421
Coronado (1935), 453
Corsican Brothers (The) (1941), 243, 249
Cost of Hatred (The) (1917), 461, 470

Counsel for Crime (1937), 453
Count of Monte Cristo (The) (1911), 228
Coupon Courtship (A) (1913), 178
Courtin' Wildcats (1929), 334
Courtship of Andy Hardy (The) (1942), 393
Covered Wagon (The) (1923), 418
Cowboy and the Prizefighter (1949), 416
Cowboy Courage (1925), 282
Cradle Buster (The) (1922), 275
Cradle of Courage (The) (1920), 116, 124
Creed of the Klan (The) (1915), 441
Crime and Punishment (1917), 274
Crime of Thought (The) (1915), 218
Criminal Code (The) (1914), 55
Crimson Canary (The) (1945), 265
Crimson Colors (1927), 80
Crimson Flash (The) (1927), 329, 333
Crimson Ghost (The) (1946), 200, 202, 205
Crimson Key (The) (1947), 288
Crimson Wing (The) (1915), 443
Crimson Yoke (The) (1916), 357
Crooked Trail (The) (1936), 19
Crook's Romance (A) (1921), 103
Cross Country Run (The) (1929), 82
Cross Purposes (1916), 357
Crossed Currents (1921), 398
Crossed Signals (1926), 105
Crossed Trails (1920), 153
Crucible of Life (1917), 293
Cruise of the Hellion (The) (1927), 369
Crusader (The) (1922), 303
Cry Havoc (1943), 327
Crystal (The) (1915), 355
Cupid and Cohen's (1916), 339
Cupid Angling (1918), 182
Cupid Beats Father (1915), 57
Cupid Takes a Taxi (1915), 55
Curse of the Desert (The) (1915), 34
Curse of the Red Man (The) (1911), 463
Custer's Last Raid (1912), 31
Custer's Last Scout (1914), 218
Custer's Last Stand (1936), 77, 86
Cycle of Fate (The) (1916), 109
Cyclone Smith Plays Trumps (1919), 192
Cyclone Smith's Comeback (1919), 192

-D-

Daddy Long Legs (1931), 474
Dad's Girls (1911), 464
Daisy Cowboy (The) (1911), 308, 312
Daisy Wins the Day (1913), 234
Dakota (1945), 72, 203
Damaged Lives (1937), 392
Damon and Pythias (1914), 115, 120, 355
Dance at Aleck Fontaine's (The) (1915), 441
Dance, Charlie, Dance (1937), 246
Dancer (The) (1914), 420
Dancer (The) (1915), 355

Dancing Craze (The) (1914), 236
Dancing Doll (The) (1915), 278
Dancing Sweeties (1930), 370
Danger Island (1931), 13, 15
Danger Rider (The) (1928), 334
Dangerous Adventure (A) (1922), 291, 293, 296
Dangerous Age (The) (1922), 359
Dangerous Intruder (1945), 253
Dangerous Love (1921), 342
Dangerous Odds (1925), 196
Dangerous Paths (1921), 60
Dangers of a Bride (1917), 91
Dante's Inferno (1917), 37
Daredevil (The) (1923), 345
Daredevil Dan (1917), 444
Daredevils of the West (1943), 4, 6, 10
Daring Change (The) (1917), 358
Darkest Hour (The) (1916), 411
Darling Dandy (1915), 442
Darling Young Person (The) (1914), 440
Daughter of Don Q (1946), 21, 66, 73
Daughter of Kings (1915), 421
Daughter of the Jungle (A) (1915), 216, 219
Daughter of the Law (A) (1921), 38
Daughter of the Nile (A) (1915), 317
Daughter of the Sioux (A) (1925), 61
Daughter of the Wilderness (A) (1913), 308, 315
Daughters of Today (1924), 366
Dawn Express (The) (1942), 374, 381
Dawn of Freedom (The) (1916), 397
Days of Buffalo Bill (1946), 431
Days of '49 (1912), 408
Days of '49 (The) (1924), 53, 61, 403
Daytime Wives (1923), 296
Dazzling Coeds (The) (1927), 80
Dead Alive (The) (1916), 274
Dead End (1937), 19
Dead Line (The) (1914), 355
Dead Man's Gold (1948), 432
Dead Men Tell (1941), 9
Dead or Alive (1921), 413
Dead-Shot Baker (1917), 337, 340
Dead Yesterday (A) (1916), 357
Deadly Battle at Hicksville (The) (1914), 179
Deadwood Dick (1940), 65, 69, 415
Deal in Diamonds (A) (1915), 55
Dean's Daughters (The) (1913), 314
Dear Old Calford (1928), 82
Dearie (1927), 369
Death Sign of High Noon (The) (1914), 409
Death Valley Scotty's Mine (1912), 177, 408
Deceiver (The) (1920), 342
Demand for Justice (A) (1913), 99
Demon of the Rails (The) (1914), 97, 101
Demon Shadow (The) (1919), 417, 422
Denver Dude (The) (1927), 39
Deputy Marshal (1949), 457

Derelict (The) (1914), 409
Desert Blossoms (1921), 302
Desert Secret (The) (1924), 280
Desert Trail (The) (1912), 176
Desert Vigilante (1949), 433
Deserted at the Auto (1915), 338
Design for Scandal (1941), 169
Desperate (1947), 47
Desperate Adventure (A) (1924), 223
Desperate Adventure (A) (1938), 259, 261
Desperate Leap (A) (1915), 102
Destiny (1916), 443
Detective Kitty O'Day (1944), 251
Detective's Sister (The) (1914), 55
Devil Dogs (1928), 282
Devil Stone (The) (1916), 469
Devil, the Servant and the Man (The) (1912), 465
Devil, the Servant, and the Man (The) (1916), 469
Devil's Bait (The) (1917), 181
Devil's Brother (The) (1933), 17
Devil's Cage (The) (1928), 447
Diamond Frontier (1940), 374, 379
Diamond Master (The) (1929), 127, 134
Diamond Queen (The) (1921). 187, 193
Diamond Runners (The) (1916), 102
Diana of Eagle Mountain (1915), 355
Dignified Family (A) (1915). 442
Dip Into Society (A) (1913). 229
Diplomatic Mission (A) (1918), 294
Disappearance of Harry Worthington (The) (1915), 180
Disappearing Necklace (The) (1915), 410
Discontent (1916), 220
Discontented Husband (1924), 296, 359
Docks of New Orleans (1948), 49
Dr. Christian Meets the Women (1940), 248
Dr. Jekyll and Mr. Hyde (1912), 418, 420
Dr. Kildare's Victory (1942), 169
Does the Woman Forget? (1915), 442
Dog of Flanders (The) (1914), 420
Dog of the Regiment (A) (1927), 80
Dollar Down (1925), 184
Dolly at the Helm (1914), 316
Dolly Plays Detective (1914), 316
Dolores D'Arada, Lady of Sorrow (1914), 353
Don Daredevil Rides Again (1951), 207, 209, 210
Don Desperado (1927), 333
Don Juan Quilligan (1945), 253
Don Juan's Three Nights (1926), 346
Don Winslow of the Navy (1941), 373, 381
Donner Pass: The Road to Survival (1978), 436
Don't Call Me Little Girl (1921), 446
Don't Get Personal (1936), 165
Don't Monkey with the Buzzsaw (1914), 179
Don't Shoot (1922), 364
Doorway of Destruction (The) (1915), 35

Dorothy Dares (1917), 444
Dorothy Vernon of Haddon Hall (1924), 451
Dottie's New Doll (1912), 419
Double Cinched (1923), 280
Double Crossed (1916), 122
Double Crossed (1921), 129
Double Dealing (1923), 299, 303
Double Harness (1933), 17
Double Speed (1920), 471
Double Trouble (1941), 285
Dove in the Eagle's Nest (The) (1913), 420
Down Argentine Way (1940), 8
Down in San Diego (1941), 249
Down to the Sea in Ships (1922), 271, 275
Dragon's Net (The) (1920), 215, 216, 223
Dream Girl (1921), 194
Dream Seekers (The) (1915), 410
Dress Reform (1913), 233
Driftwood (1912), 464
Dropped From the Clouds (1917), 189
Drummer's Note Book (The) (1913), 231
Drummer's Trunk (The) (1915), 338
Drums of the Desert (1940), 70
Du Barry Was a Lady (1943), 10
Duchess (The) (1915), 355
Dude Cowboy (1941), 105, 285
Dude Desperado (The) (1927), 79
Duffy's Tavern (1945), 137, 140
Duke of the Navy (1942), 250
Duke's Plan (The) (1910), 29, 31
Dumb Wooing (The) (1912), 312
Duped (1925), 104
Dynamite Allen (1921), 364

-E-

Eagle's Eye (The) (1918), 418, 422
Eagle's Nest (The) (1915), 188
Eagle's Talons (The) (1923), 125
East Lynn in Bugville (1914), 236
Easy Money (1914), 236
Easy Money (1919), 362
Easy Payments (1913), 439
Ebb Tide (1915), 469
Edge of the Law (The) (1917), 444
Eight Girls in a Boat (1933), 159, 164
El Paso Stampede (1953), 25
Elder Brother (The) (1913), 314
Eleanor's Catch (1916), 357
Elektra (1910), 308
Elise, the Forester's Daughter (1913), 315
Elk's Tooth (The) (1924), 38
Ella Wanted to Elope (1916), 57
Elmo, the Fearless (1920), 30, 127, 128
Elmo, the Mighty (1919), 29, 37
Elopement in Rome (An) (1912), 177, 179
Elsa Maxwell's Hotel for Women (1939), 162, 168
Elusive Enemy (The) (1916), 36

Emblems of Love (1924), 38
Emerald Pin (The) (1916), 188
Emergency Squad (1940), 337, 344
Empty Saddle (The) (1925), 403
End of the Feud (The) (1912), 438
End of the Umbrella (The) (1914), 316
Enemy of Women (1944), 415
Enemy Sex (The) (1924), 473
Engineer's Romance (The) (1910), 310
Enter Madame (1935), 390
Entertaining Uncle (1913), 178
Ermine and Rhinestones (1925), 367, 447
Escape by Night (1937), 377
Escape From Crime (1942), 456
Eternal Bond (The) (1914), 409
Eternal Flame (The) (1922), 95
Even As Eve (1920), 295
Everybody's Hobby (1939), 425, 428
Everygirl (1915), 317
Everyheart (1915), 56
Everything for Sale (1921), 472
Exclusive Rights (1926), 39
Excuse My Dust (1920), 116, 124
Exit Smiling (1926), 133
Exploits of Elaine (1914), 227, 236
Exposed (1947), 73
Extra! Extra! (1922), 364
Extravagance (1915), 356
Eye for an Eye (An) (1915), 55

-F-

Fable of Hazel's Two Husbands and What Became of Them (1915), 442
Fable of Lutie (1914), 440
Fable of the Divine Spark That Had A Short Circuit (The) (1915), 441
Fable of the Galumptious Girl (The) (1915), 441
Fable of the Highroller and the Buzzing Blondine (The) (1915), 442
Fable of the Two Sensational Failures (The) (1915), 442
Fabulous Suzanne (The) (1946), 254
Face From the Past (A) (1913), 315
Faces (1968), 78, 87
Faded Flower (The) (1916), 422
Failure (The) (1915), 91
Faith of Her Fathers (The) (1915), 355
Falcon in Hollywood (1944), 252
Falcon's Adventure (The) (1946), 47
Falcon's Brother (The) (1942), 10
Fall of the Romanoffs (1917), 278
False Alarm (The) (1914), 440
False Brands (1922), 195
False Faces (1943), 251
False Pride (1925), 447
False Prophet (1917), 412
Family Affair (A) (1937), 391
Family Honeymoon (1948), 383

Family Skeleton (The) (1914), 179
Family Tree (His) (1917), 189
Family Upstairs (The) (1926), 451
Famous Mrs. Fair (The) (1923), 303
Fangs (1927), 197
Fantomas (1920), 361, 362, 364
Farewell (1929), 82
Fargo (1952), 24
Fascination of the Fleur De Lis (The) (1915), 352, 356
Fashion Model (1945), 72
Fast Company (1918), 92
Fast Express (The) (1924), 110, 113
Fast Freight (The) (1926), 105
Fast Freight (1914), 102
Fat Bill's Wooing (1912), 177
Fatal Fortune (The) (1919), 99, 103
Fatal Legacy (The) (1913), 271
Fatal Opal (The) (1914), 409
Fatal Plunge (The) (1913), 234
Fatal Ring (The) (1917), 227, 237
Fate of America (1916), 273
Fate's Midnight Hour (1914), 272
Father's Devotion (A) (1914), 235
Fatty's Echo (1915), 180
Favorite Son (The) (1913), 31
Fearmakers (The) (1958), 257
Feathered Serpent (The) (1948), 49, 50
Feathertop (1916), 274
Federal Agents Vs. Underworld, Inc. (1949), 43, 44, 49
Federal Operator 99 (1945), 66, 71
Feet of Mud (1924), 346
Felix O'Day (1920), 422
Feud (The) (1914), 354
Fickle Blacksmith (The) (1918), 192
Fickle Freak (The) (1913), 178
Fiery Introduction (A) (1915), 356
Fifth Avenue Models (1925), 446
Fight for Love (A) (1919), 59
Fight for Millions (A) (1918), 107, 111
Fight to a Finish (1915), 220
Fighting Back (1948), 163, 170
Fighting Caballero (1935), 86
Fighting Chaplin (The) (1913), 271
Fighting Cowboy (The) (1933), 414
Fighting Fate (1921), 112
Fighting Finish (The) (1927), 80
Fighting for Love (1917), 444
Fighting for Victory (1928), 81
Fighting Fury (1924), 104
Fighting Grin (The) (1918), 111
Fighting Guide (The) (1922), 112
Fighting Heiress (The) (1917), 412
Fighting Marshal (The) (1931), 85
Fighting Ranger (1925), 196
Fighting Redhead (The) (1949), 416, 433

Fighting Spirit (1926), 79
Fighting Stallion (The) (1926), 53, 62
Fighting Three (The) (1927), 414
Fighting to Win (1926), 79
Fighting Trail (The) (1917), 337, 340
Fighting With Buffalo Bill (1926), 39
Fighting Youth (1935), 164
Figure in Black (The) (1915), 410
Figures Don't Lie (1927), 348
Filling His Own Shoes (1917), 301
Final Reckoning (A) (1929), 127, 134
Finder Keepers (1929), 306
Fingerprints (1931), 362, 363, 371
Finishing Touch (The) (1916), 91
Fire Eater (The) (1921), 130
Fire Fighters (The) (1927), 300, 306
Fire-Fighting Zowaves (The) (1913), 271
Firebrands of Arizona (1944), 41, 429
Firechief's Daughter (The) (1910), 463
Fired Cook (The) (1913), 178
Firefly of France (The) (1918), 116, 123
First Commandment (The) (1915), 269, 273
First Law (The) (1918), 422
First Love (1913), 234
First Quarrel (The) (1915), 338
Five Franc Piece (The) (1916), 110
Five-Pound Note (The) (1915), 396
Flame of the West (1918), 358
Flames of Desire (1924), 331
Flames of Passion (1923), 446
Flaming Disc (The) (1920), 127, 128
Flaming Hour (The) (1922), 303
Flash (The) (1923), 446
Flash Gordon (1936), 160, 161, 162, 165
Flash Gordon Conquers the Universe (1940), 162
Flash Gordon's Trip to Mars (1938), 162, 167
Flashing Oars (1927), 80
Flat Harmony (1917), 189
Flattery (1925), 297
Flattop (1952), 24
Flaw in the Alibi (The) (1914), 100
Flickering Light (A) (1916), 122
Flight Into Nowhere (1938), 454
Flight of a Night Bird (The) (1915), 356
Flight Of The Crow (The) (1913), 466
Flirt (The) (1917), 221
Flirt: A Namoradeira (The) (1916), 220
Flower Girl of Paris (The) (1908), 309
Flower Girl's Romance (The) (1912), 55
Flower of Faith (The) (1914), 469
Flying Disc Man From Mars (1950), 259, 266
Flying Down to Rio (1933), 17
Flying G-Men (1939), 64, 65, 67
Flying High (1929), 82
Flying Switch (The) (1913), 99
Flying to Fortune (1912), 419
Fog (1912), 313

Follow That Blonde (1946), 45, 46
Follow the Boys (1944), 264
Follow the Girl (1917), 444
Following A Clue (1915), 180
Fool's Awakening (A) (1924), 398
Footloose Heiress (1937), 377
Footprint Clue (The) (1913), 100
For a Woman (1914), 235
For Her (1912), 313
For Her Boy's Sake (1913), 420
For Her Sister's Sake (1910), 310
For High Stakes (1915), 273
For Love and Gold (1916), 110
For Sale–A Life (1912), 419
For the Commonwealth (1915), 181
For the Honor of the Name (1911), 229
Forbidden Fruit (1921), 471
Forest Rose (The) (1912), 420
Forgetful Flossie (1913), 231
Forgotten (1933), 349
Forgotten Prayer (The) (1916), 122
Forgotten Women (1931), 371
Forgotten Women (1949), 145, 255
Fort Frayne (1926), 61, 403
Fortieth Door (The) (1924), 150, 153
40-Horse Hawkins (1924), 104
Forty Thieves (1944), 287
45 Minutes From Broadway (1926), 368
Foul Play (1911), 311
Foundling (The) (1909), 309
Fourflusher (The) (1919), 445
Fourth Horseman (The) (1932), 40
Fra Diavolo (1933), 17
Framed (1927), 348
Frame-Up (The) (1915), 410
Frame-Up (The) (1937), 453
Francis Marion, the Swamp Fox (1914), 272
Frankenstein (1910), 310
Freddie Steps Out (1946). 141
Frederick the Great (1914), 316
Free, Blonde and 21 (1940), 8
Freeze-Out (The) (1921), 299, 302
Fringe of Society (The) (1917), 182
Fringe of the Glove (The) (1914), 55
From Dawn Till Dark (1913), 32
From Peril to Peril (1914), 97, 101
From the Lion's Jaws (1914), 216
From the Submerged (1912), 438
From This Day Forward (1946), 44, 46
From Tyranny to Liberty (1910), 310
From Wash to Washington (1914), 421
Frontier Gambler (1956), 244, 257
Frontier Outlaws (1944), 415
Frontier Revenge (1948), 433
Frontiersman (The) (1927), 134
Frozen Assets (1933), 388
Fruit of Folly (The) (1915), 181

Fugitive (The) (1925), 446
Fugitive (The) (1933), 387, 388
Fugitive From Justice (A) (1940), 325
Further Adventures of Stingaree (The) (1917), 407, 412
Fury (1927), 197

-G-

Gaiety Girl (The) (1924), 297
Gallant Fool (The) (1926), 404
Gallant Legion (The) (1948), 66, 74
Galloping Ghost (The) (1931), 77, 84
Galloping Hoofs (1924), 150, 154
Galloping Kid (The) (1922), 364
Gamblers (The) (1919), 301
Gambling Daughters (1941), 393
Game of Wits (A) (1914), 337
Gang Bullets (1938), 378
Gang Busters (1942), 41
Garden of Shadows (The) (1916), 318
Gasoline Buckaroo (1921), 38
Gasoline Habit (The) (1917), 189
Gauchos of El Dorado (1941), 263
Gay Blades (1946), 170
Gay Blade's Last Scrape (1916), 339
Gay Caballero (The) (1932), 386
General Bunko's Victory (1913), 178
Gentleman From America (The) (1923), 130
Gentleman of Leisure (A) (1915), 337
Gentleman of Quality (A) (1919), 294
Gertie Gets the Cash (1914), 179
Get-Away (The) (1941), 249
Get Going (1943), 263
Get Out And Get Under (1914), 235
Getting in Wrong (1915), 57
Getting Reuben Back (1914), 235
Ghost City (1921), 99, 103
Ghost of Mother Eve (The) (1914), 315
Ghost of Smiling Jim (The) (1914), 34
Ghost's Warning (The) (1911), 311
Giant Powder (1916), 188
Giant Power (1916), 110
Gift of Gab (The) (1917), 301
Gilded Cage (The) (1915), 442
Girl, a Guard, and a Garret (A) (1915), 338
Girl and the Bachelor (The) (1915), 273
Girl and the Explorer (The) (1914), 272
Girl and the Game (The) (1915), 98, 102
Girl and the Gangster (The) (1913), 408
Girl and the Judge (The) (1913), 466
Girl and the Outlaw (The) (1913), 308, 315
Girl and the Stowaway (The) (1914), 272
Girl at the Cabaret (The) (1913), 420
Girl at the Cupola (The) (1912), 465
Girl at the Throttle (The) (1914), 97
Girl Detective (The) (1915), 174, 180
Girl From Arizona (The) (1910), 226, 228
Girl From Avenue A (1940), 8

Girl From Frisco (The) (1915), 405, 411
Girl From Monterey (The) (1943), 251
Girl From Nowhere (The) (1919), 353, 358
Girl From the West (1923), 95
Girl From Thunder Mountain (The) (1914), 441
Girl In His House (The) (1918), 294
Girl In Every Port (1928), 197, 348
Girl In Lower 9 (The) (1916), 357
Girl In Pants (The) (1914), 236
Girl In Room 313 (1940), 8, 455
Girl In the Next Room (The) (1912), 229
Girl In the Saddle (1921), 193
Girl In the Taxi (The) (1921), 37
Girl Loves Boy (1937), 391
Girl Named Mary (A) (1919), 470
Girl of the Limberlost (A) (1924), 446
Girl of the People (A) (1914), 316
Girl of the Rio (1932), 371
Girl of the Secret Service (The) (1915), 34
Girl of the West (1925), 196
Girl on the Spot (1946), 261, 266
Girl on the Stairs (The) (1924), 399
Girl Reporter (The) (1913), 232
Girl Who Dared (The) (1944), 71, 251
Girl Who Feared Daylight (The) (1916), 318
Girl Who Had a Soul (The) (1915), 317
Girl Who Lost (The) (1917), 352, 358
Girl With the Lantern (The) (1912), 465
Girls About Town (1931), 13, 15
Girls Can Play (1937), 453
Girls in Chains (1943), 429
Girls in Prison (1956), 26
Girls Will Be Boys (1913), 234
Giuseppe's Good Fortune (1912), 438
Glamour for Sale (1940), 248
Glamour Girl (1948), 143
Glass Key (The) (1942), 326
Glory (1917), 91
Going Some (1914), 235
Going Some (1920), 301
Going Up (1923), 366
Gold Is Not All (1910), 463
Gold Madness (1923), 296, 353, 359
Golden Bed (The) (1925), 451
Golden Eagle Trail (The) (1917), 407, 411
Golden Hoofs (1941), 9
Golden Idiot (The) (1917), 301
Gone With the Wind (1939), 5
Good Bad Man (A) (1920), 342
Good Men and Ban (1923), 413
Good Morning Judge (1928), 81
Good Morning Nurse (1917), 189
Good Ole Summer Time (The) (1913), 178
Gopher (The) (1915), 115, 121
Gossip (1923), 342
Governor (The) (1912), 313
Governor Maker (The) (1915), 218

Governor's Daughter (The) (1913), 465
Graduation Daze (1929), 83
Grand Central Murder (1942), 393
Grateful Outcast (A) (1914), 235
Gray Wolf's Ghost (The) (1919), 413
Great Circus Mystery (The) (1925), 127, 128, 132
Great Diamond Mystery (The) (1924), 330
Great Jesse James Raid (The) (1953), 416
Great Jewel Robbery (The) (1925), 297
Great Radium Mystery (The) (1919), 187, 192, 351, 353, 359
Great Secret (The) (1917), 51, 58
Great Shadow (The) (1920), 423
Great Stagecoach Robbery (1945), 41
Great Torpedo Secret (The) (1918), 59
Great Universal Mystery (The) (1914), 34, 217, 352, 354
Greater Influence (A) (1913), 233
Greatest Menace (The) (1923), 125
Greatest Show on Earth (1952), 137, 146
Green Apples (1915), 56
Green Archer (The) (1925), 150, 151, 154
Green Hornet (The) (1939), 373, 378
Green Hornet Strikes Again (The) (1940), 373, 380
Green Rose (The) (1914), 269, 272
Greyhound Limited (The) (1929), 369
Grim Toll of War (The) (1913), 271
Grip of Circumstances (The) (1914), 439
Grouch, the Engineer (1914), 97, 101
Guide for the Married Man (A) (1967), 213
Guilty (1916), 110
Guilty One (The) (1916), 352, 357
Gulf Between (The) (1916), 292
Gulf Between (1918), 294
Gun Cargo (1949), 157
Gun Justice (1933), 389
Gun Runner (1949), 144
Gun Town (1946), 283, 288
Gunfighters of the Northwest (1954), 21, 26
Gunman (The) (1952), 24
Guns Don't Argue (1957), 212
Guns of the Pecos (1937), 376
Guys and Dolls (1955), 243, 244, 257
Gypsy Flirt (The) (1912), 229

-H-

Hair Trigger Baxter (1926), 332
Hair Trigger Casey (1922), 125
Half Breed (The) (1922), 330
Half Million Bride (The) (1916), 422
Hall Room Girls (The) (1913), 232
Ham Among the Redskins (1915), 409
Ham, the Piano Mover (1914), 180
Hand of Providence (The) (1913), 233
Hand That Rocks the Cradle (The) (1914), 439
Handle With Care (1922), 296

Hands in the Dark (1917), 111
Hands Off (1921), 280
Hands Up (1918), 174, 182
Hansel and Gretel (1909), 310
Happy Landing (1934), 453
Harbinger of Peace (The) (1912), 313
Harbor Island (1912), 459, 465
Harbor of Missing Men (1950), 208
Hard Fists (1927), 133
Hard Way (The) (1942), 456
Hardys Ride High (The) (1939), 392
Harvester (The) (1927), 348
Hash House Count (The) (1913), 178
Haunted Harbor (1944), 6, 11
Haunted Hearts (1915), 355
Haunted Island (1928), 39
Haunted Valley (1923), 175, 183
Hawk of the Hills (1927), 151, 152, 155
Hawk's Trail (The) (1920), 291, 295
Hazards of Helen (The) (1914), 97, 98, 100, 101
Hazel Kirke (1916), 237
Headin' West (1922), 130
Headline Hunters (1955), 458
Heart of a Cracksman (The) (1913), 353
Heart of a Mermaid (The) (1916), 318
Heart of an Artist (The) (1913), 234
Heart of Arizona (1921), 193
Heart of Lincoln (The) (1922), 38
Heart of Lincoln (The) (1915), 34
Heart of Mary Ann (The) (1917), 444
Heart of the Hills (1914), 316
Heart of the Law (The) (1913), 439
Heart of the Night Wind (The) (1914), 316
Heart of the Princess Marsari (The) (1915), 421
Hearts and Flowers (1914), 439 (Essanay)
Hearts and Flowers (1914), 353 (Universal)
Hearts and Masks (1914), 467
Hearts Crucible (A) (1916), 357
Heart's Desire (1915), 107, 109
Hearts Entangled (1913), 233
Heaven with a Barbed Wire Fence (1939), 162, 168
Hell Bent (1918), 59
Hell Hounds of the Plains (1926), 62
Hellion (The) (1924), 413
Hell's Crater (1918), 37, 190
Helping Him Out (1911), 228
Henry Aldrich for President (1941), 137, 138
Henry Aldrich Gets Glamour (1942), 326
Henry Aldrich's Little Secret (1944), 140
Henry and Dizzy (1942), 139
Her Better Self (1916), 35
Her Big Adventure (1926), 297
Her Bitter Cup (1916), 352, 357
Her Boy (1918), 278
Her Dangerous Path (1923), 361, 366
Her Defiance (1916), 356

Her Dream of Life (1916), 292
Her Dressmaker's Bills (1912), 229
Her Great Mistake (1917), 221
Her Husband's Women (1929), 474
Her Indian Mother (1910), 176
Her Kid Sister (1913), 229
Her Kingdom of Dreams (1920), 471
Her Man O'War (1926), 297
Her Mother's Secret (1915), 338
Her New Hat (1914), 236
Her Photograph (1910), 228
Her Sacrifice (1914), 467
Her Secretaries (1913), 234
Her Sister's Sin (1916), 36
Her Visitor (1912), 229
Her Wedding Night (1930), 349
Her Western Adventure (1921), 38
Here Come the Waves (1944), 137, 140
Here Comes Carter (1936), 373, 375
Here I Am a Stranger (1939), 8
Here Is My Heart (1934), 389
Hermit's Ruse (The) (1913), 100
Hero (The) (1923), 296
Heroes of the West (1932), 449, 452
Heroic Harold (1913), 229
Heroine of San Juan (The) (1916), 36
Hidden City (The) (1915), 35
Hidden Hand (The) (1917), 395, 397
Hidden Hand (The) (1942), 456
Hidden Love (A) (1913), 233
Hideout (1934), 17
Hideout (1949), 74
High and the Mighty (The) (1954), 458
High Cost of Starving (The) (1917), 189
High Hand (The) (1914), 55
High School Girl (1935), 391
High School Hero (1946), 141
High Tide (1947), 457
Highest Trump (The) (1919), 294
Highway of Hope (The) (1918), 470
Highway Patrol (1938), 454
Highway 301 (1950), 209
Hills of Missing Men (1922), 103
Hills of Silence (The) (1914), 353
Hiram's Hotel (1914), 179
Hired, Tired and Fired (1916), 188
His Aunt Emma (1913), 233
His Awful Daughter (1913), 231
His Big Chance (1914), 316
His Birthday (1911), 228
His Birthright (1918), 412
His Buddy's Wife (1925), 367
His College Wife (1915), 55
His Fight (1914), 467
His First Flame (1927), 347
His Foreign Wife (1927), 369
His Great Triumph (1916), 422

His Greatest Battle (1925), 282
His Guardian Angel (1915), 316
His Lost Gamble (1913), 233
His Majesty Dick Turpin (1916), 35
His Marriage Wow (1924), 346
His Mother's Hope (1912), 313
His Mysterious Profession (1915), 56
His Nemesis (1914), 101
His Pal's Request (1913), 352, 353
His Pride and Shame (1916), 91
His Private Secretary (1933), 349
His Return (1916), 356
His Squaw (1912), 31
His Weak Moment (1933), 388
His Wedding Scare (1943), 286
His Wife's Stratagem (1912), 229
His Younger Brother (1911), 418
Hobo and the Myth (The) (1913), 178
Hold That Line (1952), 255
Hold That Woman (1940), 322, 325
Hold Your Man (1929), 349
Hole in the Mountain (1917), 412
Hollywood Cowboy (1937), 391
Hollywood Goes to Bat (1950), 75
Hollywood Varieties (1949), 433
Home Maker (The) (1925), 451
Home on the Range (1946), 72
Home Run Baker's Double (1914), 272
Home Spun (1913), 439
Home Sweet Home (1911), 228
Homlock Shermes (1913), 232
Honesty–The Best Policy (1926), 297
Honeymoon (1947), 45, 47
Honeymoon Flats (1928), 81, 474
Honeymoon Ranch (1920), 149, 153
Honeymoon Surprise (The) (1917), 188
Honeymooners (The) (1911), 418
Honeymooners (The) (1915), 56
Honky Tonk (1941), 244, 249
Honor of the Ormsbys (The) (1915), 317
Honor of the Press (The) (1932), 85
Honor of the Range (1934), 389
Honor Thy Country (1916), 51, 58
Hoodoo (The) (1910), 228
Hoodooed on His Wedding Day (1913), 178
Hoosier Schoolboy (1937), 377
Hop, the Devil's Brew (1916), 220
Hope (The) (1920), 445
Hope Diamond Mystery (The) (1921), 291, 295
Horse That Wouldn't Stay Hitched (The) (1913), 178
Hospital Hoax (A) (1912), 177
Hot Cargo (1946), 170
Hot Heels (1928), 197
Hot Money (1936), 375
Hot News (1953), 256
Hot Steel (1940), 379

Hotel for Women (1939), 6, 7
Hour and the Man (The) (1914), 439
Hour of Reckoning (The) (1927), 298
Hour of Terror (An) (1913), 232
House of a Thousand Candles (1915), 292
House of Cards (The) (1909), 310
House of Hate (The) (1918), 227, 237
House of Silence (The) (1918), 123
House of the Seven Gables (The) (1910), 310
House on Hocum Hill (The) (1916), 340
House Without a Key (The) (1926), 150, 154, 155
Houses of Glass (1915), 181
How a Horseshoe Upset a Happy Family (1912), 313
How Green Paid the Rent (1914), 33
How Green Saved His Mother-in-Law (1914), 33
How Jim Proposed (1911), 176
How Texas Got Left (1911), 405, 408
How They Stopped the Run on the Bank (1911), 464
Hubby's New Coat (1913), 234
Hubby's Night Off (1914), 179
Human Hearts (1914), 396
Human Menace (1915), 355
Human Pendulum (The) (1916), 220
Human Tiger (The) (1918), 191
Humphrey Takes a Chance (1950), 266
Hungry Hearts (1922), 303
Huntress of Men (The) (1916), 318
Hush (1921), 471
Hypnotic Nell (1912), 177
Hypnotizing Mamie (1913), 178

-I-

I Am Guilty (1921), 445
I Can Explain (1922), 296
I Can Get It for You Wholesale (1951), 210
I Hate Women (1934), 389
I Love My Husband, But! (1946), 254
I Loved You Wednesday (1933), 373, 375
I Married an Angel (1942), 250
I Saw Him First (1912), 177
I Take This Oath (1940), 248
I Was a Teenage Frankenstein (1957), 26
I Was Framed (1942), 455
Idea Girl (1946), 457
Identification (The) (1914), 98, 101
Idle Wives (1916), 57
Idol of the Hour (The) (1913), 420
"If Only" Jim (1921), 342, 402
I'll Cry Tomorrow (1956), 244, 257
I'll Get Her Yet (1916), 188
I'll Wait For You (1941), 249
Immediate Lee (1916), 122
Impulse (1922), 53, 60
In a Moment of Temptation (1927), 216, 223
In Again, Out Again (1917), 395, 397

In Convict's Garb (1913), 439
In Double Harness (1915), 273
In Early Arizona (1938), 86
In His Brother's Place (1919), 422
In Old California (1929), 299, 306
In Old California, When the Gringos Came (1911), 463
In Old Cheyenne (1931), 84
In the African Jungle (1917), 470
In the Balance (1917), 293
In the Days of Buffalo Bill (1922), 402
In the Days of Chivalry (1911), 311
In the Days of Daniel Boone (1923), 195, 402
In the Fall of '64 (1914), 29, 33
In the Land of the Tortilla (1916), 340
In the Talons of an Eagle (1917), 111
In the West (1923), 60
In the Wolf's Fangs (1914), 216
In Treason's Grasp (1917), 37
In Tune with the Wild (1914), 459, 467
In Walked Charley (1932), 452
Incognito (1915), 56
Incredible Petrified World (1960), 27
Indiscretion (1921), 295
Indestructible Mr. Jenks (The) (1913), 178
Indian Legend (An) (1912), 31
Indian Maid's Warning (The) (1913), 178
Indian Scout's Vengeance (1910), 176
Indians Are Coming (The) (1930), 151, 157
Indian's Lament (1917), 216, 221
Inheritance (1915), 443
Innocent Affair (An) (1948), 382
Inside Story (1939), 162, 168
Insurance Nightmare (1915), 409
International Heart Breaker (An) (1911), 312
International Squadron (1941), 455
Into the Desert (1912), 419
Into the Net (1924), 362, 365, 366
Invaders (The) (1913), 408
Invasion USA (1953), 24, 146
Invisible Divorce (1920), 295
Invisible Hand (The) (1920), 277, 279
Invisible Informer (The) (1946), 205, 431
Invisible Monster (1950), 207, 208
Invisible Woman (The) (1941), 380
Irish Eyes Are Smiling (1944), 244, 252
Iron Claw (The) (1916), 227, 237
Iron Test (The) (1918), 337, 341
Isle of Forgotten Sins (1943), 251
Isle of Hope (The) (1925), 299, 304
It Is Never Too Late to Mend (1913), 313
It May Come to This (1914), 235
It's Cheaper to Be Married (1917), 188
It's Great to Be Married (1916), 188
It's Love I'm After (1937), 246

-J-
Jacqueline, or Blazing Barriers (1923), 275
Jade Box (The) (1930), 127, 132, 134
Jake the Plumber (1927), 343
James Brothers of Missouri (The) (1950), 137, 145
Jared Fairfax's Millions (1915), 180
Jaws of Steel (1927), 306
Jeanne of the Woods (1915), 317
Jesse James Rides Again (1947), 200, 205
Jessie, the Stolen Child (1909), 309
Jest of Talky Jones (The) (1918), 340
Jewels (The) (1912), 312
Jilted (1912), 419
Jim and Joe (1911), 463
Jimmy on the Job (1915), 55
John Needham's Double (1916), 220
Johnnie's Birthday (1916), 339
Johnny the Barber (1915), 338
Johnny's Jumble (1916), 339
Joke on Jane (The) (1914), 179
Jolt (The) (1921), 361, 364
Jones' Jonah Day (1913), 178
Joseph in the Land of Egypt (1914), 418, 420
Joyce of the North Woods (1913), 315
Judge Hardy and Son (1939), 393
Judge Hardy's Children (1938), 392
Judge Her Not (1921), 280
Judgement (1922), 195
Judgement of Men (The) (1915), 317
Judith of the Cumberlands (1916), 99, 102
Julia Misbehaves (1948), 255
Julie (1956), 212
Jungle Drums of Africa (1952), 22, 24
Jungle Girl (1941), 5, 21, 321, 322, 325
Jungle Master (The) (1914), 216, 218
Jungle Menace (1937), 307
Jungle Mystery (1932), 385, 387
Jungle Princess (The) (1923), 89, 95
Jungle Queen (1945), 259, 264, 265
Jungle Queen (The) (1915), 216, 219
Jungle Raiders (1945), 244, 253
Jungle Tragedy (A) (1917), 221
Jungle Treachery (1917), 190
Jungle Woman (1944), 264
Junior Luck (1929), 82
Junior Prom (1946), 141
Junior Year (The) (1928), 81
Just A Wife (1920), 461, 471
Just Pals (1920), 302

-K-
Kangaroo Kid (The) (1950), 244, 255
Kansas Territory (1952), 434
Kansas Terrors (The) (1939), 454
Kathleen Mavourneen (1913), 313
Kicking Through (1928), 81
Kid Boots (1926), 346

Kid Galahad (1937), 245
Kid Gloves (1929), 370
Kiddess, Kids and Kiddo (1915), 339
Kidnapped Bride (The) (1917), 221
Kill the Umpire (1916), 188
King Kong (1933), 13, 86
King Lear (1909), 309
King of Chance (1914), 409
King of Hockey (1936), 373, 376
King of the Arena (1933), 17
King of the Campus (1929), 82
King of Wild Horses (The) (1924), 366
Kings Court (1912), 98, 99
King's Game (The) (1916), 237
Kinkaid, Gambler (1916), 443
Kiss (The) (1916), 270, 274
Kiss and Make Up (1934), 453
Kiss Barrier (The) (1930), 40
Kit, the Arkansas Traveler (1914), 272
Kit Carson Over the Great Divide (1925), 418, 423
Kitchen Hero (A) (1918), 190
Kitchen Mechanic (The) (1913), 234
Knights and Ladies (1913), 231
Knockout (The) (1932), 451
Knockout Man (The) (1921), 129
Know Your Men (1921), 238

-L-

La Fiesta de Santa Barbara (1935), 391
Laddie (1926), 332
Ladies Courageous (1944), 264
Lady and the Burglar (The) (1910), 310
Lady Doctor (The) (1914), 235
Lady From the Sea (The) (1911), 419
Lady Gangster (1942), 456
Lady in a Jam (1942), 250
Lady in Distress (A) (1915), 236
Lady of Sorrows (1914), 352
Lady of the Tigers (The) (1914), 459, 468
Lady Raffles Returns (1916), 35
Lady Surrenders (A) (1930), 40
Ladybird (The) (1927), 447
Laffin' Fool (The) (1927), 281
Land o' Lizards (1916), 122
Landloper (The) (1918), 278
Landlubber (The) (1912), 177
Lass of the Lumberlands (1916), 98, 102
Last Assignment (The) (1914), 316
Last Bandit (The) (1949), 74
Last Blockhouse (The) (1913), 408
Last Dance (The) (1912), 465
Last Frontier (The) (1932), 77, 85
Last Frontier Uprising (1947), 73
Last Lap (The) (1926), 79
Last Man on Earth (The) (1924), 38
Last Man on Earth (The) (1929), 31
Last of the Duanes (1930), 13, 15

Last of the Mohicans (The) (1932), 14, 16
Last of the Night Riders (The) (1917), 190
Last of the Redmen (1947), 457
Last of Their Race (The) (1914), 354
Laugh That Died (The) (1915), 317
Laughing at Danger (1940), 248
Laundress and the Lady (The) (1913), 178
Lavender and Old Lace (1921), 423
Law Comes to Texas (The) (1936), 244, 247
Law of His Kind (The) (1914), 355
Law of the Lumberjack (The) (1914), 218
Law of the Range (1914), 218
Law of the Wild (The) (1934), 14, 18
Lawless Rider (The) (1954), 146
Leah the Forsaken (1908), 308, 309
Leatherstocking (1924), 361, 364
Legion of Lost Flyers (1939), 378
Legionnaires in Paris (1927), 134
Lena Rivers (1925), 367
Lend Me Your Name (1918), 278
Leonie (1913), 313
Leopard's Foundling (The) (1914), 459, 467
Less Than Kin (1918), 116, 123
Let No Man Escape (1914), 440
Let No Man Put Assunder (1913), 439
Let's Face It (1943), 137, 139
Let's Fight (1918), 59
Let's Make Music (1941), 162, 169
Liberty (1916), 215, 216, 221
Lieutenant Governor (The) (1915), 441
Lieutenant Jones (1913), 466
Life (1921), 398
Life in Hollywood No. 2 (1927), 298
Life in the Balance (A) (1915), 396
Life on the Border (1911), 464
Life With Blondie (1945), 253
Life Without Soul (1915), 278
Lifted Veil (The) (1913), 234
Light on Troubled Waters (A) (1913), 315
Lightnin' Flashes (1926), 196
Lightnin' in the Forest (1948), 73
Lightnin' Strikes (1926), 196
Lightnin' Wins (1926), 196
Lightning Bryce (1919), 116, 124
Lightning Express (The) (1930), 127, 129, 135
Lightning Raider (The) (1919), 227, 237
Lights Out (1923), 446
Like Wildfire (1917), 58
Lil Nor'Western (1915), 317
Limb of Satan (A) (1917), 444
Limousine Mystery (The) (1916), 318
Lines of White on a Sullen Sea (1909), 463
Lion's Claw (The) (1918), 215, 216, 222
Lion's Lair (The) (1917), 190
Lipton Cup: Introducing Sir Thomas Lipton (The) (1913), 465
Liquid Dynamite (1915), 352, 356

Little Bride of Heaven (The) (1912), 312
Little Brother of the Rich (1915), 401
Little Child Shall Lead Them (A) (1913), 465
Little Engineer (The) (1914), 97
Little Fraud (The) (1916), 318
Little Giant (The) (1926), 367
Little Johnny Jones (1929), 370
Little Mister Jim (1946), 322, 328
Little Mother (The) (1913), 439
Little Tough Guy (1938), 425, 428
Little Tough Guys in Society (1938), 425, 428
Little White Violet (The) (1915), 317
Little Woolen Shoe (The) (1912), 312
Live Wires (1921), 361, 364
Living on Love (1937), 321, 323
Lizzie and the Iceman (1914), 235
Lizzie, the Life Saver (1914), 179
Lochinvar (1909), 310
Locked Doors (1925), 473
Locked Out (1912), 229
Loggers of Hell Roarin' Mountain (The) (1921), 103
Lombardi, Limited (1919), 94
Lone Hand (The) (1922), 103
Lone Larry (1917), 189
Lone Patrol (The) (1928), 53, 62
Lone Roundup (The) (1924), 195
Lone Star Pioneers (1939), 87
Lone Wolf Spy Hunt (The) (1939), 67
Lonely Road (A) (1913), 315
Lonely Salvation (A) (1914), 316
Lonesome Trail (The) (1914), 467
Long Cold Night (The) (1914), 440
Long Loop on the Pecos (The) (1927), 332
Long Pants (1927), 347
Long Trail (The) (1917), 309, 319
Longhorn (The) (1951), 23
Look Who's Laughing (1941), 285
Lorna Doane (1911), 418
Losing Fight (The) (1914), 468
Lost–A Pair of Shoes (1914), 316
Lost at Sea (1926), 346
Lost at the Front (1927), 347
Lost Battalion (The) (1919), 301
Lost City (The) (1920), 89, 90, 93, 94
Lost Express (The) (1917), 98, 99, 103
Lost Express (The) (1926), 105
Lost in the Jungle (1911), 459, 464
Lost in the Night (1913), 233
Lost Jungle (The) (1934), 385, 386, 389, 390
Lost Ledge (The) (1915), 218
Lost Legion of the Border (The) (1917), 407, 411
Lost Necklace (The) (1911), 229
Lost Special (The) (1932), 385, 387
Lost, Strayed or Stolen (1923), 280
Louisiana Purchase (1941), 10, 326
Love Aflame (1917), 444

Love and the Law (1919), 182
Love Apple (1920), 280
Love Begins at 20 (1936), 375
Love Finds Andy Hardy (1938), 392
Love, Honor and Goodbye (1945), 253
Love in the Dark (1922), 398
Love Letters (1945), 288
Love Liar (The) (1915), 180
Love Makes 'Em Wild (1927), 347
Love Me or Leave Me (1955), 256
Love, Mumps, and Bumps (1915), 56
Love Never Dies (1916), 443
Love of Penelope (The) (1913), 466
Love Pirate (The) (1923), 343
Love Route (The) (1915), 89, 91
Love Victorious (The) (1914), 354
Lovers Three (1913), 231
Love's A-Poppin' (1953), 75
Love's Battle (1920), 192
Love's Justice (1913), 395
Love's Miracle (1912), 419
Lucile (1912), 418, 419
Lucille Love, Girl of Mystery (1914), 33, 352
Luck of Roaring Camp (The) (1910), 308, 310
Lucky Stars (1925), 346
Lullaby (The) (1924), 359
Lummox (1930), 370
Lure of the Circus (1918), 187, 190, 191, 192
Lure of the Stage (1913), 234
Lure of the West (1926), 196
Lure of the Windigo (The) (1914), 107, 109
Lure of Youth (The) (1921), 353, 359
Lurking Peril (The) (1916), 274
Luxury Liner (1948), 323, 328
Lying Wifes (1925), 367

-M-

Ma, He's Making Eyes at Me (1940), 379
McBride's Bride (1914), 179
McFadden's Flats (1927), 368
McGuire of the Mounted (1923), 131
McSweeney's Masterpiece (1914), 235
Mad Doctor of Market Street (The) (1942), 381
Mad Empress (The) (1939), 415
Mad Hermit (The) (1916), 36
Mad Monster (The) (1942), 381
Madame Cubist (1916), 318
Madcap Queen of Crona (The) (1916), 35
Madcap Queen of Gredshoffen (The) (1915), 34
Madonna (The) (1915), 55
Madonna of the Slums (The) (1913), 32
Madonna's Secret (The) (1946), 204
Maid of Niagara (The) (1910), 228
Mail Clerk's Temptation (The) (1912), 419
Making a Man of Johnny (1915), 338
Making Good (1923), 195
Making Good (1926), 79
Making Monkey Business (1917), 189

Making Over Father (1915), 57
Making the Grade (1921), 302
Mammy's Rose (1916), 57
Man About Town (1939), 428
Man and Beast (1917), 189
Man and His Other Self (1913), 466
Man Beneath (The) (1919), 278
Man Between (The) (1914), 353
Man Between (The) (1923), 365
Man for A' That (A) (1914), 440
Man for Hardpan (The) (1927), 332
Man From Downing Street (The) (1922), 330
Man From Funeral Range (The) (1918), 116, 123
Man From Medicine Hat (The) (1921), 102
Man From Rainbow Valley (1946), 72
Man From Sonora (1951), 23
Man From the West (The) (1926), 332
Man From Tia Juana (The) (1917), 412
Man Hater (The) (1921), 38
Man In Irons (The) (1915), 410
Man in Motley (1915), 441
Man-Made Monster (1941), 374, 380
Man Must Live (A) (1925), 367
Man of Might (1919), 108, 111
Man of the Forest (The) (1921), 330
Man or Mouse (1948), 143
Man Outside (The) (1913), 439
Man They Could Not Hang (The) (1939), 65, 67
Man Trackers (The) (1921), 402
Man Trailer (The) (1934), 389
Man Who Came Back (The) (1919), 294
Man Who Found Himself (The) (1915), 396
Man Who Walked Alone (The) (1945), 6, 11
Man Who Was Misunderstood (The) (1914), 396
Man Who Wouldn't Talk (1940), 162, 168
Man Who Wouldn't Tell (The) (1918), 294
Man Without a Face (1928), 156
Manager of the B & A (The) (1916), 102
Manhattan Moon (1935), 159, 164
Manhunt at San Remo (1917), 412
Manhunt of Mystery Island (1945), 199, 203
Man's Home (A) (1921), 472
Man's Soul (A) (1914), 100
Manicurist and the Mutt (The) (1913), 177
Mansion of Misery (A) (1913), 466
Marble Heart (The) (1913), 420
Marked Trails (1945), 244, 251
Marriage Clause (The) (1926), 298
Marriage Is a Private Affair (1944), 327
Marry the Girl (1937), 245
Mars Attacks the World (1938), 167
Marshal of Cedar Rock (1953), 25
Marshal of Laredo (1945), 430
Martin Chuzzlewit (1912), 313
Martyrs of the Alamo (The) (1915), 89, 91
Mary Ann in Society (1917), 444
Mary Stuart (1913), 308, 314

Mary's Duke (1915), 317
Mary's Romance (1913), 232
Mashers (The) (1914), 236
Masked Angel (1928), 39
Masked Marvel (The) (1943), 283, 287
Masked Rider (The) (1919), 437, 445
Masked Woman (1927), 184
Masked Wrestler (The) (1914), 441
Master and Pupil (1912), 312
Master Key (The) (1914), 354
Master Mummer (The) (1915), 317
Master Mystery (The) (1919), 437, 445
Master Rogue (The) (1914), 409
Matchin' Jim (1916), 122
Mating of Marcella (The) (1918), 93
Matrimonial Martry (A) (1916), 181
Maud Muller (1911), 464
Maverick (The) (1952), 24, 25
Mayblossom (1912), 229
Mayblossom (1917), 237
Maytime (1923), 450
Measure of a Man (The) (1924), 413
Medicine Bend (1916), 98, 102
Medicine Show at Stone Gulch (The) (1914), 179
Meet the Chump (1941), 380
Melody Ranch (1940), 244, 248
Melting Millions (1927), 151, 155, 333
Memories of the Past (1911), 229
Men in Exile (1937), 245
Men of Daring (1927), 414
Men, Women and Money (1924), 276
Mercy Merrick (1913), 314
Mercy Plane (1940), 322, 325
Message From Reno (A) (1917), 182
Messenger of Peace (1950), 433
Mettle of Jerry McGuire (The) (1915), 102
Mexican Spy in America (A) (1915), 219
Mexican's Last Raid (The) (1914), 355
Mexeppa (1910), 463
Michael Strogoff (1910), 310
Midnight Adventure (A) (1928), 369
Midnight Guest (1923), 296
Midnight Raiders (The) (1921), 129
Midnight Romance (A) (1919), 89, 94
Midnight Secrets (1924), 280
Midnight Thieves (1926), 297
Militant Suffragette (A) (1912), 420
Mill Stream (The) (1914), 396
Million Dollar Kid (1944), 287
Million Dollar Mystery (The) (1914), 417, 421
Million in Jewels (A), (1914), 98, 100
Millionaire Baby (The) (1915), 292
Millionaire Engineer (The) (1916), 396
Millionaire Orphan (The) (1926), 282
Mind Cure (The) (1912), 229
Mind Your Own Business (1930), 83
Mine With the Iron Door (The) (1936), 391

Minister's Temptation (The) (1913), 313
Miracle on Main Street (A) (1939), 247
Mischief and a Mirror (1915), 57
Misjudged Mr. Hartley (1915), 441
Misplaced Love (1913), 233
Miss Annie Rooney (1942), 139
Miss Freckles (1915), 443
Miss Lulu Bett (1921), 302
Miss Mink of 1949 (1949), 266
Missing Bride-Groom (The) (1910), 228
Missing Witnesses (1937), 247
Mission of a Bullet (1912), 177
Mississippi Rhythm (1949), 255
Mistaken Orders (1926), 105
Mr. Hubby's Wish (1912), 438
Mr. Pickwick's Predicament (1912), 313
Mister Scoutmaster (1953), 256
Mr. Smith Goes to Washington (1939), 322, 324
Mr. Wise, Investigator (1911), 437
Model Wife (A) (1915), 180
Modern Bianas (The) (1911), 311
Modern Cinderella (A) (1911), 311
Modern Daughters (1927), 368
Modern Lochinvar (A) (1919), 152
Mollycoddle (The) (1915), 55
Money and Mystery (1917), 190
Money Leeches (The) (1915), 410
Montana Incident (1952), 146, 434
Moon Child (The) (1914), 218
Moonlight and Cactus (1932), 135
Moonshine Menace (The) (1921), 102
Morals (1921), 472
More the Merrier (The) (1943), 105
Mother Instinct (The) (1915), 355
Mother O'Dreams (1914), 440
Mother Wore Tights (1947), 244, 254
Mother's Atonement (A) (1915), 352, 356
Mother's Busy Week (1915), 56
Motor Buccaneers (The) (1914), 440
Mountain Tragedy (A) (1912), 177
Mountain Witch (The) (1913), 408
Mountain Woman (The) (1921), 238
Mounted Stranger (The) (1930), 134
Movie Night (1929), 335
Mozart Story (The) (1948), 45, 49
Mrs. Hilton's Jewels (1913), 466
Mrs. Warren's Brother (1916), 397
Much Ado About Nothing (1913), 233
Muchly Engaged (1913), 232
Murder in the Music Hall (1946), 382, 457
Murder in Times Square (1943), 250
Music Man (1948), 144
Mutiny in the Arctic (1941), 374, 380
My Baby's Voice (1912), 419
My Heart Belongs to Daddy (1942), 326
My Lady High and Mighty (1915), 316
My Little Chickadee (1940), 379

My Man (1928), 369
My Man Godfrey (1936), 166
My Neighbor's Wife (1925), 304
My Son Is a Criminal (1939), 454
My Son Is Guilty (1939), 454
My Son the Hero (1943), 263
Mysteries of the Grand Hotel (The) (1916), 411
Mysterious Airman (The) (1928), 329, 333, 335
Mysterious Contragrav (The) (1915), 188
Mysterious Crossing (1936), 166
Mysterious Hand (The) (1914), 34
Mysterious Leopard Lady (The) (1914), 29, 33
Mysterious Mr. Valentine (1946), 205
Mysterious Pearl (The) (1921), 53, 60
Mysterious Rose (The) (1914), 34
Mystery Box (The) (1925), 53, 61
Mystery Brand (The) (1927), 62
Mystery House (1938), 377
Mystery of the Dansant (1915), 180
Mystery of the Throne Room (The) (1915), 34
Mystery of the White Car (The) (1914), 29, 33
Mystery of Wickham Hall (The) (1914), 354
Mystery Ranch (1932), 387
Mystery Ship (The) (1917), 52, 58
Mystery Squadron (1933), 14, 17
Mystery Woman (The) (1915), 355
-N-
Nabbed (1915), 35
Naked Fists (1918), 191
Naked Gun (1956), 244, 257
Nan of Music Mountain (1917), 116, 123
Nan of the North (1922), 125
Nan's Victory (1914), 109
Natural Law (The) (1917), 274
Naughty Henrietta (1915), 55
Naughty Marietta (1936), 385, 390
Naughty Nineties (The) (1945), 265
Navy Blues (1941), 9
Nazi Spy Ring (1942), 381
Near Death's Door (1914), 101
Near the Rainbow's End (1930), 128, 135
Nearly Married (1914), 441
Necklace of Rameses (The) (1914), 315
Ne'er Do Well (The) (1915), 461, 469
Neglected wife (The) (1917), 174, 181
Nell Dale's Men Folks (1916), 122
Neptune's Daughter (1912), 438
Nevada Badmen (1951), 23
Never Give a Sucker an Even Break (1941), 381
Never Say Die (1924), 304
New Exploits of Elaine (1915), 227, 236
New Faces of 1937 (1937), 321, 323
New Magdalene (The) (1910), 228
New Typist (The) (1913), 232
News Item (A) (1913), 233
Night Attack (The) (1921), 195
Night Cargo (1936), 453

Night Hawks (1914), 440
Night in Casablanca (A) (1945), 262, 264
Night in Kentucky (A) (1915), 442
Night in Town (A) (1913), 231
Night Key (1937), 162, 167
Night of Love (The) (1927), 346
Night of Nights (The) (1939), 344
Night Parade (1929), 83
Night Patrol (The), 297
Nine and Three-Fifths Seconds (1925), 304
Nine to Nine (1935), 176, 185
No Defense (1921), 112
No Sad Songs For Me (1950), 19
Nob Hill (1945), 253
Nobody's Bride (1923), 365
Nobody's Home (1915), 57
Nocturne (1946), 47
North of Shanghai (1939), 87
North Wind's Malice (The) (1920), 361, 363
Northern Pursuit (1943), 456
Not Too Thin to Fight (1917), 189
Notorious Gallagher (1916), 422
Nugget Jim's Partner (1916), 122
Number Please? (1916), 339
Number 10, Westbound (1917), 189
Number 13, Westbound (1916), 469
No. 28 Diplomat (1914), 440
Nurse's Secret (The) (1941), 455

-O-

O, My Darling Clementine (1943), 71
Oak-Lawn Handicap (The) (1915), 218
Oath of Vengeance (1944), 416
Obey the Law (1926), 332, 368
Octoroon (The) (1913), 269, 272
Officer 444 (1926), 53, 62, 404
Oh, Man! (1918), 190
Oh, Such a Night (1912), 229
Oh, Susanna (1951), 49, 75
Oh! What a Night! (1926), 368
Oh! You Mummy (1914), 236
Oh! You Pearl (1913), 234
Oh! You Puppy (1914), 235
Oh! You Scotch Lassie (1913), 233
Oil Well conspiracy (The) (1914), 101
Olana of the South Seas (1914), 217
Old Code (The) (1928), 62
Old Curiosity Shop (The) (1911), 418
Old Guard (The) (1914), 395
Old Gypsy Custom (The) (1934), 389
Old Hutch (1936), 385, 391
Old Isaacson's Diamonds (1915), 180
Old, Old Song (An) (1913), 438
Old Peg Leg's Will (1915), 34
Old Soldier's Story (The) (1909), 173, 176
On Guard (1929), 82
On Probation (1935), 18
On the Brink of Ruin (1913), 408

On the Heights (1914), 316
On the Side Lines (1929), 83
Onda of the Orient (1916), 220
One Best Bet (1914), 396
One Glorious Scrap (1927), 81
One Kind of a Friend (1915), 35
One Last Fling (1949), 255
One Million in Jewels (1923), 104
One More Tomorrow (1939), 243
One Night (1915), 396
One on Willie (1913), 178
One to the Minute (1915), 57
One Wild Time (1926), 78
One Wonderful Night (1914), 441
Only One Shirt (1914), 179
Ononko's Vow (1910), 310
Open Switch (The) (1926), 99, 105
Opened Shutters (The) (1914), 115, 120
Operator at Black Rock (The) (1914), 97, 101
Ordeal (The) (1922), 364
Oregon Trail (1923), 127, 131
Oregon Trail (1945), 430
Oriental Romance (An) (1915), 396
Orphan of War (An) (1913), 29, 32
Other Girl (The) (1914), 439
Other Man (The) (1918), 294
Otherwise Bill Harrison (1915), 442
Otto Coin's Ghost (1915), 409
Our Dancing Daughters (1928), 474
Our Enemy's Spy (1914), 218
Our Hearts Were Young and Gay (1944), 140
Our Parents-In-Law (1913), 231
Our Vines Have Tender Grapes (1945), 322, 327
Out California Way (1946), 72
Out of Petticoat Lane (1914), 107, 109
Out of the Grave (1913), 234
Out of the Money (1946), 327
Out of the Storm (1948), 266
Out of the Wreck (1917), 470
Out West With the Hardys (1938), 392
Outlaw (The) (1921), 129
Outlaw Justice (1932), 85
Outlaws of Texas (1950), 23
Outlaws of the Cherokee Trail (1941), 261
Outlaws of the Sea (1923), 275
Outwitted (1925), 38, 104
Over the Hill (1920), 361, 363
Over the Santa Fe Trail (1947), 141
Over the Wall (1938), 245, 247
Overland Bound (1930), 152, 157

-P-

Pace That Kills (The) (1935), 414
Pacific Rendezvous (1942), 169
Paddling Coeds (1928), 81
Paid Back (1922), 364
Paid to Dance (1937), 454
Painted Faces (1929), 83

Painted Flapper (The) (1925), 297, 473
Painted Post (1928), 348
Painted Veil (The) (1934), 385, 389
Pair of Fools (A) (1912), 229
Pals (1913), 234
Pals (1925), 133
Panther Girl of the Kongo (1955), 21, 26, 27
Paper Doll (The) (1913), 232
Papered Door (The) (1915), 443
Paperhanger's Revenge (The) (1917), 190
Parlor, Bedroom and Bath (1920), 445
Partners for Life (1912), 312
Partners of the Sunset (1922), 149, 153
Pasadena Peach (The) (1912), 177
Passing the Bomb (1918), 190
Pathway of Years (The) (1913), 438
Patria (1917), 215, 221
Patriot and the Spy (The) (1915), 418, 421
Patsy of the Circus (1915), 220
Pay Train (The) (1914), 101
Peace Offering (The) (1912), 177
Peach at the Beach (The) (1914), 180
Peanuts and Powder (1916), 339
Pearl and the Poet (1913), 233
Pearl and the Tramp (1913), 233
Pearl as a Clairvoyant (1913), 231
Pearl as a Detective (1913), 232
Pearl of the Army (1916), 227, 237
Pearl's Admirers (1913), 229
Pearl's Dilemma (1913), 232
Pearl's Hero (1913), 234
Pearl's Mistake (1913), 233
Pecos Dandy (The) (1934), 86
Peggy's Invitation (1913), 420
Penalty (The) (1941), 243, 244, 249
Penthouse Rhythm (1945), 265
People of the Pit (The) (1915), 356
Percy's Wooing (1913), 178
Perfect Lover (The) (1919), 271, 274
Perfect Truth (The) (1914), 315
Peril of the Rail (1926), 99, 105
Perilous Journey (A), 256
Perils of Nyoka (The) (1942), 5, 7, 9, 10, 21, 70, 321
Perils of Pauline (The) (1914), IV, 226, 227, 235, 308, 352, 417
Perils of the Jungle (1927), 329, 331, 334
Perils of the Yukon (1922), 402
Perils of Thunder Mountain (The) (1919), 337, 341
Pest From the West (1939), 67
Phantom City (The) (1928), 334
Phantom Empire (The) (1935), 43
Phantom Express (The) (1932), 85
Phantom Foe (The) (1920), 89, 91, 94
Phantom Fugitive (A) (1919), 192, 222
Phantom Gold (1938), 415

Phantom Husband (A) (1915), 443
Phantom Husband (The) (1917), 445
Phantom Island (1916), 35
Phantom Light (The) (1914), 218
Phantom Mine (1917), 412
Phantom of 42nd Street (The) (1945), 6, 11
Phantom of the Violin (1915), 34
Phantom of the West (The) (1931), 77, 84
Phantom Pinto (The) (1928), 62
Phantom Plainsmen (The) (1942), 263
Phantom Rider (The) (1946), 426, 431
Philistine in Bohemia (A) (1920), 363
'Phone Message (The) (1916), 443
Phony Singer (The) (1913), 178
Pied Piper of Hamelin (The) (1911), 418
Pilgrim (The) (1916), 115, 122
Pilgrim Lady (The) (1947), 254
Pine's Revenge (The) (1915), 352, 356
Pinto Kid (The) (1941), 283, 285
Pioneer Days (1917), 470
Pioneer Trail (1938), 415
Pirate Gold (1920), 270, 271, 275
Pirates of Panama (1929), 345, 347, 349
Pistol Point Proposal (A) (1919), 192
Pitfall (The) (1915), 405, 411
Pitfalls of a Big City (1919), 59
Pittsburgh Kid (The) (1941), 249
Play Ball (1925), 150, 154
Play Square (1921), 364
Playing It Wild (1923), 113
Pleasing Her Husband (1913), 233
Plot and Counterplot (1915), 56
Plumbers Waterloo (The) (1916), 188
Plunder (1923), 227, 239
Plunderers (The) (1948), 74
Poison (1915), 273
Police Patrol (The) (1925), 367
Police Reporter (The) (1928), 329, 334
Politician's Love Story (The) (1909), 463
Pomp of Earth (The) (1915), 181
Pony Express Rider (1926), 282
Poor Girls (1927), 447
Poppy Girl's Husband (The) (1919), 89, 94
Port of Missing Girls (The) (1928), 348
Pot O'Gold (The) (1917), 407, 412
Potter and the Clay (The) (1914), 409
Powder Trail (The) (1916), 36
Power (1928), 282
Power God (The) (1925), 53, 62
Power of Fascination (The) (1915), 352, 356
Power of Love (The) (1911), 229
Powers Girl (The) (1943), 199, 201
Practically Yours (1945), 288
Prairie Mystery (The) (1922), 280
Prairie Rustlers (1945), 416
Prejudice (1915), 273
Prejudice (1949), 383

Pressing His Suit (1915), 396
Pretender (The) (1947), 205
Price of Fame (The) (1915), 180
Price of Fear (The) (1928), 40
Price of Folly (The) (1918), 174, 182
Price of His Honor (The) (1914), 440
Price of Redemption (The) (1920), 353, 359
Price of Youth (The) (1922), 53, 60
Pride of Maryland (1951), 433
Primitive Instinct (The) (1914), 409
Primrose Path (The) (1925), 399
Prince Chap (The) (1920), 461, 471
Prince of the Saddle (1926), 282
Princely Bandit (The) (1916), 36
Princess and the Man (The) (1913), 313
Princess and the Peasant (The) (1910), 310
Princess of the Desert (A) (1914), 316
Princess O'Rourke (1943), 456
Priscilla's Prisoner (1916), 357
Prison Stain (The) (1914), 409
Prisoner for Life (A) (1919), 192
Private Banker (The) (1916), 109
Private Scandal (A) (1921), 471
Prodigal (The) (1914), 272
Prodigal Uncle (The) (1917), 340
Prodigal Widow (The) (1917), 51, 58
Professor and the New Hat (The) (1911), 311
Profligate (The) (1915), 442
Prophecy (The) (1913), 314
Public Be Damned (1917), 319
Public Wedding (1937), 246
Pulque Pete and the Opera Troupe (1912), 177
Puppy Love (1917), 444
Puppy Love (1919), 362
Purple Heart Diary (1951), 210
Purple Mask (The) (1916), 29, 31, 36
Purple Monster Strikes (The) (1945), 199, 203
Pursuit of Pleasure (The) (1915), 180
Put Yourself in His Place (1912), 419
Putting It Over (1920), 192
Putting One Over (1914), 315
Puzzle Woman (The) (1917), 37

-Q-
Quagmire (The) (1916), 122
Queen for a Day (1951), 289
Queen of the Kitchen (1912), 177
Quest of Virginia (The) (1916), 221
Question of Seconds (A) (1912), 312
Quick Triggers (1918), 190
Quicksands (The) (1914), 409

-R-
Racing Luck (1924), 304
Radar Men From the Moon (1952), 207, 209, 211
Radio King (The) (1922), 127, 130, 131
Raiders From Double L Ranch (The) (1913), 178
Raiders of the Range (1955), 263

Railroad Bandit (A) (1916), 216, 220
Railroad Raiders (The) (1917), 98, 103
Rainbow Island (1944), 137, 140
Rainbow Ranch (1933), 387
Rainbow Trail (The) (1925), 343
Rainbow Trail (1932), 386
Rainbow Valley (1935), 18
Rajah's Jewels (The) (1914), 101
Rajah's Vow (The) (1914), 409
Ramblin' Kid (The) (1923), 343
Rambling Ranger (The) (1927), 77, 80
Ramon, the Sailmaker (1920), 149, 153
Ranch Girls on a Rampage (1912), 177
Range Riders (The) (1927), 62
Ranger and the Lady (The) (1940), 455
Ranger of Lonesome Gulch (The) (1916), 122
Rawhide (1926), 404
Rawhide Romance (1934), 414
Ray of God's Sunshine (A) (1913), 439
Real Agatha (The) (1914), 440
Reaping for the Whirlwind (1914), 179
Red Ace (The) (1917), 215, 219, 221
Red Circle (The) (1915), 174, 181
Red Glove (The) (1919), 215, 216, 217, 222
Red Hot and Blue (1949), 145
Red Rider (The) (1925), 413
Red River Range (1938), 65, 67
Red River Renegades (1946), 431
Red Snow (The) (1921), 94
Redeeming Love (1916), 461, 469
Redemption (The) (1913), 408
Redemption of the Jasons (The) (1915), 55
Reel Virginian (The) (1924), 345
Reform Candidate (The) (1911), 311
Refrigerator Car's Captive (The) (1914), 101
Relay (The) (1926), 79
Reluctant Dragon (The) (1941), 322, 325
Remarkable Andrew (The) (1942), 137, 139, 326
Remember When? (1925), 346
Rendezvous at Midnight (1935), 474
Reno (1930), 176, 185
Repeating the Honeymoon (1918), 190
Reported Missing (1937), 167
Reporter (The) (1911), 229
Requited Love (1912), 438
Rescued by Her Lions (1911), 459, 464
Rescued by Wireless (1914), 217
Return (The) (1916), 469
Return of the Riddle Rider (The) (1927), 39
Return of the Twins' Double (The) (1914), 29, 34
Revenge at Monte Carlo (1933), 85
Revenge of the Zombies (1943), 251
Rhapsody in Blue (1945), 457
Rhythm Inn (1951), 267
Rich Men's Wives (1922), 342
Rich Uncle (The) (1913), 234
Riddle of the Green Umbrella (The) (1914), 272

Riddle of the Tin Soldier (1913), 271
Riddle Rider (The) (1924), 99, 104, 195
Ride, Ryder, Ride (1949), 416, 433
Rider From Tucson (1950), 244, 255
Riders of Destiny (1933), 387
Riders of the Frontier (1939), 415
Riders of the Law (1922), 413
Riders of the Plains (1924), 403
Riders of the West (1927), 62
Ridin' Down the Canyon (1942), 70
Ridin' Wild (1922), 365
Ridin' Wild (1925), 282
Riding High (1950), 323, 328
Right Man (The) (1917), 111
Right of the Strongest (The) (1924), 304
Right Way (The) (1921), 302
Rimrock Jones (1918), 116, 123
Ring (The) (1914), 235
Ring of a Spanish Grandee (The) (1912), 419
Ring of Destiny (The) (1915), 352, 356
Rio Grande Raiders (1946), 205
Risky Road (The) (1918), 93
Rivals (The) (1929), 82
River of Romance (1929), 348
Road Agent (1941), 381
Road to Paradise (1930), 474
Roaring Adventure (A) (1925), 413
Roaring Road (The) (1919), 116, 124
Robbers (The) (1913), 315
Robert's Lesson (1913), 233
Rock Island Trail (1950), 74
Rockin' Through the Rockies (1940), 69
Rogues and Romance (1920), 275
Roll Along Cowboy (1937), 385, 392
Roll, Thunder, Roll (1949), 416
Roll Your Peanut (1914), 33
Rolling Stones (1916), 270, 274
Romance of a Dry Town (The) (1911), 176
Romance of an American Duchess (The) (1915), 442
Romance of Elaine (The) (1915), 227, 236
Romance of Rowena (The) (1913), 314
Romance of Tarzan (The) (1918), 353, 358
Romance of the Night (A) (1915), 441
Romance of the Western Hills (A) (1910), 463
Romance Promoters (The) (1920), 301
Romeo and Juliet (1924), 346
Rookies (1927), 133
Room Rent and Romance (1916), 188
Roped (1919), 59
Roped and Tied (1918), 191
Rosalie (1937), 5, 7
Rosalind at Redgate (1919), 445
Rosary (The) (1915), 461, 469
Rose of Old St. Augustine (The) (1911), 463
Rose of the Bowery (1927), 368
Rose of the Tenderloin (A) (1909), 310
Rosemary (1915), 421
Rouged Lips (1923), 398
Rough and Ready (1927), 414
Rough Lover (The) (1918), 92
Rough Riders of Cheyenne (1945), 430
Rough Riders of Durango (1951), 209
Rough Riding Romance (1919), 89, 94
Rough Shod (1922), 302
Rough, Tough, and Ready (1945), 163, 170, 252
Roughneck (The) (1924), 360
Royal Rogue (A) (1917), 89, 91
Runaway Freight (The) (1913), 97, 100
Running Wild (1927), 80
Rustle of a Skirt (The) (1915), 317
Rustlers of Devil's Canyon (1947), 432
Rustlers of Red Dog (1935), 40
Ruth of the Range (1923), 183
Ruth of the Rockies (1920), 174, 183
Ruth Roland, the Kalem Girl (1912), 177

-S-

Sabre Jet (1953), 458
Saddle King (The) (1929), 63
Sagebrush Gospel (1924), 61
Sagebrush Lady (The) (1925), 196
Sagebrush Law (1917), 407, 412
Sailor's Lady (1940), 8
Saintly Sinner (1917), 444
Saleslady (The) (1912), 419
Saleslady (The) (1938), 377
Sally Ann's Strategy (1912), 313
Sally in Our Alley (1927), 473
Salute for Three (1943), 139
Samson at Calford (1927), 80
San Antonio Kid (The) (1944), 201
San Diego Exposition of 1916 (1916), 181
San Quentin (1937), 245, 246
San Quentin (1946), 47
Sands of Iwo Jima (1949), 458
Santa Fe Saddlemates (1945), 200, 203
Santa Fe Trail (The) (1923), 53, 56, 60
Sap (The) (1929), 370
Saphead (The) (1920), 342
Sarge Goes to College (1947), 141
Satin Woman (The) (1927), 447
Savage Horde (1950), 74
Savages of the Sea (1925), 423
Saved From Court Martial (1912), 177
Scared Stiff (1945), 253
Scareheads (1931), 451
Scarlet Car (The) (1917), 111
Scarlet Crystal (The) (1917), 110
Scarlet Honeymoon (The) (1925), 332
Scarlet Mark (The) (1916), 318
Scarlet Pages (1930), 306
Scarlet Shadow (The) (1919), 397
Scarlet West (The) (1925), 304, 447
Scarred Hands (1923), 195

Scheme of Shiftless Sam Smith (The) (1913), 408
Screaming Shadow (The) (1920), 52, 59
Screen Snapshots (1926), 184
Screen Snapshots No. 2 (1925), 184
Sea Flower (The) (1918), 89, 94
Sea Hornet (The) (1951), 66, 75
Sea Lion (The) (1921), 342
Sea Mystery (A) (1916), 318
Sea Squawk (The) (1924), 330
Seal of Silence (1918), 294
Sealed Lips (1941), 380
Sealed Orders (1914), 352, 353
Sealskin Coat (The) (1916), 273
Second Chance (1948), 283, 288
Second Choice (1930), 370
Second in Command (The) (1915), 421
Second Woman (The) (1951), 163, 171
Secret Agent X-9 (1937). 162, 166
Secret Code (The) (1942), 374, 376, 382
Secret Kingdom (The) (1917), 395, 397
Secret of the Lost Valley (The) (1917), 407, 411
Secret of the Submarine (The) (1916), 89, 91
Secret Room (The) (1915), 269, 273
Secret Service Saunders (1925), 125
Secret Sinners (1933), 388
Secret Well (The) (1915), 410
Secretary of Frivolous Affairs (1915), 338
Secrets of Chinatown (1935), 18
See My Lawyer (1921), 295
Send Me No Flowers (1964), 212
Sensations of 1945 (1944), 287
Servant in the House (1920), 295
Servant Question (The) (1914), 441
Seven Sweethearts (1942), 393
Seventh Commandment (The) (1915), 273
Seventh Sheriff (The) (1923), 60
Severed Hand (The) (1914), 354
Shackles of Fear (1924), 281
Shadow (The) (1939), 243, 244, 247
Shadow of Crime (The) (1914), 235
Shadow of Guilt (The) (1914), 409
Shadow of Suspicion (1921), 193
Shadow of the Cross (The) (1912), 438
Shadow of the Eagle (The) (1932), 77, 85
Shadowed (1914), 234
Shadows of Life (1913), 353
Shadows of the Night (1928), 134
Sham Reality (The) (1916), 36
Sharpshooter (The) (1913), 31
She (1911), 419
She Loved a Fireman (1937), 247, 377
She Went to the Races (1945), 322, 327
She Wolf (The) (1913), 32
She Would Be a Cowboy (1915), 180
Shenandoah (1913), 271
Sheridan's Pride (1914), 29, 33
Sheriff of Hope Eternal (The) (1921), 413
Sheriff of Las Vegas (1944), 430
Sheriff of Redwood Valley (1946), 431
Sheriff of Cimarron (1945), 203
Sheriff of Sundown (1944), 201
Sheriff's Girl (The) (1926), 62
Sherlock Bonehead (1914), 179
She's for Me (1943), 264
She's in the Army (1942), 250
Shield of Honor (The) (1927), 81
Shielding Shadow (1916), 291, 293
Shod With Fire (1920), 301
Shoot 'Em Up Kid (The) (1926), 79
Shooting High (1940), 6, 8
Shoplifter (The) (1918), 192
Should a Girl Marry (1939), 373, 378
Show Girl's Glove (The) (1914), 272
Show of Shows (The) (1929), 370
Shuttle (The) (1918), 111
Shuttle of Faith (The) (1913), 466
Sign of the Cross (The) (1932), 344
Silent Flyer (The) (1926), 127, 133
Silent Guardian (The) (1926), 133
Silent Hero (The) (1927), 369
Silent Lover (The) (1926), 346
Silent Master (The) (1917), 116, 122
Silent Peril (The) (1914), 218
Silent Selby (1916), 122
Silent Terror (The) (1916), 221
Silent Tongue (The) (1911), 311
Silent Valley (The) (1914), 396
Silent Voice (The) (1915), 421
Silent Vow (The) (1922), 112
Silver City Kid (1944), 429
Silver Comes Through (1927). 368
Sin of Olga Brandt (The) (1914), 352, 354
Singing Marine (The) (1937), 246
Single Man (A) (1929), 474
Single Standard (The) (1929), 474
Single Wives (1924), 473
Sinners in Silk (1924), 330
Sins of the Children (1936), 391
Sis (1915), 396
Si's Wonderful Mineral Spring (1912), 177, 179
Sisters (1910), 310
Sister's Love (A) (1909), 309
Six-Gun Decision (1953), 427, 435
Skeleton in the Closet (The) (1913), 408
Skelly's Skeleton (1916), 339
Skinny the Moocher (1939), 69
Skip the Maloo! (1931), 451
Sky Dragon (1949), 145
Sky Commando (1953), 323, 328
Sky Giant (1938), 322, 324
Slave Girl (1947), 266
Slavery of Foxicus (The) (1914), 179
Sleepytime Gal (1942), 429
Sliding Home (1927), 80

Slim Princess (The) (1915), 442
Smart Guy (1943), 251
Smart Politics (1948), 143
Smash-Up (1947), 141
Smashing Barriers (1919), 112
Smashing Barriers (1923), 113
Smashing the Spy Ring (1938), 67
Smoked Out (1923), 280
Smuggler (The) (1913), 99
Smugglers of Lone Isle (The) (1914), 409
Smuggler's Island (1915), 34
Snowed In (1926), 150, 154
So Long, Letty (1920), 295
So Proudly We Hail (1943), 70
So This Is Marriage (1924), 331
So You Love Your Dog (1953), 25
So You Think You Can't Sleep (1953), 26
So You Want a Television Set (1953), 25
So You Want to Be a Bachelor (1951), 23
So You Want to Be a Cowboy (1951), 23
So You Want to Be a Muscleman (1949), 22
So You Want to Be a Plumber (1951), 23
So You Want to Be an Heir (1953), 26
So You Want to Be in Politics (1948), 22
So You Want to Buy a Used Car (1951), 23
So You Want to Get It Wholesale (1952), 23
So You Want to Hold Your Husband (1950), 23
So You Want to Wear The Pants (1952), 24
So Your Wife Wants to Work (1956), 26
So You're Going to a Convention (1952), 24
So You're Having In-Law Trouble (1949), 22
So You're Having Neighbor Trouble (1954), 26
Social Pirates (The) (1916), 405, 410
Society Hypocrites (1916), 57
Society's Driftwood (1917), 37
Soldier Brothers of Susanna (The) (1912), 177
Soldier Man (1926), 346
Solitary Sin (The) (1919), 279
Some Collectors (1914), 236
Some Heroes (1916), 188
Some Night (1916), 339
Something to Do (1919), 124
Something to Shout About (1943), 10, 244, 250
Son of a Badman (1949), 145
Son of the Desert (A) (1928), 414
Son of Zorro (1946), 426, 432
Song of Life (The) (1922), 296
Song of Norway (1970), 213
Songs of Truce (1913), 466
Sons of the Northwoods (1912), 464
Sorceress (1917), 358
Soubrette (The) (1913), 234
Soul Enslaved (A) (1916), 356
Soul Mate (The) (1914), 468
Souls for Sale (1923), 472
Souls in Bondage (1923), 330, 359
Soup to Nuts (1930), 13, 15

Source (The) (1918), 116, 123
Spanish Dancer (The) (1923), 472
Sparks of Fate (1914), 440
Spawn (The) (1918), 37
Speck on the Wall (The) (1914), 467
Speed (1927), 197
Speed Limit (The) (1913), 178
Speed to Spare (1948), 163, 170
Speeding Youth (1928), 82
Spider (The) (1915), 443
Spider's Net (The) (1926), 187, 197
Spindle of Life (The) (1917), 58
Spirit of West Point (1947), 382
Splash Mates (1929), 83
Splash of Local Color (A) (1916), 318
Splashing Through (1927), 80
Splendid Dishonor (A) (1914), 440
Splendid Sin (The) (1919), 401
Spoilers (The) (1914), 459, 461, 467
Spoilers of the North (1947), 73
Sporting Courage (1929), 82
Spring Madness (1938), 454
Spy's Defeat (The) (1913), 439
Square Deal Sanderson (1919), 116, 124
Square Deceiver (The) (1917), 278
Square Shooter (1935), 453
Squatter's Right (1919), 152
Squaw Man (The) (1918), 115, 116, 123
Stage Door (1937), 321, 324
Stage Romance (A) (1911), 311
Stage to Blue River (1951), 23
Stagecoach Buckaroo (1942), 381
Stagecoach to Denver (1946), 432
Stagecoach to Monterey (1944), 429
Stage-Struck Daughter (The) (1908), 309
Stain (The) (1912), 438
Stand Up and Cheer (1934), 373, 375
Standing Room Only (1944), 139, 251
Star of Bethlehem (The) (1912), 420
Star Spangled Banner (The) (1911), 311
Star Spangled Rhythm (1942), 327
Stardust on the Sage (1942), 284, 286
Stars and Stripes Forever (The) (1913), 32
Starving for Love (1913), 232
Stay-At-Homes (The) (1915), 55
Steadfast Heart (The) (1923), 276
Steel Hearts (1917), 111, 221
Steel Trail (The) (1923), 113
Steelhart (1921), 112
Stingaree (1915), 405, 411
Stolen Actress (The) (1917), 444
Stolen Honors (1916), 318
Stolen Kisses (1929), 369
Stolen Melody (The) (1913), 466
Stolen Nickel (The) (1912), 312
Stolen Play (The) (1917), 182
Stolen Ranch (The) (1926), 133

Stolen Rembrandt (The) (1914), 100
Stop, Look, and Love (1939), 162, 168
Stork Club (The) (1945), 137, 141
Stormswept (1923), 398
Stormy (1935), 159, 162, 164
Stormy Seas (1923), 104
Story of Elias Howe (The) (1939), 19
Story of the Blood Red Rose (The) (1914), 468
Straight and Narrow Path (The) (1915), 410
Straight From the Shoulder (1921), 302
Straight Through (1925), 446
Strange Melody (A) (1914), 337
Strange Mr. Gregory (The) (1946), 170
Stranger (The) (1973), 435
Stranger From Texas (The) (1939), 68, 69
Stranger in New York (A) (1916), 292
Stranger in Town (1943), 169
Strangler's Cord (The) (1915), 410
Street Angel (1928), 348
Strenuous Life (The) (1914), 353
Strictly Business (1913), 231
String of Pearls (A) (1914), 100
Strings of Steel (1926), 38, 77, 79, 196
Strong Arm Nellie (1912), 177
Struggle (The) (1913), 408
Submarine Command (1951), 146
Submarine D-1 (1937), 247
Substitute for Pants (A) (1914), 179
Sultana (The) (1916), 181
Sultana of the Desert (A) (1915), 469
Summer Flirtation (A) (1910), 228
Sunday Punch (1942), 169
Sundaying in Fairview (1917), 301
Sundered Ties (1912), 29, 31
Sunken Silver (1925), 150, 154
Sunset Legion (The) (1928), 369
Sunshine (1912), 438
Superman (1948), 49, 137, 142, 144
Superman (1978), 147
Superman and Scotland Yard (1954), 147
Superman and the Jungle Devil (1954), 147
Superman Flies Again (1954), 147
Superman in Exile (1954), 147
Superman's Peril (1954), 147
Sure Cure (1914), 235
Surgeon Warren's Ward (1914), 441
Surgeon's Temptation (The) (1911), 311
Surprise of My Life (The) (1915), 441
Surprises of an Empty Hotel (The) (1916), 397
Surrender (The) (1915), 220
Swamp Fox (The) (1912), 271
Swearing Off (1917), 189
Sweet Alyssum (1915), 461, 469
Sweet Lady Peggy (1916), 470
Sweetheart of the Navy (1937), 392
Swellhead (The) (1927), 334
Swellhead (The) (1930), 349

Swing Shift Maisie (1943), 170
Switchman's Tower (The) (1911), 311

-T-

Tacky Sue's Romance (1917), 444
Tailor Maid (1919), 59
Tailspin Tommy and the Great Air Mystery (1935), X, 161, 164, 165
Tale of the C (The) (1915), 318
Taming of Mary (The) (1915), 317
Tammany's Tiger (1916), 220
Tangle (The) (1914), 34
Tangled Marriage (A) (1912), 229
Tannhauser (1913), 420
Tarzan and the Golden Lion (1927), 368
Tarzan, the Fearless (1933), 449, 450, 452
Tarzan, the Mighty (1928), 345, 348
Tarzan, the Tiger (1929), 345, 349
Tarzan Triumphs (1943), 321, 322, 327
Tattered Duke (The) (1914), 179
Taxi! Taxi! (1927), 306
Teeth of the Tiger (1919), 271, 274
Telephone Engagement (A) (1914), 236
Tell It to a Star (1945), 72
Tell Your Children (1938), 414
Telltale Hat Band (The) (1913), 31
Temper (1915), 442
Temperance Town (1916), 293
Tempest Cody Bucks the Trust (1919), 223
Tempest Cody Flirts With Death (1919), 222
Tempest Cody Gets Her Man (1919), 223
Tempest Cody Hits the Trail (1919), 222
Tempest Cody, Kidnapper (1919), 223
Tempest Cody Plays Detective (1919), 222
Tempest Cody Rides Wild (1919), 222
Tempest Cody Turns the Tables (1919), 223
Tempest Cody's Man Hunt (1919), 222
Temple of Terror (1917), 190, 197
Ten Nights In A Bar Room (1911), 464
Ten Scars Make a Man (1924), 150, 154
Tenderfoot (The) (1917), 337, 340
Tenderfoot's Luck (The) (1913), 178
Tenderfoot's Troubles (The) (1912), 405, 408
Terrible People (The) (1929), 151, 157
Terror (1924), 239
Terror in the Wax Museum (1972), 427, 435
Terror of the Night (A) (1914), 316
Terror Trail (1921), 194
Terrors of the Jungle (The) (1915), 216, 218
Terrors of War (The) (1917), 37
Test of a Man (1915), 219
Test of Donald Norton (The) (1926), 332
Tex Granger (1948), 427, 432
Texan (The) (1932), 17
Texas Kelly at Bay (1913), 29, 32
Texas Steer (A) (1915), 292
Texas Terror (1935), 18
That Certain Age (1938), 425, 428

That Country Gal (1915), 57
That Crying Baby (1913), 233
That Gal of Burke's (1916), 115, 122
That Other Girl (1913), 231
That Sharp Note (1916), 340
Their Best Friend (1914), 420
Their Hour (1915), 355
Their Stepmother (1913), 465
Their Vacation (1914), 33
Thief (The) (1920), 227, 238
Thing We Love (The) (1918), 461, 470
Third Commandment (The) (1915), 273
Third Hand High (1915), 441
Thirteenth Girl (The) (1915), 396
Thirteenth Man (The) (1913), 438
Thirty Days at Hard Labor (1912), 312
Thor, Lord of the Jungles (1913), 459, 467
Those High Grey Walls (1939), 69
Thou Shalt Not (1910), 463
Thou Shalt Not Covet (1915), 461, 469
Thousand-Dollar Drop (The) (1917), 189
Three Bad Men and a Girl (1915), 34
Three Cheers For Love (1936), 243, 245
Three In Exile (1925), 132
Three Legioneers (1937), 377
Three Live Ghosts (1936), 391
Three Mounted Men (1918), 59
Three Musketeers (1911), 308, 311
Three on a Ticket (1947), 288
Three Sailors and a Girl (1953), 256
Three Scraps of Paper (1913), 439
Three Snappy People (1939), 69
Three Wishes (The) (1916), 318
Thrill of a Romance (1945), 327
Through the Flames (1914), 272
Through the Window (1911), 229
Thrown to the Lions (1916), 318
Thunder in the Sun (1959), 258
Thunderbolt Jack (1920), 407, 413
Thunderbolt's Tracks (1927), 281, 404
Thundering Speed (1926), 196
Thundering Thompson (1929), 63
Thy Will Be Done (1913), 439
Tide of Destiny (The) (1913), 466
Tiger Band (The) (1920), 99, 103
Tiger Woman (The) (1944), 6, 21, 199, 200, 201, 204
Tiger Woman (The) (1945), 430
Tiger's Cub (The) (1920), 238
Tiger's Trail (The) (1919), 174, 182
Tight Shoes (1914), 179
Tight Squeeze (A) (1914), 316
Till Death Us Do Part (1914), 468
Tillie and Gus (1933), 452
Tillie, the Little Swede (1916), 358
Timber Queen (The) (1921), 174, 183
Time Out for Murder (1938), 167

Times Have Changed (1923), 153
Tin Hats (1926), 196
Tip-Off (The) (1915), 180
Tipped Off (1923), 398
Tireman, Spare My Tires (1942), 286
To a Finish (1921), 302
To Another Woman (1916), 352, 358
To the Highest Bidder (1917), 319
To the Highest Bidder (1918), 361, 362
Today and Tomorrow (1915), 181
Toil and Tyranny (1915), 181
Told in the Hills (1919), 116, 124
Toll of the Jungle (1916), 109
Toll of the Sea (1915), 219
Tomboy (The) (1911), 419
Tombstone Canyon (1932), 387
Tombstone–The Town Too Tough to Die (1942), 322, 324, 326
Tommy Gets His Sister Married (1910), 228
Tongues of Flame (1918), 222
Tonio, Son of the Sierras (1925), 61, 403
Too Much Married (1916), 339
Toodleums (1913), 232
Topeka (1953), 25
Topeka Terror (The) (1945), 203
Torrent (The) (1915), 218
Torture Ship (1937), 454
Totem Mark (The) (1911), 464
Touring With Tillie (1915), 57
Town That Tried to Come Back (The) (1916), 188
Trader Tom of the China Seas (1954), 207, 211, 212
Trading With Mother (1911), 311
Traffic in Crime (1946), 382
Tragedy of Bear Mountain (The) (1915), 405, 409
Tragedy That Lived (The) (1914), 467
Trail Breakers (The) (1914), 218
Trail Drive (The) (1933), 387
Trail of Chance (The) (1916), 318
Trail of Gold (The) (1912), 176
Trail of No Return (1918), 191
Trail of the Octopus (1919), 52, 59
Trail of Vengeance (The) (1924), 281
Trail to San Antone (1947), 432
Trailin' (1921), 342
Trail's End (The) (1919), 152
Trail's End (The) (1916), 274
Train Wreckers (The) (1925), 104
Transcontinental Limited (1926), 332
Translation of a Savage (The) (1913), 314
Trap (The) (1913), 353
Trap (The) (1947), 382
Trapped (1914), 409
Treasure Canyon (1924), 223
Treasure of Cibola (1917), 412
Treasure Train (The) (1914), 396

Tree and the Chaff (The) (1913), 466
Tree of Knowledge (The) (1919), 461, 471
Trey O'Hearts (The) (1914), 351, 352, 354
Tricksters (The) (1916), 274
Trigger Trail (The) (1921), 128
Trimmed in Scarlet (1923), 472
Trinkets of Tragedy (1914), 440
Triumph of Truth (1916), 358
Trooper Billy (1913), 408
Troopers Three (1930), 83, 84
Trouble Trail (1924), 60
Troublesome Telephone (1913), 178
True As Steel (1924), 360
True Blue (1922), 130
True Chivalry (1913), 232
True to Their Colors (1917), 37
Trunk An' Trouble (A) (1916), 339
Tucson Raiders (1944), 425, 429
Tudor Princess (A) (1913), 315
Tumbling Tumbleweeds (1935), 18
Turn in the Road (1919), 279
Turn of the Tide (The) (1914), 396
Tuxedo Junction (1941), 70
Twelfth Night (1910), 407
Twilight (1912), 438
Twin Six O'Brien (1926), 282
Twin's Double (The) (1914), 29, 33
Two Bits (1916), 122
Two-Fisted Buckaroo (1926), 282
Two-Fisted Sheriff (A) (1925), 446
Two Hearts and a Thief (1915), 57
Two in a Crowd (1936), 166
Two Lunatics (1913), 231
Two Men and a woman (1913), 465
Two Moons (1920), 342
Two Officers (1911), 311
Two Orphans (1911), 461, 464
Two Slips and a Miss (1916), 340
Two Yanks in Trinidad (1942), 244, 250

-U-

Unbeliever (The) (1918), 274
Under Colorado Skies (1947), 73
Under Desperation's Spur (1914), 101
Under Handicap (1917), 122
Under Montana Skies (1930), 83
Under Oath (1915), 410
Under Southern Skies (1915), 317
Under Texas Skies (1930), 349
Under the Big Top (1938), 377
Under the Black Flag (1913), 353
Under the Tonto Rim (1947), 45, 48
Under Two Flags (1912), 419
Undine (1912), 419
Unexpected (The) (1916), 36
Unexpected Father (1939), 378
Unexpected Fortune (An) (1912), 465
Unholy Love (1932), 474

Unjustly Accused (1914), 355
Unknown (The) (1913), 439
Unknown Guest (The) (1943), 251
Unknown Purple (The) (1923), 303
Unknown Valley (1933), 387
Unmasked (1917), 37
U. P. Trail (The) (1919), 461, 471
Unplanned Elopement (An) (1914), 440
Unseen Hand (The) (1920), 280
Unseen Hands (1924), 360
Unsigned Agreement (The) (1914), 33
Untamed (1917), 319
Untamed (1929), 40
Unto Herself Alone (1915), 180
Unusual Sacrifice (An) (1912), 312
Up and Going (1922), 342
Up in the Air (1940), 70
Up in the Air About Mary (1922), 130
Use Your Feet (1929), 83
Utah (1945), 430

-V-

Vacation Days (1947), 141
Valley of Bravery (1926), 332
Valley of Doubt (The) (1920), 397
Valley of Hate (The) (1924), 304
Valley of Hell (The) (1927), 368
Valley of the Giants (1919), 291, 294
Valley of the Rogue (The) (1921), 129
Valley of the Zombies (1946), 72
Valley of Tomorrow (The) (1920), 280
Valliants of Virginia (The) (1916), 109
Vampire (The) (1913), 272
Vampire's Ghost (The) (1945), 430
Van Thornton Diamonds (The) (1915), 109
Vanderhoff Affair (The) (1915). 273
Vanishing Dagger (The) (1920), 401
Vanishing Vases (The) (1915), 410
Vanishing West (The) (1928), 187, 197
Vanishing Westerner (The) (1950), 208
Vanity Pool (The) (1918), 413
Varsity Drag (The) (1929), 82
Varsity Show (1937), 246
Veiled Lady (The) (1913), 231
Veiled Mystery (The) (1920), 277, 279, 280
Veiled Woman (The) (1922), 423
Velvet Fingers (1920), 271, 275
Vengeance and the Woman (1917), 337, 340
Vengeance Trail (The) (1921), 280
Ventures of Marguerite (The) (1915), 270, 273
Verdict (The) (1925), 132
Vic Dyson Pays (1925), 53, 61
Vigilantes of Boomtown (1947), 432
Vigilantes of Dodge City (1944), 202
Viking Queen (The) (1914), 308, 316
Violinist (The) (1914), 337
Virgin Lips (1928), 399
Virgin Paradise (1921), 238

Virginia (1916), 357
Virginia Courtship (A) (1921), 472
Virtue of Rags (The) (1912), 438
Virtuoso (The) (1914), 316
Vision of the Shepherd (The) (1915), 469
Viva Cisco Kid (1940), 162, 168
Vivisectionist (The) (1915), 410
Vogues of 1938 (1938), 5, 7
Voice From the Sky (The) (1930), 54, 63
Voice of Hollywood No. 7 (1930), 83
Voice on the Wire (The) (1917), 52, 58
Voodoo Man (1944), 287
Vultures of Skull Mountain (The) (1917), 407, 411

-W-

Wages of Conscience (1927), 298
Wages of Sin (The) (1911), 176
Wages of Sin (The) (1922), 398
Wagon Wheels Westward (1945), 204
Waitress and the Boobs (The) (1915), 409
Walloping Kid (1926), 282
Walloping Time (1917), 445
Wanderer (The) (1926), 473
Wanderer of the Wasteland (1924), 473
Wanted, an Heir (1914), 179
War Against Mrs. Hadley (The) (1942), 169
War Correspondent (The) (1913), 269, 271
War Time Reformation (A) (1914), 33
Warrior Gap (1925), 61, 403
Wartime Siren (1913), 271
Washington at Valley Forge (1914), 29, 33
Watch Your Watch (1918), 190
Water Right War (The) (1912), 55
Way of a Man (1924), 149, 150, 153
Way of the Transgressor (The) (1923), 446
Way Out West (1937), 105, 344
Way West (The) (1967), 435
Ways of a Man (The) (1915), 355
We Americans (1928), 473
We Can't Have Everything (1918), 4, 61, 470
Web (The) (1917), 358
Webs of Steel (1925), 104
Wedding Rings (1929), 474
Weird Woman (1944), 264
Wells Fargo (1937), 425, 427
West of Cimarron (1941), 263
West of the Law (1926), 62
West of the Rainbow's End (1926), 282
West of the Rio Grande (1921), 149, 153
West Point Widow (1941), 325
Western Fate (1924), 61
Western Frontier (1935), 19
Western Vengeance (1924), 223
Westward Bound (1930), 156, 157
Westward Ho (1942), 263
Westward the Women (1952), 458
Wet Paint (1926), 346

What a Blonde (1945), 252
What Didn't Happen to Mary (1914), 235
What Every Woman Wants (1919), 294
What Happened to Mary? (1912), 241, 307, 308, 312, 352, 459
What Love Will Do (1921), 361, 364
What Papa Got (1913), 232
What Pearl's Pearls Did (1914), 236
Wheel of Fortune (1923), 296
Wheels of Destiny (1934), 414
Wheels of Justice (The) (1911), 464
When A Girl Loves (1921), 472
When A Woman Strikes (1919), 59
When Adam Had 'Em (1916), 340
When Danger Calls (1927), 197
When Danger Smiles (1922), 112
When Duty Calls (1913), 234
When East Met West in Boston (1914), 316
When Ghost Meets Ghost (1913), 420
When Greek Meets Greek (1913), 314
When Justice Sleeps (1915), 180
When Lad Comes Home (1919), 152
When Law Comes to Hades (1923), 195
When Love Is Young (1913), 232
When Love Is Young (1937), 167
When May Weds December (1913), 466
When Men Wear Skirts (1914), 179
When My Baby Smiles at Me (1948), 144
When My Lady Smiles (1915), 442
When Rogues Fall Out (1915), 102
When the Clock Strikes (1961), 435
When the Clock Went Wrong (1914), 291, 292
When the Devil Drives (1922), 398
When the Heart Rules (1912), 464
When the Right Man Comes Along (1913), 314
When the Studio Burned (1913), 420
When the Wolf Howls (1916), 352, 357
When the World Sleeps (1910), 228
When Thieves Fall Out (1915), 410
When Women Are Police (1913), 178
Where Are My Children? (1916), 220
Where Charity Begins (1913), 232
Where Men Are Men (1921), 112
Where the Worst Begins (1925), 184, 297
While Father Telephoned (1913), 178
Whirling Disc (The) (1915), 355
Whirlwind Finish (The) (1918), 222
Whirlwind Ranger (The) (1924), 61
Whispering Chorus (The) (1918), 461, 470
Whispering Smith (1916), 98, 102
Whispering Smith (1926), 105
Whistling Hills (1951), 146
Whistling in Brooklyn (1943), 170
White and Unmarried (1921), 295
White Banners (1938), 425, 428
White Eagle (1922), 174, 183, 184
White Flame (1928), 197

White Flower (The) (1923), 398
White Lies (1914), 440
White Moll (The) (1920), 238
White Moth (The) (1924), 366
White Rider (1920), 192
White Vaquero (The) (1912), 31
Who Is in the Box? (1913), 232
Who Is the Goat? (1913), 231
Who Pays? (1915), 174, 180
Who Will Marry Mary? (1913), 241, 308, 314
Who Wins? (1916), 174, 182
Whom God Hath Joined (1912), 419
Whose Baby? (1917), 92
Why Get Married (1924), 303
Why Women Remarry (1923), 343
Wide Open (1927), 298
Wide Open (1930), 370
Wife Tames Wolf (1947), 47
Wife to Spare (1947), 19
Wife Wanted (1946), 254
Wild Beauty (1946), 266
Wild Bill Hickok Rides (1942), 455
Wild Girl (The) (1925), 132
Wild Goose Chaser (The) (1924), 331
Wild Horse Stampede (The) (1926), 414
Wild Irish Rose (1915), 355
Wild Rider (The) (1919), 192
Wild to Go (1926), 332
Wild West (1946), 288
Wild West (1925), 300, 305
Wild West Show (The) (1928), 81
Wildcat Jordan (1922), 330
Wildcatter (The) (1919), 152
Wildcatter (The) (1937), 167
Wildfire (1925), 367
Wilful Youth (1927), 369
Will Power (1913), 232
Willie's Disguise (1914), 236
Willie's Great Scheme (1913), 233
Wings of Eagles (1957), 257
Winking Idol (The) (1926), 38, 77, 79, 196
Winners of the West (1940), 41, 373, 374, 379
Winners of the Wilderness (1927), 133
Winning Five (1927), 80
Winning Goal (The) (1927), 80
Winning Pair (The) (1917), 444
Winning Point (The) (1928), 82
Winning Punch (The) (1927), 80
Winning Whiskers (The) (1914), 409
Wise Old Elephant (A) (1913), 459, 465
Witch of Salem Town (A) (1915), 317
Witch of the Dark House (1916), 411
Witch of the Everglades (The) (1911), 463
With Her Rival's Help (1913), 231
With Love's Eyes (1913), 465
With Stanley in Africa (1922), 127, 130
With the Eyes of the Blind (1913), 314

Within the Law (1923), 303
Without Fear (1922), 238
Wives at Auction (1926), 367
Wives of Men (1918), 294
Wives of the Prophet (The) (1926), 447
Wives of the Rich (1916), 292
Wolf Among Lambs (A) (1913), 439
Wolf Pack (1922), 195
Wolf's Prey (The) (1915), 410
Wolves of the Desert (1926), 62, 404
Wolves of the North (1924) 108, 113
Woman and the Law (The) (1913), 233
Woman Chases Man (1937), 321, 323
Woman Hater (The) (1910), 228
Woman in Grey (A) (1920), 394, 395, 397
Woman in Room 13 (The) (1920), 422
Woman in the Case (1917), 189
Woman Laughs (A) (1914), 467
Woman of Distinction (A) (1950), 19
Woman of It (The) (1914), 467
Woman of Mystery (The) (1922), 31, 38
Woman Who Lied (The) (1915), 317
Woman Who Would Not Pay (The) (1917), 358
Woman's Debt (A) (1915), 355
Woman's Loyalty (A) (1914), 420
Woman's Revenge (A) (1913), 234
Woman's Way (A) (1913), 439
Woman's Wit (1921), 194
Woman's Woman (A) (1922), 359
Women in Bondage (1944), 382
Women of all Nations (1931), 386
Women–Past and Present (1913), 466
Won by One (1916), 57
Won in the Clouds (1914), 217
Won in the First (1914), 33
Won Ton Ton, the Dog Who Saved Hollywood (1976), 78, 87
Wood Nymph (The) (1915), 442
Woodland Paradise (A) (1913), 315
World Above (The) (1913), 439
World for Sale (The) (1918), 123
World's Applause (The) (1923), 472
Wright Idea (The) (1928), 134
Wynona's Vengeance (1913), 33
Wyoming Roundup (1952), 24

-Y-

Yankee Go-Getter (A) (1921), 60
Yellow Arm (The) (1921), 89, 90, 94, 271, 275
Yellow Cameo (1928), 156
Yellow Contraband (1928), 197
Yellow Fin (1951), 75
Yellow Star (The) (1915), 220
Yellow Streak (A) (1927), 62
Yesterday's Heroes (1940), 6, 8, 162, 168
You Came Along (1945), 457
Young As You Feel (1931), 13, 15, 385, 386
Young Bill Hickok (1940), 455

Young Hunter (The) (1913), 466
Young Mrs. Eames (The) (1913), 466
Your Friend and Mine (1923), 153
Your Girl and MIne (1914), 292
You're in the Army Now (1941), 10
You're Only Young Once (1937), 392
You're Telling Me (1932), 452
You're Never Too Young (1955), 257
Yukon Jake (1924), 345

-Z-

Zombies of the Stratosphere (1952), 207, 212
Zorro's Black Whip (1944), 199, 202
Zudora (The Twenty Million Dollar Mystery)
   (1914), 417, 421, 422